TO MARGARET HARWOOD
1885–1979
Radcliffe '07

CONTENTS

ACKNOWLEDGMENTS

I owe an enormous debt of gratitude to James Lockhart, professor of Latin American history at UCLA. More than a decade ago he showed me a copy of Molina's 1571 dictionary and engaged my interest in the language. From then on he shared with me primary Nahuatl data, drafts of work in progress, and publications, to the end that today my personal research library rivals his own. In 1974 we joined forces in writing about linguistic aspects of Nahuatl during the colonial period, and from then on, with generous foundation support to both of us, we continued joint research and publication. This dictionary is a research tool that we felt Nahuatl scholars needed in order to advance work in the field. Although the research, design, compilation, and writing have been mine, Jim devoted countless hours to providing commentary, argument, examples, and support. Without his complete reading of the entire work from beginning to end, many errors and incomprehensions would have gone undetected; it is an infinitely better product for his devotion. Ultimately and inevitably I made choices with which he did not agree, and so the conventional disclaimer that all imperfections should be attributed to the author alone is especially appropriate here.

The National Science Foundation generously supported the research, writing, and publication of the dictionary, and pilot projects were funded by the American Council of Learned Societies and the National Endowment for the Humanities. The Linguistics Research Center at the University of Texas—Winfred P. Lehmann, director—was host to the Nahuatl lexicography project, and I have especially enjoyed the friendly interest of the staff there. In particular, I enjoyed working with Robert Amsler, who provided programming support for the project. Thanks to his unfailing promptness and competence, I never missed a deadline in my work schedule. Helen Jo Hewitt generously taught me how to create and edit my files and took on the job of producing a high quality printed manuscript for me. I especially appreciated her good humor and that of Clive Dawson of the UT Computation Center, who not only provided clear, helpful advice on countless occasions, but once arranged for the computer to talk back to me in the elegantly courteous seventeenth-century Spanish of my input data. The computer's competence in older Spanish was, however, only the palest reflection of the human competence of Gilka Wara Céspedes, who undertook to check the Spanish throughout the dictionary, especially the modernization of the spelling of the oldest sources.

Among my fellow Nahuatlatos at other institutions, I have especially to thank J. Richard Andrews, who in the glossary to his book on Classical Nahuatl set the standards for this dictionary, and Arthur J. O. Anderson, who provided me with information about the original manuscript of the Clavigero grammar in Bologna. R. Joe Campbell was first my teacher at Indiana University, then a fellow worker at the computation center there, and finally another practitioner of computational

Nahuatl lexicography. We have benefited from each other's experience and enthusiasm. I also have Una Canger to thank for an important piece of advice. Early in the project she said that the exact format of the dictionary was less important than clear explanations of what I was doing, how, and why. On occasion, when I have been tempted to impose some sort of rigid and less than obvious consistency on the dictionary, I have recalled her advice and instead provided attestations and commentary.

Lauri Karttunen has shared an interest in computation with me since 1965, and I owe him a great deal for his generous help and supplementary programming support and for boundless confidence in this project.

And then there are our predecessors, all the Nahuatl grammarians from the missionary friars to the fieldworkers practicing today, first among them Horacio Carochi, whose 1645 grammar is a major source for this dictionary.

This work is dedicated to Margaret Harwood, who performed a lifetime of meticulous astronomical research, returned a full measure of honor and support to Radcliffe College, promoted scientific education within and beyond the Nantucket school system, and was my beloved friend. Without her example and encouragement I would have dared less and missed the joys of accomplishment that came into full bloom during the compilation of this dictionary. I am deeply grateful that she and I were able to share the excitement of it all in the last weeks of her ninety-fourth year.

USER'S GUIDE

Three principles have shaped the format of this dictionary. The first is adherence to established convention, the second involves justification and support for choices made, and the third is the principle of less is more. For the user's convenience I will present here the individual parts of a dictionary entry one at a time, explaining how these principles apply. Although I hope the user will also care to read the lengthier Introduction following, which provides background material in considerable detail, the basic information here is crucial to the use of the dictionary.

An entry may contain up to seven parts, although brief ones may contain as few as two. The seven parts are (1) the canonical form, (2) grammatical information, (3) the English gloss, (4) the Spanish gloss, (5) attestations, (6) commentary, and (7) reference.

CANONICAL FORM

By 'canonical' I mean that which is basic and can be related to other forms by general rules. The canonical form of a word not only regularizes the different spelling conventions of the sources for this dictionary but also predicts, insofar as possible, its inflectional paradigm—that is, what shape the word will take when prefixes and suffixes are added to it. (For details, please see the Introduction.)

The word is printed in capitals. For nouns, the absolutive suffix (-TLI, -TL, -LI, -IN) is separated from the stem by a hyphen. Vowels and consonants that are dropped in some inflected, derived, or compounded forms of the stem are parenthesized. A macron over a vowel indicates that it is a long vowel. Glottal stops are printed as H. The H of CH, UH, and HU does not indicate a glottal stop, however; these digraphs (two letters used together to represent a single sound) have their traditional Nahuatl orthographic value.

Nahuatl, Spanish, and English share the consonant represented by CH, and both Spanish and Nahuatl conventionally alphabetize it after C. But Nahuatl has additional unitary consonants that are represented by digraphs, and these are treated in the same manner as CH is with respect to C. Hence, the initial alphabetical order for the sections of the dictionary reflects Nahuatl phonology rather than English or Spanish conventions of alphabetization. The sections have the following order A, C, CH, CU, E, HU, I, M, N, O, P, QU, T, TL, TZ, X, Y, Z. (No Nahuatl words begin with L or glottal stop.) Within these sections, for the user's convenience, conventional English alphabetization is observed.

The spelling of the canonical forms here is consistent with, although not quite identical to, that used by J. Richard Andrews in his Classical Nahuatl textbook. (The Introduction discusses this in detail.) This is in the interest of ease of use, since, with the exception of the H for glottal stop and Z for common ç, the notation is as close to traditional Nahuatl orthography as possible, given the lack of orthographic standardization that has characterized Nahuatl writing through the centuries.

The use of a diacritic, the macron over long vowels, does not disturb alphabetization and poses no difficulty to the user of this dictionary. The user accustomed to the colonial-period ç may find Z an inelegant substitution, but it does, after all, follow modern Spanish spelling conventions. The use of the letter H for glottal stop, which traditionally has been indicated with a diacritic or omitted, really does make the search for Nahuatl words in this dictionary more difficult, since the presence of an H will upset the expected alphabetical order and put a word elsewhere than where one would look in the dictionaries of Molina or Siméon. If the user fails to find a word on the first search, that does not necessarily mean that the word is missing from the dictionary. The burden is on the user to search again for the word with an H at the end of the first syllable, then the second, etc., until all possibilities have been exhausted. For instance, textual *içahuia* or *izahuia* 'to frighten someone' and *iztac* 'something white' will be found under ĪZAHUIĀ and IZTĀC respectively. But *iça* or *iza* 'to wake up' will be found under IHZA.

There are quite a few pairs of words derived from a single stem by reduplication of the first consonant and vowel, one with a glottal stop and the other with a long vowel and no glottal stop, which are distinct in meaning. An example is XEHXELOĀ 'to divide something up into portions' and XĒXELOĀ 'to slice something', both from XELOĀ 'to divide something'. It would be instructive to have such pairs together for contrast, but, because of the convention of writing the glottal stop as H, they are separated in this dictionary. To compensate for this, for each member of the pair the other member is mentioned in the commentary.

The reasons for introducing H with its attendant difficulties into the dictionary are several. First of all, when Andrews made it part of his notation, he was following a venerable precedent. Although glottal stops are not consistently indicated in Molina's 1571 dictionary, he uses *h* for the ones he does indicate. The *h* convention springs up time and again in colonial Nahuatl writing, despite Carochi's authoritative use of a diacritic for what was called the *saltillo*. This reflects an accurate understanding of Nahuatl phonology. Whereas long and short vowels are distinguished by a feature of pronunciation, namely duration of the vowel in question, the *saltillo* is in fact a consonant following a vowel, not just some peculiarity of the vowel itself. As a full consonant like any other (no matter how alien it may seem to English or Spanish speakers), it can affect the shape a word assumes when affixes are added to it. Hence, vowel length is appropriately marked by a diacritic, while the glottal stop is appropriately written as a letter, and this dictionary observes phonological accuracy, recent precedent, and one vein of historical tradition in doing so. This justification notwithstanding, I appreciate the inconvenience to the user of the dictionary and hope that time and familiarity will ease the burden.

GRAMMATICAL INFORMATION

In the absence of specific grammatical information to the contrary in an entry, a word is inflected by the regular rules of Nahuatl morphology. That is, the stem retains its basic shape or changes in a way common to all stems with comparable shape and takes prefixes and suffixes as described in any Nahuatl reference grammar. If the inflection is unpredictable from the canonical form or irregular, and if the sources for this dictionary provide examples of the inflection, then this information is given here, immediately following the canonical form of the word. Typically this will involve plural and possessive forms of nouns and preterit forms of verbs. If alternative forms of these are attested, the variants are given separated by a wavy line. If a regular phonological process is reflected orthographically, then it is given here even if it is predictable. For instance, the preterit form of NEM(I) 'to live' is NEN. The change of M to N is regular and predictable, but the preterit form is given as a reminder to the dictionary user.

In the case of long words, when grammatical information concerns only the end, the whole word is not reproduced, but instead there is abbreviation to the last element, with a hyphen indicating that the preceding material remains unchanged.

The grammatical section also indicates part of speech, such as postposition, particle, exclamation, etc. If an entry is not specifically identified, the less-is-more principle is at work, and the part of speech is obvious from the gloss.

Transitive verbs are those that require a direct object; intransitive ones do not take a direct object. An example of an English transitive verb is *eat* in the sentence 'He ate the food,' while *sing* is intransitive in 'She sang beautifully.' English, however, allows some latitude in transitivity, as illustrated by 'He eats at noon every day' and 'She sang the song.' On the other hand, Nahuatl strictly distinguishes transitive from intransitive verbs, and for that reason the transitive ones are labeled here. Generally speaking, transitive verbs may be used reflexively, in which case one performs some action upon oneself or to one's own benefit or causes oneself to engage in some activity. But not all transitive verbs are in fact so used, and there are a few verbs in Nahuatl which have come to be used exclusively reflexively. For this reason, verbs are labeled not only transitive but also reflexive if that use is attested. Here a convention established by Molina is observed, and the reflexive use is indicated before the transitive use, even though the former is a special case of the latter. By the less-is-more principle a verb not labeled reflexive and/or transitive is intransitive.

ENGLISH GLOSS

The aim of the English gloss is to convey the basic meaning of the word. This has sometimes resulted in an English gloss more literal than the following Spanish one, so the two should be taken together, the Spanish gloss amplifying the English one.

If a word has more than one meaning, and they are at some distance from each other semantically, the different senses are given separated by a semicolon. On the other hand, there are some completely different words that happen to be homophonous (that is, to have identical canonical forms), and in these cases there are separate main entries.

Another use of the semicolon in the English gloss is with transitive verbs which are also used reflexively. For such verbs the reflexive sense appears first, separated from the transitive gloss by a semicolon.

For some transparent compound words no English gloss is given, but there is cross reference to the constituent parts. In the case of some common derived forms, there is also no gloss, but the reference section identifies what form it is. (Please see the section under Reference below.)

SPANISH GLOSS

Following the English gloss and separated from it by a slash is the Spanish gloss. By choice this is from Molina's dictionary and is so identified by (M) after the gloss. As an aid to the user, I have modernized Molina's Spanish spelling. Molina has separate entries for reflexive and transitive uses of verbs, with the reflexive preceding any and all others and later glosses often referring back to the reflexive gloss. I have followed the practice here, since it would be awkward to reorder them.

When a gloss from Molina is not available, I have chosen one from another source or, in the few cases where no Spanish gloss has been available, I have written one myself and indicated that I have done so with (K). Please see the list of abbreviations at the end of this guide for the other letters identifying sources.

ATTESTATIONS

Following the Spanish gloss there may be a list of attestations with the source identified by initial and the location by folio or page number. If no attestations are listed, the less-is-more principle is again at work; absence of such information means that the word is widely and consistently attested across sources.

COMMENTARY

The commentary typically contains information about inconsistency in attestation, unexpected form or meaning, other words minimally contrasting in shape and susceptible to confusion, etc. The commentary section also provides room for substantial grammatical discussion where necessary and for comparison of literal meaning with conventional usage in cases where the two are rather far apart.

Two symbols that appear in this section, always between two canonical forms, may be unfamiliar: < means that the first form is derived from the second, while > means that the first is the derivational source of the second.

REFERENCE

The references direct the user to other relevant entries in the dictionary. In the case of a compound word, the component elements are given here; in the case of a derived word, there is reference to the derivational source. In the case of applicative, causative, and nonactive verb forms, the cross reference indicates which it is and gives the basic verb from which it is formed. The reference section also identifies the source of words in which the initial syllable has been reduplicated.

This dictionary is not intended to replace the great dictionaries of Molina and Siméon. Molina's dictionary has approximately 23,600 entries, while this one has fewer than 9,000. The number of Molina's entries is inflated by his practice of making separate main entries of reflexive and transitive uses of verbs and of having plural forms, insofar as he includes them, as main entries. On the other hand, this dictionary includes relatively more applicative and nonactive verb forms.

But there are some simple, basic words that appear in Molina that are not attested in any of the sources for this dictionary. One example is *eptli* 'oyster'. About this word we cannot know if the first vowel is long or short. Another omission is *tlalalacatl* 'goose', in which any of the first three syllables might contain a short vowel, a long vowel, or a short vowel and glottal stop. Because no source provides us with information about these words, they do not appear in this dictionary.

On the other hand, many of the words Molina has that are missing from this dictionary are compound or derived forms, and the component parts are indeed in this dictionary. If the whole cannot be found here, the parts almost always can.

This dictionary is rigid in its exclusion of Spanish loanwords, more so than Molina, who admitted several hundred, including *cuentaxtli* 'rosary beads' and *hicox* 'fig' from Spanish *cuenta* and *higo*, respectively. The reason for the relentless nativism of this dictionary is that loanwords exist in the language in all stages of assimilation to the phonology of the language, as can be seen in the two examples from Molina given here. As a result, it is rather meaningless to assign canonical forms to them, existing as they do in transit from one language to the other.

To reiterate, this dictionary is not to displace Molina and Siméon. Its purpose is to provide two things not to be found in those two dictionaries: (1) modern English glosses and (2) information about long vowels and glottal stops in individual words. Spanish-based orthography for Nahuatl obscured the second, and this dictionary—the result of detailed comparative work—is a contribution to the renewed interest in the actual phonology of the language behind the traditional orthographic representation. If we are only in this decade returning to Horacio Carochi's fold, still it is better late than never.

If the user's interest is only in glosses, the detailed commentary on phonology and conflicting attestations may seem very tedious, and the fact that this dictionary is only a third as large as the previous ones may be a disappointment. I hope that the analytical aspect of the dictionary, expressed both in the English glosses and in the references between entries, will compensate. Let this dictionary join the others as fellow and companion, a means to explication and clarification; it is not intended as a competitor.

If it could be done without increasing the bulk of this volume, I would want to print on every other page an exhortation to read the Introduction, which provides further keys to understanding and using this work. Please read it and return to it from time to time.

ABBREVIATIONS

The following letters identify sources for this dictionary. With Spanish glosses they are parenthesized. For attestations they are followed by page or folio numbers, and folio numbers are in turn followed by r for *recto* or v for *verso*. Hence [(2)Cf.120v] indicates that the word is attested twice in Carochi's grammar on folio 120 verso.

B   'Huehuetlatolli.' Ms. M-M 458, Bancroft Library, University of California, Berkeley, Early seventeenth century.

C   Horacio Carochi. *Arte de la lengua mexicana con la declaración de los adverbios della*. Mexico City: Juan Ruiz, 1645.

K   Frances Karttunen. (This appears only with a small number of Spanish glosses.)

M   Fray Alonso de Molina. *Vocabulario en lengua castellana y mexicana y mexicana y castellana*. Mexico City: Porrúa, 1970. Facsimile of 1571 edition.

P   Ignacio de Paredes. *Promptuario manual mexicano*. Mexico City: Bibliotheca Mexicana, 1759.

R   Francis Xavier Clavigero. 'Regalas de la lengua mexican." Ms. Mezzofanti XXII-10, Biblioteca dell' Archiginnasio, Bologna, Mid eighteenth century.

S   Rémi Siméon. 'Diccionario de la lengua nahuatl o mexicana.' Mexico City: Siglo Veintiuno, 1977. Originally published in Paris, 1885.

T   Forrest Brewer and Jean G. Brewer. *Vocabulario de Tetelcingo, Morelos*. Mexico City: Summer Institute of Linguistics, 1971.

X   Cleofas Ramírez de Alejandro and Karen Dakin. *Vocabulario náhuatl de Xalitla, Guerrero; Cuadernos de la Casa Chata 25*. Mexico City: Centro de Investigaciones Superiores del Instituto Nacional de Antropología e Historia, 1979.

Z   Harold Key and Mary Ritchie de Key. *Vocabulario de la Sierra de Zacapoaxtla, Puebla*. Mexico City: Summer Institute of Linguistics, 1953.

The following are abbreviations of grammatical terms:

altern.	alternate
applic.	applicative
caus.	causative
nonact.	nonactive
pers.	person
poss.	possessive
postp.	postposition
pl.	plural
pres.	present
pret.	preterit
redup.	reduplicated
sg.	singular
vrefl.	reflexive verb
vt.	transitive verb

INTRODUCTION

BACKGROUND

Nahuatl is the best documented of Native American languages. At the time of the Spanish conquest of Mexico it was the dominant language of Mesoamerica, and Spanish friars immediately set about learning it. Some of them made heroic efforts to preach in Nahuatl and to hear confessions in the language. To aid in these endeavors they devised an orthography based on Spanish conventions and composed Nahuatl-language breviaries, confessional guides, and collections of sermons which were among the first books printed in the New World. Nahuatl speakers were taught to read and write their own language, and under the friars' direction the surviving guardians of oral tradition set down in writing the particulars of their shattered culture in the *Florentine Codex*[1] and other ethnographic collections of Fray Bernardino de Sahagún and his contemporaries.

Writing soon passed from the church into Indian hands. The Nahua and many of their neighbors shared an indigenous Mesoamerican literary tradition; before the conquest they had created and regularly consulted paper books in which records were kept in a partially pictorial, partially syllabic notation. It was not difficult to make the transition to alphabetic writing, and soon every substantial Central Mexican Indian town had a notary who kept the local records in written Nahuatl. This practice carried through the entire colonial period.

Because of the vigorous initial activity of the friars and the fertile environment in which it took root, Nahuatl has been thoroughly described and documented over a period of more than four hundred years. Among the monuments of this tradition are a whole series of grammars and two great dictionaries, that of Fray Alonso de Molina, published in 1571,[2] and the Nahuatl-French dictionary of Rémi Siméon, published in 1885[3] and republished in Spanish translation in 1977.[4] These dictionaries, together with Horacio Carochi's 1645 grammar,[5] are the most important reference works about Nahuatl in existence.

1. Sahagún, Fray Bernadino de. *Florentine Codex: General History of the Things of New Spain.*Ed. and trans. Arthur J. O. Anderson and Charles Dibble. 13 vols. Salt Lake City: University of Utah Press, and Santa Fe: School of American Research, 1950-1969.
2. Molina, Fray Alonso de. *Vocabulario en lengua castellana y mexicana y mexicana y castellana.*Mexico City: Antonio de Spinoza, 1571.
3. Siméon, Rémi. *Dictionnaire de la langue nahuatl ou mexicaine.* Paris: Imprimerie Nationale, 1885.
4. Siméon, Rémi. *Diccionario de la lengua nahuatl o mexicana.* Trans. Josefina Oliva de Coll. Mexico City: Siglo Veintiuno, 1977.
5. Carochi, Horacio. *Arte de la lengua mexicana con la declaración de los adverbios della.* Mexico City: Juan Ruiz, 1645.

The dictionaries are, however, like almost all colonial-period Nahuatl texts, written in a Spanish-based orthography that ignores two vital aspects of the phonology of the language—the distinction between long and short vowels and the glottal stop as a consonant. Since Spaniards had great difficulty in hearing these, while Nahuatl speakers knew, except in truly contextually ambiguous cases, where long vowels and glottal stops were located, neither group adopted spelling conventions to indicate their presence. The grammarian Carochi consistently used a system of diacritics to represent the information, but it was not widely adopted. The great dictionaries are somewhat analogous to an English dictionary lacking the letter P and failing to distinguish between I and E. Entirely different words fall together as single dictionary entries. Molina's *auatl*, for example, subsumes AHHUA-TL 'thorn', ĀHUA-TL 'oak', and ĀHUĀ-TL 'woolly caterpillar'. AHTLĀCA-TL 'cruel, inhuman person' and ĀTLAHCA-TL 'sailor, fisherman' fall together into the single entry *atlacatl* in Molina. Carochi distinguishes them and introduces ĀTLĀCA-TL 'person made of water' for a three-way contrast.

In 1975 J. Richard Andrews published *Introduction to Classical Nahuatl*[6] with a glossary in which long vowels are printed with macrons and glottal stops are printed as H. He drew his information mainly from the grammatical examples in Carochi's grammar, with additional support from the occasional orthographic indication of glottal stop in the *Florentine Codex* and from a dictionary of modern Tetelcingo Nahuatl.[7]

This analytical dictionary is based on exhaustive compilation and comparison of all the material in Carochi and the Tetelcingo dictionary plus several other sources. The most important of these are a manuscript located in the Bancroft Library of the University of California, Berkeley,[8] and a dictionary of modern Zacapoaxtla Nahuatl.[9] In these four primary sources, two early and two modern, vowel length and glottal stop are systematically represented in the orthography, although the conventions vary somewhat from source to source. Several other sources contribute secondary support, among them Francis Xavier Clavigero's eighteenth-century grammar,[10] a book of Nahuatl sermons published in the eighteenth century by Ignacio Paredes,[11] and a word list of modern Xalitla Nahuatl.[12]

6. Andrews, J. Richard. *Introduction to Classical Nahuatl.* Austin: University of Texas Press, 1975.

7. Brewer, Forrest, and Jean G. Brewer. *Vocabulario mexicano de Tetelcingo, Morelos.* Mexico City: Summer Institute of Linguistics, 1971.

8. 'Huehuetlatolli.' Ms. M-M 458, Bancroft Library, University of California, Berkeley. Early seventeenth century.

9. Key, Harold, and Mary Ritchie de Key. *Vocabulario de la Sierra de Zacapoaxtla, Puebla.* Mexico City: Summer Institute of Linguistics, 1953.

10. Clavigero, Francis Xavier. 'Reglas de la lengua mexicana.' Ms. Mezzofanti XXII-10, Biblioteca dell' Archiginnasio, Bologna. Mid eighteenth century.

11. Paredes, Ignacio de. *Promptuario manual mexicano.* Mexico City: Bibliotheca Mexicana, 1759.

12. Ramírez, Cleofas de Alejandro, and Karen Dakin. *Vocabulario náhuatl de Xalitla, Guerrero; Cuadernos de la Casa Chata 25.* Mexico City: Centro de Investigaciones Superiores del Instituto Nacional de Antropología e Historia, 1979.

THE SOURCES

In his *Arte de la lengua mexicana con la declaración de los adverbios della*, Horacio Carochi marks long vowels with a macron and short vowels with an acute accent. When a vowel is followed by a glottal stop, he uses a circumflex over the vowel if it is phrase-final and a grave accent on the vowel otherwise /ē/ = ē, /e/ = é, /eʔ/ = ê, è. In general he marks short vowels specifically short only in contrastive contexts. Otherwise, a vowel without a diacritic is intended as short with one reservation: in certain high-frequency items with long vowels, especially in grammatical particles, Carochi only uses a macron when the item itself is under direct discussion. When it is incidental to discussion of some other item or when the vowel length has been explicitly stated earlier in the section, the macron is omitted. Because of this practice, a vowel that has a macron in even a small percentage of attestations of an item in Carochi can be considered to be long if there is no evidence to the contrary. Carochi includes in his grammar a very useful list of pairs of words contrasting in vowel length and the presence or absence of glottal stop, which is an amplification of a list that first appeared in the Nahuatl grammar of Antonio de Rincón, published in 1595.[13]

A group at the University of Copenhagen has compiled the *Diccionario de vocablos aztecas contenidos en el arte de la lengua mexicana de Horacio Carochi*,[14] a work based on the 1892 edition of Carochi in the National Museum's *Colección de gramáticas de la lengua mexicana*.[15] Since many errors were introduced in that reprinting, the Danish work has not been used as a contributing source to this dictionary, which is based on the original text with its significantly higher internal consistency. Because the *Compendio del arte de la lengua mexicana del P. Horacio Carochi*[16] published by Ignacio de Paredes in 1759 is derivative and also less accurate in its diacritics, it too has not been used as a source here.

The manuscript preserved by the Bancroft Library is an exemplar of the indigenous literary genre known as *huehuetlatolli* 'sayings of the elders'. This particular text is less a set of maxims for leading a well-ordered life than a collection of dialogues written in polite conversational style illustrating how persons of different rank and age should address one another on various occasions. It consists of thirteen densely written folios, and the diacritics used are as in Carochi except that a real breve is used to mark short vowels rather than an acute accent /e/ = ĕ. The manuscript is internally consistent and consistent with Carochi. A few errors in the diacritics have been marked and corrected, and at the end is written *Estos retazos de excelente Megicano son escritos por Dn. Miguel, Mro. de P. Oracio*. It

13. Rincón, Antonio del. *Arte mexicana*. Mexico City: Pedro Balli, 1595.

14. Adrian, Karen, Una Canger, Kjeld K. Lings, Jette Nilsson, and Anne Schlanbusch. *Diccionario de vocablos aztecas contenidos en el Arte de la lengua mexicana de Horacio Carochi*. Copenhagen: University of Copenhagen, 1976.

15. Carochi, Horacio. 'Arte de la lengua mexicana con la declaración de los adverbios della,' in *Colección de gramáticas de la lengua mexicana*, pp. 396-536. Mexico City: Imprenta del Museo Nacional, 1892.

16. Paredes, Ignacio de. *Compendio del Arte de la lengua mexicana del P. Horacio Carochi*. Mexico City: Bibliotheca Mexicana, 1759.

is tempting to take this to mean that the manuscript was written by a Nahuatl speaker under Carochi's personal direction and with Carochi's own corrections.

In 1943 Angel María Garibay published this manuscript under the title 'Huehue-tlatolli, Documento A' in the first two issues of the journal *Tlalocan*,[17] but he omitted the diacritics and also folios 10v and 11r. This dictionary returns to the original manuscript as a source.

The Nahuatl of Tetelcingo, Morelos, has been thoroughly investigated by linguists Richard S. Pittman,[18] Forrest Brewer,[19] and Jean G. Brewer and has been found to preserve vowel length distinctions as vowel quality distinctions. The difference between /ī/ and /i/ is realized as a contrast between tense and lax vowels; /ē/ is distinct from /e/ by having diphthongized to [ie]; /ā/ has labialized; and /ō/ is realized as [u]. In their dictionary Brewer and Brewer use the following notation.

long vowels   *i, ie, ö, u*
short vowels   *i̠, e, a, o*

(Pittman used slightly different notation but described the values of his notation in virtually the same way.)

Although the changes in pronunciation have maximized the vowel-length distinctions, other phonological rules are a source of significant ambiguity in the Tetelcingo dictionary. Distinct from the diphthongization of long /ē/, there has been a rule of initial glide formation. EZ-TLI 'blood', which is consistently attested in other sources with a short vowel, appears as *yeztli*. No Nahuatl words in the Tetelcingo dictionary begin with *e* or *ie*. They are all together and undistinguished as *ye*. The sequence YA also often appears as *ye*; in derivations involving YAC(A)-TL 'nose' there is *yeca-*.

There has been sporadic loss of glottal stop in Tetelcingo, notably in the negative particle *amo* for AHMŌ but also within stems. Where there is a reflex of a glottal stop, it is written as *j*. This leads to ambiguity because of a rule that dissimilates adjacent identical consonants (except for the sequence LL, which simply de-geminates—*cali* for CAL-LI 'house'), *ijta* for ITTA 'to see', *mijqui* for MICQUI /mikki/ 'corpse.' Hence, a consonant preceded by *j* in the Tetelcingo dictionary may correspond to a consonant preceded by a glottal stop or to a sequence of identical consonants elsewhere.

Generally speaking, Nahuatl is very given to dropping syllable-final nasal consonants. For word-final N this has become a general rule in Tetelcingo, although in

17. Garibay, Angel María. 'Huehuetlatolli, Documento A,' *Tlalocan* 1(1):31-53 and 1(2):81-107 (1943).

18. Pittman, Richard S. *A Grammar of Tetelcingo (Morelos) Nahuatl.* Language Dissertation 50. Baltimore: Linguistic Society of America, 1954, and 'The Phonemes of Tetelcingo (Morelos) Nahuatl,' in *A William Cameron Townsend en el XXV Aniversario del Instituto de Lingüístico de Verano*, pp. 643-651. Mexico City: Summer Institute of Linguistics, 1961.

19. Brewer, Forrest. 'Morelos (Tetelcingo) Nahuatl Verb Stem Constructions' in *Aztec Studies I: Phonological and Grammatical Studies in Modern Nahuatl Dialects*,ed. Dow F. Robinson pp. 33-42. Norman: Summer Institute of Linguistics, 1969.

many cases, but not all, the missing consonants still turn up when followed by suffixes.

Despite these local complexities, the Tetelcingo dictionary is remarkably consistent with Carochi and the Bancroft manuscript. It is also internally consistent and appears to contain the same material in the Spanish-to-Nahuatl side as in the Nahuatl-to-Spanish side. For this dictionary only the Nahuatl-to-Spanish side was exhaustively surveyed.

The Nahuatl of Zacapoaxtla is a T-dialect; it has lost the characteristic lateral release of TL. Otherwise, judging from the *Vocabulario mejicano de la Sierra de Zacapoaxtla, Puebla*, by Harold Key and Mary Ritchie de Key, it is not distant, at least lexically, from the Nahuatl described by Carochi. It retains word-final nasals and apparently shortens all geminate consonants; *cali* for CAL-LI 'house', *ita* for ITTA 'to see', *miquet* for MICQUI 'corpse'. In any case, there is no evidence of dissimilation of identical consonants or qualitative distinction of short and long vowels. Short vowels in stressed syllables are often given as long, but this may be an interpretation imposed by the fieldworkers rather than a fact of local speech.

The notation used includes *j* for the local reflex of glottal stop and underlining for long vowels (so that *i* for Zacapoaxtla is the opposite of *i* for Tetelcingo).

/ī/ = *i*	/ē/ = *e*	/ā/ = *a*	/ō/ = *o*
/i/ = *i*	/e/ = *e*	/a/ = *a*	/o/ = *o*

This source is more problematical by far than the Tetelcingo dictionary. Originally only the Nahuatl-to-Spanish side was surveyed for present purposes. Serious conflicts with the other sources led to consultation of the Spanish-to-Nahuatl side, and it became immediately clear that no effort had been made to monitor internal consistency. As an example, under *bocio* 'tumor of the neck' is found *quechtamalayoj*. On the Nahuatl-to-Spanish side is given *quechtamalayoj*. The literal sense of this is apparently from QUECH-TLI 'neck' and TAMALAYOH-TLI, which according to Molina is a type of squash. This appears in the Zacapoaxtla dictionary as *tamal ayoj* and is transparently derived in its turn from TAMAL-LI 'tamale' and AYOH-TLI 'squash'. In three different places in the same dictionary are given *-tamalayoj*, *-tamalayoj*, and *tamal ayoj*. Of these, the first is wrong in terms of its constituent parts; the second is phonologically impossible, since in Nahuatl there are no long vowels before glottal stops or their reflexes; and the third agrees with other sources but should be written solid. This is perhaps one of the worst cases, but unfortunately it is not uncharacteristic. The strategy here has been to accept the Zacapoaxtla form as supporting evidence when it is consistent with other sources, to check the entry on the Spanish-to-Nahuatl side in case of inconsistency or rare attestation, and to report inconsistencies in the commentary section of an entry here. The user of this dictionary should bear in mind that a form attested only in Zacapoaxtla is not as solid as one attested in the other primary sources.

Despite the inconsistencies, the Zacapoaxtla dictionary is tremendously valuable and rewarding because there are many items shared by Molina and Zacapoaxtla and to be found nowhere else. It is endlessly gratifying to find a word attested twice at a distance of nearly four hundred years.

Francis Xavier Clavigero wrote his *Reglas de la lengua mexicana* in Italy during the latter part of the eighteenth century after the expulsion of the Jesuits from Mexico. From his examples and the wording of some grammatical discussion, it appears that he knew Carochi's grammar well, most likely in the form of Paredes' *Compendio*, but that he did not have a copy with him in exile. He uses the macron for long vowels, the acute accent for short vowels, and the grave accent and circumflex for vowels followed by glottal stops as Carochi does, but the diacritics are sparse. So many are omitted that the absence of a diacritic is not significant. Only those items specifically marked with diacritics can contribute to this dictionary and then only in a supporting role, not as definitive attestations. The grammatical examples within the text are mostly marked with diacritics that convey inflectional sense, such as preterit or plural, but the appended word list of nearly 3,500 items, which reflects Clavigero's personal interest in animals and medicinal plants, includes a significant number of words with internal diacritics.

The *Reglas* remained an unpublished manuscript in the Biblioteca dell' Archiginnasio in Bologna until Arthur J. O. Anderson published an English translation in the United States in 1973[20] and a Spanish translation in Mexico the following year.[21] Only the Mexican publication includes the word list.

In 1759, the same year that he published his *Compendio* of Carochi, Ignacio de Paredes also published *Promptuario manual mexicano*, a book of homilies in Nahuatl. In these short sermons the grave accent and the circumflex are used to mark the presence of glottal stops. Distinctive vowel length is not indicated. These diacritics serve as additional support for forms attested elsewhere.

Among modern dialects of Nahuatl, Tetelcingo and Zacapoaxtla stand at considerable distance from one another. Xalitla is a town geographically quite far from both of them, but it also preserves vowel-length distinctions. In their *Vocabulario nahuatl de Xalitla, Guerrero*, a list of approximately 1,500 items, Cleofas Ramírez de Alejandro and Karen Dakin indicate long vowels with the macron. An *h* in their notation has several sources. It is the reflex of the first of two identical consonants in forms such as *tlayōhli* for TLAŌL-LI 'shelled corn', *nahpa* for NĀPPA 'four times' (ultimately from NĀUHPA), and *mihqui* from MICQUI 'corpse'. Ramírez and Dakin also have *h* for /w/ after a long vowel. And in some inflectional suffixes *h* represents the reflex of glottal stop.

The vowel-length marking in the Xalitla word list is not exhaustive; in this respect the list resembles Clavigero's. Items with macrons can be used to support other attestations, but the absence of a macron does not guarantee that the vowel is short. Some modern dialects of Nahuatl appear to have lost vowel-length distinctions altogether and others seem to preserve only vestiges of it. Perhaps Xalitla represents a transitional stage in which some long vowels are retained in lexically frozen forms while elsewhere the distinction between short and long is neutralized.

In *Los mil elementos del mexicano clásico*[22] Morris Swadesh and Madalena

20. Anderson, Arthur J. O., ed. and trans. *Rules of the Aztec Language: Classical Nahuatl Grammar*. Salt Lake City: University of Utah Press, 1973.

21. Anderson, Arthur J. O., ed. and trans. *Reglas de la lengua mexicana con un vocabulario*. Mexico City: Instituto de Investigaciones Históricas. 1974.

22. Swadesh, Morris, and Madalena Sancho. *Los mil elementos del mexicano clásico*. Mexico City: Instituto de Investigaciones Históricas, 1966.

Sancho use the macron for long vowels and an apostrophe for glottal stops. Since their source is the 1892 edition of Carochi with its introduced printing errors, and since all of the original Carochi has been surveyed for this dictionary, their publication is not used as a contributing source here.

ORGANIZATION

The format of the dictionary entries has been described in the User's Guide; here is each section again, explained and justified at somewhat greater length.

THE CANONICAL FORM

The canonical form of each word is based on comparison of all attestations, taken together with the general rules of Nahuatl word-formation and phonology. It is printed in capitals at the head of the entry. Other canonical forms referred to within the entry are also printed in capitals. This canonical notation is very close to traditional orthography, which facilitates reference between dictionary and most Nahuatl texts. The letters used represent essentially the same sounds as they do in Spanish with the addition of TL /tˡ/, TZ /tˢ/, and X /š/. The sequence LL represents two adjacent /l/'s and not the /lʸ/ or /y/ of Spanish. A departure from older Nahuatl conventions is the use before A and O of Z and CU. What would be written in older texts as *ça* 'only' and *qualli* 'good' appear here as ZĀ and CUAL-LI. HU and CU represent /w/ and /kʷ/ respectively as in Spanish, but these sounds can be syllable-final in Nahuatl, and when they are, the order of the letters is reversed to UH, UC.

HUEL	/wel/	'fully, very, well'
IUH	/iw/	'thus'
CUAL-LI	/kʷalli/	'good'
TĒUC-TLI	/tekʷtˡi/	'lord'

In traditional Nahuatl writing, the CU was not always inverted, and this conveyed the false impression of a syllable [ku] in forms like *tecutli* for TĒUC-TLI.

With the enrichment of long-vowel marking and H for glottal stop, this close-to-traditional orthography represents Nahuatl unambiguously.

Table 1 shows the correspondence among the sounds of Nahuatl, the canonical spelling, and traditional spelling.

As mentioned in the User's Guide, the canonical forms of this dictionary are very close notationally to what J. Richard Andrews uses in his *Introduction to Classical Nahuatl*, but there are some differences. The canonical forms here are slightly more abstracted from actual pronunciation than Andrews', in that certain regular rules that affect pronunciation are not reflected in the canonical forms. A major example is the long vowel at the end of what Andrews calls Class C verbs. In his glossary they appear with final IA and OA, but here they appear as IĀ and OĀ. In actual pronunciation, the long vowels are shortened at the ends of words, but they remain long when followed by a suffix. The canonical form here indicates their underlying length, while Andrews' notation does not. In spite of this abstraction, however, the canonical form of this dictionary is not identical with a pho-

TABLE 1. Vowels

sound	canonical spelling	traditional spelling
/a/	A	*a*
/ā/	Ā	*a*
/e/	E	*e*
/ē/	Ē	*e*
/i/	I	*i, y, j*
/ī/	Ī	*i, y, j*
/o/	O	*o*
/ō/	Ō	*o,u*

Consonants

/p/	P	*p*
/t/	T	*t*
/k/	C, QU	*c,qu*
/ʔ/	H	*h* (usually omitted)
/tˢ/	TZ	*tz*
/tˡ/	TL	*tl*
/č/	CH	*ch*
/kʷ/	CU, UC	*qu, cu, uc*
/s/	C,Z	*c, ç, s, z*
/š/	X	*x*
/m/	M	*m,n*
/n/	N	*n*
/l/	L	*l*
/w/	HU, UH	*hu, u, v, o, uh*
/y/	Y	*y, i, j*

nemic or a historically prior proto-form. It leans to the conservative Nahuatl of the central Mexican highlands and includes some historical innovation of form from that area. Nonetheless, the canonical form can to a high degree be related in a regular fashion to even the most peripheral of the regional dialects of the contributing sources.

In his glossary, where stems appear as main entries and derivations as subentries, Andrews makes use of parentheses and hyphens to convey morphological information. This serves the purpose of teaching families of related words and elucidating their relationships, but it hampers search for individual words, since the user must often make guesses about the stem. TLAXCAL-LI 'tortilla', for instance is to be found only under Andrews' iXCA 'to bake something in hot coals'. Because compactness and pedagogy are not at issue for this dictionary, extensive use of cross reference replaces much of Andrews' morphological machinery. Parentheses, hyphens, and asterisks are used in canonical forms here to convey different information than in Andrews.

Parentheses enclose a segment that is regularly dropped in a predictable environment. For many nouns the possessed form drops not only the absolute suffix but also the last vowel of the stem.

YAC(A)-TL   'nose'
ĪYAC   'his nose'

Many verbs drop their final vowels in forming the preterit, and the same paren-
thesis notation is used.

YŌL(I)   'to live'
YŌLI   'he lives'
ŌYŌL   'he lived'

A third case of vowel-dropping involves initial short I. In some, but not all, stems
in which it is followed by a consonant cluster, I drops when preceded by a prefix
ending in a vowel. Since there are exceptions to this rule, Andrews distinguishes
the 'weak' vowel that is susceptible to deletion from its strong unalternating counterpart by printing it in lower case as with iXCA above. Here it is parenthesized.

(I)TTA   'to see something'
TLATTA   'he sees something'
MOTTA   'he sees himself'

An example of contrasting (I) and I is the following.

(I)ZTE-TL 'fingernail'   NOZTI 'my fingernail'
IHTE-TL   'belly'   NIHTI 'my belly'

Weak I is really problematical in Nahuatl. There is dialectal variation, with
Tetelcingo apparently going farther than the central highland dialect described by
Carochi in deleting I in individual stems. But even within the central dialect, some
stems that maintain initial I in the presence of a reflexive or possessive prefix lose
it after TLA- in derived forms. The criterion applied here is that the I is enclosed in
parentheses if the stem is attested with I-deletion after the O of a reflexive or possessive prefix.

Nahuatl nouns have always been given in citation form complete with absolutive suffix. Since the form of the suffix is not entirely predictable, this is a well-
motivated practice. Here it is given as part of the canonical form but separated from
the stem by a hyphen.

By far the most common absolutive suffix is -TLI, which drops its own final
vowel when attached to stems ending in vowels and has the form -LI when attached to stems ending in L.

TĒUC-TLI   'lord'
Ā-TL   'water'
CAL-LI   'house'

Another absolutive suffix is -IN, which is associated mainly with stems referring
to small animate things.

MICH-IN   'fish'

Many classes of derived nouns have no absolutive suffix.

TLAHTOĀNI   'speaker; king, lord' < (I)HTOĀ 'to say something'
CACCHĪUHQUI   'shoemaker' < CAC-TLI 'shoe', CHĪHU(A) 'to make
              something'
CALEH   'householder' < CAL-LI 'house'

A few exceptional basic, nonderived nouns also lack absolutive suffixes (as do
Spanish loanwords, which are not included here).

The hyphen is also used with bound forms. If a lexical item cannot occur free, but must be attached to something else, the hyphen indicates the direction of the attachment.

AH-	negative prefix
-YĀN	'customary place'
-NACAYŌ	'one's own flesh' (as contrasted with the simply possessed form of NAC(A)-TL 'meat')

Examples in construction

AHHUELI	'impossible' < HUELI 'possible'
ĪTĒTLACUĀYĀN	'his dining room' < CUĀ 'to eat something'
ĪNACAYŌ	'his own flesh' (In actual pronunciation the final vowel is shortened at the end of the word.)
ĪNAC	'his meat'

A canonical form is prefixed with an asterisk if it is not directly attested in the sources contributing to this dictionary or in Molina or Siméon but can be deduced from other attested forms. (See the section on attestations below.)

A general rule of Nahuatl is that long vowels are shortened word-finally and before glottal stop. Only some uninflected particles and nouns which lose a stem vowel in possessed form are unaffected by this rule.

AHMŌ	'no, not'
ZĀ	'only'
ĪMĀ	'his hand' < MĀ(I)-TL 'hand'

Because of context, verbs which end in IĀ and OĀ (of which there are many) do not reveal the length of the final vowel in either the singular or the plural of the present tense.

ĀLTIA	'he bathes'	ĀLTIAH	'they bathe'
CHOLOA	'he flees'	CHOLOAH	'they flee'

It comes out in the customary present and imperfect forms, however.

ĀLTIĀNI	'he customarily bathes'
ĀLTIĀYA	'he used to bathe'
CHOLOĀNI	'he customarily flees'
CHOLOĀYA	'he used to flee'

In parts of the verbal paradigm, the final Ā of these verbs drops, and the preceding vowel is compensatorily lengthened.

ĀLTĪZ	'he will bathe'
CHOLŌZ	'he will flee'

The preterit of these verbs is formed by adding a glottal stop, which has the effect of shortening the vowel again.

ŌĀLTIH	'he bathed'
ŌCHOLOH	'he fled'

All IĀ and OĀ verbs are regular after this pattern and require no additional paradigmatic information beyond the canonical form. Some verbs ending in just a single long Ā also follow this pattern, while verbs ending in long vowels other than Ā inflect like verbs ending in single short vowels.

CUĀ	'to eat something'
QUICUA	'he eats it'
QUICUAH	'they eat it'

QUICUĀNI	'he customarily eats it'
ŌQUICUAH	'he ate it'
PANŌ	'to cross a river'
PANO	'he crosses a river'
PANOH	'they cross a river'
PANŌNI	'he customarily crosses a river'
ŌPANŌC	'he crossed a river'
CHŌCA	'to cry'
CHŌCA	'he cries'
CHŌCAH	'they cry'
CHŌCANI	'he customarily cries'
ŌCHŌCAC	'he cried'

Nonactive derivations with the -LŌ suffix behave like PANŌ.

The canonical form alone conveys all the necessary paradigmatic information about verbs of the types exemplified by CHŌCA, YŌL(I), ĀLTIĀ, and CHOLOĀ. Verbs of the PANŌ and CUĀ types are, in fact, distinguished by their final vowels, but a certain amount of redundant information about preterits has been included in the grammatical information section of entries for the user's convenience.

The contextual vowel-shortening rule is pervasive; it applies to nouns as well as to verbs. A vowel-lengthening rule applies before the nonactive verbal suffix -HUA.

TOM(A)	'to loosen, untie something'
TOMĀHUA	'to bulge'
TOMĀHUAC	'something fat'

Certain sets of related words show a vowel-length alternation, with a long vowel before -NI corresponding to a short vowel elsewhere.

CACALACA	'to ring, to sound'
CACALATZA	'to ring something, to cause something to make a sound'
CALĀNI	'to jingle'

This is not to be confused with the customary present -NI, which does not affect the length of the vowel before it.

Yet another instance of the alteration of vowel length is the causative derivation of verbs. The L of the causative suffix -LTIĀ can be dropped with compensatory lengthening of the vowel before it.

| MIQUI | 'to die' |
| MIQUILTIĀ | |

~ MIQUĪTIĀ 'to cause someone to die'

A third possibility with the causative is apocope of IL.

MIQUILTIĀ > MICTIĀ

This is the most common causative form of this particular verb, but all are attested.

Regular alternations of vowel length by rules of the type illustrated here account for what might appear to be inconsistencies in canonical forms. Genuine inconsistencies between what might be expected and what is actually attested are noted in the commentary section of the entry.

GRAMMATICAL INFORMATION

The grammatical section provides information that cannot be deduced from the canonical form itself. For nouns this includes the plural and possessed forms.

Except for regular derived nouns exemplified above by TLAHTOĀNI, CAC-CHĪUHQUI, and CALEH, noun plural forms are not predictable. The plural suffix represented here as -TIN is geographically restricted; it is unknown in some peripheral areas, apparently including Zacapoaxtla. Where it is known, it is generally restricted to a subset of stems ending in consonants as in CŌL-LI 'grandfather', CŌL-TIN 'grandfathers'. It has the form -*tin* in Carochi and the Bancroft manuscript, -*teh* in Xalitla, and -*te* in Tetelcingo. The plural suffix -*tinij* of Huastecan Nahuatl seems to be the same, but it is not restricted to consonant stems.

For stems ending in vowels, for those consonant stems that do not take -TIN, and for noun stems in general where -TIN is not known, -MEH is the most common plural suffix, and there are some -TIN ~ -MEH doublets.

COYŌ-TL	'coyote'
COYŌMEH	'coyotes'
OQUICH-TLI	'man, husband'
OQUICHMEH	
~ OQUICHTIN	'men, husbands'

Some nouns simply add a glottal stop to form the plural.

TLĀCA-TL 'person'   TLĀCAH   'people'

Some plurals are formed by reduplicating the initial consonant and vowel of the noun stem as well as adding a plural suffix. Some nouns use a reduplicated plural form exclusively.

TĒUC-TLI 'lord'   TĒTĒUCTIN   'lords'

Because of this range of variation, the plural form, insofar as it is attested, is included in this section of the entry. Strictly speaking, only animate and quasi-animate nouns are overtly marked for plurality in Nahuatl, so many noun entries contain no plural information at all.

Some possessed forms of nouns are also unpredictable from their canonical forms.

ĀMA-TL	'paper'	ĪĀMAUH	'his paper'
OH-TLI	'road'	ĪOHHUI	'his road'
TĒUC-TLI	'lord'	ĪTĒUCYŌ	'his lord' (In actual pronunciation the Ō shortens word-finally.)

Information of this sort is also included in this section.

Transitive verbs in Nahuatl require an object prefix. The Tetelcingo and Zacapoaxtla dictionaries include one in the citation form of the verb, but in this dictionary, as in Molina and Siméon, just the verb stem is given, with information about transitivity following. After Molina, the order is reflexive followed by transitive.

Also in this section are given unpredictable preterit forms. Verbs exemplified by CHŌCA, YŌL(I), ĀLTIĀ, and CHOLOĀ above are predictable from their canonical forms. In principle, only entries for CUĀ type verbs need explicit information about the preterit form, but for the sake of convenience both PANŌ and CUĀ types are given here with their preterits. Also given are irregular preterits, alternate preterits, and preterits of the YŌL(I) type verbs where the consonant changes when it comes into word-final position.

      PIY(A) 'to keep something'   pret: PIX ~ PĪX
      ĀM(I) 'to go hunting'   pret: ĀN

    Part of speech is indicated in this section if it is not obvious from the gloss. Because Nahuatl morphology is different from English or Spanish morphology, some things may seem underdifferentiated, as in the case of nouns and adjectives, and others oddly overdifferentiated. An example of fine differentiation is the distinction among suffixes, postpositions, and what are here called 'compounding elements'.

    Suffixes are endings that are added to words. Inflectional suffixes indicate such things as plurality and tense, while derivational suffixes make some parts of speech into others, create abstractions from basic words, etc. English examples of inflectional suffixes are *boy-s* and *start-ed*; derivational suffixes are exemplified by *racism*, *communicat-ion*, and *class-ic*. Nahuatl is very rich in suffixes, of which only a few are given as main entries in this dictionary. For most, one must consult a reference grammar.

    Nahuatl postpositions roughly correspond to English prepositions and indicate position or movement with respect to some point in the manner of English *on, at, to*, etc. In Nahuatl the postposition must be attached to either a noun or a possessive prefix. While it is thus a bound form just as a suffix is, no suffix could simply combine with a possessive prefix, as postpositions can.

    Then there are compounding elements. These, too, look like suffixes in that they attach themselves to the ends of words. But compounding elements pluralize by reduplicating their own first consonant and vowel. An example is honorific-diminutive -TZIN-TLI.

      ICHCA-TL   'sheep'
      ICHCA-TZIN-TLI   'sheep (diminutive)'
      ICHCA-TZITZIN-TIN 'sheep (diminutive plural)'

    Finally, there are nouns that are necessarily possessed or in some other way bound but are nonetheless nouns in full standing. They also appear with an initial hyphen in the canonical form and an explanation in this section.

    Other types of grammatical information in this section are self-explanatory.

ENGLISH GLOSS

    As mentioned in the User's Guide, the English glosses strive to balance basic, rather literal meaning with conventional usage. Conversely, I have attempted to avoid awkwardness in English without being cavalier about the Nahuatl. Fidelity to the Nahuatl has had a few ramifications for this section.

    It may strike the user as odd that there are no adjectival English glosses, although the Spanish gloss may be an adjective. For example, in the Zacapoaxtla dictionary TLĪLTIC is glossed as 'negro', but the English gloss in this dictionary is not 'black' but 'something black'. The reason for this practice is that there is no morphological distinction in Nahuatl between nouns-substantives and adjectives, as there clearly is in Spanish, where nouns have gender and adjectives agree in gender with the nouns they modify. As a result, the criterion for distinguishing between nouns and adjectives in Nahuatl would be semantic, a distinction that Molina eschewed in his dictionary. His gloss of TLĪLTIC is 'cosa negra de etiopia', and in general he uses 'cosa' glosses of words we might be inclined to gloss adjectivally. (Molina did not invent this type of gloss for Nahuatl, however. Antonio de Nebrija already used it, with considerably less justification, in his Spanish-Latin dictionary of 1516, which served as Molina's model.)[23]

Throughout this dictionary there is a systematic split in glosses for two grammatically equivalent derivations. -TICAH and -TOC constructions are created from the preterit-as-present verbs CĀ and O, respectively, joined to other stems by the ligature -TI-. (-TI-OC yields -TOC by a regular rule applying to adjacent vowels.) But this dictionary glosses -TICAH constructions as though they were verbs and -TOC ones as substantives except in a few cases, such as CHICĀUHTICAH 'something strong, healthy, stable', where Molina himself has a 'cosa' gloss. The reason for this inconsistency is that these constructions are essentially complete clauses which can either stand as the main clause of a sentence and be appropriately translated verbally or serve as modifying clauses, which would be most naturally translated substantively or adjectivally. Z, which is the source of most of the -TOC constructions, almost exclusively treats them as modifiers, equivalent to Spanish adjectives, and this is reflected in the glosses. -TICAH constructions are not so limited in the sources and are given here with their more primary verbal glosses. The important thing to bear in mind is that both constructions can, in fact, be used both ways.

The glosses for some postpositions seem to have contradictory 'to' and 'from' senses. The reason for the oddity of the English gloss is that the Nahuatl simply means motion with respect to some point. The directionality is not expressed by the postposition itself, although it may be indicated by some other element in a clause containing the postposition.

As mentioned above, in the case of a verb used both reflexively and transitively, it is to avoid awkwardness in citing Spanish glosses from Molina that the reflexive gloss precedes the the transitive gloss here.

Quite a few names of plants and animals are attested in the sources for this dictionary. These are, however, merely documentary references to plants and animals; there are no actual specimens on which to base identifications and only a few cases of pictorial illustration. I have consulted several herbals and modern field guides and offer tentative identifications. Some are indubitable, but many are quite tenuous, for which I apologize and give warning. Nahuatl names for plants and animals introduced from other parts of the world should not be discredited, however, because many established themselves centuries ago and acquired names from native vocabulary stock via transference or neologism.

23. Nebrija, Antonio de. *Vocabulario de romance en latín.*Seville: Johannes Varela, 1516.

There are also cases of neologism or semantic extension involving words having to do with the Christian faith. So long as they are true to the principles of Nahuatl word formation, they have been included, along with such words reflecting innovations in material culture as TLĀLQUĪXTĪLŌNI 'wheelbarrow'.

SPANISH GLOSS

The Spanish gloss is drawn by preference from Molina. Where Siméon has a clearer gloss or has an item Molina lacks, the gloss is from Siméon. Next preference goes to Carochi, and, failing that, the gloss is taken from one of the other sources. Old Spanish spelling is modernized. For place names and personal names, the English gloss is generally not distinct from the Spanish gloss. In some cases several different glosses are provided to clarify the item or to show a range of meaning across sources. These are separated by commas. While the English gloss is intended to convey the sense of the item succinctly, the Spanish glosses, drawn from various kinds of sources, are often more elaborate. The different styles of the English and the Spanish glosses complement each other and should both be consulted.

The diversity of the sources is reflected not only in the style of the Spanish glosses, but in the format as well. This is especially evident in the glosses of verbs. Molina, Siméon, and Clavigero gloss verbs with Spanish infinitives, as do Ramírez and Dakin in the Xalitla dictionary. Since Carochi's examples are often phrases, his translations of verbs are sometimes inflected forms, while the Tetelcingo and Zacapoaxtla dictionaries gloss verbs with the Spanish third person singular present, reflecting their use of that person, tense, and number as the citation form in Nahuatl.

ATTESTATION

If a word appears in any of the sources in its basic form, in an inflected or derived form, or as a constituent element of a compound, it serves as an attestation for this dictionary. In the case of an inflected form, a derived form, or a compound, the attestation is counted if the stem can be unambiguously recovered in its full form.

If an item is abundantly and consistently attested across sources, this section is omitted. In the case of rare or restricted attestation, the number of times it occurs and its locations in sources are given. The letter code for the sources is given in the User's Guide. Addresses for attestations from Carochi are given for the 1645 original.

Table 2 indicates the correspondence between the 1645 original and the 1892 reprinting at 10-folio intervals, which may prove useful for reference.

Attestations from Clavigero's grammar are drawn from the original manuscript, but the addresses are given from Anderson's Mexican publication of the grammar, because the manuscript pages are unnumbered and irregular.

For all sources the attestations themselves are not reproduced, because the

TABLE 2

1645 folio	1892 page
1r	401
10r	409-410
20r	419
30r	429-430
40r	440-441
50r	452-453
60r	463
70r	472-473
80r	483-484
90r	494
100r	504
110r	514
120r	524
130r	533-534
132r (final folio)	536

divergent orthographic conventions of sources render them unhelpful for direct comparison.

There are entries in Molina and Siméon which do not appear here, because the items are not to be found in any sources which consistently indicate long vowels and glottal stops. On the other hand, an item which never occurs in free form in the sources for this dictionary may still have an entry here if it can be unambiguously deduced from attested compound or derived forms. If the item appears as an entry in Molina or Siméon too, it is treated as a fully attested entry here. Otherwise, it is marked with an asterisk. Despite the conservatism and care that went into writing entries for this dictionary, all canonical forms are ultimately hypothetical and of my creation; the ones marked with an asterisk are more so.

COMMENTARY

The commentary deals with inconsistencies across sources, problems of meaning, distribution in sources, and similar topics. It is both diverse and self-explanatory.

One of the most important functions of the commentary section is to point out pairs of words that are easily confused. Such confusion arises for words that are phonologically and semantically distinct but not distinguished in the traditional orthography. These pairs, and occasionally triples, such as Molina's *auatl* and *atlacatl* discussed above, have been the bane of Nahuatl scholarship, in spite of Carochi's cautionary list.

Insofar as metaphorical use of words is dealt with in this dictionary, it is also presented in the commentary section. In a process known as *difrasismo*, some words are paired to mean something other than their sum. A classic example is the pairing of TLĀLLOH 'something of earth' and ZOQUIYOH 'something of mud' to refer to the human body. But *difrasismo* really exceeds the bounds of this dictionary and is by no means exhaustively treated here. Fortunately, lists of the most common pairs and their metaphorical meanings have been published elsewhere. Given a *difrasismo* and its meaning, one can get from this dictionary the literal meaning and complete phonological shape of its component parts.

CROSS REFERENCE

Because Nahuatl makes extensive use of compounding and derivation, most entries contain cross references to other entries which are component parts or derivational sources. When the user is directed to 'see' another entry, that does not necessarily mean that it is directly involved in the formation of the entry at hand, merely that it is relevant. But in general the reference is the nearest constituent, not one many steps back. As a result, a user intent on tracing a complex word to its roots may have to go back more than one step.

The reference section may begin with something other than 'see.' The simplest kind of entry in this dictionary is a canonical form and a reference identifying it as the applicative, causative, or nonactive form of a verb. These forms are to a large extent regular and predictable but not entirely. Insofar as they are attested in the sources for this dictionary they appear here, but if they have no special gloss in the source, they appear with only a reference to the main verb from which they are derived.

For many Nahua speech communities the applicative form of the verb (which some grammarians call 'benefactive'), together with a reflexive prefix, is used honorifically rather than literally. When one intends to say deferentially, 'You do it,' one literally says, 'You do it for your own benefit.' It is for this reason that so many applicative verb forms are attested and appear in this dictionary with no gloss. Sometimes it is the causative form of the verb that is so used. Moreover, there is some overlap of use between applicative and causative suffixes. For the purposes of this dictionary, verb forms derived with the suffixes -LIĀ and -HUIĀ are called applicative, and those derived with -LTIĀ and -TIĀ are called causative. For nonliteral use of these forms one must consult a reference grammar of Nahuatl.

In some cases more than one applicative, causative, or nonactive form of a verb is attested, and these are labeled 'alternative.' There is no cross reference between alternative forms but only reference back to the main verb from which the alternatives are derived.

The other possible heading under cross reference refers to reduplication of the initial syllable of a stem. There are several types and functions of reduplication, for which one must consult a grammar. The reference heading simply directs the user back to the basic word from which the reduplicated form has been derived.

CONCLUSION

The user of a dictionary of this sort needs more information about the structure of the language than can be conveyed by the dictionary entries or in a general introduction to the work. The best possible authority in this case is Carochi's original

Arte. The two modern sources most compatible with this dictionary are Andrews' *Introduction to Classical Nahuatl* and Michel Launey's *Introduction à la langue et à la litterature azteques I.*[24]

The compilation of this dictionary involved two steps, first a maximum expansion of the data and then reduction and synthesis. In the expansion phase all the data from each source were cross-listed in their original notation under all potentially relevant canonical forms. Then the lists for the individual sources were merged into a master list of attestations from which the dictionary was written.

In the course of the writing, it turned out that some of the hypothetical canonical forms were in error, and they were corrected. In some cases a decision was ultimately arbitrary, as with internal IA and IYA. When these sequences occur inside a word and are never exposed at the end, it is not possible to chose one over the other as the correct canonical form; in some sources both IA and IYA are written *ia* and in others *iya*. Where the canonical form is arbitrary, dubious, or controversial, I have provided attestations and commentary so that the concerned user can refer to the original sources and make an independent decision.

A great many attestations are not given here because they are solidly noncontroversial. But the original exhaustive lists of attestations by source and the master list remain as by-products of the lexicography project at the Linguistics Research Center at the University of Texas at Austin. I would greatly appreciate it if users' queries, disagreements, or offers of additional data would be directed to me there. They will all be gratefully received, replied to, and incorporated into the data files. It is also possible to search the output files from which this dictionary was printed for all sorts of information, and insofar as time and funds are available, these files are open to others' research.

The beauty of computation is that update and improvement are continuous processes. This volume is an artifact of an ongoing project that remains open to input indefinitely.

24. Launey, Michel. *Introduction à la langue et à la litterature aztèques I: Grammaire.* Paris: L'Harmattan, 1978.

A

Ā *preterit-as-present verb; pret:* **ĀC** to be present See ĀC.

ĀAQU(I) to be soaked / se empapa (Z) [(3)Zp.49,139,181]. The literal sense of this is 'to water-enter.' Z has the reflex of AH instead of Ā-TL, but the sense is of Ā-TL, and Z has AH for Ā-TL elsewhere. See AQU(I).

ĀC *pl:* **ĀQUIHQUEH** (one) who; who? / ¿quién? o ¿cuál? (M) This is the preterit agentive form derived from the existential verb Ā. It contrasts in vowel length with AC, the preterit form of AQU(I) 'to enter.' See Ā, ACAH, ĀQUIN.

ĀCACHACHA-TL *pl:* **-MEH** a type of grasshopper, locust / otro género de langostas (M) [(1)Tp.169]. See ĀCA-TL, CHACHA-TL.

ĀCACHIQUIHU(I)-TL reed basket / canasto hecho de cañas (M), jícara para tortillas (X) [(3)Xp.25]. The initial vowel is not marked long in the attestation. See ĀCA-TL, CHIQUIHU(I)-TL.

ACACHTO first / primero, o primeramente (M) See ACATTO, ACATTOPA, ACHTO.

ACACHTOPA first / primero, o primeramente (M) See ACATTOPA, ACHTO.

ACACHTOPAHUIĀ to be the first to do something / soy el primero que hago algo (C for first pers. sg.) See ACHTOPA, -HUIĀ.

ACAH *pl:* **-MEH** someone / alguno (M) See ĀC.

ĀCĀHUAL-LI large, dry leaves for lighting ovens / yerbas secas y grandes para encender hornos (M) [(4)Tp.169,170,243]. The second vowel is attested long only once, but it should be long if the literal sense is 'something dehydrated.' See Ā-TL, CĀHU(A).

ĀCĀHUATŌTŌ-TL small yellow or blue bird with gray on the back / pájaro (chico, amarillo o azul con gris sobre la espalda) (T) [(3)Tp.170,243]. See ĀCĀHUAL-LI, TŌTŌ-TL.

ĀCALAQUIĀ *vrefl,vt* to dive; to submerge something / se bucea (de bucear), se mete en el agua (Z), meter algo debajo del agua, o hundirlo (M) [(2)Zp.21,167]. See Ā-TL, CALAQU(I).

ĀCAL-LI boat / navío, barca, canoa, etc. (M) The literal sense of this is 'water-house.' See Ā-TL, CAL-LI.

ACĀLOAH a type of lizard that bites / un animal que muerde—parecido a la largatija (Z) [(1)Zp.139]. Z provides a picture which appears to be of a gila monster. The final H is uncharacteristic of native Nahuatl but is common to vowel-final loanwords.

ĀCAMĀPĪCH-TLI *personal name* Acamapichtli [(2)Bf.8r,9v]. See ĀCA-TL, MĀPĪCH-TLI.

ĀCAMĀYA crayfish, crab / langostino (Z) [(2)Zp.25,139]. The attestation on Zp.139 has an uncharacteristic final H as does ACĀLOAH.

ĀCAPAH-TLI medicinal plant with radishlike leaves / planta medicinal semejante en las hojas al rábano [(1)Rp.57]. The initial vowel is not marked long in the attestation. See ĀCA-TL, PAH-TLI.

ĀCAPECH-TLI reed mat / petate de zacate (Z) [(1)Zp.139]. Z fails to mark the initial vowel long. See ĀCA-TL, PECH-TLI.

ĀCAPETL(A)-TL reed mat / acapetate, petate de carrizo (T) [(1)Tp.70]. See ĀCA-TL, PETL(A)-TL.

ĀCATEQU(I) See ĀCA-TL, TEQU(I).

ĀCA-TL reed / caña (M)

ACATTO first / primero (C) Cf.98r gives YACATTO as a variant. See ACACHTO, ACACHTOPA.

ACATTOPA first / primero (C) Cf.98r gives YACATTOPA as a variant. See ACACHTOPA.

ĀCAX(I)-TL *pl:* **-TIN** watering trough /

alberca (M), pileta para tomar agua los
animales (X) [(3)Xp.25]. X fails to mark the
initial vowel long. See Ā-TL, CAX(I)-TL.
ĀCEC-TLI icicles, ice in trees / hielo
en árbol (Z) [(2)Zp.67,141]. See Ā-TL,
CEC-TLI.
ACH *dubitative particle* possibly, one
doesn't know / part. que ordinariamente
indica duda y a veces equivale a una nega-
ción (S) Cf.125v gives ACHAH as a variant.
Zp.139 gives ACHA ~ ĀCHĀ as variants.
ACHAHNEL See ACH, AHNEL.
ĀCHĀHU(I)-TL swamp / charco, ciénaga (Z)
[(3)Zp.28,139].
ĀCHĀUHTLAH swamp / ciénaga (Z)
[(2)Zp.28,139]. See ĀCHĀHU(I)-TL,
-TLAH.
ACHCA often / a menudo, frecuentemente
(C)
ACHCĀMPA one knows not where / no sé
dónde (S) See ACH, -CĀN, -PA.
ACHCĀNIN one knows not where / no sé
dónde (S) See ACH, CĀNIN.
ĀCHCĀUH-TLI elder brother; leader of
youths / primogénito, hermano mayor de
alguien, el jefe de alguien (S) This seems to
be related to ACHTO 'first,' but there is a
vowel-length discrepancy. See ĀCH-TLI,
TĀCHCĀUH, TIĀCHCĀUH.
ACHCHICA often / a menudo, o frecuentemente (M) This is commonly written with
only a single CH. Of six attestations in C,
one has a marked long vowel in the second
syllable.
ACHCŌL-LI great-grandfather, ancestor /
bisabuelo (M for *achtontli*, which is
in apposition with ACHCŌL-LI in B)
[(4)Bf.6v,7r,8r,11v, (3)Xp.32]. All the attestations are possessed plurals with reduplication of the CŌL element: COHCŌL.
Two attestations have the first element
with a specifically marked short vowel,
two with a specifically marked long vowel.
In the paired form ACHTŌN-TLI, Bf.6v,
the vowel of the first element is specifically marked short. This is inconsistent
with the first element of ĀCHCĀUH-TLI
'elder brother,' which is without exception
marked long, but it agrees with ACHTO
'first.' X appears to have reanalyzed the
plural as a singular and dropped ACH. See
CŌL-LI.

ACHI a bit / un poco, o poca cosa, o
en alguna manera (M) This appears to
be an element in constructions where it
has the contrary sense of 'a lot, more,
very much,' as in ACHIPA 'always,'
ACHICUAL-LI 'better.' See the note with
ACHĪC. In some, but not all, constructions this has a final glottal stop, ACHIH.
See ACHIHTETZIN, ACHIHTŌN,
ACHIHTZIN.
ACHĪC just a short time / un poco de
tiempo (C) C marks the vowel of the
second syllable long in both this and the
comparative particle ACHĪC. R marks it
long only in the comparative particle and
says they are distinct. See ACHI.
ACHĪC particle used in making comparisons
/ hay diferencia entre una persona, o cosa,
y otra (C) This comparative ACHĪC may be
related in some way to the contradictory
'more' sense of ACHI. See ACHI, ĪC.
ACHICA See ACHCHICA.
ĀCHICĀHUAL-LI downpour / aguacero (X)
[(1)Xp.25]. See Ā-TL, CHICĀHU(A).
ĀCHICĀL-IN *pl:* **-TIN** ~ **-MEH** nettle / ortiga
(X) [(1)Xp.25]. See ĀTZĪTZICĀZ-TLI.
ACHICUAL-LI better / mejor (C) See ACHI,
CUAL-LI.
ACHIHTETZIN a bit / un poco, un poquito
(C) See ACHI.
ACHIHTŌN a bit / un poco (M) See ACHI.
ACHIHTŌNCA soon, a short time / un poco
de tiempo (M) See ACHI.
ACHIHTZIN a bit / un poquito, o poca cosa
(M) See ACHI.
ACHIHTZINCA soon, a short time / un
poco de intervalo, o espacio de tiempo (M)
See ACHI.
ĀCHĪHUAL-LI water used in milling,
grinding / agua que se ocupa para moler (T)
[(1)Tp.170]. See Ā-TL, CHĪHU(A).
ĀCHĪHUIĀ *vrefl* to wash one's hands while
grinding maize / se lava las manos (mujer
cuando muele) (T) [(3)Tp.164]. See Ā-TL,
CHĪHU(A).
ĀCHĪHUILŌ In the attestation of this on
Tp.164 the vowel of the second syllable
is incorrectly marked short. nonact.
ĀCHĪHUIĀ
ĀCHIO-TL *pl:* **-TIN** ~ **-MEH** a tree (Bixa
orellana) from the seeds of which is made a
paste used as a seasoning and for coloring

things orange / bija, fruto empleado en el teñido (S), achiote, fruto y árbol conocido (R) [(4)Xp.25, (1)Rp.58]. This is attested in R without diacritics. X has -TLI, implying a glottal stop at the end of the stem, but in general Nahuatl has -TL with this item.

ACHIPA always / siempre (Z) [(3)Zp.115,139,176].

ĀCHITLACŌ-TL white staff / vara blanca (T) [(1)Tp.170]. See TLACŌ-TL.

ACHTLEIN See ACH, TLEIN.

ACH-TLI *possessed form:* **-ACHYŌ** seed / pepita o semilla (C) [(2)Cf.126v, (2)Rp.58]. This seems to be related to XINĀCH-TLI 'seed,' but there is a vowel-length discrepancy. It also seems to be related to the HUACH element of AYOHHUACH-TLI 'squash seed.' It contrasts in vowel length with ĀCH-TLI 'elder brother.'

ĀCH-TLI elder brother (from the point of view of a younger sister) / hermano mayor de la hermana menor (C) [(1)Cf.126v, (1)Rp.59]. This seems to be related to ACHTO 'first,' but there is a vowel-length discrepancy. It contrasts in vowel length with ACH-TLI 'seed.'

ACHTO first / primero, o primeramente (M)

ACHTŌN-TLI great-grandfather, ancestor / bisabuelo (M) [(1)Bf.6v]. See ACHTO, ACHCŌL-LI.

ACHTOPA first / primero, o primeramente (M) See ACHTO, ACACHTOPA, ACATTOPA.

ACHTOPAHUIĀ *vt* to take the lead in some matter / guiar en alguna cosa o ser el primero en hacerla (R) [(1)Rp.48]. See ACHTOPA, -HUIĀ.

ACHTZAN often / a menudo, frecuentemente (C) Cf.105v gives the variant ACHTZAH.

ACĪL-LI nit, louse egg / liendre (M) [(1)Tp.108, (2)Zp.76,140]. Z gives a variant AHCĪLĪ-TL.

ĀCŌCĪL-IN crayfish / acosil (animal) (T) [(1)Tp.170, (1)Rp.59]. R provides the characteristic -IN absolutive suffix of small animates. See Ā-TL.

ĀCOCOĀ for a plant to suffer from overwatering / se enferma (planta) de tanta agua (T) [(1)Tp.164]. See Ā-TL, COCOĀ.

ACOCOH-TLI acocote, name of several different squash plants / dos plantas

medicinales semejante la una al nardo (R) [(1)Rp.59].

ACOHUA nonact. AQU(I)

ĀCŌLHUAH person from Acolhuacan / fuerte, es también nombre de nación (R) [(1)Bf.12v, (1)Rp.59].

ĀCŌLHUAHCĀN *place name* the realm of Texcoco [(2)Bf.4r,4v]. See Ā-TL, CŌLHUAHCĀN.

ĀCOLMĀN *place name* Acolman [(1)Cf.56v].

ĀCŌLMĒCA-TL resident of Acolman / natural de Acolman [(1)Cf.56v].

ĀCŌLMIZ-TLI *personal name* Acolmiztli [(3)Bf.81,9v,10v]. See MIZ-TLI.

ĀCŌLŌ-TL *pl:* **-MEH** crayfish / alacrán de agua (X) [(3)Xp.25]. The literal sense of this is 'water-scorpion,' as in the Spanish gloss. See Ā-TL, CŌLŌ-TL.

ĀCŌM(I)-TL water pot / tinaja de agua (M) X has the variant ĀCŌN-TLI. See Ā-TL, CŌM(I)-TL.

ĀCOMŌL-LI well, water hole / pozo (Z) [(1)Zp.139]. See ĀTLACOMŌL-LI.

ĀCONI who? / ¿quién? (Z) [(1)Zp.139]. This form appears to be peculiar to Z. See ĀC.

ĀCŌZAMĀLŌ-TL rainbow / arco iris (T) See Ā-TL, CŌZAMĀLŌ-TL.

ACTOC within / metido adentro (Z) [(1)Zp.139]. See AQU(I), the verb O.

ĀCUEYA-TL frog / rana (Z) See Ā-TL, CUEYA-TL.

ĀCUI *pret:* **-C** to swim / nada (de nadar) (Z) [(1)Zp.140]. Z has the reflex of AH rather than Ā-TL, but the sense demands the latter. See Ā-TL, CUI.

ACXOYA-TL branches used in penitential offerings; fir / planta cuyas hojas eran utilizadas por los sacerdotes para recoger la sangre que se sacaban por penitencia (S) [(1)Bf.10r, (1)Rp.58].

ĀCZĀ someone / alguien (Z) [(2)Zp.139, 145]. See ĀC, ZĀ.

ĀEHĒCA *pret:* **-C** to rain and be windy / llueve con viento (T) See Ā-TL, EHĒCA.

AH- *negative prefix* not, un-, in- / negación, usado en comp. por *amo*, no (S)

AHACHI not a little, much / abundante, hay muchos (T) [(2)Tp.221]. T gives this bound with ZAN, ZANAHACHI. It is possible that this is a case of distributive reduplication rather than negation in view of the 'more, very much' sense of ACHI in some other constructions. See AH-, ACHI.

AHACHICHI bit by bit / poco a poco (Z) [(1)Zp.139]. See ACHI.

AHAHĀHUILTIĀ double redup. ĀHUILTIĀ

AHAHCI redup. AHCI

AHAHCUI *vrefl,vt* to rise up; to raise something up / se levanta (Z); lo levanta, lo alza, lo eleva (Z) [(3)Zp.143,168,185]. The sense of this suggests that it is a reduplicated form related to AHCOCU(I).

AHAHHUA redup. AHHUA

AHAHHUALŌ nonact. AHAHHUA

AHAHHUILIĀ applic. AHAHHUA

AHAHPĀN(A) redup. AHPĀN(A)

AHĀHUIĀ *vt* to moisten something / lo moja (Z) [(1)Zp.185]. This implies *ĀHUIĀ, of which this would be the reduplicated form. This contrasts with AHĀHUIY(A) 'to take pleasure.' See Ā-TL, -HUIĀ.

AHĀHUIL-LI licentiousness / liviandades (C) [(2)Cf.72r]. See AHĀHUIY(A).

AHĀHUIY(A) *pret:* AHĀHUĪX to take pleasure / regocijarse mucho (C). This contrasts with AHĀHUIĀ 'to moisten something.' redup. ĀHUIY(A)

AHAHXĪHUA redup. AHXIHUA

AHALAC-TLI alache, a fibrous, slippery plant (Sida rhombifolia) / malva simarrona (yerba) (T) [(1)Tp.107]. See ALACTIC.

AHĀLTIĀ redup. ĀLTIĀ

AHĀLTILIĀ redup. applic. ĀLTIĀ

AHĀLTĪLŌ redup. nonact. ĀLTIĀ

AHĀMAT(I) *pret:* -MAT to get damp / se humedece (T) [(1)Tp.107]. See Ā-TL.

AHĀMĀXĒHU(I) to swell and ooze / se escalda (de comezón), se pone blanquizca (la mano, etc.), se esponja (frijol, etc.), se enlama (T) [(1)Tp.107]. See ĀMAXCUITL(A)-TL, -ĒHU(I).

AHĀM(I) [(1)Bf.10r]. redup. ĀM(I)

AHĀN(A) redup. ĀN(A)

AHAQU(I) redup. AQU(I)

AHAQUIĀ *vt* to insert something repeatedly / meter una cosa varias veces (S) [(2)Bf.71,10r]. This distributive form contrasts with AHĀQUIĀ 'to moisten something.' redup. AQUIĀ

AHĀQUIĀ *vt* to moisten something / lo moja (Z) [(1)Zp.185]. This contrasts with

AHAQUIĀ 'to insert something repeatedly.' See Ā-TL.

AHAQUĪLTIĀ redup. AQUĪLTIĀ

AHĀTĒM(I) *pret:* -TĒN to fill up with water, to flood / ser hidrópico (M for *atemi*), se inunda (T) [(1)Tp.107]. See Ā-TL, TĒM(I).

AHĀTOCŌ for things to be carried away by water / (corriente de agua) arrastra (muchas cosas) (T) [(1)Tp.107]. This is derived from the nonactive form of the verb. See Ā-TL, TOCA.

AHĀTŌLTIC something very ripe, soft / cosa muy blanda, como higo muy maduro, etc. (M), aguado, magullado (T) [(1)Tp.107]. T does not mark the vowel of the second syllable long. See ĀTŌL-LI.

AHĀY(I) redup. ĀY(I)

AHĀYĪHUA redup. ĀYĪHUA

AHĀYĪTIĀ redup. ĀYĪTIĀ

AHCĀMPA See AHCĀN, -PA.

AHCĀN nowhere / en ninguna parte o lugar (M) See AH-, -CĀN.

AHCĀNMAH See AHCĀN, MAH.

AHCAZAYĀC See AHCAZOMŌ, AYĀC.

AHCAZOMŌ perhaps not / quizá no (M) In one of two attestations R gives this with a glottal stop in the third syllable, but in four attestations in C there is no glottal stop indicated. See AH-.

AHCEH See AHZO, (Y)EH.

AHCHĪHU(A) *vrefl* to be withdrawn, taken away / se quita (Z) [(1)Zp.168]. See AH-, CHĪHU(A).

AHCHĪUHCĀYŌ-TL something badly made / cosa mal hecha o desacierto (C) [(2)Cf.121r]. The vowel of the second syllable is not marked long in either attestation. C gives AHIUHCĀYŌ-TL as a synonym of this. See AH-, CHĪHU(A).

AHCI to reach, to arrive / llegar con la mano, o alcanzar con ella a donde algo está, o llegar al lugar donde voy (M) T has lost the internal glottal stop. AHCI compounds with other verbs by means of the -CĀ- ligature to convey a sense of achievement.

AHCI *vt* to catch something with the hand, to reach for and take something / alcanzar con la mano a donde está la cosa (M) T has lost the internal glottal stop. A lexicalized reflexive form of this conveys a sense of wholeness or completeness, as in MAHXĪTIĀ 'to cause something to become complete.' M has synonymous *maxiltia* and also *macic* 'something whole,' which can bind with verbs to mean 'completely.'

AHCICĀCAQU(I) *vt* to understand something completely / comprender o alcanzar a saber enteramente la cosa o el negocio (M) [(2)Rp.43,100]. See AHCI, CAQU(I).

AHCICĀITTA *vt* to perceive something, to know something well / advertir, conocer bien (R), ver algo perfectamente (M) [(1)Rp.59]. See AHCI, (I)TTA.

AHCICĀMAT(I) *vt* to master something, to understand something completely / saber o entender algo perfectamente (M) [(1)Rp.59]. See AHCI, MAT(I).

AHCITLAH See AHZO, ITLAH.

AHCO above / arriba, o en lo alto (M)

AHCOCU(I) *vrefl,vt; pret:* **AHCOC** to rise up; to raise something up / levantarse de suelo, o empinarse el caballo, o revolar el ave, o batir las alas cuando quiere volar (M), alzar o levantar algo en alto (M) See AHCO, CUI.

AHCOCUĪHUA nonact. AHCOCU(I)

AHCOHUETZ(I) to become calm, resigned / sosegarse y consolarse (M) [(1)Rp.59]. See AHCO, HUETZ(I).

AHCOHUĪC upward / hacia arriba (M) See AHCO, -HUĪC.

AHCOL-LI shoulder / hombro (M) [(4)Tp.127,139,(3)Zp.21,68,156]. This invites analysis as a derivation from *CŌL 'something twisted, bent,' but there is a difference in vowel length. See AHCO.

AHCOLTEHTEQU(I) *vrefl* to cut oneself in the shoulder / se corta el hombro (T) [(3)Tp.139]. See AHCOL-LI, TEHTEQU(I).

AHCOMAN(A) *vrefl,vt* to get worked up, to become disturbed; to disturb others / alborotarse, o turbarse (M), alborotar a los otros (M) [(2)Rp.59,108]. See AHCO, MAN(A).

AHCOPA upward / de arriba, o hacia arriba (M) See AHCO, -PA

AHCOPAHUAH highlander / arribeño (Z) [(1)Zp.140]. See AHCOPA.

AHCOPAHUĪC upward / arriba, hacia arriba (R) [(1)Rp.59, (1)Pp.89]. See AHCOPA, -HUĪC.

AHCOPAITTA See AHCOPA, (I)TTA.

AHCOPATLACHIY(A) See AHCOPA, TLACHIY(A).

AHCOQUETZ(A) *vt* to build up something; to raise the bidding at an auction / aumentar o doblar el trabajo a otros, o pujar en almoneda (M), erigir, alivar (R) [(1)Rp.59]. See AHCO, QUETZ(A), AHQUETZ(A).

AHCOTLACHIY(A) See AHCO, TLACHIY(A).

AHCOTZICUĪN(I) to leap up, jump / brinca de abajo arriba, salta (T) See AHCO, TZICUĪN(I).

AHCUAL-LI something bad / cosa mala (M) The literal sense is 'something not good.' See AH-, CUAL-LI.

AHHUA *vt* to scold someone, to quarrel with someone, to irritate someone / reñir a otro (M)

AHHUACHHUIĀ *vt* to irrigate, sprinkle something / lo riega, lo rocia (Z) See AHHUACH-TLI, -HUIĀ.

AHHUACHIĀ *vt* to irrigate, sprinkle something / rociar a otro (M) See AHHUACH-TLI.

AHHUACHPŌC-TLI rain cloud / aguaviento (T) [(1)Tp.107]. See AHHUACH-TLI, PŌC-TLI.

AHHUACHQUIYAHU(I) to rain lightly / llovizna (M) [(2)Tp.107]. See AHHUACH-TLI, QUIYAHU(I)-TL.

AHHUACHTELĀHU(I) *pret:* **-TELĀUH** to begin to rain hard / empieza a llover de veras (T) [(1)Tp.107]. See AHHUACH-TLI, TELĀHU(I).

AHHUACH-TLI dew, drizzle, mist / rocío (K) This is implied by the many compounds of of which it is an element.

AHHUACHTZITZICUICA to rain lightly / llovizna ligera (T) [(1)Tp.107]. See AHHUACH-TLI, TZITZICUICA.

AHHUACHYOH something covered with dew / cosa que tiene rocío (M) [(1)Tp.107, (1)Rp.58]. See AHHUACH-TLI, -YOH.

AHHUALŌ nonact. AHHUA

AHHUA-TL long, slender thorn / espina (M), espina delgada (C) M puts the definition of this together with the definition of ĀHUA-TL 'oak' and ĀHUĀ-TL, a type of caterpillar.

AHHUAYOHUA to have an itch / tiene

comezón (Z) [(4)Zp.30,140]. In both
attestations Z marks the final vowel long,
which is unlikely in terms of Nahuatl verb
morphology. See AHHUA.

AHHUAYOHUALIZ-TLI itch / comezón,
picazón (Z) [(2)Zp.30,140]. Z marks the
vowel of the fourth syllable long in both
attestations. See AHHUAYOHUA.

AHHUEL impossible / no poder, no ser
posible (R), imposible, absolutamente no
(S) See AH-, HUEL(I).

AHHUEL(I) impossible / no es posible (C)
See AH-, HUEL(I).

AHHUELITI to be impossible / no es posible
(C) See AH-, HUELITI.

AHHUIĀC something fragrant / cosa
suave y olorosa, o cosa gustosa (M) See
AHHUIĀYA.

AHHUIĀCĀYŌ-TL fragrance / suavidad o
fragrancia, o olor de cosa sabrosa y gustosa
(M) See AHHUIĀYA, -YŌ.

AHHUIĀLIZ-TLI fragrance / suavidad de
olor, o de cosa gustosa y sabrosa (M) See
AHHUIĀYA.

AHHUIĀYA to be fragrant / tener o dar de sí
buen olor (M)

AHHUĪC here and there, back and forth / a
una parte y a otra (M) C contrasts this with
ĀHUĪC 'toward the water.'

AHHUĪCPA from one side to another, from
one place to another / de un lado y de otro,
de un lugar a otro (S) See AHHUĪC, -PA.

AHHUILIĀ vt to water, irrigate something /
regar (R) One would expect a long vowel
from Ā-TL 'water' here, but AH is attested
in C and R. In T the glottal stop is missing,
but the vowel is not marked long. It appears to be related to AHHUACH-TLI
'dew.' This verb is homophonous with the
applicative form of AHHUA.

AHHUILIĀ applic. AHHUA

AHHUILĪLŌ nonact. AHHUILIĀ

-AHHUITZ only attested in possessed
form wing / ala (T) [(1)Tp.127]. See
AHTLAPAL-LI.

AHIUHCĀYŌ-TL something badly made /
cosa mal hecha (C) [(2)Cf.121r]. C gives
AHCHĪUHCĀYŌ-TL as a synonym of
this. See AH-, IHU(I).

AHMAN(A) vrefl to get worked up, to be
discontent / distraerse interiormente,

turbarse, alborotarse o desasosegarse (M)
This contrasts with ĀMAN(A) 'for water to
be contained.' See AHCOMAN(A).

AHMŌ negative particle no, not / no.
adverbio para negar (M) T and Z have lost
the internal glottal stop, and this is true for
most Nahuatl outside the Valley of
Mexico, but although AHMŌ and also
AHHUEL(I) are generally attested in
modern Nahuatl without it, other forms
with the negative prefix AH- generally
retain some reflex of the glottal stop.

AHMŌACAH See AHMŌ, ACAH.

AHMŌCUAL-LI pl: -TIN something bad,
evil / mal, malo, mala, no es bueno (T)
More common in older texts is the shorter
form AHCUAL-LI, but AHMŌCUAL-LI
appears in P as well as in the modern
sources. See AHMŌ, CUAL-LI.

AHMOHUIĀ vrefl to wash with soap /
enjabonarse, lavarse la cabeza con jabón (S)
This is apparently derived from AHMŌL-
LI 'soap' with loss of L and vowel
shortening. Although T, Z, and R all attest
L-loss, M has amolhuia with the L, both
reflexive and transitive, with the sense of
'to wash with soap.' See AHMŌL-LI.

AHMŌICAH See AHMŌ, ICAH.

AHMŌL-LI soap / raíz conocida que sirve de
jabón (R) In the derived form AHMOHUIĀ
the vowel of the second syllable is short,
and the L is lost. See AHMOHUIĀ.

AHMŌNEL See AHNEL.

AHMŌQUĒN without inconvenience /
carencia de turbación, pena, y cuidado (C)
[(1)Cf.115r]. In M this does not appear as a
separate entry but as part of three phrases.
The literal sense is 'in no manner.' See
AHMŌ, QUĒN.

AHNEL negative interrogative particle neg.
interrogativa (S) See AH-, NEL.

AHNO neither / tampoco (M) See AH-.

AHNOCEH perhaps, otherwise, or / o quizá
(M) See AHNOZO, (Y)EH.

AHNOZO or, perhaps / o, quizás (S) See
AHNO, -ZO.

AHPĀN(A) vrefl to gird oneself, to be dressed
/ arrearse o ceñirse con manta de algodón,
o con otra cosa semejante (M) [(1)Cf.115r].

AHPĀX-TLI See AHPĀZ-TLI.

AHPĀZHUĒHUĒN large pan, kettle / paila

(T) [(1)Tp.107]. T does not have the reflex of a long vowel in the final syllable, but in HUĒHUĒNTŌN and HUĒHUĒNTZIN 'old man' it is long. T forms the plural of this item by adding the plural form of the compounding element -TŌN. See AHPĀZ-TLI, HUĒHUĒIHTZIN.

AHPĀZ-TLI earthen bowl, tub / lebrillo, o barreñón grande de barro (M) R has the variant AHPĀX-TLI.

AHPILŌL-LI pitcher / jarro de barro (M), el cántaro de la mano (C) [(1)Cf.105r]. Ā 'water' rather than AH is to be expected for the first element if this is literally 'liquid-pourer,' but the attestation clearly indicates a glottal stop. See PILŌL-LI.

AHPŌCHQUIYĀHUAYOHCĀN chimneyless building / casa sin chimenea (M) [(1)Bf.71r]. In B this refers to the land of the dead. See AH-, PŌCHQUIYĀHUA-TL, -YOH, -CĀN.

AHQUECHILIĀ applic. AHQUETZ(A)

AHQUĒMMAN at no time / en ningún tiempo (M), nunca (R) See AH-, QUĒMMAN.

AHQUĒN See AHMŌQUĒN.

AHQUETZ(A) to raise one's head; to rear up; to be upside down / levantar o alzar la cabeza (M), se lo empina (T), boca arriba (T) M combines the definitions of AHQUETZ(A) with ĀQUETZ(A) 'to beat liquid (such as chocolate) into a foam.' In principle, the sense of 'to lift up the head' could be derived from Ā-TL's 'crown of the head' sense, but C specifically contrasts AHQUETZ(A) with ĀQUETZ(A). See AHCO, QUETZ(A).

AHQUETZALTIĀ vt to turn something upside down / lo lleva boca arriba (T) caus. AHQUETZ(A)

AHQUETZTITLAHCAL(I) vt to knock something upside down / lo tumba boca arriba, lo tira boca arriba (T) [(3)Tp.112]. See AHQUETZ(A), (I)HCAL(I).

AHQUIMAHMATQUI idiot / el necio (C), desaliñado, torpe, que no hace cosa bien hecha (M for aquimamati) [(1)Cf.125v]. See AH-, MAT(I).

AHTĒL but / pero, y en forma interrogativa: ¿no es evidente? (S) See AH-, TĒL.

AHTLĀCA-TL bad, inhumane person / no

hombre, o tan mal hombre, que no se merece se llame hombre (C) M combines in a single entry this and ĀTLAHCA-TL 'sailor, fisherman.' They both contrast with C's ĀTLĀCA-TL 'person made of water.' See AH-, TLĀCA-TL.

AHTLĀCAYŌ-TL cruelty, inhumanity / inhumanidad o crueldad (M) [(1)Rp.62]. See AHTLĀCA-TL.

AHTLAPAL-LI wing; leaf / ala de ave, o hoja de árbol, o de yerba (M) X has MĀTLAPAL-LI 'wing,' literally 'hand-side.' See TLAPAL-LI.

AHTLA-TL spear thrower, atlatl / aparato, correa para lanzar dardos (S) [(1)Bf.10r].

AHTLE(H) nothing / nada o ninguna cosa (M) The final glottal stop drops when followed by a word beginning with a vowel. See AH-, TLE(H).

AHTLEHPIYALIZ-TLI want, need / carestía, necesidad (R) [(1)Rp.63]. R does not indicate the glottal stop of the second syllable. See AHTLE(H), PIY(A).

AHTLEHTILIĀ vt to ruin, to destroy someone, something / deshacer o apocar a otros (M), aniquilar alguna cosa o tornarla a nada (R) [(1)Rp.63]. R does not indicate the glottal stop of the second syllable. applic. AHTLEHTIY(A)

AHTLEHTIY(A) pret: -AHTLEHTĪX to come to nothing, to be ruined / tornarse en nada (M) [(1)Rp.63]. -IY(A) verbs generally have an alternation of final-syllable vowel length yielding ĪX in the preterit, although it is not attested for this item. The glottal stop of the second syllable is also not attested. See AHTLE(H).

AHTLEIN nothing / nada o no es nada (C) See AH-, TLEIN.

ĀHUACACUAHU(I)-TL avocado tree / árbol de aguacate (T,Z) See ĀHUACA-TL, CUAHU(I)-TL.

ĀHUACA-TL avocado; testicle / fruta conocida, o el campañón (M), ahuacate, fruta conocida (R)

ĀHUACĀTZIN swallow (bird) / golondrina (T) [(1)Tp.170].

ĀHUACAXIHU(I)-TL avocado leaf / hoja de aguacate (T) See ĀHUACA-TL, XIHU(I)-TL.

ĀHUACAXŌCHI-TL avocado flower /

flor de aguacate (T) See ĀHUACA-TL, XŌCHI-TL.

ĀHUAH someone who possesses, has control over water / dueño del agua (C) This is generally found in the phrase ĀHUAH TEPĒHUAH 'resident of a town' from ĀLTEPĒ-TL 'town.'

ĀHUAHUETZ(I) for one's head to droop / se baja la mollera (y se enferma) (T) [(1)Tp.170]. This involves the less common 'crown of the head' sense of Ā-TL. See Ā-TL, HUETZ(I).

ĀHUATILĀN(A) vt to jerk, shake, beat someone's head / sacude su mollera (T) [(3)Tp.117]. This involves the less common 'crown of the head' sense of Ā-TL. See Ā-TL, TILĀN(A).

ĀHUA-TL oak / encina (C) Z marks the vowel of the second syllable long, but C specifically marks it short and contrasts it with ĀHUĀ-TL 'caterpillar.' M combines the definitions of these two in a single entry along with the definition of AHHUA-TL 'thorn.'

ĀHUĀ-TL woolly caterpillar / gusano lanudo de árbol (C) [(1)Cf.126v, (1)Rp.59]. M combines in a single entry the definition of this with those of ĀHUA-TL 'oak' and AHHUA-TL 'thorn.'

ĀHUATZETZELOĀ vt to jerk, shake, beat someone's head / sacude su mollera (T) [(3)Tp.117]. This involves the less common 'crown of the head' sense of Ā-TL. See Ā-TL, TZETZELOĀ.

ĀHUĒHUĒ-TL cypress tree; ruler (by metaphor) / ciprés dístico, vulg. ciprés calvo ... jefe, señor (S) [(2)Bf.2v,4r, (1)Cf.121r]. This also appears in R but without diacritics. According to R three different types of cypress share this name.

ĀHUĒLIC something tasteless, insipid, sour / desabrido, insípido (T) [(1)Tp.169]. One would expect the reflex of AH rather than Ā and a literal meaning of 'not-tasty.' The single attestation has Ā, however. Possibly the sense is 'water-flavored,' hence 'tasteless.' See Ā-TL, HUĒLIC.

***ĀHUIĀ** See AHĀHUIĀ.

ĀHUĪC toward the water / hacia el agua (C) [(1) Cf.126v]. This contrasts with AHHUĪC 'here and there, back and forth.' See Ā-TL, -HUĪC.

ĀHUILACA someone playful, mischievous / juguetón, travieso (Z) [(1)Zp.139]. See ĀHUIY(A).

ĀHUILĀN(A) to swim / nada (T) [(3)Tp.164]. See Ā-TL, HUILĀN(A).

ĀHUIL-LI pleasure; toy / liviandad (C), juguete (T,Z) See ĀHUIY(A).

ĀHUILMACA vt to entertain someone / le complace (un niño) (Z) [(1)Zp.184]. See ĀHUIY(A), MACA.

ĀHUILNEM(I) pret: ĀHUILNEN to go about playing and wasting time / anda jugando, gastando el tiempo (Z) [(1)Zp.139, (1)Rp.60]. See ĀHUIY(A), NEM(I).

ĀHUILNENQUI idler / ocioso (T) [(1)Tp.169]. See ĀHUILNEM(I).

ĀHUILOĀ vt to waste, squander something / le desperdicia ... lo gasta (Z) [(1)Zp.184]. See ĀHUIY(A).

ĀHUILPOLHUIĀ applic. ĀHUILPOLOĀ

ĀHUILPOLOĀ vt to waste, squander something / ser pródigo y destruidor de la hacienda (M for reduplicated auilpopoloa) See ĀHUIY(A), POLOĀ.

ĀHUILPOLŌLŌ nonact. ĀHUILPOLOĀ

ĀHUILQUĪXTIĀ vrefl,vt to diminish oneself by misuse of office or property; to sell one's belongings to raise cash / infamarse o apocarse (M), lo saca (de la casa) para venderlo aunque sea barato para tener dinero (T) See ĀHUIY(A), QUĪZ(A).

ĀHUILTIĀ vrefl,vt to waste time; to entertain someone / pasar tiempo (M), dar placer a otro con algún juego regocijado, o retozar a alguna persona (M) altern. caus. ĀHUIY(A)

ĀHUI-TL aunt / tía (M)

ĀHUIY(A) pret: ĀHUĪX to be happy, content / tener lo necesario y estar contento (M) C attests the preterit twice, once with the vowel long and once with it unmarked for length. Elsewhere the lengthening of this vowel in the preterit of verbs ending in IY(A) is well attested. Derivations from ĀHUIY(A) have the somewhat divergent senses of 'contentment, happiness' and 'self-indulgence, loose behavior, waste.'

ĀHUIYALTIĀ altern. caus. ĀHUIY(A)

ĀHUIYANI courtesan, woman of pleasure / puta, o mala mujer (M) See ĀHUIY(A).

AHXĪHUA nonact. AHCI

AHXILIĀ vt to get to know something entirely; to stalk something, someone for someone / alcanzar a saber algo enteramente (M), montear, o cazar para otro (M) applic. AHCI

AHXILTIĀ *vt* to make something up, to complete something; to see someone to his place / suplir, o añadir lo que falta (M), acompañar o seguir a otro hasta su posada (M), hacer que llegue algo a alguna parte (M) altern. caus. AHCI

AHXĪTIĀ The vowel of the second syllable should be long by general rule and is consistently long in C, but it is short in T and twice specifically in B, although B also has it specifically marked long. altern. caus. AHCI

AHYĒC-TLI something bad / cosa mala (M) See AH-, YĒC-TLI.

AHZAYĀC See AHZO, AYĀC.

AHZO perhaps / por ventura, o quizá (M)

AHZOMAH See AHZO, MAH.

AHZOYEH See AHZO, (Y)EH.

AĪC never / nunca, o en ningún tiempo (M) The first element of this is from the negative particle AH- and is often written AY. See AH-, ĪC.

AĪCMAH never / jamás (C) [(1)Cf.119r]. See AĪC, MAH.

AIHHUACHMŌL-LI a stew prepared with squash seeds, ground corn, chili, and achiote / mole de pipián (T) [(1)Tp.107]. See AIHHUACH-TLI, MŌL-LI.

AIHHUACH-TLI squash seed / pepita de calabaza (X) [(1)Tp.107, (3)Xp.29]. The IH sequence of the first syllable is open to question, and X has HUĒX for HUACH. It is probably the same element as in AYOHHUACH-TLI and related to ACH-TLI 'seed.'

ĀIHĪYŌCALAQU(I) to sink / se sumerge dentro del agua (T) [(3)Tp.170]. See Ā-TL, IHĪYŌ-TL, CALAQU(I).

ĀIHĪYŌMIQU(I) to drown / se ahoga (T) [(3)Tp.117]. See Ā-TL, IHĪYŌ-TL, MIQU(I).

AITZTE-TL *possessed form:* **-AITZTEUH** gizzard / molleja en las aves (M) [(2)Zp.85,156]. See TE-TL.

ĀĪXCO on the surface of the water / encima del agua (K) [(1)Zp.177]. This seems to be synonymous with ĀTLĪXCO. See Ā-TL, ĪX-TLI, -C(O).

ALACTIC something slippery, crumbly / cosa deleznable (M) [(3)Zp.140]. Although

Z gives this with a long vowel in the second syllable, attestations of related items in T have a short vowel. Related derived forms with -HUA have the vowel long by a general lengthening rule. See AHALAC-TLI, ALAZTIC.

ALĀHU(A) *vrefl,vt* to slip; to slide something / resbalar (M)

ALĀHUILIĀ applic. ALĀHU(A)

ALĀHUAC something slippery, crumbly / lo mismo es que alactic (cosa deleznable) (M) see ALĀHU(A)

ALAXOĀ *vt* to polish something / lo afina, lo lima, lo pule, lo alisa (Z) [(1)Zp.185]. see ALAZTIC

ALAZTIC something slippery, crumbly / lo mismo es que alactic (cosa deleznable) (M) [(1)Tp.107]. Zp.140 has ALĀXTIC, which is probably the same with the vowel length of the second syllable in error, since the corresponding vowel of Z's ALAXOĀ is short.

ĀLPĪCHIĀ to spit / rocia (con la boca) (Z) [(2)Zp.203,204]. See Ā-TL, (I)LPĪCHIĀ.

ĀLTEPĒHUAH resident of a town / vecino de ciudad (M) See ĀLTEPĒ-TL.

ĀLTEPĒ-TL *pl:* **-MEH** town / pueblo, o rey (M) The literal sense of this is 'water-hill,' those two elements being fundamental necessities for a community. When possessed, the elements of the compound generally separate, with the possessive prefix attaching to each one, -ĀUH -TEPĒUH. See Ā-TL, TEPĒ-TL.

ĀLTIĀ *vrefl,vt* to bathe; to bathe someone / bañarse (M), bañar a otro, o hacer mercedes el mercader rico, o sacrificar y matar esclavos ante los idolos, o ofrecer ornamentos al templo o iglesia (M) See Ā-TL.

ĀLTZAPO-TL *pl:* **-MEH** type of sapota, the fruit of which has a narcotic effect (Lucuma salicifolia) / zapote borracho (T) [(1)Tp.170]. See TZAPO-TL.

ĀMĀC at the edge of the water / a la orilla del río (C) [(1)Cf.127r]. C contrasts this with ĀMAC (synonymous with ĀMAPAN) 'on paper.' See Ā-TL, -MĀC.

ĀMACHĪLTIĀ *vt* to over-water, over-irrigate something / lo riega demasiado, le dilata el riego (T) [(1)Tp.117]. See Ā-TL, MACHĪLTIĀ.

ĀMACUAHU(I)-TL fig tree (the inner bark

of which is used in papermaking) / amate
(árbol) (T) [(1)Tp.170]. See ĀMA-TL,
CUAHU(I)-TL.

ĀMAHUIĀ *vt* to paper something / empape-
lar algo (M) [(1)Rp.48]. R fails to mark the
initial vowel long. See ĀMA-TL, -HUIĀ.

ĀMAĪXMAT(I) to know how to read / sabe
leer (Z) [(1)Zp.140]. See ĀMA-TL,
ĪXMAT(I).

ĀMAĪZQUI-TL cherry tree / capulín (T)
[(1)Tp.170]. See ĀMA-TL, ĪZQUI-TL.

ĀMAN today / hoy (X) This is peculiar to X,
where it is abundantly attested. In phrases
it can have the sense 'immediately, right
away.'

ĀMAN(A) for water to be contained, as in a
tub or broad vessel / tener agua en lebrillo
o cosa ancha (C) [(1)Cf.127r, (1)Rp.60]. This
contrasts with AHMAN(A) 'to get worked
up, to be discontent' See Ā-TL, MAN(A).

ĀMANAL-LI pool of water, lake / alberca o
estanque de agua (M) [(1)Tp.170]. This also
appears in R but with the initial vowel
unmarked for length. X has ĀMAN-TLI.
See ĀMAN(A).

ĀMANTĒCA-TL artisan / oficial de arte
mecánica (M) [(1)Bf.10v, (2)Cf.4v,
(1)Tp.170, (1)Rp.60]. This originally referred specifically to featherworkers. In T
it has the special sense of 'healer, curandero,' while R glosses it as 'interlocutor,
speaker.'

ĀMANTĒCAYŌ-TL artisanry / arte
de oficial mecánico, o cosa que pertenece
a la dicha arte (M) [(1)Bf.10v]. See
ĀMANTĒCA-TL, -YŌ.

ĀMAN-TLI place where water collects /
arroyo, laguna (X) [(3)Xp.26]. X fails
to mark the initial vowel long. See
ĀMAN(A).

ĀMAPŌHU(A) to read (from a book or text) /
leer libro, o relatar proceso (M) [(3)Tp.170].
See ĀMA-TL, PŌHU(A).

ĀMAPŌHUALIZ-TLI reading (of books) /
leer (C) [(1)Cf.42r]. This is in a construction meaning 'to know how to read.' See
ĀMAPŌHU(A).

ĀMAQUĒMEHCĀN *place name* Amecameca See ĀMA-TL, QUĒM(I)-TL, -CĀN.

ĀMAQUĒMEHCA-TL *pl:* **ĀMAQUĒ-
MEHCAH** person from Amecameca /

natural de Amecameca (K) See ĀMA-
QUĒMEHCĀN.

ĀMA-TL *possessed form:* **-ĀMAUH** paper,
letter, book / papel (M), papel, carta, etc.
(S), papel o libro (C)

ĀMAXCUITL(A)-TL mud sludge, sediment /
lama (T) [(1)Tp.170, (2)Xp.26]. T has the
reflex of a short A in the second syllable. X
fails to mark the initial vowel long and has
Ō for A in the second syllable. M has
amaxac 'delta.' See Ā-TL, MAXAL-LI,
CUITL(A)-TL.

AMEHHUĀN you (plural) / vosotros (C) This
has a longer form AMEHHUĀNTIN. T and
Z have absorbed the article IN into the
pronoun: NAMEHHUĀN. This is a
freestanding pronoun as contrasted with
the prefixes AM- and AMĒCH- 'you
(plural).'

ĀMĒYALCO spring / manantial (T)
[(1)Tp.170]. This is a locative meaning
literally 'at the spring.' See ĀMĒYAL-LI,
-C(O).

ĀMĒYAL-LI spring, fountain / fuente de
agua (M), pozo, fuente, manantial (Z) Z has
a shortened variant: ĀMĒL. See Ā-TL,
MĒY(A).

ĀM(I) *pret:* **ĀN** to go hunting / montear, o
cazar (M) [(1)Bf.10r, (2)Cf.30v].

ĀMIC-TLI thirst / sed (T,Z) [(1)Tp.170,
(2)Zp.140]. See ĀMIQU(I).

ĀMĪL-LI irrigated field / tierra de regadío
(M) [(3)Xp.26]. This is only attested in a
compound and lacks diacritics, but it is a
transparent derivation. See Ā-TL, MĪL-LI.

ĀMĪLTOMA-TL green membrane tomato /
tomatillo de cáscara verde (X) [(3)Xp.26].
The attestation lacks diacritics, but the
derivation is transparent. See ĀMĪL-LI,
TOMA-TL.

ĀMĪN-TLI diarrhea / diarrea (Z) [(1)Zp.140].
M has *amina* 'to suffer indigestion from
drinking water after eating raw vegetables.'
See Ā-TL, MĪN(A).

ĀMIQU(I) *pret:* **ĀMIC** to be thirsty / tener
sed, o morir de sed (M) M also has an entry
amiqui 'something immortal' from the
negative prefix AH- and MICQUI, the
agentive noun derived from MIQU(I) 'to
die.' There is a contrast between ĀMIQU(I)
'to be thirsty' and AHMICQUI 'something

that does not die.' X has reduplicated
ĀMĪMIQU(I). See Ā-TL, MIQU(I).
ĀMIQUILIZ-TLI thirst / sed ardiente (S) M
combines in a single entry this sense and
that of AHMIQUILIZ-TLI 'immortality.'
See ĀMIQU(I).
ĀMOXPŌHU(A) to read (from a book or
text) / leer libro, o relatar el proceso (M)
[(1)Cf.42r]. See ĀMOX-TLI, PŌHU(A).
ĀMOXPŌHUALIZ-TLI reading (of books) /
leer (C) [(1)Cf.42r]. See ĀMOX-TLI,
PŌHU(A).
ĀMOXPŌUHQUI reader / lector (C)
[(1)Cf.52r]. M has *amoxpoani* with the
same sense. See ĀMOXPŌHU(A).
ĀMOX-TLI book / libro de escritura (M)
ĀN(A) vt to take hold of, seize something,
someone / tomar, asir, o prender (M)
ĀNĀL See Ā-TL, -NĀL.
ĀNALŌ altern. nonact. ĀN(A)
ĀNALTIĀ caus. ĀN(A)
ANCA therefore / de manera que (M), luego
(C)
ĀNEHNELOĀ redup. ĀNELOĀ
ĀNELOĀ to swim / nadar (X) [(3)Xp.26,
(1)Rp.61]. R reduplicates the initial syllable
of NELOĀ and fails to mark the Ā long.
See Ā-TL, NELOĀ.
ĀNILIĀ applic. ĀN(A)
ĀNŌ altern. nonact. ĀN(A)
ĀNQUI something long / cosa luenga o larga
(M) [(1)Tp.136].
ĀNTICAH to be at a certain distance / estar
algo lejos el lugar, o haber buen trecho
hasta él (M for *achica onantica*)
[(3)Bf.11,4v]. This progressive form is built
from the stem and the verb CĀ linked by
the ligature -TI-. CĀ is a preterit-as-present
verb with alternate preterit singular forms
CAH ~ CATQUI. *ĀN or *ĀM, the main
verb stem here, is otherwise unattested. It
is always prefixed with the directional
ON- to yield the alternate forms
ONĀNTICAH ~ ONĀNCATQUI. See CĀ.
ANTLEIN no, none / no hay (T) [(2)Tp.108].
This is a reduction of AHMŌ TLEIN. The
word-final N is dropped in T. See AHMŌ,
TLEIN.
AOC no longer, not any more / ya no (C)
This is a reduction of AH-OC and is often
written AYOC. See AH-, OC.

AOCĀC there is no longer anyone; the
person in question is no longer here / ya no
está aquí, o ya no parece (M) See AOC, ĀC.
AOCCĀMPA no longer anywhere / ya de
ninguna parte (M) See AOC, -CĀN, -PA.
AOCCĀN no longer anywhere / en ninguna
parte ya (C) See AOC, -CĀN.
AOCMŌ no longer, not anymore / ya no (M)
See AOC.
ĀOCOXŌCHI-TL a plant the foliage of
which grows all to one side / cierta planta
cuyos ramos se extienden solamente hacia
una parte (R) [(1)Rp.61]. See Ā-TL,
OCO-TL, XŌCHI-TL.
AOCTLE(H) nothing / nada ... ya no hay
nada, no más (S) The final H drops when
followed by a word beginning with a
vowel. See AOC, TLE(H).
ĀOCUIL-IN type of water animal / animal
que nada en el agua (Z) [(1)Zp.141]. The
literal sense of this is 'water-worm.' See
Ā-TL, OCUIL-IN.
AOQUĪC never again, no more / nunca más
(M) See AOC, ĪC, AĪC.
ĀPACHIHU(I) to get inundated, soaked /
remoja, está dentro del agua (T) [(1)Tp.170,
(1)Rp.61]. See Ā-TL, PACHIHU(I).
ĀPACHILHUIĀ applic. ĀPACHOĀ
ĀPACHOĀ vt to inundate something, to
soak something / echar algo en mojo, o
regar la hortaliza (M) See Ā-TL, PACHOĀ.
ĀPACHŌLŌ nonact. ĀPACHOĀ
ĀPACH-TLI roe, insect lavae, or plant that
grows in water, marsh hay / ovas que se
crían dentro del agua (M), planta que crece
dentro del río, heno (T) [(1)Tp.170]. See
Ā-TL, PACH-TLI.
ĀPANŌ pret: **ĀPANŌC** to cross, ford a body
of water / pasar a la otra parte del río o del
mar (M) See Ā-TL, PANŌ.
ĀPAN-TLI pl: **-MEH** ditch, canal, river /
acequia de agua (M), barranca, río (T), zanja
(T) [(2)Tp.170,171, (1)Rp.61]. R's gloss of
this as 'bridge' probably represents a different derivation from Ā-TL and PANŌ. In
one attestation T has a long vowel in the
second syllable. See Ā-TL, -PAN.
ĀPĪTZ(A) vrefl to have diarrhea / tener
cámaras (M), hace del excusado, depone (T)
[(3)Tp.165]. See Ā-TL, PĪTZ(A).
ĀPITZAC-TLI rivulet, small stream /

arroyo, riachuelo (Z) [(4)Zp.14,110,141]. The vowel of the second syllable should be short but is marked long in two of the four attestations. See Ā-TL, PITZAC-TLI.

ĀPĪTZAL-LI diarrhea / cámaras (M) This is implied by ĀPĪTZALPAH-TLI. See ĀPĪTZ(A).

ĀPĪTZALPAH-TLI turmeric / camotillo, planta conocida. Item otras tres plantas medicinales (R) [(1)Rp.62]. R fails to mark the vowels of the first two syllables long, but T has them long in the verb ĀPĪTZ(A) 'to have diarrhea.' See ĀPĪTZAL-LI, PAH-TLI.

ĀPĪZMIQU(I) *pret:* **ĀPĪZMIC** to be hungry / morir de hambre (M), tener hambre (C) See ĀPĪZ-TLI, MIQU(I).

ĀPĪZ-TLI hunger; hungry person / glotón; hambre (S), hambriento (Z) In T the vowel of the second syllable is short.

ĀPŌC-TLI water vapor; rain squall with wind / exhalación, vapor de agua (S), llueve con viento (T) [(1)Tp.171]. See Ā-TL, PŌC-TLI.

ĀPOHPOXOĀ to wallow in water / se revuelca en el agua (T) [(1)Tp.165]. See Ā-TL, POHPOXOĀ.

ĀPOYEC salt water / agua salada (T) [(1)Tp.171]. T has I for E. See Ā-TL, POYEC.

ĀQUETZ(A) to beat water into a foam / colgar el agua, como lo hace quien hace cacao, para que haga espuma (C) [(1)Cf.127r]. C contrasts this with AHQUETZ(A) 'to rise up, to turn upside down.' See Ā-TL, QUETZ(A).

AQU(I) *pret:* **AC** to enter, to fit in / contener, entrar en un lugar (S) In the phrase AQUI IN TŌNATIUH the sense is 'for the sun to set.' AQU(I) has two alternative nonactive forms, ACOHUA and AQUĪHUA, the second of which it apparently shares with AQUIĀ. AQUĪHUA is given with AQU(I) on Tp.108 and with AQUIĀ on Tp.140. The preterit form of this verb contrasts in vowel length with ĀC '(one) who; who?'

AQUIĀ *vrefl,vt* to adjust to something, to fit something; to cause something to be inserted, to plant something / se ajuste, se mete, se esconde, cabe (T), trasponer árboles, hincar estacas, o meter algo en

agujero (M) This apparently shares one alternative nonactive form, AQUĪHUA, with AQU(I). It contrasts with ĀQUIĀ 'to get dressed.' See AQU(I).

ĀQUIĀ *vrefl,vt* to get dressed; to do up a garment / vestirse camisa o vestidura cerrada (M) This contrasts with AQUIĀ 'to fit.'

ĀQUIHQUEH those who; who-plural? / ¿quiénes? (M) See ĀC.

AQUIHTŌN a bit / un poco (C) [(3)Cf.125v]. See ACHIHTŌN.

AQUIHTZIN a bit / un poco (C) [(1)Cf.125v]. See ACHIHTZIN.

AQUĪHUA nonact. AQU(I), AQUIĀ

AQUILIĀ applic. AQU(I)

ĀQUILIĀ applic. ĀQUIĀ

AQUĪL-LI red maize / maíz colorado (T) [(1)Tp.108]. S has the verb *aquili* with the sense of burnishing something or applying rouge.

AQUĪLŌ nonact. AQUIĀ

ĀQUĪLŌ nonact. ĀQUIĀ

AQUĪLTIĀ caus. AQUIĀ

ĀQUIN (one) who; who? / ¿quién, o a quién? (M), alguien, quien, alguno (T) See ĀC.

AQUĪTIĀ caus. AQU(I)

ĀQUĪXTIĀ to rinse clothing / enjaguar la ropa después de lavada (M) [(1)Tp.118]. See Ā-TL, QUĪXTIĀ.

ĀTECAX(I)-TL container in which mud is mixed / cajete (donde baten el lodo) (T) [(1)Tp.171]. See Ā-TL, TECAX(I)-TL.

ĀTECOM(A)-TL water gourd / calabaza redonda (M), guaje (calabazo para agua) (T) [(1)Tp.171, (6)Xp.28]. See Ā-TL, TECOM(A)-TL.

ĀTECONXŌCHI-TL *pl:* **-MEH** flower of the guaje vine (Lagenaria siceraria, Lagenaria leucantha), the fruits of which are made into water containers / flor de huaje (X) [(1)Xp.28]. X does not mark the first vowel long. See ĀTECOM(A)-TL, XŌCHI-TL.

ATEMIĀ *vrefl,vt* to delouse oneself; to delouse someone / espulgarse (M), espulgar a otro (M) See ATEM(I)-TL.

ATEMILIĀ applic. ATEMIĀ

ATEMĪLŌ nonact. ATEMIĀ

ATEM(I)-TL *possessed form:* **-ATEN** louse / piojo (M) Z has a long initial vowel, while X has the variant form ATIN-TLI.

ĀTĒNTĒNYOH shore, beach / orilla del
agua, playa (Z) [(1)Zp.142]. See ĀTĒN-TLI,
TĒNYOH.

ĀTĒN-TLI edge of a body of water / ribera de
río o de mar (M) See Ā-TL, TĒN-TLI.

ĀTĒNYOH river bank / orilla (del río) (Z)
[(1)Zp.155]. See Ā-TL, TĒNYOH.

ĀTĒQUIĀ vt to water or sprinkle water on
something, someone / regar (M), mojar a
otro echándole agua (M) See Ā-TL, TĒCA.

ĀTE-TL testicle, or rock in water /
compañón (M), piedra del río (Z)
[(1)Zp.142]. The literal sense of this is
'water-stone.' See Ā-TL, TE-TL.

ĀTEXĀ-TL pig swill / atolate (masa batida
para marranos) (T) [(3)Bf.2r,12r, (1)Tp.171].
T has O for Ā in the second syllable. See
Ā-TL, TEX-TLI.

ĀTEXPETL(A)-TL tortoise shell / su concha
(de tortuga) (T) [(1)Tp.132]. See Ā-TL,
TEXPETL(A)-TL.

ĀTĒZCA-TL surface of a body of water /
charco de agua, o nivel para nivelar agua
(M), el mar (T) [(1)Tp.171]. See Ā-TL,
TĒZCA-TL.

ĀTIC something melted, smelted / cosa
derretida, o cosa rala, o cosa trasparente
como cristal, etc. (M) [(1)Tp.171,
(1)Zp.142]. See ĀTIY(A), Ā-TL.

ĀTILIĀ applic. ĀTIY(A)

ĀTIY(A) pret: ĀTIYAC ~ ĀTĪX to melt, to
be smelted / derretirse o regalarse algo, o
pararse ralo lo espeso, o alegrarse mucho
(M) This has the vowel length alternation
in the preterit characteristic of verbs in
IY(A). See Ā-TL.

Ā-TL possessed form: -ĀUH water, liquid;
crown of the head / agua, orines, guerra, o
la mollera de la cabeza (M) In T there has
been a confusion of the possessed form of
Ā-TL 'water' with Spanish agua, and this
confusion has spread to the 'crown of
the head' sense, leading to a possessed
form -ĀHUA and three derived verbs
incorporating ĀHUA, namely
ĀHUAHUETZ(I), ĀHUATILĀN(A), and
ĀHUATZETZELOĀ.

ĀTLĀCA-TL person made of water / hombre
hecho de agua (C) [(1)Cf.57r]. C does not
write this out but describes it in prose as
contrasting with ĀTLAHCA-TL 'sailor,

fisherman' by lack of the internal glottal
stop. It also contrasts with AHTLĀCA-TL
'bad person.' See Ā-TL, TLĀCA-TL.

ĀTLACCO at the place of a gully or
stream / barranca, río (T) [(1)Tp.171]. See
ĀTLAC-TLI, -C(O).

ĀTLACOMŌL-LI well, valley with water /
pozo (M), valle (con agua) (Z) [(1)Zp.142].
Z has E for A in the second syllable. See
Ā-TL, TLACOMŌL-LI.

ĀTLACOXŌNIĀ vrefl to beat water with
one's hand / hace sonar el agua con la
mano (T) [(3)Tp.165]. See Ā-TL, COXŌN(I).

ĀTLAC-TLI pl: -MEH gully, stream /
barranca, río, arroyo, riachuelo (T)
[(1)Tp.171]. See Ā-TL, ĀTLAHU(I)-TL.

ĀTLACUI to draw water / sacar agua de
pozo o de jaguey (M) [(3)Tp.171]. See Ā-TL,
CUI.

ĀTLACUĪHUAYĀN place name Tacubaya
[(2)Cf.56v]. See ĀTLACUI, -YĀN.

ĀTLAH place of abundant water / abundancia de la cosa significada (agua) (C)
[(3)Cf.57r,127r]. See Ā-TL, -TLAH.

ĀTLAHCA-TL one who dwells in the water;
fisherman / el que vive en el agua, y el
pescador (C) [(2)Cf.57r,127r, (1)Rp.62]. M
combines the definition of this and of
AHTLĀCA-TL 'inhuman person' in a
single entry. They both contrast with C's
ĀTLĀCA-TL 'person made of water.' R
does not indicate the internal glottal stop.
See ĀTLAH.

ĀTLAHU(I)-TL valley, canyon, gully / valle,
cañada (Z) [(1)Zp.142]. The more common form is ĀTLAUH-TLI. See Ā-TL,
ĀTLAC-TLI.

ĀTLĀL-LI irrigated land / tierra de regadío
(M) [(1)Cf.118v]. See Ā-TL, TLĀL-LI.

ĀTLAPĒCH-TLI slope, side of a gully /
bajada (de la barranca) (T) [(1)Tp.171]. This
is attested with a long vowel in the third
syllable despite its apparent affinity to
TLAPECH-TLI 'bed' which consistently
has a short vowel across all sources including T. See Ā-TL.

ĀTLATLĀCATZĪCA-TL a type of ant /
hormiga (una especie) (T) [(1)Tp.171]. M
has atlatlacamani 'to bring on a storm or
torment.' Possibly T is characteristically
lacking a glottal stop, and the first element

of this compound should be ĀTLAH and
have to do with an abundance of water. See
TZĪCA-TL.

ĀTLATZCUEPŌNIĀ *vrefl* to beat water
with one's hand / hace sonar el agua con
la mano (T) [(3)Tp.165]. See Ā-TL,
TLATZĪN(I), CUEPŌNIĀ.

ĀTLATZIC something watered, watery /
aguado (Z) [(1)Zp.142]. See Ā-TL.

ĀTLAUH-TLI *pl:* **-TIN** valley, canyon, gully
/ barranca grande (M) [(3)Xp.28]. X does not
mark the first vowel long. See Ā-TL,
ĀTLAC-TLI, ĀTLAHU(I)-TL.

ĀTLĬ *pret:* **ĀTLĬC** to drink water / beber
agua o cacao (M) See Ā-TL, Ĭ.

ĀTLĬHUA nonact. ĀTLĬ

ĀTLĬHUALŌNI jug with two handles / jarro
de dos asas redondas (C) [(2)Cf.921,92v]. See
ĀTLĬ.

ĀTLĬLTIĀ caus. ĀTLĬ

ĀTLĬXCA-TL person from Atlixco / natural
de Atlixco (C) [(1)Bf.111, (1)Cf.56r]. See
ĀTLĬXCO.

ĀTLĬXCO *place name* Atlixco (literally
'surface of a body of water') / encima del
agua, o en la superficie (M) [(1)Cf.56r]. Z
has the variant ĀĪXCO. See Ā-TL, ĪX-TLI,
-C(O).

ĀTOCĀMĒCA-TL person from Atocan /
morador (de Atocan) (C) [(1)Cf.56v]. See
ĀTOCĀN.

ĀTOCĀN *place name* Atocan [(1)Cf.56v].

ĀTOHTOLOĀ to drown / se ahoga (Z)
[(1)Zp.142]. See Ā-TL, TOLOĀ.

ĀTŌLĀTZIN-TLI a bit of atole / un poquito
de atole (C) [(1)Cf.119v]. See ĀTŌL-LI,
ĀTZIN-TLI.

ĀTŌL-LI atole, a drink made from cornstarch / papilla de maíz<atole> de la cual
hacían gran consumo los indígenas prepa-
rándola de muy diversas maneras (S)

ĀTŌLOCA-TL *pl:* **-MEH** tadpole / atolocate,
atepocate (T) [(1)Tp.171]. See Ā-TL.

ĀTŌNAHU(I) *pret:* **ĀTŌNAUH** to have
chills and fever / tener calentura con frío
(M) [(1)Cf.106v]. See Ā-TL, TŌNA.

ĀTŌNAHUIZ-TLI a type of fever, malaria /
la terciana (C) [(1)Cf.107r, (1)Rp.63]. R
has this as the name of an insect. See
ĀTŌNAHU(I).

ĀTŌYĀHUIĀ *vrefl,vt* to throw oneself in
the river; to throw someone or something
in the river / echarse en el río (M), echar a
otro en el río (M), echar cualquier cosa el
río abajo (M) [(1)Bf.111r]. See ĀTŌYĀ-TL,
-HUIĀ.

ĀTŌYĀ-TL river / corriente de agua, río (S)
[(1)Bf.111r]. See Ā-TL.

ĀTZIN-TLI a bit of water, polite way of
referring to a beverage / pequeña cantidad
de agua (S) [(1)Cf.119v]. See Ā-TL.

ĀTZĪTZICĀZ-TLI water nettle / chichicastle (yerba) (Z), cierta planta semejante a
la ortiga (R) [(1)Zp.142, (1)Rp.63]. X has
ACHICĀL-IN 'nettle,' which appears to be
related. This appears in R without diacritics. See Ā-TL, TZĪTZICĀZ-TLI.

ĀTZŌTZOCOL-LI tall pitcher / cántaro (Z)
[(1)Zp.142]. M has *atzotzocolli* referring to
young men's long side locks of hair. The Z
attestation lacks an absolutive suffix. See
Ā-TL, TZŌTZOCOL-LI.

ĀTZOYŌN(I) for water to boil away / se
consume (el agua) por tanto hervir (T)
[(1)Tp.171]. See Ā-TL, TZOYŌN(I).

AUH and, but / conjunción copulativa (M)
This contrasts with ĀUH 'well, then.'

ĀUH well, then / pues (C), pues, ¿qué hay?
¿qué se hace? (M) C contrasts AUH and
ĀUH. ĀUH and its reverential form
ĀUHTZIN convey approval.

ĀXĀYAC(A)-TL a type of water insect, the
eggs of which serve as foodstuff / masca
palustre de cuyos huevos se hace el
ahuauhtli (R) [(1)Bf.111r]. This is used as a
personal name and as such generally takes
the honorific suffix -TZIN. See Ā-TL,
XĀYAC(A)-TL.

ĀXCĀCO possession, property / posesión,
propiedad (Z) [(1)Zp.156]. This appears to
be a locative with -C(O). See ĀXCĀ(I)-TL,
-C(O).

ĀXCĀHUAH a person with many possessions, someone wealthy / dueño de algo,
o rico y próspero (M) [(1)Cf.58v]. See
ĀXCĀ(I)-TL.

ĀXCĀHUAHCĀTI to make oneself
rich / hacerse rico (C) [(1)Cf.58v]. See
ĀXCĀHUAH.

ĀXCĀ(I)-TL possessions, property /

hacienda (C) This is often found in the
phrase -ĀXCĀ -TLATQUI (both elements
possessed) referring to someone's property.
ĀXCĀMPA then, thereupon / luego, desde
luego, o con tiempo (M) [(1)Cf.99r]. See
ĀXCĀN.
ĀXCĀN now, today / ahora (M)
ĀXCĀTIĀ vrefl,vt to appropriate to oneself;
to give possession of something to some-
one / aplicar, o apropiar para sí alguna cosa
(M), dar la posesión de alguna cosa a otro
(M) [(1)Bf.1v]. See ĀXCĀ(I)-TL.
ĀXĪC-TLI pl: -MEH eddy, whirlpool / remolino de agua que corre (M) [(1)Tp.171]. See
Ā-TL, XĪC-TLI.
ĀXIHU(I)-TL a type of tree / hoja santa
(árbol) (Z) [(1)Zp.142, (1)Rp.63]. R glosses
this as 'an herb' rather than a tree and fails
to mark the initial vowel long. See Ā-TL,
XIHU(I)-TL.
ĀXIL-LI river crayfish / cangrejo del río (Z)
[(1)Zp.142]. Because of the general reduction of geminate to single L in Z and the
tendency to loss of final N (general to T
but not to Z), it is possible that the absolutive form of this is ĀXIL-IN. See Ā-TL.
ĀX-IN pl: -TIN insect that secretes a substance used medicinally, and that substance itself / cierto ungüento de esta tierra (M), la grosura de ciertos gusanos que
se emplea útilmente en la medicina (R)
[(1)Tp.240, (2)Zp.34,208, (1)Rp.63]. R fails
to mark the initial vowel long, while T has
a stem-final A in the absolutive form
which is absent in the plural form.
ĀXĪX(A) vrefl to urinate or to have diarrhea / orinar o hacer cámara (M) See Ā-TL,
XĪX(A).
ĀXĪXALŌ nonact. ĀXĪX(A)
ĀXĪXILIĀ applic. ĀXĪX(A)
ĀXĪXPAH-TLI medicinal plant for treating
urinary disorders / nombre de tres plantas
medicinales (R) [(1)Rp.64]. See ĀXĪX-TLI,
PAH-TLI.
ĀXĪXPIPIHYĀC to smell like urine / huele
a orines (T) [(1)Tp.171]. See ĀXĪX(A),
PIPIHYĀC.
ĀXĪX-TLI pl: -TIN urine / meados o orines
(M) [(3)Xp.28]. See ĀXĪX(A).
ĀXŌCHI-TL pl: -MEH a marsh plant

(Erblichia odorata, Astianthus viminalis) /
asuchil (X) [(3)Xp.29]. X does not mark
the first vowel long. R has axochiatl
also referring to a water plant. See Ā-TL,
XŌCHI-TL.
ĀXŌLŌ-TL pl: -MEH axolotl, edible larval
salamander (Ambystoma tigrinum) / batra-
cio con branquias persistentes ... los mexicanos lo utilizaban y lo utilizan todavía
como alimento (S), ajolote, pez conocido
de cuatro pies, que menstrua como las
mujeres (R) [(1)Zp.142, (3)Xp.29, (1)Rp.64].
See Ā-TL, XŌLŌ-TL.
ĀXOXOCTZIN a type of bird with green
plumage / pájaro verde (X) [(3)Xp.29]. See
Ā-TL, XOXOCTIC.
ĀXOXŌHUĪL-LI deep water; beach, green
(shallow) water / abismo de agua profunda
(M), playa, agua verde (Z) [(1)Zp.142]. For M
this refers to water so deep it appears blue
green, while Z uses it for water that turns
to light green as it grows shallower and the
bottom begins to show through. See Ā-TL,
XOXŌHUIYA.
AYA not yet, no longer / aun no (C) R
consistently has a final glottal stop in this
item. See AH-, YA.
AYĀC no one / ninguno, o nadie (M) See
AH-, ĀC.
ĀYACACHCUAHU(I)-TL mahogany tree /
caoba (Z), planta de hojas como las del
algodón (R) [(1)Zp.142, (1)Rp.64]. R has X
for CH and does not mark the initial vowel
long. See ĀYACACH-TLI, CUAHU(I)-TL,
CUAUHĀYACACH-TLI.
ĀYACACHE-TL a type of bean / frijol chino
(T) [(1)Tp.172]. See ĀYACACH-TLI, E-TL.
ĀYACACHILHUIĀ applic. ĀYACACHOĀ
ĀYACACHOĀ to play the rattle / tañer
las sonajas llamadas ayacachtli (C) See
ĀYACACH-TLI.
ĀYACACH-TLI rattle / sonajas hechas a
manera de dormideras (M) The Bf.10v
attestation is at variance in its vowel
length pattern from all the other attestations, which are consistent across C,T,Z. R
and X have the variant ĀYACAX-TLI.
AYACĀN as yet nowhere / aun en nin-
guna parte o lugar (M) See AYA, -CĀN.
ĀYACAX-TLI See ĀYACACH-TLI.

AYAHUEL(I) as yet impossible / aun no es possible (M) See AYA, HUEL(I), AHHUEL(I).

ĀYĀHUIĀ *vt* to toss something in a blanket / lo sacude con ayate (p.ej. maíz) (T) See ĀYĀ-TL, -HUIĀ.

ĀYĀHUILIĀ applic. ĀYĀHUIĀ

ĀYĀHUĪLŌ nonact. ĀYĀHUIĀ

ĀYAHU(I)-TL cloud, fog / niebla, neblina, o nube del ojo (M) This has an interesting similarity to QUIYAHU(I)-TL 'rainstorm.' See Ā-TL.

AYAĪC never yet, never until now / nunca hasta ahora (C) See AYA, AĪC, YA.

ĀYAMĀNILĀ-TL tepid water / agua tibia (T) [(1)Tp.172]. See Ā-TL, YAMĀNIĀ.

AYAMŌ not yet / aun no (M) R consistently has AYAHMŌ. See AYA.

ĀYĀ-TL cotton or henequen cloak, blanket / manta delgada de algodón, o de maguey (M)

ĀYĀTLAQUĒN-TLI part of a garment, cover / bocamanga, cobija (Z) [(1)Zp.142]. The literal sense of this is 'ayate-garment.' See ĀYĀ-TL, TLAQUĒN-TLI, QUĒM(I)-TL.

ĀYAUHCŌZAMĀLŌTŌNAMĒYOHTI-MANI to shimmer in rainbow colors / está resplandeciendo a manera del arco iris (C) [(1)Cf.77r]. See ĀYAHU(I)-TL, CŌZAMĀLŌ-TL, TŌNAMĒYOĀ.

ĀYĀXCĀN with difficulty, slowly / con dificultad, o apenas (M), algo despacio, y con flema (C)

ĀYĀXCĀNYOH someone phlegmatic / el flemático (C) [(2)Cf.123v]. See ĀYĀXCĀN, -YOH.

ĀYĀXCĀNYŌ-TL slowness, dullness, apathy / lentitud, indolencia, flojedad (S) [(2)Cf.123v]. See ĀYĀXCĀN, -YŌ.

ĀY(I) *vt; pret:* ĀX to do something / hacer alguna cosa exterior (M) This verb can also be used intransitively. TLA-ĀY(I) with the indefinite object prefix means 'to cultivate land.' See TLAĀX-TLI.

AYĪC See AĪC.

ĀYĪHUA nonact. ĀY(I)

ĀYILIĀ applic. ĀY(I)

ĀYĪLTIĀ T attests this with a long vowel in the second syllable, although by general rule it should be short. altern. caus. ĀY(I)

ĀYĪTIĀ altern. caus. ĀY(I)

AYOC See AOC.

ĀYOH something that contains water / cosa aguada, como vino o miel, etc. (M) [(3)Cf.54v,126v, (1)Zp.142, (2)Rp.45,64]. C gives this twice with the absolutive suffix -TLI and contrasts it with AYOH-TLI 'squash.' See Ā-TL, -YOH.

AYOHCONĒ-TL small squash / calabacita (T) [(1)Tp.109]. See AYOH-TLI, CONĒ-TL.

AYOHCOZTIC yellow squash / calabaza de castilla (Z) [(1)Zp.142]. See AYOH-TLI, COZTIC.

AYOHHUACHMŌL-LI green mole, a sauce made from ground squash seeds / mole verde (T) [(1)Tp.109]. See AYOHHUACH-TLI, MŌL-LI.

AYOHHUACH-TLI squash seed / pepitas de calabaza (M) [(2)Tp.109, (3)Xp.29]. The HUACH elemet of this seems to correspond to the free form ACH-TLI 'seed.' X has HUĒX in place of HUACH. See AYOH-TLI, ACH-TLI.

AYOHQUIL(I)-TL squash greens / hierba de calabaza (X) [(2)Xp.29]. X lacks the glottal stop. See AYOH-TLI, QUIL(I)-TL.

AYOHTEQU(I) See AYOH-TLI, TEQU(I).

AYOHTLAH squash patch / calabazal (R) [(1)Rp.64]. See AYOH-TLI, -TLAH.

AYOH-TLI *pl:* **-MEH** squash, calabash / calabaza (M)

ĀYŌHUA to fill up with water / henchirse de agua, aguarse (C) [(1)Cf.54v]. See Ā-TL, ĀYŌ-TL.

ĀYŌHUIĀ *vt* to warm something with the breath / calentar algo con el huelgo, o echar el huelgo (M), le sopla como cuando uno calienta sus manos ... (T) This appears to be related to IHĪYŌ-TL 'breath' in some idiosyncratic way. See -HUIĀ.

AYOHXIHU(I)-TL squash greens / hierba de calabaza (X) [(2)Xp.29]. X lacks the glottal stop. See AYOH-TLI, XIHU(I)-TL.

AYOHXŌCHI-TL squash blossom / flor de calabaza (M) See AYOH-TLI, XŌCHI-TL.

AYOHYŌL-LI squash seed / pepita, semilla de calabaza (X) [(3)Xp.29]. X lacks the glottal stop. See AYOH-TLI, YŌL-LI.

ĀYŌTIĀ *vt* to irrigate something, to sprinkle water on something / aguar algo (M) [(3)Tp.118]. See Ā-TL.

ĀYŌ-TL *pl:* **-MEH** turtle, tortoise / tortuga

(M) [(1)Tp.172, (3)Xp.29]. X does not mark the initial vowel long. See Ā-TL.

ĀYŌ-TL something watery; broth, soup / caldo de alguna cosa (C) See Ā-TL, -YŌ.

ĀYŌTŌCHCACAHUA-TL armadillo shell / concha de armadillo (Z) [(1)Zp.142]. See ĀYŌTŌCH-IN, CACAHUA-TL.

ĀYŌTŌCH-IN armadillo / armadillo (Z), cuadrúpedo; especie de lagarto cubierto de escamas (S) [(2)Zp.142, (1)Rp.64]. If this means literally 'turtle-rabbit,' as it seems to, the vowel of the second syllable should be long, but in the attestations it is not so marked. R has the absolutive suffix -TLI rather than -IN. See ĀYŌ-TL, TŌCH-IN, TŌCH-TLI.

ĀYŌTZĪNCUEP(A) *vrefl* to tumble / voltear o trepar al modo de españa (M) See TZĪN-TLI, CUEP(A).

ĀZACA to draw, transport water / acarrear agua, o ser azacani y aguador (M) See Ā-TL, ZACA.

ĀZCACUAHU(I)-TL a type of tree that serves as a host for a species of ant that makes its nest within it (Cordia alliodora, Cordia gerascanthus, Cerdana alliodora) / hormiguillo (árbol) (Z) [(1)Zp.141]. See ĀZCA-TL, CUAHU(I)-TL.

ĀZCACUALOĀ to have a tingling sensation / adormecido (la mano) (Z) [(1)Zp.178]. The

first vowel is not marked long in the attestation, but the sense suggests that it is derived from ĀZCA-TL.

ĀZCAPŌTZALCO *place name* Azcapotzalco [(1)Bf.9v, (1)Cf.120v]. See ĀZCAPŌTZAL-LI, -C(O).

ĀZCAPŌTZAL-LI ant hill / hormiguero (M) [(1)Bf.9v, (1)Cf.120v, (1)Rp.65]. C has TZ where B and R have Z. See ĀZCA-TL, PŌTZAL-LI.

ĀZCA-TL ant / hormiga (M)

ĀZCAXŌCHI-TL *pl:* **-MEH** a type of flowering plant associated with ants, one of several different plants known as 'lirio.' / flor de hormiga, lirio (X) [(3)Xp.27, (1)Rp.65]. X does not mark the first vowel as long, and R has no diacritics at all, but this is a transparent compound. See ĀZCA-TL, XŌCHI-TL.

ĀZOLŌN(I) for a blister to form, for water to bubble up / hace ámpula (Z) [(1)Zp.141]. See Ā-TL, ZOLŌN(I).

ĀZOLŌNIĀ *vt* to blister something / lo ampolla (Z) [(1)Zp.185]. In the single attestation, the vowel length values of the stem are reversed, with the vowel of ZO marked long and those of the adjacent syllables not marked for length. Since this is certainly a derivation from ĀZOLŌNI, the attestation is clearly in error.

C

CA clause introductory particle / porque. conjunción para dar razon de algo (M), pues es (C), ya, cierto, dónde, porque, por qué, puesto que (S) Corresponding to the English construction 'as for (something),' followed by a clause, Nahuatl has '(something), CA' followed by the relevant clause. C gives the example *inōn calli, ca àmo tè mocal* 'as for that house, it is not yours.' The CA is not obligatory to the construction; its presence conveys emphasis. CA also combines as initial element with other particles and particle clusters; CA AHMŌ (emphatic negation), CA HUEL OC 'todavía,' CA NEL 'porque,' CA NEL NOZO 'porque' (emphatic), CA YE 'ya,' CA ZAN 'sino que,' etc. The emphatic force of CA is often negligible.

-CA *instrumental postposition* through, by, by means of / de, por, mediante (C) This binds to nouns with the ligature -TI-. The -CA of NECHCA 'from here to there,' ACHIHTŌNCA 'a short time,' and similar forms seems to be a different cliticizing particle that does not imply instrumentality and does not require -TI-.

-CĀ- *a linking element traditionally known as a ligature* This serves to bind one verb in its preterit form to a second verb. This medial -CĀ- and the final -QUI of the class of derived nouns known as preterit agentives appear to be derived from the same source. The sense of the construction is that the second verb is performed in the manner of one who is or does whatever the first verb signifies; CUALĀN(I) 'to become angry,' (I)TTA 'to see something' > CUALĀNCĀITTA 'to look upon something angrily.' Preterit agentive nouns have -CĀ- in derivations; TLAHTOHQUI 'ruler' (< TLAHTOĀ 'to speak, to give orders'), TLAHTOHCĀYŌ-TL 'kingdom.' -CĀ- also links nouns derived with the possessor

suffixes -EH and -HUAH to other elements; CALEH 'householder,' CĀHU(A) 'to give something up' > CALEH-CĀCĀHU(A) 'to turn over stewardship of a household to someone.'

CĀ *preterit-as-present verb; pret:* **CAH** ~ **CATQUI,** *pret. pl:* **CATEH** to be / estar, o ser (M) Since the preterit of this verb is used for the present tense, past tense is expressed with the pluperfect form CATCA. It is suppletive with the verb YE, which is used for the future, the imperative, and the optative. The nonactive YELOHUA is built on the YE verb. The sense of CĀ in context is generally locative or existential. In equational sentences CĀ and YE are used only as vehicles for overt tense marking other than simple present or unspecified time; otherwise they are omitted from the sentence.

CACA toad, frog / sapo (T), rana (X) [(1)Tp.112, (6)Xp.31,104]. No absolutive suffix is attested. T has this with -TŌN, and X has it with -TZIN. See CALĀ-TL.

CACAHUACA to be indisposed, disordered, feverish; to shine, to glare / tener gran destemplanza y calor en el cuerpo (M), brilla ... resplandece (Z) [(2)Zp.21,143]. See CAHUĀN(I).

CACAHUANĀN-TLI tree planted to give shade to coffee bean shrubs / árbol que se planta en las sementeras de cacao para hacerle sombra (R) [(1)Rp.65]. R fails to mark the vowel of the fourth syllable long. See CACAHUA-TL, NĀN-TLI.

CACAHUA-TL cacao, chocolate bean; shell, hard outer covering / grano de cacao (M) In Nahuatl the word for 'peanut' is specifically TLĀLCACAHUA-TL< TLĀL-LI 'earth,' CACAHUA-TL.

CACALACA to rattle / sonar el cascabel, o la vasija de barro que tiene dentro pedrezuelas, o el cacao dañado cuando lo

cuentan, o echan en el suelo, o cosa semejante (M), suena (Z) See CACALATZ(A),
CALĀN(I).

CACALACHILIĀ applic. CACALACA

CACALACHILĪLŌ nonact. CACALACA

CĀCALĀCH-IN *pl:* **-TIN** cockroach /
cucaracha (T) [(2)Tp.117]. X has
CALĀCH-IN, pl: -MEH, apparently an
apocopated form, with the same sense.
CĀCALĀCH-IN has a different vowel
length pattern from the verb CACALACA
'to rattle' and the associated noun
CACALACH-TLI, which might otherwise
be taken to be related in sense.

CACALACHTIC someone thin, gaunt /
flaco, delgado (Z) [(2) Zp.60,143]. One of
the two attestations has the vowel of the
second syllable long. In two related forms,
CACALTIC 'thin, gaunt' and CACALCUI
'to become thin,' Z does not have a
long vowel in the second syllable. See
CACALTIC, CACALCUI.

CACALACH-TLI *pl:* **-MEH ~ -TIN** rattle /
cascabel de barro (M), sonaja (T), su cascabel (de víbora) (T) See CACALACA.

CĀCALĀCHTŌTŌ-TL *pl:* **-MEH** Mexican flycatcher / avispero (pájaro) (T)
[(2)Tp.117,243]. In Spanish this is known
as a wasp (eating) bird, but in Nahuatl it is
a cockroach bird. See CĀCALĀCH-IN,
TŌTŌ-TL.

CĀCALĀN(I) redup. CALĀN(I)

CACALATZ(A) *vt* to cause something to
make a rattling noise / hacer ruido revol-
viendo jícaras, o nueces, o cosas semejantes; o abriendo y cerrando cajas, cajones, o
puertas y ventanas (M) See CACALACA,
CALĀN(I).

CACALATZALŌ nonact. CACALATZ(A)

CACALCUI to become thin, to lose weight /
se enflaquece (Z) [(2)Zp.51,143]. See
CACALTIC, CUI.

CĀCALŌ-TL *pl:* **-MEH** crow / cuervo (M)

CĀCALŌXŌCHI-TL *pl:* **-MEH** frangipanni
(Plumeria rubra) / flor de singular fragrancia que se da en racimos, en ciertos árboles
de tierra caliente (R), flor del cuervo,
cacalosuchil (X) [(1)Rp.66, (3)Xp.30]. X does
not mark the first vowel long, and R has
no diacritics at all for this item, but the
Spanish name leaves no doubt about the

derivation. See CĀCĀLŌ-TL, XŌCHI-TL.

CACALTIC someone thin, gaunt / flaco,
delgado (Z) [(2)Zp.60,143]. See
CACALACHTIC.

CACAMA-TL *pl:* **-MEH** secondary ears of
maize that form at the base of the primary
ear / mazorcas pequeñas de maíz, que
nacen cabe la mazorca mayor (M), jilote (T)
[(1)Tp.112].

CĀCANATZIN something thin / (cosa)
delgada (T) [(1)Tp.117]. See CANACTIC,
CANĀHUAC.

CACAPACA to make a slapping sound /
sonar las chinelas o alcorques cuando
andan con ellas (M) [(1)Cf.74r]. See
CAPĀN(I).

CACAPATZ(A) *vt* to cause something to
make a slapping noise / hacer ruido con los
pantuflos, o chinelas cuando andan (M)
[(3)Cf.74r]. Because of the hand slapping
that goes into it, this can be used to refer
to tortilla-making. Z has what appears to
be this verb compounded with HUETZ(I)
meaning 'to fall very hard.' In one attestation the vowels of the first two syllables
are marked long, and in the other they are
not. See CAPĀN(I).

CĀCĀX-TLI packframe / escalerillas de
tablas para llevar algo a cuestas el tameme
(M) [(5)Bf.51,5v,7r].

CĀCAXTŌLTICA every fifteen days / de
quince en quince días (C) See CAXTŌL-LI,
-CA.

CACAZŌTIC something porous / poroso
(como esponja o piedra poma) (T)
[(1)Tp.112].

CACCHĪHU(A) to make shoes / hacer
zapatos (S) [(2)Cf.51v,52r, (1)Rp.66]. None
of the attestations has the second vowel
marked long, but the compound is transparent. See CAC-TLI, CHĪHU(A).

CACCHĪHUHCĀN place where shoes are
made / zapatería (M) [(1)Cf.51v]. See
CACCHĪHU(A), -CĀN.

CACCHĪHUHQUI shoemaker / zapatero (M)
[(1)Cf.52r]. See CACCHĪHU(A).

CACHOPĪN *pl:* **-TIN** pejorative term for
Spaniard, European / gachupín (T)
[(1)Tp.112]. This is thought to be a Nahuatl
word derived from CAC-TLI 'shoe' and
CHOPĪNIĀ 'to pick at something,' but this

attestation is in a modern source, where it could be a loanword or a back loan. The term appears as early as the first half of the 18th century in Nahuatl texts.

CACTI *no preterit form given* to moderate, to calm down / se va calmando (T) [(1)Tp.112]. This is the first element of the common verb CACTIMAN(I) 'to be quiet, empty, deserted' and M's *cactiuetzi* 'to fall quiet.' The -TI- of the compound forms seems to be the -TI- 'ligature' that binds together verb stems, which makes the free form CACTI appear anomalous. Aside from this single attestation, the initial element does not occur independently. See CACTIMAN(I).

CACTIĀ *vrefl, vt* to put on one's shoes; to put shoes on someone / calzarse los zapatos, o cacles (M), calzar zapatos a otro (M) See CAC-TLI.

CACTIHUETZ(I) to fall quiet / hacer bonanza después de la tormenta, y aclarar el tiempo (M) This is not directly attested in the sources for this dictionary, but its component parts are attested. See CACTIMAN(I), HUETZ(I).

CACTILIĀ applic. CACTIĀ

CACTĪLŌ nonact. CACTIĀ

CACTIMAN(I) for there to be silence, stillness, absence of activity; for the weather to be fair / casa desamparada que se no habita, o hacer bonanza y buen tiempo, o haber silencio un poco de tiempo, o estar la ciudad asolada de repente y destruída (M) The initial element of this construction is restricted in occurrence. M has it in *cactiuetzi* 'to fall quiet,' and T has CACTI 'to moderate.' See CACTI, MAN(I).

CAC-TLI *pl: -MEH* shoe / cacles, o zapatos, sandalias, etc. (M)

CAH See the verb CĀ.

CAHCĀHU(A) *vrefl, vt* to give up, to lose; to set something, someone loose, to free someone, something / dejarse o apartarse muchas veces los casados, o pasarse los unos a los otros los que caminan, o los que trabajan y cavan la tierra a destajo (M), callarse (X), lo abandona, le permite, le da libertad (T) redup. CĀHU(A)

CAHCĀHUALŌ nonact. CAHCĀHU(A)

CAHCALĀNIĀ *vt* to beat, pound something / golpea (Z) [(2)Zp.63,204]. See CALĀN(I).

CAHCALAQU(I) redup. CALAQU(I)

CAHCAMANĀLOĀ redup. CAMANĀLOĀ

CAHCAPOLLAH place where there are cherry orchards / cerezales (C) [(1)Cf.72r]. This is given by C as the plural of CAPOLLAH 'cherry orchard.' Strictly speaking, it is the reduplicated stem of CAPOL-IN 'cherry tree' bound to -TLAH 'place where the relevant thing is found in abundance.' See CAPOL-IN, -TLAH.

CAHCATZA *vt* to tie something securely / atar fuertemente alguna cosa, o embutir o recalcar algo (M) [(1)Cf.116v].

CAHCATZILPIĀ *vt* to tie something securely / atar reciamente algo (M) [(1)Cf.116v]. See CAHCATZA, (I)LPIĀ.

CAHCAYĀHU(A) *vrefl, vt* to mock or deceive someone / burlar o escarnecer de otro, o engañarle (M) M gives this as reflexive and in construction with TĒCA 'with regard to someone,' but T, Z, and X treat it as a simple transitive verb. redup. CAYĀHU(A)

CAHTZŌ-TL jicama, an edible root (Pachyrhizus angulatus) / jícama, raíz comestible (R) [(2)Zp.73,143, (1)Rp.68]. Z marks the second vowel long in one attestation and not in the other. This appears in R without diacritics.

CĀHU(A) *vt* to leave, abandon, relinquish something, someone / dejar algo, o llevar alguna cosa a otra parte (M), dejar o desamparar a otro, o exceder y sobrepujar a los otros (M)

CAHUĀCTIC something hot / caliente (Z) [(2)Zp.24,143]. Although Z marks the vowel of the second syllable long in both attestations, the expected form would be a short vowel. See CAHUĀN(I).

CĀHUAL-LI one who is left behind, widow, widower / viudo, viuda (X) This is attested as a free form in X and Z and is abundantly attested in compounds across sources. See CĀHU(A).

CĀHUALŌ nonact. CĀHU(A)

CĀHUALTIĀ *vrefl, vt* to restrain oneself; to restrain, prohibit someone / irse a la mano o abstenerse de algo (M), vedar a otro, o irle a la mano (M) caus. CĀHU(A)

CAHUĀN(I) to catch fire / prende (Z)
[(4)Zp.24,101,143]. Two of these
attestations are in the construction
CAHUĀNTOC< CAHUĀN(I) bound to
the preterit-as-present verb O with the -TI-
ligature. See CAHUĀCTIC.

CAHUĀNTIĀ *vt* to set something afire / lo
enciende, lo calienta, hace lumbre (Z)
[(3)Zp.23,50,185]. In one of the two attestations the vowel of the first syllable is
marked long, but it is not in the other or in
related forms. See CAHUĀN(I),
CAHUĀCTIC.

CĀHUILIĀ applic. CĀHU(A)

CĀHU(I)-TL time / tiempo (M)

CAHUĪX-IN *pl:* **-MEH** osprey / quebranta-
hueso, aura (T) [(1)Tp.112]. In Campeche
CAHUĪX without the absolutive suffix is
used as the name for the female grackle.
See CUĪX-IN.

CALACĀHUIĀ *vt* to attack someone,
something / lo ataca, lo asalta (Z)
[(4)Zp.15,16,185,204].

CALĀCH-IN *pl:* **-MEH** cockroach /
cucaracha (X) [(3)Xp.31]. See
CĀCALĀCH-IN.

CALACOHUA nonact. CALAQU(I)

CALACOHUAYĀN door, entry / puerta o
entrada para entrar o salir (M) [(1)Cf.91v].
X has CALAQUIYĀN, derived from
the active form of the verb CALAQU(I)
and apparently synonymous. See
CALACOHUA, -YĀN.

CALĀMPA outside / afuera (Z) [(2)Zp.6,143].
In one of the two attestations the vowels of
both syllables are marked long; in the
other only the second is. See CALĀN, -PA.

CALĀN outside / afuera (Z)
[(6)Zp.6,112,143,185]. In two of six attestations Z marks the vowel of the first
syllable long. This is possibly derived from
CAL-LI and -TLĀN with degemination of
medial LL resulting from LTL assimilation.
See CALLĀMPA.

CALĀN(I) to jingle, to rattle / reteñir el
metal (M), hacer ruido cosas como nueces,
jícaras, cosas de madera (C) [(1)Cf.73v]. See
CACALACA, CACALATZ(A).

CALĀNQUĪXTIĀ *vt* to take something
outside / lo saca afuera [(2)Zp.112,185]. See
CALĀN, QUĪXTIĀ.

CALAQU(I) *pret:* **CALAC** to enter / entrar o
meterse en alguna parte (M) CALAQU(I)
has essentially the same sense as AQU(I)
and appears to be derived from that verb
and CAL-LI 'house.' This would mean
literally 'to house-fit, to house-enter.' The
construction has been lexicalized to the
point that the CAL element contributes
nothing literal to the construction as a
whole. See CAL-LI, AQU(I).

CALAQUIĀ *vrefl, vt* to enter into
something such as employment; to close
something up inside something / entrar
con otro asoldada (M), meter o encerrar
trigo o cosas semejantes en casa (M), meter
dentro (C) See CALAQU(I).

CALAQUILIĀ applic. CALAQUIĀ

CALĀ-TL frog / rana (Z) [(4)Zp.105,143,230].
M has *milcalatl* 'a type of frog.' See CACA.

CALCA-TL householder, resident / el que
tiene casa (C) [(3)Cf.56v]. C equates
CALQUI, CALCA-TL, and CHĀNEH in
sense. See CAL-LI.

CALCHĪHU(A) to build a house / hace una
casa (T) [(3)Tp.113]. M has *calchiualiztli*
'repairs made to a house.' See CAL-LI,
CHĪHU(A).

CALCUĀCO at the peak of the house /
encima de la casa, azotea, techo, tejado (Z)
[(2)Zp.50,143]. The expected form would
be CALCUĀC. See CAL-LI, CUA(I)-TL,
-C(O).

CALCUĒCH-TLI soot / hollín (S)
[(2)Zp.143]. Z has Ī for Ē. See CAL-LI,
CUĒCH-TLI.

CALCUĪCH-TLI See CALCUĒCH-TLI.

CALEH guardian of the household,
householder / dueño de la casa (M) See
CAL-LI.

CALEHCĀTZIN-TLI guardian of the household (honorific) / cuidador de la casa (T)
[(1)Tp.113]. T has I for E. See CALEH.

CALĪCAMPA behind the house / atrás de
la casa (Z) [(2)Zp.16,143]. Z also has a
shortened form CALĪCAN. See CAL-LI,
-ĪCAMPA.

CALIHTEC See CALIHTIC.

CALIHTIC inside the house / hacia dentro
de casa (M for *caliticpa*), dentro de casa (C)
See CAL-LI, -IHTIC.

CALĪXPAN in front of the house / delante

de la casa (S), patio (Z) [(2)Zp.95,144]. See CAL-LI, -ĪXPAN.

CALĪX-TLI entryway, patio / zaguán (M), vestíbulo, puerta (S) [(2)Zp.95,144]. See CAL-LI, ĪX-TLI.

CALLÁLIÁ *vrefl* to set up housekeeping / hace hogar (Z) [(2)Zp.68,169]. See CAL-LI, TLÁLIÁ.

CALLÁMPA corridor / corredor (Z) [(1)Zp.144]. See CAL-LI, -TLĀN, -PA.

CAL-LI *pl:* **-TIN** house / casa (M) M combines the definitions of CAL-LI and CĀL-LI 'tongs' in a single entry. R has CAL-LI and CĀL-LI as separate entries but with the vowel length values reversed.

CĀL-LI tongs / tenazuelas de palo o de caña para comer maíz tostado en el rescoldo (M) [(2)Cf.47v,127r]. This contrasts with CAL-LI 'house.' M combines the two in a single entry. R contrasts them but has the vowel length values reversed.

CALLŌTIÁ *vrefl* to reside / se aloja (T) [(3)Tp.145]. See CAL-LI.

CALLŌTĪLŌ nonact. CALLŌTIÁ

CALMECAC name of one of the academies of precolumbian Mexico / una de las academias precolombinas, donde estudiaban los nobles (K) [(1)Bf.10v]. See CAL-LI, MECA-TL, -C(O).

CALNĒNEPANIUHQUI a house of more than two stories / casa de más de uno (sobrado) (C) [(1)Cf.73r]. See CALNEPANIUHQUI.

CALNEPANIUHQUI two-story house / casa de un sobrado (C) [(3)Cf.73r]. M has *calnepanolli* for 'story of a house.' See CAL-LI, -NEPANŌL-LI.

CALPANOĀ *vt* to go visiting people / andar de casa en casa (M) [(4)Zp.130,185,219]. See CAL-LI, -PAN.

CALPATLA *vrefl* to move / se muda de lugar (Z) [(2)Zp.86,169]. See CAL-LI, PATLA.

CALPIXQUI major-domo, steward / mayordomo (M), el mayordomo, el que guarda las cosas de casa (C) See CAL-LI, PIY(A).

CALPOHPŌCHECTIC house filled with smoke / casa ahumada (T) [(1)Tp.113]. See CAL-LI, PŌCHECTIC.

CALQUI householder, resident / el que tiene casa (C) [(3)Cf.56v]. C equates CALQUI, CALCA-TL, and CHĀNEH in sense. See CAL-LI.

CALTECH next to a house, to one side / en la pared (C) See CAL-LI, -TECH.

CALTECHILHUIĀ applic. CALTECHOĀ

CALTECHOĀ *vrefl,vt* to separate, to draw aside; to set something to one side / se echa a un lado, se aparta, se ladea (T), lo echa a un lado, lo aparta, lo pone aparte (T) [(6)Tp.145,179]. See CALTECH.

CALTECHŌLŌ nonact. CALTECHOĀ

CALTECH-TLI wall of a house; walkway along the side of a house / pared, la acera de ella (M) See CALTECH.

CALTĒNCO outdoors / campo (T) [(1)Tp.113]. See CALTĒN-TLI, -C(O).

CALTĒN-TLI corridor, walkway along the side of a house / la acera de la pared de las casas (M), cerca de la puerta (Z) See CAL-LI, TĒN-TLI.

CALTĒNYOH corridor, patio / corredor, patio (Z) [(3)Zp.34,95,144]. See CALTĒN-TLI.

CALTETZON-TLI foundation of a building / cimiento de casa, hasta medio estado de pared (M) [(1)Cf.75v]. See CAL-LI, TETZON-TLI.

CALTIÁ *vrefl, vt* to build a house for oneself or someone else / hacer o edificar casa para sí (M), edificar casa a otro (M) See CAL-LI.

CALTZĀLAN-TLI street between buildings / la calle entre las casas (M) [(1)Cf.20r]. See CAL-LI, TZĀLAN-TLI.

CALXŌMIL-IN *pl:* **-MEH** bedbug / chinche (X) [(3)Xp.31]. See CAL-LI, XŌMIL-IN.

-CAMAC *necessarily bound form* place where there is an abundance of something This is attested only for T, where it is compounded with CUAHU(I)-TL 'tree,' OHUA-TL 'cane,' XĀL-LI 'sand' and other such nouns. It seems to be synonymous with -TLAH, which also occurs in T, so that there are doublets—TECAMAC, TETLAH 'pedregal (field of volcanic stones)'; CUAUHZĀHUACAMAC, CUAUHZĀHUATLAH 'place where many casaguate trees grow.' In one pair of variants T gives -CAMAC with an absolutive suffix, TLAHZOLCAMAC, TLAHZOLCAMAC-TLI 'dump, trash heap.' See CAM(A)-TL, -C(O).

CAMACĀHU(A) *vt* to let something fall from the mouth / soltársele alguna palabra, la cual no quisiera haber dicho (M), lo

suelta de la boca, lo deja caer de la boca (T)
[(3)Tp.179]. See CAM(A)-TL, CĀHU(A).

CAMACHAL-LI jaw, jawbone / quijada (M)
See CAM(A)-TL.

CAMACHALOĀ to open the mouth wide /
abrir mucho la boca (M) [(2)Zp.20,145,
(3)Xp.33]. Both Z and X give this with a
long vowel in CHAL, but in the abundant
attestations of CAMACHAL-LI elsewhere,
the vowel is short. See CAMACHAL-LI.

CAMACHALTEHTEQU(I) See
CAMACHAL-LI, TEHTEQU(I).

CAMACHALTZON-TLI beard / barba (T)
See CAMACHAL-LI, TZON-TLI.

CAMACOTOCTIC hare lip / labio leporino (T) [(1)Tp.113]. See CAM(A)-TL,
COTOCTIC.

CAMACTIC something fresh, like a newly
harvested crop / cosa tierna y reciente,
como la mazorca de maíz antes que está
del todo sazonada y seca (M), entre verde y
seco, está húmedo, está recién cortado
(frijol, mazorca, etc.) (T) [(1)Tp.113]. See
CAMĀHU(A).

CAMAC-TLI pl: **-TIN** mouth / boca (X), su
boca (T for possessed form) C gives
-CAMAC as an alternative possessed form
for CAM(A)-TL. The locative -CAMAC has
the sense 'place where there is an abundance of something.' See CAM(A)-TL.

CAMACUI vt to take something in the
mouth / lo coge con la boca (T) [(1)Cf.96r,
(3)Tp.179]. See CAM(A)-TL, CUI.

CAMĀHU(A) for maize to achieve ripeness /
pararse el maíz sarazo, o casi del todo
sarazonado (M) [(1)Tp.113, (1)Zp.144].

CAMĀHUAC something that has achieved
ripeness; a ripe ear of corn / cosa saraza
(M), mazorca fresca (pero demasiado
dura para comer como elote) (T) See
CAMĀHU(A), CAMACTIC.

CAMAHUĀCOHUA nonact.
CAMAHUĀQU(I)

CAMAHUĀQU(I) for the mouth to be dry /
tiene la boca seca (T) [(3)Tp.113]. See
CAM(A)-TL, HUĀQU(I).

CAMAHUĀQUĪTIĀ caus. CAMA-
HUĀQU(I)

-CAMANACAYŌ necessarily possessed
form one's gum (of the mouth) / su encía
(Z) [(2)Zp.50,156]. See CAM(A)-TL,
NAC(A)-TL.

-CAMANACAZTLAN necessarily possessed
form one's cheek / su mejilla, su cachete
(Z) [(3)Zp.22,83,156]. See CAM(A)-TL,
-NACAZTLAN.

CAMANĀLIHTOĀ vt to tell a joke / dice
chiste (Z) [(2)Zp.39,185]. One of the two
attestations has the second vowel marked
long as well as the third one, but in related
forms it is not long. See CAMANĀL-LI,
(I)HTOĀ.

CAMANĀLLAHTŌL-LI jest, joke, ridicule /
palabra burlesca (R) [(1)Rp.67]. See
CAMANĀL-LI, TLAHTŌL-LI.

CAMANĀL-LI boast, joke; someone who
jests, jokester / chufa, o burla de palabras
(M), charlador (Z) See CAM(A)-TL, -NĀL.

CAMANĀLOĀ to make jokes / decir
chistes, o gracias (M) See CAMANĀL-LI.

CAMANECUILHUĪTIĀ caus.
CAMANECUILIHU(I)

CAMANECUILIHU(I) to make faces / hace
gestos (T) [(3)Tp.113]. See CAM(A)-TL,
NECUILIHU(I).

CAMANECUILIHUĪHUA nonact.
CAMANECUILIHU(I)

CAMANELOĀ See TLACAMANELOĀ.

-CAMAPACH necessarily possessed
form one's beard / su barba (T)
[(2)Tp.113,128]. See CAM(A)-TL,
PACH-TLI.

CAMAPIHPĪ vrefl, vt; pret: **-PIHPĪC** to
shave one's own beard or someone else's /
rasura su barba (T), le rasura la barba (T) See
CAM(A)-TL, PIHPĪ.

CAMAPĪNĀHUA to be bashful in speech or
eating habits / se avergüenza en comer, en
hablar, etc. (T) [(5)Tp.113]. T forms the
preterit as CAMAPĪNĀUH, but elsewhere
PĪNĀHUA forms its preterit by adding -C.
See CAM(A)-TL, PĪNĀHUA.

CAMAPĪNĀUHQUI someone bashful in
speech or eating habits / vergonzoso en
hablar, en comer, etc. (T) [(2)Tp.113]. See
CAMAPĪNĀHUA.

CAMAPIY(A) vt; pret: **-PIX** ~ **-PĪX** to hold
something in one's mouth / lo tiene en la
boca (T) [(3)Tp.179]. See CAM(A)-TL,
PIY(A).

CAMAPOLOĀ vrefl to blunder in speech /
se equivoca al hablar (T) See CAM(A)-TL,
POLOĀ.

CAMAQUETZ(A) vrefl to finish eating /

para de comer (T) [(2)Tp.145]. See
CAM(A)-TL, QUETZ(A).

CAMATELICZA *vt* to kick someone in the
mouth / o patea en la boca (T) [(3)Tp.179].
See CAM(A)-TL, TELICZA.

CAMATEPĀCHOĀ *vrefl, vt* to get one's
mouth bruised; to bruise someone on
the mouth / se machuca la boca (T), le
machuca la boca (T) See CAM(A)-TL,
TEPĀCHOĀ.

CAM(A)-TL *possessed form:* -CAN mouth /
boca (M) Cf.82v gives -CAMAC as an
alternative possessed form. See
CAMAC-TLI.

CAMATLAPOLŌLTIĀ *vrefl* to blunder
in speech / se equivoca en decir (T) See
CAMAPOLOĀ.

CAMATOTŌNCĀPAH-TLI medicinal plant
with round leaves / planta medicinal y
bella de hojas casi perfectamente redondas (R) [(1)Rp.67]. The single attestation
does not mark the vowels of the fourth and
fifth syllables long. See CAM(A)-TL,
TOTŌNQUI, PAH-TLI.

CAMATOXCOĀ *vrefl* to say something
unintentionally / dice una cosa cuando
no iba a decirla (T) [(3)Tp.145]. See
CAM(A)-TL.

CAMATOXCŌLŌ nonact. CAMATOXCOĀ

CAMOHTIHTĪXIĀ *vrefl* to harvest sweet
potatoes / rejunta camotes (T) See
CAMOH-TLI, TIHTĪXIĀ.

CAMOHTIHTĪX-TLI harvested sweet
potatoes / camotes rejuntados (T)
[(1)Tp.113]. See CAMOHTIHTĪXIĀ.

CAMOHTLAH sweet potato patch / donde
hay muchas papas (Z) [(1)Zp.144]. See
CAMOH-TLI, -TLAH.

CAMOH-TLI *pl:* -MEH ~ -TIN sweet potato
/ batata, raíz comestible (M), camote, raíz
comestible bien conocida (R)

CĀMPA to where? / ¿a dónde, o a qué parte,
o por dónde? adverbio para preguntar (M)
CĀMPA can be used without a strictly
interrogative sense; ZĀ ZAN CĀMPA
means 'just anywhere,' and T gives the
meaning of CĀMPA ZĀ as 'very distant.'
See CĀN, -PA.

CAMPAXILHUIĀ applic. CAMPAXOĀ

CAMPAXOĀ *vt* to nip at something or
someone, to swallow something without

chewing / morder a alguien sin llevarse el
pedazo (S), comer apriesa, tragando sin
mascar (C) [(1)Cf.65r].

CĀN where? / ¿a dónde? adverbio para
preguntar (M)

-CĀN at some place, time, point / posp. que
indica el lugar, el tiempo, la parte (S) This
is a common element of place names. It
binds with the preterit stem of verbs, with
possessor derivations in -EH and -HUAH,
and with numbers, as well as being an element of NICĀN 'here' and ONCĀN
'there.'

CĀNACHI how much / cuánto, ¿cuánto? (Z)
[(6)Zp.36,144]. See CĀN, ACHI.

CANACTIC something thin and flat / cosa
delgada, como tabla, estera, lienzo, o cosas semejantes llanas (M), delgado (Z)
[(2)Zp.40,144]. In one attestation Z marks
the vowel of the first syllable long, but it
should not be. See CANĀHU(A).

CANAH somewhere / en alguna parte, o
lugar (M) In spite of the obvious relationship of CANAH and CĀN, they differ in
vowel length. This same pattern is true of
ĀC 'who,' ACAH 'someone' and ĪC 'when,'
ICAH 'sometimes.'

CANAHPA to or from some place / en
alguna parte (M), hacia alguna parte, o de
alguna parte (C) See CANAH, -PA.

CANĀHU(A) *vt* to make something thin and
flat / adelgazar tablas, o piedras anchas o la
losa cuando la hace, etc. (M) See
CANACTIC.

CANĀHUAC something flat and thin /
cosa delgada ... lienzo, o manta delgada
de algodón (M) See CANĀHU(A),
CANACTIC.

CANĀHUALŌ nonact. CANĀHU(A)

CANĀHU(I) for clothes to wear out / se
desgasta (ropa) (T) [(1)Tp.114]. See
CANĀHU(A).

CANĀHUILIĀ applic. CANĀHU(A)

CANAUH-TLI duck / anade (M) [(2)Rp.67].
The attestations are written without
diacritics; it is possible that one or both
vowels are long.

CANEL since / pues es así, o pues así es (M)
This contrasts with CĀNNEL 'where?'.
See CA, NEL.

CĀNIN where? to where? from where?;

somewhere, anywhere / dónde, de dónde, a dónde, por dónde (C), cualquier lugar, donde quiera (T) See CĀN.

CĀNMACH where / dónde (C) C also has emphatic CĀNINMACH with the same sense. See CĀN, MACH.

CĀNNEL where? where in the world? / ¿dónde? (S) This contrasts with CANEL 'since.' See CĀN, NEL.

CĀNNELPA to where? / dónde (S) See CĀNNEL, -PA.

CAPĀN(I) to make a cracking or slapping noise / crujir, o restallar las coyunturas de los dedos cuando los estiran (M), el ruido que se hace con la palma de la mano, o el ruido del crujir de los dedos, o el de los zapatos, y chinelas (C)

CAPĀNIĀ vt to cause something to make a creaking or slapping sound / hacer ruido con los zapatos (M) [(1)Cf.74r, (1)Zp.170]. See CAPĀN(I).

CAPOLCUAHU(I)-TL cherry tree / cerezo árbol (M) [(1) Tp.114, (1)Zp.145, (1)Rp.67]. R has capolquauhtli, but for 'tree' R has the standard CUAHU(I)-TL. See CAPOL-IN, CUAHU(I)-TL.

CAPOL-IN pl: -TIN cherry tree, cherry / cerezo, el árbol, o la fruta del (M)

CAPOLLAH cherry orchard / cerezal (M) [(2)Cf.71v,72r]. See CAPOL-IN, -TLAH.

CAPOLMECA-TL a type of bindweed, vine / capulín de bejuco (Z) [(1)Zp.145]. See CAPOL-IN, MECA-TL.

CAPOLTIC something black, dark / prieto (T) [(1)Tp.114]. See CAPOTZTIC.

CAPOTZĒHU(I) to turn black / se pone negro (T) [(1)Tp.114]. M has caputzaui with the same sense. See CAPOTZTIC, -ĒHU(I).

CAPOTZTIC something black / cosa negra (M), negro, prieto, tringueño, moreno (T) See CAPOLTIC.

CAPOTZTICTŌTŌ-TL pl: -MEH cowbird, grackle / tordo real, urraca (T) [(2)Tp.114, 243]. See CAPOTZTIC, TŌTŌ-TL.

CAQU(I) vt; pret: **CAC** to hear something / oír, entender, o escuchar (M)

CAQUĪHUA nonact. CAQU(I)

CAQUILIĀ vt to hear what others say / oír lo que otros dicen (M) applic. CAQU(I)

CAQUILTIĀ altern. caus. CAQU(I)

CAQUĪTIĀ vt to get other people to listen to something, to announce, tell something to someone / dar relación de algo a otros, o notificarles algo (M) altern. caus. CAQU(I)

CAQUIXTŌC-TLI pl: -MEH leather strap, leash / correa (T) [(1)Tp.114].

CAQUIZTI to sound, to be heard clearly / sonar, o oírse bien el que habla, o cuenta (M) [(1)Tp.114]. See CAQU(I).

CAQUIZTILIĀ vt to declare, explain something / exponer, declarar, atestigar, comentar, interpretar, anotar, explicar una cosa (S) [(1)Bf.5r]. See CAQU(I).

CAQUIZ-TLI sound, that which is heard / sonido, o persona de crédito (M) [Cf.109r]. See CAQU(I).

CATCA See the verb CĀ.

CATEH See the verb CĀ.

CĀTLEHHUĀ-TL which? / ¿cuál de ellos? preguntado (M), ¿qué? adjectivo de la misma significación de tlein (R) This has a short form CĀTLEH. The -HUĀ-TL element is that which is also found in the long forms of the personal pronouns. See TLE(H).

CATQUI See the verb CĀ.

CATZĀHUA to get dirty / pararse sucio (M) M gives CATZĀUH as an alternative preterit for this intransitive verb as well as for its transitive counterpart.

CATZĀHU(A) vrefl, vt to get oneself dirty; to get someone dirty / ensuciarse (M), ensuciar a otro (M)

CATZĀHUAC something dirty / cosa sucia (M) Catzactic is to be found in M with the same sense but is not attested in the sources for this dictionary. See CATZĀHU(A).

CATZĀHUACA-TL inalienably possessed form: -CATZĀHUACAYŌ dirtiness, filth / la suciedad (C) See CATZĀHU(A).

CĀTZĀN(A) vrefl to stretch out one's arms and legs / se despereza (el cansancio) (T) [(3)Tp.146].

CĀTZĀNALŌ nonact. CĀTZĀN(A)

CĀUHTĒHU(A) vrefl, vt to make one's will; to stop and remain somewhere; to leave, relinquish or abandon something / testar, hacer testamento, o detenerse y quedarse en algún lugar (M), dejar a otro, o a otra cosa, e irse luego a alguna parte (M) [(2)Zp.40,185]. See CĀHU(A), ĒHU(A).

CAXAHPĀZCONĒ-TL small plate / platito (Z) [(2)Zp.99,145]. See CAXAHPĀZ-TLI, CONĒ-TL.

CAXAHPĀZ-TLI plate / plato, lebillo (Z) [(4)Zp.99,145]. See CAX(I)-TL, AHPĀZ-TLI.

CAXALTIC something loose, weak, lacking in substance / flojo, suelto (Z) [(3)Zp.60,118,145]. One of the three attestations has the vowel of the second syllable marked long. See CAXĀN(I).

CAXĀN(I) to loosen, slacken; to lose courage / aflojarse lo atado (M), se ablanda, se suaviza, se afloja (T) See CAXALTIC.

CAXĀNIĀ *vrefl, vt* to relapse into sickness; to loosen, unstring something / recaer el enfermo (M), aflojar lo atado, o desarmar la ballestra, y aflojar el arco (M) See CAXĀN(I).

CAXĀNILIĀ applic. CAXĀN(I)

CAXĀNĪLŌ nonact. CAXĀN(I)

CAXĀNQUI something mild, weak, lacking in substance, loose / cosa floja o mal atada (M), blando, suave, flojo, suelta (tierra), tierno (T) [(1)Tp.115]. See CAXĀN(I), CAXALTIC.

CAXEH one who possesses a bowl, vessel / dueño, y poseedor de la cosa ... escudilla, o cajete (C) [(1)Cf.55v, (1)Rp.45]. C and R give this and CAXHUAH as synonymous. See CAX(I)-TL.

CAXHUAH one who possesses a bowl, vessel / dueño, y poseedor de la cosa ... escudilla, o cajete (C) [(1)Cf.55v, (1)Rp.45]. C and R give this and CAXEH as synonymous. See CAX(I)-TL.

CAX(I)-TL cup, bowl, vessel / escudilla (M), escudilla, plato, taza, vajilla (S) There is a printing error in M. This item appears as *caxtil* but is alphabetized for *caxitl*. T has CAX-TLI as well as CAX(I)-TL.

CAX-TLI *pl:* **-MEH** cup, vessel / cajete (T) [(3)Tp.115,171,224]. In T this short variant of CAX(I)-TL has the specialized gloss 'cup for drinking alcohol.'

CAXTŌL-LI fifteen / quince (M)

CAXTŌLOMĒY(I) eighteen / dieciocho (M) See CAXTŌL-LI, -OM-, ĒY(I).

CAXTŌLOMŌME seventeen / diesisiete (M) See CAXTŌL-LI, -OM-, ŌME.

CAXTŌLONCĒ sixteen / dieciséis (M) See CAXTŌL-LI, OM-, CĒ.

CAXTŌLONNĀHUI nineteen / diecinueve (M) See CAXTŌL-LI, -OM-, NĀHU(I).

CAYAHCIHU(I) for clothes to wear out / se desgasta (ropa) (T) [(1)Tp.115]. The single attestation in T does not have an internal glottal stop, but in view of the tendency in T to lose such glottal stops, this is a plausible derivation from (I)HCIHU(I). Compare TEOHCIHU(I) 'to be hungry.' The first element may be related to M's *cacayactic* 'something thin, with respect to a cloak or blanket.' This appears to be synonymous with CANĀHU(I).

CAYĀHU(A) *vrefl, vt* to blunder; to deceive someone, to mock someone / engañarse a sí mismo, equivocarse ... burlarse, reírse de alguien (S) S and C treat this as a reflexive verb with the object of the deception expressed in contruction with -CA. C cites *in noca timocayāhua* 'with respect to me you practice deception.' T and Z treat it as a simple transitive verb. The reduplicated form CAHCAYĀHU(A) is more common.

CAYĀHUALŌ nonact. CAYĀHU(A)

CAYĀHUILIĀ applic. CAYĀHU(A)

CAYE See CA, YE.

CAYEHUAL-LI *pret:* **-TIN** andiron / morillo (T) [(2)Tp.115,141].

CAZAN See CA, ZAN.

CĒ *pl:* **CĒMEH** one / uno o una (M) The related bound form -CĒL has a long vowel, but CEM has a short one. The plural CĒMEH has the sense 'one of several.' As an example C gives *cēmè tèhuāntin* 'one of us,' *cēmè azcihuà* 'one of you women' (Cf.85v). See CEM, -CĒL.

CECCĀN in one place / en cierta parte, o en una parte (M) [(3)Cf.91r,92r]. See CEM, -CĀN.

CECEC something cold / cosa fría (M) This is abundantly attested in Z and consistently with the vowel of the second syllable long, but as a reduplicated form of CEC-TLI, it should have a short vowel. See CEC-TLI.

CECECĀ-TL cold water / agua fresca (fría) [(2)Zp.7,202]. See CECEC, Ā-TL.

CĒCECNI here and there, in several different places / en diversas partes (M) [(2)Cf.92r]. redup. CECNI

CECECPAH-TLI cecepacle, a plant used in

treating dysentery, gall bladder complaints, and sores / nombre de tres plantas medicinales (R) [(1)Rp.68]. See CECEC, PAH-TLI.

CĒCECU(I) *pret:* **CĒCEC** to shiver, to have chills / le dan frío, tiene escalofrío (T) [(3) Tp.222]. This apparently forms its preterit in the same manner as AHCOCU(I); namely the final vowel and also the labialization of CU are lost. The delabialization is analogous to that of M in word-final position, yielding N. redup. CECU(I)

CĒCECUILIZ-TLI chills, shivers, malaria / resfrío, escalofríos, paludismo (T) [(1)Tp.222]. See CĒCECU(I).

CĒCECUĪTIĀ caus. CĒCECU(I)

CĒCĒL redup. -CĒL

CECELIĀ *vt* to cool, refresh something, someone / lo hace en frío, lo refresca (Z) [(2)Zp.107,194]. In both attestations Z has a long vowel in the second syllable, but in the related form TLACECELTIĀ, T has short vowels. See CECEC, CELIC.

CĒCEM one apiece, one for each / cada uno sendos, o a cada uno sendos, o a cada uno de ellos (M) CEHCEM with glottal stop reduplication also occurs, and both CĒCEM and CEHCEM are attested with expressions of time and period. The final nasal consonant delabializes word-finally, CĒCEN. redup. CEM

CĒCEMILHUI-TL every day / cada día (M) redup. CEMILHUI-TL

CĒCEMPŌHUAL-LI by twenties, twenty apiece, in lots of twenty / de veinte en veinte, o cada uno veinte (M) redup. CEMPŌHUAL-LI

CĒCEN See CĒCEM.

CĒCENTE-TL one apiece, one for each / cada uno sendos, o a cada uno sendos, o a cada uno de los (M) redup. CENTE-TL

CĒCENTLAPAL each person or thing on one side / cada persona, o cosa del un lado (C) redup. CENTLAPAL

CĒCENYOHUAL every night / cada noche (M) redup. CENYOHUAL

CECĒPAHTIC something very cold, something that gives one the chills / cosa muy fría ... cosa muy espantable (M) [(1)Zp.166]. The long vowel of the second syllable is questionable. See CE-TL, CEPŌHUA.

CECEPOCA to get numb, to have goose bumps / se entume (T), carne de gallina (aplicado a la piel humana) (Z) M has *cecepoctic* 'something asleep or benumbed.' This seems to include CE-TL 'ice' as an element in its derivation.

CECEPOCALŌ nonact. CECEPOCA

CECEPOQUĪTIĀ caus. CECEPOCA

CĒCEXXIUHTICA every year, annually / cada año, o de año a año (M) [(2)Cf.107r, (1)Rp.37]. Although all attestations are printed with a single *x*, the ones in C are in a section of examples formed with CĒCEM. The M assimilates to X by general rule to give the sequence XX. See CĒCEM, XIHU(I)-TL.

CECĒY(A) *pret:* **CECĒYAC** ~ **CECĒX** to cool off / enfriarse o resfriarse (M) See CE-TL.

CECI-TL something frozen / helada (T) [(1)Tp.222]. See CE-TL.

CECMIQU(I) *pret:* **-MIC** to suffer from cold / morirse de frío (M) See CEC-TLI, MIQU(I).

CECNI in some particular place, apart / en otra parte o lugar, o en cierta parte, o por sí aparte (M) See CECCĀN.

CĒCO apart, separate / aparte, separadamente (Z) Of nine attestations in Z, four have the vowel of the first syllable marked long. In principle, this could be a reduction of CECCO analogous to CECCĀN and CECNI, but it also seems to be an acceptable construction of CĒ 'one' plus the locative -C(O). See CECCĀN, CECNI, CĒ, -C(O).

CĒCOTLĀLIĀ *vt* to set something aside, apart / lo pone aparte (Z) [(2)Zp.12,194]. See CĒCO, TLĀLIĀ.

CECTIĀ *vrefl* to catch a cold; to cool off / se resfría [Zp.109,172]. See CEC-TLI.

CEC-TLI ice, snow / helado, nieve, hielo (Z) [(4) Zp.67,88,202]. This is found as a free form only in Z, where once out of four times it is given with a long vowel. Z also gives it in some compounds with a long vowel. CEC is abundantly attested in the other sources as an element of compounds, always with a short vowel. See CE-TL.

CECU(I) *pret:* **CEUC** ~ **CEC** to be cold; to have chills / tener frío (M) According to M,

the preterit of this form loses the final
vowel, but the resulting final consonant
does not delabialize, yielding CEUC, but T
gives as the preterit of CECU(I) a reduplicated form CEHCEC with delabialization.
See CE-TL, CUI.

CECUĪTIĀ caus. CECU(I)

CECUIZ-TLI *pl:* **-MEH** something cold; high
mountain place / frío (M), cerro, volcán (T)
See CECU(I).

CEH This is the reduction of the particle
sequence ZO (Y)EH, typically as the last
elements of a particle cluster such as
ZĀCEH 'once and for all,' AHNOCEH 'or
perhaps,' etc. See ZO, (Y)EH.

CEHCĒ redup. CĒ

CEHCECU(I) redup. CECU(I)

CEHCECUILIZ-TI chills, shivers / los
fríos (Z), calosfría, tiene escalofrío (Z)
[(4)Zp.24,61,189,202]. This is given without an absolutive suffix in both attestations. See CECU(I).

CEHCĒLIĀ *vrefl, vt* to cool off; to cool
something off / enfriar cosas calientes (M),
se resfría (T), lo refresca, lo resfría (T) This
contrasts with the reduplicated form of
CELIĀ glossed by M as 'to enjoy oneself.'
See CE-TL.

CEHCĒLILIĀ applic. CEHCĒLIĀ

CEHCĒLĪLŌ nonact. CEHCĒLIĀ

CEHCELTIĀ *vrefl, vt* to amuse oneself,
someone else / deleitarse (R), recrear a otro
(M) [(1) Rp.68]. M gives the corresponding
applicative *cecelia*, used reflexively as 'to
amuse oneself.' redup. CELTIĀ

CEHCEM Both CEHCEM and CĒCEM occur
with expressions of time or period. The
nasal consonant delabializes word-finally,
CEHCEN. redup. CEM

CEHCEMMĒTZTICA every month,
monthly / cada mes, o de mes a mes (M)
[(2)Cf.107r]. These attestations lack long-
vowel marking in MĒTZ. C writes *nm* as
though a word boundary intervenes between CEHCEM and MĒTZ. R has this
without diacritics but writes *mm*. See
CEHCEM, MĒTZ-TLI.

CEHCĒPANOĀ *vt* to unite, to put something together / ayuntar o recoger razones
en favor de algún negocio (M), juntar (R)
[(1)Rp.68]. R indicates the glottal stop but

fails to mark the vowel of the second
syllable long. See CĒPAN.

CĒHU(A) to be cold / hacer frío (M) See
CE-TL.

CĒHUAL-LI shadow of something / sombra
de alguna cosa (M) See CĒHU(A).

CĒHUALLŌ-TL shadow of something /
sombra de alguna cosa (M) [(2)Cf.19r]. See
CĒHUAL-LI, -YŌ.

CEHUAPĀHU(A) to get stiff with cold /
aterirse, o pararse yerto de frío (M)
[(1)Cf.101r]. See CE-TL, HUAPĀHU(A).

CEHUETZ(I) to freeze / helar (M)
[(2)Cf.88r,127r]. See CE-TL, HUETZ(I).

CEHUETZILIZPAN in winter, at the time of
cold and ice / en tiempo de fríos y hielos
(C) [(1)Cf.88r]. See CEHUETZ(I), -PAN.

CĒHU(I) to calm down, to take a rest, to
cool off / aplacarse el airado, o apagarse
el fuego o amatarse la vela, o enfriarse la
cosa caliente (M), parar, descansar (C) See
CĒHU(A).

CĒHUIĀ *vrefl, vt* to rest oneself; to get
someone else to rest, to relieve someone /
descansar (M), descansar a otro, ayudán-
dole a llevar la carga, o aplacar el enojado
(M) See CĒHU(I).

CĒHUILIĀ applic. CĒHUIĀ

CĒHUILIZ-TLI rest, relief, repose /
descanso, reposo [(1)Tp.222]. See CĒHU(I).

CĒHUĪLŌ nonact. CĒHUIĀ

CĒHUILŌNI seat, chair / silla, asiento (Z)
[(3)Zp.15,116,202]. In all three attestations,
Z fails to mark the vowel of the second
syllable long. This would be correct if the
noun is derived from CĒHU(I) rather than
CĒHUIĀ. See CĒHU(I).

-CĒL *necessarily bound form; pl:* **-TIN** alone
/ solo ... solos (C) When bound with a
possessive prefix, this means 'oneself
alone'; NOCĒL 'I alone,' TOCĒLTIN 'we
alone.' It can also be incorporated into
verbs to convey exclusivity. Z has the
variant form CĒLTI. See CĒ, CEM.

*CEL This is an element meaning 'fresh,
green.' It can also refer to heat, since
Nahuatl's use of 'green' as an intensifier
for heat is analogous to the use of 'blue'
and 'white' in English. It is only attested
bound, but Z has the form CELTZIN,
which implies a free form. Z has the vowel

marked long, but in related forms it is
consistently short.

CELIĀ *vt* to receive, accept, admit something / hospedar a otro (M), recibir alguna
cosa (M) With the nonspecific object prefix
TLA- this specifically means 'to take
communion.'

CELIC something fresh, green / cosa fresca y
verde (M) In addition to CELIC, Z also has
CELQUI with the sense of 'fresh.' See
CELIY(A).

-CELICĀ *possessed form of* **CELICĀYŌ-TL**
the freshness of something / frescura y
verdor (C) [(1)Bf.5r, (2)Cf.49r,82v]. M has
celica as a free form with the sense
'freshly.' The final vowel is shortened
word-finally but appears long in
CELICĀYŌ-TL.

CELICĀYŌ-TL *possessed form:* **-CELICĀYŌ**
~ **-CELICĀ** freshness / frescura y verdor
(C) [(3)Cf.53r,82v]. See CELIC.

CELICPAH-TLI medicinal plant that resembles nettles / cierta planta medicinal
cuyas hojas son como las de la ortiga (R)
[(1)Rp.69]. See CELIC, PAH-TLI.

CELILIĀ applic. CELIĀ

CELĪLŌ nonact. CELIĀ

CELIY(A) *pret:* **CELIYAC** ~ **CELIZ** to catch
fire; for plants to sprout, to blossom /
prender, brotar, o retoñecer la planta (M)
See CEL.

CELTIĀ caus. CELIĀ

CELTICĀYŌ-TL *possessed form:*
-CELTICĀ the delicacy of something fresh
and green / ternura de cosa reciente, fresca,
y verde (M) [(3)Cf.82v]. See CEL.

CEM one, entirely, wholly / enteramente, o
del todo, o juntamente (M) Generally
speaking CĒ is the free form meaning 'one'
and CEM is the corresponding bound form.
In word-final position the M delabializes,
yielding CEN. Within a compound the M
assimilates to adjacent nonlabial consonants. Before vowels and labial consonants
CEM retains its underlying form. In the
related forms CĒ and -CĒL the M is missing
and the vowel is long. Z consistently has
CĒM where the other sources have CEM.

CEMAHCI to be perfect, complete / ser algo
cabal, y perfecto (C) [(3) Cf.88r,88v,
(3)Rp.69]. See CEM, AHCI.

CEMAHCIC something perfect, complete /
cosa cabal (C) [(1) Cf.88r]. See CEMAHCI.

CEMAHCICĀPOHPOHTIĀ to pay back, to
even the score / recompensar algo copiosa-
mente (M for nonreduplicated verb stem),
igualar (R) [(1)Rp.69]. CEMAHCI,
POHPOHTIĀ

CEMAHCITICAH to be complete, perfect /
ser entero, puro, sin tacha (S) [(1)Rp.69]. R
glosses this as 'spirit,' i.e. that which is
complete and perfect. See CEMAHCI, the
verb CĀ.

CEMĀN(A) *vt* to resell, exchange, barter
something / lo revende, lo rescata (T)
[(3)Tp.201]. This contrasts with
CEMMAN(A) 'to sprinkle, scatter,
disseminate something.' Neither has the
sense of M's *cemana* 'to carry something
on to the end, to persevere in something.'

CEMANĀHUA-TL the world / el mundo (M)
[(4)Cf.84v,88r,99r,101v]. The vowel length
pattern and absence of locative -C< -C(O),
cf. TLĀLTICPAC-TLI 'the earth,' are
evidence against a derivation involving
CEM 'entirely' and ĀNĀHUAC< Ā-TL
'water' and NĀHUAC 'adjacent to.' A
reasonable derivation would be from the
nonactive form of M's *cemana* 'to continue
something on to the end, to persevere in
something' In this case, the single M
would probably result from a reduction of
MM. See CEMMANIYĀN.

CĒMEH See CĒ.

CEMĒLLEH disharmoniously (in construction with negation) / falta de union, y de
paz (C) This appears to have negative
polarity. S gives a positive sense of *con alegría, tranquilidad* for this without negation, but there are no nonnegative
constructions attested in the sources for
this dictionary.

CEMI once and for all, ultimately; always /
finalmente, una sola vez, de repente (S),
siempre (T), muy (Z) In Z, which has the
variant forms CEMI ~ CIMI, this has come
to be a general intensifier meaning 'very'
or 'very much.'

CEMIHCAC eternally, perpetually, forever /
para siempre, jamás (M) See CEM, IHCA.

CEMIHCACĀYŌLĪHUAYĀN place of
eternal life / lugar donde se vive eterna-

mente (C) [(1)Cf.102r]. In the single attestation the medial vowel of the sequence YŌLĪHUA is not marked long, but it should be by general rule. See CEMIHCAC, YŌL(I), -YĀN.

CEMIHCACĀYŌLIZ-TLI eternal life / vida eternal (K) [(1)Cf.102r]. See CEMIHCAC, YŌL(I).

CEMILHUITIĀ to pass a whole day somewhere, for something to take up a whole day / tardar, o estar todo el día en alguna parte (M), lo hace todo el día, pasa todo el día haciéndole (T) See CEMILHUI-TL.

CEMILHUITĪHUA altern. nonact. CEMILHUITIĀ

CEMILHUITILIĀ applic. CEMILHUITIĀ

CEMILHUITĪLŌ altern. nonact. CEMILHUITIĀ

CEMILHUI-TL a day, all day / un día (M) See CEM, ILHUI-TL.

CEMITTA vt to stare at someone, to pay close attention to something / mirar a otro de hito en hito (M), estar muy atento, o absorto en algún negocio (M), lo fija, lo admira, le hace caso, lo mira (Z) [(1)Zp.194]. In the single attestation, the initial vowel is marked long, and the M appears as n, but the derivation is transparent, and the sense is compatible with the entry in M. See CEM, (I)TTA.

CEMIZTI-TL the distance from the tip of the thumb to the tip of the forefinger, a small amount / un jeme (C) [(1)Cf.118v]. See CEM, (I)ZTE-TL.

CEMMĀCTIĀ vt to hand something over / lo entrega [(3)Tp.201]. The geminate MM is not attested. See CEM, -MĀC.

CEMMĀCTILIĀ applic. CEMMĀCTIĀ

CEMMĀCTĪLŌ nonact. CEMMĀCTIĀ

CEMMAN(A) vt to sprinkle, scatter, disseminate something (other than liquid) / esparcir, derramar, o echar algo por el suelo (M), lo riega (cosa seca), lo esparce, lo tira (T) [(7)Tp.182,201,235]. T reduces the MM sequence to M. This contrasts with CEMĀN(A) 'to resell, exchange, barter something.' See CEM, MAN(A).

CEMMANALŌ nonact. CEMMAN(A)

CEMMAN(I) to fall, to spill, to spread out, to scatter / descarriarse, o aventarse el

ganado, o apartarse los que estaban juntos, yéndose cada uno por su parte, o cosas sencillas, o cosas que estan llanas e iguales (M), cae, derrama (T) [(1)Tp.221]. The attestation is written with a single medial m, but M has it double. See CEM, MAN(I).

CEMMANILIĀ applic. CEMMAN(A)

CEMMANIYĀN ultimately, perpetually, forever / de todo en todo, o ultimadamente (M), enteramente, formalmente, finalmente, perpetuamente (S) C consistently writes the MM sequence as nm. M's cemana 'to continue something on to the end, to persevere in something' must be related to this by degemination of MM. See CEM, MAN(I), -YĀN.

CEMMAT(I) vt; pret: CEMMAH ~ CEMMAT to pay close attention to something; to agree about something / estar muy atento a algún negocio, sin divertirse a otro (M), están de acuerdo (Z) [(2)Zp.5,194]. Both attestation have n for M and have the vowel of the first syllable marked long, but the derivation is transparent. See CEM, MAT(I).

CEMPŌHUAL-LI twenty / veinte (M) In the vigesimal counting system twenty is one full count. See CEM, -PŌHUAL-LI.

CEMPŌHUALPA twenty times / veinte veces (M) [(1)Cf.106r]. See CEMPŌHUAL-LI, -PA.

CEMPŌHUALXŌCHI-TL marigold (Tagetes erecta) / flor que llaman de muertos, y otros, clavel grande de indias (R), caléndula, flor de muerto, zempasuchil (T) None of the many attestations marks the vowel of the second syllable long, but the compound is transparent. See CEMPŌHUAL-LI, XŌCHI-TL.

CEN See CEM.

CENCAH very; very much / muy o mucho, o cosa estable que no se muda (M) See CEM, the verb CĀ.

CENCĀHU(A) vrefl, vt to prepare, get ready; to ready something, to prepare something / aparejarse, apercibirse, disponer, ataviarse, o aderezarse (M), aparejar algo así (M) See CEM, CĀHU(A).

CENCĀHUALŌ nonact. CENCĀHU(A)

CENCĀHU(I) to end / termina (T) [(1)Tp.222]. See CENCĀHU(A).

CENCAQU(I) *vt; pret:* CENCAC to take heed; to take someone's advice, to admire someone / escarmentar (M), corregirse, escuchar, seguir fielmente los consejos (S), lo admira (Z) [(2)Zp.5,194]. In both attestations the initial vowel is marked long, although the derivation appears to be from ÇEM. In general Z has CĒM where the other sources have CEM. See CEM, CAQU(I).

CENCHICHILIĀ *vt* (for one's heart) to grow permanently embittered / se enoja para siempre (T) [(3)Tp.201]. All attestations are in the construction QUICENCHICHILIĀ ĪYŌLLŌ. CEM, CHICHILIĀ

CENMANIYĀN See CEMMANIYĀN.

CENNEHNEHUILIĀ *vt* to equalize things / igualar (R) [(1)Rp.70]. See CEM, NEHNEHUILIĀ.

CENNEHNEUHQUEH *plural form of a* -QUI *nominalization* equals / iguales (R) [(1)Rp.70]. See CENNEHNEHUILIĀ.

CENNOHNŌHUIYĀN everywhere / en todas partes (R) [(1)Rp.113]. See CEM, NŌHUIYĀN.

CENPEHPEN(A) See CEN-TLI, PEHPEN(A).

CENQUĪZQUI *in bound forms:* CEN-QUĪZCĀ- something perfect / cosa entera y perfecta (M) [(2)Cf.88r, (1)Zp.202]. See QUĪZQUI.

CENTETILIĀ *vrefl, vt* to join together, to become one / juntar diversas cosas en uno (M), se junta, se hace uno (T), lo junta (T) T has CENTI for CENTE, while Z lacks the TE altogether. See CENTE-TL.

CENTETILILIĀ *applic.* CENTETILIĀ

CENTETILĪLŌ *nonact.* CENTETILIĀ

CENTE-TL one, a single one / uno o una (M), único, solo (T) T has a variant CENTI-TL. Numbers suffixed with TE-TL, which literally means 'stone,' are used for enumerating objects more or less arbitrarily assigned for the purpose of counting to the class of rock-like or lump-like things. Among other things, the class includes eggs, tamales, fruits, and beans. See CEM, TE-TL.

CENTILIĀ See CENTETILIĀ.

CENTLACHIY(A) *pret:* -CHIX ~ -CHĪX to stare in surprise / mira (con sorpresa), queda mirando (Z) [(2)Zp.85,202]. The

alternative preterits given here are based on CHIY(A). See CEMI, TLACHIY(A).

CENTLAHCOL a half, a portion of something / la mitad de algo (M), mitad, fracción, porción de una cosa (S), la mitad (C) [(2)Cf.110v, (1)Rp.70]. C fails to indicate the glottal stop, but it is attested in R. See CEM, TLAHCOL.

CENTLĀLIĀ *vt* to gather people or things together in one place / ayuntar, congregar, o acaudillar gente (M), allegar, recoger, o amontonar algo (M) See CEM, TLĀLIĀ.

CENTLĀLĪLŌ *nonact.* CENTLĀLIĀ

CENTLAMAN-TLI *pl:* -TIN one / una cosa, un negocio, o una parte, o un par (M) [(3)Cf.86r,119r,124r]. Numbers suffixed with -TLAMAN-TLI are used in enumerating objects more or less arbitrarily assigned to a class of flat objects including, among other things, shoes, sheets of paper, and dishes, as well as more abstract items such as speeches and pieces of advice. See CEM, TLAMAN-TLI.

CENTLANI in the depths, the abysm / abismo, cosa muy honda o pielago (M), en el abismo, en lo más profundo (C) [(3)Cf.93v]. See CEM, TLANI.

CENTLAPAC-TLI a fragment, crumb of something / un pedazo (C) [(2)Cf.119v, 128v]. See CEM, TLAPAC-TLI.

CENTLAPAL on, belonging to one side / de un lado, o del un lado (M) See CEM, TLAPAL-LI.

CENTLEHCŌ to go up together / suben juntos (Z) [(2)Zp.74, 202]. See CEM, TLEHCŌ.

CEN-TLI dried ear of maize / mazorca de maíz curada y seca (M) C, Z, and X have the variant form CIN-TLI. R and T have CEN-TLI, and M gives both forms.

CENTOCA to omit nothing, to continue something, to pursue something / no dejar nada, o comprar todo cuanto se vende (M), lo continúa, permanece (Z) [(2)Zp.97,194]. The Z sense of this follows from the literal senses of CEM 'entirely' and TOCA 'to follow something.' This contrasts with CENTŌCA 'to plant things together.' See CEM, TOCA.

CENTŌCA *vt* to plant things together / lo siembra juntos (Z) [(1)Zp.194]. This contrasts with CENTOCA 'to continue, pursue something.' See CEM, TŌCA.

CENTZACU(A) *vt* to pay a penalty for all of one's offense / pagar todo junto (K) [(1)Cf.117v]. CEM, TZACU(A)

CENTZOMPA four hundred times / cuatrocientas veces (C) [(1)Cf.106r]. See CENTZON-TLI, -PA.

CENTZONTLAHTŌLEH brown-backed solitaire; mockingbird / pájaro que canta mucho (M), ave celebrada por su admirable canto (R) [(2)Rp.71]. R has both the full form and the shortened form CENTZONTLEH. See CENTZON-TLI, TLAHTŌL-LI.

CENTZONTLEH See CENTZON-TLAHTŌLEH.

CENTZON-TLI four hundred; a bunch of grass / cuatrocientos, o una mata de hortaliza o de yerba (M) The representation of the unit four hundred in the vigesimal counting system by a bunch of grass is probably a metaphor for a large and more or less uncountable quantity. TZON-TLI literally refers to the hairs on the head, which would embody much the same notion. See CEM, TZON-TLI.

CENYĀ *pres:* **CENYAUH** to go along well / ir el canto bien concertado y ordenado (M) [(1)Cf.102v]. See CEM, the verb YĀ.

CENYOHUAL all night, one night / toda la noche, o en toda la noche, o una noche See CEM, YOHUAL-LI.

CĒPA once, one time / una vez (Z) [(6)Zp.129,202,231]. Sources other than Z have CEPPA. See CĒ, -PA.

CĒPAN together / juntamente, o en compañía (M), significa simultaneidad o concomitancia (R) This is abundantly attested in B and C with the first vowel marked long. B also has two attestations in which the vowel is specifically marked short. CĒPAN can be incorporated into verbs to convey the sense of simultaneity. T has CĒPAYEHU(I) 'to be the same age' which seems to be derived from CĒPAN. The YEHU(I) element suggests a derivation from the verb YĀ, but it has regular rather than suppletive causative and nonactive forms. R has CEHCĒPANOĀ 'to unite things.' See CĒ, -PAN.

CEPAYAHU(I)-TL snow / nieve (M) M also

has the associated verb *cepayahui* 'to snow.' The possessed form of the noun is not attested, but by analogy with QUIYAHU(I)-TL, -CEPAYAUH is to be expected. See CE-TL.

CĒPAYEHU(I) See CĒPAN.

CĒPAYEHUĪHUA nonact. CĒPAYEHU(I)

CĒPAYEHUĪTIĀ caus. CĒPAYEHU(I)

CEPŌHUA *pret:* **CEPŌHUAC** for a part of one's body to be numb from cold or lack of circulation / estar yerto y aterido de mucho frío, o estar entumecido algún miembro del cuerpo, o adormecido (M) [(2)Zp.53,194]. M has two entries for *cepoa*. The first is this item, and the second, meaning to scrub something and forming its preterit by final vowel loss, is not attested in the sources for this dictionary. See CE-TL.

CEPŌHUIĀ *vt* to numb something / lo entume [(9) Tp.165,201]. T has contrasting CEPŌHUIĀ and CEPŌHUIY(A). See CEPŌHUA.

CEPŌHUĪHUA altern. nonact. CEPŌHUIĀ

CEPŌHUILIĀ applic. CEPŌHUIĀ

CEPŌHUĪLŌ altern. nonact. CEPŌHUIĀ

CEPŌHUĪTIĀ caus. CEPŌHUIĀ, CEPŌHUIY(A)

CEPŌHUIY(A) *pret:* **CEPŌHUIX** to get numb / se entume, se adormece (T) [(3)Tp.222]. This intransitive form contrasts with transitive CEPŌHUIĀ. See CEPŌHUA.

CEPŌHUIYALŌ nonact. CEPŌHUIY(A)

CEPPA once, one time / una vez (M) Z consistently has CĒPA where the other sources have CEPPA. See CEM, -PA.

CEPPAHUIĀ *vt* to review, revise something / lo repasa, lo revisa (T) [(3)Tp.201]. See CEPPA, -HUIĀ.

CEPPAHUILIĀ applic. CEPPAHUIĀ

CEPPAHUĪLŌ nonact. CEPPAHUIĀ

CEQUI *pl:* **CEQUĪN ~ CEQUĪNTĪN** some, a separate part / algo, o alguna parte de lo que estaba entero (M), algunos, o los unos (M for *cequintin*) The long vowel of the second syllable in plural forms is abundantly attested in B and C. The long vowel of the final syllable of the longer plural form is given here by analogy with plurals of other quantifiers. It is not directly attested as long.

CEQU(I) *vt* to toast something / lo tuesta (T)

[(3)Tp.201]. M has *tlacectli* 'something toasted.'

CEQUĪHUA nonact. CEQU(I)

CEQUILIĀ applic. CEQU(I)

CEQUĪN See CEQUI.

CEQUĪNTĪN See CEQUI.

CĒTICA *instrumental construction* with one of something / un (C), con ninguno (C for negated form) [(4)Cf.19v,86r]. M and C both give examples with CŌHU(A) 'to buy something' where CĒTICA means 'one *real*'s worth.' See CĒ, -CA.

CĒTILIĀ *vrefl, vt* to unite people, things / hacerse muchos una cosa, o unirse por la vía de amistad (M), casar los novios, o conchabar y conformar a los desconformes (M), hacer de algunas cosas una, juntándolas (M) See CĒ.

CĒTILĪLŌ nonact. CĒTILIĀ

CĒTITILIĀ *vt* to unite something / lo une, lo hace uno (T) [(3)Tp.201]. See CĒTILIĀ.

CĒTITILILIĀ applic. CĒTITILIĀ

CĒTITILĪLŌ nonact. CĒTITILIĀ

CE-TL *possessed form:* **-CEUH** ice, icicle / hielo, o carámbano (M) In compounds the element CEC is generally found instead of CE, but the free form CEC-TLI is attested only in Z, which lacks CE-TL. See CEC-TLI.

CEUC-TLI chill, shiver / escalofrío (X) [(1)Xp.81]. See CECU(I).

-CĒUHYĀN place where something reposes, rests / lugar donde remansan, y reposan las aguas (C in construction with Ā-TL) [(1)Cf.51r, (1)Rp.42]. See CĒHU(A), -YĀN.

CĒXIUHTIĀ to be at a place for a year, to pass a year somewhere / estar o tardar un año en algún lugar (M) [(1)Tp.222]. C has *cēcexiuhtica* in a section of derivations with CĒCEM. The NX sequence assimilates to XX and is printed in C as a single *x*. The item here appears to be derived not from CEM but from CĒ, hence the long vowel and the genuinely short X. See CĒ, XIHU(I)-TL.

CEY(A) *pret:* **CEZ** to consent / querer o consentir (M) This has a variant form CIY(A).

CIACATITLAN su costado (T for possessed form) [(1)Tp.133]. T has the reflex of CĒYEC corresponding to CIAC. See CIAC(A)-TL, -TLAN.

CIAC(A)-TL armpit / sobaco (M) [(2)Cf.82r]. Because the sequence is internal, it is impossible to determine if it should be IA or IYA.

CIACATLAN armpit / su sobaco (T for possessed form) [(1)Tp.133]. This appears to be a truncation of CIACATITLAN 'flank' with a specialized meaning. T has CĒYEC corresponding to CIAC. See CIAC(A)-TL.

CIAHU(I) to get tired / cansarse (M) Z has O for A. According to M the preterit of this intransitive verb is identical to the preterit form of the corresponding transitive verb. Because the sequence is internal, it is impossible to determine if it should be IA or IYA.

CIAHU(I) *vt* to attain something by labor and fatigue / adquirir con trabajo lo necesario a la vida (M)

CIAHUIC someone tired / cansado (Z) [(2)Zp.25,203]. Z has O for A. See CIAHU(I).

CIAHUĪHUA nonact. CIAHU(I)

CIAHUĪTIĀ caus. CIAHU(I)

CIAHUĪTILIĀ applic. CIAHUĪTIĀ

CIAHUIZTICA by fatigue / con mi fatiga (C for possessed form) [(1)Cf.49r]. This pairs with the instrumental form TLATEQUIPANŌLIZTICA (both elements in possessed form) to form a construction with the sense of the English phrase 'by the sweat of one's brow.' See CIAHUIZ-TLI, -CA.

CIAHUIZ-TLI fatigue, tiredness / cansancio (M) [(1)Cf.59r]. This is conventionally paired with TLATEQUIPANŌLIZ-TLI 'labor.' See CIAHU(I).

CIAMMICTIĀ *vt* to make someone get tired / cansar, fatigar o acosar a otro (M) [(2)Cf.61v,66v]. One of the attestations has the variant spelling CIANMICTIĀ. altern. caus. CIAMMIQU(I)

CIAMMIQU(I) *pret:* **-MIC** to be very tired / estar muy cansado (M) C gives the variant spelling CIANMIQU(I) See CIAHU(I), MIQU(I).

CIAMMIQUILTIĀ altern. caus. CIAMMIQU(I)

CIAMMIQUĪTIĀ altern. caus. CIAMMIQU(I)

CIANMICTIĀ See CIAMMICTIĀ.

CIANMIQU(I) See CIAMMIQU(I).

CIAUHQUECHILIĀ applic. CIAUH-QUETZ(A)

CIAUHQUETZ(A) *vt* to greet, salute someone / saludar a otro (M) [(1)Bf.131, (2)Cf.67v]. The sense of this does not follow literally from its component elements. See CIAHU(I), QUETZ(A).

CIAUHTICAH to be tired / cansado (T) [(1)Tp.222]. See CIAHU(I), the verb CĀ.

CIAUHTLĀZ(A) *vrefl* to rest from labor and fatigue / descansa (T) [(3)Tp.157]. See CIAHU(I), TLĀZ(A).

CIAUHTLĀZALŌ nonact. CIAUHTLĀZ(A)

CICUIL-LI waist / cuerpezuelo o jubón (M) [(3)Tp.131,142]. T has E for I in the first syllable.

CIH-TLI *pl:* **CIHTIN** grandmother, or sister of one's grandfather / abuela, o tía hermana de abuelo (M) M combines CIH-TLI 'grandmother' with CIH-TLI 'hare' in a single entry. C also glosses CIH-TLI as 'abuela o liebre,' but while he gives CIHTIN as the plural of this, he goes on to repeat twice that the plural of 'hare' involves reduplication, CĪCIHTIN. In this case, the two items contrast in the plural although they are homophonous in the singular. X has CĪZ-TLI for 'grandmother,' CIH-TLI for 'hare.'

CIH-TLI *pl:* **CĪCIHTIN ~ CIHTIN** hare / liebre (M) C twice gives the reduplicated form CĪCIHTIN for the plural of this, making it distinct in the plural from CIH-TLI 'grandmother,' but he also once glosses the singular form as both 'hare' and 'grandmother' and gives the plural as CIHTIN. X has CIHTIN for the plural of this item, which is not homophonous with the X word for 'grandmother.'

CIHUĀCĀHUAL-LI widow / viuda (Z) [(2)Zp.130,203]. See CIHUĀ-TL, CĀHUAL-LI.

CIHUĀCŌĀ-TL title of a high Aztec office / magistrado supremo que juzgaba en último instancia y cuyo poder igualaba casi siempre el del soberano, por cuya razón ha sido equiparado a un virrey o lugarteniente (S) [(1)Bf.10r]. The single attestation is in the honorific form CIHUĀCŌĀTZIN-TLI. The literal sense is 'female snake.' See CIHUĀ-TL, CŌĀ-TL.

CIHUĀCONĒ-TL *pl:* **-CŌCONEH** female

child / niña (de nene hasta los 9 años) (X) [(2)Xp.81]. See CIHUĀ-TL, CONĒ-TL.

CIHUĀICNĪUH-TLI female cousin / prima (Z) [(2)Zp.102,155]. See CIHUĀ-TL, (I)CNĪUH-TLI.

CIHUĀITZCUĪN-TLI bitch, female dog / perra (Z) [(1)Zp.203]. See CIHUĀ-TL, ITZCUĪN-TLI.

CIHUĀMŌN-TLI daughter-in-law / nuera, mujer de su hijo (M), novia (T) In T the possessed form has the sense 'daughter-in-law,' but the unpossessed form is glossed as 'girlfriend, fiancée.' See CIHUĀ-TL, MŌN-TLI.

-CIHUĀNACAYŌ *necessarily possessed form* one's female genitals / vulva, vagina (S) [(1)Cf.83r]. M has *ciuanacayo* 'weak, effeminate man,' which probably represents CIHUĀNACAYOH. S gives this with an absolutive suffix, but C has it only in possessed form. See CIHUĀ-TL, NAC(A)-TL.

CIHUĀPAH-TLI name applied to several medicinal plants used to induce contractions during childbirth (Montanoa tomentosa, Montanoa grandiflora, Eriocoma floribunda) / nombre de cinco o seis plantas medicinales (R) [(1)Rp.75]. See CIHUĀ-TL, PAH-TLI.

CIHUĀPIL-LI *pl:* **-PĪPILTIN** lady / señora o dueña (M) See CIHUĀ-TL, PIL-LI.

CIHUĀPITZO-TL sow, female pig / puerca (Z) [(1)Zp.203]. See CIHUĀ-TL, PITZO-TL.

-CIHUĀPOH *necessarily possessed form* female companion, kinswoman / usado en comp. *nociuapo* una mujer como yo, mi compañera, mi pariente, *teciuapo* la acompañante, la hermana, la pariente de alguien (S) [(1)Bf.4v]. S gives this with an absolutive suffix, but it is not so attested in the sources for this dictionary. See CIHUĀ-TL, -POH.

CIHUĀTEŌ-TL weeping female ghost / llorona (Z) [(2)Zp.203]. See CIHUĀ-TL, TEŌ-TL.

CIHUĀTEQUI-TL *possessed form:* **-TE-QUIUH** woman's business / oficio de mujeres (C) [(1)Cf.118r]. See CIHUĀ-TL, TEQUI-TL.

CIHUĀTĒUC-TLI *possessed form:* **-TĒUC-YŌ** noblewoman, mistress, lady / ama o señora de esclavos (M), su patrona (Z for

possessed form) [(2)Zp.95,161]. See
CIHUĀ-TL, TĒUC-TLI.

CIHUĀ-TL pl: **CIHUAH,** *possessed form:*
-CIHUĀUH woman, wife / mujer (M) T
has the variant ZOHUA-TL, which is also
in M in addition to CIHUĀ-TL. Besides the
difference of vowel in the first syllable,
there seems to be a vowel length discrepancy in the second syllable between
CIHUĀ-TL and ZOHUA-TL. In compounds Z drops the vowel of the first
syllable. When honorific -TZIN is added to
the possessed form of CIHUĀ-TL, a glottal
stop intervenes between the two elements,
ĪCIHUĀHUAHTZIN 'his wife (H).' This is
true of several other expressions of kinship
relationship as well.

CIHUĀTŌTŌ-TL pl: **-MEH** female bird /
hembra de pájaro [(3)Xp.81]. M has
CIHUĀTOTŌL-IN 'hen.' See CIHUĀ-TL,
TŌTŌ-TL.

-CIHUĀYŌ female genital secretions /
secreción de los órganos sexuales de la
mujer (S for *cihuaayotl*) [(1)Cf.83r]. S gives
this with a double vowel medially and an
absolutive suffix and analyzes it as a
compound of CIHUĀ-TL and ĀYŌ-TL, but
C has this in a section with -OQUICHYŌ
'semen,' both apparently inalienably
possessed forms of the corresponding
nouns, although it is not impossible that
-YOH is intended. M also has *cihuayotl*
'vulva.' See CIHUĀ-TL, -YŌ.

CIHUĀYŌLQUI female animal / hembra de
animal (X) [(3)Xp.82]. See CIHUĀ-TL,
YŌLQUI.

CIHUĀYŌ-TL pl: **-MEH** female genitals and
womb / la madre do concibe la mujer (M),
matriz, vulva (S) [(3)Xp.82]. See CIHUĀ-TL,
-YŌ.

CIMAPAH-TLI medicinal plant of the bean
family the root of which can be used to
induce vomiting / cierta planta medicinal
(R) [(1)Rp.75]. See CIMA-TL, PAH-TLI.

CIMA-TL a plant (Desmodium amplifolium)
the well-cooked root of which is used to
season stews / cierta raíz de yerba (M), planta
cuya raíz se usa en guisados (S) [(1)Rp.75].

CINCAL-LI corncrib / granero, troje (Z)
[(3)Zp.64,125,203]. See CIN-TLI, CAL-LI.

CINMĪL-LI cornfield / mazorcal, milpa (Z)
[(2)Zp.84,203]. See CIN-TLI, MĪL-LI.

CINTLAH cornfield / milpa [(2)Zp.84,203].
See CIN-TLI, -TLAH.

CIN-TLI dried ears of maize / mazorcas de
maíz secas y curadas Z consistently has
the stem vowel long, but it is consistently
short elsewhere. See CEN-TLI.

CĪTLALCUITL(A)-TL obsidian / la suciedad
de estrella, gusanos en la tierra (Z)
[(1)Zp.203]. Obsidian is known in Spanish
in some areas by the apparent loan translation *caca de estrella*, but another ex-
planation of Z's rather opaque gloss is the
belief reported in the *Florentine Codex*
that falling stars turn into worms that
invade animals (Bk.7,p.13). See
CĪTLAL-IN, CUITL(A)-TL.

CĪTLAL-IN pl: **CĪCĪTLALTIN** star / estrella
(M)

CĪTLALLOH something starry, filled with
stars / estrellado, cosa que tiene estrellas
(M) [(1)Cf.54v]. See CĪTLAL-IN, -YOH.

CĪTLALLOHTIHCA *preterit-as-present
verb; pret:* **-IHCAC** to stand among the
stars / está en pie lleno de estrellas (C)
[(1)Cf.54v]. See CĪTLALLOH, IHCA.

CĪTLALTI to turn into a star / volverse
estrella (C) [(1) Cf.58v]. See CĪTLAL-IN.

CIY(A) See CEY(A).

CIYACA-TL See CIACATL.

CIYĀHU(A) *vt* to soak something, to water something / remojar algo, o regar
la hortaliza (M) [(3)Tp.202]. By analogy
with the nouns ĀYAHU(I)-TL
'cloud,' CEPAYAHU(I)-TL 'snow,' and
QUIYAHU(I)-TL 'rainstorm,' one would
expect a short A in the second syllable, but
T has the reflex of Ā.

CIYĀHUALŌ nonact. CIYĀHU(A)

CIYĀHU(I) to get damp / se humedece (T)
[(1)Tp.222]. See CIYĀHU(A).

CIYĀHUILIA applic. CIYĀHU(A)

CIYALTIĀ *vt* to lure, captivate someone, to
cause someone to give in, to consent to
something / atraer a otro haciéndole querer
algo (M) [(1)Cf.117r]. caus. CIY(A), see CEY(A)

-CIYAYA *necessarily possessed form* one's
consent / la voluntad con que uno consiente (C) [(1)Cf.50r]. See CEY(A).

-C(O) *locative suffix; with stems ending in
vowels this has the form* **-C** among, in /
dentro, en, sobre, por (S) -C(O) is a suffix
which attaches to nouns. It does not take

the possessive prefixes as postpositions do. To indicate motion in the direction indicated by -C(O), -PA is suffixed to give the sequence -COPA.

-CO *centripetal verbal compounding element; pl:* **-COH** to come to do the action indicated by the verb to which it is attached This does not take the tense suffixes; it is suppletive with -QUĪHU(I) for the future tense. See -QUĪHU(I).

CŌĀMICH-IN eel / anguila (M) [(2)Zp.10,145]. See CŌĀ-TL, MICH-IN.

CŌĀNŌTZ(A) *vt* to invite someone / convidar a otro [(1)Cf.118v]. See CŌĀ-TL, NŌTZ(A).

CŌĀTĒCA-TL resident of Coatlan / natural de Coatlán (K) [(1)Bf.11v]. See CŌĀ-TL.

CŌĀ-TL *pl:* **CŌCŌAH ~ CŌĀMEH** snake, serpent, worm; twin / culebra, mellizo, o lombriz de estómago (M) This has two distinct senses, the concrete 'snake' and an abstract one involving reciprocity. This latter use is involved in the use of CŌĀ-TL to mean 'twin,' in the expression of a host-and-guest relationship in CŌĀNŌTZ(A), and in *coatequitl* 'communal work' (which is not attested in the sources for this dictionary but is transparently a compound of CŌĀ-TL and TEQUI-TL 'work'). There is no phonological contrast corresponding to the two different uses of CŌĀ-TL. Possibly the reciprocal sense derives from some belief about snakes. Otherwise there are two homophonous lexical items. Because the sequence is internal, it is impossible to determine if it should be ŌĀ or ŌHUĀ.

CŌĀTLĪCHĀN *place name* Coatlichan / casa de la culebra (C), pueblo del estado de Acolhuacan (S) [(1)Cf.56v]. The literal sense of this is 'serpent's home.' See CŌĀ-TL, CHĀN-TLI.

COCHCĀHU(A) *vrefl,vt* to oversleep; to steal away from someone who is sleeping; to neglect to do something because one has been asleep / duerme demasiado (Z), dejar durmiendo a otro e irse (M), dejar de hacer algo por se haber dormido (M) [(2)Zp.47,169]. See COCH(I), CĀHU(A).

COCHCAMACHALOĀ to yawn / bostezar (M) [(2)Zp.20,145, (3)Xp.33]. X has this

in reduplicated form. See COCH(I), CAMACHALOĀ.

COCHCAMACOYĀHU(I) to yawn / bosteza (T) [(3)Tp.115]. M has *camacoyauac* 'person with a large mouth.' See COCH(I), CAM(A)-TL, COYĀHUAC.

COCHCAMACOYĀHUĪHUA nonact. COCHCAMACOYĀHU(I)

COCHCAMACOYĀHUĪTIĀ caus. COCHCAMACOYĀHU(I)

COCHCĀYŌTIĀ *vrefl, vt* to eat supper; to serve supper to others / cenar (M), dar de cenar a otro (M) [(3)Cf.28r,54v]. See COCHCĀYŌ-TL.

COCHCĀYŌ-TL *possessed form:* **-COCHCĀYŌ ~ -COCHCĀ** supper / cena (S) This is conventionally paired with NĒUHCĀYŌ-TL 'breakfast,' both in possessed form, to mean one's daily sustenance. See COCH(I).

COCHHUIĀ *vt* to have intercourse with a woman who is asleep, to rock someone in one's arms / hacerlo a la mujer que está durmiendo (M), lo mece en los brazos (T) [(3)Tp.179]. See COCH(I).

COCHHUILIĀ applic. COCHHUIĀ

COCHHUĪLŌ nonact. COCHHUIĀ

COCH(I) to sleep / dormir (M)

COCHIHTLĒHUA for someone who has been sleeping to leap out of bed / saltar de la cama con presteza el que estaba durmiendo (M) [(2)Bf.1v,7r]. B has this as a transitive verb 'to route someone out of bed' and has as the final element -ĒHU(A), forming preterit -ĒUH. See COCH(I), ĒHUA.

COCHIHTLĒHUAL-LI dream / sueño, ensue9no (S) [(2)Cf.93v,114v]. See COCHIHTLĒHUA.

COCHĪHUA nonact. COCH(I)

COCHĪHUANI something to aid in sleeping, poppies / instrumento para dormir, como las adormideras (C) [(1)Cf.46r]. See COCH(I).

COCHIHUAYĀN bedroom, dormitory / dormitorio, mesón, celda, o cámara para dormir (M) [(1)Cf.51r]. See COCHĪHUA, -YĀN.

COCHIHZOLOĀ *vrefl, vt* to lose sleep over something; to prevent someone from sleeping / desuela (Z), quitar el sueño a

otro (M) [(2)Bf.7v,13v, (2)Zp.45,169]. In one
of the two attestations in Z the glottal stop
is missing and the preceding vowel is
marked long. In the other the glottal stop
is also missing, but the vowel is short. See
COCH(I), IHZOLOĀ.

COCHILIĀ applic. COCH(I)

COCHILIZ-TLI sleep, dream / sueño del que
duerme (M) [(2)Tp.116,135, (1)Zp.145]. One
of the Z attestations has the vowel of the
third syllable long, and the other has the
vowels of both the second and third
syllables long, but neither syllable should
contain long vowels. See COCH(I).

COCHILTIĀ altern. caus. COCH(I)

COCHINI a sleeper, someone asleep /
dormilón (M), el que duerme (C) [(1)Cf.44r].
See COCH(I).

COCHĪTIĀ vt to put someone up for the
night; to put someone to sleep / dar posada
a otro albergándolo, o hacer dormir a
alguno (M) altern. caus. COCH(I)

COCHĪTILIĀ applic. COCHĪTIĀ

COCHĪTĪLŌ nonact. COCHĪTIĀ

COCHITTA vt to dream about something /
ver alguna cosa entre sueños (M) See
COCH(I), (I)TTA.

COCHITTALIZ-TLI dream / sueño (T)
[(1)Tp.116, (1)Zp.118]. See COCHITTA.

-COCHIYĀN necessarily possessed
form one's customary sleeping place, bed /
dormitorio, cama (S) S gives this with a
-TLI absolutive suffix, but it is only
attested in possessed form. See COCH(I), -
YĀN.

COCHIZNEQU(I) pret: **-NEC** to be sleepy, to
want to go to sleep / tiene sueño (T)
[(3)Tp.116, (2)Zp.118,145]. Z has the vowel
of the second syllable long in both
attestations, but it should be short. See
COCH(I), NEQU(I).

COCHIZNEQUĪHUA nonact.
COCHIZNEQU(I)

COCHIZNEQUĪTIĀ caus.
COCHIZNEQU(I)

COCHĪZ-TLI sleep / sueño (M) [(1)Bf.7v,
(2)Xp.33, (1)Rp.76]. This is a shortened
form of COCHILIZ-TLI with compensatory lengthening of I due to loss of following LI indicated only in the attestation in
B. See COCHILIZ-TLI.

COCHMAHMAUHTIĀ vrefl to have a
nightmare, to be frightened in one's sleep /
se espanta en el sueño (T) [(3)Tp.146]. See
COCH(I), MAHMAUHTIĀ.

COCHPACHIHU(I) to have had a good sleep
/ se satisface de sueño (T) [(3)Tp.116]. See
COCH(I), PACHIHU(I).

COCHPACHIHUĪHUA nonact.
COCHPACHIHU(I)

COCHPACHIHUĪTIĀ caus.
COCHPACHIHU(I)

COCHPETL(A)-TL mattress / colchón (Z)
[(2)Zp.30,146]. See COCH(I), PETL(A)-TL.

COCHTĒMIQU(I) vt; pret: **-MIC** to dream
about something / lo sueña (T) See
COCH(I), TĒMIQU(I).

COCHTĒMIQUĪHUA nonact.
COCHTĒMIQU(I)

COCHTĒMIQUILIĀ applic.
COCHTĒMIQU(I)

COCHTĒMIQUILIZ-TLI dream / sueño
[(2)Tp.116,135]. See COCHTĒMIQU(I).

COCHTLACHIY(A) pret: **-CHIX** ~
-CHĪX to waken and go back to sleep
repeatedly / recuerda, se despierta y vuelve
a dormir repetidas veces (T) [(3)Tp.116]. M
has the noun cochtlachializtli 'conception,
vision between dreams.' Although T only
indicates that the preterit is formed with
X, this undoubtedly undergoes the same
potential vowel lengthening before the
X as CHIY(A) does. The alternative preterits given here are based on CHIY(A). T
only gives the final X. See COCH(I),
TLACHIY(A).

COCHTLACHIYALŌ nonact.
COCHTLACHIY(A)

COCHTLACHIYALTIĀ caus.
COCHTLACHIY(A)

COCHTLAMELĀHU(A) to go right to sleep
/ dormir a sueño suelto (C) [(1)Cf.98v]. T
has TLACOCHMELĀHU(A) 'to be sleeping
soundly.' See COCH(I), MELĀHU(A).

COCHTLAPECHTEPEHXIHUIĀ vrefl to
fall out of bed in one's sleep / cae de la
cama dormido (T) [(3)Tp.146]. See
COCH(I), TLAPECH-TLI, TEPEHXIHUIĀ.

COCHTLAPECHTEPEHXIHUĪHUA nonact. COCHTLAPECHTEPEHXIHUIĀ

COCHTOC someone asleep, someone lying
sleeping / estar tendido dormiendo (M),

está durmiendo (C) [(2)Cf.72v,98v, (2)Zp.47,146]. C has a reduplicated plural form of this which may be distributive. See COCH(I), the verb O.

COCOĀ *vrefl, vt* to be sick, to hurt; to hurt someone / estar enfermo (M), escocerme o dolerme alguna parte del cuerpo (M for first pers. sg. object), lastimar a otro (M) The sense of 'to be sick' may arise from confusion with COCOY(A), or it may derive from the shared sense of pain.

COCOC something that stings the mouth / cosa que quema y abrasa la boca, así como el ají o pimienta, etc. (M) [(1)Cf.127r, (1)Tp.115, (3)Zp.98,145, (1)Xp.32]. C specifically gives both vowels short and contrasts this with COCŌC 'affliction.' But only the single attestation in C is in accord with this contrast. All the other attestations have a long vowel in the second syllable. Z has a derived noun COCŌYĀLIZ 'piquancy' which is deviant as a derivation from either COCOĀ or COCOY(A). See COCO-TL, COCOĀ.

COCŌC someone, something afflicted; pain, affliction / afligido, atormentado, maltratado; dolor, pena, aflicción, trabajo, etc. (S), aflicción y trabajo (C) This is conventionally paired with TEOHPŌUHQUI with the whole construction having the sense of 'affliction.' See COCOĀ.

COCOCĀ-TL brandy, rum / agua picosa, aguadiente (Z) [(1)Zp.145]. This contrasts with COCŌCA-TL 'property.' See COCOC, Ā-TL.

COCŌCA-TL property, sustenance / hacienda o sustenación de la vida (M) [(1)Bf.12r]. In the single attestation this appears with -TZIN and an intervening glottal stop which makes the basic length of the vowel of the last syllable unrecoverable; it may be Ā. This contrasts with COCOCĀ-TL 'brandy, rum.'

CŌCOCHTICAH to be dozing / dormitar, o cabecear de sueño (M) [(2)Cf.72v]. See COCH(I), the verb CĀ.

CŌCOHPĀTZMICTIĀ *vt* to kill someone by pressing the neck, to hang someone / le aprieta el pescuezo hasta matarlo, lo ahorca (T) [(3)Tp.182]. T consistently has

the reflex of CŌCŌ for CŌCOH. See CŌCOH-TLI, PĀTZCA, MICTIĀ.

CŌCOHPĀTZMICTILIĀ applic. CŌCOHPĀTZMICTIĀ

CŌCOHPĀTZMICTĪLŌ nonact. CŌCOHPĀTZMICTIĀ

CŌCOHPOZĀHU(I) for the throat, neck to swell / se hincha el cuello (T) [(4)Tp.121]. T consistently has the reflex of CŌCŌ for CŌCOH. See CŌCOH-TLI, POZĀHU(I).

CŌCOHPOZĀHUĪHUA nonact. CŌCOHPOZĀHU(I)

CŌCOHPOZĀHUILIZ-TLI tumor of the neck / bocio (T) [(1)Tp.121]. See CŌCOHPOZĀHU(I).

CŌCOHPOZĀHUĪTIĀ caus. CŌCOHPOZĀHU(I)

CŌCOHTLAN neck, throat / su garganta, su cuello (T for possessed form) [(1)Tp.128]. T consistently has the reflex of CŌCŌ for CŌCOH. X has the variant form CŌCOHTITLAN, of which this may be a shortened form. See CŌCOH-TLI.

CŌCOH-TLI throat, windpipe / garguero (M), cuello (T) [(7)Tp.121,147]. M provides the absolutive suffix, the -TLI form of which indicates a stem-final glottal stop, but T characteristically lacks the internal glottal stop and moreover has reflexes of long vowels in both syllables.

CŌCOH-TLI dove, mourning dove / tórtola (M), tórtola mexicana (R) [(1)Rp.77, (1)Tp.121, (3)Xp.33]. R attests the stem-final glottal stop and absolutive suffix, while T's and X's CŌCOTETZIN lacks the glottal stop, but attests the long vowel in the first syllable. This is apparently homophonous with CŌCOH-TLI 'throat.' For a similar case, see COPĀCTECOLŌ-TL.

COCOLAQU(I) *pret:* **-AC** to get sick / se enferma (Z) [(4)Zp.51,169,186]. See COCOY(A), AQU(I).

COCOLAQUIĀ *vt* to make someone sick / lo enferma (Z) [(2)Zp.51,186]. See COCOLAQU(I)

COCŌLEH someone angry, irritable / colérica e impaciente persona (M) [(2)Cf.87v,109r]. See COCOĀ.

COCŌLHUIĀ *vrefl, vt* to hurt, to hurt someone / entortar algo a otro, o lastimarle, o maltratarle algo (M) [(2)Cf.65v, (3)Tp.179,219,228]. The T attestations are specifically given as derivations from COCOĀ, and neither they nor the C attestations have a long vowel in the second syllable. See COCŌL-LI, -HUIĀ.

COCOLIĀ *vt* to hate someone, to wish someone ill / aborrecer o querer mal a otro (M) applic. COCOĀ

CŌCŌLIHU(I) to have turns, curves, loops / tiene vueltas o curvas (T) [(1)Tp.121]. redup. CŌLIHU(I)

COCOLILIĀ applic. COCOLIĀ

COCOLĪLŌ nonact. COCOLIĀ

COCOLIZ-TLI illness, disease / enfermedad o pestilencia See COCOY(A).

COCŌL-LI anger, hurt / riña o enojo (M) See COCOĀ.

COCŌLŌ nonact. COCOĀ

CŌCŌLOĀ *vrefl* to coil / se tuerce (T referring to snake) [(1)Tp.147, (2)Zp.83,169]. redup. CŌLOĀ

COCOMOCA to crackle, to make a sound like a roaring fire / hace ruido la llama (M) [(1)Cf.74v, (2)Zp.109,145]. See COMŌN(I).

COCOMOTZ(A) *vrefl, vt* for a baby to make a smacking noise nursing at the breast; to make a clamour, clatter with one's feet / paladear el niño cuando mama (M), hacer estruendo con los pies (M) [(1)Cf.74v]. See COMŌN(I).

CŌCONĒCHIHCHĪHU(A) *vt* to make an effigy of someone / hace efigie de otra persona (T) [(3)Tp.182]. See CŌCONĒ-TL, CHIHCHĪHU(A).

CŌCONĒCHIHCHĪHUALŌ nonact. CŌCONĒCHIHCHĪHU(A)

CŌCONĒTIĀ to do embroidery / hace bordados, lo borda (T) [(3)Tp.182]. See CŌCONĒYOH.

CŌCONĒTILIĀ applic. CŌCONĒTIĀ

CŌCONĒTĪLŌ nonact. CŌCONĒTIĀ

CŌCONĒ-TL *pl:* **-MEH;** *possessed form:* **-CONĒUH** doll / muñeca [(1)Tp.121, (2)Zp.87,145, (3)Xp.33]. Following Spanish, X has extended the sense of this to 'wrist,' but T and Z have not. See CONĒ-TL.

CŌCONĒYOH something embroidered / el bordado (T) [(1)Tp.121]. The final glottal stop is not attested. It is hypothesized here for the sense of 'something embodying

embroidery.' The 'embroidery' sense associated with CŌCONĒ-TL is opaque. See CŌCONĒTIĀ.

CŌCONĒYŌ-TL childishness / muchacherías o niñerías (M) [(1)Bf.2r]. See CONĒ-TL.

COCOQUIL(I)-TL *pl:* **-MEH** ~ **-TIN** quausoncle, an edible plant (Chenopodium bonus henricus, Chenopodium nuttalli) / huazontle (X) [(4)Xp.33]. Because of the minimal attestation, the first element of this is unidentifiable. See QUIL(I)-TL.

CŌCOTETZIN dove / tórtola [(1)Tp.121, (3)Xp.33]. See CŌCOH-TLI.

COCO-TL sore, pimple / llaga, grano (Z) [(6)Zp.64,78,145,176]. See COCOĀ.

COCOTOCA for something to tear / quebrarse o despedazarse el hilo, la manta, o romperse la red, etc. (M) [(1)Cf.74r, (1)Rp.36]. See COTŌN(I).

COCOTOCHILIĀ applic. COCOTOTZ(A)

CŌCOTŌN(A) *vt* to cut, tear something up, to pinch, squeeze, wound something / desmenuzar o despedazar pan o cosa semejante (M), pellizcar a otro (M) [(1)Cf.72r]. redup. COTŌN(A)

COCOTOTZ(A) *vt* to cause something to be cut up, torn into pieces / cortar algo muy menudo, o hacerlo pedazos (M) See COTŌN(I).

COCOTOTZAHU(I) to be crippled / tullirse (M), se endurece, se entiesa, se dobla (T) [(3)Tp.115]. See COTOTZOĀ.

COCOTOTZAHUĪHUA nonact. COCOTOTZAHU(I)

COCOTOTZAHUĪTIĀ caus. COCOTOTZAHU(I)

COCOTOTZALŌ nonact. COCOTOTZ(A)

COCOTZALHUIĀ [(1)Tp.180]. This derived applicative form has either lost a syllable or replaced T with C. See COCOTOTZAHU(I), COTOTZAHU(I).

COCOTZIN child / sirvienta (S) This appears once in a string of epithets all of which are glossed as 'hija mía' and once unglossed in a command. S has COCO glossed as *sirvienta* and with the possessed form -COCOUH. See XŌCOYŌ-TL, XŌCOH.

COCOXCĀCUI to become sick / se enferma (Z) [(2)Zp.51,145]. See COCOY(A), CUI.

COCOXCĀNEHNEQU(I) *vrefl; pret:* **-NEC** to feign illness / me finjo enfermo (R for first person) [(1)Rp.111]. See COCOY(A), NEHNEQU(I).

COCOXOCA to make a sloshing sound / zonglotear o bazucar la vasija, o sonar el huevo menguado (M), brota (agua) (Z) [(1)Cf.74r, (2)Zp.21,145]. In one of the Z attestations the vowel of the third syllable is marked long, but this is contrary to the general patterning of verbs of this type. See COXŌN(I).

COCOXOTZ(A) *vt* to cause something to make a sloshing noise / agitar una vasija, unos huevos, etc. (S) [(1)Cf.74r]. See COXŌN(I).

COCOXQUI someone ill, something withered / enfermo, o cosa marchita (M) See COCOY(A).

COCOY(A) *pret:* **COCOX** to be sick / estar enfermo (M) See COCOĀ.

CŌCŌYEHUALOĀ *vrefl* to coil / se enrozca (T) [(1)Tp.147]. The derivation of this is opaque. Despite the absence of L, the sense seems to call for CŌL 'something twisted' as an element. The second element is probably YAHUALOĀ 'to go around something' with T's characteristic substitution of E for A.

CŌCOYOL-LI redup. COYOL-LI

COCOYŌNIĀ to get sore, chafed / se escalda (Z) [(2)Zp.54,145]. See COYŌNIĀ.

COHCOCOĀ redup. COCOĀ

COHCŌL-LI someone with twisted, crippled legs / uno que tiene los pies torcidos y no puede andar (T) [(1)Tp.116]. The single attestation is in honorific form, COHCŌLTZIN. See CŌL.

COHCOMŌNIĀ *vt* to strike something / golpea (Z) [(2)Zp.63,204]. redup. COMŌNIĀ

COHCOTOC-TLI *pl:* **-MEH** morsel, shred / cosa quebrada o despedazada (M) [(1)Tp.226]. See COHCOTŌN(A).

COHCOTŌN(A) *vt* to pluck, shred, crumble something; to cut, pinch, wound someone / desmenuzar o despedazar pan o cosa semejante (M), pellizcar a otro (M) redup. COTŌN(A)

CŌHU(A) *vt* to buy something / comprar algo (M)

CŌHUALŌ nonact. CŌHU(A)

CŌHUIĀ *vrefl* to buy something for oneself / comprar algo para sí (M) See CŌHU(A).

CŌHUILIĀ applic. CŌHU(A)

CŌHUĪLŌ nonact. CŌHU(A)

***CŌL** something twisted This is found only as an element of derivations, not in absolutive form. It is not clear whether it is derivationally related to CŌL-LI 'grandfather' or just homophonous with it.

CŌLHUAH *pl:* **CŌLHUAHQUEH** resident of Culhuacan / natural de Culhuacán (K) [(1)Cf.57r].

CŌLHUAHCĀN *place name* Culhuacan [(2)Cf.57r,107v]. See CŌL, CŌL-LI

CŌLHUAHCA-TL *pl:* **CŌLHUAHCAH** resident of Culhuacan / natural de Culhuacán (K) [(1)Cf.57r].

CŌLHUIĀ *vt* to skirt something, someone; to avoid something, someone bypassing to one side / llevar a otro por rodeos a alguna parte, o rodear por no pasar por donde está alguno (M) [(4)Tp.207,229, (3)Zp.45,94,194]. See CŌL, CŌLOĀ.

CŌLHUILIĀ applic. CŌLOĀ

CŌLIHU(I) for something to curve, turn / torcerse, o acostarse la pared (M) [(2)Zp.37,146]. This is only attested in the construction CŌLIUHTOC. In one attestation Z marks no vowels long and in the other both the first and second. See CŌLOĀ.

CŌLIUHTOC something curved / curvo (Z) [(2)Zp.37,146]. See CŌLIHU(I).

CŌL-LI *pl:* **-TIN** grandfather, ancestor / abuelo (S) This is rarely attested in nonpossessed form. The possessed plural is abundantly attested in B, always in reduplicated form, -COHCOLHUĀN. Since reduplication in plural formation involves long vowels rather than short vowel and glottal stop, the forms in B may be distributive. In X and in one attestation in B the reduplicated form has a singular sense and appears without the plural suffix.

CŌLOĀ *vrefl, vt* to twist, to change direction; to bend, fold something; to detour around something / entortarse, o encorvarse, o rodear caminando (M), encorvar o entortar algo, o rodear yendo camino (M) See CŌL, CŌLIHU(I).

CŌLŌLŌ nonact. CŌLOĀ

CŌLŌ-TL *pl:* -MEH scorpion / alacrán See
CŌLOĀ.
CŌLŌTLAH a place teeming with scorpions
/ tiene mucho alacrán (T) [(2)Tp.122]. See
CŌLŌ-TL, -TLAH.
CŌLŌTZIN vinegaroon, whip scorpion /
vinagrillo (Z) [(2)Zp.129,224]. See
TEHUITZCŌLŌ-TL, CŌLŌ-TL.
CŌLŌTZĪTZICĀZ-TLI a type of nettle /
ortiga (T) [(1)Tp.122]. See CŌLŌ-TL,
TZĪTZICĀZ-TLI.
CŌLTIĀ *vt* to offer intoxicating drink to
someone / le ofrece cerveza, mezcal (T)
[(3)Tp.183]. The literal sense of this is 'to
twist someone.' See CŌL.
CŌLTIC something twisted / cosa tuerta, o
torcida (M) See CŌL.
CŌLTILIĀ applic. CŌLTIĀ
CŌLTĪLŌ nonact. CŌLTIĀ
COMĀL-LI *pl:* -TIN griddle / comal adonde
cuecen tortillas de maíz, etc., o el bazo (M)
COM(A)-TL *pl:* -MEH; *possessed form:*
-CON vessel, container / jarro (C for
TECOM(A)-TL) This occurs mainly in the
constructions TECOM(A)-TL 'clay pot'
and CUEZCOM(A)-TL 'corn crib.' C
has *mocontzin* with the same sense as
TZONTECOM(A)-TL 'brain pan.' The
related free form is CŌM(I)-TL, which
differs from COM(A)-TL in vowel length in
the initial syllable as well as in quality of
the final vowel. See CŌM(I)-TL.
CŌM(I)-TL *pl:* CŌMIH; *possessed form:*
-CŌN pot / olla o barril de barro (M) X has
a variant CŌN-TLI. There is a related form
COM(A)-TL that differs in final vowel and
also in vowel length in the initial syllable
and which occurs in some but not all
compounds with the same sense as
CŌM(I)-TL. See COM(A)-TL.
COMĪX-IN *pl:* CŌCOMĪXTIN small lizard
/ lagartija (T) [(1)Tp.116].
COMŌL-LI gully or depression This
is implied by ĀCOMŌL-LI and
TLACOMŌL-LI and in turn implies
COMŌLIHU(I) 'to become gullied' and
COMŌLOĀ 'to create gullies,' both in M.
COMŌN(I) to crackle, crash / encenderse y
echar llama el fuego (M), hacer ruido
alguna cosa pesada que cae, como piedra
(C), suena (Z)
COMŌNIĀ *vrefl* for a crowd to become

inflamed, aroused / alterarse o alborotar la
gente (M) [(2)Zp.63,204]. This is implied by
the reduplicated form COHCOMŌNIĀ.
See COMŌN(I).
CŌNCHILI *pl:* CŌNCHILIMEH a type
of locust, grasshopper / una clase de langosta (T) [(1)Tp.122]. The plural form is
based on an absolutiveless noun. Both
*CŌNCHIL-IN and *CŌNCHIL-LI would
fail to give a vowel before the plural suffix.
In either case the expected plural form
would be *CŌNCHILTIN, possibly
*CŌNCHILMEH. However, there are
attested plurals in I-MEH for other words
that take the -IN absolutive suffix, and this
is the regular plural formation of such
words in X. This implies a loss of final N
from the absolutive suffix and reanalysis of
the remaining vowel as part of the stem.
CŌNCHĪUHCĀN place where pots are
made / ollería (C) [(1)Cf.51v]. See
CŌM(I)-TL, CHĪHU(A), -CĀN.
CONĒ-TL *pl:* CŌCONEH child, offspring of
a female / niño o niña (M)
CŌN-TLI See CŌM(I)-TL.
-COPA in the manner of / a manera de (K)
See -C(O), -PA.
COPĀCTECOLŌ-TL *pl:* -MEH
sparrowhawk / gavilancillo (X) [(3)Xp.34].
X also uses COPĀC-TLI alone to mean
'sparrowhawk,' although the literal sense
is 'palate' or 'throat.' See COPĀC-TLI,
TECOLŌ-TL.
COPĀC-TLI palate, throat / el paladar (M),
garganta (T) [(1)Tp.128].
COPALCUAHU(I)-TL *pl:* -TIN copal tree /
árbol de incienso, olinolue (X) [(3)Xp.35].
See COPAL-LI, CUAHU(I)-TL.
COPAL-LI copal, a type of incense / incienso
(M), incienso de la tierra (C)
COPALPOTZAC-TLI *pl:* -MEH candlewood
(Fouquieria formosa) or casaguate (Ipomoea
arborescens) / palo santo (X) [(3)Xp.35]. See
COPAL-LI.
COPALQUIL(I)-TL *pl:* -TIN a type of grass /
copalquelite (X) [(3)Xp.35]. See COPAL-LI,
QUIL(I)-TL.
COPALXOCO-TL *pl:* -MEH sumac / cierto
árbol resinoso, fructífero, medicinal y de
buena madera (R), ciruela berraca (X)
[(1)Rp.78, (3)Xp.35]. X is missing the
internal L. See COPAL-LI, XOCO-TL.

CŌPILIHU(I) to twine, curl, coil / se enrozca (T) [(1)Tp.123].

COPĪN(A) vrefl,vt for something to pull itself loose; to pull something out, to remove something from a mold, to copy something / se arranca (T), sacar una cosa de otra, o por otra, o sacar algo con molde así como adobes o vasos (M), lo arranca (T) See COPĪN(I).

COPĪNALŌ nonact. COPĪN(A)

COPĪN(I) for something to pull loose, get out, come unstuck / se arranca, se zafa (T) This is abundantly attested but only in T and Z. See COPĪN(A).

COPĪNIĀ vrefl for something to pull itself loose / se arranca (T) [(1)Tp.146]. See COPĪN(I).

COPĪNILIĀ applic. COPĪN(A), COPĪN(I)

COPITZTIC something narrow, tight / estrecho, angosto (Z) [(2)Zp.58,146]. In one of the two attestations the vowel of the second syllable is marked long. This may be related to COPĪN(A) and COPĪN(I), because they are associated with the sense of 'mold,' hence something very tight. M has copichtic 'something pried out.'

COTOCTIC something that lacks a fragment / cosa que le falta algo o algún pedazo (M) Z has the variant COTOLTIC. See COTŌN(A).

COTOC-TLI pl: -MEH morsel, crumb, fragment / mendrugo (M), pedazo (T) See COTŌN(A).

COTOLHUIĀ applic. COTOLOĀ

COTOLOĀ to snore, to roar / ronca (T) [(3)Tp.117].

COTOLŌLŌ nonact. COTOLOĀ

COTOLTIC See COTOCTIC.

COTŌN(A) vt to cut something, to break something off, to wound someone / cortar o despedazar algo, o coger la fruta del árbol con la mano, o coger espigas, o abreviar algo (M), pellizcar (M) See COTŌN(I).

COTŌNALŌ nonact. COTŌN(A)

COTŌN(I) for a cord, thread, or rope to snap / quebrarse la cuerda o el hilo, soga, etc. (M) See COTŌN(A).

COTŌNILIĀ vt to cut, separate something / partir algo con otro (M) applic. COTŌN(A)

COTŌNILILIĀ applic. COTŌNILIĀ

COTŌNILĪLŌ nonact. COTŌNILIĀ

COTOTZAHU(I) to be crippled / tullirse (M), se encoge (T) [(1)Tp.117]. See COTOTZOĀ.

COTOTZOĀ vrefl, vt to squat down, for something to shorten, shrink; to lengthen or shorten something / ponerse de cuclillas, encogerse o encaramarse (M), encoger la costura (M) This is related by metathesis to synonymous TOCOTZOĀ.

COTOTZŌLŌ nonact. COTOTZOĀ

COTOTZTLĀLIĀ vrefl to squat down / ponerse de cuclillas, encogerse o encaramarse (M) [(3)Tp.146]. This is related by metathesis to synonymous TOCOTZTLĀLIĀ. See COTOTZOĀ, TLĀLIĀ.

COTOTZTLĀLĪLŌ nonact. COTOTZTLĀLIĀ

CŌTZILIZ-TLI cramp / calambre (T) [(1)Tp.123]. See CŌTZ-TLI.

CŌTZIL-LI cramp / calambre (T) [(1)Tp.123].

CŌTZ-TLI calf of the leg / pantorilla (M) [(1)Bf.10r, (5)Zp.93,156]. This also appears in three attestations in T with the gloss 'la piel' instead of 'el pie,' and the gloss is repeated on the Spanish-to-Nahuatl side of T. It is either a mistake or a confusion with CUETLAX-TLI 'skin, leather.'

COXŌN(I) for a hollow vessel to make a sloshing sound / zonglotear o bazucar la vasija (M) [(1)Cf.74r].

COXŌNIĀ vt to stir something / lo agita (medicina) (T) [(6)Tp.165,180]. See COXŌN(I).

COXŌNILIĀ applic. COXŌNIĀ

COXŌNĪLŌ nonact. COXŌNIĀ

COYĀHU(A) vt to extend something, to enlarge a hole, to peel staffs / ensanchar algún agujero, o descortezar varas (M) See COYOC-TLI.

COYĀHUAC something wide / cosa ancha, así como caño de agua o ventana, etc. (M) See COYĀHU(A).

COYAME-TL pl: CŌCOYAMEH pig; peccary / puerco (M), jabalí (C)

COYOCTIC hole, something perforated / agujero o cosa agujereada (M) [(1)Tp.130, (4)Xp.36,83]. T and X have the variant COYACTIC. See COYOC-TLI.

COYOC-TLI pl: -MEH hole / hoya, agujero (T), cueva (X) See COYŌN(I).

COYŌHUAHCĀN *place name* Coyoacan
See COYŌ-TL, -CĀN.

COYOL-LI *pl:* **-TIN** jingle bell / cascabel
(M), sonaja (T), cascabel, campanita (Z) M
also gives 'fishing rod' as a sense for this,
but it is unattested in the sources for this
dictionary and may differ in vowel length.

COYOLXŌCHI-TL amarylis / cierta planta
medicinal de bellas flores (R) [(1)Rp.78].
Spanish names for this are *granadita* and
flor de sonaja. See COYOL-LI, XŌCHI-TL.

COYŌN(I) for something to get full of holes
/ se agujerea (T for PĪTZCOYŌN(I)),
perfora (Z) [(1)Tp.174, (2)Zp.97,147].

COYŌNIĀ *vt* to perforate something, to
make holes in something / agujerear, o
horadar algo (M) See COYŌN(I).

COYŌNILIĀ applic. COYŌNIĀ

COYŌNĪLŌ nonact. COYŌN(I)

COYŌNQUI something pitted, perforated,
open / horadado, agujereado, abierto,
ahondado (S) [(1)Tp.117, (3)Xp.36]. See
COYŌN(I).

COYŌ-TL *pl:* **COYŌMEH** ~ **CŌCO-
YOH** coyote / adive (M), adive, zorro (C),
coyote (T)

COYŌTOMA-TL *pl:* **-MEH;** *possessed form:*
-TOMAUH a plant of the verbena family
with bitter roots (Vitex mollis) / tomate
de coyote, jerengue (X) [(3)Xp.36]. See
COYŌ-TL, TOMA-TL.

COYŌTZIN parakeet / perico (pájaro) (Z)
[(2)Zp.97,147].

CŌZAH-TLI *pl:* **-MEH** weasel, ferret /
comadreja (M), hurón (T) [(1)Tp.123].

COZAHUIY(A) *pret:* **-HUIX** ~ **-HUIZ** to
turn yellow / pararse amarillo (M) See
COZTIC.

CŌZAMĀLŌ-TL rainbow / arco del cielo
(M), arco iris (S)

COZĀN-TLI lynx / onza (animal) (Z)
[(4)Zp.91,146].

CŌZCACHAPOL-IN *pl:* **-TIN** a type
of locust, grasshopper / una clase de langosta (T) [(1)Tp.123]. See CŌZCA-TL,
CHAPOL-IN.

CŌZCA-TL *pl:* **-MEH;** *possessed form:*
-CŌZQUI jewel, ornament, necklace /
joya, piedra preciosa labrada de forma
redonda, o cuenta para rezar (M), collar,
gargantilla (Z) This contrasts in vowel
length with COZTIC 'yellow, golden.' X
has a variant CŌZ-TLI.

COZĒHU(A) *vt* to make something turn
yellow / lo amarilla (T) [(3)Tp.180]. See
COZTIC, ĒHU(A).

COZĒHU(I) to turn yellow, to ripen / se
pone amarillo, madura (T) [(1)Tp.116,
(2)Zp.9,146]. See COZĒHU(A).

COZŌL-IN crayfish / langostino
[(2)Zp.75,146].

CŌZOL-LI cradle / cuna de niño (S)
[(1)Bf.111r, (2)Zp.37,146]. B gives only the
first vowel long. Of the two attestations in
Z, one has both vowels marked long, the
other neither. Z also has a part-Spanish
construction meaning 'net, sling' which
seems to include this element.

COZTIC something yellow, golden / cosa
amarilla (M) The COZ of this appears as an
element in some compounds.

COZTICĀTŌL-LI atole (cornstarch
beverage) flavored with unrefined sugar /
atole de piloncillo (T) [(2)Tp.108,117]. See
COZTIC, ĀTŌL-LI.

COZTICĀYŌ-TL yellowness / amarillez (C)
[(1)Cf.53r]. See COZTIC.

COZTICMECAPAH-TLI a medicinal plant /
cierta planta medicinal (R) [(1)Rp.78]. See
COZTIC, MECAPAH-TLI.

COZTICPAH-TLI name given to two
medicinal plants / nombre de dos plantas
medicinales de las cuales la una es
semejante al adianto (R) [(1)Rp.78]. See
COZTIC, PAH-TLI.

COZTICTŌTŌ-TL *pl:* **-MEH** oriole /
calandria (T) [(2)Tp.117,243]. See COZTIC,
TŌTŌ-TL.

CŌZ-TLI *pl:* **-TIN** necklace, collar / collar
(X) [(3)Xp.35]. This contrasts in vowel
length with COZ from COZTIC 'yellow,
golden.' See CŌZCA-TL.

CH

CHACHACUACA to sprinkle, for mud to splatter / salpicar el lodo, andando por lodazales (M), salpica (Z) [(2)Zp.113,150]. This is synonymous with CHACHAPACA, and they probably share a common source with substitution of one labial consonant for another. See CHACUĀN(I).

CHACHACUATZ(A) vt to splatter mud / chapotear en el lodo (M) This is implied by CHACHACUACA

CHACHALACA to chatter, especially for birds to do so / parlar mucho, o gorjear las aves (M) [(1)Cf.73v]. Z has CHACHALĀCAH as a noun for the birds known in Spanish as chachalacas (Ortalis vetula, Ortalis cinereiceps) That this is a back loan from Mexican Spanish is shown by the lengthening of the stressed vowel and by the word-final glottal stop, both of which are characteristic of Spanish loans into Nahuatl. M has chachalatli 'a type of bird,' complete with absolutive suffix. See CHALĀN(I).

CHĀCHALĀNALTIĀ caus. CHĀCHA-LĀN(I)

CHĀCHALĀN(I) to make a hubbub, create an uproar / boruca, habla en desorden (T) [(3)Tp.126]. M has only the transitive verb chachalania with the sense of to mix things up, to disturb people. redup. CHALĀN(I)

CHĀCHALĀNOHUA nonact. CHĀCHALĀN(I)

CHACHALATZ(A) vt to cause a chattering noise / se dice del que causa este ruido (C for CHACHALACA) [(1)Cf.73v]. See CHALĀN(I).

CHACHALŌ-TL pl: -MEH squirrel / ardilla (T) [(1)Tp.123, (2)Zp.13,151]. Z has E for A.

CHACHĀNTIC something furry, shaggy, hairy / velludo, lanudo (Z) [(3)Zp.75,128,150]. M has chamactic 'something thick and swollen or something massive like thick wool.' See CHAMĀHUAC.

CHACHAPACA for rain to patter down in big drops, to sprinkle / cuando las pellas son muchas (C), caer grandes gotas, llover (S), salpica, rocia (Z) [(1)Cf.74r, (3)Zp.111,113,150]. In one of the attestations in Z the vowel of the third syllable is marked long, but it should be short. See CHAPĀN(I).

CHACHAPACHILIĀ applic. CHACHA-PATZ(A)

CHACHAPĀN(I) for rain to sprinkle, patter in large drops / caer gotas grandes cuando llueve (M) [(2)Zp.111, 150]. redup. CHAPĀN(I)

CHACHAPATZ(A) vt to make something splash, spatter, get spotted / chapotear por lodazales (M), patalear en el barro, salpicar, manchar algo (S) [(1)Cf.74r, (3)Tp.184]. See CHAPĀN(I).

CHACHAPATZALŌ nonact. CHACHAPATZ(A)

CHACHA-TL pl: -MEH locust / langosta (K) [(1)Tp.169]. This is only attested in the compound ĀCACHACHA-TL, of which M has what appears to be a shortened form acachatl. See CHAPOL-IN.

CHĀCHICTE-TL a good luck stone known as a 'corn kernel' / piedra de buena suerte, 'el corazón de maíz' (T) [(2)Tp.126]. T has the variant CHĀCHTE-TL. The first element is nowhere else attested. See TE-TL.

CHĀCHTE-TL See CHĀCHICTE-TL.

CHACUĀN(I) for something to get spattered, soaked / mojarse mucho la ropa o cosa así (M) This is implied by CHACHACUACA.

-CHAHCHĀN C gives this possessed reduplicated form of CHĀN-TLI 'home' as an example of the distributive, 'each to his own home.'

CHĀHU(A) someone in an irregular, nonlegitimate relationship, someone likely to arouse jealousy, mistress / mi combleza (M for possessed form) S gives *chauatl*, but since this only appears in compounds and in possessed form, the absolutive suffix is unattested. T has the pejorative diminutive CHĀHUATŌN. M has compounds of CHĀHU(A) with COCOY(A) 'for a woman to be miserable on account of her husband's mistress, or to be gravely ill,' with NE-COCOY(A) 'to be possessed by evil,' with CONĒ-TL and PIL-LI 'stepchild,' and with NĀN-TLI 'stepmother.' See CHĀHUATI.

CHĀHUALIZ-TLI envy, jealousy, suspicion / celo (Z) [(2)Zp.27,150]. See CHĀHU(A).

CHĀHUANĀN-TLI stepmother / madrastra (M) [(1)Tp.129]. See CHĀHU(A), NĀN-TLI.

CHĀHUAPĀPĀLŌ-TL night butterfly, moth / mariposa nocturna (Z) [(2)Zp.82,150]. See CHĀHU(A), PĀPĀLŌ-TL.

CHĀHUATI to be envious, jealous, suspicious / tiene celos, encela (T) See CHĀHU(A).

CHĀHUATIĀ to incite jealousy / encela (Z) [(1)Zp.150]. See CHĀHU(A), CHĀHUATI.

CHĀHUATĪHUA nonact. CHĀHUATI

CHĀHUATILIĀ applic. CHĀHUATI

CHĀHUATŌN someone jealous, envious, suspicious / celoso (T) [(1)Tp.126]. See CHĀHU(A).

CHĀHUIZ-TLI chahuistle, a blight especially affecting wheat / plaga, enfermedad (de plantas) (Z) [(3)Zp.51,99,150]. See CHIYĀHUIZ-TLI.

CHALĀN(I) for something such as a pot or copper pot to crack or for such vessels to make a noise together; for a song or instrument to be out of tune / cascarse la vasija de barro, o de cobre, o desentonarse el canto, o el instrumento musical (M) Z gives *escurre* as a gloss for this, apparently in the sense of trickling or dripping from a crack.

CHALĀNILIZ-TLI confusion, tumult, hubbub / confusión, alboroto (T) [(1)Tp.123]. See CHALĀN(I).

CHĀLCA-TL pl: **CHĀLCAH** someone from Chalco / natural de Chalco (C) [(2)Cf.56r,107r].

CHĀLCHIHU(I)-TL precious green stone; turquoise / esmeralda basta (M), esmeralda en bruto, perla, piedra preciosa verde (S)

CHĀLCHIUHCAL-LI house of precious green stone / casa de esmeralda (C) [(1)Cf.75v]. See CHĀLCHIHU(I)-TL, CAL-LI.

CHĀLCHIUHTĒUH in the manner of precious green stones / a manera de esmeraldas (C) [(1)Cf.18v]. See CHĀLCHIHU(I)-TL, -ĒHU(I).

CHĀLCO *place name* Chalco [(1)Cf.56r].

CHĀLIĀ *vt* to inaugurate something, to handle something for the first time / estrenar alguna cosa nueva (M) [(2)Zp.58,187].

CHAMĀHU(A) *vrefl,vt* to brag, to be arrogant; to enhance someone's reputation, to flatter someone / se enorgullece, jacta (T), lo afama (T), lisonjear (M) M also has this as an intransitive verb with the gloss 'for a child to grow or for maize or cacao to ripen.' The common sense is of inflation, swelling up.

CHAMĀHUAC thick, dense / cosa gorda y crecida, o cosa vasta como lana gruesa (M), grueso (... maíz, frijol, etc.) (T) [(2)Tp.123,136]. M gives this as synonymous with *chamactic*. Z has the variant CHACHĀNTIC. See CHAMĀHU(A), CHACHĀNTIC.

CHAMĀHUALŌ nonact. CHAMĀHU(A)

CHAMĀHUILIĀ applic. CHAMĀHU(A)

-CHĀN *necessarily possessed form* at the home of / en casa del (C) This must be possessed; unlike a postposition, it cannot bind with another noun to the exclusion of a possessive prefix. Z gives ĪCHĀMPA with the stative gloss 'his vicinity,' but the suffixed -PA should convey a directional sense. When the honorific -TZIN is bound to -CHĀN, then locative -C(O) is suffixed to the whole construction, ĪCHĀNTZINCO 'at his home (H).' See CHĀN-TLI.

CHĀNEH resident, householder / el que tiene casa (C), los naturales (C for plural), habitante (Z) See CHĀN-TLI.

CHĀNQUETZ(A) *vrefl* to set up housekeeping / hace hogar (T) [(3)Tp.149]. See CHĀN-TLI, QUETZ(A).

CHĀNTI to live, to take root in a place, to

settle / mora, vive, se radica (T) [(1)Tp.126].
See CHĀN-TLI, CHĀNTIĀ.

CHĀNTIĀ *vrefl* to live, to reside in a place /
vivir o morar en algún lugar (M) See
CHĀN-TLI.

CHĀNTĪLŌ nonact. CHĀNTI

CHĀNTLĀLIĀ *vrefl* to set up housekeeping / hace hogar (T) [(3)Tp.149]. See
CHĀN-TLI, TLĀLIĀ.

CHĀN-TLI *pl:* **-MEH** home, residence / la
casa (C), casa, habitación, residencia, país,
patria, etc. (S) This contrasts with CAL-LI
as English *home* contrasts with *house*.
CAL-LI refers to the physical structure,
while CHĀN-TLI implies a human, social
connection with a location. See -CHĀN.

CHAPĀN(I) for there to be a slapping sound
like falling dough or wet clay / mojarse
mucho, o caer en tierra la masa, el lodo o
cosas semejantes (M), el ruido del barro y
masa, que cae en el suelo (C)

CHAPĀNIĀ *vt* to cause something wet and
flexible to slap to the ground / echar en el
suelo o por ahí lodo, masa, o cosa
semejante (M) M gives the preterit of this
as *chapan*, but T gives CHAPĀNIH as it
should be. See CHAPĀN(I).

CHAPĀNILIĀ applic. CHAPĀNIĀ

CHAPĀNĪLŌ nonact. CHAPĀNIĀ

CHAPOL-IN *pl:* **-TIN** a type of locust,
grasshopper / langosta (M), chapulín,
saltamontes, langosta (Z) [(2)Tp.123,
(4)Zp.38,151,182]. Z consistently gives the
vowel of the second syllable as long, but T
has a short vowel. See CHACHA-TL.

CHAPOPOH-TLI a type of tar, asphalt /
especie de betún oloroso que se usaban
como incienso; las mujeres se lavaban los
dientes con él (S), chapapote (Z) [(1)Tp.123,
(2)Zp.38,151, (1)Rp.71]. Z gives the vowel
of the first syllable as long, but the other
sources do not.

CHAYĀHU(A) *vt* to scatter, pour, sprinkle
something down / esparcir o derramar por
el suelo trigo o cosa semejante (M), lo tira,
lo derrama, lo esparce, lo riega (T) See
CHAYĀHU(I).

CHAYĀHUALŌ nonact. CHAYĀHU(A)

CHAYĀHU(I) for something to spill,
sprinkle down; for snow to fall / echarse

así trigo, o caer nieve (M) See
CHAYĀHU(A).

CHAYĀHUILIĀ applic. CHAYĀHU(A)

CHAYALTIC open-work weaving / tejido
abierto (Z) [(2)Zp.120,151].

CHAYOHQUIL(I)-TL chayote greens /
chayotera, mata de chayote (Z)
[(3)Zp.38,151]. See CHAYOH-TLI,
QUIL(I)-TL.

CHAYOH-TLI *pl:* **-MEH** chayote, a spiny,
edible squash / fruta como calabacilla
espinosa por encima o como erizo (M)

CHICACTIC something robust, strong,
powerful; someone who has attained old
age / cosa recia y fuerte, o persona anciana
(M) [(1)Tp.124]. See CHICĀHU(A).

CHICĀHU(A) to grow vigorous, to gather
strength, to live to old age / arreciar o
tomar fuerzas, o hacerse viejo el hombre o
la bestia (M) There is also a transitive verb
of the same form.

CHICĀHU(A) *vt* to strengthen, fortify,
animate something, someone / fortalecer o
guarnecer algo, y esforzar y animar (M),
esforzar a otro (M) There is also an
intransitive verb of the same form. Z gives
the additional sense of 'to ferment
something.'

CHICĀHUAC something strong, robust,
powerful; someone who has attained old
age / cosa recia o fuerte, o persona anciana
(M) See CHICĀHU(A).

CHICĀHUALIZ-TLI strength, power /
fortaleza o firmeza o esfuerzo y ani-
mosidad (M) See CHICĀHU(A).

CHICĀHUALŌ nonact. CHICĀHU(A)

CHICĀHUALTIĀ *vt* to make something
grow strong, ripen / lo arrecia, lo hace
madurar (T) [(3)Tp.185]. caus.
CHICĀHU(A)

CHICĀHUALTILIĀ applic.
CHICĀHUALTIĀ

CHICĀHUALTĪLŌ nonact.
CHICĀHUALTIĀ

CHICĀHU(I) to ripen / madura (T)
[(1)Tp.124]. Z has the variant
CHICĀHUAYA. See CHICĀHU(A).

CHICĀHUILIĀ *vt* to hasten work, to push
work to the point of exhaustion / se apura
a trabajar (T) applic. CHICĀHU(A)

CHICĀHUILILIĀ applic. CHICĀHUILIĀ
CHICĀHUILĪLŌ nonact. CHICĀHUILIĀ
CHICĀUHTICAH something strong, healthy, stable / cosa firme, estable, y permaneciente (M) [(1)Tp.124]. Z has the variant CHICĀUHTOC. See CHICĀHU(A), the verb CĀ.
CHĪCHCOCOLIZ-TLI illness brought on by sorcery / enfermedad por brujería (T) [(1)Tp.124]. See CHĪCH-TLI, COCOLIZ-TLI.
CHĪCHĪ to suckle / mamar (M) C contrasts this with CHICHI 'dog,' CHIHCHI 'saliva,' and the verb CHIHCHI 'to mend, patch something.' T and Z give both vowels as long, but T has the vowel of the second syllable short in three attestations of the derived form meaning 'breast.' X has CHĪCHĪ as a transitive verb 'to suckle something' and does not mark the vowel of the second syllable long. See CHĪCHĪHUAL-LI.
CHICHI pl: **-MEH** dog / perro o perra (M) This is commonly used with the diminutive compounding element -TŌN. Since CHICHI is an absolutiveless noun, the compound is also absolutiveless, CHICHITŌN. CHICHI contrasts with CHĪCHĪ 'to suckle' and CHIHCHI 'saliva.'
CHICHIC something bitter / cosa amarga (M) Z and X have the vowel of the second syllable long, and so does one attestation from T, although another in T has it specifically marked short. This reflects the variation of vowel length in verbs ending in -IY(A), which are attested in the preterit as both -IX and -ĪX. See CHICHIY(A).
CHICHICA-TL bile, bitterness / hiel (M) [(1)Tp.129, (2)Zp.67,157]. In one attestation Z has an internal geminate CC which is probably a typographical error. In both of the attestations in Z the vowel of the second syllable is given as long. See CHICHIC.
CHĪCHICĀUHCĀNEHNEQU(I) vrefl; pret: **-NEHNEC** to gather strength to do something / hace fuerza (aunque esté débil) para una cosa (T) [(3)Tp.148]. In these attestations the vowel of the second syllable is given as long. This is also true

of the item as it appears in a gloss on the Spanish-to-Nahuatl side of T. This must be an error, since this is a derivation from CHICĀHU(A). See CHICĀHU(A), NEHNEQU(I).
CHICHICCUAHU(I)-TL a tree from the bark of which quinine is extracted / palo amargo (Z) [(1)Zp.151, (3)Xp.41]. Another name for this plant is CHICHICTLACŌ-TL. See CHICHIC, CUAHU(I)-TL.
CHĪCHICO from one side to the other repeatedly / de un lado a otro (C) [(2)Cf.94r]. redup. CHICO
CHĪCHICOHŌME by sevens, every seven / de siete en siete, o a cada uno siete (M) [(3)Cf.107r]. In this item there are two reduplications. redup. CHICŌME
CHĪCHICOHŌMETICA every week, every seven days / cada semana (C), cada siete (días) (C) [(2)Cf.107r]. See CHĪCHICOHŌME.
CHĪCHICOHŌMILHUITICA every seven days / cada siete (días) (C) [(1)Cf.107r]. See CHĪCHICOHŌME, ILHUI-TL.
CHICHICTLACŌ-TL a tree from the bark of which quinine is extracted / palo amargo (Z) [(1)Zp.151]. This plant is also known as CHICHICCUAHU(I)-TL. See CHICHIC, TLACŌ-TL.
CHĪCHICUACEM every six, by sixes / de seis en seis, o a cada uno seis (M) [(1)Cf.107r]. This is in a compound. There is a macron over the vowel of the last syllable, but this is an error, because C has the nonreduplicated form immediately above without a macron. The final M delabializes to N before nonlabial consonants and in word-final position. See CHICUACĒ.
CHĪCHICUACEMILHUITICA every six days / cada seis (días) (C) [(1)Cf.107r]. See CHĪCHICUACEM, ILHUI-TL.
CHĪCHICUEHĒY(I) every eight, by eights / de ocho en ocho, o cada uno ocho (M) [(1)Cf.107r]. In this item there are two reduplications. See CHICUĒY(I).
CHĪCHICUEHĒYILHUITICA every eight days / cada ocho (días) (C) [(1)Cf.107r]. See CHĪCHICUEHĒY(I), ILHUI-TL.

CHICHICUEP(A) *vt* to turn someone into a
dog / os vuelve como perros (C for second
pers. plural object) [(1)Cf.113v]. See
CHICHI, CUEP(A).

CHĪCHIHCŌLOĀ *vrefl* to move like a
snake, to weave from side to side /
culebrea (Z) [(2)Zp.37,169]. redup.
CHIHCŌLOĀ

CHĪCHIHCŌLTIC something sinuous, full
of curves / sinuoso (Z) [(2)Zp.116,151]. Z
gives both this and CHIHCHIHCŌLTIC
with the same gloss. redup. CHIHCŌLTIC

CHĪCHĪHUALĀYŌ-TL breast milk / su
leche (de la mamá) (T) [(1)Tp.129]. M
has *chichiualayoatl* 'whey.' See
CHĪCHĪHUAL-LI, ĀYŌ-TL.

CHĪCHĪHUAL-LI breast, teat / teta (M), su
chiche, su pecho (de mujer) (T) A single
attestation in B has the vowel of the
second syllable long as it should be if
CHĪCHĪ is the correct form of the verb,
but T has this vowel consistently short. In
X the vowels of the first two syllables are
unmarked for length and that of the third
is marked long. See CHĪCHĪ.

CHĪCHĪHUALTECOM(A)-TL udder;
someone with large breasts / su ubre (vaca)
(T), mujer de grandes tetas (M) [(1)Tp.129].
See CHĪCHĪHUAL-LI, TECOM(A)-TL.

CHICHILAMA bitch, female dog / perra
[(1)Tp.124]. See CHICHI, ILAMA-TL.

CHĪCHĪLĀZCA-TL a type of large red ant /
hormiga arriera (Z) [(2)Zp.68,151]. See
CHĪL-LI, ĀZCA-TL.

CHĪCHĪLĒHU(I) to turn red, to blush / se
pone colorado, rojo (T), sonroja (Z) Because
the vowel of the third syllable is long, this
seems to be constructed on the verb
-ĒHU(I) rather than to be a simple case of
substitution of E for I. See CHĪCHĪLIHU(I).

CHĪCHĪLĒHUĪHUA nonact. CHĪCHĪL-
ĒHU(I)

CHĪCHĪLĒHUĪTIĀ caus. CHĪCHĪLĒHU(I)

CHICHILIĀ *vt* to make something or
someone bitter / acedar o hacer amargo
algo (M) in construction with 'one's heart'
as direct object, this has the sense of 'to
grow angry.' See CHICHIC.

CHĪCHĪLIHU(I) to become red / pararse
bermejo o colorado (M) [(1)Cf.116v]. This

implies the transitive verb CHĪCHĪLOĀ 'to
make something red,' which is in M but is
not directly attested in the sources for this
dictionary. T and Z have CHĪCHĪLĒHU(I).
See CHĪL-LI.

CHICHILILIĀ applic. CHICHILIĀ

CHICHILĪLŌ nonact. CHICHILIĀ

CHĪCHĪLOĀ to make something red / hacer algo bermejo o colorado (M) See
CHĪCHĪLIHU(I).

CHĪCHĪLTIC something red / cosa colorada
o bermeja (M) See CHĪL-LI.

CHĪCHĪLTICCIHUĀPAH-TLI a medicinal plant / cierta planta medicinal (R)
[(1)Rp.73]. The literal sense of this is 'red
female-medicine.' See CHĪCHĪLTIC,
CIHUĀPAH-TLI.

CHĪCHĪLTICCUAHU(I)-TL candlewood, a
spiny red-flowering bush (Fouquieria
splendens, Fouquieria formosa) / ocotillo
(Z) [(2)Zp.90,151]. See CHĪCHĪLTIC,
CUAHU(I)-TL.

CHĪCHĪLTZAPO-TL mamey (a type of
fruit) / zapote colorado, mamey (Z)
[(3)Zp.80,131,151]. In all three attestations
Z fails to mark the vowel of the first
syllable long. See CHĪCHĪLTIC,
TZAPO-TL.

CHĪCHĪMĒCAPAH-TLI a potent medicinal
plant / planta medicinal muy célebre, pero
demasiadamente activa (R) [(1)Rp.73]. R
does not mark the vowels of the first three
syllables long. An alternative analysis
is a compound of CHICHI 'dog,'
MECA-TL 'vine,' PAH-TLI 'medicine.' See
CHĪCHĪMĒCA-TL, PAH-TLI.

CHĪCHĪMĒCA-TL *pl:* **CHĪCHĪMĒCAH**
Chichimec, a person from one of the
indigenous groups of northern Mexico
considered barbarians by Nahuatl-
speakers. / Chichimeco de nación (C) Used
as a modifier this has both a negative
'barbarous' sense and a positive 'noble
savage' sense. By its vowel length pattern
it is clearly not derived from the words for
'dog,' 'rags, patches,' or 'bitter.' It is
possibly derivationally related to CHĪCHĪ
'to suckle.'

CHĪCHĪMĒCAYŌ-TL something partak-
ing of the nature of the Chichimecs /

lo concerniente a los chichimecos (S)
[(1)Cf.53r]. See CHĪCHĪMĒCA-TL.
CHICHIMICQUI dead dog / perro muerto
(T) [(2)Tp.124,142]. See CHICHI, MICQUI.
CHICHĪN(A) *vt* to soak something up, to
suck something in, to smoke something /
chupar algo, o tomar sahumerio de olores
con cañas (M), rezumarse la vasija embe-
biéndose en ella algún licor ... lo mismo se
dice de la esponja o de cosa semejante que
embebe en sí algún licor (M)
CHICHINACA to hurt, to suffer pain /
escocer la llaga (M), tener dolor, pena o
aflicción (M) [(1)Cf.75r]. See CHINOĀ.
CHICHINAQUIZ-TLI pain, exhaustion /
dolor o fatiga (M) [(1)Bf.6v]. See
CHICHINACA.
CHICHINATZ(A) *vt* to cause someone to
suffer pain / afligir o atormentar a otro (M)
[(3)Cf.52r,75r]. See CHINOĀ.
CHICHĪNILIĀ applic. CHICHĪN(A)
CHICHINOĀ *vrefl,vt* to scorch, burn oneself; to scorch, burn something / cham-
uscarse, o quemarse (M), chamuscar o
quemar a otro (M) *Flo. Codex* has
chîchina. [(3)Zp.38,104,187]. See CHINOĀ.
CHICHIPAHTIC something very bitter /
cosa muy amarga (M) [(2)Zp.9,151]. In one
of the two attestations the vowel of the
second syllable is marked long. R has
related CUAUHCHICHICPAH-TLI with
the internal C which is missing in this
item. See CHICHIC, PAH-TLI.
CHICHIPICA to drip, sprinkle / gotear algo
(M) [(1)Cf.74r, (2)Zp.64,151]. See CHIPĪN(I).
CHICHIPITZ(A) *vt* to sprinkle something,
to cause something to drip / derramar algo
a gotas en abundancia (C) [(1)Cf.74r]. See
CHIPĪN(I).
CHICHIQUIL-LI crest; guiding feathers on a
spear, vane / flecha arpón (M) [(2)Tp.129].
The two attestations are in compounds
meaning 'spine' and 'cock's crest.'
CHĪCHĪTIĀ *vt* to cause someone to suckle /
le da de mamar (T) caus. CHĪCHĪ
CHĪCHĪTILIĀ applic. CHĪCHĪTIĀ
CHĪCHĪTĪLŌ nonact. CHĪCHĪTIĀ
CHICHITLĀCAMAZĀTEH rabid dog /
perro con rabia (T) [(2)Tp.124]. See
CHICHI, TLĀCAMAZĀTEH.

CHICHITOCA to sparkle, crackle, explode /
saltar muchas chispas, etc. (C), centellear,
crepitar, estallar (S) [(2)Cf.75r,Tp.124]. See
CHITŌN(I).
CHICHITOTZ(A) *vt* to cause something to
sparkle, crackle, explode / hacer saltar las
astillas, chispas, etc. (C) [(1)Cf.75r]. See
CHITŌN(I).
CHĪCHIUCNĀHU(I) every nine, by nines /
de nueve en nueve (S) [(1)Cf.107r]. See
CHIUCNĀHU(I).
CHĪCHIUCNĀHUILHUITICA every nine
days / cada nueve (días) (C) [(1)Cf.107r]. See
CHĪCHIUCNĀHU(I), ILHUI-TL.
CHICHIY(A) *pret:* CHICHIX ~ CHICHĪX
to become sour, bitter / acedarse algo, o
tornarse amargo (M) The alternating vowel
length in the preterit is not attested but is
based on analogy with other verbs in IY(A).
See CHICHIC.
CHICHIZĀYŌL-IN *pl:* **-TIN** a type of fly /
mosca que se para en el aire volando (T)
[(1)Tp.124]. The literal sense of this is 'dog-
fly.' See CHICHI, ZĀYŌL-IN.
CHĪCH-TLI *pl:* **-MEH** owl; a type of
whistle; sorcerer / lechuza, o pito que
tañen los muchachos (M), brujo, bruja (T)
CHĪCHYŌ-TL sorcery / brujería (T)
[(1)Tp.124]. See CHĪCH-TLI.
CHICO to one side, indirectly, perversely /
aviesamente (M), a un lado (C) T has the
variant CHICUA.
CHICOCAQU(I) *vt; pret:* **-CAC** to mis-
understand something / entender al revés
algo (M) [(1)Cf.94r]. See CHICO, CAQU(I).
CHICOCCĀN in seven parts / en (siete)
partes (C) [(1)Cf.91r]. See CHICŌME,
-CĀN.
CHICOCHĪHU(A) *vt* to despise something,
someone / lo desprecia (Z) [(2)Zp.44,187].
See CHICO, CHĪHU(A).
CHĪCOH-TLI See XĪCOH-TLI.
CHICOIHTOĀ *vt* to speak ill of someone,
to slander someone / murmurar o decir
mal de otro (M) [(3)Cf.17v,42v,94r]. See
CHICO, (I)HTOĀ.
CHICOILHUIĀ *vt* to malign, curse some-
one / lo maldice (T) [(3)Tp.185]. T has CUA
for CO. See CHICO, (I)LHUIĀ, CHICO-
IHTOĀ.

CHICŌME seven / siete (M)

CHICŌMEPA seven times / siete veces (T) [(1)Tp.124]. In the single attestation there is the reflex of a glottal stop preceding the -PA. See CHICŌME, -PA.

CHICOPETŌN(I) for something to be out of line, protruding sideways / se desconcierta uno, y se sale a un lado (C) [(1)Cf.94r]. See CHICO, PETŌN(I).

CHICOQUĪZ(A) to move aside; to fall from virtue; to surpass, exceed / se sale a un lado (C), apartarse de la virtud (M), sobresale (T) [(1)Cf.94r, (1)Tp.124]. T has CUA for CO. See CHICO, QUĪZ(A).

CHICOTIYA for something to tilt sideways, turn to one side / se ladea (Z) [(2)Zp.75,151]. See CHICO.

CHICOTLAHTOĀ to rave, to blaspheme, to speak cagily / desvariar el enfermo, o blasfemar el blasfemo, o hablar cautelosamente (M) [(1)Cf.94r, (3)Tp.124]. The literal sense of this is to speak in a less than forthright manner. T has CUA for CO. See CHICO, TLAHTOĀ.

CHICOTLAHTŌLŌ nonact. CHICOTLAHTOĀ

CHICOTLAHTŌLTIĀ caus. CHICOTLAHTOĀ

CHICOTLAMAT(I) pret: **-TLAMAH** to be suspicious / ser sospechoso (M) [(1)Cf.94r]. See CHICO, TLAMAT(I).

CHICOTLANĀHUAC off to one side / a un lado (K) [(1)Bf.7v]. See CHICO, -NĀHUAC.

CHICOYŌLLŌHUA to be suspicious / sospechar (M) [(1)Cf.94r]. See CHICO, YŌL-LI.

CHICUACĒ in compounds **CHICUACEM-** six / seis (M) X has CHICUACEN as the free form.

CHICUACECCĀN in six places / en seis partes (M) [(1)Cf.91r]. See CHICUACĒ, -CĀN.

CHICUACEPPA six times / seis veces (M) [(1)Tp.124]. M forms this from CHICUACEM- with assimilation of M to P, but T forms it from CHICUACĒ. See CHICUACĒ, -PA.

CHĪCUAH-TLI pl: **-MEH** barn owl / lechuza (M) [(1)Cf.5r, (1)Rp.74, (1)Tp.124]. In the attestation in T the vowel of the first

syllable is specifically marked short, but C marks it long.

CHĪCUAHTŌTŌ-TL a bird that resembles a barn owl / cierta ave semejante a la lechuza (R) [(1)Rp.74]. See CHĪCUAH-TLI, TŌTŌ-TL.

CHICUĒXCĀN in eight places or portions / en ocho partes u ocho raciones (M) [(1)Cf.91r]. See CHICUĒY(I), -CĀN.

CHICUĒXPA eight times / ocho veces (M) [(2)Tp.124]. M forms this with the regular compounding form of CHICUĒY(I). T has two variants. In one the final stem vowel is retained and the reflex of a glottal stop intervenes between stem and -PA. The other variant is like M's but with the X weakened before -PA. See CHICUĒY(I), -PA.

CHICUĒY(I) in compounds: **CHICUĒX-** eight / ocho (M)

CHIHCHA to spit / escupir

CHIHCHALHUIĀ applic.CHIHCHA

CHIHCHAL-LI spittle / escupitajo (T) [(1)Tp.124]. See CHIHCHA.

CHIHCHALŌ nonact. CHIHCHA

CHIHCHALTIĀ caus. CHIHCHA

CHIHCHI vt to mend, patch something / remendar vestidura o zapato, etc. (M) C contrasts this with CHICHI 'dog' and CHĪCHĪ 'to suckle.' It is homophonous with the stem of CHIHCHI-TL 'saliva.'

CHIHCHICĀHU(A) redup. CHICĀHU(A)

CHIHCHICŌLTIC something sinuous, full of curves / sinuoso (Z) [(2)Zp.116,152]. Z gives both this and CHĪCHIHCŌLTIC with the same gloss. redup. CHIHCŌLTIC

CHIHCHIHCOP(I) to blink, to wink / parpadea (T) [(3)Tp.124]. In T this has characteristically lost an internal glottal stop. It is to be found in the nonreduplicated form CHIHCOPILIĀ, also in T. See IHCOP(I).

CHIHCHIHCOPĪHUA nonact. CHIHCHIHCOP(I)

CHIHCHIHCOPILIĀ applic. CHIHCHIHCOP(I)

CHIHCHĪHU(A) vrefl,vt to adorn, dress oneself, to get ready; to adorn, dress someone, to adorn, embellish something / aderezarse, componerse, o ataviarse (M), aderezar de esta manera otro (M), aderezar alguna cosa (M) This contrasts with M's *chichiua* 'nursemaid,' which is derived from CHĪCHĪ 'to suckle.'

CHIHCHĪHUILIĀ applic. CHIHCHĪHU(A)
CHIHCHĪHUILĪLŌ nonact. CHIH-CHĪHUILIĀ
CHIHCHĪMOLŌN(I) for something to burst open while boiling / se revienta (p.ej. papa, frijol, nixtamal, etc., hirviendo, etc.) [(1)Tp.125]. See MOLŌN(I).
CHIHCHINOĀ See CHICHINOĀ.
CHIHCHI-TL saliva / saliva o bofes (M) See CHIHCHA.
CHIHCHĪUHTOC something made, constructed / hecho, constrúido (Z) [(2)Zp.33,152]. See CHĪHU(A), the verb O.
CHIHCŌLOĀ *vrefl,vt* to twist, to move in a serpentine manner; to twist something / entortar algo (M), culebra (Z), se encorva (Z) This is abundantly attested but only in Z. In the direct attestations of the verb and in the derivation CHIHCŌLTIC there is inconsistency, but overall this pattern holds, contrasting with CHICO 'to the side' and incorporating CŌL 'turn, curve.'
CHIHCŌLTIĀ caus. CHIHCŌLOĀ
CHIHCŌLTIC something bent, twisted, bowed / cosa tuerta como garabato (M), torcido, chueco, desparejo, de lado (Z) See CHIHCŌLOĀ.
CHIHCŌLTILIĀ applic. CHIHCŌLTIĀ
CHIHCOPILIĀ *vt* to wink at someone, to catch someone's eye / hace señas con los ojos, le parpadea (T) [(3)Tp.185]. See IHCOP(I).
CHIHCOPILILIĀ applic. CHIHCOPILIĀ
CHIHCOPILĪLŌ nonact. CHIHCOPILIĀ
CHĪHU(A) *vt* to make, do something; to engender, beget someone / hacer algo (M), engendrar a otro (M) The reflexive use of this has the lexicalized sense 'to happen.'
CHĪHUALIZ-TLI something feasible / cosa factible (M), trabajo (Z) [(4)Zp.20,124,151,159]. See CHĪHU(A).
CHĪHUALŌ nonact. CHĪHU(A)
CHĪHUALTIĀ caus. CHĪHU(A)
CHĪHUALTILIĀ applic. CHĪHUALTIĀ
CHĪHUĀLTĪLŌ nonact. CHĪHUALTIĀ
CHĪHUIĀ This is attested twice in the compound PAHCHĪHUIĀ used reflex-

ively 'to avail oneself of medicine.' See CHĪHU(A).
CHIHUIHCOYŌ partridge / perdiz (pájaro) (Z) [(2)Zp.96,152]. Z also has COYŌTZIN 'parakeet.'
CHĪHUILIĀ applic. CHĪHU(A)
CHĪHUILILIĀ applic. CHĪHUILIĀ
CHĪHUILĪLŌ nonact. CHĪHUILIĀ
CHILACAYOH-TLI a type of soft squash (Cucurbita filicifolia) / especie particular de calabaza (R) [(1)Rp.74, (3)Xp.42]. See TZILACAYOH-TLI.
CHĪLACH-TLI chili pepper seed / pepita de chile (C) [(1)Cf.126v]. See CHĪL-LI, ACH-TLI.
CHĪLATLĀHUIC a type of mild chili pepper / chile pasilla (T) [(1)Tp.125]. Because of the characteristic reduction in T, the intervocalic L may represent a geminate. Possibly the second element is related to TLĀHUIĀ and has to do with redness. See CHĪL-LI.
CHĪLĀTŌL-LI cornstarch beverage flavored with chili / chile atole (Z) [(2)Zp.38,152]. See CHĪL-LI, ĀTŌL-LI.
CHĪLĀZCA-TL a type of red ant / hormiga picahuye (Z) [(2)Zp.68,152]. See CHĪL-LI, ĀZCA-TL.
CHĪLCHŌ-TL green chili pepper / ají o chile verde (M) [(2)Zp.38,152]. It would make sense for the second element of this to be XŌ, referring to greenness, but M and Z agree on CH rather than X.
CHĪLHUĀC dried, smoked chili pepper / chilpocle (Z) [(1)Zp.152]. M has *chiluacmulli* 'sauce or stew seasoned with smoked chilies.' See CHĪL-LI, HUĀQU(I).
CHĪLHUIĀ *vt* to season something with chili peppers / lo pica (con picante), lo enchila (Z) [(3)Zp.51,98,187]. See CHĪL-LI, -HUIĀ.
CHĪLIĀ T gives this as the applicative form of CHIY(A). It is noteworthy that the vowel of the first syllable is long in the absence of YA.
CHĪLLACUĒCHŌL-LI sauce, paste of ingredients very finely ground together / mole, salsa (Z) [(2)Zp.113,152]. Z does not give the absolutive suffix. See CHĪL-LI, TLACUĒCHŌL-LI.

CHĪLLAPĪTZAL-LI enchilada, tortilla and chili dish / enchilada (T) [(1)Tp.125]. See CHĪL-LI, TLAPĪTZAL-LI.

CHĪL-LI chili pepper / ají, o pimienta de las indias (M) In compounds CHĪL- often conveys the sense 'red.'

CHĪLLŌTIĀ *vt* to season something with chili peppers / lechar ají en algún manjar o guisado (M) [(3)Tp.185]. See CHĪL-LI.

CHĪLLŌTILIĀ applic. CHĪLLŌTIĀ

CHĪLLŌTĪLŌ nonact. CHĪLLŌTIĀ

CHĪLPACH profusion or scattering of chili peppers / desperdicio de chile (Z) [(2)Zp.44,152]. Z uses the element PACH without an absolutive suffix in this and in TOMAPACH with the sense of 'profusion,' possibly 'waste.' It may be related to PACH-TLI 'moss.' See CHĪL-LI.

CHĪLPAH-TLI plant with toxic milky sap / cierta planta medicinal y lactifera, cuya leche es venenosa (R) [(1)Rp.74]. R fails to mark the vowel of the initial syllable long. See CHĪL-LI, PAH-TLI.

CHĪLPĀN *pl:* **-TIN** a type of wasp / avispa (T)

CHĪLPOPŌ-TL *pl:* **-MEH** a type of leguminous plant (Parosela diffusa) / escoba colorada (T) [(1)Tp.125]. See CHĪL-LI, POPŌ-TL.

CHĪLTAMAL-LI tamale containing chili peppers / tamal de chile (T) [(1)Tp.125]. See CHĪL-LI, TAMAL-LI.

CHĪLTECAX(I)-TL mortar for grinding chili peppers / cajete, molcajete (Z) [(3)Zp.23,85,152]. See CHĪL-LI, TECAX(I)-TL.

CHĪLTECPIN *pl:* **-TECPINMEH** a tiny, very hot chili pepper pod known in Spanish as *chiltipiquín* / chiltepín, chilpiquín (Z) [(1)Tp.125, (2)Zp.38,152]. In the plural the final N may assimilate to the M of the plural suffix. See CHĪL-LI, TECPIN-TLI.

CHĪLTLEMŌLLOH soup or stew seasoned with chili peppers / temolote (Z) [(2)Zp.120,152]. The more usual Spanish form of this is clemole. See CHĪL-LI, TLEMŌL-LI.

CHĪLTŌTŌ-TL *pl:* **-MEH** cardinal (bird) / cardenal (T) [(2)Tp.125,243]. See CHĪL-LI, TŌTŌ-TL.

CHĪMAL-LI shield / rodela, adarga pavés, o cosa semejante (M), escudo (Z)

CHĪMALQUĪZA-TL piece of gypsum, plaster of Paris / piedra de yeso [(1)Tp.125]. The derivation of this is opaque. See CHĪMAL-LI, QUĪZ(A).

CHĪMALTIĀ *vrefl,vt* to shield oneself; to use something or someone as a shield / hacer rodela para sí, o guarecerse con ella del sol y del agua (M), te tomo por mi escudo, me sirves de escudo (C for first pers. sg. subject, second pers. sg. object) [(1)Cf.58r]. See CHĪMAL-LI.

CHĪNAH-TLI *pl:* **-MEH** vermin / coruco, bicho (T) [(1)Tp.125].

CHINĀM(I)-TL fence of cane or cornstalks, an area so enclosed, or the canes or stalks themselves / seto o cerca de cañas (M), cañuela de maíz, chinámil (T) Z has the variant CHINĀN-TLI with the sense 'pyramid,' while X has it with the sense 'hovel.' It also is a term of social organization referring to a unit closely equivalent to a *calpolli*. The sense all share to some degree is 'enclosure.'

CHINĀMPEHPEN(A) to gather cane or cornstalks / junta chinamíl (T) [(2)Tp.125,196]. See CHINĀM(I)-TL, PEHPEN(A).

CHINĀNCAL-LI house or enclosure built of cane or cornstalks / casa de cañuela de maíz (T) [(1)Tp.125]. See CHINĀM(I)-TL, CAL-LI.

CHINĀNTEQU(I) to cut cane or cornstalks / corta chinamíl (T) [(2)Tp.125,204]. See CHINĀM(I)-TL, TEQU(I).

CHINĀN-TLI See CHINĀM(I)-TL.

-CHINĀNYŌ *necessarily possessed form* the stalks (of a canebrake or cornfield) / su caña (de la milpa) (T) [(1)Tp.129]. See CHINĀM(I)-TL.

CHINOĀ *vt* to burn off land / quemar los campos (M) [(4)Tp.149,231]. All attestations are of the prefixed stem (I)HCHINOĀ. In fact, since as an intransitive verb this must always take an object prefix, and since in such cases the (I)H element is only detectable in sources that indicate glottal stop, it is possible that (I)HCHINOĀ also underlies M's entry *chinoa*. See (I)HCHINOĀ.

CHINŌLŌ nonact. CHINOĀ
CHINOLTIĀ caus. CHINOĀ
CHIPACTIC something clean, pure / blanco, limpio, güero, huero, rubio (T) [(2)Tp.125]. Z has the variant CHIPACTZIN. M has *chipaccaltic* with the same sense. Both are virtually synonymous with CHIPĀHUAC. See CHIPĀHU(A).
CHIPĀHUA *pret:* **CHIPĀHUAC** for something to become clean, pure / pararse limpio, o pararse clara el agua turbia, o purificarse algo (M) This contrasts in the preterit form with the corresponding transitive verb. T has the intransitive form CHIPĀHU(I).
CHIPĀHU(A) *vrefl,vt* to purify oneself; to purify something,someone / alimpiarse o purificarse (M), alimpiar o purificar a otro (M), alimpiar, purificar, o afinar algo (M) This contrasts in the preterit with intransitive CHIPĀHUA.
CHIPĀHUAC something clean, pure / cosa limpia, hermosa, o clara (M) See CHIPĀHUA.
CHIPĀHUACĀYŌ-TL purity, cleanliness / la limpieza en abstracto (C) [(2)Cf.49v]. See CHIPĀHUAC, -YŌ.
CHIPĀHUALIZ-TLI cleanliness, purity, clarity / limpieza, hermosura, y lindeza, o claridad de agua no turbia (M) [(2)Zp.15,206]. See CHIPĀHUA.
CHIPĀHUALŌ nonact. CHIPĀHU(A)
CHIPĀHU(I) for something to become clean / se limpia (T) [(1)Tp.125]. This is a variant intransitive verb form with the same sense as intransitive CHIPĀHUA and contrasting with transitive CHIPĀHU(A). See CHIPĀHU(A).
CHIPĀHUILIĀ applic. CHIPĀHU(A)
CHIPETLACTIC scar tissue / cicatriz (T) [(1)Tp.125].
CHIPĪN(I) to drip / gotear o caer gota (M) T has a variant TLACHIPĪN(I) with the same gloss. M has a corresponding transitive verb *chipinia* 'to scatter something in droplets.'
CHIQUIHU(I)-TL *pl:* **-MEH** basket / cesto o canasta (M)
CHIQUILĒUHTZAHTZI to cry out loudly / grita fuerte (T) [(3)Tp.125]. M has *chi-*

quilitzatzi with the same sense. See TZAHTZI.
CHIQUILĒUHTZAHTZĪHUA nonact. CHIQUILĒUHTZAHTZI
CHIQUILĒUHTZAHTZĪTIĀ nonact. CHIQUILĒUHTZAHTZI
CHIQUILĪCH-TLI cicada / cigarra (M), chicharra (Z) [(2)Zp.38,152]. The Z form of this item appears to retain a relic of the -IN absolutive suffix, while M has the -TLI absolutive.
CHĪTAH-TLI net, sling, hammock, hanging cradle / redecilla para llevar de comer por el camino (M), hamaca, cuna (T) [(3)Tp.125].
CHITŌN(I) for sparks, chips to fly; for a story to be told in an animated manner; for a fire to flare and sparkle / saltar el astilla, o la cuenta cuando la quieren ensartar, o centellear la lumbre o el fuego (M), bota, tira, salta (T)
CHIUCNĀHU(I) nine / nueve (M)
CHIUCNĀHUILHUI-TL nine days / nueve (días) (C) [(2)Cf.107r]. See CHIUCNĀH J(I), ILHUI-TL.
CHIUCNĀUHCĀN in nine places or portions / en nueve partes, o nueve raciones (M) [(1)Cf.91r]. See CHIUCNĀHU(I), -CĀN.
CHĪUHQUI someone in authority, someone with power / mayor (Z), autoridad, poderoso (Z) [(5)Zp.17,82,100,152,155]. This item is abundantly attested with an incorporated object, for example CACCHĪUHQUI 'shoemaker,' but only in Z does it appear as a free form. See CHĪHU(A).
CHIXCĀCAH *vrefl* to be expecting something good / tener confianza, o esperar algún beneficio (M) [(3)Bf.2v,3r,5v, (1)Cf.107r]. One of the B attestations has a long vowel in the first syllable which reflects the general variation of preterit CHIX ~ CHĪX. See CHIY(A), the verb CĀ.
CHIYA See CHIYAN-TLI.
CHIY(A) *vt; pret:* **CHIX** ~ **CHĪX** to wait for someone, something / esperar a alguno (M) This has a variant with E for A. The preterit shows an alternation in vowel length characteristic of verbs in IY(A).

CHIYĀHUA to get greasy / mancharse alguna cosa (M), se engrasa (T) [(2)Tp.125]. This contrasts in the preterit with transitive CHIYĀHU(A). See CHIYAN-TLI.

CHIYĀHU(A) *vt* to get something greasy / manchar algo (M) [(1)Tp.125]. This contrasts in the preterit with the corresponding intransitive verb form. See CHIYĀHUA.

CHIYĀHUAC something greasy, grimy, filthy / cosa grasienta (M) [(3)Zp.64,150]. Z has the shortened form CHĀHUAC. See CHIYĀHUA.

CHIYĀHUALTIĀ to make something dirty, greasy / lo hace grasiento (Z) [(2)Zp.64,187]. Z has the shortened form CHĀHUALTIĀ. Both attestations give the vowel of the second syllable as long, but it should probably be short. See CHIYĀHUAC.

CHIYĀHUIZ-TLI fatness, bloat, blight / humor (M), enfermedad de planta (T), gordura, grasa (X) Z has the shortened form CHĀHUIZ-TLI. See CHIYĀHU(A).

CHIYALIĀ applic. CHIY(A)

CHIYĀLŌ nonact. CHIY(A)

CHIYALTIĀ caus. CHIY(A)

CHIYAN See CHIYAN-TLI.

CHIYAN-TLI chia, a plant (Salvia chian) from the seed of which oil is pressed; the seed is also used in making a refreshing beverage / chía, semilla común en México de que hacen bebidas frescas y sacan un buen aceite (R) [(1)Rp.72]. M has *chia* and *chian* without an absolutive suffix. From the single attestation it is not possible to establish beyond doubt that there is an intervocalic Y or that both vowels are short. See CHIYĀHUA.

CHIY(E) See CHIY(A).

CHIYELIĀ applic. CHIY(E)

CHIYELTIA caus. CHIY(E)

CHŌCA to weep, cry, howl, to utter one's characteristic sound / llorar, balar la oveja, bramar el león o el toro, cantar el buho o las otras aves (M)

CHŌCALIZ-TLI tears, weeping / llanto (T) [(1)Tp.126, (2)Zp.78,152]. See CHŌCA, CHŌQUILIZ-TLI.

CHŌCALTIĀ caus. CHŌCA

CHŌCANI weeper / llorador (M), llorón (T) See CHŌCA.

CHŌCHŌCA to go on crying, to weep repeatedly / llorar repetidas veces (R) [(1)Rp.36]. redup. CHŌCA

CHOCHOPITZ fake, phony / no sabe en realidad (tocar), mentiroso (T) [(1)Tp.125].

CHOCHOPOCA to boil furiously / hierve muy fuerte (Z) [(2)Zp.67,152]. T has TZOTZOPOCA with the closely related sense of 'for something to bubble as it ferments.' M has *chochopoca* with a different sense 'to itch, to have a rash.' See CHOPŌN(I).

CHŌCOHUĀ nonact. CHŌCA

CHOCOLĀĀTŌL-LI cornstarch beverage flavored with chocolate / atole de cacao (T) [(2)Tp.108,125]. See CHOCOLĀ-TL, ĀTŌL-LI.

CHOCOLĀTIC something the color of chocolate, dark brown / color de café (Z) [(2)Zp.23,152]. See CHOCOLĀ-TL.

CHOCOLĀ-TL chocolate / alimento hecho con almendras de cacao y semillas del árbol llamado *pochotl*, en partes iguales (S), chocolate (R) This is not attested in M, B, or C, but it is attested in R as well as in the modern sources. Possibly the initial element is related to M's *xocolia* 'to make something bitter or sour' and to XOCOC 'something sour.' The substitution of CH for X is not uncommon. See Ā-TL.

CHŌCTIĀ altern. caus. CHŌCA

CHŌCTILIĀ applic. CHŌCTIĀ

CHŌCTĪLŌ nonact. CHŌCTIĀ

CHŌCUETLĀN june bug grub / gallina ciega (gusano) [(2)Zp.62,152]. In one attestation the vowel of the first syllable is marked long, and in the other it is unmarked.

CHOHCHOC a type of bird / pájaro arriero (Z) [(2)Zp.93,152]. The literal sense of the Spanish gloss is 'muleteer bird.' Since neither attestation marks the vowel of the second syllable long, there does not seem to be a connection with CHŌCA 'to cry.'

CHOHCHŌCA redup. CHŌCA

CHOLHUIĀ *vt* to jump over something / saltar arroyo o acequia (M) [(2)Zp.94,145]. applic. CHOLOĀ

CHOLOĀ to flee; to run swiftly, to leap along / huir, saltar, o ausentarse, o saltar o chorrear el agua (M)

CHOLŌLLĀN *place name* Cholula [(1)Cf.56v]. See CHOLŌLŌ, -TLĀN.

CHOLŌLŌ nonact. CHOLOĀ

CHOLŌLTĒCA-TL person from Cholula / de Cholula (C) [(1)Bf.11r, (1)Cf.56v]. See CHOLŌLLĀN.

CHOLŌLTIĀ *vrefl,vt* to throw oneself into flight; to make someone flee / echar a huir (M), hacer huir a otro (M) caus. CHOLOĀ

CHOPĪNIĀ *vt* to pick at something, to prick someone / picar la víbora, o comer el pájaro (M) This is only indirectly and weakly attested in CACHOPĪN, but synonymous TZOPĪNIĀ is well attested.

CHOPŌN(I) to spatter / salpica, busea (Z) [(1)Zp.152].

CHŌQUILIĀ applic. CHŌCA

CHŌQUILIZ-TLI tears, weeping, cries, howls, the characteristic sound of an animal / lloro o llanto, balido de oveja, bramido de león o otro, aullido de perro o de lobo, o canto de buho y de las otras aves (M) This is attested across sources, including C. Z gives CHŌCALIZ-TLI and CHŌQUILIZ-TLI together as synonyms. CHŌQUIZ-TLI is also synonymous. See CHŌCA.

-CHŌQUILLŌ *only attested in possessed form* sap, juice / su savia [(2)Zp.114,157].

CHŌQUILTIĀ altern. caus. CHŌCA

CHŌQUĪTIĀ altern. caus. CHŌCA

CHŌQUĪTILIĀ applic. CHŌQUĪTIĀ

CHŌQUIZHUĒHUETZCA to laugh with tears in one's eyes / se ríe llorando (T) [(3)Tp.126]. See CHŌCA, HUĒHUETZCA.

CHŌQUIZHUĒHUETZCOHUA nonact. CHŌQUIZHUĒHUETZCA

CHŌQUIZHUĒHUETZQUĪTIĀ caus. CHŌQUIZHUĒHUETZCA

CHŌQUIZTILIĀ *vt* to make someone feel pain (about spendng money) / le da dolor gastar (T) [(3)Tp.186]. This draws its sense from the T sense of 'miser' for the related noun. See CHŌQUIZ-TLI.

CHŌQUIZTILILIĀ applic. CHŌQUIZTILIĀ

CHŌQUIZTILĪLŌ nonact. CHŌQUIZTILIĀ

CHŌQUIZTLAHTLAHTOĀ to speak while weeping / habla llorando (T) [(3)Tp.126]. See CHŌQUIZ-TLI, TLAHTOĀ.

CHŌQUIZTLAHTLAHTŌLŌ nonact. CHŌQUIZTLAHTLAHTOĀ

CHŌQUIZTLAHTLAHTŌLTIĀ caus. CHŌQUIZTLAHTLAHTOĀ

CHŌQUIZ-TLI tears, weeping, cries, howls, the characteristic sound of an animal / lloro o llanto, etc. (K) According to M and C, this is synonymous with CHŌQUILIZ-TLI, of which, in fact, it is a shortened form. T glosses it as a substantive 'a miserable person, someone indigent, a miser.' See CHŌQUILIZ-TLI.

CU

CUĀ *vt; pret:* **CUAH** to eat something, someone / comer algo (M), morder o comer a otro (M) T has a short final vowel in derived forms where other sources have a long one. But across sources CUĀ appears in some derived forms with a short vowel where a long one is to be expected.

CUĀĀTĒQUIĀ *vrefl,vt* to sprinkle water on one's head, to wash one's head, to receive baptism; to wash someone's head, to baptize someone / echar agua sobre la cabeza, o lavársela, o bautizarse (M), lavar a otro la cabeza de esta manera (M), lo bautiza (T) M has almost identical glosses for CUĀTĒQUIĀ, which results from the compression of the two adjacent long vowels into one. See CUĀ(I)-TL, ĀTĒQUIĀ.

CUACEMMAN(A) *vrefl,vt* for something to spill, scatter, sprinkle; to spill, scatter, sprinkle something (other than liquid) / se derrama, se esparce, se riega (cosa seca) (T), lo derrama, lo esparce, lo riega (T) [(4)Tp.146,182]. Intransitive CUACEMMAN(I) has the same sense as CUACEMMAN(A) used reflexively. See CEMMAN(A).

CUACEMMAN(I) for something (other than liquid) to scatter / se esparce (T) [(1)Tp.120]. See CUACEMMAN(A).

CUĀCHCAL-LI canopy, awning / pabellón, cielo de cama, paramento, o tienda de mantas enceradas (M) [(1)Cf.92v]. See CUĀCH-TLI, CAL-LI.

CUĀCHCALTŌPĪL-LI canopy pole, support / las varas del palio (C) [(1)Cf.92v]. See CUĀCHCAL-LI, TŌPĪL-LI.

CUĀCHICHIQUIL-LI feather crest / cresta de pluma (M) [(1)Tp.129]. See CUĀ(I)-TL, CHICHIQUIL-LI.

CUĀCHIPĀHU(A) *vt* to brush someone's hair / lo cepilla (Z) [(2)Zp.27,186]. See CUĀ(I)-TL, CHIPĀHU(A).

CUĀCHPĀM(I)-TL standard, banner / estandarte, bandera, o pendón (M) [(3)Cf.82v]. See CUĀCH-TLI, PĀM(I)-TL.

CUĀCH-TLI large cotton blanket, sheet / manta grande de algodón (M) This is attested indirectly in CUĀCHPĀM(I)-TL and CUĀCHCALTŌPĪL-LI.

CUACUĀ *vt; pret:* **CUACUAH** to chew or gnaw at something / mascar pan, carne, etc., o roer el ratón papel, manta, etc. (C) [(1)Cf.127v]. This contrasts with CUAHCUĀ 'to snap, nip at something' M combines both senses in a single entry with the gloss 'to nip something or for a sheep to ruminate.' redup. CUĀ

CUĀCUAHUEH ox, cow, bull, or other horned animal / toro, o animal que tiene cuernos (M) Z has a -MEH plural, implying that this has been lexicalized and is not recognized as a derivation with the possessor suffix -EH, which forms its plural as -EHQUEH. See CUĀCUAHU(I)-TL.

CUĀCUAHUEHCĀHUAH keeper of cattle, horned animals / señor de los que tienen cuernos ... el señor de éste ganado mayor (C) [(1)Cf.56r]. See CUĀCUAHUEH.

CUĀCUAHUEHHUAH keeper of cattle, horned animals / señor de los que tienen cuernos ... el dueño de éste ganado mayor (C) [(1)Cf.56r]. C gives this as an alternative to the longer form CUĀCUAHUEHCĀHUAH. See CUĀCUAHUEH.

CUĀCUAHU(I)-TL horn, antler / cuerno de animal, o astas (M) [(2)Cf.9v,56r]. The literal sense of this is 'head-tree.' See CUĀ(I)-TL, CUAHU(I)-TL.

CUACUALACA to make a thundering sound or a sound like water boiling in a pot or boiling over / tronar o hacer ruido lo que hierve en la olla a borbollones (M) [(1)Cf.74v]. See CUALĀN(I).

CUACUALATZ(A) *vt* to cause something to make a thundering sound or a sound like water boiling over / levantar semejante ruido (C referring back to CUACUALACA) [(1)Cf.74v]. According to C this item was little used. See CUALĀN(I).

CUACUALŌ By general rule this should be CUĀCUALŌ, but it is attested in T with the reflex of short A in the second syllable (p.180). nonact. CUACUĀ

CUACUALŌC something pitted (such as wood) / picada (madera) (T) [(1)Tp.119]. See CUACUĀ.

CUACUALTIĀ caus. CUACUĀ

CUĀCUALTZIN someone, something pretty, attractive / bonito, agradable, hermoso, lindo (T) [(2)Tp.122,136]. See CUAL-LI.

CUĀCUAUHCHŌCA to bellow like a bull / brama (el toro) (T) [(1)Tp.122]. CUĀCUAUH here is apparently a truncation of CUĀCUAHUEH 'animal with horns.' See CUĀCUAHU(I)-TL, CHŌCA.

CUĀCUAUHCONĒ-TL calf / becerro (Z) [(2)Zp.19,147]. CUĀCUAH here is apparently a truncation of CUĀCUAHUEH 'animal with horns.' See CUĀCUAHU(I)-TL, CONĒ-TL.

CUĀCUAUHNAC(A)-TL beef / carne de res (T) [(2)Tp.122,166, (2)Zp.109,147]. CUĀCUAUH here is apparently a truncation of CUĀCUAHUEH 'animal with horns.' See CUĀCUAHU(I)-TL, NAC(A)-TL.

CUĀCUAUHPIXQUI cowherd / boyerizo o vaquero (M), pastor de ganado de bueyes (T) [(1)Tp.122]. In M the UHP sequence assimilates to PP. See CUĀCUAUHPIY(A).

CUĀCUAUHPIY(A) *pret:* **-PIX ~ -PĪX** to herd cattle / cuida bueyes (T) [(4)Tp.122,231]. CUĀCUAUH here is apparently a truncation of CUĀCUAHUEH 'animal with horns.' The long-vowel variant preterit form is not directly attested but is established for component PIY(A). See CUĀCUAHU(I)-TL, PIY(A).

CUĀCUAUHTZON-TLI ox bristles / cerda (de buey) (T) [(1)Tp.122]. CUĀCUAHUEH here is apparently a truncation of CUĀCUAHUEH 'animal with horns.' See CUĀCUAHU(I)-TL, TZON-TLI.

CUĀĒHUAYŌ-TL scalp; dandruff / el cuero de la cabeza (M), su cuero cabelludo (T) for possessed form), su caspa (Z for possessed form) [(1)Tp.129, (2)Zp.26,157]. See CUĀ(I)-TL, ĒHUAYŌ-TL.

CUAHCUĀ *vt; pret:* **CUAHCUAH** to snap, nip at something; for stock to graze / dar bocados o dentelladas a otro (M), pacer el ganado (M) [(4)Cf.50v,127v,128r]. M combines this item with CUACUĀ in a single entry with the gloss 'to nip something or for a sheep to ruminate.' redup. CUĀ

CUAHCUA *vt; pret:* **CUAHCUAC** for something (such as rheumatism) to cause someone pain / le duele (T) [(3)Tp.182]. This appears nearly synonymous with CUAHCUĀ in the sense of causing a gnawing pain, but this item has a short vowel in the last syllable, and the preterit is distinct from that of CUĀ.

CUAHCUACUĀ *vt; pret:* **CUAHCUACUAH** to masticate, to chew interminably / mascar el enfermo lo que no puede tragar, o el sano lo que está ... duro (C) [(2)Cf.128r, (3)Rp.125]. redup. CUACUĀ

CUAHCUACUAHTIMAN(I) *vrefl* for things to be scraping against each other / se están rascando los unos a los otros (C) [(1)Cf.128r]. According to C this can refer to a dog biting at fleas, horses scratching each other, and the like. See CUAHCUACUĀ, MAN(I).

CUAHCUAHU(I) to be a woodcutter, to cut, gather firewood / ser leñador (M), leña, junta leña (T) [(3)Tp.119, (2)Zp.76,147]. See CUAHU(I)-TL.

CUAHCUAHUĪHUA nonact. CUAHCUAHU(I)

CUAHCUAHUĪTIĀ caus. CUAHCUAHU(I)

CUAHCUALTIĀ caus. CUAHCUA

CUAHCUAUHTI to get stiff, tired / envararse o pararse yerto (M), se cansa (T) [(1)Tp.119]. For the gloss M refers from *quaquauhti* to *quaquappitzaui* but the latter does not occur in M, and the gloss is to be found with unreduplicated *quappitzaui*. redup. CUAUHTI

CUAHCUAUHTIC someone large, tall, full grown / personas ya adultas, altas o largas (M for plural), grande, fuerte, adulto (S) [(1)Cf.71r]. redup. CUAUHTIC

CUAHCUAUHTĪHUA nonact. CUAH-
CUAUHTI

CUAHCUAUHTĪTIĀ caus. CUAH-
CUAUHTI

CUAHNĀMIQU(I) vt; pret: **-NĀMIC** to
oppose, contradict, attack, resist someone,
to meet someone head on / le opone, le
contradice, le afrente, le ataca, le asalta,
lo resiste (T), unirse, hablando de
dos extremos (S) [(6)Tp.182, 229]. See
CUĀ(I)-TL, NĀMIQU(I).

CUAHNĀMIQUĪHUA nonact. CUAH-
NĀMIQU(I)

CUAHNĀMIQUILIĀ applic. CUAH-
NĀMIQU(I)

CUĀHUĪHUĪCA vrefl to nod, to shake one's
head / cabecea ... lo menea (la cabeza)
(Z) [(3)Zp.22,83,169]. See CUĀ(I)-TL,
HUĪHUĪCA.

CUAHUINENETZIN a type of insect, possibly the walking stick (Aplopus mayeri) /
palillo (insecto) (T) [(1)Tp.118]. This appears to have CUAHU(I)-TL 'wood' and
NENE-TL 'image' as constituent elements.

CUĀHUĪTEQU(I) vrefl,vt to strike one's
head; to beat someone on the head / se
pega en la cabeza (T), le pega en la cabeza
(T) [(6)Tp.147,183]. M combines this in a
single entry with CUAUHHUĪTEQU(I) 'to
strike something with a stick, to work
land with a hoe, stick.' See CUĀ(I)-TL,
HUĪTEQU(I).

CUAHU(I)-TL tree, wood, stick, staff, beam /
árbol, madero, o palo (M)

CUĀIHUINTIC someone giddy, faint, lightheaded / desvanecido de la cabeza (M),
mareado (Z) [(2)Zp.82,147]. Z lacks the
final -C, although it is present in Z's
ĪXHUINTIC. Z consistently has the
vowel of HUIN marked long although it
is consistently short elsewhere. See
CUĀ(I)-TL, IHUINTI.

CUĀILPIĀ vrefl,vt to receive confirmation
(in the church); to bind one's head; to bind
someone's head / atarse la frente, ... recibir
la confirmación (S), se confirma (en
la iglesia); se amarra la cabeza (T), le
amarra la cabeza (T) [(6)Tp.147,183]. See
CUĀ(I)-TL, (I)LPIĀ.

CUĀILPILIĀ applic. CUĀILPIĀ

CUĀILPĪLŌ nonact. CUĀILPIĀ

CUĀ(I)-TL head; top, summit, peak / extre-
midad de algo, o la cabeza ... lo alto de ella
como es la superficie del casco, vértice (M)
In the derived form CUAHNĀMIQU(I),
this has the alternate stem form CUAH-,
making it analogous to MĀ(I)-TL ~ MAH.

CUĀĪTZTILIĀ vrefl for one's head to
get chilled / se le enfría la cabeza (T)
[(3)Tp.147]. See CUĀ(I)-TL, ĪTZTILIĀ.

CUĀĪXHUINTIĀ vt to make someone dizzy
/ lo marea (Z) [(2)Zp.82,147]. Z consistently marks the vowel of HUIN long, but
elsewhere it is short. See CUĀ(I)-TL,
ĪXHUINTIĀ.

CUĀIZTĀC someone gray-haired / cana,
canosa (T) [(1)Tp.123]. See CUĀ(I)-TL,
IZTĀC.

CUĀIZTAY(A) for one's hair to be turning
gray / encanecer o tornarse cana de la
cabeza (M) [(1)Cf.93r]. See CUĀ(I)-TL,
IZTAY(A).

CUALĀNALTIĀ caus. CUALĀN(I)

CUALĀNCĀNAHUATIĀ vt to give an or-
der to someone angrily / le ordena con ira
(Z) [(2)Zp.91,186]. See CUALĀNQUI,
NAHUATIĀ.

CUALĀNCĀQUIQUINACA to speak angrily / habla con ira (Z) [(2)Zp.66,147]. See
CUALĀNQUI, QUIQUINACA.

CUALĀN(I) to get angry / enojarme (M for
first pers. sg. subject)

CUALĀNILIZ-TLI anger / enojo (M), enojo,
coraje (T) [(1)Tp.120]. See CUALĀN(I).

CUALĀNINI pl: **-MEH** someone irritable,
easily angered / enojón (T) [(1)Tp.120]. See
CUALĀN(I).

CUALĀNOHUA nonact. CUALĀN(I)

CUALĀNQUI someone angry / el que está
enojado (M) This follows from CUALĀN(I)
but is attested in the sources for this
dictionary only as the first element
in CUALĀNCĀNAHUATIĀ and
CUALĀNCĀQUIQUINACA. In the form
CUALĀNCĀ- it is the first element in
several more verbs in M. See CUALĀN(I).

CUALĀNTIĀ vrefl,vt for someone to get
angry, peevish; to anger, irritate someone /
enojar a otro (M), se enoja (T), le hace
enojar, le causa molestia, lo enoja, lo
ofende, le provoca (T) caus. CUALĀN(I)

CUALĀNTILIĀ applic. CUALĀNTIĀ

CUALĀNTĪLŌ nonact. CUALĀNTIĀ

CUALĀN-TLI anger / enojo (M) See
CUALĀN(I).

CUALĀNTOC someone angry, irritated,
enraged / enojado, irritado, coraje (Z)
[(4)Zp.34,52,73,147]. See CUALĀN(I), the
verb O.

CUALCĀN a good place or proper time /
lugar abrigado y decente, o buen tiempo, o
a buen tiempo y sazón (M) CUAL-LI,
-CĀN

CUALCO early / temprano (T) [(1)Tp.120].
See CUAL-LI, -C(O).

CUĀLIĀ applic. CUĀ

CUALITTA vt to be pleased with something
/ parecerme bien, o agradarme alguna
persona (M for first pers. sg. subject), le
gusta, le agrada, le parece, le tiene cariño
(T) See CUAL-LI, (I)TTA.

CUAL-LI something good / cosa buena (M)
In the modern Nahuatl of Morelos and
Tlaxcala the Spanish phrase está bien has
been translated as CUALLI CAH, and this
has been lexicalized so that the stress may
fall on -LI.

CUALLŌ-TL goodness / bondad, mode-
ración, discreción (S) [(1)Bf.10r]. See
CUAL-LI, -YŌ.

CUALNĒC(I) to look good / parecer bien (C)
[(4)Cf.49v]. In M this is given only as a
substantive qualneci 'something fine-
looking, beautiful.' See CUAL-LI, NĒC(I).

CUALNEQU(I) vt to praise, recommend
someone / lo afama, lo recomienda (Z)
[(3)Zp.5,106,186]. See CUAL-LI, NEQU(I).

-CUALNĒZCĀ necessarily possessed
form one's good appearance, beauty / tu
buen parecer, tu hermosura (C for second
person singular possessor) [(3)Cf.49v]. See
CUALNĒZCĀYŌ-TL.

CUALNĒZCĀYŌ-TL good appearance,
beauty / belleza, gracia, elegancia (S), tu
buen parecer, tu hermosura (C for possessed form) [(2)Cf.49v]. See CUALNĒC(I).

CUALŌ The expected form would be
CUĀLŌ. nonact. CUĀ

CUĀLŌHUA for an eclipse to take place /
eclipse (Z) [(2)Zp.48,147]. This appears to
be derived from the nonactive form of
CUĀ 'to eat something' In two related
derived forms T has CUALO with short

vowels in place of CUĀLŌ. See CUALŌ,
CUĀ.

CUALOMĒTZ-TLI lunar eclipse / eclipse de
luna [(1)Tp.120]. T also has MĒTZCUALO
with the same sense. If this is derived from
the nonactive stem of CUĀ 'to eat something,' the vowel of the second syllable
corresponds to a long vowel in the verb
form, but this vowel shortens word-finally,
and the compound may be based on the
short form. See CUALŌ, MĒTZ-TLI.

CUALQUETZ(A) vt to praise, esteem,
recommend someone / lo estima, lo
recomienda, lo alaba, lo afama (Z)
[(5)Zp.5,8,57,106,186]. See CUAL-LI,
QUETZ(A).

CUALTI to become good / hacerse bueno (C)
[(2)Cf.57v,60r]. See CUAL-LI.

CUALTIĀ caus. CUĀ

CUALTILIĀ vt to restore, repair something
damaged / restaurar o aderezar lo dañado (M) [(1)Cf.60r]. applic. CUALTIY(A),
CUALTI

CUALTIY(A) pret: CUALTIX ~
CUALTIYAC to recover, to get better /
restaurarse y hacerse bueno lo que estaba
dañado (M) [(3)Cf.57v]. See CUAL-LI.

CUALTZIN someone or something pretty,
attractive / bonito, hermoso, fino, lindo,
puro, precioso (Z) [(7)Zp.20,60,67,77,
101,103,147]. T has synonymous
CUĀCUALTZIN. See CUAL-LI.

CUĀMAN(A) vt to lie to someone, to deceive someone / le miente, lo engaña (T)
[(6)Tp.183,229].

CUĀMĀTL(A)-TL pl: -MEH hairnet, cap,
bonnet / albanega o cofia de red (M),
gorro (T) [(2)Tp.123]. See CUĀ(I)-TL,
MĀTL(A)-TL.

CUĀMELĀHU(A) vrefl,vt to straighten, raise
the head; to brush someone's hair / se endereza la cabeza; le endereza la cabeza (T),
lo cepilla (Z) [(6)Tp.147,183, (2)Zp.27,186].
See CUĀ(I)-TL, MELĀHU(A).

CUĀMOMOTZALHUIĀ applic.
CUĀMOMOTZOĀ

CUĀMOMOTZOĀ vt to depilate someone,
to pluck the hairs from someone's head /
mesar a otro (M), arrancar los cabellos a
alguien (S) [(2)Cf.65r]. See CUĀ(I)-TL,
MOMOTZOĀ.

CUĀMŌTLA *vt* to throw something at someone's head / le tira en la cabeza (T) [(3)Tp.183]. See CUĀ(I)-TL, MŌTLA.

CUĀNACA chicken, rooster / gallo o gallina de castilla (M) [(2)Cf.104r,117v, (1)Tp.123, (1)Rp.124]. With the absolutive suffix, CUĀNACA-TL refers literally to the comb of a chicken. The absolutiveless form refers to the animal itself. R has final glottal stop. See CUĀ(I)-TL, NAC(A)-TL.

CUĀNACAYŌ-TL the skin of the scalp / la carne del casco de la cabeza (M), su cresta (Z for possessed form, referring to chicken's comb) [(2)Zp.35,157]. See CUĀ(I)-TL, NAC(A)-TL, -YŌ, CUĀNACA.

CUANHUĀCOHUA nonact. CUAN-HUĀQU(I)

CUANHUĀCQUI something thin, frail / débil, debilitado, enclenque, delgado (S), delgado, flaco, (animal u hombre) (T) [(1)Tp.119]. T has lost the internal N. See CUANHUĀQU(I).

CUANHUĀQU(I) to grow thin, frail / estar débil, enclenque, delgado, seco (M), se adelgaza, se enflaquece (T) [(3)Tp.119, (1)Rp.124]. T has lost the internal N. M has CUANHUĀQU(I), the associated noun CUANHUĀCQUI, and also CUANHUĀTZ(A) 'to make someone get thin, weak,' but only in the Spanish-to-Nahuatl side, associated with the verb *enflaquecer*. They are synonymous with HUĀQU(I), HUĀCQUI, and HUĀTZ(A) respectively. See HUĀQU(I).

CUANHUĀQUĪTIĀ caus. CUANHUĀQU(I)

CUANHUĀTZ(A) See CUANHUĀQU(I).

CUĀPAHPĀC(A) *vrefl* to scrub one's head / se lava la cabeza (Z) [(2)Zp.76,169]. See CUĀ(I)-TL, PAHPĀC(A).

CUĀPATLACHILHUIĀ applic. CUĀPATLACHOĀ

CUĀPATLACHOĀ *vrefl,vt* for one's head to get crushed; to crush someone's head / se aplasta la cabeza (T), le aplasta la cabeza (T) [(6)Tp.148,184]. See CUĀ(I)-TL, PATLACHOĀ.

CUĀPATLACHŌLŌ nonact. CUĀ-PATLACHOĀ

CUĀPEHPETZTIC someone bald / pelón (T) [(1)Tp.123]. See CUĀ(I)-TL, PEHPETZTIC, CUĀPETZOĀ.

CUĀPETZOĀ *vrefl,vt* to cut the hair very short, to shave the scalp / se corta el pelo muy corto, se alisa el pelo (T), le corta el pelo muy corto, le alisa el cabello (T) [(6)Tp.148,184]. See CUĀ(I)-TL, PETZOĀ.

CUĀPETZOLHUIĀ applic. CUĀPETZOĀ

CUĀPETZŌLŌ nonact. CUĀPETZOĀ

-CUĀPĪCCA *only attested in possessed form* cap, bonnet / gorra (Z) [(2)Zp.63,157]. See CUĀ(I)-TL, PĪCCA-TL.

CUĀPIHPĪ *vrefl,vt* to cut one's hair; to cut someone's hair / se corta el pelo (T), le corta el pelo (T) See CUĀ(I)-TL, PIHPĪ.

CUĀPIHPĪHUA nonact. CUĀPIHPĪ

CUĀPIHPILIĀ applic. CUĀPIHPĪ

CUĀPĪLOĀ *vt* to taper something to a point by twisting and drawing it out / le adelgazo la punta, torciéndole (C for first pers. sg. subject) [(1)Cf.127v]. See CUĀ(I)-TL, PĪLOĀ.

CUĀPINTIC something pointed or drawn out at the ends / puntiagudo, ovalado (T) [(1)Tp.123]. See CUĀ(I)-TL, PINTIC.

CUĀPĪPINALHUIĀ applic. CUĀPĪPINOĀ

CUĀPĪPINOĀ *vt* to draw something out into a point, to taper something / le saca punta (T) [(3)Tp.184]. See CUĀ(I)-TL, PĪPINOĀ.

CUĀPĪPINŌLŌ nonact. CUĀPĪPINOĀ

CUĀPĪQUILŌNI cap, bonnet / gorra (Z) [(2)Zp.63,157]. See CUĀ(I)-TL, PĪQU(I).

CUĀPOCHICTIC someone gray-haired / canoso, cano (Z) [(2)Zp.25,147]. See CUĀ(I)-TL, POCHICTIC.

CUAPPITZĀHU(I) See CUAUH-PITZĀHU(I).

CUAPPITZOĀ See CUAUHPITZOĀ.

CUĀQUEPI someone crazy / loco (Z) [(1)Zp.147]. See CUĀ(I)-TL, QUEP(A).

CUĀQUEPTOC someone crazy / azorado, loco (Z) [(3)Zp.17,77,147]. See CUĀ(I)-TL, QUEPTOC.

CUĀTATACA *vrefl* to scratch one's head / se rasca la cabeza (T) [(3)Tp.148]. See CUĀ(I)-TL, TATACA.

CUĀTATAPAH *pl:* **-TIN** someone disheveled / desmelenado (C), (1)Rp.125 [(2)Cf.5v, (1)Rp.125]. See CUĀ(I)-TL, TATAPAH-TLI.

CUĀTENEXTIC someone gray-haired / canoso, cano (Z) [(2)Zp.25,147]. In one of the attestations Z mistakenly marks the vowel of the second syllable long. See CUĀ(I)-TL, TENEX-TLI.

CUĀTENEX-TLI dandruff, crust, scabs on the scalp / caspa, tiña (T) [(1)Tp.123]. See CUĀ(I)-TL, TENEX-TLI.

CUĀTEPĒHU(I) to go bald / es calvo, se le cae el cabello (T) [(1)Tp.123]. See CUĀ(I)-TL, TEPĒHU(I).

CUĀTEPĒHUĪHUA nonact. CUĀ-TEPĒHU(I)

CUĀTEPĒHUĪTIĀ caus. CUĀTEPĒHU(I)

CUĀTEPOLTIC something abbreviated at the top, lacking its top / sin sombrero, árbol sin follage, cosa que no tiene punta (T) [(1)Tp.123]. See CUĀ(I)-TL, TEPOLTIC.

CUĀTĒQUIĀ See CUĀĀTĒQUIĀ.

CUATETE type of long-tailed lizard / chintete [(1)Tp.120].

CUĀTEXOCO caterpillar / oruga [(2)Zp.92,147].

CUĀTEX-TLI *possessed form:* **-CUĀTEXYŌ** brains / sesos (T) [(1)Tp.123, (2)Zp.115,157]. Z has TĪX for TEX. See CUĀ(I)-TL, TEX-TLI.

CUĀTLACUĀHUAC hardheaded / duro de la cabeza (Z) [(1)Zp.147]. See CUĀ(I)-TL, TLACUĀHUAC.

CUĀTLAPĀN(A) *vrefl,vt* for one's head to break, be crushed; to smash, crush someone's head / quebrarse o quebrantarse la cabeza (M), quebrantar a otro la cabeza (M) See CUĀ(I)-TL, TLAPĀN(A).

CUĀTLAPECH-TLI pillow / almohada (Z) [(2)Zp.9,147]. In one of the two attestations Z mistakenly marks the vowel of PECH long. See CUĀ(I)-TL, TLAPECH-TLI.

CUĀTLAPOLŌLIZ-TLI madness, confusion / locura, confusión (Z) [(3)Zp.32,77,147]. The second element is a shortened form of TLAPOLŌLTILIZ-TLI. See CUĀ(I)-TL, TLAPOLŌLIZ-TLI.

CUĀTLAPOLŌLTIĀ to be stunned, confused / se ataranta (Z) [(2)Zp.16,147]. See CUĀ(I)-TL, TLAPOLŌLTIĀ.

-CUĀTLAYŌLLOH *only attested in possessed form* the crown of one's head, the top of a tree / su coronilla; la punta de su cabeza, la punta del árbol (T) [(1)Tp.129]. See CUĀ(I)-TL, TLAYŌLLOH-TLI.

CUĀTŌHUITZTIC something pointed /

puntiagudo (T) [(1)Tp.123]. M has the synonymous reflexive verbs *tohuitzoa* and *tonhuitzoa* 'to rise, to lift oneself up.' See CUĀ(I)-TL.

CUĀTOTŌNIĀ *vrefl* to get angry / se enoja (Z) [(2)Zp.52,169]. See CUĀ(I)-TL, TOTŌNIĀ.

CUĀTOTŌNILIĀ *vrefl* to study / estudia (T) [(3)Tp.148]. See CUĀ(I)-TL, TOTŌNILIĀ.

CUĀTZETZELOĀ *vrefl* to shake one's head / sacude la cabeza (T), lo menea (la cabeza) (Z) See CUĀ(I)-TL, TZETZELOĀ.

CUĀTZETZELŌLŌ nonact. CUĀ-TZETZELOĀ

CUĀTZONĀHUIĀ *vrefl* to wash one's hair / se lava la cabeza con agua (T) [(3)Tp.148]. See CUĀTZON-TLI, Ā-TL, -HUIĀ.

CUĀTZON-TLI head hair (as contrasted with body hair) / cabellos, o pelos de la cabeza (M) [(3)Tp.148]. This is attested as an element of the construction CUĀTZONĀHUIĀ. See CUĀ(I)-TL, TZON-TLI.

CUAUHĀYACACH-TLI mahogany tree / caoba (árbol) (Z) [(2)Zp.25,147]. Z also has ĀYACACHCUAHU(I)-TL with the same meaning. In one attestation Z incorrectly marks the vowel of CUAUH long. See CUAHU(I)-TL, ĀYACACH-TLI.

CUAUHAYOH-TLI *pl:* **-MEH** a type of squash used in making mole / calabaza para mole (T) [(2)Tp.109,119]. See CUAHU(I)-TL, AYOH-TLI.

CUAUHCAL-LI wooden cage, jail / jaula grande de palo, a donde estaban los presos por sus delitos (M) [(1)Cf.97v]. A common variant is HUAUHCAL-LI. See CUAHU(I)-TL, CAL-LI.

CUAUHCALPIXQUI custodian, jailer / los que le guardaban (C for plural) [(1)Cf.97v]. See CUAUHCAL-LI, PIY(A).

CUAUHCAMAC forest / lugar de árboles, arboledo, bosque, selva (T) [(1)Tp.119]. M has *quauhcamac* with the sense of 'fissure or knothole in wood.' See CUAHU(I)-TL, -CAMAC.

CUAUHCAMOH-TLI cassava, a woody root used in making tapioca and cassava flour (manioc) / yuca (T,Z) [(1)Tp.119, (2)Zp.131,149]. See CUAHU(I)-TL, CAMOH-TLI.

CUAUHCEC-TLI ice in trees, snow / hielo en árbol, nieve (Z) [(5)Zp.67,88,149]. See CUAHU(I)-TL, CEC-TLI.

CUAUHCUĒCH-TLI wood debris, wood shavings, sawdust / basura de palos, que trae la creciente, viruta, aserrín (T) [(1)Tp.119]. See CUAHU(I)-TL, CUĒCH-TLI.

CUAUHHUAUHCAL-LI cage / jaula (Z) [(4)Zp.73,149,225]. Z has characteristic CUO for CUAUH. M has *quauacalli* and *quauhacalli*, both meaning a measure for grain, and also *quauacal* referring to a person with a narrow head. These are probably CUAUHĀCAL-LI and CUĀHUACAL respectively, and not synonymous with this item. A more common synonymous form is CUAUHCAL-LI. See CUAHU(I)-TL, CUAUHCAL-LI.

CUAUHHUĀTZAL dead, dried out tree / árbol seco (Z) [(2)Zp.13,149]. See CUAHU(I)-TL, HUĀTZ(A).

CUAUHHUEXŌ-TL tree which produces pods of seeds in an edible pulp (Inga jinicuil) / jinicuile (árbol) (Z) [(2)Zp.73,147]. See CUAHU(I)-TL, HUEXŌ-TL.

CUAUHHUIĀ *vt* to hit someone, something with a stick / le pega con palo, le da una paliza (T) [(3)Tp.182]. See CUAHU(I)-TL, -HUIĀ.

CUAUHHUILIĀ applic. CUAUHHUIĀ

CUAUHHUĪLŌ nonact. CUAUHHUIĀ

CUAUHHUĪTEQU(I) *vt* to beat something, someone with a stick; to break large clumps of earth into small clumps by beating with a hoe, stick / dar de palos a otro, o herirle en la cabeza con palo, o desboronar terrones con azadón o con palo (M) This is attested in its constituent parts in the sources for this dictionary. M combines the senses of this and of CUĀHUĪTEQU(I) in the first part of the gloss reproduced here. See CUAHU(I)-TL, HUĪTEQU(I).

CUAUHHUĪZTIC splinter, chip / astilla (Z) [(1)Zp.149]. The second element is probably HUITZ 'thorn' in spite of the Z for TZ and the discrepancy in vowel length. See CUAHU(I)-TL.

CUAUHMĀPAN up in a tree / arriba en el árbol [(1)Zp.149]. This is based on a compound of CUAHU(I)-TL 'tree' and MĀ(I)-TL 'hand' referring to the outspread branches of the crown of the tree. MĀ(I)-TL by itself is used to mean 'branch' as well as 'hand.' See CUAHU(I)-TL, MĀ(I)-TL, -PAN.

CUAUHMAXAL-LI *pl:* -TIN forked stick / horqueta, horcón (Z) [(2)Zp.69,148, (3)Xp.34]. See CUAHU(I)-TL, MAXAL-LI.

CUAUHMĀYAHUĪLLAH place where trees have been felled / lugar desmontado (Z) [(1)Zp.149]. See CUAHU(I)-TL, MĀYAHU(I), -TLAH.

CUAUHMECAEXŌ-TL vanilla bean plant (Vanilla planifolia) / vainilla (Z) [(2)Zp.127,149]. See CUAUHMECA-TL, EXŌ-TL.

CUAUHMECAPAH-TLI sarsaparilla / zarzaparrilla (R) [(1)Rp.125]. See CUAUHMECA-TL, PAH-TLI.

CUAUHMECA-TL Mexican creeper (Antigonon leptopus), hairbrush vine (Combretum farinosum), sarsaparilla; vine or ivy in general / bejuco, enredadera, trepador (Z), zarzaparrilla (R) [(6)Zp.19,52,125,127, 149, (2)Rp.125]. See CUAHU(I)-TL, MECA-TL.

CUAUHMŌCHIPEHPEN(A) See CUAUHMŌCHI-TL, PEHPEN(A).

CUAUHMŌCHITEQU(I) See CUAUHMŌCHI-TL, TEQU(I).

CUAUHMŌCHI-TL tamarind / guamuchil (T) [(2)Tp.196,204]. This is only attested in compounds; the absolutive suffix is attested in the work on Mexican natural history by Francisco Hernández. T has CUE for CUAUH. See CUAHU(I)-TL.

CUAUHNĀHUAC *place name* Cuernavaca (literally: 'near the trees') / cerca de los árboles (C) [(1)Cf.20v]. See CUAHU(I)-TL, -NĀHUAC.

CUAUHNELHUIĀ applic. CUAUHNELOĀ

CUAUHNELOĀ *vrefl,vt* for something to be stirred; to stir something (with a stick) / se revuelve (T), lo revuelve (T) [(4)Tp.146,182]. See CUAHU(I)-TL, NELOĀ.

CUAUHNELŌLŌ nonact. CUAUHNELOĀ

CUAUHNENECUIL-LI *pl:* **-TIN** tree which produces pods of seeds in an edible pulp (Inga jinicuil) / jinicuil (árbol) (T) [(1)Tp.119]. M has the reflexive verb *nenecuiloa* 'to stagger around.' See CUAHU(I)-TL.

CUAUHNEPANŌL-LI cross / cruz (C) [(3)Cf.20r,67r]. See CUAHU(I)-TL, -NEPANŌL-LI.

CUAUHNEPANTLAH in the middle of the forest / en el medio de los árboles de bosque (C) [(1)Cf.20r]. See CUAHU(I)-TL, NEPANTLAH.

CUAUHNEX-TLI ash / ceniza (Z) [(2)Zp.27,149]. See CUAHU(I)-TL, NEX-TLI.

CUAUHPACH-TLI Spanish moss / moho, musgo, paxtle (Z), paxtle de árboles (Z) [(4)Zp.85,87,148,149]. See CUAHU(I)-TL, PACH-TLI.

CUAUHPAHZOL-LI briarpatch / maraña (Z) [(2)Zp.81,149]. See CUAHU(I)-TL, PAHZOL-LI.

CUAUHPAMPILOĀ *vt* to hang something in a tree / cuelga en un árbol (Z) [(2)Zp.30,187]. See CUAHU(I)-TL, -PAN, PILOĀ.

CUAUHPAN-TLI stretcher, litter / lecho, camilla (Z) [(4)Zp.24,76,149]. See CUAHU(I)-TL, -PAN.

CUAUHPEHPEN(A) See CUAHU(I)-TL, PEHPEN(A).

CUAUHPILCATICAH to be hanging from a tree / está colgado del árbol (T) [(1)Tp.119]. See CUAHU(I)-TL, PILCA, the verb CĀ.

CUAUHPITZA someone, something weak / flaco (T) [(1)Tp.119]. M has *quauhpitzactli* 'thin stick, wand.' See CUAHU(I)-TL, PITZAC-TLI.

CUAUHPITZĀHU(I) to get hard, tough; to get thin / envararse o pararse yerto (M), endurece (tortilla, carne), se adelgaza, se enflaquece (T) [(3)Tp.119]. In this compound T has a short vowel in the third syllable coresponding to the long vowel of the free form. M also has a variant of this in which the sequence UHP assimilates to PP. See CUAHU(I)-TL, PITZĀHU(I).

CUAUHPITZĀHUĪHUA nonact. CUAUHPITZĀHU(I)

CUAUHPITZĀHUĪTIĀ caus. CUAUHPITZĀHU(I)

CUAUHPITZOĀ *vrefl,vt* for someone to become stiff, to become stiff, to be steadfast; to stiffen someone's resolve, to give someone courage / pararse yerto como palo (M), le da valor (para hacer o no hacer una cosa (T) [(9)Tp.146,153,182]. The sequence UHP can assimilate to PP, as it does in M. See CUAHU(I)-TL, PITZOĀ.

CUAUHPITZŌLŌ nonact. CUAUHPITZOĀ

CUAUHPITZO-TL *pl:* **-MEH** peccary, wild pig / jabalí (T,Z) [(1)Tp.119, (2)Zp.73,149]. See CUAHU(I)-TL, PITZO-TL.

CUAUHPITZTIC someone or something thin, tough, stiff / delgado (animal u hombre), duro, macizo, tieso, paralítico (T) [(1)Tp.119]. See CUAUHPITZĀHU(I).

CUAUHQUEQUĒX woodpecker / pájaro carpintero (Z) [(2)Zp.93,149]. Despite the discrepancy in vowel length, the second element appears to be related to QUEQUEXQUIYA 'to have an itch,' possibly 'to scratch' or 'to be eaten away.' See CUAHU(I)-TL, QUEQUEXQUIC.

CUAUHTEMA *Z has this as both transitive and intransitive.* to beat someone with a stick / le pega (Z), le da una paliza, le aporrea (con palo) (Z) [(5)Zp.12,93, 95,150,187]. M has *quauhtema* 'to roof a house with wood; to board, plank, floor a house,' which is clearly derived from TĒM(A) 'to fill up,' while none of the Z attestations have the vowel of TE long. The verb TEM(A) 'to take a sweat bath' has a short vowel and refers to an activity involving beating oneself with leafy branches. Since Z never drops the stem vowel in verbs of this type, it cannot be determined whether the preterit of this would be -TEN, as in the case of TEM(A). See CUAHU(I)-TL, TEM(A).

CUAUHTĒN-TLI edge of the woods, stump or trunk of a tree / halda o orilla de monte (M), tronco (Z) [(2)Zp.125,148]. See CUAHU(I)-TL, TĒN-TLI.

CUAUHTEPAHZOL-LI briarpatch / lugar de barañas (T) [(1)Tp.119]. See CUAHU(I)-TL, TEPAHZOL-LI.

CUAUHTEPEHXIHUIĀ *vrefl,vt* to fall from

a tree; to throw something or someone down from a tree / se derrumba del árbol (T), lo derrumba del árbol (T) [(6)Tp.146,182]. See CUAHU(I)-TL, TEPEHXIHUIÃ.

CUAUHTEPEHXIHUILIÃ applic. CUAUHTEPEHXIHUIÃ

CUAUHTEPEHXIHUÍLŌ nonact. CUAUHTEPEHXIHUIÃ

CUAUHTEQU(I) See CUAHU(I)-TL, TEQU(I).

CUAUHTĒTECOHUA altern. nonact. CUAUHTĒTEQU(I)

CUAUHTĒTEQU(I) to trim the branches off a tree / derrama (ramas del árbol) (T) [(3)Tp.119]. See CUAHU(I)-TL, TĒTEQU(I).

CUAUHTĒTEQUÍHUA altern. nonact. CUAUHTĒTEQU(I)

CUAUHTĒTEQUILIÃ applic. CUAUHTĒTEQU(I)

CUAUHTI to get stiff, tired / se cansa (T for reduplicated form) See CUAHU(I)-TL.

CUAUHTIC someone tall, something long or someone tired and stiff / hombre alto de cuerpo, o de gran estatura (M), cosa larga como palo o árbol (C), cansado (Z) Height and stiffness are both attributes of trees, hence the distinct senses of this. See CUAHU(I)-TL, CUAUHTI.

CUAUHTĪHUA nonact. CUAUHTI

CUAUHTILIÃ applic. CUAUHTI

CUAUHTILILIÃ applic. CUAUHTILIÃ

CUAUHTILILĪLŌ nonact. CUAUHTILIÃ

CUAUHTITLAN *place name* Cuauhtitlan (literally: 'adjacent to woodland') / nombre de otro pueblo, y significa junto al árbol o arboleda (C) [(1)Bf.11r, (6)Cf.22r,56v]. See CUAHU(I)-TL, -TLAN.

CUAUHTLAĀQUĪLLŌ-TL fruit-bearing tree / árbol que produce fruta (Z) [(1)Zp.150]. See CUAHU(I)-TL, TLAĀQUĪLLŌ-TL.

CUAUHTLĀCA-TL man of wood / hombre de palo (C) [(1)Cf.57r]. C contrasts this with CUAUHTLAHCA-TL 'highlander, mountain dweller, savage.' See CUAHU(I)-TL, TLĀCA-TL.

CUAUHTLACHIHCHĪUHQUI carpenter / carpintero (Z) [(2)Zp.26,149]. See CUAHU(I)-TL, CHIHCHĪHU(A).

CUAUHTLAH mountain, wilderness, forest / montaña, arboleda o bosque (M) See CUAHU(I)-TL, -TLAH.

CUAUHTLAHCA-TL highlander, mountain dweller, savage / salvaje o montañés (C) [(1)Cf.57r]. C contrasts this with CUAUHTLĀCA-TL 'man of wood.' See CUAUHTLAH.

CUAUHTLAHOCUIL-IN wild animal (as contrasted with a domestic animal) / animal salvaje (Z) [(2)Zp.11,150]. See CUAUHTLAH, OCUIL-IN.

CUAUHTLAHQUIT-TLI wooden loom / telar (Z) [(2)Zp.120,150]. In one of the attestations the reflex of the glottal stop is printed as *g*. See CUAHU(I)-TL, TLAHQUIT-TLI.

CUĀUHTLĀN *place name* Cuautla, Morelos [(2)Tp.119,123]. Although T loses word-final -N, the remaining reflex of the long vowel in -TLĀN aids in distinguishing this from CUAUHTLAH. T gives variants with a short vowel and a long vowel in the initial syllable but treats the long-vowel variant as basic, taking this to be derived from CUĀUH-TLI 'eagle,' not CUAHU(I)-TL 'tree.' See CUĀUH-TLI, -TLĀN.

CUAUHTLAPĀN(A) to split kindling-wood / raja madero (M), raja leña (T) See CUAHU(I)-TL, TLAPĀN(A).

CUAUHTLAPĀNALŌ nonact. CUAUHTLAPĀN(A)

CUAUHTLAPĀNILIÃ applic. CUAUHTLAPĀN(A)

CUAUHTLAPAN-TLI *pl*: -MEH bower, shelter of branches, platform / arbolado, casa en el campo hecha de ramitas del árbol, enramada, tapanco (T) [(1)Tp.119]. See CUAHU(I)-TL, TLAPAN-TLI.

CUAUHTLAPECH-TLI *pl*: -MEH scaffold, platform; litter, stretcher / tablado o andamio (M), camilla (T) See CUAHU(I)-TL, TLAPECH-TLI.

CUAUHTLAPOÃ to clear woods / desmonta (T) [(3)Tp.119]. See CUAHU(I)-TL, TLAPOÃ.

CUAUHTLAPOLHUIÃ applic. CUAUHTLAPOÃ

CUAUHTLAPŌLŌ nonact. CUAUHTLAPOÃ

CUAUHTLATĪL-LI firewood / leña (Z) [(2)Zp.76,150]. See CUAHU(I)-TL, TLATIĀ.

CUAUHTLEHCAHUIĀ applic.
CUAUHTLEHCŌ

CUAUHTLEHCŌ to climb up in a tree / gatear, trepar, subir por el árbol (M) [(3)Tp.119]. See CUAHU(I)-TL, TLEHCŌ.

CUAUHTLEHCŌHUA nonact.
CUAUHTLEHCŌ

CUĀUH-TLI eagle / águila (M)

CUAUHTLĪL-LI half burned charcoal / tizo (Z) [(2)Zp.123,150]. See CUAHU(I)-TL, TLĪL-LI.

CUAUHTŌCQUECHIĀ *vt* to stake something out / lo estaca (Z) [(2)Zp.56,187]. See CUAUHTŌC-TLI, QUECHIĀ.

CUAUHTŌC-TLI *pl:* **-MEH** stake, forked stick set in the ground / árbol o estaca para plantar (M), horcón, horqueta (T) [(1)Tp.119, (4)Zp.56,150,187]. In one attestation Z fails to mark the vowel of the second syllable long. See CUAHU(I)-TL, TŌCA.

CUAUHTŌPĪL-LI *pl:* **-MEH** cross decorated with flowers / cruz floreada (que usan en el casamiento) (T) [(2)Tp.120]. See CUAHU(I)-TL, TŌPĪL-LI.

CUAUHTŌQUIĀ *vt* to stake something out / lo estaca (Z) [(2)Zp.56,187]. See CUAUHTŌC-TLI.

CUAUHTŌTOL-IN crested guan, a bird somewhat pheasant-like in appearance (Penelope purpurascens) / cojolite, totola silvestre (Z) [(3)Zp.29,124,150]. See CUAHU(I)-TL, TŌTOL-IN.

CUAUHTOZAN a type of pocket gopher / tusa de monte (Z) [(2)Zp.126,150]. See CUAHU(I)-TL, TOZAN.

CUAUHTZĀLAN-TLI road or path among trees / camina o senda entre árboles (C) [(1)Cf.20r]. M has *quauhtzalan* as a locative 'among trees.' See CUAHU(I)-TL, TZĀLAN-TLI.

CUAUHTZAPO-TL *pl:* **-MEH** annona, a plant that produces a fruit with sweet pulp and black seeds (Annona glabra) / anona (T) [(1)Tp.120]. See CUAHU(I)-TL, TZAPO-TL.

CUAUHTZAYĀN(A) to split kindling-wood

/ raja leña [(3)Tp.120]. See CUAHU(I)-TL, TZAYĀN(A).

CUAUHTZAYĀNALŌ nonact.
CUAUHTZAYĀN(A)

CUAUHTZAYĀNILIĀ applic.
CUAUHTZAYĀN(A)

CUAUHTZICALHUIĀ applic.
CUAUHTZICOĀ

CUAUHTZĪCA-TL *pl:* **-MEH** type of ant that lives in trees / hormiga (las que habitan en el árbol) (T) [(1)Tp.120]. See CUAHU(I)-TL, TZĪCA-TL.

CUAUHTZICOĀ *vt* to connect, hitch, hang something / lo engancha (T) [(3)Tp.182]. See CUAHU(I)-TL, TZICOĀ.

CUAUHTZICŌLŌ nonact.
CUAUHTZICOĀ

CUAUHTZIC-TLI parrot flower (Psittacanthus calyculatus), a parasitic plant / injerto del árbol, goma del árbol (T) [(2)Tp.120]. See CUAUHTZICOĀ.

CUAUHTZICTŌTŌ-TL a type of oriole that eats sap / calandria (pájaro que come goma de los árboles), avispero (T) [(2)Tp.120,243]. See CUAUHTZIC-TLI, TŌTŌ-TL

CUAUHTZONTECOPĪN(A) to uproot trunks of trees, to pull out stumps / arranca troncos (T) [(3)Tp.120]. See CUAUHTZONTE-TL, COPĪN(A).

CUAUHTZONTECOPĪNALŌ nonact.
CUAUHTZONTECOPĪN(A)

CUAUHTZONTECOPĪNILIĀ applic.
CUAUHTZONTECOPĪN(A)

CUAUHTZONTE-TL *pl:* **-MEH** trunk or stump of a tree, a piece of a timber or a beam / tronco de árbol o de madera (M), pedazo de palo o de viga (T) [(4)Tp.120]. See CUAHU(I)-TL, TZONTE-TL.

CUAUHXAXACA a type of horned owl / tecolote, buho (Z) [(3)Zp.21,120,150]. See CUAHU(I)-TL, XAXACA.

CUAUHXĀYAC(A)-TL *pl:* **-MEH** a type of wasp, hornet that builds a large nest / avispa de campo (en los árboles), mascarón (panal grande) (T) [(1)Tp.120]. See CUAHU(I)-TL, XĀYAC(A)-TL.

CUAUHXIHU(I)-TL fronds, branches of trees; a type of palm tree / ramos de árboles (M), palma (árbol) (Z)

[(2)Zp.93,150]. See CUAHU(I)-TL, XIHU(I)-TL.

CUAUHXĪLŌ-TL *pl:* **-MEH** tropical tree and its edible fruit (Parmentiera edulis) / cuajilote (T,Z,X) See CUAHU(I)-TL, XĪLŌ-TL.

CUAUHXĪM(A) *pret:* **-XĪN** to do carpentry, to work wood / carpintear, labrar madera (M) [(1)Bf.10v, (2)Zp.74,150]. See CUAHU(I)-TL, XĪM(A).

CUAUHXĪMALIZ-TLI carpentry / carpintería (K) [(1)Bf.10v]. See CUAUHXĪM(A).

CUAUHXĪNQUI carpenter, sawyer, someone who saws wood / carpintero (M), aserrador (Z) [(2)Zp.15,148]. See CUAUHXĪM(A).

CUAUHYOH mountain, forest, wilderness / monte, bosque, montaña (Z) [(5)Zp.20,43,86,150,215]. There is inconsistency across attestations; in two the vowel of -YOH is mistakenly marked long. See CUAHU(I)-TL, -YOH.

CUAUHYŌLLOH-TLI heart of wood, pith / corazón de palo (T) [(1)Tp.120]. See CUAHU(I)-TL, YŌLLOH-TLI.

CUAUHZĀHUACAMAC place where there are many casaguate trees / lugar de muchas cazaguates (T) [(1)Tp.120]. See CUAUHZĀHUA-TL, -CAMAC.

CUAUHZĀHUACAPOTZ-TLI a type of casaguate tree / cazaguate prieto (árbol) (T) [(1)Tp.120]. See CUAUHZĀHUA-TL, CAPOTZTIC.

CUAUHZĀHUACUAHU(I)-TL *pl:* **-MEH** casaguate tree / cazaguate (árbol) (T) [(1)Tp.120]. See CUAUHZĀHUA-TL, CUAHU(I)-TL.

CUAUHZĀHUA-TL *pl:* **-MEH** casaguate, a tree popularly believed to be poisonous to people and animals (Ipomoea murucoides, Ipomoea arborescens) / cazaguate (árbol) (T) [(6)Tp.120, (3)Xp.38]. This may ultimately be derived from CUAHU(I)-TL 'tree' and ZAHUA-TL 'pox, rash, disease,' despite the descrepancy in vowel length. T has lost the final labial consonant of the first syllable.

CUAUHZĀHUATLAH place where there are many casaguate trees / lugar de

muchos cazaguates (T) [(1)Tp.120]. See CUAUHZĀHUA-TL, -TLAH.

CUAUHZĀHUAXŌLĒ-TL *pl:* **-MEH** a type of mushroom / hongo (T) [(1)Tp.120]. See CUAUHZĀHUA-TL, XŌLĒ-TL.

CUĀXAHXAMĀNILIĀ *vt* to shatter someone's head to pieces / se la hizo pedazos (la cabeza) (C for past tense) [(1)Cf.75r]. redup. CUĀXAMĀNILIĀ

CUĀXAMĀNIĀ *vrefl,vt* for one's head to break; to break someone's head / quebrantarse o quebrarse la cabeza (M), quebrantar la cabeza a otro (M) This is indirectly attested in CUĀXAMĀNILIĀ. See CUĀ(I)-TL, XAMĀNIĀ.

CUĀXAMĀNILIĀ *vt* to break someone's head / le quebró la cabeza (C for past tense) [(1)Cf.75r]. applic. CUĀXAMĀNIĀ

CUĀXAXAMACHILIĀ applic. CUĀXAXAMATZ(A)

CUĀXAXAMATZ(A) *vt* to make someone's head crumble / desmenuzó la cabeza (C for past tense) [(2)Cf.75r]. See CUĀ(I)-TL, XAXAMATZ(A).

CUAXELOĀ *vrefl,vt* for animals and the like to scatter, separate; to scatter trash, manure, corn, etc. / se riegan, se desperdigan (animal, etc.) (T), lo riega (basura, abono, maíz, etc.), lo desperdiga, lo alborota, lo frota (T) [(6)Tp.146,182]. This contrasts with CUĀXELOĀ in the same source, but what the first element is, if not CUĀ(I)-TL, is not clear. It would appear to be the same as the first element in CUACEMMAN(A). See XELOĀ.

CUĀXELOĀ *vrefl,vt* to spill out (as from of an overflowing sack); to pour the excess of something out / se quita (p.ej. de un costal que tiene demasiado, etc.) (T), lo quita, lo riega, lo saca (lo que sobra del maíz, etc., del bote, costal, etc.) (T) This is abundantly attested and within T contrasts with CUAXELOĀ 'to scatter something.' See CUĀ(I)-TL, XELOĀ.

CUĀXĒPOHHUIĀ *vt* to lie to someone, to deceive someone / le miente (T) [(7)Tp.184,229]. This opaque construction may incorporate the Spanish word *sebo* 'tallow' and have some literal sense of dripping candle-wax on someone's head.

CUĀXĒPOHHUILIĀ applic. CUĀ-
XĒPOHHUIĀ

CUĀXĒPOHHUĪLŌ nonact. CUĀ-
XĒPOHHUIĀ

CUĀXĪCAL-LI skull, cranium / casco de la
cabeza, o calavera (M) [(2)Tp.123,129,
(3)Zp.24,96,148]. See CUĀ(I)-TL,
XĪCAL-LI.

CUĀXĪCALTIC someone bald / calvo,
pelón, cabeza de jícara (T) [(1)Tp.123,
(3)Zp.24,96,148]. See CUĀXĪCAL-LI.

CUĀXILHUĀZ-TLI hairbrush / cepillo (para
peinarse) (Z) [(2)Zp.27,157]. See CUĀ(I)-TL,
XILHUĀZ-TLI, XELOĀ.

CUĀXĪPETZTIC someone bald / calvo,
pelón (T) [(1)Tp.123]. See CUĀ(I)-TL,
XĪPETZTIC.

CUĀYACAPITZTIC something pointed /
puntiagudo (Z) [(2)Zp.103,148]. See
CUĀ(I)-TL, YACAPITZTIC.

CUĀYECACHOĀ *vrefl* to nod one's
head / cabecea (T) [(3)Tp.148]. The second element here may be derived from
YAC(A)-TL 'nose, ridge, summit' or
may conceivably be a reduction of
ĀYACACHOĀ 'to play the rattle,' namely,
for one's head to bob up and down like a
rattle. See CUĀ(I)-TL.

CUĀYETIC someone with his head hanging,
drooping, a tree drooping with heavy fruit,
or a wilted plant / se cuelga (la cabeza o la
punta) (por tener mucha fruta, o por estar
marchitada) (T) [(1)Tp.123]. See CUĀ(I)-TL,
ETIC.

CUĀYŌLCUEPTOC confused, agitated /
atontado, azorado (Z) [(1)Zp.148]. This
appears just once in Z and seems to be a
variant of CUĀYŌLQUEPTOC, with more
standard CUEP(A) for Z's characteristic
QUEP(A). See CUĀ(I)-TL, YŌLCUEP(A).

CUĀYŌLLOH-TLI the crown of one's head,
the crown of a tree, treetop / la coronilla,
o el medio de la cabeza (M), su coronilla, la punta del árbol (T) [(1)Tp.129].
The attestation is a locative derivation
that seems to be built on YŌLLŌ-TL
rather than YŌLLOH-TLI, as in M. See
CUĀ(I)-TL, YŌLLOH-TLI.

CUĀYŌLQUEPI someone crazy / loco (Z)
[(2)Zp.77,148]. See CUĀYŌLQUEPTOC.

CUĀYŌLQUEPTOC someone confused,
crazy / atontado, loco (Z) [(2)Zp.77,148].
See CUĀ(I)-TL, YŌLQUEPTOC.

CUE *mild exclamation* [(2)Bf.8v,9r].

CUECHĀHU(A) to get moist, damp /
pararse algo húmedo o liento (M) This is
indirectly attested in CUECHĀHUAC,
CUECHĀHUALIZ-TLI, and CUE-
CHĀHUALLŌ-TL

CUECHĀHUAC something moist,
damp / cosa lienta y húmeda (M) See
CUECHĀHU(A).

CUECHĀHUALIZ-TLI humidity, damp-
ness / humedad (Z) [(2)Zp.69,148]. See
CUECHĀHU(A).

CUECHĀHUALLŌ-TL humidity, damp-
ness / humedad (T) [(1)Tp.121]. See
CUECHĀHU(A), -YŌ.

CUECHĀHUAXTOC rusty, damp / oxidado,
humediciendo (Z) [(2)Zp.92,148]. See
CUECHĀHUAY(A), the verb O.

CUECHĀHUAY(A) *pret:* -HUAX ~
-HUAYAC to get moist, damp / se
humedece (Z) [(2)Zp.69,148]. See
CUECHĀHU(A).

CUECHĀHU(I) to get moist, damp, wet
through / trasmina, se humedece (T)
[(2)Tp.121,229]. See CUECHĀHU(A).

CUECHĀHUIĀ *vt* to get something
damp / lo humedece (T) [(3)Tp.182]. See
CUECHĀHU(I).

CUECHĀHUILIĀ applic. CUECHĀHUIĀ

CUECHĀHUĪLŌ nonact. CUECHĀHUIĀ

CUECHAQUIĀ *vrefl,vt* to twist, sprain a
body part / se tuerce (mano, pie, etc.)
(T), le lastima el pie (al otro) (T for
(I)CXICUECHAQUIĀ) This is abundantly
attested, but only in T.

CUECHAQUILIĀ applic. CUECHAQUIĀ

CUECHAQUĪLŌ nonact. CUECHAQUIĀ

CUĒCHILHUIĀ nonact. CUĒCHOĀ

CUĒCHOĀ *vrefl,vt* to get ground up, ground
to powder; to grind something fine / se
muele (T), heñir la masa, o moler mucho
alguna cosa (M)

CUĒCHŌLŌ nonact. CUĒCHOĀ

CUĒCHPAH-TLI medicine in powdered
form / medicina en polvo (T) [(1)Tp.122].
See CUĒCHOĀ, PAH-TLI.

CUĒCHTIC something ground fine,

powdered / cosa muy molida (M)
[(2)Tp.122,240]. See CUĒCHOĀ.

*CUĒCH-TLI This is the second element of CALCUĒCH-TLI 'soot' and CUAUHCUĒCH-TLI 'sawdust' and apparently means 'residue.' It contrasts in meaning and possibly in phonological form with M's *cuechtli* which refers to a type of snail or spiral shell.

CUĒC-TLI fox / zorro (Z) [(2)Zp.132,148]. Although this is suggestive of CUETLĀCH-TLI 'wolf,' there is a vowel-length discrepancy.

CUĒCUĒLIHU(I) to bend, to be flexible / entortarse o torcerse (M for unreduplicated form), se tuerce, es flexible (T) [(1)Tp.121]. M has this in unreduplicated form only, with the same sense as T. This intransitive verb is synonymous with the reflexive verb CUĒCUĒLOĀ. See CUĒCUĒLOĀ.

CUĒCUĒLOĀ *vrefl* to bend, twist / se tuerce (T) [(3)Tp.147, (2)Zp.37,169]. M has *cuecuel* as an element in compounds having to do with twisting.

CUĒCUĒLŌLŌ nonact. CUĒCUĒLOĀ

CUĒCUĒLTIC something flexible / flexible (T) [(1)Tp.122]. See CUĒCUĒLIHU(I).

CUĒCUEP(A) *vrefl* to be disturbed, upset / se turba (T) [(4)Tp.147,164]. This contrasts in T with CUĒCUĒP(A) 'to turn something over repeatedly.' redup. CUEP(A)

CUĒCUĒP(A) *vt* to turn something over repeatedly, to plow land / volver muchas veces alguna cosa lo de arriba abajo, o probar y experimentar alguna cosa, o ser vario en lo que dice (M), lo barbecha (prepara terreno para la siembra) (T) [(3)Tp.183]. In sense this appears to be the reduplicated form of CUEP(A) 'to turn,' in which the vowel of the second syllable should be short. In T this contrasts with CUĒCUEP(A) 'to be disturbed, upset.' See CUEP(A).

CUĒCUEPALŌ nonact. CUĒCUEP(A)
CUĒCUĒPALŌ nonact. CUĒCUĒP(A)
CUĒCUĒPILIĀ applic. CUĒCUĒP(A)

CUECUEPOCA for many flowers to bloom at once, to break out in a rash / brotar las flores o cosa semejante, o sarpullirse (M), brotar muchas flores juntas (C) [(1) Cf.73v]. See CUEPŌN(I).

CUECUEPOTZ(A) *vt* to cause many flowers to bloom at once / hacer que brotan las flores, etc. (C) [(1) Cf.73v]. See CUEPŌN(I).

CUECUETLACA for a fire to make a loud noise; to shake, tremble / hacer mucho ruido la llama (M), estremece, tiembla (T) [(1)Tp.121, (3)Zp.40,58,148]. See CUETLĀN(I).

CUECUETLACHILIĀ applic. CUECUETLATZ(A)

CUECUETLATZ(A) *vt* to shake something, make something tremble; to brandish a spear / lo estremece (T), blandear lanza o cosa así (M) [(3)Tp.182]. See CUETLĀN(I).

CUECUETLATZALŌ nonact. CUECUETLATZ(A)

CUĒCUETLAXTIC something flexible / flexible (T,Z) [(2)Tp.45,121, (2)Zp.60,148]. In the Spanish-to-Nahuatl side, T has the reflex of CUĒCUETLAXTIC, while the Nahuatl-to-Spanish side has a variant form with I for E in the first two syllables. Z does not mark the vowel of the first syllable long. redup. CUETLAXTIC

CUEHCHAHUIĀ *vt* to go over something without stepping on it / pasa sobre él sin que pisa (T) [(3)Tp.182]. This has the same gloss as CUEHCHOLHUIĀ.

CUEHCHAHUILIĀ applic. CUEHCHAHUIĀ

CUEHCHAHUĪLŌ nonact. CUEHCHAHUIĀ

CUEHCHOLHUIĀ *vt* to go over something without stepping on it / pasa sobre una cosa sin pisar en ella (T) [(3)Tp.182]. M has *cuecxolhuia, cueacxolhuia,* and *cuencholhuia* all with the sense of jumping over a ditch or something of the sort. See CHOLOĀ.

CUEHCHOLHUILIĀ applic. CUEHCHOLHUIĀ

CUEHCHOLHUĪLŌ nonact. CUEHCHOLHUIĀ

CUEHCIHU(I) to hurry / se apura (T) [(4)Tp.121]. T has lost the internal glottal stop. See (I)HCIHU(I).

CUEHCIHUĪHUA nonact. CUEHCIHU(I)
CUEHCIHUĪTIĀ caus. CUEHCIHU(I)

CUEHCIUHQUI someone intelligent, nimble, lightweight, mischievous / inteligente, ligero, liviano (T) [(1)Bf.11v,

(1)Tp.121]. In the B attestation the sense seems to be 'disobedient.' See CUEHCIHU(I).

CUEHCUELPACHTIC something wrinkled, crumpled, folded / arrugado (Z) [(2)Zp.14,148]. M has *cuecuelpachoa* 'to double over or fold something repeatedly' redup. CUELPACHTIC

CUEHMOLĪHUIC someone worried, disturbed / preocupado (Z) [(2)Zp.101,232]. Both attestations mark the vowel of the third syllable long. This implies intransitive CUEHMOLIHU(I) corresponding to transitive CUEHMOLOĀ, but the I should be short. See CUEHMOLOĀ.

CUEHMOLĪUHTOC someone irritated, annoyed / impaciente (Z), excitado, molestado (Z) [(3)Zp.70,148,232]. All attestations mark the vowel of the third syllable long. This implies intransitive CUEHMOLIHU(I) corresponding to transitive CUEHMOLOĀ, but the I should be short. See CUEHMOLOĀ.

CUEHMOLOĀ *vrefl,vt* to become disturbed, worried, upset; to bother, upset, disturb someone / se preocupa, se turba, se trastorna (Z), lo molesta, lo alborota, lo trastorna, lo distrae (Z) This is abundantly attested, but only in Z.

CUEHMOLŌLIZ-TLI trouble, annoyance, bother / molestia (Z) [(5)Zp.6,85,148,232]. See CUEHMOLOĀ.

CUEHZOĀ *vrefl,vt* to be disturbed, bothered; to disturb, bother someone / se turba (Z), lo molesta (Z) [(6)Zp.85,126,169,186,220].

CUĒITIĀ *vrefl* to get dressed / se viste (Z) [(2)Zp.129,169]. See CUĒTIĀ.

CUĒ(I)-TL *pl*: -MEH skirt, petticoat / saya, faldellín, faldillas, o naguas (M), falda, chincuete, vestido (T) Since despite a vowel length discrepancy -CUEXĀNCO 'lap' is clearly related, it is possible that this should be CUĒY(I)-TL, with the Y appearing as X in the derivation.

CUĒL already / ya (C)

CUĒLIHU(I) to bend, twist / entortarse o torcerse (M) This is attested in the sources for this dictionary only in the reduplicated form CUĒCUĒLIHU(I). See CUĒLOĀ.

CUĒLOĀ *vt* to fold or bend something /

doblegar vara o cosa semejante (M) [(1)Tp.162]. CUĒLOĀ and CUELPACHOĀ appear to be synonymous in spite of the vowel length discrepancy attested in T.

CUELPACHIHU(I) to fold over, bend / se dobla [(1)Tp.121]. This intransitive verb is synonymous with the verb CUELPACHOĀ used reflexively. See CUELPACHOĀ.

CUELPACHILHUIĀ applic. CUELPACHOĀ

CUELPACHIUHTOC something folded, bent / doblado (Z) [(2)Zp.47,148]. See CUELPACHIHU(I).

CUELPACHOĀ *vrefl,vt* to bend, fold over; to bend something, to fold something over / se dobla (T), doblar o plegar mantas o cosa semejante (M) See CUĒLOĀ, PACHOĀ.

CUELPACHŌLŌ nonact. CUELPACHOĀ

CUELPACHTIC something bent, folded over / doblado (T) [(1)Tp.121]. See CUELPACHOĀ.

CUEM(I)-TL *pl*: **CUEMIH;** *possessed form*: **-CUEN** field, cultivated land; furrow, soil turned up with a hoe or plow / heredad, tierra labrada, o camellón (M), surco (T)

CUEMŌCHICUAHU(I)-TL tamarind tree / guamuchil (árbol) (T) [(1)Tp.121]. See CUEMŌCHI-TL.

CUEMŌCHIPEHPEN(A) See CUEMŌCHI-TL, PEHPEN(A).

CUEMŌCHITEQU(I) See CUEMŌCHI-TL, TEQU(I).

CUEMŌCHI-TL tamarind / guamuchil (T) [(4)Tp.121]. This is a variant of CUAUHMŌCHI-TL.

CUEMŌN(I) for a fire to flame, blaze up; to have a fever / flaméa mucho, arde mucho (la flama), tiene el cuerpo calenturiento (T) [(3)Tp.121].

CUEMŌNĪHUA nonact. CUEMŌN(I)

CUEMŌNĪTIĀ caus. CUEMŌN(I)

CUENTLĀLIĀ *vrefl,vt* to become furrowed; to plow, turn up furrows / se surca (T), lo surca (T) [(4)Tp.147,182]. See CUEM(I)-TL, TLĀLIĀ.

CUEP(A) *vrefl,vt* to turn, to turn back, to turn into something, to become something; to turn something, to return something / volverme de donde iba, o volverme de lado, o de la otra parte (M for first pers. sg. subject), volver a otro del camino (M), volver algo, o dar razon de sí, o excusarse (M) In T the stem of this verb has the form CUEC- before TZ and TL; MO-CUEC-TZINOĀ, TLACUEC-TLI. Z has a variant form QUEP(A).

CUEPALŌ nonact. CUEP(A)

CUEPILIĀ *vrefl,vt* to vomit; to return something to someone, to restore someone else's property / vomita, lo devuelve (T), vengarse o restituir lo ajeno (M) applic. CUEP(A)

CUEPILILIĀ applic. CUEPILIĀ

CUEPILĪLŌ nonact. CUEPILIĀ

CUEPOH-TLI causeway / calzada (M) [(1)Cf.72r].

CUEPŌNALTIĀ caus. CUEPŌN(I)

CUEPŌNCĀYŌ-TL *possessed form:* **-CUEPŌNCĀ** the opening, blooming of flowers / abrimiento de flor, o el acto de brotar la dicha flor (M), el abrirse de las flores (C) [(1)Bf.4r, (1)Cf.49r]. See CUEPŌN(I).

CUEPŌN(I) to shine, glow; for flowers to burst into bloom; for something to burst, explode / dar estallido el huevo o la castaña cuando la asan, o abrirse y abrotar la flor o la rosa, o resplandecer alguna cosa (M) Nahuatl also has XŌTLA, which associates blooming with bursting into flame.

CUEPŌNIĀ *vt* to cause something to make a thundering sound / lo truena (T) This is abundantly attested, but only in T. See CUEPŌN(I).

CUEPŌNILIĀ applic. CUEPŌNIĀ

CUEPŌNILILIĀ applic. CUEPŌNILIĀ

CUEPŌNILĪLŌ nonact. CUEPŌNILIĀ

CUĒTIĀ *vrefl* to get dressed, to put on a skirt / se viste, se pone el chincuete (T) [(6)Tp.147,214]. S gives a different gloss for this 'to be a person of rank,' but derives it from CUĒ(I)-TL nonetheless. Z has the variant CUĒITIĀ See CUĒ(I)-TL.

CUĒTĪLŌ nonact. CUĒTIĀ

CUETLĀCH-TLI *pl:* **CUĒCUETLĀCH-TIN** wolf / lobo (M) [(2)Cf.5r]. C fails to mark the vowel of the first syllable long in the reduplicated plural form. This also appears in P, but the long vowel is not marked there either.

CUETLAHU(I) to wither, crumple, weaken /

mustiarse, ajarse, debilitarse, decaer (S), marchita ... se desmaya ... se debilita (Z) [(3)Zp.43,148,232]. This implies CUETLAHUIY(A)

CUETLAHUIC something withered / marchito (Z) [(2)Zp.82,148]. See CUETLAHUIY(A).

CUETLAHUIY(A) *pret:* **CUETLAHUIX** ~ **CUETLAHUIYAC** to get withered, crumpled easily / mustiarse, ajarse fácilmente (S) This is indirectly attested in CUETLAHU(I).

CUETLĀN(I) to abate; to flicker, to tremble / mitigarse, o aflojarse la enfermedad, o amansarse el viento recio, o arder el fuego echando de sí gran llama (M), se mueve, tiembla (T) [(1)Tp.121].

CUETLĀNIĀ *vrefl,vt* for something to collapse; to break something up, disjoint, dislocate something / se cae (de debilidad, etc.) (T), quebrar palos, o cosas largas (M), lo disloca (Z) See CUETLĀN(I).

CUETLĀNĪLŌ nonact. CUETLĀNIĀ

CUETLAXCŌL-LI earthworm / lombriz de la tierra (Z) [(2)Zp.77,148]. Z also has CUITLAXCOL-LI 'intestines,' shared with T. The two items differ in the vowel length of the third syllable. The variation CUETLAX-TLI ~ CUITLAX-TLI is common across Nahuatl dialects. See CUETLAX-TLI, CŌLOĀ.

CUETLAXCUAHU(I)-TL type of tree (Ampelocera hottlei) / cuerillo (árbol) (Z) [(2)Zp.36,148]. See CUETLAX-TLI, CUAHU(I)-TL.

CUETLAXHUIĀ *vt* to cover or bind something with cured leather / encorar algo con cuero adobado (M), lo pega con cuero (Z) [(2)Zp.95,149]. The Z attestations are in intransitive form without an object prefix. See CUETLAX-TLI, -HUIĀ.

CUETLAXIHU(I) to be weak, feeble, faint / desmayar o emperezar (M) [(1)Tp.129]. This implies CUETLAXOĀ. See CUETLAHU(I).

CUETLAXIHUĪHUA nonact. CUE-TLAXIHU(I)

CUETLAXIHUĪTIĀ caus. CUETLAXIHU(I)

CUETLAXOĀ *vrefl,vt* to be weak, faint, swooning; to cause someone to be weak, faint, swooning / desmayarse, o amortecerse de tristeza (M), desmayarse a otro (M) This is implied by CUETLAXIHU(I). See CUETLAHU(I).

CUETLAXTIC something withered, weak / suelta (que no tiene fuerza) (T referring to a crippled hand) [(1)Tp.164]. See CUETLAHU(I).

CUETLAX-TLI pl: -MEH; inalienably possessed form: -CUETLAXYŌ leather, cured hide, skin / cuero adobado (M), piel, cuero (T) T has I for E in the initial syllable, which is a common variation for this item. See CUETLAHUIY(A).

CUETZPAL-IN pl: -TIN ~ -MEH ~ CUECUETZPALTIN ~ CUĒCUETZPALTIN lizard, iguana / lagartija (S), iguana (T) [(4)Tp.110,121, (6)Xp.27,38]. S also gives the alternate absolutive form CUETZPAL-LI. X has QUETZPAL-IN. T also the alternates CUETZPAL-IN, HUETZPAL-IN, and HUĒHUETZPAL-IN and gives reduplicated plural forms with both long and short vowels in the initial syllable.

-CUEXĀNCO necessarily possessed form one's lap / su regazo (Z for third pers. sg. possessor) [(3)Bf.2v,3v,6v, (2)Zp.107,157]. See CUEXĀN-TLI.

CUEXĀN-TLI skirts, packing bags / haldas para llevar en ellas algo (M) [(3)Xp.37]. This appears to be related to CUĒ(I)-TL 'skirt,' but the vowel is not marked long in X and also is not so marked in Z's attestations of -CUEXĀNCO. In B's attestations of -CUEXĀNCO, the vowel is specifically marked short.

CUEYA-TL pl: CUEYAMEH ~ CUĒ-CUEYAH frog / rana (M) M also has the variant form cuiyatl.

CUĒYEH someone who possesses a skirt, woman / mujer que tiene o lleva faldas (S) [(1)Cf.55r]. See CUĒ(I)-TL.

CUEZA vt to baste a garment together / lo medio cose (T) [(3)Tp.183]. S has cuecueço 'to put together, baste, make a provisional seam in something' In spite of the similarity to coser, this does not have the characteristic structure of a Spanish loanword in Nahuatl.

CUEZALHUIĀ applic. CUEZA

CUEZALŌ nonact. CUEZA

CUEZCOM(A)-TL pl: -MEH granary / troja o alfolí de pan (M), cozcomate, troje, granero (T) [(1)Cf.72r, (2)Tp.110,121]. See COM(A)-TL.

CUI vt; pret: CUIC to take something or someone / tomar algo, o tener parte el hombre con la mujer (M) For all sources, with the exception of T, this verb consistently has a long stem vowel before the applicative and causative suffixes, but the vowel is never marked long before preterit -C.

CUĪCA to sing / cantar el cantor, o chirriar las aves (M)

CUĪCATIĀ vrefl,vt to sing; to make music for others / canta (T), dar música a otros (M) See CUĪCA-TL.

CUĪCATILIZ-TLI song / canción, himno (T) [(1)Tp.121]. See CUĪCA.

CUĪCATĪLŌ nonact. CUĪCATIĀ

CUĪCA-TL song / canto o canción (M) This is conventionally paired with XŌCHI-TL 'flower' to refer to poetry.

CUĪCAYŌ-TL song / canción, himno (T) [(1)Tp.121]. See CUĪCA-TL, -YŌ.

CUĪCUĪCAYŌTZIN pl: CUĪCUĪCA-YŌTZITZIN a type of cricket, grasshopper / grillo (T) [(1)Tp.121]. See CUĪCA-TL.

CUICUINACA to make a low sound in the throat; for a person to hum or a dog to growl / canturrea (gente), gruñe (perro) [(3)Tp.121].

CUICUINACALTIĀ caus. CUICUINACA

CUICUINACOHUA nonact. CUICUINACA

CUĪCUITLAHUILTIĀ vt to force, persuade someone / aconsejar, convencer, obligar a alguien, seducir, violar (S) [(2)Cf.72v]. See CUITLAHUIĀ.

CUĪCUĪTZCĀNI See CUĪCUĪTZCA-TL.

CUĪCUĪTZCA-TL pl: -MEH swallow (bird) / golondrina (M) [(2)Cf.4r, (2)Zp.63,149]. Z has the variant CUICUĪTZCĀNI, once with the vowels of the second and third syllable marked long and once with no vowels marked long.

CUIHCUI vrefl,vt to get ready, to be prepared; to take something away, to work wood or stone by chipping off the surface, to clean up a surface / se dispone ... se prepara (Z), lo trae (T), labro piedra o madera, como hace el escultor (C for first pers. sg. subject), entallar en madera, o alimpiar el suelo quitando lo que echan de la mesa (M) With reference to sculpting and cleaning, the indefinite object prefix TLA- may be absorbed into the stem. M also gives *cuicui* with a gloss about copulation, but there is no way to know if the form has short vowel, long vowel, or vowel-plus-glottal stop reduplication. redup. CUI

CUIHCUĪCATIĀ redup. CUĪCATIĀ

CUIHCUĪLIĀ *vt* to take things, to take something from others; to commit robbery / tomar algunas cosas a otro o una cosa a varios (C), robar (C) This reduplicated form has a distributive sense. redup. CUĪLIĀ

CUIHCUĪLIĀ *vrefl* to hold out against entreaties or advances, to resist / hacerse de rogar, o negar el débito la mujer, o resistir (M) [(3)Cf.52r]. This appears to be the applicative form of CUIHCUI, but the sense is not clearly derived in that way.

CUIHCUILTIC something painted / pintado (T) [(2)Zp.98,149]. Z marks the vowels of the first and second syllables long in one attestation and those of the second and third syllables long in the other, but none should be long. See (I)HCUILOĀ.

CUĪHUA For CUI, but not for compounded or reduplicated forms with CUI, T has the nonactive form CŌHUA, or because of potential ambiguity of the notation, possibly COHUA. altern. nonact. CUI

CUĪLIĀ *vrefl,vt* to take something for oneself; to take something for or from someone / tomar algo para sí, sin que nadie se lo de (M), tomar algo a otro (M) The applicative form of CUI consistently has a long vowel preceding the applicative suffix in all sources but T, where the vowel is specifically marked short. applic. CUI

CUĪLILIĀ applic. CUĪLIĀ

CUĪLĪLŌ nonact. CUĪLIĀ

CUĪLŌ altern. nonact. CUI

CUILŌ-TL *pl:* **-MEH** stick / palo (T) [(1)Tp.122].

CUĪLTIĀ altern. caus. CUI

CUĪLTILIĀ applic. CUĪLTIĀ

CUĪLTĪLŌ nonact. CUĪLTIĀ

CUILTŌNOĀ *vrefl,vt* to be wealthy and happy; to live happily and enjoy something; to enrich someone / abundar en hacienda o gozarse mucho (M), fruir y gozar de algo (M), enriquecer a otro (M)

CUINACHILIĀ applic. CUINATZ(A)

CUINATZ(A) *vt* to cause something to creak, resound / le gruñe, lo suena (T) [(3)Tp.183]. See CUICUINACA.

CUINATZALŌ nonact. CUINATZ(A)

CUITCŌĀ-TL tapeworm / lombriz (Z) [(2)Zp.77,149]. The first element is a reduction of CUITL(A)-TL. Z has T for TL. In other dialects the expected form would be CUITLACŌĀ-TL. See CUITL(A)-TL, CŌĀ-TL.

CUITCOTOLTIC something bobtailed, docked / rabón (Z) [(3)Zp.105,149]. Z gives an abbreviated alternate form CUITCOLTIC. The first element is a reduction of CUITL(A)-TL. In other dialects, the expected form would be CUITLACOTOCTIC. See CUITL(A)-TL, COTOCTIC.

CUĪTIĀ *vrefl,vt* to acknowledge one's failings, to be called something; to name someone / conocer o confesar a otro por señor, o conocer el delito que cometió (M), se llama, es llamado (T), lo llama (T) This is an element of two compounds; YŌLCUĪTIĀ 'to make confession, to confess someone' and ĪXCUĪTIĀ 'to reproach, blame someone.' altern. caus. CUI

CUITIHUECHILIĀ applic. CUITIHUETZ(I)

CUITIHUETZ(I) *vrefl,vt* to turn back or retreat quickly; to take something quickly, to snatch something, to assault something / tornar, o volver sobre sí, o espantarse el trueno o de cosa semejante (M), tomar o arrebatar algo de priesa (M), apechugar o arremeter contra alguno (M) See CUI, HUETZ(I).

CUĪTILIĀ applic. CUĪTIĀ

CUĪTĪLŌ nonact. CUĪTIĀ

CUITLACHAPĀN(I) for a pustule or boil to throb / punza, palpita (grano, etc.) (T) [(1)Tp.122]. See CUITL(A)-TL, CHAPĀN(I).

CUITLACHICHIQUIL-LI backbone / su espina dorsal, su espinazo (T) [(1)Tp.129]. See CUITL(A)-TL, CHICHIQUIL-LI.

CUITLACOCH-IN an ear of maize infected

with a fungus that turns the kernels dark gray and deforms them, edible and considered a delicacy / mazorca de maíz degenerada y diferente de las otras (M) [(1)Tp.122]. See CUITL(A)-TL.

CUITLACUAHU(I)-TL night jasmine, a tree with flowers that are fragrant by night (Cestrum nocturnum, Cestrum lanatum) / huele de noche (árbol) (Z) [(2)Zp.69,149]. See CUITL(A)-TL, CUAHU(I)-TL.

CUITLACUEP(A) *vrefl* to flee, retreat / huir atrás (M) [(1)Cf.106r, (2)Zp.126,149]. Z has this with QUEP(A) for CUEP(A). See CUITL(A)-TL, CUEP(A).

CUITLAHUIĀ *vrefl,vt* to invite oneself to a feast or gathering, to be responsible for someone, something; to care for, raise someone; to fertilize the soil with manure / convidarse en convite (M), tener cuidado o cargo de algo (M), tener cuidado de otros (M), estercolar la tierra (M) Simple transitive CUITLAHUIĀ is derived from CUITL(A)-TL 'excrement' and -HUIĀ. When this has the sense of 'to care for someone, something,' it is a double object verb requiring both a transitive and a reflexive prefix.

CUITLAHUĪLTIĀ *vt* to oblige someone to do something, to make someone responsible for something / provocar o constreñir a otro para que haga algo (M) caus. CUITLAHUIĀ

CUITLAHUĪLTILIĀ caus. CUITLA-HUĪLTIĀ

CUITLAHUĪLTILILIĀ applic. CUITLA-HUĪLTILIĀ

CUITLAHUĪLTILĪLŌ nonact. CUITLA-HUĪLTILIĀ

CUITLĀLŌLŌ a type of beetle / escarabajo (Z) [(2)Zp.54,149]. In both attestations the vowels of all syllables beyond the first are marked long. See CUITL(A)-TL.

-CUITLAPAN *necessarily bound locative* behind someone / a las espaldas (C), mi trasera, y tras de mí, a mis espaldas (C for first pers. sg. possessor) See CUITL(A)-TL, -PAN.

CUITLAPANCHIHCŌLTIC someone hump-backed / jorobado (Z) [(2)Zp.73,149]. See CUITLAPAN-TLI, CHIHCŌLTIC.

CUITLAPANHUIĀ *vrefl,vt* to carry some-

thing on one's back; to bring up the rear / se cargaba (C for imperfect reflexive), ser trasero caminando con otros, o en la virtud (M) [(1)Cf.90r]. See CUITLAPAN-TLI, -HUIĀ.

CUITLAPANOMI-TL *inalienably possessed form:* **-CUITLAPANOMIYŌ** backbone / su espinazo, su espina dorsal (Z) [(2)Zp.56,157]. See CUITLAPAN-TLI, OMI-TL.

CUITLAPANTEHTEQU(I) See CUITLAPAN-TLI, TEHTEQU(I).

CUITLAPAN-TLI back, shoulders / espaldas (M) See -CUITLAPAN.

CUITLAPANTZOTZON(A) *vrefl* for people to clap each other on the back while embracing / se dan papachos (palmadas) en la espalda al abrazarse (T) [(3)Tp.147]. See CUITLAPAN-TLI, TZOTZON(A).

CUITLAPANTZOTZONALŌ nonact. CUITLAPANTZOTZON(A)

CUITLAPANXĪLŌ-TL *inalienably possessed form:* **-CUITLAPANXĪLŌYŌ** backbone / su espina dorsal, su espinazo (T for third person possessor) [(1)Tp.129]. See CUITLAPAN-TLI, XĪLŌ-TL.

CUITLAPĀYO-TL a type of beetle / escarabajo (insecto) (T) [(1)Tp.122]. M has *payatl* 'a small woolly caterpillar,' and elsewhere T has PĀYĀ-TL 'moyote, flying beetle.' The O here seems idiosyncratic. See CUITL(A)-TL, PĀYĀ-TL.

CUITLAPILCOTOL something bobtailed, docked / rabón (Z) [(2)Zp.105,149]. See CUITLAPIL-LI, COTOLTIC.

CUITLAPIL-LI tail / cola o rabo de animal o de ave (M) This is frequently attested in B with the vowel of the last syllable specifically marked short, but also twice with the vowel marked long, both times before the plural suffix -HUĀN. It is marked short in T but long in Z. See the discussion under PIL-LI.

CUITLAQUEP(A) See CUITLACUEP(A).

CUITLAQUĪXOHUA nonact. CUITLA-QUĪZ(A)

CUITLAQUĪXTIĀ caus. CUITLAQUĪZ(A)

CUITLAQUĪZ(A) to burst forth / sale con fuerza, con rapidez (p.ej. agua) (T) [(3)Tp.122]. See CUITL(A)-TL, QUĪZ(A).

CUITL(A)-TL excrement, residue, excrescence / mierda (M), excremento, fiemo, inmundicia, residuo; llaga, tumor, absceso (S) By extension this has the sense of 'back, rump, behind' in compounds.

CUITLATZĪCA-TL *pl:* **-MEH** a type of ant associated with excrement / hormiga de mierda (T) [(1)Tp.122]. See CUITL(A)-TL, TZĪCA-TL.

CUITLAXCOL-LI intestines / tripas (M) [(1)Tp.129, (1)Zp.157]. The second element seems related to CŌLOĀ 'to curve, twist' in spite of the vowel-length discrepancy. See CUITL(A)-TL.

CUITLAXIHU(I) to get loose, to go weak / se suelta (el pie, la mano, etc.), se debilita (T) [(3)Tp.122]. This is a variant of CUETLAXIHU(I), which is also in T.

CUITLAXIHUĪHUA nonact. CUITLA-XIHU(I)

CUITLAXIHUĪTIĀ caus. CUITLAXIHU(I)

CUITLAXŌCHI-TL poinsetta / noche buena, flor de pascua (K) This is not directly attested in the sources for this dictionary, but its component parts are. The name probably refers to the growth of the plant on dungheaps. See CUITL(A)-TL, XŌCHI-TL.

CUITLAX-TLI See CUETLAX-TLI.

CUITLĀZCA-TL a type of ant associated with excrement / hormiga de mierda (Z) [(2)Zp.68,149]. In the Nahuatl-to-Spanish side this is identified as 'hormiga pepehua,' but it is glossed as 'hormiga de mierda' in the other side of the dictionary. See CUITL(A)-TL, ĀZCA-TL.

CUIX *introductory particle for questions which can be appropriately answered with 'yes' or 'no.'* is it the case that ...? / ¿porventura?* (M) T and Z have the variant form COX.

CUĪX-IN *pl:* **-MEH** large bird of prey, hawk / milano (M), gavilán grande (X) [(3)Xp.39]. X also has what appears to be the reflex of CUAUHHUĪX-IN< CUAHU(I)-TL and HUĪX-IN and meaning 'lizard.'

E

ECACAHUA-TL bean pod / cáscara de frijol (Z) [(1)Zp.153]. See E-TL, CACAHUA-TL.

ECAHUĪLLAH a shadowed place, place in the shade / sombreado (Z) [(2)Zp.117,153]. See ECAHUĪL-LI, -TLAH.

ECAHUĪL-LI *pl:* **-TIN** shadow, shade / sombra (Z) This is abundantly attested in Z, where three of nine attestations mark the vowel of the second syllable long, although it probably should be short. On the other hand, Z fails to mark the vowel of the third syllable long, but it is long in T's synonymous TLAECAHUĪLLŌ-TL. There is an internal glottal stop in the synonymous EHCAUHYŌ-TL, and there should probably be one here as well. See EHCAUHYŌ-TL.

ECAPOTZI-TL black bean / frijol negro (T) [(1)Tp.248]. See E-TL, CAPOTZTIC.

ECHĪCHĪLE-TL red bean / frijol colorado (T) [(2)Tp.46,248]. In one of the rare inconsistencies in T, the entry on the Nahuatl-to-Spanish side has the vowels of the second and third syllables marked short, while the Spanish-to-Nahuatl side correctly has them long. See E-TL, CHĪCHĪLTIC, CHĪL-LI.

ECOPĪN(A) to pick beans / arranca frijol (T) [(3) Tp.248]. See E-TL, COPĪN(A).

ECUĀTLAHTLAPĀN mashed beans / frijol quebrado (T) [(1) Tp.248]. See E-TL, CUĀ(I)-TL, TLAPĀN(A).

ECUETLAX-TLI bean pod / vaina (de frijol) (Z) [(1)Zp.153]. The Z attestation lacks an absolutive suffix. See E-TL, CUETLAX-TLI.

EH See (Y)EH, (Y)EHHUĀ-TL.

-EH *possessor suffix; pl:* **-EHQUEH** Added to nouns this means 'possessor of' the word in question. It is only added to noun stems ending in consonants; for stems ending in vowels -HUAH is used instead. -HUAH is also used with some consonant stems,

yielding pairs such as ZĀYŌLEH ~ ZĀYŌLHUAH 'one who has flies.'

EHCAHUIĀ caus. EHCŌ

EHCAMALACŌ-TL dust devil / remolinito (T) [(1)Tp.249]. The first element of this seems to have lost a syllable, and the final syllable has the reflex of Ō instead of expected A. See EHĒCA-TL, MALACA-TL.

EHCAUHTIC something trifling, light / liviano, no pesa (Z) [(1)Zp.153]. See EHCAUHTILIĀ.

EHCAUHTILIĀ *vt* to lighten something / lo hace menos pesado (Z) [(2)Zp.97,187]. It seems plausible to relate this in sense to EHCAUHYŌ-TL, referring to shadows and light, insubstantial things. It is opposite in sense from ETIY(A) 'to be heavy.'

EHCAUH-TLI a type of plant / acahuale (yerba), una verdura (Z) [(3)Zp.4,153]. See ĀCĀHUAL-LI, EHCAUHTIC.

EHCAUHYŌ-TL shadow, shade / sombra (M) [(2) Bf.2v,5v, (2)Cf.19r]. See EHCAUHTILIĀ.

EHCŌ to arrive / llegar, usarse en tierra caliente (C)

EHĒCA *pret:* **EHĒCAC** to blow lightly, for there to be a breeze, to be windy / hacer viento, o aire (M) An unreduplicated verb stem related to this is to be expected, but none is attested. This verb and the related noun have identical stems. R has a short vowel and glottal stop in the second syllable in place of a long vowel, EHEHCA. See EHĒCA-TL.

EHĒCACŌĀ-TL a type of venomous snake noted for its swiftness / cierto serpiente venenosa y muy ligera (R) [(1)Rp.81]. There is disagreement about whether this is a constrictor or a pit viper. Sahagún and Clavijero both believe it is called a 'wind serpent' because of its swiftness, but it is also more directly associated with wind. M has the phrase *eecacoayo mixtli* 'storm cloud with whirlwind,' and T has EHQUETZALCŌĀ-TL, 'whirlwind.' See EHĒCA-TL, CŌĀ-TL.

EHĒCAHUILŌ a child possessed by evil spirits / niño que le cogen los malos espíritus (T) [(1) Tp.249]. This is attested without an absolutive suffix and appears to be a substantive use of the nonactive form of a verb derived from EHĒCA-TL 'evil spirit' and -HUIĀ. If this is the case, the vowel of the fourth syllable should be long. Possibly this should be EHĒCAHUĪLLŌ-TL. See EHĒCA-TL.

EHĒCAMŌTLA *vt* to bewitch someone; to make spirits visible / lo embruja [(2)Zp.49,187]. See EHĒCA-TL, MŌTLA.

EHĒCAPAH-TLI medicine against sorcery / una medicina contra brujería (Z) [(1)Zp.153, (2)Rp.81,158]. Possibly this is wild senna (Casia laevigata), a plant used medicinally to relieve the symptoms of syphilis. R has EH instead of Ē in the second syllable. See EHĒCA-TL, PAH-TLI.

EHĒCA-TL *pl: -MEH* breeze, wind, bad spirit, ghost / viento, o aire (M), aire, viento; espíritu malo, malos aires (T) B, C, and T agree in the glottal stop and vowel length pattern, although it is slightly obscured in T by initial glide formation and the ambiguity in T of YE and Ē. Z does not mark the vowel of the second syllable long. R has a short vowel and a glottal stop in the second syllable in place of a long vowel, EHEHCA-TL. This is clearly related to IHĪYŌ-TL 'breath,' and some dialects of Nahuatl have A for E. Since intervocalic glottal stops only arise in Nahuatl through reduplication of vowel-initial stems, this must be derived from *ĒCA-TL, but the unreduplicated form is unattested in the sources for this dictionary.

EHECOĀ See YEHYECOĀ.

EHĒHUĪTA *vt* to consider something unimportant, to deprecate someone, something / no importa, lo achica, lo apoca, no le da importancia (Z) [(4)Zp.12,70,187]. In two of four attestations the vowel of the second syllable is marked long, and in three the vowel of the third is so marked. Because Z lacks the lateral release of TL, it is ambiguous whether the last syllable is TA or TLA.

EHĒLCĪM(A) redup. ĒLCĪM(A)

EHHUĀN See (Y)EHHUĀ-TL.

EHHUĀ-TL See (Y)EHHUĀ-TL.

EHPŌTZ(A) See IHPŌTZ(A).

EHQUETZALCŌĀ-TL whirlwind, dust devil / remolino (T) [(1)Tp.249]. This seems to have lost two syllables. Compare EHCAMALACŌ-TL. See EHĒCA-TL, QUETZALCŌĀ-TL, EHĒCACŌĀ-TL.

ĒHUA to depart, to rise to go / partirse (C) Intransitive ĒHUA and transitive ĒHU(A) are distinguished in the preterit as ĒHUAC and ĒUH respectively. See -ĒHU(I).

ĒHU(A) *vrefl, vt* to get up, to get out of bed; to raise someone or something / levantarse de dormir, o de donde está echado (M), levantar al que está echado (M) Transitive ĒHU(A) and intransitive ĒHUA are distinguished in the preterit as ĒUH and ĒHUAC respectively.

ĒHUALŌ C twice writes this *eōhua* (Cf.36r). nonact. ĒHUA

ĒHUALTIĀ altern. caus. ĒHUA

ĒHUATICAH to be seated / estar asentado (M) [(1)Tp.249]. ĒHUA here and in some derived forms means 'seated,' which is just the opposite of its reflexive sense of 'to get up.' X has ĒHUATOC with the same sense. See ĒHUA, the verb CĀ.

ĒHUA-TL *possessed form: -ĒHUAYŌ* skin, hide, husk, rind / cuero por curtir, o mondadura y cáscara de fruta (M) There is ambiguity in T between initial E and Ē. Of nine attestations in Z, four have the vowel of the first syllable marked long.

ĒHUATOC See ĒHUATICAH.

ĒHUAYŌ-TL skin, leather; husk, rind / pellejo, y cáscara, o mondadura de fruta (M) [(3)Tp.138,249, (2)Zp.98,158]. See ĒHUA-TL, -YŌ.

-ĒHU(I) *verbal compounding element* to turn out in a particular manner, to become / pararse (K) This is attested in T and Z. It corresponds to the intransitive verb ĒHUA, which also appears in compounds. Both correspond to transitive ĒHU(A).

ĒHUILIĀ applic. ĒHUA

ĒHUILTIĀ altern. caus. ĒHUA

-ĒHUILTIHTICAH someone seated / estar sentado (C) [(1)Cf.78v]. This takes the reflexive prefixes and serves as the honorific of ĒHUATICAH.

ĒHUĪTIĀ altern. caus. ĒHUA

ĒHUITIQUETZ(A) *vt* to put something to rights; to raise and straighten something bent or out of place / lo endereza, levanta una cosa que está doblada (niño dormido, vela, planta, etc.) (T) [(6)Tp.142,186]. See ĒHUA, QUETZ(A).

ĒLCHIQUIHU(I)-TL chest, breast, bosom / los pechos o el pecho (M) See ĒL-LI, CHIQUIHU(I)-TL.

ĒLCIHCIHU(I) *pret:* **ĒLCIHCIUH** to sigh / suspirar (M) Z has YŌLNEHCIHU(I) with the same sense. See ĒL-LI, (I)HCIHU(I).

ĒLCIHCIHUĪHUA nonact. ĒLCIHCIHU(I)

ĒLCIHCIHUĪTIĀ caus. ĒLCIHCIHU(I)

ĒLCĪM(A) *vrefl; pret:* **ĒLCĪN** to choke, suffocate / atravesárseme el bocado en los gaznates (M) [(3)Tp.141]. See ĒL-LI.

ĒLCĪMALŌ nonact. ĒLCĪM(A)

ĒLCĪMIĀ *vrefl* to choke, suffocate / se ahoga (Z) [(2)Zp.7,169, (3)Xp.56]. This is a variant of ĒLCĪM(A). X has TZ for C.

ĒLĒHUIĀ *vt* to desire someone or something / desear o codiciar algo (M), codiciar a alguna persona (M) This is attested three times in C with a long vowel in the initial syllable. Elsewhere in C and without exception in B the vowel is not marked long. In T and Z there is short E. T has an intensifier meaning 'great, very' which may be derived from this. It would correspond to a canonical form LALEHUIZ, but since Nahuatl morpheme structure excludes initial L, the one in this item must result from vowel loss or be excrescent. See ĒL-LI, ĒHUA.

ĒLĒHUĪLŌNI desirable person or thing / cosa deseable (M), persona o cosa deseable (C) [(1)Cf.44v]. See ĒLĒHUIĀ.

ĒLHUĒHUETZCA to laugh with the mouth closed / se ríe con la boca cerrada (T) [(3)Tp.249]. The T form is ambiguous between EL and ĒL, but the sense seems to call for ĒL with its broad reference to internal organs and strong emotion. See ĒL-LI, HUĒHUETZCA.

ĒLIMIQU(I) *pret:* **ĒLIMIC** to till the soil / labrar o arar la tierra (M) [(1)Bf.10v].

-ĒLLELAHCI *verb that takes possessive rather than subject prefixes* to suffer greatly / recibir o tener mucha pena y aflicción (M) The first element of this is apparently an incorporated noun which is

necessarily possessed with the possessive prefix expressing the person and number of the subject; 'he suffers' is expressed as IĒLLELAHCI. See ĒL-LI, AHCI.

ĒLLELQUĪXTIĀ *vrefl, vt* to relax, to enjoy oneself; to entertain someone, make someone relax / recrearse (M), recrear a otro (M) caus. ĒLLELQUĪZ(A)

ĒLLELQUĪZ(A) to relax and enjoy oneself; to suffer / recrearse, espaciarse o desenfadarse, y recibir o tener gran aflicción (M) This verb has two completely contradictory senses, although both involve feelings manifesting themselves or being drawn forth. See ĒL-LI, QUĪZ(A).

ĒL-LI liver / el hígado (M) In compounds this has a broader sense of 'internal organs' and is also associated with emotions, especially strong or unpleasant ones.

ĒLMĪMIQU(I) *pret:* **-MIC** to stutter, to stammer / ser tartamudo o tartamudear (M) [(5)Xp.106]. See ĒL-LI, MĪMIQU(I).

ĒLMĪMIQUINI stutterer, stammerer / tartamudo (X) [(2)Xp.106]. M has *elmimicqui* with the same sense. See ĒLMĪMIQU(I).

ĒLMOYĀHU(I) to be disgusted / tiene asco (T) [(3)Tp.249]. See ĒL-LI, MOYĀHU(A).

ĒLMOYĀHUĪHUA nonact. ĒLMOYĀHU(I)

ĒLMOYĀHUĪTIĀ caus. ĒLMOYĀHU(I)

ĒLŌĀTŌL-LI maize atole (a type of beverage) / atole de elote (T) [(2)Tp.108,249]. See ĒLŌ-TL, ĀTŌL-LI.

ĒLŌNAMACA See ĒLŌ-TL, NAMACA.

ĒLŌOCUIL-IN *pl:* **-TIN** maize worm / gusano de elote (T) [(1)Tp.249]. See ĒLŌ-TL, OCUIL-IN.

ĒLŌTEQU(I) See ĒLŌ-TL, TEQU(I).

ĒLŌTIC something the color of fresh young maize / color de elote (T) See ĒLŌ-TL.

ĒLŌ-TL ear of fresh young maize with the kernels already formed, corn on the cob / mazorca de maíz verde, que tiene ya cuajados los granos (M) The first vowel is long in Z and ambiguous in T. There are no attestations in B or C. ĒLŌ-TL contrasts with XĪLŌ-TL, which is the still-soft, semi-formed green ear.

ĒLŌTZON-TLI corn tassel / cabello de elote (Z) [(2)Zp.22,153]. This contrasts with ĒLTZON-TLI 'a turkey's chest tassel.' See ĒLŌ-TL, TZON-TLI.

ÉLPAN-TLI breast, bosom / el pecho o los pechos (M) [(2)Zp.95,158]. See ÉL-LI, -PAN.

ÉLTLAPECH-TLI protector for a chest-strap or tumpline / protector para la correa o mecapale (Z) See ÉL-LI, TLAPECH-TLI.

ÉLTLATLAC(I) to cough to attract attention / tose a propósito para que le vea el otro (T) [(3)Tp.249]. See ÉL-LI, TLATLAC(I).

ÉLTZON-TLI the beard of a turkey, the tassel of hair-like feathers that grow from a turkey's chest / su escobeta (de guajolote) (T) [(1)Tp.138]. This contrasts with ÉLÓTZON-TLI 'corn tassel' See ÉL-LI, TZON-TLI.

EMÓL-LI bean porridge / guisado de frijoles, o de habas (M) [(1)Tp.249, (1)Zp.153]. See E-TL, MÓL-LI.

EMOLÓNIÁ to weed beans / escarda frijol (T) [(3)Tp.249]. See E-TL, MOLÓNIÁ.

ENAMACA See E-TL, NAMACA.

EPA-TL *pl:* **-MEH** skunk / cierto animalejo que hiede mucho (M), zorrillo (T,Z,X)

ÉPATZAC-TLI lentil / lantejas, o legumbres (C) [(1)Cf.125v]. This is apparently not derived from E-TL, as S thought it to be.

EPAZÓ-TL epazote, a type of seasoning herb (Chenopodium ambrosiodes) / yerba buena de está Nueva España (M) [(2)Cf.118r,122v, (1)Zp.153, (2)Xp.107]. T has absolutive -TLI, implying a variant with a stem-final glottal stop.

EPAZÓYOH something redolent of epazote / con mucho epazote (C) [(2)Cf.118r,122v]. See EPAZÓ-TL, -YOH.

EPITZÁHUAC string bean / frijol delgado (T) [(1)Tp.249]. See E-TL, PITZÁHUA.

ÉQUIMI-TL coral tree, colorín (Erythrina americana, Erythrina corallides) / gásparo (árbol) (Z) [(2)Zp.62,153]. In one of two attestations Z marks the vowel of the first syllable long, but since the tree produces pods of bean-shaped seeds, the first element is probably E-TL.

ETEQU(I) See E-TL, TEQU(I).

ETIC something heavy / cosa pesada (M) See ETIY(A).

ETIY(A) *pret:* **ETÍX** to become heavy / hacerse pesado (M) [(1)Bf.7v]. Like other verbs in IY(A), this probably has alternate preterit forms with long and short vowels. See ETIC.

E-TL bean / frijol, o haba (M) The common variant YE-TL is caused by regular glide formation affecting word-initial E in certain dialects, of which T and X are two.

ETLAH bean patch / heredad de frijoles, o habas (M), frijolar (Z) [(1)Zp.153]. See E-TL, -TLAH.

EUCXOÁ to sneeze / estornudar (M) [(3)Xp.106]. X lacks the labiality of the final consonant of the initial syllable. See IUCXOÁ.

ÉUHTÉHUA to leave, go / partirse con aceleramiento y corriendo para alguna parte (M), sale ... se va (Z) [(1)Zp.153]. This consists of two instances of the verb ÉHUA joined by the -TI- ligature. Such constructions are not incongruous in Nahuatl. See ÉHUA.

ÉXCÁMPA from or to three places / de tres, o a tres partes (C) [(1)Cf.91r]. This also has a variant form YÉXCÁMPA. See ÉXCÁN, -PA.

ÉXCÁN in three places / en tres partes (M) [(4)Cf.91r]. This also has a variant form YÉXCÁN. See ÉY(I), -CÁN.

-ÉXCÁNIXTI *necessarily possessed form* in all three parts of something / en todas tres (partes) (C) [(1)Cf.91v]. See ÉXCÁN, -IXTI.

EXIXITAMAL-LI a type of tamale / tamales pintos (Z) [(3)Zp.119,154,210]. In two of three attestations Z marks the vowel of the first syllable long. See E-TL, TAMAL-LI.

EXÓTEQU(I) See EXÓ-TL, TEQU(I).

EXÓ-TL green bean / frijol o haba verde (M) See E-TL, XÓ-.

EXÓYAMÁN-TLI a type of bean / frijol gordo (Z) [(1)Zp.154]. The literal sense of this is 'soft green bean.' See EXÓ-TL, YAMÁNIÁ.

ÉXPA three times / trez veces (M) [(1)Cf.117r]. This single attested form does not have the first vowel marked long, but ÉX 'three' is attested abundantly elsewhere. See ÉY(I), -PA.

EXQUIQUIL(I)-TL a type of plant / mafafa cimarrón (blanco) (Z) [(2)Zp.79,154]. This may be a back formation from Spanish *exquite*< ÍZQUI-TL 'popcorn,' often used to describe plants with clusters of white flowers. This plant may be *Colocasia mafaffa*, one of a group of plants from the

roots of which an edible starch can be
extracted. See QUIL(I)-TL.

ĒY(I) three / tres (M) A variant form is
YĒY(I). The internal Y reveals itself in
forms like YĒXCĀN, where it undergoes
spirantization, Y > X. In other compounds
this has the form Ē- with no final consonant. See (Y)ĒY(I).

EZCOCOLIZ-TLI dysentery / disentería (Z)
[(1)Zp.153]. See EZ-TLI, COCOLIZ-TLI.

EZCUAHU(I)-TL medicinal plant, the bark
of which produces a red dye (Jatropha
spatulata) / sangre de grado (árbol) (Z)
[(2)Zp.113,153]. R has EZPAH-TLI. See
EZ-TLI, CUAHU(I)-TL.

EZHUIĀ vrefl, vt to bloody oneself; to
bloody someone, something / ensangren-
tarse (M), ensangrentar algo (M) [(2)Cf.6ov].
See EZ-TLI, -HUIĀ.

EZMĒY(A) pret: **EZMĒX** to spurt blood /
brota sangre (Z) [(1)Zp.153]. See EZ-TLI,
MĒY(A).

EZŌTLA See IHZŌTLA.

EZPAH-TLI medicinal plant, the bark of
which produces a red dye (Jatropha spatulata) / cierto arbusto medicinal, que destila
por incisión un licor como sangre (R)
[(1)Rp.82]. Z has EZCUAHU(I)-TL See
EZ-TLI, PAH-TLI.

EZQUĪXTIĀ caus. EZQUĪZ(A)

EZQUĪZ(A) to bleed, to menstruate / tener su costumbre la mujer (M), sale sangre, sangra, se desangra (T) See EZ-TLI,
QUĪZ(A).

EZTIC something red / colorado, rojo (T)
[(1)Tp.249]. See EZ-TLI.

EZTLATLA for a blood blister to form / hace
ámpula (de sangre) (Z) [(2)Zp.10,153]. See
EZ-TLI, TLATLA.

EZ-TLI inalienably possessed form: **-EZYŌ**
~ **-EZZŌ** blood / sangre (M) The ZY
sequence of the possessed form commonly
assimilates to ZZ.

-EZYŌ necessarily possessed form one's
own blood / sangre The ZY sequence
commonly assimilates, -EZZŌ.

EZYOH See EZZOH.

EZZOH someone, something bloody, blood-
thirsty / sangriento (M) [(2)Zp.113,153,
(1)Rp.82]. In Z the ZY sequence fails to
assimilate to ZZ. See EZ-TLI, -YOH.

-EZZOHCĀPOHTZIN necessarily possessed
form one's blood fellow / (ha tomado)
sangre ... humana como nosotros (C)
[(1)Cf.84r]. This is said of Christ in an
affirmation that he is flesh of our flesh,
blood of our blood. See EZYOH, -POH.

HU

HUĀCCĀTLATLAXIZ-TLI consumption, tuberculosis / tisis (Z) [(2)Zp.122,154]. See HUĀCQUI, TLATLAXIZ-TLI.

HUĀCHILIĀ applic. HUĀTZ(A)

HUACH-TLI seed / semilla (X) This appears to be a variant form of ACH-TLI 'seed.' It is attested as a free form in X, and elsewhere it appears in AYOHHUACH-TLI and AIHHUACH-TLI, both meaning 'squash seed.' X has E, marked long in one set of attestations and not in the other, for A.

HUĀCOHUA nonact. HUĀQU(I)

HUĀCQUI something dry, desiccated / cosa seca, enjuta, o enmagrecido (M) [(2)Tp.127,239, (2)Xp.100]. See HUĀQU(I).

HUĀCTZIN a large bird with a distinctive call known in Spanish as *pájaro vaquero* (Herpetotheres cochinans) / cierta ave canora, grande como la gallina; es también nombre de otra ave de la misma magnitud, pero no canora (R) huaco (X) [(1)Rp.82, (3)Xp.100].

-HUAH *possessor suffix; pl:* **-HUAH-QUEH** See -EH.

HUAHHUALTZ(A) *vt* to bark at someone / ladra el perro a alguno (M) [(2)Cf.75r]. One of the attestations has a glottal stop at the end of the first syllable, and the other does not. This would appear to be a mistake in diacritics, with the simple short vowel reduplication being the intended one. There is a related verb HUAHHUANOĀ, however, which is attested in T with a glottal stop.

HUAHHUANILHUIĀ applic. HUAH-HUANOĀ

HUAHHUANOĀ *vt* to bark at someone / le ladra (T) [(3)Tp.186].

HUAHHUĀQU(I) redup. HUĀQU(I)

HUAHUAN(A) *vt* to scratch, scrape something, to incise lines on something / es-carbar o hacer rayas en la tierra, reglar papel, trazar o dibujar algo (M), lo raspa (T) Z has a long vowel in the second syllable and in one attestation has the reflex of a glottal stop at the end of the first syllable. X consistently has a long vowel in the second syllable, while T consistently has a short one.

HUAHUANALŌ nonact. HUAHUAN(A)

HUAHUANILIĀ applic. HUAHUAN(A)

HUĀHUĀ-TL *pl:* **-MEH** type of caterpillar also known as *chinahuate* / azotador (gusano) (T) [(1)Tp.127]. See ĀHUĀ-TL.

HUĀL- *directional prefix* hither, in this direction / hacia acá (M)

HUĀLAHCI to arrive / llegar (C), sobrevenir, sorprender (S) See HUĀL-, ACHI.

HUĀLAQUILIĀ *vt* to be capable of doing something / tiene capaz hacer, les cabe a todos (Z) [(1)Zp.188]. See HUĀL-, AQU(I).

HUĀLCAH much more / mucho más (M) This is generally preceded by OC 'yet,' although it is once attested in C without. C gives the literal sense of the phrase 'to be in this direction, to be more this way, to be more.' See HUĀL-, the verb CĀ.

HUĀLCUI *vt* to bring something / llevar, traer una cosa (S) [(2)Zp.124,147]. With the third pers. singular object prefix, Z alternatively has QUIHUĀLCUI or shortens the sequence C-HUĀL to CUĀL. See HUĀL-, CUI.

HUĀLĒHU(A) to come from somewhere, to come forth, to flee / venimos (C for first pers. plural subject), sale, se viene de allí para acá (T), huir (S) [(2)Cf.90r,121v, (3)Tp.127]. T has an idiosyncratic short vowel in HUĀL-. See HUĀL-, ĒHU(A).

HUĀLĒHUALŌ nonact. HUĀLĒHU(A)

HUĀLĒHUALTIĀ caus. HUĀLĒHU(A)

HUĀLHUĪCA *vrefl,vt* to come, to arrive, to reach a place; to bring something /

traer (C), aportar algo (S) T has the
common variant form HUALĪCA. See
HUĀL-, HUĪCA.

HUĀLHUĪCALŌ nonact. HUĀLHUĪCA

HUĀLHUĪQUILIĀ applic. HUĀLHUĪCA

HUĀLHUĪQUILILIĀ applic. HUĀL-
HUĪQUILIĀ

HUĀLHUĪQUILĪLŌ nonact. HUĀL-
HUĪQUILIĀ

HUĀLITTA vt to come to visit someone /
me ha visitado (C for first pers. sg. object)
[(1)Cf.106v]. See HUĀL-, (I)TTA.

HUĀLLĀ to come hither, to approach / venir hacia acá (M) This is a compound
of HUĀL- and the verb YĀ, but the
HUĀL- has been absorbed into the stem so
that no other prefixes can intervene, and
there is assimilation of the Y to preceding
L. The YĀ element behaves like free YĀ,
being suppletive with HU(I). The present singular form is HUĀLLAUH, and
the present plural is HUĀLHUIH. See
HUĀL-, the verb YĀ.

HUĀLLĀLIZ-TLI arrival / advenimiento o
venida (M) [(2)Cf.85r,97r]. See HUĀLLĀ.

HUĀLNĒC(I) to come into view / se parece
(C) [(1)Cf.89v]. See HUĀL-, NĒC(I).

HUĀLQUĪZ(A) to emerge, to come hither
out of some place / salir de lo profundo
del agua así (M), salir hacia acá (M)
[(3)Cf.20r,101r,106r]. See HUĀL-, QUĪZ(A).

HUĀLTEMŌ to come down, to descend /
abajar o descender de alto (M) This is
implied by HUĀLTEMŌLIZ-TLI See
HUĀL-, TEMŌ.

HUĀLTEMŌLIZ-TLI descent; something
lowered / descendimiento así (M), bajado
(Z) [(2)Zp.18,154]. This implies the verb
HUĀLTEMŌ. See HUĀLTEMŌ.

HUĀLTOHTOCA vt to come following after someone, to drive someone away /
viene siguiendo (Z), desterrar (R) See
HUĀL-, TOHTŌCA.

-HUĀMPOH necessarily possessed form
one's countryman, companion, equal,
relative / ser uno de la misma naturaleza,
estado, o condición que otro (C), nuestro
pariente (S) See -HUĀN, -POH.

-HUĀN necessarily possessed form and,
with / junto y en compañía de otro (C) T

has lost the final N by general rule, and the
vowel has shortened in word-final position.
T and Z use HUĀN without a possessive
prefix to mean 'and,' contrasting with
ĪHUĀN 'with him ~ her ~ it.'

HUĀNTI vt to invite someone / le convida,
le invita (Z) [(4)Zp.33,147,188]. With the
third pers. singular object prefix Z alternatively has QUIHUĀNTI or shortens the
sequence C-HUĀNTI to CUĀNTI. See
-HUĀN.

-HUĀNYŌLQUI necessarily possessed
form relative / pariente cercano, unido por
la sangre (S) [(3)Cf.86r]. S has an alternate
form without the N. This almost always
appears in plural possessed form, 'one's
relatives.' Only the -HUĀN is actually
bound with the possessive, so no plural
possessive suffix appears after YŌLQUI.
See -HUĀN, YŌLQUI.

HUAPĀHU(A) vrefl,vt to grow up, to gain in
strength; to raise children / crecer en edad,
o esforzarse y animarse (M), criar niños,
o esforzar y animar a otro (M) T has
the variant form HUEPĀHU(A). M also
has intransitive HUAPĀHUA, preterit
HUAPĀHUAC, 'to become hard, stiff,
numb.' See HUAPAL-LI.

HUAPĀHUALŌ nonact. HUAPĀHU(A)

HUAPĀHUILIĀ applic. HUAPĀHU(A)

HUAPAL-LI board, small beam / viga o
viga pequeña (M) [(1)Cf.47v, (1)Tp.110,
(5)Zp.19,119,154]. In three of five attestations Z marks the vowel of the first
syllable long. T has the variant form
HUEPAL(I)-TL.

HUAPALTLAPĀCALŌNI wooden trough,
pan / batea (Z) [(2)Zp.19,154]. See
HUAPAL-LI, TLAPĀCALŌNI.

HUĀQU(I) to dry out, evaporate, wither /
secarse, enjugarse al sol, mermar las cosas
líquidas o pararse flaco (M)

HUĀQUĪTIĀ caus. HUĀQU(I)

HUĀTZ(A) vrefl,vt to get dried out; to dry
something / enjugarse (M), secar o enflaquecer a otro (M), enjugar o secar algo
(M) In T the vowel of the first syllable is
consistently short, while in Z it is long. In
one of three attestations in C it is marked
long. See HUĀQU(I).

HUĀTZALŌ nonact. HUĀTZ(A)

HUAUHCAL-LI This is a variant of CUAUHCAL-LI.

HUĀUHQUIL(I)-TL wild amaranth, greens which are boiled and eaten as a vegetable / una verdura (Z), huajquelite (X) [(1)Zp.154, (3)Xp.100]. In the Z attestation the vowel is not marked long. See HUĀUH-TLI, QUIL(I)-TL.

HUĀUH-TLI amaranth / bledos (M), huatle, una semilla que comen tostada (Z) [(2)Zp.154, (2)Rp.72,82, (3)Xp.100]. Only in X is the vowel of the stem marked long.

HUĀXCUAHU(I)-TL guaje tree / guaxi (árbol) (Z) [(2)Zp.65,154]. See HUĀX-IN, CUAHU(I)-TL.

HUĀX-IN large tropical tree that produces edible pods (Leucaena diversifolia, Crescentia alata) / cierto árbol que da unas como algarrobas comestibles, de tierra caliente (C), guaje (T) In C, Z, and X the vowel of the stem is long. In T it is consistently short.

HUĀXPEHPEN(A) See HUĀX-IN, PEHPEN(A).

HUĀXPĪTZ-TLI dried seed of the guaje tree / semilla seca de guaje (T) [(1)Tp.127]. See HUĀX-IN, PĪTZ-TLI.

HUĀXTEPĒC place name Oaxtepec See HUĀX-IN, TEPĒ-TL.

HUĀXTEQU(I) See HUĀX-IN, TEQU(I).

HUĀXYŌ-TL [(1)Cf.53r, (1)Rp.44]. This appears in C as an example of derivation with -YŌ. The base is HUĀX-IN 'guaje,' and no gloss is given for the derived form. The sense would be approximately 'essence of guaje.' See HUĀX-IN, -YŌ.

HUĀYIC something dry / seco (Z) [(7)Zp.14,114,124,154,217,219]. See HUĀQU(I), HUĀTZ(A).

HUECHILIĀ This is an applicative form of HUETZ(I) only used bound to the verb CUI by the ligature -TI-.

HUECHOHUA altern. nonact. HUETZ(I)

HUECPAL-LI pl: -TIN digging stick / coa (T) [(1)Tp.109]. T also has synonymous HUEHCOL-LI. M has *huictli* with the same sense.

HUEHCA far away, distant / lejos (M) See HUĒ(I).

HUEHCACAYŌ-TL something brought

from afar; someone who has come from afar, wanderer / cosa que se trae de acarreo (M), peregrino (Z) [(1)Zp.154]. See HUEHCA.

HUEHCACHĀNEH foreigner, stranger / extranjero o advenedizo (M) [(2)Zp.58,154]. See HUEHCA, CHĀNEH.

HUEHCACONĒ-TL someone adopted / adoptado (Z) [(2)Zp.5,158]. See HUEHCA, CONĒ-TL.

HUEHCĀHU(A) vt to retain something for a long time, to detain someone for a long time, to postpone doing something / detener largo tiempo alguna cosa ajena, no la tornando con tiempo a su dueño, o diferir y dilatar algún negocio (M), detener por largo espacio a otro (M), diferir o dilatar algo, o tardarse en hacer algo (M) See HUEHCA, HUEHCĀHUA, CĀHU(I)-TL.

HUEHCĀHUA pret: HUEHCĀHUAC ~ HUEHCĀUH to attain great age or to remain for a long time in one place / tener mucha edad o detenerse y tardar en algún lugar (M) See HUEHCĀHU(A).

HUEHCĀHUALTIĀ caus. HUEHCĀHU(A)

HUEHCĀHU(I) to last, endure, delay, procrastinate / dilata, dura, demora, tarda, retrasa (T) [(6)Tp.108,109]. This is synonymous with intransitive HUEHCĀHUA. See HUEHCA, CĀHU(I)-TL.

HUEHCĀHUĪHUA nonact. HUEHCĀHU(I)

HUEHCĀHUĪLTIĀ A short vowel in the third syllable is to be expected, but it is attested long in T. caus. HUEHCĀHU(I)

HUEHCĀHUĪLTILIĀ applic. HUEHCĀHUĪLTIĀ

HUEHCĀHUĪLTĪLŌ nonact. HUEHCĀHUĪLTIĀ

HUEHCĀHUĪTIĀ caus. HUEHCĀHU(I)

HUEHCAITTA vt to see something from afar / ver de lejos (R) [(1)Rp.83]. This also appears in P with the glottal stop marked. See HUEHCA, (I)TTA.

HUEHCAPA to, from afar / de lejos (M), desde lejos (C) See HUEHCA, -PA.

HUEHCAPAHUIĀ vt to keep one's distance from something, someone / seguir a otro de lejos (M), apartarse de algo (R) [(1)Rp.83]. See HUEHCAPA, -HUIĀ.

HUEHCAPAN something high, elevated /

cosa alta (M), alto, arriba, elevado (T) The general loss of word-final N makes this homophonous with HUEHCAPA in T. See HUEHCA, -PAN.

HUEHCAPANCAYŌ-TL height, stature / altura (R) [(1)Rp.83]. See HUEHCAPAN, -YŌ.

HUEHCAPANIHU(I) to gain honor and high estate / subir o crecer en honor, dignidad y estado (M) This is implied by HUEHCAPANIUHQUI

HUEHCAPANILHUIĀ applic. HUEHCAPANOĀ

HUEHCAPANIUHQUI someone of honor and high estate / ensalzado y sublimado en honra y estado (M) [(1)Rp.83]. This implies HUEHCAPANIHU(I). HUEHCAPANIUHQUI also appears in P with the glottal stop marked. See HUEHCAPAN.

HUEHCAPANOĀ vrefl,vt to rise up, to become enlarged; to raise, enlarge something / ensalzarse o agrandecerse (M), sublimar y engrandecer a otro (M) See HUEHCAPAN.

HUEHCAPANŌLŌ nonact. HUEHCAPANOĀ

HUEHCAPANTIC height / altura (Z) [(2)Zp.9,155]. See HUEHCAPAN.

HUEHCATLAN something deep, abysm / cosa honda y profunda (M), hondo, abismo, profundo (Z) Although Z marks the vowel of the last syllable long, X does not. In T the vowel is short, and the final N is missing. Although the N is present in HUEHCATLANOĀ, as attested in T, the vowel before it is still short. See HUEHCA, -TLAN.

HUEHCATLANOĀ vt to submerge, sink something / lo hunde (T) [(1)Tp.177]. See HUEHCATLAN.

HUEHCATLANTLĀLIĀ vt to deepen something / lo ahonda (T) [(3)Tp.177]. The N of the third syllable is missing in T. See HUEHCATLAN, TLĀLIĀ.

HUEHCATLĀZ(A) vrefl,vt to withdraw; to defer, postpone something / ponerse lejos (R), diferir, aplazar, dejar para más tarde (S) [(2)Rp.83]. See HUEHCA, TLĀZ(A).

HUEHCĀUH a long time; something old / largo tiempo (C), viejo (S) This occurs

frequently in the phrases YE HUEHCĀUH 'long ago,' OC HUEHCĀUH 'a long time from now,' and their negations AYAMŌ HUEHCĀUH 'recently' and AOCMŌ HUEHCĀUH 'in a little while, shortly.' See HUEHCĀHU(A).

HUEHCĀUHCĀYŌ-TL old age, antiquity; ancestor / antigüedad o vejez (M), antecesor, ancestro (Z) [(2)Zp.11,155]. See HUEHCĀHU(A), -YŌ.

HUEHCĀUHPA later, after a while / mas tarde, después de un rato, hace tiempo (T) [(2)Tp.109]. See HUEHCĀUH, -PA.

HUEHCĀUHTĀTAH ancestor / antecesor, ancestro (Z) [(2)Zp.11,155]. Z also has the variant HUEHCĀUHTĒTĀT. See HUEHCĀUH, TAH-TLI.

HUEHCĀUHTICA a long time / largo tiempo, muy gran rato See HUEHCĀUH, -CA.

HUEHCOL-LI digging stick / coa (T) [(1)Tp.109]. T also has synonymous HUECPAL-LI.

HUEHHUEHCA far away, with respect to several things / distantes unas de otras (R), distancia de cosas apartadas unas de otras (M) [(2)Rp.83]. This is the distributive of HUEHCA. C and T have HUĒHUEHCA with long-vowel reduplication but the same meaning. M's entry is ambiguous between the two. redup. HUEHCA

HUEHHUEHCAPAN redup. HUEHCAPAN

HUEHHUEHCĀUHTICA sometimes, now and then / de tarde en tarde o raramente (M) [(1)Rp.83]. redup. HUEHCĀUHTICA

HUEHHUĒI pl: **HUEHHUĒINTIN** great, grand, large things / cosas grandes (M) M gives this a plural gloss in the absence of the plural suffix, which is consistent with the fact that Nahuatl in general does not overtly mark the plurals of inanimate objects. redup. HUĒ(I)

HUEHHUELIHU(I) to go to pieces, to collapse / se destruirá (C for future) [(1)Cf.102r, (3)Xp.101]. The glottal stop in the first syllable is not attested in C or X but is attested in transitive HUEHHUELOĀ.

HUEHHUELOĀ vt to destroy, undo, lay waste something / deshacer, desbaratar o derrocar algo (M) The internal glottal stop is not attested in X but does appear in Z and R. redup. HUELOĀ

HUEHHUETZCA to smile / sonreírse (C) [(3)Cf.70v,127r, (1)Rp.83]. C contrasts this with HUEHUETZCA 'to laugh a great deal.' In general, reduplication with glottal stop implies a reiterated act, so HUEHHUETZCA would seem more proper to 'to laugh' than HUEHUETZCA, but C's contrast is explicitly the opposite. R has *huehuetzca* as a modifier of TLAHTOĀ and TLAHTŌL-LI with the sense of 'to blaspheme' and 'blasphemy' respectively, but it is multiply ambiguous and may represent HUEHHUETZCA, HUEHUETZCA, or HUĒHUETZCA. redup. HUETZCA

HUEHHUETZ(I) redup. HUETZ(I)

HUEHHUETZQUĪTIĀ caus. HUEH-HUETZCA

HUEHPĀM(I)-TL a large hewn beam / viga grande desbastada y por labrar (M), las vigas (C) [(1)Cf.93r]. M has the form *ve-pantli*. See HUĒ(I), PĀM(I)-TL.

HUEHPĀN-TLI See HUEHPĀM(I)-TL.

HUEHPŌLHUIĀ *vrefl* to be in love with one's brother-in-law / tiene a su cuñado por querido (T) [(3)Tp.144]. See HUEHPŌL-LI, -HUIĀ.

HUEHPŌLHUĪLŌ nonact. HUEHPŌLHUIĀ

HUEHPŌL-LI in-law of opposite sex, same generation; brother-in-law of woman, sister-in-law of man / cuñada de varón o cuñado de mujer (M)

HUĒHUEH pl: **HUĒHUETQUEH;** *singular possessed form:* **-HUĒHUETCĀUH** old man / viejo o anciano (M) This has T before the plural suffix but a glottal stop word-finally in the singular, except in Z, which has T throughout. Before -TZIN and -TŌN this has the form HUĒHUĒN. See HUĒHUĒNTŌN, HUĒHUĒNTZIN.

HUĒHUEHCA distance between more than two things / distancia entre más de dos cosas (C), distancia de cosas apartadas unas de otras (M) See HUEHHUEHCA.

HUĒHUEHCĀUHTICA occasionally, rarely / de tarde en tarde o raramente (M) [(4)Cf.99v,100r,131r]. redup. HUEHCĀUHTICA

HUĒHUEHHUAH master of old men /

dueño de viejos (C) [(1)Cf.55v]. This appears as a grammatical example in a discussion of the possessor suffixes and may have no real referent. It contrasts with HUĒHUĒHUAH 'master of drums.' See HUĒHUEH.

HUĒHUEHTI to grow old / hacerse viejo (M) [(1)Bf.12r, (3)Tp.110, (1)Rp.43]. See HUĒHUEH.

HUĒHUEHTĪHUA nonact. HUĒHUEHTI

HUĒHUEHTILIĀ *vrefl,vt* to age; to age something / se envejece (T), lo envejece (T) applic. HUĒHUEHTI

HUĒHUEHTILILIĀ applic. HUĒHUEHTILIĀ

HUĒHUEHTILĪLŌ nonact. HUĒHUEHTILIĀ

HUĒHUĒHUAH master of drums / dueño de atabales, o guitarras (C) [(1)Cf.55v]. C contrasts this with HUĒHUEHHUAH 'master of old men.' Only C glosses HUĒHUĒ-TL as 'guitar.' It specifically means the indigenous upright drum. See HUĒHUĒ-TL.

HUĒHUEHYŌ-TL age; something pertaining to old people / vejedad o costumbre y propiedad de viejos (M) [(2)Tp.110,111, (2)Zp.128,154]. See HUĒHUEH.

HUĒHUĒIHTZIN something middling large / grandecito (T) [(2)Tp.111]. This is one of the cases where glottal stop intervenes between the stem and -TZIN. See HUĒ(I).

HUĒHUELATZIN cripple, one who drags himself around / uno que no puede andar, no más se arrastra, cojo (T) [(2)Tp.110,111]. This is derived from HUILĀN(A). T has E for I and LA for LĀN. This is a reduplicated form of T's HUELATZIN, but the reduplication has to do with the action of the verb, 'to drag oneself around in various places,' rather than with the whole derived noun. See HUELATZIN.

HUĒHUĒNTŌN little old man; character in a comical traditional 'old men's' dance / vejezuelo (M), cómico, payaso (Z) [(3)Zp.30,95,154]. M lacks the final N. See HUĒHUEH.

HUĒHUĒNTZIN old man / anciano, viejo, viejito (T) In T the vowel of the second syllable is short. See HUĒHUEH.

HUĒHUET See HUĒHUEH.

HUĒHUETCĀYŌ-TL old age / edad
de viejos o vejedad (M), vejez (T)
[(2)Tp.110,111]. See HUĒHUEH.

HUĒHUĒ-TL *possessed form:* **-HUĒ-
HUĒUH** upright drum / atabal (M)

HUEHUETZCA to laugh a lot / reirse mucho (C) [(1)Cf.127r]. C contrasts this with
HUEHHUETZCA 'to smile.' The vowel of
the first syllable is specifically marked
short, and in the text it is also said to be
short. redup. HUETZCA

HUĒHUETZCA to laugh with a good will,
to laugh hard / me río con mucha gana (C
for first pers. sg. subject), se ríe (T) This is
abundantly attested in T and Z and also
once in C, making a three-way contrast
with HUEHUETZCA and HUEH-
HUETZCA. See HUETZCA.

HUĒHUETZCALIZ-TLI guffaw / carcajada
(Z) [(2)Zp.25,140]. This suggests that M's
veuetzca, glossed in Spanish as *dar
carcajadas de risa*, is HUĒHUETZCA. Z
marks the vowel of the third syllable long,
but it should not be. See HUETZCA.

HUĒHUETZCOHUA nonact. HUĒ-
HUETZCA

HUĒHUETZPAL-IN iguana / iguana (T)
[(2)Tp.110,111]. See HUETZPAL-IN,
CUETZPAL-IN.

HUĒHUETZQUĪTIĀ caus. HUĒHUETZCA

HUEHXŌLŌCUEP(A) *vrefl* to turn into a
turkey cock / se vuelve guajolote (T)
[(3)Tp.144]. See HUEHXŌLŌ-TL,
CUEP(A).

HUEHXŌLŌCUEPALŌ nonact. HUEH-
XŌLŌCUEP(A)

HUEHXŌLŌHUĒHUEH old turkey cock /
guajolote macho viejo (T) [(1)Tp.110]. See
HUEHXŌLŌ-TL, HUĒHUEH.

HUEHXŌLŌILAMA turkey hen / guajolota, totola, pava (T) [(1)Tp.110]. See
HUEHXŌLŌ-TL, ILAMA-TL.

HUEHXŌLŌNAC(A)-TL turkey meat /
carne de guajolote (T) [(2)Tp.110,166]. See
HUEHXŌLŌ-TL, NAC(A)-TL.

HUEHXŌLŌ-TL *pl:* **HUĒHUEHXŌLOH ~
HUEHXŌLŌMEH** turkey / gallo de la
tierra (C), guajolote, pavo (Z) T and X lack
the internal glottal stop. Z has the form
HUEHUEHCHO.

HUĒ(I) *pl:* **HUEHHUĒIN ~ HUEH-**

HUĒINTIN something big, great, large /
grande (M) In related forms such as
HUEHCA 'far away,' HUEHCĀHU(A) 'to
detain someone, postpone something for a
long time,' and HUĒHUEH 'old man' the
stem has the form HUEH. HUĒHUEH also
has the variant stem forms HUĒHUET and
HUĒHUĒN.

HUĒIĀ-TL river, sea / río, mar (Z)
[(3)Zp.81,110,155, (3)Xp.49,100]. See
HUĒ(I), Ā-TL.

HUĒICA in a grand, noble manner; for a
long time / alta y soberanamente (M), largo
tiempo (Z) [(7)Zp.10,25,41,75,141,155,206].
See HUĒ(I).

HUĒICHĪHU(A) *vrefl,vt* to grow large, to
aggrandize oneself, to be vain; to enlarge,
augment, exaggerate something / se da por
maravilla (esta fruta) (C), jacta, se enorgullece, es egoísta, se hace grande (T), lo en-
grandece (T) See HUĒ(I), CHĪHU(A).

HUĒICHĪHUALŌ nonact. HUĒICHĪHU(A)

HUĒICHĪHUILIĀ applic. HUĒICHĪHU(A)

HUĒIHCĀYŌ-TL greatness of station and
dignity / grandeza de estado y dignidad (M)
[(1)Cf.53v]. In the same grammatical
discussion C gives OHUIHCĀYŌ-TL
'difficulty and danger' derived from
OHUIH 'something difficult,' in both
cases with a glottal stop followed by
-CĀ-, implying a deverbal derivation. See
HUĒ(I), -YŌ.

HUĒILIĀ *vrefl,vt* to aggrandize oneself or
someone else; to enlarge, augment something, to start bidding in a game of chance
/ estimarse, engrandecerse o ensoberbe-
cerse (M), engrandecer a otro (M), hacer
mayor lo pequeño o alargar y añadir o
envidar en juego (M) See HUĒ(I).

HUĒILILIĀ applic. HUĒILIĀ

HUĒILĪLŌ nonact. HUĒILIĀ

HUĒIMAHPIL-LI thumb / dedo pulgar de la
mano (M) [(2)Zp.103,158]. See HUĒ(I),
MAHPIL-LI.

HUĒIMAT(I) *vrefl,vt* to hold oneself in high
regard; to have a high opinion of someone
or something / tenerse y estimarse en
mucho (M), estimar o tener en mucho alguna cosa (M) [(2)Cf.79r,79v]. See HUĒ(I),
MAT(I).

-HUĒINĀN *only attested in possessed form* grandmother / su abuelita (Z for possessed form) [(1)Zp.158]. Z also has several other permutations of NĀN-TLI and HUĒ(I) in possessed form with the same sense. This is peculiar to Z; the common Nahuatl word for 'grandmother' is CIH-TLI. See HUĒ(I), NĀN-TLI.

HUĒINEQU(I) *vrefl* to hold oneself in high regard / tenerse en mucho (M), arrogante, orgulloso (Z) [(5)Zp.14,69,92,169]. See HUĒ(I), NEQU(I).

-HUĒITĀTAH *only attested in possessed form* grandfather / su abuelito (Z for possessed form) [(2)Zp.4,158]. Z also has the phrase TĀTAH HUĒ(I) with the same sense. This is peculiar to Z; the common Nahuatl word for 'grandfather' is CŌL-LI. See HUĒ(I), TAH-TLI.

HUĒITŌTOL-IN a type of wild bird, probably the wild turkey / totola silvestre (Z) [(2)Zp.124,155]. See HUĒ(I), TŌTOL-IN.

HUĒIY(A) *pret:* **HUĒĪX ~ HUĒIYAC** to grow; to gain in honor and dignity / hacerse grande o crecer en honra y dignidad (M) See HUĒ(I).

HUĒIYAC something long / cosa larga o luenga (M) [(3)Zp.75,77,155, (3)Xp.49,101]. The I is only hypothesized from HUĒIY(A). X marks the vowel of the last syllable long in all attestations, and Z marks it long once. See HUĒIY(A).

HUEL well; able, possible; more, very / bien (M) This often serves as an intensifier without contributing any distinct lexical meaning of its own in phrases that do not always translate well into English with 'very,' HUEL ĀXCĀN 'right now,' CA HUEL MOCHĪNTĪN 'all, every single one,' HUEL IHUI 'vigorously.' See HUEL(I).

HUELĀN(A) See HUILĀN(A).

HUELATZIN cripple, one who drags himself around / cojo, uno que no puede andar, no más se arrastra (T) [(4)Tp.110,111]. This is derived from HUILĀN(A). T has E for I and LA for LĀN. See HUILĀN-TLI.

HUEL(I) to be able to / puede (Z) S gives this as an alternate of HUEL, but it does not appear in M. In the sources for this dictionary HUEL(I) is abundantly at-

tested across sources with negation, as in AHHUEL(I) 'impossible,' AOC HUEL(I) 'no longer possible,' AYA HUEL(I) 'not yet possible' and in Z as a shortened form of the verb HUELITI 'to be able to do something' In view of the verb HUELITI 'to be able to do something,' HUEL is probably a truncation of more basic HUEL(I). See HUEL.

HUĒLIC something delicious, pleasing / cosa sabrosa y gustosa (M) Z and X mark the vowel of the second syllable long, but T has it short.

HUĒLILIYA for food to taste good / está sabroso (X) [(3)Xp.100]. M has transitive *uelilia* 'to make food taste good,' which forms its preterit as a regular -IĀ verb, while this intransitive verb adds -C in the preterit. See HUĒLIC.

HUELĪLIZ-TLI power, ability / poder, capacidad, habilidad (Z) [(5)Zp.25,65,100,155]. This is a shortened form of HUELITILIZ-TLI. Z consistently marks the vowel of the second syllable long, which may be in compensation for the elided syllable. M's *veliliztli* is derived from HUĒLILIYA 'for food to taste good' which has a long vowel in the first syllable in contrast with this item. See HUELITILIZ-TLI.

HUELITI to be able to do something, to be sufficient for something / poder hacer algo, o tener suficiencia y ser bastante para algo (M) See HUEL(I).

HUELITĪHUA nonact. HUELITI

HUELITILIĀ applic. HUELITI

HUELITILIZ-TLI possibility; power and authority to do something / posibilidad, facultad, poder y autoridad para hacer algo (M) [(1)Tp.110]. See HUELITI.

HUELITTA *vrefl,vt* to enjoy oneself; to find something pleasing and good, to approve of something / se goza, se regocija (Z), agradarme y parecerme bien alguna cosa (M for first pers. sg. subject) [(5)Zp.8,64,107,169,188]. See HUEL, (I)TTA.

HUELIYOH someone powerful, vigorous / poderoso, activo (R) [(1)Rp.84]. See HUEL(I), -YOH.

HUELIZ perhaps, possibly / quizá, quizás, tal vez (T), posible, puede que sí (Z) This is

abundantly attested but only in T and Z.
See HUEL(I).

HUELLAHCAH late in the day / tarde (C)
[(1)Cf.98r]. See HUEL, TLAHCAH.

HUELLAMACHTIĀ vt to please someone / dar contentamiento a otro (M)
[(3)Bf.2r,5v,6r]. See HUEL, TLAMACHTIĀ.

HUELMAT(I) vt for something to taste good
to someone / saberme bien el manjar (M
for first pers. sg. subject), le gusta mucho,
lo saborea (T) See HUEL, MAT(I).

HUELOĀ vrefl,vt to be dislocated; to consume, undo, demolish something / se disloca (Z), desboronar, deshacer, o derribar
algo (M) This also has a reduplicated form
with the same sense, HUEHHUELOĀ

HUĒLTĪUH-TLI elder sister / hermana
mayor (M) [(2)Bf.4v, (1)Cf.63v]. The possessed form adds a glottal stop before
-TZIN, -HUĒLTĪHUAHTZIN.

HUELYEHHUĀ-TL the very same one /
el mismo en persona (M), él mero (T)
[(6)Tp.110]. See HUEL, (Y)EHHUĀ-TL.

HUENCHĪHU(A) vrefl to make an offering / pone ofrenda (T) [(3)Tp.144]. See
HUEN-TLI, CHĪHU(A).

HUENTLĀLIĀ to set an offering on the altar
/ pone ofrenda (en el altar) (T) [(3)Tp.110].
See HUEN-TLI, TLĀLIĀ.

HUENTLĀLILIĀ applic. HUENTLĀLIĀ

HUENTLĀLĪLŌ nonact. HUENTLĀLIĀ

HUEN-TLI offering / ofrenda (M)
[(7)Tp.110,144].

HUEPĀHU(A) See HUAPĀHU(A).

HUEPĀHUALŌ See HUAPĀHUALŌ.

HUEPAL(I)-TL See HUAPAL-LI.

HUETZCA to laugh / reírse (M)

HUETZCALIZ-TLI laughter / risa (Z)
[(2)Zp.110,155]. See HUETZCA.

HUETZCANI a laughing person, or something amusing / risueño, o cosa que se
suele reír naturalmente (M) [(1)Tp.135]. See
HUETZCA.

HUETZCOHUA altern. nonact. HUETZCA

HUETZ(I) to fall / caer (M)

HUETZĪHUA nonact. HUETZ(I)

HUETZILTIĀ altern. caus. HUETZ(I)

HUETZĪTIĀ altern. caus. HUETZ(I)

HUETZPAL-IN pl: HUĒHUETZPALTIN
iguana / iguana (T) [(2)Tp.110,121]. See
CUETZPAL-IN, HUĒHUETZPAL-IN.

HUETZQUILIĀ vt to laugh at something,
with someone / reírse de alguno (M), reírse
a la risa de otro (M) applic. HUETZCA

HUETZQUILILIĀ applic. HUETZQUILIĀ

HUETZQUILĪLŌ nonact. HUETZQUILIĀ

HUETZQUĪLTIĀ vt to make someone
laugh / le hace reír (T) [(3)Tp.178]. T has a
long vowel in the second syllable where a
short one is to be expected. altern. caus.
HUETZCA

HUETZQUĪLTILIĀ applic. HUETZ-
QUĪLTIĀ

HUETZQUĪLTĪLŌ nonact. HUETZ-
QUĪLTIĀ

HUETZQUĪTIĀ vt to make someone laugh
/ hacer reír a otro o hacer algo por donde se
rían de mí (M) [(1)Cf.61v, (3)Tp.126]. altern.
caus. HUETZCA

HUETZTOC to be lying down, stretched
out / estar echado (M), acostado (Z)
[(2)Zp.5,155]. T has the variant forms
HUETZTICAH and HUETZTOTICAH
derived with the verb CĀ and with the
same sense. See HUETZ(I), the verb O.

HUEXŌ-TL willow tree / sauce (M)

HUEXŌTLAH willow grove (a common
place name) / sauceda o arboleda de sauces
(M) [(2)Cf.57r]. See HUEXŌ-TL, -TLAH.

HUEXŌTLAHCA-TL someone from
Huejutla / natural de Huejutla (K)
[(1)Cf.57r, (1)Rp.46]. See HUEXŌTLAH.

HUEXŌTZINCA-TL someone from
Huejotzingo / natural de Huejotzingo (K)
[(3)Bf.11r]. See HUEXŌ-TL.

HUEZHUAH-TLI possessed form: -HUEZ-
HUI a woman's sister-in-law / cuñada de
mujer (M) [(1)Cf.81v, (1)Tp.127]. C has
stem-final Z, but this is probably a typographical error, since Z is absent in M and
in the possessed form attested in T.

HUI exclamation for attracting someone's
attention or expressing surprise or distress válgame Dios (C), hao, hola, oyes
... para llamar a otro, o interjección para
hacer exclamación o para quejarse (M)
[(1)Cf.103v].

HU(I) suppletive verb with YĀ to go / ir (K)
In view of HUĪLOHUA, and possibly of
HUĪCA, HUĪTZ, and HUĪCATZ, a case
might be made for basic HUĪ, but the I is
short in the imperfect and optative, and it

disappears in the construction YĀ-HU(I) > YAUH. Only short vowels are susceptible to such deletion, but there is clearly irregularity in the whole suppletive relationship of YĀ and HU(I). See YĀ.

-HUIĀ *transitive verb-forming suffix* This suffix is added to nouns to create verbs with an essentially applicative sense — to wield, use, or apply the thing named by the noun in relation to someone or something, or to bring forth, produce the thing for someone Such verbs are generally paired with intransitive verbs in -OĀ, so that the -HUIĀ verbs may be considered the applicative forms of the corresponding -OĀ verbs.

-HUĪC *postposition* toward, in the direction of / hacia y contra (C) C contrasts ĀHUĪC 'toward the water' with AHHUĪC 'to and fro, in no one direction.' This can also indicate direction from a point.

HUĪCA *vrefl,vt* for people to go together, hence to get married; to take, carry something; to accompany others / se llevan, se casan (T), llevar algo (M), ir con otros, o ir acompañando o en compañía de otros (M)

HUĪCALŌ altern. nonact. HUĪCA

HUĪCALTIĀ *vrefl,vt* to conform to what others do; to send something with someone, to cause someone to go accompanied by others, to charge someone with something / seguir el hilo de la gente, haciendo lo que los otros hacen (M), hacer que alguno lleve a otra persona o a algún animal consigo (M), hacer que vaya acompañada una cosa con otra (M), dar quien acompañe a otro (M), lo encarga (un favor) (T) caus. HUĪCA

HUĪCALTILIĀ applic. HUĪCALTIĀ

HUĪCALTĪLŌ nonact. HUĪCALTIĀ

HUĪCATZ See HUĪTZ.

HUICCI to cook; to ripen / se cuece, se cocina, madura (T) This is the T variant of IUCCI. The CC represents the phonetic sequence [ks]. X has lost the initial HU.

HUICCIC ripened; cooked / maduro, cocido (T) [(1)Tp.110, (1)Xp.45]. See HUICCI.

-HUĪCCOPA *postposition* toward, in the direction of / hacia y contra (C) [(2)Cf.20r].

C gives -HUĪC, -HUĪCPA, and -HUĪC-COPA as synonyms. See -HUĪC, -COPA.

HUĪCŌ altern. nonact. HUĪCA

HUĪCŌLLOH something (specifically a pitcher) having handles / jarro de dos asas redondas como anillos (C for construction with TECOM(A)-TL) [(2)Cf.92r,92v]. M has *vicollotl* 'handle of a pitcher.' The attestations in C do not mark the vowel long. See HUĪCŌLTIC, -YOH.

HUĪCŌLTIC something curved, twisted / cosa tuerta como asa de jarro o persona cenceña y enjuta (M) [(2)Zp.37,155]. See CŌLTIC.

-HUĪCPA *postposition* toward, in the direction of / hacia y contra (C) [(5)Cf.20r,116r]. C gives -HUĪC, -HUĪCPA, and -HUĪCCOPA as synonyms. See -HUĪC, -PA.

HUĪCTLA See HUĪPTLA.

HUĪCTLATICA See HUĪPTLATICA.

HUICXITIĀ *vt* to cook something / lo coce, lo cocina (T) [(3)Tp.178, (3)Xp.69]. Although the vowel of the second syllable before causative -TIĀ is long in X, as it should be, it is short in T and also in C's corresponding IUCXITIĀ. caus. HUICCI

HUICXITILIĀ applic. HUICXITIĀ

HUICXITĪLŌ nonact. HUICXITIĀ

HUIHHUĪCALTIĀ *vt* to curse, slander someone / lo maldice (Z) [(2)Zp.80,188]. This is the causative form of unattested *HUIHHUĪCA, which in turn would be a reduplicated form of HUĪCA 'to take, carry something.' See TLAHUIHHUĪCALTIĀ.

HUIHHUĪLOHUA redup. HUĪLOHUA

HUIHHUĪTEQU(I) *vt* to beat someone; to beat clothes, mats, etc., with a stick / apalear a otro (M), sacudir ropa, esteras o cosa así con vara (M) [(1)Cf.71r, (2)Zp.17,188]. redup. HUĪTEQU(I)

HUIHHUITŌN(I) to stagger / se tambalea (T) [(1)Bf.12r, (3)Tp.111]. M has *viuitomi* 'to be sick and unable to stand.' In the attestation in B the final vowel is deleted, and the nasal agrees with the adjacent T, hence it is ambiguous between basic M(I) and N(I). T has N(I).

HUIHHUITŌNĪHUA nonact. HUIH-HUITŌN(I)

HUIHHUITŌNĪTIĀ caus. HUIHHUITŌN(I)
HUIHHUITZTLAH briar patch / lugar lleno
de espinas o puyas (M) [(1)Tp.111]. M also
has the unreduplicated form HUITZTLAH.
See HUITZ-TLI, -TLAH.

HUIHHUITZYOH something covered with
thorns / espinosa cosa, o llena de puyas
(M), trae muchas espinas en la ropa o en el
pelo (del animal), espinudo (T) [(1)Tp.111].
See HUITZ-TLI, -YOH.

HUIHHUĪXTILIĀ *vt* to weaken someone /
lo debilita (Z) [(2)Zp.40,188]. M has *vi-
uixcatilia* 'to weaken someone so that he
staggers.' The Z form seems to be the
same verb with one syllable elided.
See HUIHHUITŌN(I), HUIHUIXCA,
HUĪHUĪCA.

HUĪHUĪCA *vrefl,vt* to stagger; to go along
with other people repeatedly / bambolea
(Z), seguir muchas a algunas veces yéndo-
los acompañando (M) [(2)Zp.18,169]. redup.
HUĪCA

HUĪHUILATZIN See HUĒHUELATZIN.

HUĪHUĪLOHUA redup. HUĪLOHUA

HUĪHUĪLOHUATZ redup. HUĪLOHUATZ

HUIHUITILIĀ *vt* to weed, dig up something
/ lo desyerba [(2)Zp.45,188]. altern. applic.
HUIHUITLA

HUIHUITLA *vt* to pull up weeds; to pluck
feathers / pelar o desplumar aves, o coger
yerbas con la mano sin arrancar, o arrancarlas de raíz (M), coger matas de frijoles
(M) X marks the vowel of the second
syllable long.

HUIHUITLALHUIĀ altern. applic.
HUIHUITLA

HUIHUITLALŌ nonact. HUIHUITLA

HUIHUITLĀTZOĀ *vt* to rock something / lo mece (Z) [(2)Zp.83,188]. See
HUIHUIXOĀ.

HUĪHUĪTZ redup. HUĪTZ

HUIHUIXALHUIĀ applic. HUIHUIXOĀ

HUIHUIXCA to tremble, shake / temblar
(M) [(3)Tp.110, (3)Zp.58,120,155]. See
HUIHUIXOĀ.

HUIHUIXCALŌ nonact. HUIHUIXCA

HUIHUIXCALTIĀ caus. HUIHUIXCA

HUIHUIXOĀ *vt* to shake or rock someone
or something / sacudir o menear el árbol, o
mecer la cuna al niño, o menear al que

duerme porque despierte, o prender por
pena (M) [(3)Tp.178].

HUIHUIXŌLŌ nonact. HUIHUIXOĀ

HUIHUIYOCA to tremble, shiver / temblar o tiritar de frío (M) [(6)Tp.110,140,
(2)Zp.120,155]. In one attestation Z marks
the O long, but elsewhere it is short and
conforms to the pattern of this type of
verb. See HUIYŌN(I).

HUIHUIYOCOHUA nonact. HUIHUIYOCA

HUIHUIYŌNIĀ *vrefl,vt* to shake, shiver; to
shake something / se mece (T), lo mece (T)
[(6)Tp.144,178]. See HUIYŌN(I).

HUIHUIYŌNILIĀ applic. HUIHUIYŌNIĀ

HUIHUIYŌNĪLŌ nonact. HUIHUIYŌNIĀ

HUIHUIYOQUĪTIĀ caus. HUIHUIYOCA

HUILAC(A) *pl:* -MEH a type of snail /
caracol de monte (X) [(3)Xp.101]. See
HUILĀN(A).

HUILĀN(A) *vrefl,vt* to drag oneself along; to
drag something / andar arrastrando y a
gatas por el suelo (M), arrastrar algo
(M) T has HUILĀN(A) in the compound
ĀHUILĀN(A) 'to swim' but elsewhere the
variant HUELĀN(A). T also has the derived
nouns HUELATZIN, HUĒHUELATZIN
'cripple, one who drags himself around.'
See HUILĀN-TLI.

HUILĀNALŌ nonact. HUILĀN(A)

HUILĀNILIĀ *vrefl,vt* for people to want to
take something away from one another; to
haul something for someone / quieren
quitárselo uno a otro (T), se lo jala (T) [(6)
Tp.144,177]. T has E for I in the first syllable. applic. HUILĀN(A)

HUILĀNILILIĀ applic. HUILĀNILIĀ

HUILĀNILĪLŌ nonact. HUILĀNILIĀ

HUILĀNTIHUETZ(I) *vt* to snatch
someone,something / arrebatar (K)
[(1)Cf.100v]. See HUILĀN(A), HUETZ(I).

HUILĀNTIQUĪXTIĀ *vt* to drag, shove
someone out / echar o sacar a otro de
casa a empujones, o arrastrándolo (M)
[(2)Cf.78r]. See HUILĀN(A), QUĪXTIĀ.

HUILĀN-TLI cripple, one who drags himself
around / tullido que anda a gatas (M)
[(4)Tp.110,111]. T has E for I and LA for
LĀN. See HUILĀN(A).

HUĪLOHUA for leavetaking to take place /
todos van (M) B marks the O long twice

and leaves it unmarked for length once. C
and T share a notation which appears to
represent OHUA but possibly represents
ŌHUA. nonact. HU(I)

HUĪLOHUALIZ-TLI the act of general
leavetaking, departure / el acto de partirse
todos a alguna parte (M) [(1)Cf.40r]. See
HUĪLOHUA.

HUĪLOHUATZ *special honorific form* to
come / viene (T) [(2)Tp.128]. This is only
attested in T. The plural is formed by
reduplication, HUIHUĪLOHUATZ. This
appears to be related to HUĪTZ 'to come.'
See HUĪLOHUA.

HUĪLŌ-TL *pl:* **-MEH** dove, pigeon / paloma (M)

HUĪPĀN(A) *vrefl,vt* to form a line; to line
people up, to put something in order /
se forma en cola (T), poner por orden y
concierto la gente, cuando hay procesión,
etc. (M), poner orden y concierto en las
cosas o en la república (M), lo forma
en línea o cola, lo pone en línea (T) See
HUĪPĀN-TLI.

HUĪPĀNALŌ nonact. HUĪPĀN(A)

HUĪPĀNILIĀ applic. HUĪPĀN(A)

HUĪPĀNTICAH to be lined up / están
formando en cola (T for plural) [(1)Tp.111].
See HUĪPĀN(A), the verb CĀ.

HUĪPĀN-TLI file, line, row / fila (T)
[(1)Tp.111]. See PĀM(I)-TL.

HUĪPĪL-LI *pl:* **-TIN** ~ **-MEH** indigenous
woman's blouse / camisa de india (M)
[(1)Tp.174, (4)Xp.101]. T has P for HU. X
marks only the second syllable long.

HUĪPTLA day after tomorrow / después de
mañana (M) This often appears in the
phrase MŌZTLA HUĪPTLA 'in the future,'
literally 'tomorrow, day after tomorrow.'

HUĪPTLATI to return on the day after
tomorrow / llegar a después de mañana (C)
[(2)Cf.59r]. See HUĪPTLA.

HUĪPTLATICA on the third day, every third
day / a tercer día (M), cada tercer día (C)
[(4)Cf.107r]. See HUĪPTLA.

-HUĪPTLAYŌC *necessarily possessed form*
two days later / dos días después (M for
iuiptlayoc), dos días después, a los dos días
(S) [(1)Cf.97v]. This takes the third person
singular prefix. See HUĪPTLA.

HUĪQUILIĀ *vt* to take, carry something for
someone; to owe something to someone /

lo lleve a él, lo debe a él (T) The sense of
'to owe' this verb has in modern Nahuatl
appears already in C on f.101r and is
common in colonial-period texts. applic.
HUĪCA

HUĪQUILILIĀ applic. HUĪQUILIĀ

HUĪQUILĪLŌ nonact. HUĪQUILIĀ

HUĪTECŌC bolt of lightning / rayo (T)
[(1)Tp.111]. See HUĪTEQU(I).

HUĪTECŌNI chisel; something deserving of
whipping / escoplo, o cosa semejante (M),
el digno de ser azotado (C) [(1)Cf.45v]. C
contrasts HUĪTECŌNI with TĒHUĪ-
TECŌNI 'instrument for whipping, beating someone.'

HUĪTEQU(I) *vrefl,vt* to get whipped; to
whip, beat someone; to thresh grain / se
azota, se arroja (T), herir o castigar a otro
(M), desgranar semillas con varas o palos
(M)

HUĪTEQUĪHUA nonact. HUĪTEQU(I)

HUĪTEQUILIĀ applic. HUĪTEQU(I)

HUĪTŌLIHU(I) to arch, to form an arc /
entortarse o torcerse la vara o cosa semejante (M), torcerse algo ... en forma de arco
(C) [(2)Cf.76v]. This implies transitive
HUĪTŌLOĀ 'to bend, arch something.'

HUĪTŌLOĀ *vt* to bend, arch something /
enarcar sin tirar flecha, o doblegar vara o
cosa semejante (M) This is implied by
HUĪTŌLIHU(I) See TŌLOĀ.

HUĪTZ *defective verb; pl:* **HUĪTZEH** to
come / venir (M) This is a preterit-as-
present verb, the preterit being HUĪTZ,
and the pluperfect HUĪTZA. It appears to
be related to HU(I), which enters into a
suppletive paradigm with YĀ 'to go.'

HUITZACATZIN hummingbird / colibrí,
chuparrosa (X) [(3)Xp.101]. See HUĪ-
TZIL-IN.

HUITZHUIĀ *vt* to prick something with a
thorn / punzar con puya o espina (M)
[(2)Zp.56,188]. See HUITZ-TLI, -HUIĀ.

HUĪTZILIHHUI-TL *personal name* hummingbird feather / pluma de colibrí (K)
[(1)Bf.11r]. See HUĪTZIL-IN, IHHUI-TL.

HUĪTZIL-IN hummingbird / pajarillo que
zumba (S), chuparrosa, chupamirto, colibrí,
chupamiel (T) [(2)Bf.10r,11r, (1)Tp.111,
(3)Zp.30,39,156]. M has *vitzitzilin* with an
additional syllable in the stem. T has the

variant HUĪTZTZĪTZIQUIH, and Z has
the variant HUĪTZIQUITZIN. Despite the
thorn-like shape of the hummingbird's
beak, B and T agree that the vowel of the
first syllable is long, hence contrasting
with HUITZ-TLI 'thorn.' Z does not mark
the the vowel long, and neither does X in
synonymous HUITZACATZIN.

HUĪTZILŌPŌCH-TLI *personal name*
Huitzilopochtli [(1)Bf.10r]. There is much
disagreement on the meaning of this name.
Contrary to some hypotheses, the first
element, HUĪTZIL 'hummingbird,' modi-
fies the second, ŌPŌCH-TLI 'left-hand
side.' See HUĪTZIL-IN, ŌPŌCH-TLI.

HUĪTZIQUITZIN See HUĪTZIL-IN.

HUITZŌC-TLI hoe / palanca de roble
puntiaguda para arrancar céspedes y abrir
la tierra (M) [(3)Xp.101]. See HUITZ-TLI.

HUITZPATLĀX-TLI broad thorn / espino
ancho (X) [(3)Xp.101]. See HUITZ-TLI,
PATLĀHUAC.

HUITZPEHPEN(A) See HUITZ-TLI,
PEHPEN(A).

HUITZTLAH See HUIHHUITZTLAH.

HUITZ-TLI thorn, spine / espina grande o
puya (M)

HUĪTZTZĪTZIQUIH *pl:* **-MEH** hummingbird / chuparrosa, chupamirto, colibrí, chupamiel (T) [(1)Tp.111]. The final
consonant of this appears only before
-MEH and could represent the weakening
of some consonant other than H, possibly
N. M has *tzitzicuini* 'something light, free,
nimble,' which, somewhat reduced,
could be the second element of this. See
HUĪTZIL-IN.

HUĪX-IN See CUĪX-IN.

HUIYŌN(I) for something to move / moverse, se mueve (X) [(3)Xp.101]. See
HU(I).

HUIYŌNIĀ *vt* to move something / mover
(X) [(4)Xp.78]. See HUIYŌN(I).

I

Ī *vt; pret:* ĪC to drink something / beber mazamorra, cacao, pinol, o cosa semejante (M) The evidence for a long vowel rests on a future tense form in B that has ĪZ (f.11v) and on C's nominalization TLAĪ-TL. Z also makes a contrast between ĀTIC 'something melted' and ĀTĪC< Ā-TL 'water' and Ī 'to drink,' which is possible only because TL and T do not contrast in Z.

*IĀ *preterit-as-present verb; pret:* IH to exist / ser (K) This is a hypothetical element included in ĀQUIHQUEH 'who are they?', the plural of ĀC, and of IN IHQUEH ĪN (or ŌN) 'these (or those) present.' See INIHQUEH.

ĪC when? / ¿en qué tiempo? (M) This frequently appears in the construction ZAN ĪC 'frequently, repeatedly.'

ĪC with, by means of, thereby / con (M), con, hacia, por, en (S) This often fuses with IN to form INĪC with the same sense. It is abundantly attested across sources, especially in C where, in keeping with C's practice of not marking the noncontrastive and the obvious, the vowel is marked long only half the time. See ĪCA.

ĪCA by means of something / con ... o por (M) This is the third person singular possessive prefix Ī- and the postposition -CA 'means, reason, cause.' Two common phrases with ĪCA are TLE ĪCA 'why?' and YEH ĪCA 'because of something, since.'

ICAH sometime, on some occasion / en algún tiempo o alguna vez (M)

-ĪCAMPA *postpositon* behind, behind one's back / detrás de algo (M), detrás de mí (M for first pers. sg. possessor), detrás de algunos (M), detrás de las espaldas de algo (C) C fails to mark the vowel of the first syllable long in seven attestations on a single page. Some of the other attestations

can be understood as possessive Ī- added to -ICAMPA, yielding a single long Ī. But a half dozen cases with a marked long vowel remain. Z consistently marks the vowel of the second syllable long as well and has a nominal reading 'one's shoulders' for the gloss of one attestation. For the locative sense 'behind something' Z has the alternate forms TLAĪCAMPA and TLAĪCAN. This conventionally pairs with -TEPOTZCO 'at one's back,' the whole phrase meaning 'when one is dead.'

ĪCANCHIHCŌLTIC someone hunchbacked / jorobado (Z) [(2)Zp.73,156]. See -ĪCAMPA, CHIHCŌLTIC.

ICCĀUH-TLI younger brother / hermano menor (M) [(2)Bf.11r,12r, (1)Cf.106v]. S has the absolutive suffix, which is unattested in the sources for this dictionary. See TĒICCĀUH.

ICCEMMANIYĀN forever / siempre, para siempre, para siempre jamás (S) [(2)Cf.102r,102v]. C gives this as synonymous with CEMMANIYĀN. It is sometimes written with only a single M. See ICCEN, CEMMANIYĀN.

ICCEN once and for all / ultimadamente (M) The CEN element of this is undoubtedly CEM 'one,' but the IC element never occurs with a marked long vowel, so this is apparently not a simple compound of ĪC and CEM.

ICHCACUAHU(I)-TL *pl:* -TIN silk-cotton tree, ceiba (Ceiba pentandra) / árbol de algodón (X) [(3)Xp.45]. See ICHCA-TL, CUAHU(I)-TL.

ICHCANAC(A)-TL lamb, mutton / carne de borrego o carnero (Z) [(2)Zp.26,157]. See ICHCA-TL, NAC(A)-TL.

ICHCA-TL *pl:* ICHCAMEH ~ ĪICHCAMEH cotton, wool, or (by extension) sheep / algodón o oveja (M), algodón, lana (T) C

provides the reduplicated plural as an
alternative to the simple -MEH plural.
ICHCAYŌL-LI *pl:* **-TIN** cotton seed /
semilla de algodón (X) [(3)Xp.46]. See
ICHCA-TL, YŌL-LI.
(I)CHCUA *vt* to remove earth with a hoe, to
dig something / sacar tierra con el azadón
(C)
(I)CHPĀHU(A) See (I)CHPĀN(A).
(I)CHPĀN(A) *vt* to sweep something /
lo barre (T) M has an entry *chpana* to
be used with the prefix TLA- and also
TLACHPĀN(A), where the object prefix has been absorbed into the stem
and the verb is treated as intransitive.
(I)CHPĀN(A) may be related by metathesis
to CHIPĀHU(A) 'to purify something' Z
has the variant (I)CHPĀHU(A) and also two
attestations of OCH for (I)CH, which
appears to relate this to M's *ochpantli*
'road,' in the sense that a road is kept
swept clean.
(I)CHPĀNALŌ nonact. (I)CHPĀN(A)
(I)CHPĀNILIĀ applic. (I)CHPĀN(A)
(I)CHPOCA-TL See (I)CHPOCATZIN-TLI.
(I)CHPOCATZIN-TLI very young girl,
maiden / mozuela (M), joven (mujer) (Z for
(I)CHPOCA-TL) [(1)Bf.4v,(2)Zp.73,157]. Z
has a long vowel in the second syllable,
but B specifically marks it short. See
(I)CHPŌCH-TLI.
(I)CHPŌCHCĀHUAL-LI spinster / soltera
(T) [(1)Tp.129]. See (I)CHPŌCH-TLI,
CĀHUAL-LI.
(I)CHPŌCH-TLI *pl:* **(I)CHPŌPŌCHTIN**
maiden, young woman / virgen o mujer
por casar (M) (I)CHPŌCH-TLI and also
TĒLPŌCH-TLI 'young man' both form the
plural by reduplicating the PŌCH element,
which suggests that *PŌCH-TLI, although
it does not appear as a free form, is a stem
in its own right, and (I)CH is a modifier.
A variant form of (I)CHPŌCH-TLI is
(I)CHPOCA-TL, corresponding to the
variants TĒLPŌCH-TLI and TĒLPOCA-TL
'young man.'
ICHTACA secretly / secretamente o a
escondidas (M) T has the variant form
ICHTECA. With -TZIN there is an intervening glottal stop which does not appear

in compounds. The alternation Ā ~ AH
is to be found elsewhere, suggesting that
this should be ICHTACĀ, but even in
compounds where it is not word-final,
the final vowel is never attested long in
the sources for this dictionary. See
(I)CHTEQU(I).
ICHTACACONĒ-TL illegitimate offspring / hijo bastardo o hija bastarda (M)
[(1)Tp.129]. See ICHTACA, CONĒ-TL.
ICHTACANAMACA *vt* to sell something
in secret / lo vende (a escondidas de la
familia) (T) [(3)Tp.185]. See ICHTACA,
NAMACA.
ICHTACANOHNŌTZ(A) *vrefl* to whisper / cuchichea (Z) [(2)Zp.36,170]. T has
ICHTACANŌNŌTZ(A). See ICHTACA,
NOHNŌTZ(A).
ICHTACANŌNŌTZ(A) *vrefl,vt* to whisper,
to converse in secret; to speak to someone
in secret / cuchichea, platica en secreto (T),
le habla en secreto (T) [(6)Tp.149,185]. See
ICHTACA, NŌNŌTZ(A).
ICHTACATŌNAHUIZ-TLI malaria /
paludismo (Z) [(2)Zp.93,158]. See
ICHTACA, TŌNAHUIZ-TLI.
(I)CHTECQUI thief / ladrón (M) See
(I)CHTEQU(I).
(I)CHTEQU(I) *vt; pret:* **-TEC** to steal
something / hurtar (C), lo roba (T)
(I)CHTEQUĪHUA nonact. (I)CHTEQU(I)
(I)CHTEQUILIĀ *vt* to steal something
from someone / se lo roba (T) applic.
(I)CHTEQU(I)
(I)CHTEQUILILIĀ applic. (I)CHTEQUILIĀ
(I)CHTEQUILIZ-TLI robbery / el acto
de hurtar (M) [(3)Cf.62v,113r]. See
(I)CHTEQU(I).
ĪCH-TLI *pl:* **-TIN** thread made from maguey
fiber / cerro o copo de maguey (M), ixcle
(de pita, maguey), hilo (T)
ICI here / aquí (S) This has a short
form IZ. T's ICI 'morning' is related to
IHCIUHCĀPAN and not to this item.
ICI morning / mañana (del día) (T)
[(2)Tp.133]. This appears to be a reduction
of IHCIUHCĀPAN with a loss of the
glottal stop characteristic of T. See
IHCIUHCĀPAN.
(I)CNĒLIĀ *vrefl,vt* to look after one's own

---

welfare; to do a favor for someone, to be charitable to someone / hacer bien a sí mismo (M), hacer bien a otro (M) See (I)CNŌ-TL, (I)CNĪUH-TLI.

(I)CNĒLILIĀ applic. (I)CNĒLIĀ

(I)CNĒLĪLMAT(I) *vrefl,vt* to be grateful; to thank someone / ser agradecido (M), agradecer algo a otro (M) [(1)Cf.62r]. By regular derivational process, the vowel of the third syllable should be long, but it is unmarked for length in C. See (I)CNĒLIĀ, MAT(I).

(I)CNĒLILŌ C specifically says that the I of the third syllable is short by contrast with the Ē of the preceding syllable, but this is probably the result of some secondary shortening. By general rule this should be (I)CNĒLĪLŌ. nonact. (I)CNĒLIĀ

(I)CNĪUHTLA *vrefl,vt* to become friends; to cause people to befriend each other / hacerse amigos o tomar amistad unos con otros (M), dar a conocer a otros para que se amen o hacer amigos a los enemistados (M) [(1)Cf.81r]. See (I)CNĪUH-TLI.

(I)CNĪUH-TLI friend, sibling / amigo (M), su hermano, hermana (T for possessed form) The 'sibling' sense extends to 'cousin' in the phrase HUEHCA ICNĪUH-TLI, literally 'distant sibling.' See (I)CNĒLIĀ, (I)CNŌ-TL.

(I)CNŌCIHUĀ-TL widow, spinster / viuda (M), solterona, viuda (T for ICNŌZOHUA-TL) [(1)Tp.128]. See (I)CNŌ-TL, CIHUĀ-TL.

(I)CNŌITTA *vt* to have pity on someone, to regard someone with compassion / apiadarse de otro (M) In one attestation in T the initial vowel is not deleted in the presence of a reflexive prefix. See (I)CNŌ-TL, (I)TTA.

(I)CNŌITTALIZ-TLI compassion / misericordia (T) [(1)Tp.128]. See (I)CNŌITTA.

(I)CNŌMAT(I) *vrefl* to humble oneself / humillarse (M) [(2)Cf.79v,87r]. See (I)CNŌ-TL, MAT(I).

(I)CNŌOQUICH-TLI bachelor, widower / viudo (M), solterón, viudo (T) [(1)Tp.128]. M writes the two elements as separate words, while T writes them solid and

reduces the sequence ŌO to Ō. See (I)CNŌ-TL, OQUICH-TLI.

(I)CNŌPILHUIĀ *vt* to obtain something by entreaty / alcanzar o impetrar algo (M), recibir mercedes o alcanzar lo deseado o cosa provechosa (M with fused TLA-) [(4)Bf.2v,5r,5v, (1)Cf.17v]. See (I)CNŌPIL-LI, -HUIĀ.

(I)CNŌPILLAHUĒLĪLŌC someone ungrateful / ingrato (M) [(2)Cf.58v]. See (I)CNŌPIL-LI, TLAHUĒLĪLŌC.

(I)CNŌPILLAHUĒLĪLŌCAT(I) *pret:* **-CAT ~ -CATIC** to be ungrateful / ser desagradecido e ingrato (M) [(1)Cf.58v]. See (I)CNŌPILLAHUĒLĪLŌC.

(I)CNŌPIL-LI fatherless child, person deserving of compassion; one's fate, future, lot in life / huérfano de padre (M), su suerte (T) See (I)CNŌ-TL, PIL-LI.

(I)CNŌPILTI *irregular verb* to prosper in life, to be favored, to attain one's desires / obtener lo que se desea, ser feliz, recibir favores, enriquecerse (S) This has only a singular form and takes possessive prefixes rather than subject prefixes, AMOCNŌPILTI 'you are favored, you prosper.' The preterit is (I)CNŌPILTIC, the future (I)CNŌPILTIZ. No other forms are used. See (I)CNŌPIL-LI.

(I)CNŌ-TL orphan, someone or something poor, humble, worthy of compassion and aid / huérfano (M), pobre o huérfano (C) See (I)CNĒLIĀ.

(I)CNŌTLĀCAYŌ-TL poverty, misery / orfandad o miseria (M) [(1)Cf.118v]. See (I)CNŌ-TL, TLĀCAYŌ-TL.

(I)CNŌZOHUA-TL spinster, widow / solterona, viuda (T) [(1)Tp.128]. See (I)CNŌ-TL, ZOHUA-TL.

ĪCŌL-LI See ĪCŌLTIĀ.

ĪCŌLTIĀ *vrefl,vt* to long for, desire something, someone / antojárseme alguna cosa o codiciarla (M for first pers. sg. subject), codiciar algo (M) T consistently has the O short, although it is long elsewhere. S has an associated noun ĪCŌL-LI 'something desirable.'

ĪCŌLTILIĀ applic. ĪCŌLTIĀ

ĪCŌLTĪLŌ nonact. ĪCŌLTIĀ

-(I)CPAC *postposition* on or at the head of,

above / encima de lo alto, o en lo alto de alguna cosa (M), sobre, encima, en la cima, sobre la cabeza, delante (S)

(I)CPAL-LI seat, specifically a certain type of seat for persons of authority, hence by extension such a person himself or the authority of such a person / asentadero (M), sillón con respaldo, signo de poder de los antiguos jefes, los únicos que tenían el derecho de usarlos; ... protector, jefe, gobernador, padre, madre, etc. (S) [(8)Bf.4r,4v,6v,7v,12v,13r, (1)Rp.148]. See -(I)CPAC.

ĪCPA-TL thread, hemp fiber / hilo (M), hilo, pita, cáñamo (T) [(1)Tp.128]. See ĪCH-TLI.

(I)CPOĀ *vt* to reseed something / lo siembre de nuevo (T) [(3)Tp.180].

(I)CPOHUILIĀ applic. (I)CPOĀ

(I)CPŌLŌ nonact. (I)CPOĀ

(I)CXEH possessor of a foot or feet / que tiene pies (K) [(1)Cf.55v, (1)Rp.45]. C and R give this without a gloss as an example of the possessor derivation. See (I)CXI-TL.

(I)CXICOTOC lame, crippled / rengo, cojo See (I)CXICOTŌN(A).

(I)CXICOTŌN(A) *vrefl,vt* to cut one's foot; to cut someone in the foot / se mocha el pie (T), le mocha el pie (T) [(4)Tp.148,184]. See (I)CXI-TL, COTŌN(A).

(I)CXICOTŌNALŌ nonact.(I)CXICOTŌN(A)

(I)CXICOTŌNILIĀ applic. (I)CXICOTŌN(A)

(I)CXICUAUHTI for one's legs to get tired / se cansa los pies, se cansa el pie (T) [(3)Tp.129]. See (I)CXI-TL, CUAUHTI.

(I)CXICUAUHTĪHUA nonact. (I)CXI-CUAUHTI

(I)CXICUAUHTILIĀ applic. (I)CXI-CUAUHTI

(I)CXICUECHAQUIĀ *vrefl,vt* to sprain one's ankle, break one's leg; to injure someone in the leg / se tuerce el pie, se zafa (T), le lastima el pie (al otro) (T) [(6)Tp.148,184]. See (I)CXI-TL, CUECHAQUIĀ.

(I)CXICUECHAQUILIĀ applic. (I)CXI-CUECHAQUIĀ

(I)CXICUECHAQUĪLŌ nonact. (I)CXI-CUECHAQUIĀ

(I)CXICUETLAXIHU(I) for one's foot to become weakened, paralyzed / se suelta el

pie, se debilita el pie (T) [(3)Tp.129]. See (I)CXI-TL, CUETLAXIHU(I).

(I)CXICUETLAXIHUĪHUA nonact. (I)CXI-CUETLAXIHU(I)

(I)CXICUETLAXIHUĪTIĀ caus. (I)CXI-CUETLAXIHU(I)

(I)CXIMŌTLA *vt* to throw something at the legs of someone, something / le tira a los pies (T) [(3)Tp.184]. See (I)CXI-TL, MŌTLA.

(I)CXIPOZTEQU(I) *vrefl* to break a leg / se quiebra la pata, la pierna (T) [(3)Tp.148]. See (I)CXI-TL, POZTEQU(I).

(I)CXIPOZTEQUĪHUA nonact. (I)CXI-POZTEQU(I)

(I)CXIQUECHCOCHTITLAN instep / su empeine (de pie) (T for possessed form) [(1)Tp.129]. T drops the -TI- and word-final N. See (I)CXI-TL, QUECHCOCHTITLAN.

(I)CXITEPĀCHOĀ *vrefl,vt* to bruise one's leg; to bruise someone in the leg / se machuca el pie (T), le machuca el pie (T) [(4)Tp.148,184]. See (I)CXI-TL, TE-PĀCHOĀ.

(I)CXI-TL foot / pie (M)

-(I)CXITLALHUAYŌ *only attested in possessed form* tendon of one's leg / su tendón del pie (T) [(1)Tp.129]. See (I)CXI-TL, TLALHUA-TL.

-(I)CXITLAN *compound postposition* at the foot of / a sus pies (T), en sus pies (T), al pie de (Z) [(2)Tp.129, (2)Zp.98,157]. Z marks the vowel of the last syllable long. See (I)CXI-TL, -TLAN.

(I)CXITLANĪTZ-TLI shinbone, shank / su canilla (del pie) (T for possessed form) [(1)Tp.129]. See (I)CXI-TL, TLANĪTZ-TLI.

(I)CXITOHMI-TL *inalienably possessed form:* **-TOHMIYŌ** leg hair / su pelo de la pierna (T for possessed form) [(1)Tp.129]. See (I)CXI-TL, TOHMI-TL.

ICXŌ altern. nonact. ICZA

ICXOĀ See IUCXOĀ.

(I)CXOPAL-LI sole of the foot / su planta de pie (T for possessed form) [(7)Tp.129,148,184]. This contrasts with (I)CXOPIL-LI 'toe.' See (I)CXI-TL, XO-, -PAL.

(I)CXOPALTEHTEQU(I) See (I)CXOPAL-LI, TEHTEQU(I).

(I)CXOPIL-LI toe / su dedo del pie (T for possessed form) This is abundantly attested but only in T. It is not attested in absolutive form, and the -LI here is by analogy with MAHPIL-LI. This contrasts with (I)CXOPAL-LI 'sole of the foot.' See (I)CXI-TL, XOPIL-LI.

(I)CXOPILTEHTEQU(I) See (I)CXOPIL-LI, TEHTEQU(I).

(I)CXOPILTEPĀCHOĀ *vrefl,vt* to bruise one's toe; to bruise someone's toe / se machuca el dedo del pie (T), le machuca el dedo del pie (T) [(6)Tp.148,184]. See (I)CXOPIL-LI, TEPĀCHOĀ.

ICZA *vt* to step on or trample something / hollar o pisar algo (M) There is potential minimal contrast with ĪCZĀN 'once upon a time, long ago' in case the latter loses its final N, but the transitive verb will always have object prefixes.

ICZALŌ altern. nonact. ICZA

ĪCZAN once upon a time, long ago / desde hace tiempo, alguna vez (en tiempo pasado) (T) [(3)Tp.128,227, (4)Zp.8,129,156]. In cases where this loses its final N, it contrasts with the verb ICZA 'to step on something,' but the verb will always have object prefixes. See ĪC, ZAN.

ICZŌ-TL a type of yucca (Yuca aloifolia) / palmera de las montañas ... la fibra de ese árbol se utilizaba en el tejido de paños (S) This is attested in the compound ICZŌXŌCHI-TL.

ICZŌXŌCHI-TL yucca flower / flor de yuca, flor de iczote (Z) [(2)Zp.60,157]. See ICZŌ-TL, XŌCHI-TL.

IHCA *preterit-as-present verb; pret:* **IHCAC** to be on foot, to be standing / estar en pie (M)

IHCAC See IHCA.

(I)HCAHUACA for people or birds to make a lot of noise / gorjear, cantar, hablando de pájaros (S), el ruido y el murmullo que hace la gente en la plaza (C) [(2)Cf.75v, (1)Tp.130].

(I)HCAHUATZ(A) *vt* to cause a noise, hubbub / alzar alboroto (K) This is indirectly attested in C's substantive TLAHCAHUATZA 'those that make such a noise' (referring to the verb IHCAHUACA).

(I)HCAL(I) *vrefl,vt* to engage in skirmishing; to contest with someone / escaramuzar o batallar (M), pelear contra otros (M), pelear unos con otros o escaramuzar (M)

(I)HCALIĀ applic. (I)HCAL(I)

(I)HCALĪHUA altern. nonact. (I)HCAL(I)

(I)HCALĪLŌ altern. nonact. (I)HCAL(I)

IHCATICAH to be standing, to be on foot / está de pie, está parado (T) [(7)Tp.130]. See IHCA, the verb CĀ.

IHCATILTIĀ altern. caus. IHCA

IHCATOC someone standing, on foot / parado, está de pie (Z) [(7)Zp.94,98,107,129,158]. See IHCA, the verb O.

(I)HCHĪHUIĀ See TLAHCHĪHUIĀ.

(I)HCHINILHUIĀ applic. (I)HCHINOĀ

(I)HCHINOĀ *vrefl,vt* to burn; to scorch, set fire to, burn something / se chamusca, se quema (T), lo chamusca, lo enciende, lo quema (T) [(7)Tp.149,187,231]. See CHINOĀ.

(I)HCHINŌLŌ nonact. (I)HCHINOĀ

(I)HCHIQU(I) *vt* to scrape the core of a maguey plant to collect its liquid / raspar el corazón del maguey para sacar miel (M) [(1)Cf.97v, (2)Zp.123,207].

IHCĪCA to pant, to be winded, to palpitate / carlear, acezar, o jadear (M) [(1)Bf.11v, (1)Tp.133, (3)Zp.73,109,158]. Z consistently has a long vowel in the second syllable, but the single attestation in B leaves it unmarked for length. T has it long but has lost the internal glottal stop. See (I)HCIHU(I).

(I)HCIHU(I) to hurry / apresurarse o darse priesa (M) Z has a reflexive form in which the initial I does not drop after reflexive prefixes, but in some other derived forms it appears that the vowel is weak and is deleted when adjacent to another vowel. See IHCĪCA.

(I)HCIHUIC something hurried, rapid / apriesa, rápido (Z) [(2)Zp.105,158]. See (I)HCIHU(I).

(I)HCIHUĪHUA nonact. (I)HCIHU(I)

(I)HCIHUILIĀ applic. (I)HCIHU(I)

(I)HCIHUĪTIĀ caus. (I)HCIHU(I)

(I)HCIUHCĀ quickly, promptly, swiftly / presto o de presto o prestamente (M) See (I)HCIHU(I)

(I)HCIUHCĀCHĪHU(A) *vt* to do something swiftly, violently / le hace violentemente (Z) [(2)Zp.129,188]. See (I)HCIUHCĀ, CHĪHU(A).

IHCIUHCĀPAN early / por la mañana (K) [(1)Tp.133]. This is attested in the phrase IHCIUHCĀPAN TŌNALLI 'morning, in the morning.' See ICI, (I)HCIUHCĀ, -PAN.

(I)HCIUHCĀQUIYAHU(I)-TL downpour / lluvia violenta y pertinaz [(2)Zp.79,159]. See (I)HCIUHCĀ, QUIYAHU(I)-TL.

(I)HCIUHCĀYŌ-TL hastiness, speed, promptness / apresuramiento o presteza y diligencia (M), rápido, pronto, inmediatemente (Z) [(3)Zp.71,102,105]. See (I)HCIUHCĀ, -YŌ.

(I)HCIUHTOC something or someone hurried / apurado (Z) [(2)Zp.13,159]. See (I)HCIHU(I), the verb O.

IHCOCH-IN a type of earthworm / un gusano de tierra (Z) [(3)Zp.65,158,208].

IHCOHUA nonact. IHCA

IHCOP(I) to wink, blink, close the eyes / cerrar los ojos (M), pestañea ... cierra los ojos (Z) [(3)Zp.27,98,158].

IHCOYOCA to roar, whir, crackle / hacer ruido la llama del fuego o la avenida recia del río, o el viento o huracán, o zumbar (M) [(2)Zp.109,158].

IHCUĀC when (noninterrogative), then / cuando, afirmando alguna cosa, entonces (M) T has lost the initial syllable.

(I)HCUANIĀ *vrefl,vt* to withdraw; to move someone or something from one place to another / dar lugar apartándose (M), apartar a otro, o deponerlo y privarlo de su oficio (M), mudar o apartar algo de una parte a otra (M) T has the variant form (I)HCUENIĀ

(I)HCUANILIĀ applic. (I)HCUANIĀ

(I)HCUANĪLŌ nonact. (I)HCUANIĀ

IHCUĀQUINŌN at that moment, then / en ese tiempo, en ese momento; en esa ocasión (T) [(2)Tp.123]. See IHCUĀC, INŌN.

(I)HCUENIĀ See (I)HCUANIĀ.

(I)HCUILHUIĀ *vt* to write something to or for someone / se lo escribe (T) [(1)Cf.65v, (4)Tp.187]. applic. (I)HCUILOĀ

(I)HCUILHUILIĀ applic. (I)HCUILHUIĀ

(I)HCUILHUĪLŌ nonact. (I)HCUILHUIĀ

(I)HCUILIHU(I) for something to get written / están escritas (C for construction with the verb O) [(1)Cf.92r]. See (I)HCUILOĀ.

(I)HCUILOĀ *vrefl,vt* for something to get written; to write or paint something, to sign or inscribe someone's name / se escribe (T), inscribir a alguien, escribir su nombre ... escribir, pintar una cosa (T) In Z the initial I does not drop before the reflexive prefix. M has this as *cuiloa* 'to write or paint something,' the initial syllable being lost to the orthography, because the weak intial vowel drops after the object prefix TLA- and the glottal stop is not written.

(I)HCUILŌLŌ nonact. (I)HCUILOĀ

IHCUINACA to buzz, whir / rezumba (T) [(1)Tp.130].

IHCUIXALHUIĀ applic. IHCUIXOĀ

IHCUIXOĀ to sneeze / estornuda (T) [(3)Tp.130]. See IUCXOĀ.

IHCUIXŌLŌ nonact. IHCUIXOĀ

(I)HCUIY(A) *vrefl, pret:* **(I)HCUIX** to wrap or coil oneself, to coil one's hair up / coger o revolver los cabellos la mujer a la cabeza, o ceñir la culebra por el árbol o por el cuerpo de hombre (M) This is implied by TEHCUIY(A) 'to wrap or entangle something.'

IHHUI-TL *possessed form:* **-IHHUIUH,** *inalienably possessed form:* **-IHHUI-YŌ** feather, down / pluma menuda (M)

IHICHTEQU(I) to go from house to house committing robbery / voy a hurtar a casas ajenas, de casa en casa (M for first pers. sg. subject) [(1)Cf.72r]. This reduplicated form has a frequentative sense. The intervocalic glottal stop arises from reduplication of initial I. redup. (I)CHTEQU(I)

IHĪCŌLTIĀ *vrefl,vt* to be arbitrary, tyrannical; to entice and then disappoint someone / tiranizar (M), se lo muestra, se lo enseña para que lo quiera y después no se lo da (T) [(3)Tp.187]. redup. ĪCŌLTIĀ

IHĪCŌLTILIĀ applic. IHĪCŌLTIĀ

IHIHTOĀ *vt* to criticize, slander someone / lo critica, habla de otro (malo) (Z) [(5)Zp.27,35,66,188]. redup. (I)HTOĀ

(I)HILNĀMIQU(I) *vt* to daydream, to indulge in fantasies / me divierto en mil disparatadas imaginaciones (C)

[(1)Cf.115v]. This reduplicated form has a frequentative sense. redup. (I)LNĀMIQU(I)
(I)HILPIĀ redup. (I)LPIĀ

IHITTA *vt* to watch, observe others, to pick out or choose something / estar mirando a los otros (M), lo escoge, lo selecciona, lo elige (Z) [(4)Zp.49,55,114,188]. redup. (I)TTA

IHITZTOC to be wakeful / estoy desvelado (C for first pers. sg. present), estaba despierto (C for imperfect) [(2)Cf.100r,104r]. redup. ITZTOC

IHIXHUIC someone full, satisfied after a meal / harto (C) [(1)Cf.118r]. redup. IXHUIC

IHĪY(A) *vrefl,vt; pret:* **IHĪX ~ IHĪYAC** to be in a bad mood, to be peevish; to hate someone, something / aborrecerse estando mohino (M), aborrecer a otro (M) [(2)Cf.32r].

IHĪYŌCĀHUALTIĀ *vrefl,vt* to suffer exhaustion, prostration; to drive someone to exhaustion, collapse, to cause someone to faint / perdais el aliento (M for second pers. plural subject); hacer desfallecer a otro el huelgo de mucho trabajar o de enfermedad (M) [(1)Cf.120r]. See IHĪYŌ-TL, CĀHUALTIĀ.

IHĪYŌCUI to have something to eat, take some refreshment / comer ... un bocado (C) [(1)Cf.104v]. See IHĪYŌ-TL, CUI.

IHĪYŌCUĪTIĀ *vrefl,vt* to take a rest, to have some refreshment; to give someone something to eat and a chance to rest / coma usted (C for imperative), refocilar o dar de comer a otro (M) [(1)Cf.98r, (1)Rp.89]. caus. IHĪYŌCUI

IHĪYŌHUIĀ *vt* to endure hardship, to labor hard in order to subsist, to acquire something by one's own hard effort / padecer necesidad el pobre, o adquirir con trabajo lo necesario a la vida (M), padecer trabajos (M) See IHĪYŌ-TL, -HUIĀ.

IHĪYŌHUILIĀ applic. IHĪYŌHUIĀ

IHĪYŌHUILIZ-TLI torment, misery / tormento (C) [(1)Cf.102r]. See IHĪYŌHUIĀ.

IHĪYŌHUĪLŌ nonact. IHĪYŌHUIĀ

IHĪYŌHUILTIĀ caus. IHĪYŌHUIĀ

IHĪYŌMICOHUA nonact. IHĪYŌMIQU(I)

IHĪYŌMICTIĀ *vt* to choke, strangle, suffocate someone / atapar el huelgo a otro (M) [(2)Zp.57,188]. caus. IHĪYŌMIQU(I)

IHĪYŌMIQU(I) *pret:* **-MIC** for someone to suffocate, to be strangled / se sofoca, se estrangula [(3)Tp.131]. See IHĪYŌ-TL, MIQU(I).

IHĪYŌMIQUĪTIĀ altern. caus. IHĪYŌMIQU(I)

IHĪYŌPEXŌNTIĀ *vt* to inflate something / lo infla (Z) [(2)Zp.71,189]. See IHĪYŌ-TL, PEXŌNTIĀ.

IHĪYŌQUĪZ(A) to evaporate, to breath, and by extension, to give an order / vaporiza, sale de aire (T), vahear ... mandar alguna cosa (M) [(1)Tp.131]. See IHĪYŌ-TL, QUĪZ(A).

IHĪYŌTĒM(A) *vrefl,vt; pret:* **-TĒN** to inflate, to fill up with air; to inflate something / infla, se llena de aire (T), henchir algo con viento (M) [(4)Tp.142,188]. See IHĪYŌ-TL, TĒM(A).

IHĪYŌTIĀ *vrefl* to inhale or exhale loudly, to break wind; to do something breathtaking / refollarse o peerse o tomar aliento, o resplandecer y lucir con ricas vestiduras (M) This is abundantly attested across sources. T fails to mark the vowel of the first syllable short. See IHĪYŌ-TL.

IHĪYŌTĪLŌ nonact. IHĪYŌTIĀ

IHĪYŌ-TL breath, respiration, hence one's life, sustenance / aliento huelgo, o soplo (M) In T and Z the second vowel has been absorbed into the following Y, reducing the stem by a syllable to (I)HYŌ. This is a reduplicated form that implies an unattested *ĪYŌ-TL or an unattested verb *IHĪ 'to breath' ultimately from Ī 'to take a breath,' but Ī exists as a verb in Nahuatl with the sense 'to drink.' IHĪYŌ-TL appears to be related to EHĒCA-TL 'wind,' which in some dialects of Nahuatl even has A in the first two syllables. The long vowel of the second syllable of IHĪYŌ-TL is abundantly attested in C.

IHĪYŌTZACU(A) *vrefl,vt* to choke, suffocate; to choke, strangle someone / enmudecer o atravesársele el bocado (M), atapar el huelgo a otro (M) [(3)Tp.142, (1)Rp.89]. T gives the preterit of this as -TZACUAC, but M drops the final vowel.

M also has *ihiomotzaqua* 'to suffer from
asthma.' Z has an intransitive form based
on IHĪYŌTZACU(I) meaning 'to close.' See
IHĪYŌ-TL, TZACU(A).

IHĪYŌTZACUALŌ nonact. IHĪYŌ-
TZACU(A)

IHIZTĀC redup. IZTĀC

IHMATCĀCHĪHU(A) *vt* to make, do
something carefully / hago con cordura (C
for first pers. sg. subject) [(2)Cf.77v,
(1)Rp.91]. One of the two attestations in
C is unclear; apparently TC has been
reversed. See IHMAT(I), CHĪHU(A).

IHMATCĀNEM(I) *vrefl; pret:* **-NEN** to live
circumspectly / vivir recatadamente y
sobre aviso (M), vive con cordura (C)
[(1)Cf.99r]. See IHMAT(I), NEM(I).

IHMAT(I) *vrefl,vt; pret:* **IHMAH**, *pret. pl:*
IHMATQUEH to be careful in what one
does; to know how to do something well,
to be deft, expert in something / ser prudente y avisado, o ir convaleciendo el
enfermo (M), proveer o disponer lo que se
ha de hacer (M), travesear ... hacer algo de
habilidad (C) The form TLAHMAT(I) 'to
know how to do something well, etc.' has
absorbed the nonspecific object prefix
TLA- and essentially become an intransitive verb 'to be expert.' Although the
initial I is lost in TLAHMAT(I), it is retained in the presence of reflexive prefixes.
See MAT(I).

(I)HNECU(I) *vt* to smell something / oler
algo (M)

(I)HNECUĪHUA nonact. (I)HNECU(I)

(I)HNECUILTIĀ caus. (I)HNECU(I)

(I)HNECUĪTIĀ altern. caus. (I)HNECU(I)

(I)HNECUIZTI to smell, stink / huele (T)
[(1)Tp.130]. See (I)HNECU(I).

*(I)HPIY(A) See TLAHPIY(A).

IHPOTOCA to vaporize, to turn to
steam / vaporiza (Z) [(2)Zp.127,158]. See
IHPOTOC-TLI.

IHPOTOCALIZ-TLI vapor, steam / vapor (Z)
[(2)Zp.127,158]. Z marks the vowel of the
fourth syllable long, but it should not be.
See IHPOTOCA.

IHPOTOC-TLI vapor, steam, exhalation,
breath / vaho (M), humo, vapor, exhalación
(S) [(6)Zp.127,158].

IHPOTOQUĪLCA-TL vapor, steam / vapor
(Z) [(2)Zp.127,158]. Z marks the vowel of
the last syllable long, but it should not be.
See IHPOTOCA.

IHPŌTZ(A) *vrefl* to belch / regoldar (M),
eructa (Z) [(3)Tp.141, (2)Zp.54,170]. T has E
for I. X has ILPŌTZ(A). See PŌTZ(A).

IHPŌTZALŌ nonact. IHPŌTZ(A)

IHQUILTIĀ altern. caus. IHCA

(I)HQUITI to weave cloth / tejer tela
(M) [(7)Zp.120,150,188,208]. See
TLAHQUITĪL-LI.

IHTAC(A)-TL provisions / provisión, mochila, o despensa de camino o matalotaje
(M), comestibles, comida, lonche, taco,
itacate (T)

IHTALHUIĀ *vt* to say something about
someone / decir algo de alguno (C) In
TLAHTALHUIĀ 'to speak for someone,
etc.,' the prefix TLA- has been absorbed
into the stem with the loss of initial I, but
in B and C it is not lost when preceded by
reflexive prefixes. It is lost, however,
in T, where initial I deletion is more
widespread. applic. (I)HTOĀ

-IHTEC *postposition* within, inside / dentro
de algo (M for -IHTIC) A common variant
is -IHTIC. The I may drop or be retained
after possessive prefixes, NOHTIC ~
NIHTIC 'inside me.' See IHTE-TL, -C(O).

-IHTECCOPA *compound postposition* to
within / en sí mismo, dentro de uno (T)
[(3)Tp.130]. N intervenes between this and
-TZINCO in an attestation in T, but the
final element here should definitely be
-PA, not -PAN. See -IHTEC, -C(O), -PA.

IHTECHŌCA for one's stomach to growl /
gruñe el estómago (T) [(3)Tp.130]. See
IHTE-TL, CHŌCA.

IHTECHŌCOHUA nonact. IHTECHŌCA

IHTECHŌQUĪTIĀ caus. IHTECHŌCA

IHTECOYOCTIC something hollow /
hueco, no tiene nada (T) [(1)Tp.130]. T
has YA for YO. T also has a variant
IHTECOYOCTICAH. See IHTE-TL,
COYOC-TLI.

-IHTECPA *compound postposition* out of or
into one's belly / de su vientre (C for
-IHTICPA) [(1)Cf.21v]. See -IHTEC, -PA.

IHTEH possessor of a belly / obeso,

ventrudo, ventruda, que tiene vientre (S)
[(1)Cf.55v, (1)Rp.45]. See IHTE-TL.
IHTEMĒTZOCUIL-IN tapeworm /
lombriz (T) [(1)Tp.130]. See IHTE-TL,
MĒTZOCUIL-IN.
-IHTEPĀCHYŌ *only attested in possessed
form* pith, soft interior of something /
migaja, la parte interior de bolillo, de la
caña de la milpa, etc. (T) [(2)Tp.130]. See
IHTE-TL.
IHTETEHTEQU(I) See IHTE-TL,
TEHTEQU(I).
IHTE-TL belly / barriga o vientre (M) A
common variant of this is IHTI-TL.
IHTETLAPĀN(A) See IHTE-TL,
TLAPĀN(A).
IHTETZACQUI something hard at the
center / sólido o duro por dentro (T for
possessed form) [(1)Tp.130]. See IHTE-TL,
TZACU(A).
IHTETZACTIC something hard at the
center / sólido o duro por dentro (T)
[(1)Tp.130]. See IHTE-TL, TZACU(A).
IHTEXAHUACA for one's stomach to
rumble / corre el gruñimiento de un lado al
otro, gruñe la barriga (T) [(3)Tp.131]. See
IHTE-TL, XAXAHUACA.
IHTEXAHUACOHUA nonact. IHTE-
XAHUACA
IHTEXAHUAQUĪTIĀ caus. IHTE-
XAHUACA
IHTEXOCO See IHTEXOCOTIC.
IHTEXOCOTIC someone with a big belly /
barrigón, panzón (T for possessed form)
[(1)Tp.131]. The second element of this is a
reduction of XOCOTETIC 'something
round in form.' T has the further reduction
IHTEXOCO with the same sense. See
IHTE-TL, XOCOTETIC.
-IHTEYŌ *necessarily possessed form*
entrails / entrañas (Z for -IHTIYŌ)
[(2)Zp.53,159]. Z regularly has IHTI for
IHTE. This is the inalienably possessed
form of IHTE-TL. See IHTE-TL, -YŌ.
IHTEZŌNĒHU(I) for one's belly to swell up
/ se avienta la barriga (T) [(4)Tp.130]. See
IHTE-TL, ZŌNĒHU(I).
IHTEZŌNĒHUĪHUA nonact. IHTE-
ZŌNĒHU(I)
IHTEZŌNĒHUILIZ-TLI a swollen belly / su

barriga aventada (T for possessed form)
[(1)Tp.130]. See IHTEZŌNĒHU(I).
IHTEZŌNĒHUĪTIĀ caus. IHTEZŌNĒHU(I)
-IHTIC This is a common variant of -IHTEC
'inside.' See IHTE-TL.
-IHTICPA See -IHTECPA.
IHTI-TL See IHTE-TL.
-IHTIYŌ See -IHTEYŌ.
(I)HTLACAHU(I) to go wrong, to be ruined
or corrupted, to injure oneself, to spoil /
corromperse, dañarse, o estragarse algo ... o
empollarse el huevo (M) This has the same
sense as (I)HTLACOĀ used reflexively.
(I)HTLACALHUIĀ to ruin something for
someone / dañar algo a otro (M) applic.
(I)HTLACOĀ
(I)HTLACALHUILIĀ applic. (I)HTLA-
CALHUIĀ
(I)HTLACALHUĪLŌ nonact. (I)HTLA-
CALHUIĀ
(I)HTLACOĀ *vrefl,vt* to be corrupted,
spoiled, damaged; to spoil, damage
something / se empeora (la cosa), se
envicia (T), enfermar por se dar mucho
a mujeres (M), estragar o dañar algo (M)
In Z the I does not drop after the reflexive
prefixes.
(I)HTLACŌLŌ nonact. (I)HTLACOĀ
IHTLAN(I) *vt* to ask, request, beg some-
thing / pedir algo (M) Attestations are very
mixed about loss of the initial vowel before
prefixal vowels.
IHTLANIĀ *vrefl,vt* to beg, to ask for alms;
to question, examine someone / mendigar,
pedir limosna (S), le pregunta, le pide (T)
See IHTLAN(I).
IHTLANĪHUA nonact. IHTLAN(I)
IHTLANILIĀ *vt* to make a request on some-
one's behalf / le pide para otra persona (T)
[(3)Tp.187]. applic. IHTLANIĀ
IHTLANILILIĀ applic. IHTLANILIĀ
IHTLANILĪLŌ nonact. IHTLANILIĀ
IHTLANĪLŌ nonact. IHTLANIĀ
IHTLAPOĀ See TLAIHTLAPOĀ.
(I)HTOĀ *vrefl,vt* to speak up, to volunteer;
to say something, to speak well or ill of
someone / comedirse u ofrecerse a hacer
alguna cosa (M), decir alguna cosa (M),
decir bien o mal de otro (M)
(I)HTŌLŌ nonact. (I)HTOĀ

(I)HTŌLTIĀ caus. (I)HTOĀ

(I)HTOPŌLOĀ *vt* to say something,
to criticize something / decir algo (K)
[(1)Cf.70r]. When -PŌLOĀ is added to a
verb, it contributes a sense of deprecation
or reproach, as in this attestation where
the object of (I)HTOĀ is the speaker's sins.
See (I)HTOĀ, -PŌLOĀ.

IHTŌTIĀ *vrefl,vt* to dance; to get someone
to dance / bailar o danzar (M), hacer bailar
a otro (M)

IHTŌTILIĀ *vt* to dance for someone / se lo
baila (T) [(4)Tp.187]. applic. IHTŌTIĀ

IHTŌTILILIĀ applic. IHTŌTILIĀ

IHTŌTILĪLŌ nonact. IHTŌTILIĀ

IHTŌTILIZ-TLI a dance / baile (X)
[(1)Xp.58]. X lacks the glottal stop. See
IHTŌTIĀ.

IHTŌTĪLŌ nonact. IHTŌTIĀ

(I)HTZOM(A) *vrefl,vt; pret:* **-TZON** for
something to get sewn; to sew something / coser (C), se cose (T), lo cose (T)
The nonspecific object prefix TLA- has
been absorbed to form intransitive
TLAHTZOM(A) 'to sew.'

(I)HTZOMALŌ nonact. (I)HTZOM(A)

IHTZŌMIĀ *vrefl* to blow one's nose / so-
narse las narices (M) [(2)Cf.71v]. This stem
also appears with fused TLA-, meaning
'to snort,' which is then reduplicated to
form frequentative TLAHTLAHTZŌMIĀ
'to snort repeatedly.' T has the variant
(I)LTZŌMIĀ. There is inconsistency about
the strength of the initial I. It is retained in
the presence of the reflexive prefix in
M and C but not in T. With TLA- it is
dropped in M and C as well. M also has a
derived form with NE- in which the I is
dropped.

(I)HTZOMILIĀ applic. (I)HTZOM(A)

ĪHUA nonact. Ī

IHUĀ *vt; pret:* **IHUAH** to send someone,
something / enviar a otro a alguna parte o
dar de mano el preso (M), enviar mensajero
(M) The long vowel of the second syllable
is evident in the applicative form, which is
abundantly attested in B. C, R, and M agree
on the preterit form above, but S also gives
IUH and IHUAC (with vowel length in-
determinate) as alternate preterits.

IHUĀLIĀ applic. IHUĀ

ĪHUĀN in the company of something or
someone else, and / y, y también (M) The
third person singular possessed form of the
postposition -HUĀN has virtually the
function of a conjunction. In T and Z it has
lost the possessive prefix Ī- and has been
lexicalized as HUĀN 'and.' In T the final
N is also lost by general rule. See -HUĀN.

IHU(I) *singular present and preterit only,
plus derivations* to be or become a certain
way; thus, such, so / de ésta manera o así
(M) Although this is transparently verbal
with its present and regular preterit forms
and the derived agentive IUHQUI 'someone, something of a particular nature,' it
has been lexicalized in an essentially
adverbial role of 'thus, such, so.' The
optative phrase MĀ ZO IHUI 'let it be
so' has been lexicalized as MĀCIHUI
'though, however.' Other particle compositions with IHU(I) are HUEL IHUI 'greatly,
grandly, vigorously,' ZAN YE NŌ IHUI 'in
like manner,' IHUI ĪN 'in this way,' IHUI
ŌN 'in that way.' The preterit form IUH is
often misleadingly spelled *yuh.*

IHUĪHUIH with great difficulty / con mucha dificultad, a mucha costa (C) This is
related to OHUIH 'with difficulty, danger'
in some not entirely direct way. The first
element is probably IHU(I) 'thus, such, so.'

IHUĪHUIHCĀYŌTICA at great cost, with
great difficulty / mucho me ha costado (C),
con sentimiento, con pena, dificultad (S)
[(2)Cf.121v]. See IHUĪHUIHCĀYŌ-TL,
-CA.

IHUĪHUIHCĀYŌ-TL difficulty, cost / pena,
dificultad, sentimiento, impotencia (S)
[(2)Cf.121v]. See IHUĪHUIH.

IHUINTI to get drunk / se emborracha, se
ataranta, se embriaga (T), estar ébrio,
embriagarse (S) [(3)Tp.127]. Intransitive
IHUINTI has the same sense as IHUINTIĀ
used reflexively.

IHUINTIĀ *vrefl,vt* to get drunk; to get
someone drunk / emborracharse (M),
emborrachar a otro (M) T and Z have lost
the initial vowel. There is a related form
ĪXHUINTIĀ 'to make someone dizzy,'
which even in C has lost the initial I of the

stem, being compounded with ĪX-TLI
'face.' See IHUINTI.
IHUINTĪHUA nonact. IHUINTI
IHUINTILIĀ applic. IHUINTIĀ
IHUINTĪLŌ nonact. IHUINTIĀ
IHUINTILTIĀ T has a long vowel before
-LTIĀ where a short one is to be expected.
caus. IHUINTI
IHUINTITICAH to be drunk / está borracho
(T) [(1)Tp.111]. See IHUINTI, the verb CĀ.
IHUINTITOC someone drunken / borracho
(Z) [(2)Zp.20,156]. See IHUINTI, the verb O.
ĪHUĪPTLAYŌC See -HUĪPTLAYŌC.
ĪHUIYĀN calmly, peacefully, moderately, a
little at a time / mansamente o con tiento
(M), pacíficamente (C), poco a poco (C)
IHXĀMIĀ vrefl,vt to wash one's face; to
wash someone's face / lavarse la cara (M),
lavar a otro la cara (M) [(1)Cf.103v]. See
XĀMIĀ.
(I)HXĪCA for something to leak, ooze,
trickle / rezumarse o salirse la vasija (M)
[(2)Cf.75r, (4)Tp.136,248, (2)Zp.55,159]. In
the Z attestations the vowel of the second
syllable is marked long, while in C it is
unmarked for length. T has ĪXĪCA.
IHXĪTIĀ caus. IHZA. C has a short vowel in
the second syllable.
(I)HXĪTZA vt to distill, separate something /
destilar, esparcir una cosa (S) [(1)Cf.75v]. C
does not mark the vowel of the second
syllable long. See (I)HXĪCA.
(I)HXOHUA nonact. IHZA
IHYĀC something foul, stinking / cosa
hedionda (M) See (I)HYĀYA.
-IHYĀCA necessarily possessed form the
stench of something / hediondez (C)
[(2)Cf.49v]. This contrasts with the element ĪYACA- to be found in some compounds and having to do with noses or
points, as in M's iyacamecayo '(horse's)
bridle.' The latter is formed from
YAC(A)-TL 'nose' with the possessive
prefix Ī-. See (I)HYĀYA.
IHYĀCXIHU(I)-TL night jasmine (Cestrum
nocturnum) / huele de noche (árbol) (T)
[(2)Tp.131,248]. See IHYĀC, XIHU(I)-TL.
(I)HYĀLILIĀ vt to let something turn foul,
rotten / lo hace que apeste (la carne, etc.,
por no atenderla luego) (T) [(3)Tp.188]. See
(I)HYĀYA.

(I)HYĀLILILIĀ applic. (I)HYĀLILIĀ
(I)HYĀLILĪLŌ nonact. (I)HYĀLILIĀ
(I)HYĀN(A) vrefl,vt to hide, conceal oneself; to hide, conceal, deny something /
se esconde, se oculta (T), lo esconde, lo
niega, lo oculta (T), esconder algo (M)
[(7)Tp.150,188].
(I)HYĀNALŌ nonact. (I)HYĀN(A)
(I)HYĀNILIĀ applic. (I)HYĀN(A)
(I)HYĀYA to stink / heder o tener
mal olor (M) [(3)Tp.131,230,244
(7)Zp.12,34,54,66,227]. This drops the
initial I after the reflexive prefixes but
retains it after the nonspecific object prefix
TLA-.
(I)HYEHUILIĀ vt to peel something / lo
descascara, levanta la cáscara (de árbol,
yerba, etc.) (T) [(3)Tp.188]. Since T charac-
teristically has YE for YA, this may be
related to M's iyauilia 'to raise something
up in sacrifice.'
(I)HYEHUILILIĀ applic. (I)HYEHUILIĀ
(I)HYEHUILĪLŌ nonact. (I)HYEHUILIĀ
(I)HYŌHUIĀ See IHĪYŌHUIĀ.
(I)HYŌHUĪLŌ See IHĪYŌHUĪLŌ.
(I)HYŌHUILTIĀ See IHĪYŌHUILTIĀ.
(I)HYŌMICTIĀ See IHĪYŌMICTIĀ.
(I)HYŌTZACU(I) See IHĪYŌTZACU(A).
IHZA to wake up / despertar (M)
IHZAC someone awake / despierto (Z)
[(2)Zp.44,158]. See IHZA.
IHZACTOC someone awake / despierto (Z)
[(2)Zp.44,158]. See IHZA, the verb O.
IHZALIZ-TLI wakefulness / despierto (Z)
[(2)Zp.144,158]. See IHZA.
(I)HZANACA to make a rustling noise like
dry leaves / hacer ruido las hojas secas, etc.
(C) [(1)Cf.75v, (1)Tp.133]. M has this as a
substantive, something that makes such a
noise. T has lost the glottal stop.
(I)HZANATZ(A) vt to cause something to
make a rustling noise / hace ... ruido
con hojas secas, pliegos de papel, etc. (C)
[(1)Cf.75v].
IHZOLIHU(I) for things to get old, wear out
/ envejecerse la ropa, los libros, las esteras,
o cosas semejantes (M) This is implied by
IHZOLOĀ.
IHZOLOĀ vrefl,vt to abase oneself; to
mistreat, wear out things like clothes,
books, mats, etc. / deshonrarse (M), maltra-

tar o envejecer las cosas dichas (la ropa, los libros, las esteras, o cosas semejantes) (M) [(2)Bf.7v,13v]. This implies intransitive IHZOLIHU(I) 'for things to get old, wear out.' There is a derived form TLAHZOL-LI in which the initial I drops after the prefix TLA-, but M has strong, undeleting I for the verb. See -ZOL-LI.

IHZŌTLA *vrefl* to vomit / vomitar (M) [(4)Tp.141, (2)Zp.130,170, (3)Xp.57]. T has E for IH.

ĪICHTEQU(I) redup. (I)CHTEQU(I)

ĪIHTECCAH to be within something / está adentro (T) [(1)Tp.130]. This is a fusion of the preterit-as-present verb CĀ with the postposition -IHTEC prefixed with the third person singular possessive prefix. T treats the sequence CC as though no morpheme boundary intervenes and probably shifts stress accordingly as in CUALLICAH 'for something to be good.' T also has ĪIHTICCAH 'for something to be done correctly; to be empty, to be without work,' apparently with the same derivational history. See -IHTEC, the verb CĀ.

ĪIHTICCAH See ĪIHTECCAH.

ILACATZIHU(I) to twist, entwine / torcerse alguna cosa así, como la punta de alesna o cosa semejante (M), torcerse (C) [(2)Cf.76r,76v, (1)Tp.131].

ILACATZILHUIĀ applic. ILACATZOĀ

ILACATZOĀ *vrefl,vt* to turn one's back on someone, to wrap oneself around something; to roll up blankets, mats, paper, thread, etc. / volver el cuerpo por no ver ni mirar al que aborrece, o ceñir la culebra al árbol (M), arrollar manta, estera, papel o cosa así, o coger y revolver hilo o cordel al dedo, etc. (M) See ILACATZIHU(I).

ILACATZŌLŌ nonact. ILACATZOĀ

ILACATZTIC something twisted, wound / cosa torcida o tuerta (M) [(1)Tp.131, (3)Zp.20,39,163]. See ILACATZOĀ.

ILAMA-TL *pl:* **ILAMATQUEH;** *possessed form* **-ILAMATCĀUH** old woman / vieja (M) M gives this with an absolutive suffix and in its more common form without the suffix. A T appears in the plural and possessed forms, but there is no attestation of a corresponding stem-final glottal stop in the singular as in HUĒHUEH 'old man.'

The shape of the absolutive suffix in M's entry requires that the stem end in a vowel. From the plural and possessed forms, ILAMA seems to be a truncation of *ILAMATQUI. T and Z have lost the initial vowel.

ILAMATZAPO-TL *pl:* **-MEH** custard-apple (Anona glabra) / anona, chicozapote (X) [(3)Xp.50]. See ILAMA-TL, TZAPO-TL.

(I)LCĀHU(A) *vt* to forget something / olvidarse de alguna cosa (M) A common variant has E for I. See (I)LCĀHU(I).

(I)LCĀHUALŌ nonact. (I)LCĀHU(A)

(I)LCĀHU(I) to be forgotten / se olvida (T) [(1)Tp.131]. See (I)LCĀHU(A).

(I)LCĀHUILIĀ applic. (I)LCĀHU(A)

(I)LCHĪN(A) *vt* to suck something up, to consume something / lo chupa, lo consuma (T) [(3)Tp.188]. M has *chichina* 'to suck something.'

(I)LCHĪNALŌ nonact. (I)LCHĪN(A)

(I)LCHĪNILIĀ applic. (I)LCHĪN(A)

(I)LHUIĀ *vrefl* to grow in strength, violence (as with a storm or epidemic) / arreciar (C) [(3)Cf.79r].

(I)LHUIĀ *vrefl,vt* to take counsel with oneself, to make a complaint; to say something to someone, to reveal something to someone / quejarse a la justicia (M), consultar algo consigo mismo (M), decir algo a otro o descubrir el secreto (M) Because this is an inherently applicative verb, it takes both a direct and an indirect object prefix. NITĒTLALHUIĀ 'I say something to someone,' NINOTLALHUIĀ 'I consult myself about something.'

ILHUICAC in heaven / en el cielo (S) See ILHUICA-TL, -C(O).

ILHUICACAYŌ-TL something pertaining to heaven, celestial / cosa celestial (M) [(2)Cf.53r,53v]. M gives the alternatives *ilhuicacayotl* and *ilhuicaccayotl* with identical sense. See ILHUICA-TL, -YŌ.

ILHUICACCOPAHUĪC heavenwards / hacia el cielo (C) [(1)Cf.20r]. This is synonymous with ILHUICACOPAHUĪC. It is apparently built on ILHUICAC rather than ILHUICA.

ILHUICACHĀNEH someone who resides in heaven / morador del cielo (M) [(1)Rp.90]. See ILHUICA-TL, CHĀNEH.

ILHUICACOPAHUĬC heavenwards / hacia
el cielo [(1)Cf.93v]. See ILHUICA-TL,
-COPA, -HUĬC.
ILHUICACPAHUĬC heavenwards / hacia el
cielo (C) [(1)Cf.20r]. See ILHUICAC, -PA,
-HUĬC.
ILHUICAHUAH lord of heaven / señor
del cielo (C), Diós (C) [(5)Cf.7r,55r,112r,
(1)Rp.45]. See ILHUICA-TL.
ILHUICA-TL heaven, sky / cielo (M)
ILHUICAYŌ-TL something of or pertaining
to heaven / cosa celestial (M for *ilhuicacayotl*), cosas de cielo (R) [(1)Rp.44]. See
ILHUICA-TL, -YŌ.
ILHUICEH much more, especially / mucho
más (M), especialmente o mucho más (C)
[(4)Cf.113v,114r,131v, (2)Rp.90,99]. See
ILHUIZ.
(I)LHUILIĀ applic. (I)LHUIĀ
(I)LHUIL-LI merit, due reward / merecimiento (C) [(3)Cf.59r].
(I)LHUĪLŌ C specifically states that the
vowel of the second syllable is short
through the influence of the preceding two
consonants, but this is probably due to
some superficial neutralization of length
distinctions. In T there is the reflex of
a long vowel in this position. nonact.
(I)LHUIĀ
(I)LHUILTI *irregular verb* to be deserving of
something, to be worthy / merecedor de
algo (M) This verb is always in the singular
and takes the possessive prefixes instead of
the subject prefixes, NOLHUILTI 'I am
worthy,' but its tense inflection is regular.
See (I)LHUIL-LI.
ILHUIPAN at the fiesta, celebration / en la
fiesta (T) [(1)Tp.131]. See ILHUI-TL, -PAN.
ILHUI-TL day, festival day, holiday / fiesta
de guardar, o cualquier día de la semana
(M) In some derived forms this loses the
initial vowel.
-ILHUIYŌC *preceded by possessive prefix
and quantifier* (a certain number of) days
after / días después (C) An example with a
number is ĪCHICŌMILHUIYŌC 'seven
days after that'; one with a nonnumeral
quantifier is ĪQUĒZQUILHUIYŌC 'several
days after that.' With a month or year, the
expression means on the designated day of
that unit of time. See ILHUI-TL, -YŌ,
-C(O).

ILHUIZ much more, especially / especialmente o mucho más (C)
ĪLIHUIZ inconsiderately / sin consideración
y desvariadamente (M), fuerte, fuertemente
(Z) C marks the initial vowel long in only
two of fourteen attestations; in the others
it is unmarked for length. Z has E for I in
the initial syllable and does not mark it
long but consistently marks the vowel of
the final syllable long. This is synonymous
with TLALHUIZ, and often forms the
phrase ZAN ĪLIHUIZ with the same sense.
This may be related to an intensifier in
T, the canonical form for which would
probably be LALEHUIZ.
ĪLIHUIZCIHUĀ-TL good-for-nothing
woman / mujer de no nada (C) [(1)Cf.77r].
See ĪLIHUIZ, CIHUĀ-TL.
ĪLIHUIZHUIĀ *vt* to do something inconsiderately / hago algo inconsi-
deradamente (C for first person subject)
[(1)Cf.60v, (1)Rp.48]. See ĪLIHUIZ, -HUIĀ.
ĪLIHUIZTLAHTOĀ to speak carelessly,
unguardedly / hablar cosas sin tiento ni
consideración (M) [(1)Cf.77r, (1)Rp.90]. See
ĪLIHUIZ, (I)HTOĀ.
ĪLIHUIZTLAHTŌL-LI careless speech /
palabras inconsideradas (R) [(1)Rp.90]. See
ĪLIHUIZTLAHTOĀ.
ĪLIHUIZTZAHTZI to cause a scandal / le
escandaliza (Z) [(1)Zp.159]. See ĪLIHUIZ,
TZAHTZI.
ĪLĪ-TL alder tree / aliso (M) [(2)Zp.9,159].
(I)LNĀMICTIĀ *vt* to remind someone of
something / traer a la memoria, o acordar
algo a otro (M) [(3)Tp.208]. altern. caus.
(I)LNĀMIQU(I)
(I)LNĀMICTILIĀ applic. (I)LNĀMICTIĀ
(I)LNĀMICTĪLŌ nonact. (I)LNĀMICTIĀ
(I)LNĀMICTINEM(I) *vt; pret:* **-NEN** to go
along recalling, thinking on something / ve
... pensando (C for imperative) [(1)Cf.68r].
See (I)LNĀMIQU(I), NEM(I).
(I)LNĀMIQU(I) *vrefl,vt; pret:* **(I)LNĀMIC** for
memory to return, sharpen; to remember,
reflect on something / se refrescará la
memoria de esto (C for future tense),
acordarse de una cosa, imaginar, pensar,
reflexionar, considerar (S) A common
variant has EL for (I)L.
(I)LNĀMIQUĪHUA nonact. (I)LNĀMIQU(I)
(I)LNĀMIQUILIĀ applic. (I)LNĀMIQU(I)

(I)LNĀMIQUĪTIĀ altern. caus. (I)LNĀ-
MIQU(I)

ĪLŌCHTIĀ *vt* to turn something, someone back, to set back a clock, to revoke a
sentence, to sell something at a loss /
tornar a otro, desde donde le había ido a
acompañar (M), achicar o acortar algo (M),
tornar atrás el reloj, o tornar a enviar algo
al que me le envío, o mudar o revocar la
sentencia que se había dado, o vender algo
por menos de lo que vale (M) [(1)Bf.6v,
(2)Cf.61v, (1)Rp.33]. See ĪLŌT(I).

ĪLŌT(I) to return whence one came; for an
illness to abate / volverse o tornarse de
donde iba (M), aflojarse la enfermedad (M)
[(1)Bf.7r, (2)Cf.61v,102v, (1)Rp.33].

(I)LPIĀ *vrefl,vt* to gird oneself; to tie something or someone up, to take someone into
custody / ceñirse (M), atar alguna cosa (M),
atar a alguno o prenderlo y encarcelarlo (M)

(I)LPĪCHIĀ *vt* to inflate something with
water / lo resopla con agua (T) [(3)Tp.117].
See (I)LPĪTZ(A).

(I)LPĪCHILIĀ applic. (I)LPĪCHIĀ, applic.
(I)LPĪTZ(A)

(I)LPĪCHĪLŌ nonact. (I)LPĪCHIĀ

ILPIHTICAH to be bound / está amarrado,
está atado (T) [(1)Tp.131]. T is missing the
internal glottal stop. See (I)LPIĀ, the verb
CĀ.

ILPIHTIHU(I) to go in bonds / va amarrado
(T) [(1)Tp.131]. T shortens this to ILPIHTI
and is missing the glottal stop. See (I)LPIĀ,
HU(I).

(I)LPILIĀ applic. (I)LPIĀ

ILPILIZ-TLI the act of tying something,
someone up / acción de amarrar (Z)
[(2)Zp.159,207]. See (I)LPIĀ.

(I)LPĪLŌ nonact. (I)LPIĀ

ILPITOC someone, something bound / amarrado, atado, nudo (Z) [(4)Zp.10,16,89,159].
See (I)LPIĀ, the verb O.

(I)LPĪTZ(A) *vt* to blow something up, to
inflate something / soplar (M), soplar a otro
(M), lo sopla (T) See PĪTZ(A).

(I)LPĪTZALŌ nonact. (I)LPĪTZ(A)

ILPŌTZ(A) *vrefl* to belch / eructar (X)
[(3)Xp.57]. T and Z have synonymous
IHPŌTZ(A). See PŌTZ(A).

(I)LTEQU(I) *vt* to sip, suck, drink something
/ sorber algo (M), lo bebe (caldo, huevo,
etc.) (T) [(1)Bf.11v, (3)Tp.188].

(I)LTEQUĪHUA nonact. (I)LTEQU(I)

(I)LTEQUĪTIĀ caus. (I)LTEQU(I)

ĪLTIĀ caus. Ī

ĪLTILIĀ applic. ĪLTIĀ

ĪLTILĪLŌ nonact. ĪLTILIĀ

(I)LTZŌMIĀ *vrefl* to blow one's nose / se
suena (la naríz) (T) [(3)Tp.150]. See
IHTZŌMIĀ.

(I)LTZŌMĪLŌ nonact. (I)LTZŌMIĀ

ĪMACAC(I) *vt; pret:* **ĪMACAZ** to hold
someone in awe, to fear someone, to be
respectful toward someone / temer a
alguno (M), tener respeto o temor rever-
encial (M)

ĪMACAXILIĀ applic. ĪMACAC(I)

ĪMACAXILTIĀ caus. ĪMACAC(I)

ĪMACAXŌ nonact. ĪMACAC(I)

ĪMACAX-TLI someone worthy of being held
in awe, someone of authority and dignity /
digno de ser temido, o persona grave y de
autoridad (M) See ĪMACAC(I).

IMMAN to be high time for something /
es hora y tiempo This is also written
INMAN, reflecting its origin of IN
MAN(I). M also has *immani*, which
may represent IMMANĪN rather than
IMMAN(I). This generally occurs with YE
'already.' See IMMANĪN.

IMMĀNEL however, given that, inasmuch,
since / aunque, desde que, o puesto que
(M) This is a fusion of MĀNEL with the
particle IN and is synonymous with
MĀNEL. This also combines with the
cliticizing element -(Y)EH with no change
of sense.

IMMĀNELEH See IMMĀNEL.

IMMĀNELYEH See IMMĀNEL.

IMMANI See IMMAN.

IMMANĪN at this time / a esta hora (C) See
IMMAN, ĪN.

IMMANTI for the right moment to be at
hand / ser ya hora y tiempo oportuno para
hacer algo, o venir y cumplirse el tiempo
y hora que se esperaba (M) [(3)Cf.59r,
(1)Rp.47]. See IMMAN.

IMMANYEH at this time / a estas horas (T)
[(1) Tp.131]. T has multiple ambiguity
involving Ē, YE, and IYE. Possibly this
should be from IMMANĪNYEH with T's
characteristic loss of syllable-final N. See
IMMAN.

ĪMONEQUIYĀN at the right time / en

tiempo y sazón, o en buen tiempo y coyuntura (M) [(2)Cf.42v]. This is prefixed with the third person singular possessive prefix Ī-. See MONECYĀN.

ĪMŌZTLAYŌC the following day, the next day / el día siguiente (C), un día antes que (C) This is prefixed with the third person singular possessive prefix Ī-. When preceded by OC, it means the day before. See MŌZTLA, -YŌ, -C(O).

ĪN proximal particle this, these / ésto (C) This is often postposed after the element it refers to and becomes bound to it as a suffix, YEHHUĀTLĪN 'this one, this person,' INĪN 'this,' IMMANĪN 'at this very time.' It contrasts with the distal particle ŌN 'that, those.' The phrase IN IHQUEH ĪN is used for the plural.

IN This particle is pervasive in Nahuatl and appears yet more so in texts in which IN and ĪN are not distinguished. Moreover, it tends to lose N, which leads to confusion with possessive Ī-. Alternatively, in high-frequency items it may lose I, with the N then being reanalyzed as part of the following item, as in NICI< IN ICI and NAN- 'we'< IN AN-. IN is generally translated as 'the' or left untranslated, especially when in construction with a whole phrase. While it has no lexical sense of its own (unlike the proximal particle ĪN 'this'), its grammatical sense can be conveyed with the English phrases 'as for' or 'with reference to.' IN tends to fuse with time adverbials and other particles, sometimes yielding lexicalized forms of slightly different sense; ICI 'here,' INICI 'recently.'

ĪNĀNTZĪCA-TL pl: -MEH coral snake / coralillo (X) [(2)Xp.46]. According to popular belief, this snake resides in ant hills and protects the ants. See NĀN-TLI, TZĪCA-TL.

ĪNĀY(A) vrefl, vt; pret: ĪNĀX to hide or take refuge somewhere; to hide something / esconderse o guarecerse en algún lugar (M), encubrir o esconder algo (M)

ĪNĀYILIĀ vt to hide something from someone / esconder y encubrir algo a otro (C) [(1)Cf.64r]. applic. ĪNĀY(A)

ĪNĀYILILIĀ applic. ĪNĀYILIĀ

INĪC with, by means of, so that / con qué o para qué (M) See IN, ĪC.

INICI recently / tiempo recién pasado (C) [(5)Cf.95v,96r]. See ICI. The initial vowel can drop, yielding NICI, which C accepts as an alternate form. See IN, ICI.

INIHCUĀC then / entonces (M) See IN, IHCUĀC.

INIHQUEH these, those / éstos o éstas [(6)Cf.15v,16r,16v, (1)Rp.92]. When followed by ĪN, this means 'these' and when followed by ŌN, 'those'; such phrases are equivalent to the plurals of INĪN 'this one' and INŌN 'that one.' See IN, IĀ.

INĪN this one / éste, ésta, ésto (M) See IN, ĪN.

INIUH like, in such a fashion / así como (M), de la manera que (C) According to C's examples, this is used with verbal constructions, while INIUHQUI is used with substantives. See IN, IHU(I).

INIUHQUI like, in such a fashion / así, como (M), de la manera que (C) According to C's examples, this is used with substantives, while INIUH is used with verbal constructions. See IN, IUHQUI.

INMAN See IMMAN.

INMĀNEL See IMMĀNEL.

INOC while / mientras que, o en tanto que (M) [(2)Cf.98v,131r, (1)Rp.83]. See IN, OC.

INŌN that one / ésta, éste, éso (S) See IN, ŌN.

INTLĀ if / si, conjuntión condicional (M) There are two homophonous particles, TLĀ 'let it be so that' (synonymous with MĀ) and TLĀ 'if.' This form with fused IN is more common across sources than simple TLĀ 'if.' See IN, TLĀ.

INTLĀCA if not, otherwise / y si no (M), para negar, si no (C) [(7)Cf.27r,27v]. See INTLĀ.

INTLĀCAĪC if never / si en ningún tiempo, y si nunca (M) [(2)Cf.27r,103r]. One of the two attestations has an additional syllable intlācayaīc. See INTLĀCA, AĪC.

INTLĀCAMŌ if not, otherwise / y si no (M), para negar, si no (C) [(4)Cf.27r,27v,59v,119r]. See INTLĀCA, MŌ.

INTLĀCATLE(H) if nothing / si no hay nada (S) [(1)Cf.27r]. See INTLĀCA, TLE(H).

INTLĀCAYĀC if no one / si nadie (C) [(3)Cf.27r,27v]. See INTLĀCA, AYĀC.

INTLĀNEL though, however / y aunque, o

dado que (M) [(3)Cf.119r]. See INTLĀ, NEL.

ĪOCCĀMPAIXTI *possessed form, prefixed with third person singular possessive* **Ī-** to or from both places / de ambas partes (C) [(1)Cf.91v]. See ĪOCCĀNIXTI, -PA.

ĪOCCĀNIXTI *possessed form, prefixed with third person singular possessive* **Ī-** in both places / en ambas partes (C), de ambas partes (C) [(2)Cf.91r,91v]. See OCCĀN, -IXTI.

ĪŌNTLAPALIXTI *possessed form, prefixed with third person singular possessive* **Ī-** on both sides / de ambos lados (C) [(2)Cf.92v]. See ŌNTLAPAL, -IXTI.

ĪPAL *possessed form, prefixed with third person singular possessive* **Ī-** for, by means of something or someone / por él, o mediante él (M) see -PAL

ĪPALNEMOHUALŌNI See ĪPAL-NEMOHUANI.

ĪPALNEMOHUANI *possessed form, prefixed with third person singular possessive* **Ī-** that one through whom living goes on, giver of life / por quien se vive, el que da vida (C), Diós, por quien se vive (C) There are three attestations (Bf.11,21,71) of a longer form ĪPALNEMOHUALŌNI. NEMOHUA is the nonactive form of NEM(I) 'to live,' and an alternate, through infrequent, nonactive form is with -HUALŌ. B also has attestations in which the HU is not written and the A, the preceding O, or both are marked long, but this is an -OHUA, not an -OĀ derivation, in spite of the fact that it is almost always spelled *ipalnemoani*. The possessive prefix is bound with -PAL, not with the whole construction. See -PAL, NEM(I).

ĪPAMPA *possessed form, prefixed with third person singular possessive* **Ī-** because of something, for some reason / por esto, dando razón o causa porque se hizo la cosa (M) See -PAMPA.

ĪPAN *possessed form, prefixed with third person singular possessive* **Ī-** on, on top of, at or for something / encima de algo (M), por (C) See -PAN.

ĪPANTI to hit the mark with an arrow or shot / dar la saeta o arcabuz en el blanco (M) This is implied by ĪPANTILIĀ

ĪPANTIĀ *vt* to hit the mark, to be right in what one says / acertar o atinar en lo que

dice (M) [(1)Cf.115r]. T has what appears to be an attestation of this with incorporated YŌL-, but the vowel corresponding to Ī is short. Elsewhere this takes TLA- as object prefix. See ĪPAN.

ĪPANTILIĀ *vt* to hit upon what one is searching for; to fall upon one's enemies / hallar lo que se busca o dar sobre los enemigos (M) [(1)Cf.115r]. applic. ĪPANTIĀ

ĪQUIN when? / ¿cuándo? o ¿en qué tiempo? preguntando (M) See ĪC.

ITCŌ nonact. ITQUI

-ITCŌCA *necessarily possessed form* that which someone carries, that for which someone is responsible / vasallos, gente menuda o súbditos (M for *itconi*) [(6)Bf.2v,4r,7r,12v,13r,13v]. B does not indicate the presence of the possessive prefix Ī- by vowel length marking, but this is conventionally paired with possessed forms of other deverbal constructions about carrying something or someone,. hence governing and being responsible for someone. See (I)TQUI.

ĪTECH *possessed form, prefixed with third person singular possessive* **Ī-** next to, on, attached to something, someone / en, en él, o de él (M), junto a él, pegado a él (T) See -TECH.

ITHUA *vt* to see something / ver (usarse en tierra caliente) (C) This is cognate with (I)TTA, which developed an unusual geminate TT corresponding to this item's more historically conservative sequence THU.

ITHUAL-LI patio, interior yard / patio generalmente (M) See ITHUA.

ĪTIĀ *vt* to have someone drink something / dar a beber algún brebaje (M) caus. Ī

ITLAH *pl:* **-MEH** something / algo o alguna cosa (M) Although it is abundantly attested short in other sources, B marks the initial vowel long in sixteen attestations.

ĪTLOC *possessed form, prefixed with third person singular possessive* **Ī-** by, with, next to something, someone / par de él, o junto a él (M) [(4)Tp.134]. T has A for O in -TLOC. See -TLOC.

ĪTŌNAL-LI sweat / sudor (M) In the Nahuatl-to-Spanish side of T there is Ī-TŌNAL-LI 'one's shadow, spirit, soul,' but the Spanish-to-Nahuatl side has

ĪTŌNAL 'sweat (third pers. sg. possessor),' which represents a consolidation of Ī-ĪTŌNAL. M has absolutive *ytonalli* 'sweat.' See ĪTŌNIĀ.

ĪTŌNIĀ *vrefl* to sweat, perspire / sudar (M) [(3)Tp.143, (2)Zp.118,167]. This appears only in the Spanish-to-Nahuatl side of M. See TŌNA.

ĪTŌNĪLŌ nonact. ĪTŌNIĀ

(I)TQUI *vt* to carry something, to govern people (by extension of meaning) / llevar algo (M), regir o gobernar a otros (M) This verb is abundantly attested in B and C.

(I)TQUĪHUA nonact. (I)TQUI

(I)TQUILIĀ applic. (I)TQUI

(I)TQUITIĀ *vt* to send something with someone / enviar algo con otro a algún cabo (M) [(2)Cf.62r]. By general rule the vowel of the second syllable should be long, but C specifically marks it short. caus. (I)TQUI

(I)TTA *vrefl,vt* to look at oneself; to see something or someone / mirarme (M for first pers. sg. subject), ir a visitar a otro, o mirar a otro (M), hallar lo que se había perdido o lo que se procura y busca, o mirar a otro (M) This verb has an unusual internal geminate consonant. See ITHUA, (I)TZ-.

(I)TTALŌ altern. nonact. (I)TTA

(I)TTALTIĀ altern. caus. (I)TTA

(I)TTILIĀ *vt* to take aim at, point out, look after something / lo apunta (una cosa), lo cuida, lo atina (T) applic. (I)TTA

(I)TTILILIĀ applic. (I)TTILIĀ

(I)TTILĪLŌ nonact. (I)TTILIĀ

(I)TTĪTIĀ *vrefl,vt* to appear to someone, to reveal oneself to someone; to show something or someone to others, to get others to see something / aparecer a otro o mostrársele (M), dar a conocer a otro o mostrárselo (M), mostrar algo a otros (M), hallar o procurar algo para sí (M) By general rule the vowel of the second syllable should be long, but T consistently has a short vowel and C leaves it unmarked. In one of four entries in M there is an extra TI syllable, but its place in alphabetical order and its sense make it clear that this is a printing error. altern. caus. (I)TTA

(I)TTITILIĀ applic. (I)TTITIĀ

(I)TTITĪLŌ nonact. (I)TTITIĀ

(I)TTŌ altern. nonact. (I)TTA

(I)TTŌNI something that can be seen / cosa visible (M) [(4)Zp.125,176]. See (I)TTA.

(I)TZ- This appears as a variant stem form of (I)TTA in a number of constructions, especially before the ligature -TI-. Although (I)TTA is transitive, (I)TZ- appears in some constructions with no object prefix.

ITZCUĪN-TLI native Mexican dog / perro, perra (S) [(1)Cf.85v, (3)Zp.97,162,203, (3)Xp.86]. Z consistently has the vowel of the second syllable long, while C and X leave it unmarked for length. This commonly occurs without the abs. pref.

ITZMĪN(I) *vrefl,vt* to receive an injection; to inject someone / se inyecta (T), lo inyecta (T) This is abundantly attested but only in T. In T the initial vowels drops after reflexive prefixes but not after the prefix TLA-. See MĪN(A).

ITZMĪNILIĀ applic. ITZMĪN(I)

ITZMĪNĪLŌ nonact. ITZMĪN(I)

(I)TZMOLĪN(I) to sprout again, to grow, to appear / retoñecer (C), retoña (T), nacer, crecer, reverdecer, hablando de vegetales ... ser juicio, discreto, razonable, rico, no carecer de nada (S) [(1)Bf.5r, (2)Cf.36v, (1)Tp.135]. T has the reflex of Ō although B and C do not mark the vowel long.

ITZTAPALĀPAN *place name* Iztapalapa [(2)Cf.56v]. The literal sense of this has to do with paving stones in the vicinity of water. See ITZTAPAL-LI, Ā-TL, -PAN.

ITZTAPALĀPANĒCA-TL someone from Iztapalapa / natural de Iztapalapa (K) [(1)Cf.56v]. See ITZTAPALĀPAN.

ITZTAPAL-LI paving stone, flagstone / adoquín, piedra labrada para pavimentar (S) [(2)Cf.56v]. TAPAL- occurs as an element in compounds having to do with flat stones. ĪTZ-TLI 'obsidian' would make sense as the first element here, but C does not mark the initial vowel long in either attestation of ITZTAPAL-LI, while the single attestation of ĪTZ-TLI in T does have a long vowel.

(I)TZTĒHU(A) to go away out of sight / ir, salir (S) [(2)Cf.68r,91v]. See (I)TZ-, ĒHU(A).

ĪTZTI See ĪTZTIYA.

ĪTZTIC something cold / frío, fría (S) [(1)Tp.135]. See ĪTZTIYA, ĪTZ-TLI.

(I)TZTICAH *vt* to be looking at someone / está mirando (T) [(1)Tp.215]. See (I)TZ-, the verb CĀ.

(I)TZTIHU(I) to go seeking, contemplating / ir a ver, buscar, mirar, considerar (S) [(4)Cf.68r,90r,105v,124v]. See (I)TZ-, HU(I).

(I)TZTILIĀ This is used in place of applicative (I)TTILIĀ in constructions with the ligature -TI-. There is a discussion of this in C on f.68r. (I)TZTILIĀ contrasts with ĪTZTILIĀ 'to chill something.' See (I)TZ-.

ĪTZTILIĀ *vrefl,vt* to get cold; to chill something / se le enfría la cabeza (T for CUĀĪTZTILIĀ), refrescarse (S), enfriar, refrescar a alguien (S), enfriar una cosa (S), lo enfría (T) This is abundantly attested, but only in T. It contrasts with (I)TZTILIĀ< (I)TTA. See ĪTZTIC, ĪTZTIYA.

(I)TZTILIHTICAH *vrefl* to be looking at something / estoy mirando (C) [(2)Cf.68r, (1)Tp.215]. See (I)TZTILIĀ, the verb CĀ.

(I)TZTILIHTIHU(I) This applicative form is attested in use only as an honorific form. applic. (I)TZTIHU(I)

ĪTZTILILIĀ applic. ĪTZTILIĀ

ĪTZTILĪLŌ nonact. ĪTZTILIĀ

(I)TZTILTIĀ This is used in place of causative (I)TTALTIĀ or (I)TTĪTIĀ in constructions with the ligature -TI-.

(I)TZTINEM(I) *vt; pret:* **-NEN** to go along looking at something, someone; to consider something / considerar, estar atento (S) [(1)Cf.68r]. See (I)TZ-, NEM(I).

ĪTZTIYA to get cold / refrescarse (S), se enfría (T) [(1)Tp.135]. R has *itzti* and *itztia*, and S gives them with the preterits *itztic* and *itzti* respectively, implying ĪTZTI and ĪTZTIĀ as well as ĪTZTIYA. See ĪTZTIC, ĪTZTILIĀ.

(I)TZTIYE See (I)TZTICAH.

ĪTZ-TLI obsidian / obsidiana o fragmentos de obsidiana utilizados como cuchillos, navajas de afeitar, lancetas, flechas, espejos, etc. (S) [(1)Tp.224]. See ĪTZTIC.

ITZTOC something visible / visible (Z), lo observa (Z) [(4)Zp.90,130,174,199, (1)Rp.83]. In Z this appears with reflexive and object prefixes, while in R it appears as an intransitive verb glossed as 'to be sleepless.' See (I)TZ-, the verb O.

IUCCI to ripen, to cook / madurarse la fruta

o cocerse algo (M) [(4)Cf.32r, (1)Rp.32]. T has a variant form HUICCI, X has ICCI, and Z has YOCCI. The UCC sequence here represents [k^{w}s], not [ukk]. This is often misleadingly spelled *icuci*.

IUCCIC something ripened or cooked / cocido, maduro (X) [(1)Xp.45]. See IUCCI.

IUC-TLI a younger sibling / mi hermano o hermana menor (dice la hermana mayor) (M for first pers. sg. possessor), mi hermana menor (dice el hermano mayor) (M for first pers. sg. possessor) [(1)Bf.11v, (1)Cf.119v]. S provides the absolutive suffix. This is only attested in possessed form. M's gloss is ambiguous; it may mean that this term is used for 'younger sibling of the opposite sex' and also for 'little sister' by older sisters. Or it may mean that it is used by both sexes for 'little sister' and also for 'brother' by sisters in general. The possessed form of this is often misleadingly spelled *-icuh*.

IUCXITIĀ By general rule the vowel of the second syllable should be long, but C specifically marks it short. caus. IUCCI

IUCXOĀ to sneeze / estornuda (M) Z has delabialized the final consonant of the first syllable and has the form ICXOĀ. T has the form IHCUIXOĀ. X has ECXOĀ, which M also has in addition to IUCXOĀ.

IUCXŌLIZ-TLI sneeze / estornudo (M for *ecuxoliztli*) [(1)Zp.157]. See IUCXOĀ.

IUH *preterit form of* IHU(I) thus, so, such / así (M) This is often misleadingly spelled *yuh*. See IHU(I).

IUHCAH thus, so, such / así (C) [(1)Cf.120v]. See IHU(I), the verb CĀ.

IUHCĀN in or with reference to such a place / de la misma manera que ésta (C) [(2)Cf.89v,90r]. See IUH, -CĀN.

IUHQUI thus, in such a way, like / semejante o así o de essa manera (M) This is often misleadingly spelled *yuhqui*. See IHU(I).

IUHQUIN like, in the manner of / como (C) See IUHQUI, IN.

IUHQUINMAH like, as though it were / como, a manera (C) The NM sequence may assimilate to MM. See IUHQUIN, MAH.

IUHTOC something established, appearing to be a certain way / parece, establecido (Z) [(3)Zp.56,94,162]. See IHU(I), the verb O.

ĪX- This is a modifier common in T but also attested in B which conveys the sense of 'somewhat, middling.' Although it is homophonous with the stem of ĪX-TLI 'face,' the sense suggests that it might be a reduction from ĪXQUICH 'all.'

ĪXACA face down / boca abajo, invertido (Z) This is abundantly attested in Z and also appears in X. In one attestation the vowel of the second syllable is marked long, and in three the vowel of the third syllable is marked long, but otherwise Z is consistent. See ĪX-TLI.

ĪXACAHUILĀN(A) vrefl to drag oneself along, to crawl / se arrastra ... gatea (Z) [(3)Zp.14,63,170]. See ĪXACA, HUILĀN(A).

ĪXACAMAN(A) to stretch out face down / acostarse ... boca abajo (X) [(6)Xp.58]. X marks the vowel of the fourth syllable long, but it should not be. See ĪXACA, MAN(A).

ĪXACANEHNEM(I) pret: -NEN to crawl / gatea (Z) [(2)Zp.63,163]. See ĪXACA, NEHNEM(I).

ĪXACATLAMŌTLA vt to throw someone face downwards, headlong / lo tira boca abajo (Z) [(2)Zp.122,199]. See ĪXACA, MŌTLA.

ĪXACATLAPACHOĀ vt to upset someone, to mix someone up / lo trabuca (Z), lo pone boca abajo (Z) [(3)Zp.124,189,199]. See ĪXACA, PACHOĀ.

IXACHI pl: IXACHĪN ~ IXACHĪNTIN much, great in number, very many / mucho o grande en cantidad (M), muy muchos en número (M for plural) [(1)Bf.11v, (3)Cf.5v].

ĪXĀCOZTIC possessed form, prefixed with third person singular possessive Ī- someone yellowish, jaundiced / amarillento de la cara (Z) [(2)Zp.9,163]. This is a reduction of ĪXĀYACCOZTIC and is analogous to ĪXĀIZTĀC 'someone pallid.' See XĀYAC-TLI, COZTIC.

ĪXAHCI vt to approach something, someone closely, to comprehend something completely / acercarse mucho, agarrar, alcanzar por completo algo (S) [(2)Zp.106,190]. This also appears in P with the glottal stop marked. See ĪX-, ĪX-TLI, AHCI.

ĪXAHMŌL someone undependable / incon-

stante, variable (Z) [(3)Zp.71,128,163]. Z also has a variant ĪXNĀMŌL. The literal meaning of this seems to be 'someone with a soapy face.' See ĪX-TLI, AHMŌL-LI.

ĪXĀHUIĀ vt to rinse or whitewash something / lo enjuaga, lo lava (T), embarrar o enjalbegar (M) [(3)Tp.217, (2)Zp.52,199]. See ĪX-TLI, XĀHUIĀ.

ĪXĀHUILIĀ applic. ĪXĀHUIĀ

ĪXĀHUĪLŌ nonact. ĪXĀHUIĀ

ĪXĀHUILTIĀ vt to make signals with one's eyes / hace seños con los ojos (Z) [(1)Zp.170]. See ĪX-TLI, ĀHUILTIĀ.

ĪXĀIZTĀC possessed form, prefixed with third person singular possessive Ī- someone pale, pallid / pálido (Z) [(2)Zp.93,163]. This appears to be a reduction of ĪXĀYACIZTĀC. Z only marks the vowel of the second syllable long in one of two attestations. See XĀYAC(A)-TL, IZTĀC.

ĪXĀNQUI someone with a long face / cara larga (T) [(1)Tp.136]. See ĪX-TLI, ĀNQUI.

ĪXĀYŌCHŌCA to cry, weep / lagrimea (T) [(3)Tp.136]. See ĪXĀYŌ-TL, CHŌCA.

ĪXĀYŌCHŌCOHUA nonact. ĪX-ĀYŌCHŌCA

ĪXĀYŌCHŌQUĪTIĀ caus. ĪXĀYŌCHŌCA

ĪXĀYŌPOHPŌHU(A) vt to wipe someone's tears away / enjugar a otro las lágrimas (R) [(1)Rp.94]. See ĪXĀYŌ-TL, POHPŌHU(A).

ĪXĀYŌTEPĒHU(I) for tears to come in floods / derrama las lágrimas (T) [(3)Tp.136]. See ĪXĀYŌ-TL, TEPĒHU(I).

ĪXĀYŌTEPĒHUĪHUA nonact. ĪXĀYŌ-TEPĒHU(I)

ĪXĀYŌTEPĒHUĪTIĀ caus. ĪXĀYŌ-TEPĒHU(I)

ĪXĀYŌ-TL tears / lágrimas (M) There is also nearly synonymous ĪXXĀYŌ-TL derived from ĪX-TLI 'eye' and XĀYŌ-TL 'discharge, excrement.' It is possible that the frequently attested ĪXĀYŌ-TL is a reduction or reanalysis of ĪXXĀYŌ-TL, which is attested just once. The simplification of XX to X is common in the modern sources and may extend to B and C too in this case. On the other hand, ĀYŌ-TL 'watery substance' is as plausible for a second element here as XĀYŌ-TL 'discharge.' See ĪX-TLI, ĀYŌ-TL.

(I)XCA *vt* to bake something; to fire pottery / cocer loza o asar huevos, batatas, o cosa semejante (M) [(1)Cf.47r]. This is also abundantly attested in the derived form TLAXCAL-LI 'bread.'

ĪXCAHCAYĀHU(A) *vt* to deceive, mislead someone, to falsify something / lo engaña (T), falsifica (T) [(6)Tp.215,230]. See ĪX-TLI, CAHCAYĀHU(A).

IXCAHUIĀ *vrefl,vt* to be single-minded, preoccupied with one's own affairs; to have or do just one thing to the exclusion of others / hacer algo a solas o entender solamente lo que mc toca (M), no tener más de una cosa (M), comérmelo yo todo (M), aprovecharse él solo de alguna cosa, sin partirla con otros (M), entender en sola una sola cosa (M) [(1)Cf.111v]. It is possible that C fails to mark a long initial vowel and that this is derived from ĪX-TLI and CĀHU(A).

ĪXCALAQUIĀ See TLAĪXCALAQUIĀ.

ĪXCAPOTZTIC something gray, dark, swarthy, someone with a black face / (negro claro), gris, medio negro, trigueño, moreno (T), cara negra (Z) This is also attested in Z in the shortened form ĪXCAPOTZ. See ĪX-TLI, CAPOTZTIC.

ĪXCAUH-TLI tick / garrapata (Z) [(2)Zp.62,163].

ĪXCAUHTŌTŌ-TL ani, a bird that eats ticks off domestic animals / tordo garrapatero (pájaro) (Z) [(2)Zp.124,163]. Z idiosyncratically has a P corresponding to the UH of the second syllable. This may reflect a confusion between ĪXCAUH-TLI 'tick' and ĪXCAPOTZTIC 'black,' since the bird is glossy black. See ĪXCAUH-TLI, TŌTŌ-TL.

ĪXCHAMĀHUAC something rather thick / medio grueso (T) [(1)Tp.136]. See ĪX-, CHAMĀHUAC.

ĪXCHICĀHU(A) *vrefl* to take courage / se hace valiente (Z) [(2)Zp.127,170]. See ĪX-TLI, CHICĀHU(A).

ĪXCHICĀHUAC someone compelling, hypnotic / hipnótico (Z) [(2)Zp.68,163]. Z's gloss is not the literal sense implied by the verb, which would be 'someone brave, dauntless.' See ĪXCHICĀHU(A).

ĪXCHĪCHĪLĒHU(I) to blush, flush, turn red in the face / sonroja (Z) [(2)Zp.117,163]. M

has reflexive *ixchichiloa* with the same sense. See ĪX-TLI, CHĪCHĪLĒHU(I).

ĪXCHĪCHĪLTIC something rather red / medio rojo (T) [(1)Tp.136]. See ĪX-, CHĪCHĪLTIC.

ĪXCHICOTIC someone cross-eyed / bizco, bisojo (Z) [(2)Zp.20,163]. Z also gives the shortened form ĪXCHICO. See ĪX-TLI, CHICO.

ĪXCHIYANTIC something dappled, splotched / medio habado (color) [(1)Tp.136]. See ĪX-TLI, CHIYAN-TLI.

ĪXCHŌCA to cry / llora (Z) [(2)Zp.78,163]. See ĪX-TLI, CHŌCA.

-ĪXCO *compound postposition* on one's face, on the surface of / en la cara o en la sobrehaz (M), en su superficie (T) See ĪX-TLI, -C(O).

ĪXCOCH(I) to nap / duerme un poco (Z) [(2)Zp.47,163]. See ĪX-, COCH(I).

ĪXCOCHILIZ-TLI sleep, dream, nap / sueño (T) [(1)Tp.135]. See ĪXCOCH(I).

ĪXCOCHTĒMIQUILIZ-TLI dream, sleep, nap / sueño (T) [(1)Tp.135]. See ĪXCOCH(I), TĒMIQU(I).

ĪXCOCOĀ *vrefl* to have something the matter with one's eyes / tiene mal de ojo [(1)Tp.143]. M has *ixcocoya* with the same sense, and in compounds T has the element ĪXCOCOX derived from ĪXCOCOY(A), although T does not have the verb independently. See ĪX-TLI, COCOĀ.

ĪXCŌCOCH(I) to nap / cabecea (Z) [(2)Zp.22,163]. redup. ĪXCOCH(I)

ĪXCOCOLIZ-TLI infection, disease of the eyes / enfermedad de ojos (M) [(1)Tp.135]. M gives *ixcocoyaliztli* as a synonym. See ĪXCOCOĀ.

ĪXCOCŌLŌ nonact. ĪXCOCOĀ

ĪXCOCOXCĀTIĀ *vrefl* to go blind / se vuelve ciego (T) [(3)Tp.135,143]. This appears in T as a reflexive verb and also as an intransitive verb. See ĪXCOCOXQUI.

ĪXCOCOXCĀTILIĀ *vt* to blind someone / le ciega (T) [(3)Tp.215]. applic. ĪXCOCOXCĀTIĀ

ĪXCOCOXCĀTILILIĀ applic. ĪXCOCOXCĀTILIĀ

ĪXCOCOXCĀTILĪLŌ nonact. ĪXCOCOXCĀTILIĀ

ĪXCOCOXCĀTĪLŌ nonact. ĪXCO-
COXCĀTIĀ
ĪXCOCOXQUI someone blind / enfermo de
ojos (M), ciego (T) [(1)Tp.135]. See
ĪXCOCOY(A).
ĪXCOCOY(A) *pret:* **COCOX** ~ **COCOYAC**
to have something the matter with one's
eyes / tener enfermedad de ojos (M) See
ĪX-TLI, COCOY(A).
ĪXCOHCOYOCTIC someone with
sunken eyes / tiene los ojos sumidos (T)
[(1)Tp.135]. See ĪXCOHCOYOC-TLI.
ĪXCOHCOYOC-TLI someone with
sunken eyes / tiene los ojos sumidos
(T) [(1)Tp.135]. T has COYAC-TLI
for COYOC-TLI 'hole.' See ĪX-TLI,
COYOC-TLI.
-ĪXCOHTIYĀN C gives this as a less common variant of -ĪXCOHYĀN.
-ĪXCOHYĀN *necessarily possessed form*
something of one's own, something
personally owned, proper to oneself or its
purpose / propio, personal, particular (S),
solo (Z) This is abundantly attested in C
where it is given as synonymous with
NOHMAH. Bf.11v has *īxcocà*, which from
context appears to mean 'one's business,
one's own responsibility.' It would seem to
be derived in some indirect way from
-ĪXCO. See ĪX-TLI, -C(O), -YĀN.
ĪXCOMACA *vrefl,vt* to confess to having
done something; to tell another person his
faults to his face, to give evidence / confesar y conocer haber hecho algo (M), decir a
alguno sus tachas o faltas en la cara (M),
comprueba (Z) [(3)Tp.143, (2)Zp.31,199]. In
M this appears as a double transitive verb,
taking a direct and an indirect object
prefix, while it is attested as simply reflexive in T and transitive in Z and has to
do with clarification, verification, and
proof. See -ĪXCO, MACA.
ĪXCOMACALŌ nonact. ĪXCOMACA
ĪXCOPITZOTIC someone with a dirty,
messy face / cara sucia (Z) [(2)Zp.25,163].
See -ĪXCO, PITZOTIC.
ĪXCOZTIC something clear yellow, somewhat yellow, tending to yellow / amarillo
claro, amarillento, medio amarillo (T)
[(1)Tp.135]. See ĪX-TLI, COZTIC.
ĪXCUĀCUALTZIN someone with an

attractive face / con cara bonita (T)
[(1)Tp.136]. See ĪXCUĀ(I)-TL, CUAL-LI.
ĪXCUAHMŌL-LI eyebrow / las cejas (M)
[(1)Bf.8v, (9)Tp.135,143]. See ĪXCUĀ(I)-TL.
ĪXCUAHMŌLQUEHQUETZ(A) *vrefl* to
frown / para las cejas de coraje, frunce el
ceño (T) [(3)Tp.143]. See ĪXCUAHMŌL-LI,
QUEHQUETZ(A).
ĪXCUAHMŌLQUEHQUETZALŌ nonact.
ĪXCUAHMŌLQUEHQUETZ(A)
ĪXCUAHMŌLTEHTEQU(I) See ĪX-
CUAHMŌL-LI, TEHTEQU(I).
ĪXCUAHMŌLTZON-TLI eyebrow / su ceja
(T for possessed form) [(1)Tp.135]. See
ĪXCUAHMŌL-LI, TZON-TLI.
ĪXCUĀHUIĀ *vt* to cut the heads of grain
with a sickle; to carry something with a
tumpline across the forehead / arrasar trigo
o cosa semejante (M), lo carga en la frente
(T) [(3)Tp.215]. See ĪXCUĀ(I)-TL, -HUIĀ.
ĪXCUĀHUILIĀ applic. ĪXCUĀHUIĀ
ĪXCUĀHUĪLŌ nonact. ĪXCUĀHUIĀ
ĪXCUĀ(I)-TL forehead / la frente de la cara
(M) Z has the locative construction
ĪXCUĀCO with the same sense. M also
has the variant *ixquatl*. In compounds this
often appears as ĪXCUAH rather than
ĪXCUĀ. See ĪX-TLI, CUĀ(I)-TL.
ĪXCUĀTEHTECŌ altern. nonact.
ĪXCUĀTEHTEQU(I)
ĪXCUĀTEHTEQU(I) See ĪXCUĀ(I)-TL,
TEHTEQU(I).
ĪXCUĀTEHTEQUĪHUA altern. nonact.
ĪXCUĀTEHTEQU(I)
ĪXCUĀTEHUIĀ *vrefl,vt* to hit one's fore-
head; to hit someone in the forehead / se
pega en la frente (T), le pega en la frente (T)
[(6)Tp.143,216]. See ĪXCUĀTE-TL,
-HUIĀ.
ĪXCUĀTEHUILIĀ applic. ĪXCUĀTEHUIĀ
ĪXCUĀTEHUĪLŌ nonact. ĪXCUĀTEHUIĀ
ĪXCUĀTE-TL *pl:* **-MEH;** *possessed form:*
-TEUH forehead / su frente, su rostro (T
for possessed form) [(1)Tp.136, (3)Xp.102].
See ĪXCUĀ(I)-TL, TE-TL.
-ĪXCUĀTLACUAXĒL *only attested in
possessed form* the part in one's hair / su
raya (del pelo) (T) [(1)Tp.136]. This should
be derived ultimately from XELOĀ 'to
divide something,' but the attestation has
the reflex of a long vowel in the last

syllable, suggesting XĒLOĀ 'to spread something out' instead. See ĪXCUĀ(I)-TL, CUAXELOĀ.

ĪXCUĀTZON-TLI forelock / su copete (de caballo, persona, etc.) (T) [(1)Tp.136]. See ĪXCUĀ(I)-TL, TZON-TLI.

ĪXCUECHĀHUAC something damp / está mojado, húmedo (T) [(1)Tp.135]. See ĪX-, CUECHĀHUAC.

ĪXCUEHCHOLHUIĀ *vt* to beckon to someone with one's head / le hace seña (con la cabeza que venga) (T) [(3)Tp.215]. M has *ixcuechoa* 'to nod one's head in agreement' and *ixcuechilhuia* 'to wink at someone.' See ĪX-TLI, CUEHCHOLHUIĀ.

ĪXCUEHCHOLHUILIĀ applic. ĪX-CUEHCHOLHUIĀ

ĪXCUEHCHOLHUĪLŌ nonact. ĪX-CUEHCHOLHUIĀ

ĪXCUEP(A) *vrefl,vt* to lose one's way and get confused; to deceive someone, to turn something inside out or upside down / errar el camino o andar descarriado (M), embaucar o engañar a otro (M), volver lo de dentro a fuera (M), lo trabuca, lo pone boca arriba, le tiene dos caras (T) See ĪX-TLI, CUEP(A).

ĪXCUICUIL-LI someone with a dirty face / tiene la cara sucia (T) [(1)Tp.136]. M has *cuicuilchapultic* 'something painted in many colors.' See ĪX-TLI.

ĪXCUĪTIĀ *vrefl,vt* to follow someone's example; to set a good example to others, to reproach someone / tomar ejemplo de otras (M), dar buen ejemplo (M), le reprocha (T) [(3)Tp.215]. M gives the reflexive use of this in composition with TĒTECH 'next to someone.' See ĪX-TLI, CUĪTIĀ.

ĪXCUĪTILIĀ applic. ĪXCUĪTIĀ

ĪXCUĪTĪLŌ nonact. ĪXCUĪTIĀ

ĪXCUITLA someone blear-eyed / lagañoso (M) [(3)Cf.7v]. See ĪXCUITL(A)-TL.

ĪXCUITL(A)-TL discharge from the eyes / lagañas (M) [(4)Cf.7v]. See ĪX-TLI, CUITL(A)-TL.

ĪXEH someone intelligent and wise / que tiene cara, ojos, buena vista, cabeza, inteligencia (S) The literal sense of this is 'someone who has a face' or 'someone who has eyes.' It is conventionally paired with

NACACEH 'someone who has ears,' the whole phrase meaning 'someone who is prudent.' See ĪX-TLI.

ĪXĒHUA-TL *inalienably possessed form:* -ĪXĒHUAYŌ eyelid / su párpado (T for possessed form) [(1)Tp.138]. See ĪX-TLI, ĒHUA-TL.

ĪXĒHUIĀ *vrefl* to take a risk, to expose oneself to hazard / se atreve ... se arriesga (Z) [(3)Zp.14,16,170]. See ĪX-TLI, ĒHU(A).

ĪXĒLĒHUIĀ *vt* to desire someone / codiciar a alguna persona (M), lo desea, lo codicia (T) See ĪX-TLI, ĒLĒHUIĀ.

ĪXĒLĒHUILIĀ applic. ĪXĒLĒHUIĀ

ĪXĒLĒHUĪLŌ nonact. ĪXĒLĒHUIĀ

ĪXĒLŌTIC something dappled / color granizo, color habado (T) [(1)Tp.138]. See ĪX-TLI, ĒLŌ-TL.

IXHUA for a seed to sprout, germinate; for a plant to come up / nacer la planta o brotar la semilla (M) [(2)Cf.31v, (4)Zp.21,87,163,164]. The attestations in Z are inconsistent, with *ixoa*, *īxōa*, *ixua* and *īxua*, but C's attestations are consistent with each other and with M. See IZHUA-TL.

ĪXHUĒHUETZCA to smile / se sonríe (T) [(1)Tp.135]. T also has unreduplicated ĪXHUETZCA. See ĪX-TLI, HUĒHUETZCA.

ĪXHUĒ(I) someone with enlarged eyes / un ojo grande, los dos ojos grandes (T) [(1)Tp.135]. See ĪX-TLI, HUĒ(I).

ĪXHUETZCA to smile, to gesture laughingly / sonreírse o hacer gestos con risa (M) [(1)Tp.135, (2)Zp.117,164]. T also has reduplicated ĪXHUĒHUETZCA. See ĪX-TLI, HUETZCA.

ĪXHUETZCALIZ-TLI smile / sonrisa (Z) [(2)Zp.117,164]. M has *ixhuetzquiliztli* with the same sense. See ĪXHUETZCA.

ĪXHUETZCANI someone who smiles, someone agreeable and good-natured / el que así se sonríe (M), risueño (T) [(1)Tp.135]. See ĪXHUETZCA.

ĪXHUETZQUI someone who smiles, someone agreeable and good-natured / risueño (Z) [(2)Zp.110,164]. Both attestations of this have a final *s* which seems out of place. See ĪXHUETZCA.

(I)XHUI to satisfy one's appetite for food, to

become full / hartarse de vianda (M) In a reversal of the prevailing pattern, C has this with I deleted in the presence of the reflexive prefix, and T retains I.

ĪXHUIĀ *vt* to level something, to make something even, to cross something, to put something crossways / nivelar con el ojo o con astrolabio (M), lo cruza, lo atraviesa (T) [(3)Tp.215]. See ĪX-TLI, -HUIĀ.

IXHUIC someone satisfied, full after a meal / harto de vianda (M) [(2)Zp.78,164, (1)Rp.99]. See (I)XHUI.

ĪXHUICCI someone with a splotchy face, something showing signs of ripeness / paño (mancha de la piel en la cara), empieza a madurar (T) [(1)Tp.135]. The CC sequence here represents [ks], not [kk]. See the verb ĪXHUICCI.

ĪXHUICCI to blush, flush / se sonroja (Z) [(2)Zp.117,163]. This is in a phrase with *de huetzca*, hence 'to flush from laughing.' In Z HUICCI has the variant form YOCCI, and here the initial Y assimilates to the X of ĪX-. Z's reduction of geminate consonants shortens the resulting XX, and the resulting local form is ĪXOCCI. T has ĪXHUICCI as a substantive. See ĪX-TLI, HUICCI.

(I)XHUĪHUA nonact. (I)XHUI

ĪXHUĪHUĬCA *vrefl* to shake one's head back and forth / menea (la cabeza) [(2)Zp.83,170]. See ĪX-TLI, HUĪHUĬCA.

ĪXHUILIĀ applic. ĪXHUIĀ

ĪXHUĪLŌ nonact. ĪXHUIĀ

ĪXHUĪLTIĀ *vt* to feed someone to satisfaction, to nurture someone / lo nutre, le sacia (T) [(3)Tp.215]. By general rule the vowel of the second syllable should be short, but it is consistently long in T. T also retains the initial I in the presence of reflexive prefixes, although M has weak (I) in the basic verb from which this is derived. M and T also have an alternate causative form (I)XHUĪTIĀ used reflexively with the sense of 'to be overwhelmed by food.' altern. caus. (I)XHUI

IXHUĪLTILIĀ applic. IXHUĪLTIĀ

IXHUĪLTĪLŌ nonact. IXHUĪLTIĀ

ĪXHUINTIĀ *vt* to get someone dizzy, to make someone seasick / lo marea (Z for CUĀĪXHUINTIĀ) [(1)Cf.96r, (2)Zp.82,147]. M has *ixihuinti* 'to be confused, stupified'

and *ixihuintia* 'to confuse, bewilder someone.' See ĪX-TLI, IHUINTI.

ĪXHUINTIC someone dizzy, seasick / mareado (Z) [(2)Zp.82,164]. See ĪXHUINTIĀ.

(I)XHUĪTIĀ *vrefl,vt* to stuff oneself, to be overwhelmed by food; to feed someone to surfeit / ser destemplado en comer o ahitarse (M), ahitar a otro (M) In T the initial vowel does not drop before reflexive prefixes, and the second vowel, which should be long before -TIĀ is short. In a single attestation in C the vowel is unmarked for length. Z is inconsistent. T has an alternative causative (I)XHUĪLTIĀ where by general rule the corresponding vowel should be short but is given as long. altern. caus. (I)XHUI

(I)XHUĪTILIĀ applic. (I)XHUĪTIĀ

(I)XHUĪTĪLŌ nonact. (I)XHUĪTIĀ

(I)XHUĪUHCIHUĀPIL-LI granddaughter / nieta (Z) [(2)Zp.88,164]. See (I)XHUĪUH-TLI, CIHUĀPIL-LI.

(I)XHUĪUH-TLI grandchild / nieto o nieta (S) This is abundantly attested in B and is also in T and Z. In B the vowel of the second syllable is consistently marked long when the plural possessed affix -HUĀN immediately follows, and the same vowel is specifically marked short elsewhere. In T and Z the vowel is long in all attestations.

ĪXĪCA to run, drip, ooze, bleed / rezumarse o salirse la vasija (M), se escurre (T), sangrar (X) [(4)Tp.136,248, (3)Xp.49]. See (I)HXĪCA.

ĪXĪCALTIĀ caus. ĪXĪCA

ĪXĪCOHUA caus. ĪXĪCA

ĪXIHIZTĀC something somewhat white / medio blanco (T) [(1)Tp.136]. See ĪX-, IHIZTĀC.

ĪXILACATZTIC someone cross-eyed / bizco, bisojo (Z) [(2)Zp.20,163]. M has reflexive *ixilacatzoa* 'to shake one's head in irritation.' See ĪX-TLI, ILACATZTIC.

ĪXILCĀHU(A) *vt* to forget someone's face, to forget what someone looks like / se le olvida la cara de otro (T) [(3)Tp.216]. See ĪX-TLI, (I)LCĀHU(A).

ĪXILCĀHUALŌ nonact. ĪXILCĀHU(A)

ĪXILCĀHUILIĀ applic. ĪXILCĀHU(A)

ĪXILPĪCHILIĀ applic. ĪXILPĪTZ(A)

ĪXILPĪTZ(A) *vt* to blow in someone's eye / le sopla en el ojo (T) [(3)Tp.216]. T fails to mark the vowel of the second syllable short, but it is so marked in the Spanish-to-Nahuatl side of T. See ĪX-TLI, (I)LPĪTZ(A).

ĪXILPĪTZALŌ nonact. ĪXILPĪTZ(A)

ĪXIMACHILIĀ applic. ĪXIMAT(I)

ĪXIMACHŌ altern. nonact. ĪXIMAT(I)

ĪXIMAT(I) *vrefl,vt; pret:* **ĪXIMAH** to know oneself; to recognize someone, to know something in general / conocer a sí mismo (M), conocer a otro (M), conocer algo generalmente (M) Z has the variant ĪXMAT(I). See ĪX-TLI, MAT(I).

ĪXIMATĪHUA altern. nonact. ĪXIMAT(I)

ĪXĪPTLAYŌ-TL image, likeness, representation / imagen, retrato (R) [(1)Cf.94v, (1)Rp.95]. M has *ixiptlayotia* 'to stand in for someone' and 'to make something in one's image,' while S has *ixiptlatl* 'representative.' See ĪX-TLI, XĪP-, -YŌ.

IXITIĀ *vrefl,vt* to wake up, to come to, to recall something; to wake someone up, to remind someone of something / despertarse (M), despertar a otro (M), le despierta, le hace acordar (T) [(3)Tp.216]. In T the initial I is deleted in the presence of reflexive prefixes, but in M it is retained.

IXITILIĀ applic. IXITIĀ

IXITĪLŌ nonact. IXITIĀ

ĪXIUHQUI something like, resembling / parecido (Z) [(2)Zp.94,163]. See ĪX-TLI, IUHQUI.

ĪXIZTĀC something whitish; the whites of one's eyes / medio blanco, el ojo se le puso blanco (T) [(2)Tp.136,137]. There are two derivations here. The sense of 'something whitish' involves the modifier ĪX- 'somewhat,' while 'whites of one's eyes' is a compound with IX-TLI. See ĪX-, ĪX-TLI, IZTĀC.

ĪXMAHUIZTIC someone pleasant, agreeable / agradable, respetable (Z) [(3)Zp.6,109,163]. Z has MO for MA See ĪX-TLI, MAHUIZTIC.

ĪXMALACACHIHU(I) to get dizzy, bewildered / se marea, se ataranta (T) [(3)Tp.136]. See ĪXMALACACHOĀ.

ĪXMALACACHIHUĪHUA nonact. ĪXMALACACHIHU(I)

ĪXMALACACHIHUĪTIĀ caus. ĪXMALACACHIHU(I)

ĪXMALACACHOĀ *vrefl,vt* to get dizzy, to make someone dizzy / se marea (T), lo marea (T) [(1)Cf.96r, (6)Tp.143,217]. Intransitive ĪXMALACACHIHU(I) is synonymous with ĪXMALACACHOĀ used reflexively. See ĪX-TLI, MALACACHOĀ.

ĪXMALACACHŌLŌ nonact. ĪX-MALACACHOĀ

ĪXMALACACHTIC something oval, egg-shaped / ovalado (T) [(1)Tp.136]. See ĪX-TLI, MALACACHTIC.

ĪXMALACAHILHUIĀ applic. ĪX-MALACACHOĀ

ĪXMAN(A) *vt* to level, even something / igualar suelo o cosa semejante (M), lo aplana, lo empareja (T) [(3)Tp.217]. This implies ĪXMANI 'something equal or level,' which appears in M. See ĪX-TLI, MAN(A).

ĪXMANQUI something level, even / cosa llana e igual (M), parejo, plano (T) [(1)Tp.136]. See ĪXMAN(A).

ĪXMANTITI openly, clearly / abiertamente, claramente (T) [(1)Tp.136]. See ĪXMAN(A).

ĪXMAT(I) See ĪXIMAT(I).

ĪXMATILHUIĀ applic. ĪXMATILOĀ

ĪXMATILOĀ *vt* to scrub someone's face; to blindfold someone / refregar la cara a otro (M), no se deja ver el ojo (T) [(3)Tp.217]. See ĪX-TLI, MATILOĀ.

ĪXMĀTLATIC brave, gallant / valeroso (Z) [(2)Zp.127,163]. The second element of this is obscure. See ĪX-TLI.

ĪXMAUHTIĀ *vrefl,vt* to feel giddy or intimidated; to intimidate someone / tener algún negocio arduo entre manos, o desvanecerse la cabeza pasando por algún lugar hondo o puente estrecha y alta (M), le da miedo (de no ser capaz para hacerlo) (T) [(3)Tp.217]. This seems to be homophonous with and in fact the same derivation as ĪXMAUHTIĀ 'to poke someone in the eye.' See ĪX-TLI, MAUHTIĀ.

ĪXMAUHTIĀ *vt* to poke someone in the eye / le pica en el ojo, le tienta el ojo (T) [(3)Tp.217]. This seems to be homophonous with and in fact the same derivation as ĪXMAUHTIĀ 'to frighten someone.' See ĪX-TLI, MAUHTIĀ.

ĪXMAUHTILIĀ applic. ĪXMAUHTIĀ

ĪXMAUHTĪLŌ nonact. ĪXMAUHTIĀ
ĪXMELACTIC someone, something upright
/ recto (cosa parada, como un hombre,
árbol, etc.) (T) [(1)Tp.136]. See ĪX-TLI,
MELACTIC.
ĪXMELĀHU(A) vt to straighten something /
lo endereza (Z) [(2)Zp.51,199]. See ĪX-TLI,
MELĀHU(A).
ĪXMICOHUA nonact. ĪXMIQU(I)
ĪXMICTIĀ vt to dazzle someone / lo encandila (T) [(3)Tp.217]. M has reduplicated
ixmimictia with the same sense. altern.
caus. ĪXMIQU(I)
ĪXMIHMIQU(I) pret: -MIC to be dazzled,
blinded by strong light, to squint /
encandilarse o cegarse con la gran lumbre o
claridad (M) [(1)Cf.99r, (3)Zp.43,57,163].
redup. ĪXMIQU(I)
ĪXMIQU(I) pret: -MIC to be blinded by the
sun or a bright light / lastima los ojos el sol
o una luz fuerte (T) [(3)Tp.136]. See ĪX-TLI,
MIQU(I).
ĪXMIQUĪTIĀ altern. caus. ĪXMIQU(I)
ĪXMIXTLACHIY(A) to have cataracts, for
one's vision to be clouded / catarata (Z)
[(2)Zp.26,163]. In one of the attestations
the final vowel is missing, and in the other
the vowel of the second syllable is marked
long. See ĪX-TLI, MIX-TLI, TLACHIY(A).
ĪXMŌN-TLI pl: -TIN eyelash / cejas, pes-
tañas (X) [(3)Xp.103]. See ĪX-TLI.
ĪXNAHUATIĀ vrefl,vt to make an assertion;
to condemn or dismiss someone,
something / proponer firmemente alguna
cosa (M), condenar o despedir a otro ... o
desahuciar al enfermo (M), reprochar
o despedir a alguno (M) [(1)Cf.126r]. See
ĪX-TLI, NAHUATIĀ.
ĪXNĀMIQU(I) vrefl,vt; pret: -MIC for people
to have differences among themselves, to
have a confrontation; to have differences
with someone, to contradict or resist
someone / contender o tener diferencias
unos con otros (M), juntar los rostros
mirándose el uno al otro (M), contender o
risar con otro o resistirle (M) P has this in
reduplicated form ĪXNAHNĀMIQU(I). See
ĪX-TLI, NĀMIQU(I).
ĪXNĀMŌL See ĪXAHMŌL.
ĪXNECUILTIC cross-eyed / bizco (T)
[(1)Tp.136]. T also has the truncated form

ĪXNECUIL glossed as 'squint.' See ĪX-TLI,
NECUILTIC.
ĪXNEHNEMILTIĀ vrefl for one's eyes to
swim, for one's vision to be blurred /
menea la vista (Z) [(2)Zp.83,170]. Both
attestations lack the glottal stop. See
ĪX-TLI, NEHNEM(I).
ĪXNEHNEXTIC someone gray-eyed / tiene
ojos zarcos, gris (T) [(1)Tp.136]. redup.
ĪXNEXTIC
ĪXNĒHUALLOH pl: -MEH idol, image /
ídolo, imagen (T) [(1)Tp.136]. The vowel of
the second syllable is attested long, but
unless there has been loss of a syllable
with compensatory lengthening, the vowel
should not be long, assuming that this
is related to ĪXNENEHUILIĀ. See
ĪXNENEHUILIĀ.
ĪXNĒMPOLIHU(I) to go astray, to get lost /
se extravía, se pierde (T) [(3)Tp.136]. See
ĪX-TLI, NĒMPOLIHU(I).
ĪXNĒMPOLIHUĪHUA nonact. ĪX-
NĒMPOLIHU(I)
ĪXNĒMPOLIHUĪTIĀ caus. ĪX-
NĒMPOLIHU(I)
ĪXNENEHUILIĀ vt to resemble someone, to
estimate something, to examine something / parecer a otro en el rostro (M), lo
calcula, lo examina (T) [(3)Tp.217]. See
ĪX-TLI, NENEHUILIĀ.
ĪXNENEHUILILIĀ applic. ĪXNENEHUILIĀ
ĪXNENEHUILĪLŌ nonact. ĪXNENEHUILIĀ
ĪXNEQU(I) See TLAĪXNEQU(I).
ĪXNEXTIC someone gray-eyed, something
grayish / tiene ojos zarcos; gris (T)
[(1)Tp.136]. See ĪX-TLI, NEXTIC.
ĪXNEXTLACHIY(A) to have cataracts, for
one's vision to be clouded / catarata, ve
como nublado (Z) [(2)Zp.26,163]. In both
the attestations the vowel of the second syllable is marked long. See ĪX-TLI,
NEX-TLI, TLACHIY(A).
ĪXOCUIL-IN acne / espinilla (de la cara) (T)
[(1)Tp.136]. See ĪX-TLI, OCUIL-IN.
ĪXOMITIC thin-faced, boney of face / flaco
de la cara (Z) [(2)Zp.60,163]. See ĪX-TLI,
OMI-TL.
ĪXŌTIĀ vrefl,vt to keep watch; to take care
of something, to look after something, to
make a record of something / se cuida, se
vigila (T), lo cuida, lo recuerda, lo vigila

(T), poner en escrito todo el tributo (M) In
the sources for this dictionary, this is only
attested in T, but there it is abundantly
attested. See ĪX-TLI.
ĪXŌTILIĀ applic. ĪXŌTIĀ
ĪXŌTĪLŌ nonact. ĪXŌTIĀ
ĪXPACHIHU(I) for a swelling or inflammation to subside / se desinflama (Z)
[(2)Zp.43,163]. In one of the two attestations the vowel of the third syllable is
marked long. See ĪX-TLI, PACHIHU(I).
ĪXPAHPĀL-LI someone whose eyes see
nothing, someone blind / no ven nada los
ojos, se ciega (T) [(1)Tp.136]. The verb PĀ
means 'to dye something' The common
associated noun is TLAPAL-LI 'dye' with a
short vowel. M has simple *palli*, presumably PAL-LI, referring specifically to black
clay used in dying. In spite of the vowel
length discrepancy, these probably share a
common origin with the second element of
this item. See ĪX-TLI, PĀ.
ĪXPAHPĀLTIC someone whose eyes see
nothing, someone blind / no ven nada los
ojos, se ciega (T) [(1)Tp.136]. Note that this
is not a reduplicated form of ĪXPALTIC
'something damp, wet,' which has a short
vowel in the next to last syllable. See
ĪXPAHPĀL-LI..
ĪXPAHTĒQUILIĀ *vt* to put medicine in
someone's eyes / le pone medicina en los
ojos (T) [(3)Tp.217]. See ĪX-TLI, PAH-TLI,
TĒQUILIĀ.
ĪXPALTIC something damp, wet / está
mojado, húmedo (T) [(1)Tp.136]. See ĪX-,
PALTIC.
-ĪXPAMPA *compound postposition* from
or toward the front of / de delante (C),
de la presencia (C) See -ĪXPAN, -PA.
-ĪXPAN *compound postposition* before, in
front of, in the presence of, in the time of /
ante mí o en mi tiempo (M for first pers.
sg.), delante (C) See ĪX-TLI, -PAN.
ĪXPANTIĀ *vrefl,vt* for something to present,
manifest itself; to present, reveal, confide
something / se presenta (T), proponer,
manifestar, o dar noticia de algún negocio
a otros (M), descubrir algo al amigo (M), lo
revela (T) [(6)Tp.143,217]. See -ĪXPAN.
ĪXPANTILIĀ applic. ĪXPANTIĀ
ĪXPANTĪLŌ nonact. ĪXPANTIĀ

-ĪXPATCA *compound postposition* for, in
place of / de parte, por parte, en lugar de (Z)
[(3)Zp.77,94,158]. See ĪX-TLI, PATCA.
ĪXPATLĀHU(A) *vrefl,vt* to widen, to spread
out; to widen something / se ensancha (T),
lo ensancha (T) [(6)Tp.143,217]. See ĪX-TLI,
PATLĀHU(A).
ĪXPATLĀHUALŌ nonact. ĪXPATLĀHU(A)
ĪXPATLĀHUILIĀ applic. ĪXPATLĀHU(A)
ĪXPATZAC someone with one eye / tuerto
de un ojo (M) [(3)Cf.7v]. See ĪX-TLI,
PATZAC-TLI.
ĪXPEHPEN(A) *vt* to choose or select some-
thing, to pick something out on the basis of its appearance / escoger a algunos
por los rostros o caras (M), lo elige, lo
escoge, lo selecciona (T) [(3)Tp.217]. See
ĪX-TLI, PEHPEN(A).
ĪXPEPETŌNALTIĀ caus. ĪXPEPETŌN(I)
ĪXPEPETŌN(I) for one's eyes to bulge from
anger / se le saltan los ojos (por enojarse)
(T) [(3)Tp.136]. See ĪX-TLI, PETŌN(I).
ĪXPEPETŌNILŌ nonact. ĪXPEPETŌN(I)
ĪXPETLĀN(I) to revive, sober up, return to
one's senses / vuelve, se le pasa la borra-
chera (Z) [(2)Zp.130,163]. M has transitive
ixpetlania 'to sprinkle something out of
a cup or to scandalize people.' See ĪX-TLI,
PETLĀN(I).
ĪXPETLĀNTOC to be in possession of one's
senses / en su juicio (Z) [(2)Zp.74,163]. See
ĪXPETLĀN(I), the verb O.
ĪXPETZALHUIĀ *vt* to plane, smooth, polish
something for someone / se lo alisa (T)
[(4)Tp.217]. applic. ĪXPETZOĀ
ĪXPETZALHUILIĀ applic. ĪXPETZALHUIĀ
ĪXPETZALHUĪLŌ nonact. ĪXPETZALHUIĀ
ĪXPETZOĀ *vrefl,vt* to be involved in scru-
tinizing something; to plane, smooth,
polish something / mirar con diligencia
escudriñando alguna cosa (M), acepillar o
bruñir o alisar algo (M) [(3)Tp.217]. See
ĪX-TLI, PETZOĀ.
ĪXPETZTIC something smooth, polished /
liso (T) [(1)Tp.136]. See ĪXPETZOĀ.
ĪXPIHPITZŌTIC someone with small eyes /
con ojos chicos (T) [(1)Tp.137]. M has
ixpitzictic 'someone squint-eyed.' See
ĪX-TLI, PITZŌTIC.
ĪXPILCATOC someone, something bent
over, leaning / agachado, inclinado (Z)

[(3)Zp.6,71,163]. See ĪX-TLI, PILCATOC.
ĪXPILCUETLAX-TLI *possessed form:*
-ĪXPILCUETLAXYŌ eyelid / su párpado
(Z for possessed form) [(2)Zp.94,163]. See
ĪXPIL-LI, CUETLAX-TLI.
ĪXPILHUI-TL *possessed form:* -ĪX-
PILHUIYŌ eyelash / su pestaña
(Z for possessed form) [(2)Zp.98,163].
This is apparently a shortened form of
ĪXPILIHHUI-TL, which would literally
mean 'eyelash feather.' See ĪXPIL-LI,
IHHUI-TL.
ĪXPIL-LI eyelash / su pestaña (Z for
possessed form) [(5)Zp.98,163]. Since all
the attestations are in possessed form, the
absolutive suffix is not directly attested,
and Z marks the vowel of the second
syllable long. The citation form given here
is by analogy with MAHPIL-LI 'finger.' See
ĪX-TLI, PIL-LI.
ĪXPILOĀ *vrefl* to bend over, to lean / se
agacha ... se inclina (Z) [(3)Zp.6,71,170]. M
has intransitive *ixpoloa* 'to lower one's
eyes.' See ĪX-TLI, PILOĀ.
ĪXPINTETIC someone with a naturally
small face or a face made gaunt by illness /
tiene el rostro chico (por naturaleza), tiene
el rostro flaco (por la enfermedad) (T)
[(1)Tp.137]. See ĪX-TLI, PINTIC.
ĪXPOHPOLIHU(I) to go blind / se ciega (Z)
[(2)Zp.27,163]. See ĪX-TLI, POHPOLIHU(I).
ĪXPOHPOLTIC someone blind / ciego (X)
[(2)Xp.49]. See ĪXPOHPOLIHU(I).
ĪXPOLHUIĀ applic. ĪXPOLOĀ
ĪXPOLIHU(I) to disappear / desaparece (T)
[(1)Tp.137, (2)Zp.44,164]. See ĪX-TLI,
POLIHU(I).
ĪXPOLOĀ *vrefl,vt* to dissemble, to be mis-
leading about what one is doing, to go
astray; to confuse someone, to conceal
something / disfrazarse o no acertar en lo
que hace (M), encandila (Z), se pierde
(T), desperdiciar o echar a perder algo
(M), lo distrae, lo pierde de vista (T)
[(6)Tp.143,218, (1)Zp.170]. See ĪX-TLI,
POLOĀ.
ĪXPOLŌLŌ nonact. ĪXPOLOĀ
ĪXPOPOYACTIC something smudged,
murky / (color de) medio borrado (T)
[(1)Tp.137]. See ĪX-, POPOYACTIC.
ĪXPOPOYŌT(I) to go blind / cegar (M)

[(2)Cf.57v]. R has this with a short vowel
and glottal stop in the fourth syllable instead of a long vowel. See
ĪXPOPOYŌ-TL.
ĪXPOPOYŌ-TL someone blind / ciego
(M) [(6)Cf.7v,57v,122v]. See ĪX-TLI,
POPOYŌ-TL.
ĪXPOYĀHU(I) to get dizzy / mareado (Z)
[(2)Zp.82,164]. Z glosses this as an adjec-
tive, but in form it is a verb. M has transi-
tive *ixpoyahua* 'to dazzle, bewilder some-
one.' See ĪX-TLI, POYĀHU(I).
ĪXQUĒNTATACA *vrefl* to scratch, rub one's
eyelids / rasca los párpados (T) [(3)Tp.143].
The first element of this is also the first
element of M's *ixquempalli* 'inner side
of the eyelid.' See ĪX-TLI, QUĒM(I)-TL,
TATACA.
ĪXQUĒNTATACALŌ nonact. ĪXQUĒN-
TATACA
ĪXQUEP(A) This is the Z variant of
ĪXCUEP(A)
ĪXQUEP-TLI someone deceitful / dos caras, hombre falso (Z) [(2)Zp.47,164]. See
ĪXCUEP(A).
-**ĪXQUI** *only attested in possessed form*
the front edge of the eyelid / parte de
adentro y de la orilla de su párpado (T)
[(2)Tp.137,138]. See ĪX-TLI.
ĪXQUICH all, a certain amount / todo (M)
This is abundantly attested with a long
vowel in B, C, and Z. When ĪXQUICH
appears in paired or serial phrases, the
sense is 'an equal amount of each.'
ĪXQUICHCA up to or from a point, until or
from a certain time / hasta tanto o hasta
tal tiempo (M), desde aquí, desde allí, y
desde allá (C) See ĪXQUICH.
ĪXQUICHCĀHUITIĀ to be detained /
estar detenido (K) [(1)Cf.109r]. See
ĪXQUICHCĀHU(I)-TL.
ĪXQUICHCĀHU(I)-TL up until a certain
point in time, meanwhile, during a certain
period / todo el tiempo pasado, hasta el
tiempo presente, hasta éste tiempo (S)
[(5)Cf.103r,109r,123v]. This is often written separated, ĪXQUICH CĀHUITL. See
ĪXQUICH, CĀHU(A).
ĪXQUICHCAPA up to or from a certain
point / desde donde (C) [(1)Cf.43r]. See
ĪXQUICHCA, -PA.

ĪXQUICHCĀUH See ĪXQUICH-
CĀHU(I)-TL.
ĪXQUIHQUĪZ(A) to stumble around in a
daze / ser atochado y tonto, andando de
acá para allá (M) [(1)Cf.113v]. redup.
ĪXQUĪZ(A)
ĪXQUĪZ(A) to go about aimlessly and
without rest; for dye to wash out of
something, for something to get defaced /
andar sin reposo de una parte a otra (M),
destiñe ... se despinta (Z) [(3)Zp.44,164].
See ĪX-TLI, QUĪZ(A).
ĪXTALECTIC someone jaundiced, yellowish
of face / amarillez de la cara (T) [(1)Tp.137].
See ĪX-TLI, IZTALECTIC.
ĪXTALĒHU(I) to turn yellowish in the face /
se pone amarillo de la cara, amarillento (T)
[(1)Tp.137]. See ĪX-TLI, IZTALĒHU(I).
ĪXTECOHCOYOC pl: -TIN someone who
has very sunken eyesockets / el que tiene
muy hundidas las cuencas de los ojos (M)
[(2)Cf.5v]. M has the same gloss for ixco-
coyoc. See ĪXTECOHCOYOC-TLI.
ĪXTECOHCOYOC-TLI very sunken eye
socket / la cuenca del ojo muy hundida (M)
[(1)Cf.5v]. See ĪXTE-TL, COYOC-TLI.
ĪXTEHTĒZCATIC something silvery, blue-
gray like the surface of a mirror / gris-azul
(T) [(1)Tp.137]. See ĪX-TLI, TĒZCA-TL.
ĪXTEHUIHHUITZACAL-LI someone cross-
eyed / hombre bizco (T) [(2)Tp.137]. The
second element is obscure. Possibly it is
related to HUIHHUĪXTILIĀ and has
something to do with weakness. See
ĪXTE-TL.
ĪXTELOLOH-TLI eye, eyeball / ojo (M)
[(1)Cf.116v, (1)Tp.137, (1)Rp.96]. Z has
the variant ĪXTOLOLOH. See ĪX-TLI,
TELÓLOH-TLI.
ĪXTĒM(A) vt; pret: ĪXTĒN to fill something
up, to level something, to top something
off / lo rellena, lo empareja (T), alla-
nar hinchendo de tierra los hoyos (M)
[(6)Tp.218,230]. See ĪX-TLI, TĒM(A).
ĪXTĒMALŌ nonact. ĪXTĒM(A)
ĪXTEMEHMĒTZTIC someone who goes
about looking angry / uno que anda con la
cara como enojada (T) [(1)Tp.137]. The
second element is opaque. Possibly it
has to do with MĒTZ-TLI 'moon.' See
ĪXTE-TL.

ĪXTĒMILIĀ applic. ĪXTĒM(A)
ĪXTĒMOĀ vrefl,vt to long for children of
one's own; to scrutinize something very
carefully, to search for something every-
where / desear tener hijos (M), escudriñar
bien o buscar por todas partes alguna cosa
(M) [(3)Tp.218]. See ĪX-TLI, TĒMOĀ.
ĪXTENEHNECUIL-LI someone cross-eyed /
hombre bizco (T) See ĪX-TLI, NECUILTIC.
ĪXTENEXĒHU(I) for one's eye to be clouded
/ tiene nube en el ojo (T) [(1)Tp.137]. See
ĪXTENEXTIC, -ĒHU(I).
ĪXTENEXĒHUĪHUA nonact. ĪXTE-
NEXĒHU(I)
ĪXTENEXĒHUĪTIĀ caus. ĪXTENEXĒHU(I)
ĪXTENEXTIC someone pale from illness,
pregnancy, or chill; someone showing only
the whites of the eyes / descolorido por
enfermedad, preñez, o frío (M), el ojo se le
puso blanco (T) [(1)Tp.137]. See ĪX-TLI,
TENEX-TLI.
ĪXTĒN-TLI inalienably possessed form:
-ĪXTĒNYŌ the edge of the eyelid / los
bezos de los párpados de los ojos (M)
[(8)Zp.40,61,97,101,103,164,170,202]. In Z
the possessed form of this functions as a
postposition 'in front of, in the presence
of.' M has ixtentla with the same function
and sense. See ĪX-TLI, TĒN-TLI.
ĪXTEPATLACHTIC someone with a round
face / con cara redonda (T) [(1)Tp.137]. See
ĪXTE-TL, PATLACHTIC.
ĪXTEPETLA pl: -MEH someone blind by
reason of having flesh cover the eyes;
someone stupid and unenlightened / ciego
del todo con carnaza en los ojos (M), ciego
con carnaza en los ojos, tonto (C) See
ĪX-TLI, TEPETL(A)-TL.
ĪXTEPĪTZTIC something hard / está dura
(T) [(1)Tp.137]. See ĪX-, TEPĪTZOĀ.
ĪXTE-TL pl: -MEH; possessed form
-TEUH eye, eyeball / ojo (X) [(5)Xp.49].
Although this appears as a free form only
in X, it is an element of a number of
compounds across sources. See ĪX-TLI,
TE-TL.
ĪXTETZĪLTIC someone cross-eyed / bizco,
bisojo (Z) [(2)Zp.20,164]. See ĪX-TLI,
TETZĪLTIC.
ĪXTETZOHTZOYŌNTIC someone with
small eyes / con ojos chicos (T) [(1)Tp.137].

T is missing the syllable-final N in the next to last syllable. See ĪXTE-TL, TZOYŌN(I).

-IXTI *postposition* in all of a certain number of parts or from all of a certain number of directions / en ambas partes (C in construction with 'two'), en todas diez partes (C in construction with 'ten') [(8)Cf.91r,91v,92v]. This enters into more complex constructions than an ordinary postposition. It requires a possessive prefix, a number, and either -CĀN or -TLAPAL; ĪEXCĀNIXTI 'in all three places,' ĪONTLAPALIXTI 'on both sides.' The TI is possibly a lexicalized instance of plural -TIN that has lost the final N.

ĪXTIĀ *vrefl,vt* to keep watch, to observe; to face someone / atalayar o asechar (M), advertir y mirar diligentemente (M), hacer rostro a los enemigos (M), se asoma (T) [(3)Tp.143]. See ĪX-TLI.

ĪXTICĒHU(I) to be pale from shock or illness, for only the whites of one's eyes to show / tener mancillada la cara o estar descolorido por enfermedad (M for *ixticeua*), el ojo se puso blanco (T) [(3)Tp.137]. See ĪXTE-TL, CĒHU(I).

ĪXTICĒHUĪHUA nonact. ĪXTICĒHU(I)

ĪXTICĒHUĪTIĀ caus. ĪXTICĒHU(I)

ĪXTILIĀ *vrefl,vt* to hold oneself in high regard, to be vain; to have respect for someone / estimarse en mucho con presunción (M), respetar a otro (M) [(2)Cf.119r,123v]. applic. ĪXTIĀ

ĪXTĪL-LI person of authority / persona de autoridad (C) [(1)Cf.119r]. By regular derivation from ĪXTIĀ, the vowel of the second syllable should be long, but C fails to so mark it. See ĪXTIĀ.

ĪXTĪLŌ nonact. ĪXTIĀ

ĪXTLACCHICHI coyote / coyote (T) [(1)Tp.137]. The first element, which also appears in ĪXTLACMIZ-TLI 'wildcat,' apparently means 'wild.' See CHICHI.

ĪXTLACMIZ-TLI wildcat / gato del campo, gato montés (T for ĪXTLACMIZTŌN) [(1)Tp.137]. The first element, which also appears in ĪXTLACCHICHI 'coyote,' apparently means 'wild.' See MIZ-TLI.

-ĪXTLAH *postposition* before, in the presence of, contemporary with / en mi presencia o en mi tiempo (M for first pers. sg.), delante (C) [(4)Cf.21r,21v, (4)Zp.94,207]. M has a printing error and reads *ixila*. -ĪXTLAH is synonymous with -ĪXTLAN, which is attested in C but does not appear in M. Because of the general loss of final N and H in T, attestations from that source are ambiguous between the two. See ĪX-TLI, -TLAH.

ĪXTLAHPACH upside down / boca abajo (T), estar echado boca abajo o de bruces, o estar alguna cosa atravesada (M in construction with the verb O) See ĪX-TLI, -TLAHPACH.

ĪXTLAHPACHHUETZ(I) to fall headlong, upside down / cae boca abajo (T) [(4)Tp.137]. See ĪXTLAHPACH, HUETZ(I).

ĪXTLAHPACHHUETZĪHUA nonact. ĪXTLAHPACHHUETZ(I)

ĪXTLAHPACHHUETZĪTIĀ caus. ĪXTLAHPACHHUETZ(I)

ĪXTLAHPACHHUETZTICAH to be upside down / está boca abajo (T) [(1)Tp.137]. See ĪXTLAHPACHHUETZ(I), the verb CĀ.

ĪXTLAHPACHTĒCA *vt* to turn something, someone upside down / lo pone boca abajo (T) [(3)Tp.218]. See ĪXTLAHPACH, TĒCA.

ĪXTLAHPACHTĒCALŌ nonact. ĪXTLAHPACHTĒCA

ĪXTLAHPACHTĒQUILIĀ applic. ĪXTLAHPACHTĒCA

ĪXTLAHPACHTLAHCAL(I) *vt* to hurl something or someone headlong, upside down / lo tira boca abajo (T) [(3)Tp.218]. See ĪXTLAHPACH, (I)HCAL(I).

ĪXTLAHPACHTLAHCALILIĀ applic. ĪXTLAHPACHTLAHCAL(I)

ĪXTLAHPACHTLAHCALILŌ nonact. ĪXTLAHPACHTLAHCAL(I)

-ĪXTLAHTLĀLLOH *necessarily possessed form* someone with a dirty face / tiene la cara sucia (T) [(1)Tp.137]. See -ĪXTLAH, TLĀLLOH.

ĪXTLAHTLAYOHUA for it to get dark / no ver bien por ser ya muy noche (M), anoche, obscurece (T) [(1)Tp.137]. See ĪX-TLI, TLAYOHUA.

(I)XTLĀHU(A) *vrefl,vt* for payment to take place; to repay a debt, to pay for something / se paga (T), pagar lo que se debe (M) C and Z have transitive TLAXTLĀHUIĀ with the same sense. See (I)XTLĀHU(I).

IXTLĀHUA-TL plain, field, savanna / vega o tierra llana, sabana (M) [(2)Bf.4v,7r, (6)Zp.78,95,101,164]. Z has a long initial vowel, but B specifically marks it short.

IXTLĀHUAYOH something flat, level, unobstructed / llano, llanura (Z) [(2)Tp.78,164]. See IXTLĀHUA-TL, -YOH.

ĪXTLAHUĒLMIQU(I) *pret:* **-MIC** to look angry / tiene cara enojada (T) [(1)Tp.137]. See ĪX-TLI, TLAHUĒLMIQU(I).

(I)XTLĀHU(I) to be restored or satisfied, to prosper / restituirse o satisfacerse algo (M) [(7)Bf.1v,2r,4v,6r,9r,9v,12v]. This has the same sense as (I)XTLĀHU(A) used reflexively.

(I)XTLĀHUIĀ See TLAXTLĀHUIĀ.

ĪXTLĀLIĀ *vrefl,vt* to fall in love; to fix something in one's mind / se enamora (T), se fija en cuánto había de una cosa para saber después si se perdió; se fija en una cosa para no olvidarse de ella (T) [(6)Tp.143,218]. See ĪX-, TLĀLIĀ.

ĪXTLĀLILIĀ applic. ĪXTLĀLIĀ

ĪXTLĀLĪLŌ nonact. ĪXTLĀLIĀ

ĪXTLĀLTIC something earth-colored / color de tierra (T) [(1)Tp.137]. See ĪX-, TLĀL-LI.

ĪXTLĀLTZIN someone with earth on his face / una persona que tiene tierra en la cara (T) [(1)Tp.137]. See ĪX-TLI, TLĀL-LI.

ĪXTLAMACHĪTIĀ caus. ĪXTLAMAT(I)

ĪXTLAMAT(I) *pret:* **ĪXTLAMAT** to exercise reason and prudence, to make gestures with one's hands and face, to be familiar with a place / ser experimentado usar de razón y prudencia, o hacer gestos y visajes (M), conoce (un lugar) (T) There are two distinct senses of ĪXTLAMAT(I). One literally has to do with the surface appearance of something conveying information, while the other involves the lexicalized sense of 'prudence.' See ĪX-TLI, MAT(I).

ĪXTLAMATĪHUA nonact. ĪXTLAMAT(I)

ĪXTLAMATILICEH someone prudent / prudente (K) [(1)Rp.45]. See ĪXTLAMATILIZ-TLI.

ĪXTLAMATILIZ-TLI prudence / prudencia, razón natural, o gestos y visajes (M) [(1)Rp.96]. See ĪXTLAMAT(I).

-ĪXTLAN *compound postposition* before, in the presence of / delante, delante de los ojos de alguno, en su presencia (C) [(4)Cf.21r,21v, (4)Tp.137,167]. This is synonymous with -ĪXTLAH, also attested in C. T is ambiguous between the two, since it loses both N and H word-finally. Where additional suffixes are added to form the honorific, T has the form with N, -ĪXTLANTZINCO. See ĪX-TLI, -TLAN.

-ĪXTLANTZINCO *honorific compound postposition* with one's indulgence, permission, pardon / con su permiso (T for third pers. sg. possessor) [(2)Tp.143,167]. See -ĪXTLAN.

ĪXTLAPAL sideways, across / de través o de lado (M) [(1)Bf.7v]. See ĪX-TLI, TLAPAL-LI.

ĪXTLAPOLŌLTIĀ *vrefl,vt* to be confused; to mislead, confuse someone / confunde (T), le hace equivocarse, lo distrae, lo confunde (T) [(6)Tp.143,218]. See ĪX-TLI, POLŌLTIĀ.

ĪXTLAPOLŌLTILIĀ applic. ĪXTLA-POLŌLTIĀ

ĪXTLAPOLŌLTĪLŌ nonact. ĪXTLA-POLŌLTIĀ

ĪXTLAPŌPOYĀHU(I) to get dark / se obscurece (T) [(1)Tp.137]. See ĪX-TLI, TLAPOYĀHUA.

ĪXTLAQUĒZ someone or something bent / inclinado (Z) [(2)Zp.71,164]. This is not a regular derivation. It appears to be a truncation of some deverbal form. See ĪX-TLI, TLAQUĒZŌLTIĀ.

ĪXTLĀYI See TLAĪXTLĀYI.

ĪXTLAYOHUA to get dark, for night to fall; to be bewildered, dazzled, stunned / anochece, obscurece (T), encandilarse o cegarse con la mucha claridad (M) [(1)Tp.137, (2)Zp.16,164]. See ĪX-TLI, TLAYOHUA.

ĪXTLAZOLHUIĀ *vt* to injure someone with one's gaze / por mirar le hace daño al otro (a propósito), le hace mal de ojo (T) [(3)Tp.218]. See ĪX-TLI, ZOLOĀ.

ĪXTLAZOLHUILIĀ applic. ĪXTLA-ZOLHUIĀ

ĪXTLAZOLHUĪLŌ nonact. ĪXTLA-ZOLHUIĀ

ĪXTLEHCŌ See TLAĪXTLEHCŌ.

ĪX-TLI face, surface, eye / la haz o la cara, o el nudo de la caña (M), faz, rostro, por ext. ojo (S)

ĪXTLĪLXŌCHI-TL a type of vine / una

planta voluble (K) [(1)Bf.11v]. According to
Hernández, this plant is used to treat
diseases of the eye. TLĪLXŌCHI-TL is the
vanilla orchid. ĪXTLĪLXŌCHI-TL is used
as a personal name. See ĪX-TLI, TLĪL-LI,
XŌCHI-TL.

ĪXTOHMI-TL *inalienably possessed form:*
-ĪXTOHMIYŌ eyebrow / su ceja (Z for
possessed form) [(2)Zp.27,164]. See ĪX-TLI,
TOHMI-TL.

ĪXTOMĀHUA to get rather fat, to be silly /
atochado o tonto, o cordel algo gordo o
grueso (M for substantive) [(1)Bf.7v]. See
ĪX-, ĪX-TLI, TOMĀHUA.

ĪXTŌNĒHU(I) for one's eyes to burn, hurt /
arde de ojo (T) [(3)Tp.137]. M has reflexive
ixtoneua 'to get red in the face from being
teased.' See ĪX-TLI, TŌNĒHU(I).

ĪXTŌNĒHUĪHUA nonact. ĪXTŌNĒHU(I)

ĪXTŌNĒHUĪTIĀ caus. ĪXTŌNĒHU(I)

ĪXTŌZOĀ to keep vigil, to stay awake
through the night / pasa toda la noche en
vela (C) [(1)Bf.7v, (1)Cf.97r]. See ĪX-TLI,
TŌZOĀ.

ĪXTZACU(A) *vrefl* to cover the face, to
have one's eyes stuck shut with tissue or
discharge / tapa la cara, tiene los ojos pegados con lagañas (T) [(6)Tp.144]. See
ĪX-TLI, TZACU(A).

ĪXTZACUALŌ nonact. ĪXTZACU(A)

ĪXTZACUILIĀ *vrefl* to cover the face, to
have one's eyes stuck shut with tissue or
discharge / tapa la cara, tiene los ojos
pegados con lagañas (T) [(3)Tp.144]. T's
gloss for this applicative form is identical with that for ĪXTZACU(A). applic.
ĪXTZACU(A)

ĪXTZACUILĪLŌ nonact. ĪXTZACUILIĀ

ĪXTZOHCUIL someone with a dirty face /
cara sucia (Z) [(2)Zp.25,164]. See ĪX-TLI,
TZOHCUILTIC.

ĪXTZOPĪNIĀ *vrefl* to get poked in the eye /
se pica en el ojo (T) [(3)Tp.144]. See ĪX-TLI,
TZOPĪNIĀ.

ĪXTZOPĪNĪLŌ nonact. ĪXTZOPĪNIĀ

ĪXTZOTZŌLOĀ *vrefl* to make faces /
hace gestos (Z) [(2)Zp.63,170]. Z does not
mark the vowel of the third syllable
long in either attestation. See ĪX-TLI,
TZOTZŌLOĀ.

ĪXXACUALOĀ *vrefl,vt* to rub one's eyes;

to scrub, rub, scour something / refri-
ega los ojos (T), lo restriega, lo friega, lo
frota (Z) [(3)Tp.143, (4)Zp.61,109,199].
T gives this with an internal glottal
stop ĪXAHCUALOĀ, but elsewhere in T
XACUALOĀ appears without a glottal
stop. The XX sequence is reduced to X in T
and Z. See ĪX-TLI, XACUALOĀ.

ĪXXACUALŌLŌ nonact. ĪXXACUALOĀ

ĪXXAHUACA to make a noise as of rushing,
spouting water / ruido del chorro de agua
(T) [(1)Tp.135]. If this is a compound with
ĪX-TLI, then the XX sequence shortens to
X. Another possibility is that T has Ī for
IH, and this should be IHXAHUACA. See
ĪX-TLI, XAXAHUACA.

ĪXXĀYŌ-TL tear / lágrima (K) [(1)Bf.11r].
The literal sense of this would be 'eye-
excrement' or 'eye-discharge.' Either this
makes a minimal pair with synonymous
ĪXĀYŌ-TL, or the latter is a reduction
or reanalysis of this word. See ĪX-TLI,
XĀYŌ-TL.

ĪXXŌHUA to bloom, burst forth / brota (Z)
[(2)Zp.21,163]. There is a single X in the
attestations in Z, presumably a reduction
of XX. See ĪX-TLI, XŌ-.

ĪXXŌTIĀ *vrefl,vt* to keep watch, to be
vigilant; to watch over or guard something / se cuida, se vigila (T), cuida (T)
[(6)Tp.144,230]. The transitive form is
attested only with the prefix TLA-, which
may be fused to form an intransitive verb.
See ĪXXŌ-TL.

ĪXXŌ-TL prudence, moderation / la cordura,
la prudencia (C) [(1)Cf.54r]. There is only a
single X in the attestation, but C also gives
synonymous ĪXYŌ-TL with unassimilated Y.

ĪXXOXOCTIC something blue / azul (T)
[(1)Tp.137]. See ĪX-, XOXOCTIC.

ĪXYAHUALTIC someone with a round face
/ con cara redonda (T) [(1)Tp.138]. T has YE
for YA. See ĪX-TLI, YAHUALTIC.

ĪXYEHYECOĀ *vt* to examine, test, certify or
judge something / lo examina, lo califica,
lo tienta (T), lo considera, lo examina, lo
calcula (Z) This is abundantly attested in T
and Z. With the prefix TLA- M glosses this
as 'to be judicious in one's activities.' See
ĪX-TLI, YEHYECOĀ.

ĪXYEHYECOLHUIĀ applic. ĪXYEHYECOĀ
ĪXYEHYECŌLŌ nonact. ĪXYEHYECOĀ
ĪXYŌTIĀ See ĪXXŌTIĀ.
ĪXYŌ-TL prudence, moderation / la cordura,
la prudencia (C) [(1)Cf.54r]. In this variant
the Y fails to assimilate to X. See IXXO-TL.
ĪXZĀLOĀ vrefl to have one's eyes stuck
together with discharge or tissue / tiene los
ojos pegados con lagañas (T) [(3)Tp.143].
See ĪX-TLI, ZĀLOĀ.
ĪXZĀLŌLŌ nonact. ĪXZĀLOĀ
*IYOĀ preterit-as-present verb; pret: IYOH
to be alone, to act alone / solo (K) This
takes subject prefixes and has a regular
preterit form; the singular is IYOH and the
plural IYOHQUEH. Third person singular
IYOH is lexicalized to the oint that it
functions adverbially. It commonly occurs
in the phrase ZAN IYOH 'only.' T has two
instances of what appears to be the reflex
of YĀUH incorporated with reflexive verbs
and conveying the sense of 'to oneself
alone.'
IYOH dolorous interjection guay interjección (M) [(1)Bf.8v, (1)Cf.112v, (1)Rp.97].
The glottal stop is attested only in R.
IYOH only / solo, solamente (S) This is the
lexicalized third person singular preterit
form of the verb IYOĀ.
IYOHPA only (in reference to time) / solo (C)
According to C, this is limited to the
constructions ZĀ IYOHPA 'just once and
no more,' ZAN IYOHPA 'only once,' and
QUIN IYOHPA 'the first time.' See IYOĀ,
-PA.
IYOHYAHUE dolorous interjection guay ...
o, interjección (M for iyoiyaue) [(1)Bf.6v,
(5)Cf.112r,112v,131v, (3)Rp.97]. See IYOH.
ĪYŌLIC gradually, pacifically / poco a poco,
mansamente, y con tiento (M)
IZ here / aquí (M) See ICI.
ĪZAHUIĀ vrefl,vt to be overawed; to
frighten, outrage someone / admirarse o
espantarse (M), espantar o escandalizar a
otros (M) [(1)Bf.10r, (1)Cf.104r].
IZCAH here it is / helo aquí, he aquí, o
toma esto (M) [(2)Cf.89r,124v]. A common
variant form of this is IZCATQUI. See IZ,
the verb CĀ.
(I)ZCALIĀ vrefl,vt to hatch, to revive, to be
restored; to revive someone or to teach and

nurture someone / avivar, tornar en sí, o
resuscitar (M), avivar así a otro, doctrinarlo
o corregirlo de palabra o con castigo (M)
(I)ZCALILIĀ applic. (I)ZCALIĀ
(I)ZCALĪLŌ nonact. (I)ZCALIĀ
(I)ZCALTIĀ vt to raise children / criar niño
(M), crio a personas, como a niños (C for
first pers. sg. subject) caus. (I)ZCALIĀ
IZCATQUI See IZCAH.
IZHUA-TL inalienably possessed form:
-IZHUAYŌ leaf, foliage / hoja (M), su hoja
(de la caña de la milpa) (T for possessed
form) [(2)Tp.134,135, (4)Xp.48]. This is
historically related to XIHU(I)-TL 'grass.'
ĪZOLOCA for water to make a rushing
sound / el agua hace ruido corriendo (T)
[(1)Tp.133].
ĪZQUI pl: ĪZQUĪNTĪN as much, as many,
so much, so many (referring to flat things)
/ tantas en número, dicese de tablas o
esteras o de cosas llanas (M) In the single
attestation of the plural form C marks·the
vowel of the third syllable long but not
the second. But by analogy with other
quantifiers, there should be alternate plural
forms ĪZQUĪN and ĪZQUĪNTĪN.
ĪZQUICĀN so many places as there are, an
equal number of places / de todas partes
o de todos lugares (M for izquicampa)
[(2)Bf.9v]. See ĪZQUI, -CĀN.
ĪZQUĪNTĪN See ĪZQUI.
ĪZQUIPA as many times, so many times /
tantas veces See ĪZQUI, -PA.
ĪZQUI-TL popcorn (used to describe many
plants and trees that produce clusters of
white flowers) / maíz tostado; flor muy
olorosa (S) [(1)Tp.170, (3)Xp.40]. M has
izquiatl 'drink made of ground popcorn.'
ĪZQUIXŌCHI-TL pl: -MEH a tree that
produces fragrant white flowers (Bourreria
huanita), or any of a number of plants and
trees that produce clusters of white flowers / cuéramo (X) [(3)Xp.47]. The literal
sense of this is 'popcorn-flower.' X fails to
mark the initial vowel long although X
has it long in ĪZQUI-TL. See ĪZQUI-TL,
XŌCHI-TL.
IZTAĀ-TL salt water / agua salada (Z)
[(2)Zp.7,161]. See IZTA-TL, Ā-TL.
IZTĀC something white / cosa blanca (M)
See IZTA-TL.

IZTĀCĀTŌL-LI white atole (a beverage made of cornstarch) / atole blanco (T) [(2)Tp.108,134]. See IZTĀC, ĀTŌL-LI.

IZTĀCĀYŌ-TL the white of an egg / clara (de huevo) (T) [(1)Tp.134, (1)Zp.161]. Z fails to mark A long, and T has a short vowel and postvocalic glottal stop in the third syllable. M has *iztacayotl* 'whiteness,' which is probably derived simply from IZTĀCĀ- (the compounding form of ĪZTĀC) and -YŌ. See IZTĀC, ĀYŌ-TL.

IZTĀCTILIĀ *vt* to bleach something / lo blanquea (Z) [(2)Zp.20,194]. See IZTĀC.

IZTĀCTZAPO-TL white zapote, the fruit of which is narcotic (Casimiroa edulis) / zapote blanco [(1)Tp.134, (2)Zp.131,161]. See IZTĀC, TZAPO-TL.

IZTACUACUĀ for animals to eat salt / comen sal los animales (T) [(1)Tp.133]. T has CA for CUA in the third syllable. See IZTA-TL, CUACUĀ.

(I)ZTAHUIĀ *vt* to salt something / salar algo, o echar sal al manjar o guisado (M) [(2)Cf.60v, (3)Tp.202, (1)Rp.48]. See IZTA-TL, -HUIĀ.

(I)ZTAHUILIĀ applic. (I)ZTAHUIĀ

(I)ZTAHUĪLŌ nonact. (I)ZTAHUIĀ

IZTALECTIC someone pale from chill, fear, or illness / descolorido o blanquecino de frío, o de temor, o de enfermedad (M) [(1)Tp.133]. Z has IZTĀLTIC, which seems to be a shortened form of this, possibly with compensatory lengthening of the vowel caused by loss of a syllable. See IZTALĒHU(A).

IZTALĒHU(A) to turn pale from chill, fear, or illness / pararse descolorido de esta manera (de frío, o de temor, o de enfermedad) (M) [(1)Cf.76v]. This appears to be synonymous with T's IZTALĒHU(I). See IZTA-TL, ĒHU(A).

IZTALĒHU(I) to turn pale / se pone pálido, anémico, está descolorido (T) [(3)Tp.133]. This appears to be synonymous with C's and M's IZTALĒHU(A). See IZTA-TL, -ĒHU(I).

IZTALĒHUĪHUA nonact. IZTALĒHU(I)

IZTALĒHUĪTIĀ caus. IZTALĒHU(I)

IZTĀLTIC someone anemic-looking, palid / anémico, pálido (Z) [(2)Zp.10,161]. Z marks the vowel of the second syllable long, but

it should not be, unless it is lengthened in compensation for the loss of a syllable. See IZTALECTIC.

IZTAPINOLHUIĀ *vt* to salt something / salo (C for first pers. sg. subject) [(1)Cf.60v]. See IZTAPINOL-LI, -HUIĀ.

IZTAPINOL-LI ground salt / sal molida (M) [(2)Cf.60v]. See IZTA-TL, PINOL-LI.

IZTĀQUĒHU(A) *vrefl,vt* for something to bleach out; to bleach something / se blanquea (T), lo blanquea (T) [(4)Tp.149,202]. See IZTĀC, ĒHU(A).

IZTĀQUĒHUALŌ nonact. IZTĀQUĒHU(A)

IZTĀQUĒHUILIĀ applic. IZTĀQUĒHU(A)

IZTĀQUE-TL white bean / frijol blanco (T) [(1)Tp.134]. T has I for E. See IZTĀC, E-TL.

IZTA-TL salt / sal (M) In verbal derivations the initial I is weak and deleted when preceded by a prefixal vowel.

IZTAY(A) *pret:* IZTAZ ~ IZTAYAC for something to turn white, to appear white because of being at a distance / pararse blanca alguna cosa, o blanquear algo de lejos (M), pararse blanco (M) [(4)Cf.32v,93r]. See IZTA-TL.

IZTAYOH something salted / salado (Z) [(5)Zp.7,112,161,177]. M has *iztayotl* 'brine' derived with -YŌ rather than -YOH. See IZTA-TL, -YOH.

IZTAYOHĀ-TL salt water / agua salada (Z) [(2)Zp.7,161]. See IZTAYOH, Ā-TL.

(I)ZTECUI *vt* to scratch, pinch something / lo rasguña, lo pellizca (Z) [(3)Zp.96,105,194]. See (I)ZTE-TL, CUI.

(I)ZTEHUETZ(I) *vt* to burst forth from a place / sale rápidamente, violento (Z) [(2)Zp.113,194]. See (I)ZTE-TL, HUETZ(I).

(I)ZTETIĀ See OZTETIĀ.

(I)ZTETIĀ See OZTETIĀ.

(I)ZTE-TL fingernail, toenail, a very small unit of length measurement / uña (M), jeme (C) This has a variant form (I)ZTI-TL. Both are often used in metaphors referring to offspring as parts of one's own body, especially when conventionally paired with TZON-TLI 'hair.'

(I)ZTI-TL See (I)ZTE-TL.

IZTLACA- something false / falso (M), vano y no verdadero (M) This does not appear as a free form but only in compounds and derivations.

(I)ZTLĀCALHUIĀ applic. (I)ZTLĀCOĀ
IZTLACATĒTEOH false gods / falsos dioses (K) [(2)Bf.10r,10v]. See IZTLACA-, TEŌ-TL.
(I)ZTLACAT(I) to lie / mentir (M) See IZTLACA-.
(I)ZTLACATĪHUA nonact. (I)ZTLACAT(I)
(I)ZTLACATILIĀ *vt* to lie to someone / le miente (T) [(4)Tp.133,202]. applic. (I)ZTLACAT(I)
(I)ZTLACATILILIĀ applic. (I)ZTLACATILIĀ
(I)ZTLACATILĪLŌ nonact. (I)ZTLACATILIĀ
(I)ZTLACATILIZ-TLI lie / mentira o falsedad (M) [(1)Cf.34v, (1)Tp.133, (1)Rp.98]. R has the shortened free form IZTLACALIZ-TLI but has the full form in a compound. See (I)ZTLACAT(I).
(I)ZTLACATINI *pl:* **-MEH** someone mendacious, a liar / mentiroso (M) [(1)Tp.133]. See (I)ZTLACAT(I).
(I)ZTLACATLAHTŌL-LI lie / mentira (T) [(1)Tp.133]. M has *iztlacatlatoliztli* 'the art of lying.' See IZTLACA-, TLAHTŌL-LI.
(I)ZTLACATQUI someone mendacious,

a liar / mentiroso (M) [(1)Tp.133]. See (I)ZTLACAT(I).
IZTLACMĒY(A) *pret:* **-MĒX** to drool / babea (T) [(2)Tp.133,142]. See IZTLAC-TLI, MĒY(A).
IZTLACMĪN(A) *vt* for a snake to bite someone / morder la víbora (M) [(1)Cf.96r]. See IZTLAC-TLI, MĪN(A).
(I)ZTLĀCOĀ *vrefl,vt* to consult one's own judgement; to examine and judge something, especially without appearing to do so / examinar o tomar consejo consigo mismo (M), mirar con cautela, y notar lo que otro dice o hace, acechándole (M) [(1)Bf.7v, (1)Cf.121v, (6)Tp.202,230]. T has a vowel length discrepancy; half its attestations have a long vowel in the initial syllable.
(I)ZTLĀCŌLŌ nonact. (I)ZTLĀCOĀ
IZTLAC-TLI saliva / baba (M), su saliva (T for possessed form) [(3)Tp.133,142]. By extension of meaning, this has the sense 'poison.'

M

MĀ *introductory particle for clauses expressing wishes, commands, admonitions; negative form:* **MĀCA ~ MĀCAMŌ** let it be that ... , may ... / es partícula de optativo ... y de imperativo, y del avisativo, vetativo, y entonces quiere decir no (M) Preceding a verb in the optative or vetative form, this particle implies that a wish is being expressed rather than a direct command. The negative sense mentioned in M's gloss is not inherent in MĀ but in the vetative form of the verb, which warns against doing something (Or M may be combining the senses of MĀ and MAH in a single entry.) MĀNĒN is more emphatic with the vetative. With negative wish clauses, MĀCA ~ MĀCAMŌ occurs in place of the sequence *MĀ AHMŌ. TLĀ may occur in place of MĀ with the optative and TLĀCA ~ TLĀCAMŌ in corresponding negative wish sentences.

MĀ *vt; pret:* **MAH** to hunt, catch something, to take captives / cazar o cautivar (M) [(3)Cf.31r,32v]. It is possible that this shares a common root with MĀ(I)-TL 'hand, arm.'

-MĀĀCAYŌ *necessarily possessed form* one's forearm / su antebrazo (Z) [(2)Zp.11,159]. See MĀ(I)-TL, ĀCA-TL.

MĀAHCI *vt* to reach something with one's hand / lo alcanzar (T), alcanza con la mano (Z) [(3)Tp.191, (2)Zp.8,165]. Z gives this as an intransitive verb. See MĀ(I)-TL, AHCI.

MĀAHXĪHUA nonact. MĀAHCI

MĀAHXILIĀ applic. MĀAHCI

MĀĀZCACUALŌ for one's hand or arm to tingle because of reduced circulation / adormecida (la mano) (Z) [(2)Zp.5,178]. The literal sense of this is 'for one's hand or arm to be eaten by ants.' One of the attestations gives it with final -C, 'something that tingles as though an arm were being eaten by ants.' The other attestation has a final A, which is surely an error. See MĀ(I)-TL, ĀZCA-TL, CUALŌ.

-MĀC *necessarily possessed form* in the hands of / en, por mi mano o mis manos (S for first pers. sg. possessor), en las manos de alguien (S for TĒMĀC) Although this commonly takes only possessive prefixes, in C's ĀMĀC 'at the brink of the river,' it appears to be bound to a noun in the manner of a full postposition. An alternative analysis is ĀMĀ(I)-TL (M has amaitl 'inlet, bay') plus -C(O), but in either case, the component elements are the same. See MĀ(I)-TL, -C(O).

MACA *vrefl,vt* to dose oneself, to take something like medicine; to give something to someone / tomar medicina (M); dar algo a otro o restituír (M) Because of the inherent applicative nature of this verb, it takes two object prefixes, one direct and the other oblique reflexive or indirect. X has this as a simple intransitive verb.

MĀCA *negated form of* MĀ See MĀCAMŌ.

MĀCACAPATZ(A) *vrefl* to clap, applaud / dar palmadas (M) [(1)Cf.74r]. See MĀ(I)-TL, CACAPATZ(A).

MĀCAHCĀHU(A) *vt* to let something fall / deja caer (Z) [(2)Zp.40,189]. redup. MĀCĀHU(A)

MĀCAHCAPĀN(I) to make tortillas / tortillea (Z) [(2)Zp.124,165]. This refers to the slapping motion of shaping a tortilla. See MĀCAPĀNIĀ.

MĀCĀHU(A) *vt* to drop something, let go of something; to concede something, to give consent, to agree to something / dar licencia a otro (M), otorgar algo o conceder o soltar algo de la mano (M) Z has derived forms with MAH in place of MĀ. See MĀ(I)-TL, CĀHU(A).

MĀCĀHUALŌ nonact. MĀCĀHU(A)

MĀCĀHUALTIĀ caus. MĀCĀHU(A)

MĀCĀHUILIĀ *vt* to concede something to

someone / otorgar o conceder algo a otro
(M) [(1)Tp.191]. applic. MĀCĀHU(A)
MĀCAĬC may it never be that ... / ojalá que
nunca (C) [(4)Cf.26v,271,103r]. See MĀCA,
AĬC.
MACALŌ nonact. MACA
MĀCAMŌ *negated form of* **MĀ** let not ... ,
may it not be that ... / no ... se haga, etc.
(M) This contrasts with MAHCAMŌ 'as
though it weren't' the negated form of
MAH 'such that.' Each has a synonymous
short form, MĀCA 'let not ...' contrasting
with MAHCA 'as though it weren't.' R
twice attests this with a glottal stop in the
second syllable, but C repeatedly attests
the second syllable with a specifically
short vowel and with no glottal stop. See
the particle MĀ.
MĀCANAH if only somewhere, let it be
that somewhere ... / sea o no sea en alguna
parte o lugar (M) [(2)Cf.91v]. See MĀ,
CANAH.
MĀCAOQUĬC let ... no longer / no ... ya
más (C) [(1)Cf.103r]. See MĀCA, AOQUĬC.
MĀCAPĀNIĀ *vrefl* to make a noise with
one's hands, to applaud / si el ruido (de las
palmadas) es poco, y con sola una mano
(C), aplaude (Z) [(1)Cf.74r, (2)Zp.12,170].
See MĀ(I)-TL, CAPĀNIĀ.
MĀCĀUHTOC something loose, separate /
suelto (Z) [(3)Zp.118,165,227]. Z has MĀ in
the verb MĀCAHCĀHU(A), and there is
agreement across sources on MĀCĀHU(A),
but in two of the three attestations of this
in Z, there is MAH instead of MĀ. See
MĀCĀHU(A), the verb O.
MĀCCUAHU(I)-TL hand sword of wood
edged with obsidian / macana, especie
de espada de madera guarnecida por ambos lados de cuchillos de obsidiana (S)
[(1)Bf.10r]. The single attestation has locative MĀC 'in the hand' as the initial element, although S assumes it is MĀ 'hand.'
See MĀ(I)-TL, -C(O), CUAHU(I)-TL.
MĀCECĒPAHTIC someone with cold, damp
hands / sudoroso de las manos, frío de
las manos (Z) [(1)Zp.166]. See MĀ(I)-TL,
CECĒPAHTIC.
MĀCECEPOC-TLI *pl:* **-MEH** elbow / codo
(X) [(4)Xp.52]. M has *macecepoa* 'for one's
arm to go to sleep, to tingle from lack of

circulation.' This seems to specifically
refer to one's funny bone. See MĀ(I)-TL,
CECEPOCA.
MĀCEH *particle cluster used in place
of simple* **MĀ** *to introduce clauses expressing wishes, commands, admonitions*
[(3)Cf.25v]. See MĀ, ZO, (Y)EH.
MĀCĒHUAL-LI *pl:* **-TIN** subject, commoner; indigenous person, speaker of
Nahuatl / vasallo (M), hombre plebeyo
(C), mejicano, azteca, uno que habla
nahuat, trigueño (Z) This contrasts with
MAHCĒHUAL-LI 'merit, recompense,
fortune.' T glosses this as specifically
referring to the language as well as to a
speaker of the language. M gives as a gloss
for the plural form 'vassals or plebians.'
MĀCĒHUALTIĀ *vrefl,vt* to make others
vassals to oneself; to provide someone
with vassals / hacer a otros vasallos míos
(M for first pers. sg. reflexive); dar vasallos
a otro, o echar algo a la rebatiña (M) This
is not directly attested in the sources
for this dictionary, but it can be derived
from MĀCĒHUAL-LI. It contrasts with
MAHCĒHUALTIĀ 'to give someone his
due,' and M gives them in separate contiguous entries. Because it is inherently
applicative, this takes both a direct and an
indirect or oblique reflexive object prefix.
See MĀCĒHUAL-LI.
MĀCĒHUALTLĀCA-TL indigenous Mexican / hombre mexicano, indígena azteca (T) [(1)Tp.165]. See MĀCĒHUAL-LI,
TLĀCA-TL.
MĀCEPŌHUIĀ for the hand or arm to
tingle because of reduced circulation / se
adormece la mano (T) [(3)Tp.165]. See
MĀ(I)-TL, CEPŌHUIĀ.
MĀCEPŌHUĪHUA nonact. MĀCEPŌHUIĀ
MĀCEPŌHUĪTIĀ caus. MĀCEPŌHUIĀ
MACH it is said that, it appears that ... /
dizque o dicen que (M), parece que (C)
Bound to an interrogative particle, this
serves as an intensifier. C gives its
equivalent in Spanish as *diablos*, hence
TLEINMACH 'what the devil?' In a ques-
tion this implies perplexity; in confirming
something, it leaves room for doubt.
MACH very much, indeed, positively /
mucho, en gran manera (C), mucho, en

extremo, ciertamente, positivamente (S) This is generally accompanied by antecessive Ō- or by NEL or is used in the extended form MACHEH, all of which serve to distinguish it from dubitive MACH.

MACHEH very much, especially / mucho, en gran manera (C), especialmente (C) See MACH, (Y)EH.

MACHIĀ to be known, to be apparent / ser conocido, descubierto (S), se sabe, se siente (T) [(2)Tp.108,139]. T has E for I and gives no preterit form. S gives a preterit form implying that this is a verb ending in IĀ. M has *tlamachia* to do something well, to arbitrate for people,' which appears to be this verb used transitively and fused with the prefix TLA-. See MAT(I).

MACHILIĀ *vt* to be aware of defects in someone or something, to discriminate among things by their quality / saber defectos ajenos (M), disponer o repartir algo a otros conforme a la calidad de cada uno (M) applic. MAT(I)

MACHILILIĀ applic. MACHILIĀ

MACHILĪLŌ nonact. MACHILIĀ

MACHĪLTIĀ This causative form of MAT(I) should by general rule have a short vowel before -LTIĀ, but the vowel is specifically marked long in B, is consistently the reflex of a long vowel in T, and is marked long once in C. It is so conventionally used as an honorific form that the reflexive object can be taken as fused with the verb. Z has the variant form MATĪLTIĀ.

MACHĪLTILIĀ applic. MACHĪLTIĀ

MACHĪLTĪLŌ nonact. MACHĪLTIĀ

MACHĪTIĀ *vrefl,vt* to reveal oneself, to make oneself known; to inform or notify someone / mostrarse, darse a conocer (S), hacer saber o notificar algo a otros (M) altern. caus. MAT(I)

MACHIYŌTIĀ *vrefl,vt* to make a sign upon oneself, as in making the sign of the cross; to make a sign on someone or something or to set an example to someone / se persigna (T), dar buen ejemplo, incitar a la virtud a alguien (S), confirmar o crismar (M), reglar papel o dibujar algo (M) [(3)Tp.150, (2)Zp.97,170]. T has E for I

in the second syllable. One of Z's two attestations has the vowel of the second syllable marked long. See MACHIYŌ-TL.

MACHIYŌTĪLŌ nonact. MACHIYŌTIĀ

MACHIYŌ-TL sign, example / señal, comparación, ejemplo o dechado (M) This is implied by the verb MACHIYŌTIĀ. See MAT(I), -YŌ.

MACHIZTIĀ *vrefl,vt* to say that one knows or believes something, to meddle; to announce something, to make something known to others / decir que sabe o entiende alguna cosa ... o entremeterse sin ser llamado (M), publicar, notificar, o hacer saber algo a otros (M) Because this is inherently applicative or causative, it takes both a direct object prefix and an oblique reflexive or indirect object prefix. M also has *machizti* and *machiztia* 'for something to be known or believed.' Both form the preterit by adding -C, which shows that the latter represents MACHIZTIYA rather than MACHIZTIĀ. See MAT(I).

MACHIZTILIĀ applic. MACHIZTIĀ

MACHIZTĪLŌ nonact. MACHIZTIĀ

MACHŌ nonact. MAT(I)

MACHTIĀ *vrefl,vt* to learn, to study; to teach someone / aprender o estudiar (M), enseñar o predicar (M) X has X for CH and glosses the reflexive use of this as 'to pray.' altern. caus. MAT(I)

MACHTILIĀ applic. MACHTIĀ

MACHTILIZ-TLI *pl:* **-TIN** prayer / rezo (X) [(3)Xp.52]. X has X for CH. See MACHTIĀ.

MACHTĪLŌ nonact. MACHTIĀ

MACH-TLI nephew, or niece (from the point of view of an uncle) / sobrino, de varón (M) [(7)Bf.4v,51,12r,12v]. S glosses this as specifically 'nephew,' but according to the Spanish-to-Nahuatl side of M, it applies equally to nephews and nieces.

MĀCIHUI although, granted that / aunque o dado que o puesto caso (M) This is attested once in B with MAH in place of MĀ, but it is clearly a shortened form of MĀZO IHUI. See MĀZO, IHU(I).

MĀCIUHQUI no matter, nonetheless, however that may be / aunque sea tal, o tal cual es (M), no importa, aunque (T) [(1)Tp.165, (3)Zp.17,166]. This shortened form of MĀZO IUHQUI has undergone further syncopation in T, Z and other modern Nahuatl speech communities, and in the form MĀZQUI or MĀZQUE has become a conventional leave-taking phrase in some localities. See MĀCIHUI, MĀZO, IUHQUI.

MĀCO fist, grasp / puño (Z) [(7)Zp.81,103,159,160]. This only occurs in Z. By general rules, MĀ(I)-TL plus -C(O) yields MĀC. See MĀ(I)-TL, -C(O).

MĀCOHCŌLTZIN someone with crippled hands / paralítico de las manos (T) [(1)Tp.164]. See MĀ(I)-TL, COHCŌL-LI.

MĀCOHCOZTIC paw or foot of an animal colored yellow / pata (de animal) amarillo (T) [(1)Tp.164]. See MĀ(I)-TL, COZTIC.

MĀCOTOCTIC See MĀCOTOLTIC.

MĀCOTOLTIC person who has had a hand or arm cut off / manco de la mano por se la haber cortado (M for *macotoctic*) [(2)Zp.81,165]. Z has COTOLTIC for COTOCTIC elsewhere. See MĀ(I)-TL, COTOCTIC.

MĀCOTŌN(A) *vt* to cut off someone's hand, to injure a hand / cortar a otro la mano (M), le mocha la mano (T) [(4)Tp.191]. T provides an additional gloss 'to make *memelas* (a type of thick, oblong tortilla).' In this sense it probably means to section something off by hand. See MĀ(I)-TL, COTŌN(A).

MĀCOTŌNALŌ nonact. MĀCOTŌN(A)

MĀCOTŌNILIĀ applic. MĀCOTŌN(A)

-MĀCPA *compound postposition* from or by one's hands / de mis manos o por mis manos (M for first person possessor) [(1)Cf.104v]. See -MĀC, -PA.

MĀCPAL-LI the palm of the hand / palma de la mano (M) [(1)Tp.131, (3)Zp.93,159,189]. See MĀ(I)-TL, -C(O), -PAL.

MĀCPALXŌCHI-TL a type of plant (Chiranthodendron pentadactylon) / manita, mano de león (K) This is not directly attested in the sources for this dictionary, but its component elements are. It has a diversity of medicinal uses as an anti-inflammatory agent, an anti-epileptic, and for heart ailments. See MĀCPAL-LI, XŌCHI-TL.

MĀCTIĀ *vrefl,vt* to surrender, submit; to hand something over / se entrega, se rinde (T), lo pone en la mano, lo entrega (T) [(6)Tp.152,191, (2)Zp.53,197]. See -MĀC.

MĀCTILIĀ applic. MĀCTIĀ

MĀCTĪLŌ nonact. MĀCTIĀ

MĀCUAUHPITZOĀ *vrefl* to extend the arm or hand and hold it rigid, to exert force with the arm / extiende la mano y la detiene rígida, endurece las manos, se hace fuerza con las manos (T) [(3)Tp.153]. See MĀ(I)-TL, CUAUHPITZOĀ.

MĀCUAUHTI for the hands, arms to tire, grow stiff / se cansa las manos (T) [(3)Tp.164]. See MĀ(I)-TL, CUAUHTI.

MĀCUAUHTĪHUA nonact. MĀCUAUHTI

MĀCUAUHTILIĀ *vt* to tire out someone's arms / le cansa las manos (T) [(4)Tp.164,191]. applic. MĀCUAUHTI

MĀCUAUHTILILIĀ applic. MĀCUAUHTILIĀ

MĀCUAUHTILĪLŌ nonact. MĀCUAUHTILIĀ

MĀCUĒLEH *compound introductory particle for clauses expressing strong wishes and exhortations* let it be that ... , on with ... / ea ea, alto a ello, suso (M), ojalá (C) [(3)Cf.26v,27r,29r]. See MĀ, CUĒL, (Y)EH.

MĀCUĒLOĀ *vrefl,vt* to twist, dislocate one's hand or arm; to twist someone's hand or arm, to pull down the branch of a tree / torcérseme o desconcertárseme la mano (M for first pers. sg. subject), torcer a otro la mano o el brazo (M), abajar la rama del árbol, tirando de la (M) This is implied by MĀ(I)-TL, CUĒLOĀ, and MĀCUELPACHYĀN.

MĀCUELPACHYĀN elbow / ángulo del codo (Z) [(2)Zp.10,165]. See MĀ(I)-TL, CUELPACHOĀ, -YĀN.

MĀCUEP(A) *vrefl,vt* to recoup one's losses, to get square; to return, restore something / se desquita, se venga (Z), lo recompensa (Z), lo devuelve (Z) [(5)Zp.44,45,128,189]. Z has this as both MĀCUEP(A) and MĀQUEP(A), apparently synonymous. See MĀ(I)-TL, CUEP(A).

MĀCUETLAXTIC someone lacking strength in an arm, someone with a withered arm / mano suelta (que no tiene

fuerza) (T) [(1)Tp.164]. M has *macuetlaxtli*
for a type of bracelet, possibly one of cured
leather. See MĀ(I)-TL, CUETLAXTIC.

MĀCUI *vt* to grasp something, to take
something in one's hand / lo coge en
la mano, lo agarra con la mano (T)
[(3)Tp.191]. Z has MAHCUI 'to baptize'
and TLAMAHCUĪLIZ-TLI 'baptism' which
may be variants of this verb in the sense of
faith taking one into its hands or being
bestowed by the laying on of hands. See
MĀ(I)-TL, CUI.

MĀCUĪLCĀN in five places or parts / en
cinco lugares o partes (M) [(1)Cf.91r]. See
MĀCUĪL-LI, -CĀN.

MĀCUILIĀ applic. MĀCUI

MĀCUILĪLŌ nonact. MĀCUI

MĀCUĪL-LI five / cinco (M)

MĀCUĪLPA five times / cinco veces (M)
[(2)Cf.106r, (1)Tp.164]. See MĀCUĪL-LI,
-PA.

MAH *negated form:* **MAHCA** as though, as
though it were / como que (K) According to
C, with negated locatives such as AHCĀN
'nowhere' MAH emphasizes the negation
(Cf.90v). With IUHQUI, MAH may precede
or follow, and the sense is 'as, like.'

MAHCA *negated form of* **MAH** such that
not, as though it weren't / y que no (C), no
(M) This has a counterfactual implication
'not as things in fact are.' Double negations
with MAHCA affirm; the sense of AHMŌ
MAHCA is 'without doubt' (Cf.123v). This
contrasts with MĀCA, the negative counterpart of the clause-introductory particle
MĀ. See MAH.

MAHCAMŌ such that not, as though it
weren't / y que no (C) [(6)Cf.123v,131v]. C
specifically contrasts this with MĀCAMŌ,
the extended negated form of MĀ which is
exclusively used with the optative and
vetative forms of the verb (Cf.123v). See
MAHCA, MAH.

MAHCĒHU(A) *vt* to obtain or to des_rve
what one desires; to do penance / con-
seguir o merecer lo deseado (M), hacer
penitencia (M) The penitential sense of
MAHCĒHU(A) probably has the object
prefix TLA- fused and can be regarded as
an intransitive verb. M has intransitive
maceua 'to dance,' but it is not attested in

the sources for this dictionary, so it cannot
be determined whether there is an internal
glottal stop and what the vowel length
pattern is.

MAHCĒHUAL-LI merit, recompense,
fortune / mérito, recompensa (S) This
contrasts with MĀCĒHUAL-LI 'subject,
commoner, indigenous person.' See
MAHCĒHU(A).

-MAHCĒHUALTI *irregular verb* to be
fortunate, to attain what one deserves, to
be worthy / ser dichoso o alcanzar lo que
desea (M), ser merecedor (C) This takes
possessive rather than subject prefixes
and is paradigmatically limited to third
person singular form. The preterit is
-MAHCĒHUALTIC. See MAHCĒHUAL-
LI.

MAHCĒHUALTIĀ *vt* to give someone his
due, or to assign penance to someone / dar
a merecer o dar penitencia a otro (M) caus.
MAHCĒHU(A)

MAHCĒHUIĀ applic. MAHCĒHU(A)

MAHCIC something whole, solid, certain /
cosa entera o maciza (M) This is implied
by MAHCITICAH and MAHCITOC. See
AHCI.

MAHCITICAH something whole, something unadulterated / cosa entera, fina, o
pura (M) [(1)Rp.100]. See AHCI, the verb
CĀ.

MAHCITOC something whole / entero (Z)
[(2)Zp.53,165]. See AHCI, the verb O.

MAHCUEXTIĀ *vt* to bedeck something
with a bracelet / enjoyar (K) [(1)Bf.6r].
M has *macuextli* 'bracelet or string
of precious stones for the wrist.' See
MĀ(I)-TL.

MAHCUEX-TLI See MAHCUEXTIĀ.

MAHCUI *vt* to baptize someone / lo bautiza
(Z) [(4)Zp.19,189,209]. See MĀCUI.

MAHIUHQUI as, in the manner of / como, a
manera (C) [(2)Cf.121r]. Both attestations of
this occur in the phrase IN MAHIUHQUI.
See MAH, IUHQUI.

MAHMACA *vt* to divide something up
among several people; to handle something
/ repartir algo a otros (M), repartir algo
entre sí o hacer algo a veces (M), lo toca (T)
[(1)Cf.44r, (3)Tp.189]. redup. MACA

MAHMACALŌ nonact. MAHMACA

MAHMACHILIĀ *vt* to test something / lo prueba (Z) [(2)Zp.102,189]. redup. MACHILIĀ

MAHMĀIHCIHU(I) to gather things together quickly and leave / coge cosas rápidamente y va (T) [(3)Tp.140]. See MĀ(I)-TL, (I)HCIHU(I).

MAHMĀIHCIHUĪHUA nonact. MAH-MĀIHCIHU(I)

MAHMĀIHCIHUĪTIĀ caus. MAH-MĀIHCIHU(I)

MAHMAN(I) for things to be individually spread out / para significar la multitud de cosas que están tendidas (R) [(1)Rp.101]. This is a distributive use of MAN(I) 'to spread out.' redup. MAN(I)

MAHMAQUILIĀ applic. MAHMACA

MAHMAT(I) This is the distributive reduplicated form of MAT(I).

MAHMAUHTIĀ *vrefl,vt* to get frightened; to frighten or threaten someone / se espanta (T), espantar o amenazar a otro (M) redup. MAUHTIĀ

MAHMAUHTILIĀ applic. MAHMAUHTIĀ

MAHMAUHTĪLŌ nonact. MAHMAUHTIĀ

MAHPĒHU(A) *vt* to shove something aside, cast something down with disgust, to hold something in contempt / dar empujón a otro o echar a alguno por ahí con desdén (M), lo desprecia (Z) [(2)Zp.44,189]. See MĀ(I)-TL, PĒHU(A).

MAHPILCOTŌN(A) See MAHPIL-LI, COTŌN(A).

MAHPILCUECHAQUIĀ *vrefl* to twist, sprain one's finger / se tuerce el dedo (T) [(3)Tp.150]. See MAHPIL-LI, CUECHAQUIĀ.

MAHPILCUECHAQUĪLŌ nonact. MAHPILCUECHAQUIĀ

MAHPILHUIĀ *vt* to signal to someone with one's finger, to point something out to someone with one's finger / mostrar o señalar a otro con el dedo o escoger o elegir a alguno (M), señalar algo con el dedo mostrándolo a otros (M) [(3)Tp.189, (2)Zp.115,189]. See MAHPIL-LI, -HUIĀ.

MAHPILHUILIĀ applic. MAHPILHUIĀ

MAHPILHUĪLŌ nonact. MAHPILHUIĀ

MAHPIL-LI finger / dedo de la mano (M) See MĀ(I)-TL, PIL-LI.

MAHPILPIPITZOĀ *vt* to suck some-

one's finger / lo chupa a un dedo (Z) [(2)Zp.39,189]. See MAHPIL-LI, PIPITZOĀ.

MAHPILTEHTEQU(I) *vrefl* to cut one's finger / se corta el dedo (T) [(3)Tp.150]. See MAHPIL-LI, TEHTEQU(I).

MAHPILTEPĀCHOĀ *vrefl,vt* to bruise one's finger; to bruise someone's fingers / se machuca el dedo (T), le machuca el dedo (T) [(6)Tp.152,189]. See MAHPIL-LI, TEPĀCHOĀ.

MAHPILTOMĀHUAC thumb / dedo pulgar (X) [(4)Xp.52]. X has MĀ for MAH. See MAHPIL-LI, TOMĀHUAC.

MAHPILZAHZĀLIHUIYĀN-TLI finger joint, knuckle / conjunturas de los dedos de las manos (M), artejo (Z) [(2)Zp.14,159]. See MAHPIL-LI, ZĀLIUHYĀN-TLI.

MAHTĒL *conventional leave-taking phrase* así se responde cuando otro saluda y se va de nuevo (T) [(2)Tp.140,141]. The literal sense of this is 'well anyway, though so it is.' C has abundant attestations of MĀTĒL, a clause introductory compound particle used with the optative and implying doubt or difficulty, which contrasts phonologically with MAHTĒL. In T MAHTĒL is used as MĀCIUHQUI is in some other communities. See MAH, TĒL.

MAHTEQUIĀ *vrefl* to wash one's hands / lavarse las manos (M) [(3)Cf.98r,127r, (3)Xp.58]. C contrasts this with the imperfect form of MĀTEQU(I) 'to cut one's hand.' This would seem to be from MĀ(I)-TL 'hand' and ĀTĒQUIĀ 'to sprinkle water on something,' but the vowel length pattern is completely wrong. Even deriving it with MAH, the alternative stem of MĀ(I)-TL, and TĒQUIĀ 'to sprinkle something,' there remains a discrepancy. X has MĀ for MAH.

MAHTLACCĀN in ten places / en diez partes (M) [(2)Cf.91v]. See MAHTLAC-TLI, -CĀN.

-MAHTLACCĀNIXTI *necessarily possessed form* in all ten parts of something / en todas diez partes (M) [(1)Cf.91v]. See MAHTLACCĀN, -IXTI.

MAHTLACPA ten times / diez veces (M) [(1)Tp.140]. See MAHTLAC-TLI, -PA.

MAHTLAC-TLI ten / diez (M) This is abundantly attested across sources, and with the exception of X (which has MĀ) and R (which fails to indicate either vowel length or glottal stop), all agree on MAH for the first syllable. But in reduplicated form it is attested twice, both times as *mātlātlaquilhuitica* (Cf.19v,107r). This reduplication is unusual in that it is the second syllable that reduplicates, as well as in the occurrence of MĀ for expected MAH.

MAHTZOLCUI *vt* to seize something with the hands, talons / lo agarra con las manos, con las uñas (T) [(3)Tp.189]. M has *matzoloa* 'to take a handful of something.' See MĀ(I)-TL, CUI.

MAHTZOLCUĪHUA nonact. MAHTZOLCUI

MAHTZOLCUILIĀ applic. MAHTZOLCUI

MĀHU(A) *vrefl,vt* for illness to spread; to infect someone, to spread contagion to others / se contagia, infecta (T), inficionar o pegar enfermedad contagiosa a otro (M)

MĀHUALŌ nonact. MĀHU(A)

MAHU(I) to be frightened / temer (M) Z has O for A in the first syllable, and this substitution in this particular item is common in modern Nahuatl, although not in T. X gives *u*, which is not the local reflex of either O or Ō. In both cases the labial vowel represents an assimilation of A to following HU.

MĀHUILIĀ This contrasts with MAHUILIĀ 'to fear someone, something.' applic. MĀHU(A)

MAHUILIĀ *vt* to fear something, someone / lo teme, le teme [(3)Tp.188]. This contrasts with MĀHUILIĀ, the applicative form of MĀHU(A). applic. MAHU(I)

MAHUILILIĀ applic. MAHUILIĀ

MAHUILĪLŌ nonact. MAHUILIĀ

MAHUILIZ-TLI fear / miedo, temor (Z) [(1)Tp.139, (3)Zp.84,120,169]. Z has O for A. This appears to be synonymous with MAHUIZ-TLI. See MAHUILIĀ.

MĀHUILTIĀNI *pl:* **-MEH** someone playful / juguetón (T) [(1)Tp.164]. See ĀHUILTIĀ.

MĀHUILTIHQUI someone playful / juguetón (Z) [(2)Zp.74,165]. S has the variant *mauiltiani* with the same sense. See ĀHUILTIĀ.

MĀHUILTILIZ-TLI play, game / juego (Z) [(2)Zp.74,165]. By general deri-

vational processes this should be NEĀHUILTILIZ-TLI, which is the form to be found in M. See ĀHUILTIĀ.

MAHUINI *pl:* **-MEH** someone fearful, frightened / miedoso, temeroso (T) [(1)Tp.139]. See MAHU(I).

MAHUIZALHUIĀ applic. MAHUIZOĀ

MAHUIZCUĪTIĀ *vrefl,vt* to learn from experience; to correct someone, to inspire a respectful attitude in someone / se escarmienta (T), lo escarmienta (T) [(6)Tp.150,188]. M has intransitive *mahuizcui* 'to take fear, become frightened.' See MAHUIZ-TLI, CUĪTIĀ.

MAHUIZCUĪTILIĀ applic. MAHUIZCUĪTIĀ

MAHUIZCUĪTĪLŌ nonact. MAHUIZCUĪTIĀ

MAHUIZOĀ *vt* to marvel at something, to observe something / admirarse (M), estar sorprendido (S), lo divierte (T) lo observa (Z) This is abundantly attested across sources. It contrasts with intransitive MAHUIZOHUA 'to receive honor' not only in preterit formation but also in that in C the intransitive is sometimes represented with a geminate ZZ. This may be the basic form, with the single Z the result of degemination. S combines the transitive and intransitive verbs in a single entry, while M separates them in contiguous entries. See MAHUIZ-TLI.

MAHUIZOH something or someone honorable and glorious / cosa honorosa y gloriosa (M), cosa o persona que tiene honra y gloria (C) [(4)Cf.6r,7r, (2)Rp.44,100]. This appears to be a reduction of MAHUIZZOH by degemination, but it is possible that a different derivation is involved. See MAHUIZ-TLI, -YOH.

MAHUIZOHUA to become renowned, to receive honor / afamarse o recibir honra (M), hacerse ilustre (C) This appears to be a reduction of MAHUIZZOHUA by degemination. It contrasts with transitive MAHUIZOĀ. See MAHUIZZOHUA.

MAHUIZŌLŌ nonact. MAHUIZOĀ

MAHUIZŌLTIĀ See TLAMAHUIZŌLTIĀ.

MAHUIZŌTIĀ *vt* to divert or observe someone / lo divierte, lo observa (T) [(6)Tp.188,232]. caus. MAHUIZOĀ

MAHUIZŌTILIĀ applic. MAHUIZŌTIĀ

MAHUIZŌTĪLŌ nonact. MAHUIZŌTIĀ
MAHUIZŌ-TL honor / honra o dignidad de
grandes (M) [(1)Bf.2v, (3)Cf.71,31v,66r,
(1)Tp.131]. This is apparently a reduction
of MAHUIZZŌ-TL by degemination. See
MAHUIZ-TLI, -YŌ.
MAHUIZPIY(A) vt to hold someone in
respect / lo respeta (Z) [(2)Zp.109,190]. See
MAHUIZ-TLI, PIY(A).
MAHUIZPOLOĀ vrefl,'vt to disgrace oneself; to defame, insult someone / disfa-
marse o deshonrarse (M), disfamar o
deshonrar a otro (M) [(4)Zp.71,72,90,190].
See MAHUIZ-TLI, POLOĀ.
MAHUIZTI to be held in esteem, respect / ser estimado (M) [(1)Cf.57v]. See
MAHUIZ-TLI.
MAHUIZTIC something marvelous, awesome, worthy of esteem / cosa maravillosa
y de estima (M) See MAHUIZTI.
MAHUIZTILIĀ vt to honor, respect someone, to hold someone in awe, to adore
someone / honrar y respetar a otro (M), lo
adora (Z) applic. MAHUIZTI
MAHUIZTILILIĀ applic. MAHUIZTILIĀ
MAHUIZTILĪLLANI vrefl to desire to be
honored, respected, held in awe / desear ser
honrado y respetado (M) [(1)Cf.119r]. By
general derivational rules the vowel of the
fourth syllable should be long, but it is not
marked long in the single attestation. See
MAHUIZTILIĀ, TLANI.
MAHUIZTILIZ-TLI adoration / adoración
(Z) [(2)Zp.5,170]. See MAHUIZTILIĀ.
MAHUIZ-TLI awe, or person worthy of awe
and respect / miedo o persona digna de
honra (M) [(1)Cf.57v]. See MAHU(I).
MAHUIZYOH See MAHUIZZOH.
MAHUIZYŌTILIĀ See MAHUIZZŌTILIĀ.
MAHUIZYŌ-TL See MAHUIZZŌ-TL.
MAHUIZZOH someone who is the em-
bodiment of honor / persona de honra (C)
[(2)Cf.54v,119r]. In one of the attestations,
the ZY sequence of this derived form
remains unassimilated. This also appears
as MAHUIZOH, apparently by degemination. See MAHUIZ-TLI, -YOH.
MAHUIZZOHUA to become renowned, to
receive honor / afamarse o recibir honra
(M), recibo honra y dignidad (C) [(1)Bf.2r,
(3)Cf.31v,54v]. The preterit of this intransitive verb is MAHUIZZOHUAC, which

contrasts with preterit MAHUIZOH from
transitive MAHUIZOĀ. Neither attestation of MAHUIZZOHUA marks the vowel
before -HUA long, although by derivation
from MAHUIZZŌ-TL it should be. Cf.31v
has this as a stem and in its preterit form,
both spelled with a single rather than a
geminate consonant, although on Cf.54v it
has two consonants. See MAHUIZZŌ-TL.
MAHUIZZŌTIĀ vt to render honor and
glory to someone / dar honra y gloria a
otro (C) [(1)Bf.2v, (2)Cf.54v,119r]. The B
attestation and one of the C attestations
are in applicative form derived from this.
Although M spells this with a single consonant between the second and third syllables, B and C have a geminate, and C also
spells it with the unassimilated ZY sequence. See MAHUIZZŌ-TL.
MAHUIZZŌTILIĀ applic. MAHUIZZŌTIĀ
MAHUIZZŌ-TL honor / honra (C)
[(3)Bf.3v,5v,8v, (1)Cf.54v, (3)Zp.32,109,170].
The ZY sequence of MAHUIZ-YŌ-TL
assimilates to ZZ, and then apparently
optionally degeminates to yield alternative
MAHUIZŌ-TL, which is the form represented in M. See MAHUIZ-TLI, -YŌ.
MAHXĪTIĀ vt to complete something, to
make something whole / lo completa (2)
[(2)Bf.6v, (2)Zp.13,189]. M has maxiltia 'to
supply something that was missing,' which
is clearly an alternate causative form of a
verb that underlies this verb too. It appears
to be a reflexive form of the verb AHCI 'to
arrive, reach' with the reflexive prefix
fused to the stem. M also has macic 'something whole.' See AHCI.
-MĀICNĪUH only attested in possessed
form one's comrade, fellow laborer /
su compañero de trabajo (T) [(1)Tp.131,
(2)Zp.31,159]. See MĀ(I)-TL, (I)C-
NĪUH-TLI.
MĀ(I)-TL compounding form: MĀ ~
MAH hand or arm, branch, dependency /
mano (M), mano. por ext. brazo, rama (S) In
addition to the alternating stem forms MĀ
and MAH, the reduplicated form MĀMĀ is
used in some compounds. In referring to a
tree's branches the inalienably possessed
form is -MĀYŌ or -MĀMĀYŌ. MĀYEH
'someone with hands' has -EH as the
possessor suffix, which is the form used

with stems ending in consonants. Perhaps
the Y is from I, or possibly this should be
MĀY(I)-TL. X gives *mātli*, which also
implies a stem-final consonant. MĀH-TLI,
however, is impossible in terms of Nahuatl
phonology, because vowels before glottal
stops are always short.

MĀITZMĪN(I) *vrefl,vt* to receive an injection in the arm; to inject someone in
the arm / se vacuna en el brazo, se injecta
en el brazo (T), lo inyecta en el brazo, lo
vacuna en el brazo (T) [(6)Tp.153,191]. See
MĀ(I)-TL, ITZMĪN(I).

-MĀIXCO *compound postposition* in the
palm of one's hand / palma de la mano (Z)
[(2)Zp.93,159]. See MĀ(I)-TL, -ĪXCO.

MĀIXNŌTZ(A) *vt* to beckon to someone
with one's hand / lo llama con la mano (Z)
[(2)Zp.78,189]. See MĀ(I)-TL, ĪX-TLI,
NŌTZ(A(.

MALACACHIHU(I) to spin, revolve /
girar (K) [(3)Tp.136]. This intransitive
verb is only attested in the compound
ĪXMALACACHIHU(I) 'to be dizzy, bewildered' and in derived forms in M. See
MALACACHOĀ.

MALACACHIHUĪHUA nonact. MALA-
CACHIHU(I)

MALACACHIHUĪTIĀ caus. MALA-
CACHIHU(I)

MALACACHILHUIĀ applic. MALA-
CACHOĀ

MALACACHOĀ *vrefl,vt* to turn, revolve; to
turn, spin something / volverse al derredor
estando en pie, o dar vueltas al rededor (M),
volver algo al derredor (M) P has this in
reduplicated form, MAHMALACACHOĀ,
used reflexively. See MALACA-TL.

MALACACHŌLŌ nonact. MALACACHOĀ

MALACACHTIC something round, circular
/ redondo, circular (S) [(2)Tp.136,140,
(1)Zp.165]. See MALACACHOĀ.

MALACAEHĒCA-TL whirlwind / viento (Z)
[(2)Zp.120,191]. This occurs in a phrase
meaning 'rain squall with wind.' See
MALACA-TL, EHĒCA-TL.

MALACA-TL spindle, bobbin, spiral / huso
(M)

MALCOCHILHUIĀ applic. MALCOCHOĀ

MALCOCHOĀ *vt* to embrace something, to
carry something in one's arms / abarcar

algo (M), lo lleva en los brazos, lo coge en
las manos (T) [(3)Tp.189].

MALCOCHŌLŌ nonact. MALCOCHOĀ

MALHUIĀ *vrefl,vt* to be careful with one's
appearance or reputation; to handle something delicately, to take care of something /
regalarse, tratarse bien, o tener cuenta con
su honra (M), tratar bien y delicadamente
alguna cosa (M), lo guarda, lo ahorra, lo
asegura (T) [(9)Tp.152,153,189].

MALHUILIĀ applic. MALHUIĀ

MALHUĪL-LI *pl:* **-TIN** ~ **-MEH** something
protected, hallowed / cosa guardada, cosa
consagrada (T) [(1)Tp.140]. See MALHUIĀ.

MALHUĪLŌ nonact. MALHUIĀ

MALĪN(A) *vrefl,vt* to wind, twist; to wind,
twist, sprain something / se tuerce (T), lo
tuerce (T), torcer cordel encima del muslo
(M) Fused with the prefix TLA-, this means
'to make rope.'

MALĪNALŌ nonact. MALĪN(A)

MALĪNILIĀ applic. MALĪN(A)

MĀL-LI *pl:* **-TIN** captive, prisoner / cautivo
en guerra o cautivado (M) [(1)Cf.58v]. M
also has a reduplicated plural *mamaltin*
and the same form missing the final consonant *mamalti*. See the verb MĀ.

MĀLTI to be a captive / cautivado ser (M)
[(2)Cf.58v]. See MĀL-LI.

MĀMĀ *vt; pret:* **MĀMAH** to bear something, to carry something on one's shoulders, to govern someone / llevar carga a
cuestas (M), llevar a cuestas a otro, o regir
y gobernar a otros (M) Although there is
agreement across sources that the vowel of
the second syllable is long (as it must be to
form the preterit as it does), the corresponding vowel in TLAMĀMAL-LI
'burden' is short, and B also marks
the corresponding vowel short in
TLAMĀMALŌNI 'someone who bears a
burden.' T gives doublets for derived forms
with long and short vowel variants. This
vowel length variation in verb and derived
nouns parallels that in the verb CUĀ 'to
eat' and TLACUAL-LI 'food.' MĀMĀ may
be derivationally related to the verb MĀ 'to
take someone captive,' since captives were
bound and borne on the shoulders. The
preterit is homophonous with that of
MĀMAT(I) 'to be embarrassed.'

MĀMĀCUĪLILHUITICA every five days / cada cinco días (C) [(2)Cf.107r]. See MĀCUĪL-LI, ILHUI-TL.

MĀMĀCUĪL-LI by fives, five apiece / de cinco en cinco, o cada uno cinco (M) This is implied by MĀMĀCUĪLILHUITICA. redup. MĀCUĪL-LI

MĀMALACACHOĀ redup. MALA-CACHOĀ

MĀMALHUĀZ-TLI gear for carrying something on the shoulders / mochila (K) [(1)Bf.3v]. This is paired with CUEXĀN-TLI 'packing bags,' the whole phrase meaning 'under the protection of someone' M has *mamalhuaztli* 'the constellation of Castor and Pollux' (literally 'the Drill'), which would contrast with this item in vowel length of the first syllable. See TLAMĀMAL-LI, MĀMĀ.

MĀMALHUIĀ *vrefl* to acknowledge one's sins, to load something on oneself / se acusa, se carga (T) [(3)Tp.153]. Although this would appear to be an alternative applicative form of the verb MĀMĀ, it makes better sense as a truncation of TLAMĀMAL-LI plus -HUIĀ.

MAMAL(I) *vt* to drill a hole through something / taladrar o barrenar algo (M) [(3)Bf.4r,5v,6r, (1)Cf.47v, (1)Rp.41]. This verb is easily confused with forms derived from the verb MĀMĀ 'to bear, carry something.'

MĀMĀLIĀ applic. MĀMĀ

MĀMĀLŌ nonact. MĀMĀ

MĀMALTIĀ *vrefl,vt* to assume a burden, to take something on one's conscience, to take a load onto one's shoulders; to burden someone with responsibility for something / tomar algo sobre su conciencia, encargarse de algo, o tomar algo a cuestas (M), tomar la carga a cuestas (M), cargar a otro o encargarle algo (M), abonar a otro en la hacienda (M), le carga, lo acusa (T) [(2)Bf.1v,11v, (7)Tp.153,191]. The vowel of the second syllable is short here, although it is long in the verb MĀMĀ 'to bear something' and in the applicative derivation from MĀMĀ. Derived forms of MĀMĀ with L are easily confused with MAMAL(I) 'to drill a hole through something.' caus. MĀMĀ

MĀMALTILIĀ applic. MĀMALTIĀ

MĀMALTĪLŌ nonact. MĀMALTIĀ

MĀMĀPĒHU(A) *vrefl* to keep pushing oneself away / se empuja mucho (T) [(3)Tp.153]. redup. MĀPĒHU(A)

MĀMĀPĒHUALŌ nonact. MĀMĀPĒHU(A)

MĀMAT(I) *vrefl,vt; pret:* **MĀMAH** to be timid, embarrassed; to be embarrassed by others / ser empacho o vergonzoso (M), tener empacho de otros (M) [(2)Cf.44r]. The preterit is homophonous with that of MĀMĀ 'to bear something' R attests this with MAH in place of MĀ for the first syllable. See MAT(I).

MĀMATILOĀ *vt* to confound someone, to ensnare someone / enredar (X) [(3)Xp.70]. See MĀMAT(I).

-MĀMĀYŌ *necessarily possessed form* the branches of a tree / su rama (T) [(1)Tp.131]. M has this in *mamatlapaltia* 'for a tree to to come into leave.' redup. -MĀYŌ

MĀMELĀHU(A) *vrefl* to extend one's hand / extiende la mano (Z) [(2)Zp.58,170]. See MĀ(I)-TL, MELĀHU(A).

-MĀMOMOLOC *only attested in possessed form* one's elbow / su codo (T) [(1)Tp.131]. In the Spanish-to-Nahuatl side this has the reflex of a long vowel in the last syllable. See MĀ(I)-TL, MOLIC-TLI.

-MĀN *locative suffix* [(2)Cf.56v]. This appears to be derived from MAN(I) 'to extend over a surface,' but both attestations in C, ĀCŌLMĀN and ŌZTŌMĀN, have a specifically marked long vowel. Unlike a postposition, this combines only with full stems, not with possessive prefixes.

MAN(A) *vt* to spread something out flat and smooth, to pat out tortillas / poner en el suelo plato o cosas llanas, o hacer tortillas de maíz antes que las cuezan en el comalli (M) M also glosses this as 'to make an offering,' presumably by laying something out on a surface. See MAN(I).

MĀNĀHUAL-LI coverlet for a cradle, protection / manta de cuna de niño (M) [(1)Bf.7r]. This appears in M and B in possessed form. S provides the absolutive suffix.

MĀNAHUATIĀ *vt* to cast something or someone away / se despide de él (con la mano) (Z) [(1)Zp.189]. See MĀNAHUIĀ.

MĀNAHUIĀ *vrefl,vt* to extricate oneself; to extricate someone from a dispute or to take leave of people who are quarreling / defenderse (M), defender a otro o departir a los que riñen (M) [(3)Tp.156]. M also glosses reflexive *manauia* as 'to suffer from diarrhea.'

MĀNAHUĪLŌ nonact. MĀNAHUIĀ

MANALŌ nonact. MAN(A)

MĀNĀMIC-TLI *pl:* **-TIN** tool, instrument / instrumento (Z), herramienta (Z) [(4)Zp.67,72,165]. See MĀ(I)-TL, NĀMIC-TLI.

MANCA See MAN(I).

MĀNEHNENQUI something that goes on all fours / cuadrúpedo (R) [(1)Rp.101]. R fails to mark the vowel of the first syllable long. See MĀ(I)-TL, NEHNEM(I).

MĀNEL although / aunque (M), si quiera (C) See MĀ, NEL-LI.

MĀNELIHU(I) to be stirred, mixed, beaten together / mezcla ... se revuelve (Z) [(4)Zp.84,110,165]. Z marks the vowel of the third syllable long, but by general rule it should be short. See MĀNELOĀ.

MĀNELIUHTOC something beaten together, mixed by hand / revuelto (Z) [(2)Zp.110,165]. See MĀNELIHU(I), the verb O.

MĀNELOĀ *vt* to mix something together by hand, to swim / nadar o revolver algo con la mano (M), lo mueve, lo revuelve, lo mezcla, lo bate (con la mano) (Z) See MĀ(I)-TL, NELOĀ.

MĀNĒN *compound introductory particle for clauses expressing admonition* let it not be that ... , let it be in vain that ... / mirad que no ... se haga tal cosa, advertiendo, ... mirad bien y advertid (M) This serves as a more emphatic introductory particle than simple MĀ with the admonitive. If the following clause includes explicit negation, in addition to the admonitive construction itself, MĀNĒN creates a double negative which serves to affirm rather than to negate. See MĀ, NĒN.

MAN(I) *irregular verb; pret:* **MANCA** for something flat to cover a surface, as water in a shallow pan, etc. / estar cosas llanas (C) M has the phrase *nican mani* with the gloss 'here is the book, plate, or pan of water.' There is a locative suffix -MĀN which, though close in sense, has a long vowel in its attestations in C. Z consistently has the corresponding vowel in MAN(I) long, but there is agreement across the other sources that the verb has a short vowel. See MAN(A).

MANILIĀ *vt* to spread something before someone / ofrecer o poner algo ante otro (M) C has one attestation of this with a long vowel in the initial syllable. applic. MAN(A), MAN(I)

MANILILIĀ applic. MANILIĀ

MANILĪLŌ nonact. MANILIĀ

MĀNOCEH nor, or else / ni (C), o (C), sirve algunas veces ... de lo mismo que *mā* (C) [(7)Cf.102v,111v,115v,124r, (1)Rp.101]. Although C glosses this as 'or,' he elsewhere specifically says that it has the sense of Spanish *ni* rather than *o* in the presence of negation and is synonymous with NOCEH. It is also used as a compound introductory particle for clauses expressing wishes, commands, and admonitions in place of simple MĀ. C marks the vowel of the first syllable long in only one attestation. This is also attested in P, where the glottal stop is indicated but not the long vowel. See MĀ, NOCEH.

MĀNŌTZ(A) *vt* to beckon to someone with one's hand / lo llama con la mano (Z) [(2)Zp.78,189]. See MĀ(I)-TL, NŌTZ(A).

MĀNOZO *compound introductory particle for clauses expressing wishes, commands, or admonitions* or else / sirve ... de lo mismo que *mā* (C) [(1)Bf.4r, (3)Cf.111v]. Only B marks the vowel of the first syllable long. B specifically marks the vowel of the second syllable short. See MĀ, NOZO.

MANQUI something smooth, flat / de nivel, plano (T) [(2)Tp.136,140]. M has *manqui* 'advanced in years, aged,' which may have a different derivation, possibly from ĀN(A), since M has *ana*, used reflexively, 'to grow in bodily size.' See MAN(I).

MANTIMAN(I) to lie in a place, to be located somewhere / hay (C) [(1)Cf.121r]. See MAN(I).

MĀNTZOCO child unwilling to be separated from its mother / niño que no quiere dejar a su mama (T) [(1)Tp.165]. S has *tzo-*

coton 'something very small.' The first element may be from ĀN(A), used reflexively, 'to grow in bodily size.' See TZOCO.

MĀOLĪNIĀ *vrefl* to move one's hand / mueve la mano (Z) [(2)Zp.86,171]. There is a vowel length discrepancy between -OLĪNIĀ in compounds and ŌLĪNIĀ as a free form. See MĀ(I)-TL, ŌLĪNIĀ.

MĀPACH-IN *pl:* **-TIN ~ -MEH** raccoon; thief (by extension) / el que hurta, ladrón (T), mapache (animal) (Z) This apparently can extend to coatis and ringtails. See MĀPACHOĀ.

MĀPACHOĀ *vt* to seize something, lay hold of something or press something with the hand / tomar, asir, apretar algo con las manos (S) [(3)Tp.191]. See MĀ(I)-TL, PACHOĀ.

MĀPAHPĀC(A) *vrefl* to wash one's hands / se lava las manos (Z) [(3)Tp.153, (2)Zp.76,171]. See MĀ(I)-TL, PĀC(A).

MĀPAHPĀCO *nonact.* MĀPAHPĀC(A)

MĀPAHPAZOL something rough, irritating / es muy tentón (T) [(1)Tp.165]. See MĀ(I)-TL, PAHPAZOL.

MĀPĀTILIĀ In this applicative form of MĀPĀTLA, there is T rather than expected TL before the applicative suffix -ILIĀ.

MĀPĀTLA *vrefl,vt* to defend oneself, to put up resistance; to beat something with one's hand, to mix something by hand / defenderse o resistir (M), lo bate con la mano, lo revuelve con la mano (T) [(3)Tp.191]. See MĀ(I)-TL, PĀTLA.

MĀPĀTLALŌ *nonact.* MĀPĀTLA

MĀPĒHU(A) *vt* to push something / lo empuja [(3)Tp.191, (3)Xp.70]. See MĀ(I)-TL, PĒHU(A).

MĀPĪCCA-TL glove / guante (Z) [(2)Zp.65,159]. This is only attested in third person singular possessed form, but S has *piccatl*. See MĀ(I)-TL, PĪCCA-TL, MĀPĪQU(I).

MĀPĪCH-TLI *pl:* **-TIN ~ -MEH** fist / puño de la mano (X) [(2)Bf.8r,9v, (3)Xp.51]. X has X before the absolutive suffix and CH elsewhere. See MĀPĪQU(I).

MĀPĪCTŌN a small handful / puñadillo (C) [(1)Cf.125v]. See MĀPĪCH-TLI, -TŌN.

MĀPĪQU(I) *vrefl,vt* to close the hand, make a fist; to grip something in one's fist /

cerrar la mano (M), empuñar o apretar algo en el puño (M) [(1)Cf.125v]. See MĀ(I)-TL, PĪQU(I).

MĀPIY(A) *vt; pret:* **-PIX ~ -PĪX** to hold something in one's hand / lo tiene en la mano (T) [(3)Tp.191]. See MĀ(I)-TL, PIY(A).

MĀPŌCH *pl:* **-TIN** left hand / mano izquierda (X) [(4)Xp.52,62]. See MĀ(I)-TL, ŌPŌCH-TLI.

-MĀPŌCHCOPA *necessarily possessed form* to one's left-hand side / a la izquierda (X) [(2)Xp.46]. See MĀPŌCH, -COPA.

MĀPOHPŌHU(A) *vrefl* to clean one's hands / lavarse las manos (S) [(2)Cf.45v, (1)Rp.102]. See MĀ(I)-TL, POHPŌHU(A).

MĀQUECHTLAN-TLI wrist / muñeca del brazo (T) [(1)Tp.131, (3)Zp.87,159]. M has *maquechtli* with the same sense. See MĀ(I)-TL, QUECHTLAN-TLI.

MĀQUEP(A) See MĀCUEP(A).

MAQUILIĀ *applic.* MACA

MĀQUĪTZQUIĀ *vt* to detain someone or to seize something with one's hand / lo detiene con la mano, lo agarra con la mano, lo coge con la mano (T) [(3)Tp.191]. See MĀ(I)-TL, QUĪTZQUIĀ.

MĀQUĪTZQUILIĀ *applic.* MĀQUĪTZQUIĀ

MĀQUĪTZQUILŌ *nonact.* MĀQUĪTZQUIĀ

MĀQUĪXTIĀ *vrefl,vt* to escape, free oneself from danger or harm; to deliver someone from danger, to free someone, to redeem someone / escaparse o librarse de algún peligro o daño (M), librar o salvar a otro (M) *caus.* MĀQUĪZ(A)

MĀQUĪZ(A) to escape, free oneself from danger or harm / escaparse o librarse de algún peligro o daño (M) See MĀ(I)-TL, QUĪZ(A).

MĀQUĪZTE-TL bracelet, ornament / brazalete, adorno (K) [(3)Bf.6r,9r]. See MĀQUĪZ-TLI, TE-TL.

MĀQUĪZ-TLI bracelet / ajorca o cosa semejante (M) [(8)Bf.4r,5r,5v,6r,9r]. There is a typographical error in M; this is spelled *mequiztli* but alphabetized as *maquiztli*. See MĀ(I)-TL.

MĀTAHTAPAYOLTIC someone broken out with bumps on the arms / tiene bolas en el brazo (T) [(1)Tp.165]. See MĀ(I)-TL, TAPAYOLTIC.

MATCĀ gradually, peacefully / apacible-

mente, con dulzura (S), poco a poco (C)
[(5)Cf.109v,119v,120r]. M has this in the
construction *matcanemini* 'someone
peacable, tranquil.' See TLAMATCĀ.

MĀTĒCA *vt* to pull up weeds / arranca
(yerba), roza (T), desyerba (Z) [(3)Tp.233,
(2)Zp.45,210]. The nonspecific object prefix
TLA- appears to be fused to the stem in
this verb. See MĀ(I)-TL, TĒCA.

MĀTECHĀN(A) *vt* to seize something with
the hand, to direct something with one's
hand / lo agarra con la mano, lo coge con la
mano, lo guía con la mano, lo lleva con
la mano (T) [(3)Tp.191]. See MĀ(I)-TL,
-TECH, ĀN(A).

MĀTECHĀNALŌ nonact. MĀTECHĀN(A)

MĀTECHĀNILIĀ applic. MĀTECHĀN(A)

MĀTECOCHTŌN a small handful / puñadillo (C) [(1)Cf.125v]. See MĀ(I)-TL,
TECOCH-TLI, -TŌN.

MĀTEHTEQU(I) See MĀ(I)-TL,
TEHTEQU(I).

MĀTĒL *compound introductory particle for
clauses with implied doubt, difficulty* let
it be ... after all, anyway / cuando uno tuvo
duda, ... en resolviéndose, dice *mātēl* (C)
[(5)Cf.25v,119v]. See MĀ, TĒL.

MATELĪN(A) *vrefl* to twist / se tuerce (T)
[(1)Tp.152]. See MATELOĀ.

MATELOĀ *vrefl* to bruise one's foot by
stepping on a stone / se magulla el pie por
pisar en piedra, etc. (T) [(6)Tp.152,158].
Both M and S have transitive *mateloa*
referring to striking things with the hand,
and S believes it to be derived from
MĀ(I)-TL, but if so the initial syllable
would be MĀ or MAH. Conceivably T has
characteristically lost a glottal stop. See
MATILOĀ.

MATELŌLŌ nonact. MATELOĀ

MĀTEPĀCHOĀ *vrefl,vt* to bruise one's
hand, to bruise someone's hand / se
machuca la mano (T), le machuca la
mano (T) [(6)Tp.153,192]. See MĀ(I)-TL,
TEPĀCHOĀ.

MĀTEPOZ-TLI ring (for the finger) / anillo
(Z,X) [(2)Zp.11,159, (4)Xp.52]. M glosses
this as 'adze, a hand-held cutting tool.' The
literal sense is 'hand metal.' See MĀ(I)-TL,
TEPOZ-TLI.

MĀTEQU(I) *vrefl,vt* to cut one's hand; to
cut someone's hand, to prune trees / cortar

o herirse la mano con cuchillo (M), corta la
mano a otro así (M), podar vides o árboles
(M) [(1)Cf.127r]. C contrasts the present
reflexive form of this with the preterit of
reflexive MAHTEQUIĀ 'to wash one's
hands.' See MĀ(I)-TL, TEQU(I).

MĀTETLAHTLATZCUEPŌNIĀ *vt* to beat
someone or something with one's hand /
lo pega con la mano (T) [(3)Tp.192]. See
MĀ(I)-TL, TLAHTLATZCUEPŌNIĀ.

MĀTETLAHTLATZCUEPŌNILIĀ applic.
MĀTETLAHTLATZCUEPŌNIĀ

MĀTETLAHTLATZCUEPŌNĪLŌ nonact.
MĀTETLAHTLATZCUEPŌNIĀ

MAT(I) *vt; pret:* **MAH ~ MAT** to know
something / saber algo (M) There are many
lexicalized constructions built on MAT(I),
and in many cases it is difficult to distinguish derivations from MAT(I) and derivations from IHMAT(I) 'to know how to do
things deftly, cleverly.' In their extensive
glossing of this item both M and S inter-
sperse derivations from both of these.
MAT(I) used reflexively can mean 'it
seems, it is thought that ...,' and when
this is in other than in third person, as in
'It seems to me,' the subject prefix is
omitted, hence NOMAT(I) rather than
NINOMAT(I). ONMAT(I) with the
directional particle ON- means 'to know
the way to a place.'

MĀTIĀ *vt* to equip something with hands or
arms / poner manos a la estatua o figura
(C) [(1)Cf.127v]. C contrasts this with
MATIYA, the imperfect form of MAT(I).
See MĀ(I)-TL.

MATĪHUA altern. nonact. MAT(I)

MATILHUIĀ applic. MATILOĀ

MATILIĀ This applicative form of
MAT(I) is attested only in the construction
TLAZOHCĀMATILIĀ on Tp.210,
but T also has the applicative form
TLAZOHCĀMACHILIĀ on p.209. See
MAT(I).

MATILOĀ *vt* to injure something or someone by rubbing or abrading / lo lastima
(T) [(6)Tp.190,217]. This is a variant of
MATELOĀ. M has them both with glosses
about the rubbing on of ointment. In T, the
reflexive form has E in the second syllable
and the transitive form has I.

MATILŌLŌ nonact. MATILOĀ

MATĪLTIĀ *vt* to inform someone, to make something known / lo entera, lo anuncia (Z) [(6)Zp.11,53,71,190,197]. This corresponds to MACHĪLTIĀ in the other sources. altern. caus. MAT(I)

-MATIYĀN *necessarily possessed form* one's time, span of personal experience / en mi tiempo (M for first pers. sg. possessor) [(3)Cf.99v,115r]. See MAT(I), -YĀN.

MĀTLAHPALTIC someone very strong / bracero que tira mucho (M), es en gran manera fuerte (C) [(1)Cf.110v]. See MĀ(I)-TL, TLAHPALTIC.

MĀTLAHTLANIĀ *vt* to interrogate someone / lo interroga (Z) [(2)Zp.72,190]. See MĀ(I)-TL, TLAHTLANIĀ.

MĀTLAHUĒL-LI *pl: -TIN ~ -MEH* large knife / machete (X) [(4)Xp.52]. See MĀ(I)-TL, TLAHUĒL-LI.

MĀTLALHUA-TL *inalienably possessed form:* **-MĀTLALHUAYŌ** tendon of the hand, arm / su tendón de la mano (T for possessed form) [(1)Tp.132]. See MĀ(I)-TL, TLALHUA-TL.

MĀTLĀL-IN the color dark green / color verde oscuro (M) [(2)Zp.130,166]. This is attested in Z in MĀTLĀLZAHUA-TL (literally 'green pox') and possibly in MĀTLĀLPAN, although the sense of the latter would be obscure from its gloss, which appears to have something to do with lowness of stature. Conceivably it is derived instead from TLĀLPAN 'on the ground.'

MĀTLĀLZAHUA-TL pox / viruela (Z) [(2)Zp.130,166]. This is literally 'green pox.' See MĀTLĀL-IN, ZAHUA-TL.

-MĀTLAN *necessarily possessed form* in the hand of, under the power of / en su mano (en su poder) (T) [(1)Tp.131]. See MĀ(I)-TL, -TLAN.

MĀTLANĪTZ-TLI the long bone of the arm / su canilla (de brazo) (T) [(1)Tp.132]. See MĀ(I)-TL, TLANĪTZ-TLI.

MĀTLAPAL-LI *pl: -TIN* wing / ala (X) [(4)Xp.52]. This is synonymous with AHTLAPAL-LI. See MĀ(I)-TL, TLAPAL-LI.

MĀTLAPECH-TLI glove / guante (Z) [(2)Zp.65,166]. See MĀ(I)-TL, TLAPECH-TLI.

MĀTLAPĪCHILIĀ applic. MĀTLAPĪTZ(A)

MĀTLAPĪTZ(A) to make a whistle with the hands and mouth / silbar con las manos y boca (M) [(3)Tp.165]. See MĀ(I)-TL, PĪTZ(A).

MĀTLAPOĀ *vrefl,vt* to be injected intravenously; to give someone an intravenous injection / se inyecta intravenosamente (T), lo inyecta intravenosamente (T) [(6)Tp.153,192]. The literal sense of this is 'to open the arm.' See MĀ(I)-TL, TLAPOĀ.

MĀTLAPOLŌLTIĀ *vrefl* to make a slip of the hand / se equivoca con la mano (T) [(3)Tp.153]. See MĀ(I)-TL, TLAPOLOĀ.

MĀTLAPOLŌLTĪLŌ nonact. MĀTLA-POLŌLTIĀ

MĀTLAQUECHIĀ *vrefl* to lean on something, support oneself with something / se apoya (T for ĪTECH MOMĀTLAQUECHIĀ) [(4)Tp.153]. This is used in construction with a possessed form of the postposition -TECH. See MĀ(I)-TL, TLAQUECHIĀ.

MĀTL(A)-TL net, sling / red generalmente (M) M has this in the Spanish-to-Nahuatl section of the dictionary, but it is missing from the Nahuatl-to-Spanish side.

MĀTLĀTLAC-TLI This reduplicated form is implied by MĀTLĀTLAQUILHUITICA. See MAHTLAC-TLI.

MĀTLĀTLAQUILHUITICA every ten days / de diez en diez días (M), cada diez (días) (C) [(2)Cf.19v,107r]. See MAHTLAC-TLI, ILHUI-TL.

MĀTLAXCALHUIĀ *vt* to applaud something or someone / lo aplaude (S) [(3)Tp.192]. applic. MĀTLAXCALOĀ

MĀTLAXCALOĀ *vrefl* to applaud / aplaude (T) [(3)Tp.153, (2)Zp.12,171]. The literal sense of this is to slap one's hands together as in making tortillas. M has the reduplicated form *matlatlaxcaloa* with the same sense. See MĀ(I)-TL, TLAXCAL-LI.

MĀTLĀXILIĀ *vt* to signal to someone, to beckon to someone with the hand / le hace señas con la mano, lo llama con la mano (T) [(3)Tp.192]. See MĀ(I)-TL, TLĀXILIĀ.

MĀTLĀXILILIĀ applic. MĀTLĀXILIĀ

MĀTLĀXILĪLŌ nonact. MĀTLĀXILIĀ

MĀTLEQUIQUIZTLĀZQUI musketeer / los arcabuceros (C for plural) [(1)Cf.120r]. M has *matlequiquiztli* 'harquebus.' See MĀ(I)-TL, TLEQUIQUIZ-TLI, TLĀZ(A).

MĀTOCA *vrefl,vt* to fondle oneself, to

masturbate; to touch, feel, fondle someone
or something / palpar o tocar sus partes
vergonzosas (M), palpar a otro así (M), tocar
o tentar algo con la mano (M) [(3)Tp.192,
(2)Zp.121,190]. M gives a specifically
sexual interpretation that is lacking in the
literal Nahuatl 'to hand-follow.' See
MĀ(I)-TL, TOCA.

MĀTOCALŌ nonact. MĀTOCA

MĀTOHMI-TL *inalienably possessed form:*
-MĀTOHMIYŌ the hair of one's hands
and arms / su pelo de la mano o del brazo
(T) [(1)Tp.132]. See MĀ(I)-TL, TOHMI-TL.

MĀTOQUILIĀ applic. MĀTOCA

MATZAH-TLI pineapple / piña, fruta de la
tierra (M) [(1)Rp.103]. R marks the glottal
stop. The vowel of the first syllable is
unmarked for length.

-MĀTZĀLAN *compound postposition* between the hooves, paws of an
animal / entre las patas del animal (T)
[(1)Tp.132]. See MĀ(I)-TL, -TZĀLAN.

MĀTZOCUITLANELTIC something dirty /
sucio (T) [(1)Tp.165]. M has *tzocuitlatl*
'thick sweat of the body.' See MĀ(I)-TL,
TZO-TL, CUITL(A)-TL, NELTIC.

MAUHCĀCĀHU(A) *vt* to keep one's silence
out of fear / tu callas por miedo (R for
second pers. sg. subject) [(1)Rp.31]. R fails
to mark the vowel of the third syllable
long. See MAHU(I), CĀHU(A).

MAUHCĀHUIHUIYOCA to tremble,
shake with fear / estremece, tiembla (T)
[(3)Tp.140]. See MAHU(I), HUIHUIYOCA.

MAUHCĀHUIHUIYOCOHUA nonact.
MAUHCĀHUIHUIYOCA

MAUHCĀHUIHUIYOQUĪTIĀ caus.
MAUHCĀHUIHUIYOCA

MAUHCĀITTA *vt* to regard someone,
something with fear, respect / ver a alguien
con temor, respeto (S), prestar atención a
una cosa, mirarla con temor (S) [(3)Tp.189].
See MAHU(I), (I)TTA.

MAUHCĀMAHUILIZ-TLI fright, fear /
susto, miedo (T) [(1)Tp.140]. See MAHU(I),
MAHUILIZ-TLI.

MAUHCĀMICOHUA nonact. MAUHCĀ-
MIQU(I)

MAUHCĀMICTIĀ *vt* to frighten
someone / lo espanta, le da un susto
(T) [(6)Tp.189,232]. altern. caus.
MAUHCĀMIQU(I)

MAUHCĀMICTILIĀ applic. MAUHCĀ-
MICTIĀ

MAUHCĀMICTĪLŌ nonact. MAUHCĀ-
MICTIĀ

MAUHCĀMIQU(I) *pret:* -MIC to get scared,
to take fright; to faint or urinate from fear /
mearse o amortecerse de temor (M), se
espanta, se asusta, tiene miedo (T)
[(3)Tp.140]. See MAHU(I), MIQU(I).

MAUHCĀMIQUĪTIĀ altern. caus.
MAUHCĀMIQU(I)

MAUHCĀTIC someone timid, easily
frightened / tímido (Z) [(2)Zp.122,174]. See
MAUHCĀ-TL.

MAUHCĀ-TL someone fearful, cow-
ardly / miedoso (Z), temeroso (Z)
[(4)Zp.84,120,170,174]. MAUHCĀ-, the
verb MAHU(I) plus the ligature -CĀ-,
is an element in a large number of
constructions, but MAUHCĀ-TL as a free
nominal form with an absolutive suffix
appears only in Z. See MAHU(I).

MAUHCĀTOCA *vt* to put someone to flight
by scaring him / lo corretea, lo ahuyenta
(T) [(3)Tp.189]. See MAHU(I), TOCA.

MAUHCĀTOCALŌ nonact. MAUH-
CĀTOCA

MAUHCĀTOQUILIĀ applic. MAUH-
CĀTOCA

MAUHCĀTZAHTZI to cry out in fear /
grita de espanto (T) [(3)Tp.140]. See
MAHU(I), TZAHTZI.

MAUHCĀTZAHTZĪHUA nonact.
MAUHCĀTZAHTZI

MAUHCĀTZAHTZĪTIĀ caus.
MAUHCĀTZAHTZI

MAUHCĀYACĀN(A) *vt* to flee ahead of
someone / va adelante huyendo (el otro
le sigue) (T) [(3)Tp.189]. See MAHU(I),
YACĀN(A).

MAUHCĀYACĀNALŌ nonact. MAUH-
CĀYACĀN(A)

MAUHCĀYACĀNILIĀ applic. MAUH-
CĀYACĀN(A)

MAUHCĀYŌ-TL fear, terror / temor,
timidez; terror, espanto, miedo (S) [(6)Zp.72,84,119,169,175]. See
MAUHCĀ-TL, -YŌ.

MAUHTIĀ *vrefl,vt* to be frightened; to
frighten someone / haber miedo (M),
espantar a otro (M) caus. MAHU(I)

MAUHTILIĀ applic. MAUHTIĀ

MAUHTĪLŌ nonact. MAUHTIĀ

MAXAC-TLI thighs, crotch / entre mis piernas o en la horcajadura (M for first pers. sg. possessor), parte interior de las piernas (X) [(2)Xp.52]. See MAXAL-LI.

MAXAL-LI *pl:* **-TIN** earwig (Psalis americana), something forked / tijerilla (animalito) (T), horqueta, horcón (Z,X for CUAUHMAXAL-LI) [(1)Tp.140, (4)Zp.69,122,148,149]. Despite the vowel length discrepancy, this appears to be related to MĀXTLA-TL 'breechclout.' M has *maxaltic* 'something divided like a road or the crotch of a tree.' The absolutive form is attested in the compound CUAUHMAXAL-LI. It is possible that the insect name should take absolutive -IN rather than -TLI. T is ambiguous between the two.

MAXAUHTINEM(I) to go about with one's crotch exposed / anduvieras con las carnes defuera (C for second pers. sg. subject, future tense) [(1)Cf.105r]. M has reflexive *mamaxauia* 'to undress, to expose oneself' in the Spanish-to-Nahuatl side only. See MAXAL-LI, NEM(I).

MĀXITTOMŌN(I) for blisters or bumps to appear on the hand / se ampolla la mano (T) [(3)Tp.165]. See MĀ(I)-TL, XITTOMŌN(I).

MĀXITTOMŌNĪHUA nonact. MĀXITTOMŌN(I)

MĀXITTOMŌNTIĀ caus. MĀXITTOMŌN(I)

MĀXIXITTOMŌNIĀ *vrefl* for blisters or bumps to appear on the hand / le levantan ampollas en la mano, ampolla la mano (T) [(3)Tp.153]. Because of the distributive sense of this, a glottal stop is to be expected in the reduplication of XITTOMŌNIĀ, but none is attested, perhaps due to T's characteristic tendency to lose internal glottal stops. See MĀXITTOMŌN(I).

MĀXIXITTOMŌNĪLŌ nonact. MĀXIXITTOMŌNIĀ

MĀXOXOCOTETIC someone with blistered hands or arms / tiene bolas en el brazo (T) [(1)Tp.165]. See MĀ(I)-TL, XOCOTETIC.

MĀXTLA-TL *possessed form:* **-MĀXTLI** breechclout / bragas o cosa semejante (M)

[(1)Bf.111r, (3)Cf.82v]. Without the absolutive suffix, this may serve as a personal name. The sequence *max* appears in many entries in M and S having to do with bifurcation, but the length of the vowel is in question, since it is attested short in MAXAL-LI and MAXAC-TLI 'crotch, something forked' and long in MĀXTLA-TL.

MĀYAHU(I) *vrefl,vt* to fall; to hurl something down, to dash someone down to his death / se tumba (T), lo tumba, lo mata (T), echar o arrojar por ahí (M), derribar a otro en el suelo (M), arrojar o echar algo por ahí (M)

MĀYAHUĪHUA nonact. MĀYAHU(I)

MĀYAHUILIĀ applic. MĀYAHU(I)

MAYĀN(A) to be hungry / tener hambre (M)

MAYĀNALIZ-TLI hunger, famine / hambre general (M) [(2)Zp.66,166]. See MAYĀN(A).

MAYĀNALŌ nonact. MAYĀN(A)

MAYĀNALTIĀ caus. MAYĀN(A)

MAYĀNCĀCUI to get hungry / le da hambre (Z) [(2)Zp.66,166]. See MAYĀN(A), CUI.

MAYĀNMIQU(I) *pret:* **-MIC** to be very hungry, to be perishing of hunger / se muere de hambre (Z) [(2)Zp.86,166]. This is attested without assimilation of the NM sequence to MM. See MAYĀN(A), MIQU(I).

MAYĀN-TLI hunger / hambre (Z) [(4)Zp.66,166]. See MAYĀN(A).

-MĀYĒCCĀNCOPA *necessarily possessed form* at one's right hand / a tu mano derecha (C for second pers. sg. possessor) [(1)Cf.94v]. See MĀYĒCCĀN-TLI, -C(O), -PA.

MĀYĒCCĀN-TLI the right hand / mano derecha (M) [(1)Cf.94v]. See MĀ(I)-TL, YĒC-TLI, -CĀN.

-MĀYĒCMĀ *necessarily possessed form* one's right-hand side / su lado derecho (T) [(3)Tp.132]. See MĀ(I)-TL, YĒC-TLI.

MĀYECUĒLEH *compound introductory particle for clauses expressing strong wishes and exhortations* let it be that ... , on with ... / ojalá (C) [(1)Cf.26v]. M glosses this as synonymous with MĀCUĒLEH.

MĀYEH someone with hands / el que tiene manos (C) [(1)Cf.55r, (2)Zp.24,166,

(1)Rp.45]. The Y of this form may be the stem-final I of MĀ(I)-TL, or it may be an intrusive intervocalic glide between the stem and the possessor suffix. See MĀ(I)-TL.

MĀYEHCHIQUIHU(I)-TL handbasket / canasta (de mano) (T) [(2)Zp.24,166]. See MĀYEH, CHIQUIHU(I)-TL.

MAYĪ *leavetaking phrase used in T* se responde así cuando otro dice que ya se va (T) [(4)Tp.140,141]. This may be a further reduction of MĀCIUHQUI, which is used as a leave-taking phrase in some Nahuatl-speaking communities.

-MĀYŌ *inalienably possessed form of* **MĀ(I)-TL** a tree's crown, its branches and foliage / su rama (Z) [(1)Tp.131, (4)Zp.52,105,159,193]. T has this in reduplicated form -MĀMĀYŌ. M has *imamainquauitl* 'branches of a tree,' which represents the phrase ĪMĀMĀ IN CUAHUITL, literally 'its-branches the tree,' where the suffix -YŌ indicating inalienable possession is not used. See MĀ(I)-TL.

MĀZĀ *compound introductory particle for clauses expressing wishes, commands, admonitions* let it be that ... / ojalá que (K) [(1)Cf.25v]. C mentions this as one example of numerous such clause-introductory particles without specifically glossing it. See MĀ, ZĀ.

MAZĀCŌĀ-TL *pl:* **-MEH** a type of horned caterpillar or a type of large, nonvenomous snake, a boa / gusano gordo con cuernos o culebra grande que no hace mal (M), culebra mazacuate (Z) [(2)Zp.37,166, (3)Xp.52]. Several Spanish sources remark that the snake of this name is large enough to feed on four-legged animals. The literal sense of the name 'deer snake' probably refers to its alleged diet rather than to any aspect of its appearance. The caterpillar, on the other hand, takes its name from its antler-like projections. See MAZĀ-TL, CŌĀ-TL.

MĀZANNEL even if / aunque (C) [(1)Bf.4v, (2)Cf.119v]. See MĀ, ZAN, NEL.

MAZĀ-TL *pl:* **MĀMAZAH ~ MAZĀ-MEH** deer / venado (M), ciervo (C)

MĀZO if only even, howsoever / aunque (C) [(1)Bf.4v, (6)Cf.119r,119v]. See MĀ, -ZO.

MĀZOIHUI although it were so that ... / aunque, dado que, o puesto caso (M) [(1)Cf.119v]. This is commonly shortened to MĀCIHUI. See MĀZO, IHU(I).

MĀZOLHUIĀ *vt* to make gestures while talking to someone / habla agitando las manos enfrente de otra persona (Z) [(1)Zp.189]. This appears to have the literal sense 'to wear someone out with gesturing,' and Z has what seems to be a secondary derived form MĀZOL 'someone who goes about touching things.' See MĀ(I)-TL, ZOLOĀ.

MĀZONELIHUI although it were so that ... / aunque, dado que, o puesto caso o puesto caso que sea así (M) [(1)Cf.119v]. See MĀZOIHUI, NEL-LI.

MĀZOTĒL given that, no matter if / demos caso que (C) [(6)Cf.118r,131v]. See MĀZO, TĒL.

MECAHUĪTEQU(I) *vrefl,vt* to flagellate oneself; to beat someone with a whip / azotarse a sí mismo (M), azotar a otro (M) [(1)Cf.112v]. See MECA-TL, HUĪTEQU(I).

MECĀNIĀ *vrefl,vt* to hang oneself; to hang someone / ahorcarse (M), ahorcar a otro (M) [(3)Bf.11r, (2)Zp.126,190]. Z has the sense of 'to stumble, to trip' for this verb. The sense common to M and Z is 'to be brought up short by a rope.' See MECA-TL.

MECĀNĪLŌ This is attested twice (Bf.11r), both times with the vowel of the third syllable marked short, although by regular derivational processes it should be long. nonact. MECĀNIĀ

MECAPAH-TLI sarsaparilla / la zarzaparrilla (R) [(1)Rp.104]. See MECA-TL, PAH-TLI.

MECAPAL-LI *pl:* **-MEH ~ -TIN** tumpline, rig for carrying a load on the back supported by a band across the forehead / mecapal, cordel para llevar carga a cuestas (M) [(1)Cf.103v, (2)Tp.133,141, (3)Xp.52]. See MECA-TL, -PAL.

MECA-TL *pl:* **-MEH** cord or rope, whip made of knotted cords, vine / cordel o soga o azote de cordeles (M)

MECAYŌ-TL lineage / abolorio o parentesco de consanguinidad (M) This is indirectly attested in MECA-TL. See MECA-TL, -YŌ.

MECEYŌCAYEHUAL-LI *pl:* **-TIN** flowering stalk of the maguey / quiote (T) [(1)Tp.141]. See MECEYŌ-TL, CAYEHUAL-LI.

MECEYŌ-TL wild maguey / maguey del
campo (T) [(1)Tp.141]. M has *mecellotl*
'maguey heart, crown before it has
sprouted.' See ME-TL.
MECHŌNTIC someone bandylegged /
perniabierto (T) [(1)Tp.141].
MEHCACEHUIZ-TLI fleabites, rash / sarpullido, erupción (T) [(1)Tp.141].
MELACTIC something long and straight /
cosa derecha y luenga (M) [(2)Tp.136,141].
T also has MELAC as an internal component of OHUAMELAC-TLI 'long, whole
stalk of cane.' There is a variant in T,
MELAZTIC, which appears to be synonymous. See MELĀHU(A).
MELĀHU(A) *vrefl,vt* to stretch oneself out
on a surface; to straighten something out,
to get directly to a point or destination. /
tenderme en el suelo (M for first pers. sg.
subject), enderezar alguna cosa tuerta, o
exponer y declarar la escritura o lo que es
dificultoso de entender (M), caminar
derecho, pasando de largo sin detenerse en
algún lugar o enderezar alguna cosa tuerta
(M) See MELACTIC.
MELĀHUAC something straight, true,
genuine, honest / vertical, recto (Z),
verdadero, cierto, derecho, positivo (S)
C gives the phrase *ca huel melahuac* 'it
is very true.' The negation AHMŌ
MELĀHUAC means 'false.' As variants of
this, Z has MELĀUH, which has the form
of the preterit of the verb MELĀHU(A),
and MELĀN with N replacing the final
-UH. See MELĀHU(A).
MELĀHUALŌ nonact. MELĀHU(A)
MELĀHUILIĀ applic. MELĀHU(A)
MELĀUHCĀPŌHU(A) *vt* to relate, declare,
explicate something / narrar, exponer algo
fielmente, exactamente (S), lo afirma, lo
declara, lo explica, testifica (T) [(3)Tp.190].
See MELĀHU(A), PŌHU(A).
MELAZOĀ *vrefl* to stretch out, extend / se
estira (T) [(3)Tp.152]. See MELAZTIC,
MELĀHU(A).
MELAZŌLŌ nonact. MELAZOĀ
MELAZTIC something straight, vertical /
derecho (se dice de palo, etc.), vertical,
recto (T) [(2)Tp.141,175]. See MELACTIC.
MEME-TL cultivated maquey / maguey
cultivado (T) [(1)Tp.141]. redup. ME-TL
ME-TL century plant, maguey, member of

the Agave family of plants (most commonly those cultivated for the production
of pulque and mezcal) / maguey (M) T has
the reduplicated form MEME-TL for cultivated maguey, presumably referring to a
field of plants.
METLAMĀ(I)-TL stone rolling pin used to
grind cornmeal on the metate / metlapile,
la mano de metate (Z) [(3)Zp.81,84,167].
A more common name for this is
METLAPĪL-LI. See METL(A)-TL,
MĀ(I)-TL.
METLAPĪL-LI *pl:* **-MEH ~ -TIN** stone
rolling pin used to grind cornmeal on the
metate / moledor con que muelen el maíz
(M) [(1)Tp.141, (6)Xp.53]. See METL(A)-TL.
METLAPĪLTETZOTZONTZIN road-
runner / correcaminos (X) [(1)Xp.53]. See
METLAPĪL-LI, TE-TL, TZON-TLI.
METLATE-TL type of stone used in making
metates / piedra de metate (Z) [(1)Zp.98]. Z
also has TEMETL(A)-TL with the same
gloss. See METL(A)-TL, TE-TL.
METL(A)-TL *pl:* **-TIN ~ -MEH** stone slab for
grinding cornmeal, metate / piedra donde
muelen el maíz, etc. (M), metate (T)
METLAXELHUĀZ-TLI scrubbing brush
for the metate / escobeta para metate
(Z) [(1)Tp.141]. See METL(A)-TL,
XELHUĀZ-TLI.
-METZĀCAYŌ *necessarily possessed
form* one's shin bone / su tibia, su canilla,
su espinilla (Z) [(4)Zp.25,56,122,159]. See
METZ-TLI, ĀCA-TL.
METZCAMOH someone barefoot / descalzo
(Z) [(2)Zp.42,167]. The second element
appears to be CAMOH-TLI 'sweet potato,'
but the sense would be obscure. See
METZ-TLI.
METZCOCOXQUI someone lame / rengo
(Z) [(2)Zp.108,167]. See METZ-TLI,
COCOXQUI.
METZCOHCŌLTIC someone lame / rengo
(Z) [(2)Zp.108,167]. See METZ-TLI,
COHCŌL-LI.
METZCOPĪN(A) *vrefl* to dislocate one's
hip / se disloca (Z) [(2)Zp.46,171]. See
METZ-TLI, COPĪN(A).
METZCOPĪN(I) for one's hip to be-
come dislocated / se zafa (el pie) (Z)
[(2)Zp.131,167]. See METZ-TLI, COPĪN(I).
METZCOTOLTIC someone lame / rengo (Z)

[(2)Zp.108,167]. This would seem to mean 'someone lame by virtue of having lost a leg.' See METZ-TLI, COTOLTIC.

METZCOTŌNI someone crippled by loss of a leg or foot / cojo (falta un pie) (Z) [(2)Zp.29,168]. See METZ-TLI, COTŌN(I).

MĒTZCUALO eclipse of the moon / eclipse de luna (T) [(1)Tp.142]. T also has CUALOMĒTZ-TLI with the same sense. If the second element is the nonactive form of the verb CUĀ 'to eat something,' the final vowel should be basically long, but it is not long in the synonymous construction CUALOMĒTZ-TLI. See MĒTZ-TLI, CUĀ, CUALŌ.

METZCUAUHYOH *pl:* **-MEH** thigh, inner side of the leg / el muslo o el largor de toda lo pierna (M) [(3)Xp.53]. See METZ-TLI, CUAHU(I)-TL, -YOH.

METZHUEHHUELOĀ *vrefl* to dislocate one's hip / se disloca (Z) [(2)Zp.46,171]. See METZ-TLI, HUEHHUELOĀ.

METZICXIPIL-LI toe / dedo (del pie) (Z) [(2)Zp.40,159]. See METZ-TLI, (I)CXI-TL, (I)CXOPIL-LI.

METZIHCATOC someone on foot / está de pie (Z) [(2)Zp.98,168]. See METZ-TLI, IHCA, the verb O.

METZIUHQUI someone barefoot / descalzo (Z) [(2)Zp.42,168]. See METZ-TLI, IUHQUI.

-METZĪXCO *necessarily possessed form* sole of one's foot / planta del pie (Z) [(2)Zp.99,159]. This is a locative expression 'at the sole of one's foot' and implies a noun METZĪX-TLI. See METZ-TLI, ĪX-TLI, -C(O).

METZĪX-TLI See -METZĪXCO.

MĒTZOCUIL-IN *pl:* **-TIN** earthworm, tapeworm / lombriz (T) [(1)Tp.142]. See MĒTZ-TLI, OCUIL-IN.

METZOHOHUICĀN a road, path very hard on the legs, rocky and difficult / el camino muy fiero (Z) [(1)Zp.168]. See METZ-TLI, OH-TLI, OHUIHCĀN.

METZQUECHZĀLIUHYĀN-TLI ankle / su tobillo (Z for possessed form) [(2)Zp.123,159]. See METZ-TLI, QUECH-TLI, ZĀLIUHYĀN-TLI.

METZTELOĀ *vrefl* to stumble / tropieza (Z) [(2)Zp.126,171]. See METZ-TLI, TELOĀ.

METZTETZĪLOĀ *vrefl* to twist, sprain one's foot / se tuerce (el pie) (Z) [(2)Zp.123,171]. See METZ-TLI, TETZĪLOĀ.

-METZTLAMPA *necessarily possessed form* sole of one's foot / planta de pie (Z) [(2)Zp.99,160]. This is a locative construction rather than a noun and has the literal sense 'to, from under one's foot.' See METZ-TLI, -TLAN, -PA.

METZTLAPACH-TLI *pl:* **-TIN ~ -MEH** groin / ingle (X) [(5)Xp.53]. See METZ-TLI, TLAPACH-TLI.

MĒTZ-TLI moon, month / luna o mes (C) M combines the glosses of MĒTZ-TLI and METZ-TLI 'thigh, leg' in a single entry.

METZ-TLI thigh, leg / muslo o pierna (C) M combines the glosses of METZ-TLI and MĒTZ-TLI 'moon, month' in a single entry.

MĒTZTŌNA for the moon to be up and shining / hace luna (T) [(1)Tp.142, (2)Zp.78,210]. See MĒTZ-TLI, TŌNA.

-METZTZĀLAN *compound postposition* between the legs of / entre sus piernas (Z) [(1)Tp.131]. See METZ-TLI, -TZĀLAN.

METZXOCPAL-LI sole of one's foot / planta del pie (Z) [(2)Zp.99,160]. See METZ-TLI, XOCPAL-LI.

MEXCALĀ-TL sap, juice of the maguey used as an unfermented drink / agua o jugo de maguey (Z) [(2)Zp.7,168]. In both attestations this is bound with -TZIN. See MEXCAL-LI, Ā-TL.

MEXCALCOHCOHYOC drunkard / borracho (T) [(1)Tp.141]. M has *cocoyonenemi* 'to crawl on all fours,' which may contain another instance of what is the second element here. See MEXCAL-LI.

MEXCALHUIĀ *vrefl,vt* to rub alcohol, mezcal on oneself; to rub mezcal on someone / se unta con alcohol (T), lo unta con alcohol (T) [(6)Tp.152,190]. See MEXCAL-LI, -HUIĀ.

MEXCALHUILIĀ applic. MEXCALHUIĀ
MEXCALHUĪLŌ nonact. MEXCALHUIĀ
MEXCAL-LI mezcal, distilled alcoholic drink made by cooking the heart of the maguey plant / cierta planta comestible de la clase de los magueyes o áloes de la cual se saca un licor fortísimo (R), mezcal (T) T has MEZ for MEX and a long vowel in the

second syllable in this and all derivations, probably by receiving it from Spanish as a back loan and interpreting the Spanish stressed syllable as containing a long vowel. A possible derivation is from ME-TL 'maguey' and (I)XCA 'to bake something' Distilling was a late introduction, and the earliest attestation of this item among the sources for this dictionary is R.

MĒXIHCA-TL *pl:* **MĒXIHCAH** resident of Mexico-Tenochtitlan / Mexicano, natural de Mexico (C) See MĒXIHCO.

MĒXIHCAYŌ-TL the essence of Mexica community and culture / el imperio mexicano (C), el señorio de Mexico (C), la nobleza o republica de los Mexicanos (C), cosa de México (C) [(7)Cf.5 31,82v,102r, 1151,121v]. See MĒXIHCA-TL, -YŌ.

MĒXIHCO Mexico / México (C) [(4)Bf.2r,9v,11r, (4)Cf.56r,79r,102r,104r, (1)Tp.142]. The etymology of this is opaque. Because of the difference in vowel length, it cannot be derived from ME-TL 'maguey.' The sequence XIH also differs in vowel length from XĪC-TLI 'navel,' which has been proposed as a component element. The final element is locative -C(O).

MEX-TLI See MIX-TLI.

MĒY(A) *pret:* **MĒX** to gush, bubble up / manar la fuente o cosa semejante (M)

MĒYAL-LI spring, fountain, place where something comes gushing forth / manantial (T) [(2)Tp.170]. This is only attested as ĀMĒYAL-LI 'water spring, water fountain.' See MĒY(A).

MĒYYŌ-TL rays of light, lightning / luz (los rayos), rayo (Z) [(3)Zp.78,106,168]. See MĒY(A), -YŌ.

MIAC *pl:* **MIAQUĪN** ~ **MIAQUĪNTĪN** ~ **MIACTĪN** ~ **MĪMIAC** very much, many; the constellation Pleiades (by extension) / mucho en cantidad, o las siete cabrillas, constelación (M for *miec*) This varies greatly in form. B, C, and R have MIEC, while Z and X have MIAC. T has MEYAC. M has both *miac* and *miec*. The A is probably basic to the form, with MIEC the result of the prevalent vowel-raising that affects A in Nahuatl. Because they are

stem-internal, it cannot be determined if there is a segmental Y between the I and the A. T has the reflex of a long vowel in the plural suffix -TIN with this item, as B, C, and T do with MOCH(I) and C does with ĪZQUI.

MIACCĀN in many places / en muchas partes (M for *mieccan*) [(2)Cf.91v, (3)Zp.77,94,168]. See MIAC, -CĀN.

MIACPA many times / muchas veces (M for *miecpa*) [(1)Tp.141, (3)Zp.86,129,168]. See MIAC, -PA.

MIACTILIĀ *vt* to augment, multiply something / lo aumenta, lo multiplica (Z) [(3)Zp.17,87,190]. See MIAC.

MIĀHUATI See MIYĀHUATI.

MIĀHUA-TL See MIYĀHUA-TL.

MIAQUILIĀ *vrefl,vt* to increase, multiply; to augment, multiply something / se aumenta, multiplica, produce (T), lo aumenta, lo multiplica (T) [(3)Tp.190]. This has the same sense as MIACTILIĀ. applic. MIAQUIYA

MIAQUILILIĀ applic. MIAQUILIĀ

MIAQUILĪLŌ nonact. MIAQUILIĀ

MIAQUIYA to abound / abundarse (X) [(3)Xp.53]. See MIAC.

MICCĀ- This has two sources. It is the compounding form of the derived noun MICQUI 'corpse, dead person,' and it also arises directly from the verb MIQU(I) 'to die' followed by the -CĀ- ligature.

MICCĀCĀHU(A) *vrefl* to faint / se desmaya (Z) [(2)Zp.43,171]. Z idiosyncratically raises the Ā to Ē. See MICCĀ-, CĀHU(A).

MICCĀCĀHUAL-LI orphan, stepdaughter / huérfano (Z), entenada (Z) [(1)Zp.160]. The literal sense of this is 'someone left behind by someone who has died.' Z also has a variant in which the vowel of the second syllable is idiosyncratically raised to Ē. See MICCĀ-, CĀHUAL-LI.

MICCĀCHĪHU(A) *vrefl* to faint / se desmaya (Z) Z idiosyncratically raises Ā to Ē. See MICCĀ-, CHĪHU(A).

MICCĀCOYOC-TLI *pl:* **-MEH** grave / sepulcro, tumba (T) [(2)Tp.142, (3)Zp.115,126,167]. Z also has a variant in which the second vowel is idiosyncratically raised to Ē. See MICCĀ-, COYOC-TLI.

MICCĀTĒCA *vrefl,vt* to be stunned, dazed, unconscious; to daze, stun someone / se priva, está inconsciente (T), lo priva (T) [(6)Tp.152,190]. See MICCĀ-, TĒCA.

MICCĀTLATLAXIZ-TLI whooping cough / tosferina (T) [(1)Tp.142, (2)Zp.124,167]. Z has a variant with the Ā idiosyncratically raised to Ē. See MICCĀ-, TLATLAXIZ-TLI.

MICCĀTLATZILĪN(I) for the bell for the dead to toll / repica la campana para el muerto (T) [(3)Tp.142]. See MICCĀ-, TZILĪN(I).

MICCĀTLATZILĪNILIĀ applic. MIC-CĀTLATZILĪN(I)

MICCĀTLATZILĪNĪLŌ nonact. MIC-CĀTLATZILĪN(I)

MICCĀTŌNAHUIZ-TLI malaria / paludismo (Z) [(2)Zp.93,167]. Z idiosyncratically raises Ā to Ē. See MICCĀ-, TŌNAHUIZ-TLI.

MICCĀTZONTECOM(A)-TL skull / calavera (T) [(1)Tp.142, (2)Zp.23,167]. Z idiosyncratically raises Ā to Ē. See MICCĀ-, TZONTECOM(A)-TL.

MICCĀXŌCHI-TL marigold (Tagetes erecta) / flor de muerto (Z) [(2)Zp.60,167]. This is a translation from Spanish. The indigenous name for the large native marigold associated with precolumbian rituals and today specifically with All Souls Day is CEMPŌHUALXŌCHI-TL. Z idiosyncratically raises Ā to Ē. See MICCĀ-, XŌCHI-TL.

MICCĀYEHYECOĀ *vrefl* to be in terminal agony / está en agonía (T) [(3)Tp.152]. The literal sense of this is 'to sample death.' T also has MIQUILIZYEHYECOĀ 'to have a brush with death.' See MICCĀ-, YEHYECOĀ.

-MICECUIL *only attested in possessed form* one's rib / su costilla (T) [(2)Tp.131]. One of these attestations reduplicates the initial syllable. See OMICICUIL-LI.

MICHCOZ-TLI codfish / bacalao (T) [(1)Tp.141]. See MICH-IN, COZTIC.

MICHHUAH possessor of fish, person from Michoacan / dueño de pescado (C), natural de Michoacán (C) [(6)Cf.18v,53r,57r, (4)Rp.45,46]. See MICH-IN.

MICHHUAHCĀN *place name* Michoacan [(1)Cf.57r]. See MICHHUAH, -CĀN.

MICHHUAHCA-TL resident of Michoa-

can / natural de Michoacán (K) [(1)Cf.57r, (1)Rp.46]. See MICHHUAH.

MICHHUAHCAYŌ-TL quality, thing pertaining to Michoacan / cosa de Michoacán (C) [(1)Cf.53r]. See MICHHUAHCA-TL, -YŌ.

MICH-IN *pl:* **MĪMICHTIN** fish / pescado (M) This is commonly reanalyzed so that the stem is taken to be MICHI or MICHIN. X has the plural form MICHIMEH, but in X this is the general way in which stems that take the -IN absolutive suffix form their plurals.

MICHPAH-TLI walnut tree / nogal (Z) [(2)Zp.89,168]. The literal sense of this, 'fish potion,' refers to its use in fishing, the leaves having a narcotic effect rendering the fish easier prey. See MICH-IN, PAH-TLI.

MICHTLAHZOL-LI small fresh water fish abundant in Michoacan / charal (T) [(1)Tp.141]. Despite the literal sense of its name 'trash fish,' this fish is caught and dried and is important to the local economy. T has lost the glottal stop. See MICH-IN, TLAHZOL-LI.

MICOHUA C has the O before -HUA marked long twice. nonact. MIQU(I)

MICOHUANI deadly weapon, instrument / cosa mortífera o ponzoñosa (M), instrumento para morir (C) [(2)Cf.45v]. See MICOHUA.

MICOHUAYĀN place of death / donde se muere (C) [(1)Cf.51r]. C marks the O long in the single attestation. See MICOHUA, -YĀN.

MICQUI dead person or animal, corpse / muerto o difunto (M) Since in texts the medial geminate is often written as though there were only a single consonant, nominal MICQUI is often confused with the verb MIQU(I). See MIQU(I).

MICTIĀ *vrefl,vt* to commit suicide, to mistreat oneself; to kill or injure someone / matar o maltratar a sí mismo (M), matar o maltratar a otro (M) M provides additional glosses of 'to be unable to procreate' and 'to engage in blood sacrifice' for this with the object prefix TLA-. M also has an opaque gloss of the reflexive as 'to choose the best.' altern. caus. MIQU(I)

MICTILIĀ applic. MICTIĀ

MICTĪLŌ nonact. MICTIĀ
MICTLĀNCAL-LI the house of the dead / infierno, purgatorio (T) [(1)Tp.141]. See MICTLĀN-TLI, CAL-LI.
MICTLĀNCAYŌ-TL something pertaining to the realm of the dead / cosa infernal o del infierno (M) [(1)Cf.53v, (1)Rp.44]. C also gives the synonymous short form MICTLĀNYŌ-TL. See MICTLĀN-TLI, -YŌ.
MICTLĀN-TLI the realm of the dead / infierno o en el infierno o al infierno (M), infierno, purgatorio (T) This is consistently attested across sources with a long vowel in the second syllable. M gives it both with and without the absolutive suffix. It is more common without and does not take the suffix when used as a locative expression. See MIQU(I), -TLĀN.
MICTLĀNYŌ-TL something pertaining to the realm of the dead / cosa infernal o del infierno (K) [(1)Cf.53v, (1)Rp.44]. C gives this as synonymous with MICTLĀNCAYŌ-TL. See MICTLĀN-TLI, -YŌ.
MIEC See MIAC.
MIECCĀN See MIACCĀN.
MIECPA See MIACPA.
MIHMATCĀTLĀCA-TL a prudent person / prudente y avisado (M), cuerdo (C) [(1)Cf.113v]. See IHMAT(I), TLĀCA-TL.
MIHMILHUIĀ applic. MIHMILOĀ
MIHMILOĀ vt to spill something / trastornar o derrocar cántaro o cosa semejante (M), lo vierte, lo derrama (T) [(3)Tp.190, (2)Zp.41,107]. This contrasts with MĪMILOĀ 'to trample about' and MIMILOĀ 'to revolve, turn something' Z has a form COCHMIHMIL 'sleepyhead,' which may be derived from this. In both attestations of the verb in Z the internal glottal stop is omitted.
MIHMILŌLŌ nonact. MIHMILOĀ
MIHMIQU(I) redup. MIQU(I)
MIHTOH-TLI dance / baile (R) [(1)Rp.105]. See IHTŌTIĀ.
MIHTŌTIĀNI dancer / danzante (M) [(1)Zp.39]. Z glosses this as 'dance' rather than 'dancer,' but from a derivational viewpoint, M's gloss is the correct one. See IHTŌTIĀ.
MIHTŌTIHQUI dancer / danzante (M),

bailador (Z) [(1)Tp.150, (2)Zp.18,168]. T has the variant MOHTŌTIHQUI. See IHTŌTIĀ.
MĪHUAH possessor of arrows / el que tiene flechas, el dueño de las flechas (K) [(1)Cf.55v]. See MĪ-TL.
MĪLCHIPĀHU(A) to clear land for cultivation / limpia un sembrado (milpa) (Z) [(2)Zp.76,166]. See MĪL-LI, CHIPĀHU(A).
MĪLEH possessor of cultivated land / el dueño de la sementera (C) [(4)Cf.55v,81v,84r, (1)Rp.45]. See MĪL-LI.
MILĪN(I) to shine, sparkle, flare / brilla (Z) [(4)Zp.21,60,166,167].
MILĪNTIĀ vt to set something afire / lo prende (Z) [(2)Zp.101,190]. caus. MILĪN(I)
MĪLLAH place where there is an abundance of cultivated land / lugar de sementeras (C), milpa (Z) [(2)Cf.57r, (2)Zp.84,168]. See MĪL-LI, -TLAH.
MĪLLAHCA-TL field laborer / labrador o aldeano (M) [(1)Cf.57r, (1)Rp.46]. R fails to indicate the glottal stop, but it is attested in C. See MĪLLAH.
MĪL-LI cultivated land, field / heredad (M), sementera (C)
MĪLTEPĀN-TLI boundary, landmark, wall separating sections of cultivated land / linde entre heredades de muchos (M), la señal que indica las secciones de la milpa (T) [(1)Tp.142]. See MĪL-LI, TEPĀN-TLI.
MĪLTIĀ vrefl to prepare a cultivated field for oneself / hago sementera para mí (C for first pers. sg. subject) [(1)Cf.57v]. See MĪL-LI.
MĪLZACA-TL forage, fodder / forraje (Z) [(2)Zp.60,166]. See MĪL-LI, ZACA-TL.
MĪMIAC T attests this reduplicated form with a plural sense (p.141). redup. MIAC
-MIMICECUIL See -MICECUIL.
-MIMICECUILYŌ See -MICECUIL.
MĪMICOHUA nonact. MĪMIQU(I)
MIMILAHU(I) to swell, spill, overflow / desparrama (Z), rebosa (Z) [(3)Zp.44,106,167]. Z consistently marks the vowel of the third syllable long, but it should not be. This appears to be a characteristic case of Z representing a stressed syllable with a long vowel. See MIMILIHU(I).
MIMILHUIĀ applic. MIMILOĀ
MIMILICA to shine, sparkle, flare / brilla (Z) [(2)Zp.21,167]. See MILĪN(I).

MIMILIHU(I) to round out or swell, to
unroll or unfold / abotonarse la flor o
crecer el vientre de la que está preñada (M),
rodar (X) [(3)Xp.54]. Z has the variant
MIMILAHU(I).
MIMILĪN(I) to flame up / flamea ... la lumbre flamea (Z) [(3)Zp.60,167]. This form
should have long-vowel reduplication or
vowel and glottal stop reduplication, but
the attestations indicate neither. redup.
MILĪN(I)
MIMILOĀ vrefl,vt to roll over and over; to
roll or revolve something / rodar por el
suelo (M), lo rueda (T) C contrasts this
with MĪMILOĀ 'to trample about.' They
both contrast with MIHMILOĀ 'to spill
something' M combines the reflexive
glosses of MIMILOĀ and MĪMILOĀ in a
single entry.
MĪMILOĀ vrefl to trample about / se revuelca como una bestia (C) [(1)Cf.127v].
C contrasts this with MIMILOĀ 'to roll
over and over; to roll something.' They
both contrast with MIHMILOĀ 'to spill
something.'
MIMILŌLŌ nonact. MIMILOĀ
MIMILTIC something round, columnar /
rollizo (T) [(1)Tp.142, (1)Zp.167]. See
MIMILOĀ.
MĪMIQUI(I) pret: **-MIC** to have an attack / le
da ataque (T) [(3)Tp.142]. redup. MIQU(I)
MĪMIQUĪTIĀ caus. MĪMIQU(I)
MIMITE-TL pl: **-MEH** bone / hueso (T)
[(1)Tp.142]. T has this and also -MICECUIL
~ -MIMICECUIL ~ -MIMICECUILYŌ
'rib.' These latter all correspond to
OMICICUIL-LI, which is derived from
OMI-TL 'bone.' Here too T has lost the
initial vowel of OMI-TL and performs
reduplication on the resulting form. See
OMI-TL, TE-TL.
MIMIYĀHUATZIN a type of brightly
colored bird / dominico (pájaro) (Z)
[(2)Zp.47,166]. M has mimiauatl for a type
of honeycomb and the bee that makes it.
In both attestations Z has the vowel of the
fourth syllable marked long instead of
the vowel of the third. The derivation is
questionable. See MIYĀHUA-TL.
MĪMIZQUICUAHU(I)-TL pl: **-MEH**
mesquite tree / mesquite (T) [(1)Tp.142].
See MIZQUI-TL, CUAHU(I)-TL.

MĪMIZQUI-TL redup. MIZQUI-TL
MĪN(A) vt to shoot arrows, to pierce
someone with arrows / tirar saeta
o garrocha (M), asaetar a alguno
(M) [(1)Cf.96r]. The variant MĪN(I) is
abundantly attested in T.
MĪN(I) vt to prick, pierce something / le
quema (el sol), le pica (abeja, etc.) (T) This
is abundantly attested in T. The preterit is
MĪN, not MĪNIC, but T's nonactive form
consistently has the reflex of a long vowel
in the second syllable. This is a variant of
MĪN(A). See MĪ-TL.
MĪNILIĀ vt to inject someone with
something / se lo inyecta (T) applic. MĪN(I)
MĪNILILIĀ applic. MĪNILIĀ
MĪNILĪLŌ nonact. MĪNILIĀ
MĪNILŌ By general rule the vowel of the
second syllable should be short, but T
consistently has the reflex of a long vowel.
nonact. MĪN(I)
MIQU(I) pret: **MIC** to die / morir (S) There
are a number of verbs built on MIQU(I)
which do not have the literal sense of
'to die,' but rather 'to suffer,' such as
ĀPĪZMIQU(I) 'to be hungry,' CECMIQU(I)
'to suffer from cold.' Other verbs with
MIQU(I) as second element are even further removed from the literal sense of 'to
die,' such as TĒMIQU(I) 'to dream.'
MIQUILIĀ applic. MIQU(I)
MIQUILIZ-TLI death, mortality /
muerte o mortandad (M) The short form
MIQUIZ-TLI is more common, but this is
abundantly attested across sources. See
MIQU(I).
MIQUILIZYEHYECOĀ vrefl to have a
brush with death / está para morir (pero
revive) (T) [(3)Tp.152]. T also has
MICCĀYEHYECOĀ 'to be in terminal
agony.' See MIQUILIZ-TLI, YEHYECOĀ.
MIQUILIZYEHYECŌLŌ nonact.
MIQUILIZYEHYECOĀ
MIQUILTIĀ altern. caus. MIQU(I)
MIQUĪTIĀ altern. caus. MIQU(I)
MIQUIZCUAHU(I)-TL pl: **-TIN** casaguate
(Ipomoea murucoides, Ipomoea arbores-
cens) / palo de muerto (X) [(3)Xp.54].
This tree is believed to be poisonous to
people and animals. See MIQUIZ-TLI,
CUAHU(I)-TL.
MIQUIZ-TLI death / muerte (M) X glosses

this as 'corpse,' which is more appropriate to MICQUI. See MIQU(I).

MĪ-TL arrow, dart / saeta o flecha (M) [(1)Bf.10r, (2)Cf.55v]. This is also abundantly attested in the verbs MĪN(A) and MĪN(I) 'to prick, pierce something.'

MIXĀEHĒCA-TL wind and drizzle / llovizna con viento (Z) [(2)Zp.79,167]. See MIXĀ-TL, EHĒCA-TL.

MIXĀ-TL mist, drizzle / llovizna (Z) [(4)Zp.79,167]. See MIX-TLI, Ā-TL.

MĪXCUEPANI pl: **-MEH** hypocrite / hipócrita (T) [(1)Tp.143]. This specifically refers to someone other than oneself. Presumably it could also take first person prefixes, but it is not attested with them. See ĪX-TLI, CUEP(A).

MIXHUĀQU(I) for fog or clouds to lift / se levanta la neblina (Z for preterit form) [(2)Zp.88,167]. See MIX-TLI, HUĀQU(I).

MĪXIHU(I) to give birth / parir la mujer (M), le da a luz, pare su hijo (T) [(1)Cf.99v, (3)Tp.190, (3)Xp.70]. In T and X this is a transitive verb, but in M and C it is intransitive. See ĪX-TLI.

MĪXĪHUIĀ vrefl to use an intoxicating herb, to get drunk / se emborrachó (C for preterit form) [(1)Cf.60v]. This is conventionally paired with TLĀPĀHUIĀ, the whole phrase meaning 'to become intoxicated.' This verb contrasts with intransitive MĪXIHU(I) 'to give birth' both in the final syllable and in being reflexive. See MĪXĪ-TL.

MĪXIHUĪHUA nonact. MĪXIHU(I)
MĪXIHUILIĀ applic. MĪXIHU(I)

MĪXĪ-TL intoxicating herb, possibly jimsonweed / hierba que altera el cerebro (S) [(4)Cf.60v,116v,121r]. C gives the vowel of the second syllable long. According to S, the possessed form is -MĪX, but this is unlikely, since long stem-final vowels do not drop. This is conventionally used in the phrase IN MĪXĪ-TL, IN TLĀPĀ-TL 'intoxication.'

MIXMOLŌN(I) for clouds to build up / se levantan las nubes atrás de los cerros, está nublado (T) [(1)Tp.41]. See MIX-TLI, MOLŌN(I).

MIXQUIYAHU(I) to drizzle / llovizna (Z) [(2)Zp.79,167]. See MIX-TLI, QUIYAHU(I).

MIXTĒM(I) to be cloudy / está nu-

blado [(4)Zp.88,89,210]. Z treats this as a transitive verb and prefixes it with TLA-. See MIX-TLI, TĒM(I).

MIXTETEICA to drizzle / llovizna (Z) [(2)Zp.79,167]. The literal sense of this is for a cloud to get ground up, chewed up. See MIX-TLI, TETEICA.

MIXTLAH an abundance of clouds / está nublado (T) [(2)Zp.89,167]. See MIX-TLI, -TLAH.

MIXTLAYOHUA to be dark because of heavy clouds / medio se obscurece por estar muy nublado (T) [(1)Tp.141]. See MIX-TLI, TLAYOHUA.

MIX-TLI cloud / nube (M) T has the variant form MEX-TLI.

MIYAC See MIAC.

MIYĀHUAPAH-TLI a parasitic plant used to stimulate the appetite / cierta planta parásita y medicinal (R) [(1)Rp.104]. R fails to mark the vowel of the second syllable long. See MIYĀHUA-TL, PAH-TLI.

MIYĀHUATI for a cornstalk to produce tassels and flowers / echar espiga y flor la caña del maíz (M) [(2)Cf.108r,114v]. In one of the attestations C has a glottal stop before verbal -TI, but since the noun stem ends in a vowel, this is probably an error. See MIYĀHUA-TL.

MIYĀHUA-TL inalienably possessed form: **-MIYĀHUAYŌ** the tassel and flower of maize / la espiga y la flor de la caña de maíz (M) B attests this once with the vowel of the second syllable specifically marked short. Because the sequence is stem-internal and unalternating, it is impossible to determine whether this is MIYĀ or MIĀ.

MĪYEX(I) to break wind / despide pedos, ventosea (T) [(3)Tp.144]. M has miexini 'flatulent.'

MĪYEXĪHUA nonact. MĪYEX(I)
MĪYEXĪTIĀ caus. MĪYEX(I)

MIZILAMA female cat / gata (hembra) (T) [(1)Tp.142]. See MIZ-TLI, ILAMA-TL.

MIZQUI-TL mesquite / árbol de goma para tinta (M), mesquite (T) [(1)Bf.4r, (2)Tp.142, (5)Xp.54,86]. X marks the vowel of this long, while T reduplicates it to yield MĪMIZQUI-TL.

MIZ-TLI pl: **MĪMIZTIN** feline, mountain lion / león (M) The diminutive of this,

MIZTŌN, is used for the domestic cat.

MŌ *particle which combines with negative particles to form* **AHMŌ** *'no,not,'* **AOCMŌ** *'no longer,'* **AYAMŌ** *'not yet,'* *etc.* MŌ can serve as a negative particle on its own in questions expressing doubt; in such a context MŌ is synonymous with AHMŌ, and MŌNEL is synonymous with AHMŌ NEL (Cf.121v).

MO- *non-first person reflexive prefix* In addition to its literal sense of '-self,' this is used in combination with the applicative and the causative forms of verbs and also paired with -TZINOĀ for honorific address. Nahuatl speech communities vary greatly in degree of elaboration of the honorific system and means of expressing it. The combination of MO- with the applicative of verbs is pervasive in Classical Nahuatl and in varieties of Nahuatl most closely akin to it. Some dialects have simplified the reflexive paradigm and make no distinction between first person reflexive prefixes and non-first person, but the honorific use of the reflexive prefix should not refer back to the speaker. Reflexive MO- and possessive MO- are homophonous, but the former binds with verbals, while the latter binds with nominals.

MO- *second person singular possessive prefix* your / tu (K) Possessive MO- and reflexive MO- are homophonous, but the former binds with nominals, and the latter binds with verbals.

MOĀN(A) to flame up / flamea (T) [(2)Tp.154]. T gives the variant MĀN(A). This appears to be ĀN(A) used reflexively, which in M is glossed as 'to grow in bodily size.' See ĀN(A).

MOCA full of / lleno de (C) [(7)Cf.118r,122r, 122v,131v].

MOCĀHU(A) to cease, to remain behind / cesar de llover, o de llorar, o de hacer algo (M) This reflexive use of CĀHU(A) has become lexicalized and is commonly used only in the third person singular. See CĀHU(A).

MOCĒLOQUICH-TLI soldier, warrior / soldado (C) [(3)Cf.86r,109v,118v]. This is attested only in the vocative, and even in

the plural vocative the possessive prefix remains MO-. This suggests a lexicalization of MOCĒL- as 'peerless.' See -CĒL, OQUICH-TLI.

MOCH See MOCH(I).

MOCHAHCHAMĀHUANI someone arrogant and self-important / el que se jacta y alaba (M), arrogante, orgulloso (T) [(1)Tp.148]. This is specifically non-first person. Presumably it could also take first person prefixes. See CHAMĀHU(A).

MOCHEH all of something not named but understood / todo (K) [(1)Cf.119r]. See MOCH(I), (Y)EH.

MOCH(I) *pl:* **MOCHĪN ~ MOCHĪNTĪN ~ MOCHTĪN** all / todo (M) M lists this under *muchi*, but the initial vowel is not long. The plural suffix with this item, as with MIAC and ĪZQUI is attested as -TĪN rather than -TIN, in this case in B, C, and T. T, Z, and X have NOCH(I) for MOCH(I), as do many communities peripheral to the central dialect area. X uses the plural suffix -MEH with NOCH(I).

MOCHĪHU(A) to occur, to come about / sucede, acontece, ocurre (Z) [(2)Cf.50v,117r, (5)Zp.4,90,118,169,224]. This is the non-first person reflexive form of the verb CHĪHU(A) 'to make or do something.' See CHĪHU(A).

-MOCHĪHUAYĀN *necessarily possessed form* proper time or place for something to come about, as for fruit trees to bear fruit / tiempo o lugar ... donde o cuando se da (C) [(1)Cf.50v, (1)Rp.43]. C also has the shorter form -MOCHĪUHYĀN with the same sense. See MOCHĪHU(A), -YĀN.

MŌCHILIĀ applic. MŌTLA

MOCHĪN See MOCH(I).

MOCHIPA always, continually / siempre, de contínuo (C) [(7)Cf.105v,106r,116v,131v]. T and Z have NOCHIPA with the same sense. See MOCH(I), -PA.

-MOCHĪUHYĀN *necessarily possessed form* the proper time for something to come about / es tiempo de (C) [(2)Cf.51r, (1)Rp.42]. See -MOCHĪHUAYĀN.

MOCHTĪN See MOCH(I).

MOCUĀNI *pl:* **-MEH** something edible / se come, es comestible (T) [(1)Tp.147]. See CUĀ.

MOCUIHCUĪLIĀNI someone who makes another entreat him, someone who resists / el que se hace de rogar o el que resiste (M) [(1)Cf.52r]. This is synonymous with MOCUIHCUĪLIHQUI. See CUIHCUĪLIĀ.

MOCUIHCUĪLIHQUI someone who makes another entreat him, someone who resists / el que se hace de rogar o el que resiste (M) [(1)Cf.52r]. This is synonymous with MOCUIHCUĪLIĀNI. See CUIHCUĪLIĀ.

MOHCIHUIĀ vrefl,vt to suffer, agonize, be troubled; to bother, upset someone / congojarse, trafagar o agonizar (M), se molesta, se fastidia (T), ser importuno o desasosegar a otro (M) [(1)Bf.11r, (6)Tp.152,191]. T has lost the internal glottal stop. See (I)HCIHU(I).

MOHCIHUILIĀ applic. MOHCIHUIĀ

MOHCIHUĪLŌ nonact. MOHCIHUIĀ

MOHMŌTLA vt to stone someone, to throw rocks at someone / apedrear a otro (M) [(3)Zp.12,122,190]. redup. MŌTLA

MOHMOTZALTIC something rough, scratchy / rasposa (T) [(1)Tp.149]. Related forms in T and C lack the internal glottal stop. See MOMOTZOĀ.

MOHMOXTIC something torn open, tattered / rasgado, rasgón, roto (Z) [(3)Zp.105,111,170]. The related verbs MOMOXTIYA and MOMOTZOĀ lack the internal glottal stop. See MOMOXTIĀ.

MOHMOYĀHU(A) vt to deflate something / lo deshincha (T) [(3)Tp.190]. redup. MOYĀHU(A), see MOHMOYĀHU(I)

MOHMOYĀHU(I) to emit air or fluid, to deflate / se deshincha (T) [(1)Tp.149]. See MOYĀHU(A).

MOHTŌTIHQUI See MIHTŌTIHQUI.

MŌLA vrefl,vt to get ground up; to grind something / se muele (chile, tomate, etc.) (T), lo muele (chile, tomate, etc.) (T) [(4)Tp.153,192]. See MŌL-LI.

MŌLALŌ nonact. MŌLA

MŌLCA-TL secondary ear of maize that remains small and does not develop fully / mazorca chiquita o segunda, inferior (Z) [(4)Zp.80,82,170]. In one attestation the vowel of the second syllable is marked long.

MŌLCATLAŌL-LI inferior maize / maíz segundo (Z) [(2)Zp.80,170]. Z has TLAGŌL

for TLAŌL. See MŌLCA-TL, TLAŌL-LI.

MŌLCAX(I)-TL pl: -MEH ~ -TIN stone mortar, soup bowl / escudilla (M), molcajete (T) [(1)Bf.11r, (1)Tp.166].

MŌLĒHU(A) vt to root about in the ground, to break up soil / amollentar la tierra (M), hocica (Z) [(2)Zp.68,211]. Neither attestation has the first vowel marked long. This is attested only with the object prefix TLA-, which may be fused to the stem. See MŌL-LI, ĒHU(A).

MOLICPI-TL elbow / codo (M) [(2)Cf.82v]. See MOLIC-TLI.

MOLIC-TLI elbow / codo (M), su codo (parte del cuerpo) (Z), codo (medida) (Z) [(1)Bf.10r, (4)Zp.29,160,202]. Z has a long vowel in the first syllable, but B specifically marks it short, and it is also short in MOLICPI-TL. Z has extended this to mean a unit of length measurement on the model of Spanish codo.

MŌLILIĀ applic. MŌLA

MŌLĪNIĀ See ŌLĪNIĀ.

MŌL-LI sauce, broth, gravy, mole / salsa, guiso, potaje (S), mole (T) See MŌLA.

MOLŌN(I) to waft, to rise and drift on air currents, to effervesce / manar la fuente o cosa así o levantarse muchas nubes, o levantarse con el aire las plumas, o extenderse o oler mucho los perfumes o olores suaves (M) [(1)Cf.74v, (2)Tp.141,150, (3)Zp.67,170].

MOLŌNIĀ vt to lighten something or to fill something with air by boiling, carding, tilling, etc. / mullir lana o pluma (M), labra (tierra), hocica, escarba (T for reduplicated form), lo hierva (T) This is abundantly attested, but only in T. See MOLŌN(I).

MOLŌNILIĀ applic. MOLŌNIĀ

MOLŌNĪLŌ nonact. MOLŌNIĀ

MOLŌNTOC something boiling / hirviendo (Z) [(2)Zp.68,170]. See MOLŌN(I), the verb O.

MOMACA to come to blows / se pega, se pelea (T) [(3)Tp.150]. This is a lexicalized use of the reflexive of MACA 'to give.' See MACA.

MOMACHTIHQUI student, follower / aprendiz o estudiante (M), discípulo, alumno, estudiante (Z) [(4)Zp.9,46,58,170]. See MACHTIĀ.

MOMĀMATINI someone timid, embarrassed / el que tiene empacho (C) [(1)Cf.44r]. See MĀMAT(I).

MOMAT(I) *pret:* **MOMAT** it appears, it is thought, it happens that / se halla, se engríe, se acostumbra, se impone (T) [(4)Tp.152, (4)Zp.5,66,171]. This is a lexicalized use of the third person reflexive form of MAT(I) 'to know something' The first person reflexive is also lexicalized and means 'it seems (to me) that ...' See MAT(I).

MOMOLOCA to bubble up, to waft up on air currents / burbujear el agua, o levantarse gran polvo de cosas secas y livianas así como harina, cal, o de cosas semejantes (M) See MOLŌN(I).

MOMOLOTZ(A) *vt* to mix something with air / hacer espuma en el agua, meneándola (M), levantar ... polvo (C) [(1)Cf.74v]. See MOLŌN(I).

MOMOTZALHUIĀ *vt* to pluck, clean feathers or something of the sort / rozar o repelar pluma o cosa semejante (M), mesar a otro (C) [(1)Cf.65r, (1)Tp.206]. altern. applic. MOMOTZOĀ

MOMOTZOĀ *vrefl,vt* to scrape, scratch oneself; to scrape, scratch or pluck something or someone / rasguñarse o rascarse (M), rasguñar o rascar a otro (M), rozar o coger yerbas sin arrancarlas (C)

MOMOTZOLHUIĀ altern. applic. MOMOTZOĀ

MOMOTZŌLŌ nonact. MOMOTZOĀ

MOMOXTIYA to come apart, to get tattered / se desmorona (Z) [(2)Zp.43,171]. Z also has MOHMOXTIC 'something torn, tattered' with an internal glottal stop. See MOMOTZOĀ.

MOMOYOCA This is only attested in YACAMOMOYOCA 'for one's nose to itch' in T. See MOYŌN(I).

MOMOYOCOHUA nonact. MOMOYOCA

MOMOYOQUĪTIĀ caus. MOMOYOCA

MŌMŌZTLAEH every day / cada día (M) T omits the final -EH; Z has it unreduplicated as MŌZTLAH. See MŌZTLA.

MONECQUI someone arrogant / arrogante (T) [(1)Tp.154]. See NEQU(I).

-MONECYĀN *necessarily possessed form* the proper time or place for something / su

lugar (C) [(1)Cf.96r]. This is a short form of -MONEQUIYĀN. See NEQU(I), -YĀN.

MŌNEL *interrogative particle conveying doubt* is it really so that ... ? / ¿no lo verás? (C for *mōnel tiquittaz*) [(6)Cf.120r,121v,122r,131v]. MŌNEL is synonymous with AHMŌ NEL. See MŌ, NEL-LI.

MONENEPILTIĀ See NENEPILTIĀ.

MONEQU(I) to be necessary or wanting, to be useful / es necesario, se necesita (Z), serme útil, ventajoso, usarse en provecho mío, hablando de una cosa (S for construction with NOTECH) The person or thing experiencing lack or need is expressed with -TECH in construction with this lexicalized use of the reflexive of the verb NEQU(I) 'to want something' In Z the negation AHMŌ MONEQU(I) is glossed as 'it does not matter.' M glosses *monequiatle notech* as 'to live in poverty,' but *atle monectoc* 'for there to be an abundance of whatever is necessary.' See NEQU(I).

MONEQUINI *pl:* **-MEH** someone arrogant, proud / orgulloso (T) [(1)Tp.154]. T also has MONECQUI with the same sense. M has MONEQUINI with its more literal sense of 'something necessary.' See NEQU(I).

-MONEQUIYĀN *necessarily possessed form* the proper time or place for something / la sazón y tiempo (C) [(1)Cf.42v]. C also has the short form -MONECYĀN. See NEQU(I), -YĀN.

MŌNNĀN-TLI *pl:* **-TIN** mother-in-law / suegra, madre de mujer casada (M) See MŌN-TLI, NĀN-TLI.

MŌNTAH-TLI *pl:* **-TIN** father-in-law / suegro, padre de la mujer casada (M) See MŌN-TLI, TAH-TLI.

-MŌNTĒZYŌ *only attested in possessed form* mother-in-law of a man / su suegra (del hombre) (T) [(1)Tp.131]. See MŌN-TLI.

MŌNTIĀ *vrefl* to take a father-in-law by marrying his daughter, for a prospective son-in-law to do work in the household of the father of the bride / tomar yerno casando su hija (M), está sirviendo de novio (trabaja dos meses en la casa del suegro) (T) [(4)Tp.154]. All attestations are in complex progressive form. See MŌN-TLI.

MŌNTĪHUA nonact. MŌNTIĀ

MŌNTĪLTIĀ T has a long vowel in the second syllable, although by general rule it should be short. caus. MŌNTIĀ

MŌNTIQUI son-in-law, daughter-in-law / yerno, nuero (Z) [(3)Zp.89,131,171]. See MŌN-TLI.

MŌN-TLI son-in-law / yerno, marido de hija (M) In general MŌN carries the sense of 'related by marriage.' CIHUĀMŌN-TLI is 'daughter-in-law,' MŌNNĀN-TLI 'mother-in-law,' and MŌNTAH-TLI 'father-in-law.' T has the reflex of a short vowel in this item, but in C and Z it is long. M provides an additional gloss 'mousetrap,' which probably belongs to a different lexical item which is not attested in the sources for this dictionary.

MOPĪCHAQUIĀNI someone compliant, meek, humble / sumiso, humilde (T) [(1)Tp.155]. See PĪCHAQUIĀ.

-MOPILOĀYĀN *necessarily possessed form* place where something hangs, gathers, or looms / lugar donde se arman los aguaceros (C referring in context to rain) [(1)Cf.50v]. See PILOĀ, -YĀN.

MOPĪTZNEQUI a sulky child / un niño berrinchudo, se enoja pronto (T) [(1)Tp.155]. See PĪTZ(A), NEQU(I).

MOPŌHUANI someone proud, arrogant / soberbio (M) [(1)Cf.44r]. See PŌHU(A).

MOPOLOH something destroyed / perdido (Z) [(2)Zp.96,172]. See POLOĀ.

MOQUEQUETZ(A) See QUEQUETZ(A).

-MOTĒCAYĀN *necessarily possessed form* place where something spreads itself out on a surface / lugar donde el aguacero descarga y cae (C referring in context to rain) [(1)Cf.50v]. R glosses this as 'place where rain clouds form,' which is the gloss C provides for -MOPILOĀYĀN. See TĒCA, -YĀN.

MOTĒCUITLAHUIĀNI guardian of someone / el que cuida de ellas (C) [(1)Cf.44r]. C contrasts this with MOTLACUITLAHUIĀNI 'guardian of something.' See CUITLAHUIĀ.

MOTĒICNŌITTILIĀNI someone compassionate / misericordioso (C) [(1)Cf.44v]. See (I)CNŌITTA.

MOTĒNĒHUANI someone arrogant,

boastful / arrogante (T) [(1)Tp.158]. See TĒNĒHU(A).

MOTĒTLAPOHPOLHUILIĀNI pardoner, one who forgives / perdonador (C) [(1)Cf.44r]. See POHPOLHUILIĀ.

MOTĒTLATZONTEQUILIĀNI judge / juez (C) [(1)Cf.101v]. See TZONTEQUILIĀ.

MOTĒUCZŌMA *personal name* Montezuma / Moctezuma (C) [(2)Cf.109r]. Because word-final vowels are subjected to shortening, and because this is not attested in suffixed or compounded form, the basic length of the final vowel cannot be determined. See TĒUC-TLI, ZŌMĀ.

MŌTLA *vt* to stone someone, to throw a rock at someone or something, to hunt something / dar pedrada a otro (M), tirar con piedra (M), caza (Z)

MOTLACUITLAHUIĀNI guardian of something / el que cuida de algo (C), hombre cuidadoso (M) [(1)Cf.44r]. C contrasts this with MOTĒCUITLAHUIĀNI 'guardian of someone.' See CUITLAHUIĀ.

MOTLAHTLAIHTLANI beggar, one who seeks alms / mendicante que pide limosna (M) [(1)Tp.159]. See TLAHTLAIHTLAN(I).

MOTLAHYELTIĀNI someone experiencing nausea / asqueroso (T) [(1)Tp.159]. See TLAHYELTIĀ.

MŌTLALŌ nonact. MŌTLA

MOTLĀTIHTOC something hidden, covert / escondido, oculto (Z) [(3)Zp.55,90,173]. See TLĀTIĀ, the verb O.

MŌTOH-TLI *pl:* **-MEH** squirrel / ardilla (C) [(1)Cf.21, (1)Rp.106, (3)Xp.55].

MOTTA to be visible / se ve, visible (Z) [(5)Zp.72,90,128,130]. Two of the attestations in Z have a long vowel in the first syllable, but it should be short, since this is the reflexive form of (I)TTA. AHMŌ MOTTA has the sense 'to be invisible, hidden.' See (I)TTA.

MOTTITIĀ *vt* to see something in a dream / lo revela (lo ve en un sueño) (T) [(3)Tp.190]. The reflexive prefix MO- has been absorbed into the stem, so this receives a second MO- when used honorifically. See MOTTA.

MOTTITILIĀ applic. MOTTITIĀ

MOTTITĪLŌ nonact. MOTTITIĀ

MOTZOLIHU(I) to huddle / acurrucarse (X)

[(4)Xp.84]. M has *motzoloa* to hold on to someone, to grapple with someone.'

MOXĪCOĀNI devil; jealous, invidious person / diablo, satanás, el envidioso (T) [(1)Tp.162]. M has *moxico* 'someone envious.' See XĪCOĀ.

MOXĪCOHCĀTLĀCA-TL diabolical, jealous person / el hombre envidioso, diablo (T) [(1)Tp.162]. See XĪCOĀ, TLĀCA-TL.

MOXĪX(A) to rust / se oxida ... se enmohece (metal) (Z) [(5)Zp.52,92,175]. See XĪX(A).

MOXĪXAC something rusted / oxidado (Z) [(2)Zp.92,175]. See MOXĪX(A).

MOYĀHU(A) *vt* to disseminate or disperse something, to deflate something / echar fama de algo, o enturbiar el agua (M), desbaratar o hacer alzar el cerco a los enemigos o ahuyentar gente o ganado (M), enturbiar el agua o otra cosa líquida (M), lo deshincha (T)

MOYĀHUALŌ nonact. MOYĀHU(A)

MOYĀHUILIĀ applic. MOYĀHU(A)

MŌYŌCOCO-TL insect bite / grano de mosca (Z) [(2)Zp.64,175]. See MŌYŌ-TL, COCO-TL.

MOYŌLĒHUANI someone with an interest, preoccupation / tiene interés (T) [(1)Tp.164]. M has *moyoleuhqui* 'someone in love, someone driven by internal motivation.' See YŌLĒHU(A).

MOYŌLĪCAHTZIN See -YŌLĪCAHTZIN.

MOYŌN(I) to swarm / brullir las hormigas, gusanos o cosa semejante (M) [(2)Zp.8,175].

This appears to be related to MŌYŌ-TL 'mosquito, flying insect,' but there is a vowel length discrepancy in the first syllable.

MŌYŌ-TL *pl:* **MŌYŌMEH ~ MŌ-MŌYOH** mosquito, flying insect / mosquito (M)

MŌYŌTZIN gnat / jején, chaquistle (Z) [(2)Zp.73,175]. See MŌYŌ-TL.

MŌZŌ-TL plant that produces indigo dye and from which an antidysentery medicine is made / mozote (Z) [(5)Zp.86,175].

MŌZTICA See MŌZTLATICA.

MŌZTLA tomorrow / mañana (M) This is conventionally paired with HUĪPTLA 'day after tomorrow,' the sense of the phrase being 'in the future, from this day forward.'

MŌZTLAH See MŌMŌZTLAEH.

MŌZTLATI to see another day, to survive until tomorrow / llegar a mañana (C) [(2)Cf.59r]. See MŌZTLA.

MŌZTLATICA the following day, in the future / el día siguiente, el día próximo, en el futuro (T) [(1)Tp.166]. Z has a shortened form MŌZTICA, which is only attested in possessed form. See MŌZTLA, -CA.

-MŌZTLAYŌC *necessarily possessed form* the day following something / el día siguiente (S) [(6)Cf.85r,97r,97v]. All attestations are in possessed form. In construction with preceding OC, this means 'the day before something.' See MŌZTLA, -YŌ, -C(O).

N

NACACEH something possessing ears / que tiene orejas, ángulos (S), jarro de dos asas, pero no redondas (C for NECOC NACACEH) [(1)Cf.92r]. This combines with ĪX-TLI 'eye' to form the phrase NACACEH ĪXEH 'someone prudent,' literally 'someone with ears and eyes.' It is also attested in P, where the glottal stop is marked but not the long vowel. See NACAZ-TLI.

NACACIC on the side / de lado (M) This is attested in Z's NACACICAHUĪCA and T's NACACICATĒCA. In M it appears as an initial element of seven different entries, although it does not appear independently. Since this is not derived from a verb, it is probably a locative construction based on a stem form *NACACI rather than NACAZ. See NACAZ-TLI, -C(O).

NACACICAHUĪCA vt to make something get out of line, to carry something on its side / lo desploma ... lo lleva de lado (Z) [(2)Zp.44,190]. See NACACIC, HUĪCA.

NACACICATĒCA vrefl,vt to sleep on one's side; to lay something down on its side / duerme del lado (T), lo acuesta de lado (T) [(6)Tp.153,192]. See NACACIC, TĒCA.

NACACICATĒCALŌ nonact. NACACICATĒCA

NACACICATĒQUILIĀ applic. NACACICATĒCA

NACACITTA vt to gaze upon someone with affection, to cast someone a sidelong glance / mirar a otro con afición (M), lo ve del lado (T) [(3)Tp.192]. See NACAZ-TLI, (I)TTA.

NACACITTALŌ nonact. NACACITTA

NACACITTILIĀ applic. NACACITTA

NACACUĀ to eat flesh / comer carne (K) [(1)Cf.98r]. M has *nacaqualizpan* 'period during which one may eat meat,' i.e. a nonfast day. See NAC(A)-TL, CUĀ.

NACAMŌL-LI meat stew / guisado o potaje de carne (M) [(1)Tp.166]. See NAC(A)-TL, MŌL-LI.

NACANAMACAC meat vendor / carnicero que pesa y vende carne (M) [(1)Cf.51v]. See NAC(A)-TL, NAMACA.

NACAOCUIL-IN pl: -TIN maggot or cataract of the eye / gusano de carne dañada (M), catarata (T) [(1)Tp.166]. See NAC(A)-TL, OCUIL-IN.

NACAPALAX-TLI rotten meat / carne podrida [(1)Cf.49v]. See NAC(A)-TL, PALĀN(I).

NACATAMAL-LI meat tamale / empanada de carne o cosa semejante (M) [(1)Tp.223, (3)Zp.119,176,210]. See NAC(A)-TL, TAMAL-LI.

NAC(A)-TL inalienably possessed form: **-NACAYŌ** flesh, meat / carne (M) The inalienably possessed form means 'one's own flesh, one's body.'

NACAYOH something, someone fleshy, of flesh and blood, incarnate / cosa carnuda y gorda (M), cosa o persona que tiene carne en sí (C) See NAC(A)-TL, -YOH.

-NACAYOHCĀPOH necessarily possessed form sharing flesh and blood with another, a human being like oneself / el que tiene cuerpo como yo (C for first person possessor) [(2)Cf.84r]. See NACAYOH, -POH.

NACAYŌTIĀ vrefl,vt to assume flesh, to grow fat; to give someone a fleshly form, to fatten animals / encarnar o pararse gordo (M), cebar o engordar aves o puercos, etc. (M) [(1)Bf.1v, (4)Cf.21v,22r,109v,129r]. M also gives this as a double object verb with a direct object and an oblique reflexive prefix and meaning 'to get used to something.' See NACAYŌ-TL.

NACAYŌ-TL something pertaining to flesh / cosa que pertence a la carne (M) In the sources for this dictionary all instances of -NACAYŌ are instances of the inalienably possessed form of NAC(A)-TL, but this is indirectly attested in the derived verb NACAYŌTIĀ. See NAC(A)-TL, -YŌ.

NACAZCŌLŌ-TL *pl:* **-MEH** divi-divi, a tree that produces curved pods resembling a scorpion's tail which are high in tannic acid and used for making black dye (Caesalpinia coriacea) / oreja de alacrán, cascalote (X) [(3)Xp.55]. See NACAZ-TLI, CŌLŌ-TL.

NACAZCOTOCTIC something, someone with a cropped ear / oreja mocha (T) [(1)Tp.166]. See NACAZ-TLI, COTOCTIC.

-NACAZCOYOC *necessarily possessed form* one's hearing / su oído, su auditivo (Z) [(2)Zp.91,160]. M has the necessarily possessed locative form *nacazco* 'in one's ears.' See NACAZ-TLI, COYOC-TLI.

NACAZCOYŌNIĀ *vrefl,vt* for one's ear to get pierced; to pierce someone's ear / se agujera la oreja (T), le agujera la oreja (T) [(6)Tp.153,192]. See NACAZ-TLI, COYŌNIĀ.

NACAZCUEHZOĀ *vt* to impede someone's hearing / molesta el oído (Z) [(2)Zp.85,220]. See NACAZ-TLI, CUEHZOĀ.

NACAZCUIHCUITL(A)-TL earwax / cera de los oídos (M) [(1)Zp.175]. The single attestation in Z has CHI for the third syllable instead of CUIH. See NACAZTECUIHCUITL(A)-TL.

NACAZMAHU(I) to live in fear with one's ears cocked / tienen temores (y) sobresaltos (C for third person plural subject) [(1)Cf.120r]. See NACAZ-TLI, MAHU(I).

NACAZPACHŌNTIC someone, something shaggy, with a great deal of hair on the head / mechudo, le crece mucho el pelo (T) [(1)Tp.166]. See NACAZ-TLI, PACHŌNTIC.

NACAZQUEHQUETZ(A) *vrefl* to prick up one's ears / aguza las orejas (Z) [(2)Zp.7,171]. redup. NACAZQUETZ(A)

NACAZQUETZ(A) *vrefl* to listen., to pay attention [(3)Tp.153]. See NACAZ-TLI, QUETZ(A).

NACAZQUETZALŌ nonact. NACAZ-QUETZ(A)

NACAZTAPAL someone deaf / sordo (M) [(2)Zp.117,175]. See NACAZ-TLI.

NACAZTĀTAPA *pl:* **-MEH** a type of locust,

grasshopper / una clase de langosta (T) [(1)Tp.166]. See NACAZTAPAL.

NACAZTECUIHCUITL(A)-TL earwax / su cerilla (T for possessed form) [(2)Tp.132,166]. See NACAZTE-TL, CUITL(A)-TL.

NACAZTEHTEQU(I) See NACAZ-TLI, TEHTEQU(I).

NACAZTEPOLTIC something, someone with a cropped ear / oreja mocha (T) [(1)Tp.166]. See NACAZ-TLI, TEPOLTIC.

NACAZTE-TL Although this does not occur as a free form, it is an element in a number of entries in M having to do with the ear. See NACAZ-TLI, TE-TL.

NACAZTILĀN(A) *vt* to pull someone's ear / le jala la oreja (T) [(3)Tp.192, (2)Zp.73,190]. See NACAZ-TLI, TILĀN(A).

NACAZTITĪCA earache / dolor de oído (Z) [(2)Zp.47,176]. One of the attestations is missing the Z. M has reflexive *nacastititza* 'to have a buzzing in the ears.' See NACAZ-TLI.

-NACAZTLAN *compound postposition* next to, beside, near / junto a él, a lado de, proximidad (Z) [(1)Tp.132, (4)Zp.74,75, 103, 160]. See NACAZ-TLI, -TLAN.

NACAZTLAPILŌL-LI earring / arete (Z) [(2)Zp.13,160]. See NACAZ-TLI, PILOĀ.

NACAZ-TLI ear / oreja (M)

NACAZTZACU(I) to become deaf / sordo, ensordece, remolino, torbellino (Z) [(4)Zp.53,108,117,175]. See NACAZ-TLI, TZACU(I).

NACAZTZATZA someone deaf / sordo (Z) [(2)Zp.117,175]. In one attestation Z gives this with a preterit suffix, although the gloss does not suggest that it is a verb, and M's verb *tzatzati* 'to go deaf' is derived from the noun TZATZA. See NACAZ-TLI, TZATZA.

NAHNACAZQUETZ(A) redup. NACAZ-QUETZ(A)

NAHNAHUATIĀ *vrefl* to take leave / se despide (Z) [(2)Zp.44,171]. redup. NAHUATIĀ

NAHNALTIC someone with a hoarse voice / habla de ronco, con voz ronca (T) [(2)Tp.166,241]. See NANALCA.

NAHNAMACA redup. NAMACA

*NĀHUA- This element enters into many

derivations with divergent meanings. The basic sense appears to be 'audible, intelligible, clear,' from which different derivations extend to 'within earshot, near,' 'incantation' (hence many things to do with spells and sorcery), and 'language.'

-NĀHUAC *postposition* near to, adjacent to, within earshot / par de mí o conmigo (M for first pers. sg. possessor) See NĀHUA-,

NĀHUAHTEQU(I) *vrefl,vt* to hug oneself, to embrace someone / abrazar a sí mismo (M), abrazar a otro (M) [(3)Tp.194]. The attested final consonant of the second syllable is ambiguous in T between glottal stop and the reduction of some other consonant before T. Conceivably this should be NĀHUA-CTEQU(I). See NĀHUA-, TEQU(I).

NĀHUAHTEQUĪHUA nonact. NĀHUAH-TEQU(I)

NĀHUAHTEQUILIĀ applic. NĀHUAH-TEQU(I)

NĀHUALAHCI *vt* to take someone by surprise, stealth / le agarra con sorpresa (T) [(6)Tp.194,233]. See NĀHUAL-LI, AHCI.

NĀHUALCOCO-TL sore caused by sorcery / llaga de brujería (Z) [(2)Zp.21,176]. See NĀHUAL-LI, COCO-TL.

NĀHUALHUIĀ *vt* to put a spell on someone / lo embruja (Z) [(2)Zp.49,190]. See NĀHUAL-LI, -HUIĀ.

NĀHUALIZ-TLI sorcery / brujería (X) [(1)Xp.56]. X marks the vowel of the second syllable long instead of the first. See NĀHUAL-LI.

NĀHUAL-LI *pl:* **NĀNĀHUALTIN ~ NĀHUALTIN** sorcerer, one who uses spells and incantations / bruja (M), nagual, brujo (T) See NĀHUA-.

NĀHUALLŌ-TL sorcery / nigromancia o cosa semejante (M), brujería, mágico (Z) [(3)Zp.21,79,176]. See NĀHUAL-LI, -YŌ.

NĀHUALPOLOĀ *vrefl,vt* to go into danger unwittingly; to lure someone into danger / vas a la muerte sin saber lo que haces (C for second pers. singular subject), llevar con cautela a otro a algún lugar peligroso, para hacerle mal (M) [(1)Cf.118v]. See NĀHUAL-LI, POLOĀ.

NĀHUALTLAHCACAQUĪTIĀ *vt* to offend someone / lo ofende (T) [(3)Tp.194]. See NĀHUAL-LI, CAQUĪTIĀ.

NĀHUALTLAHCACAQUĪTILIĀ applic. NĀHUALTLAHCACAQUĪTIĀ

NĀHUALTLAHCACAQUĪTĪLŌ nonact. NĀHUALTLAHCACAQUĪTIĀ

NĀHUAQUEH the one that is close to all things, god / con quien está el ser de todas las cosas, dios (M), nombre que se da a Dios, y significa aquel en quien están todas las cosas; se usa ordinariamente con el Tloquê, que expresa casi lo mismo (R) This is conventionally paired with TLOQUEH< -TLOC, which also has the sense of vicinity, the whole phrase being an epithet for divine presence. See -NĀHUAC.

NĀHUAT(I) to speak clearly, to make a clear sound, to answer or respond / hablar alto o tener buen sonido la campana o cosa así (M), responde, contesta (T) See NĀHUA-TL.

NAHUATIĀ *vt* to give orders to someone / mandar algo a otros, o pedir licencia o darla para hacer algo, o para ir a alguna parte, o citar a otro, o despedir y echar los criados de casa, o despedirse de algunos el que quiere partirse para algún lugar (M) Although this would appear to be related to NĀHUAT(I) 'to speak clearly,' it is attested with a long vowel in the first syllable only in X. Elsewhere, across sources, it is nowhere marked long. In T, NĀHUAT(I) has the reflex of a long vowel in the first syllable, and NAHUATIĀ a short one. This is attested twice in C, once in B with the first vowel marked short, three times in X, and abundantly in T and Z. See NĀHUA-, NĀHUAT(I).

NĀHUATILIĀ applic. NĀHUAT(I)

NAHUATILIĀ applic. NAHUATIĀ

NAHUATĪL-LI law, obligation, constitution / ley o constitución (M) [(2)Cf.84r,87v]. See NAHUATIĀ.

NAHUATĪLŌ nonact. NAHUATIĀ

NĀHUA-TL something that makes an agreeable sound, someone who speaks well or speaks one's own language / cosa que suena bien; así como campana, etc., o hombre ladino (M) This is not attested as a free form in the sources for this dictionary. As a language name the compound NĀHUATLAHTŌL-LI is attested rather than simple NĀHUA-TL. See NĀHUA-.

NĀHUATLĀCAH *plural form* Nahuatl-

speaking people / nombre que se dió
a las naciones cultas que hablaban la
lengua mexicana (R) [(1)Rp.107]. See
NĀHUA-TL, TLĀCA-TL.

NĀHUATLAHTALHUIĀ *vt* to serve as
interpreter for someone / ser nahuatlato o
intérprete de otro (M) [(1)Cf.65r]. applic.
NĀHUATLAHTOĀ

NĀHUATLAHTOĀ to serve as interpreter /
tener oficio de faraute (M), hago oficio de
intérprete (C for first pers. sg. subject)
[(2)Cf.65r]. See NĀHUA-TL, (I)HTOĀ.

NĀHUATLAHTŌL-LI one's native language,
Nahuatl / lengua mexicana (R) [(1)Rp.107].
See NĀHUA-TL, TLAHTŌL-LI.

NĀHU(I) four / cuatro (M) M glosses *naui* as
'four or my aunt,' the second part of the
gloss being the first pers. sg. possessed
form of ĀHUI-TL 'aunt.'

-NĀL *postposition* across, through, to the
other side / allende (C) This is nearly
exclusively restricted to compositions with
Ā-TL 'water'; ĀNĀL ~ ĀNĀLCO 'across
the water, on the other side of the river.' In
Z, ĀNĀL simply means 'on the other side,'
and to convey the sense of 'across water'
ĀNĀL is further compounded with Ā-TL
to yield ĀNĀLĀ-TL.

NĀL- This is the initial element of a number of verbs having to do with crossing,
travelling through, and being at a distance.
See -NĀL.

NĀLCAQU(I) *vt* to hear something from a
distance / lo está oyendo de afuera o de
lejos (Z for construction with the verb O)
[(1)Zp.190]. See NĀL-, CAQU(I).

NĀLĪXAHCI *vt* to recognize someone from
a distance / lo reconoce (Z) [(2)Zp.106,190].
See NĀL-, ĪXAHCI.

NĀLPANOHUA to cross to the other
side / lo cruza ... lo atraviesa (Z)
[(3)Zp.16,36,176]. See NĀL-, PANŌ.

NĀLQUĪZ(A) for something to be traversed,
penetrated, torn in half / traspasarse o
penetrarse alguna cosa (C), se rompe de
lado a lado (Z) [(1)Cf.18r, (1)Tp.168]. In M
this is compounded to other verbs with
the ligature -CĀ- to convey the sense of
'entirely, thoroughly.' See NĀL-, QUĪZ(A).

NĀLTLACHIY(A) to gaze from afar / mira
(para afuera, a otro lado) (Z) [(2)Zp.85,176].

M has the longer form *nalquizcatlachia* 'to
see completely, to observe, to take notice.'
In both attestations in Z, CHIY(A) has
been reduced to CHA, once with the vowel
marked long. See NĀL-, CHIY(A).

NĀLTOCTIC something transparent /
transparente (Z) [(2)Zp.125,176]. M has
naltonac with the same sense. See
NĀLTŌNA.

NĀLTŌNA to be entirely clear, transparent / hacer claro por todas partes (M), estar traspasado de luz y trasparente (C)
[(1)Cf.18r]. See NĀL-, TŌNA.

NĀLTŌNI something transparent / transparente (Z) [(2)Zp.125,176]. See NĀLTŌNA,
NĀLTOCTIC.

NAMACA *vt* to sell something / vender
algo (M) This verb commonly incorporates objects, yielding such constructions as OCNAMACA 'to sell pulque,'
ĒLŌNAMACA 'to sell corn,' etc.

NAMACALŌ altern. nonact. NAMACA

NAMACŌ altern. nonact. NAMACA

NAMACŌYĀN place where something is
sold / la taberna (C for OCNAMACŌYĀN)
[(1)Cf.105v]. See NAMACŌ, -YĀN.

NAMAQUILIĀ applic. NAMACA

NAMAQUILTIĀ T consistently has a long
vowel in the third syllable, although by
general rule it should not be long. C and R
do not mark it long. caus. NAMACA

NAMAQUILTILIĀ applic. NAMAQUILTIĀ

NAMAQUILTĪLŌ nonact. NAMAQUILTIĀ

NĀMICOHUA altern. nonact. NĀMIQU(I)

NĀMICTIĀ *vrefl,vt* to get married, to come
together with someone for some purpose;
to marry someone off, to join two things
together or to even things off / casarse (M),
casar a otro (M), contender o tener bragas
con otro (M), juntar o igualar una cosa con
otra o declarar sueños (M) altern. caus.
NĀMIQU(I)

NĀMICTILIĀ applic. NĀMICTIĀ

NĀMICTĪL-LI marriage / casamiento (X)
[(1)Xp.56]. X fails to mark the vowel of the
third syllable long. See NĀMICTIĀ.

NĀMICTĪLŌ nonact. NĀMICTIĀ

NĀMIC-TLI *pl:* **NĀNĀMICTIN** spouse /
casado o casada (M) See NĀMIQU(I).

NĀMIQUEH one who has a spouse / casado
o casada (M) [(1)Cf.61v, (5)Zp.26,116,176,

(1)Rp.108]. M has a separate entry for *namiqueque* 'spouses,' the regular plural of this. See NĀMIC-TLI.

NĀMIQU(I) *vt; pret:* **NĀMIC** to go to meet someone or find something, to have a confrontation or to incur a penalty under the law / salir a recibir al que viene, o encontrar con alguno, o contender con otros (M), incurrir en pena puesta por la ley (M)

NĀMIQUĪHUA altern. nonact. NĀMIQU(I)

NĀMIQUILIĀ applic. NĀMIQU(I)

NĀMIQUILTIĀ *vt* to make something even, equal with something else / aparear e igualar una cosa con otra (C) [(1)Cf.62r]. altern. caus. NĀMIQU(I)

NĀMIQUĪTIĀ altern. caus. NĀMIQU(I)

NĀMOYĀ *vt; pret:* **NĀMOYĀC** to rob someone / robar a alguno (M) [(2)Cf.64r]. C gives an applicative form of this with the vowel of the third syllable marked long.

NĀMOYĀLIĀ *vt* to rob something from someone / robar algo a alguno (C) [(1)Cf.64r]. applic. NĀMOYĀ

NANAC(A)-TL *pl:* **-MEH** mushroom / hongo (M) This is attested in all sources except B. Z has the vowel of the first syllable long, but C specifically marks it short. R has this as NAHNAC(A)-TL. See NAC(A)-TL, NANATZOĀ.

NĀNĀHUACOCO-TL sore caused through sorcery / llaga (de brujería) (Z) [(2)Zp.78,176]. Although this looks like a reduplicated form of NĀHUALCOCO-TL, which has the same gloss, there is no L in either attestation. If this is instead derivationally related to NĀNĀHUA-TL 'bubo, swollen gland,' then Z has confused two similar but distinct items. See NĀHUAL-LI, COCO-TL.

NĀNĀHUAPAH-TLI medicinal plant used to alleviate syphilis / cierta planta medicinal, especialmente contra la gálico (R) [(1)Rp.108]. See NĀNĀHUA-TL, PAH-TLI.

NĀNĀHUA-TL bubo, swollen gland / bubas (M) [(2)Rp.108]. This is attested without diacritics in R. Z's NĀNĀHUACOCO-TL suggests long vowels in the first two syllables.

NĀNĀHU(I) by fours, four apiece / cuatro en cuatro (C) [(4)Cf.19v,107r,120r]. M has *nanauin* with the same sense. redup. NĀHU(I)

NANALCA for various animals to make their characteristic low noises, or to make a sound like a cracked bell or vessel / graznar el ansar, ladrar o regañar y gruñir el perro o el puerco, o sonar aquebrada la campana o la olla (M) [(3)Zp.20,21,176]. T has related NAHNALTIC with an internal glottal stop. In two of three attestations in Z the vowel of the second syllable is marked long. See NAHNALTIC, NANATZCA.

NĀNĀNQUILIĀ *vt* to respond to someone's criticism with impatience; to oppose someone / responder con impaciencia el que es reprehendido o corregido (M), le opone, le hace oposición (T) redup. NĀNQUILIĀ

NĀNĀNQUILILIĀ applic. NĀNĀNQUILIĀ

NĀNĀNQUILĪLŌ nonact. NĀNĀNQUILIĀ

NANATZALHUIĀ applic. NANATZOĀ

NANATZCA to creak / rechinar o crujir algo (M), rechina (Z) [(2)Zp.107,176]. In both attestations Z has an intrusive O, NANATZOCA.

NANATZOĀ *vrefl,vt* to get fat; to bother someone / pararse gordo o engordarse (M), lo molesta (T) [(3)Tp.192]. This may be related to NAC(A)-TL 'flesh.'

NANATZOCA See NANATZCA.

NANATZŌLŌ nonact. NANATZOĀ

NĀNĀUHTE-TL by fours, four apiece / de cuatro en cuatro, o a cada uno cuatro (M) [(1)Tp.168]. This attestation is affixed with the diminutive -TZIN, and T glosses it as *poquito*. redup. NĀUHTE-TL

NĀNQUILIĀ *vt* to respond to someone, to answer someone; to recite the responses in a ceremony such as the Mass / responder o ayudar a misa o a otra cosa (M), le contesta, le responde (T)

NĀNQUILILIĀ applic. NĀNQUILIĀ

NĀNQUILĪLŌ nonact. NĀNQUILIĀ

NĀNTĒNĒHU(A) *vrefl,vt* to curse, swear; to curse someone by insulting his mother / mienta la autora de sus días, mienta la madre (T), le mienta la madre (T) [(6)Tp.154,194]. See NĀN-TLI, TĒNĒHU(A).

NĀNTĒNĒHUALŌ nonact. NĀN-
TĒNĒHU(A)

NĀNTĒNĒHUILIĀ applic. NĀN-
TĒNĒHU(A)

NĀNTIĀ *vrefl* to take someone as one's
mother or godmother, or to take up residence / tomar a alguna por madre o por
madrina o avecindarse (M) [(1)Cf.58r]. See
NĀN-TLI.

NĀN-TLI mother / madre (M) This can be
used in the extended sense of 'protector.'
A tree planted to shade crops is called
NĀN-TLI, and the coral snake is called an
'ant-mother,' because it is believed to live
in ant hills and protect the insects.

NĀNYŌ-TL motherhood, the responsibilities of motherhood / matriz generalmente (M), maternitas, oficio de madre (C)
[(2)Cf.53r]. See NĀN-TLI, -YŌ.

NĀPALHUIĀ *vt* to carry something in one's
arms for someone / llevar algo en las
manos o en los brazos para otro (M)
[(1)Bf.6v, (1)Tp.194]. P has this with NAH
in place of NĀ. applic. NĀPALOĀ

NĀPALOĀ *vt* to carry something in one's
arms / tomar o llevar algo en los brazos (M)
This is abundantly attested across sources.
P has this with NAH in place of NĀ.

NĀPALŌLŌ nonact. NĀPALOĀ

NĀPPA See NĀUHPA.

NĀPPŌHUAL-LI See NĀUHPŌHUAL-LI.

NATZCUĀLTIĀ *vt* to bruise, pound something / lo apresa, lo machuca, lo machaca
(Z) [(2)Zp.79,190].

NĀUHCĀN in four places or parts / en
cuatro partes o lugares (M) [(3)Cf.91r]. See
NĀHU(I), -CĀN.

NĀUHPA four times / cuatro veces (M
NĀPPA) [(1)Cf.98r, (2)Tp.168,
(2)Zp.36,176]. The UHP sequence often
assimilates to PP. See NĀHU(I), -PA.

NĀUHPŌHUALLAHTŌL-LI court of justice held every eighth day / tribunal que
celebraba audiencia cada ochenta días
(S) [(1)Bf.10v]. See NĀUHPŌHUAL-LI,
TLAHTŌL-LI.

NĀUHPŌHUAL-LI eighty / ochenta (M for
nappoalli) [(1)Bf.10v]. The UHP sequence
often assimilates to PP. See NĀHU(I),
-PŌHUAL-LI.

NĀUHTE-TL four / cuatro (M) [(2)Tp.168]. T
glosses this as 'a bit.' See NĀHU(I), TE-TL.

NĒ there; that one / ahí (T), aquel, aquella
(Z) This is abundantly attested in T, Z, and
X but not in the older sources. See
NECHCA.

NE- *nonspecific reflexive object prefix* The
nonactive form of reflexive verbs and
nominals derived from reflexive verbs take
this prefix. For example, NĀMICTIĀ used
reflexively has the sense 'to get married,'
and NENĀMICTILIZ-TLI 'marriage' is a
derived nominal, while the nonactive form
is NENĀMICTĪLŌ 'people get married.'
NEHCALILIZ-TLI 'battle, engagement' is
derived from (I)HCAL(I) 'to engage in
skirmishing.' CĒHUIĀ used reflexively has
the sense 'to rest,' and -NECĒHUIĀYĀN
means 'someone's resting place.'

NEAHCOMANALIZ-TLI uprising, distur-
bance / alboroto de gente (M) [(1)Rp.108].
See AHCOMAN(A).

NĒCAH to be there (distant) [(5)Tp.167].
This is a compound of the deictic particle
NĒ and the verb CĀ. It appears to have
been lexicalized to function as a demon-
strative particle, but its plural retains the
verbal plural form of -CĀ, -CATEH. See
NĒ, the verb CĀ.

-NECĀUHCĀ *necessarily possessed
form* relic, remainder of someone,
something / reliquia (C) [(1)Bf.8r, (2)Cf.49r].
M has unpossessed *necauhcayotl* with the
same sense. See CĀHU(A).

-NECĒHUIĀYĀN *necessarily possessed
form* one's resting place / lugar para
descansar o de descanso (M for *nece-
uiloyan*) [(1)Bf.1v]. M's form is derived
from the nonactive form of CĒHUIĀ 'to
rest,' while B's derivation is from the
active form. See CĒHUIĀ, -YĀN.

NECHCA there / allí (M) According to C,
this points to a place in sight, albeit distant
(f.89v).

NECHCAPA to, from there / allí (M)
[(2)Cf.89v]. See NECHCA, -PA.

NECHICALHUIĀ applic. NECHICOĀ

NECHICOĀ *vrefl,vt* to be collected; to
collect something / se cobra (T), lo cobra
(T), ayuntar o recoger algo (M)

NECHICŌLŌ nonact. NECHICOĀ
NĒC(I) *pret:* **NĒZ** to appear, to reveal one-self, to become visible / parecer ante otros o descubrirme a los que no me hallaban (M) Referring to money or assets, this means 'to be produced, gotten together.'
NECŌ altern. nonact. NEQU(I)
NECOC on both sides, from or to one side and the other / de ambas partes, o a una parte y a otra, o a un lado y a otro (M)
NECOCCĀMPA from or toward both sides / de ambas, o desde ambas, o hacia ambas partes (M) [(3)Cf.92r]. See NECOC, -CĀN, -PA.
NECŌNI something that is necessary, beneficial, advantageous / cosa que es menester y es provechosa (M), lo que es digno de quererse y desearse (C) [(1)Cf.44v, (2)Zp.66,177]. Z postposes YA 'already' and cliticizes it to this. See NEQU(I).
NECPACHILHUIĀ applic. NECPACHOĀ
NECPACHOĀ *vrefl,vt* to rise above some-thing, to exalt oneself; to place something on top, to raise something on high / se enciman, se sobreponen (T), lo encima (T) This shares some common meaning with MONECQUI and MONEQUINI 'some-one proud, arrogant,' suggesting that the first element is derived from the verb NEQU(I) 'to want something.' See NEQU(I), PACHOĀ.
NECPACHŌLŌ nonact. NECPACHOĀ
NECTIĀ *vt* to desire something for oneself; to get someone to desire something to court someone / codiciar algo para sí (M), hacer querer algo a otro (M), requebrarse con alguna persona procurando ser de ella codiciado (M) This takes both a direct object prefix and an indirect object or oblique reflexive prefix. altern. caus. NEQU(I)
NECTILIĀ applic. NECTIĀ
NECTĪLŌ nonact. NECTIĀ
NECUĀĀTĒQUILIZ-TLI baptism / bau-tismo que se recibe (M) [(1)Cf.35r]. The sequence ĀĀ is conventionally written with a single letter. See CUĀĀTĒQUIĀ.
NECUALTIC mesh of a net / malla (Z) [(2)Zp.80,177].
NECUĀ-TL unfermented maguey juice /

agua miel (Z) [(2)Zp.7,177]. See NEUC-TLI, Ā-TL.
NECUILHUIĀ applic. NECUILOĀ
NECUILIHU(I) to twist, bend / encorvarse, torcerse (K) [(1)Tp.113]. This is only at-tested in CAMANECUILIHU(I) 'to make gestures with the mouth.' See NECUILOĀ.
NECUILIHUĪHUA nonact. NECUILIHU(I)
NECUILOĀ *vrefl,vt* to bow or bend; to bend or twist something, to engage in commerce / se echueca (T), contratar, regatonear, o entortar alguna cosa (M) With the nonspe-cific object prefix TLA- and in construc-tion with -TECH, this means to make a loan with interest to someone Z glosses the reflexive as 'to get dislocated.' See NECUILIHU(I).
NECUILŌLŌ nonact. NECUILOĀ
NECUILTIC someone bow-legged / chueco (T) [(1)Tp.167]. NECUILOĀ
NECUILTŌNŌL-LI wealth / riqueza (M), riqueza, prosperidad, y gozo (C) [(2)Cf.46v,114v]. See CUILTŌNOĀ.
-NECUITLAHUĪLŌCĀ *necessarily pos-sessed form* the care with which one is looked after / el cuidado con que se cuida de mi (C for first person possessor) [(1)Cf.48v]. This is derived from the nonac-tive form of CUITLAHUIĀ 'to care for, nurture someone.'
NECUITLAHUĪLŌNI someone or some-thing deserving to be cared for / merecedor que se tenga del cuidado (M) [(1)Cf.45r]. See CUITLAHUIĀ.
-NEĒLLELQUĪXTIĀYA *necessarily pos-sessed form* that with which one enter-tains oneself / instrumento con que yo me recreo (C for first person possessor) [(1)Cf.50v]. M has *neellelquixtiliztli* 'pas-time, recreation.' See ĒLLELQUĪXTIĀ.
NEH *first person singular pronoun* I, me / yo, pronombre (M) This is a freestand-ing pronoun, as contrasted with the per-sonal prefixes NI- 'I' and NĒCH- 'me.' See NEHHUĀ-TL.
NEHCALILIZ-TLI battle, engagement, fight / batalla o pelea (M) [(3)Cf.211,100r,107v]. M also has the shorter form *necaliztli* with the same sense. See (I)HCAL(I).
NEHHUĀ-TL *first person singular pronoun,*

long form I, me / yo, pronombre (M) When this appears without the absolutive suffix, the Ā is subject to the general rule of word-final shortening. The sequence NEH, NEHHUĀ, NEHHUĀ-TL represents increasingly emphatic 'I, me.' See NEH.

-NEHHUIYĀN *necessarily possessed form* oneself, one's own, personally / mi propia (cosa), de mi propio (S for first person singular possessor) M also has the noun *neuhyantli* 'something personal, created of one's own will, voluntary.'

NEHHUIYĀNHUIĀ *vrefl* to be the occasion or cause of something happening to oneself / sucederme algo dando yo la oración, o siendo yo la causa (M for first pers. sg. subject), doy yo la causa a lo que me sucede de mal (C for first pers. sg. subject) [(1)Cf.60v]. See -NEHHUIYĀN, -HUIĀ.

NEHMACHYŌ-TL prudence, proper deportment / la prudencia, y el estar sobre aviso (C) [(1)Cf.54r]. See IHMAT(I), -YŌ.

NEHNECOC redup. NECOC

NEHNECTIĀ *vrefl* to volunteer oneself, to meddle, to aspire to do something one is not equipped for / se acomide, se entremete, pretende hacer una cosa (sin poder hacerlo bien) (T) [(3)Tp.154]. redup. NECTIĀ

NEHNECTĪLŌ nonact. NEHNECTIĀ

NEHNECUIL-LI something displaced, dislocated, twisted / desplazado, torcido (K) [(2)Tp.137]. This is only attested in ĪXTENEHNECUIL-LI 'someone cross-eyed.' It implies NEHNECUILOĀ. See NECUILOĀ.

NEHNECUILOĀ *vrefl* to totter along / bambanearse a una parte y a otra (M) This is implied by ĪXTENEHNECUIL-LI. redup. NECUILOĀ

NEHNEHNEM(I) *pret:* **-NEN** to walk, stroll, wander about / pasearse por las calles, por las plazas, etc. (S) [(1)Cf.71v]. redup. NEHNEM(I)

NEHNEHNENTINEM(I) redup. NEHNENTINEM(I)

NEHNEHUILIĀ *vt* to equal something else, to make things equal or paired with one another, to compare things / ser igual a otros (M), emparejar o igualar algunas

cosas o hacer comparación o concordancias de unas cosas a otras (M) [(2)Rp.70,110]. P also attests this with a glottal stop in the first syllable, while C has NĒNEHUILIĀ and T has NENEHUILIĀ 'to weigh, consider, imagine something,' which is probably just this item with T's characteristic loss of glottal stop. See NĒNEHUILIĀ, NENEHUILIĀ.

NEHNELOĀ *vt* to stir something, to disorder things, to make a mess / mezclar o revolver unas cosas con otras o desordenar lo bien ordenado (M) [(1)Rp.111]. See NELOĀ.

NEHNEM(I) *pret:* **-NEN** to wander about / andar o caminar (M) This is a reduplicated form of NEM(I), which in the free form generally means 'to live' but here and in compounds 'to go about.'

NEHNEMILIĀ *vt* to mull something over, to imitate or copy someone, something / juzgar (Z for TLANEHNEMILIĀ), lo imita, lo remeda (Z) [(6)Zp.70,74,108,191,211]. redup. NEMILIĀ

NEHNEMILIZ-TLI the act of walking about, travel / el acto de andar o caminar (M), viaje (R) [(1)Rp.111]. See NEHNEM(I).

NEHNEMILTIĀ By general derivational rules the vowel of the third syllable should be short. It is unmarked for length in C and long in T. altern. caus. NEHNEM(I)

NEHNEMĪTIĀ altern. caus. NEHNEM(I)

NEHNEMOHUA nonact. NEHNEM(I)

NEHNENQUI walker, foot traveler, pilgrim, one who comes to a fiesta from a distance / caminante (M), andariego, los invitados en la fiesta (T) [(1)Tp.167, (1)Rp.101]. See NEHNEM(I).

NEHNENTINEM(I) *pret:* **-NEN** to wander / andar vagueando (R) [(2)Rp.99,111]. See NEHNEM(I).

NEHNEQU(I) *vrefl,vt* to pretend to be something one is not, to try to pass for someone else; to get a craving for something, to be capricious / hacerse de rogar, o contrahacer y arrendar a los de otra nación (M), antojárseme algo, o ser tirano (M for first pers. sg. subject) The reflexive form incorporates the name of what one is posing as, NINOCOCOXCĀNEQUI 'I pretend to be someone sick.' See NEQU(I).

NEHNEUHCĀ equally / igualmente (M) [(1)Cf.114r]. This is also attested in P with the glottal stop marked. See NEHNEHUILIĀ.

NEHNEUHQUI something equal, on par with, like another / cosa igual o pareja, o cosa que es semejante a otra (M) [(1)Rp.70]. The attestaton is in the plural, for which M has a separate entry with the gloss 'equals, with respect to people or animals.' This also appears in P. See NEHNEHUILIĀ.

NEHTŌL-LI vow, promise, vote / voto (M) [(1)Rp.112]. By general derivational rules the vowel of the second syllable should be long, but it is unmarked for length in R. In derived NEHTŌLTIĀ T has the reflex of a long vowel. See (I)HTOĀ.

NEHTŌLTIĀ *vrefl* to make a vow, promise / hacer voto (M), prometer (R), se encomienda a las imágenes (T) [(1)Cf.122r, (3)Tp.154, (1)Rp.112]. T has the reflex of a long vowel in the second syllable; the other sources do not mark the vowel for length. See NEHTŌL-LI.

NEHTŌLTĪLŌ nonact. NEHTŌLTIĀ

NEHUĀN both together / ambos a dos o juntamente ambos a dos (M) M gives as a separate entry the plural form *neuantin*. T has a short vowel in the second syllable, but B and C mark it long. This is generally, but not necessarily, possessed, ĪNNEHUĀN 'the two of them.' The phrase NEHUĀN ĒHUAH appears in C and M meaning 'they are siblings.' See NE-, -HUĀN.

NEHUĀNTILIĀ *vt* to join something / lo junta (T) [(3)Tp.193]. T has a short vowel in the second syllable, but NEHUĀN has a long syllable elsewhere. See NEHUĀN.

NEHUĀNTILILIĀ applic. NEHUĀNTILIĀ

NEHUĀNTILĪLŌ nonact. NEHUĀNTILIĀ

NEHUILTIĀ *vt* to compare something / lo compara (Z) [(2)Zp.31,190]. An unattested verb *NEHUILIĀ underlies the reduplicated forms NEHNEHUILIĀ and NĒNEHUILIĀ, and this appears to be the causative form of it.

NEHUILTILIZ-TLI comparison / comparación (Z) [(2)Zp.31,177]. In both attestations Z marks the first vowel long. There should

be an object prefix, but Z has a tendency to drop them. M has *tlaneneuililiztli*. See NEHUILTIĀ.

NĒHUĪN there / ahí, por ahí (Z) [(4)Zp.3,7,177,212]. Z gives this as synonymous with NĒPA.

NĒHUĪNTLANI there below / para allá abajo (Z) [(2)Zp.3,212]. See NĒHUĪN, TLANI.

NEĪXCUĪTĪL-LI example, model, pattern / dechado o ejemplo (M), señal, demostración, prueba, maravilla, milagro (Z) [(6)Zp.41,82,84,103,115,178]. In Z the sequence NEĪX has been consolidated to NĒX. See ĪXCUĪTIĀ.

NEL This is a particle that combines with the other particles and contributes the sense of 'in truth, indeed,' although in some lexicalized constructions it appears to contribute no sense of its own at all. According to C, in conjunction with an interrogrative particle -NEL implies that there is no other choice (f.91r), but this does not seem to hold in all cases, CĀMPANEL 'where in the world?' Among common constructions are AHNEL 'isn't it so?,' CANEL (NOZO) 'because,' CĀNNEL 'where?,' MĀNEL 'however,' MŌNEL 'isn't it so?,' NELNOZO ~ NOZONEL 'how could it be otherwise?' and QUĒNNEL 'how else?' See NEL-LI.

NELCHĪHU(A) This is implied by the applicative form NELCHĪHUILIĀ. M gives it as a reflexive verb with the sense of 'to take something from someone as a joke and then keep it.' See NEL-LI, CHĪHU(A).

NELCHĪHUILIĀ *vt* to demand something, to insist on something, to struggle for something / lo exige, insiste, lucha (T) [(3)Tp.193]. applic. NELCHĪHU(A)

NELCOHCOCOĀ *vrefl* to seriously injure oneself / se lastima gravemente (Z) [(2)Zp.75,171]. See NEL-LI, COHCOCOĀ.

NELHUA-TL *pl:* -MEH root / raíz (T) [(2)Tp.167,237, (2)Zp.105,176]. Z has Ā in the first syllable in place of E. The inalienably possessed form is probably -NELHUAYŌ, but there are no unambiguous attestations. See NELHUAYŌ-TL.

NELHUAYŌTIĀ *vrefl,vt* to take root, settle down; to base a discourse on a particular authority / arraiga o echar raíces (M), fundar platica o sermón sobre alguna autoridad de escritura (M) See NELHUAYŌ-TL.

NELHUAYŌ-TL *pl:* -**MEH** base, foundation, starting point, root or vein / principio, fundamento, o comienzo (M), raíz (T), vena (X) [(3)Tp.132,154,167, (3)Xp.56]. This is an abstract derivation from NELHUA-TL 'root,' but apparently it can be used concretely and hence synonymously with NELHUA-TL itself. It is not clear whether the possessed form attested in T is the simple possessed form of this or the inalienably possessed form of NELHUA-TL. M also has *nelhuayo*, which represents NELHUAYOH 'something that has a root,' which also appears in P.

NELHUIĀ *vt* to stir up something, to disorder something, to make a mess of something for someone / remar a otro o mecerle y revolverle alguna cosa (M), agitar, sacudir a alguien, desordenarle, revolverle alguna cosa (S) applic. NELOĀ

NELHUILIĀ applic. NELHUIĀ

NELHUĪLŌ nonact. NELHUIĀ

NELIHU(I) This is only attested in the construction PITZONELIHU(I) 'to get dirty.' NELIHU(I) is the intransitive verb corresponding to transitive NELOĀ 'to stir up something, to make a mess of something.' See NELOĀ.

NELIZTAYOH something very salty / salado (tiene mucho sal) (Z) [(2)Zp.112,177]. See NEL-LI, IZTA-TL, -YOH.

NEL-LI something true, certain / cierto, ciertamente o de verdad (M) In five attestations, B twice marks the E long, although other derivations from NEL-LI in B have the vowel specifically marked short. It is abundantly attested in C with no length marking at all. T has the reflex of a short vowel, while Z consistently has it long. This often occurs in the phrase HUEL NEL-LI 'something very true and certain,something genuine.'

NELNOZO This is attested four times in C and NOZONEL, with the elements in reverse order, three times. All are on Cf.91r with no gloss. It should probably be treated as a phrase composed of NEL and NOZO in optional order with a sense of 'how could it be otherwise?' See NEL-LI, NOZO.

NELOĀ *vrefl,vt* to get mixed together; to stir up something, to beat something, to make a mess of something / se revuelve, se mezcla (T), remar, mecer, o batir algo (M) **NELŌLŌ** nonact. NELOĀ

NELŌLTIĀ *vrefl,vt* to get mixed together; to mix something / se mezcla (T), lo revuelve, lo mezcla (T) [(4)Tp.154,193, (3)Xp.71]. On p.193 T gives the nonactive form of this verb as NELTĪLŌ, but this is clearly a typographical error involving the omission of two letters. The nonactive form should be NELŌLTĪLŌ. caus. NELOĀ

NELŌLTILIĀ applic. NELŌLTIĀ

NELŌLTĪLŌ See NELŌLTIĀ.

NELTI to prove true, to be verified, to be realized / verificarse algo (M), hacerse verdadero ... verificarse, cumplirse (C) [(1)Bf.5r, (2)Cf.58v,110v]. C gives NELTIĀ with the same sense. See NEL-LI.

NELTIĀ to prove true, to be verified, to be realized / hacerse verdadero ... verificarse, cumplirse (C) [(2)Cf.58v,110v]. C gives this as synonymous with NELTI. S provides the preterit form *onelti*. If this is correct, assuming the vowel of the second syllable to be unmarked for length rather than specifically short, the future form *neltiz* on Cf.110v is ambiguous between the two. On the other hand, a verb with the form NELTIĀ should be transitive. B's NELTIY(A) would be the intransitive, and S's preterit form, on which this entry is based, may simply be an error. See NELTI, NELTIY(A).

NELTIC This is only attested in the constructions PITZONELTIC and MĀTZOCUITLANELTIC, both meaning 'something dirty.' It is related to NELIHU(I) 'to get messy' and NELOĀ 'to make a mess of something.'

NELTILIZ-TLI truth / verdad (M) [(4)Cf.11r,112v,123r,124v]. See NELTI, NELTIĀ.

NELTIY(A) *pret:* **NELTIX** to prove true, to be verified, to be realized / hacerse verdadero

(K) [(1)Bf.3r]. The single attestation is in preterit form. C's *neltia*, given as synonymous with NELTI, may represent NELTIY(A) rather than NELTIĀ, in which case the future form *neltiz* on Cf.110v is unambiguously the future form of NELTI alone. S assumes that it represents NELTIĀ with the preterit form NELTIH. If this were correct, then there are would be three nearly synonymous verbal derivations from NEL-LI 'something true, certain,' namely NELTI, NELTIĀ, and NELTIY(A), each with a different paradigm, but NELTIĀ is questionable. See NELTI, NELTIĀ.

NELTLAHTLAN(I) to request, demand / lo exige (Z) [(2)Zp.58,177]. See NEL-LI, TLAHTLAN(I).

NELTLAMATQUI someone wise / sabio (Z) [(2)Zp.112,177]. See NEL-LI, TLAMATQUI.

NELTLANAHU(I) to be in a bad way, to be gravely ill / se pone grave (Z) [(2)Zp.64,177]. See NEL-LI, TLANAHU(I).

NELTOCA *vrefl,vt* to hold a belief; to believe in something / cree (T), creer algo (M) See NEL-LI, TOCA.

NELTOCALŌ altern. nonact. NELTOCA

NELTOCŌ altern. nonact. NELTOCA

-NELTOCŌCĀ *necessarily possessed form* the faith others have in one / la fé con que me creen (C for first person possessor) [(2)Cf.48v]. S has *neltococayotl* 'faith, belief.' C distinguishes between -NELTOCŌCĀ, the faith others have in one, and TLANELTOQUILIZ-TLI, the faith one has in something else, which is the general distinction between nonactive derivations in -CĀYŌ-TL and active ones in -LIZ-TLI. See NELTOCA.

NELTOQUILIZ-TLI faith / fé (T) [(1)Tp.167]. This appears to be a truncated form of TLANELTOQUILIZ-TLI. M has *neltoquiztli* 'something worthy of belief.' See NELTOCA.

NELTOQUĪTIĀ caus. NELTOCA

NELYŌLCOCOLIZ-TLI sadness / tristeza (Z) [(2)Zp.125,177]. Z also has NEYŌLCOCOLIZ-TLI 'affliction, trouble, grief,' which is formed with the nonspecific reflexive prefix NE- rather than with NEL. See NEL-LI, YŌL-, COCOLIZ-TLI.

NELYŌLQUĪZALIZ-TLI great happiness / muy gozoso (Z) [(2)Zp.64,177]. See NEL-LI, YŌLQUĪZAC.

NEMACHTIĀ *vrefl,vt* to prepare, to accustom oneself; to become accustomed to something, to use something / apercebirse o aparejarse (M), se acostumbre (T), lo acostumbre (T) See MAT(I).

NEMACHTILIĀ applic. NEMACHTIĀ

NEMACHTĪL-LI study, learning / el estudio, el aprender (C) [(1)Cf.46r]. C marks the vowel of the first syllable long, which is incorrect. See NEMACHTIĀ.

NEMACHTĪLŌ nonact. NEMACHTIĀ

NEMACTIĀ *vt* to give a portion, endowment, dowry to someone / dar algo de balde o dotar a otro (M) [(2)Bf.1v,2r, (2)Zp.90,191]. With the oblique reflexive, this means 'to obtain a portion, gift, dowry.' See NEMAC-TLI.

NEMACTILIĀ applic. NEMACTIĀ

NEMAC-TLI inheritance, gift, portion / don, o merced que se recibe (M) [(1)Bf.1v, (1)Cf.125v].

NEMĀPOHPŌHUALŌNI towel for wiping the hands / instrumento para limpiarse las manos (C), paño de manos o toalla (M for *nemapopoaloni tilmatli*) [(1)Cf.45v]. See MĀPOHPŌHU(A).

NEMĀQUĪXTILIZ-TLI redemption, salvation / rescate, salvación (T) [(1)Tp.167]. See MĀQUĪXTIĀ.

NEMAUHTĪL-LI fear, dread / espanto, susto (Z) [(3)Zp.55,119,177]. Z has O for A in this item and no absolutive suffix. M has the longer form *nemauhtiliztli* with the same sense. See MAUHTIĀ.

NEM(I) *pret:* NEN to live / vivir o morar (M) In compound constructions NEM(I) also has the sense 'to go about doing something,' but as a free form it is generally reduplicated, NEHNEM(I) 'to go along, to walk, to wander.' The preterit form contrasts in vowel length with NĒN 'in vain.'

NEMILIĀ *vrefl,vt* to provide one's own sustenance, to support oneself, to be resolved; to consider, ponder, or look into something / mantenerse con su industria (M), se resuelve (Z), pesquisar o inquirir vida ajena (M), pensar o deliberar algo (M)

There are divergent senses here, between concrete support and sustenance of life on one hand and mental provision of life through imagination and investigation on the other. applic. NEM(I)

NEMILICEH something, someone with a life / el que tiene vida (C) [(1)Cf.55v, (1)Rp.45]. See NEMILIZ-TLI.

NEMILILIĀ applic. NEMILIĀ

NEMILĪLŌ nonact. NEMILIĀ

NEMILIZ-TLI life / vida (C), vida, conducta, manera de vivir (S) See NEM(I).

NEMILTIĀ vt to raise, maintain someone or something / le crio o sustento (C for first pers. sg. subject) [(1)Cf.61r, (1)Rp.32]. altern. caus. NEM(I)

NEMILTILIĀ T has the reflex of a long vowel in the second syllable, but it is not marked long in C. applic. NEMILTIĀ

NEMILTĪLŌ T has the reflex of a long vowel in the second syllable, but it should not be. nonact. NEMILTIĀ

NEMINI resident / el que vive o mora en algún lugar (M) [(1)Cf.59r]. The attestation is of a verb form which is, however, homophonous with the noun. See NEM(I).

NEMĪTIĀ vt to maintain, nurture someone or something / mantener o sustentar a otro (M), tener o sustentar criado o caballo (M) altern. caus. NEM(I)

NEMĪTILIĀ applic. NEMĪTIĀ

NEMĪTĪLŌ nonact. NEMĪTIĀ

-NEMIYĀN necessarily possessed form the place or time in which one lives / lugar donde yo vivo (C for first pers. sg. possessor), duración, tiempo de vida (S) [(2)Cf.50v]. See NEM(I), -YĀN.

NEMOHUA for living or residence to go on / todos viven o todos moran en alguna parte (M) [(3)Tp.167,242]. This is only attested in the spelling nemoa, but M's preterit form nemoac shows that it is an -OHUA verb rather than an -OĀ one. nonact. NEM(I)

NEMOHUAYĀN place where people reside / lugar donde algunos moran o habitan, o población (M) [(1)Rp.42]. R fails to mark the vowel of the last syllable long. See NEMOHUA.

NĒMPANCAH something without a clear outcome or benefit, something in vain / cosa sin provecho o por demás (M) usarse

cuando uno pretende hacer algo y dudando si le ha de salir bien, se resuelve a cometerle (C) [(5)Cf.122r,123r,131v]. See NĒN, -PAN, the verb CĀ.

NĒMPĒHUALTIĀ vt to mistreat someone for no good reason / maltratar a otro sin causa (M) [(1)Cf.77r, (3)Tp.193]. See NĒN, PĒHUALTIĀ, NĒMPĒHU(I).

NĒMPĒHUALTILIĀ applic. NĒM-PĒHUALTIĀ

NĒMPĒHUALTĪLŌ nonact. NĒM-PĒHUALTIĀ

NĒMPĒHU(I) to begin to have some feeling of apprehension for no good reason / empieza (a tener miedo, etc.) sin causa (T) [(3)Tp.167]. See NĒN, PĒHU(A).

NĒMPĒHUĪHUA nonact. NĒMPĒHU(I)

NĒMPĒHUĪTIĀ caus. NĒMPĒHU(I)

NĒMPOLIHU(I) to spoil, to get stale, to be ruined / desperdiciarse algo (M), se echa a perder, se pierde (T) [(3)Tp.167]. See NĒN, POLIHU(I).

NĒMPOLOĀ vt to waste, spoil or damage something, to kill someone / desperdiciar o echar a perder (M), lo pierde, lo echa a perder, lo asesina (T) [(3)Tp.193]. See NĒN, POLOĀ, NĒMPOLIHU(I).

NĒMPOTI-TL stutterer / tartamudo (T) [(2)Tp.167]. T gives the variants NĒMPOTI-TL and NĒMPOTE and a plural form NĒMPOTEMEH.

NĒN in vain, futilely, profitlessly / en vano, por demás, o sin provecho (M) This commonly occurs bound with ZAN. It contrasts in vowel length with the preterit form of NEM(I).

NENĀMICTILIZ-TLI wedlock / casamiento o desposorio (M) [(4)Bf.3r,3v, (2)Zp.26,176]. Z lacks the reflexive NE-. See NĀMICTIĀ.

NENĀMICTĪLŌYOH marriage / matrimonio, casamiento (T) [(1)Tp.167]. It seems that this should be derived with -YŌ or -YĀN rather than -YOH, but T's form has no absolutive suffix as -YŌ would and has the reflex of O rather than Ā. T would not retain final H or N in any case. M has nenamictiliztli 'marriage, wedlock' and also nenamictiloni 'something pertaining to marriage.' See NĀMICTIĀ.

NĒNCAH to be idle, without profit, in vain, futile / estar ocioso y sin alguna ocupación

(M) [(2)Tp.167,221, (4)Zp.18,64,127,177]. T
and Z both have this in composition with
ZAN, either before or after NĒNCAH, the
phrase functioning adverbially. See NĒN,
the verb CĀ.

NĒNCĀHU(A) *vrefl,vt* to be negligent; to
leave something undone through negligence / ser desdichado (M), dejar de hacer
algo por negligencia o dejar de castigar algún delito (M) This is implied by
-NĒNCĀUHYĀN and NĒNCĀHU(I). Its
preterit form contrasts in vowel length
with -NENCĀUH 'one's servant.'

NĒNCĀHU(I) to be in vain / ser en balde (K)
[(2)Tp.167]. T only gives a gloss for the
negation of this, AHMŌ NĒNCĀHU(I)
'not to be in vain, hopeless.' The preterit of
this verb contrasts in vowel length with
-NENCĀUH 'one's servant.' See NĒN-
CĀHU(A).

-NENCĀUH *necessarily possessed form; pl:*
-NENCĀHUĀN one's servant / mi criado
(M for first pers. sg. possessor) [(1)Cf.119v].
This contrasts in vowel length with the
preterit forms of the verbs NĒNCĀHU(A)
'to leave something undone' and NĒN-
CĀHU(I) 'to be in vain.' See NENQUI.

-NĒNCĀUHYĀN *necessarily possessed*
form one's negligence / negligencia (K)
[(2)Bf.7r,9r]. See NĒNCĀHU(A), -YĀN.

NENCĀYŌ-TL *possessed form:* **-NENCĀ**
sustenance, what one needs to support
life / mantenimiento humano (M)
[(3)Cf.49r,54r]. This conventionally appears
in the phrase -YŌLCĀ -NENCĀ (both
possessed) with the sense 'one's daily
sustenance.' The possessed form -NENCĀ
contrasts with NĒNCAH 'for something to
be in vain' both in vowel length and in the
presence or absence of a final glottal stop.
See NEM(I), -YŌ.

NĒNCHĪHU(A) *vt* to do something in vain
or without profit / hacer algo en vano o sin
algún provecho (M) [(3)Tp.194]. See NĒN,
CHĪHU(A).

NĒNCHĪHUALŌ nonact. NĒNCHĪHU(A)
NĒNCHĪHUILIĀ applic. NĒNCHĪHU(A)
NENCUAH See NŌNCUAH.

NĒNCUEP(A) *vrefl,vt* to go somewhere for
naught; to restore, return something to no
avail / va en balde, va en vano (T), lo

devuelve en vano (T) [(6)Tp.154,194]. See
NĒN, CUEP(A).

NĒNCUEPALŌ nonact. NĒNCUEP(A)
NĒNCUEPILIĀ applic. NĒNCUEP(A)
NĒNECOC on, to or from both sides, both
sides of several things / a una parte y a
otra, o de una parte y de otra, o al un lado
y al otro, o a ambos lados (M), pluralidad
de cosas que tienen los dos lados (C)
[(4)Cf.92r,92v]. redup. NECOC

NENECUIL-LI *pl:* **-TIN** a type of tree
(Inga jinicuil) / jinicuil (K) This is attested
only as the second element of CUAUH-
NENECUIL-LI 'jinicuil tree.' It is certainly
related to M's *nenecuiloa* 'to stagger,
meander this way and that.' It is possible
that the absolutive suffix should be -IN,
because this is attested only in T, where
there is an ambiguity between absolutive
-LI and -IN in cases where the stem ends in
L. See NECUILOĀ.

NENEHTŌLTILIZ-TLI vow, pledge / voto
(M) [(1)Rp.111]. R fails to mark the
vowel of the third syllable long. See
NEHTŌLTIĀ.

NĒNEHUILIĀ *vt* to equal something else; to
pair things, to compare things / ser igual a
otros (M), emparejar o igualar algunas
cosas o hacer comparación o concordancias
de unas cosas a otras (M) [(1)Cf.121v]. T
has NENEHUILIĀ with the closely related
sense of 'to consider, imagine something'
but with a short vowel in the initial
syllable. R has NEHNEHUILIĀ with a
glottal stop in the first syllable. This
implies an unattested verb *NEHUILIĀ
with all the possible kinds of initial-
syllable reduplication. M has the verb
neuiuilia 'to be equal to something,
someone else.' See NEHNEHUILIĀ,
NENEHUILIĀ.

NENEHUILIĀ *vt* to weigh, consider,
imagine something / lo piensa, lo considera, lo imagina, lo opina, lo prueba,
lo supone (T) [(6)Tp.193,217]. This is
probably NEHNEHUILIĀ with loss of the
glottal stop, which is characteristic of T.
See NEHNEHUILIĀ, NĒNEHUILIĀ.

NENEHUILILIĀ applic. NENEHUILIĀ
NENEHUILILŌ nonact. NENEHUILIĀ
NĒNEMIZQUI someone invited / el in-

vitado (T) [(2)Tp.167,232]. In one of two attestations T gives a plural gloss to a singular form and a different form as the plural. See NEM(I).

NENEPIL-LI *pl:* **-TIN** tongue / lengua (M) See NENE-TL, PIL-LI.

NENEPILTIĀ *vrefl,vt* for ears of corn to bud; to serve as a spokesman or translator / brotar la marzorca de maíz en la caña (M), (se sirve como) lengua ... hablar por ellos (C) [(1)Cf.58r]. The literal sense of this has to do with becoming like or serving as a tongue. See NENEPIL-LI.

NĒNETECH close together (of more than two objects) / muy juntos unos de otros (C), cercanía de cosas ... más de dos (C) [(3)Cf.93r]. redup. NETECH

NENE-TL female genitals; image, doll / la natura de la mujer, ídolo, o muñeca de niños (M) In the sources for this dictionary this is only attested as the first element of NENEPIL-LI 'tongue' and the second element of CUAHUINENETZIN (the name of an insect). Since the two senses of this item are at some distance from each other and both distant from the senses of the attestations, it is possible that more than one lexical item is represented here, and they may differ phonologically.

NENĒTZ twin / cuate, gemelo (Z) [(4)Zp.36,63,177]. Z gives NENĒTZTIC as an alternative form. Relationship to NĒNETECH 'close together' is plausible, but the vowel length values are reversed.

NĒNMANIYĀN ordinary day, day between festivals / entre semana (C) [(3)Cf.106r,114r]. M has *nemayan* with the same sense. There is no assimilation of the NM sequence in the attestations. The sequence IY is provided here on the model of analogous CEMMANIYĀN. It is written only as *y* in the attestations. See NĒN, MAN(I), -YĀN.

NENOHMAHHUILIZ-TLI free will / libre albedrío (M) [(1)Rp.111]. This is also attested in P with the glottal stops marked. See NOHMAHHUIĀ.

NĒNQUĒN right away, immediately / inmediatemente, prisa, apurado, aprisa (Z) This is abundantly attested, but only in Z. See NĒN, QUĒN.

NĒNQUĒNTI to improve / mejora (Z)

[(2)Zp.83,177]. The sense of this may be related to that of the phrase AHMŌ QUĒN CAH 'for nothing to be the matter with something.' See NĒNQUĒN.

NENQUI resident of some place, someone who lives / morador de alguna parte (M), el que vive (R) Z marks the vowel of the first syllable long in two attestations of the compound OHNENQUI 'traveler,' but NENQUI is clearly derived from NEM(I) 'to live,' which has a short vowel. The possessed form -NENCĀUH is glossed by M and C as 'one's servant.' See NEM(I).

NĒNQUĪZCĀYŌ-TL vanity, something nonsensical, inane / vanidad (C) [(1)Cf.114v]. S has *nenquizqui* 'something useless, futile, profitless,' and M has *nenquiça* 'to labor in vain.' See NĒN, QUĪZ(A), -YŌ.

NĒNTEQUITI to labor in vain, to no end / trabaja en balde, en vano (T) [(3)Tp.167]. T forms the preterit of this by dropping the final vowel, but M forms the preterit of TEQUITI by adding -C. See NĒN, TEQUITI.

NĒNTEQUITĪHUA nonact. NĒNTEQUITI

NĒNTEQUITILIĀ applic. NĒNTEQUITI

NĒNTI for something to turn out to be in vain, to be frustrated / salir vana una cosa, frustrarse (C) [(2)Cf.58v, (1)Rp.47]. See NĒN.

NĒNTLĀCA-TL worthless person, good for nothing / hombre sin provecho (C) [(2)Cf.59r,77r]. See NĒN, TLĀCA-TL.

NĒNTLAMACHILIZ-TLI anxiety, distress / congoja, angustia, o aflicción (M), determinación (Z) [(2)Zp.45,177]. Z's gloss does not seem to follow directly from the component parts of this item. See NĒN, TLAMACHTILIZ-TLI.

NĒNYĀN in vain, to no end / en vano, inútilmente, sin provecho (S) [(6)Cf.112v,113v]. Both C and S provide a variant of this without the final N. See NĒN, -YĀN.

NĒPA there, at some distance in space or time / allí o allá o de allí o de allá (M), antiguamente (C for IN YE NĒPA), en aquel tiempo, en aquellos días (T for CA YE NĒPA) According to C this is close in sense to NECHCA but does not require the point in question to be visible, as

NECHCA does (f.89v). C also says that this is close in sense to NIPA 'over there, on the other side' (which has a short vowel in the initial syllable) but NIPA does not specifically point at a location (f.90r).

NĒPACAH to be at a distance / helo allí o helo allá o allí está (M), de aquel lado (Z) [(1)Cf.16v, (5)Zp.75,82,143,177]. See NĒPA, the verb CĀ.

NĒPACATICA in the future / en futuro (Z) [(2)Zp.62,177]. Since Z does not mark the vowel of the third syllable long or have a glottal stop, the first element may not be NĒPACAH but rather NĒPA and -CA, and that in turn suffixed by the sequence -TI-CA. See NĒPACAH.

NEPAN- This appears only as an element of compounds and derivations and conveys a sense of mutuality or reciprocity. See NE-, -PAN.

NEPANOĀ *vrefl,vt* for things to intersect, unite, join together; to join, unite something, to examine something / reunir, juntarse (S), juntar, unir, amontonar; averiguar, examinar algo (S) [(1)Cf.90v, (1)Zp.10]. See NEPAN-.

NEPANŌHUILIĀ *vt* to pile something up / lo amontona (Z) [(1)Zp.191]. In the Spanish-to-Nahuatl side of Z, NEPANOĀ is given instead of NEPANŌHUILIĀ. This may not be derived from the verb NEPANOĀ but from NEPANŌ-TL and -HUIĀ. In either case the vowel of the third syllable should be long but is not so marked in the single attestation. See NEPANOĀ.

-NEPANŌL-LI something joined, crossed, formed by placing one thing on top of another / cruzado (K) [(3)Cf.20r,67r]. This is not attested as a free form but only as the second element of CUAUHNEPANŌL-LI 'cross.' M has *calnepanolli* 'two-story house, attic of a house' and *tlanepanolli* 'something collated or investigated.' See NEPANOĀ.

NEPANŌ-TL mutuality, reciprocity / unos a otros, o unos con otros, o los unos a los otros (M) [(5)Cf.35v,125r]. The NY sequence NEPANYŌ-TL apparently undergoes assimilation of Y to N and then degemination of the resulting NN. This is mainly used in adverbial constructions

with the sense 'mutually, reciprocally.' See NEPAN-, -YŌ.

NEPANTLAH in the middle of something / en el medio, o en medio, o por el medio (M) See NEPAN-, -TLAH.

NEPANTLAHTIC late in the morning, near to noon / se hace tarde (en la mañana) (Z) [(2)Zp.119,177]. In one attestation this appears with YA 'already' postposed and cliticized to the end, with a spelling change that makes the construction opaque. The other attestation, which is not written solid, clarifies the situation and confirms this analysis. See NEPANTLAH.

NEPANTLAHTILIĀ *vrefl* for it to get late in the morning, to draw near to noon / se hace tarde (en la mañana) (Z) [(2)Zp.119,171]. See NEPANTLAH.

NEPANTLAHTITOC late in the morning, near to noon / atardece la mañana (Z) [(2)Zp.16,177]. This appears with YA 'already' postposed and cliticized to the end, with a spelling change that makes the construction opaque. The analysis is supported by Z's paired phrase TEŌTLACTOC YA 'late in the afternoon,' which is not written solid (p.16). See NEPANTLAH, the verb O.

NEPANTLAHTŌNATIUH at midday / a medio día (C) [(3)Cf.95r,95v]. See NEPANTLAH, TŌNATIUH.

NEPANTLAHYŌ-TL lunch, midday meal / comida, de medio día (Z) [(2)Zp.30,177]. See NEPANTLAH, -YŌ.

NEPĀPAN various different, discrete things / cosas diversas y diferentes (M) [(5)Bf.10r,10v]. redup. NEPAN-

NEPECHTĒQUILIZ-TLI prostration, genuflection, bow / inclinación (C) [(1)Cf.67v]. M has *nepechtecaliztli*. See PECHTĒCA.

NEPŌHUALIZ-TLI haughtiness, arrogance / la soberbia (C) [(1)Cf.48r]. See PŌHU(A).

NEQUETZALIZ-TLI raising up, resurrection, raising of doubt / levantamiento del que estaba asentado, o duda del que la tiene, o resurrección el que resuscita (M), estatura, apariencia, presentación (Z) [(3)Zp.12,57,177]. See QUETZ(A).

NEQU(I) *vt; pret: NEC* to want or use something, to engage, accept, or want someone in some enterprise (M) / querer algo o gastar y emplear alguna cosa (M),

admitir a otro para algún negocio (M) In construction with a verb in the future tense form, NEQU(I) means 'to want to ...' Used reflexively with an incorporated noun, NEQU(I) means 'to pretend to be ...'
NEQUÍHUA altern. nonact. NEQU(I)
NEQUILIĀ applic. NEQU(I)
NEQUILIZ-TLI pride / orgullo (Z for HUĒINEQUILIZ) [(2)Zp.92,155]. Z appears to have lost a necessary prefix, probably NE-. See MONECQUI, MONEQUINI.
NEQUILTIĀ *vt* to want something for someone else or to make someone want something / desear algo a otro o hacerle querer alguna cosa (M) With the oblique reflexive this means 'to want something for oneself.' altern. caus. NEQU(I)
NEQUÏTIĀ altern. caus. NEQU(I)
NETECH close together, adjacent (with respect to two objects) / entre sí (M), cercancia de cosas ... solas dos (C) [(4)Cf.93r, (1)Tp.132]. For more than two objects, the reduplicated form NĒNETECH is used. See NE-, -TECH.
NETECHILHUIĀ applic. NETECHOĀ
NETECHOĀ *vrefl,vt* for things to join or stick together; to get two things together, to join things / se junta, se acerca, se pega uno junto al otro (T), hacer llegar o juntar una cosa con otra (M) [(6)Tp.154,193]. See NETECH.
NETECHŌLŌ nonact. NETECHOĀ
NETĒCUITLAHUILIZ-TLI care of someone / cuidado de personas (K) [(1)Cf.48r]. C contrasts this with NETLACUITLAHUILIZ-TLI 'care of something.' See CUITLAHUIĀ.
NETĒCUITLAHUĪLŌNI means of caring for someone / instrumento para cuidar de alguno (C) [(1)Cf.45v]. See NETĒCUITLAHUILIZ-TLI.
NETEQUIPACHŌLIZ-TLI affliction, suffering / aflicción y angustia del que la padece (M) [(5)Zp.6,48,125,178]. See TEQUIPACHOĀ.
NETĒYEHYECALIZ-TLI temptation, experiment / tentación, prueba (R) [(1)Rp.112]. See YEHYECOĀ.
NETLĀCATILIZPAN nativity, Christmas / navidad (T) [(1)Tp.167]. See TLĀCATILIZ-TLI, -PAN.
NETLACUITLAHUILIZ-TLI care of

something / cuidado de algo (C) [(1)Cf.48r]. C contrasts this with NETĒCUITLAHUILIZ-TLI 'care of someone.' See CUITLAHUIĀ.
NETLAMACHCUILTŌNOLŌYĀN place of well-being / lugar de ... bienaventuranza (C) [(1)Cf.102r]. See TLAMACHTIĀ, CUILTŌNOĀ.
NETLAMACHTĪL-LI riches, good fortune / riqueza, prosperidad, y gozo (C) [(1)Cf.46r]. See TLAMACHTIĀ.
-NETLAQUECHIĀYA *necessarily possessed form* staff, crutch, support / bordón o muleta (C) [(1)Cf.50r, (1)Rp.43]. See QUETZ(A).
NETLATLĀTLAUHTILIZ-TLI prayer, request / súplica (Z) [(2)Zp.118,178]. See TLATLĀTLAUHTILIZ-TLI.
NETLAZOHTLALIZ-TLI love of people for one another or of someone for himself / amor con que algunos se aman, o amor propio (M), estimación (Z) [(2)Zp.57,178]. M contrasts this with *netlaçotiliztli* 'exaggeration of worth.' See TLAZOHTLA.
NETLOC close to / juntamente (M), muy juntos, cerquita, junto a (T) [(1)Tp.132]. T treats this as a postposition -NETLOC and has A for O in the second syllable. See NE-, -TLOC.
NETOLĪNILIZ-TLI poverty, misery / pobreza o miseria (M) [(1)Cf.88r]. See TOLĪNIĀ.
NEUCCHĪUHPAN *pl:* **-MEH** beehive / colmena de abeja (X) [(3)Xp.57]. X has L for UH. M has *necuchiua* 'for bees to make honey.' See NEUC-TLI, CHĪHU(A), -PAN.
NEUC-TLI honey / miel (M) T and Z have lost the labialization of the stem-final consonant, NEC-TLI.
NĒUHCĀYŌ-TL *possessed form:* **-NĒUH-CĀ** sustenance, a meal taken upon rising, breakfast / el sustento necesario (C), lo que se come después de levantarse (C), víveres, alimentos, nutrición, subsistencia (S) This is conventionally paired with COCHCĀYŌ-TL 'evening meal,' both possessed, the whole phrase meaning 'one's daily bread.' See ĒHU(A).
NEXĀ-TL lime water (used in preparing maize for grinding) / lejía (M), el agua de nixtamal, nijayote, agua encalada (T) [(1)Tp.167]. See NEX-TLI, Ā-TL.

NEXCŌMEH type of small wasp / una clase de avispa más chiquita (Z) [(2)Zp.17,178]. The literal meaning of this is 'possessor of a nixtamal pot.' Presumably this is a wasp that builds a pot-shaped nest. See NEXCŌM(I)-TL.

NEXCŌM(I)-TL vessel for soaking maize in lime water / olla para poner nixtamal (T) [(1)Tp.167, (1)Zp.178]. Z has a gloss that seems to refer to the process of preparing nixtamal rather than to the container which is its literal referent. See NEX-TLI, CŌM(I)-TL.

NEXHUA pl: **-MEH** a type of gray snake that inhabits rocky places / cierta víbora (M), culebra nezua (color gris) (T) [(1)Tp.167, (3)Xp.57]. See NEX-TLI.

NEXHUĪTĪL indigestion, intestinal cramps / enfermo del estómago, descompuesto del estómago, indigestión (Z) [(4)Zp.42,51,71,178]. M has *nexuitiliztli* with the same sense. See (I)XHUĪTIĀ.

NEXĪCŌLHUIĀ vt to envy someone / lo envidia (Z) [(2)Zp.54,191]. See NEXĪCŌL-LI, -HUIĀ.

NEXĪCŌLHUILIZ-TLI envy, jealousy / envidia (Z) [(2)Zp.54,178]. See NEXĪCŌLHUIĀ.

NEXĪCŌLITTA vt to be jealous of someone / le tiene envidia (X) [(1)Xp.71]. See NEXĪCŌL-LI, (I)TTA.

NEXĪCŌLIZ-TLI envy, jealousy / envidia (M) [(1)Tp.167]. See XĪCOĀ.

NEXĪCŌL-LI vanity, envy / egoísmo (T), envidia (X) [(1)Tp.132, (2)Zp.54,178, (1)Xp.57]. See XĪCOĀ.

NĒXILTIĀ vt to make something appear, to show something / le hago parecer, le muestro (C for first pers. sg. subject) [(1)Cf.62r]. altern. caus. NĒC(I)

NĒXĪTIĀ vt to make something appear, to show something / le hago parecer, le muestro (C for first person subject) [(1)Cf.62r]. altern. caus. NĒC(I)

NĒXOHUA nonact. NĒC(I)

NEXPĪQU(I) vrefl,vt to be put under coals, ashes; to put something under coals, ashes / se pone debajo del rescoldo (T), lo mete debajo del rescoldo (T) [(4)Tp.154,193]. See NEX-TLI, PĪQU(I).

NEXQUETZ(A) to soak maize in lime water / pone el nixtamal, encala el maíz (T) [(3)Tp.167]. See NEX-TLI, QUETZ(A).

NEXTAMAL-LI maize soaked in lime water and then ground for making tortillas, tamales, and other cornmeal-based dishes / nixtamal (T,Z) [(1)Tp.167, (2)Zp.88,178, (2)Xp.57]. See NEX-TLI, TAMAL-LI.

NEXTECUIL-IN pl: **-TIN** type of large, whitish caterpillar that eats the roots of plants; a deranged person / gusano de muladar, o persona desatinada y loca (M), nextecuil, gallina ciega (gusano) (T) See NEX-TLI, OCUIL-IN.

NĒXTIĀ vrefl,vt to reveal oneself; to reveal someone, something; to eke out a living / descubrirse o manifestarse (M), manifestar a otro (M), descubrir o manifestar algo, o buscar lo necesario a la vida (M) altern. caus. NĒC(I)

NEXTIC something gray, ashen / gris, de color ceniciento (S), gris, pardo, color de plomo (T) See NEX-TLI.

NĒXTILIĀ vrefl,vt to reveal oneself to others; to reveal, teach something to someone, to tell something to someone in confidence / aparecer o manifestarse a otros (M), revelar o descubrir algo a otro (M), descubrir secreto al amigo (M) applic. NĒXTIĀ

NĒXTILILIĀ applic. NĒXTILIĀ

NĒXTILĪLŌ nonact. NĒXTILIĀ

NĒXTĪLŌ nonact. NĒXTIĀ

NEX-TLI ashes, cinders / ceniza (M)

NEYŌLCOCOLIZ-TLI affliction, trouble, grief / duelo (Z) [(2)Zp.48,178]. The pairing of NE- with COCOLIZ-TLI is irregular. Possibly this is derived instead from the reflexive use of YŌLCOCOĀ 'to suffer.' For this alternative analysis it may be significant that in both attestations the vowel of the fourth syllable is marked long. Z also has NELYŌLCOCOLIZ-TLI 'sadness.' See YŌL-, COCOLIZ-TLI.

NEYŌLCUĪTILIZ-TLI confession / confesión (M) [(1)Cf.77r]. In the single attestation, the vowel of the third syllable is not marked long, but the vowel in the corresponding verb is long. See YŌLCUĪTIĀ.

NEZAHUALCOYŌ-TL personal name Nezahualcoyotl [(2)Bf.8r,10v, (1)Cf.97r]. The honorific form of this is NEZAHUALCOYŌTZIN. See NEZAHUALIZ-TLI, COYŌ-TL.

NEZAHUALIZ-TLI fast, hunger / ayuno de
la iglesia o voluntario (M) [(1)Zp.201,
(2)Xp.57]. See ZAHU(A).

NEZAHUALPIL-LI *personal name*
Nezahualpilli [(5)Bf.8r,9v,111, (1)Cf.85r].
The honorific form of this is
NEZAHUALPILTZIN-TLI. The sense here,
in spite of truncation, is 'son of Neza-
hualcoyotl.' See NEZAHUALIZ-TLI,
PIL-LI.

NEZCALILIZ-TLI resurrection; prudence or
profit / resurrección, cordura, o aprovecha-
miento del que va aprovechando en algo
(M) [(1)Cf.97r]. See (I)ZCALIĀ.

NĒZCĀYŌTIĀ *vt* to mean, denote, indicate
something / denotar, figurar, o significar
algo (M) [(1)Cf.101v]. See NĒZCĀYŌ-TL.

NĒZCĀYŌ-TL sign, token, gift / marca,
señal (S), regalo, propina (Z)
[(3)Zp.102,107,177]. See NĒC(I), -YŌ.

NEZOHUAHTĪLŌYŌ-TL marriage /
matrimonio, casamiento (T) [(1)Tp.167].
This implies an otherwise unattested
reflexive use of ZOHUAHTIĀ, which in its
transitive (and literal) sense means 'for a
man to take a wife.' See ZOHUAHTIĀ.

NICĀN here / aquí, acá, de aquí, o por aquí
(M) See -CĀN.

NICCA *exclamation used for hailing
someone, getting someone's attention*
hola, hao, oyes, para llamar a alguno (M)
[(1)Cf.124v].

NICI here, nearby / aquí (S) [(1)Bf.9v,
(2)Cf.95v,96r]. This form arises from a
reanalysis of IN ICI as IN NICI. See ICI.

NIMAN then, right away / luego, o incon-
tinenti (M)

NIPA over there, the other way / acullá, o a
ésta parte (M), por ahí, a otra parte (C)
[(6)Cf.89r,90r,131r]. C remarks that this is
close in sense to NĒPA 'at some distance,'
which however has two senses not shared
by NIPA, namely to point out a particular
spot or to refer to a remote time. NIPA is
indefinite and does not point to a particular spot. Rather, the sense is 'away from
here, anywhere but here,' which somewhat
resolves the apparent conflict between M's
'this way' and C's 'the other way.'

NO See NŌ.

NŌ also / también, conjunción y (M) This
particle bonds with others in various
clusters incorporating the sense of 'also,'
but there appears to be another clitic NO
with a short vowel, which is a component of NOCEH 'or else,' NOZO 'either,'
AHNOZO 'or, perhaps' and NOZAN
'still, up until now.' In these the vowel of
NO is specifically marked short or left unmarked for length; it is never marked long.
This is abundantly attested in B and C and
also appears in R and X but not at all in T
and Z.

NOCEH or, nor / o ... ni (C) This is abundantly attested in B and C. The vowel
of the initial syllable is unmarked for
length in C and is specifically marked
short in B (f.7v,10r,10v). C says that
NOCEH is a syncopated form of NOZO
(Y)EH (f.111v), which implies that neither
NOCEH or NOZO has NŌ 'also' as a
component part, although it would be
compatible with their senses. See NOZO,
(Y)EH.

NOCHEHHUĀ-TL all of a set of things,
something homogeneous and consisting
entirely of one thing / todo eso así lo uno
como lo otro, o cosa se cuenta con lo
demás, o que es de la misma cosa (M), solo,
puro, nada más (T) [(1)Tp.168]. M combines
the gloss of this with that for 'the fruit of a
prickly pear cactus'< NŌCH-TLI. M also
has *mucheuatl* derived from corresponding
MOCH(I). See NOCH(I), (Y)EHHUĀ-TL.

NOCH(I) *pl:* **NOCHTĪN ~ NOCHIMEH**
all / todo (T) T, Z, and X have NOCH(I)
for MOCH(I) as do many other Nahuatl
speech communities. See MOCH(I).

NŌCHILIĀ *applic.* NŌTZ(A)

NOCHIPA forever / eterno, siempre (T)
[(1)Tp.168, (1)Xp.58]. See MOCHIPA.

NOCHTĪN See NOCH(I).

NŌCH-TLI fruit of the prickly pear cactus /
tuna, fruta conocida (M) [(1)Tp.168]. See
NOHPAL-LI.

NŌCUĒL again / otra vez (C) This often has
a lexically empty final (Y)EH added to it. It
may also be preceded by YE 'already.'
Notice that although they may be spelled
alike in a text, these are different particles.
The extended form YE NŌCUĒLYEH
occurs on Cf.108r. See NŌ, CUĒL.

NŌCUĒLYEH See NŌCUĒL.
NOHMAH spontaneously, still / aún todavía (M), todavía, mismo, siempre, espontáneamente (S) M contrasts this with NOMĀ 'my hand' by giving them in separate contiguous entries, although he spells them identically. See -NOHMAH.
-NOHMAH necessarily possessed form; pl: -NOHMAH ~ NOHMATCAH personally, in person, oneself / mismo (C) C gives a full paradigm of this for all persons singular and plural. The free form and the necessarily possessed form share the sense of spontaneity, internal control. Some sort of reanalysis relates this to IYOĀ 'to be alone' and IYOH 'only.' See IYOĀ.
NOHMAHHUIĀ vrefl to act of one's free will / hacer algo de su propio albedrío y voluntad (M) [(2)Bf.10r,11r, (2)Cf.60v, (2)Rp.111]. See NOHMAH, -HUIĀ.
NOHMAHHUILIĀ applic. NOHMAHHUIĀ
-NOHMATCAH See NOHMAH.
NOHNŌHUIYĀN redup. NŌHUIYĀN
NOHNŌNCUAH apart, with respect to a number of discrete objects / aparte o de por sí, hablando de muchas cosas (R) [(1)Rp.114]. This also appears in P with the glottal stop marked but not the long vowel. C has the reduplicated form NŌNONCUAH for the distributive plural. redup. NŌNCUAH
NOHNŌNCUAHITTA vt to discriminate, divide something / discernir, dividir (R) [(1)Rp.114]. See NOHNŌNCUAH, (I)TTA.
NOHNŌNCUAHQUĪXTIĀ vt to divide, separate things, to set things apart / dividir, separar (R) [(1)Rp.114]. This also appears in P with the glottal stop marked but not the long vowels. redup. NŌNCUAHQUĪXTIĀ
NOHNŌNCUAHTLĀLIĀ vt to divide, separate things, to set things apart / dividir, separar (R) [(1)Rp.114]. redup. NŌNCUAHTLĀLIĀ
NOHNŌQUIHU(A) to spread out, to be scattered, to leak / derramarse (R) [(1)Rp.114]. This also appears in P with the glottal stop marked but not the long vowel. M has nonoquiuhtiuh with the same sense. See NŌQUIĀ, NŌNŌQUIHU(I).

NOHNŌTZ(A) vt to speak with someone, to have a conversation / parlo con él (C for first pers. sg. subject), habla con otro ... consultar ... advertir (R) This is abundantly attested across sources. It is difficult to distinguish in sense from NŌNŌTZ(A), although the latter seems to have the sense of 'to advise, instruct' not shared by NOHNŌTZ(A). Since M does not distinguish between the two, the glosses are probably mixed. M's gloss for nonotza with the directional prefix ON- 'to go to chat with others' is undoubtedly this one; M's other glosses appear here under NŌNŌTZ(A). redup. NŌTZ(A)
NOHPAL-LI prickly pear cactus / nopal, cactus del que se cuenta con dos especies principales: opuntia vulgaris, que da la mejor nochtli, y opuntia cochinillifera, en el cual vive la cochinilla (S) [(3)Tp.168, (3)Zp.22,89,179]. M gives NOHPAL-LI as part of a phrase meaning to cultivate the plant. T has the variant form NOHPALI-TL.
NŌHUIYĀMPA to, from everywhere / de todas partes (M) [(1)Cf.117r]. See NŌHUIYĀN, -PA.
NŌHUIYĀN everywhere / en todas partes (M) In C the vowel of the initial syllable is marked long, but in B it is specifically marked short. T has the reflex of a short vowel, and in Z the vowel is unmarked for length. See -YĀN.
NŌHUIYĀNYOH something common, universal / común, universal (R) [(1)Rp.113]. See NŌHUIYĀN, -YOH.
NŌIUH in the same way / de la misma manera (M) [(3)Cf.120v]. This often appears in the phrase ZAN NŌIUH. See NŌ, IUH.
NOMATI it seems that ..., I think that ... / parece que (M), paréceme (C) [(4)Cf.126r,126v]. This is a lexicalized syncopated form of NINOMAT(I). See MAT(I).
NŌNCUAH apart, separate / aparte, o por sí aparte (M) This is abundantly attested in C and R. T has the variant NENCUAH.
NŌNCUAHCAH to be separate, apart / está aparte, está apartado (T) [(1)Tp.167]. See NŌNCUAH, the verb CĀ.
NŌNCUAHQUĪXTIĀ vt to set something

apart, to make an exception of something / poner aparte por sí lo que se escoge, o sacar de regla general algo (M) This is implied by the reduplicated form NOHNŌNCUAHQUĪXTIĀ and is abundant in P, where the glottal stop is marked but not the long vowels. See NŌNCUAH, QUĪXTIĀ.

NŌNCUAHTLĀLIĀ *vrefl,vt* for something to be set apart; to set something apart, to make an exception of something / se pone aparte (T), poner aparte por sí lo que se escoge, o sacar de regla general algo (M) [(1)Cf.94v, (3)Tp.154]. C also gives NŌNCUAH TLĀLIĀ as separate words with verbal prefixes attached to TLĀLIĀ alone. M gives this as synonymous with NŌNCUAHQUĪXTIĀ. See NŌNCUAH, TLĀLIĀ.

NŌNCUAHXELOĀ *vrefl,vt* to be separated, set apart; to separate something, to set something apart / se aparta, se separa (T), lo aparta, lo separa (T) [(6)Tp.154,193]. In the attestations in T the final glottal stop of the first element is missing. See NŌNCUAH, XELOĀ.

NŌNŌCHILIĀ applic. NŌNŌTZ(A)

NŌNŌHUIYĀN redup. NŌHUIYĀN

NŌNŌNCUAH apart, with respect to several discrete objects / de más de dos personas o cosas que cada una esté aparte (C) [(3)Cf.94v]. R has NOHNŌNCUAH for the distributive plural of NŌNCUAH. redup. NŌNCUAH

NŌNŌQUIĀ *vt* to sprinkle, scatter, spill something / lo desparrama, lo derrama, lo riega (agua, leche, etc.), lo vacía (líquido), lo vuelca (T) [(3)Tp.194]. See NŌQUIĀ.

NŌNŌQUIHU(I) to spill, scatter, overflow, leak / se tira (de una cosa llena), derrama, se desborda, se riega, se desparrama (T) [(1)Tp.168]. M has *nonoquiuhtiuh* 'to go about spreading or scattering.' See NŌQUIĀ.

NŌNŌQUILIĀ applic. NŌNŌQUIĀ

NŌNŌQUĪLŌ nonact. NŌNŌQUIĀ

NŌNŌTZ(A) *vrefl,vt* to take counsel with oneself, to converse, consult, come to agreement; to caution, correct or inform others, to relate things / consultar o tratar algo consigo mismo, o enmendarse (M), amonestrar o hablar con otros, o corregir, castigar y aconsejar (M), informar o contar y relatar historia, o tratar del precio que vale lo que se ha de comprar (M) It is hard to separate the senses of NŌNŌTZ(A) from NOHNŌTZ(A). Both are attested across sources. NŌNŌTZ(A) seems to carry more of the sense of 'to advise, instruct,' while NOHNŌTZ(A) is more neutrally 'to converse.' C contrasts serious discussion of business (NŌNŌTZ(A)) with casual chat (NOHNŌTZ(A)) (f.73r). redup. NŌTZ(A)

NŌN-TLI someone mute / mudo (M) [(2)Zp.86,179, (2)Xp.59].

NŌQUIĀ *vt* to upset, spill something / lo trastorna, lo derrama (T) [(3)Tp.194, (5)Zp.43,127,130,191,199].

NŌQUILIĀ applic. NŌQUIĀ

NŌQUĪLŌ nonact. NŌQUIĀ

NŌTZ(A) *vt* to call or summon someone, to talk to someone / citar o llamar a alguno, o hablar con otro (M)

NŌTZALŌ nonact. NŌTZ(A)

NOZAN still, up until now / todavía, hasta ahora (C) [(5)Cf.126r]. This seems to have as a component the element NO with a short vowel rather than NŌ 'also.' See NŌ, ZAN.

NOZO or, either ... or / o (C) With CA, CA NEL, and INĪC this has the sense of 'because.' According to C, CA NELNOZO indicates stronger causality, to the point of necessity.

NOZONEL See NELNOZO.

O

O *preterit-as-present verb; pret:* **OC** to be lying, to stretch out / estar echada o tendida alguna persona, o madero, o cosa semejante que sea larga (M for *onoc*) This verb as a free form always appears with the directional ON-, which in this case does not convey any distal sense but gives more substance to an otherwise rather minimal verb and distinguishes the verb from OC 'again.' The directional ON- is not included in the common construction in which another verb is bound to this one by the -TI- ligature. The resulting sequence -TI-OC is reduced to -TOC. Constructions with -TOC are of high frequency in Nahuatl and convey a progressive sense.

Ō exclamation that conveys admiration or surprise that something is contrary to expectation, or initiates a vocative, or is used as an expression of pain / exclamación de él que se admira de oír o saber lo que no sabía (C), interjección del que está afligido y hace exclamación (M) In B this is generally marked long except when it is capitalized, while in C it is never marked long. In a discussion of Ō on f.124r,124v, C remarks that this particle can compound with honorific -TZIN for greater formality.

Ō- antecessive particle indicating completion of some action prior to some point / señal ... de los pretéritos (M) This particle generally cliticizes to preterit and pluperfect verb forms, sometimes to the imperfect, and serves as a redundant past tense marker. However, especially in early sources, other constituents can intervene between Ō (which is then freestanding) and the verb complex. It can also be found with verbs in the future tense conveying the sense that the action in question will be complete at some point in the future.

OC still, yet, another / aun todavía (M)

Despite the discrepancy in vowel length, this is probably related to ŌME 'two.'

OCACHI a bit more / otro poco más (M) [(2)Cf.87v]. See OC, ACHI.

OCCĀMPA to or from two places or directions / de dos o a dos partes (C) [(2)Cf.91r]. See OCCĀN, -PA.

OCCĀN in two places / en dos partes o en dos lugares, o dos raciones de comida (M) See OC, -CĀN.

OCCĒ another, one more / otro o otra, o otro más (M) See OC, CĒ.

OCCECNI in another place / en otro lugar (C) [(2)Cf.92r]. See OC, CECNI.

OCCENCAH principally, especially / mayormente o principalmente (M) [(3)Cf.87r,87v]. See OC, CENCAH.

OCCENCAHYEH principally, especially / mayormente o especialmente (M) [(1)Cf.87r]. See OCCENCAH, -YEH.

OCCENTE-TL other, the next thing / otro (M), próximo, otro (T) [(4)Tp.168,222, (1)Xp.61]. See OC, CENTE-TL.

OCCENTLAMAN-TLI another thing altogether, in another way / otra cosa, en otra manera o de otra manera (M), diferente concepto (C) [(1)Cf.124r]. See OC, CENTLAMAN-TLI.

OCCENTLAPAL other side, on or from the other side / el otro (lado) (C), del otro (lado) (C) [(2)Cf.92v]. See OC, CENTLAPAL.

OCCEPPA again / otra vez (M) T has a variant OCZAPPA. See OC, CEPPA.

OCCEQUI *pl:* **OCCEQUĪN ~ OC-CEQUĪNTĪN** something more, something additional, a bit more / más, o un poco, o otras cosas (M) See OC, CEQUI.

OCCEQUĪNTĪN others / otros (M) [(1)Cf.5v]. This also appears in the short form OCCEQUĪN in C and Z. The long vowel of TĪN here is provided by analogy with other quantifiers. See OCCEQUI.

ŌCĒLMOTLAHUĒLILTIC Oh how
wretched you are. Woe to you. / o desven-
turado de tí, guay de tí (M), desdichadísimo
(C) [(1)Cf.59v]. This is specifically second
person singular, but the MO- could be
replaced with any of the other possessive
prefixes with a corresponding change in
reference. See Ō, -CĒL, TLAHUĒLILTIC.

ŌCĒLŌ-TL *pl:* **-MEH** jaguar (Felis onca),
ocelot (Felis pardalis) / tigre (M)
[(3)Bf.2v,3r, (2)Cf.4v]. B marks the first
vowel long, but C fails to.

ŌCĒLŌXŌCHI-TL Aztec lily, tiger flower
(Tigridia pavonia), the bulbs of which are
used as food and to treat fevers and infer-
tility / cacomite, flor de tigre (K) This is
not directly attested in the sources for this
dictionary, but the component parts are.
See ŌCĒLŌ-TL, XŌCHI-TL.

OCHPAHUĀZ-TLI broom / escoba para
barrer (M) [(2)Zp.55,179]. This appears only
in the Spanish-to-Nahuatl side of M. See
OCHPĀN(A).

OCHPĀN(A) *vt* to sweep something / lo
barre (Z) [(2)Zp.19,145]. M has an entry
chpana 'to sweep' requiring the prefix
TLA- and yielding TLACHPĀN(A). See
(I)CHPĀN(A).

OCMĀ This shortened form of OCMĀYA is
only attested in the phrase TLĀ OCMĀ
'wait a minute.' See OCMĀYA.

OCMĀYA a bit further on, a bit ahead, soon
/ de aquí a un poco, o aguarda un poco (M)
The phrase TLĀ OCMĀYA and its short
form TLĀ OCMĀ mean 'wait a minute,'
and OCMĀYA alone can also be used with
this sense. See OC, MĀ.

OCNAMACAC pulque vendor / tabernero o
tabernera (M), el pulquero, que vende
pulque (C) [(1)Cf.51v]. See OC-TLI,
NAMACA.

OCNAMACŌYĀN place where pulque is
sold / taberna (M), taberna donde se vende
pulque (C) [(2)Cf.51r,105v]. See OC-TLI,
NAMACA, -YĀN.

OCNŌ in addition, more, too / y más, y
también (M) [(2)Cf.92r]. See OC, NŌ.

OCNŌCECNI in another place / en otro
lugar (C) [(2)Cf.92r]. See OCNŌ, CECNI.

OCOCIN-TLI pine seed / semilla de ocote
(Z) [(1)Zp.179]. See OCO-TL, CIN-TLI.

OCOPETL(A)-TL fern / helecho (S)
[(1)Bf.10r]. The literal meaning of this is
'pine-mat,' probably referring to ferns as
ground cover in pine forests. See OCO-TL,
PETL(A)-TL.

OCO-TL pine tree; torch made of pine / tea,
raja o astilla de pino (M), ocote (árbol) (Z) Z
marks the vowel of the second syllable
long, and it is so marked in half the attestations in X, but other sources have it
consistently short.

OCOTZOCUAHU(I)-TL gum tree (Liqui-
dambar styraciflua) / ocozol, liquidámbar
(Z) [(3)Zp.77,90,179]. The gum from this
tree is cooked and formed into tablets that
are used for medicinal purposes. Burned,
they produce a smoke used for fumigation.
See OCOTZO-TL, CUAHU(I)-TL.

OCOTZO-TL pine pitch, turpentine / re-
sina de pino o trementina (M) [(1)Tp.168,
(2)Zp.125,179]. See OCO-TL, TZO-TL.

OCOXĀL-IN carpet of decayed pine needles
that collects on the floor of pine forests /
ocoxale (Z) [(4)Zp.90,179]. Z gives this
twice with the -IN absolutive and twice
with no absolutive suffix. See OCO-TL,
XĀL-LI.

OCPA two times / dos veces (X) [(1)Xp.61].
See OC, -PA, ŌPPA.

OC-TLI pulque / vino (M), pulque (C) Z has
a long vowel in this item, but in abundant
attestation elsewhere it is short.

ŌCUĒL very quickly, soon / tan presto (C)
[(2)Cf.107v]. See Ō-, CUĒL.

OCUIL-IN *pl:* **-TIN** worm, caterpillar /
gusano generalmente, o cebo para pescar
(M) Z also uses OCUIL-IN with the sense
'wild animal.'

OCUILLŌ-TL something pertaining to
worms / cosa de gusanos (M) [(1)Cf.53r].
See OCUIL-IN, -YŌ.

OCUILOĀ to become wormy, worm-eaten /
se agusana (T) [(1)Tp.169]. See OCUIL-IN.

OHCHĪUHQUI one who builds, maintains
roads / uno que hace caminos, repara
caminos (Z) [(1)Zp.180]. See OH-TLI,
CHĪHU(A).

OHHUITIĀ *vt* to guide someone, to show
someone the way / lo encamina, lo guía (T)
[(1)Tp.116]. See OH-TLI.

OHHUITILIĀ applic. OHHUITIĀ

OHHUITĪLŌ nonact. OHHUITIĀ

OHHUIYŌ-TL matters having to do with roads / cosa de caminos (K) [(1)Cf.53r, (1)Rp.44]. This is an abstract noun derived from OH-TLI. Neither attestation is specifically glossed, but the gloss given here parallels the others in the same section in C. This contrasts with OHUIHCĀYŌ-TL 'danger, difficulty.' See OH-TLI, -YŌ.

OHMACA to guide / guía (Z) [(3)Zp.180,191,212]. See OH-TLI, MACA.

OHMACALIZ-TLI advice / consejo (Z) [(1)Zp.180]. See OHMACA.

OHMACTIĀ vt to guide someone, to show someone the way / lo encamina (Z) [(1)Zp.191]. The single attestation of this has a long vowel in the second syllable, but this is undoubtedly the causative form of OHMACA. See OHMACA.

-OHMI-TL pelt, downy fur / pelo de conejo (M for *tochomitl*) [(1)Bf.10v]. This contrasts with OMI-TL 'bone, awl.' -OHMI-TL is only attested compounded with TŌCH-TLI 'rabbit.' TOHMI-TL 'down' occurs as a free form.

OHNENQUI traveler / pasajero, viajero (Z) [(1)Zp.180]. See OH-TLI, NEM(I).

OHŌME each two, two by two, two apiece / cada dos, o de dos en dos, o cada uno dos (M) redup. ŌME

OHŌMEILHUITICA every other day, every second day / cada dos (días) (R) [(1)Rp.37]. This appears in R without diacritics. See OHŌME, ILHUI-TL.

OHONOC redup. ONOC

OHŌYALŌ redup. ŌYALŌ

OHPITZAC-TLI pl: **-MEH** path, narrow way / vereda, senda (T) [(1)Tp.169, (1)Zp.180]. Z has a long vowel in the second syllable, but it is inconsistent with the derivation. See OH-TLI, PITZAC-TLI.

OHTĒNYŌ-TL roadside / orilla (del camino) (Z) [(1)Zp.180]. See OH-TLI, TĒN-TLI.

OHTLATOCA to travel a road, to go along in life, for a stain to spread / caminar, o ir cundiendo mucho la mancha (M) Z has a short form OHTOCA attested twice, once with a long vowel in TOCA. See OH-TLI, TOCA.

OHTLATOCTIĀ caus. OHTLATOCA

OH-TLI *possessed form:* **-OHHUI** road / camino generalmente (M)

OHTLĪCA along or in the road / por el camino (C) [(1)Cf.19v, (1)Rp.65]. See OH-TLI, ĪCA.

OHTLĪPANQUETZ(A) vrefl to set out on the road / se pone en camino (Z) [(1)Zp.171]. In the single attestation the second vowel is not marked long, but the structure of the first part of this is parallel to OHTLĪCA. See OH-TLI, -PAN, QUETZ(A).

OHUAĀ-TL juice pressed from sugar cane / jugo de caña (Z) [(1)Zp.179]. See OHUA-TL, Ā-TL.

OHUACAMAC canebreak / cañaveral (T) [(1)Tp.169]. See OHUA-TL, -CAMAC.

OHUAMELAC-TLI long canes / cañas largas enteras (T) [(1)Tp.169]. See OHUA-TL, MELACTIC.

OHUAMĪL-LI cane field / cañaveral (Z) [(1)Zp.179]. See OHUA-TL, MĪL-LI.

OHUANEUC-TLI cane syrup, corn syrup / miel de cañas de maíz, que parece arrope (M) [(1)Zp.179]. OHUA-TL, NEUC-TLI

OHUAPACH-TLI remains of sugar cane after pressing / bagazo (Z) [(1)Zp.179]. See OHUA-TL, PACH-TLI.

OHUATEQU(I) See OHUA-TL, TEQU(I).

OHUA-TL green maize stalks, sugar cane / caña de maíz verde (M), caña de azúcar (Z)

OHUATLAH canebreak / cañaveral (Z) [(1)Zp.179]. See OHUA-TL, -TLAH.

OHUIH something difficult or dangerous / cosa dificultosa o peligrosa (M) R marks the glottal stop on the wrong syllable, but the other sources are in agreement.

OHUIHCĀN dangerous place, situation / lugar dificultoso y peligroso, o escondrijo de fieras, o lugar oscuro y espantoso (M) [(1)Bf.111, (1)Zp.180]. See OHUIH, -CĀN.

OHUIHCĀYŌ-TL danger, difficulty / dificultad o peligro (M) [(1)Cf.53v, (1)Rp.44]. See OHUIH, -YŌ.

OHUIHTITOC something laborious, difficult / trabajoso (Z) [(2)Zp.124,180]. In one attestation Z marks the vowel of the third syllable long. See OHUIH.

OHXILIĀ vt to put salve on something, to annoint something, someone / lo unta (Z) [(2)Zp.126,191]. M has *oxitl* 'salve made of turpentine' and *oxiutia* 'to anoint something with this salve.' This also appears in P with the glottal stop marked. See OHZA.

OHYĀNQUI traveler / viajero, pasajero (Z) [(2)Zp.129,180]. See OH-TLI, YĀ.

OHZA *vt* to put salve on something, to annoint something, someone / untar o embijar a otro (M)

ŌILIĀ *vt* to shell something for someone / desgranarle algo (K) [(2)Cf.64r, (1)Tp.233]. T has a medial glide *w* between the first two vowels, which conclusively demonstrates that the Y of the stem is dropped in this form. applic. ŌY(A)

*ŌLĪN(I) See ŌLĪNIĀ.

ŌLĪNIĀ *vrefl,vt* to move; to move something / menearse, o moverse (M), lo mueve, lo menea (T) The basic intransitive verb *ŌLĪN(I) is not attested in the sources for this dictionary. As a free form in T and Z, ŌLĪNIĀ has a long vowel in the initial syllable, but derived forms have a short initial vowel. A single attestation of the verb in B is a freestanding reflexive in which the vowel is unmarked for length. X, however, has a long vowel even in derived forms.

ŌLĪNILIĀ applic. ŌLĪNIĀ
ŌLĪNĪLŌ nonact. ŌLĪNIĀ

OLŌCHTLATZOTZONANIH *This is a plural, which is formed by adding* -H. group of musicians / grupo de músicos (Z) [(2)Zp.64,180]. In one of the attestations, the vowel of the next to last syllable is marked long. See OLŌCH-TLI, TLATZOTZONANIH.

OLŌCH-TLI a group / grupo, unidos (Z) [(5)Zp.64,180]. See OLOLOĀ.

OLOLHUIĀ applic. OLOLOĀ

OLOLOĀ *vt* to roll something into a ball; to collect something / hacer alguna cosa redonda como bola, o cosa semejante esférica, o arrebañar y ayuntar algo (M) The vowel of the second syllable is consistently short in T but long in 4 of 6 attestations in Z.

OLOLŌLŌ nonact. OLOLOĀ

OLOLTĒNTOC heap, pile / montón (Z) [(1)Zp.180]. See OLOLOĀ, TĒM(I).

OLOLTIC something ball-shaped, spherical / bola (Z) [(2)Zp.20,221]. The single attesta-

tion has both the second and third vowels long. See the note about attested vowel length in OLOLOĀ. A long vowel in -TIC is idiosyncratic to Z. See OLOLOĀ.

ŌLŌTETZONTE-TL *pl:* **-MEH** instrument for removing kernels from corncobs / olotera (para desgranar) (T) [(1)Tp.245]. See ŌLŌ-TL, TE-TL, TZON-TLI.

ŌLŌ-TL corncob with kernels removed / el corazón o espiga desgranada de la mazorca de maíz (M) [(2)Tp.245, (1)Zp.180].

ŌLŌXŌCHI-TL maize flower / flor de olote (X) [(3)Xp.61]. See ŌLŌ-TL, XŌCHI-TL.

OM- *prefix used in adding digits to larger numbers in the Nahuatl vigesimal number system* and, plus / y, más (K) Despite the vowel length discrepancy, this appears to be related to both ŌME 'two' and OC 'another, again.' Regular nasal assimilation gives this the form ON- with numbers beginning with a nonlabial consonant. See ŌME, OC.

ŌMACH- a great deal / mucho (C) [(2)Cf.116v]. This is MACH inserted between antecessive Ō- and the rest of the verb complex. See Ō-, MACH.

ŌME *pl:* **ŌMENTIN ~ ŌMEMEH** two / dos (M) Z has a single attestation of ŌMEN as a plural form, and C forms the plural of OMŌME 'twelve' by adding -N too. In compounds the final vowel is lost, and before nonlabial consonants there is nasal assimilation yielding the alternation ŌM- ~ ŌN-. B has an attestation of an honorific form in which a glottal stop intervenes between ŌME and -TZIN. See OM-.

ŌMEQUIL(I)-TL a fragrant white lily-like flower (Polyanthes tuberosa, Polyanthes mexicana) / omequelite (yerba) (Z) [(2)Zp.91,180]. This is another name for OMIXŌCHI-TL. Possibly the ŌME element is a substitution for OMI. See ŌME, QUIL(I)-TL.

OMICICUIL-LI rib / costilla (M) [(3)Tp.131,142]. T has lost the initial O and has a reduplicated form based on the truncated form. T also has CE for CI. The possessive of the reduplicated form ends in -YŌ. M has this in the Spanish-to-Nahuatl side, while in the Nahuatl-to-Spanish side it occurs only in a compound. See OMI-TL, CICUIL-LI.

OMI-TL bone, awl / hueso, alesna, o punzón (M) The vowels are both consistently short except in Z where the first vowel is long in three attestations of six and the second vowel is given long twice. This contrasts with -OHMI-TL 'pelt, down.'

OMIXŌCHI-TL a fragrant white lily-like flower (Polyanthes tuberosa, Polyanthes mexicana) / azucena (M), flor de hechura de hueso (C) [(1)Cf.76r]. R has the variant OMIYŌXŌCHI-TL See OMI-TL, XŌCHI-TL.

-OMIYŌ necessarily possessed form one's own bones / sus huesos (K) See OMI-TL.

-OMIYOHCĀPOHTZIN necessarily possessed form someone who shares one's own type of bones / ha tomado ... huesos ... como nosotros (C for first pers. plural possessed form with MOCHĪHU(A)) This is said of Christ's incarnation. It is paired with -EZYOHCĀPOHTZIN 'sharing one's own type of blood.' See -OMIYŌ, -POH.

OMŌME pl: **OMŌMEN** twelve / doce [(1)Cf.110r]. C marks the vowel of the last syllable long in the plural form. See ŌME.

ŌMPA there (distal) / allá, o de allá (C) T consistently has a short vowel in the first syllable. See ŌN, -PA.

ON- prefix for verbs primarily indicating direction of action away from the speaker; sometimes used for formality without literal directional sense partícula que se junta a verbos para significar distancia de lugar, o por vía o manera de ornato y buen sonido, etc. (M) Although this shares the distal sense with the particle ŌN found in ŌMPA, INŌN, etc., they differ in vowel length.

ŌN distal particle / adj. que indica la distancia, la lejanía (S) This particle contrasts with the proximal particle ĪN to form such pairs as INŌN 'that, those' and INĪN 'this, these.' The vowel length is generally left unmarked in C because of this item's high frequency. C does mark the long vowel part of the time, and T is consistent in having the reflex of Ō. The directional

verbal prefix ON- differs from the particle ŌN in vowel length despite the similarity of meaning.

ONCĀN there, middle distance / ahí, allí (C) This sometimes has the sense 'within sight,' closer than ŌMPA. One would expect the ON to have a long vowel as ŌMPA does, and in fact B marks the vowel long in two out of six attestations, and X has u for O. Elsewhere it is consistently short. See ON-, -CĀN.

ONĪ See the verb Ī.

ONOC See the verb O.

ONOLTIĀ caus. of the verb O

ŌNTE-TL two (of a class of lump-shaped things) / dos (M) See ŌME, TE-TL.

ŌNTLAPAL on, from both sides / de dos lados (M), de ambos lados (C) [(4)Cf.92v]. C does not mark the vowel of the first syllable long in any of the attestations. See ŌME, TLAPAL-LI.

ŌNTLAPALIXTI on, from both sides / de dos lados (M) [(2)Cf.92v]. See ŌNTLAPAL, -IXTI.

-ŌPŌCHCOPA only attested in possessed form at one's left hand / a tu mano izquierda (C for second pers. sg. possessor) [(1)Cf.94v]. C does not mark the first and second vowels long in the single attestation. See ŌPŌCH-TLI, -COPA.

ŌPŌCHEHĒCA-TL pneumonia / pulmonía (Z) [(2)Zp.103,180]. Z fails to mark the long vowels in this item. See ŌPŌCH-TLI, EHĒCA-TL.

ŌPŌCHMĀ(I)-TL the left hand / mano izquierda (M) [(2)Cf.82r, (2)Zp.81,180]. ŌPŌCH-TLI, MĀ(I)-TL

ŌPŌCH-TLI left, left-hand side / izquierdo (Z) There is inconsistency across sources in vowel length marking. In a single entry in B both vowels of the stem are long; in three out of four attestations in C only the first vowel is marked long, with both vowels unmarked in the fourth attestation. Z consistently leaves the first vowel unmarked and twice out of six times marks the second long. M's alternative spelling opuch suggests a long second vowel, but M is not consistent in using this convention only for long Ō.

ŌPPA two times / dos veces (M) In two attestations C does not mark the initial vowel long, but T consistently has the reflex of Ō, and Z marks it long once out of two times. In T ŌPPA has been reanalyzed as a unitary lexical item and a second -PA attached to yield ŌPPAPA. In Z ŌPPA also seems to have been lexicalized and from it has been derived ŌPPATICA 'for a second time.' X has a different derivation, OCPA< OC 'another' and -PA, but with the same sense. See ŌME, -PA.

OQUĪC while, as long as / mientras que, o entretanto (M) The sense of this appears to be the combined sense of OC and ĪC, but the second vowel is attested marked long only a single time in B. C does not mark it long in any of abundant attestations. OC, ĪC

OQUICHCONĒ-TL male child / niño (de nene hasta los 9 años) (X) [(2)Xp.69]. See OQUICH-TLI, CONĒ-TL.

-OQUICHNACAYŌ necessarily possessed form one's male genitals / de sus partes, hablando honestamente ... de las del varón (C) [(1)Cf.83r]. See OQUICH-TLI, NAC(A)-TL.

OQUICHPIL-LI boy, youth / niño o muchacho (M for honorific oquichpiltzintli) [(5)Zp.86,88,128,180]. Z idiosyncratically has PĪL where other sources have PIL. See OQUICH-TLI, PIL-LI.

OQUICHPĪPILOC youth / juventud (Z) [(2)Zp.74,180]. Z idiosyncratically has PĪL where other sources have PIL. The long vowel of the reduplication is standard. The derivation is opaque; perhaps it should be from PĪPIL, -YŌ, and -C(O). See OQUICHPIL-LI.

-OQUICHTIHUAHTZIN necessarily possessed form honorific form of -OQUICHTIUH

-OQUICHTIUH necessarily possessed form older brother (from the point of view of a sister) / la hermana dice de su hermano mayor (C) [(2)Cf.81v]. See OQUICH-TLI.

OQUICHTLAĪCŌLTIĀ vrefl to have lovers / tiene queridos (T) [(3)Tp.156]. T has COL for CŌL here, but there should be the reflex of a long vowel. See OQUICH-TLI, ĪCŌLTIĀ.

OQUICH-TLI pl: -TIN ~ MEH; possessed form: -OQUICHHUI man, male, husband / varón, o macho en cada especie (M) The possessed honorific form is -OQUICHHUAHTZIN with a glottal stop intervening between the possessed noun form and -TZIN.

-OQUICHXINĀCHYŌ necessarily possessed form one's semen / el semen genital (C) [(1)Cf.83r]. See OQUICH-TLI, XINĀCH-TLI.

-OQUICHYŌ necessarily possessed form one's semen / semen genital (C) [(1)Cf.83r]. See OQUICH-TLI.

OTLA-TL bamboo / caña maciza y recia (M) [(1)Tp.169, (2)Zp.92,180]. In one attestation Z has both vowels long, the first followed by the reflex of a glottal stop (a phonologically impermissable sequence), whereas T has both vowels short.

OTOMI-TL pl: -H a member of the group of people who speak Otomi (a language unrelated to Nahuatl) / de nación Otomí (C) [(2)Cf.4r].

ŌTZTIĀ vrefl,vt to become pregnant; to impregnate someone / embarazarse, concebir (la mujer) (X), engendrar (el hombre) (X) M and X have an intransitive verb 'to become pregnant' in addition to a transitive verb 'to cause someone to become pregnant,' while T has this as a reflexive verb 'to conceive.' M and X give the preterit as onotztic, but T has it as a regular -IĀ verb. X has Z for TZ. See ŌTZ-TLI.

ŌTZTĪLŌ nonact. ŌTZTIĀ

ŌTZTITOC pregnant / embarazada (Z) [(2)Zp.49,180]. This is not directly derived from ŌTZTIĀ but rather from M's related intransitive verb, which forms its preterit with -C. See ŌTZTIĀ.

ŌTZ-TLI pl: ŌŌTZTIN someone pregnant / preñada (M), encinta, embarazada (T) [(1)Tp.245, (2)Xp.61]. X has Z for TZ.

ŌY(A) vt; pret: ŌX to shell something (corn, peas, etc.) / desgranar (C) T has a reduplicated form that loses the Y and forms the preterit as a regular -OĀ verb, OHOĀ. T

also has lost the Y where ŌY(A) is bound
with the prefix TLA-, while C gives an
applicative form that also loses the Y,
ŌILIĀ.
ŌYALŌ nonact. ŌY(A)
***OZTETIĀ** vrefl to germinate, sprout /
germina, brota (T) [(1)Tp.157]. If this is the
correct analysis, this would seem to be
related in an idiosyncratic way involving
vowel length and consonant discrepancies
to ŌTZTIĀ 'to conceive, to become pregnant.' A possible alternate derivation is

from a reflexive verb *(I)ZTETIĀ having to
do with becoming powerful, taking command. See also TĒIZTI 'someone's fingernail' as a metaphor for 'child, offspring.'
See ŌTZTIĀ, (I)ZTE-TL.
ŌZTŌMĀN *place name* Oztoman
[(1)Cf.56v]. See ŌZTŌ-TL.
ŌZTŌMĒCA-TL *pl:* **-H** a type of merchant;
person from Oztoman / tratante o mercader (C) [(3)Cf.4r,56v]. See ŌZTŌ-TL.
ŌZTŌ-TL *pl:* **-MEH** cave / cueva o caverna
(M)

P

-PA This indicates movement toward or from a point and, with numerals, how many times; MĀCUĪLPA 'five times'< MĀCUĪL-LI 'five.'

PĀ *vt; pret:* **PAH** to dye something / teñir algo con tinta o colores de tintoreros (M) [(6)Cf.3ɪr,32v,64v,128v, (2)Zp.121,192]. M only gives the nonspecific object prefix as compatible with this verb, and it is exclusively so attested in C, but Z gives it as a full transitive verb. T has a synonymous full transitive verb TLAPALLŌTIĀ derived from TLAPAL-LI 'dye.'

PĀC(A) *vrefl,vt* to bathe; to wash, launder something / se lava, se asea (T), lavar algo o batanar paños o sayales (M) In a section on the preterits of verbs represented by MACA and TOCA which retain their stem-final vowels, C points out that PĀC(A) follows the rules of vowel-dropping but leaves it open that it may have an alternate preterit PĀCAC (Cf.3ɪv). M gives alternative preterits -PĀC and -PĀCAC for TLAHTLAPĀC(A) 'to wash something repeatedly.' This verb preserves the Proto-Uto-Aztecan initial *P which has been lost in Ā-TL 'water, liquid.'

PĀCALŌ altern. nonact. PĀC(A)

PĀCALTIĀ caus. PĀC(A)

PĀCCĀ happily, contentedly, pacificly, without struggle / alegremente (M), con quietud y sosiego (C), poco a poco, etc. (C) [(4)Cf.2v,70v,119v, (6)Tp.176]. See PĀQU(I).

PĀCCĀCOCH(I) to sleep to one's content / duerme a gusto (T) [(3)Tp.176]. See PĀCCĀ, COCH(I).

PĀCCĀCOCHĪHUA nonact. PĀC-CĀCOCH(I)

PĀCCĀCOCHĪTIĀ caus. PĀCCĀCOCH(I)

PĀCCĀPOLIHU(I) to be weak, faint, sickly / tiene flojera, se desmaya, tiene poca salud (T) [(3)Tp.176]. See PĀCCĀ, POLIHU(I).

PĀCCĀYŌHUIĀ *vt* to suffer something / lo sufre (dolor, enfermedad, etc.) (T) [(3)Tp.199]. See PĀCCĀ.

PĀCCĀYŌHUILIĀ applic. PĀCCĀYŌHUIĀ

PĀCCĀYŌHUĪLŌ nonact. PĀCCĀYŌHUIĀ

PACHAYOH-TLI *pl:* **-TIN** chayote, a spiney edible squash / chayote, pachayota (X) [(3)Xp.62]. See PACH-TLI, AYOH-TLI.

PACHIHU(I) to collapse, for a building to settle / hundirse algo así como la sepultura, el atabal, la casa, o la troja (M), hacer asiento el edificio (M) See PACHOĀ.

PACHIHU(I) to eat one's fill, to be satisfied / hartarse de vianda o estar satisfecho (M) [(3)Cf.85r,114r,124v, (3)Tp.116]. With YŌLLŌ this means to satisfy someone about some matter in doubt. This may be an extension of PACHIHU(I) 'to collapse, settle' in the sense that one is satisfied when one's meal has settled. See PACHOĀ.

PACHIHUIĀ *vt* to waylay or spy on someone / asechar o espiar a otro (M) [(1)Cf.127v]. This takes a direct object plus an oblique reflexive prefix. C contrasts this with PAHCHĪHUIĀ 'to benefit from medicine.'

PACHIHUĪHUA nonact. PACHIHU(I)

PACHIHUĪTIĀ caus. PACHIHU(I)

PACHILHUIĀ *vt* to press something down on someone / apretar o apesgar algo a otro (M) [(2)Bf.4v, (1)Cf.65v]. applic. PACHOĀ

PACHOĀ *vrefl,vt* to bow down; to press down on someone, to govern or control someone, or for a hen to sit on her eggs / abajarse, inclinando el cuerpo, o apretarse la barriga, etc. (M), regir o gobernar a otros, o apretar a alguna persona (M), gobernar o apretar algo, o estar la gallina sobre los huevos (M) There are two homophonous verbs PACHOĀ with homophonous derived forms. This one has to do with pressing down on something, while the other has to do with gathering something.

PACHOĀ *vrefl,vt* to be gathered; to reap something to oneself / se arrima, se acerca (T), lo arrima, lo acerca (T), aplicar o allegar algo junto a sí (M for construction with -TECH) [(6)Tp.154,195, (4)Zp.33,164,232]. As a transitive verb this occurs in construction with -TECH to express 'oneself' as the recipient. This may be an extension of PACHOĀ 'to press something' in that in gathering, one presses something to oneself.

PACHŌHUĀZHUIĀ *vrefl,vt* to comb, groom oneself; to comb, groom someone / se peina, se acepilla (T), lo peine, lo acepilla (T) [(6)Tp.154,195]. See PACHŌHUĀZ-TLI.

PACHŌHUĀZHUILIĀ applic. PACHŌHUĀZHUIĀ

PACHŌHUĀZHUĪLŌ nonact. PACHŌHUĀZHUIĀ

PACHŌHUĀZ-TLI *pl:* **-MEH** comb / peine (T) [(7)Tp.154,172,195]. T's notation is ambiguous between OHUA and ŌHUA, but by general rule the sequence here should be ŌHUA. See PACHOĀ.

PACHŌLŌ nonact. PACHOĀ

PACHŌNTIC something hairy, woolly / lanudo, velludo (T) [(2)Tp.166,172, (3)Zp.75,128,181]. See PACH-TLI.

PACH-TLI mistletoe, hay, refuse of plants / malojo o cierta yerba que se cria y cuelga en los árboles (M), heno (T) [(3)Tp.128,172, (10)Zp.44,85,87,148,149,152,179,181,224]. CUAUHPACH-TLI is Spanish moss. The sense common to the many uses of PACH-TLI is of worthlessness, parasitism, or refuse with respect to plants.

PĀCŌ altern. nonact. PĀC(A)

PĀCOHUA This nonactive form of PĀQU(I) 'to be happy' contrasts with PĀCALŌ ~ PĀCŌ, the alternative nonactive forms of PĀC(A) 'to bathe, wash.'

PĀCTIĀ *vt* to enjoy, take pleasure in something; to give someone pleasure / fruir de algo o tener mucho placer y contentamiento con alguna cosa (M), dar placer a otro (M) altern. caus. PĀQU(I)

PĀCTICAH to be happy and content / estar alegre y contento (M) [(1)Tp.176]. See PĀQU(I), the verb CĀ.

PĀCTILIĀ applic. PĀCTIĀ

PĀCTĪLŌ nonact. PĀCTIĀ

PĀCTOC someone, something healthy / sano, saludable, buena salud (Z) [(4)Zp.113,181, (2)Xp.62]. See PĀQU(I), the verb O.

PACYŌ-TL weft of cloth, fabric, web / trama (M) [(2)Zp.124,181]. This appears only in the Spanish-to-Nahuatl side of M. Z appears to have an intrusive vowel between the first and second syllables, PAQUIYŌ-TL.

PAHCHĪHUIĀ *vt* to avail oneself of something as medicine / me aprovecho de algo, como de medicina (C for first pers. sg. subject) [(1)Cf.127v, (1)Rp.119]. This takes a direct object plus an oblique reflexive object. C contrasts it with PACHIHUIĀ 'to spy on someone, to waylay someone.' See PAH-TLI, CHĪHU(A).

PAHCUALTIĀ *vrefl,vt* to take poison; to poison someone / se envenena (T), lo envenena (T) [(6)Tp.155,195]. See PAH-TLI, CUALTIĀ.

PAHCUALTILIĀ applic. PAHCUALTIĀ

PAHCUALTĪLŌ nonact. PAHCUALTIĀ

PAHHUIĀ *vrefl,vt* to take poison; to poison someone or something / se envenena (Z), lo envenena (Z), lo fumiga (T) [(3)Tp.195, (4)Zp.54,171,192]. M has *pauia* 'for a mother to chew food for her child.' See PAH-TLI, -HUIĀ.

PAHHUILIĀ applic. PAHHUIĀ

PAHHUĪLŌ nonact. PAHHUIĀ

PAHĪ *pret:* **PAHĪC** to drink medicine / tomar o beber purga o jarabe (M) [(1)Cf.62v]. See PAH-TLI, Ī.

PAHĪTIĀ *vrefl,vt* to take medicine or poison; to administer medicine or poison to someone / tomar o beber purga o ponzoña jarabe o cosa así (M), dar purga o ponzoña a otro (M) [(1)Cf.62v]. caus. PAHĪ

PAHMICTIĀ *vrefl,vt* to take poison; to poison someone / tomar ponzoña para matarse (M), matar con veneno (R) [(1)Rp.119]. caus. PAHMIQU(I)

PAHMIQU(I) *pret:* **-MIC** to die of poisoning / morir con veneno (R) [(2)Rp.119]. See PAH-TLI, MIQU(I).

PAHNAMACAC apothecary / boticario o vendedor de medicinas (M) [(1)Cf.51v]. See PAH-TLI, NAMACA.

PAHPĀC(A) *vrefl,vt* to bathe; to bathe someone, scrub something / lavarse (M), enjabonar ... a otra (M), fregar o lavar vasos, o quitar y limpiar heces (M) This contrasts with PĀPĀC(A) 'to insult someone' M combines them in a single entry. redup. PĀC(A)

PAHPACHOĀ *vt* to knead, pummel something / soba (Z) [(2)Zp.116,192]. redup. PACHOĀ

PAHPĀCŌ nonact. PAHPĀC(A)

PAHPĀCOHUA nonact. PAHPĀQU(I)

PAHPAHZOL *pl:* **-TIN** something, someone bothersome, uncomfortable, rough / travieso, molesto (T) [(3)Tp.165,172]. M has the transitive verb *papaçoloa* 'to snare, perplex, entangle something or to make impertinent remarks.' T has lost the glottal stop in the second syllable. See PAHZOLOĀ.

PAHPAHZOLTIC something or someone rough, bothersome / tentón, travieso (T) [(1)Tp.172]. T has lost the glottal stop in the second syllable. Z has PĀPAHZOLTIC 'something disordered, messed up.' See PAHPAHZOL.

PAHPĀL-LI something black, dark / negro, oscuro (K) [(3)Tp.136]. This is only attested in compounds with ĪX-TLI 'eye,' the construction having the sense 'blind.' Although TLAPAL-LI 'dye' has a short vowel in the second syllable, this item and the verb from which they are both derived have the corresponding vowel long. See PĀ, TLAPAL-LI.

PAHPALOĀ *vrefl,vt* to lick one's lips; to lick something, to touch something lightly / lamerse o relamerse (M), lamer algo (M), lamer a otro (M) redup. PALOĀ

PAHPĀLTIC something dark, black / negro, oscuro (K) [(1)Tp.136]. See PAHPĀL-LI.

-PAHPANI redup. -PANI

PAHPĀQU(I) to enjoy oneself, to take great pleasure / tomar placer y alegrarse (M) M also has transitive *papaqui* 'to repeatedly enjoy something' R consistently has PAHPAHQU(I) for PAHPĀQU(I) and its derivations. redup. PĀQU(I)

PAHPĀQUILIZ-TLI joy, rejoicing / allegría o gozo (M), recogio grande (R) [(1)Rp.120]. See PAHPĀQU(I).

PAHPĀQUILTIĀ *vt* to cause someone to be happy / alegro a otros (C for first pers. sg. subject) [(3)Cf.511, (1)Rp.120]. caus. PAHPĀQU(I)

PAHPĀT(I) to melt, dissolve, be consumed / deshacernos (C for first pers. plural subject) [(1)Cf.18v]. redup. PĀT(I)

PAHPATLA large leaf, frond / hoja grande (como el plátano), papatla (Z) [(3)Zp.68,93,181]. This seems to describe foliage rather than to refer to a specific plant. T has PĀPATLA. See PATLĀHUA.

PAHPATLĀHUAC something broad / ancho (T) [(1)Tp.237]. redup. PATLĀHUAC

PAHPĀTZ(I) to get creased, dented, bruised / se abolla (T) [(2)Tp.172]. See PĀTZIHU(I).

PAHPĀTZTIC something creased / abollado (T) [(1)Tp.172]. See PAHPĀTZ(I).

PAHTĒQUILIĀ *vt* to give medicine to someone / le pone medicina (T) [(3)Tp.195]. See PAH-TLI, TĒQUILIĀ.

PAHTĒQUILILIĀ applic. PAHTĒQUILIĀ

PAHTĒQUILĪLŌ nonact. PAHTĒQUILIĀ

PAHTI to recover one's health / convalecer y sanar el enfermo (M) The preterit of this, PAHTIC, contrasts with the preterit of PĀT(I) 'to melt, dissolve, be consumed,' which is PĀT. See PAH-TLI.

PAHTIĀ *vt* to cure someone, to restore someone to health, to restore or fix something / curar o sanar a otro (M), restaurar, adobar, o enmendar algo (M) See PAH-TLI.

PAHTĪHUA nonact. PAHTI

PAHTILIĀ applic. PAHTIĀ

PAHTILIZ-TLI cure, restoration of health / cura o sanidad (M), restablecimiento de la salud (R) [(1)Rp.120]. See PAHTIĀ.

PAHTĪLŌ nonact. PAHTIĀ

PAHTĪLTIĀ By general rule the vowel of the second syllable should be short here but is attested as long in both T and Z. caus. PAHTIĀ

PAHTIYOH something with medicinal properties / medicina eficaz (R) [(1)Rp.120]. This contrasts with PATIYOH 'something costly.' See PAH-TLI.

PAHTLĀLILIĀ *vrefl,vt* to recover with the aid of medicine; to cure someone, to administer medicine to someone / se medicina, se cura (T), lo cura, lo medi-

cina, lo sana (T) [(9)Tp.155,195,234]. See
PAH-TLI, TLĀLIĀ.
PAHTLĀLILILIĀ applic. PAHTLĀLILIĀ
PAHTLĀLILĪLŌ nonact. PAHTLĀLILIĀ
PAH-TLI medicine, potion / medicina
generalmente, emplasto, ungüento, etc.
(M) This often has the sense of 'poison' as well
as beneficial medicine.
PĀHUAC(I) vt; pret: **PĀHUAZ** to cook
something in a pot, to stew something /
cocer algo en olla o en cosa semejante (M)
[(7)Cf.46v,62v,64r]. The initial syllable
of this is probably cognate with Ā-TL
'water, liquid' and preserves the Proto-Uto-
Aztecan initial *P.
PĀHUAXILIĀ applic. PĀHUAC(I)
PĀHUAXĪLTIĀ By general rule the vowel of
the third syllable should be short but is
attested long in C. It is unmarked for
length in R. caus. PĀHUAC(I)
PAHUETZ(A) See PANHUETZ(I).
-PAHUĪC compound postposition to or from
a direction / hacia, a (K) The order of
elements appears to be optional. -HUĪCPA
also occurs with the same sense.
PAHZOLHUIĀ vt to be bothered by
something, someone / se lo molesta (T)
[(5)Tp.195,196,220]. applic. PAHZOLOĀ
PAHZOLHUILIĀ applic. PAHZOLHUIĀ
PAHZOLHUĪLŌ nonact. PAHZOLHUIĀ
PAHZOL-LI briarpatch / maraña (Z for
CUAUHPAHZOL) [(4)Tp.119,225,
(2)Zp.81,149]. M has paçoltic 'something
tangled, matted, thick.' In TEPAHZOL-LI
T and X have lost the internal glottal stop.
See PAHZOLOĀ.
PAHZOLOĀ vrefl,vt to bristle, to be
bothered, troubled; to snarl, entangle,
bother, or trouble someone / erizársele el
pelo al gato o al perro (M), se molesta, se
estorba (T), reburujar, enhetrar, o marañar
algo (M), lo molesta, lo estorba (T) This is
abundantly attested in T, where the glottal
stop has been lost. Z has it in reduplicated
form and with the glottal stop present.
PAHZOLŌLŌ nonact. PAHZOLOĀ
-PAL postposition for, by means of, for the
sake of / por, y mediante, como (C), por,
por medio de, cerca, con, etc. (S)
PALĀCTIC something rotten / podrido,
pudrido (Z) [(2)Zp.100,181]. By general rule

the vowel of the second syllable should be
short, but is attested as long in Z. See
PALĀN(I).
PALĀNALTIĀ vt to rot something / lo pudre
(T) [(4)Tp.172,195, (2)Zp.100,192]. M has
palaniltia with the same sense. caus.
PALĀN(I)
PALĀNALTILIĀ applic. PALĀNALTIĀ
PALĀNALTĪLŌ nonact. PALĀNALTIĀ
-PALĀNCĀ necessarily possessed form
one's unworthiness, one's sins, one's
rottenness / nuestra podredumbre (C for
first pers. plural possessor) [(1)Cf.49v]. See
PALĀNQUI.
PALĀNCĀNAC(A)-TL rotten flesh / carne
podrida (C) [(1)Cf.76v]. C fails to mark the
vowels of the second and third syllables
long. See PALĀNQUI, NAC(A)-TL.
PALĀNCĀPAH-TLI name of several medicinal plants / nombre de dos o tres plantas
medicinales (R) [(1)Rp.119]. R indicates the
glottal stop but not the long vowels. See
PALĀNQUI, PAH-TLI.
PALĀN(I) to rot / podrecerse (M)
PALĀNOHUA nonact. PALĀN(I)
PALĀNQUI something rotten / cosa podrida (M) [(1)Cf.76v, (1)Tp.172]. Z has
PALĒNQUI (once with the vowels of both
the first two syllables long) with the sense
'distillery of aguadiente.' This may be a
variant of PALĀNQUI and refer to the
fermentation process. See PALĀN(I).
PALAX-TLI something festering or rotten, a
wound, sore, or tumor / carne podrida (C
for nacapalaxtli), llaga, herida, tumor (S)
[(1)Cf.49v]. This implies an unattested verb
*PALAY(A) 'to fester, become infected.' See
PALĀN(I).
***PALAY(A)** See PALAX-TLI.
PĀLCHICHĪN(A) vt to suck something in,
to inhale / lo chupa (T) [(3)Tp.199]. See
CHICHĪN(A).
PĀLCHICHĪNALŌ nonact. PĀL-
CHICHĪN(A)
PĀLCHICHĪNILIĀ applic. PĀLCHICHĪN(A)
PALĒHUIĀ vrefl,vt to look after one's own
interests; to help someone, for something
to favor someone / favorecer y ayudar a mí
mismo (M), ayudar a otro (M), serme
favorable y provechosa alguna cosa (M
with first pers. sg. object)

PALĒHUĪHUA altern. nonact. PALĒHUIĀ
PALĒHUILIĀ applic. PALĒHUIĀ
PALĒHUĪLŌ altern. nonact. PALĒHUIĀ
PALHUIĀ applic. PALOĀ
PĀLIĀ applic. PĀ
PAL-LI black clay used in dying cloth / barro
negro para teñir ropa (M) This is indirectly
attested in TLAPAL-LI 'dye.' The verb PĀ
'to dye something' has a long vowel, while
the corresponding vowel of TLAPAL-LI is
short. By analogy, the vowel of PAL-LI
is probably also short, but T has
ĪXPAHPĀL-LI 'blind,' also derived from PĀ
and with the reflex of a long vowel. See PĀ.
PALOĀ vt to sip, taste something; to sop
bread in soup or gravy / gustar algún
manjar o mojar el pan en algún potaje o
salsa (M), probar alguna bebida o manjar
(C), lo sopea (T) The reduplicated form of
this, PAHPALOĀ, has among its senses 'to
lick something.'
PALŌLŌ nonact. PALOĀ
PALTI See PALTIY(A).
PALTIĀ vt to wet, soak something / lo
moja (T) [(3)Tp.195]. This contrasts with
intransitive PALTIY(A) 'to get wet, soaked.'
PALTIC something wet, soaked / cosa mojada (M) [(2)Tp.136,172, (2)Zp.85,181]. T
consistently has a short vowel in the initial
syllable and Z a long one. See PALTIY(A).
PALTILIĀ vrefl,vt to get wet, soaked; to wet,
soak something / se moja (T), mojar a otro
(M), mojar algo (M), se lo moja (T) applic.
PALTI
PALTILILIĀ applic. PALTILIĀ
PALTILĪLŌ nonact. PALTILIĀ
PALTĪLŌ nonact. PALTIĀ
PALTIY(A) pret: PALTIX ~ PALTIYAC to
get wet, soaked / mojarme (M for first pers.
sg. subject) T consistently has a short
vowel in the initial syllable and Z a long
one. The initial P is a survival of Proto-
Uto-Aztecan *P, and this item is related to
PĀC(A) 'to wash something,' PĀT(I) 'to
dissolve,' and Ā-TL 'water, liquid.' M also
has the variant palti.
PĀM(I)-TL possessed form: **-PĀN** flag, banner / bandera, estandarte (S) [(4)Cf.82v,93r,
(2)Tp.244]. A variant of this is PĀN-TLI,
which is homophonous with the word for
'row, wall.' The possessed form -PĀN
contrasts in vowel length with locative

-PAN 'at (surface or time).' M has this in
the compounded forms quachpamitl,
quachpantli and quachpanitl.
-PAMPA compound postposition for, for the
sake of, through, because of / por, por
amor, a causa de (S) See -PAN, -PA.
PAMPILOĀ vt to suspend, hang something / lo cuelga, lo suspende (Z)
[(4)Zp.30,119,192]. See -PAN, PILOĀ.
-PAN postposition on the surface of, for or
at a particular time / dentro, sobre, en,
durante, por (S) Z consistently has a long
vowel, while there is agreement across
other sources that the vowel is short.
PANAHAQU(I) to sink / hunde (Z)
[(1)Zp.181]. -PAN, AQU(I)
PANAHUIĀ vt to surpass, cross something,
to transport someone over water / vencer o
sobrepujar a otros, o ser mayor que ellos, o
pasar a los que van adelante caminando, o
pasar de la otra parte del río a alguno, en
barca, o acuestas (M), traspasar mandamiento o ley (M), lo cruza, los pasa (T) See
PANŌ.
PANAHUILIĀ applic. PANAHUIĀ
PANAHUĪLŌ nonact. PANAHUIĀ
PANCALAQU(I) to sink / se hunde, se sume
(Z) [(2)Zp.70,181]. See -PAN, CALAQU(I).
PANHUETZ(I) to climb upward, to scale the
heights, to attain honor / alcanzar honra
o encumbrar sierra o cuesta (M), encum-
bra, va cuesta arriba, va subiendo (T)
[(6)Tp.172,195, (1)Rp.119]. This has the
opposite sense from HUETZ(I) 'to fall.'
T has the variant form PAHUETZ(I).
M has entries for both forms. See -PAN,
HUETZ(I).
PANHUETZĪHUA nonact. PANHUETZ(I)
PANHUETZĪTIĀ vt to climb, scale some-
thing / lo sube, lo saca para arriba (T)
[(4)Tp.172,195]. caus. PANHUETZ(I)
PANHUETZĪTILIĀ applic. PAN-
HUETZĪTIĀ
PANHUETZĪTĪLŌ nonact. PAN-
HUETZĪTIĀ
PANI on top, on the outside or surface /
encima, o por de fuera, en la sobre haz (M)
See -PAN.
-PANI irregular verb; pret: **-PANIC** to go
well with / convenir, ir bien (S) [(3)Cf.123r].
This item takes possessive rather than sub-
ject prefixes and is always sg. in form.

PANILHUIĀ applic. PANOĀ

PANIYĀN place on top, at the summit / encima de él (Z) [(1)Bf.131, (2)Zp.50,181]. See PANI, -YĀN.

PANŌ *pret:* **PANŌC** to ford, cross a river / pasar el río a pie, o nadando, o en barca (M) Z has intransitive PANOĀ 'to go by, cross over' and transitive PANŌHUIĀ 'to cross something' X has PANOHUA but drops the HUA and adds C to form the preterit.

PANOĀ *vt* to transport something / lo lleve (T) [(3)Tp.214, (1)Rp.68]. Z has this as an intransitive verb 'to go by, cross over' and has PANŌHUIĀ as the corresponding transitive verb 'to cross something.' See PANO.

PANŌHUA nonact. PANŌ

PANŌLIZ-TLI crossing, habit or life style / travesía (S), costumbre (modo de vivir) (Z) [(2)Zp.35,160]. See PANŌ.

PANŌLŌ nonact. PANOĀ

PANŌLTIĀ *vt* to pass, convey something, someone from one place to another / lo pasa (T) This is abundantly attested in T and is also in Z. caus. PANŌ

PANŌLTIH *salutation directed to a stranger, someone not local* saludo entre el mexicano (el de pueblo) y la persona de afuera (T) [(2)Tp.173]. This is most commonly used in honorific form, PANŌLTIHTZINOH. See PANŌLTIĀ.

PANŌLTILIĀ applic. PANŌLTIĀ

PANŌLTĪLŌ nonact. PANŌLTIĀ

PANQUĪXTIĀ *vt* to make something clear, manifest / lo aclara, lo manifiesta (T) [(3)Tp.195]. T consistently has a short vowel in the first syllable of QUĪXTIĀ. By general rule the vowel should be long, and it is so marked in other constructions of this type from other sources. caus. PANQUĪZ(A)

PANQUĪZ(A) to rise, revive, bloom forth, issue / sube, mana, brota, resucita, encumbra (Z) [(6)Zp.51,81,109,118,181]. See -PAN, QUĪZ(A).

PANTIĀ *vt* to blame someone for something / se lo achaca (Z) [(2)Zp.5,192]. See -PAN.

PANTLĀLIĀ *vt* to mount something / lo monta (Z referring to a horse) [(2)Zp.86,192]. See -PAN, TLĀLIĀ.

PANTLAMŌTLA *vt* to hurl something from above / lo arroja (de arriba abajo), lo tira (de arriba abajo) (Z) [(2)Zp.14,192]. See -PAN, MŌTLA.

PĀN-TLI row, wall / muro, línea, hilera (S), grupo (Z) [(4)Zp.64,87,94,181]. This is also abundantly attested in T in TEPĀN-TLI 'stone wall.' PĀM(I)-TL 'flag, banner' has a variant form that is homophonous with this.

PANTZICUĪN(I) to leap down from above; for water to fall, cascade / brinca de arriba abajo (Z), salto de agua, cascada (Z) [(4)Zp.21,113,181]. See -PAN, TZICUĪN(I).

PĀPĀC(A) *vt* to ridicule, insult someone / baldonar una mujer a otra (M), lo escarnece (T) [(1)Cf.127v, (3)Tp.199]. C contrasts this with PAHPĀC(A) 'to scrub something.'

PĀPĀCALŌ nonact. PĀPĀC(A)

PAPACHCA to curdle, to separate / cortarse el almendrada o otra cosa semejante (M), trasmina (T) [(1)Tp.173]. In the Spanish-to-Nahuatl side T has PAHPACHCA.

PĀPACHOĀ *vt* to caress, massage someone / lo papacha (T) [(3)Tp.199]. See PACHOĀ.

PAPACTIC something greasy, sticky / pegajoso, se siente el cabello pegajoso, grasiento (T) [(1)Tp.173].

PĀPAHZOLOĀ *vt* to mess something up, to disorder something / marañar o enhetrar algo o mezclar pláticas impertinentes (M), desordena (Z) [(4)Zp.41,43,181]. T has two related forms with PAH instead of PĀ for the initial syllable. redup. PAHZOLOĀ

PĀPAHZOLTIC something disordered, messed up / desarreglado (Z) [(2)Zp.41,181]. T has PAHPAHZOLTIC 'something rough, bothersome.' See PĀPAHZOLOĀ.

PĀPĀLŌCUAHU(I)-TL tropical elm tree (Ulmus mexicana) / papalote (árbol) (Z) [(1)Zp.181]. See PĀPĀLŌ-TL, CUAHU(I)-TL.

PĀPĀLŌQUIL(I)-TL edible plant used for food and medicinally for rheumatism / papaloquelite (T) [(1)Tp.176, (2)Zp.93,181]. In T the third syllable has been elided. See PĀPĀLŌ-TL, QUIL(I)-TL.

PĀPĀLŌ-TL *pl: -MEH* butterfly / mariposa (M)

PĀPĀQUILIĀ applic. PĀPĀC(A)

PĀPATLA large leaf, frond / papatla (hoja grande), quequesque (T) [(1)Tp.176]. This seems to describe foliage rather than refer to a specific plant. Z has PAHPATLA. See PATLĀHU(A).

PAPATLACA to flutter, palpitate, tremble / revolar el ave, o temblar y tiritar de frío (M), revolotear el ave, temblar el corazón, etc. (C) [(1)Cf.75r]. See PATLĀN(I).

PAPATLATZ(A) *vrefl* for something to beat its wings / se pega con sus alas (Z) [(1)Zp.172]. Z gives this as though it were a preterit-as-present verb, although verbs of this type are otherwise regular. See PAPATLACA, PATLĀN(I).

PĀPĀYĪN(I) to pace nervously / anda por aquí y por allá, inquieto (Z) [(3)Zp.10,71,181]. In one of the attestations the vowels of the first two syllables are unmarked for length.

PĀQU(I) to be happy, to experience pleasure / alegrarse y tener placer (M) M also gives this as a transitive verb 'to enjoy something, to lead a happy life.' It contrasts with PAQUI 'now and then.'

PAQUI sometimes, now and then / a veces, de vez en cuando (T) [(1)Tp.173]. This contrasts with the verb PĀQU(I) 'to be happy.' R consistently has PAH for PĀ. See -PA.

PĀQUILIĀ applic. PĀQU(I)

PĀQUILIZMACA *vt* to give someone pleasure, enjoyment / le complace, le da gozo (T) [(3)Tp.199, (2)Zp.64,192]. See PĀQUILIZ-TLI, MACA.

PĀQUILIZ-TLI pleasure, happiness / gozo y alegría (M) See PĀQU(I).

PĀQUILTIĀ *vt* to make someone happy, to give someone pleasure / alegrar a otro (M), le alegro (C for first pers. sg. subject) [(1)Bf.1r, (1)Cf.61v, (1)Rp.33]. M gives this as synonymous with *papaquiltia*, which is only to be found in the Spanish-to-Nahuatl side of the dictionary. altern. caus. PĀQU(I)

PĀQUĪTIĀ *vt* to make someone happy, to give someone pleasure / lo alegra (T) [(4)Tp.172,199]. altern. caus. PĀQU(I)

PĀQUĪTILIĀ applic. PĀQUĪTIĀ

PĀQUĪTĪLŌ nonact. PĀQUĪTIĀ

PĀQUITTA *vrefl* to rejoice, to take delight / se regocija (Z) [(2)Zp.107,172]. See PĀQU(I), (I)TTA.

PATCA substitute; mistress or concubine / de parte de, por parte de, en lugar de (Z for -ĪXPATCA), su querida (del hombre casado)

(T) [(3)Tp.132, (2)Zp.77,94,158]. M has *patcayotia* 'to substitute for someone, to succeed someone in office.'

PĀT(I) to dissolve, melt / deshacerse la sal, nieve, o hielo y carámbano o hacerse agua y derretirse (M) [(5)Cf.3v,18v,127v, (2)Zp.41,182]. This verb preserves the Proto-Uto-Aztecan initial *P which has been lost in Ā-TL 'water, liquid.' C contrasts this with PAHTI 'to recover one's health.' See PĀTLA.

*PATI This is implied by PATIUH-TLI, and PATIYOH. It has to do with worth or price and may also be related to PATLA 'to exchange something'

PĀTILIĀ *vt* to dissolve, melt something for someone / se lo derrite (para otra persona), se lo revuelve (T) [(2)Cf.3v,64v, (3)Tp.199]. The applicative forms of intransitive PĀT(I) 'to dissolve' and transitive PĀTLA 'to dissolve something' appear to have fallen together in T. applic. PĀT(I)

PATILIĀ *vrefl,vt* to change; to misdirect someone, to change, exchange, or barter something with someone / se cambia (T), errar a otro en el camino (M), vender, trocar ... una cosa (S) [(2)Bf.5v, (3)Cf.3v,64v,114r, (6)Tp.155,160]. C contrasts this with PĀTILIĀ, the applicative form of PĀT(I) 'to dissolve.' S confuses this with PAHTILIĀ 'to cure someone' and PĀTILIĀ 'to dissolve something for someone.' applic. PATLA

PĀTILILIĀ applic. PĀTILIĀ

PĀTILĪLŌ nonact. PĀTILIĀ

PATIUH-TLI price, worth of something / paga, precio de lo que se vende, o soldada (M) This is almost always used in possessed form, and the UH of the second syllable is probably the possessive suffix absorbed into the stem. See PATI.

PATIYOH something costly / cosa que tiene precio o que vale tanto (M), precio alto, caro, costoso (Z) This is abundantly attested in T and Z. T has a variant with E for I. It contrasts with PAHTIYOH 'something with medicinal properties.' See PATI, -YOH.

PATIYOHTILIĀ applic. PATIYOHTIYA

PATIYOHTIYA to rise in price / se encarece (Z) [(2)Zp.50,182]. See PATIUH-TLI, PATIYOH.

PATIYŌHUA to rise in price, to be expensive / costar o valer tanto, o cosa que tiene precio (M), se encarece, sube el precio (T) [(1)Tp.173]. See PATIUH-TLI, PATIYOHTIYA.

PATIYŌTIĀ *vt* to raise the price of something / lo encarece (T) [(3)Tp.196]. See PATIUH-TLI, PATIYOHTIYA.

PATIYŌTILIĀ applic. PATIYŌTIĀ

PATIYŌTĪLŌ nonact. PATIYŌTIĀ

PATLA *vt* to change, exchange something / cambiar o trocar algo (M) M combines the glosses of this and PĀTLA 'to dissolve, melt something' in a single entry. C contrasts the two.

PĀTLA *vt* to dissolve, melt something / desleir o deshacer algo, como azúcar, sal, nieve, carambano, etc. (M) M combines the glosses of this and PATLA 'to change, exchange something' in a single entry. C contrasts the two. See PĀT(I).

PĀTLA *vrefl* to lose hope, to weary of waiting / enfadarse o cansarse de espera o desconfiar (M) [(1)Cf.127v, Rp.120]. If this is just a reflexive use of PĀTLA 'to dissolve, decompose, melt something,' it is considerably removed in sense. C contrasts both this and transitive PĀTLA with PATLA 'to change, exchange something.'

PATLACHIHU(I) to become flat, to collapse / se aplasta (T) [(1)Tp.173]. This is synonymous with the reflexive use of PATLACHOĀ. See PATLACHOĀ.

PATLACHILHUIĀ applic. PATLACHOĀ

PATLACHOĀ *vrefl,vt* to become flat, to collapse; to flatten, press, crush something / se aplasta (T); lo aplasta, lo prensa (T) This is abundantly attested but only in T, Z, and X.

PATLACHŌLŌ nonact. PATLACHOĀ

PATLACHTIC something broad / cosa ancha, así como mesa, viga, etc. (M) [(2)Tp.137,173]. See PATLACHOĀ.

PATLĀHUA to widen / ensancharse lo angosto y estrecho (M) M has intransitive and transitive *patlahua* and gives no preterit form for the transitive verb. It is likely that the preterit of this item is PATLĀHUAC, contrasting with the transitive preterit PATLĀUH, but this is not adequately attested.

PATLĀHU(A) *vt* to widen something /

ensanchar camino, mesa, lecho, o cosa semejante (M) See PATLĀHUA.

PATLĀHUAC something broad, wide / cosa ancha (M) See PATLĀHUA.

PATLĀHUALŌ nonact. PATLĀHU(A)

PATLĀHUILIĀ applic. PATLĀHU(A)

PATLALŌ nonact. PATLA

PĀTLALŌ nonact. PĀTLA

PATLĀNALTIĀ *vt* to make something fly / lo hace volar (T) [(4)Tp.173,196]. caus. PATLĀN(I)

PATLĀNALTILIĀ applic. PATLĀNALTIĀ

PATLĀNALTĪLŌ nonact. PATLĀNALTIĀ

PATLĀN(I) to fly / volar (M)

PATLĀNOHUA nonact. PATLĀN(I)

PATOĀ to throw dice, gamble, play patole / jugar a los dados, o a juego de fortuna (M) [(4)Cf.34v,65v]. M glosses *patolli* as 'dice' although it is actually a game played with colorín seeds.

PATOHUIĀ to gamble with someone / jugar con otro a los dados o a juego de fortuna (M) [(1)Cf.65v]. applic. PATOĀ

PATŌLŌ nonact. PATOĀ

PĀTZ- This element is a constituent of many constructions having to do with liquid; PĀTZCA 'to squeeze liquid out of something,' PĀTZIHU(I) 'for a swelling to subside,' PĀTZCALAQU(I) 'to sink,' PĀTZTŌCA 'to submerge something,' etc. This preserves the Proto-Uto-Aztecan *P that has been lost in Ā-TL 'water, liquid.'

PATZAC-TLI something mildewed, blighted, smutted / trigo, maíz, o cacao añublado o helado o cosas semejantes (M for *patzactic*) [(4)Cf.7v,125v]. M has *patzac* in a phrase referring to mildewed maize.

PĀTZCA *vrefl,vt* to express, give forth liquid; to squeeze liquid out of something, to wring out wet clothes / se exprime, se aprensa, se oprime (T), exprimir o sacar zumo de alguna cosa o torcer ropa mojada (M), exprimir cosa que da aqua o zumo (C) PĀTZCA is an element of CŌCOHPĀTZMICTIĀ and QUECHPĀTZCA 'to choke, strangle someone.' See PĀTZ-.

PĀTZCALACOHUA nonact. PĀTZCALAQU(I)

PĀTZCALAQU(I) to sink, submerge / se hunde, se sume, se sumerge (T) [(3)Tp.176]. See PĀTZ-, CALAQU(I).

PĀTZCALAQUIĀ *vt* to sink, submerge something / lo hunde (T) [(3)Tp.199]. See PĀTZCALAQU(I).
PĀTZCALAQUILIĀ applic. PĀTZCALAQUIĀ
PĀTZCALAQUĪLŌ nonact. PĀTZCALAQUIĀ
PĀTZCALŌ nonact. PĀTZCA
PĀTZCALTIĀ caus. PĀTZCA
PĀTZIHU(I) for something to get crushed, bruised, dented in, or for a swelling to subside / abollarse alguna cosa o deshincharse el encordio (M) [(1)Tp.176]. See PĀTZOĀ.
PĀTZILHUIĀ applic. PĀTZOĀ
PĀTZOĀ *vt* to bruise something, to mash fruit, to crush someone, to make light of what someone says or does / abollar algo, o ablandar fruta o cosa semejante entre los dedos (M), apretar a otro, o deshacer y apocar lo que otro dice o hace (M) See PĀTZ-.
PĀTZŌLŌ nonact. PĀTZOĀ
PĀTZQUILIĀ *vt* to squeeze, wring out excess liquid from something for someone / sacar, estrujar o exprimir zumo de alguna cosa para otro (M) applic. PĀTZCA
PĀTZQUILILIĀ applic. PĀTZQUILIĀ
PĀTZQUILĪLŌ nonact. PĀTZQUILIĀ
PĀTZTIC something dripping wet, something juicy; something bruised, mashed, soft / cosa abollada o cosa blanda, así como fruta muy madura (M), mojado (X) [(1)Tp.176, (3)Xp.63]. X has reduced TZT to TZ. See PĀTZ-, PĀTZOĀ.
PĀTZTŌCA *vrefl,vt* to submerge, sink; to submerge something, to sink something / se sume, se sumerge, se hunde (Z), lo hunde, lo sume, lo sumerge (Z) [(4)Zp.70,118,172,192]. See PĀTZ-, TŌCA.
PAYĀN(A) *vrefl,vt* for something to get pulverized; to break up, crumble, grind something / se muele (T), quebrantar terrones o desmenuzar algo (M)
PAYĀNALŌ nonact. PAYĀN(A)
PAYĀNILIĀ *vrefl,vt* to grind something for someone / se lo muele (T), se lo muele (el nixtamal a otra persona) (T) [(7)Tp.155,196]. applic. PAYĀN(A)
PAYĀNILILIĀ applic. PAYĀNILIĀ
PAYĀNILĪLŌ nonact. PAYĀNILIĀ

PĀYĀ-TL *pl:* **-MEH** woolly caterpillar or insect / cierto gusanillo velloso (M), moyote (T)
PAZOLOĀ See PAHZOLOĀ.
PĒCHILHUIĀ applic. PĒCHOĀ
PĒCHOĀ *vrefl,vt* to squat, crouch, bend over; to lower something, to bend something down / se encorva, se agacha (T), lo agacha, lo encorva (T) [(6)Tp.155,197]. Only T has PĒCHOĀ as an independent verb, and in T the first syllable contains the reflex of a long vowel. The other sources have items involving prostrating oneself with PECH as an element, and the vowel is consistently short.
PĒCHŌLŌ nonact. PĒCHOĀ
PECHTĒCA *vrefl* to bow low, to humble oneself / humillarse, inclinando mucho el cuerpo (M) [(1)Cf.66r]. This is abundantly attested in applicative form. See PĒCHOĀ, TĒCA.
PECHTĒQUILIĀ to bow down in reverence before someone / hacer a otro gran inclinación y reverencia (M) applic. PECHTĒCA
PECH-TLI sleeping mat, petate / petate de zacate (Z for ĀCAPECH-TLI) [(1)Zp.139]. This is not attested as a free element. It appears as prefixed TLAPECH-TLI, reduplicated PEHPECH-TLI, and in compounds. See PĒCHOĀ.
PEHPECH-TLI mattress, bedclothes; saddle, riding tack / colchón o ropa sobre que nos echamos a dormir (M), avío (de las bestias), silla, fuste (T) [(1)Tp.173, (2)Zp.17,160]. See PĒCHOĀ.
PEHPEN(A) *vt* to pick, choose someone, to gather, collect, or glean something / elegir o escoger a alguno (M), escoger algo o arrebañar y recoger lo esparcido por el suelo (M) This is abundantly attested with incorporated objects across all sources but especially in T where it appears with more than a dozen different harvestable or collectable items such, such as CUAUHPEHPEN(A) 'to gather firewood,' TLAŌLPEHPEN(A) 'to harvest maize,' XĪTOMAPEHPEN(A) 'to pick tomatoes,' etc.
PEHPENALŌ altern. nonact. PEHPEN(A)

PEHPENILIĀ applic. PEHPEN(A)
PEHPENŌ altern. nonact. PEHPEN(A)
PEHPETLA *vrefl,vt* to groom oneself; to
groom someone or to stroke, pat, or pet
something / peinarse (M), peinar a otro, o
halagarle trayéndole la mano sobre la
cabeza y asentándole el cabello con ella
(M), lo acaricia (animal), lo alisa (Z)
[(2)Zp.4,192]. See PETLĀN(I).
PEHPETZILHUIĀ applic. PEHPETZOĀ
PEHPETZOĀ *vt* to rid oneself entirely of
something / lo quita todo (T) [(3)Tp.196].
As a reduplicated form of PETZOĀ 'to
polish something, to make something
shine,' this seems to arrive at its meaning
in T by way of the sense of losing one's
hair or shaving one's head and hence
having a shiny bald pate. See PETZOĀ,
PEHPETZTIC.
PEHPETZŌLŌ nonact. PEHPETZOĀ
PEHPETZTIC something smooth,
shiny / cosa muy alisa que reluce (M)
[(2)Tp.123,173, (1)Xp.63]. M has *pepetzca*
'for silk or fine plumage to shimmer.'
redup. PETZTIC
PĒHU(A) to begin / tener comienzo o principio, o comenzar, o hacer algo (M) There is
a typographical error in M so that this
appears as a transitive verb with the nonspecific human object prefix TĒ-, but
M's preterit form in the entry is correct.
With the directional prefix ON- this verb
has the sense 'to go forth, depart, take
one's leave.'
PĒHU(A) *vt* to drive something ahead of
oneself, to vanquish one's enemies / lo
arrea (T), conquistar o vencer a los enemi-
gos (M) [(6)Tp.197,234, (2)Zp.14,192].
PĒHUALŌ nonact. PĒHU(A)
PĒHUALTIĀ *vt* to begin, initiate something
/ comenzar o principiar algo (M) caus.
PĒHU(A)
PĒHUALTILIĀ applic. PĒHUALTIĀ
PĒHUALTĪLŌ nonact. PĒHUALTIĀ
PĒHUILIĀ applic. PĒHU(A)
*****PEPECHIHU(I)** See PEPECHIUHTOC.
PEPECHILHUIĀ applic. PEPECHOĀ
PEPECHIUHTOC something affixed,
permanent / pegado, fijo (Z)
[(3)Zp.60,95,182]. This implies intransitive
*PEPECHIHU(I) 'to stick, to become

attached,' although only the transitive
PEPECHOĀ 'to affix something' is attested. See PEPECHOĀ, the verb O.
PEPECHOĀ *vt* to cover or patch something,
to affix something, to attach something
permanently / atapar o cerrar algún agujero
de pared a piedra lodo (M), lo pega, lo
suelda (T), lo pega (con goma), lo conecta
(Z)
PEPECHŌHUILIĀ *vt* to hook something up,
to harness something / lo engancha (Z)
[(2)Zp.51,192]. See PEPECHOĀ.
PEPECHŌLŌ nonact. PEPECHOĀ
PĒPĒHUALTIĀ *vt* to offend, injure someone
/ provocar a saña a otro (M), lo ofende (T),
lo injuria (T) [(4)Tp.197]. The sense of this
reduplicated form is at some distance from
the sense of unreduplicated PĒHUALTIĀ
'to initiate something.' redup. PĒHUALTIĀ
PĒPĒHUĀNI a type of ant / hormiga
pepehua (Z) [(2)Zp.68,182]. See
PĒPĒHUALTIĀ.
PEPETLACA to shimmer, to reflect light, to
be resplendent / resplandecer o relumbrar
(M) R has this with a glottal stop in the
first syllable, but there should not be
one, and C, T, and Z agree on this. See
PETLĀN(I).
PEPETLACHILIĀ applic. PEPETLATZ(A)
PEPETLAQUILIZ-TLI shimmer, gleam /
resplandor (M) [(1)Rp.121]. See
PEPETLACA.
PEPETLATZ(A) *vt* to sprinkle, to scatter
water / riega agua (T) [(3)Tp.196]. This
should share with PEPETLACA and
PETLĀN(I) the sense of 'to shimmer, to
reflect light.'
PEPETLATZALŌ nonact. PEPETLATZ(A)
PEPETŌN(I) redup. PETŌN(I)
PĒPETZOĀ *vt* to pat or stroke something /
lo acaricia (el perro, etc.) (T) [(3)Tp.197].
redup. PETZOĀ
PĒPETZOLHUIĀ applic. PĒPETZOĀ
PĒPETZŌLŌ nonact. PĒPETZOĀ
PĒPETZTOLOĀ *vt* to lap or slurp something
/ beber a lengüetadas (K) [(1)Bf.11v]. redup.
PETZTOLOĀ
PEPEYACA to spill, spread, scatter / des-
parrama (Z) [(2)Zp.44,182]. M has *pepeyoca*
'for water or fields to shine in the light of
the sun or moon.' This is probably the

same verb with the sense referring to the scattering of light.

PEPEYOCHILIĀ applic. PEPEYOTZ(A)

PEPEYOTZ(A) *vt* to give someone the shivers, to make someone's skin crawl / le hace cosquillas, siente andar algo en la piel (T) [(3)Tp.196]. This should relate in some regular way to M's *pepeyoca* 'for something to shimmer with reflected light.'

PETLĀCAL-LI woven wicker hamper / petaca a manera de arca que hacen de cañas tejidas (M) [(2)Bf.7r,9r, (1)Cf.113v]. The vowel of the second syllable is marked long in all attestations. Possibly this is a compound of PETL(A)-TL 'woven mat' and ĀCAL-LI 'boat'< Ā-TL 'water' and CAL-LI 'structure' and partially analogous to CUAUHCAL-LI 'cage.'

PETLĀHU(A) *vrefl, vt* to disrobe; to undress someone, to uncover something, to polish or burnish something / despojarme o desnudarme (M), despojar o desnudar a otro (M), bruñir, lucir, o acicalar algo (M) This makes the same connection between 'bare' and 'shiny' that PEHPETZOĀ and PEHPETZTIC do. See PETLĀN(I).

PETLAHUAH possessor of mats, petates / dueño de esteras [(3)Cf.56r]. In one of three attestations C marks the vowel of the second syllable long. See PETL(A)-TL.

PETLAHUAHCĀHUAH master of the possessors of mats, petates / señor de los dueños de las esteras y petates (C) [(1)Cf.56r]. See PETLAHUAH.

PETLĀHUALŌ nonact. PETLĀHU(A)

PETLĀHUILIĀ *vt* to undress someone, to uncover something for someone / se lo descubre (T) [(4)Tp.196]. applic. PETLĀHU(A)

PETLĀHUILILIĀ applic. PETLĀHUILIĀ

PETLĀHUILĪLŌ nonact. PETLĀHUILIĀ

PETLĀN(I) for something to scatter, glisten, reflect / derramarse alguna cosa líquida (M), derramarse algo y relumbrar (C), brilla, reluce, relumbra (T)

PETLĀNIĀ to scatter or sprinkle something / derramar cosa líquida o acicalar y lucir algo (M), lo tira, lo riega (T) [(3)Tp.196]. See PETLĀN(I).

PETLĀNILIĀ applic. PETLĀNIĀ

PETLĀNĪLŌ nonact. PETLĀNIĀ

PETL(A)-TL *pl:* **-MEH** woven mat, petate / estera generalmente (M), petate (T)

PETLAZOL-LI *pl:* **-TIN** centipede / ciempiés (T) [(1)Tp.173]. M has *petlaçolcoatl* with the same sense. It is possible that the absolutive suffix here should be -IN, since T's notation is ambiguous for -LI and -IN with stems ending in L.

PETLAZŌYĀ-TL petate woven of palm fronds / petates de palma (T) [(1)Tp.173]. See PETL(A)-TL, ZŌYĀ-TL.

PETŌNALTIĀ caus. PETŌN(I)

PETŌN(I) to dislocate, to move out of place / desencasarse algún hueso del cuerpo o cosa semejante, o salir fuera a la pared los canes de madera o el tablamento, etc. (M) [(1)Cf.94r, (4)Tp.136,173]. T gives as a nonactive form of this PETŌNĪLŌ with the reflex of a long vowel in the third syllable, which is clearly wrong.

PETZALHUIĀ altern. applic. PETZOĀ

PETZALHUILIĀ applic. PETZALHUIĀ

PETZALHUĪLŌ nonact. PETZALHUIĀ

PETZCAHUI to slip, slide / se resbala (T) [(1)Tp.173]. T gives the preterit of this as PETZCAHUIC even though it pairs with transitive PETZCOĀ as -HU(I) verbs in general pair with -OĀ verbs. See PETZCOĀ.

PETZCALHUIĀ applic. PETZCOĀ

PETZCOĀ *vrefl,vt* to slip, slide; to slide something along / resbalar, deslizarse, o descabullirse de entre otros (M), se resbala (T), lo resbala (T) This seems to be related to PETZOĀ 'to make something smooth, to polish something.'

PETZCŌHUĪX-IN *pl:* **-MEH** a type of venomous lizard / aspia, tipo de lagartija muy brillosa y venenosa (X) [(3)Xp.64]. See PETZCOĀ, CUĪX-IN.

PETZCŌLŌ nonact. PETZCOĀ

PETZIHU(I) to be smooth, slippery, shiny / pararse muy lucio lo bruñido o acicalado (M), se resbala, se alisa (T) [(2)Tp.173,248]. See PETZOĀ.

PETZOĀ *vt* to polish, burnish something, to make something smooth and shiny / acicalar, bruñir, o lucir algo (M) [(9)Tp.148]. See PETZ-TLI.

PETZOLHUIĀ altern. applic. PETZOĀ
PETZŌLŌ nonact. PETZOĀ
PETZTIC something smooth, shiny, slippery / pulido, brillante, reluciente, barnizado, fino, liso (S) [(2)Tp.136, (1)Xp.63]. X has reduced TZT to ZT. See PETZIHU(I).
PETZ-TLI *pl:* **-MEH** pyrite, material used in making mirrors / piedra de espejos (M) [(1)Tp.225]. See PETZOĀ.
PETZTOLHUIĀ applic. PETZTOLOĀ
PETZTOLOĀ *vt* to swallow something soft, slippery / lo traga (cosa lisa) (T) [(3)Tp.197, (2)Zp.124,192]. See PETZOĀ, TOLOĀ.
PETZTOLŌLŌ nonact. PETZTOLOĀ
PEXŌN(I) to fill up with liquid / henchirse o rebosar la medida de cosa líquida (M), llena (Z) [(2)Zp.78,182].
PEXŌNTIĀ *vt* to fill something up with liquid / henchir mucho alguna medida de cosas líquidas (M), lo llena (Z) [(4)Zp.71,78,189,192]. caus. PEXŌN(I)
PEXŌNTOC something full / lleno (Z) [(2)Zp.78,182]. See PEXŌN(I), the verb O.
PEYĀHU(I) to slip / resbalarse (X) [(3)Xp.64].
PEYO-TL mescal cactus (Lophophora lewinii, Lophophora williamsii), the button-shaped segments of which are consumed as an intoxicant / cierta planta medicinal de que abusan para la superstición (R) [(1)Rp.121]. This appears in R without diacritics. M has *peyutl* 'cocoon.'
PĒZOH-TLI *pl:* **-TIN** ~ **-MEH** badger / cierto animalejo (M), tejón (T,Z) [(1)Tp.173, (2)Zp.120,182, (4)Xp.63].
PĪ *vt; pret:* **PĪC** to gather plants without disturbing the roots, to pluck something / pelar o sacar de raíz los pelos o coger yerbas sin arrancar las raíces de las (M) The evidence for the vowel of this verb being long is circumstantial. The verb is abundantly attested in C but not in the modern sources, which have only CUI and PEHPEN(A). C does not mark the vowel long in several attestations of the preterit but does consistently mark it long in causative PĪLTIĀ. This is weak evidence, because there is some variation over verbs in general between short and lengthened vowels before -LTIĀ. For CUI there is more evidence of a short stem vowel, but its

attested causative is nonetheless CUĪLTIĀ. In the attested applicative form of reduplicated PIHPĪ T has the reflex of a short vowel before -LIĀ. See PIY(A), PĪQU(I).
PĪCCA-TL wrapping / envoltura (K) [(4)Zp.63,65,157,159]. This is attested in the possessed forms -MĀPĪCCA 'glove' and -CUĀPĪCCA 'bonnet.' M has *picca*, also in possessed form, referring to the vulva, and S gives *piccatl* as the absolutive form. S is the only authority for the absolutive form. The attestations from the sources for this dictionary are compatible with this being the possessed form of PĪCQUI 'something wrapped up.' See PĪQU(I).
PĪCHAQUIĀ *vrefl,vt* to humble oneself; to humble someone, to bring someone low / es humilde, se humilla (T), lo humilla (T) [(6)Tp.155,197]. See PĒCHOĀ, AQUIĀ.
PĪCHAQUĪHUA This is the nonactive form attested for the transitive use of PĪCHAQUIĀ.
PĪCHAQUILIĀ applic. PĪCHAQUIĀ
PĪCHAQUĪLŌ This is the nonactive form attested for the reflexive use of PĪCHAQUIĀ.
PĪCHĒHUA-TL skin, complexion / cutis (Z) [(2)Zp.37,182]. Z also has PĪTZĒHUA-TL. See ĒHUA-TL.
PĪCHILIĀ *vt* to blow or snort at someone / se lo sopla (T) This is abundantly attested in T. applic. PĪTZ(A)
PĪCHILILIĀ applic. PĪCHILIĀ
PĪCHILĪLŌ nonact. PĪCHILIĀ
PICICTIC someone fat, stout / gordo (T) [(1)Tp.174].
PICĪLIHU(I) for something to get worn down, diminished, ground fine / hacerse menudo lo que era grueso y redondo (M) This is implied by PICĪLTIC.
PICĪLOĀ *vt* to wear something down, to make large, round things smaller, to grind something fine / desbastar o achicar cosas grandes y redondas (M) This is implied by PICĪLTIC. X has TLAPICĪLOĀ 'to rain' and a derived noun meaning '(rain)drop.'
PICĪLTIC something small or fine, something ground down to small size / cosas menudas así como chinas o aljofar (M),

tejido apretado (de tela, ayate, zaranda, etc.) (T), picado, pequeño (Z) [(2)Tp.174, (3)Zp.96,98,183]. Z also has the shortened form PICĪL referring to gravel. This implies PICĪLOĀ and PICĪLIHU(I).

PĪCQUI something wrapped up, firm, solid / cosa maciza (M) This is indirectly attested in MĀPĪCTŌN 'handful,' MĀPĪCCA-TL 'glove,' and -CUĀPĪCCA 'bonnet.' In the sources for this dictionary and in M there is only possessed -PĪCCA, which would seem to be the possessed form of this, but S has *piccatl* as well as *picqui*, assuming two lexical items distinct in their absolutive forms. See PĪQU(I).

PIHPĪ *vt* to pluck, gather something in quantity / coger muchas y varias (C) This reduplicated form is the distributive of PĪ 'to pluck, gather something' In T it is attested with incorporated objects referring to hair and beard, hence 'to cut one's hair' and 'to shave.' Although there is some evidence that PĪ has a long stem vowel, the attested applicative form in T has a short vowel before -LIĀ and -TZĪNOĀ. redup. PĪ

PIHPĪHUA nonact. PIHPĪ
PIHPILIĀ applic. PIHPĪ
PIHPĪLTIĀ caus. PIHPĪ

PIHPĪTZCUA *vt* for something to make one's skin itch / le cosquillea la piel (p. ej. cuando ha andado en la yerba o en la milpa, etc.) (T) [(3)Tp.197]. redup. PĪTZCUA

PIHPĪTZCUALŌ nonact. PIHPĪTZCUA
PIHPĪTZCUALTIĀ caus. PIHPĪTZCUA

PIHPIY(A) *vt; pret:* PIHPIX to spy on someone, to lurk in wait for someone / espiar o acechar a otro (M) [(2)Zp.56,193]. Z has PIHPĪX as the name of a thrush (tordo real). If this is derived from the verb, then the preterit form of the verb is also PIHPĪX. See PIY(A) for more about the alternation of long and short I in preterits ending in X. redup. PIY(A)

PIH-TLI older sister (from the point of view of a woman), lady's maid / hermana mayor o dama o criada que acompaña a su señora (M) [(1)Bf.111, (2)Cf.83v]. C comments that the honorific form -PIHTICĀTZIN is more affectionate than simple -PIHTZIN.

PĪHUA nonact. PĪ

PĪHUIC something extra given over and above what is paid for / lo que se da más de lo pesado cuando uno está comprando (T) [(1)Tp.173]. TLAPĪHUILIĀ

-PIL *necessarily possessed form* one's offspring, son or daughter / hijo, hija (S) To mean the offspring of someone, this is used in possessed form, and the plural is necessarily suffixed with plural possessive -HUĀN. Unlike PIL-LI 'noble person,' this plural does not reduplicate, NOPILHUĀN 'my children' contrasts with NOPĪPILHUĀN ~ NOPĪPILLŌHUĀN 'my lords,' the latter forms rather unlikely without the honorific -TZIN. Honorific -TZIN is generally but not universally used with 'offspring' too, *nopiltzin* 'my child' (Cf.55v). Although PIL with the sense of child rarely occurs in absolutive form, the diminutives PILTŌN-TLI and PILTZIN-TLI do, and in these the plural stem does reduplicate in just the same form as PIL-LI 'noble person,' PĪPILTZITZINTIN. See PIL-LI.

-PĪL *diminutive compounding element; pl:* -PIPĪL C gives the difficult example of PILPĪL 'little boy,' the plural of which (to be found in M as well) is PĪPILPIPĪL, with reduplication of both the stem and the diminutive element. Since PIL 'child' has a short vowel in the stem and a long vowel in its reduplication, while diminutive -PĪL has a long vowel with short-vowel reduplication, this leads to mirrored relative vowel length (long-short, short-long) which has been confused in the 1892 reprinting of Carochi. It is correct in the original printing.

PILĀHUILTIĀ to look after children, to play with a child / hace por cuidar a las criaturas, juega con el niño (T) [(3)Tp.174]. See -PIL, ĀHUILTIĀ.

PILĀHUILTILIĀ applic. PILĀHUILTIĀ
PILĀHUILTĪLŌ nonact. PILĀHUILTIĀ

PILALACCONĒ-TL *pl:* PILALACCŌCONEH little boy / niñito, niño, chamaquito, chamaco, muchachito (T) [(1)Tp.174]. T has the possessed form -PĪPILANCONĒ and the plural possessed form -PĪPILANCŌCONĒHUĀN. See PILALAC-TLI, CONĒ-TL.

PILALAC-TLI *pl:* **-MEH** boy / muchacho, chamaco (T) [(2)Tp.174]. T has the variants PILAN- and PĪPILAN- in compounds. See -PIL.

PILCA *preterit-as-present verb; pret:* **PIL-CAC** to be hanging / estar colgado o ahorcado (M) See PILOĀ.

PILCATICAH to be hung up / está colgado (T) [(1)Tp.174]. M has *pilcaticac* with the same sense. See PILCA, the verb CĀ.

PILCATOC something hung up / colgado (Z) [(5)Zp.6,30,71,163,182]. In three of the attestations Z marks the vowel of the initial syllable long, but it should not be. See PILCA, the verb O.

PILCHĪHU(A) *vt* to commit a sin / pecar o hacer algún defecto (M) [(1)Bf.9v]. See CHĪHU(A).

PILHUAH one who has children / persona que tiene hijos (M) See -PIL.

PILHUAHTIĀ *vrefl,vt* to conceive children; to provide someone with children / hacer hijos o engendrarlos (M), le engendra hijos (T) [(3)Tp.197]. See PILHUAH.

PILHUAHTILIĀ applic. PILHUAHTIĀ

PILHUAHTĪLŌ nonact. PILHUAHTIĀ

PILHUĒHUEHCA someone who has children separated by long intervals / tiene hijos de vez en cuando, no continuamente (T) [(1)Tp.174]. See -PIL, HUĒHUEHCA.

PILHUIĀ *vt* to hang something up for someone / colgar algo a otro de algún palo, etc. (M) applic. PILOĀ

PILĪN(I) to wither, to deflate / se marchita, se deshincha (T) [(1)Tp.174].

PILĪNQUI something wrinkled, withered / arrugado, marchitado (T) [(1)Tp.174]. M has *pilinqui* 'someone bushy-haired.' See PILĪN(I).

PILIZOL *pl:* **-TIN** blanket, sarape / cobija, sarape (T) [(1)Tp.174].

PIL-LI *pl:* **PĪPILTIN;** *possessed form:* **-PILLŌ** noble person / caballero o noble persona (M), los cortesanos del Rey (C for possessed form) There is a variation in vowel length across sources. C and T consistently have a short vowel in the stem; Z consistently has a long one. B in general has the vowel unmarked for length or specifically marks it short but commonly marks it long when the vowel of an

adjacent syllable is long. This is not consistent; B has both *cihuāpīpīltin* and *cihuāpīpíltin*. B marks the corresponding vowel long in TĒCPILLŌ-TL 'nobility' and TĒCPILCAL-LI 'court.' (The same assimilation appears when B marks the vowel of the last syllable of CUITLAPIL-LI 'tail' short when followed by -LI but long when followed by plural possessive -HUĀN.) The honorific vocative form has two full honorific -TZIN's, NOPILTZINTZINE 'my noble person,' etc. This best makes sense if thought of as the iterative addition of -TZINE to PILTZIN; it is not reduplication, which would give -TZITZINE. PIL-LI is neutral with respect to sex or masculine by default. 'Lady' has the modified form CIHUĀPIL-LI. M has *nopilo* 'my nephew (from the point of view of a woman),' which is probably a different and contrasting item, since both times that it occurs in M it is spelled with a single *l*. See -PIL.

-PIL-LI This component element of CUITLAPIL-LI 'tail,' NENEPIL-LI 'tongue,' MAHPIL-LI 'finger,' and (I)CXOPIL-LI 'toe' appears to have the general sense 'appendage,' hence it is not unreasonable to associate it in sense with -PIL 'offspring.' On the other hand, it can also be reasonably connected with PILOĀ 'to hang.' The vowel of the stem is short across sources except in Z where PIL is always long, whether as 'lord,' 'child,' 'appendage,' or the diminutive compounding element. Z also has this compounded with TĒN-TLI 'beak' to mean 'stinger' and with TZON-TLI 'head' to mean 'cold, respiratory infection.' Despite the affinity of meaning, it is apparently not a component of TŌPĪL-LI 'staff, rod' or METLAPĪL-LI 'rolling pin,' since it differs in vowel length.

PILLŌ-TL nobility / nobleza tal (M) [(4)Cf.81v]. M also gives 'childishness,' which is derived from -PIL 'child.' See PIL-LI, -YŌ.

PILOĀ *vrefl,vt* to hang oneself; to hang something up, to hang someone / ahorcarse o colgarse (M), ahorcar o colgar a otro (M), colgar alguna cosa de alto, así como ropa, etc. (M) This contrasts with PĪLOĀ 'to make something thinner.'

PĪLOĀ *vt* to make something thinner, to taper something / adelgazar algo (C) [(4)Cf.127v]. This contrasts with PILOĀ 'to hang something up.'

PILŌHUILIĀ *vt* to connect something, to hook something up / lo conecta, lo engancha (Z) [(3)Zp.32,51,193]. Only one of the three attestations marks the O long. See PILOĀ.

PILŌL-LI pitcher / cántaro (C) [(1)Cf.105r, (1)Tp.247]. See PILOĀ.

PILŌLŌ nonact. PILOĀ

-PILPĒHUAYĀN *necessarily possessed form* childhood / niñez (C) [(1)Cf.100r]. See -PIL, PĒHU(A), -YĀN.

PILQUĪTIĀ caus. PILCA

PĪLTIĀ caus. PĪ

PILTIC something, someone noble / hombre gentil (M), cosa ahidalgada y noble (C) [(3)Cf.127v]. This contrasts with PĪLTIC 'something thin or tapered to a point.' See PIL-LI.

PĪLTIC something thin or tapered to a point / hilo adelgazado (C) [(1)Cf.127v, (1)Rp.122]. This contrasts with PILTIC 'something or someone noble.' See PĪLOĀ.

-PILTIYĀN *necessarily possessed form* one's childhood / mi niñez o el tiempo de mi niñez (R for first pers. sg. possessor) [(1)Rp.43]. This implies *PILTI 'to be a child.' R fails to mark the vowel of the final syllable long. See -PIL, -YĀN.

PILTŌN-TLI child / niño o niña, muchacho o muchacha (M) See -PIL.

PILTZIN-TLI child / niño o niña (M) See -PIL.

PĪNACA-TL large nonflying, reddish beetle / escarabajo grande y bermejo que no vuela (M) [(1)Cf.122v].

PĪNĀHUA to be ashamed / tener vergüenza (M) T has preterit PĪNĀUH rather than PĪNĀHUAC. M also has transitive *pinahua* 'to be embarrassed to appear or to do something before others' with the same preterit form as T's intransitive.

PĪNĀHUAC, embarrassed, bashful / vergonzoso, tímido (Z) [(3)Zp.122,128,182]. See PĪNĀHUA, PĪNĀUHQUI.

PĪNĀHUALIZ-TLI shame, embarrassment / vergüenza (M) [(1)Tp.174, (2)Zp.129,182]. See PĪNĀHUA.

PĪNĀHUALŌ nonact. PĪNĀHUA

PĪNĀHUALTIĀ caus. PĪNĀHUA

PĪNĀHUIĀ *vt* to ridicule, embarrass someone / le hace burla, se burla de uno (T) [(3)Tp.197]. See PĪNĀHUA.

PĪNĀHUILIĀ applic. PĪNĀHUIĀ

PĪNĀHUĪLŌ nonact. PĪNĀHUIĀ

PĪNĀHUIZ-TLI shame, embarrassment / vergüenza (M) [(1)Bf.9v]. See PĪNĀHUA.

PĪNĀUHQUI *pl:* PIHPĪNĀUHQUI someone embarrassed, timid / vergonzoso (M) [(2)Tp.174]. See PĪNĀHUA.

PĪNĀUHTIĀ *vrefl,vt* to be ashamed; to shame or insult someone / tiene vergüenza, se avergüenza (T), avergonzar o afrentar a otro (M) caus. PĪNĀHUA.

PĪNĀUHTILIĀ applic. PĪNĀUHTIĀ

PĪNĀUHTĪLŌ nonact. PĪNĀUHTIĀ

PINOLĪYŌ sheep tick / garrapata chiquita, coloradilla (Z) [(3)Zp.30,62,182]. Because of word-final shortening, the length of the final vowel is ambiguous. This seems to be related to PINOL-LI 'flour.'

PINOL-LI flour, something ground / la harina de maíz y chía antes que la deslian (M), sal molida (C for IZTAPINOL-LI) [(2)Cf.60v, (2)Xp.64].

PINTETIC something small, pointed / chico (T) [(1)Tp.137]. See PINTIC.

PINTIC something small, pointed / puntiagudo (T) [(2)Tp.123,174]. S has *pinton* 'something very small.' See PĪPINOĀ, XIPINTIC.

PIPĪCTIC something tough, hard, sinewy / correoso, duro (un palo que se raja con trabajo) (T) [(1)Tp.174, (4)Zp.48,183,232]. Z marks the vowel of the second syllable long, but T marks it short. See PĪCQUI.

PIPIHYĀC something with a strong scent / perfumado (T), huele a orines (T for ĀXĪXPIPIHYĀC) [(2)Tp.171]. M has *pipiyaliztli* 'underarm odor.' T has YOC for YĀC. See IHYĀC.

PĪPILANCONĒ-TL *pl:* PĪPILANCŌCONEH small child, little boy / niñito, chamaco (T) [(2)Tp.133,174]. See PILALACCONĒ-TL.

PĪPILLŌ-TL childishness / niñería (M) [(1)Bf.1v]. See PILLŌ-TL, -PIL.

PĪPĪNA *vt* to suck on something / comer y chupar cañas (M) [(1)Zp.39]

PĪPINALHUIĀ applic. PĪPINOĀ

PĪPINOĀ *vt* to draw something out into a point, to sharpen something / le saca punta (T) [(3)Tp.197].

PĪPINŌLŌ nonact. PĪPINOĀ

PIPĪTZ(A) *vt* to blow on something with bellows, to blow on something repeatedly / follar o soplar muchas veces (M) [(2)Zp.117,193]. redup. PĪTZ(A)

PĪPITZATZIN something drawn into a point, something or someone thin, narrow / delgado (hombre), estrecho, angosto (T) [(2)Tp.123,174]. See PITZA.

PIPITZCA to whinny, shriek, squeak / brama el ciervo, relinchar el caballo, o chillar el ratón (M), rechina (T) [(1)Tp.174].

PIPITZOĀ *vt* to suck or gnaw something / chupar o roer algo (M) T specifically marks the vowel of the reduplicated syllable short. redup. PITZOĀ

PĪPIXAHU(I) to drizzle or to snow / lloviznar, cerner, o caer nieve (M) [(2)Bf.6v]. M also has unreduplicated *pixaui* with the same sense.

PĪQU(I) *vt* to invent or fabricate something, to wrap something up or enclose something / forgicar o fingir e inventar alguna cosa o mentir a sabiendas, o envolver tamales en hojas cuando los hacen, o cosa semejante (M), lo envuelve (Z) See PĪ.

PĪQUĪHUA nonact. PĪQU(I)

PĪQUILIĀ applic. PĪQU(I)

PĪQUILŌNI wrapper, container / envoltura (K) This is attested in CUĀPĪQUILŌNI 'bonnet' and TLAXCALPĪQUILŌNI 'napkin for wrapping tortillas.' See PĪQU(I).

PĪTZ(A) *vrefl,vt* to huff and puff with anger; to blow on something, to play a wind instrument / pararse bermejo o encenderse de enojo (M), tañer o tocar trompeta, chirimía, flauta o otro instrumento semejante o soplar el fuego (M) This contrasts with PITZA 'something thin, tough.'

PITZA something thin, tough / flaco (T for CUAUHPITZA) [(5)Tp.119,174]. This contrasts with the transitive verb PĪTZ(A) 'to blow on something.' See PITZĀHU(I).

PITZAC-TLI something thin and long / cosa delgada y larga así como vara, soga, o cosas semejantes (M) Z marks the vowel of the first syllable long, but it is short elsewhere. See PITZĀHUAC.

PĪTZAHTZI to talk in a high, thin voice, to squeak / habla en voz delgadita, chilla (garganta, puerta, etc.) [(3)Tp.174]. Despite the discrepancy in vowel length, this appears to be related to PIPITZCA 'to

whinny, shriek, squeak.' See PĪTZ(A), TZAHTZI.

PĪTZAHTZĪHUA nonact. PĪTZAHTZI

PĪTZAHTZĪTIĀ caus. PĪTZAHTZI

PITZĀHUA to get thin / pararse delgado y flaco (M) This is implied by PITZĀHUAC and is synonymous with PITZĀHU(I).

PITZĀHU(A) *vt* to make something thin, to cut boards or lengths of rope / adelgazar palos o sogas (M) This is implied by PITZĀHUAC and PITZĀHU(I). M combines this gloss in one entry with another referring to a high-pitched voice, which is derived from PĪTZ(A).

PITZĀHUAC something thin, slender / cosa delgada, así como varas, pilares, columnas, sogares, y cosas largas y rollizas, o el camino, el viento delgado y sutil, los frijoles pequeños, lentejas, o cosas semejantes (M) This implies intransitive PITZĀHUA 'to get thin' and transitive PITZĀHU(A) 'to make something thin.' See PITZĀHU(I).

PITZĀHUAQUE-TL long bean / frijol delgado (Z) [(2)Zp.61,183]. See PITZĀHUAC, E-TL.

PITZĀHU(I) to get thin / se adelgaza (T) [(4)Tp.119,175]. In a compound with CUAUH T has a short vowel in the second syllable but in the free form T has a long one. M has synonymous *pitzaua*, which forms its preterit by adding -C. It is apparently the same verb with an idiosyncratic vowel-length variation.

PITZALHUIĀ applic. PITZOĀ

PĪTZALHUIĀ applic. PĪTZ(A)

PĪTZALŌ nonact. PĪTZ(A)

PITZĀUHCĀCECU(I) to have chills, to shiver / tiene calofríos, tiene escalofríos (T) [(3)Tp.175]. See PITZĀUHQUI, CECU(I).

PITZĀUHCĀCECUĪHUA This is attested in T, which has CŌHUA for CUĪHUA. nonact. PITZĀUHCĀCECU(I)

PITZĀUHCĀCECUĪTIĀ caus. PITZĀUHCĀCECU(I)

PITZĀUHCĀN *pl:* **-MEH** waist, belt / cintura (X) [(3)Xp.65]. See PITZĀHU(I), -CĀN.

PITZĀUHQUI something thin, weak, lean / delgado, flaco, y magro (M) [(1)Tp.175]. See PITZĀHU(A).

PITZCOTŌN(A) *vt* to pinch something / lo

pellizca (T) [(3)Tp.198]. T has a long vowel
in the first syllable of PĪTZCUA 'to pinch
something' and a short vowel here. See
PITZĀHUA, COTŌN(A).
PITZCOTŌNALŌ nonact. PITZCOTŌN(A)
PITZCOTŌNILIĀ applic. PITZCOTŌN(A)
PĪTZCOYŌN(I) to become pierced /
se agujera (T) [(1)Tp.174]. See PĪTZ-
COYŌNQUI.
PĪTZCOYŌNQUI something pierced,
something with a narrow opening /
estrecha cosa así como agujero o cosa
semejante (M), agujerado (T) [(1)Tp.174].
Despite the vowel length discrepancy, this
appears to be related to PITZĀHU(A)
'to make something thin.' See PĪTZ-
COYŌN(I).
PĪTZCUA vt; pret: **PĪTZCUAC** to pinch
something / lo pellizca (T) [(3)Tp.198]. T
has a short vowel in the first syllable of
PITZCOTŌN(A) 'to pinch something' and
a long vowel here. See PITZĀHU(A).
PĪTZCUALŌ nonact. PĪTZCUA
PĪTZĒHUA-TL inalienably possessed form:
-PĪTZĒHUAYŌ skin / su cutis (Z for
possessed form) [(2)Zp.37,160]. Z also has
PĪCHĒHUA-TL with the same sense. See
ĒHUA-TL.
PITZĪN(I) for something to burst / quebrarse
el huevo, machucarse la fruta, o quebrarse
el ojo, o reventar el encodio o cosa semejante (M), se exprime (T) [(1)Tp.174].
PITZĪNILIĀ vt to squeeze something out for
someone / se lo exprime (T) [(3)Tp.198].
applic. PITZĪN(I)
PITZĪNILĪLŌ nonact. PITZĪNILIĀ
PITZOĀ vt to kiss someone or something /
lo besa (T) [(3)Tp.198, (3)Xp.72]. This seems
to have to do with extending or puckering
the lips. See PITZĀHU(A).
PITZOEHĒCA-TL pl: **-MEH** malicious
spirit, ghost / espíritu malo, mal aire (T)
[(1)Tp.175]. See PITZO-TL, EHĒCA-TL.
PITZOILAMA sow / puerca, marrana (T)
[(1)Tp.174]. In T the initial I of ILAMA
drops after the final vowel of PITZO-TL,
but elsewhere ILAMA retains its initial I
adjacent to preceding vowels. PITZO-TL,
ILAMA-TL
PITZŌLIZ-TLI kiss / beso (T) [(1)Tp.175].
See PITZOĀ.

PITZŌL-LI kiss / beso (T) [(2)Tp.175,235].
See PITZOĀ.
PITZONAC(A)-TL pork / carne de puerco (C)
[(1)Cf.60v, (2)Tp.166,174]. See PITZO-TL,
NAC(A)-TL.
PITZONELHUIĀ applic. PITZONELOĀ
PITZONELIHU(I) to get dirty / se ensucia
(T) [(1)Tp.174]. See PITZONELOĀ.
PITZONELOĀ vrefl,vt to get dirty, to get
something dirty / se ensucia (T), lo en-
sucia, lo mancha (T) [(6)Tp.155,198]. See
PITZO-TL, NELOĀ.
PITZONELŌLŌ nonact. PITZONELOĀ
PITZONELTIC something dirty /
mugriento, sucio (T) [(1)Tp.174]. See
PITZONELOĀ.
PITZONEM(I) pret: **-NEN** to go about dirty /
andar sucio (Z) [(2)Zp.118,183]. See
PITZO-TL, NEM(I).
PITZOTIC something ugly, dirty, repul-
sive / feo, escabroso, cosa inmunda, sucio,
terrible (T) This is attested twice in T
and abundantly in Z. It contrasts with
PITZŌTIC 'narrow.' See PITZO-TL.
PITZŌTIC something narrow, squeezed
together / angosto, reducido (T)
[(2)Tp.137,175]. See PITZOĀ PITZĀHU(A).
PITZOTILIĀ vrefl,vt to soil oneself; to
make something ugly, to defile something /
se ensucia (Z), lo hace feo, lo afea, lo mancha (T) See PITZO-TL.
PITZOTILILIĀ applic. PITZOTILIĀ
PITZOTILĪLŌ nonact. PITZOTILIĀ
PITZO-TL pl: **-MEH** pig / puerco (M) There
is agreement across sources that both
vowels are short except for Z in which
about half the attestations mark that of
the second syllable long. Association of
PITZO-TL with filth and defilement is
limited to T and Z. See PITZOĀ.
PITZOTLAHTOĀ to speak in a crude manner / habla sucio (T) [(4)Tp.174]. See
PITZO-TL, TLAHTOĀ.
PITZOTLAHTOĀNI someone who speaks
in a gross or obscene way / uno que
habla sucio, grosero (T) [(1)Tp.175]. See
PITZOTLAHTOĀ.
PITZOTLAHTŌL-LI obscene or gross
speech / palabra sucia, grosería (T)
[(2)Tp.112,175]. See PITZOTLAHTOĀ.
PITZOYŌ-TL uncleanliness, defilement,

something unclean / cosa inmunda, suciedad (T) [(1)Tp.175]. See PITZO-TL, -YŌ.

PĪTZQUILIĀ applic. PĪTZCUA

PITZTIC something lean, tough / delgado (animal o hombre), duro, macizo, tieso, paralítico (T for CUAUHPITZTIC) [(2)Tp.119,137, (4)Xp.38,64]. This is not attested as a free form but only as the second element of two compounds in T. X reduces TZT to ZT. See PITZAC-TLI.

PĪTZ-TLI pit, stone of a fruit / cuesco o hueso de cierta fruta (M) [(1)Tp.127].

PIXCA to harvest maize or wheat / coger el maíz o segar el trigo (M) See PIY(A).

PIXĪCAH pl: **PĪPIXĪCAHTIN** balloon / globo (T) [(1)Tp.175].

-PIXQUI necessarily bound form keeper, custodian of something. That which is kept or guarded is bound to this as an incorporated object of the verb PIY(A). B and Z attest this with a long vowel in the first syllable. See PIY(A).

PIXQUI-TL harvest / cosecha, lo que se coge, o siega de la heredad o sementera (M) [(2)Cf.47r,113r, (1)Rp.41]. See PIXCA.

PIY(A) vrefl; pret: **PIX** ~ **PĪX** to protect oneself from something; to take care of someone or something, to have stewardship of something, to hold something / guardarse de algo (M), guardar a otro (M), guardar alguna cosa (M) T consistently has a short I throughout the verbal paradigm, and Z has a long vowel. B and C have a short vowel throughout except in the preterit, where the I is followed by X. In these cases the vowel is sporadically marked long. The incidence of TLAHPIY(A) implies a virtually synonymous derived verb (I)HPIY(A). A common variant of PIY(A) is PIY(E).

PIYĀCILHUIĀ applic. PIYĀZOĀ

PIYALIĀ vt to keep something for someone, to care for something for someone / guardar algo a otro (M) A common variant of this is PIYELIĀ. T reduces it further to PILIĀ in compounds and PĪLIĀ as a free form. applic. PIY(A)

PIYALILIĀ applic. PIYALIĀ

PIYALĪLŌ nonact. PIYALIĀ

PIYALŌ nonact. PIY(A)

PIYALTIĀ vrefl,vt to entrust oneself to

someone; to deposit something with someone for safekeeping / encomendarme a otro o fiar mi persona del que pienso que me aprovechará (M for first pers. sg. subject), depositar o dar guardar algo a otro (M) [(3)Tp.197]. caus. PIY(A)

PIYALTILIĀ applic. PIYALTIĀ

PIYALTĪLŌ nonact. PIYALTIĀ

PIYĀZOĀ vt to make something long and straight / hacer una cosa larga, derecha, y redonda como una vara (C) [(2)Cf.65v]. T has YO for YĀ, and C does not write the intervocalic Y. C gives this as a metaphor for 'to urinate' and T glosses it as 'to defecate,' while M has reflexive piazoa 'to steal off, to slip away' and also piaztli 'long, thin gourd used as a pipe to conduct liquid.' The basic meaning probably has to do with liquid running in a narrow course. With the senses 'to urinate' and 'to defecate,' this takes the prefix TLA-.

PIYĀZTĒTĒCA vrefl,vt to lie stretched out; to lay something straight / se acuesta estirado (T), lo acuesta bien derecho (T) [(6)Tp.155,198]. T has YOZ for YĀZ See PIYĀZTIC, TĒTĒCA.

PIYĀZTIC something straight, narrow, vertical / cosa larga y delgada así como hombre, columna, o cosa semejante, o cosa estrecha así como mesa, lecho, o cosa así (M), derecho (vertical—se dice de palo) (T) [(1)Tp.175, (2)Xp.64]. T has YOZ for YĀZ. See PIYĀZOĀ.

PIY(E) See PIY(A).

PIYELIĀ See PIYALIĀ.

PIYELTIĀ See PIYALTIĀ.

PIYELTĪLŌ See PIYALTĪLŌ.

-PŌCH This element of (I)CHPŌCH-TLI 'young woman' and TĒLPŌCH-TLI 'young man' forms its plural by reduplication, -PŌPŌCHTIN, implying that (I)CH and TĒL are modifiers, but these elements do not appear independently in other constructions.

PŌCH See PŌC-TLI.

PŌCHECTIC something sooty, smoke-blackened / tiznado, ahumado (T) [(2)Tp.113,176]. M has pochectilia 'to smoke something.' See PŌC-TLI.

PŌCHĒHU(A) vrefl,vt to get smoky; to smoke something, to fill something with

smoke / se ahuma (T), ahumar algo (M)
[(6)Tp.156,199]. M also has intransitive
pocheua, preterit formed with -C, 'for a
house to fill up with smoke, for bread to
scorch.' See PŌC-TLI, ĒHU(A).

PŌCHĒHUALŌ nonact. PŌCHĒHU(A)

PŌCHĒHU(I) to get smoky / se tizna (T)
[(1)Tp.176]. This has the same sense as
PŌCHĒHU(A) used reflexively.

PŌCHĒHUILIĀ applic. PŌCHĒHU(A)

POCHICTIC something raveled, frayed,
spongy; something pale in color, blonde /
cosa carmenada, fofa, o esponjada (C),
huero, blonde, blanco (Z) [(1)Tp.175,
(9)Zp.20,25,69,112,147,161,162,183]. The
sense in Z points to PŌC-TLI 'smoke'
rather than POCHĪN(A) 'to unravel
something,' but in only one of the nine
attestations is the vowel of the initial syllable marked long. Z also has
POHPŌCTIC 'smoke colored' derived
from PŌC-TLI. There are two typographical errors in Z's attestations. In one the
final C of the second syllable is omitted,
and in the other there is S in place of word-
final C.

POCHĪN(A) *vt* to unravel something, to card
wool, cotton / cardar o carmenar lana,
algodón, o cosa semejante (M) This is
implied by POHPOCHĪN(I). Z has
what appears to be the causative form
POCHĪNALTIĀ with the sense of 'to
whiten something,' possibly because fibers
become lighter in color as they are carded.

POCHĪNALTIĀ *vt* to make something
white / lo blanquea (Z) [(2)Zp.20,193]. In
both attestations the vowel of the first
syllable is marked long, and this seems to
contain the element PŌCH 'smoke,' but Z
also has POCHICTIC 'something pale in
color, blonde' in which the vowel is not
marked long in eight of nine attestations.
This also appears to be the causative form
of the verb POCHĪN(A) 'to unravel something, to card fiber.' See POCHICTIC,
POCHĪN(A).

PŌCHMĀCOCOPA at the left-hand side /
mano izquierda (Z) [(2)Zp.81,160]. See
PŌCHMĀ(I)-TL, -C(O), -COPA.

PŌCHMĀ(I)-TL left hand / mano izquierda
(Z) [(3)Zp.73,81,160]. See PŌCH-TLI,
MĀ(I)-TL.

PŌCHŌ-TL silk-cotton tree / árbol hermoso
y grande, de cuyas raíces se sacaba un jugo
que se utilizaba como febrífugo (S), árbol
grande (C) [(1)Bf.4r, (1)Cf.121r].

PŌCHQUIYĀHUA-TL chimney, smoke
hole, window / ventana que da claridad (M)
[(1)Bf.7r]. See PŌC-TLI, QUIYĀHUA-TL.

PŌCHTĒCA-TL *pl:* **PŌCHTĒCAH** long
distance trader, merchant / mercader (C)
[(1)Bf.11r, (2)Cf.4r]. This is a regular derivation from a place name, which in this case
would be PŌCHTLAN, probably related to
PŌC-TLI 'smoke, vapor.'

PŌCH-TLI left, left-hand side / izquierda,
mano izquierda (S) S has this as a free
form, and it appears as an element of Z's
PŌCHMĀ(I)-TL, but Z also has OPŌCH.
Since C and M have exclusively OPŌCH,
PŌCH can be thought of as a variant
which has lost the initial vowel. No absolutive form of it is attested in the sources
for this dictionary, although S gives it in
absolute form.

PŌCHUIĀ *vt* to smoke, fumigate some-
thing / lo ahuma (Z) [(3)Zp.8,193,213].
This derivation with the form PŌC
'smoke' is apparently synonymous with
T's POPŌCHHUIĀ with PŌCH. See
PŌC-TLI, -HUIĀ.

PŌCTĒM(I) See TLAPŌCTĒM(I).

PŌCTĒMĪTIĀ *vt* to fill something up with
smoke / lo llena de humo (T) [(3)Tp.199].
See TLAPŌCTĒM(I).

PŌCTĒMĪTILIĀ applic. PŌCTĒMĪTIĀ

PŌCTĒMĪTILŌ nonact. PŌCTĒMĪTIĀ

PŌC-TLI smoke, vapor, fumes / humo (M)
In compounded and derived forms there is
generally the form PŌCH in place of PŌC,
but Z retains PŌC, and T has both.

PŌCYOH something smoked / cosa que
tiene humo (M), ahumado (Z) [(2)Zp.7,183].
Z has an intrusive I between the two
syllables, PŌQUIYOH. See PŌC-TLI,
-YOH.

PŌCYOHUA to become smoked / se ahuma
(Z) [(2)Zp.8,183]. The vowel of the second
syllable of PŌCYOHUA is not marked
long in Z, but it probably should be. See
POCYOH.

-POH *necessarily possessed form* one's
equal, another like oneself / su igual, o su
compañero (M), igualdad o semejanza (C)

This is abundantly attested in C, R, and P. Modifying elements may intervene between the possessive prefix and the verb, NOPOH 'my equal, someone like me,' NOTLĀCAPOH 'a human being like myself,' NOCNŌPOH 'someone poor like me.' This can be thought of as a preterit-as-present verb of the irregular type which takes possessive rather than subject prefixes and occurs only in singular form, in which case, it implies *POĀ 'to be, become like someone' S has absolutive *potli*, but it is nowhere attested in the sources for this dictionary.

POHPŌCHECTIC something smoky / ahumada (T) [(1)Tp.113]. See PŌC-TLI.

POHPOCHĪN(I) to ravel, fray / se deshilacha (lazo, etc.), se enmaraña (T) [(1)Tp.175]. This implies transitive POCHĪN(A) 'to unravel something, to card fiber.'

POHPŌCTIC something the color of smoke / color ahumado (Z) [(1)Zp.183]. See PŌC-TLI.

POHPOHTIĀ *vt* to pair off, unite, join one thing with another / parear, hermanar, o conchabar una cosa con otra (M) [(1)Cf.84r, (2)Rp.69,123]. In one attestation in R this takes a direct object plus an oblique reflexive object prefix. redup. POHTIĀ

POHPŌHU(A) *vt* to clean something / alimpiar algo (M) M combines this with PŌPŌHU(A) 'to pay something' in a single entry.

POHPŌHUALŌ nonact. POHPŌHU(A)
POHPŌHUILIĀ applic. POHPŌHU(A)
POHPOLHUIĀ *vt* to pardon someone for something; to destroy something for someone / perdonar a otro la ofensa o destruirle alguna cosa (M) POHPOLHUIĀ as the applicative of POHPOLOĀ has a literal sense of destruction, but it also has the lexicalized sense of specifically obliterating someone's sins or guilt. applic. POHPOLOĀ

POHPOLHUILIĀ applic. POHPOLHUIĀ
POHPOLHUĪLŌ nonact. POHPOLHUIĀ
POHPOLIHU(I) redup. POLIHU(I)
POHPOLOĀ *vt* to consume, destroy, obliterate something / gastar la hacienda (M), destruir combatiendo o conquistando (M), desperdiciar o destruir algo, o hacer costa, borrar alguna cosa, o oscurecer la

claridad grande a la pequeña (M) redup. POLOĀ

POHPOLŌN(I) to stammer, stutter, speak unintelligibly / ser tartamundo o impedido de la lengua (M) [(1)Cf.74v]. redup. POLŌN(I)

POHPOXOĀ *vrefl,vt* to get turned over, to undergo upheaval; to turn something over, to prepare ground for sowing / se revuelca (T), barbechar o mollir la tierra (M) [(4)Tp.161,165]. T has this modified by TLĀL with the sense 'to roll in the dirt' and by Ā 'to wallow about in water.'

POHPOXŌN smallpox / viruela (Z) [(2)Zp.130,183]. In one of the attestations Z marks the vowel of the second syllable long. This appears to be related to POHPOXOĀ 'to turn something over' and implies *POHPOXŌN(I). M's *puxactic* 'something spongy' may also be relevant.

POHPOZTEQU(I) *vt; pret:* **-TEC** to chop, break up, smash something / quebrar muchas veces palos o cosas semejantes (M) [(1)Cf.18v]. This appears as a transitive verb in M, but C gives it as intransitive 'to get broken.'

POHTIĀ *vt* to pair off, join one thing with another / parear, hermanar, o conchabar una cosa con otra (M) [(3)Cf.83v]. This appears in P as a reflexive verb. See -POH.

PŌHU(A) *vt* to count something, to read something, to recount, relate, or give account of something, to assign something / contar a algunos o encartarlos (M), contar cosa de cuenta o número, o relatar proceso e historia, o leer, o dar cuenta el mayordomo de su mayordomía o cosa semejante (M) There is an apparently lexicalized use of PŌHU(A) with the sense 'to be haughty,' which appears here as a separate entry. M also has a transitive use meaning 'to sow seed again' which is not attested in the sources for this dictionary.

PŌHU(A) *vrefl,vt* to be lofty, haughty, arrogant; to hold someone in respect / ser soberbio (M), tener respeto a otro (M) [(8)Cf.35r,44r,48r]. M combines the gloss of the transitive use of this with that of the verb 'to count,' and the sense of putting oneself or someone else first is a reasonable extension of 'to count.'

-PŌHUAL-LI *necessarily bound form; pl:*

-TIN a unit of twenty in the vigesimal counting system / veinte (M for CEMPŌHUAL-LI) This is prefixed by a number which multiplies the twenty, CEMPŌHUAL-LI 'twenty,' ŌMPŌHUAL-LI 'forty' (two times twenty), etc. TLAPŌHUAL-LI means 'something countable,' and the negated phrase AHMŌ ZAN TLAPŌHUAL-LI 'an infinite number.' See PŌHU(A).

PŌHUALŌ nonact. PŌHU(A)

PŌHUANI pl: **-MEH** someone lofty, haughty, arrogant / soberbio (C) [(2)Cf.44r]. This belongs to a group of deverbal nouns derived from the customary present form of the verb. The verb in this sense is reflexive and retains a relexive prefix corresponding to the person and number of the referent, although the plural also takes an absolute (i.e., nonpossessed) plural suffix, MOPŌHUANI 'he is haughty,' TITOPŌHUANIMEH 'we are haughty' (Cf.44r). See PŌHU(A).

PŌHU(I) intransitive verb form, object expressed as possessive bound with **-TECH.** to pertain to something, to belong to someone, to go with someone / pertenecer a alguna persona (M), partidario, con él pertenece, lo acompaña (Z) [(5)Zp.97,103,158,162,183]. On the Spanish-to-Nahuatl side Z once has yohui corresponding to PŌHU(I) on the other side. See PŌHU(A).

PŌHUILIĀ vrefl,vt to count, to talk, to discourse; to count something, to discuss something, to report something to someone / platica, cuenta (T), lo cuenta, lo platica, lo entera (T) This is abundantly attested but only in T. applic. PŌHU(A)

PŌHUILILIĀ applic. PŌHUILIĀ

PŌHUILĪLŌ nonact. PŌHUILIĀ

-PŌL derogative compounding element implying large size, great degree; pl: **-POPŌL** acrecienta la significación in malam partem de ordinario (C) [(7)Cf.7r,8r,59v].

POLACTIĀ vt to submerge something in water / anegar o sumir algo en el agua (M) [(3)Tp.198]. M also has polacqui 'something submerged,' which implies *POLAQU(I) 'to sink, to submerge.'

POLACTILIĀ applic. POLACTIĀ

POLACTĪLŌ nonact. POLACTIĀ

POLHUIĀ vt to lose or destroy something for someone / perder cosa ajena o borrarle algo de otro (M) applic. POLOĀ

POLHUILIĀ applic. POLHUIĀ

POLHUĪLŌ nonact. POLHUIĀ

POLIHU(I) to perish, to disappear, to be missing or consumed / perecer o desaparecer o perderse y destruirse (M) This is the intransitive verb corresponding to transitive POLOĀ 'to lose, ruin, destroy something.'

POLIHUĪHUA nonact. POLIHU(I)

POLIHUĪTIĀ caus. POLIHU(I)

POLIUHCĀYŌ-TL condemnation / mi perdimiento, mi perdición (C for first pers. sg. possessor) [(1)Cf.49r]. This is only attested in possessed form. See POLIHU(I).

POLIUHQUI something lost, condemned / cosa que se perdió (M) [(1)Cf.49r].

-PŌLOĀ derogative verbal compounding element added directly to the preterit stem significa menosprecio y vituperio (C) [(6)Cf.7or]. See -PŌL.

POLOĀ vrefl,vt to perish, to be destroyed; to destroy, squander or spend something, to lay waste something or someone / perderse y destruirse (M), perder o destruir a otros con guerra o conquistarlos (M), gastar hacienda (M), perder algo (M), perder el juicio y desatinarse, borrar algo, o quitarla señal que estaba puesta en alguna parte (M) This contrasts with PŌLOĀ 'to mix flour, earth, etc., with water.' M combines the glosses of both in a single entry. With the prefix TLA-, POLOĀ means to lose one's senses or to make errors.

PŌLOĀ vt to mix flour, bran, earth, etc., with water / hacer lodo o barro (M), revolver harina o salvado o tierra con agua (C) [(3)Cf.64v,127v, (1)Rp.123]. This contrasts with POLOĀ 'to lose, destroy something.'

POLOCHTIC someone with curly, nappy hair / chino (T), cabello chino, pelo chino (T for TZON-TLI POLOCHTIC) [(3)Tp.175,244].

POLŌLŌ nonact. POLOĀ

POLŌLTIĀ caus. POLOĀ

POLŌN(I) to stutter, to talk unintelligibly /

POPŌCA to smoke, to give off vapor / hacer humo (M), humear, echar humo de sí (M) R has POHPŌCA, as does *Flor. Codex.* See PŌC-TLI.

POPŌCACĪTLAL-IN comet / cometa (T) [(1)Tp.175]. See POPŌCA, CĪTLAL-IN.

POPŌCHCAX(I)-TL censer, vessel for incense / vasija para quemar incienso (Z) [(1)Zp.183]. See POPŌCH-TLI, CAX(I)-TL.

POPŌCHHUIĀ *vrefl,vt* to be smoked; to smoke, fumigate something / se sahuma (T), lo sahuma (T) This is abundantly attested in T and also appears in B and R. R has a glottal stop in the first syllable. This may be derived from POPŌCH-TLI 'incense,' but it seems to be synonymous with Z's PŌCHUIĀ and may also be a reduplicated derivation from PŌCH 'smoke.' See PŌC-TLI, -HUIĀ.

POPŌCHHUILIĀ applic. POPŌCHHUIĀ
POPŌCHHUĪLŌ nonact. POPŌCHHUIĀ
POPŌCH-TLI incense / perfumes (M), sahumerio, incensario (T) [(1)Tp.175]. See POPŌTZ(A).

PŌPŌHU(A) to pay something, to make restitution for something / restituir lo ajeno (M), pagar una cosa (S) M combines this with POHPŌHU(A) 'to clean something' in a single entry. This is not directly attested in the sources for this dictionary but is implied by intransitive PŌPŌHU(I). redup. PŌHU(A)

PŌPŌHU(I) to be restored, discharged / se ha cumplido con la obligación (C for phrase with paired (I)XTLĀHU(A)) [(7)Bf.1v,2r,4v,6r,9r,9v,12v, (1)Cf.53r]. redup. PŌHU(I)

POPOLOCA to speak a language badly, to speak a foreign language, to speak unintelligibly / hablar languaje bárbaro (M) See POLŌN(I).

POPOLOCOHUA nonact. POPOLOCA
POPOLOQUĪTIĀ caus. POPOLOCA
POPOLOTZ(A) *vt* to speak in such a way that others fail to understand, to make one's speech unintelligible, to say something in a foreign language / no hacerse comprender, hablar una lengua bárbara (S) [(2)Cf.74v]. See POLŌN(I), POPOLOCA.

POPŌ-TL *pl:* **-MEH** plant used to make

brooms; broom, straw / escoba (T) [(2)Tp.125,176].

POPŌTZ(A) *vt* to smoke something / hace humo (para alguna cosa, p.ej. hacer salir al conejo) (T) [(2)Cf.75r, (1)Tp.235]. See PŌC-TLI.

POPŌTZOĀ *vrefl* to puff out, thicken, swell / hinchar los carillos, apretarse la gente, o espesarse las yerbas (M) [(2)Zp.103,160]. In one of the two attestations Z marks the vowel of the second syllable long and in the other leaves it unmarked for length. Z glosses this as a noun 'lung.'

POPOYACTIC something gray, dark, cloudy / gris, pardo (T) [(2)Tp.137,175]. T omits the C of the third syllable in one attestation, but it is present in the other and in the entries of the Spanish-to-Nahuatl side. See POYĀHU(I).

POPOYŌTIĀ to rot / se pudre (T) [(1)Tp.175]. See POPOYŌ-TL.

POPOYŌTIC something rotten / medio podrido (T) [(1)Tp.175]. M has *pupuyuctic* referring to blighted grain. See POPOYŌ-TL.

POPOYŌ-TL rottenness, decay / podre, podredumbre (T) [(4)Cf.57v,122v, (2)Tp.175].

POPOZOCA to boil hard, to foam / hervir la olla o cosa así (M), hervir con mucho ruido (C) [(1)Cf.73v, (1)Tp.175, (2)Zp.56,183]. See POZŌN(I).

POPOZOC-TLI foam / espuma (T) [(1)Tp.175]. See POPOZOCA.

PŌPOZŌNALIZ-TLI foam / espuma (T) [(1)Tp.175]. M has *popoçoniliztli* 'the bubbling, boiling of a pot; great anger.' See POZŌN(I).

POPOZOTZ(A) *vt* to boil something hard, to make something foam / hacer hervir mucho una cosa (S) [(1)Cf.73v]. See POZŌN(I).

PŌQU(I) to give off smoke / fumar (X) [(3)Xp.65]. See PŌC-TLI.

POTŌN(I) to stink / heder o oler mal (M) [(3)Cf.49r]. T has this compounded with TLĀL-LI with the sense of 'for it to be dusty (weather).' This would appear to be a homophonous but separate item, yet M provides a gloss about dust for related POTŌNQUI.

POTŌNQUI something stinking, rotten /

cosa olorosa o hedionda (M) [(2)Cf.49r,49v].
M has the additional gloss 'very fine dust
or sifted flour.' This would seem to be a
separate item, but T provides a gloss for
POTŌN(I) referring to dust. See POTŌN(I).

PŌTZ(A) to throw up earth, to burrow /
echa tierra, tusa (Z for TLĀLPŌTZ(A))
[(2)Zp.126,213]. One of the attestations is
TLĀLPŌTZ(A), while the other appears
to be TLAPŌTZ(A). See IHPŌTZ(A),
ILPŌTZ(A).

PŌTZAL-LI mound / terrero (K) This is attested as an element of ĀZCAPŌTZAL-LI
'ant hill' and the place name ĀZCA-
PŌTZALCO. See PŌTZ(A).

-PŌX attested only in possessed form and in
compounds, not in absolute form pot
belly / barrigón, panzón (Z) This is abundantly attested but only in Z. It may be related to POZĀHU(I) 'to swell.'

POXĀHUAC something spongy / fofo (T)
[(1)Tp.176, (1)Zp.183]. M has poxactic with
the same sense. See POCHICTIC.

POXĀHU(I) to fall, to get out of plumb / se
cae, se desploma (T) [(1)Tp.176].

POXCAHU(I) to get moldy, dank / enmohe-
cerse o henchirse alguna cosa de orín (M)
[(2)Zp.52,183]. See POXCAHUIYA.

POXCAHUIYA to get covered with
slime / se enlama (T) [(1)Tp.176]. See
POXCAHU(I).

PŌXIHCATOC someone with a pot belly /
panzón (Z) [(2)Zp.93,184]. In one attestation PŌX is written out as a separate word.
See -PŌX, IHCA, the verb O.

-PŌXNACAZTLAN attested only in possessed form one's side, flank / su
lado, su costado (Z for possessed form)
[(2)Zp.35,160]. See -PŌX, -NACAZTLAN.

PŌXPAMPILCAC someone with a pot belly
/ panzón (Z) [(2)Zp.93,184]. One of the
attestations omits the final C. See -PŌX,
-PAN, PILCA.

PŌXTOMĀHUAC someone with a pot belly
/ panzón (Z) [(2)Zp.93,184]. See -PŌX,
TOMĀHUAC.

POYĀHU(A) vt to darken something / mati-
zar en pintura (M) [(1)Cf.97r]. M also has
poyahuac 'something shaded, something dark,' which implies intransitive
*POYĀHUA.

POYĀHU(I) to darken / obscurecerse (K)
[(1)Tp.137, (2)Zp.82,164]. This is attested
in Z in the form ĪXPOYĀHU(I) 'to be
dizzy' and in T in ĪXTLAPŌPOYĀHU(I) 'to
get dark.' See POYĀHU(A).

POYEC something salted / cosa que tiene
sal, así como el manjar o el agua (M)
[(2)Tp.171,176, (2)Zp.112,184]. T has I for
E.

POYELIĀ vrefl,vt to get salty; to add salt to
something / se pone salado (T), le echa sal
(T) [(4)Tp.156,198]. See POYEC.

POYELILIĀ applic. POYELIĀ

POYELĪLŌ nonact. POYELIĀ

POYŌMICQUI victim of treachery or evil
design / víctima de traición (K) [(1)Bf.12v].
See POYŌMIQU(I).

POYŌMIQU(I) pret: -MIC to die by
treachery or evil design of others / morir
por traición (K) [(1)Bf.12v]. This is implied
by POYŌMICQUI. See POYŌ-TL,
MIQU(I).

POYŌ-TL something evil / cosa mala, algo
mal (K) [(1)Bf.12v]. This is more common in reduplicated form POPOYŌ-TL
'rottenness, decay.'

POZĀHU(A) vt to inflate something /
hinchar ... a otro (M), se lo hincha (T)
[(6)Tp.198]. M has intransitive poçaua,
preterit poçahuac, 'for one's body to swell
up,' while T's corresponding intransitive is
POZĀHU(I).

POZĀHUAC something inflated, swollen / hinchado (Z) [(2)Zp.68,183]. See
POZĀHU(A).

POZĀHUALŌ nonact. POZĀHU(A)

POZĀHUALTIĀ caus. POZĀHU(A)

POZĀHUALTILIĀ applic. POZĀHUALTIĀ

POZĀHUALTĪLŌ nonact. POZĀHUALTIĀ

POZĀHUAYA to swell, to become inflamed
/ se hincha ... inflama (Z) [(3)Zp.68,71,183].
See POZĀHU(A).

POZĀHU(I) to swell / se hincha, está
hinchado (T) [(3)Tp.176, (3)Xp.65]. See
POZĀHU(A).

POZĀHUĪHUA nonact. POZĀHU(I)

POZĀHUILIĀ applic. POZĀHU(A)

POZĀHUILIZ-TLI swelling, inflammation /
hinchazón, inflamación (T) [(1)Tp.176]. See
POZĀHU(I).

POZĀHUĪLLŌ-TL swelling, inflammation /

hinchazón (Z) [(2)Zp.68,183]. This implies
*POZĀHUIĀ. See POZĀHU(I), -YŌ.
POZĀHUĪTIĀ caus. POZĀHU(I)
POZOC-TLI *pl:* **-TIN** foam / espuma (Z)
[(4)Zp.56,183, (3)Xp.65]. Z gives this with
and without the absolutive suffix. See
POZŌN(I).
POZOL-LI pork and hominy stew / pozole
(X) [(2)Xp.65]. See POZŌN(I).
POZŌN(I) for something to boil, for the sea
to be turbulent and covered with foam; to
get very angry / hervir la olla o la mar (M),
enojarse mucho (M) [(1)Cf.73v].
POZŌNIĀ *vt* to boil something / lo hierve
(T) [(6)Tp.198, (3)Xp.73]. See POZŌN(I).
POZŌNILIĀ applic. POZŌNIĀ
POZŌNĪLŌ nonact. POZŌNIĀ

POZŌNQUI something boiled / chiltejate,
agua de orchata, una cosa hervida (T)
[(1)Tp.176]. See POZŌN(I).
POZTECPAH-TLI plant used in treating fractures / nombre de dos plantas
medicinales (R), bejuco, huesero (X)
[(1)Rp.123]. See POZTEQU(I), PAH-TLI.
POZTEQU(I) *vrefl,vt; pret:* **-TEC** to split, to
break lengthwise; to break something
lengthwise / se quiebra, quiebra la dirección en que va (T), quebrar palo o cosa así
(M), lo quiebra (T) T also gives this as an
intransitive with the same meaning as the
reflexive.
POZTEQUĪHUA nonact. POZTEQU(I)
POZTEQUILIĀ applic. POZTEQU(I)

QU

QUECHCOCHTITLAN *pl:* **-MEH** nape
of the neck / nuca (X) [(2)Zp.89,160,
(3)Xp.66]. T has possessed -QUECHTLAN,
which may be a truncation of
QUECHCOCHTITLAN. M has the shorter
form with an absolutive suffix, *quech-
tlantli*. See QUECHTLAN-TLI.

QUECHCOTOCTIC someone without
a head, decapitated / sin cabeza (T)
[(1)Tp.177]. See QUECH-TLI, COTOCTIC,
QUECHCOTŌN(A).

QUECHCOTŌN(A) *vt* to cut off the head of
someone or something / degollar, o cortar la cabeza a otro (M), coger espigas o
cosa semejante con la mano (M) See
QUECH-TLI, COTŌN(A).

QUECHCOTŌNQUI someone without a
head, decapitated / degollado, o descabe-
zado (M), un muerto sin cabeza (Z) [(1)
Zp.184]. See QUECHCOTŌN(A).

QUECHCŌZCA-TL collar, necklace / la
asillas de la olla de la garganta, o cuentas y
piedras preciosas, joyas que se ponen en la
garganta o en el cuello (M), collar, gargantilla (T) [Tp.177]. See QUECH-TLI,
CŌZCA-TL.

QUECHCUAUHTI for one's head to get
tired / cansa el cerebro (T) [(3)Tp.177]. See
QUECH-TLI, CUAUHTI.

QUECHCUAUHYŌ *pl:* **-MEH** the throat,
neck, nape of the neck, neck of an animal / su cuello, su pescuezo, su nuca (T),
su pescuezo (de animal) (Z) [(1)Tp.133,
(2)Zp.97,160, (3)Xp.66]. No attestation
indicates a final glottal stop, indicating
-YOH rather than -YŌ, but this does not
take an absolutive suffix, and since vowels
shorten word-finally, the length of the final
vowel is ambiguous. See QUECH-TLI,
CUAUH(I)-TL, -YŌ.

QUECHIĀ *vt* to support something / se
apoya (T for refl. MĀTLAQUECHIĀ)

[(2)Cf.50r, (4)Tp.153, (2)Zp.56,187]. This
appears without TLA- only in Z, where
CUAUHTŌC 'stake' is incorporated into
the verb. See TLAQUECHIĀ, QUETZ(A).

QUECHILACATZOĀ *vt* to twist the neck,
to wring someone's neck, to strangle
someone / descervigado (M for *quechila-
catztic*), estaba torciendo el pescuezo
(C) [(1) Cf.104v]. See QUECH-TLI,
ILACATZOĀ.

QUECHILIĀ applic. QUETZ(A)

QUECHILŌ nonact. QUETZ(A)

QUECHMALĪN(A) *vt* to wring the neck /
le tuerce el cuello (de gallina, etc.) (T)
[(3)Tp.200]. See QUECH-TLI, MALĪN(A).

QUECHNĀHUAHTEQU(I) *vt; pret:* **-TEC** to
hug someone around the neck / lo abraza
por el cuello (T) [(3)Tp.200]. See QUECH-
TLI, NĀHUAHTEQU(I).

QUECHŌL-LI bird with red plumage;
flamingo or roseate spoonbill; the plumage
of such a bird / pájaro de pluma rica (M),
pájaro de brillante plumaje muy solicitado;
algunos autores lo han llamado flamenco;
pluma de dicho pájaro (S) [(1)Cf.76v]. This
attestation is of TLĀUHQUECHŌL-LI 'red
flamingo,' which is redundant in English
translation but not in Nahuatl, since
QUECHŌL refers not to the color of the
bird but apparently to the characteristic
sweeping motion of its neck. Elsewhere in
Nahuatl literature QUECHŌL-LI often
appears without the modifying TLĀUH
without alteration of sense, as illustrated
in the gloss in S. It commonly occurs
without the absolutive suffix. See
QUECH-TLI.

QUECHPANOĀ *vt* to carry someone or
something on the shoulders / llevar a otro
encima de los hombros (M), llevar otra
cualquier cosa encima de los hombros (M)
This is indirectly attested in the causa-

tive form QUECHPANŌLTIĀ. See
QUECH-TLI, PANOĀ.

QUECHPANŌLTIĀ *vrefl* for something to
be carried on the shoulders / se pone en el
hombro (Z) [(1)Zp.172]. This implies
QUECHPANOĀ, which is not directly
attested in the sources for this dictionary.
caus. QUECHPANOĀ

QUECHPĀTZCA *vt* to strangle someone / lo
estrangula, lo ahorca (Z) [(3)Zp.7,57,193].
See PĀTZCA, QUECHPĀTZOĀ.

QUECHPĀTZOĀ *vt* to strangle some-
one / lo estrangula (T) [(3)Tp.200]. Z has
QUECHPĀTZCA with the same sense. See
QUECH-TLI, PĀTZOĀ.

QUECHPILOĀ *vt* to hang someone / colgar
a alquien por el cuello (S) [(2)Rp.48,49]. See
QUECH-TLI, PILOĀ.

QUECHQUĒM(I)-TL an indigenous Mesoamerican garment consisting of a cloth
with a neck hole cut in the center; it is
pulled on over the head and usually falls to
a point in front and back. This literally
means 'neck-garment.' / papahigo (M), re-
bozo (T), huipil, bufanda (Z) [(1)Tp.177,
(3)Zp.21,69,184]. None of the glosses
cited conveys a true sense of QUECH-
QUĒM(I)-TL. See QUECH-TLI, QUĒM(I)-
TL.

QUECHTAMALAYOH-TLI tumor of the
neck / bocio (Z) [(2)Zp.20, 184]. In one of
the attestations Z has the first and fourth
syllables of TAMALAYOH long, and in the
other the second and third, but on the
basis of M's *tamalayutli* meaning a type of
squash, it appears that the constituents of
this compound are indeed TAMAL-LI
and AYOH-TLI and that there are no
long vowels at all. See QUECH-TLI,
TAMALAYOH-TLI.

QUECHTECOYĀHU(A) *vt* to make a hole in
something (a huipil or quechquemitl) in
order to pull it on over the head / lo agujera
para ponérselo por la cabeza (T) [(3)Tp.200].
See QUECH-TLI, COYĀHU(A).

QUECHTEHTEQU(I) See QUECH-TLI,
TEHTEQU(I).

-QUECHTEMĒMECAPAL *only attested in
possessed form* tendons of the neck
and head / sus tendones del cerebro (T)

[(1)Tp.133]. T has a reflex of a long vowel
in the second syllable, but it should not be.
As attested, this is a possessed form with
reduplicated stem but no plural suffix.
The absolute singular should probably
be QUECHTEMECAPAL-LI. See
QUECHTE-TL, MECAPAL-LI.

QUECHTEPOL-LI nape of the neck / la
cerviz (M), su nuca (T) [(1)Tp.133]. See
QUECH-TLI, TEPOL-LI.

QUECHTE-TL neck / cuello (K) This is only
attested as the first element of several
compounds. See QUECH-TLI, TE-TL.

QUECHTETZOM(I)-TL shawl, protection
for neck / cabello o pelo (M for *tzontli*),
lana, seda, crin (S for *tzomitl*) [(1)Bf.7r].
This entry is questionable in both form
and gloss. Because the single attestation is
in possessed form, the final element may
be either TZON-TLI or TZOM(I)-TL.
This occurs in a metaphor with
MĀNĀHUAL-LI 'coverlet, blanket,' and
the sense of the whole construction is
'protection.' See QUECHTE-TL,
TZOM(I)-TL.

QUECHTLAN-TLI throat, neck / cuello
o pescuezo (M) [(2)Tp.131,133]. X has
QUECHCOCHTITLAN 'nape of the neck.'
See QUECH-TLI, -TLAN.

QUECHTLAPĀN(A) *vrefl* to have a tumor of
the neck / bocio (Z) [(2)Zp.20,172]. See
QUECH-TLI, TLAPĀN(A).

QUECHTLAZĀL-LI shawl, scarf / bufanda
(Z) [(2)Zp.21,184]. See QUECH-TLI,
TLAZĀL-LI.

QUECH-TLI throat, neck / cuello o pescuezo (M) Z is inconsistent, with a long
vowel in some attestations. The rest agree
with the other sources in having a short
vowel.

QUECHTOMĀHUAC someone with a
swollen neck, a tumor of the neck / bocio (Z) [(2)Zp.20,184]. See QUECH-TLI,
TOMĀHUA.

QUECHTZON-TLI mane / crin (de caballo)
(Z) [(2)Zp.35,160]. Z is inconsistent. In one
attestation both stem vowels are long, in
the other only the second. The latter form
is consistent with other sources since Z
regularly has a long vowel corresponding to

the short one in TZON-TLI elsewhere. See
QUECH-TLI, TZON-TLI.

QUĒCĪZQUIPA how many times each? /
cuántas veces cada uno (C) [(2)Cf.117r]. C
contrasts this with QUĒZQUIPA which
means simply 'how many times?.' See
QUĒZQUI, -PA.

QUEHQUEHQUETZTINEM(I) *vrefl; pret:*
-NEN to wander about stopping in one
place and another / andarse parando en una
parte y otra (C) [(1)Cf.71v, (1)Rp.37]. See
QUEHQUETZ(A), NEM(I).

QUEHQUELEH someone ticklish, irritable /
cosquilloso (Z) [(2)Zp.35,184]. Z lacks the
glottal stop of the first syllable in both
attestations. See QUEHQUEL-LI.

QUEHQUELHUIĀ *vt* to tease, ridicule
someone / burlar, o escarnecer de alguno
(M) [(1)Tp.200]. See QUEHQUELOĀ.

QUEHQUELHUĪTIĀ T has an alternation between QUEHQUELHUĪTIĀ
and QUEHQUELIHUĪTIĀ. caus.
QUEHQUELIHU(I)

QUEHQUELIHU(I) to be ticklish, irri-
table / tiene cosquillas, hace cosquillas
(Z) [(3)Tp.177, (1)Zp.184]. See QUEH-
QUELOĀ.

QUEHQUELIHUĪHUA nonact. QUEH-
QUELIHU(I)

QUEHQUELIHUĪTIĀ caus. QUEH-
QUELIHU(I)

QUEHQUEL-LI tickling, teasing, irritation;
someone ticklish, irritable / cosquillas
(M), cosquilloso (T) [(1)Tp.177]. Z has
this without the absolutive suffix
with the sense of 'jester, joker.' See
QUEHQUELOĀ.

QUEHQUELOĀ *vt* to tease, mock, ridicule
someone / hacer cosquillas a otro, o escarnecer y burla a alguno (M) T lacks a
glottal stop in the first syllable, and it is
only present in some of Z's attestations of
QUEHQUELOĀ and its derivations. See
QUEHQUEL-LI.

QUEHQUELÔLIZ-TLI joke, hoax, mockery / burla (Z) [(2)Zp.21,184]. See
QUEHQUELOĀ.

QUEHQUELÔLÔ nonact. QUEHQUELOĀ

QUEHQUETZ(A) *vrefl,vt* to pace about
aimlessly, wasting time; to kick out at

something in anger / espaciarse, o perder
tiempo (M), dar patadas de coraje (C)
[(2)Cf.71v,128r, (2)Zp.7,171, (1)Rp.128]. Z
has this in a phrase about ears standing up,
a literal distributive sense of QUETZ(A).
C contrasts QUEHQUETZ(A) with
QUEQUETZ(A) 'to trample on something.'
redup. QUETZ(A)

QUEHTZOM(A) to bite something, someone
/ adentallar, morder a otro, o dar bocados
(M) [(4)Tp.200,235, (2)Zp.86,193]. T has
lost the internal glottal stop. This may be
related to (I)HTZOM(A) 'to sew, stitch
something.'

QUĒMAH yes / si, afirmando algo (M)

QUĒMAHCA yes / si, afirmando algo (M)
[(2)Cf.98r,110v]. According to C, this is
more polite than QUĒMAH alone.

QUĒMAHCATZIN yes / si, afirmando algo
(M) [(2)Cf.110v,125r, (2)Zp.115,184]. According to C this is yet more reverential
than QUĒMAHCA

QUĒM(I) *vt* to put on or wear clothes /
ponerse manta o capa, o traerla puesta (M),
vestirse de una vestidura (C) This most
often occurs with the nonspecific object
prefix TLA- with the sense 'to be dressed.'
With a particular item of clothing, the
specific object marker is used.

QUĒMĪHUA nonact. QUĒM(I)

QUĒMILOĀ *vt* to wrap something up, to
cover something / lo envuelve, lo cubre (Z)
[(3)Zp.36,54,193]. T has QUIMELOĀ See
QUĒM(I), QUĒM(I)-TL.

QUĒMILTIĀ altern. caus. QUĒM(I)

QUĒM(I)-TL garment / vestidura, vestido,
manto, etc. (S) The variant QUĒN-TLI co-
occurs with QUĒM(I)-TL IN C, T, and Z.
When not modified by QUECH, this form
is prefixed with TLA- in all attestations.
See TLAQUĒM(I)-TL, QUĒM(I).

QUĒMMACH how is it possible? / ¿como es
posible? ... ¿es posible? (M) See QUĒN,
MACH.

QUĒMMAN at times; at what time? /
algunas veces, a tiempos, o a ratos, vel. ¿a
que hora? (M) See QUĒN.

QUĒMMANIYĀN sometimes, at times,
someday / algunas veces, o a tiempos (M),
algún día, alguna vez (T), cuando (Z) Z has

a variant with ME for MA; T has variants
in -EYA, -EYO, and -O for IYĀN. See
QUĒMMAN.
QUĒN how? in what manner? / ¿de que
manera? o ¿como? (M)
QUĒNAMIH pl: **QUĒNAMIHQUEH** how?
in what manner or condition? / ¿de qué
manera? o ¿de qué condición es? o ¿qué
arte o condición tiene? (M) [(6)Cf.115v,
(1)Bf.6r, (2)Zp.15,190]. B and Z end in
-MEH rather than -MIH. Z has QUI for
QUĒ. AMIH is separable to the point that
MACH can be inserted to form
QUĒMMACHAMIH. See QUĒN.
QUĒNAMIHCĀTZINTLI a respectful
greeting / ¿de qué manera es su merced
o señoría? (M) [(2)Cf.115v,116r]. See
QUĒNAMIH.
QUĒNIN how? in what manner? / ¿de qué
manera? o ¿cómo es eso? (M) Z has this
with QUĒN and QUIN variants and
also QUEMEH with the same sense. See
QUĒN.
QUĒNMACH See QUĒMMACH.
QUĒNMAN See QUĒMMAN.
QUĒNMANIYĀN See QUĒMMANIYĀN.
QUĒNNEL what is to be done (of something
irreversible)? / ¡hecho es, qué hemos de
hacer? o ¿qué remedio hay? (M) [(1)Cf.91r].
See QUĒN, NEL.
QUĒNOCYEH all the more, how much
more? / ¿cuanto más? (M) [(1)Cf.88r]. C
gives this together with QUĒNOQUEH to
show the variation -YEH ~ -EH. The literal
sense is approximately 'how-still-that?' See
QUĒN, OC, (Y)EH.
QUĒNOQUEH all the more; how much
more? / ¿cuanto más? (M) [(1)Cf.88r]. See
QUĒNOCYEH.
QUĒNTĒL somewhat, in some way /
algún tanto, o en alguna manera (M)
[(6)Cf.125r,131v, (2)Bf.12v,13r]. See QUĒN,
TĒL.
QUĒNTIĀ altern. caus. QUĒM(I)
QUEP(A) Z has this form instead of CUEP(A)
elsewhere. It appears to represent loss of
labialization of the initial consonant. Since
Z does not drop stem-final vowels in the
preterit, the last vowel of the stem is
parenthesized here only because it corre-

sponds to a vowel that drops in other dialects. See CUEP(A).
QUEPTOC turned over, backwards / volteado, a revés (Z) [(3)Zp.110,130,184]. See
QUEP(A), the verb O.
QUEQUETZ(A) vrefl,vt for birds to copulate;
to trample on something / de las aves, que
se toman (C), pisar y trillar (C) [(3)Cf.128r].
C contrasts this with QUEHQUETZ(A) 'to
stand up, to pace, to kick out at something' M has moquetza 'for animals to
mate.' See QUETZ(A).
QUEQUEXIHU(I) to have an itch, mange /
tiene comezón (T) [(3)Tp.177]. Since
this is only attested for T and since T
has a tendency to lose internal glottal
stops, this probably corresponds to
QUEHQUEXIHU(I) and is in some way
related to QUEHQUELOĀ.
QUEQUEXIHUĪHUA nonact. QUE-
QUEXIHU(I)
QUEQUEXIHUĪTIĀ caus. QUEQUEXIHU(I)
QUEQUEXQUIC something that causes an
itch / cosa que da comezón (M) [(1)Tp.177].
See QUEQUEXQUIYA.
QUEQUEXQUILIĀ applic. QUE-
QUEXQUILIĀ
QUEQUEXQUIYA to have an itch, mange /
tener comezón (M) [(1)Tp.177, (3)Xp.67].
See QUEQUEXIHU(I).
QUĒQUĒZQUILHUITICA at an interval
of how many days? / ¿de cuantos a cuantos dias? (C) [(1)Cf.107r]. See QUĒZQUI,
ILHUI-TL.
QUETZ(A) vrefl,vt to stand up; to stop
someone or to raise someone or something
/ levantarse el que estaba asentado (M),
detener o hacer parar al que camina o hacer
levantar al que está asentado (M)
QUETZALCŌĀ-TL personal name Quetzalcoatl (a major deity, also the name
associated with the office of a high priest) /
dios del aire (S) [(1)Bf.10r, (1)Tp.249]. T has
a form EHQUETZALCŌĀ-TL meaning
'whirlwind,' suggesting a blend of this with
EHĒCACŌĀ-TL 'wind serpent.' S has a
long description of Quetzalcoatl drawn
from Sahagún. See QUETZAL-LI,
CŌĀ-TL.
QUETZALHUĪTŌLIHU(I) to twist, writhe

in the manner of quetzal plumes / se va ... retorciendo a manera de quetzal (C) [(1)Cf.76r]. See QUETZAL-LI, HUĪ-TŌLIHU(I).

QUETZALILACATZIHU(I) to weave in and out in the manner of quetzal plumage / se va entretejiendo ... a manera de quetzal (C) [(1)Cf.76r]. See QUETZAL-LI, ILACATZIHU(I).

QUETZAL-LI plumage of the quetzal bird, a trogon with long green tail feathers (Pharomachrus mocinno) / pluma rica, larga y verde (M)

QUETZALŌ nonact. QUETZ(A)

QUETZALTEUH in the manner of quetzal feathers, as something very precious / a manera de quetzales (C) [(1)Cf.18v]. See QUETZAL-LI, -TEUH.

QUETZALTIĀ caus. QUETZ(A)

QUETZOM(A) See QUEHTZOM(A).

QUETZOMALŌ nonact. QUETZOM(A)

QUETZOMILIĀ applic. QUETZOM(A)

QUEXAHPĀZ-TLI large earthenware tub / apastle, lebrillo (de barro) (Z) [(3)Zp.12,76,184]. The first element may be related to QUEXĪL-LI 'groin' or QUECH-TLI 'neck.' See AHPĀZ-TLI.

QUEXĪLIHU(I) to suffer pain in the groin / está malo de la ingle (T) [(4)Tp.177]. See QUEXĪL-LI.

QUEXĪLIHUĪHUA nonact. QUEXĪLIHU(I)

QUEXĪLIHUĪTIĀ caus. QUEXĪLIHU(I)

QUEXĪL-LI groin / la ingre (M), su ingle (T for possessed form) [(5)Tp.133,177].

QUĒXQUICH pl: **-TIN** how much, how many? / ¿qué tanto? (M) See QUĒN, ĪXQUICH.

QUĒXQUICHCA how far? / ¿qué tanto trecho habrá hasta tal parte? (M), interrogativo del espacio que hay de un lugar a otro (C) [(6)Cf.93v,94v,131r]. See QUĒXQUICH.

QUĒXQUICHPA how many times? / ¿cuántas veces? (T) [(1)Tp.186]. See QUĒXQUICH, -PA.

QUĒXQUICHTZOCOTZIN a bit / un poco (C) [(1)Cf.125v]. See QUĒXQUICH, TZOCO.

-QUĒZ only attested in possessed form and in compounds thigh, leg / su muslo, su pierna (T,Z) [(5)Tp.133,156, (1)Zp.160].

This seems to be related to QUEXĪL-LI 'groin' but differs in vowel length in the first syllable. See QUEXĪL-LI.

-QUĒZCUAUHYŌ only attested in possessed form and compounds thigh, leg / su muslo, su pierna (T) [(4)Tp.133,156]. See -QUĒZ, CUAHU(I)-TL, -YŌ.

QUĒZCUAUHYŌTEHTEQU(I) See -QUĒZCUAUHYŌ, TEHTEQU(I).

-QUĒZPAN postposition in or on someone's legs / en sus piernas (T) [Tp.133]. See -QUĒZ, -PAN.

QUĒZQUI pl: **QUĒZQUIMEH ~ QUĒZQUĪN ~ QUĒZQUĪNTĪN** how many? how much? / ¿qué tanto? (C) ¿cuántos o cuántas son? (M for plural forms), un poco (T) The noninterrogative sense of QUĒZQUI and its derivatives is 'a bit, a few.' Other quantifiers with -QUĪN plurals also have -QUĪNTĪN as a longer plural form. The vowel of the last syllable of the longer form for QUĒZQUI is unmarked for length and is given long here by analogy with MOCH(I) 'all' and MIAC 'many.' See QUĒN, ĪZQUI.

QUĒZQUICĀN in how many places? / ¿en cuántas partes o lugares? o ¿cuántas raciones son? (M) [(4)Cf.91v]. The noninterrogative sense of QUĒZQUICĀN is 'in a few places.' See QUĒZQUI, -CĀN.

QUĒZQUIPA how many times? / ¿cuántas veces? (M) The noninterrogative sense of QUĒZQUIPA is 'few times, seldom.' See QUĒZQUI, -PA.

QUĒZQUITE-TL a bit of something / una poca (C) [(1)Cf.118v]. See QUĒZQUI, TE-TL.

QUĒZZANNEL what is to be done? / ¿qué remedio hay, qué se ha de hacer? (C) [(2)Cf.116r]. See QUĒN, ZAN, NEL, QUĒNNEL.

-QUI pl: **-QUIH** to come to do something / venir a (K) This is the optative form related to -QUĪHU(I) and -CO.

QUIĀHUA-TL See QUIYĀHUA-TL.

QUIAHUĀ-TL See QUIYAHUĀ-TL.

QUIAHU(I)-TL See QUIYAHU(I)-TL.

QUICHPĀYA-TL pl: **-PĀPĀYAMEH** a type of bird / agarista (pájaro) (T) [(2)Tp.185,243]. T has the reflex of Ō for Ā

in the reduplicated syllable of the plural
form. Possibly the first element of this is a
truncation of OQUICH-TLI 'male.' See
PĀYĀ-TL.

-QUICHTŌN *necessarily possessed form; pl:*
-TOTŌN the size of something / su tamaño (T) [(3)Tp.111,133]. See ĪXQUICH.

QUIHQUILPĪ *pret:* **-C** to gather edible
plants by hand without pulling up the root
/ coger con la mano yerbas comestibles, sin
las arrancar de raíz (M) [(3)Cf.62v]. Here
QUIL(I)-TL is the incorporated object of PĪ,
and there is vowel plus glottal stop reduplication. See QUIL(I)-TL, PĪ.

QUIHQUILPĪLTIĀ [(2)Cf.62v]. caus.
QUIHQUILPĪ

QUIHQUĪZ(A) redup. QUĪZ(A)

QUIHTŌZNEQU(I) to mean (of words,
phrases) / quiere decir (M) This frozen form
includes the specific object prefix. See
(I)HTOĀ, NEQU(I).

-QUĪHU(I) *centripetal verbal compounding
element; sg:* **-QUĪUH,** *pl:* **-QUĪHUIH** to
come to do something. This form is used
in future constructions. It is attested nineteen times in C, and in three of these
attestations the vowel of the first syllable
is marked long. The corresponding vowel
of -TĪHU(I) 'to go to do something' is more
abundantly attested long. See -CO.

QUIL it is said that / dicen que, o dizque (M)
This is abundantly attested in C.

QUILĀ-TL a type of vegetable soup /
caldo de quelite (Z) [(2)Zp.23,189]. See
QUIL(I)-TL, Ā-TL.

QUILCHĪUHQUI vegetable gardener / el
hortelano (C) [(1)Cf.99r]. See QUIL(I)-TL,
CHĪHU(A).

QUIL(I)-TL greens, quelite (the name of
several edible grass-like plants) / verdura, o
yerbas comestibles (M) There is great
inconsistency in Z with one or the other of
the vowels long as well as with both short.
C and T are consistent with both vowels
short.

QUILMACH it is said that / dicen que, o
dizque (M) [(5)Cf.122r,123r,131v]. In one of
five attestations the vowel of QUIL is
marked long; elsewhere it is short. See
QUIL, MACH.

QUILTŌNĪL greens, vegetables / verdura (Z)
[(2)Zp.128,189]. The second element is not
attested elsewhere. Z often omits absolutive suffixes. The full form should probably
be QUILTŌNĪL-LI. See QUIL(I)-TL.

QUIMELOĀ See QUIMILOĀ.

QUIMICHCUITLAXŌCHI-TL a type of
flower / flor de ratón (X) [(3)Xp.70].
QUIMICH-IN 'mouse' is sometimes used
as a diminutive, so this may mean 'dwarf
CUITLAXŌCHI-TL, lesser poinsetta.' The
Spanish gloss treats the name literally. See
QUIMICH-IN, CUITLAXŌCHI-TL.

QUIMICH-IN *pl:* **QUIMICHTIN** ~
QUIQUIMICHTIN ~ **QUIMICHI-
MEH** mouse / ratón (M) The alternate
plural QUIMICHIMEH from M is the
standard one for X and is built on MICHIN
as a unitary stem rather than stem plus -IN
absolutive suffix. It probably represents
QUIMICHIMMEH with nasal assimilation
and reduction of the resulting geminate
consonant. QUIMICH-IN is used as a
diminutive meaning 'small, dwarf, baby,' as
in Z with the local word for opossum to
mean 'baby opossum.'

QUIMICHPAH-TLI white-flowered lily used
as a purgative / cebadilla, hierba purgante
(R) [(1)Rp.128]. See QUIMICH-IN, PAH-TLI.

QUIMILCĒHUIĀ *vt* to relieve someone
of his burden / compartirle la carga (K)
[(2)Bf.5v]. See QUIMIL-LI, CĒHUIĀ.

QUIMILHUIĀ *vt* to wrap or bundle
something for someone / envolverle, o
liarle algo a otro (M) [(1)Tp.200]. applic.
QUIMILOĀ

QUIMIL-LI bundle of clothes, blankets / lío
de mantas, o de ropa (M) [(6)Bf.5r,5v,7r,
(4)Tp.200]. M has *quimili* without the
geminate, but elsewhere it behaves as a
regular stem ending in L followed by the
-LI form of the absolutive suffix.

QUIMILOĀ *vt* to wrap someone or something in a blanket, to enshroud someone /
amortajar muerto, o envolver, enmantar, o
vestir a otro (M), liar, o envolver algo en
manta, o en cosa semejante (M) T has
ME for MI. Z has QUĒMILOĀ with the
same sense, and it appears derived from
QUĒM(I)-TL 'garment.'

QUIMILŌLŌ nonact. QUIMILOĀ
QUIMILPATLA *vt* to change someone's burden / trocarle la carga (K) [(1)Bf.5v]. See PATLA.
QUIN afterwards, then; just now / después (M) This is abundantly attested in C but also appears in B. Z has YĒQUĪNPA 'recently, a while ago,' which appears to be related despite the vowel length discrepancy.
QUINACHĪC a little while ago / ahora poco ha, o denantes (M) [(1)Cf.96r]. See QUIN, ACHĪC.
QUINIHCUĀC when (noninterrogative) / entonces (M) [(6)Cf.100v,101r,131r, (2)Rp.92]. According to C, QUINIHCUĀC is distinct from IHCUĀC in that it implies some prior event (f.100v). See QUIN, IHCUĀC.
QUINIUH recently, for the first time / una cosa recién hecha, y que se acaba de hacer (C), ser la primer vez que acaeció algo (M for *quiniuhti*) [(3)Cf.90r,96r, (2)Zp.30,191]. See QUIN, IUH.
QUINĪZQUI a short time ago / poco tiempo ha, o no ha mucho tiempo (M) [(1)Cf.96r]. The vowel of the second syllable is not marked long in the single attestation. See QUIN, ĪZQUI.
QUIQUIC(I) *pret:* QUIQUIZ to whistle, to hiss / chifla, silba (Z) [(3)Zp.38,116,193, (1)Rp.28, (3)Xp.92]. The vowel of the second syllable is marked long in X and in one attestation in Z. This is synonymous with TLANQUIQUIC(I).
QUIQUINACA *pret:* **-C** to talk through clenched teeth because of pain or anger; to growl, grunt, squeal, buzz / gemir con dolor, o zumbar el abejón, gruñir el puerco, regañar el perro, o hablar entre dientes (M) [(1)Cf.75r, (4)Zp.66,147,193]. In one attestation Z has a long vowel in NA, but elsewhere it is short. See QUIQUINATZ(A).
QUIQUINATZ(A) *vt* to make various grunting, squealing, buzzing sounds at someone / rifar el caballo (M), me gruñe el perro (C), lo platica (Z) See QUIQUINACA.
QUIQUIZ-TLI conch shell trumpet / bocina de caracol, o caracol que sirve de bocina o de trompeta (M) [(3)Cf.104r,109r,120r]. See QUIQUIC(I).

QUITELMATI someone competent / competente (Z) [(2)Zp.31,196]. See YECTELTLAMATQUI.
QUĪTZQUIĀ *vt* to grasp, seize something / lo detiene con la mano, lo agarra (T) This is abundantly attested, but only for T and Z.
QUĪTZQUILIĀ applic. QUĪTZQUIĀ
QUĪTZQUILŌ nonact. QUĪTZQUIĀ
-QUĪUH See -QUĪHU(I).
QUĪXOHUA nonact. QUĪZ(A)
QUĪXOHUAYĀN main exterior door, exit / puerta, o lugar por donde salen de casa (M) [(1)Cf.91v]. The single attestation does not provide the HU or the long vowel of -YĀN, but the form is built on QUĪXOHUA, the nonactive form of QUĪZ(A), which is elsewhere attested, and the locative suffix -YĀN is abundantly attested with a long vowel. See QUĪZ(A), -YĀN.
QUĪXTIĀ *vrefl,vt* to relieve oneself; to cause someone to leave, go out, withdraw / excusarse (M), sacar algo fuera de casa, o desempeñar algo (M), echar de casa a la mujer o al criado, o desterrar a alguno, o parecer el hijo a sus padres (M) T has the exceptional variant QUIXTIĀ with a short vowel. All the other sources agree that the long vowel of QUĪZ(A) is maintained in this derivation. In construction with -HUĪC, the reflexive of QUĪXTIĀ means to discharge one's obligation to someone. See QUĪZ(A).
QUĪXTILIĀ applic. QUĪXTIĀ
QUĪXTILĪLŌ nonact. QUĪXTILIĀ
QUĪXTĪLŌ nonact. QUĪXTIĀ
-QUIYĀHUAC *compound postposition* outside (with respect to a building) / fuera de casa (M) C glosses the construction TĒCPANQUIYĀHUAC, literally 'outside the palace,' as *la plaza*. See QUIYĀHUA-TL, -C(O).
QUIYAHUĀEHĒCA-TL rainstorm with wind / llueve con viento (Z) [(2)Zp.79,191]. M has *quiauhyo ehecatl* 'south wind.' See QUIYAHUĀ-TL, EHĒCA-TL.
QUIYĀHUATĒMPAN at the door, outside / en el lugar del portal, de la puerta (T), afuera (X) [(1)Tp.219, (1)Xp.67]. See QUIYĀHUATĒN-TLI, -PAN.
QUIYĀHUATĒN-TLI entrance / portal(T) [(2)Tp.219]. X has locative

QUIYĀHUĀTENCO 'patio.' See
QUIYĀHUA-TL, TĒN-TLI.

QUIYĀHUA-TL entrance, vestibule / puerta
o entrada de alguna casa o lugar (M),
zaguán (R) This is abundantly attested,
but because the sequence is stem-internal
and invariant, there is no evidence to decide between QUIĀHUA-TL and
QUIYĀHUA-TL. C has IĀ, T has IYĀ, and
B has it both ways. This contrasts with
QUIYAHUĀ-TL 'rainstorm.'

QUIYAHUĀ-TL rainstorm / lluvia, aguacero
(Z) [(2)Zp.155,191]. This contrasts with
QUIYĀHUA-TL 'entrance.' It is attested
only for Z, which has O for A in the
second syllable. See QUIYAHU(I)-TL,
Ā-TL.

QUIYAHUĀTLAH rainy season / tiempo de
aguas, temporal (Z) [(2)Zp.120,191]. See
QUIYAHUĀ-TL, -TLAH.

QUIYAHU(I) to rain / llover (M)
[(2)Zp.79,167]. This is to be found only in
the Spanish-to-Nahuatl side of M. See
QUIYAHU(I)-TL.

QUIYAHU(I)-TL rainstorm / lluvia o
aguacero (M) Because the sequence is
stem-internal and invariant, there is no
evidence to decide between QUIAHU(I)-TL
and QUIYAHU(I)-TL. Z has O for A. X
has the variant QUIYAUH-TLI. Although

this does not appear to be a compound
word, there are the related forms
such as ĀYAHU(I)-TL 'cloud, fog,'
and CEPAYAHU(I)-TL 'snow.' See
QUIYAHU(I).

QUIYAUHMĀNAHUIĀ *vrefl* to take shelter
from the rain / se quita de la lluvia (bajo de
techo, árbol, petate, etc.), se ataja de la
lluvia (T) [(3)Tp.156]. See QUIYAHU(I)-TL,
MĀNAHUIĀ.

QUIYAUHTŌTŌ-TL a type of bird / una
especie de pájaro (T) [(1)Tp.218]. See
QUIYAHU(I)-TL, TŌTŌ-TL.

QUĪZ(A) to come out, to emerge, to
conclude or finish / salir de casa (M),
concluirse o acabarse alguna obra, o correr
el arroyo, o escampar, o sazonarse lo que se
sembró, o acabarse la fruta, por haber ya
pasado el tiempo de ella (M)

-QUĪZAYĀN *necessarily possessed form*
place from which something comes forth /
lugar de donde sale una cosa, comienzos
(S) [(1)Xp.47]. This is attested in a phrase
with TONAL-LI 'day,' the whole phrase
meaning 'east.' See QUĪZ(A), -YĀN

QUĪZQUI something set apart / separado,
sacado, extraído (S) This is indirectly
attested in CENQUĪZQUI 'something
perfect.' See QUĪZ(A).

T

TĀCHCĀUH See TIĀCHCĀUH.

TAHTIĀ *vt* to take someone as one's father / tomar a otro por padre (M) [(2)Rp.129]. M gives this with a direct object prefix plus an oblique reflexive prefix, while R has only a direct object. R also gives this as an intransitive meaning 'to become a father.' See TAH-TLI.

TAH-TLI *pl:* **TAHTIN, TĀTAHTIN** father / padre (M) This contrasts with TLAH-TLI 'uncle.' For 'father' T and Z also have TĀTAH, a form widespread in modern Nahuatl. M has *tata* specifically as the term of address used by a child.

TAHYŌ-TL fatherhood, paternity / oficio de padre, y paternidad (C) [(2)Cf.53r]. The phrase IN TAHYŌ-TL, IN NĀNYŌ-TL refers to parental responsibility. See TAH-TLI, -YŌ.

TALA-TL *pl:* **-MEH** a type of ant / talata (T) [(2)Tp.223].

TALATLĀL-LI *pl:* **-TIN** ant hill, colony of a certain type of ant / talatero (T) [(1)Tp.223]. See TALA-TL, TLĀL-LI.

TAMACHĪHU(A) *vrefl,vt* to be measured or weighed; to weigh or measure something / se mide (T), medir algo (M), medir, pesar (X) [(9)Tp.158,203,236, (3)Xp.73]. T has E for A in the first syllable.

TAMACHĪHUALŌ nonact. TAMA-CHĪHU(A)

TAMACHĪHUILIĀ applic. TAMACHĪHU(A)

TAMACHĪUHTOC border, boundary / límite, lindero (Z) [(2)Zp.76,209]. See TAMACHĪHU(A).

TAMALAYOH-TLI *pl:* **-MEH** a type of squash / cierto género de calabazas comestibles y muy buenas (M), calabaza para dulce (T) [(2)Tp.109,223, (2)Zp.20,184, (1)Rp.129]. See TAMAL-LI, AYOH-TLI.

TAMALEPĀHUAX tamale with bean filling / tamal de frijol (T) [(1)Tp.223]. See TAMAL-LI, E-TL, PĀHUAC(I).

TAMAL-LI bread made of steamed corn-meal, tamale / pan de maíz envuelto en hojas y cocido en olla (M) By extension TAMAL-LI often refers to soft, unstructured things.

TAMALOĀ to make tamales / hacer este pan, tamales (M) This is implied by TAMALŌLIZ-TLI.

TAMALŌLIZ-TLI the making of tamales / el hacer tamales (K) [(1)Bf.10v]. See TAMAL-LI, TAMALOĀ.

TAMALTE-TL a tamale with no filling / tamal toloche (pura masa y sal) (T) [(1)Tp.223]. See TAMAL-LI, TE-TL.

TAMALXOC-TLI pot for steaming tamales / olla para poner tamales (T) [(1)Tp.223]. See TAMAL-LI, XOC-TLI.

TAMAZOL-IN *pl:* **-TIN ~ -MEH** toad / sapo (M) [(2)Tp.224, (2)Zp.114,210, (3)Xp.84]. For 'big toad' T has TAMAZOLHUĒHUEH, forming the plural by adding the reduplicated plural form of the diminutive compounding element -TŌN. X has -LI for the absolutive suffix and E for A in the first syllable.

TĀMPILHUIĀ applic. TĀMPILOĀ

TĀMPILOĀ *vrefl,vt* to swing, to rock; to swing or rock something / se columpia (T), lo columpia, lo mece (T) [(6)Tp.161,213].

TĀMPILŌLŌ nonact. TĀMPILOĀ

TĀNAH-TLI basket with a handle, woven of palm / espuerta hecha de palmas (M)

TAPACHICHI green grasshopper / grillo verde, langosta (T) [(1)Tp.224].

TAPACH-TLI sea shell, coral / coral, concha, o venera (M), concha (del mar) (Z) [(2)Zp.32,212].

TAPAHZOLCĀN briar patch / maraña (Z) [(2)Zp.81,212]. See TAPAHZOL-LI, -CĀN.

TAPAHZOL-LI bird's nest / nido de pájaros (M), nido de aves (M) [(5)Zp.81,88,212]. M also has *tapaçolloa* 'to tangle something.' See PAHZOL-LI.

TAPAHZOLYĀN briar patch / maraña (Z) [(2)Zp.81,212]. See TAPAHZOL-LI, -YĀN.

TAPALCA-TL *pl:* **-MEH** potsherd, broken tile / casco de vasija de barro quebrada, o teja quebrada (M) [(1)Tp.224, (1)Zp.212]. In the compound ITZTAPAL-LI 'paving stone' this occurs without final CA.

TAPAYOLTIC something round like a ball, something broken out in bumps / cosa redonda como pelota o bola (M), boludo (T) [(2)Tp.165,224].

TATACA *vrefl,vt* to scratch oneself; to scratch something, to dig in the earth / rascarse (M), rascar a otro (M), cavar o escarbar tierra (M)

TATACALŌ altern. nonact. TATACA

TATACŌ altern. nonact. TATACA

TĀTAH See TAH-TLI.

TĀTAHHUĒ(I) grandfather / abuelo (Z) [(2)Zp.4,214]. The more usual word for 'grandfather' is CŌL-LI. See TAH-TLI, HUĒ(I).

TATAPAH-TLI *pl:* **-TIN ~ -MEH** worn and mended fabric, rag / maṇta gruesa, traída y remendada (M), ropa, tela, trapo, género; cosa vieja (T) [(3)Cf.5v, (2)Tp.224,243, (2)Rp.125,129].

TATAQUILIĀ applic. TATACA

TĒ- *nonspecific human object prefix* By extension of its primary grammatical function, this nonspecific human prefix 'someone' appears as the initial element of many nouns derived from transitive verbs which take human objects, TĒMICTIĀNI 'murderer'< MICTIĀ 'to kill someone'; TĒMACHTIHQUI 'teacher'< MACHTIĀ 'to teach someone'; TĒCUILTŌNOHCĀN 'place of recreation, pleasure'< CUIL-TŌNOĀ 'to enrich someone' TĒ- also occurs as a possessive prefix to convey a generic sense as in M's *tenantzin* 'someone's mother'< NĀN-TLI, *tepiltzin* 'son or daughter of someone'< -PIL 'offspring,' P's *tetâtzin* referring to God the Father, etc.

TEĀCHCĀUH See TIĀCHCĀUH.

TĒĀXCĀ something belonging to another / cosa ajena (M) [(2)Cf.131,58r, (4)Zp.8,101,219]. This is conventionally paired with TĒTLATQUI, the whole phrase meaning 'someone else's property.' See ĀXCĀ(I)-TL.

TĒCA *vrefl,vt* to stretch oneself out, to lie down, to settle; to stretch something out, to spread something on a flat surface / echarse o acostarse en la cama (M), asentar piedras en el edificio o poner maderos o cosa semejante en el suelo tendidos, o envasar alguna cosa líquida (M), tender (C)

TĒCA through the agency of someone, in the company of someone / de alguno, o de alguna (M), con él (T) [(1)Tp.227]. This is homophonous with the verb TĒCA 'to stretch something out,' but the verb is transitive and always appears with an object prefix. The attestation is in honorific form, TĒCATZINCO. See TĒ-, -CA.

TĒCĀHUILIĀ *vt* to rent something / lo alquila (Z) [(2)Zp.9,196]. See CĀHU(A).

TĒCALŌ nonact. TĒCA

TĒCALPANOHQUI visitor / visita, visitante (Z) [(2)Zp.130,219]. See CALPANOĀ.

TECALTIĀ *vt* to stone someone or something / lo apedrea, lo avienta con piedra (T) [(3)Tp.203]. Possibly a glottal stop has been lost, and the second element here is derived from (I)HCAL(I) 'to skirmish with someone.' See TE-TL.

TECALTILIĀ applic. TECALTIĀ

TECALTĪLŌ nonact. TECALTIĀ

TECAMAC place where there is an abundance of stone / pedregal, lugar de mucha piedra (T) [(1)Tp.224]. See TE-TL, -CAMAC.

-TĒCA-TL *pl:* **-TĒCAH** This ending replaces -TLĀN in place names to yield 'resident of, person from' that place, TEPOZTĒCA-TL 'person from Tepoztlan.'

TECAX(I)-TL *pl:* **TECAXMEH** stone trough or bowl for grinding, mortar / pila de piedra o cosa semejante (M), molcajete (Z) A variant form is TECAX-TLI. M has *tecaxtli* in the Spanish-to-Nahuatl side and *tecaxitli* in the Nahuatl-to-Spanish side. See TE-TL, CAX(I)-TL.

TECAX-TLI See TECAX(I)-TL.

TECĀYĀ-TL a type of flower / tecayate (flor) (Z) [(1)Zp.219]. See ĀYĀ-TL.

TĒCCIZ-TLI conch, the shell of which was used as a trumpet, or shell in general; egg / caracol grande (M) [(1)Cf.85r].

TĒCEMĪXPAN in public / delante de todos, en público (C) [(1)Cf.21r]. See CEM, -ĪXPAN.

-TECH *postposition* adjacent to, together with, adhering or attached to / junta con otra (C)

-TECHCOPA *compound postposition* concerning / de, acerca de (C) [(2)Cf.20r]. See -TECH, -COPA.

TECHICHICŌ-TL *pl:* **-MEH** a type of lizard with blue neck markings / lagartija rasposa que tiene el cuello azul (T) [(1)Tp.224].

TĒCHICHINA a caterpillar that inflicts a painful bite / una oruga que pica muy recio, fuerte (Z) [(2)Zp.92,219]. In both attestations in Z the vowels of the second and third syllables are marked long. But C attests TĒCHICHINATZ with short vowels, and this is clearly related. See CHICHINATZ(A).

TĒCHICHINATZ something that causes pain / cosa que aflije y atormenta (M) [(1)Cf.52r]. See CHICHINATZ(A).

TĒCHICOIHTOĀ See CHICOIHTOĀ.

TĒCHĪHUANI creator, engenderer, steward / hacedor, criador, engendrador (M) [(2)Bf.4r,6r]. See CHĪHU(A), TĒCHĪUHQUI.

TĒCHĪUHQUI one who governs, exercises control over people, one who creates or engenders people / el que gobierna, dirige a la gente (S) This is abundantly attested but only in B. All attestations are in possessed form, and this may be in suppletive relationship with absolutive TĒCHĪHUANI. See CHĪHU(A).

TECHTIĀ *vrefl* to become possessor or custodian of something / se hace poseedor, se hace dueño (T) [(3)Tp.158]. M has this as a double object verb taking both a reflexive prefix and a specific object prefix and with the sense 'to take something as one's own, to appropriate something.' See -TECH.

TECHTĪLŌ nonact. TECHTIĀ

TEC(I) *pret:* **TEZ** to grind something like corn meal / moler maíz o cosa semejante en piedra (M), muele (T) This verb and its derivative TEX-TLI 'flour, meal' are abundantly attested with the vowel of the initial syllable short. Hence it is a clear mistake that on Cf.33r this verb and its nonactive form appear with the vowel marked long. T has this as a transitive verb 'to grind something.'

TECIHU(I) to hail / granizar (M) [(1)Tp.226].

TECIHUI-TL *pl:* **-TIN** hail / granizo (M) Z has a variant with a glottal stop in the first syllable. X has the variant form TECIUH-TLI. See TECIHU(I).

TECŌ altern. nonact. TEQU(I)

TĒCŌ nonact. TĒCA

TECOĀ *vt* to entrust someone with something safekeeping / lo encarga (Z) [(2)Zp.50,196]. M has this used reflexively in construction with ĪC and meaning 'to do something on purpose.'

TECOCH-TLI grave, pit; sweet-basil (an herb) / sepultura, hoyo, o mata de albahaca, etc. (M), agujero, hoyo, sepultura (Z) [(1)Cf.125v, (4)Zp.7,69,219, (6)Xp.83]. X has TECOCHCUITLAPIL-LI as the name of a plant, possibly the same as in M's gloss. X glosses TECOCH-TLI itself as 'woodpecker,' and as the name of the plant has TECOCHCUITLAPIL-LI, literally 'woodpecker-tail.' See COCH(I).

TĒCOCOH something painful, anguish / cosa que escuece y duele (M), sufrimiento (T) See COCOĀ.

TĒCOCOHCĀYŌ-TL pain or itching / pena u escocimiento (M), dolor, dolencia (Z) [(2)Zp.47,219]. See TĒCOCOH, -YŌ.

-TĒCOCOLIHCĀ *only attested in possessed form* one's enemy / los que mal me quieren (C for first pers. sg. possessor, plural) [(1)Cf.111v]. M has synonymous absolutive *tecocoliani*, which may be suppletive with this possessed form. See COCOLIĀ.

TĒCOCOLIZ-TLI pain, injury / daño causado a alguien (S), dolor, dolencia (Z) [(2)Zp.47,219]. M has *tecocoliztli* with the sense 'hatred, malice,' which is derived from COCOLIĀ and contrasts with this. See COCOLIZ-TLI.

TECOHCOYŌ-TL *pl:* **-MEH** mouse / ratón (T) [(1)Tp.224]. S has *tecocon* and *tecocoton* 'house mouse, rat.'

TECOL-LI *pl:* **-TIN** charcoal / carbón (M) [(1)Tp.224, (2)Zp.25,219, (3)Xp.83].

TECOLŌ-TL *pl:* **TĒTECOLOH** ~ **TECOLŌMEH** owl; louse / buho o piojo blanco del cuerpo (M) The compound TLĀCATECOLŌ-TL< TLĀCA-TL 'person' and TECOLŌ-TL means 'devil, monster.'

TECOM(A)-TL *pl:* **TECOMAMEH;** *possessed form* **-TECON** clay pot / vaso de barro, como taza honda (M) T gives the inalienably possessed form -TECOMAYŌ when referring to the husk of a green tomato, but for the inalienably possessed form of the compound TZONTECOM(A)-TL 'skull,' T does not add -YŌ. Z and X compound TE-TL with CŌM(I)-TL rather than COM(A)-TL, but the sense remains the same. See TE-TL, COM(A)-TL.

TECOMAXŌCHI-TL a member of the nightshade family, cup of gold (Solandra nitida) or wild cotton (Cochlospermum vitifolium) / nombre de dos flores de figura particular (R), copa de oro, tecomaxochitl (K) [(1)Rp.130]. R has MAC for MA. See TECOM(A)-TL, XŌCHI-TL.

TECŌM(I)-TL See TECOM(A)-TL.

TECŌNI something in need of cutting / cosa que se debe cortar (C) [(1)Cf.45v]. This is derived from the nonactive form of TEQU(I) 'to cut' and is opposite in meaning from TLATECŌNI 'cutting instrument.'

TECONTIC something deep (used with respect to vessels) / hondo (jícara, bandeja, plato, etc.) (T) [(1)Tp.224]. See TECOM(A)-TL.

TECOPĪN(A) *vt* to uproot something / lo arranca (T) [(6)Tp.203,224]. See COPĪN(A), TECOPĪN(I).

TECOPĪN(I) to pry out stones, boulders / arranca piedra (T) [(1)Tp.224]. See TE-TL, COPĪN(I).

TECOYACTIC something hollow, perforated / agujerado, socavón (T) [(1)Tp.224]. See TECOYĀHU(A).

TECOYĀHU(A) *vt* to perforate something / lo agujera (T) [(3)Tp.203]. See COYĀHU(A).

TECOYĀHU(I) to be pierced through / se perfora (T) [(1)Tp.224]. See TECOYĀHU(A).

TECOYĀHUILIĀ applic. TECOYĀHU(A)

TECOYĀHUILĪLŌ nonact. TECOYĀHUILIĀ

TĒCPAN palace / casa o palacio real, o de algún señor de salva (M) In this derivation the final consonant of the stem TĒUC 'lord' loses its labiality or has it absorbed into the following labial consonant, and the result is spelled TĒC. TĒCPAN can refer to the organization or household as well as to the structure. See TĒUC-TLI, -PAN.

TECPĀN(A) *vrefl,vt* to line up; to line something up, put something in a queue, set something in order / fila (Z), poner en orden la gente (M), poner algo por orden y concierto o establecer o ordenar algo (M) [(3)Tp.203, (4)Zp.8,60,196]. See PĀN-TLI.

TECPĀNALŌ nonact. TECPĀN(A)

TĒCPANCAL-LI palace / casas reales, o de grandes señores (M) [(2)Bf.9v,111]. See TĒCPAN, CAL-LI.

TECPĀNILIĀ applic. TECPĀN(A)

TĒCPANTLĀCA-TL *pl:* **-TLĀCAH** courtier, member of a palace household or staff / cortesano (M), gente de palacio, o consagrada al servicio inmediato de príncipe (R) [(1)Rp.130]. R gives this in plural form, and the only diacritic that appears is the final glottal stop. See TĒCPAN, TLĀCA-TL.

TECPĀN-TLI See TLATECPĀN-TLI.

TECPĀNTOQUI line, column / fila (Z) [(2)Zp.60,219]. See TECPĀN(A), the verb O.

TECPA-TL *pl:* **-MEH** flint / pedernal (M) [(1)Tp.224].

TĒCPILCAL-LI court, royal reception hall / sala del palacio donde se reunían los soldados nobles y donde el rey juzgaba los delitos de adulterio de esos guerreros (S) [(1)Bf.9v]. See TĒCPIL-LI, CAL-LI.

TĒCPIL-LI nobleman / hidalgo, persona noble, caballero (C) [(2)Bf.5v,9v, (4)Cf.57v,80r]. See TĒUC-TLI, PIL-LI.

TĒCPILLŌ-TL nobility, good breeding / hidalguía, nobleza, buena crianza y cortesía (M) [(1)Bf.5v]. See TĒCPIL-LI, -YŌ.

TĒCPILTIC someone noble, well bred / cortés y bien criado (M) [(2)Cf.57v]. See TĒCPIL-LI.

TECPINTLAH place infested with fleas / lugar lleno de pulgas (M) [(1)Bf.7r, (1)Tp.224]. See TECPIN-TLI, -TLAH.

TECPIN-TLI *pl:* **-TIN** ~ **-MEH** flea / pulga (M) M gives this both with and without the absolutive suffix -TLI.

TECPOĀ to resow, replant / resiembra (Z) [(2)Zp.109,219].

TECPŌLIZ-TLI resowing / la resiembra (Z) [(2)Zp.109,219]. See TECPOĀ.

TĒC-TLI *pl:* **-MEH** rattlesnake / ví-

bora, serpiente, culebra de cascabel (T)
[(1)Tp.227]. See TĒCUĀNCŌĀ-TL.

TĒCTOC to lie spread out in a body /
estancada (Z referring to water)
[(6)Zp.7,38,75,144,219]. see TĒCA, the verb
O

TĒCUĀNCŌĀ-TL *pl:* **-MEH** rattlesnake /
víbora (C), culebra, víbora de cascabel (X)
[(1)Cf.96r, (3)Xp.83]. See TĒCUĀNI,
CŌĀ-TL.

TĒCUĀNI *pl:* **-MEH** wild beast / una fiera
(C), animal fiero (onza, tigre, león, etc.) (T)
The literal sense of this is 'maneater.' See
CUĀ.

TECUEH a type of large venomous lizard /
cierta lagartija grande y venenosa (R)
[(1)Rp.131]. This may be an element of the
personal name TECUEPOHTZIN, but in
the name B indicates just a short E, not
EH, in the second syllable.

TECUEPOHTZIN *personal name* Tecuepo-
tzin [(2)Bf.10r,10v]. See TECUEH, -POH.

TĒCUILTŌNOH someone or something
that enriches someone / el que enriquece a
otro, o cosa que enriquece a otro (M)
[(2)Cf.6v]. See CUILTŌNOĀ.

TĒCUILTŌNOHCĀN place of recreation,
enjoyment, pleasure / luga de recreación y de alegría (C) [(2)Cf.18v,51v]. See
TĒCUILTŌNOH, -CĀN.

TECUĪNALTIĀ *vt* to seize, capture someone
/ lo prende (T) [(3)Tp.203]. M has *tecuinal-
tia* 'to cause a fire to flame up,' which is
the causative form of TECUĪN(I) and
homophonous with this item. See
TETECUĪNOĀ.

TECUĪNALTILIĀ applic. TECUĪNALTIĀ

TECUĪNALTĪLŌ nonact. TECUĪNALTIĀ

TECUĪN(I) for a fire to flare up or for one's
heart to pound / encenderse el fuego
echando llama, o batir y dar golpes el
corazón (M) [(1)Cf.74v, (1)Tp.236].

-TĒCUIYŌ *necessarily possessed form* lord,
lordship / mi señor (C for first pers. sg.
possessor), cortesanos (C for plural) This
slightly idiosyncratic or conservative
possessed form of TĒUC-TLI is over-
whelmingly attested as TOTĒCUIYŌ 'our
Lord' with Christian reference. P has an
internal glottal stop, -TĒCUIHYŌ. See
TĒUC-TLI.

TĒĒLLELQUĪXTIHCĀN place of recre-

ation, enjoyment, pleasure / lugar apla-
cible y de recreación (M) [(1)Cf.51v]. See
ĒLLELQUĪXTIĀ, -CĀN.

TĒEZZŌ someone well born / hijo o hija de
nobles caballeros (M), bien nacido (C)
[(1)Cf.99r]. This is conventionally paired
with TĒTLAPALLŌ, the whole phrase
referring to good breeding. See EZ-TLI.

TEH *second person singular pronoun* you
(singular) / tu (C) This is a freestanding
pronoun as contrasted with the personal
prefixes TI- and MITZ- 'you (singular).' See
TEHHUĀ-TL.

TEHCUILIĀ *vt* to wrap something up for
someone, to entangle something for
someone / se lo envuelve (T) [(3)Tp.203].
applic. TEHCUIY(A)

TEHCUILILIĀ applic. TEHCUILIĀ

TEHCUILĪLŌ nonact. TEHCUILIĀ

TEHCUIY(A) *vt; pret:* **TEHCUIX** to wrap
something, to entangle something /
devanar, envolver, o liar algo (M), lo
envuelve, lo enreda (T) [(3)Tp.203]. See
(I)HCUIY(A).

TEHCUIYALŌ nonact. TEHCUIY(A)

TEHHUĀN *first person plural pronoun* we,
us ¿ nosotros (C) This contrasts with
TĒHUĀN 'in the company of someone'
TEHHUĀN has a long form, TEH-
HUĀNTIN. It is a freestanding pronoun as
contrasted with the personal prefixes TI-
'we' and TĒCH- 'us.'

TEHHUĀ-TL *second person singular
pronoun, long form* you (singular) / tu (C)
When this appears without the absolutive
suffix, the Ā is subject to the general rule
of word-final shortening. The sequence
TEH, TEHHUĀ, TEHHUĀ-TL represents
increasingly emphatic 'you (singular).' See
TEH.

TEHTĒCA *vrefl* to lie down / nos acostamos
(C for first pers. plural subject) [(1)Cf.117v].
M also has transitive *teteca* 'to warp cloth
or to make a bed' and intransitive *teteca*
'to lie with a woman,' which may represent either TEHTĒCA or TĒTĒCA. redup.
TĒCA

TEHTECOPĪN(A) to clear land of boulders /
arranca piedras (T) [(3)Tp.224]. redup.
TECOPĪN(A)

TEHTECOPĪNALŌ nonact. TEH-
TECOPĪN(A)

TEHTECOPĪNILIĀ applic. TEH-
TECOPĪN(A)
TEHTEĪN(I) redup. TEĪN(I)
TEHTELICZA redup. TELICZA
TEHTĒM(A) *vt; pret:* **-TĒN** to cast
something down, to throw something into
something, to scatter something / echar y
poner algo en vulgar (M), lo derrama, lo
riega (T) [(3)Tp.203]. M combines this in a
single entry with TETĒM(A) 'to fill
something with rocks.' It also contrasts
with TĒTĒM(A) 'to stack or pile something.' redup. TĒM(A)
TEHTĒMALŌ nonact. TEHTĒM(A)
TEHTĒMILIĀ applic. TEHTĒM(A)
TEHTĒMIQU(I) redup. TĒMIQU(I)
TEHTĒMOĀ redup. TĒMOĀ
TEHTĒMOLIĀ The vowel of the third
syllable is specifically marked long on
Cf.126r, although it is short in unreduplicated TĒMOLIĀ. redup. TĒMOLIĀ
TEHTEPOL-LI something dull, blunted,
stumpy / desafilado (T referring to a knife)
[(2)Tp.224]. See TEPOL-LI.
TEHTEQU(I) *vt; pret:* **-TEC** to cut, hack
someone, something to pieces / des-
cuartizar, hacer pedazos a otro, o sajar a
alguno (M), depedazar o cortar algo en
muchas partes (M) This contrasts with
TĒTEQU(I) 'to divide, distribute something' M has reflexive *tetequi* 'to practice
ritual bleeding.' redup. TEQU(I)
TEHTEQUIHUIĀ See TĒTEQUIHUIĀ.
TEHTĒQUILIĀ applic. TEHTĒCA
TEHTEQUILIĀ applic. TEHTEQU(I)
TEHTETLAH place of abundant stones /
lugar pedregoso, o pedregal (M)
[(2)Cf.18v,71v, (2)Tp.224,226]. redup.
TETLAH
TEHTĒZCATIC something blue gray / gris-
azul (T) [(1)Tp.137]. This is attested only
with prefixed ĪX- 'somewhat, rather.' See
TĒZCA-TL.
TĒHUĀN in the company of someone / con
otro o con otros (M) [(2)Tp.227]. This
contrasts with the pronoun TEHHUĀN
'we.' See -HUĀN.
TĒHUĀNYŌLQUI relative or close associate
/ deudo o pariente de otro (M) [(2)Bf.3r,3v].
In M the N of the second syllable is missing, *teuayolqui.* See -HUĀNYŌLQUI.
TĒHUĒINĀNAH great-grandmother /

bisabuela (Z) [(2)Zp.20,219]. See HUĒ(I),
NĀN-TLI.
TĒHUĒITĀTAH great-grandfather /
bisabuelo (Z) [(2)Zp.20,219]. See HUĒ(I),
TAH-TLI.
TEHUIĀ *vrefl,vt* to get struck with stones;
to strike, pound something with stones /
se topetea (T), dar golpes con piedra, pisar
con pisón, o bruñir mantas, papel, o cosa
así (M) See TE-TL, -HUIĀ.
TEHUĪHUĪPĀN-TLI a band of stones / una
cinta de piedras (T) [(1)Tp.224]. See TE-TL,
HUĪPĀN(A).
TEHUILIĀ applic. TEHUIĀ
TEHUĪLŌ nonact. TEHUIĀ
TEHUĪLŌCOTOC-TLI shard of glass /
pedazo de botella (T) [(1)Tp.224]. See
TEHUĪLŌ-TL, COTOC-TLI.
TEHUĪLŌ-TL *pl:* **-MEH** glass, crystal /
cristal o vidrio (M) [(1)Tp.224].
TĒHUĪTECŌNI whip, lash / el instrumento
para azotar y dar de palos (C) [(1)Cf.45v].
See TĒHUĪTEQU(I).
TĒHUĪTEQU(I) *vrefl, pret:* **TĒHUĪTEC** to
scourge oneself, to shed blood / se azota, se
arroja (T) [(3)Tp.158]. T has a short vowel
in the first syllable, but C has a long one in
derived TĒHUĪTECŌNI. See HUĪTEQU(I).
TĒHUĪTEQUĪHUA nonact. TĒHUĪTEQU(I)
TEHUITZCŌLŌ-TL *pl:* **-MEH** vinegaroon,
whip scorpion / vinagrillo (insecto) (T)
[(1)Tp.224]. See TEHUITZ-TLI, CŌLŌ-TL.
TEHUĪTZO-TL a type of lily / tehuitzote
(planta para fiestas) (Z) [(1)Zp.219]. This
has only a single attestation in Z. If it is
derived from TEHUITZ-TLI, the vowel of
the second syllable should be short.
TEHUITZ-TLI bill, beak, pointed stone / su
pico (pájaro, etc.) (T for possessed form),
piedra puntiaguda (S) [(2)Tp.134,224]. If
this is derived from TE-TL 'stone' and
HUITZ-TLI 'thorn,' as the glosses imply,
the vowels of both syllables should be
short, but in one of two attestations T has
them both long. See TE-TL, HUITZ-TLI.
TĒICCĀUH younger brother / hermano
menor (M) [(2)Bf.11r,12r, (1)Cf.106v]. This
basically possessed form, TĒ-ICCĀUH,
literally 'younger brother of someone,' has
been lexicalized and can take a further
possessive prefix, NOTĒICCĀUH 'my
younger brother.' See ICCĀUH-TLI.

TĒICNĒLILIZ-TLI compassion, mercy, aid / beneficio hecho a otro (M) [(1)Cf.59v, (6)Zp.31,33,75,85,219]. See (I)CNĒLIĀ.

TĒICNĒLĪL-LI compassion, mercy, aid / beneficio hecho a otro (M) [(2)Bf.5v,13r]. By general rule the vowel of the fourth syllable should be long, but it is unmarked for length in both attestations. See (I)CNĒLIĀ.

TĒICNĒLTIH someone sad, woeful / lastimero, lastimoso (Z) [(2)Zp.76,219]. See (I)CNĒLIĀ.

TĒICNĒLTIHQUI someone unfortunate / desgraciado (Z) [(2)Zp.42,219]. See (I)CNĒLTIĀ.

TĒICNŌITTANI someone compassionate, pious / piadoso (M), el misericordioso (C) [(1)Cf.44v]. See (I)CNŌITTA.

TĒILHUIĀ vrefl,vt to bring a complaint; to accuse someone, to bring a complaint against someone, to reveal something to someone / quejarse a la justicia (M), acusar a otro dando queja contra él (M), descubrir secreto (M) [(3)Tp.158]. See (I)LHUIĀ.

TĒILHUĪLŌ nonact. TĒILHUIĀ

TĒILNĀMIQUILIZ-TLI recollection of someone / recordación o memoria que de otro se tiene (M) [(1)Bf.11v]. See (I)LNĀMIQU(I).

TĒILPILŌYĀN prison, place of confinement / cárcel (M) [(1)Cf.106v]. See (I)LPIĀ, -YĀN.

TEĪN(I) to shatter / quebrarse algún vaso, saltando con ruido algún pedazo de él (M) [(4)Cf.18v,73v,74r,105r].

TEĪNIĀ vt to break something into pieces, to shatter something / quebrar vaso (M), cambiar, lo cambia (dinero) (X) [(3)Xp.73]. X marks the E long rather than the following I. See TEĪN(I).

TEĪTZ-TLI glass / vidrio (T) [(1)Tp.224]. See TE-TL, ĪTZ-TLI.

TĒĪXTĒNYOH something done in public / publicamente (Z) [(2)Zp.103,220]. See ĪXTĒN-TLI, -YOH.

TĒIZCALIĀNI tutor, one who instructs someone / el que industria y doctrina a otro (M) [(1)Cf.52v]. See (I)ZCALIĀ.

TĒIZCALIH something instructive, didactic / cosa que da doctrina y aviva y da entendimiento (M) [(2)Cf.52v]. M also has *teizcalti* with the same sense. See (I)ZCALIĀ.

TĒIZTI offspring / hijo, hija, descendiente

(K) [(2)Bf.4v,6v]. The literal sense of this is 'someone's fingernail.' It is conventionally paired with TĒTZON 'someone's hair,' the whole phrase meaning 'offspring' in a generic sense. See (I)ZTE-TL.

TĒL but, however, nonetheless (implying difficulty or doubt) / conjunción adversativa (M), duda si haría algo, o dificultad de hacerlo (C), pero (C) This frequently binds with other particles, AHTĒL 'is it not clear?,' MĀTĒL 'although,' MĀZOTĒL 'supposing that,' TĒLYEH 'but,' QUĒNTĒL 'somehow.'

TELAC-TLI pl: -MEH thick oblong tortilla / memela (T) [(1)Tp.224]. See TELĀHUAC.

TELĀHUAC something thick, bulky / grueso (p. ej. libro, tabla, pared, etc.) (T) [(4)Tp.224,226].

TELĀHU(I) to rain hard, to pour / llueve fuerte, cae aguacero (T) [(4)Tp.107,224,226]. See TELĀHUAC.

TELĀN(A) See TILĀN(A).

TELĀNALŌ See TILĀNALŌ.

TELĀNILIĀ See TILĀNILIĀ.

TELCHĪHU(A) vt to undervalue, dismiss, malign someone, something / menospreciar a otro (M), abominar o maldecir alguna cosa (M) See TELCHI-TL.

TELCHI-TL pl: -MEH satisfaction in someone's misfortune, feeling that someone has received his just deserts / endemal, del que se goza mal de otro (M) This is aundantly attested but only in C. See TELCHĪHU(A).

TELICXILIĀ applic. TELICZA

TELICZA vt to kick something, someone / dar de coces a otro o tirar coz (M)

TELICZALŌ altern. nonact. TELICZA

TELICZŌ altern. nonact. TELICZA

TĒLILHUIĀ vt to accuse someone / lo tacha, lo acusa (Z) [(3)Zp.5,119,196]. See (I)LHUIĀ.

TELOĀ vrefl to stumble / topetea (Z) [(3)Zp.123,126,174].

TELOCHCŌ altern. nonact. TELOCHCUI

TELOCHCUI vrefl,vt to be taken by surprise; to diminish or drain something / sobresalta, se sorprende (T), lo achica (p. ej. agua cuando hay poca en la tinaja) (T) [(7)Tp.158,203].

TELOCHCUĪHUA altern. nonact. TELOCHCUI

TELOCHCUILIĀ applic. TELOCHCUI

TĒLOHUIH something difficult / difícil [(2)Zp.46,220]. See TĒL, OHUIH.

TELOLOH-TLI pellet / bodoque de piedra (M) [(1)Cf.116v, (1)Tp.137, (1)Rp.96]. See TE-TL, OLOLOĀ.

TĒLPOCA-TL youth, young man / mancebete (M), joven (hombre) (Z) [(1)Cf.113r, (4)Zp.73,74,220, (1)Rp.132]. Z has both TĒLPOCA-TL and TĒLPŌCH-TLI, which according to R are synonymous. This corresponds to the variants (I)CHPOCA-TL and (I)CHPŌCH-TLI 'young woman.'

TĒLPŌCHCAL-LI house of youths, an institution of education for young men / casa en la que se educaba a los niños a los que se encargaba diversos cuidados en las ceremonias religiosas (S) [(1)Bf.10v]. See TĒLPŌCH-TLI, CAL-LI.

TĒLPŌCH-TLI pl: **TĒLPŌPŌCHTIN** youth, young man / mancebo (M) This appears to be synonymous with TĒLPOCA-TL, which differs in the length of the vowel of the second syllable. The plural is formed by reduplication of the second syllable rather than the first. This and the fact that 'young woman' is (I)CHPŌCH-TLI imply that PŌCH is a compounding element and TĒL a modifier.

TĒLYEH but / pero (C) [(1)Cf.118r]. See TĒL, (Y)EH.

TĒM(A) vt; pret: **TĒN** to cause something to fill up, to pour something into a container / echar o poner algo en alguna parte así como maíz, etc., o cocer algo en hornillo pequeño (M) This contrasts with TEM(A) 'to bathe in a sweat house.' See TĒM(I).

TEM(A) vrefl,vt; pret: **TEN** to bathe in a sweathouse; to bathe someone in a sweathouse / bañarse en temazcalli (M), bañar a otro así (M) [(2)Cf.30v, (6)Tp.158,203]. In T the preterit of the reflexive is given as TEMAC, but the preterit of the transitive as TEN, while C gives the preterits of both the reflexive and the transitive as TEN. TEM(A) contrasts with TĒM(A) 'to cause something to fill up.' See TEMĀZCAL-LI.

TĒMĀC in someone's hands, at the hands of someone / en las manos de alguno (M), en manos de la justicia o de mis enemigos (C) [(1)Cf.115v]. See -MĀC.

TĒMACA vrefl,vt to surrender, to give oneself up; to give something to someone /

darse alguno así mismo y entregarse a otro (M), dar algo a otro (M) See MACA.

TĒMACALŌ There should be an alternative form of this TĒMACŌ. nonact. TĒMACA

TĒMACHIĀ vrefl,vt to expect or have confidence in someone or something; to have expectations of someone / confiar o esperar algo (M), confiar o esperar en otro (M) [(3)Bf.2v,5v, (1)Cf.87v]. See MACHIĀ.

TĒMACHTIĀ to teach or preach / yo predico, yo enseño (C for first pers. sg. subject) C uses this verb in an illustrative paradigm and glosses it throughout as though the nonspecific human object prefix TĒ- were fused with the stem to form an intransitive verb. See MACHTIĀ.

TĒMACHTIĀNI pl: **-MEH** teacher, preacher / enseñador, predicador, o maestro (M) See MACHTIĀ.

TĒMACHTIĀNITI to be a teacher, to serve as a teacher / ser maestro (K) [(1)Cf.58v]. See TĒMACHTIĀNI.

-TĒMACHTIĀYĀN necessarily possessed form place where one gives instruction / lugar donde enseño (C) [(1)Cf.82r]. See TĒMACHTIĀ, -YĀN.

TĒMACHTIHCĀTI to be a teacher, to serve as a teacher / ser maestro (K) [(1)Cf.58v]. See TĒMACHTIĀ.

TĒMACHTIHQUI teacher / enseñador, predicador, o maestro (M) [(2)Cf.66r,98v, (1)Xp.84]. M has synonymous temachtiqui and temachti. X has reduplicated TĒMAMACHTIQUI. See TĒMACHTIĀ.

TĒMACHTĪL-LI something taught to someone, something instructive or didactic, a sermon / enseñanza tal (M), cosa que se enseña a personas, como plática, sermón (C) [(1)Cf.46r]. See TĒMACHTIĀ.

TĒMACHTĪLŌYĀN place where people are instructed, school / púlpito, cátedra, o lugar donde enseñan a otros (M) [(2)Cf.82r,129r]. Neither attestation marks the vowel of the third syllable long, but it is marked long elsewhere in attestations of the nonactive form of MACHTIĀ. See TĒMACHTIĀ, -YĀN.

TĒMĀCTIĀ vrefl,vt to surrender; to hand something over / se rinde, se entrega (M), lo entrega (M) [(6)Tp.158,205]. See TĒMĀC.

TĒMĀCTILIĀ applic. TĒMĀCTIĀ
TĒMĀCTĪLŌ nonact. TĒMĀCTIĀ
TĒMAHMAUHTIHCĀN frightening place / lugar espantoso y temoroso (M) [(1)Tp.227]. The reflex of the glottal stop in the fourth syllable is missing in T on p.227, but it does appear in the Spanish-to-Nahuatl side of T on p.42. See MAHMAUHTIĀ, -CĀN.
TĒMAL-LI pus, infection / materia o podre (M), pus, infección (T) [(3)Tp.227, (6)Zp.71,104,220, (2)Xp.84]. M also has *timalli*. See TĒMALOĀ.
TĒMALLOH something infected / tiene pus (T), infección (Z) [(1)Tp.227, (2)Zp.71,220]. Z is inconsistent in the vowel length pattern but has a reflex of the final glottal stop; T is reliable about the vowel length but has lost the final glottal stop. See TĒMAL-LI, -YOH.
TEMALŌ This nonactive form of TEM(A) 'to bathe in a sweathouse' contrasts with TĒMALŌ, the nonactive form of TĒM(A) 'to cause something to fill up,' and with TĒMALLOH 'something infected.'
TĒMALŌ This nonactive form of TĒM(A) 'to cause something to fill up' contrasts with TEMALŌ, the nonactive form of TEM(A) 'to bathe in a sweathouse,' and with TĒMALLOH 'something infected.'
TĒMALOĀ to become infected / infecta (T) [(1)Tp.227, (4)Zp.71,220]. M has *temalloa* and *timalloa* 'for an abscess to form.' The preterit of these is formed by adding -C, and they are given with medial *ll* except in the preterit of *temalloa*, which appears as *otemaloac*. See TĒMAL-LI, TĪMALIHU(I).
TĒMALOHTOC something infected / infección (Z) [(2)Zp.71,220]. See TĒMALOĀ, the verb O.
TĒMĀQUĪXTIĀNI saviour, deliverer / librador, salvador, o redentor (M) [(3)Cf.7r]. See MĀQUĪXTIĀ.
TĒMĀQUĪXTIHQUI saviour, deliverer / salvador (Z) This is abundantly attested, but only in Z does it appear without the honorific element -TZIN. Elsewhere it has the invariant form TOTĒMĀQUĪXTIHCĀTZIN 'our Savior (honorific)' and with Christian reference. TĒMĀQUĪXTIĀNI is usually used in place of this as a free form. See MĀQUĪXTIĀ.

TĒMĀQUĪXTILIZ-TLI salvation, deliverance / salvación tal o redención (M) [(3)Zp.109,113,220]. In all three attestations the vowel of the fourth syllable is marked long, although by general rule it should be short. See MĀQUĪXTIĀ.
TEMATELOĀ *vrefl* to stumble, to stub one's toe / topetea, pisa en un piedra y se magulla el pie (T) [(3)Tp.158]. See TE-TL, MATELOĀ.
TEMATELŌLŌ nonact. TEMATELOĀ
TĒMAUHCĀITTANI someone timid, shy / temeroso, huraño (T) [(1)Tp.227]. See MAUHCĀITTA.
TĒMAUHTIH something frightening / cosa que espanta y pone temor a otros (M) [(1)Tp.227, (2)Xp.84]. See MAUHTIĀ.
TEMAZĀ-TL red deer / temasate (animal) (Z) [(2)Zp.120,220]. See TE-TL, MAZĀ-TL.
TEMĀZCAL-LI *pl:* -TIN sweathouse for bathing / casilla como estufa a donde se bañan (M), temascal (T) [(1)Tp.225, (2)Zp.18,220, (3)Xp.84]. See TEM(A), CAL-LI.
TEMECA-TL *pl:* -MEH vine, shoot, sucker, coral vine (Cissus cucurbitina) / guía, bejuco, trepador (T) [(1)Tp.224]. See TE-TL, MECA-TL.
TEMECAYOH vineyard, place where there are many vines / lugar de muchos bejucos (T) [(1)Tp.225]. The final glottal stop is not attested because of the general loss of word-final glottal stop in T. See TEMECA-TL, -YOH.
TEMETL(A)-TL type of stone from which metates are made / piedra de metate (Z) [(2)Zp.98,220]. Z has TEMETL(A)-TL and METLATE-TL, both glossed as 'piedra de metate.' See TE-TL, METL(A)-TL.
TĒM(I) to fill up, to be full / estar harto y repleto, o henchirse la vasija de algún licor, o estar juntos gatillos, perrillos, o cosas semejantes, así como maíz, cacao, calabazas (M) See TĒM(A).
TĒMIĀ *vt* to fill something, to stuff something / lo llena bien, lo empaca bien lleno (T for YĒCTĒMIĀ) [(9)Tp.211,212,238]. See TĒM(I).
TĒMICTIĀNI murderer or someone who assaults others, something mortal, harmful or poisonous / matador, o el que maltrata a

otro, o cosa mortífera y venenosa (M) [(2)Cf.44r,117r, (2)Xp.84]. See MICTIĀ.

TĒMICTIH murderer or someone who assaults others,, something mortal, harmful or poisonous / matador, o el que maltrata a otro, o cosa mortífera y venenosa (M), veneno (T) [(1)Tp.227, (4)Zp.15,68,82,220]. Z has the longer form TĒMICTIHQUI. See MICTIĀ.

TĒMIC-TLI dream / sueño (M) [(3)Cf.93v,101v,114v]. See TĒMIQU(I).

TEMILIĀ applic. TEM(A)

TĒMILIĀ *vt* to throw something onto something, to fill in on top of something / se lo echa (cosa seca) (T) This is homophonous with the applicative form of TĒMIĀ. applic. TĒM(A)

TĒMILIĀ This is homophonous with the applicative form of TĒM(A). applic. TĒMIĀ

TĒMILILIĀ applic. TĒMILIĀ

TĒMILĪLŌ nonact. TĒMILIĀ

TĒMĪLŌ nonact. TĒMIĀ

TĒMIQU(I) *vt; pret:* **TĒMIC** to have a dream about something / soñar algo (M) M has this as an intransitive verb, but B, C, and T have it as transitive.

TĒMIQUĪHUA nonact. TĒMIQU(I)

TĒMIQUILIĀ applic. TĒMIQU(I)

TĒMIQUILIZ-TLI the act of dreaming / sueño (M) [(2)Tp.116,135]. See TĒMIQU(I).

TĒMĪTIĀ *vt* to fill something, to satisfy someone / hartar a otro (M), henchir algo (M) [(6)Tp.199,205]. caus. TĒM(I)

TĒMĪTILIĀ applic. TĒMĪTIĀ

TĒMĪTĪLŌ nonact. TĒMĪTIĀ

TEMŌ *pret:* **TEMŌC** to descend / descender o abajar (M)

TĒMOĀ *vt* to seek something / buscar algo, o inquirir de algún negocio. This contrasts with TEMŌHUA, the nonactive form of TEMŌ 'to descend.'

TEMŌHUA for descent to take place, for people to descend / todos descienden o abajan (M) This nonactive form of TEMŌ with its preterit TEMŌHUAC has an entry of its own in M. It contrasts with TĒMOĀ 'to seek something'. The notation of the attestations is ambiguous for the vowel of the second syllable, but by analogy with TLEHCŌ, it should be long. nonact.

TEMŌ

TEMOHUIĀ *vt* to lower something / descender o abajar algo (M) The vowel of the second syllable here contrasts in length with that in TEMŌ 'to descend.' T has one attestation with a reflex of a long vowel, but it is abundantly attested in T and elsewhere with a short vowel. See TEMŌ.

TEMOHUILIĀ applic. TEMOHUIĀ

TEMOHUĪLŌ nonact. TEMOHUIĀ

TĒMOLIĀ *vt* to seek something for someone, or to make inquiry of someone / buscar algo para otro, o hacer inquisición de vida ajena (M) applic. TĒMOĀ

TEMŌLIZ-TLI descent / descendimiento o el acto de descender y abajar (M) [(5)Zp.18,220]. See TEMŌ.

TĒMŌLŌ nonact. TĒMOĀ

TEMŌLO-TL stone for grinding chilies / temolote, para moler (Z) [(4)Zp.120,152,220]. Z marks the vowel of the second syllable long in only one of four attestations. See TE-TL, MŌLA.

TEMŌLTIĀ caus. TEMŌ

TEMOMOX gravel / grava (Z) [(2)Zp.64,220]. No absolutive suffix is attested for this. See TE-TL, MOMOXTIYA.

TĒMŌX-TLI illness, disease / enfermedad o pestilencia (M for phrase with EHĒCA-TL) [(9)Bf.11,4v,8r,8v,12r,12v,,13r]. B is inconsistent in marking vowel length in the second syllable. In three attestations it is marked long, in one it is specifically marked short, and in five it is unmarked for length. This is conventionally paired with EHĒCA-TL, the whole phrase meaning 'pestilence, disease.'

TĒMPAHPALHUIĀ applic. TĒMPAHPALOĀ

TĒMPAHPALOĀ *vrefl,vt* to lick one's lips; to lick someone's lips / se lame la boca (T), le lame la boca (T) [(6)Tp.158,205]. See TĒN-TLI, PAHPALOĀ.

TĒMPAHPALŌLŌ nonact. TĒMPAHPALOĀ

TĒMPANHUETZOĀ *vt* to mention something, to let something fall in conversation / lo pronuncia, lo menciona (Z) [(3)Zp.83,102,197]. See TĒN-TLI, PANHUETZ(I).

TĒMPATILIĀ *vrefl* to mix up one's words, to

stammer / trastrocar las palabras o trastra-
billarseme la lengua (M) [(1)Cf.114r]. See
TĒN-TLI, PATILIĀ.

TĒMPĒHUALTIĀ *vt* to incite some-
one to speak / lo provoca a hablar
(Z) [(2)Zp.103,197]. See TĒN-TLI,
PĒHUALTIĀ.

TĒMPIPITZOĀ *vt* to suck something in
one's mouth / lo chupa en la boca (Z)
[(2)Zp.39,197]. See TĒN-TLI, PIPITZOĀ.

TĒMPITZAC *pl:* **-MEH** a type of insect /
chupón (insecto) (T) [(1)Tp.227]. See
TĒMPIPITZOĀ.

TĒMPOHPOLHUIĀ applic. TĒM-
POHPOLOĀ

TĒMPOHPOLOĀ *vt* to dull, blunt something / lo embota, lo desafila (T)
[(3)Tp.205]. See TĒN-TLI, POHPOLOĀ.

TĒMPOHPOLŌLŌ nonact. TĒM-
POHPOLOĀ

TĒMPOLOĀ *vrefl* to stammer / tartamudea
(T) [(3)Tp.158]. See TĒN-TLI, POLOĀ.

TĒMPOLŌLŌ nonact. TĒMPOLOĀ

TENA to complain of discomfort / quejarse
el enfermo (M), se queja (de dolor) (T)
[(3)Tp.225, (2)Zp.104,220, (3)Xp.85].

TĒNACAZCUEHZOĀ See NACAZ-
CUEHZOĀ.

TĒNĀCECĒC something tasteless,
insipid / insípido, desabrido, soso (Z)
[(4)Zp.41,72,117,220]. Z consistently has a
long vowel in the final syllable. If the
literal meaning of this is 'something that
tastes like cold water,' the final element
should be CECEC with both vowels short
See TĒN-TLI, Ā-TL, CECEC.

TENALŌ nonact. TENA

TENALTIĀ caus. TENA

TENAMAZ-TLI *pl:* **-TIN ~ -MEH** the
configuration of three hearth stones for
supporting pots over fire; by extension,
triplets / piedras sobre que ponen la olla al
fuego, o tres criaturas nacidas de un
vientre (M) [(1)Tp.224, (2)Zp.120,220,
(3)Xp.84]. In T and X this is metathesized
to TEMANAZ-TLI. M gives only the plural
form *tenamaztin*. See TE-TL.

TĒNĀMIQUILIZ-TLI meeting, encounter,
reception / recibimientos (C), encuentro
fortuito (S) [(1)Cf.108r]. See NĀMIQU(I).

TENĀM(I)-TL *possessed form:* **-TENĀN** wall
/ cerca o muro de ciudad (M) [(2)Cf.58r].

TENANAC(A)-TL *pl:* **-MEH** a type of
mushroom / una especie de hongo (T)
[(1)Tp.225]. See TE-TL, NANAC(A)-TL.

TENĀNTIĀ *vt* to wall something in, to
encircle something with a wall or trench /
cercar de mura la ciudad o hacer albarrada
(M) [(1)Cf.58r]. See TENĀM(I)-TL.

TĒNĀYŌ-TL saliva / su saliva, su baba (Z
for possessed form) [(2)Zp.113,162]. See
TĒN-TLI, ĀYŌ-TL.

TĒNCĀHUAL-LI crumb, remnant, leaving / relieves o sobras de la mesa (M)
[(3)Zp.84,116,162]. See TĒN-TLI,
CĀHUAL-LI.

TĒNCAQU(I) *vt* to listen to someone, to
court someone / lo escucha (T), lo enamora
(Z) [(3)Tp.205, (2)Zp.50,197]. See TĒN-TLI,
CAQU(I).

TĒNCHAL-LI chin, beard / barba, no los
pelos (M), su barba (T for possessed form)
[(7)Tp.134,158]. The CHAL element also
occurs in CAMACHAL-LI 'jaw.' Although
M specifically excludes individual hairs, in
T TĒNCHAL is compounded with verbs of
plucking and cutting. See TĒN-TLI.

TĒNCHALPIHPĪ *vrefl* to shave one's beard /
rasura la barba (T) [(3)Tp.158]. PIHPĪ literally means 'to pluck' rather than 'to shave.'
See TĒNCHAL-LI, PIHPĪ.

TĒNCHALPIHPĪHUA nonact. TĒNCHAL-
PIHPĪ

TĒNCHALTEHTECŌ nonact. TĒN-
CHALTEHTEQU(I)

TĒNCHALTEHTEQU(I) *vrefl; pret:* **-TEC** to
cut, trim one's beard / se corta la barba (T)
[(3)Tp.158]. See TĒN-TLI, TEHTEQU(I).

TĒNCHICHINOĀ *vrefl* to burn one's mouth
/ se quema de la boca (Z) [(1)Zp.174]. See
TĒN-TLI, CHICHINOĀ.

-TĒNCO *compound postposition* at the edge
of something / su orilla (T for third pers.
sg. possessor) See TĒN-TLI, -C(O).

-TĒNCOPA *compound postposition* at the
order of / a la orden de (K) [(1)Bf.111]. See
TĒN-TLI, -COPA.

TĒNCUALAC-TLI saliva / babas (M), su
saliva (T for possessed form) [(1)Tp.134]. X
marks the vowel of the second syllable
long in TĒNCUALCAX(I)-TL 'jaw.' See
TĒN-TLI, TĒNCUĀTZIN.

TĒNCUALCAX(I)-TL *pl:* **-TIN** jaw / quijada
(X) [(3)Xp.85]. This is literally 'saliva box.'

X marks the vowel of the second syllable long, but it is short in T's TĒNCUALAC-TLI. See TĒNCUALAC-TLI, CAX(I)-TL, TĒNCUĀTZIN.

TĒNCUĀTZIN someone with a hare lip / labio leporino (Z) [(2)Zp.74,220]. M has *tenquapol* 'someone lacking a lip.' In both attestations of TĒNCUĀTZIN Z indicates a long vowel in the second syllable followed by a glottal stop, which is not possible in Nahuatl. See TĒN-TLI.

TĒNCUI *vrefl, vt* to be in dispute; to copy something / se dispute (Z), lo imita (Z) [(4)Zp.46,70,174,197]. In both attestations of the reflexive Z gives this with a final glottal stop, and there is no information about the preterit form. The second element of the transitive form is given as CUI, preterit CUIC. See TĒN-TLI, CUI.

TĒNEH something sharp, something with a cutting edge / cosa aguda, como espada, etc. (M) [(1)Cf.92r, (2)Zp.60,220, (1)Rp.109]. See TĒN-TLI.

TĒNĒHU(A) *vrefl,vt* for something to be mentioned, named; to endorse, give recognition to someone, to express, mention, praise something / nombrarse, ser llamado (S), afamar a otro o dar voto en elección o encartar a alguno (M), prometer o expresar algo (M) See TĒN-TLI, ĒHU(A).

TĒNĒHUALŌ nonact. TĒNĒHU(A)

TĒNĒHUILIĀ applic. TĒNĒHU(A)

TENEXCŌN-TLI *pl:* **-TIN** lime kiln / horno para cocer la cal (X) [(3)Xp.85]. See TENEX-TLI, CŌM(I)-TL.

TENEXTE-TL limestone / piedra de cal (M) [(2)Zp.98,221]. See TENEX-TLI, TE-TL.

TENEXTIC something gray, leaden / gris, plomo (Z) [(3)Zp.64,100,221]. See TENEX-TLI.

TENEX-TLI lime / cal (M) This is abundantly attested in Z and also appears in T. See TE-TL, NEX-TLI.

TĒNHUĒHUEHCA open-work weaving / tejido abierto (T) [(1)Tp.227]. See TĒN-TLI, HUĒHUEHCA.

TĒNHUĪTEQU(I) *vrefl; pret:* **TĒNHUĪTEC** to make an outcry / dar alaridos (M) [(1)Bf.11v]. See TĒN-TLI, HUĪTEQU(I).

TĒNIHZA to eat breakfast / almorzar (M) See TĒN-TLI, IHZA.

TĒNNAC(A)-TL *inalienably possessed form:*

-TĒNNACAYŌ gum of the mouth / su encía (Z for possessed form) [(2)Zp.50,162]. See TĒN-TLI, NAC(A)-TL.

TĒNNĀMIQU(I) *vt* to kiss someone / besar a otro (M) See TĒN-TLI, NĀMIQU(I).

TĒNNĀMIQUILIĀ applic. TĒNNĀMIQU(I)

TĒNNEHNEMILIĀ *vt* to imitate, mimic someone's voice / lo remeda (con voz) (Z) [(2)Zp.108,197]. See TĒN-TLI, NEHNEMILIĀ.

TENOCHCA-TL *pl:* **TENOCHCAH** person from Tenochtitlan / natural de Tenochtitlán (K) [(1)Bf.5r]. See TENOCHTITLAN.

TENŌCHTIC something painted, mottled / pintado [(1)Tp.225]. This contrasts with the initial element of TENOCHTITLAN in vowel length of the second syllable.

TENOCHTITLAN Tenochtitlan, the capital of the Mexica / (Tenochtitlán), en el tunal de la piedra, o nacido en la piedra (R) [(4)Bf.4r,9v,11r, (1)Rp.144]. B specifically marks the vowels of the first three syllables short. This contrasts with TENŌCHTIC 'something painted, mottled' as attested in T. NŌCH-TLI 'fruit of the prickly pear cactus' is often cited as a constituent of this name, but it contrasts in vowel length.

TĒNOHOTOTIYA to stammer / tartamudea (Z) [(2)Zp.120,221]. One of the two attestations is truncated, TĒNOHOTO, which would seem to be an associated noun, but it has the same gloss as the longer item. See TĒN-TLI.

TĒNŌNŌTZALIZ-TLI advice, discourse, sermon / amonestación, plática, reprehensión o sermón (M) [(1)Cf.90r]. See TĒN-TLI, NŌNŌTZ(A).

TĒNQUĪXTIĀ *vt* to declare something / declarar o pronunciar algo (M) [(1)Bf.5v, (1)Tp.227]. T consistently has the reflex of a short vowel in the first syllable of QUĪXTIĀ and all its compounds, but B marks it long for this item, as it should be by general rule. caus. TĒNQUĪZ(A)

TĒNQUĪZ(A) to enunciate clearly / pronuncia las palabras bien claras (T) [(3)Tp.227]. T gives the preterit of this as -QUĪZAC rather than -QUĪZ, although T elsewhere has QUĪZ from QUĪZ(A). See TĒN-TLI, QUĪZ(A).

TĒNTIĀ *vrefl,vt* to interfere; to sharpen

something, to give something an edge, to tune an instrument / hablar alguno o entremeterse donde no llaman, o en negocio ajeno (M), amolar o afilar cuchillo o cosa semejante, o echar ribete o floradura o franja a la vestidura (M), lo afila, lo afina (guitarra, violín) (T) With the oblique reflexive in addition to a direct object prefix, this means 'to make someone serve as a voice for someone else.' See TĒN-TLI.

TĒNTICAH to be full / está lleno (T) [(1)Tp.227]. See TĒM(I), the verb CĀ.

TĒNTILĀN(A) *vt* to haul, drag something (by a bit or ring in the lip) / lo jala (burro, etc.) (T) [(3)Tp.205]. See TĒN-TLI, TILĀN(A).

TĒNTILIĀ applic. TĒNTIĀ

TĒNTĪLŌ nonact. TĒNTIĀ

TĒNTLAHTLATIĀ *vrefl* to burn one's mouth / se quema de la boca (Z) [(1)Zp.174]. See TĒN-TLI, TLAHTLATIĀ.

-TĒNTLAN *compound postposition* before someone's lips / por delante de ... nuestros labios (C for first pers. plural possessor) [(1)Cf.21v]. See TĒN-TLI, -TLAN.

TĒNTLĀN(I) *vt* to surpass someone in speaking or eating / le gana hablando (o comiendo) (Z) [(2)Zp.62,197]. See TĒN-TLI, TLĀN(I).

TĒNTLAPĪQUIĀ *vt* to give false testimony about someone / levantar testimonio a otro (M) [(1)Cf.113r]. See TĒN-TLI, PĪQU(I).

TĒNTLAPOĀ *vt* to uncover something / lo destapa [(2)Zp.44,197]. See TĒN-TLI, TLAPOĀ.

TĒN-TLI lip, mouth, edge, and (by extension) word / los labios, o el borde, o orilla de alguna cosa (M)

TĒNTOC something filled up, something heaped, thrown together in a place / cosa que está llena o cosa que está puesta en algún lugar (M) [(1)Zp.221, (2)Xp.85]. See TĒM(A), the verb O.

-TĒNTZACCĀ *only attested in possessed form* cover or stopper for something / tapón, tapadera (Z) [(2)Zp.119,162]. See TĒNTZACU(A).

TĒNTZACU(A) *vrefl,vt* to be stifled, silenced; to force someone to be quiet, to imprison someone / ataparse o cubrirse la boca, o enmudecer (M), hacer callar a otro

confundiéndolo y convenciéndolo (M), lo encierra, le aprisiona (Z) [(5)Zp.13,50,197]. See TĒN-TLI, TZACU(A).

TĒNTZONEH someone with a beard / hombre barbado (M) [(1)Cf.120v, (1)Tp.227, (1)Zp.221]. In the Spanish-to-Nahuatl side M has this for 'sheep, goat.' It contrasts with CUĀCUAHUEH 'steer, cow.' T has I for EH. See TĒNTZON-TLI.

TĒNTZONPIHPĪ *vrefl* to shave one's beard / rasura la barba (T) [(3)Tp.159]. See TĒNTZON-TLI, PIHPĪ.

TĒNTZONPIHPĪHUA nonact. TĒNTZONPIHPĪ

TĒNTZONQUĪXTIĀ *vrefl* to shave one's beard / se afeita, se rasura (Z) [(3)Zp.6,105,174]. M has *tentzonquiça* 'to be growing out one's beard, to be unshaven.' One of the three attestations is prefixed with TLA- instead of a reflexive prefix. See TĒNTZON-TLI, QUĪXTIĀ.

TĒNTZON-TLI beard / barba (M) See TĒN-TLI, TZON-TLI.

TĒNTZONYŌHUA for one's beard to grow / se hace la barba (Z) [(2)Zp.18,221]. See TĒNTZON-TLI.

TĒNXĪM(A) *vrefl; pret:* TĒNXĪN to shave / se rasura (Z) [(2)Zp.105,174]. M has *tentzonxima* with the same sense. See TĒN-TLI, XĪM(A).

TĒNXĪPAL-LI *pl:* **-TIN** ~ **-MEH** lip / labio o bezo (M) [(2)Tp.134,159 (2)Zp.74,162, (5)Xp.85]. In T the NX sequence assimilates to XX, which is then degeminated, yielding X. See TĒN-TLI, XĪPAL-LI.

TĒNXĪPALTEHTEQU(I) *vt; pret:* **TĒNXĪPALTEHTEC** to cut someone's lip / le corta el labio (T) [(6)Tp.159,206]. See TĒNXĪPAL-LI, TEHTEQU(I).

TĒNYOH someone of fame, a person of repute / persona afamada o encumbrada en honra (M) [(1)Cf.54v, (3)Rp.44,45,133]. See TĒNYŌ-TL.

TĒNYOH edge, shore / orilla (Z) [(6)Zp.92,162,166]. See TĒN-TLI, -YOH.

TĒNYŌHUA to become famous / hacerse afamado (C) [(3)Cf.32r,54v]. See TĒNYŌ-TL.

TĒNYŌTIĀ *vrefl,vt* to become famous; to make someone famous / afamarse (M), afamar y dar honra a otro (M) [(2)Cf.54v]. See TĒNYŌ-TL.

TĒNYŌ-TL fame, repute / fama (M) See TĒN-TLI, -YŌ.

TEŌĀMOXIHCUILOĀNI writer of sacred scripture / el Escritor Sagrado (C) [(1)Cf.92r]. See TEŌĀMOX-TLI, (I)HCUILOĀ.

TEŌĀMOXPAN in sacred scripture / en los libros divinos (M) [(1)Cf.92r]. See TEŌĀMOX-TLI, -PAN.

TEŌĀMOX-TLI sacred scripture / libro divino, libro sagrado. Especie de recopilación general escrita en caracteres jeroglíficos que contenía las leyes, las costumbres, la religión, el rito, lo cronología, la astronomía, etc. (S) [(2)Cf.92r]. See TEŌ-TL, ĀMOX-TLI.

TEŌCHĪHU(A) *vrefl,vt* to celebrate divine ritual; to bless someone or something / hacer oración, darse a dios, o celebrar los oficios divinales (M), absolver o echar o darle bendición a otro (M), bendecir ornamentos eclesiasticos o otra cualquier cosa (M) See TEŌ-TL, CHĪHU(A).

TEŌCHĪHUILIĀ applic. TEŌCHĪHU(A)

TEŌCUITLAHUIĀ *vt* to gild or silver plate something / dorar algo (M), platear algo (C) [(1)Cf.60v]. See TEŌCUITL(A)-TL, -HUIĀ.

TEŌCUITL(A)-TL gold, silver, precious metal / oro o plata (M) See TEŌ-TL, CUITL(A)-TL.

TEOHCAL-LI temple, church / casa de dios o iglesia (M) [(1)Bf.10r, (2)Cf.81r,100v]. B and C agree that a glottal stop intervenes between TEŌ and CAL-LI shortening the final vowel of the first element. See TEŌ-TL, CAL-LI.

TEOHCIHU(I) to be hungry / tener hambre o tener gana de comer (M) [(2)Cf.36r, (3)Tp.225]. M also has transitive *teociui* 'to crave something material or spiritual.' T has lost the internal glottal stop.

TEOHCIHUĪHUA nonact. TEOHCIHU(I)

TEOHCIHUĪTIĀ caus. TEOHCIHU(I)

TEOHCIŌHUA for there to be hunger, for people to be starving / tener todos gana de comer o hambre (M) [(1)Cf.36r]. C states that intransitive verbs ending in -HU(I) and -HU(A) form the impersonal by replacing those endings with -ŌHUA (f.36r), and this is one such case. nonact. TEOHCIHU(I)

TEOHPŌHU(A) *vrefl,vt* to suffer, be

afflicted; to torment, afflict, offend someone / angustiarse o afligirse (M), angustiar o afligir a otro (M) [(1)Bf.9v, (2)Cf.72v,108v]. This is attested in applicative form only.

TEOHPŌHUILIĀ applic. TEOHPŌHU(A)

TEOHPŌUHQUI something or someone sad, painful / cosa afligida y angustiada (M) [(1)Bf.1r, (2)Cf.115r,127r]. Conventionally paired with COCŌC, this forms a phrase meaning 'affliction and travail.' See TEOHPŌHU(A).

TEŌMAT(I) *vrefl,vt; pret:* **TEŌMAH** to think oneself a god; to be engaged in, concerned with spiritual matters / se tiene por Dios (C), ocuparse en cosas espirituales y divinas (M) [(4)Cf.30v,79v]. M's gloss is for this with the prefix TLA-, which may be a lexicalized form in which the prefix has been absorbed to form an intransitive verb TLATEŌMAT(I). See TEŌ-TL, MAT(I).

TEŌPANCALIHTIC inside a church / dentro de la iglesia (C) [(1)Cf.21v]. See TEŌPANCAL-LI, -IHTEC.

TEŌPANCAL-LI temple, church / iglesia o templo (M) [(2)Cf.21v]. M separates this as *teopan calli*. See TEŌPAN-TLI, CAL-LI.

TEŌPAN-TLI *pl: -TIN ~ -MEH* temple, church / iglesia (M) M gives this both with and without the absolutive suffix and with no difference in meaning. See TEŌ-TL, -PAN.

TEŌPIXCĀTI to be or become a priest or a member of a religious order / ser eclesiastico o ministro de la iglesia (M), hacerse sacerdote o religioso (C) [(1)Cf.58v]. See TEŌPIXQUI.

TEŌPIXCĀYŌ-TL religious orders, priesthood / sacerdocio, orden sacra, o dignidad eclesiastica (M) [(2)Cf.53v]. See TEŌPIXQUI, -YŌ.

TEŌPIXQUI priest, religious, member of a religious order / eclesiastico, clerigo, o religioso (M) See TEŌ-TL, PIY(A).

TEŌTI to be, become a god / hacerse Dios (C) [(1)Cf.58r]. See TEŌ-TL.

TEŌTIĀ *vrefl,vt* to create gods for oneself, to be an idolater; to take something to be a god / hago dioses para mí, y usarse por idolatrar (C for first pers. sg. reflexive), tener o adorar alguna cosa por dios (M) [(3)Cf.58r]. Used transitively, this takes a direct object prefix and an oblique reflexive prefix. See TEŌ-TL.

TEŌ-TL *pl:* **TĒTEOH** god / dios (M) Z has the variant TIŌ-TL

TEŌTLAC afternoon, evening / la tarde del día, a puesta de sol (M), anoche (T) This is abundantly attested in C with Ō, but T, Z, and X have the vowel short. Z has I for E.

TEŌTLACCO evening / noche (T) [(1)Tp.225]. See TEŌTLAC, -C(O).

TEŌTLACPA in the afternoon / por la tarde (Z) [(2)Zp.119,223]. See TEŌTLAC, -PA.

TEŌTLAHTŌL-LI divine word, doctrine / palabras divinas (M) [(1)Cf.33v]. This also appears in P with the glottal stop marked but not the long vowels. See TEŌ-TL, TLAHTŌL-LI.

TEŌTLAQUILIĀ applic. TEŌTLAQUIYA

TEŌTLAQUILIZ-TLI evening / noche (T) [(2)Tp.225]. In one of the two attestations T has suffixed *-pa*, which probably represents -PAN. See TEŌTLAQUIYA.

TEŌTLAQUILTIĀ caus. TEŌTLAQUIYA

TEŌTLAQUILTIHTZINOH *greeting* good afternoon / buenas tardes (Z) [(2)Zp.119,223]. See TEŌTLAQUIYA.

TEŌTLAQUIYA to grow late, to get dark / hacerse tarde o anochecer (M) [(2)Zp.119,174]. This is attested in applicative form in Z.

TEŌTOCA *vrefl,vt* to think oneself a god; to take something as a god / se tiene por Dios (C), idolatrar (M) [(4)Cf.67v,79v, (1)Rp.83]. See TEŌ-TL, TOCA.

TEŌXIHU(I)-TL turquoise, precious green stone, gem / turquesa fina y preciosa (M) [(1)Bf.4r, (4)Cf.53v,82v]. M also gives *teoxiuh* with no absolutive suffix as 'generous son or son of generous parents,' probably by metaphor. See TEŌ-TL, XIHU(I)-TL.

TEŌXIUHYŌ-TL C gives this without a gloss as an example of a derivation with -YŌ. The sense would be something like 'the quality of being a turquoise.' See TEŌXIHU(I)-TL, -YŌ.

TEŌYOH something invested with divinity / cosa que tiene en sí divinidad (C) [(1)Cf.54r]. See TEŌ-TL, -YOH.

TEŌYŌ-TL divinity, spirituality / cosa

espiritual o cosa divina (M) See TEŌ-TL, -YŌ.

TEPĀCHILHUIĀ applic. TEPĀCHOĀ

TEPĀCHOĀ *vt* to bruise someone or something, to pound something / apezgar o emprensar algo (M), lo azota, lo quiebra (frijol, haba, etc.) ... lo martilla (T) This is abundantly attested but only in T. It contrasts with TEPACHOĀ 'to stone someone.'

TEPACHOĀ *vt* to stone someone / apedrear a otro (M), tirar piedra (M) [(1)Bf.11r]. This contrasts with TEPĀCHOĀ 'to pound something, to bruise something.' See TE-TL, PACHOĀ.

TEPĀCHŌLŌ nonact. TEPĀCHOĀ

TEPACHŌLŌ nonact. TEPACHOĀ

TĒPAHPĀQUILTIHCĀN place of pleasure, enjoyment / lugar deleitoso y placentero (M), lugar donde alegra (C) [(1)Cf.51r]. See PAHPĀQUILTIĀ, -CĀN.

TĒPAHTIĀ to cure people / curar (gente) (X) [(6)Xp.85]. This also appears in P with the glottal stop marked but not the long vowel. See PAHTIĀ.

TĒPAHTIĀNI doctor, curer / medico que cura (M) [(3)Xp.85]. See TĒPAHTIĀ.

TĒPAHTIHQUI doctor, curer / doctor, curandero, médico (Z) [(4)Zp.37,47,83,221]. M has *tepati* with the same sense. See TĒPAHTIĀ, TĒPAHTIĀNI.

-TEPAHYŌ *necessarily possessed form* it serves one right (expression of satisfaction in just punishment) / cuando uno se huelga del mal de otro, o muestra que tiene u merecido (C), tanto mejor, bien hecho (S) [(7)Cf.122r,125r,125v,131v].

TEPAHZOLIHU(I) to get caught, entangled / se enreda, se enmaraña (T) [(1)Tp.225]. See TEPAHZOL-LI.

TEPAHZOL-LI *pl:* **-TIN ~ -MEH** nest, tangle / nido (T) [(4)Tp.119,225, (3)Xp.85]. See PAHZOL-LI.

TEPAHZOLTIC something tangled / maraña, desordenado, enmarañado (como nido, leña, etc.) (T) [(1)Tp.225]. See TEPAHZOL-LI.

TĒPALĒHUILIZ-TLI aid, favor / favor, ayuda, o socorro (M) [(3)Cf.59v,106v,113r]. With the possessive prefix MO- and the honorific suffix -TZIN, this is used as a request for aid. See PALĒHUIĀ.

TEPĀM(I)-TL See TEPĀN-TLI.

TĒPAN after someone, afterwards / sobre alguno o sobre algunos (M), después (C for *çatēpan*) This is abundantly attested in C, mainly in construction with QUIN, ZĀ, or both and meaning 'afterwards.' It contrasts with TEPĀN-TLI 'wall.' See -PAN.

TEPĀNCALCO in a walled garden / en la huerta (C) [(1)Cf.118v]. See TEPĀNCAL-LI, -C(O).

TEPĀNCAL-LI enclosure, corral, house with stone or adobe walls / corral o cosa cercada de paredes (M), casa de piedra, de tabique, de adobe (T) [(1)Cf.118v, (1)Tp.226, (2)Zp.26,221]. See TEPĀN-TLI, CAL-LI.

TEPĀNCHĀN-TLI house with stone walls / casa de piedra (Z) [(3)Zp.26,162,221]. See TEPĀN-TLI, CHĀN-TLI.

TEPĀNCHĪHU(A) to build a wall / hace pared (T) [(3)Tp.226]. See TEPĀN-TLI, CHĪHU(A).

TEPĀNCHĪHUALŌ nonact. TEPĀN-CHĪHU(A)

TEPĀNCHĪHUILIĀ applic. TEPĀN-CHĪHU(A)

TEPĀNCHĪUHQUI mason, bricklayer / albañil (Z) [(2)Zp.8,221]. See TEPĀN-CHĪHU(A).

TEPĀNCOHCOTOC-TLI pl: **-MEH** piece of standing wall / pedazo de paredón (T) [(1)Tp.226]. See TEPĀN-TLI, COHCOTOC-TLI.

TEPĀN-TLI pl: **-TIN** ~ **-MEH** wall, boundary / pared (M), pared, muro (T) See TE-TL, PĀN-TLI.

TEPĀNTZICUĪNALTIĀ caus. TEPĀN-TZICUĪN(I)

TEPĀNTZICUĪN(I) to jump over a wall / brinca sobre la pared (T) [(3)Tp.226]. See TEPĀN-TLI, TZICUĪN(I).

TEPĀNTZICUĪNOHUA nonact. TE-PĀNTZICUĪN(I)

TEPĀNXITOC-TLI old, ruined wall / pared vieja, paredón, muro viejo (T) [(1)Tp.226]. See TEPĀN-TLI, XITĪN(I).

TEPĀX-IN pl: **-MEH** chameleon / camaleones (X) [(3)Xp.86].

TEPĒCOYOC-TLI cave / cueva (Z) [(2)Zp.36,221]. See TEPĒ-TL, COYOC-TLI.

TEPĒCUĀCO crest of a hill / sumo, cumbre, punta del cerro (Z) [(3)Zp.103,118,221]. See TEPĒ-TL, CUĀ(I)-TL, -C(O).

TEPEHPECH-TLI base of a column, stone foundation / base de columna (M), empedrado (T) [(1)Tp.225]. See TE-TL, PEHPECH-TLI.

TEPEHPEN(A) See TE-TL, PEHPEN(A).

TEPĒHU(A) vt to scatter, sow something / esparcir o echar algo por el suelo, así como tomines, cacao (M), lo siembra (Z) See TEPĒHU(I).

TEPĒHUAH This possessor derivation from TEPĒ-TL 'hill' is conventionally paired with the ĀHUAH, the possessor derivation of Ā-TL, the whole phrase meaning 'resident of a town.'

TEPĒHUALŌ nonact. TEPĒHU(A)

TEPĒHUĀQU(I) pret: **TEPĒHUĀC** to be preserved by drying / se seca y no se pudre (T) [(1)Tp.225]. See TEPĒ-TL, HUĀQU(I).

TEPĒHUĀX-IN pl: **-MEH** a type of acacia tree / huaje de cerro (X) [(2)Xp.86]. See TEPĒ-TL, HUĀX-IN.

TEPĒHU(I) for a multitude of small objects to fall, spill / caerse las hojas de los árboles, o esparcirse y derramarse trigo o otras semillas por el suelo (M) See TEPĒHU(A).

TEPĒHUĪHUA nonact. TEPĒHU(I)

TEPĒHUILIĀ vt to scatter something for someone or on someone / se lo echa (maíz, zacate, etc.) (T) [(3)Tp.204]. applic. TEPĒHU(A)

TEPĒHUILILIĀ applic. TEPĒHUILIĀ

TEPĒHUĪTIĀ caus. TEPĒHU(I)

TEPEHXIHUIĀ vrefl,vt to fling oneself headlong; to throw something, someone down from a height, or down a ravine / despeñarse (M), despeñar a otro (M) This is abundantly attested in T, where the internal glottal stop is missing. B has a single attestation with the glottal stop (f.1v). The high frequency in T is due to compounding with many possible locations, CUAUHTEPEHXIHUIĀ 'to hurl something down from a tree,' TLAPECHTEPEHXIHUIĀ 'to knock someone out of bed,' etc. See TEPEHXI-TL, -HUIĀ.

TEPEHXIHUĪHUA altern. nonact. TEPEH-XIHUIĀ

TEPEHXIHUILIĀ applic. TEPEHXIHUIĀ

TEPEHXIHUĪLŌ altern. nonact. TEPEH-XIHUIĀ

TEPEHXI-TL precipice, large rock, cliff, ravine / peñasco (M), roca, peñasco, altura, precipicio (S), barranca, precipicio (Z) This is abundantly attested in T and also appears in B and Z. T lacks the internal glottal stop, but it remains in B and Z. See TEPĒ-TL.

TEPEHXIYOH ravine / barranca, una peña que tiene pura piedra (Z) [(2)Zp.18,221]. See TEPEHXI-TL, -YOH.

TEPĒIHTIC valley or ravine among mountains / valle o quebrada de sierras (M) [(1)Cf.21v]. See TEPĒ-TL, -IHTEC.

TEPĒĪXCO face, slope of a hill, ridge / ladera del monte (C), frente del cerro (Z) [(1)Cf.89v, (2)Zp.61,221]. See TEPĒ-TL, ĪX-TLI, -C(O).

TEPĒMIZQUI-TL pl: **-MEH** a type of mesquite tree / mesquite de cerro (X) [(3)Xp.86]. See TEPĒ-TL, MIZQUI-TL.

TEPĒ-TL pl: **-MEH;** possessed form: **-TEPĒUH** hill, mountain, precipice / sierra (M), el monte, y cerro (C) This is conventionally paired with Ā-TL 'water,' the whole phrase meaning 'town.' The phrase may be further reduced to ĀLTEPĒ-TL, but the possessed form often remains separated, TOTĀUH TOTEPĒUH 'our town.'

TEPĒTLĀL-LI unirrigated land / (tierra) de temporal (C) [(1)Cf.118v]. The literal sense of this is 'hill(side) land.' See TEPĒ-TL, TLĀL-LI.

TEPETL(A)-TL pl: **-MEH** a type of porous rock used in construction; someone rough, uncouth / tierra dura (C), peña, tepetate (T), tosca o cucilla (M) See TE-TL, PETL(A)-TL.

TEPĒTOMA-TL pl: **-MEH** a type of tomato / tomate de cerro (X) [(3)Xp.86]. See TEPĒ-TL, TOMA-TL.

TEPETZ-TLI pl: **-MEH** smooth stone / piedra lisa (T) [(1)Tp.225]. See TE-TL, PETZ-TLI.

TEPĒXĪLŌXŌCHI-TL a shrub (Calliandra anomala) with reddish purple tassel-shaped flowers, used in treating inflammations and dysentery. / cierta planta (R), cabeza de ángel (K) [(1)Rp.134]. R fails to mark the long vowels. See TEPĒ-TL, XĪLŌXŌCHI-TL.

TEPĪCHILIĀ applic. TEPĪTZOĀ

TEPICĪL-LI gravel, debris / ripio, piedrezuelas pequeñas (M), grava (Z) [(3)Zp.26,64,221]. See TE-TL, PICĪLOĀ.

TEPIL-LI vulva / natura de hembra (M), pudenda muliebria (C) [(1)Cf.128r]. C contrasts the honorific of this, TEPILTZIN, with TĒPILTZIN 'offspring.' The word for 'penis' is TEPOL-LI.

TĒPILŌLŌYĀN place where people are hanged / lugar donde ahorcan (M) [(1)Cf.51r]. See PILOĀ, -YĀN.

TĒPILTZIN offspring, someone wellborn / hijo o hija de alguno (M), bien nacido (C) [(2)Cf.99r,128r]. This is -PIL 'offspring' prefixed with the prefix TĒ-, which imparts a generic sense 'offspring of someone,' and the honorific element -TZIN. C contrasts this with TEPILTZIN, the honorific form of TEPIL-LI 'vulva.' See -PIL.

TEPĪNIĀ vt to punch someone, to hit something with one's fist, to strike something with one's elbow / dar coscorrón con los artejos o dar de codo (M), dar puñete con la mano cerrada o dar de codo (M), lo toca (T), lo picotea (Z)

TEPĪNILIĀ applic. TEPĪNIĀ

TEPĪNĪLŌ nonact. TEPĪNIĀ

TEPITŌN pl: **TEPITOTŌN** something small, insignificant / cosa pequeña o poca cosa (M) In M the final N is missing. This compounds with nouns to form diminutives, CALTEPITŌN 'small house'< CAL-LI 'house.' See TEPITZIN.

TEPĪTZAHU(I) for something to become tough, hardened / endurecerse alguna cosa (M) [(1)Tp.225]. See TEPĪTZOĀ.

TEPĪTZĪLTIC something closely woven / cerrado el tejido (de tela, ayate, zarando, etc.) (T) [(1)Tp.225]. See TEPĪTZAHU(I).

TEPITZIN pl: **TEPITZITZIN** something small / un poco, un poquito (C) Z also has the variant TIPITZIN. See TEPITŌN.

TEPITZINTIĀ to diminish, grow smaller / disminuye (Z) [(2)Zp.46,223]. Z has I for E in the initial syllable. See TEPITZIN.

TEPĪTZOĀ vt to harden something / endurecer alguna cosa (M) [(3)Tp.204]. See TE-TL.

TEPĪTZŌLŌ nonact. TEPĪTZOĀ

TĒPOHPOLHUĪLŌNI deed or guilt which

can or should be pardoned / cosa y culpa que se puede o debe perdonar (C) [(2)Cf.45r]. See POHPOLHUIĀ.

TĒPŌHUALTIĀ *vrefl* to associate with someone / asocia (Z) [(2)Zp.15,174]. See PŌHU(A).

TEPOL-LI penis / miembro de varón (M) [(7)Tp.123,133,166,224,225,243]. In compounds this has the sense 'stump, trunk, something blunt.' In one attestation T has the reflex of a long vowel in the second syllable, but in the six other attestations T has it short. The word for 'vulva' is TEPIL-LI.

TEPOLTIC something docked, stumpy / rabón (T) [(3)Tp.167,225,243]. See TEPOL-LI.

TEPONĀCILHUIĀ *applic.* TEPONĀZOĀ

TEPONĀZOĀ to play the teponastle / tañer teponaztli (M) [(4)Cf.65v,67r]. See TEPONĀZ-TLI.

TEPONĀZ-TLI lateral log drum, teponastle / cierto palo hueco que tañen y hacen son con el cuando bailan o cantan (M) [(4)Cf.65v,67r]. One sense of TEPOL-LI is 'stump,' and since this type of drum is carved from a short log, there may be some relationship between the two words.

TEPŌTLAMIĀ *vrefl* to stumble / tropezar sin caer en el suelo (M) [(1)Cf.94r, (3)Tp.158, (2)Zp.126,174]. C fails to mark the vowel of the second syllable long, but it is given as long in T and Z.

TEPŌTLAMĪLŌ *nonact.* TEPŌTLAMIĀ

-TEPOTZCO *compound postposition* behind, behind someone's back / detrás, a las espaldas (C) [(6)Cf.22r]. See TEPOTZ-TLI, -C(O).

TEPOTZOHTĒCA-TL person from Tepotzotlan / natural de Tepotzotlán (C) [(3)Cf.41r,56v]. See TEPOTZOH-TLI.

TEPOTZOHTLĀN *place name* Tepotzotlan [(2)Cf.56v,104v]. See TEPOTZOH-TLI.

TEPOTZOH-TLI *pl: -MEH ~ -TIN* hunchback / giboso o corcovado (M) This is abundantly attested in C and also appears in X. See TEPOTZ-TLI, -YOH.

TEPOTZ-TLI back, shoulders / trasera o espalda de persona (M)

TEPOTZTOCA *vt* to pursue, to follow someone, to pursue a matter, to insist on

something / seguir a alguien, andar detrás de él (S), le pregunta, lo exija, lo insiste (Z) [(1)Cf.72v, (3)Tp.204, (3)Zp.58,72,197]. C marks the vowel of the first syllable long, which is an error. In one of three attestations Z marks the vowel of the second syllable long, which is also incorrect. See TEPOTZ-TLI, TOCA.

TEPOTZTOCALŌ *nonact.* TEPOTZTOCA

TEPOTZTOQUILIĀ *applic.* TEPOTZTOCA

TEPOZCAC-TLI *pl: -MEH* horse shoe / herradura (T) [(1)Tp.225]. See TEPOZ-TLI, CAC-TLI.

TEPOZCUAHU(I)-TL *pl: -MEH* earring / arete (T) [(1)Tp.225]. See TEPOZ-TLI, CUAHU(I)-TL.

TEPOZMECA-TL metal chain / cadena de hierro (C) [(1)Cf.75v]. See TEPOZ-TLI, MECA-TL.

TEPOZQUECHILIĀ *vt* to brand an animal / lo marca (al animal) con el hierro (T) [(3)Tp.204]. See TEPOZ-TLI, QUECHIĀ.

TEPOZQUECHILILIĀ *applic.* TEPOZ-QUECHILIĀ

TEPOZQUECHILĪLŌ *nonact.* TEPOZ-QUECHILIĀ

TEPOZTĒCA-TL someone from Tepoztlan / natural de Tepoztlán (K) [(1)Cf.56v]. This is also the name of a character in folk tales from the Tepoztlan area. See TEPOZTLĀN.

TEPOZTLĀL-LI iron filings, rust / limaduras de hierro (M), moho (T) [(3)Tp.226]. See TEPOZ-TLI, TLĀL-LI.

TEPOZTLĀLLOH something rusted / oxidado (T) [(1)Tp.226]. The final glottal stop is not attested due to the general loss of word-final glottal stop in T. See TEPOZTLĀL-LI, -YOH.

TEPOZTLĀLLŌTIĀ *vt* to rust, oxidize something / lo enmohece, lo oxida (T) [(3)Tp.204]. See TEPOZTLĀLLOH.

TEPOZTLĀLLŌTILIĀ *applic.* TEPOZ-TLĀLLŌTIĀ

TEPOZTLĀLLŌTĪLŌ *nonact.* TEPOZ-TLĀLLŌTIĀ

TEPOZTLĀLOĀ to rust / se oxida, enmohece (T) [(3)Tp.226]. See TEPOZ-TLI, TLĀLOĀ.

TEPOZTLĀN *place name* Tepoztlan [(1)Cf.56v]. See TEPOZ-TLI, -TLĀN.

TEPOZTLAPŌHUAL-LI clock / reloj
(C) [(1)Cf.61v]. See TEPOZ-TLI,
TLAPŌHUAL-LI.

TEPOZTLATOPŌN firearm / arma de
fuego (Z) [(2)Zp.13,221]. See TEPOZ-TLI,
TLATOPŌN.

TEPOZ-TLI workable metal, copper or iron,
device made from metal / cobre o hierro
(M)

TEQU(I) vt; pret: **TEC** to cut something /
cortar algo (M)

TĒQUIĀ vrefl,vt to sprinkle something on
someone, something / derramar, echar (K)
This is abundantly attested in T but always compounded with Ā-TL 'water' or
CUĀ(I)-TL 'head' and generally having to
do with baptism. See TĒCA.

TEQUIH- verbal intensifier very much /
adv. que se intercala entre los verbos y
significa mucho (S) [(1)Cf.121r]. This is
prefixed directly to the stem; all other
prefixes precede it. See TEQUI-TL.

TEQUIHMACA vt to drink to excess /
bebeis demasiado (C for second pers. plural
subject) [(1)Cf.121]. This is a double object
verb which takes both an object prefix
and a reflexive prefix. It contrasts with
TEQUIMACA 'to assign tribute or labor.'
See TEQUIH, MACA.

TEQUĪHUA altern. nonact. TEQU(I)

TEQUIHUIĀ vrefl,vt to volunteer oneself; to present something, to beg something of someone / se ofrece (Z), lo
ofrece (Z), importunar algo a otro (M)
[(4)Zp.90,174,197]. See TEQUI-TL, -HUIĀ.

TĒQUILIĀ C contrasts this with TEQUILIĀ,
the applicative form of TEQU(I) 'to cut
something.' applic. TĒCA

TEQUILIĀ C contrasts this with TĒQUILIĀ,
the applicative form of TĒCA. applic.
TEQU(I)

TĒQUILILIĀ applic. TĒQUILIĀ

TĒQUILĪLŌ nonact. TĒQUILIĀ

TĒQUILIZ-TLI diarrhea / diarrea (T)
[(1)Tp.227]. See TĒCA.

TĒQUĪLŌ nonact. TĒQUIĀ

TEQUIMACA vt to assign tribute, tasks, or
posts to people, to cost someone effort /
repartir tributo o oficio, o tarea a otros (M),
le cuesta (T) [(3)Tp.204]. This contrasts

with C's TEQUIHMACA 'to drink to
excess.' See TEQUI-TL, MACA.

TEQUIPACHOĀ vrefl,vt to be anxious; to
inflict worry or pain on someone / estar
ocupando, descontento, y con pena (M),
angustiar, dar pena o afligir a otro (M) See
TEQUI-TL, PACHOĀ.

TEQUIPACHŌLIZ-TLI affliction, suffering / tristeza (T) [(1)Tp.226]. This
has lost the reflexive prefix NE-. See
NETEQUIPACHŌLIZ-TLI.

TEQUIPACHŌL-LI affliction, suffering /
tristeza (T) [(1)Tp.226]. This has lost the
reflexive prefix NE-. See TEQUIPACHOĀ.

TEQUIPACHŌLMACA vt to cause someone
to grieve / le da tristeza, lo entristece (T)
[(3)Tp.204]. caus. TEQUIPACHŌL-LI,
MACA

TEQUIPACHŌLŌ nonact. TEQUIPACHOĀ

TEQUIPACHŌLTIĀ vt to cause someone to
grieve / lo hace triste, lo entristece (T)
[(3)Tp.204]. caus. TEQUIPACHOĀ

TEQUIPACHŌLTILIĀ applic. TEQUI-
PACHŌLTIĀ

TEQUIPACHŌLTĪLŌ nonact. TEQUI-
PACHŌLTIĀ

TEQUIPANILHUIĀ applic. TEQUIPANOĀ

TEQUIPANOĀ vt to work, to serve someone / trabajar (M), lo sirve (T) This verb occurs as both intransitive and transitive.
The intransitive form and the transitive
form with the nonspecific object prefix
TLA- have the sense 'to work, to hold
office, to fulfill responsibilities, while with
specific object prefixes it has the sense 'to
serve someone, to work for someone.' See
TEQUI-TL, PANOĀ.

TEQUIPANOĀNI laborer / trabajador (X)
[(3)Xp.86]. See TEQUIPANOĀ.

TEQUIPANŌLIZ-TLI labor, public works /
trabajo (trabajo comunal) (X) [(2)Xp.86]. In
one of the two attestations there is an
additional LI syllable. See TEQUIPANOĀ.

TEQUIPANŌLŌ nonact. TEQUIPANOĀ

TEQUIPANŌLTIĀ caus. TEQUIPANOĀ

TEQUIPOLHUIĀ applic. TEQUIPOLOĀ

TEQUIPOLOĀ vt to serve, attend someone, to labor for someone / lo atiende,
le sirve (a otro) (T) [(3)Tp.204]. See
TEQUI-TL, POLOĀ.

TEQUIPOLŌLŌ nonact. TEQUIPOLOĀ
TEQUITI to work or to pay tribute / trabajar
o tributar (M) T forms the preterit by
dropping the final vowel, but according
to M it is formed by adding -C. See
TEQUI-TL.
TEQUITĪHUA nonact. TEQUITI
TEQUITILIĀ applic. TEQUITI
TEQUITILIZ-TLI work, servitude / trabajo,
servidumbre (M) [(2)Zp.124,222]. See
TEQUITI.
TEQUITILTIĀ vt to put someone, something to work, to use something / le hace
trabajar, lo ocupa, lo usa (T) [(3)Tp.204]. By
general rule the vowel of the third syllable
should be short, but it is attested long in T.
caus. TEQUITI
TEQUITILTILIĀ applic. TEQUITILTIĀ
TEQUITILTĪLŌ nonact. TEQUITILTIĀ
TEQUITINI pl: -MEH laborer, worker, one
who delivers tribute / trabajador o tributario (M) [(1)Tp.226]. See TEQUITI.
TEQUI-TL possessed form: -TEQUIUH
tribute, labor, duty, quota, term (of office) /
tributo o obra de trabajo (M), trabajo, obra,
ocupación (T) This appears to be related to
the verb TEQU(I) 'to cut something.'
TEQUITLĀL-LI pl: -TIN communal land /
terreno comunal (X) [(3)Xp.86]. See
TEQUI-TL, TLĀL-LI.
TEQUITQUI laborer, worker, one who pays
tribute / pechero, trabajador o tributario
(M) [(1)Tp.226]. Z has the variant form
TEQUITIQUI.
TEQUIUHTIĀ vt to entrust something to
someone, to make someone responsible
for something / tomar algo a su cargo o
encargarse de algún negocio (M with
additional reflexive object), te encargo (C
for second pers. sg. object) [(2)Cf.87r,115v].
M gives this as a double object verb with
a direct object prefix plus an oblique
reflexive prefix. See TEQUI-TL.
TEQUĪXQUI-TL a naturally occurring
efflorescent carbonate of soda used in
laundry, preparation of food, and medicinally / tequesquite, polvo para limpiar
(Z) [(1)Tp.226, (2)Zp.121,222]. T has a
short vowel in the second syllable. This
is probably related to the fact that T

idiosyncratically has a short vowel in
QUĪXTIĀ< QUĪZ(A) 'to come out.' M has
tequizqui 'something petrified, solidified.'
See TE-TL, QUĪZ(A)
TEQUIYOH something invested with labor,
something difficult / cosa que tiene o da
trabajo (M), trabajoso, difícil (T) [(1)Tp.226].
The final glottal stop is not attested due to
the general loss of word-final glottal stop
in T. T has E for I in the second syllable.
See TEQUI-TL, -YOH.
TEQUIYŌ-TL work, labor, payment of
tribute labor / trabajo de imposición de
tributario (M), ejercicio de trabajo o el
mismo trabajo (M), trabajo, obra, ocupación
(T) [(1)Tp.226]. T has E for I in the second
syllable. See TEQUI-TL, -YŌ.
TĒTAH See TAH-TLI.
TĒTĒCA vrefl,vt to lie down, stretch out;
to stretch something out / se acuesta
estirado (T), lo acuesta bien derecho (T
for PIYĀZTĒTĒCA) [(6)Tp.155,198,
(6)Xp.56,58]. X does not mark the vowel of
the first syllable long, but T does have the
reflex of a long vowel. M has transitive
teteca 'to make a bed or warp cloth' and
intransitive *teteca* 'to lie with a woman,'
which may respresent either TĒTĒCA or
TEHTĒCA. redup. TĒCA
TĒTECH of, by, with someone / de alguno o
en alguno (M) [(1)Cf.88r]. See -TECH.
TĒTECOHUA nonact. TĒTEQU(I)
TETECUECHILIĀ applic. TETECUITZ(A)
TETECUICA to roar, thunder, resonate,
throb / hacer gran ruido la llama de fuego,
o escocer, dar latidos, y doler mucho
la llaga o el encordio o la hinchazón, o
zumbar y hacer ruido alguna cosa así
como el viento, o reteñir el metal (M)
[(3)Cf.74v,86r]. See TECUĪN(I).
TETECUĪNOĀ vrefl,vt to become en-
meshed, tangled; to catch something, to
wrap or roll up something / se enreda, se
revuelca (Z), lo enreda, lo enrolla, lo rueda
(Z) [(7)Zp.52,110,111,174,197]. This does
not seem to be related to TECUĪN(I) 'for a
fire to roar, for one's heart to pound.' See
TECUĪNALTIĀ.
TETECUĪNŌL-LI roll, bundle / enrollar (Z)
[(2)Zp.52,222]. Z glosses this derived noun

as though it were a verb. M has *tetecuintic* 'something trimmed down, with all projections removed.' See TETECUĪNOĀ.

TETECUITZ(A) *vt* to stomp, to make noise with one's feet / hacer estruendo con los pies (M) [(3)Cf.74v,121v]. This is attested with TLA- and as an intransitive with no object prefix at all. See TECUĪN(I).

TETEICA to crumble, shatter, crunch, or for something to come apart from use / crujir algo entre los dientes (M), quebrarse vidrio o otras cosas delicadas … si los pedazos son muchos (C), se desmorona (Z) [(1)Cf.74r, (4)Zp.43,79,167,222]. See TEĪN(I).

TETEITZ(A) *vt* to shatter something, to grind something to bits / roer hueso o cosa semejante (M), quebrar estas cosas (vidrio o otras cosas delicadas) en muchas pedazos (C), lo desmorona (Z) [(1)Cf.74r, (2)Zp.43,197]. See TEĪN(I).

TETĒLIC someone grabby / agarroso (Z) [(2)Zp.6,222]. M has *teteloa* 'to elbow.'

TETĒM(A) *vt; pret:* **TETĒN** to fill something with rocks / henchir algo de piedras, así como cimiento de pared (M) This is implied by TE-TL 'stone' and TĒM(A) 'to fill something' It contrasts with TEHTĒM(A) 'to cast down, scatter something' and TĒTĒM(A) 'to stack something,' but M combines them all in a single entry.

TĒTĒM(A) *vt; pret:* **TĒTĒN** to stack or pile something / componer leña, o echar y poner algo en vulgar (M), lo amontona, lo apila (Z) [(3)Zp.10,12,197]. This contrasts with TETĒM(A) 'to fill something with rocks' and TEHTĒM(A) 'to cast down, scatter something.' redup. TĒM(A)

TĒTEMĀTL(A)-TL *pl:* **-MEH** sling / honda (T) [(1)Tp.134]. M has *tematlatl* 'slingshot,' of which this seems to be a reduplicated form. Despite the affinity of sense, this does not contain AHTLA-TL 'spear thrower' as an element of the compound. See TE-TL, MĀTL(A)-TL.

TĒTEMETL(A)-TL gizzard, crop / molleja de ave (M), su molleja (T for possessed form) [(1)Tp.134, (3)Xp.87]. M has *tememetlatl* with reduplication of the second element of the compound instead of the first. X

fails to mark the vowel of the first syllable long, but T does have the reflex of a long vowel. T has I for E. See TE-TL, METL(A)-TL.

TĒTEPITŌN See TĒTEPITZIN.

TETEPITZ(A) *vt* to peck something / lo picotea (Z) [(2)Zp.98,197]. See TEPĪNIĀ.

TĒTEPITZIN something very small / chiquillo (C) [(1)Cf.125v]. M has *tetepito* which represents TĒTEPITŌN with the same meaning. redup. TEPITZIN

TĒTEPIZCANTZIN something very small (pejorative) / chiquillo … con menosprecio (C) [(1)Cf.125v]. See TEPITZIN.

TETEQU(I) *vt; pret:* **TETEC** to gnaw on something / roe (Z) [(2)Zp.111,215]. This is only attested with the object prefix TLA-. It contrasts with TĒTEQU(I) 'to slice something' and TEHTEQU(I) 'to hack something.' redup. TEQU(I)

TĒTEQU(I) *vt; pret:* **TĒTEC** to slice something evenly, to divide and distribute something / rebano (C for first pers. sg. subject), derrama (T) [(1)Cf.72r, (8)Tp.119,205,236]. This contrasts with TEHTEQU(I) 'to hack something to pieces' and TETEQU(I) 'to gnaw on something.' redup. TEQU(I)

TĒTEQUIHUIĀ to make entreaties / ruega (Z) [(2)Zp.111,215]. One attestation in Z has a long vowel in the first syllable and the other a short vowel and a glottal stop. Both are prefixed with TLA-. M has *tetequiuia*, but the initial *te* in M's entry represents the object prefix TĒ-. Since Z's verbs take an additional prefix TLA-, their TĒ appears to be reduplication rather than a prefix. redup. TEQUIHUIĀ

TĒTEQUILIĀ applic. TĒTEQU(I)

TĒTEQUILĪLŌ nonact. TĒTEQU(I)

-TETETZOL *only attested in possessed form* one's heel / su talón (T) [(1)Tp.134].

TETEXILHUIĀ applic. TETEXOĀ

TETEXOĀ *vt* to gnaw, chew something / lo roe, lo masca (el pie, la mano, etc.) (T) [(1)Tp.205]. Possibly T has lost a glottal stop, and this should be TEHTEXOĀ. See TEC(I).

TETEXŌLŌ nonact. TETEXOĀ

TETEXTIC something rough, unpol-

ished / escabroso (Z) [(2)Zp.54,222]. See
TETEZ-TLI, TEXCAL-LI.

TETEZTIC something very hard / muy
duro (T) [(1)Tp.226]. See TETEZ-TLI,
TEZONTIC.

TETEZ-TLI something hard, tough / cosa
dura (K) [(1)Tp.220]. This is attested in the
compound ZACATETEZ-TLI, a type of
grass. See TE-TL, TETEZTIC, TETEXTIC.

TETIĀ *vrefl* to lay eggs; to collect stones /
ovar los peces o poner huevos las aves o
allegar y recoger piedras para edificar (M)
This is not directly attested, but it is
implied by its derivation from TE-TL
'stone, egg' and the preterit form given in
M. It contrasts with TETIY(A) 'to become
hard as stone.' See TE-TL.

TETIC something very hard, hard as stone /
cosa dura como piedra (M) [(1)Cf.57v,
(1)Rp.47]. See TE-TL.

TETIY(A) *pret:* TETIX ~ TETIYAC to
become as hard as stone / endurecerse
como piedra (M) [(3)Cf.57v]. This contrasts
with TETIĀ 'to lay eggs, to collect stones.'
See TE-TL.

TE-TL *possessed form:* **-TEUH** stone / piedra
generalmente (M) By extension this can
mean 'gem' or 'ornament' and in another
direction, any solid discrete object.
TŌTOLTE-TL 'egg' is literally 'bird-stone,'
and it is often shortened to TE-TL.
ĀTE-TL 'testicle' is literally 'water-stone.'
TE-TL is used as a numeral classifier in
counting small objects, CENTE-TL 'one'<
CEM, ŌNTE-TL 'two'< ŌME, etc. It also
often compounds with the names of body
parts with no apparent change of meaning
as in QUECH-TLI ~ QUECHTE-TL 'neck.'

TĒTLĀCACHĪHUALIZ-TLI friendship,
esteem / amistad, acción de apreciar (Z)
[(2)Zp.10,222]. See TLĀCACHĪHU(A).

TĒTLĀCACHĪUHQUI someone respected,
esteemed / respetable (Z) [(2)Zp.109,222].
See TLĀCACHĪHU(A).

TĒTLACUIHCUĪLIĀNI thief / robador
público o arrebatador (M) [(1)Cf.44r]. See
CUIHCUĪLIĀ.

TETLAH stony ground, lava bed / pedregal
(M) See TE-TL, -TLAH.

TĒTLAHPALŌLIZ-TLI greeting, salutation /

salutación (M), saludo (en la fiesta) (T)
[(1)Cf.108r, (1)Tp.227, (2)Zp.113,222]. See
TLAHPALOĀ.

TĒTLAHTOHUIHCĀTZIN saviour /
salvador (Z) [(2)Zp.113,222]. See
TĒTLAHTOHUIHQUI.

TĒTLAHTOHUIHQUI mediator, advocate,
defender / licenciado, abogado, mediador,
defensor (Z) [(5)Zp.3,40,76,83,222]. See
TLAHTOĀ.

TĒTLAHYELTIH something that nauseates
people / da asco (T) [(1)Tp.227]. See
TLAHYEL-LI.

TĒTLAIHĪYŌHUILTILIZ-TLI torment,
punishment inflicted on someone / tormento que se da a otro, o castigo (M)
[(1)Cf.115r]. See IHĪYŌHUIĀ.

TĒTLAMACANI someone who serves at
table / el que sirve a la mesa (M) [(1)Cf.44r].
See TLAMACA.

TĒTLAMACHTIH someone or something
that enriches or gives joy to others / cosa o
persona que enriquece o alegra a otro (M)
[(2)Cf.6v,18v]. M has *tetlamachtiani* with
the same sense. See TLAMACHTIĀ.

TĒTLAMACHTIHCĀN place of recreation and enjoyment / lugar de recreación
y de alegría (C) [(2)Cf.18v,51v]. See
TĒTLAMACHTIH, -CĀN.

TĒTLAMAHMACANI distributor, someone
who assigns shares / el que sirve a otros
de algo y les da recaudo (M), el que da
repartiendo a varios (C) [(1)Cf.44r]. See
MAHMACA.

TĒTLAN near someone, abreast of someone
/ con otros o par de los, o cerca de los, o
con otro (M) [(3)Bf.9v,111]. See -TLAN.

TĒTLANIHTOĀ *vt* to borrow money
against property / pide dinero sobre una
propiedad (T) [(3)Tp.206]. See TĒTLAN,
(I)HTOĀ.

TĒTLANIHTŌLŌ nonact. TĒTLANIHTOĀ
TĒTLANIHTŌLTIĀ caus. TĒTLANIHTOĀ
TĒTLAŌCOLILIZ-TLI compassion /
misericordia (M) [(1)Cf.123v]. X
has TĒTLAŌCOLIZ-TLI 'gift.' See
TLAŌCOLIĀ.

TĒTLAŌCOLĪL-LI tip, charitable
gift / propina, regalo, ofrenda (Z)
[(4)Zp.90,102,107,222]. See TLAŌCOLIĀ.

TĒTLAŌCOLTIH something that causes
grief, pity / se da lástima (T) [(1)Tp.227].
Because of general loss of final glottal
stop in T, the H is not attested. See
TLAŌCOLTIĀ.

TĒTLAPALLŌ someone well born / hijo o
hija de noble linaje (M) [(1)Cf.99r]. This is
conventionally paired with TĒEZZŌ, the
whole phrase referring to good breeding.
See TLAPAL-LI.

TĒTLAPOHPOLHUILIZ-TLI the act
of pardon / perdón o dispensación
hecha a otro (M) [(3)Cf.48r,48v,59v]. See
POHPOLHUILIĀ.

TĒTLAPOHPOLHUĪLŌNI means of
dispensing pardon / instrumento con
que se perdona, como la confesión (C)
[(1)Cf.45v]. See POHPOLHUIĀ.

TĒTLAPOHPOLHUĪLŌYĀN place
where pardon is dispensed / lugar de perdón o indulgencia (R) [(1)Rp.42]. See
POHPOLHUIĀ, -YĀN.

TĒTLATQUI something belonging to
another / hacienda ajena (M) [(2)Cf.13r,58r].
This conventionally pairs with synonymous TĒĀXCĀ, the whole phrase meaning
'someone else's property.'

TĒTLATZACUILTĪLŌNI means of inflicting punishment / instrumento para castigar (C) [(1)Cf.45v]. The vowel of the fifth
syllable should be long by general rule but
is not so marked in C. M has *tetlatzacuil-
tiani* 'someone who inflicts punishment.'
See TZACUILTIĀ.

TĒTLAXXĪMALIZ-TLI adultery / adultero
(M) [(1)Bf.111]. M has this with a single *x*,
but B has *xx*. See TLAXXĪM(A).

TĒTLAZOHTLALIZ-TLI love, charity towards others / amor o caridad que con otro
se tiene (M) [(3)Cf.47v,59v, (2)Zp.10,222].
See TLAZOHTLA.

TĒTLAZOHTLALŌYĀN place of human
charity, love / lugar donde se ama (C)
[(1)Cf.51r]. See TLAZOHTLA, -YĀN.

TĒTLECHIPĀHUALŌYĀN purgatory, place
of purification by fire / purgatorio (C)
[(1)Cf.93v]. See TLE-TL, CHIPĀHU(A),
-YĀN.

TĒTLOC by, close to, next to someone / con
alguno o par de alguno (M) [(3)Bf.4v,9r,9v].
See -TLOC.

TĒTOLĪNIH something that causes
affliction, injury / cosa penosa y aflic-
tiva (M), cosa que lastima y aflige (C)
[(1)Cf.52v]. See TOLĪNIĀ.

TĒTŌNĒHUALŌYĀN hell, inferno /
que se dice del infierno (R) [(1)Rp.42].
This appears in R without diacritics. See
TŌNĒHU(A), -YĀN.

TĒTŌNĒUH something that causes
pain / cosa que atormenta (M) [(1)Cf.52r,
(1)Tp.227]. T has lost the final consonant.
See TŌNĒHU(A).

TĒTOQUILIZ-TLI pursuit / seguimiento
(C) [(1)Cf.48r]. This contrasts with
TĒTŌQUILIZ-TLI 'burial.' See TOCA.

TĒTŌQUILIZ-TLI burial / enterramiento de
muerto (M) [(1)Cf.48r]. This contrasts with
TĒTOQUILIZ-TLI 'pursuit.' See TŌCA.

TĒTZACUILTĪLŌNI punishable offense / la
culpa digna de castigar (C), digno de ser
castigado (C) [(2)Cf.45r]. The vowel of the
fourth syllable should be long by general
rule but is not so marked in the attestations. See TZACUILTIĀ.

TETZĀHU(A) *vt* to condense, thicken,
solidify something / espesar o cuajar algo
(M), lo hace espeso, lo espesa, lo condensa
(T) [(3)Tp.205, (3)Zp.32,56,197]. M also has
intransitive *tetzaua* 'to condense, thicken,
congeal,' the preterit of which is formed by
adding -C.

TETZĀHUAC something thick, sticky,
congealed, hardened / cosa espesa (M),
viscoso, pegajoso, espeso (T) [(1)Tp.226,
(3)Zp.56,130,222]. See TETZĀHU(A).

TETZĀHUALŌ nonact. TETZĀHU(A)

TETZĀHUATEM(I)-TL body louse / piojo blanco del cuerpo (M) [(3)Xp.87]. See
TETZĀHUAC, ATEM(I)-TL.

TETZĀHU(I) to condense, thicken, congeal /
queda espeso, se espesa (T) [(1)Tp.226].
This is synonymous with M's intransitive
tetzaua and contrasts with TĒTZĀHUIĀ
'to be beset by forboding; to augur ill for
someone.'

TĒTZĀHUIĀ *vrefl,vt* to be beset by forboding; to frighten others, for something to
augur ill for someone / tener alguna cosa
por agüero, o espantarse mucho y escanda-
lizarse (M), escandalizar a otros (M), es mal
agüero para él (T) [(3)Tp.206]. This con-

trasts with TETZĀHU(I) 'to condense, thicken, congeal' See TĒTZĀHUI-TL.

TĒTZĀHUĪHUA nonact. TĒTZĀHUIĀ

TĒTZĀHUILIĀ applic. TĒTZĀHUIĀ

TĒTZĀHUI-TL something extraordinary, frightening, supernatural; an augury, a bad omen / cosa escandalosa o espantosa, o cosa de agüero (M) [(1)Tp.227, (3)Zp.7,102,222].

TĒTZĀHUITTA vt to marvel at something / lo maravilla, lo admira (T) [(6)Tp.206,236]. See TĒTZĀHUI-TL, (I)TTA.

TĒTZĀHUITTALŌ nonact. TĒTZĀHUITTA

TĒTZĀHUITTILIĀ applic. TĒTZĀHUITTA

TETZAPO-TL sapodilla (Achras zapota) / zapotillo, olopío (árbol) (Z) [(2)Zp.132,222]. See TE-TL, TZAPO-TL.

TETZĀUHQUIYAHU(I)-TL heavy rainstorm, deluge / tempestad, diluvio (Z) [(3)Zp.46,120,222]. Z also has a variant form that has lost the final UH of the first element. See TETZĀHU(I), QUIYAHU(I)-TL.

TETZCOHCA-TL pl: **TETZCOHCAH** someone from Texcoco / natural de Tetzcoco (C) [(4)Cf.4r,56r,107r, (1)Rp.23]. See TETZCOHCO.

TETZCOHCO place name Texcoco [(4)Bf.4r,4v,9v,11v, (2)Cf.56r,97r].

TETZĪCA-TL pl: **-MEH** a type of ant / hormiga (T) [(2)Tp.226]. M has tetzicatl 'someone sterile, incapable of reproduction.' Since there is no information about vowel length and glottal stop, it cannot be known if it is homophonous. See TE-TL, TZĪCA-TL.

TETZĪCATLĀL-LI pl: **-TIN** ant hill of a particular type of ant / hormiguero (T) [(1)Tp.226]. See TETZĪCA-TL, TLĀL-LI.

TETZĪLHUIĀ applic. TETZĪLOĀ

TETZĪLOĀ vt to twist something ropelike / torcer mucho cordel, soga, etc. (M)

TETZĪLŌLŌ nonact. TETZĪLOĀ

TETZĪLPITICAH to be fastened with a knot / nudo, está bien amarado (T) [(1)Tp.226]. TETZĪLOĀ, (I)LPIĀ, the verb CĀ

TETZĪLTIC something twisted / retorcido (T) [(1)Tp.226, (3)Zp.110,123,222]. See TETZĪLOĀ.

TETZĪLTLALPĪL-LI hard knot / nudo

duro (T) [(1)Tp.226]. See TETZĪLOĀ, TLALPĪL-LI.

TETZMOLĪN(I) to sprout again, to reappear / retoña (Z) [(2)Zp.110,222]. See TETZMOL-LI, (I)TZMOLĪN(I).

TETZMOL-LI sprout, sucker / retoño (Z), carrasco verde (M) [(2)Zp.110,222]. See TETZMOLĪN(I).

TĒTZON offspring / hijo, hija, descendiente (K) [(2)Bf.4v,6v]. This contrasts with TETZON-TLI 'stone foundation.' TĒTZON literally means 'someone's hair' and is conventionally paired with TĒIZTI 'someone's fingernail,' the whole phrase meaning 'offspring' in a generic sense. See TZON-TLI.

TETZONQUIL(I)-TL nettle / mala mujer, ortiga (planta) (Z) [(3)Zp.80,92,220]. In all three attestations Z has a glottal stop in the first syllable, but since nettles characteristically grow along walls and fences, the first element is most likely TETZON-TLI 'stone foundation.' See QUIL(I)-TL.

TETZON-TLI stone foundation / cimiento (C) [(2)Cf.75v]. See TE-TL, TZON-TLI.

TĒUCTLAHTOĀ to hold court, public hearing, council / tener audiencia o entender en su oficio el presidente, oidor, alcalde, etc. (M) This is implied by TĒUCTLAHTOĀYĀN. See TĒUC-TLI, TLAHTOĀ.

TĒUCTLAHTOĀYĀN court of justice / tribunal (C) [(1)Cf.101v]. See TĒUCTLAHTOĀ, -YĀN.

TĒUC-TLI pl: **TĒTĒUCTIN;** possessed form: **-TĒCUIYŌ** lord, member of the high nobility / caballero o principal (M), republicano (C) In older Nahuatl texts this is misleadingly written tecutli or tecuhtli, which suggests a bisyllabic stem with a stem-final glottal stop when in fact it is a monosyllabic stem with a final labialized velar consonant. The possessed form -TĒCUIYŌ contrasts with TĒUCYŌ-TL 'lordship, dominion.' In compounds the final consonant of TĒUC tends to delabialize, yielding TĒC. T and Z have -TĒCŌ as the possessed form.

TĒUCYŌ-TL lordship, dominion / señoría de estado o dignidad (M) This is abundantly attested in B and also appears in C. It contrasts with -TĒCUIYŌ, the possessed form of TĒUC-TLI. See TĒUC-TLI,-YŌ.

-TEUH *necessarily bound form* in the manner of / a manera de (C) [(2)Cf.18v].

TEUH-TLI dust / polvo (M) This appears to be related to TEX-TLI 'flour' and TEC(I) 'to grind.' X has the variant TEUC-TLI.

TEUHYOH something full of dust, dusty / cosa polvorienta (M) [(4)Cf.54v, (3)Rp.45,137]. See TEUH-TLI, -YOH.

TEUHYOHTICAH to be dusty / está lleno de polvo (C) [(1)Cf.54v]. See TEUHYOH, the verb CĀ.

TEUHYOHTIHU(I) to go along covered with dust / va lleno de polvo (C) [(1)Cf.54v, (1)Rp.45]. See TEUH-TLI, -YOH, the verb HU(I).

TEUHYOHTIHUĪTZ to come covered with dust / viene lleno de polvo [(1)Cf.54v, (1)Rp.45]. See TEUH-TLI, -YOH, the verb HUĪTZ.

TEUHYŌHUA to get covered with dust / henchirse de polvo (M) [(1)Cf.54v]. C does not mark the vowel of the second syllable long. See TEUHYOH.

TEUHYŌHUAC something covered with dust / cubierta de polvo (C) [(1)Cf.122v]. C does not mark the vowel of the second syllable long. See TEUHYŌHUA.

TEXAHCALLAH area strewn with rocks, boulders / pedregal, peña (Z) [(3)Zp.95,96,223]. See TEXAHCAL-LI, -TLAH.

TEXAHCAL-LI rocky cliff, boulder / roca (Z) [(4)Zp.95,96,111,222]. See TE-TL, XAHCAL-LI.

TEXĀL-LI sandstone used for sharpening tools / piedra arenisca como mollejón para amolar herramienta (M) This is implied by TEXĀLTE-TL. See TE-TL, XĀL-LI.

TEXĀLTE-TL *pl:* **-MEH** whetstone, sandstone / piedra arenosa, piedra para afilar (T) [(1)Tp.227]. M has *texalli* 'sandstone used for sharpening tools.' See TEXĀL-LI, TE-TL.

TEXCAL-LI oven; outcropping of volcanic rock / peñasco, risco, o horno (M), piedra volcánica (Z) [(2)Zp.98,223]. TE-TL, (I)XCA

TEXCALNAHNAC(A)-TL mushroom-shaped coastal rock formation / cierta piedra que se forman a orillas del mar a manera de hongo (R) [(1)Rp.137]. See TEXCAL-LI, NANAC(A)-TL.

TĒXCAN *pl:* **-MEH** ~ **-TIN** bedbug / chinche (C) [(3)Cf.51]. M has *texca* 'large bedbug,' which may represent either TĒXCA-TL without the absolutive suffix or TĒXCAN with a characteristically missing final N. See TĒXCA-TL.

TĒXCA-TL *pl:* **-MEH** bedbug / chinche (T) [(1)Tp.227]. See TĒXCAN.

TEXĪHUA nonact. TEC(I)

TEXILIĀ *vt* to grind something for someone / se lo muele (T) [(5)Tp.204,205,226]. applic. TEC(I)

TEXILILIĀ applic. TEXILIĀ

TEXILĪLŌ nonact. TEXILIĀ

TEXILIZ-TLI mill, or the act of grinding / molienda o el acto de moler algo (M) [(1)Bf.10v]. See TEC(I).

TEXIXĪCTŌN *pl:* **-TOTŌN** cañon wren (Catherpes mexicanus) / saltapared (pájaro) (T) [(2)Tp.226,243].

TEXŌ nonact. TEC(I)

TEXOCO-TL *pl:* **-MEH** tree of the Rosaceae family (Crataegus mexicana) and its fruit / tejocote (fruta) (T) [(1)Tp.226, (3)Xp.87]. See TE-TL, XOCO-TL.

TEXŌLŌ-TL *pl:* **-MEH** grinding stone, pestle / tejolote (T) [(1)Tp.227]. See TEC(I), ŌLŌ-TL.

TEXPETL(A)-TL *pl:* **-MEH** mixing trough; shell / batea (T), su concha (T for possessed form) [(5)Tp.132,134,227]. See TEX-TLI, PETL(A)-TL.

TEXTI to crumble, to become flour / hacer harina y desmenuzarse (M) [(3)Cf.6or]. See TEX-TLI.

TEXTILIĀ *vt* to grind something into flour, to crumble or mince something / hacer algo harina, desmenuzarlo, y picarlo menudo [(2)Cf.6or]. applic. TEXTI

TEX-TLI flour / masa de harina (M) This appears to be related to TEUH-TLI 'dust' and TEC(I) 'to grind' and contrasts with TĒX-TLI 'brother-in-law.' M combines TEX-TLI and TĒX-TLI in a single entry. Z and X have the variant form TIX-TLI.

TĒX-TLI brother-in-law of a man / cuñado

de varón (M) [(3)Cf.3r,128r, (2)Zp.37,162, (1)Rp.137]. This contrasts with TEX-TLI 'flour,' but M combines them in a single entry.

TĒXXĪPAL-LI See TĒNXĪPAL-LI.

TĒXXĪPALTEHTEQU(I) See TĒN-XĪPALTEHTEQU(I).

-TĒXXŌMA *only attested in possessed form* one's muzzle, snout / su hocico (T) [(4)Tp.134,206]. The first element of this should be TĒN 'lip, mouth.' The N would assimilate to X, yielding XX, which T degeminates to X. See TĒN-TLI.

TĒXXŌMATELICXILIĀ applic. TĒX-XŌMATELICZA

TĒXXŌMATELICZA *vt* to kick someone or something in the snout / lo patea en la trompa (T) [(3)Tp.206]. See -TĒXXŌMA, TELICZA.

TĒXXŌMATELICZŌ nonact. TĒX-XŌMATELICZA

TĒYACĀNQUI leader, ruler, boss / guiador o gobernador (M) [(1)Cf.116v]. See YACĀN(A).

TĒYACAPAN-TLI someone firstborn / primero engendrado o nacido, o primero nacida y engendrada, primogénito o primogénita (M) [(2)Tp.134,227]. M has the variant forms *tiacapan* and *tiyacapan*, where TĒ- has shortened and changed vowel quality, as in TIĀCHCĀUH. T has E for A in the second syllable. See TĒ-, YACAPAN-TLI.

TĒYŌCOYANI creator (of humanity) / creador, autor de los hombres (S) [(2)Bf.4r,6r]. See YŌCOY(A).

TEYOH place full of stones, lava bed / pedregal (Z) [(2)Zp.95,223]. M has *teyo otli* 'stony road.' See TE-TL, -YOH.

-TĒYŌLCUĪTIĀYĀN *necessarily possessed form* one's confessional / lugar donde yo confieso, mi confesionario (C) [(1)Cf.50v, (1)Rp.43]. M has *teyolcuitiloyan* 'confessional.' See YŌLCUĪTIĀ, -YĀN.

TĒYŌLICNĒLILIZ-TLI compassion / compasión (Z) [(2)Zp.31,223]. Z is inconsistent in two attestations. In one the vowel of the initial syllable is not marked long, and in the other the vowel of the fourth is not. Both attestations mark the vowels of the

last two syllables long, although by general rule they should not be. See YŌL-, (I)CNĒLIĀ.

TĒYŌLLĀLIĀNI someone who gives consolation / consolador (M) [(1)Cf.52v]. See YŌLLĀLIĀ.

TĒYŌLLĀLIH something that consoles / cosa que da consuelo (M) [(3)Cf.52r,52v, (2)Rp.44]. See YŌLLĀLIĀ.

TĒYŌLLĀLIHQUI someone who gives consolation / consolador (C) [(1)Cf.52v, (1)Rp.44]. See YŌLLĀLIĀ.

TEYŌLLŌ-TL *pl:* **-MEH** pebble / piedrita (T) [(1)Tp.227]. See TE-TL, YŌLLŌ-TL.

TEZACA to transport rock / acarrea piedra (T) [(1)Tp.201]. See TE-TL, ZACA.

TEZĀHUA-TL *pl:* **-MEH** mite / clalsahuate (insecto rojo) (T) [(1)Tp.226].

TĒZCAPAH-TLI a shrub or small tree with clusters of yellow flowers (Senecio praecox), used in treating wounds and rheumatism / cierta planta (R), palo loco (K) [(1)Rp.137]. See TĒZCA-TL, PAH-TLI.

TĒZCA-TL *pl:* **-MEH** mirror, glass / espejo parar mirarse en él (M), vidrio, espejo, cristal (T)

TĒZCATLEPŌCA *personal name* Tezcatlipoca (a major deity) / gran dios mexicano (S) [(1)Bf.10r]. Conventionally this is written with I in the third syllable, but in the single attestation the vowel is E and is specifically marked short. A commonly accepted analysis of this name takes PŌCA to be a constituent modifying TĒZCA-TL 'mirror' with the sense 'smoking.' Although PŌC is a stem form of PŌCH-TLI 'smoke,' there is no corresponding verb PŌCA. However, for reflexive IHPŌTZ(A) 'to belch,' there should be a corresponding intransitive verb IHPŌCA 'to give forth an exhalation,' conceivably 'to give forth smoke.' T has E for initial I in IHPŌTZ(A), so its corresponding intransitive would be EHPŌCA. B's attestation, however, specifically excludes a glottal stop. S provides a lengthy description of Tezcatlipoca drawn from Sahagún. See TĒZCA-TL.

TEZOMŌN(I) to snore, to growl / gruñe, ronca [(3)Tp.226].

TEZOMŌNĪHUA nonact. TEZOMŌN(I)

TEZOMŌNĪTIĀ caus. TEZOMŌN(I)

TEZONTIC something rough, coarse / áspera cosa, así como piedra o cosa semejante (M) [(1)Tp.226]. See TEZON-TLI.

TEZON-TLI porous red volcanic rock used in construction / piedra tosca, llena de agujericos y liviana (M for *teçontli*) [(1)Bf.11r, (2)Tp.226]. See TE-TL.

TEZONTZAPO-TL *pl:* **-MEH** mamey (a type of fruit) / mamey (T) [(1)Tp.226]. See TEZON-TLI, TZAPO-TL.

TEZONYOHCĀN place covered with porous red rock / pedgregal de tezontle (K) [(1)Bf.11r]. See TEZON-TLI, -YOH, -CĀN.

TIĀCHCĀUH elder brother or something superior, better, more / hermano mayor, y persona o cosa aventajada, mayor, y mas excelente que otras (M) Weakening of the first vowel of what was originally the prefix TĒ- leads to the form TIĀCHCĀUH with vowel length and quality change and ultimately to TĀCHCĀUH with vowel loss. TIĀCHCĀUH contrasts with TIAHCĀUH 'someone valiant,' although they are probably cognates. See ĀCHCĀUH-TLI.

TIAHCĀUH someone brave, valiant / valiente hombre, animoso y esforzado soldado (M) [(1)Bf.8r, (3)Cf.109v,120r]. This contrasts with TIĀCHCĀUH 'older brother,' although they are probably cognates.

TIĀMICŌ nonact. TIĀMIQU(I)

TIĀMIQU(I) *pret:* **TIĀMIC** to buy and sell, to engage in commerce / negociar en comprar y vender (C) See TIĀNQUIZ-TLI.

TIĀMIQUILIĀ applic. TIĀMIQU(I)

TIĀNQUIZCO (at the) market place / en el mercado (M), mercado, plaza (T) [(1)Tp.225]. T has EO for IĀ. See TIĀNQUIZ-TLI, -C(O).

TIĀNQUIZOĀ to engage in commerce / negociar, ir al mercado (K) [(1)Bf.1v]. With the directional ON- this means 'to go to market.' See TIĀNQUIZ-TLI.

TIĀNQUIZ-TLI marketplace / mercado (M) Because the sequence is internal, it is impossible to know if it is IĀ or ĪYĀ. See TIĀMIQU(I).

TĪCI-TL *pl:* **TĪTĪCIH** physician, prognosticator, healer / médico o agorero y echador de suertes (M) [(4)Cf.4v,65v,116v].

TIHTICUĪNALTIĀ *vt* to puncture, perforate something / lo punza (Z) [(2)Zp.103,198]. Both attestations in Z mark the vowel of the fourth syllable long, although by general rule it should be short. caus. TIHTICUĪN(I)

TIHTICUĪN(I) to bore, to punch / punza (Z) [(4)Zp.103,223,232].

TIHTILĀN(A) *vrefl* to stretch one's arms and legs / se despereza (Z) [(2)Zp.44,174]. redup. TILĀN(A)

TIHTĪTLAN(I) redup. TĪTLAN(I)

TIHTĪXIĀ *vrefl* to glean after a harvest / rebuscar después de la vendimia o cosecha (M), racimar, espigar (S), rejunta (T) [(6)Tp.145,159]. See TIHTĪX-TLI.

TIHTĪXĪLŌ nonact. TIHTĪXIĀ

TIHTĪX-TLI something gleaned / rejuntado (T) [(3)Tp.113,237]. See TIHTĪXIĀ.

-TĪHU(I) *centrifugal purposive verbal compounding element; singular* **-TĪUH**, *plural* **-TĪHUIH**; *pret:* **-TO**, *pret. pl:* **—TOH** to go to do something. This contrasts with the verb-final sequence -TIUH which is the progressive construction formed by joining a truncated form of HU(I) 'to go' to the preterit form of a verb with the ligature -TI-.

TILĀHUAC something thick / grueso (Z) [(2)Zp.64,223].

TILĀN(A) *vt* to haul, pull something / estirar o tirar de algo (M), lo jala (T) This abundantly attested verb is subject to considerable variation in T, where the vowel of the initial syllable varies from I to E to complete deletion, and the L varies with R. See ĀN(A).

TILĀNALŌ nonact. TILĀN(A)

TILĀNILIĀ applic. TILĀN(A)

TĪLĪN(I) to tighten, constrict / apretarse (M) In T the medial L varies with R. See TĪLĪNIĀ.

TĪLĪNIĀ *vrefl,vt* to exert effort; to press on something or to tighten something / ceñirse fuertemente o echar o poner fuerzas cuando trabajan (M), tirar de algo, estirar, apretar ñudo o atadura, flechar o enarcar

arco (M) In T the medial L varies with R.
See TĪLĪN(I).

TĪLĪNILIĀ applic. TĪLĪNIĀ

TĪLĪNĪLŌ nonact. TĪLĪNIĀ

TĪLĪNTIĀ caus. TĪLĪN(I)

TĪLĪNTICAH to be tightened, pressed down,
constricted / está apretado (T) [(1)Tp.242].
See TĪLĪN(I), the verb CĀ.

TĪLĪNTIMOMAN(A) for something to
remain at high tension / duró la fuerza (C
for preterit) [(1)Cf.100r]. See TĪLĪN(I),
MAN(A).

TĪLĪNTOC something tightened, com-
pressed / apretado (Z) [(2)Zp.13,223]. See
TĪLĪN(I).

TILMAHHUAH possessor of a cloak / dueño
de manta (K) [(1)Cf.55v, (1)Rp.45]. This is
given in C and R without gloss as an
example of the possessor derivation. See
TILMAH-TLI.

TILMAH-TLI cloak, blanket, an indigenous
man's garment fastened on one shoulder /
manta (M)

TĪLTLĀLIĀ vt to flatten, crush something /
lo aplasta (Z) [(2)Zp.12,198]. See TĪLĪN(I),
TLĀLIĀ.

TĪMALIHU(I) to swell, to well up / henchirse (K) [(1)Bf.7v]. See TĪMALOĀ.

TĪMALOĀ vrefl,vt to aggrandize oneself, to
be vain; to exhalt someone or to swell or
increase something / alegrarse, vanagloria-
rse (S), elogiar, exaltar, honrar a alguien (S)
[(6)Bf.2v,3r,6r,8v]. M's intransitive timalloa
and temalloa 'to swell up with infection'
form their preterits by adding -C, and the ll
implies that they are derived from the
noun TĒMAL-LI 'infection, pus.' Hence
they are different from this verb, although
S assumes that it is just a matter of variant
spelling. In B TĪMALOĀ is always paired
with MAHCĒHU(A) 'to obtain what one
deserves,' the whole phrase having to do
with abundance. See TĒMALOĀ.

TIMOMOTZILHUIĀ applic. TIMO-
MOTZOĀ

TIMOMOTZOĀ vrefl,vt to scratch oneself;
to scratch something / se rasguña (T),
rasguña (T) [(6)Tp.159,236].

TIMOMOTZŌLŌ nonact. TIMOMOTZOĀ

TITĪCHAUHQUI something snug, tight /

vestidura estrecha y corta (M), tupido,
ajustado (Z) [(2)Zp.126,224]. Z has lost the
final consonant of the third syllable. See
TITĪTZ(A)

TITĪCHILIĀ applic. TITĪTZ(A)

TITILATZ(A) vrefl,vt to creep along; to drag
something along / se arrastra, gatea (Z), lo
arrastra (Z) [(5)Zp.14,63,174,198]. See
TILĀN(A).

TĪTĪTLAN(I) vt to throw something / lo tira
(T) [(3)Tp.206]. redup. TĪTLAN(I)

TĪTĪTLANILIĀ applic. TĪTĪTLAN(I)

TĪTĪTLANĪLŌ nonact. TĪTĪTLAN(I)

TITĪTZ(A) vrefl,vt to stretch; to stretch
something / desperezarse y estirarse,
bocezando (M), lo estira (liga, etc.) (T)
[(6)Tp.159,206].

TITĪTZALŌ nonact. TITĪTZ(A)

TĪTLAN(I) vt to send someone as a messenger, envoy / enviar o hacer mensajero
(M) See TĪTLAN-TLI.

TĪTLANIĀ vt to send someone / lo
despacha, lo manda (Z) [(1)Tp.206,
(3)Zp.43,81,198]. See TĪTLAN(I).

TĪTLANĪHUA altern. nonact. TĪTLAN(I)

TĪTLANILIĀ vt to send something with
someone, to hurl something at someone /
lo manda con él, se lo arroja, se lo tira (T)
[(3)Tp.206]. applic. TĪTLAN(I)

TĪTLANILILIĀ applic. TĪTLANILIĀ

TĪTLANILĪLŌ nonact. TĪTLANILIĀ

TĪTLANILŌ altern. nonact. TĪTLAN(I)

TĪTLANŌ altern. nonact. TĪTLAN(I)

TĪTLAN-TLI pl: -TIN messenger, envoy /
mensajero o embajador (M) M also has
tititlantli with the same sense. See
TĪTLAN(I).

TĪZAHUIĀ vt to whitewash something /
embarnizar con barniz blanco (M)
[(1)Cf.60v]. See TĪZA-TL, -HUIĀ

TĪZA-TL whitewash, white earth, chalk,
cierto barniz o tierra blanca (M)
[(5)Cf.57r,60v].

TĪZAYOH See TĪZAYOHCA-TL.

TĪZAYOHCĀN place name Tizayocan
[(1)Cf.57r, (1)Rp.46]. See TĪZA-TL, -YOH,
-CĀN.

TĪZAYOHCA-TL someone from Tizayocan / natural de Tizayocán (K) [(2)Cf.57r,
(1)Rp.46]. This has a short form TĪZAYOH.
C states the principle that in general place

names in -YOHCĀN have alternative
'resident' forms with -YOHCA-TL and
-YOH. See TĪZAYOHCĀN.

-TO See -TĪHU(I).

TOCA *vt* to follow, pursue someone / seguir
a alguno (M) M combines this with TŌCA
'to bury someone, to sow something' in a
single entry.

TŌCA *vt* to bury someone or something, to
sow something / enterrar a otro (M), sembrar algo a mano así como pepitas, calabazas, melones, pepinos, o cosa semejante, o
soterrar algo (M) For the forms with the
nonspecific human object prefix TĒ-, M
combines this with TOCA 'to follow,
pursue someone' in a single entry.

TŌCA to sow / sembrar como maíz o
habas o cosas semejantes (M) [(1)Bf.10v,
(2)Cf.91v,123r]. Intransitive TŌCA appears
only in the Spanish-to-Nahuatl side of M.

TŌCĀITIĀ *vt* to name someone / lo nombra
(Z) [(2)Zp.89,198]. See TŌCĀ(I)-TL.

TŌCĀ(I)-TL name, reputation / nombre,
fama, y honra (M) Z retains the I in
possessed form. This contrasts with
TOCA-TL 'spider.'

-TŌCĀITZIN *only attested in possessed
form* one's godmother / su madrina (Z)
[(4)Zp.79,162]. See TŌCĀ(I)-TL.

TŌCALĒ-TL *pret:* **-MEH** cicada / chicharra
(T) [(1)Tp.242].

TŌCALŌ nonact. TŌCA

TOCALŌ nonact. TOCA

TŌCĀPATLA *vrefl,vt* to change one's name;
to rename someone / se cambia el nombre
cuando se casa la mujer por lo civil o por la
iglesia o por los dos (T), le cambia su nombre (T) [(6)Tp.161,213]. See TŌCĀ(I)-TL,
PATLA.

TOCATĒHU(A) *vt* to run someone off / lo
corretea (Z) [(2)Zp.34,198]. See TOCA,
ĒHU(A).

TOCA-TL *pl:* **-MEH** spider / araña generalmente (M) [(2)Tp.241, (2)Zp.13,224]. Z
marks the vowel of the second syllable
long, but T has the reflex of a short vowel.
This contrasts with TŌCĀ(I)-TL 'name.'

TŌCĀYOH a signed document, or one's
namesake / firmada escritura (M), su
tocayo, su nombre (T for possessed form)
[(1)Tp.135]. The single attestation is

ambiguous between TŌCĀYOH and
TŌCĀYŌ, but the sense appropriate to
TŌCĀYOH 'something invested with a
name' seems to agree with both M's gloss
and with *tocayo* as it has been absorbed
into Mexican Spanish as 'namesake.' See
TŌCĀ(I)-TL, -YOH.

TŌCĀYŌTIĀ *vt* to give a name or value to
someone or something, to spread someone's renown, to call someone by name /
empadronar a alguno, o matricular, o engrandecer y afamar a otro, o poner nombre,
o nombrar a alguno, o llamarle por su
nombre (M), tasar o poner precio a lo
que se vende, o nombrar (M) [(1)Bf.111,
(3)Tp.213]. Z has the variant TŌCĀITIĀ.
See TŌCĀ(I)-TL, -YŌ.

TŌCĀYŌTILIĀ applic. TŌCĀYŌTIĀ

TŌCĀYŌTĪLŌ nonact. TŌCĀYŌTIĀ

TŌCH-IN See TŌCH-TLI.

TŌCHMŌCHILIĀ applic. TŌCHMŌTLA

TŌCHMŌTLA to hunt rabbits / caza
conejos (T) [(3)Tp.242]. See TŌCH-TLI,
MŌTLA.

TŌCHMŌTLALŌ nonact. TŌCHMŌTLA

TŌCHNAC(A)-TL rabbit flesh / carne de
conejo (T) [(2)Tp.166,242]. See TŌCH-TLI,
NAC(A)-TL.

TŌCHOĀ *vrefl,vt* to lean over; to bend
something down / se inclina ... se agacha
(Z), lo agacha (Z) [(5)Zp.6,71,174,198].

TŌCHOHMI-TL rabbit fur / pelo de conejo
(M) [(1)Bf.10v]. See TŌCH-TLI, -OHMI-TL.

TŌCHTECOLŌ-TL ringdove / paloma
torcaz (Z) [(2)Zp.93,224]. Since neither of
the birds generally known as ringdoves are
indigenous to Mexico, the gloss does not
make a clear identification among the
many doves and pigeons of the area. Possibly this is Columba fasciata, a dove with
a ring-like marking on the neck. See
TŌCH-TLI, TECOLŌ-TL.

TŌCH-TLI *pl:* **TŌTŌCHTIN** ~ **TŌCHMEH**
rabbit / conejo (M) There is variation of
absolute suffix with this, the alternative
being TŌCH-IN. M has an entry for each.

-TŌCMĀYŌ *necessarily possessed form*
leaf, foliage / su hoja (de la caña de la
milpa) (T), su hoja (del chinamíl) (T)
[(2)Tp.134,135]. See TŌC-TLI, -MĀYŌ.

TOCOTZOĀ *vrefl,vt* to humble oneself, to

make oneself smaller; to shrink or shorten something, to take something in / se encoge (Z), lo encoge (Z) [(4)Zp.50,174,198]. This is related by metathesis to synonymous COTOTZOĀ.

TOCOTZTIC something shrunken, shortened / encogido (Z) [(2)Zp.50,224]. In one of two attestations, Z marks the vowel of the second syllable long but does not so mark the corresponding vowel in the related verb TOCOTZOĀ. See TOCOTZOĀ.

TOCOTZTLĀLIĀ *vrefl,vt* to sit down, to sink; to seat someone / se sienta (Z), lo sienta (Z) [(4)Zp.114,174,198]. This is related to synonymous COTOTZTLĀLIĀ by metathesis. See TOCOTZTIC, TLĀLIĀ.

TOCOTZYETOC someone seated / sentado (Z) [(2)Zp.114,224]. In one of two attestations Z marks the vowel of the second syllable long but does not so mark the corresponding vowel of the verb TOCOTZOĀ 'to make oneself smaller.'

TŌCTI to be buried / estar enterrado (K) [(1)Cf.102r]. This is attested just once in construction with the verb O, bound by the ligature -TI-. The absence of notation for a glottal stop before the ligature implies that the verb is TŌCTI rather than TŌCTIĀ. See TŌCA.

TOCTIĀ *vrefl,vt* to hide or shelter oneself behind something or someone, to reside with or accompany someone, to put something under the protection of someone / esconderse o ampararse detrás de algo (M), se aloja con él, se acompaña (T), fortificar una cosa con otra (M), le encarga con el otro (T) [(8)Tp.161,212, (2)Zp.50,198]. caus. TOCA

TOCTILIĀ applic. TOCTIĀ

TOCTĪLŌ nonact. TOCTIĀ

TŌCTITOC something buried / enterrado (C) [(1)Cf.102r, (2)Zp.53,224]. In Z this has the shortened form TŌCTOC. See TŌCTI, the verb O.

TŌC-TLI young maize plant, stalk, or cane / porreta o mata de maíz antes que espigue (M), la caña (C) see TŌCA

TŌCZACA-TL stubble / rastrojo (T) [(1)Tp.242]. See TŌC-TLI, ZACA-TL.

TOHMI-TL *inalienably possessed form:*

-TOHMIYŌ fur, fleece, down / pelo o lana o vello sotil (M) T has E for I in the second syllable. See -OHMI-TL.

TOHPOCHILHUIĀ applic. TOHPOCHOĀ

TOHPOCHOĀ *vrefl,vt* to bend, to double over; to bend something so that it cannot be straightened / se encoge, se agacha (forzosamente) (T), lo encorva y no se puede enderezarse (T) [(6)Tp.161,212].

TOHPOCHŌLŌ nonact. TOHPOCHOĀ

TOHPOCHTIC someone hunchbacked / jorobado (T) [(1)Tp.241]. T has lost the internal glottal stop. See TOHPOCHOĀ.

TOHPOL-LI terrace / bordo (T) [(3)Tp.240,241].

TOHPOLTIC something terraced / bordo (T) [(2)Tp.240,241]. See TOHPOL-LI.

TOH-TLI sparrow hawk / gavilán (T) [(1)Tp.241, (1)Rp.151]. See TLOH-TLI.

TOHTOCA *vt* to put someone to flight, to evict, dismiss, or exile someone / perseguir a otro, echarle a puertas, o despedirle o desterrarle (M) Z is inconsistent in marking vowel length, but the other sources agree. This contrasts with intransitive TOTŌCA 'to run' and TOHTŌCA 'to plant things.' redup. TOCA

TOHTŌCA to plant things individually in different places / sembrar en varias partes (C) [(1)Cf.129r, (1)Tp.241]. This contrasts with transitive TOHTOCA 'to chase someone' and with intransitive TOTŌCA 'to run.' redup. TŌCA

TOHTOCATINEM(I) *vt; pret: -NEN* to go along pursuing someone / lo anda siguiendo (Z) [(2)Zp.10,198]. See TOHTOCA, NEM(I).

TOHTOHUIĀ *vt* to set a dog to barking / hace ladrar al perro (T) [(3)Tp.212].

TOHTOHUILIĀ applic. TOHTOHUIĀ

TOHTOHUĪLŌ nonact. TOHTOHUIĀ

TOHTOLCA something harsh, rough in sound / ronquido (T) [(1)Tp.241].

TOHTOLĪNA to crave many different things to eat / antojársele a uno varias cosas de comer (C) [(2)Cf.32r]. redup. TOLĪNA

TOHTOLOĀ redup. TOLOĀ

TOHTOM(A) *vrefl,vt; pret: TOHTON* to undress; to unfasten or loosen something, to undress someone / desabrocharse (M), desenvolver o desfajar criatura, o desabrochar a otro (M), desenvolver o desatar algo (M) redup. TOM(A)

TOHTOMALŌ nonact. TOHTOM(A)

TOHTOM(I) *pret:* **TOHTON** to come loose, to come untied / (ser) desatado ... de manos y pies (C) [(1)Cf.71r]. redup. TOM(I)

TOHTOMIC something loosened, unfastened / desatado (Z) [(2)Zp.41,224]. See TOHTOM(I).

TOHTOMILIĀ *vt* to loosen, unfasten something for someone, to remove a baby's diaper or swaddling clothes / desabrochar a otro o desenvolver la criatura (M), se lo desata, se lo suelta (T) [(3)Tp.212]. This also appears in P with the glottal stop marked. applic. TOHTOM(A)

TOHTOMILILIĀ applic. TOHTOMILIĀ

TOHTOMILĪLŌ nonact. TOHTOMILIĀ

TŌHUITZTIC something pointed / puntiagudo (T for compound with CUĀ(I)-TL) [(1)Tp.123].

TŌLCAL-LI arch (structure) / arcos (C) [(1)Cf.93r]. See TŌLOĀ, CAL-LI.

TOLHUIĀ applic. TOLOĀ

TŌL-IN sedge grass, reeds / juncia o espadaña (M), planta como cañas para hacer petates (Z) [(6)Cf.56v,57r,107r, (1)Zp.224]. This appears in M with geminate *ll* before the absolutive suffix -IN, but that is contrary to the rules of Nahuatl morphology, and in compounds M writes the stem with only a single *l*. This is abundantly attested in place names as well as the attestations in C and Z.

TOLĪNA to crave some particular thing to eat / antojarseme alguna cosa de comer sin la poder haber (M for first pers. sg. subject) [(4)Cf.32r]. See TOLĪNIĀ.

TOLĪNIĀ *vrefl,vt* to suffer, to be impoverished; to inflict suffering and travail on someone / ser pobre (M), afligir o maltratar a otro (M) See TOLĪNA.

TOLĪNILIĀ applic. TOLĪNIĀ

TŌLLĀN *place name* Tula [(1)Cf.56v]. See TŌL-IN, -TLĀN.

TŌLLĀNTZINCA-TL *pl:*

TŌLLĀNTZINCA-TL *pl:* **TŌLLĀN-TZINCAH** someone from Tulancingo / los de Tullantzinco (C for plural) [(1)Cf.107r]. See TŌLLĀN, -TZIN-TLI.

TŌLLOH someone from Toluca / natural de Toluca (C) [(1)Cf.57r]. See TŌLLOHCĀN.

TŌLLOHCĀN *place name* Toluca [(1)Cf.57r]. See TŌL-IN, -YOH, -CĀN.

TŌLOĀ to lower, bend down one's head / abajar o inclinar la cabeza (M) [(1)Bf.12r, (4)Zp.174,198]. In Z this is given with reflexive and transitive prefixes, while in B and M it is intransitive. It contrasts with transitive TOLOĀ 'to swallow something.'

TOLOĀ *vrefl,vt* to swallow something / tragar algo (M) This contrasts with TŌLOĀ 'to lower, bend down one's head.'

TOLŌLŌ nonact. TOLOĀ

TOLOLOH owl / tecolote, buho (Z) [(3)Zp.21,120,224]. In one of three attestations Z marks all vowels long, although by general rule the vowel of the last syllable is necessarily short. In the other two attestations no vowels are marked long.

TOLŌLTIĀ *vt* to make someone swallow something / le hace tragarlo (T) [(2)Cf.68r, (4)Tp.212,236]. M has *tololtia* 'to make someone bow his head,' which represents the causative of TŌLOĀ and which contrasts with TOLŌLTIĀ. caus. TOLOĀ

TOLŌLTILIĀ applic. TOLŌLTIĀ

TOLŌLTĪLŌ nonact. TOLŌLTIĀ

TŌLTĒCA-TL *pl:* **TŌLTĒCAH** someone from Tula / natural de Tula (C) [(3)Bf.10r,10v,11r, (1)Cf.56v]. See TŌLLĀN.

TŌLTITLAN *place name* Toltitlan [(1)Cf.56v]. See TŌL-IN, -TLAN.

TOM(A) *vrefl,vt; pret:* **TON** for something to come loose, to undo one's clothing; to loosen, free, unwrap something / desatarse algo o abrirse (M), desatarse o desceñirse (M), desatar o soltar a otro de la prisión (M), desatar o descoger algo o abrir carta (M) See TOM(I).

TOMACHĪL-LI sauce of tomatoes and chili peppers / salsa de tomate con chile (T) [(1)Tp.241]. See TOMA-TL, CHĪL-LI.

TOMĀHUA to grow fat, to swell / engordar o crecer o pararse gordo (M) This is synonymous with the reflexive use of transitive TOMĀHU(A).

TOMĀHU(A) *vrefl,vt* to grow fat, to swell; to fatten something / engordarse o pararse grueso o querer vomitar (M), apacentar o

pensar algún ganado o habla con voz gorda
(M) See TOMĀHUA.

TOMĀHUAC something plump, thick, fat /
cosa gorda, gruesa o corpulenta (M) See
TOMĀHUA.

TOMĀHUALIZ-TLI fatness, corpulence /
gordura o corpulencia (M) [(2)Zp.63,224]. In
both attestations Z marks the vowel of the
third syllable long, although by general
rule it should not be. See TOMĀHUA.

TOMĀHUALŌ nonact. TOMĀHU(A)

TOMĀHU(I) to grow fat, to swell / engorda
(T) [(1)Tp.241]. This is synonymous with
TOMĀHUA and the reflexive use of
TOMĀHU(A).

TOMĀHUILIĀ applic. TOMĀHU(A)

TOMANAMACA See TOMA-TL,NAMACA.

TŌMĀNEHNEM(I) *pret:* **-NEN** to go on all
fours, to crawl / anda en cuatro pies, gatea
(T) [(3)Tp.242]. M has synonymous *ma-
nenemi* and *mamanenemi*. See MĀ(I)-TL,
NEHNEM(I).

TŌMĀNEHNEMILIĀ caus. TŌMĀ-
NEHNEM(I)

TŌMĀNEHNEMOHUA nonact. TŌMĀ-
NEHNEM(I)

TOMAPACH profusion or scattering of
tomatoes / desperdicio de jitomate (Z)
[(2)Zp.44,224]. Z uses the element PACH
without an absolutive suffix in this and in
CHĪLPACH with the sense of 'profusion,'
possibly 'waste.' It may be related to
PACH-TLI 'moss.' See TOMA-TL.

TOMAPEHPEN(A) See TOMA-TL,
PEHPEN(A).

TOMAPIY(A) See TOMA-TL, PIY(A).

TŌMĀQUETZ(A) *vrefl,vt* to get down on all
fours; to set someone, something on all
fours / se pone en cuatro pies (T), le pone
en cuatro pies (T) [(6)Tp.161,213]. See
MĀ(I)-TL, QUETZ(A).

TOMAQUIL(I)-TL type of greens /
yerba mora, tomate quelite (Z)
[(3)Zp.123,131,224]. See TOMA-TL,
QUIL(I)-TL.

TOMATEQU(I) See TOMA-TL, TEQU(I).

TOMA-TL *pl:* **-MEH** tomato / cierta fruta
que sirve de agraz en los guisados o salsas
(M), tomate (T) The large red tomato is
specifically named XĪTOMA-TL. In gen-

eral, unmodified TOMA-TL refers to the
green husk tomato.

TOM(I) for something to come open, to
come loose / desatarse algo o abrirse la
carta, o descoserse algo (M) [(2)Cf.71r]. This
is synonymous with the reflexive use of
TOM(A).

TOMŌN(I) to break out in blisters / levantarse ampolla, vejiga, etc. (C) [(1)Cf.73v,
(1)Tp.246].

TOMŌNIĀ *vrefl,vt* to break out in blisters,
to feel nauseated; to raise bumps, bruises /
se levantan ampollas en la mano (T for
MĀXIXIHTOMŌNIĀ), quiere vomitar,
tiene ganas de vomitar, tiene asco (T),
hacer chichones (M) [(6)Tp.153,161]. See
TOMŌN(I).

TOMŌNĪLŌ nonact. TOMŌNIĀ

TOMPIAH-TLI cylindrical or conical
container woven of palm and used for
transporting goods / esportilla honda,
hecha de palmas (M), tompiate (canasta de
palma en forma de racimo de uvas) (T)
[(2)Tp.241]. Because the sequence is stem-
internal, it cannot be determined whether
there is a segmental Y between the second
and third vowels.

TŌNA to be warm, for the sun to shine /
hacer calor o sol (M)

TŌNACĀYŌ-TL produce, human sustenance, one's daily nourishment / mantenimiento humano o los frutos de la tierra
(M) [(1)Bf.1v, (1)Cf.123r]. This often specifically refers to maize. It contrasts with
TONACAYŌ 'our flesh,' the first person plural inalienably possessed form of
NAC(A)-TL 'flesh.' See TŌNA, -YŌ.

TŌNAHU(I) to have a fever / he tenido frios
y calenturas (C for first pers. sg. of
ĀTŌNAHU(I)) [(1)Cf.106v]. See TŌNA.

TŌNAHUIZ-TLI malaria / paludismo (Z)
[(6)Zp.93,158,224]. See TŌNAHU(I).

TŌNALCĀHU(A) *vrefl,vt* to get frightened; to frighten someone / deja el
ánima al espantarse (T), le espanta (T)
[(6)Tp.161,213]. The literal sense of this
has to do with going cold or having chills,
as with fright. See TŌNAL-LI, CĀHU(A).

TŌNALCĀHUALŌ nonact. TŌNAL-
CĀHU(A)

TŌNALCĀHUILIĀ applic. TŌNAL-CĀHU(A)

TŌNALCALAQUIYĀMPA west, point where the sun sets / oeste, occidente, poniente (Z) [(3)Zp.90,100,224]. See TŌNALCALAQUIYĀN, -PA.

TŌNALCALAQUIYĀN sunset / la caída del sol (Z) [(5)Zp.23,90,100,224]. See TŌNAL-LI, CALAQU(I), -YĀN.

TŌNALCĒHU(I) to be overcast, cloudy so that the sun does not shine / ya no hace sol (T) [(1)Tp.242]. See TŌNAL-LI, CĒHU(I).

TŌNALCĒHUIĀ vrefl,vt to rest in the shade from the heat of the day; to put someone, something in the shade / tener la siesta o descansar el que camina (M), se sombrea, descansa en la sombra (T), le pone a la sombra (T) [(6)Tp.162,213, (2)Zp.72,174]. Z glosses this as insola, which is apparently antithetical to its literal sense. See TŌNAL-LI, CĒHUIĀ.

TŌNALCĒHUILIĀ applic. TŌNALCĒHUIĀ

TŌNALCĒHUĪLŌ nonact. TŌNALCĒHUIĀ

TŌNALCĒUHYOH shadow, place in the shade / sombra (T) [(2)Tp.242]. Because of word-final vowel shortening and the general loss of word-final glottal stop in T, it cannot be determined if this ends in -YŌ or -YOH, but the fact that it does not take an absolutive suffix is evidence in favor of -YOH. See TŌNALCĒHU(I).

TŌNALHUĀQU(I) pret: **TŌNALHUĀC** to dry in the sun / se asolea (ropa y tierra) (Z) [(2)Zp.15,224]. See TŌNAL-LI, HUĀQU(I).

TŌNALLĀLIĀ vt to put something in the shade / le pone la sombra (T) [(4)Tp.213,237]. See TŌNAL-LI, TLĀLIĀ.

TŌNALLĀLILIĀ applic. TŌNALLĀLIĀ

TŌNALLĀLĪLŌ nonact. TŌNALLĀLIĀ

TŌNALLATIĀ vrefl to dry in the sun, to sunburn / se asolea ... está quemado por el sol (Z) [(3)Zp.15,116,174]. This contrasts with TŌNALLĀTIĀ 'to conceal oneself by day.' See TŌNAL-LI, TLATIĀ.

TŌNALLĀTIĀ vrefl to conceal oneself by day, to protect oneself from the sun / se esconde en el día (Z) [(1)Zp.174]. This contrasts with TŌNALLATIĀ 'to dry in the sun.' See TŌNAL-LI, TLĀTIĀ.

TŌNAL-LI pl: **-TIN** warmth of the sun, summertime, day / calor del sol o tiempo

de estío (M), día, astro, sol (T) See TŌNA.

TŌNALMICOHUA nonact. TŌNAL-MIQU(I)

TŌNALMIQU(I) pret: **TŌNALMIC** to be overwarm, to suffer from the heat / tiene calor (T) [(3)Tp.242]. See TŌNAL-LI, MIQU(I).

TŌNALMIQUĪTIĀ caus. TŌNALMIQU(I)

TŌNALPOLIHUIYĀMPA west, point of sunset / occidente, poniente, oeste [(4)Zp.90,100,224]. See TŌNAL-LI, POLIHU(I), -YĀN, -PA.

TŌNALQUĪZAYĀMPA east, point of sunrise / este, oriente (Z) [(3)Zp.57,92,224]. In two of three attestations in Z the constituent parts are separated by spaces, but they should not be. See TŌNAL-LI, QUĪZ(A), -YĀN, -PA.

TŌNALTEQUITIQUI day laborer / jornalero (Z) [(3)Zp.73,224]. In two of three attestations, this is shortened to TŌNAL-TEQUITI. See TŌNAL-LI, TEQUITQUI.

TŌNALTIĀ cause. TŌNA

TŌNALTZAHTZILIĀ vt to call down harm on the head of an enemy, mentioning him by name / nombra a la persona a quien quiere hacer maldad (T) [(3)Tp.213]. See TŌNAL-LI, TZAHTZI.

TŌNALTZAHTZILILIĀ applic. TŌNAL-TZAHTZILIĀ

TŌNALTZAHTZILĪLŌ nonact. TŌNAL-TZAHTZILIĀ

TŌNAMĒYOĀ to shimmer, to shine in rays / está resplandeciendo (C for compound with MAN(I)), resplandecer el sol, echando rayos de sí (M for tonameyotia) [(1)Cf.77r]. See TŌNA, MĒY(A).

TŌNATIUH sun / el sol (M) See TŌNA.

TŌNAYĀHUIĀ vrefl,vt to dry in the sun; to dry something in the sun / se asolea (T), lo solea, lo asolea (T) [(6)Tp.162,213]. See TŌNA.

TŌNAYĀHUILIĀ applic. TŌNAYĀHUIĀ

TŌNAYĀHUĪLŌ nonact. TŌNAYĀHUIĀ

TŌNAYĀN the heat of the day, daytime / de día (Z) [(2)Zp.45,224]. M has this in tonayampa ehecatl and tonayan vitz ehecatl 'warm wind from the east or south.' See TŌNA, -YĀN.

TŌNAYOH something permeated with the heat of the sun / en el sol (T) [(1)Tp.242].

Because of the shortening of word-final
vowels and the general loss of word-final
glottal stop in T, it cannot be determined if
this ends in -YŌ or -YOH, but the absence
of an absolutive suffix and the sense of the
word are evidence for -YOH. See TŌNA,
-YOH.

TŌNĒHU(A) *vt* to inflict burning pain on
someone / atormentar o afligir a otro (M)
See TŌNĒHUA.

TŌNĒHUA to suffer burning pain / padecer
dolor, escocimiento o aflicción (M)
[(2)Bf.7r,7v, (1)Cf.111v]. The preterit of
this, TŌNĒHUAC, contrasts with
TŌNĒUH, the preterit of transitive
TŌNĒHU(A) 'to make someone suffer.' See
TŌNA.

TŌNĒHU(I) to ache, burn / arde, duele (T)
[(4)Tp.137,242, (2)Zp.13,224]. See
TŌNĒHU(A).

TŌNĒHUĪHUA nonact. TŌNĒHU(I)

TŌNĒHUILIZ-TLI hotness, fever / ardor (T)
[(1)Tp.242, (2)Zp.13,224]. M has
tonehualiztli 'burning pain,' *tonehuiztli*
'torment,' and *tonehuiliztli* 'weakness
from hunger.' See TŌNĒHU(I).

TŌNĒHUĪTIĀ caus. TŌNĒHU(I)

-TŌN-TLI *compounding element conveying
the sense of smallness, insignificance; pl:*
-TOTŌNTIN Although necessarily bound,
this behaves in a manner distinct from
suffixes and postpositions. It has its own
absolutive suffix and forms the plural by
reduplication of itself plus addition of the
plural suffix -TIN. If the noun with which
it compounds does not itself take an
absolutive suffix, then the compound does
not either, and -TIN is omitted in the
plural; CHICHI 'dog,' CHICHITŌN,
CHICHITOTŌN 'dogs.'

TOPĒHU(A) *vrefl,vt* to press forward, to
impel oneself forwards; to push, shove
someone or something / se empuja (T),
empujar a otro (M), empujar otra cosa, o
atizar el fuego allegandole los tizones (M)

TOPĒHUALŌ nonact. TOPĒHU(A)

TOPĒHUILIĀ applic. TOPĒHU(A)

TŌPĪLEH constable, minor official, holder
of a staff of office / alguacil (M), el que
tiene vara (C) See TŌPĪL-LI.

TŌPĪLEHCĀHUAH chief of constables / el

señor de alguaciles (C) [(1)Cf.56r]. This also
appears in P with the internal glottal stop
marked but not the long vowels. See
TŌPĪLEH.

TŌPĪLEHCĀTI to be, become a constable /
ser alguacil (C) [(1)Cf.58v]. See TŌPĪLEH.

TŌPĪL-LI staff of office, shaft / bordón, hasta
de lanza, o vara de justicia (M)

TOPŌN(I) to make an explosive noise, to
thunder, for a firearm to discharge / estalla,
truena (Z) [(2)Zp.56,225].

TOPŌNIĀ *vt* to make a thunderous noise,
to discharge a firearm, to make an
explosive sound / truena (el cielo), truena
la boca al comer cosa dura, truena el
pollito saliendo del huevo (T), lo truena
comiéndolo (T) [(6)Tp.212,237,
(4)Zp.122,125,216]. See TOPŌN(I).

TOPŌNILIĀ applic. TOPŌNIĀ

TOPŌNĪLŌ nonact. TOPŌNIĀ

TŌP-TLI chest, container, wrapper / ídolo o
funda de cáliz tejida con hilo de maguey, o cosa de esta manera (M), cofre (C)
[(2)Bf.7r,9r, (3)Cf.18r,113v]. Idols were
transported wrapped in bundles, which
accounts for the extension of meaning
from 'container, wrapper' to 'idol.'

TOQUIĀ *vt* to stoke a fire / atizar el fuego
(M) [(3)Tp.212, (4)Zp.60,69,216]. This is
homophonous with TOQUIĀ 'to draw
someone or something to oneself.'

TOQUIĀ *vrefl,vt* to draw near; to draw
someone or something to oneself /
se arrima (Z), lo arrima, le acerca (Z)
[(5)Zp.4,14,174,198]. This is homophonous
with TOQUIĀ 'to stoke a fire.' See TOCA.

TOQUILIĀ applic. TOCA, TOQUIĀ

TŌQUILIĀ applic. TŌCA

TOQUĪLŌ nonact. TOQUIĀ

TŌQUILTIĀ *vt* to sow something for
someone / se lo siembra (T) [(3)Tp.213].
The vowel of the second syllable of this
should be short by general rule but is
attested long in T. caus. TŌCA

TŌQUILTILIĀ applic. TŌQUILTIĀ

TŌQUILTĪLŌ nonact. TŌQUILTIĀ

TOTĒCUIYŌ *first pers. plural possessed
form of* **TĒUC-TLI** Our Lord God / Dios
(C), Nuestro Señor (C) See TĒUC-TLI.

TOTŌCA to run, to hurry, for illness to
worsen / ir de priesa o correr, empeorar o

crecer la enfermedad (M) Despite the apparent affinity of meaning, this is not derived by reduplication from TOCA 'to pursue someone,' since they differ in transitivity and in vowel length. C contrasts this with with TŌTOCA 'to run after something,' which is a genuine reduplicated derivation from TOCA.

TŌTOCA *vt* to run along after something, to go skirmishing with someone / andar corriendo trás de alguna cosa o escaramuceando (C) [(2)Cf.93r,128v]. This contrasts with TOTŌCA 'to run, to hurry.' redup. TOCA

TOTOCHALHUIĀ applic. TOTOCHOĀ

TOTOCHOĀ *vrefl,vt* to be forward, importunate; to push, shove someone or something to the front / se empuja, es muy intruso (T), lo empuja (delante de los demás para que le toque regalo, etc.) (T) [(6)Tp.161,212].

TOTOCHŌLŌ nonact. TOTOCHOĀ

TOTŌCOHUA nonact. TOTŌCA

TOTOCTIC something hot / caliente (Z) [(2)Zp.24,225]. See TOTŌNIY(A).

TŌTŌCUAUHCAL-LI birdcage / jaula (para pájaro) (Z) [(2)Zp.73,225]. See TŌTŌ-TL, CUAUHCAL-LI.

TŌTOLCŌZCA-TL a type of mushroom / hongo (Z) [(2)Zp.68,225]. See TŌTOL-IN, CŌZCA-TL.

TŌTOL-IN domestic fowl / gallina (M), guajalote (Z) From its basic meaning 'turkey' this has been extended to chickens and doves. It contrasts in vowel length in the second syllable with TŌTŌ-TL 'bird.'

TŌTOLONTIC someone fat / gordito (T) [(1)Tp.242]. M has unreduplicated *tolontic* 'something round like a ball,' which suggests a connection with synonymous OLOLTIC.

TŌTOLTECACAHUA-TL egg shell / cascarón de huevo (T) [(1)Tp.242]. M has *totoltecacalli* with the same sense. See TŌTOLTE-TL, CACAHUA-TL.

TŌTOLTENAMACA See TŌTOLTE-TL, NAMACA.

TŌTOLTEPŌHU(A) to count eggs / cuento huevos (C for first pers. sg. subject) C provides a paradigm of this as an example

of object incorporation. See TŌTOLTE-TL, PŌHU(A).

TŌTOLTE-TL *pl: -MEH* egg / huevo (M) See TŌTOL-IN, TE-TL.

TŌTOM(I) *pret:* TŌTON to ravel / se deshila (T) [(1)Tp.242]. redup. TOM(I)

TOTOMOCA to break out in many blisters / levantarse muchas (ampollas) juntas (C) [(1)Cf.73v, (2)Zp.58,232]. See TOMŌN(I).

TŌTOMŌCH-TLI dried corn husk / hojas secas de la mazorca de maíz (M), totomoxtle, hoja de mazorca (Z) [(1)Tp.242, (3)Zp.124,225]. T has the reflex of Ā for Ō in the third syllable.

TOTOMOTZ(A) *vt* to cause blisters to appear / levantarlas (ampollas) (C) [(1)Cf.73v]. See TOMŌN(I).

TOTŌNCĀMACA *vrefl* to get warm, overheated, excited / se acalora (Z) [(2)Zp.4,174]. See TOTŌNQUI, MACA.

TOTŌNIĀ *vrefl,vt* to warm oneself; to heat something / calentarse a la lumbre o al sol (M), asolear o calentar algo al sol o a la lumbre (M) The reflexive use of this is synonymous with intransitive TOTŌNIY(A). See TŌNA.

TOTŌNIC See TOTŌNQUI.

TOTŌNILIĀ applic. TOTŌNIĀ

TOTŌNĪLŌ nonact. TOTŌNIĀ

TOTŌNIY(A) *pret:* TOTŌNIX ~ TOTŌNIYAC to grow hot, to run a fever / calentarse el agua o otra cosa (M), tener ardor o calentura (M) [(3)Cf.32r, (3)Tp.241, (2)Zp.23,216]. This contrasts with transitive TOTŌNIĀ. T has the variant form TOTŌNEYA. With the prefix TLA- Z glosses this as 'to be hot (weather).' See TŌNA.

TOTŌNIYALIZ-TLI fever / calentura, fiebre (T) [(2)Tp.241]. T has E for I in the third syllable. See TOTŌNIY(A).

TOTŌNQUI something hot, fever / fiebre o cosa caliente (M) [(2)Tp.240,241, (8)Zp.4,24,59,174,209,225]. Z has the variant form TOTŌNIC. See TOTŌNIY(A).

TŌTOPĒHU(A) *vt* to swing something, to rock something / lo mece, lo columpia (Z) [(3)Zp.30,83,198]. redup. TOPĒHU(A)

TOTOPOCA to thunder, to make a loud

cracking noise / truena (p.ej. cuando se oyen las vigas que quieren quebrarse) (T) [(1)Tp.241, (2)Zp.125,225]. See TOPŌN(I).

TOTOPOCHILIĀ applic. TOTOPOTZ(A)

TOTOPOCHTIC something toasted, crunchy / cosa muy tostada, así como pan, tortillas de maíz, etc. (M) [(3)Zp.114,124,225]. See TOTOPOTZ(A).

TOTOPOCH-TLI something toasted, crunchy, noisy to eat / tostado (T) [(2)Tp.238,241]. See TOTOPOTZ(A).

TOTOPOTZ(A) vt to make something crunchy by toasting it or chewing it loudly / roer o tostar algo (M), lo mastica (haciendo ruido) (T) [(3)Tp.213]. The sense of making or noisily eating crunchy food is at some remove from TOPŌN(I) 'to make an explosive noise, to thunder, to discharge a firearm,' but this is clearly derivationally related to TOPŌN(I) and TOTOPOCA in a morphologically unexceptional way.

TOTOPOTZALŌ nonact. TOTOPOTZ(A)

TOTŌQUILTIĀ altern. caus. TOTŌCA

TOTŌQUĪTIĀ altern. caus. TOTŌCA

TŌTŌ-TL pl: **-MEH** bird / pájaro (M) This differs from related TŌTOL-IN 'domestic fowl,' in the length of the vowel of the second syllable.

TOTŌTZ(A) vt to hurry someone along, to advance something, to cause worsening of an illness / adelantar o aguijar el reloj (M), aguijar y dar priesa a él que camina, o empeorar el médico al enfermo (M), empeorar, o dar priesa a otra cualquier cosa (M) [(1)Cf.75r]. See TOTŌCA.

TOXĀHU(I) to collapse / se cae, se desploma (T) [(1)Tp.241]. M has transitive *toxaua* 'to spill something on the ground.'

TOYĀHU(I) to leak, to spill, to sprinkle water / derramarse cosas líquidas o hundirse el montón de harina (M), riega (Z) [(2)Zp.107,225]. Analogous QUIYAHU(I) 'to rain' and a number of comparable nominal forms have short A.

TOZAN gopher / topo, animal, o rata (M) [(1)Tp.240, (4)Zp.126,150,225]. M has the gloss 'mole,' but the animal currently known in Mexican Spanish as *tuza* is the gopher, which is also in keeping with the rest of M's gloss.

TOZCAC throat / su garganta (Z for possessed form) [(2)Zp.62,162]. M has *totozcac* 'palate, pharynx.' See TOZQUI-TL, -C(O).

TOZCATZACU(I) to become hoarse, for one's throat to be constricted / enronquece (Z) [(2)Zp.52,225]. See TOZQUI-TL, TZACU(I).

TOZCAZĀZAHUATIC someone hoarse / ronco (Z) [(2)Zp.111,225]. See TOZQUI-TL, ZĀZAHUATIC.

TŌZOĀ to stay awake, to keep vigil / velar (K) [(2)Bf.1v,2r, (1)Cf.97r]. M has *toçoani* 'one who keeps vigil.'

TOZQUIHUAH someone with a voice / el que tiene voz (K) [(1)Cf.55v]. C gives this without gloss as an example of the possessor derivation. See TOZQUI-TL.

TOZQUINAHNALTIC someone with a hoarse voice / tiene la voz ronca (T) [(1)Tp.241]. See TOZQUI-TL, NAHNALTIC.

TOZQUI-TL compounding form: **TOZCA-** throat, voice / la voz del que canta (M), la voz y la garganta (C)

TL

TLA- *nonspecific nonhuman object prefix* This nonspecific nonhuman prefix 'something' can be absorbed into a verb stem, changing it from a transitive verb into an intransitive one. In some cases the transitivity does not change, and the resulting verb redundantly takes another object prefix before the fused TLA-. With a given verb it is often difficult to determine whether the stem and prefix have been fused or not. If the verb never appears with a specific object or reflexive prefix, if with TLA- it has a meaning distinct from its literal sense, or if there is a reduplicated form that involves the TLA- rather than the first consonant and vowel of the verb stem, then fusion has taken place. Many verbs with TLA- are ambiguous in this respect. TLA- also functions in two ways as something other than an object prefix. With intransitive verbs it conveys an impersonal sense, while with nouns and postpositions it functions as an indefinite, nonspecific possessive prefix. This parallels the use of the corresponding human object prefix TĒ- with nouns and postpositions.

-TLA *verbal compounding element* See -TLANI.

TLĀ *introductory particle for clauses expressing wishes, commands, admonitions; negative form:* **TLĀCA** ~ **TLĀCAMŌ** let it be that / partícula que se junta al imperativo y al optativo; indica más cortesía, más insistencia que *ma* (S) TLĀ may substitute for MĀ as a clause introductory particle and conveys greater courtesy and deference. T and Z have TLA- 'if, should it be that, perhaps' which can be identified both with this and with INTLĀ 'if,' which is abundantly attested in B and C. See MĀ.

TLAAHAHHUILIZ-TLI *expression of annoyance* regaño (T) [(1)Tp.230]. See AHHUA.

TLAAHCICĀCAQUILIZ-TLI complete knowledge, understanding of something / entera y perfecta inteligencia de la cosa (M) [(1)Rp.140]. See AHCICĀCAQU(I).

-TLAAHCICĀCAQUIYA *necessarily possessed form* one's comprehension / mi entendimiento (R for first pers. sg. possessor) [(1)Rp.43]. See AHCICĀCAQU(I).

TLAAHHUILIĀ *vt* to water something / riega (C) [(1)Cf.107r, (3)Tp.230]. T and C have AHHUILIĀ as a simple transitive verb which may take specific object prefixes or nonspecific TLA-, but C also has this with a specific object prefix preceding the TLA- implying that the TLA- has been absorbed into the stem without altering the verb's transitivity. T has lost the internal glottal stop. See AHHUILIĀ.

TLAALĀHU(I) for things to be slippery / resbaloso (T) [(1)Tp.232]. See ALĀHU(A).

TLAĀLPĪCHIĀ to snort (water) / resopla (T) [(3)Tp.233]. See ĀLPĪCHIĀ.

TLAĀLPĪCHILIĀ applic. TLAĀLPĪCHIĀ

TLAĀLPĪCHĪLŌ nonact. TLAĀLPĪCHIĀ

TLAĀLPĪTZ(A) to snort (water) / resopla (T) [(3)Tp.233]. See ĀLPĪCHIĀ.

TLAĀLPĪTZALŌ nonact. TLAĀLPĪTZ(A)

TLAĀQU(I) *pret:* **TLAĀC** for a fruit tree to produce / fruticarse el árbol o cosa así (M in construction with ĪTECH) [(7)Zp.34,102,128,150,204,224]. In all attestations Z marks the second vowel long. If this is correct, then the basic verb stem cannot be AQU(I) 'to enter.'

TLAĀQUĪLLŌ-TL fruit, produce, harvest / árbol con fruta o cosa semejante (M) [(5)Zp.34,128,150,204,224]. In two attestations out of five Z marks the vowel of the third syllable long, and in three Z consolidates AĀ to Ā. See TLAĀQU(I), -YŌ.

TLAĀX-TLI plowed, cultivated land / tierra

arada o labrada (M) [(1)Cf.47v, (1)Rp.41].
This appears in R without diacritics. C
specifically marks both A's short, which
would be wrong if this is derived from
ĀY(I) 'to do something.' M has *tlaay*,
preterit *onitlaax*, 'to work land,' and C
clearly assumes that the basic verb is ĀY(I)
by glossing this noun as 'something ac-
complished, such as land plowed and cultivated.' Either C's diacritic is incorrect,
or the verb for cultivation of land is not
derived from ĀY(I).

TLĀCA See TLĀCAMŌ.

TLĀCACĀHUAL-LI widower / viudo (Z)
[(2)Zp.130,204]. This contrasts with
TLACAHCĀHUAL-LI 'loose animal.' See
TLĀCA-TL, CĀHUAL-LI.

TLĀCACCO peacefully, with tranquility /
segura y pacíficamente, o sin sobras (M)
[(2)Cf.120r]. C attests this with geminate
CC, while M has a single consonant. See
CACTI.

TLĀCACCONEM(I) *pret:* **TLĀCAC-
CONEN** to live peaceably / viven con ...
quietud (C for third pers. plural subject)
[(1)Cf.120r]. See TLĀCACCO, NEM(I).

TLĀCACHĪHU(A) *vrefl,vt* to do favors, to
give help; to hold someone in esteem /
lo apoya (se encarga de ayuda), hace favor (T), lo aprecia, lo adora, lo respeta (Z)
[(3)Tp.160, (8)Zp.5,10,12,109,194,222]. M
also has intransitive *tlacachiua* 'to engender, to give birth.' The prefix string *nitla*
implies that it is transitive, but the preterit
form *onitlacachiuh* and the entry in the
Spanish-to-Nahuatl side of M show this to
be an error. The associated prefix string
should be simply *ni*, not *nitla*. See
TLĀCA-TL, CHĪHU(A).

TLĀCACHĪHUALŌ nonact. TLĀCA-
CHĪHU(A)

TLACAH that is to say / así (C), palabra del
que cae en la cuenta y emienda lo que dice
(C) This is abundantly attested in C as a
free form and also bound with the particles
ZO and CEH< ZO (Y)EH, all used as
interjections. It contrasts with TLĀCAH,
the plural form of TLĀCA-TL 'person' and
with TLAHCAH 'at midday.'

TLACAHCĀHUAL-LI loose animal / desatado (animal) (Z) [(2)Zp.41,204]. This contrasts with TLĀCACĀHUAL-LI 'widower.'

In one attestation Z marks the vowel of
TLA- long, but it should not be. See
CAHCĀHU(A).

TLACAHCAYĀHUALIZ-TLI lie, deception /
engaño, mentira (Z) [(3)Zp.52,84,204]. See
CAHCAYĀHU(A).

TLACAHCAYĀHUANI *pl:* **-MEH** liar,
deceiver / charlatán, engañador (T)
[(1)Tp.228]. See CAHCAYĀHU(A).

TLACAHCAYĀUHQUI liar, deceiver /
mentiroso (Z) [(2)Zp.84,204]. See
CAHCAYĀHU(A).

TLACAHCEH *expression of surprise at a
discovery* / god's sake / valgame dios (C)
[(6)Cf.101r,108r,114r,124r, (2)Rp.138]. See
TLACAHZO, (Y)EH.

TLĀCAHUAH master, someone who owns
or employs other people / señor o dueño de
esclavos (M), señor, hombre que tiene
criados (R) [(1)Rp.139]. See TLĀCA-TL.

TLĀCĀHUALTIĀ *vrefl,vt* to abstain, to
restrain oneself; to restrain, impede, delay
someone / abstenerse de algo e irse a la
mano (M), ir a la mano a otro, y estorbarle
algo (M), lo suspende (Z) [(2)Zp.119,194]. In
one attestation Z marks the vowel of the
third syllable long, but it should not be.
See CĀHU(A).

TLĀCAHUAPĀHU(A) to raise children, to
be a tutor for children / criar niños o ser
tutor y ayo de ellos (M) [(4)Bf.24r,31,9v,
(1)Cf.44v]. See TLĀCA-TL, HUAPĀHU(A).

TLĀCAHUAPĀHUAL-LI child raised or
instructed by a tutor at home / pupilo o
niño criado en casa (M) [(1)Bf.21r]. See
TLĀCAHUAPĀHU(A).

TLĀCAHUAPĀHUANI tutor, instructor of
children / el que las (personas) cría (C)
[(1)Cf.44v]. M has *tlacauapauhqui* with the
same sense. See TLĀCAHUAPĀHU(A).

TLACAHZO *expression of surprise at a
discovery* / god's sake / valgame Dios,
adverbio de que usa el que con admiración
cae en la cuenta de algo que no había
reparado, o a lo menos se confirma en
aquella verdad (C) This is abundantly
attested in C and also appears in R. See
TLACAH, ZO.

-TLĀCAICNĪUH *only attested in possessed
form* one's neighbor / su vecino (T)
[(1)Tp.135]. T has lost the word-final
consonant. See TLĀCA-TL, (I)CNĪUH-TLI.

TLĀCAITTA *vt* to consider someone a human being, to acknowledge, tolerate, accept, or admit someone / te miramos ... como a hombre (C for first pers. plural subject, second pers. singular object), le permite entrar, le consiente, lo admite (T) [(1)Cf.119r, (3)Tp.211]. M has derivations from this involving hypocrisy and deception. See TLĀCA-TL, (I)TTA.

TLACALAQUILIĀ *vt* to transplant something / lo replanta, lo transplanta (T) [(3)Tp.206]. See CALAQUIĀ.

TLĀCAMACHILTIĀ altern. caus. TLĀCAMAT(I)

TLĀCAMACHĪTIĀ altern. caus. TLĀCAMAT(I)

TLĀCAMACHTIĀ altern. caus. TLĀCAMAT(I)

TLACAMANELHUIĀ applic. TLACAMANELOĀ

TLACAMANELOĀ to mumble, to fail to speak clearly / no habla claro (T) [(3)Tp.228]. See CAM(A)-TL, NELOĀ.

TLACAMANELŌLŌ nonact. TLACAMANELOĀ

TLĀCAMAT(I) *vrefl,vt; pret:* **TLĀCAMAH,** *pret. pl:* **TLĀCAMATQUEH** to be rich and prosperous; to obey someone / ser rico y próspero (M), obedecer a otro (M) See TLĀCA-TL, MAT(I).

TLĀCAMAZĀTEH *pl:* **-MEH** someone or something that has rabies / rabia (T), perro con rabia (T for compound with CHICHI) [(4)Tp.124,228]. T has a variant form with short A in the first syllable. M has *tlacamaçatl* 'someone rabid or vicious.' Compare this compound of TLĀCA-TL 'person' and MAZĀ-TL 'deer' with TLĀCATECOLŌ-TL 'devil' where the second element is TECOLŌ-TL 'owl.'

TLĀCAMAZĀ-TL someone rabid, vicious / hombre bruto y bestia (M) See TLĀCAMAZĀTEH.

TLĀCAMICTIĀNI murderer / matador (M), el que mata a personas (C) [(1)Cf.44r]. See TLĀCA-TL, MICTIĀ.

TLĀCAMŌ *negative form of the clause introductory particle* **TLĀ** if not / sino (S) [(6)Cf.101r,104v,108v,113r,119r]. This has a short form TLĀCA. See TLĀ.

TLACAMPAXOĀ See CAMPAXOĀ.

TLĀCANACAYOH something invested with human flesh / tiene carne humana (C) [(1)Cf.54v]. M has *tlacanacatl* 'human flesh.' See TLĀCA-TL, NAC(A)-TL, -YOH.

-TLĀCAPOH *necessarily possessed form* someone sharing the quality of being human / uno de nosotros (C for first pers. plural possessor) [(2)Cf.119r]. This also appears in P with the glottal stop marked but not the long vowel. See TLĀCA-TL, -POH.

TLACAQU(I) *pret:* **TLACAC** to listen, to understand, to hold a hearing / oir o entender o tener audiencia (M) [(1)Bf.12v]. This is attested in a distributive form that reduplicates the TLA- rather than CA, indicating that the prefix TLA- has been fused with the stem. See CAQU(I).

TLACAQUILTIĀ *vt* to make a complaint to someone / regaña, lo hace sentir todas las cosas (Z) [(1)Zp.194]. In the single attestation the vowel of the third vowel is marked long, although by general rule it should be short. caus. TLACAQU(I)

TLĀCATĒCCO residence of a member of the high nobilty, the name of a particular temple dedicated to the god Huitzilopochtli / templo dedicado al dios *Uitzilopochtli*, cuya consagración tuvo lugar bajo el reinado del monarca *Ahuitzotl* (S) [(2)Bf.10r,10v]. See TLĀCATĒUC-TLI, -C(O).

TLĀCATECOLŌNŌTZ(A) to invoke the devil / idolatrar o invocar al demonio (M) This is implied by the derived form TLĀCATECOLŌNŌTZQUI. See TLĀCATECOLŌ-TL, NŌTZ(A).

TLĀCATECOLŌNŌTZQUI one who invokes the devil / invocador del demonio (C) [(1)Cf.52r]. See TLĀCATECOLŌNŌTZ(A).

TLĀCATECOLŌ-TL *pl:* **TLĀTLĀCATECOLOH** devil / demonio o diablo (M) P gives the plural with TLAH in place of TLĀ for the reduplication. See TLĀCA-TL, TECOLŌ-TL.

TLĀCATĒM(I) *pret:* **TLĀCATĒN** for a crowd of people to gather / se congrega mucha gente, se junta mucha gente, multitud (T) [(1)Tp.240]. See TLĀCA-TL, TĒM(I).

TLĀCATĒUC-TLI patron, protector, boss / señor, dueño, soberano (S), su patrón, su amo (Z for possessed form) [(1)Bf.5v, (2)Zp.95,161]. This was originally a title of high nobility. See TLĀCA-TL, TĒUC-TLI.

TLĀCAT(I) to be born / nacer (M) See TLĀCA-TL.

TLĀCATĪHUA nonact. TLĀCAT(I)

TLĀCATILIĀ *vt* to engender, give birth to someone, for a bird to brood, to give form and shape to something, to treat someone humanely / engendra a otro, o tratar bien y humanamente a otro (M), engendra algo, formar o reducir a cierta forma, o sacar pollos las aves (M) applic. TLĀCAT(I)

TLĀCATILILIĀ applic. TLĀCATILIĀ

TLĀCATILĪLŌ nonact. TLĀCATILIĀ

TLĀCATILIZ-TLI birth, generation / nacimiento o generación humana (M) [(1)Cf.97r, (2)Zp.87,204]. See TLĀCATILIĀ.

TLĀCA-TL *pl:* **TLĀCAH,** *possessed form:* **-TLĀCAUH** person / hombre, persona, o señor (M) The plural of this contrasts with TLACAH 'that is to say' and TLAHCAH 'at midday.' TLĀCA-TL has contradictory uses. In older texts IN TLĀCA-TL is a respectful term of address, while the possessed form -TLĀCAUH conventionally means 'slave' and is used in place of the possessed form of TLĀCOH-TLI.

TLĀCATLAH densely populated area / (hay) mucha gente (C) [(1)Cf.100v]. See TLĀCA-TL, -TLAH.

TLĀCATZĪNTILIZTLAHTLACŌL-LI original sin / pecado original (C) [(1)Cf.75v]. This also appears in P. See TLĀCA-TL, TZĪNTILIZ-TLI, TLAHTLACŌL-LI.

TLACATZOĀ *vt* to pull, haul something / lo estira, lo jala (Z) [(2)Zp.57,194]. Since Z is a T-dialect, and this is attested nowhere else, it is possible that this should be TACATZOĀ.

TLACATZTILĀN(A) *vt* to pull something / lo estira (Z) [(2)Zp.57,194]. See TLACATZOĀ, TILĀN(A).

TLACĀUH-TLI space, capacity, something relinquished or left over / espacio de lugar, o cosa dejada o sobras (M) [(6)Zp.25,55,77,204]. See CĀHU(A).

TLĀCAXINĀCH-TLI *inalienably possessed form:* **-TLĀCAXINĀCHYŌ** semen, human seed / simiente de varón o de mujer (M), el semen genital (C) [(1)Cf.83r]. M gives a derivation of this with -YŌ meaning 'human generation, lineage' and a plural form with -TIN for 'first human generation, progenitors of the human race.' See TLĀCA-TL, XINĀCH-TLI.

TLĀCAYELICEH someone possessing human nature / que tiene naturaleza humana (K) [(1)Cf.84r]. See TLĀCAYELIZ-TLI.

TLĀCAYELIZ-TLI human nature / naturaleza humana (C) [(1)Cf.84r]. See TLĀCA-TL, the verb YE.

TLĀCAYŌ-TL humanity, multitude of people / cosa humana y piadosa o la humanidad (M), gente, multitud (Z) [(5)Zp.32,63,87,168,204]. See TLĀCA-TL, -YŌ.

TLĀCAZCALTIĀ to raise and instruct children / criar hijos o niños y doctrinarlos (M) [(3)Bf.3r,9v,11v, (2)Cf.44v]. See TLĀCA-TL, (I)ZCALTIĀ.

TLĀCAZCALTIĀNI tutor, guardian of children / ama de niño, ayo o aya, o tutor (M) [(1)Cf.44v]. See TLĀCAZCALTIĀ.

TLĀCAZCALTILIZ-TLI rearing of children / crianza o doctrina de estos (niños) (M) [(1)Bf.11v]. See TLĀCAZCALTIĀ.

TLĀCAZCALTĪL-LI child being raised and instructed by a tutor at home / niño o pupilo criado en la casa (M) [(2)Bf.2r,3r]. B does not mark the vowel of the fourth syllable for length, but it should be long. See TLĀCAZCALTIĀ.

TLĀCAZOL-LI See TLĀCAZOLYŌ-TL.

TLĀCAZOLYŌ-TL gluttony / glotonía o gula (M for *tlacaçollotl*) [(1)Bf.10r]. In general the sequence LY would assimilate to LL as it does in M, but in B it remains unassimilated. In the Spanish-to-Nahuatl side M has *vey tlacaçolli* 'glutton.'

TLACECĒHUILIĀ *vt* to conciliate someone / aplacar al enojado (M), se reconcilia con el (T) [(3)Tp.209]. See CĒHUIĀ.

TLACECĒHUILILIĀ applic. TLACECĒHUILIĀ

TLACECĒHUILĪLŌ nonact. TLACECĒHUILIĀ

TLACECELTIĀ *vt* to beg someone's pardon, to calm someone, to cool someone's emotions / se le pide disculpas, se le ofrece algo para calme ... lo convence (T) [(3)Tp.209]. See CECELIĀ.

TLACECELTILIĀ applic. TLACECELTIĀ

TLACECELTĪLŌ nonact. TLACECELTIĀ

TLACECĒY(A) *pret:* TLACECĒX ~ TLACECĒYAC to be cold / hacer frío o fresco (M) [(1)Cf.79r, (4)Zp.72,184,214]. Z has this with QUĒMMAN, the phrase meaning 'winter, at the time when it is cold.' See CECĒY(A).

TLACECĒYALIZ-TLI cold, winter / frescor ... o frío (M), invierno (Z) [(1)Zp.72]. See TLACECĒY(A).

TLACEHCĒUHYOH cool weather, shade / fresco (clima), sombra (T) [(1)Tp.235]. Because of general word-final vowel shortening and the loss of final glottal stop in T, it cannot be determined whether this ends in -YOH or -YŌ, but the absence of an absolutive suffix is evidence for -YOH. See CĒHU(I).

TLACĒHUAL-LI *pl:* -TIN shade, shadow / sombra (X) [(3)Xp.93]. X also has this without the absolutive suffix as 'hat.' See CĒHUAL-LI.

TLACELIĀ to receive communion / comulgar (C) This contrasts with TLACELIY(A) 'for new growth to take place.' See CELIĀ.

TLACELIY(A) *pret:* TLACELIZ ~ TLACELIYAC for new growth to take place, for leaves to come out / todo reverdece (C) [(2)Cf.36v,51r]. This contrasts with TLACELIĀ 'to receive communion.' See CELIY(A).

TLACELIYAYĀN verdant spot, place where new growth takes place / lugar fresco, así como prado verde que se está riendo (M) [(1)Cf.51r]. See TLACELIY(A), -YĀN.

TLACELLŌ-TL pasture / pasto (Z) [(2)Zp.95,214]. M has *tlaceliayan* 'cool, fresh place such as a pleasant meadow.' See CELIC, CELIY(A).

TLACELTIĀ to receive communion / comulgar (T) [(3)Tp.235]. This contrasts with M's *tlaceltia* 'for a place to be cool and refreshing,' which is derivationally related to TLACELIY(A). See TLACELIĀ.

TLACEMPANAHUIĀ to be superlative in some quality / cosa que excede y sobrepuja a toda lo demás (M) [(5)Cf.88r,88v]. See CEM, PANAHUIĀ.

TLACEMPANAHUILIĀ applic. TLACEMPANAHUIĀ

TLACENCĀHUAL-LI something prepared, equipped, embellished / cosa aparejada, aderezada, ataviada, o adornada (M) [(1)Cf.47v]. See CENCĀHU(A).

TLACHCUA to dig holes, to excavate / mina (Z) [(2)Zp.84,205]. See (I)CHCUA.

TLACHCUI-TL piece of sod / césped (M) [(1)Cf.47r, (1)Rp.40]. See (I)CHCUA, TLACHCUA.

TLACHICŌMETILIĀ *vt* to hold a novena for someone, to make something the object of prayers for nine days for someone / le hace el novenario (T) [(3)Tp.207]. See CHICŌME.

TLACHICŌMETILILIĀ applic. TLACHICŌMETILIĀ

TLACHICŌMETILĪLŌ nonact. TLACHICŌMETILIĀ

TLACHIHCHĪHUAL-LI something embellished, adorned, forged, counterfeit / cosa aderezada y ataviada, o cosa contrahecha, fingida, y falsificada (M) [(1)Cf.46v, (2)Zp.66,206]. See CHIHCHĪHU(A).

TLACHIHCHĪHUILIĀ *vrefl* to arrange one's own food, for a chicken to make its nest / hace su propia comida, (gallina) hace su propio nido (T) [(3)Tp.159]. See CHIHCHĪHU(A).

TLACHIHCHĪHUILĪLŌ nonact. TLACHIHCHĪHUILIĀ

TLACHIHCHĪUH-TLI something embellished, adorned, forged, counterfeit / cosa aderezada y ataviada, o cosa fingida y falsa, así como moneda contrahecha o cosa semejante (M) [(1)Cf.46v, (1)Tp.229]. See CHIHCHĪHU(A).

TLACHĪHUAL-LI creation, accomplishment, offspring / criatura o hechura (M), cosa hecha, obra, criatura (C) See CHĪHU(A).

TLACHĪLIĀ *vrefl,vt* to keep watch, vigil; to watch or spy on someone / vigila (T), lo vela, lo vigila, lo espía (T) [(6)Tp.159,207]. applic. TLACHIY(A)

TLACHĪLĪLŌ nonact. TLACHĪLIĀ

TLACHIPĀHUAL-LI something purified,

cleansed / cosa purificada o alimpiada (M) [(1)Cf.47v]. See CHIPĀHU(A).

TLACHIPĀUHCĀN clearing, cleared ground, clean place / desmonte, lugar limpio (Z) [(3)Zp.43,77,206]. See CHIPĀHU(A), -CĀN.

TLACHIPĀUH-TLI something purified, cleansed / cosa purificada o alimpiada (M) This is attested in the derived forms TLACHIPĀUHYOH, TLACHIPĀUHCĀN, and TLACHIPĀUHYĀN.

TLACHIPĀUHYĀN clearing, cleared ground, clean place / desmonte, lugar limpio (Z) [(2)Zp.77,206]. See CHIPĀHU(A), -YĀN.

TLACHIPĀUHYOH clean place / lugar limpio (T) [(1)Tp.230]. Because of general shortening of word-final vowels and the loss of final glottal stop in T, it cannot be determined whether the final element here is -YOH or -YŌ, but the absence of an absolutive suffix is evidence for -YOH. See TLACHIPĀUH-TLI.

TLACHIPĪN drop of liquid / gota (T) [(1)Tp.229]. Because of the general loss of word-final N in T, the final consonant here is unattested but can be restored from the related verb form. See CHIPĪN(I).

TLACHIY(A) *pret:* **TLACHIX ~ TLA-CHĪX** to see, to look or gaze / mirar o ver (M) M and C treat this as an intransitive verb resulting from the fusion of the nonspecific human object prefix TLA- with the verb stem CHIY(A) 'to await something' A common variation is E for A, usually written *tlachie*. The long-vowel variant preterit form is not directly attested for this item but is abundantly attested for basic CHIY(A).

TLACHIYALIĀ applic. TLACHIY(A)

TLACHIYALIZ-TLI observation, vision, sight, lookout / atalayadora o el acto de mirar o ver algo (M), vista, mirada (Z) [(3)Zp.84,130,205]. See TLACHIY(A).

TLACHIYALŌ nonact. TLACHIY(A)

TLACHIYALTIĀ caus. TLACHIY(A)

-TLACHIYAYA *necessarily possessed form* one's vision / mi vista, potencia visiva (C for first pers. sg. possessor) [(1)Cf.50r, (1)Rp.43]. See TLACHIY(A).

TLACHIY(E) See TLACHIY(A).

TLACHIYELIĀ See TLACHIYALIĀ.

TLACHIYELIZ-TLI See TLACHIYALIZ-TLI.

TLACHIYELTIĀ See TLACHIYALTIĀ.

TLACHPĀN(A) to sweep / barrer (M) There is variation across sources about whether the prefix TLA- has been fused to the verb stem in this item. See (I)CHPĀN(A).

TLACHPĀNALTIĀ caus. TLACHPĀN(A)

TLACHPĀNHUĀZ-TLI broom / escoba (X) [(3)Xp.91]. X fails to mark the vowel of the second syllable long. See TLACHPĀN(A).

TLACHPĀN-TLI a place that has been swept / lugar barrido (T) [(1)Tp.230]. See TLACHPĀN(A).

TLACHTEQUINI *pl:* **-MEH** thief / ladrón (X) [(2)Xp.95]. See (I)CHTEQU(I).

TLACOCHITTALIZ-TLI dream / un sueño (Z) [(2)Zp.118,204]. See COCHITTA.

TLACOCHMELĀHU(A) to be sound asleep / está bien durmiendo (T) [(3)Tp.228]. See COCH(I), MELĀHU(A).

TLACOCHMELĀHUALŌ nonact. TLA-COCHMELĀHU(A)

TLACOCHMELĀHUILIĀ applic. TLA-COCHMELĀHU(A)

TLACOCHYĀN place for sleeping, nest / nido, dormitorio (Z) [(3)Zp.47,88,204]. See COCH(I), -YĀN.

TLACOHCOCŌL-LI someone injured, wounded / herido, lastimado, o llagado de otros (M for unreduplicated *tlacocolli*), lastimado (Z) [(2)Zp.75,204]. X has unreduplicated TLACOCŌL-LI but glosses it as 'wound' rather than as 'someone wounded.' See COHCOCOĀ.

TLĀCOHTI to serve, to be a slave / trabajar como esclavo (M) [(1)Bf.6r, (3)Cf.58v,66v, (2)Rp.46,140]. See TLĀCOH-TLI.

TLĀCOHTILIĀ applic. TLĀCOHTI

TLĀCOH-TLI *pl:* **TLĀTLĀCOHTIN** slave / esclavo o esclava (M) This contrasts with TLACŌ-TL 'staff, pole.' See TLĀCA-TL.

TLACŌHUALIZ-TLI purchase, the act of buying something / el acto de comprar algo (M) [(1)Zp.204]. See CŌHU(A).

TLACŌHUAL-LI a purchase, something bought / cosa comprada (M) [(2)Zp.31,204]. See CŌHU(A).

TLACŌLHUIĀ *vt* to deflect something from its path, to change a trajectory / el corta la vuelta (una piedra, etc.) (T), se da vuelta, pasa a un lado (Z) [(4)Tp.207,229, (3)Zp.45,94,194]. See CŌLHUIĀ.

TLACŌLHUILIĀ applic. TLACŌLHUIĀ

TLACŌLHUĪLŌ nonact. TLACŌLHUIĀ

TLACŌLIUHYOH something with many curves / tiene muchas curvas, camino quebrado (T) [(1)Tp.229]. Because of the general shortening of word-final vowels and the loss of final glottal stops in T, it cannot be determined whether this ends in -YOH or -YŌ, but the absence of an absolutive suffix is evidence for -YOH. See CŌLIHU(I).

TLACOMŌL-LI large pit, ravine, hole in the earth / hoyo grande o barranco (M) [(3)Zp.95,99,204]. The vowel of the last syllable is marked long in only one of three attestations. M has *comoloa* 'to make holes, ravines.' See COMŌL-LI..

TLACONEXNELHUIĀ applic. TLA-CONEXNELOĀ

TLACONEXNELOĀ *vrefl,vt* to get full of ashes; to fill or cover something with ashes / se llena de ceniza (T), lo enceniza (T) [(6)Tp.159,206]. See TLACONEX-TLI, NELOĀ.

TLACONEXNELŌLŌ nonact. TLA-CONEXNELOĀ

TLACONEX-TLI ashes, cinders / ceniza (T) [(7)Tp.159,206,228]. See NEX-TLI.

TLACŌPAH-TLI pelican flower (Aristolochia grandiflora) / cierta planta medicinal (R), guaco (K) [(1)Rp.140]. R only indicates the glottal stop in PAH-TLI. Although TLACŌ-TL 'staff, pole' seems more likely for the first element, TLĀCOH-TLI 'slave' is equally possible. See PAH-TLI.

TLACŌPAN *place name* Tacuba [(3)Cf.56v,104r]. See TLACŌ-TL, -PAN.

TLACŌPANĒCA-TL someone from Tacuba / natural de Tacuba (K) [(1)Cf.56v]. See TLACŌPAN.

TLACOPITZCĀN narrow, constricted place / reducido (Z) [(2)Zp.107,204]. Possibly Z has lost a glottal stop, and the first element of this should be TLAHCO 'middle.' See PITZAC-TLI, -CĀN.

TLACŌ-TL *pl:* **-MEH** staff, stick, switch / vara, vardasca (M) This contrasts with TLĀCOH-TLI 'slave.'

TLACOTŌNALTIĀ *vt* to prohibit someone from doing something / le prohibe (Z) [(2)Zp.102,194]. See COTŌN(A).

TLACŌUHQUI buyer / el que compra algo (M) [(2)Zp.31,204]. See CŌHU(A).

TLACOYOC-TLI hole, den, cupboard / agujero o armario o alacena (M) [(2)Tp.228]. See COYOC-TLI.

TLACOYŌNĪL-LI something perforated, full of holes / cosa agujereada u horadada (M) [(2)Zp.7,204]. See COYŌNIĀ.

TLACPA- This compounding element combines with kinship terms to convey the sense of indirect relationship; TLACPACONĒ-TL 'stepchild,' TLACPAICHPŌCH-TLI 'stepdaughter,' TLACPATĒLPŌCH-TLI 'stepson,' TLACPAICNĪUH-TLI 'stepbrother, stepsister,' TLACPANĀN-TLI 'stepmother,' TLACPATAH-TLI 'stepfather.' See -TLOCPA.

TLACPAC above, on top / arriba, en lo alto, o encima de algo (M) [(1)Cf.93v, (3)Tp.228, (3)Xp.90]. See -(I)CPAC.

TLACPACNĒCA-TL *pl:* **-MEH** highlander / arribeño (T) [(1)Tp.228]. See TLACPAC.

TLACPAL-LI *pl:* **-MEH** pillow, cushion / almohada (T) [(1)Tp.228]. See (I)CPAL-LI.

TLĀC-TLI torso / el cuerpo de hombre desde la cinta arriba (M) [(2)Cf.55v, (3)Xp.90].

TLACUĀ *pret:* **TLACUAH** to eat / comer (C) In the Nahuatl-to-Spanish side M gives only transitive CUĀ 'to eat something,' but in the Spanish-to-Nahuatl side this is given as the gloss for intransitive *comer* 'to eat.' C treats TLACUĀ as an intransitive verb resulting from the fusion of the nonspecific object prefix TLA- with the stem.

TLACUĀĀTĒQUIĀ to perform baptism / bautiza (T) [(6)Tp.229]. It is unusual that the nonspecific nonhuman object prefix TLA- is involved here rather than its human object counterpart TĒ-. Because of the specialized, nonliteral sense, it appears that TLA- is fused with the stem in this item. The sequence ĀĀ is generally written with a single letter, as it is in T. See CUĀĀTĒQUIĀ.

TLACUĀĀTĒQUĪLCALCO baptistry / bautisterio (T) [(1)Tp.229]. See TLACUĀĀTĒQUĪL-LI, CAL-LI, -C(O).

TLACUĀĀTĒQUILIZ-TLI baptism / bautismo (T) [(1)Tp.229]. See CUĀĀTĒQUIĀ.

TLACUĀĀTĒQUĬL-LI someone baptized / bautizado (T) [(1)Tp.229]. See CUĀĀTĒQUIĀ.

TLACUAHCUĀ to graze / pacer como oveja (M) [(2)Cf.50v]. See CUAHCUĀ.

-TLACUAHCUĀYĀN *necessarily possessed form* grazing place / lugar donde se apacientan (C) [(1)Cf.50v]. See TLACUAHCUĀ, -YĀN.

TLACUAHNĀMIQU(I) *pret:* **TLA-CUAHNĀMIC** to set oneself up in opposition / se opone (T) [(3)Tp.229]. The prefix TLA- has been absorbed into the compound verb stem to form an intransitive verb. See CUAHNĀMIQU(I).

TLACUĀHUA to harden / endurecerse o empedernirse algo (M) Z has the variant TLACUĀHUAYA. The long vowel of the second syllable is attested in B, C, and Z, which is evidence against derivational relationship to CUAUHTI 'to stiffen' despite the affinity of meaning. M also has this as a transitive verb 'to harden something.' The intransitive and transitive verbs contrast in the preterit with TLACUĀHUAC and TLACUĀUH respectively.

TLACUĀHU(A) *vt* to harden something / endurecer algo (M) See TLACUĀHUA.

TLACUĀHUAC something hard / cosa dura o empedernida (M) [(2)Zp.61,205]. See TLACUĀHUA.

TLACUĀHUAQUE-TL hard bean / frijol duro, frijol cimarrón (Z) [(2)Zp.61,205]. See TLACUĀHUAC, E-TL.

TLACUALCĀN a good place / buen lugar (K) [(2)Zp.71,144]. Z has this only in negated form, AHMŌ TLACUALCĀN 'hell.' See CUALCĀN.

TLACUALCHĪHU(A) to prepare food / hace comida (T) [(6)Tp.207,229, (2)Zp.29,205]. M has reduplicated *tlaqualchichiua* with the same sense. See TLACUAL-LI, CHĪHU(A).

TLACUALCHĪHUALŌ nonact. TLA-CUALCHĪHU(A)

TLACUALCHĪHUILIĀ *vt* to prepare food for someone / le hace la comida (T) [(2)Cf.63v,64r, (3)Tp.207]. applic. TLA-CUALCHĪHU(A)

TLACUALCHĪHUILILIĀ applic. TLA-CUALCHĪHUILIĀ

TLACUALCHĪHUILĪLŌ nonact. TLA-CUALCHĪHUILIĀ

TLACUALIZPAN mealtime / hora o tiempo de comer (M) [(1)Cf.42r, (1)Xp.90]. See TLACUALIZ-TLI, -PAN.

TLACUALIZ-TLI the act of eating / el acto de comer (M) [(2)Cf.42r]. See TLACUĀ.

TLACUAL-LI food / comida o vianda (M) Although the verb CUĀ 'to eat something' has a long vowel, the corresponding vowel of this derived form is short in B, C, and T. In X and Z it is consistently marked long. See CUĀ.

TLACUALMĪMIQU(I) *pret:* **-MIC** to choke on food / ahogarse (con comida) (X) [(3)Xp.90]. See TLACUAL-LI, MIQU(I).

TLACUALŌ The expected nonactive form of TLACUĀ 'to eat' would be TLACUĀLŌ, but it is attested with a short vowel in the second syllable except in Z.

TLACUALŌNI eating utensil / artículos para ayudar a comer (Z) [(1)Zp.205]. See TLACUALŌ.

TLACUALŌYĀN dining place, refectory / refectorio o lugar para comer (M) [(1)Bf.12r]. See TLACUALŌ, -YĀN.

TLACUALTIĀ *vt* to feed someone / dar de comer a otro (M) The expected causative from TLACUĀ would have a long vowel in the second syllable, but it is consistently attested short. See TLACUAL-LI.

TLACUALTILIĀ applic. TLACUALTIĀ

TLACUALTĪLŌ nonact. TLACUALTIĀ

TLACUALTZOHTZOMAH-TLI napkin / servilleta (T) [(1)Tp.229]. T has lost the internal glottal stop of TZOH-TZOMAH-TLI. See TLACUAL-LI, TZOHTZOMAH-TLI.

TLACUĀMAN(A) to lie, deceive / engaña, miente (T) [(4)Tp.229]. Here the prefix TLA- appears to have fused with the stem, converting it into an intransitive verb. See CUĀMAN(A).

TLACUĀMANANI *pl:* **-MEH** liar / mentiroso (T) [(1)Tp.229]. See TLACUĀMAN(A).

TLACUĀNI *pl:* **-MEH** someone or something that eats things, glutton / comedor (M), comilón, el que come (S) [(1)Cf.44v, (1)Tp.229]. This contrasts with TĒCUĀNI 'wild beast, maneater,' in that it has the nonspecific nonhuman object prefix 'something' rather than the nonspecific human object prefix 'someone.' See TLACUĀ.

TLACUĀPAN on top / cima, cumbre, sumo (Z) [(4)Zp.28,37,118,205]. See CUĀ(I)-TL, -PAN.

TLACUĀTZIN opposum / tlacuache, zarigüeya (T) [(1)Tp.229, (3)Zp.103,123,205, (3)Xp.90]. T has a short vowel in the second syllable, while Z marks it long, as it should be if derived from the verb CUĀ 'to eat something' Z gives this for 'opposum' and also for 'porcupine.' M has *tlaquatl* 'a type of animal.' See TLA-CUĀNI, CUĀ.

TLACUĀUH very, especially, strongly, hard / fuertemente, con fuerza, bien, mucho, positivamente, especialmente (S) [(1)Cf.117v, (9)Zp.32,56,59,121,205]. See TLACUĀHU(A).

TLACUAUHTILIĀ to have an erection of the penis / arrechar o levantar el miembro (M) [(1)Cf.60r]. See CUAUHTI.

TLACUAUHTILIZPAH-TLI a medicinal plant / cierta planta medicinal (R) [(1)Rp.147]. The name of this plant suggests that it is used to treat impotence. It literally means 'medicine or potion for stiffening something.' See TLA-CUAUHTILIĀ, PAH-TLI.

TLACUĀUHTLAMAT(I) *pret:* **TLACUĀUHTLAMAH,** *pret. pl:* **TLACUĀUHTLAMATQUEH** to be certain, confident, firm in one's belief / tiene confianza, lo confía (Z) [(7)Zp.32,56,59,121,205]. M has this with -TECH 'to depend on or have confidence in someone.' See TLACUĀUH, TLAMAT(I).

TLACUĀUHTLAMATILIZ-TLI confidence, faith, trust / confianza, fe, esperanza (Z) [(4)Zp.32,56,59,205]. S has this with the entirely different sense of 'deception,' which is apparently an error. M has several synonymous phrases with -TECH and involving the element *tlaquauh* and meaning 'to have confidence in someone.' See TLACUĀUHTLAMAT(I).

TLACUĀXĒPOHHUIĀ to lie / miente [(3)Tp.229]. See CUĀXĒPOHHUIĀ.

TLACUĀXĒPOHHUIĀNI liar / mentiroso (T) [(1)Tp.229]. See TLACUĀXĒPOHHUIĀ.

-**TLACUĀYĀN** *necessarily possessed form* one's place or time for eating / lugar o tiempo donde o cuando como (C for first pers. sg. possessor) [(1)Cf.50v]. See TLACUĀ, -YĀN.

TLACUĒCHŌL-LI something finely ground, something ground to a paste or liquid / cosa muy molida (M), mole, salsa (Z) [(2)Zp.113,152]. See CUĒCHOĀ.

TLACUEHZŌLIZ-TLI noise, turmoil, uproar / ruido (Z) [(1)Zp.205]. See CUEHZOĀ.

TLACUEP(A) to invert something, to regurgitate, to appeal a sentence, to engage in translation / volver alguna cosa lo de arriba abajo, apelar de sentencia, o excusarse, y no estar por lo que otro dice ... o traducir algo de una lengua en otra (M), vomita (Z) [(4)Zp.130,214]. Z has QUEP(A) for CUEP(A) See CUEP(A).

TLACUEPALIZ-TLI appeal of a sentence; vomit / apelación (de sentencia) (M), vómito (Z) [(2)Zp.130,214]. The two senses share the literal one of 'to reverse, turn back.' See TLACUEP(A).

TLACUEPŌN(I) for things to bud and burst into bloom / todo brota (C) [(1)Cf.36v]. See CUEPŌN(I).

TLACUEP-TLI *pl:* -**MEH** something turned over or sent back, something vaulted / cosa vuelta lo de arriba abajo o cosa vuelta a quien la envió (M), volteado (T) T has C for P as in other derivations from CUEP(A) with TL and TZ. The C persists before -MEH in the plural. See CUEP(A).

TLACUETLĀNHUITZ-TLI briar / zarza (Z) [(2)Zp.132,205]. M has *tlacuetlaniliztli* 'to twist or bend wood' and *tlacuetlanilli* 'twisted wood,' which are appropriately descriptive of a briar patch. See CUE-TLĀNIĀ, HUITZ-TLI.

TLACUIĀ *vrefl,vt* to borrow; to borrow for someone / tomar algo prestado (M), lo pide prestado por otro (M) [(6)Tp.159,207]. Outside the sources for this dictionary this sometimes appears written as *tlahcuia*, suggesting that T has lost an internal glottal stop. See CUI.

TLACUIHCUI to work wood or stone by chipping or planing off the surface, to clear off a surface / desbastar madera o limpiar el suelo quitando cosas (C), labro piedra o

madera como hace el escultor (C for first
pers. sg. subject) [(3)Cf.31r]. See CUIHCUI.
TLACUIHCUĪLIĀ *vt* to relieve someone of
something, to take something away from
from something (as in culling kernels or
planing wood), to practice a type of healing
in which objects said to be causing the illness appear to be drawn from the body. /
robar alguna cosa a otros, echar granzas, o
hacer cierta hechicería dando a entender
que sacan del cuerpo pedernales, navajas,
etc., las cuales eran causas de la enfermedad del enfermo (M), alimpiar pozo, gar-
banzos, arroz, o cosas semejantes (M) This
is abundantly attested in C where the
vowel of the third syllable is marked
long and in T where it is short. applic.
TLACUIHCUI
TLACUIHCUĪLŌ-TL opposum / zarigüeya,
macebillo (animal) (Z) [(4)Zp.132,205]. In
two of four attestations Z marks the vowel
of the third syllable long and in two does
not. Z lacks the reflex of a glottal stop in
the second syllable, but by derivation there
should be one. See TLACUIHCUĪLIĀ.
TLACUIHCUI-TL piece of worked wood or
cut stone / cosa labrada o esculpida en madera o en piedra (M) [(1)Cf.47r, (1)Rp.41]. R
has a long vowel in the second syllable
rather than a short vowel and glottal stop
as C does. See TLACUIHCUI.
TLACUILIĀ applic. TLACUIĀ
TLACUIL-LI something used / usado (Z)
[(4)Zp.127,205]. See CUI.
TLACUĪLŌ nonact. TLACUIĀ
TLACUĪLTIĀ *vt* to lend something to
someone / se lo presta [(3)Tp.207]. See
TLACUIĀ.
TLACUĪLTILIĀ applic. TLACUĪLTIĀ
TLACUĪLTĪLŌ nonact. TLACUĪLTIĀ
TLACUI-TL something taken, seized / cosa
tomada (C) [(1)Cf.47r]. See CUI.
TLACZA to move fast, to run / ir muy de
priesa o correr (M) This is implied by the
derived form TLACZALIZ-TLI. See ICZA.
TLACZALIZ-TLI fast marching, running,
stomping, making tracks / el acto de
aguijar mucho o correr (M), pisada (Z)
[(2)Zp.99,205]. See TLACZA.
TLAECAHUĪLHUIĀ to make a shadow /
hace sombra (Z) [(2)Zp.117,206]. See
ECAHUĪL-LI, -HUIĀ.

TLAECAHUĪLLŌCHTIĀ *vt* to shade some-
thing / lo sombrea (T) [(3)Tp.211]. See
TLAECAHUĪLLŌ-TL.
TLAECAHUĪLLŌCHTILIĀ applic.
TLAECAHUĪLLŌCHTIĀ
TLAECAHUĪLLŌCHTĪLŌ nonact.
TLAECAHUĪLLŌCHTIĀ
TLAECAHUĪLLŌ-TL shade / sombra (de un
árbol) (T) [(4)Tp.211,239]. M has *ecauillotl*
'shade,' reflexive *ecauilia* 'to put oneself
in the shade,' and transitive *ecauillotia* 'to
shade something' In T the vowel of the
prefix TLA- has idiosyncratically as-
similated to the vowel of the stem. See
ECAHUĪL-LI, -YŌ.
TLAEHĒCA to blow, to be windy / hace
viento, sopla el aire (Z) [(3)Zp.66,129,206].
See EHĒCA.
TLAELĒHUILIZ-TLI desire, craving / codicia o deseo de algo, apetito o antojo de
alguna cosa (M) [(1)Cf.93v]. In the single
attestation the vowel of the second syllable
is marked long. See ĒLĒHUIĀ.
-TLAH *locative compounding element conveying the sense of abundance* Some
examples from C are TETLAH 'rocky
place'< TE-TL 'stone,' CUAUHTLAH 'forest'< CUAHU(I)-TL 'tree,' XŌCHITLAH
'garden'< XŌCHI-TL 'flower.' The plural
or distributive is formed by reduplication with glottal stop of the first element, TEHTETLAH, XOHXŌCHITLAH
(Cf.71v,72r). Because of the trend
throughout Nahuatl to lose final nasal
consonants and the general rule to that
effect in T, -TLAH often falls together with
locative -TLĀN and -TLAN.
TLAHCACAQUĪTIĀ *vt* to harm or offend
someone / le ofende (T) [(6)Tp.194,207]. M
has *tlanaualcaquitilli* 'mocker, scoffer.'
See CAQUĪTIĀ.
TLAHCACAQUĪTILIĀ applic. TLAH-
CACAQUĪTIĀ
TLAHCACAQUĪTĪLŌ nonact. TLAH-
CACAQUĪTIĀ
TLAHCAH at midday / de día (M) M combines this in a single entry with TLĀCAH,
the plural form of TLĀCA-TL 'person.'
TLAHCAH also contrasts with TLACAH
'that is to say.' See TLAHCAH-TLI.
TLAHCAHTI to get late in the morning,
towards noon / se va haciendo tarde (C

for progressive construction) [(1)Cf.95v, (2)Tp.230, (1)Rp.139]. This contrasts with TLĀCAT(I) 'to be born.' See TLAHCAH-TLI.

TLAHCAHTILIĀ *vrefl* to be behind schedule / (se) retrasa (Z) [(2)Zp.110,173]. There appears to be an attestation of this used intransitively but the vowel of the second syllable is difficult to make out (Bf.12r). See TLAHCAH-TLI.

TLAHCAHTLACUĀ *pret:* **-CUAH** to eat at midday, to dine late / ayunar (M), come al mediodía (T) [(3)Tp.230]. T has lost the glottal stop of the second syllable. See TLAHCAH-TLI, TLACUĀ.

TLAHCAH-TLI daytime, midday / día, desde que sale el sol hasta que se pone (C), mediodía (T) Without the absolutive suffix TLAHCAH commonly means 'at midday,' while with the absolutive suffix it refers to the middle of the day itself. See TLAHCO.

TLAHCAHUATZA someone who raises a hubbub / los que hacen semejante ruido (alboroto) (C) [(1)Cf.75v]. See (I)HCAHUATZ(A).

TLAHCALHUĀZ-TLI blow gun / cerbatana (S) [(1)Bf.10r]. See (I)HCAL(I).

TLAHCAL(I) *vrefl,vt* to lie down, to fling oneself down; to fling, cast, pitch something / se acuesta, se tira (T), lo tira, lo bota, lo tumba, lo vuelca (T) [(12)Tp.159, 207,218, (9)Xp.34,47,62,75]. See (I)HCAL(I).

TLAHCHICQUI someone who collects unfermented maguey sap (tlachique) as a beverage / oficiales encargados de raspar el maguey y preparar el pulque que se daba a beber durante las ceremonias religiosas consagradas al dios (S for plural), tlachiquero (Z) [(2)Zp.123,207]. See (I)HCHIQU(I).

TLAHCHĪHUIĀ *vt* to bewitch someone / lo embruja (T) [(3)Tp.207]. See CHĪHU(A).

TLAHCHĪHUILIĀ applic. TLAHCHĪHUIĀ

TLAHCHĪHUILŌ nonact. TLAHCHĪHUIĀ

TLAHCO middle, center, half / mediano, que ocupa el centro, que está a la mitad, en medio (S) The first element of this contrasts with TLĀC-TLI 'torso' in vowel length as well as final consonant, despite the affinity of meaning. M has this in compounds involving 'middle' but not as an

independent entry. It contrasts with TLACŌ-TL 'staff, pole' and TLĀCOH-TLI 'slave.' T also has TLAHTLAHCO with the same sense.

TLAHCOCUETLAX-TLI broad belt, sash / su cinturón (Z for possessed form) [(2)Zp.28,161]. See TLAHCO, CUETLAX-TLI.

-TLAHCOILPICA *necessarily possessed form* broad belt, sash / su cinturón (Z) [(2)Zp.28,161]. See TLAHCO, (I)LPIĀ.

TLAHCOILPILŌNI broad belt, sash / ceñidor (Z) [(2)Zp.27,207]. See TLAHCO, (I)LPIĀ.

TLAHCOL half / mitad (K) [(2)Cf.110v, (1)Rp.70]. This is only attested compounded as CENTLAHCOL 'one half.' See TLAHCO.

TLAHCOPĀC(A) *vrefl* to bathe the upper half of one's body / baña la mitad (de la cintura arriba) (T) [(3)Tp.159]. See TLAHCO, PĀC(A).

TLAHCOPĀCŌ nonact. TLAHCOPĀC(A)

-TLAHCOTEYŌ *necessarily possessed form* one's waist / su cintura (T) [(1)Tp.134]. This implies TLAHCOTE-TL, one of many names for body parts with TE-TL 'stone' in a completely nonliteral sense. See TLAHCO.

TLAHCOXĒLIUHTOC something divided in half / dividido (Z) [(2)Zp.47,207]. See TLAHCOXĒLOĀ.

TLAHCOXĒLOĀ *vt* to divide something in half / lo divide (Z) [(2)Zp.47,194]. See TLAHCO, XĒLOĀ.

TLAHCOYĀN waist / cintura (Z) [(2)Zp.28,207]. See TLAHCO, -YĀN.

TLAHCOYĀNILPIĀ *vrefl* to gird oneself, to wrap one's skirt and secure it with a sash / se faja (Z) [(2)Zp.59,173]. See TLAHCOYĀN, (I)LPIĀ.

TLAHCOYOHUAC midnight / medianoche (T) [(1)Tp.231]. See TLAHCO, YOHUAC.

TLAHCUALQUILIĀ *vrefl,vt* to curse, blaspheme; to insult someone, to quarrel with someone / mienta la autora de sus días, mienta la madre (T), reñir, rifar, o contender con otro (M), lo blasfema, lo maldice (Z), le mienta la autora de sus días, le mienta la madre (T) [(6)Tp.159,207, (1)Zp.195]. Z also has two attestations of

TLAHCUALTILILIĀ with the same sense. See AHCUAL-LI.

TLAHCUALQUILILIĀ applic. TLAH-CUALQUILIĀ

TLAHCUALQUILĪLŌ nonact. TLAH-CUALQUILIĀ

TLAHCUALTILILIĀ See TLAH-CUALQUILIĀ.

TLAHCUILOĀ to write or paint / pintar y escribir (C) M only has an entry for transitive (I)HCUILOĀ, but C treats this as a case where the nonspecific object prefix TLA- has fused with the stem to form an intransitive verb. See (I)HCUILOĀ.

TLAHCUILOH one who writes or paints / escribano o pintor (M) [(3)Cf.71,52r, (1)Rp.43]. Z has a variant TLAH-CUILOHQUI with the same sense, while M has *tlacuiloani*. See TLAHCUILOĀ.

TLAHCUILOHHUILIĀ *vt* to reply to someone in writing / le contesta por escrito (Z) [(2)Zp.33,195]. The glottal stop of the third syllable is not attested, and the vowel before it is unmarked for length. If there is no glottal stop, then the O should be long. See TLAHCUILOH, -HUIĀ.

TLAHCUILŌLIZ-TLI the act of writing or painting / el acto de escribir o pintar (M) [(1)Bf.10v, (3)Cf.42r,47v]. See TLAHCUILOĀ.

TLAHCUILŌL-LI writing or painting / escritura o pintura (M) [(1)Cf.77r, (3)Xp.91]. This also appears in P with the glottal stop marked but not the long vowel. In X the long vowel is marked, but the glottal stop is missing. See TLAHCUILOĀ.

TLAHHUĒLTAMACA to cultivate land a second time / barbecha la segunda vez (T) [(3)Tp.231].

TLAHHUĒLTAMACALŌ nonact. TLAHHUĒLTAMACA

TLAHHUĒLTAMAQUILIĀ applic. TLAHHUĒLTAMACA

TLAHMACH-TLI embroidery, skill in doing something / labor de manta labrada, o buena maña para hacer algo, o brosladura de ropa (M) [(1)Bf.10v, (1)Cf.46v]. See IHMAT(I), TLAHMAT(I).

TLAHMACHYOH something embroidered / manta labrada o lienzo con labores (M), bordado (Z) [(2)Zp.20,208]. Z spells the Y

as I, which may represent an intrusive vowel yielding the sequence IY, or it may be some sort of hypercorrection. M spells this *tlamacho*, implying assimilation of the CHY sequence to CHCH and then degemination to CH. See TLAHMACH-TLI, -YOH.

TLAHMAH physician or surgeon, someone competent in a specialty / médico o cirujano (M), el médico, o oficial de habilidad (C) [(1)Cf.128v]. A variant of this is TLAHMATQUI. R has TLAMAH 'someone who knows something,' which apparently contrasts with this. IHMAT(I)

TLAHMAT(I) *pret:* **TLAHMAT** to jest, to practice trickery and deception, to be quick-witted / embaucar a otro el hechicero (M), travesear (M) [(2)Cf.128v]. Although IHMAT(I) retains the intial I after reflexive prefixes, it loses it with fused TLA-. This contrasts with TLAMAT(I) 'to know something'< MAT(I). There is a double meaning to TLAHMAT(I). On the one hand it has to do with being skillful and quick-witted and on the other with being deceptive and tricky. Although the preterit of IHMAT(I) is given by M as -MAH, the preterit of TLAHMAT(I) is given as -MAT. See IHMAT(I).

TLAHMATILIZ-TLI trick, joke, deception / embaucamiento (M), travesura (R) [(1)Rp.144]. M combines this in a single gloss with TLAMATILIZ-TLI 'wisdom.' See TLAHMAT(I).

TLAHMATQUI physician or surgeon, someone competent in a specialty, trickster / embaucador (M), es el médico o oficial de habilidad (C) A variant of this is TLAHMAH. See TLAHMAT(I).

TLAHMATTINEM(I) *pret:* **TLAH-MATTINEN** to go about jesting and practicing trickery and deception / anda traveseando (C) [(1)Cf.128v]. C gives the additional gloss 'to practice a specialty' which goes back directly to IHMAT(I) rather than to TLAHMAT(I). See TLAHMAT(I), NEM(I).

TLAHMOLŌ-TL *pl:* **-MEH** paddle for stirring corn meal / clamolote de nixtamal (palo de nixtamal) (T) [(2)Tp.119,231].

-TLAHNECUIYA *necessarily possessed form* one's sense of smell / mi olfato (C for first pers. sg. possessor) [(1)Cf.50r]. see (I)HNECU(I)

TLAHNĒHUIĀ *vt* to mistake something or someone for another / tomar una cosa por otra, pensando que era suya la capa, siendo de otro, o pensando que hablaba con Pedro, no siendo él sino otro, etc. (M) [(4)Bf.11,2v,4r, (1)Cf.128v, (1)Rp.145]. M gives this gloss for *tlahneuia* and repeats it in briefer form for *tlaneuia*. In M this is a double object verb when it involves another person, but C treats it as a simple transitive verb for persons and things alike. This contrasts with TLANĒHUIĀ 'to borrow something.'

TLAHNĒHUILIĀ applic. TLAHNĒHUIĀ

-TLAHPACH upside down / boca abajo (T for ĪXTLAHPACH) [(6)Tp.137]. This is only attested compounded with ĪX-TLI. M has *tlapachoa* 'for a wall to fall on one and knock one over.'

TLAHPALHUIĀ applic. TLAHPALOĀ

TLAHPALIHUIZ-TLI expenditure of effort / mucho cuidado (C) [(1)Cf.112r]. M has *tlapaliuhcauia* 'to earn one's subsistence by labor.'

TLAHPAL-LI courage, vigor, spirit, effort / esfuerzo (C) The possessed form of this, generally but not necessarily with honorific -TZIN, serves as a greeting or part of a conventional salutation. TLAHPAL-LI contrasts with -TLAPAL 'side' and TLAPAL-LI 'dye.'

TLAHPALOĀ *vrefl,vt* to be forward, daring; to greet someone / atreverse o osar (M), saludar a otro (M) This contrasts with TLAPALOĀ 'to sop bread in sauce or gravy.' See TLAHPAL-LI.

TLAHPALŌLŌ nonact. TLAHPALOĀ

TLAHPALTIC something very strong / cosa recia y fuerte (M) [(1)Cf.110v]. See TLAHPAL-LI.

TLAHPIXQUI caretaker, guardian, one who keeps watch / el que guarda algo (M), vigilante, velador (T), pastor (Z) [(4)Cf.6r,52r,85v, (1)Tp.231, (2)Zp.95,105,208,213]. Z has two attestations without the internal glottal

stop, which may possibly contrast with TLAHPIXQUI, but this is not reflected in the attendant glosses. See TLAHPIY(A).

TLAHPIXTINEM(I) *pret:* **-NEN** to serve as shepherd or pastor / pastorea (Z) [(2)Zp.95,213]. Z omits the internal glottal stop in both attestations. It is possible that this should be TLAPIXTINEM(I), derived directly from PIY(A). See TLAHPIY(A), NEM(I).

TLAHPIY(A) *pret:* **TLAHPIX** to take care of things, to stand watch / cuida (cosas) (Z) This is attested across all sources and implies a verb *(I)HPIY(A) to which the nonspecific object prefix TLA- has become fused to form an intransitive verb. See PIY(A).

TLAHPIYALIĀ applic. TLAHPIY(A)

TLAHPIYAL-LI See TLAPIYAL-LI.

TLAHPIYELIĀ See TLAHPIYALIĀ.

TLAHQUITĪL-LI something woven / tejido (Z) [(2)Zp.120,208]. This implies a transitive verb *(I)HQUITIĀ 'to weave something.' See TLAHQUIT-TLI.

TLAHQUIT-TLI something woven / tejida cosa (M) [(3)Zp.120,150,208]. Z also has TLAHQUITĪL-LI as a variant of this and glosses CUAUHTLAHQUIT-TLI as 'loom.' TLAHQUIT-TLI only appears in the Spanish-to-Nahuatl side of M, with *yquittli* as a synonym. See (I)HQUITI.

TLAHTALHUIĀ *vt* to speak in behalf of someone; to malign someone / ser procurador de otros o hablar por ellos, favoreciéndolos y ayudándolos (M), lo ultraja, lo insulta (Z) [(1)Bf.5v, (1)Cf.65r, (3)Zp.72,126,196]. M and Z have contradictory senses, but both are derivable from the literal sense of IHTALHUIĀ, as the applicative form of (I)HTOĀ. Z omits the glottal stop. See IHTALHUIĀ.

TLAHTIC inside / dentro de lo interior de alguna cosa (M), dentro, sin decir de que (C) [(2)Cf.21v]. See -IHTEC.

TLAHTLACALHUIĀ applic. TLAHTLACOĀ

TLAHTLĀCANEQU(I) *vrefl; pret:* **TLAHTLĀCANEC** to pretend to be brave, to put up a brave front / se hace valiente (Z) [(2)Zp.127,173]. M has unreduplicated reflexive *tlacanequi* with -TECH 'to have faith in someone.' See TLĀCA-TL, NEQU(I).

TLAHTLACAQU(I) *pret:* **TLAHTLACAC** to hear or listen to various things / oir, escuchar varias cosas (K) [(1)Bf.12v]. This distributive form reduplicates the TLA- rather than the first consonant and vowel of CAQU(I), indicating that the prefix TLA- has fused with the stem. redup. TLA-CAQU(I)

TLAHTLACAQUĪTIĀ *vt* to contradict someone / lo contradice (T) [(3)Tp.208]. caus. TLAHTLACAQU(I)

TLAHTLACAQUĪTILIĀ applic. TLAHTLACAQUĪTIĀ

TLAHTLACAQUĪTĪLŌ nonact. TLAHTLACAQUĪTIĀ

TLAHTLACOĀ to sin, to do wrong / pecar, hacer mal (M) M also includes in the entry 'to damage, ruin something,' which is the literal sense of transitive (I)HTLACOĀ with the nonspecific object prefix TLA-. See (I)HTLACOĀ.

TLAHTLACOĀNI sinner / pecador (M) See TLAHTLACOĀ.

TLAHTLACŌLĀ-TL strong liquor, spirits / aguardiente (X) [(2)Xp.94]. See TLAHTLACŌL-LI, Ā-TL.

TLAHTLACŌLCĀHU(A) to forsake one's sins / dejares tus pecados (C for second pers. sg. subject) [(1)Cf.59v]. M has *tlatlacolcaualtia*, the causative of this verb. See TLAHTLACŌL-LI, CĀHU(A).

TLAHTLACŌLCHĪHU(A) to sin / peca (T) [(3)Tp.231]. See TLAHTLACŌL-LI, CHĪHU(A).

TLAHTLACŌLCHĪHUALŌ nonact. TLAHTLACŌLCHĪHU(A)

TLAHTLACŌLCHĪHUILIĀ applic. TLAHTLACŌLCHĪHU(A)

TLAHTLACŌLCUĪTIĀ *vrefl,vt* to confess one's sins; to lead someone into sin [(1)Rp.147]. See TLAHTLACŌL-LI, CUĪTIĀ.

TLAHTLACŌLEH sinner / pecador (C) [(1)Cf.123v, (2)Zp.95,208]. See TLAHTLACŌL-LI.

TLAHTLACŌL-LI sin, fault / pecador, culpa, o defecto (M) In possessed form with ne-

gation, this is a denial of responsibility, AHMŌ NOTLAHTLACŌL 'It is not my fault.' See TLAHTLACOĀ.

TLAHTLACŌLMACA *vrefl,vt* to sin; to corrupt someone / peca (Z), lo corrompe, lo envicia (Z) [(5)Zp.34,54,95,173,195]. See TLAHTLACŌL-LI, MACA.

TLAHTLACŌLMECA-TL the bonds of sin / la soga de los pecados (C) [(1)Cf.71r]. See TLAHTLACŌL-LI, MECA-TL.

TLAHTLACŌLPEHPEN(A) See TLAHTLACŌL-LI, PEHPEN(A).

TLAHTLACŌLPOHPOLHUILIZ-TLI forgiveness of sins / el perdón de los pecados (R) [(1)Rp.147]. M has *tlatlacolpopolhuia* 'to pardon sins, to grant absolution.' See TLAHTLACŌL-LI, POHPOLHUIĀ.

TLAHTLACŌLQUĪXTIĀ *vrefl* to apologize / disculparse (R) [(1)Rp.147]. See TLAHTLACŌL-LI, QUĪXTIĀ.

TLAHTLACŌLTIĀ *vt* to envy, reproach, blame someone / lo envidia, le culpa, le echa la culpa (Z) [(2)Zp.37,195]. See TLAHTLACŌL-LI.

TLAHTLACUALTIĀ to graze, feed animals / se apacienta a los animales, da de comer a los animales (T) [(3)Tp.231]. In this distributive form the fused prefix TLA- is reduplicated instead of the initial consonant and vowel of the verb stem CUĀ. redup. TLACUALTIĀ

TLAHTLACUALTILIĀ applic. TLAHTLACUALTIĀ

TLAHTLACUALTĪLŌ nonact. TLAHTLACUALTIĀ

TLAHTLAHCO in the middle / en medio de (T) [(2)Tp.231]. T does not give the glottal stop of the second syllable in the Nahuatl-to-Spanish side, but it does appear in the Spanish-to-Nahuatl side. redup. TLAHCO

TLAHTLAHCOTŌNAL-LI midday / mediodía (T) [(1)Tp.231]. In the Nahuatl-to-Spanish side of T the second glottal stop is omitted, and in the Spanish-to-Nahuatl side the first glottal stop is. See TLAHTLAHCO, TŌNAL-LI.

TLAHTLAHCUANIĀ to take things away / quita (T) [(3)Tp.231]. T has E for A in the third syllable. Here the fused prefix TLA-is reduplicated instead of the verb stem itself. See (I)HCUANIĀ.

TLAHTLAHCUANILIĀ applic. TLAH-TLAHCUANIĀ

TLAHTLAHCUANĪLŌ nonact. TLAH-TLAHCUANIĀ

TLAHTLAHTOĀ to chatter, babble / parlar o hablar mucho, o gorjear las aves (M) This is abundantly attested in T. This distributive form reduplicates the fused prefix TLA- instead of the verb stem itself. redup. TLAHTOĀ

TLAHTLAHTŌLTIĀ caus. TLAH-TLAHTOĀ

TLAHTLAHTZŌMIĀ to snort or bellow repeatedly / dar muchos (bufidos) (C) [Cf.71v]. This distributive form reduplicates the fused prefix TLA- rather than the verb stem itself. redup. TLAHTZŌMIĀ

TLAHTLAHUĒLĪLŌCĀT(I) to do evil at every turn, to be mean and cunning / hacer ruindades (C) [(2)Cf.95v,100r]. M glosses *tlatlauelilocati* as a noun 'someone who is mean and cunning.' redup. TLAHUĒLĪLŌCĀT(I)

TLAHTLAIHTLAN(I) *vrefl* to beg / mendigar (K) [(1)Tp.159]. This is indirectly attested in T's nominalization MOTLAHTLAIHTLANI 'beggar.' M has reflexive *tlaitlania* and, in the Spanish-to-Nahuatl side only, the reduplicated form, both meaning 'to beg.' This distributive form reduplicates the fused prefix TLA- rather than the verb stem itself. See IHTLAN(I).

TLAHTLĀLIĀ *vt* to set various things in order, to compose music or copy out writing / poner algo en orden, poner recaudo para decir misa, o poner algo en diversas partes, o poner la mesa con sus manteles, pan, cuchillo, salero, etc., o componer canto, o hacer tractado de escritura (M) [(2)Bf.6v,7r]. This is a distributive form and is not an instance of a fused prefix. redup. TLĀLIĀ

TLAHTLĀLILIĀ *vrefl,vt* to make a definite proposition; to arbitrate for others or to lay out plans for their activities, to fix something / proponer de hacer alguna cosa, haciendo ley para sí, y obligándose a ella (M), arbitrar o determinar y sentenciar entre

partes o dar orden y traza de lo que los otros han de hacer (M), remienda algo o añadir alguna cosa a la escritura que alguno compone o a lo que se cuenta (M), remendar algo o añadir alguna cosa a otra (M) [(2)Bf.6v,7r]. applic. TLAHTLĀLIĀ

TLAHTLĀLLOH something full of dirt, dust / tiene polvo (T), tiene la cara sucia (T for compound with ĪX-TLI) [(2)Tp.137,231]. Because of the general loss of final glottal stop in T, the final H is not attested in this item. See TLĀL-LI, -YOH.

TLAHTLALOĀ *vrefl* for several people to run in the same direction but in an unorganized way / corremos hacia una parte (C for first pers. plural subject) [(2)Cf.72v]. This distributive form contrasts with TLĀTLALOĀ 'to run in an orderly, sequential fashion.' redup. TLALOĀ

TLAHTLAMĀ *pret:* **TLAHTLAMAH** to hunt or fish, to take captives in war / pescar o cazar algo con redes (M), cazar o cautivar en la guerra (C) [(2)Cf.64v, (4)Tp.231]. This distributive form reduplicates the fused prefix TLA- rather than the verb stem itself. See TLAMĀ.

TLAHTLAMAHQUI fisherman / pescador (T) [(1)Tp.231]. M has synonymous *tlatlama* in the Spanish-to-Nahuatl side only. See TLAHTLAMĀ.

TLAHTLAMĀLIĀ *vt* to hunt or fish for someone; to delouse someone / cazo o pesco algo para él, o le espulgo (C for first pers. sg. subject) [(1)Cf.64v, (4)Tp.208,231]. applic. TLAHTLAMĀ

TLAHTLAMĀLILIĀ applic. TLAH-TLAMĀLIĀ

TLAHTLAMĀLĪLŌ nonact. TLAH-TLAMĀLIĀ

TLAHTLAMĀLŌ nonact. TLAHTLAMĀ

TLAHTLAMĀNI fisherman / pescador (X) [(2)Xp.94]. X fails to mark the glottal stop. See TLAHTLAMĀ.

TLAHTLAMANILIĀ *vt* This is transitive in M and X, and T's unreduplicated TLAMANILIĀ is transitive, but T gives this reduplicated form as intransitive. / remienda (T) [(3)Tp.231, (3)Xp.76]. redup. TLAMANILIĀ

TLAHTLAMANILILIĀ applic. TLAH-TLAMANILIĀ

TLAHTLAMANILĪLŌ nonact. TLAH-
TLAMANILIĀ

TLAHTLAM(I) *pret:* **TLAHTLAN** to
conclude, to come to an end / concluir (K)
[(2)Bf.6v]. redup. TLAM(I)

TLAHTLAN(I) to ask questions, to inquire /
preguntar (C) This also appears in P. See
IHTLAN(I).

TLAHTLANIĀ *vrefl,vt* to examine one's
own conscience, to practice introspection;
to ask a person questions, to interrogate
someone / examinarse el pecador para se
confesar algo así mismo, o recurrir la
memoria (M), preguntar algo a otro, e inquirir o pesquisar a algún negocio (M)
[(4)Zp.72,80,190,196]. See TLAHTLAN(I).

TLAHTLANILIZ-TLI investigation, inquiry
/ investigación, interrogación (S) [(2)Bf.131,
(2)Zp.95,208]. See TLAHTLAN(I).

TLAHTLAŌYOH a tortilla wrapped around
beans / clacloyo, tortilla con frijol adentro
(T) [(1)Tp.231]. This seems to be missing
an L before the suffix -YOH, but it is attested without one on the Spanish-to-
Nahuatl side of T too, and there is no L
in the hispanized form *clacloyo*. See
TLAŌL-LI, -YOH.

TLAHTLAPĀC(A) *pret:* **TLAHTLAPĀC** ~
TLAHTLAPĀCAC to wash something repeatedly or to do laundry in several different places / lavar alguna cosa muchas
veces o lavar en diversas partes (M)
[(1)Cf.71v, (1)Rp.37]. This distributive form
reduplicates the fused prefix TLA- rather
than the verb stem itself. redup. TLA-
PĀC(A)

TLAHTLAPALOĀ to sip, taste a number of
different beverages / probar muchos vinos
o cosa semejante (M), probar varias bebidas
y vinos, bebiendo poco de cada uno (C)
[(1)Cf.71v]. This distributive form reduplicates the fused prefix TLA- instead of the
verb stem itself. See PALOĀ.

TLAHTLAPĀQUILIĀ applic. TLAH-
TLAPĀC(A)

TLAHTLAPOĀ *vrefl* for various things to
open / se abre (C) [(1)Cf.72v]. This distributive form contrasts with TLĀTLAPOĀ 'to
open and shut continuously.' M has
tlatlapoa 'to open something' which represents an unfused instance of TLAPOĀ and

the nonspecific object prefix TLA-. redup.
TLAPOĀ

TLAHTLĀTIĀ *vrefl,vt* to hide in various
places; to hide things / esconder algo (M)
[(1)Bf.11v, (1)Cf.71v, (1)Zp.195]. This
contrasts with TLAHTLATIĀ 'to build a
fire,' although M combines them in a single entry. redup. TLĀTIĀ

TLAHTLATIĀ *vrefl,vt* to burn, to be
scorched; to burn or scorch something or
someone, to start a fire / se quema (gente
solamente) (T), hacer fuego (M), lo quema,
lo chamusca (Z) [(1)Bf.10r, (3)Tp.159,
(5)Zp.38,104,173,195]. This contrasts with
TLAHTLĀTIĀ 'to hide things,' although M
combines them in a single entry. B has a
marginal note contrasting TLAHTLATIĀ
'to scorch someone in various places' with
unreduplicated TLATIĀ 'to burn someone
up entirely.' redup. TLATIĀ

TLAHTLATĪLŌ nonact. TLAHTLATIĀ

TLAHTLATZCUEPŌNIĀ *vt* to hit something or someone repeatedly / lo pega (T)
[(6)Tp.192,214]. This is attested in two
compounds, one with MĀ-TE- 'to hit
someone repeatedly with one's hand,' and
the other with TZĪN-TE- 'to hit someone
repeatedly on the buttocks.' TZĪNTE-TL
'buttocks' is elsewhere attested, but
*MĀTE-TL is not, and it is not clear
whether the -TE- here is the 'body part' use
of TE-TL or some sort of modifier of the
verb. See TLATZCUEPŌNIĀ.

TLAHTLATZCUEPŌNILIĀ applic. TLAH-
TLATZCUEPŌNIĀ

TLAHTLATZCUEPŌNĪLŌ nonact. TLAH-
TLATZCUEPŌNIĀ

TLAHTLAXCALHUIĀ redup. TLAX-
CALHUIĀ

TLAHTLAXCALOĀ redup. TLAXCALOĀ

TLAHTLAYOHUA to get dark / se obscurece, está obscuro (T) [(1)Cf.99r,
(2)Tp.137,231]. redup. TLAYOHUA

TLAH-TLI uncle / tío, hermano de padre o
de madre (M) [(1)Bf.11v, (4)Cf.2v,83v,125r,
(2)Tp.135, (1)Rp.148]. This displays a stem
alternation of short vowel and glottal stop
TLAH with long vowel TLĀ. The absolutive suffix -TLI implies stem-final H, and
the glottal stop is specifically marked with
a diacritic in B, C, and R. Yet C uses the

possessed form meaning 'my uncle' to illustrate that final syllables ending in a long vowel have low tone. If the only attestation of the long vowel were in C, it might be taken for a mistake, albeit a disturbing one, since it would not be simply an incorrect diacritic, but an ill chosen example atypical of C. But T also gives two possessed forms, one plural and the other honorific, both with a long vowel rather than a short vowel and glottal stop. In three attestations, however, (one from B and two from C) there is a short vowel and glottal stop in honorific possessed forms. A case might be made for taking the long vowel variant as basic and the vowel-shortening glottal stop as intrusive, as it is in some cases between stem and honorific -TZIN (ACHIHTZIN 'a bit,' ĪCIHUĀHUAHTZIN 'his wife'), but it would not help here, since the glottal stop precedes even the absolutive suffix -TLI, on the one hand, and since -TZIN is preceded by the long vowel variant in one attestation from T on the other. TLAH-TLI 'uncle' contrasts with TAH-TLI 'father,' which is also exceptional in view of the early and general historical change *TA > TLA which should prevent such contrasts.

TLAHTOĀ to speak, to issue proclamations and commands, for birds to chatter / hablar algo o chirriar, gorjear, o cantar las aves (M) The prefix TLA- has been fused with the verb stem to form an intransitive verb. See (I)HTOĀ.

TLAHTOĀNI ruler, governor, one who issues proclamations and commands / hablador o gran señor (M), el rey (C), el gobernador (C), autoridad (del pueblo), jefe, presidente (T) Except in R and Z, which have them both in free singular form, TLAHTOĀNI and TLAHTOHQUI are suppletive, with the former as a free singular and the latter in inflected and compounded forms. See TLAHTOĀ.

TLAHTOHCĀCAL-LI palace / palacios (C) [(2)Cf.71r]. See TLAHTOHQUI, CAL-LI.

TLAHTOHCĀICPAL-LI throne / silla real, o cosa semejante (M) [(1)Rp.148]. See TLAHTOHQUI, (I)CPAL-LI.

TLAHTOHCĀTEQUI-TL possessed form: **-TEQUIUH** the task of governing / oficio de gobernar (C) [(2)Cf.76v,114r]. See TLAHTOHQUI, TEQUI-TL.

TLAHTOHCĀT(I) to be a ruler / ser señor o príncipe (M) [(4)Cf.58v,66v,107v, (2)Rp.148]. See TLAHTOHQUI.

TLAHTOHCĀTILIĀ applic. TLAHTOHCĀT(I)

TLAHTOHCĀYŌTIĀ to reign / reinar (R) [(1)Rp.148]. M has this as a transitive verb 'to crown someone king.' See TLAHTOHCĀYŌ-TL.

TLAHTOHCĀYŌ-TL kingdom, realm, rulership / señorío, reino, corona real, o patrimonio (M) T has lost the glottal stop in the second syllable. See TLAHTOHQUI, -YŌ.

TLAHTOHQUI possessed form: **-TLAHTOHCĀUH** ruler / señores, caciques, o principales (M for plural) This is abundantly attested but, with the exception of R and Z, not in the free-standing singular form, where TLAHTOĀNI is used instead. This item appears in the plural form TLAHTOHQUEH, the possessed singular form -TLAHTOHCĀUH, and its compounding forms TLAHTOHCĀ- and shortened -TLAHTOH. TLAHTOHQUI contrasts with TLATŌCQUI 'sower.' See TLAHTOĀ.

TLAHTŌLCHIY(A) pret: **TLAHTŌLCHIX ~ TLAHTŌLCHĪX** to await someone's order / esperar mandato de otro (M) [(1)Bf.4v]. The long-vowel preterit form is not directly attested for this, but is abundantly attested for the constituent element CHIY(A). See TLAHTŌL-LI, CHIY(A).

TLAHTŌLCHIYALIĀ applic. TLAHTŌLCHIY(A)

TLAHTŌLCOTŌN(A) vt to interrupt someone / atajar la palabra a otro (M) [(1)Cf.76r, (3)Tp.208]. See TLAHTŌL-LI, COTŌN(A).

TLAHTŌLCUAUHTIC someone with a strong, commanding voice / voz fuerte, voz respetuosa (T) [(1)Tp.231]. See TLAHTŌL-LI, CUAUHTIC.

TLAHTŌLCUEP(A) vrefl,vt to contradict oneself; to contradict someone / desdecirse a retratarse (M), desdecir a otro, diciéndole que es falso lo que dice (M) [(1)Rp.148]. See TLAHTŌL-LI, CUEP(A).

TLAHTŌLĪXNĀMIQU(I) *vt; pret:* **-MIC** to contradict, oppose someone / le contradice, lo afrenta, lo riñe (Z) [(6)Zp.6,33, 91,108,195,208]. Z attests this as an intransitive verb 'to set oneself up in opposition' where a reflexive would be expected. See TLAHTŌL-LI, ĪXNĀMIQU(I).

TLAHTŌL-LI word, speech, statement, language / palabra, plática, o habla (M) See TLAHTOĀ.

TLAHTŌLMACA *vt* to advise, counsel someone / lo aconseja, lo amonesta (T) [(3)Tp.208, (3)Zp.4,10,195, (1)Rp.148]. See TLAHTŌL-LI, MACA.

TLAHTŌLMACALIZ-TLI advice / consejo (Z) [(2)Zp.32,208]. See TLAHTŌLMACA.

TLAHTŌLMACALŌ nonact. TLAHTŌLMACA

TLAHTŌLMAQUILIĀ applic. TLAHTŌLMACA

TLAHTŌLŌ nonact. TLAHTOĀ

TLAHTŌLTĒNCUĒCUĒP(A) *vt* to respond verbally / le contesta con palabras (Z) [(3)Zp.33,195]. In one attestation Z marks the vowel of the first syllable of CUĒCUĒP(A) long but not the second. In the other neither vowel is marked long. Elsewhere, T has reflexive CUĒCUEP(A) 'to be upset' as well as transitive CUĒCUĒP(A) 'to turn things over.' The last element here could conceivably be a transitive use of CUĒCUEP(A) rather than CUĒCUĒP(A). See TLAHTŌL-LI, TĒN-TLI, CUĒCUĒP(A).

TLAHTŌLTIĀ *vrefl,vt* to intercede, to speak in favor of someone; to cause someone to talk or confess, to interrogate someone, to read something / hablar, interceder por alguien (K), hacer hablar a otro, o tomar el dicho al reo o al testigo, o darle tormento para que confiese la verdad (M), lo lee (T) caus. TLAHTOĀ

TLAHTŌLTILIĀ applic. TLAHTŌLTIĀ

TLAHTŌLTĪLŌ nonact. TLAHTŌLTIĀ

TLAHTZOM(A) *pret:* **TLAHTZON** to sew / coser (C) [(3)Cf.42r, (8)Zp.7,34,208]. See (I)HTZOM(A).

TLAHTZOMALIZ-TLI the act of sewing / el acto de coser (C) [(2)Cf.42r, (1)Zp.208]. See (I)HTZOM(A).

TLAHTZOMAL-LI something sewn / cosido

(Z) [(2)Zp.34,208]. Z is inconsistent. In one attestation the vowels of the second and third syllables are marked long, and in the other they are not. By general rules of derivation, all vowels in this item should be short. See (I)HTZOM(A).

TLAHTZOMALŌNI needle / aguja (Z) [(2)Zp.7,208]. Z is inconsistent. In one attestation the vowels of the second, third, and fourth syllables are marked long, and in the other the vowels of the third and fourth. By general rules of derivation only the vowel of the fourth syllable should be long. See TLAHTZOM(A).

TLAHTZŌMIĀ to snort or hiss, as in anger / bufar el gato, o cosa semejante (M), dar un bufido, como caballo o persona enojada (C) [(2)Cf.71v, (3)Tp.248]. C gives this once in distributive form, reduplicating the fused prefix TLA- rather than the verb stem itself. It contrasts with TLAHTZOMIĀ 'to sew something for someone.' T has Z for TZ. See IHTZŌMIĀ.

TLAHTZOMIĀ *vrefl,vt* to sew something for oneself, to sew something for someone / coser algo para sí (M), cósote algo (C for first pers. sg. subject and second pers. sg. object) [(1)Cf.64v]. This item with fused prefix TLA- is implied by an applicative form in C. It contrasts with with TLAHTZŌMIĀ 'to snort or hiss.' See (I)HTZOM(A).

TLAHTZŌMILIĀ applic. TLAHTZŌMIĀ

TLAHTZOMILIĀ applic. TLAHTZOMIĀ

TLAHTZŌMĪLŌ nonact. TLAHTZŌMIĀ

TLAHTZON-TLI something sewn / cosa cosida (C) [(1)Cf.47r]. See TLAHTZOM(A).

TLAHUĀCQUI drought / sequía (T) [(1)Tp.230]. The vowel of the second syllable should be long but is short in T. See TLAHUĀQU(I).

TLAHUAHHUĀQU(I) to dry out / se seca (T) [(1)Tp.230]. See HUĀQU(I).

TLAHUAHHUIĀ to bark / ladra (Z) [(4)Zp.75,206]. One attestation of four lacks the internal glottal stop. See HUAHHUANOĀ.

TLAHUAHHUILIZ-TLI barking, uproar / ladrido (Z) [(2)Zp.75,206]. See TLAHUAHHUIĀ.

TLĀHUĀN(A) to get drunk / beber vino o

emborracharse templadamente (M), se emborracha, se embriaga (T)

TLĀHUĀNALTIĀ *vt* to intoxicate someone / le emborracho, le doy de beber (C for first pers. sg. subject), lo emborracha, lo embriaga (T) [(1)Cf.61v, (4)Tp.211,240]. T is inconsistent in marking the vowel length of the second syllable. T has the reflex of a long vowel in one of four attestations, and C also marks the vowel long. altern. caus. TLĀHUĀN(A)

TLĀHUĀNALTILIĀ applic. TLĀHUĀNALTIĀ

TLĀHUĀNALTĪLŌ nonact. TLĀHUĀNALTIĀ

TLĀHUĀNCĀTEQUI-TL *possessed form:* **-TEQUIUH** drunkenness seen as an occupation / vuestra ocupación de borrachera (C for second pers. plural possessor) [(1)Cf.114r]. This is attested as a slip of the tongue or pun on TLAHTOHCĀTEQUI-TL 'occupation of governing.' See TLĀHUĀNQUI, TEQUI-TL.

TLĀHUĀNCĀTZAHTZI drunken shout / grito de borracho (T) [(1)Tp.240]. In form this appears to be a verb 'to shout drunkenly' rather than a nominalization. See TLĀHUĀNQUI, TZAHTZI.

TLĀHUĀNŌ nonact. TLĀHUĀN(A)

TLĀHUĀNQUI drunkard / borracho o beodo así (M) See TLĀHUĀN(A).

TLĀHUĀNTIĀ altern. caus. TLĀHUĀN(A)

TLAHUĀQU(I) for everything to dry up, for there to be a drought / haber sequedad o agostarse todo cuanto hay (M) [(2)Cf.36v]. See HUĀQU(I).

TLAHUĀTZALIZ-TLI desiccation / secada (Z) [(2)Zp.114,206]. See HUĀTZ(A).

TLAHUEHCA something spacious, roomy / amplio, espacio (T) [(1)Tp.228]. Z has TLAHUĒICA with virtually the same sense. See HUEHCA.

TLAHUEHHUELŌLIZ-TLI destruction / destrucción (Z) [(2)Zp.44,206]. In one attestation Z marks the vowel of the third syllable long, but it should not be. See HUEHHUELOĀ.

TLAHUĒICA something spacious, capacity / capacidad, amplio (Z) [(3)Zp.10,25,206]. T has TLAHUEHCA with virtually the same sense. See HUĒICA.

TLAHUĒLAHHUA *vt* to scold, chide someone angrily / lo reprende con enojo (T) [(3)Tp.206]. See TLAHUĒL-LI, AHHUA.

TLAHUĒLAHHUALŌ nonact. TLAHUĒLAHHUA

TLAHUĒLAHHUILIĀ applic. TLAHUĒLAHHUA

TLAHUĒLCĀHU(A) *vrefl,vt* to be irrational with anger; to forsake something, someone in anger / dejar de entender en lo que le es necesario por estar enojado o desesperar (M), lo deja con coraje, lo abandona (T) [(3)Tp.206, (2)Zp.3,194]. See TLAHUĒL-LI, CĀHU(A).

TLAHUĒLCĀHUALŌ nonact. TLAHUĒLCĀHU(A)

TLAHUĒLCĀHUILIĀ applic. TLAHUĒLCĀHU(A)

TLAHUĒLCUEPILIĀ *vt* to reject someone or something / lo rechaza (T) [(3)Tp.206]. See TLAHUĒL-LI, CUEPILIĀ.

TLAHUĒLCUEPILILIĀ applic. TLAHUĒLCUEPILIĀ

TLAHUĒLCUEPILĪLŌ nonact. TLAHUĒLCUEPILIĀ

TLAHUĒLCUI to become enraged, angry / apitunarse, amohinarse, o enojarse (M) [(4)Cf.62v,114r,115v]. See TLAHUĒL-LI, CUI.

TLAHUĒLCUĪTIĀ *vt* to cause someone to be angry or enraged / airar a otro, o amohinarlo, y enojarlo, o provocarlo a ira y embravecerlo (M) [(1)Cf.62v]. caus. TLAHUĒLCUI

TLAHUĒLEH someone fierce, enraged / sañudo, iracundo, y bravo (M), muy bravo (C) [(1)Cf.81r, (2)Rp.141,145]. See TLAHUĒL-LI.

TLAHUĒLIĀ *vt* to be enraged at someone / tener enojo con otro y aborrecimiento (M) There is a typographical error in M which substitutes *h* for *li*, but the preterit citation is spelled correctly, and it is correctly alphabetized. See TLAHUĒL-LI.

TLAHUĒLĪLŌC *compounding form:* **TLAHUĒLĪLŌCĀ-** someone malicious, a villain or rogue / malvado o bellaco (M) B attests this twice with the vowel of the second syllable specifically marked short, and C marks the vowel long in only one of twelve attestations, but TLAHUĒL-LI definitely has the corresponding vowel long. Possibly B and C reflect a contextual shortening of this vowel when followed by two subsequent syllables containing long vowels, but C does mark the vowel long in YŌLLOHTLAHUĒLĪLŌCĀCUEP(A). See TLAHUĒLIĀ.

TLAHUĒLĪLŌCĀT(I) to become a wicked, malicious person / hacerse malo y bellaco (M) [(6)Cf.58v,60r,100r]. See TLA-HUĒLĪLŌC.

TLAHUĒLĪLŌCĀTILIĀ vt to pervert and corrupt others / hacer vellaco a otro o pervertirle (M), pervertir y malear a los otros (M) [(3)Cf.60r]. applic. TLA-HUĒLĪLŌCĀT(I)

-TLAHUĒLILTIC irregular verb to be unfortunate / ser desgraciado, infeliz (S) [(1)Bf.6v, (4)Cf.59v,112v,125v,130v]. The vowel of the second syllable is not marked long in the attestations. This verb occurs only in the third person singular preterit form and takes possessive rather than subject prefixes, NOTLAHUĒLILTIC 'woe is me.' See TLAHUĒL-LI.

TLAHUĒLITTA vt to hate someone / aborrecer y mirar con enojo a otro (M) [(3)Tp.208, (6)Zp.3,33,51,108,194,222, (3)Xp.76]. In this item, but not in other derivations from TLAHUĒL-LI, T has Y for HU. See TLAHUĒL-LI, (I)TTA.

TLAHUĒLITTALŌ nonact. TLAHUĒLITTA

TLAHUĒLITTILIĀ applic. TLAHUĒLITTA

TLAHUĒLĪXNĀMIQU(I) pret: -MIC to set oneself in opposition / se opone (Z) [(2)Zp.91,206]. M has transitive TLA-HUĒLNĀMIQU(I) 'to set oneself in opposition to someone' The intransitivity of this item in Z is idiosyncratic. See TLAHUĒL-LI, ĪXNĀMIQU(I).

TLAHUĒL-LI rage, fury, indignation / indignación, enojo o furia del que está airado y lleno de saña (M), coraje, enojo, ira (C) M marks the vowel of the second syllable long in less than a third of the attestations, and B marks it specifically short in two derived forms, but T consistently has the reflex of a long vowel and Z generally agrees.

TLAHUĒLMICOHUA nonact. TLA-HUĒLMIQU(I)

TLAHUĒLMIQU(I) pret: -MIC to be enraged / se enoja (T) [(6)Tp.137,228]. See TLAHUĒL-LI, MIQU(I).

TLAHUĒLMIQUILIZ-TLI rage / enojo, coraje, ira (M) [(1)Tp.228]. See TLA-HUĒLMIQU(I).

TLAHUĒLMIQUINI someone easily enraged / enojón (T) [(1)Tp.228]. See TLA-HUĒLMIQU(I).

TLAHUĒLMIQUĪTIĀ caus. TLA-HUĒLMIQU(I)

TLAHUĒLNĀMIQU(I) See TLA-HUĒLĪXNĀMIQU(I).

TLAHUĒLNŌNŌCHILIĀ applic. TLA-HUĒLNŌNŌTZ(A)

TLAHUĒLNŌNŌTZ(A) vt to address someone angrily / le habla con enojo (T) [(6)Tp.206,236]. See TLAHUĒL-LI, NŌNŌTZ(A).

TLAHUĒLNŌNŌTZALŌ nonact. TLAHUĒLNŌNŌTZ(A)

TLAHUĒLPOZŌN(I) to boil over with anger / se enfureció (C for third pers. sg. preterit) [(1)Cf.115v]. M has the derived form tlauelpoçoniliztica 'with exceedingly great wrath,' and S has causative tlauelpoçonaltia. See TLAHUĒL-LI, POZŌN(I).

TLAHUĒLTLAHTLAHTOĀ to rant, to speak with anger / habla con coraje (T) [(3)Tp.228]. See TLAHUĒL-LI, TLAHTLAHTOĀ.

TLAHUĒLTLAHTLAHTŌLŌ nonact. TLAHUĒLTLAHTLAHTOĀ

TLAHUĒLTLAHTLAHTŌLTIĀ caus. TLAHUĒLTLAHTLAHTOĀ

TLAHUETZQUĪTIĀ vt to entertain someone / decir donaires y gracias para hacer reir a otros, o hacer cosa por donde se rían de mi (M) [(2)Zp.39,206]. In Z this appears as an intransitive verb with fused TLA-. See HUETZQUĪTIĀ.

TLAHUETZQUĪTIH someone witty / chistoso (Z) [(2)Zp.39,206]. See TLAHUETZQUĪTIĀ.

TLAHUETZQUĪTILIZ-TLI joke / chiste (Z) [(2)Zp.39,206]. See TLAHUETZQUĪTIĀ.

TLĀHUIĀ to light a candle, to light the way for people with tapers or torches / alumbrar la candela (M), alumbrar a otros con candela o hacha (M) M also has a related verb with the prefix TLA- meaning 'to redden something with ochre, to turn red, to blush.' TLĀHUIĀ is apparently a reduction of TLĀUHHUIĀ< TLĀHU(I)-TL 'red ochre' and -HUIĀ, and refers specifically to red light, including the light of dawn as well as firelight.

TLAHUĪCALIZ-TLI debt / deuda (Z) [(2)Zp.45,206] See HUĪCA.

TLAHUICXITĪL-LI something cooked / cocido (T) [(1)Tp.228]. See HUICXITIĀ.

TLAHUIHHUĪCALIZ-TLI curse / maldición (Z) [(2)Zp.80,206]. See TLAHUIH-HUĪCALTIĀ.

TLAHUIHHUĪCALTIĀ vrefl,vt to curse; to curse someone / se maldice (T), lo maldice (T) [(6)Tp.159,206]. See HUIHHUĪCALTIĀ.

TLAHUIHHUĪCALTILIĀ applic. TLA-HUIHHUĪCALTIĀ

TLAHUIHHUĪCALTĪLŌ nonact. TLA-HUIHHUĪCALTIĀ

TLĀHUIHPOCH-IN pl: **-TIN** sorcerer / bruja (M), brujos (C for plural) [(1)Cf.112v]. This appears only in the Spanish-to-Nahuatl side of M. It is conventionally paired with NĀHUAL-LI, which is a different kind of sorcerer, according to M. This would seem to be related to TLAHUIHHUĪCALTIĀ 'to curse someone,' but there is a vowel length discrepancy in the first syllable.

TLĀHUILIĀ vrefl,vt to light one's way with a candle; to light someone's way with a candle / alumbrarse con candela (M), alumbrar a otro así (M) applic. TLĀHUIĀ

TLĀHUILICŌCOCOTOC-TLI piece of pine used as a torch / pedazo de ocote (T) [(1)Tp.239]. See TLĀHUILICŌ-TL, COCOTOCA, COTOC-TLI.

TLĀHUILICŌCUAHU(I)-TL pine tree of a type used for making torches / ocote (árbol) (T) [(1)Tp.239]. See TLĀHUILICŌ-TL, CUAHU(I)-TL.

TLĀHUILICŌ-TL pine torch / antorcha, ocote (T) [(3)Tp.239]. The vowel of the second syllable is consistently attested short, although elsewhere in T it is attested long in TLĀHUĪL-LI 'torchlight.' The gloss implies OCO-TL 'ocote, torch pine' for the second element, but there is I

for O in one syllable and the reflex of Ō for O in the other.

TLĀHUILILIĀ vt to illuminate something for someone / se lo alumbra, se lo aluza (T) [(3)Tp.211]. applic. TLĀHUILIĀ

TLĀHUILILILIĀ nonact. TLĀHUILILIĀ

TLĀHUILILĪLŌ nonact. TLĀHUILILIĀ

TLĀHUILĪLŌ nonact. TLĀHUILIĀ

TLĀHUĪL-LI pl: **-MEH** ~ **-TIN** candlelight, lamplight, torchlight / claridad o luz de candelas (M), lámpara, luz, candil (T) If this is derived from TLĀHUIĀ, the vowel of the second syllable should be long, but B specifically marks it short. In T two of four attestations have a long vowel, and two have the corresponding vowel short. In Z and X the vowel is consistently long. See TLĀHUIĀ.

TLĀHUĪLŌ nonact. TLĀHUIĀ

TLAHUILTEQU(I) pret: **TLAHUILTEC** to go the shortest route, to cut corners / atajar o ir por camino más breve o atravesar (M) [(1)Bf.2v]. Since B specifically marks the vowels of the first three syllables short, the otherwise unattested first element of this contrasts with TLĀHUĪL-LI 'candlelight.' M has this with the directional prefix ON-. verb. TEQU(I)

TLĀHUILTIĀ caus. TLĀHUIĀ

TLAHUĪQUILIĀ vt to owe someone, to be in debt to someone / le debe a alguien (Z) [(2)Zp.40,194]. See HUĪQUILIĀ.

TLĀHU(I)-TL red ochre / almagre (M) This is indirectly attested in the verb TLĀHUIĀ having to do with red firelight and TLĀHUIZCAL-LI 'the rosy light of dawn.'

TLAHUITŌM(I) pret: **TLAHUITŌN** for things to collapse / se derrumba (Z) [(4)Zp.41,101,206]. See HUIHHUITŌN(I).

TLAHUITŌN-TLI something knocked down or undone / cosa derrocada, desbaratada, o desecha (M) [(2)Zp.101,206]. The direct derivational basis of this is M's vituma 'to demolish a building or to release dammed up water.' See TLAHUITŌM(I).

TLĀHUIZCAL-LI the rosy light of dawn / el alba, o el resplandor del alba (M) [(1)Bf.12v]. See TLĀHU(I)-TL, (I)ZCALIĀ.

TLAHXĪCA to leak, to drip / haber goteras o lloverse la casa (M) [(1)Tp.238]. T has

lost either a long vowel or, more likely, a
glottal stop. See ĪXĪCA, (I)HXĪCA.
TLAHXILLACAL-LI ward, barrio / barrio
(M) [(1)Rp.149]. This appears in R with no
diacritics, but is attested with the internal
glottal stop in the first syllable in a testa-
ment from Culhuacan, 1577.
TLAHXI-TL something reached, taken hold
of, seized / cosa cogida (C) [(1)Cf.47r,
(1)Rp.41]. See AHCI.
TLAHYELITTA *vt* to hate someone or
something / aborrecer a otro (M), lo
aborrece, lo odia (T) [(3)Tp.208]. See
TLAHYEL-LI, (I)TTA.
TLAHYELLAHTŌL-LI gross, obscene
speech / palabras obscenas (R) [(1)Rp.141].
See TLAHYEL-LI, TLAHTŌL-LI.
TLAHYEL-LI something foul, dysentery /
cosa sucia o cámaras de sangre (M) M has
this as *tlaelli*, *tlahilli*, and *tlailli*, but
the glottal stop and Y are consistently attested across sources. Z has Ā for E. See
(I)HYĀYA.
TLAHYELMICTOC someone afflicted with
nausea / tiene asco (Z) [(2)Zp.15,208]. See
TLAHYEL-LI, MIQU(I), the verb O.
TLAHYELOĀ *vt* to soil something / en-
suciar algo (M) [(1)Rp.149]. R places the
diacritic on the wrong syllable. It appears
on the second, but it belongs on the first.
See TLAHYEL-LI.
TLAHYELTIĀ *vrefl,vt* to suffer nausea; to
make someone suffer nausea / tener asco
de alguna cosa sucia (M), poner asco a otro
(M) [(1)Bf.12r, (3)Tp.208, (2)Zp.15,195]. See
TLAHYEL-LI.
TLAHYELTIĀNI something nauseating,
loathsome / asqueroso (T) [(1)Tp.159]. See
TLAHYELTIĀ.
TLAHYELTILIĀ applic. TLAHYELTIĀ
TLAHYŌHUIĀ to suffer, to fast / ayuna (T),
padece, sufre (Z) This is abundantly attested in T and Z, where IHĪYŌ-TL reduces to IHYŌ-TL. The nonspecific object
prefix TLA- has been fused to the verb
stem to form an intransitive verb. M has
corresponding derived forms with the full
TLAIHĪYŌ- element. Z does not mark the
vowel of the second syllable long. See
IHĪYŌHUIĀ.

TLAHYŌHUIH someone long-suffering,
someone who has suffered / sufrido (Z)
[(2)Zp.118,208]. See TLAHYŌHUIĀ.
TLAHYŌHUILIĀ applic. TLAHYŌHUIĀ
TLAHYŌHUILIZ-TLI misery, suffering /
tormento, fatiga o pena que se padece (M
for *tlayhiouiliztli*), afán, angustia, miseria,
sufrimiento (Z) [(5)Zp.6,10,85,118,208]. See
TLAHYŌHUIĀ.
TLAHYŌHUĪL-LI fast / ayuno (Semana
Santa) (T) [(1)Tp.232]. See TLAHYŌHUIĀ.
TLAHYŌHUĪLŌ nonact. TLAHYŌHUIĀ
TLAHYŌHUILTIĀ *vt* to torment, mistreat
someone, to make someone suffer /
atormentar y fatigar a otro (M for
tlayhiouiltia), le tormenta, le maltrata,
le angustia (Z) [(3)Zp.10,80]. caus.
TLAHYŌHUIĀ
TLAHZANATZA someone who makes a
crackling sound with something / el
que hace ... ruido con hojas secas, pliegos
de papel, etc. (C) [(1)Cf.75v]. See
(I)HZANATZ(A).
TLAHZOLCAMAC-TLI dumping place
for trash / lugar de mucha basura (T)
[(2)Tp.235]. T has lost the internal glottal
stop. See TLAHZOL-LI, -CAMAC.
TLAHZOLHUIĀ *vt* to do harm to someone
/ por mirar le hace daño a otro (a propósito), le hace mal de ojo (T for compound
with ĪX-TLI) [(3)Tp.218]. T has lost the
internal glottal stop. See IHZOLOĀ.
TLAHZOLHUILIĀ applic. TLAHZOLHUIĀ
TLAHZOLHUILĪLŌ nonact. TLAH-
ZOLHUIĀ
TLAHZOL-LI trash / basura que echan en el
muladar (M) T has lost the glottal stop. See
IHZOLOĀ.
TLAHZOLPEHPEN(A) See TLAHZOL-LI,
PEHPEN(A).
TLAHZOLZACA See TLAHZOL-LI, ZACA.
TLAĪ to drink a beverage / beber poleadas,
cacao, pinolli, purga o cosa semejante (M),
desayuna, toma atole en la mañana (T)
[(3)Tp.239, (2)Zp.19,123]. M gives an inde-
pendent entry for this as an intransitive
verb, implying that the nonspecific object
prefix TLA- has been fused with the stem.
See the verb Ī.
TLAĪCAMPA behind, in the back / detrás de

algo, allende los montes, sierras, o puertos (M) [(3)Zp.16,45,207]. Z also has the short variant TLAĪCAN. In all attestations Z marks the vowel of the third syllable long, but it is short in attestations of -ĪCAMPA across other sources. See -ĪCAMPA.

TLAĪCHĀN(A) to draw fiber from maguey / saca ixcle del maguey (T) [(3)Tp.230]. See ĪCH-TLI, ĀN(A).

TLAĪCHĀNALŌ nonact. TLAĪCHĀN(A)

TLAĪCHĀNILIĀ applic. TLAĪCHĀN(A)

TLAICHTACAYĀN hiding place / escondite (Z) [(2)Zp.55,207]. See ICHTACA, -YĀN.

TLAICNĒLILIZ-TLI charity, kindness towards others / caridad (Z) [(2)Zp.25,207]. Although the intial I of (I)CNĒLIĀ drops in other contexts when preceded by a prefixal vowel, it is retained here. M has virtually synonymous *teicneliliztli*. See (I)CNĒLILIĀ.

TLAIHIHTŌLIZ-TLI criticism, the saying of various things / acción de criticar (Z) [(1)Zp.207]. Z fails to indicate the second glottal stop. See IHIHTOĀ.

TLAIHITTALIZ-TLI something chosen, choice / escogido (Z) [(1)Zp.207]. See IHITTA.

TLAIHITTAL-LI something chosen, choice / escogido (Z) [(1)Zp.55]. See IHITTA.

TLAIHTIC inside / dentro, adentro (Z) [(3)Zp.5,41,207]. See -IHTEC.

TLAIHTLAPOĀ for something to open / abre (la puerta, la casa) (T) [(3)Tp.230]. T fails to mark the I short, but it must be so before the glottal stop. T also gives a nonactive form of this appropriate to a verb ending in OHUA rather than OĀ. See TLAPOĀ.

TLAIHTLAPOLHUIĀ applic. TLA-IHTLAPOĀ

TLAĪHUA nonact. TLAĪ

TLAĪL-LI beverage (especially an alcoholic beverage) / bebida como vino, pulque, etc., bebida alcohólica (T) [(3)Cf.47r,67v,96r, (1)Tp.230]. M has *tlailli* referring to dysentery, which is a variant of TLAH-YEL-LI, and which contrasts with this item. See the verb Ī.

TLAILPILIZ-TLI the action of untying something / acción de amarrar [(1)Zp.207]. Z also has ILPILIZ-TLI with the same sense. See (I)LPIĀ.

TLAĪNĀX-TLI something hidden, put away / cosa escondida o solapada (M) [(1)Cf.46v]. See ĪNĀY(A).

TLAĪNĀYAL-LI something hidden, put away / cosa escondida o solapada (M) [(1)Cf.46v]. See ĪNĀY(A).

TLAĪTIĀ caus. TLAĪ

TLAĪ-TL beverage / lo que se bebe (C) [(1)Cf.47r]. See the verb Ī.

TLAĪUHTICAH for there to be no one around, for a place to be deserted / no hay gente (T) [(1)Tp.230]. M has *ça iuhticac* 'vacant house' and under words for 'vacant' on the Spanish-to-Nahuatl side several other constructions with the sequence *iuhti*. If this is derived from IHU(I) 'to be or become in a certain way,' the vowel of the second syllable should be short, but T has it long. See IHU(I), the verb CĀ.

TLAĪXCALAQUIĀ to intertwine / entreteje (Z) [(2)Zp.53,207]. See ĪX-TLI, CALAQUIĀ.

TLAĪXCO on the surface, in the front / en la sobrehaz, o en la delantera (M) [(1)Cf.21r]. M and C both have this in construction with the verb CĀ with the sense of 'on top, first out.' See -ĪXCO.

TLAĪXCUEPANI hypocrite, someone who turns things inside out and falsifies things / el que vuelve la ropa lo de dentro afuera, o el falsario (M), tiene dos caras, es hipócrita (T) [(1)Tp.230]. T also has this in a phrase with the reflexive prefix M-< MO- rather than TLA- but with the sense remaining the same. See ĪX-TLI, CUEP(A).

TLAĪXĒLĒHUIĀ to lust, desire / codicia, desea (T) [(3)Tp.230, (3)Zp.29,80,207]. See ĪXĒLĒHUIĀ.

TLAĪXELĒHUILIĀ applic. TLAĪXELĒHUIĀ

TLAĪXELĒHUĪLŌ nonact. TLAĪXELĒHUIĀ

TLAĪXĪPTLAYŌ-TL portrait, painted image / imagen pintado (M) [(1)Cf.94v]. See ĪXĪPTLAYŌ-TL.

TLAĪXNĀMIQUILIZ-TLI confrontation / ataque (Z) [(2)Zp.16,207]. M has *tlaixnamictiliztli* with essentially the same meaning. See ĪXNĀMIQU(I).

TLAĪXNEQU(I) pret: TLAĪXNEC to lust, desire / codicia, quiere otra mujer (T) [(3)Tp.230, (3)Zp.29,80,207]. See ĪX-TLI, NEQU(I).

TLAĪXNEQUĪHUA nonact. TLAĪXNEQU(I)

TLAĪXNEQUĪTIĀ caus. TLAĪXNEQU(I)

TLAĪXPAN before, in front of / en la delantera de alguna cosa (M), en frente (T)
[(1)Tp.230, (3)Zp.5,51,207]. See -ĪXPAN.

TLAĪXTEMŌ to descend an incline / va de
bajada, baja uno en el camino, bajada de
camino (T) [(1)Tp.230]. See TLAĪX-TLI,
TEMŌ.

TLAĪXTLAHTZAYĀNAL-LI something
divided, partitioned / partido (Z)
[(2)Zp.94,207]. The absolutive suffix is
unattested. See -ĪXTLAH, TZAYĀN(A).

TLAĪXTLAPĀNAL-LI something divided /
partido [(2)Zp.94,207]. See ĪX-TLI,
TLAPĀN(A).

TLAĪXTLĀY(I) pret: TLAĪXTLĀX to break
land with a hoe / barbecha (con azadón) (Z)
[(2)Zp.18,207]. See ĪX-TLI, TLĀY(I).

TLAĪXTLEHCŌ to ascend an incline / va de
subida (T) [(1)Tp.230]. See TLAĪX-TLI,
TLEHCŌ.

TLAĪX-TLI uphill stretch, rise / subida del
camino, cuesta arriba (T) [(1)Tp.230]. See
ĪX-TLI.

TLAĪXTOPĒHUALIZ-TLI disregard,
contempt / desprecio (Z) [(2)Zp.44,207]. See
ĪX-TLI, TOPĒHU(A).

TLAĪXTZACUILŌNI veil / velo (Z)
[(2)Zp.128,207]. See ĪX-TLI, TZACU(I).

TLAĪXYEHYECOHQUI judge / juez (Z)
[(2)Zp.74,207]. See ĪXYEHYECOĀ.

TLAĪXYEHYECŌLIZ-TLI judgement,
opinion / consideración, plan, opinión (Z)
[(4)Zp.32,91,99,207]. See ĪXYEHYECOĀ.

TLAIZHUATĒCA to make hay / zacatea (T)
[(3)Tp.236]. T shortens the sequence
TLAIZ to TLAZ. See IZHUA-TL, TĒCA.

TLAIZHUATĒCALŌ nonact. TLAIZ-
HUATĒCA

TLAIZHUATĒQUILIĀ applic. TLAIZ-
HUATĒCA

TLĀLACATE-TL pl: -MEH dove / paloma
(X) [(3)Xp.91]. See TLĀL-LI.

TLĀLAQUIĀ vrefl,vt for something to get
buried; to bury something, to set something in the earth, to plant something /
enterrarse (M), enterrar a otro (M) See
TLĀL-LI, AQUIĀ.

TLĀLAQUILIĀ applic. TLĀLAQUIĀ

TLĀLAQUĪLŌ nonact. TLĀLAQUIĀ

TLĀLĀX-IN pl: -TIN small bedbug, mite /

chinche pequeña (M), clalaje (insecto) (T),
coruco, pipiol (animalito, insecto) (Z)
[(1)Tp.240, (2)Zp.34,208]. The word-final
nasal consonant is missing in M. T has the
variant singular form TLĀLĀX(A). See
TLĀL-LI, ĀX-IN.

TLĀLAYOH-TLI a type of squash /
calabacilla silvestre (M), planta medicinal
que lleva unas calabacillas comestibles (R)
[(1)Rp.142]. See TLĀL-LI, AYOH-TLI.

TLĀLCACAHUACOPĪN(A) to pull up,
harvest peanuts / arranca cacahuates (T)
[(3)Tp.240]. See TLĀLCACAHUA-TL,
COPĪN(A).

TLĀLCACAHUACOPĪNALŌ nonact.
TLĀLCACAHUACOPĪN(A)

TLĀLCACAHUACOPĪNILIĀ applic.
TLĀLCACAHUACOPĪN(A)

TLĀLCACAHUAPEHPEN(A) See
TLĀLCACAHUA-TL, PEHPEN(A).

TLĀLCACAHUA-TL peanut / cacahuate (T)
[(6)Tp.196,240, (2)Zp.22,208]. See TLĀL-LI,
CACAHUA-TL.

TLĀLCĀHU(A) vt to forsake land, to make
room for someone / dejar la tierra (K)
This is implied by B's TLĀLCĀHUILIĀ
and TLĀLCĀHUALTIĀ and by C's
TLĀLCĀHUIĀ. It contrasts with
TLA-LCĀHU(A)< (I)LCĀHU(A) 'to forget
something' M has tlalcaualli with the
glosses 'something forgotten' and 'unculti-
vated land,' representing derivations from
(I)LCĀHU(A) and TLĀLCĀHU(A) respectively. See TLĀL-LI, CĀHU(A).

TLĀLCĀHUALTIĀ caus. TLĀLCĀHU(A)

TLĀLCĀHUIĀ to relinquish one's place to
someone / dar lugar a otro, apartándose de
el (M) [(1)Cf.27v]. See TLĀLCĀHU(A).

TLĀLCĀHUILIĀ applic. TLĀLCĀHU(A)

TLALCĀHUĪL-LI something forgotten /
cosa olvidable (T) [(1)Tp.232]. In the
Spanish-to-Nahuatl side T has the more
accurate gloss cosa olvidada. See
(I)LCĀHU(A).

TLĀLCAMOH-TLI sweet potato / camote (Z) [(2)Zp.24,208]. See TLĀL-LI,
CAMOH-TLI.

TLĀLCĒHUĪL-LI fallow land / la tierra en
descanso (T) [(1)Tp.240]. See TLĀL-LI,
CĒHUIĀ.

TLĀLCHI on or towards the ground, down /

en el suelo (M), en o hacia el suelo (C) This is abundantly attested in C as the opposite of AHCO. See TLĀL-LI.

TLĀLCHIHUĪC in the direction of the ground / hacia la tierra (C) [(3)Cf.8ov,93v]. This is conventionally paired with AHCOHUĪC together with the verb (I)TTA, the whole phrase meaning 'to look someone up and down,' that is, to make much of someone and thereby to honor that person. See TLĀLCHI, -HUĪC.

TLĀLCHIPA in the direction of the ground / hacia la tierra o hacia el suelo (M) [(2)Cf.93v,129r]. See TLĀLCHI, -PA.

TLĀLCHIPĀUHYOH earth swept clean / está barrido (T) [(1)Tp.240]. Because of general word-final vowel shortening and the loss of final glottal stop in T, it cannot be determined if this item ends in -YOH or -YŌ, but the absence of an absolutive suffix is evidence for -YOH. See TLĀL-LI, CHIPĀHU(A).

TLĀLCHIQUIHU(I)-TL pl: **-TIN** strainer for maize soaked in lime water / colador para nixtamal (X) [(3)Xp.91]. See TLĀL-LI, CHIQUIHU(I)-TL.

TLĀLCHITLĀZ(A) vrefl to do obeisance, to prostrate oneself / humillarse y abatirse hasta el suelo (M) [(2)Cf.93v,120v]. See TLĀLCHI, TLĀZ(A).

TLĀLCOCONĒ-TL pl: **-MEH** type of venomous lizard / talcoconete, tipo de lagartija venenosa (X) [(3)Xp.91]. See TLĀL-LI, CONĒ-TL.

TLĀLCUALCĀN scenic spot / lugar bonito (Z) [(2)Zp.77,208]. See TLĀL-LI, CUALCĀN.

TLĀLCUĒCHTIC dust / polvo (de tierra) (T) [(1)Tp.240]. See TLĀL-LI, CUĒCHTIC.

TLĀLCUEP(A) vrefl to turn to dust / se vuelve como tierra (Z) [(1)Zp.173]. M has the derived form tlalcuepalli 'worn-out soil.' See TLĀL-LI, CUEP(A).

TLĀLCUEPŌNIĀ vrefl to fall to the ground / se cae al suelo (T) [(3)Tp.160]. This seems to imply making a thundering noise in falling. See TLĀL-LI, CUEPŌNIĀ.

TLĀLCUĪLIĀ to take land from someone / quitar(le) ... sus tierras (C) [(1)Cf.117v]. See TLĀL-LI, CUĪLIĀ.

TLĀLEPA-TL pl: **-MEH** fox / zorra (T) [(1)Tp.240]. See TLĀL-LI, EPA-TL.

TLALHUA-TL inalienably possessed form: **-TLALHUAYŌ** tendon / nervio (M), su tendón (Z for possessed form) [(4)Tp.132,134,232, (2)Zp.121,161]. T also has TLALHUAYŌ-TL in absolutive form. Z has only possessed forms, once with -YŌ and once without.

TLALHUAYŌ-TL blood vessel, tendon / vena, tendón (T) [(1)Tp.232]. See TLALHUA-TL.

TLĀLHUĒHUĒ-TL pl: **-MEH** tarantula / tarántula (araña) (T) [(1)Tp.240]. In the absolutive form the second element appears to be HUĒHUĒ-TL 'upright drum,' but the somewhat peculiar plural form would make sense as the reflex of TLĀLHUĒHUĒN-MEH, and 'old man' seems more appropriate to a large hairy spider than 'drum' in any case. See TLĀL-LI, HUĒHUEH.

TLĀLHUIĀ vrefl,vt to get covered with dirt; to heap dirt on something, to cultivate something / se atierra (T), allegar o echar tierra a alguna cosa (M), echar tierra a una planta, para que crezca (C) [(1)Bf.10v, (1)Cf.128v, (6)Tp.161,211]. C contrasts this with TLALHUIĀ< (I)LHUIĀ 'to summon, advise, or warn someone.' applic. TLĀLOĀ

TLALHUIĀ vt to summon or invite someone, to advise someone or warn someone to be on time / muñir o apercibir a alguno para algún negocio, o convidar a otro (M), apercibir o prevenir a alguno para que haga algo a su tiempo (C) [(1)Cf.128v]. C contrasts this with TLĀLHUIĀ 'to heap dirt on something.' See (I)LHUIĀ.

TLĀLHUILIĀ applic. TLĀLHUIĀ

TLĀLHUĪL-LI pl: **-TIN** someone invited / el invitado (T) [(1)Tp.232]. See TLALHUIĀ.

TLĀLHUĪLŌ nonact. TLĀLHUIĀ

TLALHUIQUĪXTIĀ caus. TLALHUIQUĪZ(A)

TLALHUIQUĪXTĪLŌ nonact. TLALHUIQUĪZ(A)

TLALHUIQUĪZ(A) for a fiesta to take place / se hace la fiesta (T) [(1)Cf.95r, (4)Tp.232]. M has causative tlaluiquixtia 'to hold a fiesta.' See ILHUI-TL, QUĪZ(A).

TLĀLHUĪTEQU(I) vt; pret: **-TEC** to beat something or someone down / lo golpea (Z) [(1)Zp.63,195]. See TLĀL-LI, HUĪTEQU(I).

TLALHUIZ inconsiderately, without thought for the consequences / inconsideramente, sin qué, ni para qué (C) [(1)Bf.11v, (8)Cf.113v]. See ĪLIHUIZ.

TLĀLIĀ *vrefl,vt* to sit down, to settle; to seat someone, to put something down, to set down statutes and ordinances, to set things in order / asentarse (M), dar a siento a otro (M), componer, poner algo en alguna parte, o hacer estatutos y ordenanzas (M) TLĀLIĀ is a high frequency verb used with a wide range of more or less figurative senses. It also enters in compound constructions with other verbs in invariant reflexive form and with the -TI- ligature, -TIMOTLĀLIĀ. These constructions convey the sense of putting oneself in the attitude expressed by the other verb or, in the case of weather, to set in as the type expressed by the other verb. See TLĀL-LI.

TLĀLICHPĀN(A) *vrefl,vt* to drag oneself along; to drag something / se arrastra (T), lo arrastra (T) [(6)Tp.161,211]. See TLĀL-LI, (I)CHPĀN(A).

TLALICHTIC something tough / cosa dura, como ave mal cocida o por manir (M), correoso (T) [(1)Tp.232].

TLĀLIHCOCH-IN earthworm / gusano de la tierra (Z) [(2)Zp.65,208]. See TLĀL-LI, IHCOCH-IN.

TLĀLIHTIC underground / dentro de la tierra (R) [(1)Rp.93]. See TLĀL-LI, IHTEC.

TLĀLILIĀ applic. TLĀLIĀ

TLĀLĪLŌ nonact. TLĀLIĀ

TLĀLILTIĀ caus. TLĀLIĀ

TLĀLĪXTLAHYOHUAYĀN darkness on the face of the earth / está obscuro en el suelo (Z) [(1)Zp.208]. The internal glottal stop is not attested in Z. -ĪXTLAH and -ĪXTLAN 'before, in the presence of' are synonymous, and either could be the second constituent of this construction. See TLĀL-LI, -ĪXTLAH, YOHUA, -YĀN.

TLĀL-LI *inalienably possessed form:* -TLĀLLŌ earth, land, property / tierra o heredad (M) This has the full range of senses from physical ground or soil to parcels of land to the abstract idea of 'earth.'

TLĀLLOH something covered with earth, dirt / cosa llena de tierra (C) [(2)Cf.54r, (1)Tp.137, (1)Rp.44]. This is conventionally paired with ZOQUIYOH, the phrase refer-

ring to one's earthly body. See TLĀL-LI, -YOH.

TLĀLLŌTIĀ *vrefl,vt* to get dirty; to dirty something / se ensucia con tierra (T), echar tierra en algo (M) [(3)Tp.161]. M has further glosses about separating things, perhaps in the sense of partitioning land or providing each entity with its own location. See TLĀL-LI, -YŌ.

TLĀLLŌTĪLŌ nonact. TLĀLLŌTIĀ

TLĀLMACA *vt* to give someone land / le da tierra (T) [(3)Tp.211]. See TLĀL-LI, MACA.

TLĀLMACALŌ nonact. TLĀLMACA

TLĀLMANIC surface of the earth / tierra (superficie de la tierra) (Z) [(2)Zp.122,208]. See TLĀLMANQUI.

TLĀLMANQUI plain, level ground / llano, llanura (T) [(1)Tp.240]. M has *tlalmantli* 'leveled ground.' See TLĀL-LI, MAN(I).

TLĀLMAQUILIĀ applic. TLĀLMACA

TLĀLNĀMICŌYĀN border, property line / lindero (entre terrenos) (Z) [(2)Zp.77,209]. Z fails to mark the vowel of the fourth syllable long, but it should be. See TLĀL-LI, NĀMIQU(I), -YĀN.

TLALNĀMICTIĀ *vt* to remind someone of something / traer a la memoria, o acordar algo a otro (M), lo recuerda, le hace acordar (T) [(3)Tp.208]. See (I)LNĀMICTIĀ.

TLALNĀMIQUILIZ-TLI recollection, memory / pensamiento o memoria (M) [(1)Cf.68r, (4)Zp.72,96,107,209]. See (I)LNĀMIQU(I).

-TLALNĀMIQUIYA *necessarily possessed form* one's memory / mi memoria (R for first pers. sg. possessor) [(1)Rp.43]. See (I)LNĀMIQU(I).

TLĀLNELHUIĀ *vt* to mix something together with dirt for someone / se lo revuelca con tierra (T) [(1)Tp.211]. applic. TLĀLNELOĀ

TLĀLNELHUILIĀ applic. TLĀLNELHUIĀ

TLĀLNELHUĪLŌ nonact. TLĀLNELHUIĀ

TLĀLNELOĀ *vrefl,vt* to get dirty; to dirty something, to mix something together with dirt / se ensucia con tierra (T), lo revuelca con tierra (T) [(6)Tp.161,211]. See TLĀL-LI, NELOĀ.

TLĀLNELŌLŌ nonact. TLĀLNELOĀ

TLĀLNEPANTLAH *place name* center of the earth / en el medio de la tierra (C) [(1)Cf.20v]. See TLĀL-LI, NEPANTLAH.

TLĀLNEXTIC crust of calcium carbonate and gravel on the earth / tierra caliche (barro de color de cal) (T) [(1)Tp.240]. See TLĀL-LI, NEXTIC.

TLĀLNEX-TLI dust / polvo de tierra (Z) [(2)Zp.100,209]. See TLĀL-LI, NEX-TLI.

TLALOĀ vrefl to run, to flee / correr o huir (M) This contrasts with TLĀLOĀ 'to get soiled.'

TLĀLOĀ to get soiled / se entierra, se ensucia de tierra (T) [(1)Tp.240]. M has synonymous tlalloa, forming its preterit by adding -C. See TLĀL-LI.

TLĀLOC personal name; pl: **TLĀLOH-QUEH** Tlaloc, the god of water and rain; the host of rain gods (plural) / dios del agua o de la lluvia (S), los dioses del agua (C for plural) [(1)Bf.10r, (1)Cf.112v]. The derivation of this name is unclear. The singular form, which is the personal name of one deity, is not related in a regular way to the plural form, which refers to the company of rain gods. The plural form could be based on TLĀLLOH 'something covered with earth' if geminate reduction were to apply, reducing the LL to L, , but the final -C of the singular would remain unaccounted for.

TLALŌCHTIĀ vt to drive someone, to make someone run / hacer aguijar a otro, llevando asido y haciéndolo correr (M), lo empuja adelante de uno andando(lo) (como carretilla, etc.), lo arrea, le hace correr (T) [(3)Tp.208, (3)Zp.14,34,195, (3)Xp.75]. See TLALOĀ.

TLALŌCHTILIĀ applic. TLALŌCHTIĀ

TLALŌCHTĪLŌ nonact. TLALŌCHTIĀ

TLĀLOCOTZITZIN candlewood, ocotillo (Fouquieria splendens, Fouquieria formosa) / ocotillo (planta) (Z) [(2)Zp.90,209]. This is a plural form, perhaps reflecting the way this plant branches away from its base. See TLĀL-LI, OCO-TL.

TLĀLOCUIL-IN pl: **-TIN** earthworm / gusano (cualquier) de la tierra (T) [(1)Tp.240]. See TLĀL-LI, OCUIL-IN.

TLĀLOLĪN(I) for the earth to quake / temblar la tierra (M) [(4)Zp.120,209, (3)Xp.91]. The O of the free-standing verb ŌLĪNIĀ is long, but it is attested short in derived forms in T and Z. In this item Z

has the vowel short, and X has it long. See TLĀL-LI, ŌLĪNIĀ.

TLĀLŌLĪNILIZ-TLI earthquake / temblor [(3)Xp.91]. X retains the long vowel of the first syllable of ŌLĪNIĀ here, although elsewhere it appears short in compounds. See TLĀL-LI, ŌLĪNIĀ.

TLĀLOLĪNĪLLŌ-TL earthquake / terremoto, temblor de tierra (Z) [(2)Zp.120,209]. In the related verb ŌLĪNIĀ, attested in T, the O is long. See TLĀL-LI, ŌLĪNIĀ.

TLĀLOLŌL-LI clod, lump of dirt / terrón (Z) [(2)Zp.122,209]. See TLĀL-LI, OLOLOĀ.

TLĀLOMĪTŌN a type of worm / gusano de alambre, tlalomite (T) [(1)Tp.240]. The second element of this suggests OMI-TL 'bone,' but there is a vowel length discrepancy. See TLĀL-LI.

TLĀLŌTIĀ caus. TLĀLOĀ

TLĀLPACHIHU(I) to be buried / se entierra (T) [(2)Tp.240]. This is synonymous with the reflexive use of TLĀLPACHOĀ. See TLĀL-LI, PACHIHU(I).

TLĀLPACHILHUIĀ applic. TLĀLPACHOĀ

TLĀLPACHIUHTICAH to be buried / enterrado (T) [(1)Tp.240]. M has tlalpachiuhtoc 'something covered with dirt.' See TLĀL-PACHIHU(I), the verb CĀ.

TLĀLPACHOĀ vrefl,vt to be buried; to bury something, someone / se entierra, se sepulta (T), cubrir algo con tierra o aporcar (M), lo sepulta, lo entierra (T) [(6)Tp.161, 211]. See TLĀL-LI, PACHOĀ.

TLĀLPACHŌLŌ nonact. TLĀLPACHOĀ

TLĀLPAN on the ground, throughout the land / en el suelo (M), por toda la tierra (C) See TLĀL-LI, -PAN.

TLALPĪCHILIĀ applic. TLALPĪTZ(A)

TLALPĪL-LI something knotted or tangled, a knot, a nest, or a tangle of branches / cosa atada o añudada o prisionero de otro (M), amarradijo, nudo, manojo (T) [(2)Tp.226,232]. See (I)LPIĀ.

TLALPĪTZ(A) to blow, to huff / sopla (T) [(3)Tp.232]. The nonspecific object prefix TLA- has fused with the verb stem to form an intransitive verb. M has the derived form tlalpitzaliztli 'gust, puff.' See (I)LPĪTZ(A).

TLALPĪTZALŌ nonact. TLALPĪTZ(A)

TLĀLPITZO-TL *pl:* **-MEH** cochineal insect (Dactylopius cacti), the bodies of which produce a scarlet dye; armadillo / cochinilla (Z), armadillo (X) [(2)Zp.29,209, (3)Xp.91]. See TLĀL-LI, PITZO-TL.

TLĀLPOHPOXOĀ *vrefl* to roll about in the dirt as birds do / se revuelca en la tierra (p.ej. gallina) (T) [(1)Tp.161]. See TLĀL-LI, POHPOXOĀ.

TLĀLPOTŌN(I) to make dust / hace polvo (T) [(1)Tp.240]. See TLĀL-LI, POTŌN(I).

TLĀLPŌTZ(A) to throw up earth, to burrow / echa tierra, tusa (Z) [(1)Zp.213]. Z also has what appears to be TLAPŌTZ(A) with the nominal gloss 'gopher.' See TLĀL-LI, PŌTZ(A).

TLĀLQUĪXTĪLŌNI wheelbarrow / carretilla, parihuela (Z) [(2)Zp.26,209]. The vowel of the third syllable is not attested long but should be by general rule. See TLĀL-LI, QUĪXTIĀ.

TLĀLTATACA to scratch, score, dig the earth / rasca la tierra, escarba la tierra, cava la tierra (T) [(4)Tp.240]. M has *tlaltatactli* 'earth dug up for making adobe.' See TLĀL-LI, TATACA.

TLĀLTATACALŌ altern. nonact. TLĀL-TATACA

TLĀLTATACŌ altern. nonact. TLĀL-TATACA

TLĀLTATAQUILIĀ applic. TLĀLTATACA

TLĀLTĒMIĀ *vt* to fill something in with dirt / le echa tierra (T) [(3)Tp.211]. See TLĀL-LI, TĒMIĀ.

TLĀLTĒMILIĀ *vt* to fill something in with dirt for someone / le echa tierra para él (T) [(4)Tp.211,212]. applic. TLĀLTĒMIĀ

TLĀLTĒMILILIĀ applic. TLĀLTĒMILIĀ

TLĀLTĒMILĪLŌ nonact. TLĀLTĒMILIĀ

TLĀLTĒMĪLŌ nonact. TLĀLTĒMIĀ

TLĀLTEPEHXI-TL gorge, ravine / barranca (Z) [(2)Zp.18,209]. See TLĀL-LI, TEPEHXI-TL.

TLĀLTE-TL *pl:* **-MEH** clod, lump of earth / terrón grande (M) [(1)Tp.240, (2)Zp.122,209]. See TLĀL-LI, TE-TL.

TLĀLTEUH-TLI dust / polvo (X) [(2)Xp.92]. M has reflexive *tlalteuhnemitia* 'for a sick person to turn ashen.' X has TEUC for TEUH. See TLĀL-LI, TEUH-TLI.

TLĀLTIĀ *vrefl,vt* for someone to receive

land; to give someone land / le dan terreno (T), le da terreno (T) [(6)Tp.161,211]. There is a better gloss for the reflexive use of this verb, *recibe tierra*, in the Spanish-to-Nahuatl side of T. M has intransitive *tlaltia* 'to turn to earth,' which probably represents TLĀLTIYA. See TLĀL-LI.

TLĀLTICA set in the earth / está metido en la tierra (T) [(1)Tp.240]. See TLĀL-LI, -CA.

TLĀLTICPAC the earth, on the earth, of the earth / el mundo, o en el mundo, o encima de la tierra (M) This is literally a locative construction, but C, R, and X have it as a noun with the absolutive suffix, TLĀLTICPAC-TLI. See TLĀL-LI, -(I)CPAC.

TLĀLTICPACAYŌ-TL mundane, earthly matters / cosas mundanas y terrenales (M) [(4)Cf.34r,53r,53v]. See TLĀLTICPAC, -YŌ.

TLĀLTICPACTLĀCA-TL *pl:* **TLĀLTICPACTLĀCAH** earthly being, person of this world / hombres de éste mundo (M for plural) [(1)Cf.54r]. See TLĀLTICPAC, TLĀCA-TL.

TLĀLTICPAQUEH lord of the earth (deity) / señor de la tierra (C) [(4)Cf.71,55r, (1)Rp.45]. See TLĀLTICPAC.

TLĀLTILIĀ applic. TLĀLTIĀ

TLĀLTĪLŌ nonact. TLĀLTIĀ

TLĀLTITECHYĀ *irregular verb; singular present:* **-YAUH** to fall to the ground / caerse o ir el edificio por tierra (M) [(1)Cf.102r]. M has the component *tlaltitech* 'on the ground, to the ground.' See TLĀL-LI, -TECH, the verb YĀ.

TLĀLTLACUECHĀHUAC damp ground / húmedo (el suelo) (Z) [(2)Zp.69,209]. See TLĀL-LI, CUECHĀHUAC.

TLĀLTŌCA *vrefl,vt* to be buried; to bury, plant something / enterrarse (M), enterrar a otro (M), soterrar algo (M), lo entierra, lo planta, lo sepulta (T) [(6)Tp.161,212, (3)Zp.53,99,195]. See TLĀL-LI, TŌCA.

TLĀLTOHPOL-LI terrace / lomita, bordos en el suelo (T) [(2)Tp.240]. See TLĀL-LI, TOHPOL-LI.

TLĀLTOHPOLTIC something terraced / bordos (T) [(1)Tp.240]. See TLĀL-TOHPOL-LI.

TLĀLTOTŌNQUI warm earth / el suelo está caliente (T) [(1)Tp.240]. See TLĀL-LI, TOTŌNQUI.

TLĀLTZACTIC clay soil, mud / barro, está muy pegajosa la tierra (T) [(1)Tp.240]. M has *tlaltzacutli* 'fuller's earth, plaster.' T has lost the labiality of the final consonant of the second syllable. See TLĀL-LI, TZAUC-TLI.

TLĀLXELŌLIZ-TLI division, allotment of land / repartición (Z) [(2)Zp.108,209]. See TLĀL-LI, XELOĀ.

TLĀLZACA to transport dirt / acarrea tierra (T) [(2)Tp.201,240]. See TLĀL-LI, ZACA.

TLAMĀ *pret:* **TLAMAH** to go hunting, to take game, to make captives / cazar o cautivar algo (M) In the sources for this dictionary this is attested in the reduplicated form TLAHTLAMĀ, where the reduplication demonstrates that the prefix TLA- is fused to the stem. See MĀ.

TLAMACA *vt* to serve someone food / servir a la mesa o administrar la comida y manjares (M) [(3)Tp.208, (3)Zp.8,30,195]. This contrasts in transitivity with TLAMACA 'to give blows.' See MACA.

TLAMACA to give blows / pega (T) [(3)Tp.232]. This contrasts in transitivity with TLAMACA 'to serve someone food.' See MACA.

TLAMACALŌ nonact. TLAMACA

TLAMACAZQUI one who served in a (preconquest) religious establishment, penitent / ministros y servidores de los templos de los ídolos (M for plural), penitente (R) [(1)Bf.10r]. See TLAMACA.

TLAMACH quietly, without conflict / mansamente, quedo o quedito (M) This is attested across sources except for Z, which has TLAMATCĀ, while M has both. TLAMACH also serves as a modifying element meaning 'much, many,' especially in T and Z. See TLAMAT(I).

TLAMACHCUI *vt* to take a great deal of something / coge mucho (T) [(3)Tp.208]. The idiomatic sense of Spanish *coger mucho* is 'to engage in sexual intercourse.' In view of other similar constructions with CUI, this may be a calqued euphemism. M has *tlamachcui* 'to imitate others, to forge someone's signature or handwriting,' which probably represents TLAHMACHCUI and has as its first element TLAHMAT(I) 'to practice trickery and deception.' See TLAMACH, CUI.

TLAMACHCUĪHUA nonact. TLAMACHCUI

TLAMACHCUILIĀ applic. TLAMACHCUI

TLAMĀCHIHCHĪUH-TLI something made by hand / hecho a mano (Z) [(2)Zp.66,209]. See MĀ(I)-TL, CHIHCHĪHU(A).

TLAMĀCHĪLIĀ applic. TLAMĀCHIY(A)

TLAMACHILILIZ-TLI test, temptation / tentado, acción de tentar (Z) [(2)Zp.121, 209]. In one of two attestations Z marks the vowel of the second syllable long, but it should not be. See MACHILIĀ.

TLAMACHĪLIZPATLA *vt* to convince someone, to change someone's mind / lo convence, lo convierte (Z) [(3)Zp.33,195]. See TLAMACHĪLIZ-TLI, PATLA.

TLAMACHĪLIZ-TLI wisdom / la sabiduría (C) This is abundantly attested in Z and three times in C with the vowel of the third syllable marked long. See MACHIĀ.

TLAMACHĪLIZYŌ-TL wisdom, matters having to do with wisdom / el abstracto de sabiduría (K) [(2)Cf.54r]. C has two variant forms, one in which the sequence ZY assimilates to ZZ and one in which it does not. See TLAMACHĪLIZ-TLI, -YŌ.

TLAMACHĪLIZZŌ-TL See TLAMACHĪLIZYŌ-TL.

TLAMĀCHIY(A) *pret:* **TLAMĀCHIX** ~ **TLAMĀCHĪX** to wait / espera (T) [(3)Tp.232]. The long-vowel preterit form is not directly attested for this but is for the constituent element CHIY(A). See CHIY(A).

TLAMĀCHIYALŌ nonact. TLAMĀCHIY(A)

TLAMACHQUĪTZQUIĀ *vt* to seize a great deal of something / agarra mucho, agarra un gran mucho (T) [(3)Tp.208]. In the Spanish-to-Nahuatl side T has the somewhat more revealing gloss *agarra un gran manojo*. See TLAMACH, QUĪTZQUIĀ.

TLAMACHQUĪTZQUILIĀ applic. TLAMACHQUĪTZQUIĀ

TLAMACHQUĪTZQUĪLŌ nonact. TLAMACHQUĪTZQUIĀ

TLAMACHTĒNTICAH to be piled up in a heap / amontonado (naranjas, piedras, etc.) (T) [(1)Tp.232]. See TLAMACH, TĒM(I), the verb CĀ.

TLAMACHTIĀ *vrefl,vt* to be rich, to enjoy oneself; to enrich someone, to make someone prosperous / ser rico de hacienda o gozarse mucho (M), enriquecer a otro y hacerlo próspero (M) M also has this as a double object verb, taking a reflexive prefix and an object prefix, with the sense 'to enjoy something, to take pleasure in something' This is homophonous with TLAMACHTIĀ< MACHTIĀ 'to teach something.' See TLAMACH.

TLAMACHTIĀ to preach / predica (Z) [(2)Zp.101,209]. This is homphonous with transitive TLAMACHTIĀ 'to enrich someone.' See MACHTIĀ.

TLAMACHTIHQUI teacher / maestro, profesor (Z) [(2)Zp.79,209]. See MACHTIĀ.

TLAMACHTILIZ-TLI instruction / enseñanza (T) [(1)Tp.232, (3)Zp.28,52,209]. See MACHTIĀ.

TLAMACHTĪL-LI *pl:* **-TIN** ~ **-MEH** follower, student, disciple / discípulo o el que es enseñado de otro (M) See MACHTIĀ.

TLAMACHTLĀLIĀ *vrefl,vt* to pile up; to pile something up / se amontona (T), lo amontona, lo recoge (T) [(4)Tp.159,208]. M glosses this as 'to set something in order,' which draws on the other sense of TLAMACH 'quietly, without conflict.' See TLAMACH, TLĀLIĀ.

TLAMACHTLĀLILIĀ applic. TLAMACH-TLĀLIĀ

TLAMACHTLĀLĪLŌ nonact. TLAMACH-TLĀLIĀ

TLAMAH someone knowledgeable / sabio (R) [(1)Rp.144]. This apparently contrasts with TLAHMAH 'physician, specialist.' See MAT(I).

TLAMAHCĀHUAL-LI something unfettered, free / anda suelto, desenfrenado (Z) [(1)Zp.209]. Z also has MAHCĀUH-TOC as a variant of MĀCĀUHTOC 'something loose, separate.' See MĀCĀHU(A).

TLAMAHCĒHU(A) to do penance / hacer penitencia (M) [(1)Bf.10v, (1)Cf.108v, (2)Zp.9,209, (1)Rp.144]. Transitive MAHCĒHU(A) means 'to merit what one desires,' but with the fused nonspecific object prefix TLA- it has the lexicalized sense 'to do penance.' Z has this with the entirely different sense 'to eat the first meal of the day' (perhaps in some ritual manner). See MAHCĒHU(A).

TLAMAHCĒHUALIZ-TLI penitence / penitencia, o merecimiento, o el acto de dar sacomano (M) [(1)Rp.144]. See MAHCĒHU(A).

TLAMAHCĒHUALTIĀ *vt* to punish someone, to mortify the flesh / dar aflicción al cuerpo, o hacerle hacer algunas cosas de abstinencia y penitencia (M), castigar (R) [(1)Rp.144]. R has misplaced a diacritic. The diacritic that belongs to the second syllable appears on the third. caus. TLAMAHCĒHU(A)

TLAMAHCĒUHQUI penitent / penitente, o el que hace algunos ejercicios para merecer, hermitaño o beata, etc. (M) [(1)Bf.10v]. See TLAMAHCĒHU(A).

TLAMAHCUĪLIZ-TLI baptism / bautismo (Z) [(2)Zp.19,209]. See MAHCUI.

TLAMAHCUĪL-LI someone baptized / bautizado (Z) [(2)Zp.19,209]. See MAHCUI.

TLAMAHMĀCĀHUILIĀ *vrefl* to fall because one has lost one's grip on a support / pierde equilibrio (por no haberse cogido bien con la mano y cae) (T) [(3)Tp.159]. See MĀ(I)-TL, CĀHU(A).

TLAMAHMĀCĀHUILĪLŌ nonact. TLAMAHMĀCĀHUILIĀ

TLAMĀHUANI something that spreads disease, someone contagious / contagioso (T) [(1)Tp.232]. See MĀHU(A).

TLAMĀHUIHUITLA to pull up weeds by hand / desyerba (Z) [(2)Zp.45,209]. See MĀ(I)-TL, HUIHUITLA.

TLAMAHUILĪL-LI something awesome, frightening / temible, terrible, espantoso (Z) [(3)Zp.120,122,210]. See MAHUILIĀ.

TLAMAHUIZALHUIĀ applic. TLAMAHUIZOĀ

TLAMAHUIZOĀ to be distracted, preoccupied, or entertained, to behold things / se divierte (Z) [(3)Tp.232, (2)Zp.47,210]. See MAHUIZOĀ.

TLAMAHUIZŌLIZ-TLI distraction, amusement / diversión (Z) [(2)Zp.47,210]. See TLAMAHUIZOĀ.

TLAMAHUIZŌL-LI miracle, something astonishing / milagro o maravilla (M) [(2)Cf.80r,122r]. See MAHUIZOĀ.

TLAMAHUIZŌLŌ nonact. TLAMAHUIZOĀ

TLAMAHUIZŌLTIĀ *vt* to divert or entertain someone / lo divierte (Z)

[(2)Zp.47,195]. In both attestations the vowel before -LTIĀ is marked long. See MAHUIZOĀ.

TLAMAHUIZŌTIĀ to worship / observa, adora (T) [(3)Tp.232]. See MAHUIZŌ-TL.

TLAMAHUIZŌTILIĀ applic. TLAMA-HUIZŌTIĀ

TLAMAHUIZŌTĪLŌ nonact. TLAMA-HUIZŌTIĀ

TLAMAHUIZPOLŌLIZ-TLI shame, insult / infamia o deshonra (M), insulto (Z) [(2)Zp.72,211]. In both attestations the vowel of the second syllable is marked long, but it should not be. See MA-HUIZPOLOĀ.

TLAMALĪN(A) to make rope / torcer cordeles (C) [(1)Cf.52r]. See MALĪN(A).

TLAMALĪNQUI rope maker / cordonero (C) [(1)Cf.52r]. See TLAMALĪN(A).

TLAMALĪN-TLI rope, cord, something twisted / torzal o cordel o soga torcida, o cosa semejante (M), torcido (T) [(1)Tp.232]. See TLAMALĪN(A).

TLAMĀMĀ pret: **TLAMĀMAH** to bear fruit / carga, se da fruta (T) [(1)Tp.232]. With the prefix TLA- fused, this has the specialized sense 'to bear fruit.' Otherwise, TLA-MĀMĀ has the literal sense 'to bear something.' See MĀMĀ.

TLAMĀMAH someone who bears a load, porter / el que lleva carga a cuestas (M) This short form is more common than Z's TLAMĀMAHQUI even though it does not happen to be attested in the sources for this dictionary. A common variant form is S's tlameme. See MĀMĀ.

TLAMĀMAHQUI someone who bears a load, porter / cargador (Z) [(2)Zp.25,210]. In both attestations Z marks the vowel of the third syllable long before the glottal stop, which is impossible in terms of Nahuatl morphology. See MĀMĀ.

TLAMĀMAL-LI burden, load / la carga que lleva a cuestas el tameme (M) This contrasts with TLAMĀMAL-LI 'something drilled through.' M combines the two items in a single entry. T has a variant in which the vowel of the third syllable is long, as it is in the verb stem. T also has TLAMĀMAL-LI with the vowel short, which agrees with the other sources. X

marks the vowel of the third syllable long instead of the second. See MĀMĀ.

TLAMAMAL-LI something drilled through, perforated / cosa barrenada (M), cosa taladrada y barrenada (C) [(2)Cf.47v,128v, (2)Rp.41,144]. This contrasts with TLAMĀMAL-LI 'burden, load.' See MAMAL(I).

TLAMĀMALŌNI gear for carrying things / instrumento para cargar (K) [(2)Bf.7r]. B specifically marks the vowel of the third syllable short in both attestations. This is paired in context with CĀCĀX-TLI 'packframe.' See MĀMĀ.

TLAMĀMALQUĪXTIĀ vt to remove a burden from someone / lo descarga [(2)Zp.42,195]. In one of two attestations Z marks the vowel of the third syllable long. See TLAMĀMAL-LI, QUĪXTIĀ.

TLAMĀMALTIHQUI someone who bears a load / cargador (Z) [(2)Zp.25,210]. In both attestations Z marks the vowel of the third syllable long. Z also has synonymous TLAMĀMAHQUI. See MĀMALTIĀ.

TLAMANCHĪHU(A) vt to scorn something, to lay something aside / lo desprecia (Z) [(2)Zp.44,195]. See TLAMAN-TLI, CHĪHU(A).

TLAMAN(I) for things to be a particular way / había buen orden y gobierno (C for imperfect construction with CUALLI ĪC) [(1)Cf.99v]. This is further attested in derived forms such as TLAMANILIĀ 'to lay things out for someone, to mend something' (i.e. to restore something to its proper state), and TLAMAN-TLI 'member of a class of things.' See MAN(I).

TLAMANILIĀ vt to set things in order with respect to one another, to lay things out for someone, to mend something / poner alguna cosa ante otro, o hacerle tortillas, o ofrecerle algún don o ofrenda (M), lo remienda (T) [(3)Tp.208]. See TLAMAN(I).

TLAMANILILIĀ applic. TLAMANILIĀ

TLAMANILĪLŌ nonact. TLAMANILIĀ

TLAMANILTIĀ to make things be a certain way, to behave in a certain way / se portaron (C for third pers. plural preterit) [(1)Bf.10v, (1)Cf.124v]. B specifically marks the vowel of the third syllable long, although it should be short before the suffix

-LTIĀ, and C leaves the vowel unmarked for length. caus. TLAMAN(I)

TLAMANIZOĀ *vt* to smooth, plane something / lo aplana ... lo alisa (Z) [(2)Zp.12,195]. See TLAMANIZ-TLI.

TLAMANIZ-TLI plane, flat surface / plano (Z) [(2)Zp.99,210]. See MAN(I).

TLAMANTIC something separate, distinct, different / diverso, distinto, diferente (Z) [(4)Zp.46,47,210]. See TLAMAN-TLI.

TLAMAN-TLI a separate entity, a member of a class or set / cosa (S), para contar platicas, sermones, pares de zapatos o cacles, papel, platos, escudillas, trojes, o cielos ... cuando está una cosa sobre otra doblada o cuando una cosa es diversa o diferente de otra (M) This compounds with quantifiers for counting members of an arbitrary class of objects that includes but is not limited to flat things that can be folded or layered one on top of another. It is also an element of other derivations and occurs in free form in Z meaning 'something distinct and separate.' Z consistently marks the vowel of the second syllable long, but it is short across other sources. See TLAMAN(I).

TLAMANXELOĀ *vrefl,vt* to be set aside; to separate something, to set something aside / se aparte (Z), lo separa (Z) [(4)Zp.12,115,173,195]. See TLAMAN-TLI, XELOĀ.

TLAMĀOLOLŌL-LI something rolled together, a roll / rollo (Z) [(2)Zp.111,210]. M has *tlamaolololiztli* 'the act of gathering something together with one's fingers.' See MĀ(I)-TL, OLOLOĀ.

TLAMAQUILIĀ applic. TLAMACA

TLAMATCĀ patiently, calmly / mansa y prudentemente (M) This is abundantly attested but only in Z. C has synonymous MATCĀ, and synonymous TLAMACH is attested across sources. M has all three, although MATCĀ appears in M only as a bound form. See TLAMATQUI.

TLAMATCĀCENTILIĀ *vrefl* to unite, to assemble calmly, quietly / se junta con paciencia o con calma (Z) [(1)Zp.173]. See TLAMATCĀ, CENTETILIĀ.

TLAMATCĀNEM(I) *pret:* **-NEN** to live quietly, peaceably / vivir quieta, pacífica y

sosegadamente (M) [(1)Zp.210]. M also has *matcanemini* 'someone calm, peacable.' See TLAMATCĀ, NEM(I).

TLAMATCĀYETOC someone patient, calm, tranquil / paciente, pacífico, quieto, tranquilo (Z) [(4)Zp.92,104,124,210]. See TLAMATCĀ, YETOC.

TLAMAT(I) *pret:* **TLAMAT ~ TLAMAH** to be knowledgeable, to go somewhere / saber algo o ir a alguna parte (C) [(1)Cf.128v, (1)Rp.144]. C and R concur that TLA-MAT(I) can mean 'to go somewhere' but disagree on the verb's transitivity. C gives it as transitive, and R as intransitive. In addition to independent TLAMAT(I), both C and R illustrate this sense of going somewhere with intransitive TLAMATTĪUH, where -TĪHU(I) itself implies 'to go to do.' In derivations including TLAMATCĀ and TLAMACH there is the additional sense of 'peace, tranquility, calm.' This contrasts with TLAHMAT(I) 'to be competent, quick-witted.' See MAT(I).

TLAMATILIĀ *vrefl,vt* to calm down, to grow quiet; to calm, quiet someone, something / se calla (Z), lo calma, le hace callar, lo pacifica, lo sosiega (Z) [(6)Zp.24,92,117,173,195]. applic. TLAMATIYA

TLAMATILIZ-TLI wisdom / sabiduría (M) [(2)Cf.79v,87v]. M combines this in a single entry with TLAHMATILIZ-TLI 'deception, trickery.' See TLAMAT(I).

TLAMATINI wise person, sage, scholar / sabio (M) [(6)Cf.87v,111r]. See MAT(I).

TLAMATIYA to have respite from pain / se calma (de dolor) (Z) [(2)Zp.24,210]. See TLAMATCĀ, TLAMAT(I).

TLAMATQUI someone wise, prudent / prudente, sabio, listo (T) [(1)Tp.232, (7)Zp.70,103,112,177,210]. M has *tlamatqui* 'someone deceitful, trickster,' which is derived from TLAHMAT(I) and contrasts with this. See TLAMAT(I), TLAMATINI.

TLAMĀTZOHUAL-LI folded tortilla / tortillas dobladas, plegadas o sobajadas (M) [(5)Bf.2r,6r,12r,13r]. B attests this both with and without *hu* between the third and fourth syllables. Since it is stem-internal and invariant, it is impossible to determine whether there is a segmental intervocalic [w] or not. M has *matzoa* and *matoloa* having to do with squeezing.

TLAMĀYAHUIĀNI murderer / homicida (T) [(1)Tp.233]. This implies *MĀYAHUIĀ rather than MĀYAHU(I) 'to dash someone down to his death.' See TLAMĀYAHUINI.

TLAMĀYAHUINI someone given to throwing things down on the ground, troublemaker or killer / el que tira, esparce algo en el suelo (S), matón (T) [(1)Tp.233]. See MĀYAHU(I).

TLAMĀYĒCCĀMPA to the right-hand side / a mano derecha (M) [(2)Cf.94v]. See MĀYĒCCĀN-TLI, -PA.

TLAMĀYĒCCĀNCOPA to the right-hand side / a mano derecha (C) [(1)Cf.94v]. See MĀYĒCCĀN-TLI, -COPA.

TLAM(I) *pret:* **TLAN** to come to an end, to finish, to bring an activity to an end / acabarse o consumirse y gastarse algo, o fenecer (M), acabar de hacer o de concluír alguna obra (M)

TLAMIĀ *vrefl,vt* to end, conclude; to conclude something, to finish something / se acaba (Z), lo termina, lo acaba, lo concluye (T), consumir o acabar toda la comida y bebida que tenía delante (M) In construction with -TECH this has the sense 'to accuse someone of something,' hence to slander someone. See TLAM(I).

TLAMIC something finished; a complete measure of twenty / veinte mazorcas de maíz o de cosas semejantes (M), acabado (Z) [(1)Bf.7r, (2)Zp.4,210]. M has *tlanqui* for 'something finished,' and *tlamic* as a measure of twenty, but the latter is consistent with the sense of 'something (a count, a unit) completed.' See TLAM(I).

TLAMICHĪHU(A) *vt* to accomplish something / lo cumple (Z) [(2)Zp.37,195]. See TLAM(I), CHĪHU(A).

TLAMICTIĀNI butcher / el que mata bestias, como el carnicero (C) [(1)Cf.44r, (1)Tp.232]. M glosses this as 'murderer,' which should be TĒMICTIĀNI, as in C. See MICTIĀ.

TLAMILIĀ *applic.* TLAMIĀ

TLAMILIZ-TLI the end of things, the close of life / fin de cada cosa (M), fin de la vida (Z) [(2)Zp.60,210]. This appears only in

the Spanish-to-Nahuatl side of M. See TLAM(I).

TLAMĪLŌ *nonact.* TLAMIĀ

TLAMĪN(I) for things like insects to bite or sting / pica (T) [(1)Tp.232]. M has *tlamintli* 'something wounded by a barbed weapon.' MĪN(I)

TLAMĪNINI something that bites / pica (T) [(1)Tp.232]. T also has a short variant TLAMĪNI. See TLAMĪN(I).

TLAMIXTĒM(I) *pret:* **-TĒN** to cloud over / viene la neblina (Z) [(2)Zp.88,210]. See MIX-TLI, TĒM(I).

TLAMIXTĒNTOC cloudy weather / nublado (Z) [(2)Zp.89,210]. See TLAMIXTĒM(I), the verb O.

-TLAMIYĀMPA *necessarily possessed form* to the end of something / a fines de (Z) [(2)Zp.60,161]. See -TLAMIYĀN, -PA.

-TLAMIYĀN *necessarily possessed form* the end of something / fin, término (Z) [(2)Zp.60,161]. See TLAM(I), -YĀN.

TLAMOCHĪHU(A) for things to abound / fructificar o llevar fruta el árbol (M in construction with ĪTECH), abunda (T) [(1)Tp.232]. See MOCHĪHU(A).

TLAMOHMOLŌNIĀ to work land, to aerate the soil / labra (tierra), hocica, escarba (T) [(3)Tp.232]. See MOLŌNIĀ.

TLAMOHMOLŌNILIĀ *applic.* TLAMOHMOLŌNIĀ

TLAMOHMOLŌNĪLŌ *nonact.* TLAMOHMOLŌNIĀ

TLAMOLŌNĪL-LI something boiled / hervido (T) [(1)Tp.232]. Z has the variant TLAMOLŌNTĪL-LI See MOLŌN(I).

TLAMŌLTZIN stick, wooden spoon for stirring food / palo para revolver comida (X) [(3)Xp.92]. See MŌLA.

TLAMŌTLANI *pl:* **-MEH** someone who chases something or someone away by throwing stones; slingshot / aventador (T), honda (X) [(1)Tp.233, (3)Xp.92]. See MŌTLA.

TLAMŌTQUI hunter / cazador (Z) [(2)Zp.26,211]. See MŌTLA.

-TLĀN place of, at / junto (C), entre (T) This commonly forms place names. It contrasts with the postposition -TLAN in vowel length and because -TLAN binds to other elements with the ligature -TI- in forming place names and -TLĀN does not. Because

of the tendency to lose final nasal consonants and glottal stops and because
of the shortening of vowels when they
come into word-final position, -TLĀN is
often indistinguishable from -TLAH 'place
where there is an abundance of something' -TĒCA-TL replaces -TLĀN to
mean 'person from' the place so named,
TEPOZTĒCA-TL 'someone from Tepoztlan'< TEPOZTLĀN.

-TLAN *postposition* below, next to (the base
of), among / junto a ... entre ... debajo de ...
en (C) When used to form place names,
this is bound to the preceding element
with the ligature -TI-, but in ordinary
postpositional constructions (including
compound postpositions) it attaches to
the preceding element directly. With
body parts there are some doublets with
-TI-TLAN and -TLAN. This contrasts in
vowel length with -TLĀN, which
combines directly without the ligature.
Because of the tendency to lose final nasal
consonants and glottal stops, -TLAN could
be confused with -TLAH, but the latter
does not bind to stems with the ligature
-TI-. See TLANI.

TLANACAZTECQUI *pl:* **-TECTIN** someone
or something with an ear cut off / cortada
la oreja (C) [(1)Cf.92v]. See NACAZ-TLI,
TEQU(I).

TLANĀHUAC on all sides / en todas partes,
por todos lados, enteramente, de lado,
alrededor, en derredor (S) [(1)Bf.7v]. This
appears in several phrases in M but not as a
separate entry. See -NĀHUAC.

TLANĀHUALAHCI to seize things by
surprise, to take someone by surprise /
agarra con sorpresa (T) [(3)Tp.233]. See
NĀHUALAHCI.

TLANĀHUAL-LI armful / brazado (Z),
brazada (Z) [(2)Zp.21,211]. Z marks the
vowel of the third syllable long in both
attestations, but it probably should not be.
See NĀHUAHTEQU(I), NĀHUALAHCI.

TLANAHUATIHQUI envoy, messenger /
enviado, mensajero (Z) [(5)Zp.10,54,
83,161,211]. See NAHUATIĀ.

TLANAHUATILIZ-TLI notice, orders,
regulation / orden, aviso, mandamiento,
mandato (Z) [(3)Zp.17,81,211]. See
NAHUATIĀ.

TLANAHUATĪL-LI someone cited, charged,
or dismissed; a notice, order, regulation, or law / citado, mandado, despedido, o licenciado (M), noticia, aviso,
ley, mandamiento, mandato (Z)
[(5)Zp.17,76,81,89,211]. See NAHUATIĀ.

TLANAHU(I) for a sick person's condition to
worsen, to be terminally ill / estar muy
enfermo (M), se pone grave, se empeora (T)
Z and X have a long vowel in the second
syllable, but the other sources have it
short. M has the derived noun *tlanauhqui*
'person close to death.' The basic sense of
this is 'to worsen, to go from bad to worse.'

TLANAHUĪHUA nonact. TLANAHU(I)

TLANAHUĪTIĀ caus. TLANAHU(I)

TLANAMACAC shopkeeper, vendor /
tendero o vendedor de algo (M) [(1)Cf.51v].
Z has the variant form TLANAMAQUI.
See NAMACA.

TLANAMACALIZ-TLI sale, action of selling something / acción de vender (Z)
[(1)Zp.211]. M has synonymous *tlanamaquiliztli.* See NAMACA.

TLANAMACAQUI merchant, vendor / comerciante, vendedor (Z)
[(4)Zp.30,128,211]. See TLANAMACAC.

TLANAMAC-TLI something sold, merchandise / cosa vendida (M), mercancía, venta
(Z) [(5)Zp.84,128,211]. See NAMACA.

TLANĀMIQUILIZ-TLI encounter, meeting / encuentro (Z) [(2)Zp.51,211]. See
NĀMIQU(I).

TLANĀNQUILIZ-TLI response, answer /
respuesta, contestación (Z) [(2)Zp.109,211].
Z has lost the syllable-final N of the second syllable. M has synonymous *tenanquiliztli.* See NĀNQUILIĀ.

TLANĀPALŌL-LI armful / brazado (Z)
[(2)Zp.21,211]. See NĀPALOĀ.

TLANAUHTOC someone weak, debilitated
/ débil (X) [(3)Xp.92]. See TLANAHU(I), the
verb O.

TLANCALLAMPAQUĪZ(A) for teeth to
project forward / dientes salidos (Z)
[(1)Zp.211]. Z has a long vowel in the third
syllable, but this appears to be the postposition -TLAN 'under.' See TLAN-TLI,
CAL-LI, -TLAN, -PA, QUĪZ(A).

TLĀNCHO marten, sable / marta (animal)
[(2)Zp.82,211]. This is attested with a long
vowel in the first syllable, but it seems

possible to associate it with TLANCHOĀ 'to chew,' especially since Z idiosyncratically has a long vowel in TLAN-TLI 'tooth.'

TLANCHOĀ *vrefl* to chew, to masticate / remuele con los dientes (una cosa), masca (T) [(3)Tp.160]. See TLAN-TLI.

TLANCHŌLŌ nonact. TLANCHOĀ

TLANCOCH-TLI molar tooth / muela de la boca (M) C and Z agree with M that this refers to molar teeth, but I glosses it as 'eyetooth, canine tooth.' See TLAN-TLI.

TLANCUACUĀ *vt; pret:* **-CUAH** to chew something / lo roe (T) [(3)Tp.208]. See TLAN-TLI, CUACUĀ.

TLANCUACUALŌ nonact. TLANCUACUĀ

TLANCUACUALTIĀ caus. TLANCUACUĀ

-TLANCUACUAYŌ *only attested in possessed form* one's molar tooth / su muela (T) [(1)Tp.134]. See TLANCUACUĀ.

TLANCUĀIHCA *preterit-as-present verb; pret:* **-IHCAC** to kneel, to be kneeling / se hinca de rodillas (Z) [(2)Zp.68,211]. See TLANCUĀ(I)-TL, IHCA.

TLANCUĀ(I)-TL knee / la rodilla de la pierna (M) The constituent structure is not clear. It appears to consist of CUĀ(I)-TL 'head' and either -TLAN or a truncation of -TLANI 'below.' TLANCUĀ(I)-TL 'knee' appears to be related to TLANĪTZ-TLI 'shinbone.' X has apparently metathesized this, as it appears in a compound and a derived noun as TLACUĀN.

TLANCUĀQUETZ(A) *vrefl* to kneel down / hincarse de rodillas (M) See TLANCUĀ(I)-TL, QUETZ(A).

TLANCUĀQUETZTOC someone kneeling / hincado (X) [(2)Xp.59]. See TLANCUĀQUETZ(A).

TLANCUĀTEHTECŌ nonact. reflexive TLANCUĀTEHTEQU(I)

TLANCUĀTEHTEQU(I) *vrefl,vt; pret:* **-TEHTEC** to get cut on the knee; to cut someone on the knee / se corta la rodilla (T), le corta la rodilla (T) [(6)Tp.160,208]. See TLANCUĀ(I)-TL, TEHTEQU(I).

TLANCUĀTEHTEQUĪHUA nonact. transitive TLANCUĀTEHTEQU(I)

TLANCUĀTEHTEQUILIĀ applic. TLANCUĀTEHTEQU(I)

TLANCUITZAHU(I) to grimace / hace

gestos (T) [(3)Tp.233]. M has *tlancuitzoa* 'for a dog to snarl and show its teeth' and *tlancuicuitztic* 'something toothy.' See TLAN-TLI.

TLANCUITZAHUĪHUA nonact. TLANCUITZAHU(I)

TLANCUITZALHUIĀ applic. TLANCUITZAHU(I)

TLANECHICŌL-LI *pl:* **-TIN** something gathered together, offering, alms / cosas ayuntadas y recogidas, o amontonadas (M), limosna (X) [(3)Xp.92]. See NECHICOĀ.

TLANĒC(I) *pret:* **TLANĒZ** for day to break, to get light / hacer claridad o amanecer (M) [(5)Cf.36v,79r, (2)Zp.9,211]. See NĒC(I).

TLANĒCITIĀ for dawn to break / alba (Z in construction with QUĒMMAN 'when') [(3)Zp.8,211]. This seems to be idiosyncratic to Z, which also has TLANĒXTIĀ 'to shine.' See TLANĒC(I).

TLANEHNEMILIĀ to exercise judgement, to have an opinion / juzgar (Z) [(2)Zp.74,211]. See NEHNEMILIĀ.

TLANĒHU(I) *vt* to borrow something / pide alquilado, lo pide prestado (Z) [(3)Zp.9,95, (3)Xp.75]. See TLANĒHUIĀ.

TLANĒHUIĀ *vrefl,vt* to borrow something; to borrow something for someone / tomar algo prestado para volverlo en la misma especie, o arrendar viña (M), lo pide prestado (T), lo pide prestado para otro (una cosa) (T) [(1)Cf.128v, (3)Tp.208]. With a direct object prefix plus an oblique reflexive prefix this has the sense 'to benefit from the transitory presence of someone' and is so used in B to refer to one's offspring and elsewhere to the reign of a ruler. This contrasts with TLAHNĒHUIĀ 'to mistake one thing for another.' See TLANĒHU(I).

TLANĒHUILIĀ applic. TLANĒHUIĀ

TLANĒHUĪLŌ nonact. TLANĒHUIĀ

TLANELTOCA to believe, to have faith / creer (C) [(4)Cf.48r,84v]. M does not have an entry for this, but C treats it as an intransitive verb with the nonspecific object prefix TLA- fused to the verb stem. See NELTOCA.

TLANELTOCALIZ-TLI faith, belief / fé, creencia (Z) [(3)Zp.35,59,211]. See TLANELTOQUILIZ-TLI.

TLANELTOCAQUI someone faithful, a believer / creyente (Z) [(2)Zp.35,211]. M has *tlaneltocac* with the same sense. See TLANELTOCA.

TLANELTOCTIĀ *vt* to convince someone / lo convence (Z) [(2)Zp.33,195]. See TLANELTOCA.

TLANELTOQUILIZ-TLI faith, belief / fé o creencia (M) Across sources there is inconsistency about the length of the vowel in the fourth syllable. B marks it long, as C does in two of five attestations. T has the reflex of a short vowel. Z has the variant form TLANELTOCALIZ-TLI. See TLANELTOCA.

TLANEMILIĀ to deliberate / tratar negocios de importancia, tomando consejo o consigo o con otros sobre lo que conviene hacer, etc. (M) [(1)Cf.63v]. See NEMILIĀ.

TLANEMILILIZ-TLI opinion / opinión, pensamiento (Z) [(3)Zp.91,96,211]. See TLANEMILIĀ.

TLANĒMPOLHUILIĀ *vt* to ruin things for someone / se lo echa a perder (T) [(3)Tp.209]. See NĒMPOLOĀ.

TLANĒMPOLHUILILIĀ applic. TLA-NĒMPOLHUILIĀ

TLANĒMPOLHUILĪLŌ nonact. TLA-NĒMPOLHUILIĀ

TLANEQUILIZ-TLI will, desire / voluntad o el acto de querer algo (M) [(2)Tp.134]. See NEQU(I).

-TLANEQUIYA *necessarily possessed form* one's will, one's desire / mi voluntad con que quiero algo (C for first pers. sg. possessor) [(1)Cf.50r, (1)Rp.43]. See NEQU(I).

TLANĒUHTIĀ *vrefl,vt* to be for rent, to prostitute oneself; to lend or rent something out / se presta, se alquila (T), putañear la mujer (M), lo presta, lo arrienda, lo alquila, lo da prestado (T) [(7)Tp.160,205,208, (3)Zp.9,101,197, (3)Xp.74]. M has this with a direct object prefix plus an indirect object prefix with the sense 'to lend someone something that must be returned in kind, or to lease property to someone.' See TLANĒHU(I).

TLANĒUHTILIĀ applic. TLANĒUHTIĀ

TLANĒUHTĪLŌ nonact. TLANĒUHTIĀ

TLANĒUH-TLI something borrowed /

emprestado o cosa prestada (M) [(2)Zp.101,211]. See TLANĒHU(I).

TLANEXĪCŌLHUILIZ-TLI envy / envidia (Z) [(2)Zp.54,212]. See NEXĪCŌLHUIĀ.

TLANĒXILIĀ to get up in the morning / amanece (persona) (T) [(3)Tp.233]. It is the gloss in the Spanish-to-Nahuatl side of T that distinguishes this from *amanecer* 'to dawn.' See TLANĒC(I).

TLANĒXTIĀ *vt* to illuminate something / lo alumbra (Z) [(2)Zp.9,195]. M has synonymous *tlanextilia*, of which this transitive form must be a truncation. See TLANĒC(I).

TLANĒXTIĀ to emit light, to shine / resplandecer, lucir, o relumbrar (M) [(3)Tp.233, (2)Zp.77,212]. Z also has this as a transitive verb 'to illuminate something.' See TLANĒC(I).

TLANĒXTILĪLIZ-TLI revelation, admonition / lección, revelación (Z) [(3)Zp.76,110,212]. M has *tlanextiliztli* 'clarity, light.' This implies TLANĒXTILIĀ 'to illuminate something or someone,' which appears in M and perhaps as Z's transitive TLANĒXTIĀ if the latter is a truncated form. See TLANĒXTIĀ.

TLANĒX-TLI light, radiance / luz, claridad, o resplandor (M) See TLANĒC(I).

TLANĒXYŌ-TL radiance / resplandor (C) [(1)Cf.53r]. See TLANĒX-TLI, -YŌ.

TLANHUĒHUEHCA open-work weaving / tejido abierto (de tela, ayate, etc.) (T) [(2)Tp.227,233]. See TLAN-TLI, HUĒHUEHCA.

TLANI below, underneath / abajo o debajo (M)

-TLANI *verbal compounding element* to order, wish, or request something, to aspire to something, to work to bring something about / mandar, desear, pedir ... pretender lo que el precedente verbo significa (C) There is said to be a related compounding element -TLA, which according to the grammarian Rincón is synonymous with -TLANI. C claims unfamiliarity with this usage but points out that some verbs are derived from nouns by a suffixed -TLA, as in YĀŌTLA 'to make war on someone' and (I)CNĪUHTLA 'to befriend someone.'

TLĀN(I) *vt* to win something, to defeat

someone at gambling / ganar algo en juego (M), ganar a otro jugando o en juego (M)

TLANICĀHU(A) *vt* to leave someone below as one is ascending / dejarlo debajo adelantándose (C) [(1)Cf.93v]. See TLANI, CĀHU(A).

TLANIHTALHUIĀ applic. TLANIHTOĀ

TLANIHTOĀ *vrefl,vt* to lose something at gambling / perder algo en el juego (M) This is implied by TLANIHTALHUIĀ. In light of TLĀN(I) 'to defeat someone at gambling,' one would expect a long vowel in the first syllable. TLANIHTOĀ and TLANIHTALHUIĀ are based on a single attestation (Cf.118v) in which the vowel of the first syllable is not marked for length. C may have omitted a diacritic.

TLĀNĪHUA nonact. TLĀN(I)

TLANIHUAH lowlander / abajeño (Z) [(2)Zp.3,212]. See TLANI.

TLANIHUĬC downwards / hacia abajo (M) [(1)Cf.93v]. See TLANI, -HUĬC.

TLĀNILIĀ applic. TLĀN(I)

TLANIPA downwards / hacia abajo (M), norte, lado de abajo (Z) [(2)Cf.93v, (2)Zp.89,212]. See TLANI, -PA.

TLANITLĀZ(A) *vrefl,vt* to hurl oneself down, to abase oneself; to hurl down or humiliate someone / abatir así mismo y humillándose (M), humillar y abatir a otro (M) [(1)Cf.93v]. See TLANI, TLĀZ(A).

TLANĪTZTEHTECŌ T gives this as the nonactive form of TLANĪTZTEHTEQU(I) used reflexively and gives TLANĪTZ-TEHTEQUĪHUA for the nonactive form of the same verb used transitively.

TLANĪTZTEHTEQU(I) *vrefl,vt; pret:* **-TEHTEC** to cut one's shin bone; to cut someone on the shin bone / se corta la espinilla (T), le corta la espinilla (T) [(6)Tp.160]. See TLANĪTZ-TLI, TEHTEQU(I).

TLANĪTZTEHTEQUĪHUA T gives this as the nonactive form of TLANĪTZ-TEHTEQU(I) used transitively and gives TLANĪTZTEHTECŌ for the nonactive of the same verb used reflexively.

TLANĪTZTEHTEQUILIĀ applic. TLANĪTZTEHTEQU(I)

TLANĪTZ-TLI shin bone / espinilla de la pierna (M) This is abundantly attested

but only in T. It appears to be related to TLANCUĀ(I)-TL 'knee.'

-TLANNACATOL *only attested in possessed form* the gum of one's mouth / su encía (T) [(1)Tp.134]. T reduces geminate NN to N. See TLAN-TLI, NAC(A)-TL.

TLANŌTZAL-LI someone called, cited, corrected, punished / doctrinado, corregido, castigado o reprehendido de otros (M), visita, visitante (Z) [(1)Cf.47r, (2)Zp.130,212]. See NŌTZ(A).

TLANŌTZ-TLI someone called, cited / llamado o citado (C) [(1)Cf.47r, (1)Rp.40]. According to C and R this is synonymous with TLANŌTZAL-LI. See NŌTZ(A).

TLANQUIQUIC(I) to whistle, to hiss / silbar o chiflar (M) See TLAN-TLI, QUIQUIC(I).

TLANQUIQUIXOHUA nonact. TLAN-QUIQUIC(I)

TLAN-TLI tooth / diente (M) Z idiosyncratically has Ā.

TLANTZITZILCA for one's teeth to chatter / castañetear (Z) [(2)Zp.26,212]. Z has C for TZ and marks the vowel of the third syllable long once. M has *tzitzilca* 'to shiver with cold' and reflexive *tlantzitzilitza* 'for one's teeth to chatter with cold.' See TLAN-TLI, TZITZILICA.

TLANTZITZILITZ(A) *vrefl* for one's teeth to chatter / dar tenazadas o crujir los dientes de frío (M), pega diente con diente (T) [(3)Tp.160]. T has E for I in the second and third syllables. See TLAN-TLI, TZITZILITZ(A).

TLANTZITZILITZALŌ nonact. TLAN-TZITZILITZ(A)

TLANTZOPŌNIĀ *vrefl* to hiss, to make a sound with one's tongue against the back of one's teeth / truena la boca (dice Tz. Tz.) (T) [(3)Tp.160]. See TLAN-TLI, TZOPŌNIĀ.

TLANXAXALTIC open-work weaving / tejido abierto (de tela, ayate, etc.) (T) [(3)Tp.233,245]. See TLAN-TLI, XAXALTIC.

TLAŌCOLIĀ *vrefl,vt* to be merciful to oneself; to be merciful with someone, to aid and benefit someone / usar de misericordia consigo mismo (M), hacer misericordia a otro (M), le regala, le obsequia, lo

socorre (T) T consistently has the reflex of
a long vowel in the initial syllable instead
of the second. applic. TLAŌCOY(A)
TLAŌCOLILIĀ applic. TLAŌCOLIĀ
TLAOCOLĪLŌ nonact. TLAŌCOLIĀ
TLAŌCOL-LI mercy, favor / favor, piedad,
misericordia (S) [(7)Bf.2r,3r,4r,6r,6v,7v,8v].
This is further attested in many derived
forms. In these derivations T has the reflex
of ĀO instead of AŌ. See TLAŌCOY(A).
TLAŌCOLTIĀ *vrefl,vt* to feel pity; to give
someone reason to feel pity toward one /
tiene lástima (T), entristecer a otro o poner
compasión a otro (M), dar ocasión a otro
para que se compadezca de mí (M for first
pers. sg. subject) [(1)Cf.108r, (6)Tp.161,212,
(1)Zp.173]. caus. TLAŌCOY(A)
TLAŌCOLTILIĀ applic. TLAŌCOLTIĀ
TLAŌCOLTĪLŌ nonact. TLAŌCOLTIĀ
TLAŌCOY(A) *pret:* **TLAŌCOX** to be sad /
estar triste (M) [(3)Bf.2r,6v, (1)Cf.121r,
(3)Zp.121,125,218]. Z has an intrusive
glide Y between the first two syllables
in derivations from this, and so does
B, although B does not indicate one in
TLAŌCOY(A) itself. In derivations from
this verb T has the reflex of ĀO instead of
AŌ.
TLAŌCOYALŌ nonact. TLAŌCOY(A)
TLAŌCOYANI someone sad / triste (M)
[(2)Bf.5v,9r]. See TLAŌCOY(A).
TLAOHMACAC See TLAOHMACAQUI.
TLAOHMACAQUI guide / guía (Z)
[(2)Zp.65,212]. In this type of derivation the
QUI ending with stems ending is vowels is
peculiar to Z. Elsewhere this would have
the form TLAOHMACAC. See OHMACA.
TLAŌHUILIĀ applic. TLAŌY(A)
TLAŌLCŌHU(A) to buy maize / compra
maíz (T) [(3)Tp.237]. See TLAŌL-LI,
CŌHU(A).
TLAŌLCŌHUALŌ nonact. TLAŌL-
CŌHU(A)
TLAŌLCŌHUIĀ *vrefl* to buy maize for
oneself / se compra maíz (T) [(3)Tp.160].
See TLAŌLCŌHU(A).
TLAŌLCŌHUILIĀ applic. TLAŌLCŌHU(A)
TLAŌLCŌHUĪLŌ nonact. TLAŌLCŌHUIĀ
TLAŌLCUĒCHOĀ to grind maize / moler
(maíz, chile, etc.) (X) [(3)Xp.95]. Although
the literal meaning of this is 'to grind

maize,' X apparently has generalized it to
the grinding of other things as well. See
TLAŌL-LI, CUĒCHOĀ.
TLAOLĪN(I) for there to be an earthquake /
tiembla la tierra (T) [(1)Tp.233]. The literal
sense of this is 'things move,' but in use it
is synonymous with TLĀLOLĪN(I) 'for the
earth to move.' The O of the free-standing
verb ŌLĪNIĀ is consistently long in T and
Z, but the corresponding vowel in derived
forms is attested short. See ŌLĪNIĀ.
TLAOLĪNILIZ-TLI earthquake, tremor,
movement in general / meneamiento de
algo, o el acto de menear o mover algo (M),
temblor, terremoto (T) [(1)Tp.233]. See
TLAOLĪN(I), TLĀLŌLĪNILIZ-TLI.
TLAŌL-LI dried kernels of maize / maíz
desgranado, curado, y seco (M) See ŌY(A).
TLAŌLNAMACA to sell maize / vende
maíz (T) [(4)Tp.192,237]. See TLAŌL-LI,
NAMACA.
TLAŌLNAMACŌ nonact. TLAŌL-
NAMACA
TLAŌLNAMAQUILIĀ applic. TLAŌL-
NAMACA
TLAOLOLŌLIZ-TLI the act of gathering
something together, heaping something up
/ el acto de arrebañar, ayuntar, o amonto-
nar algo (M) [(2)Zp.106,212]. See OLOLOĀ.
TLAŌLPEHPEN(A) See TLAŌL-LI, PEH-
PEN(A).
TLAŌLTEX-TLI cornstarch, used in prepar-
ing beverages / pinole (T) [(1)Tp.237]. See
TLAŌL-LI, TEX-TLI.
TLAŌLTIHTĪX-TLI maize gleaned after the
harvest / maíz rejuntado (T) [(2)Tp.237].
See TLAŌL-LI, TIHTĪX-TLI.
TLAŌLTŌTŌ-TL *pl:* **-MEH** a type of bird /
maizero (pájaro) (T) [(2)Tp.237,243]. See
TLAŌL-LI, TŌTŌ-TL.
TLAŌLTZETZELHUIĀ applic. TLAŌL-
TZETZELOĀ
TLAŌLTZETZELOĀ to separate bran
from maize kernels / sacude maíz (T)
[(3)Tp.237]. See TLAŌL-LI, TZETZELOĀ.
TLAŌLTZETZELŌLŌ nonact. TLAŌL-
TZETZELOĀ
TLAŌLXONELHUA-TL maize stubble /
tamo (basura que queda de maíz) (T)
[(1)Tp.237]. See TLAŌL-LI, XO-, NEL-
HUA-TL.

TLAŌMEPIY(A) *pret:* **-PIX** to be a bigamist, to keep more than one woman / tiene más de una mujer (T) [(3)Tp.27]. See ŌME, PIY(A).

TLAŌMEPIYALIĀ T shortens this to TLAŌMEPILIĀ applic. TLAŌMEPIY(A)

TLAŌMEPIYALŌ nonact. TLAŌMEPIY(A)

TLAŌPŌCHCOPA at, to the left hand / a mano izquierda o hacia la mano izquierda (M) [(1)Cf.94v]. See -ŌPŌCHCOPA.

TLAŌX-TLI kernels of maize removed from the cob / maíz desgranado o cosa semejante (M) [(1)Cf.46v, (1)Rp.40]. O is not marked long in C or R, but R derives this directly from ŌY(A) 'to shell something,' where the vowel is attested long. See ŌY(A).

TLAŌY(A) *pret:* **TLAŌX** to remove the kernels from dried ears of maize / desgrana (T) [(3)Tp.233]. T appears to have the reflex of a short vowel in this verb and in its nonactive form, but the vowel is long in basic ŌY(A) 'to shell something' and is attested long in T in the applicative form TLAŌHUILIĀ

TLAŌYAL-LI dried kernels of maize removed from the cob / maíz desgranada o cosa semejante (M) [(1)Cf.46v, (1)Rp.40]. C and R fail to mark the O long. See TLAŌY(A).

TLAŌYALŌ nonact. TLAŌY(A)

TLAPĀ *pret:* **TLAPAH** to dye / teñir (C) [(2)Cf.32v]. In the same section C also treats the TLA- as an unfused nonspecific object prefix, TLA-PĀ 'to dye something.' See PĀ.

TLAPĀC(A) to do the laundry, washing / he lavado (C for first pers. sg. subject, perfect) [(1)Cf.31v]. See PĀC(A).

TLAPĀCALŌNI laundry tub, wash basin, trough / batea (Z for compounds with CUAHU(I)-TL and HUAPAL-LI) [(3)Zp.19,154]. See PĀC(A).

TLAPACHILHUIĀ applic. TLAPACHOĀ

TLAPACHOĀ *vrefl,vt* to cover oneself; to cover something, to roof something over / cubrirse con algo (M), cubrir a otro (M) M also has TLAPACHOĀ as an intransitive verb 'to govern, rule.' M and T both gloss TLAPACHOĀ as 'for a hen to brood,' while M and Z have derived forms with the sense 'a setting hen.' See PACHOĀ.

TLAPACHOHQUI setting hen, brooding hen / gallina que está sobre los huevos o la que cría pollos (M for *tlapacho*), clueca (Z) [(2)Zp.28,183]. See TLAPACHOĀ.

TLAPACHŌL-LI subject, someone or something which is ruled, pressed down, oppressed / súbdito, regido o gobernado, o cosa apesgada y apretada (M) [(1)Cf.87v]. See PACHOĀ.

TLAPACHŌLŌ nonact. TLAPACHOĀ

TLAPACH-TLI scales / escama (Z) [(2)Zp.54,161]. See TLAPACHOĀ.

TLAPĀCQUI laundress, one who washes things / lavandera (Z) [(2)Zp.76,212]. M has synonymous *tlapacani*. See PĀC(A).

TLAPACTIC something cracked, shredded, or broken / agrietado, roto, rasgado, rajado (Z) [(4)Zp.6,105,111,212]. See TLAPĀN(I).

TLAPAC-TLI something split, a fragment / cosa partida (C), pedacito (C for *centlapactzin*) [(3)Cf.119v,128v]. This contrasts with TLAPĀC-TLI 'something laundered or washed.' It commonly compounds to form CENTLAPAC-TLI 'morsel.' See TLAPĀN(I).

TLAPĀC-TLI something laundered or washed / cosa lavada o batanada (M) [(1)Cf.128v]. This contrasts with TLAPAC-TLI 'fragment.' See PĀC(A).

TLAPAHHUILŌNI poison / veneno (Z) [(2)Zp.128,212]. See PAHHUIĀ.

TLAPĀHUAZ-TLI something cooked in a pot / cosa cocida en olla (M) [(1)Cf.46v]. M also has *tlapauaxtli* with the same meaning. See PĀHUAC(I).

TLĀPĀHUIĀ *vrefl* to become intoxicated / se emborrachó (C for preterit) [(1)Cf.60v]. This is conventionally paired with MĪXĪHUIĀ, the whole phrase meaning 'to become intoxicated.' See TLĀPĀ-TL.

-TLAPAL side / lado (K) When this compounds with a quantifier to form a directional construction, as in ŌNTLAPAL 'from both sides,' it does not take an absolutive suffix, but it is apparently the second element of AHTLAPAL-LI 'leaf, wing' which does take one.

TLAPALĀNALTIĀ to cause things to rot, to suffer from venereal disease / el que tiene podrido el miembro genital (M), lo pudre (Z) [(2)Zp.100,212]. See PALĀNALTIĀ.

TLAPALĀN-TLI rot, filth, manure / estiércol, suciedad, abono (Z) [(7)Zp.3, 57,118,212]. M has *tlapalanaltiliztli* 'venereal disease.' See PALĀN(I).

TLAPALĒHUIĀNI someone helpful / el que da favor y ayuda (M) [(1)Tp.234]. See PALĒHUIĀ.

TLAPALĒHUIHQUI someone helpful / ayudador y favorecedor (M) [(2)Zp.17,212]. See PALĒHUIĀ.

TLAPALĒHUILIZ-TLI aid, help / ayuda y favor (M) [(1)Tp.234, (3)Zp.17,116,212]. See PALĒHUIĀ.

-TLAPALEZZŌ *necessarily possessed form* one's blood / su sangre (T) [(1)Tp.134]. This is more commonly expressed in the phrase -EZZŌ, -TLAPALLŌ 'one's blood.' See TLAPAL-LI, EZ-TLI.

TLAPALHUĀX-IN *pl:* **-MEH** a type of fruit-bearing tree / huaje rojo (X) [(3)Xp.93]. See TLAPAL-LI, HUĀX-IN.

TLAPALHUIĀ *vt* to paint, dye something / lo pinta, lo mancha, lo tiñe (Z) [(4)Zp.81,99,121,195]. See TLAPAL-LI, -HUIĀ.

TLAPĀLIĀ *vt* to dye something for someone / tíñote algo (C for first pers. sg. subject, second pers. sg. object) [(1)Cf.64v]. applic. TLAPĀ

TLAPĀLIZ-TLI the art of dyeing / el acto de teñir alguna ropa (M) [(1)Bf.10v]. B marks the vowels of the second and third syllables both long but then indicates that the diacritic over the I is incorrect. See PĀ.

TLAPAL-LI *inalienably possessed form:* **-TLAPALYŌ ~ TLAPALLŌ** dye, ink, something dyed / color para pintar o cosa teñida (M), tinta, pintura, tintura (T) This also metaphorically refers to blood. TLAPAL-LI contrasts with TLAHPAL-LI 'courage,' which also serves as a greeting. See PĀ.

-TLAPALLŌ *inalienably possessed form of* **TLAPAL-LI** one's blood / nuestra sangre (C for first pers. plural possessor) [(2)Cf.99r,115r]. This is conventionally paired with -EZZŌ, the whole phrase meaning 'one's blood.' See TLAPAL-LI.

TLAPALLOH something splattered, painted / manchado, pintado (Z) [(3)Zp.81,98,212]. M has *tlapalloa* 'something dyed in colors.' T has a possessed form which is am-

biguous between -TLAPALYOH and -TLAPALYŌ meaning 'one's color, tint, hue.' The LY sequence would optionally assimilate to yield either -TLAPALLOH, as here, or -TLAPALLŌ, which would be identical to the inalienably possessed form of TLAPAL-LI 'dye, ink.' See TLAPAL-LI, -YOH.

TLAPALLŌTIĀ *vt* to dye or paint something / lo tiñe, lo tinta, lo pinta (T) [(3)Tp.209, (3)Xp.76]. See TLAPALLOH.

TLAPALLŌTILIĀ applic. TLAPALLŌTIĀ

TLAPALLŌTĪLŌ nonact. TLAPALLŌTIĀ

TLAPALOĀ to sop bread in broth / mojar el pan en el potaje cuando comen (M), sopear (Z) [(1)Cf.128v, (2)Zp.117,212]. This contrasts with TLAHPALOĀ 'to greet someone.' See PALOĀ.

TLAPALŌL-LI food, meal / comida (Z) [(2)Zp.30,212]. M has *tlapaloliztli* 'the act of sopping bread in broth.' See TLAPALOĀ.

TLAPALQUĪZ(A) to fade / se despinta (T) [(1)Tp.234]. See TLAPAL-LI, QUĪZ(A).

TLAPALTILIĀ *vt* to soak something / lo empapa (T) [(3)Tp.219]. In the Nahuatl-to-Spanish side of T this only appears bound with YĒC- 'well, good,' but in the Spanish-to-Nahuatl side it occurs independently. See TLAPALOĀ.

TLAPALTILILIĀ applic. TLAPALTILIĀ

TLAPALTILĪLŌ nonact. TLAPALTILIĀ

TLAPALTŌTŌ-TL *pl:* **-MEH** a type of bird / maizero (pájaro) (T) [(1)Tp.234]. See TLAPAL-LI, TŌTŌ-TL.

-TLAPALYŌ T has a possessed form that is ambiguous between -TLAPALYOH and -TLAPALYŌ meaning 'one's color, tint, hue.' If it is the latter, then it is identical to the inalienably possessed form of TLAPAL-LI 'dye, ink' without assimilation of LY to LL. Otherwise it is a variant form of TLAPALLOH 'something painted.'

TLAPĀN(A) *vt* to break or split something open, to break something open, to hatch chicks / quebrar algo, sacar pollos las aves, o descascarar mazorcas de cacao o de cosa semejante (M) See TLAPĀN(I).

TLAPĀNALŌ nonact. TLAPĀN(A)

TLAPĀNALTIĀ caus. TLAPĀN(A)

TLAPANCO loft, storage platform under the roof / en el azotea (M), sarzo, tapanco (Z)

[(2)Zp.119,212]. See TLAPAN-TLI, -C(O).

TLAPĀN(I) for something like pottery or eggshells to break into pieces / quebrarse algo (M), quebrarse vasijas de barro, tecomates, o otras cosas delicadas (C) M combines this verb in a single entry with TLAPĀNI 'someone who dyes cloth.' See TLAPĀN(A).

TLAPĀNI someone, something that dyes cloth / el tintorero que tiñe paños (M), M combines this in a single gloss with the verb TLAPĀN(I) 'for something to break into pieces.' It is not directly attested in the sources for this dictionary, but the basic verb TLAPĀ is.

TLAPĀNIC something broken up, split / agrietado [(2)Zp.6,212]. See TLAPĀNQUI.

TLAPĀNILIĀ applic. TLAPĀN(A)

TLAPĀNŌ nonact. TLAPĀN(I)

TLAPĀNQUI something broken / cosa quebrada (M) [(1)Tp.235]. Z has a less regular variant TLAPĀNIC. See TLAPĀN(I).

TLAPAN-TLI pl: -MEH flat roof / azotea o terrado (M) Z marks the vowel of the second syllable long, but it is consistently short in the other sources. See -PAN.

TLAPĀNTOC something split, broken / rajado (Z) [(2)Zp.105,212]. See TLAPĀN(I), the verb O.

TLAPATILIĀ vrefl to barter, exchange, or do business, to change clothes / feriar, trocar, o contratar (M), se muda de vestido (Z) [(2)Zp.86,173]. See PATLA.

TLĀPĀ-TL intoxicating plant, also used medicinally / yerba ... que comidas trastornan la cabeza ... se toman por pulque y vino (C), quiebra-platos, planta medicinal especie de estramonio (R), huevo de perro (X) [(4)Cf.60v,116v,121r, (1)Rp.146, (3)Xp.93]. This is conventionally paired with MĪXĪ-TL, another intoxicating plant, the whole phrase referring to inebriation.

TLAPATLĀHUA to withdraw / se aleja ... se retira (Z) [(2)Zp.8,212]. M has *tlapatlaua* 'someone who widens something.' See PATLĀHUA.

TLAPATLALIZ-TLI change, exchange, barter / el acto de trocar unas cosas con otras o de cambalachear (M), cambio, vuelto (Z) [(2)Zp.24,213]. See PATLA.

TLAPATLAL-LI something exchanged for something else, exchange, barter / cosa trocada (M), vuelto, cambio (Z) [(2)Zp.130,212]. In the same entry M has the additional gloss 'something dissolved, diluted,' which is derived from contrasting PĀTLA. See PATLA.

TLAPATLALŌNI change (money) / cambio, vuelto (Z) [(2)Zp.24,213]. See PATLA.

TLAPĀTZCALIZ-TLI action of pressing something, expressing liquid from something / acción de prensar (Z) [(1)Zp.213]. See PĀTZCA.

TLAPĀTZCAL-LI juice, milk, something expressed or wrung out / zumo, jugo, todo lo que se exprime, leche (S) [(1)Cf.47r]. See PĀTZCA.

TLAPĀTZCALŌNI press (for extracting liquid) / prensa para esprimir algo (M), trapiche (Z) [(2)Zp.125,213]. See PĀTZCA.

TLAPĀTZCATOQUI press (for extracting liquid) / trapiche (Z) [(1)Zp.213]. See PĀTZCA, the verb O.

TLAPĀTZQUI-TL milk or other liquid obtained by expressing it / leche ordeñada o zumo de yerbas o de otra cosa estrujada (M) [(1)Cf.47r]. See PĀTZCA.

TLAPAYAHU(I) to rain gently for a long time / llover mansamente y sin cesar (M) [(1)Tp.234, (5)Xp.93]. X has a long vowel in the second syllable, where T has a short one. If the vowel were basically long, then this could be understood to contain *PĀ 'water,' retaining the initial P which has been lost in Ā-TL. See QUIYAHU(I), ĀYAHU(I)-TL.

TLAPECHHUIĀ to carry something in a litter / llevar algo en andas o en angarillas (M) [(1)Cf.60v]. See TLAPECH-TLI, -HUIĀ.

TLAPECHTEPEHXIHUIĀ vt to throw someone out of bed onto the floor / lo derriba de la cama (T) [(3)Tp.209]. See TLAPECH-TLI, TEPEHXIHUIĀ.

TLAPECHTEPEHXIHUILIĀ applic. TLAPECHTEPEHXIHUIĀ

TLAPECHTEPEHXIHUĪLŌ nonact. TLAPECHTEPEHXIHUIĀ

TLAPECH-TLI pl: -MEH litter, stretcher, bed, platform / tablado, andamio, cama de tablas, andas de difuntos, o cosa semejante (M) See PECH-TLI.

TLAPEHPEN(A) *vt* to select the best from a quantity of things (such as seeds) / escoge semillas (lo bueno de entre todo) (T) [(3)Tp.209, (4)Xp.76]. X has this as TLAPEHPENIĀ. See PEHPEN(A).

TLAPEHPENAL-LI something picked, selected, elected / cosa elegida (M) [(1)Cf.46v, (3)Rp.40,121]. This also appears in P with the glottal stop marked. See PEHPEN(A).

TLAPEHPENALŌ nonact. TLAPEHPEN (A)

TLAPEHPENILIĀ applic. TLAPEHPEN(A)

TLAPEHPEN-TLI something picked, selected, elected / cosa escogida ... o cosas halladas que las perdieron o se les cayeron a otros (M) [(1)Cf.46v, (3)Rp.40,121]. See PEHPEN(A).

TLAPĒHU(A) to plow land (by driving a draft animal) / arrea, ara (T) [(3)Tp.234]. See PĒHU(A).

TLAPĒHUAL-LI trap or pit for catching animals; land or animals that have been brought under control / trampa para tomar y cazar animalias, o cosa ojeada, o tierra conquistada, o orzuelo (M), jacal (T) [(1)Tp.234]. See TLAPĒHU(A).

TLAPĒHUALŌ nonact. TLAPĒHU(A)

TLAPĒHUILIĀ applic. TLAPĒHU(A)

TLAPEPECHŌLŌNI glue / goma, cola, pegamento (Z) [(4)Zp.29,63,95,213]. See PEPECHOĀ.

TLAPETLĀHUALIZ-TLI act of polishing / acción de bruñir (K) [(1)Bf.10v]. See PETLĀHU(A).

TLAPETLĀN(I) for lightning to flash / relampaguear (M) [(2)Zp.108,213, (3)Xp.93]. See PETLĀN(I).

TLAPETLĀNIL-LI lightning / relámpago (X) [(1)Xp.93]. M has this as 'something scattered.' See TLAPETLĀN(I).

TLAPETLĀNĪLLŌ-TL lightning, flash / relámpago, centella (Z) [(2)Zp.107,213]. See TLAPETLĀN(I), PETLĀNIĀ.

TLAPETZCŌLTIĀ *vt* to make something come loose, slip down / lo desprende (Z) [(2)Zp.44,196]. See PETZCOĀ.

TLAPĒUHQUI driver of animals / arriero (Z) [(2)Zp.14,213]. See TLAPĒHU(A).

TLAPĪC in vain, purposelessly, falsely / en vano o sin propósito (M), con fal-

sedad y mentira (C) [(5)Cf.73r,106v,113r, (1)Tp.221]. This is usually but not exclusively preceded by ZAN.

TLAPICĪLOĀ to rain / lloviznar (X) [(3)Xp.93]. See PICĪLOĀ.

TLAPIHPĪ-TL something plucked, gathered / arrancado, cortado, recogido (S) [(1)Cf.47r, (1)Rp.41]. The vowel of the third syllable is not marked long in either attestation. See PIHPĪ.

TLAPĪHUILIĀ *vt* to add something above the amount purchased, to adjust or enlarge something / añadir algo más al peso o a la medida (M), lo ajusta, lo aumenta (T) [(3)Tp.209]. M has *tlapiuia* 'for something to grow, increase, or multiply.' applic. TLAPĪHUIY(A)

TLAPĪHUILILIĀ applic. TLAPĪHUILIĀ

TLAPĪHUILĪLŌ nonact. TLAPĪHUILIĀ

TLAPĪHUIY(A) *pret:* **TLAPĪHUIX** ~ **TLAPĪHUIYAC** for something to grow, enlarge, multiply / crecer o aumentarse y multiplicarse alguna cosa (M) B attests this once and specifically marks the vowel of the second syllable short (f.9v), but it is abundantly attested in T with a long vowel, and it is also long in T's PĪHUIC 'something added in over and above what is paid for.'

TLAPILCHĪHUAL-LI sin, failing / pecado o defecto (M) [(1)Bf.9v]. See PILCHĪHU(A).

TLAPILŌLIZ-TLI the act of hanging something / el acto de colgar algo de alguna cosa (M) [(2)Zp.30,213]. See PILOĀ.

TLAPILŌL-LI something hung, suspended / cosa colgada ... o ahorcada (M) [(2)Zp.13,160]. See PILOĀ.

TLAPIPĪNALŌNI instrument for sucking things / chupón (Z) [(2)Zp.39,213]. M has *pipina* 'to suck on sweet cane.'

TLAPĪPĪTZALŌNI fan / aventador (Z) [(2)Zp.17,213]. See PĪTZ(A).

TLAPĪQUIĀ to slander someone / levantar algo a otro falsamente y con calumnia (M) [(1)Cf.113r]. See PĪQU(I).

TLAPĪ-TL something plucked, gathered / arrancado, recogido, levantado (S) [(1)Cf.47r, (1)Rp.41]. The vowel of the second syllable is not marked long in either attestation. See PĪ.

TLAPĪTZALIZ-TLI the act of playing a wind

instrument or of forging metal with the aid of bellows / el acto de tañer flauta o otro instrumento semejante, o el acto de fundir y derretir metales (M) [(2)Zp.123,213]. See PĪTZ(A).

TLAPĪTZAL-LI pl: **-MEH** ~ **-TIN** flute, wind instrument / flauta, chirimía, orlo (M) [(1)Cf.47v, (1)Tp.234, (2)Zp.60,213]. Z has the abbreviated form TLAPĪTZ-TLI. See PĪTZ(A).

TLAPĪTZALŌNI flute; crucible / flauta (Z), crisol para fundir oro (M) [(2)Zp.60, 213]. The literal sense these share is of something worked by blowing into it. See PĪTZ(A).

TLAPITZHUIĀ to make a high pitched sound like an alarmed turkey or a crying child / hace ruido el guajolote al ver un gavilán, llora niño con voz delgadita (T) [(1)Tp.234]. See PIPITZCA.

TLAPITZOTEYOH ugly place / lugar muy feo (T) [(1)Tp.234]. The TEYOH of this is opaque. This would make better sense with TI-YĀN in its place. This contrasts with TLAPITZŌTEYOH 'narrow place.' See PITZOTIC.

TLAPITZŌTEYOH narrow place / lugar angosto, angostura (T) [(1)Tp.235]. The TEYOH of this is opaque. This would make better sense with TI-YĀN in its place. This contrasts with TLA-PITZOTEYOH 'ugly place.' See PITZŌTIC.

TLAPITZOTIĀ to become ugly / se pone feo (T) [(1)Tp.234]. See PITZO-TL.

TLAPIXCALIZ-TLI harvest / siega, cosecha (Z) [(2)Zp.115,213]. See PIXCA.

TLAPIXCAL-LI something harvested / lo cosechado (K) [(2)Zp.82,203]. This appears in Z in construction with CIN-TLI with the sense 'shucked maize.' See PIXCA.

TLAPIYAL-LI pl: **-MEH** domestic animal / bestia, animal, ganado (doméstico) (Z) [(4)Zp.11,19,62,213]. In view of TLAHPIXTINEM(I) 'to serve as shepherd,' it seems that this should be TLAHPIYAL-LI, but Z has no glottal stop in any attestation. See PIY(A).

TLAPIYĀZOĀ to excrete / hace el excusado, depone (T) [(3)Tp.235]. The gloss is ambiguous between urination and defecation, and moreover *deponer* can also mean 'to

vomit.' T has O for Ā in the third syllable. See PIYĀZOĀ.

TLAPIYĀZŌLŌ nonact. TLAPIYĀZOĀ

TLAPIYĀZŌLTIĀ caus. TLAPIYĀZOĀ

TLAPOĀ vt to open something / ser portero o desatapar, descubrir, o abrir algo (M) This contrasts with intransitive TLAPŌHU(A) 'to count, to read.'

TLAPŌCHUIĀ to produce smoke / hace humo (Z) [(2)Zp.69,213]. See PŌCHUIĀ.

TLAPŌCTĒM(I) pret: **TLAPŌCTĒN** for a place to fill up with smoke / se llena de humo, lleno de humo (T), humea, está lleno de humo (Z) [(1)Tp.235, (2)Zp.69,213]. See PŌCTĒM(I).

TLAPOHPŌHU(A) to clean, clear ground, mow / limpia, roza, siega (T) [(3)Tp.235, (3)Xp.93]. X lacks the internal glottal stop. See POHPŌHU(A).

TLAPOHPŌHUALŌ nonact. TLA-POHPŌHU(A)

TLAPOHPŌHUILIĀ applic. TLA-POHPŌHU(A)

TLAPOHPŌHUILIZ-TLI something clean / limpia (X) [(1)Xp.93]. X fails to mark the glottal stop. See TLAPOHPŌHU(A).

TLAPOHPOLHUIĀ vt to pardon someone / perdonar a otro, o dispensar con alguno (M) [(4)Zp.96,196,222]. See POHPOLHUIĀ.

TLAPOHPOLHUILIĀ applic. TLA-POHPOLHUIĀ

TLAPOHPOLHUILIZ-TLI pardon / perdón (T) [(1)Tp.235, (2)Zp.96,213]. See POHPOLHUIĀ.

-TLAPOHPOLHUILŌCĀ *necessarily possessed form* pardon dispensed to someone / el perdón con que me perdonan (C for first pers. sg. possessor) [(1)Cf.48v]. See POHPOLHUIĀ.

TLAPOHPOLHUILŌNI someone deserving of pardon / digno de perdón (C) [(2)Cf.45r]. See POHPOLHUIĀ.

TLAPŌHU(A) to count, to read, to pray / leer (C), reza, cuenta (T) M does not have a separate entry for this, but C, T, and Z treat it as an intransitive verb with the nonspecific object prefix TLA- fused to the verb stem. This contrasts with transitive TLAPOĀ 'to open something.'

TLAPŌHUALIZ-TLI counting, reckoning, reading / el acto de numerar o contar algo,

o el acto de echar suertes el hechicero o
el agorero, o el acto de dar lección el
estudiante a su maestro, o el acto de leer
algo (M) [(2)Zp.36,213]. See PŌHU(A).

TLAPŌHUAL-LI someone or something
counted, something read / cosa numerada
y contada o cosa leída (M), cosa o persona
contada (C) [(9)Cf.46r,46v,106v,123v]. See
PŌHU(A).

TLAPŌHUALPA a countable number of
times / veces que se pueden contar (C)
[(5)Cf.106r,106v]. This is only attested in
negated form with the sense 'countless
times.' See TLAPŌHUAL-LI, -PA.

TLAPOHU(I) for something to open / abrirse
la puerta o la carta (M) [(4)Cf.78v,79r,99r,
(2)Tp.235]. See TLAPOĀ.

TLAPŌHUIĀ vt to relate something
to someone, to testify about someone, to
cast fortunes / le cuenta (un suceso)
(Z), testifica (Z), echar suertes a otro
el hechicero o agorero con maíz
(M) [(4)Zp.33,122,196,222]. applic.
TLAPŌHU(A)

TLAPOHUILIĀ vt to unbutton, unfasten
something / lo desbotona, lo desabrocha
(Z) [(2)Zp.41,196]. applic. TLAPOHU(I)

TLAPŌHUILIZ-TLI recitation / recitación,
rezo (T) [(1)Tp.235]. M has tlapouiliztli
'opening, the act of unfastening,' which is
derived from TLAPOHU(I) and contrasts
with this. See TLAPŌHU(A).

TLAPOLHUIĀ vt to open something for
someone / se lo abre (T) applic. TLAPOĀ

TLAPOLHUILIĀ applic. TLAPOLHUIĀ

TLAPOLHUĪLŌ nonact. TLAPOLHUIĀ

TLAPOLIHU(I) for all to be lost / todo se
pierde (C) [(1)Cf.36v]. M has this in a
phrase about starvation and thirst. See
POLIHU(I).

TLAPŌLŌ nonact. TLAPOĀ

TLAPOLOĀ for the harvest to fail / se pierde
la cosecha (T) [(1)Tp.235]. See POLOĀ,
TLAPOLIHU(I).

TLAPOLOH something destroyed / perdido,
vencido (Z) [(2)Zp.128,213]. See POLOĀ.

TLAPOLŌLIZ-TLI loss / el acto de perder
alguna cosa (M), locura, confusión (Z
for compound with CUĀ(I)-TL)
[(3)Zp.32,77,147]. See POLOĀ.

TLAPOLŌLTIĀ vrefl, vt to become dis-

tracted or disoriented; to cause someone
to become distracted or disoriented /
descuidarse o desatinarse y turbarse (M),
desatinar a otro así (M) See POLOĀ.

TLAPOLŌLTILIĀ applic. TLAPOLŌLTIĀ

TLAPOLŌLTĪLŌ nonact. TLAPOLŌLTIĀ

TLAPŌPOYĀHU(I) to get dark / se obsurece
(T for compound with ĪX-TLI) [(1)Tp.137].
T also has POPOYACTIC 'gray, dark,
cloudy,' and M has tlapoyahua 'for night to
fall.' See POYĀHU(I).

TLAPOUHQUI something open / abierto (T)
[(1)Tp.235]. See TLAPOHU(I).

TLAPOUHTICAH to be open / estar abierto
(T) [(1)Tp.235]. See TLAPOHU(I), the verb
CĀ.

TLAPŌUHTICAH to recite, to count / reza,
cuenta (T) [(1)Tp.235]. See TLAPŌHU(A),
the verb CĀ.

TLAPŌUH-TLI something counted / cosa
contada y numerada (M) [(1)Cf.46v]. See
PŌHU(A).

TLAPOUHTOC something open / abierto
(X) [(2)Xp.93]. See TLAPOHU(I), the verb
O.

TLAPOXCAHUĪLLŌ-TL moss / musgo,
moho (Z) [(1)Zp.213]. Z marks the vowel of
the second syllable long, but it is not long
in the related verb. Z also has O for A in
the third syllable. See POXCAHU(I).

TLAPOYĀHUA for night to fall, to get
dark / hacerse ya noche o anochecer (M)
[(1)Cf.97r]. See POYĀHU(I).

TLAPOZŌNAL-LI something boiled / hervido (T) [(1)Tp.235]. See POZŌN(I).

TLAPOZTEC-TLI something broken,
snapped, fractured / cosa quebrada así
como palo o pierna, brazo, etc. (M)
[(2)Zp.111,213]. See POZTEQU(I).

TLAQUECHIĀ vrefl to support oneself on a
crutch, staff / estribar o sustentarse sobre
algún bordón o muleta (M) [(2)Cf.50r,
(4)Tp.153]. See QUECHIĀ.

TLĀQUEH someone, something with a body
/ cosa que tiene cuerpo (M) [(1)Cf.55v,
(2)Rp.45,147]. See TLĀC-TLI.

TLAQUEHQUELOHQUI joker, mocker /
burlador (Z) [(2)Zp.21,214]. See QUEH-
QUELOĀ.

TLAQUEHQUELŌLIZ-TLI mockery,
tickling, tormenting / acción de hacer

cosquillas (Z) [(1)Zp.214]. Z fails to mark the internal glottal stop. See QUEHQUELOĀ.

TLĀQUĒHU(A) *vt* to hire someone / alquilar a otro (M), lo alquila, lo arrienda, lo renta (Z) [(3)Zp.9,14,196]. Z has apparently extended this to the hiring of things as well as people and services.

TLĀQUĒHUAL-LI hired help, paid servant; something rented / alquilado o mercenario (M), criado, mozo, servidor, siervo, peón, sirviente (Z), alquilado (Z) [(7)Zp.9,35,86,96,115,214]. In all but two attestations, Z marks the vowels of the second and third syllables long. In one the vowels of the first and third syllables are marked long, and in the other the vowels of the first and second are marked long. This last pattern is the only correct one if this item is derived from TLĀQUĒHU(A), as it is according to M's gloss.

TLĀQUĒHUIĀ *vt* to hire someone to do something to or for someone / buscar o alquilar a alguno para que haga mal a otro (M), se preocupa por otra persona para llamarle a un doctor, a un curandero; le busca padrino, guía, etc. (T) [(3)Tp.212]. applic. TLĀQUĒHU(A)

TLĀQUĒHUILIĀ applic. TLĀQUĒHUIĀ

TLĀQUĒHUĪLŌ nonact. TLĀQUĒHUIĀ

TLĀQUĒMILTIĀ *vt* to have someone get dressed / hago a otro que se vista de algo, y doyle de vestir (C for first pers. sg. subject) [(1)Cf.62v]. This is synonymous with TLAQUĒNTIĀ. They are alternative causative forms of unattested *TLAQUĒM(I). See QUĒM(I).

TLAQUĒM(I)-TL *possessed form:* **-TLAQUĒN** garment, wrap / vestidura o ropa (M) TLAQUĒM(I)-TL and TLAQUĒN-TLI co-occur in C, T, Z, and R with no apparent distinction in meaning. In possessed form, even with honorific -TZIN, T has lost the final nasal consonant. See QUĒM(I).

TLAQUĒNQUĪXTIĀ *vrefl,vt* to get undressed; to undress someone / se desviste, se desabriga (Z), lo desnuda (Z) [(4)Zp.43,45,173,196, (3)Xp.60]. See TLAQUĒM(I)-TL, QUĪXTIĀ.

TLAQUĒNTIĀ *vrefl,vt* to get dressed; to dress someone / vestirse o arroparse (M),

vestir a otro así (M) T has short I for Ē in the second syllable. This is synonymous with TLAQUĒMILTIĀ. They are alternative causative forms of unattested *TLAQUĒM(I). See QUĒM(I).

TLAQUĒNTILIĀ applic. TLAQUĒNTIĀ

TLAQUĒNTĪLŌ nonact. TLAQUĒNTIĀ

TLAQUĒN-TLI See TLAQUĒM(I)-TL.

TLAQUEQUETZ(A) for a male bird to copulate with the female / de las aves que se toman ... del macho (C) [(1)Cf.128r]. C contrasts this with TLA-QUEHQUETZ(A) 'to kick out at something in anger.' See QUEQUETZ(A).

TLAQUĒZŌLTIĀ *vt* to cross over something, to go through something / lo atraviesa (Z) [(2)Zp.16,196]. Z also has ĪXTLAQUĒZ 'something or someone bent.'

TLAQUIN-TLI garment / vestido, traje, abrigo, ropa (T) [(4)Tp.209,235]. This is a variant of TLAQUĒM(I)-TL ~ TLAQUĒN-TLI in T. Although T has possessed forms of TLAQUĒN-TLI with the reflex of a long vowel in the second syllable, it also has short-vowel variants TLAQUEN-TLI and TLAQUIN-TLI. TLAQUINTIĀ is the T variant of derived TLAQUĒNTIĀ See TLAQUĒM(I)-TL.

-TLĀQUIXCUĀC *only attested in possessed form* one's groin / su empeine (del vientre), su vientre (T) [(1)Tp.135]. T marks the vowel of the second syllable short, while it is long in ĪXCUĀ(I)-TL 'forehead,' making it questionable whether it is a constituent of this compound. See TLĀC-TLI, ĪXCUĀ(I)-TL, -C(O).

TLAQUĪZ(A) for the rains to end, for the weather to clear / acaba el temporal, se compone (el tiempo), escampa (termina el temporal, entran las secas) (T) [(1)Tp.235, (7)Zp.4,28,31,44,54,214]. M has *tlaquizcayotl* 'end of something.' See QUĪZ(A).

TLAQUĪZCĀTLAH profusion of fruit out of season / venturera (T) [(3)Tp.235]. M has *tlaquizcayotl* 'end or conclusion of something.' See TLAQUĪZ(A), -TLAH.

TLAQUĪZCĀXŌCHI-TL bell flower / quiebraplato (T) [(1)Tp.235]. See TLAQUĪZ(A), XŌCHI-TL.

TLAQUĪZTOC clear weather / hace buen tiempo, un día muy claro (Z)

[(4)Zp.28,122,214]. See TLAQUĪZ(A), the verb O.

TLATAMACHĪHUALIZ-TLI measurement / medición (Z) [(2)Zp.83,214]. See TAMACHĪHU(A).

TLATAMACHĪHUALŌNI measure, guage, standard / medida (Z) [(2)Zp.83,209]. In one of the two attestations the initial syllable has been dropped. See TAMACHĪHU(A).

TLATAMACHĪHUANI inchworm, caterpillar / oruga (Z) [(2)Zp.92,214]. See TAMACHĪHU(A).

TLATAMACHĪUHQUI someone who measures things / el que mide algo (M), medidor (Z) [(2)Zp.83,214]. M also has synonymous *tlatlamachiuani*. See TAMACHĪHU(A).

TLATCŌNI gear for carrying something / instrumento para cargar (K) [(2)Bf.7r]. This is paired in context with CĀCĀX-TLI 'packframe.' See TLATQUI-TL.

TLATECALTIĀNI someone who fans something away, drives something off / aventador (T) [(1)Tp.236]. See TECALTIĀ.

TLATECŌNI cutting instrument / hacha para cortar algo o instrumento semejante (M) [(1)Cf.45v]. This is opposite in sense from TECŌNI 'something in need of cutting.' C states that TLATECŌNI is not used in possessed form but is suppletive with synonymous -TLATEQUIYA. See TEQU(I).

TLATECPĀNALIZ-TLI alignment, order, the act of lining something or someone up / orden y concierto de alguna cosa … el acto de poner la gente o otra cosa en procesión o por sus rengleras (M) [(2)Zp.8,215]. See TECPĀN(A).

TLATĒCPANOĀ to attend court / voy a palacio (C for first pers. sg. subject with directional ON-) [(1)Cf.107r]. See TĒCPAN.

TLATECPĀN-TLI something set in order, a queue, file, or tail / cosa ordenada (M), alineado, cola (de gente, de cosas), por turno (T for CA TLATECPĀN-TLI) [(2)Tp.236]. See TECPĀN(A).

TLATEC-TLI something cut, a wound or scar / cosa cortada (M), herida, cortadura (Z), su cicatriz (Z for possessed form) This contrasts with TLATĒC-TLI 'something spread out,' but M combines them in a single gloss. See TEQU(I).

TLATĒC-TLI something spread or poured out; fabric / guirnalda o cosa escanciada o echada en algo (M), tela (Z) [(2)Zp.120,215]. This contrasts with TLATEC-TLI 'something cut,' but M combines them in a single gloss. M also has *teteca* 'to warp cloth.' See TĒCA.

TLATECUĪN(I) to thunder / truena (el cielo) (T) [(1)Tp.236]. See TECUĪN(I).

TLATEHTEC-TLI something cut, hacked, a wound / cosa descuartizada y hecha pedazos o cosa hecha rebanadas o tajadas (M), herida (T) [(1)Tp.236, (2)Zp.34,215]. M combines the gloss for this with glosses for a form derived from TEHTĒCA 'to spread out' in a single entry. This contrasts with TLATĒTEC-TLI 'something sliced.' See TEHTEQU(I).

TLATEHTEQUILŌNI instrument for chopping, hacking / machete, cortador (Z) [(2)Zp.79,215]. See TEHTEQU(I).

TLATEHUIĀ to engage in combat / pelea (Z) [(6)Zp.19,65,96,215]. See TEHUIĀ.

TLATEHUILIZ-TLI combat, battle, war / pelea, guerra, batalla (Z) [(4)Zp.19,65,96, 215]. See TLATEHUIĀ.

TLATELCHĪHUALIZ-TLI words of scoffing or reproach, curse / escarnecimiento o reproche (M), maldición, condenación (Z) [(3)Zp.32,80,215]. See TELCHĪHU(A).

TLATELCHĪHUAL-LI someone scoffed at, reproached, cursed / escarnecido y reprochado … o reprobado (M), maldecido (Z) [(2)Zp.80,215]. See TELCHĪHU(A).

TLATELOĀ to rush forward / embiste (Z) [(2)Zp.49,215]. See TELOĀ.

TLATĒMIĀ *vt* to feed stock / le da de comer (animal) (Z) [(2)Zp.30,196]. See TĒMIĀ.

TLATĒMOLIĀ *vrefl,vt* to examine oneself for faults, to practice introspection; to carry out an investigation of someone / examinarse, trayendo a la memoria sus pecados, o lo hizo para se confesar (M), hacer inquisición, pesquisa, o información contra alguno (M), lo esculca (T) [(3)Tp.210]. See TĒMOLIĀ.

TLATĒMOLILIĀ applic. TLATĒMOLIĀ
TLATĒMOLĪLŌ nonact. TLATĒMOLIĀ
TLATĒNTOCANI someone given to answering back, someone disrespectful / respondón, rezongón (T) [(1)Tp.236]. See TĒN-TLI, TOCA.

TLATĒNYOH bank, edge, shore / orilla (Z) [(5)Zp.92,215]. See TĒN-TLI, -YOH.

TLATEŌCHĪHUALIZ-TLI blessing, the act of blessing something / el acto de consagrar o bendecir algo (M), bendición (Z) [(2)Zp.19,216]. See TEŌCHĪHU(A).

TLATEŌCHĪHUAL-LI something blessed, consecrated, a blessing / cosa bendita o consagrada (M), bendición (T) [(1)Tp.236, (2)Zp.19,216]. See TEŌCHĪHU(A).

TLATEŌCHĪHUALŌNI instrument of benediction / cosa para bendecir (Z) [(1)Zp.216]. See TEŌCHĪHU(A).

TLATEŌCHĪUH-TLI something blessed, consecrated / cosa bendecida o consagrada (M) [(1)Tp.236, (2)Zp.19,216]. See TEŌCHĪHU(A).

TLATEŌMATILIZ-TLI religious devotion / devoción, ejercicio spiritual, o ceremonia eclesiástica (M) [(1)Cf.79v]. C marks the vowel of the fifth syllable long, although by general rule it should be short. This is immediately followed in context by TLATEŌTOQUILIZ-TLI, where C also marks the corresponding vowel long. See TEŌMAT(I).

TLATEŌTOCANI idolater / idólatra (M) [(1)Cf.67v]. See TEŌ-TL, TOCA.

TLATEŌTOQUILIZ-TLI idolatry / idolatría (M) [(1)Cf.79v]. C marks the vowel of the fifth syllable long, although by general rule it should not be. This is immediately preceded in context by TLA-TEŌMATILIZ-TLI, where C also marks the corresponding vowel long. See TEŌ-TL, TOCA.

TLATEPĒUHQUI sower, scatterer / esparcidor (M), sembrador (persona) (Z) [(2)Zp.114,215]. See TEPĒHU(A).

TLATEPOTZTOCALIZ-TLI investigation, inquiry / exigencia (Z) [(2)Zp.58,215]. Z's gloss 'requirment' does not accurately convey the literal sense of this. See TEPOTZTOCA.

TLATEQUILIZ-TLI the act of cutting something / el acto de cortar alguna cosa (M) [(1)Zp.215]. See TEQU(I).

TLATEQUILŌNI saw, scissors, cutting instrument / sierra, tijeras (Z) [(3)Zp.115,122,215]. See TEQU(I).

TLATEQUIPANOH worker, servant / trabajador (M), siervo, sirviente (T)

[(1)Tp.236]. Because of general loss of final glottal stops in T, the glottal stop in this item is not attested, but it is predicted by regular derivational rules. See TEQUIPANOĀ.

TLATEQUIPANŌLIZTICA by means of labor / con ... trabajo (C) [(1)Cf.49r]. This conventionally pairs with CIAHUIZTICA 'by fatigue,' both in possessed form, the sense of the phrase being equivalent to the English phrase 'by the sweat of one's brow.' See TLATEQUIPANŌLIZ-TLI, -CA.

TLATEQUIPANŌLIZ-TLI work, labor / el acto de trabajar en alguna obra (M) [(1)Cf.49r]. See TEQUIPANOĀ.

-TLATEQUIYA *necessarily possessed form* one's cutting instrument / el intrumento con que yo corto algo, mi cuchillo, mi hacha (C for first pers. sg. possessor) [(2)Cf.50r,82r]. C states that this possessed form is suppletive with the absolute form of synonymous TLATECŌNI. See TEQU(I).

-TLATEQUIYĀN *necessarily possessed form* the cutting edge of something / filo de cuchillo (X) [(4)Xp.48]. See TEQU(I), -YĀN.

TLATĒTEC-TLI someone wounded, cut up / herida, tiene cortadas (T) [(1)Tp.236]. The literal sense of this should be 'something sliced in orderly fashion.' It contrasts with TLATEHTEC-TLI 'something hacked.' See TĒTEQU(I).

TLATETECUECHILIĀ to stamp one's feet to get attention / hago ruido con los pies, para que mire hacia acá (C for first pers. sg. subject) [(1)Cf.74v]. See TETECUITZ(A).

TLATETECUĪNŌL-LI roller / rollo (Z) [(2)Zp.111,215]. See TETECUĪNOĀ.

TLATĒTZAUHHUIĀ augury, premonition / agüero, mal agüero (T) [(1)Tp.236]. See TĒTZĀHUI-TL, -HUIĀ.

TLATETZĪLŌL-LI thread, cord, something twisted / torcido, torzal (Z) [(3)Zp.123,124,216]. See TETZĪLOĀ.

TLATHUI to dawn, to get light / amanecer (C) M has this bound with YE 'already' with the same meaning. See TLATHUĪTIĀ.

TLATHUILTIĀ The applicative of this used reflexively constitutes a reveren-

tial morning greeting in B. Once in
seven attestations B marks the vowel of
the second syllable long. altern. caus.
TLATHUI
TLATHUINĀHUAC close to dawn / cerca
del alba (M) [(1)Cf.109r]. See TLATHUI,
-NĀHUAC.
TLATHUĪTIĀ This is attested twice in B,
and in both cases the vowel of the second
syllable is not marked long, although by
general derivational processes it should be.
Like TLATHUILTIĀ, the other causative
form of TLATHUI, this is used as part of a
formal morning greeting, but it is also used
to simply inquire about someone's general
state upon arising, implying that the basic
verb TLATHUI 'to dawn' has an extended
meaning 'to get up in the morning.' altern.
caus. TLATHUI
TLATIĀ *vrefl,vt* to burn; to burn someone,
something / quemarse (M), quemarle (M)
This contrasts with TLĀTIĀ 'to hide
something,' but M combines them in a
single entry. See TLATLA.
TLĀTIĀ *vrefl,vt* to hide oneself; to hide
someone, something, to kill someone /
esconderse (M), esconder a otro (M), lo
mata (T) The literal sense 'to hide someone' extends metaphorically to 'to kill
someone' in the sense of 'to put someone
out of sight.' TLĀTIĀ contrasts with
TLATIĀ 'to burn something,' but M combines the two in a single entry.
TLATILĀNALŌNI gear for hauling things /
jaladero (Z) [(2)Zp.73,216]. See TILĀN(A).
TLATILĀNIZ-TLI the act of hauling, tug-
ging, pulling / jaladera (Z) [(1)Zp.216]. See
TILĀN(A).
TLATILĀNQUI hauler / jaladero, jalador (Z)
[(1)Zp.73]. See TILĀN(A).
TLATILIĀ applic. TLATIĀ
TLĀTILIĀ applic. TLĀTIĀ
TLATĪLŌ nonact. TLATIĀ
TLĀTĪLŌ nonact. TLĀTIĀ
TLATĪTLANIĀ *vt* to have someone sent for
/ lo manda llamar (Z) [(2)Zp.78,196]. See
TĪTLAN(I).
TLATLA to burn / arder, abrasarse, o que-
marse (M)
TLATLAC something burned / cosa que-
mada (M) [(2)Zp.104,214]. See TLATLA.
TLĀTLACALHUIĀ *vt* to mimic someone,

to mock someone / lo imita burlándose (T)
[(3)Tp.212].
TLĀTLACALHUILIĀ applic. TLĀTLA-
CALHUIĀ
TLĀTLACALHUĪLŌ nonact. TLĀ-
TLACALHUIĀ
TLATLĀCAMAT(I) *pret:* **TLATLĀCAMAH,**
pret. pl: **TLATLĀCAMATQUEH** to obey /
obedecían (C for third pers. plural, imperfect) [(2)Cf.89v,113r]. The nonspecific
object prefix TLA- has fused with the
stem to form an intransitive verb. See
TLĀCAMAT(I).
TLATLĀCAMATILIZ-TLI obedience /
obediencia (Z) [(2)Zp.90,214]. M has
tetlacamatiliztli 'obedience.' The distinction is that M's entry represents
TĒTLĀCAMATILIZ-TLI 'obedience of
someone,' while this is 'obedience of
something (such as a rule or order).' See
TLĀCAMAT(I).
TLĀTLĀCA-TL humane person / piadosa persona y humana (M) [(1)Tp.241,
(1)Rp.147]. R has a short vowel and glottal
stop in the reduplicated syllable instead of
a long vowel. redup. TLĀCA-TL
TLATLAC(I) *pret:* **TLATLAZ** to have a
cough / tener pechuguera o tos (M)
TLĀTLACŌ-TL *pl:* **-MEH** boil, swelling /
tlacote, clacote (T) [(1)Tp.241]. M has
tlacoton 'boil, sore, pustule.' This appears
to be related to TLACŌ-TL 'staff, stick,'
although the common meaning is not
evident.
TLĀTLACUĀLIZ-TLI feast / banquete (Z)
[(2)Zp.18,214]. The vowel of the third
syllable is marked long in both attestations. See TLACUĀ.
TLĀTLACUĀLŌYĀN banquet hall / lugar
de boda (Z) [(2)Zp.20,214]. See TLACUĀ,
-YĀN.
TLATLACUĀNI table companion / co-
mensal, comedor (Z) [(2)Zp.30,214]. See
TLACUĀ.
TLATLAHCALHUĀZHUIĀ to shoot a
blowgun / disparar con cerbatana (K)
[(1)Bf.10r]. See TLAHCALHUĀZ-TLI,
-HUIĀ.
TLĀTLAHCONECUILOĀ *vrefl* to twist
from side to side / se tuerce (de un lado
a otro) (T) [(3)Tp.161]. See TLAHCO,
NECUILOĀ.

TLĀTLAHCONECUILŌLŌ nonact.
TLĀTLAHCONECUILOĀ

TLATLAHCOYĀN center, middle / centro, entre, en medio de (Z) [(4)Zp.27,53,83,214]. See TLAHCO, -YĀN.

TLATLAHTLANIĀ *vt* to curse someone / lo maldice (Z) [(2)Zp.80,196]. See TLAHTLANIĀ.

TLATLAHTLATILIZ-TLI scorching / quemada (Z), quemado (Z) [(2)Zp.104,214]. See TLAHTLATIĀ.

TLĀTLAHTŌL-LI prolix speech / palabras prolijas (C) [(2)Cf.73r]. redup. TLAHTŌL-LI

TLATLAHZOLCĀN dump, rubbish heap / desaseado (Z) [(2)Zp.41,214]. See TLAHZOL-LI, -CĀN.

TLATLAHZOLTIĀ to pollute, to get things dirty / ensucia (Z) [(2)Zp.53,214]. See TLAHZOL-LI.

TLATLĀLCHIPĀHUA for dawn to break, to get light / alborear o amanecer (M) [(1)Cf.95v]. See TLĀL-LI, CHIPĀHUA.

TLATLĀLIĀ to make arrangements / poner precio a lo que se vende o hacer constituciones y ordenanzas o poner algo en algún lugar, o industriar, fabricar, y componer algo (M) This is implied by TLATLĀLĪL-LI. See TLĀLIĀ.

TLATLĀLĪL-LI something arranged, ordered, established / cosa industriada y fabricada o cosa establecida o ordenada (M), ramillete, plazo (T) [(1)Tp.236]. See TLĀLIĀ.

TLATLĀLĪLTIĀ *vt* to give someone a deadline / le da plazo (T) [(3)Tp.210]. See TLATLĀLĪL-LI.

TLATLĀLĪLTILIĀ applic. TLATLĀLĪLTIĀ

TLATLĀLĪLTĪLŌ nonact. TLATLĀLĪLTIĀ

TLĀTLALOĀ *vrefl* to run in an orderly, sequential fashion / corro de aquí para allí (C for first pers. sg. subject), corremos de la misma manera como los que corren cañas (C) [(2)Cf.72v]. With a singular subject this means for a person to run from a starting point in a set direction. With a plural subject it means for people to run in an organized manner, as in pairs or relays. This contrasts with TLAHTLALOĀ 'for several people to run in the same direction but in an unorganized way.' redup. TLALOĀ

TLĀTLAMANTIC something different,
distinct / diferente (Z) [(2)Zp.46,215]. In both attestations Z marks the vowel of the third syllable long, but it should not be. In one of two attestations Z marks the vowel of the first syllable long. redup. TLAMANTIC

TLATLAMATCĀYETOC something tranquil, peaceful, undisturbed / tranquilo, sosiegado (Z) [(2)Zp.124,215]. See TLAMATCĀ, YETOC.

TLATLAMŌTLA to discharge, fire, shoot / tira (Z) [(2)Zp.122,215]. See MŌTLA.

TLATLAMPA beneath, underneath / debajo de (Z) [(2)Zp.40,215]. Z has a long vowel in the postposition -TLAN, but the other sources agree that it is short. See -TLAN, -PA.

TLATLAMPACUĒ(I)-TL petticoat / su enaguas (Z for possessed form) [(2)Zp.50,161]. See TLATLAMPA, CUĒ(I)-TL.

-TLATLĀN *only attested in possessed form* income, gain from an investment / su redito (T) [(1)Tp.134]. This implies unattested *TLATLĀN-TLI 'gain, winnings at gambling.' See TLĀN(I).

TLĀTLANĒC(I) *pret:* **TLĀTLANĒZ** to be luminous / transparente (T for a ĪIHTEC TLĀTLANĒC(I)) [(2)Tp.241]. The literal sense of the phrase in T is 'to be luminous inside.' redup. TLANĒC(I)

TLATLANĒXTIHTOC something lustrous / resplandece (Z) [(2)Zp.109,215]. See TLANĒXTIĀ, the verb O.

TLATLĀN(I) to win (in gambling) / gana (T) [(3)Tp.236]. redup. TLĀN(I)

TLATLĀNIC someone defeated / vencido (Z) [(2)Zp.128,215]. See TLĀN(I).

TLATLĀNĪHUA nonact. TLATLĀN(I)

TLATLĀNILIĀ applic. TLATLĀN(I)

TLATLAPACA for something to break into bits / hacerse pedazos el pan o las vasijas de barro o de vidrio (M) [(1)Cf.74r]. See TLAPAC-TLI, TLAPĀN(I).

TLATLAPATZ(A) *vt* to break something to bits / despedazar o quebrantar algo en muchas partes (M) [(1)Cf.74r]. See TLAPĀN(I).

TLĀTLAPOĀ *vrefl* to keep coming open / ábrese y cerrada se vuelve a abrir continuadamente (C) [(1)Cf.72v]. This contrasts

with TLAHTLAPOĀ 'for various things to
open.' redup. TLAPOĀ
TLATLAPOUHTOC something open,
aperture / abierto, abertura (Z)
[(2)Zp.3,215]. Z has PŌ for POUH. See
TLAPOHU(I), the verb O.
TLATLĀTIĀNI someone who hides
something, murderer / el que ... esconde
alguna cosa (M), matón (T) [(1)Tp.236]. See
TLĀTIĀ.
TLATLATILIĀ *vrefl,vt* to build a fire to
warm oneself; to burn something in the
course of laying a curse on someone /
hacer lumbre para se calentar (M), lo
quema (aceite para que le caiga maldad) (T)
[(3)Tp.210]. See TLATIĀ.
TLATLATILILIĀ applic. TLATLATILIĀ
TLATLATILĪLŌ nonact. TLATLATILIĀ
TLATLATILIZ-TLI the act of burning
something / quemada (Z) [(2)Zp.104,215].
Z's gloss does not precisely reflect the
literal sense of this item. This contrasts
with TLATLĀTILIZ-TLI 'the act of hiding
something.' See TLATIĀ.
TLATLĀTILIZ-TLI the act of hiding
something / escondite (Z) [(2)Zp.55,215].
Z's gloss does not precisely reflect the
literal sense of this item. This contrasts
with TLATLATILIZ-TLI 'the act of burning something.' See TLĀTIĀ.
TLATLĀTLAUHTILIĀ *vt* to pray for
someone / ruega (por otro) (Z)
[(2)Zp.111,222]. See TLĀTLAUHTIĀ.
TLATLĀTLAUHTILIZ-TLI prayer, suppli-
cation / oración, ruego, o suplicación (M)
[(1)Cf.47v, (4)Zp.91,118,178,215]. See
TLĀTLAUHTIĀ.
TLATLATZĪN(I) for it to thunder / tronar
cuando llueve o cae rayo (M) [(1)Cf.109r,
(1)Zp.125]. See TLATZĪN(I).
TLATLATZĪNILIZ-TLI thunderclap /
trueno de rayo (M) [(1)Cf.109r]. See
TLATLATZĪN(I).
TLATLATZĪNĪLLŌ-TL thunderclap / trueno
(Z) [(2)Zp.126,215]. See TLATZĪNIĀ, -YŌ.
TLĀTLAUHTIĀ *vrefl,vt* to pray; to pray to
someone or implore someone for something, to plead with someone / ruega, ora
(T), hacer oración o rezar (M), rogar por
otro (M) T's reflexive use of this is synonymous with M's use of it with the prefix

TLA-. In polite speech this is an overblown
but conventional way of saying 'to address
someone.' Z marks the A of the second
syllable long as well as that of the first, but
the other sources agree that it is short.
TLATLAXĪHUA nonact. TLATLAC(I)
TLATLAXĪTIĀ caus. TLATLAC(I)
TLATLAXIZ-TLI cough / tos (T) [(1)Tp.236,
(2)Zp.124,215, (2)Xp.95]. See TLATLAC(I).
TLATLĀX-TLI something cast or hurled
down, something rejected, aborted, plowed
under (of land) / cosa arrojada o que se le
cayó a alguno, o tierra arada y labrada, o
criatura abortada y echada a sabiendas (M)
[(1)Cf.47r]. C and M also have the variant
TLATLĀZ-TLI, and moreover, this is
synonymous with TLATLĀZAL-LI. See
TLĀZ(A).
TLATLĀZ(A) to lay eggs / poner huevos la
gallina (M) See TLĀZ(A).
TLATLĀZAL-LI something cast down /
cosa arrojada (C) [(1)Cf.47r]. This is
synonymous with TLATLĀX-TLI and
TLATLĀZ-TLI. See TLĀZ(A).
TLATLĀZCĀTZAHTZI to cackle / clo-
quea, cacarea (Z) [(3)Zp.22,28,215]. See
TLATLĀZ(A), TZAHTZI.
TLATLAZOHTLAL-LI someone, something beloved / cosa o persona amada (C)
[(1)Cf.46r]. See TLAZOHTLA.
TLATLĀZ-TLI something cast or hurled
down, something rejected, aborted, or
plowed under (of land) / cosa arrojada por
hay o cosa que se le cayó a alguno o criatura abortada y echada voluntariosamente
(M) [(1)Cf.47r]. C and M also have the
variant TLATLĀX-TLI, and moreover, this
is synonymous with TLATLĀZAL-LI. See
TLĀZ(A).
TLATLEHUĀTZ something broiled, toasted
/ asado, tostado (Z) [(3)Zp.14,124,215]. See
TLEHUĀTZ(A).
TLATLĪLĒUHTOC for something to be so
far away that it appears as a dark object /
lejos, lejano está negreando [(1)Zp.216]. See
TLĪL-LI, ĒHU(A), the verb O.
TLATOCA to sow / siembra (T) [(1)Tp.237].
See TŌCA.
TLATŌCALIZ-TLI the act of sowing /
siembra (Z) [(2)Zp.115,216]. See
TLATŌCA.

TLATŌCALLAH sown cornfield / campo sembrado de maíz (Z) [(1)Zp.216]. See TLATŌCA, -TLAH.

TLATŌCALŌNI staff for punching holes for sowing seed / sembrador (palo), punzón (Z) [(2)Zp.114,216]. See TLATŌCA.

TLATŌCCUAHU(I)-TL staff for punching holes for sowing seed, digging stick / sembrador (palo), coa (Z) [(2)Zp.114,216]. See TLATŌCA, CUAHU(I)-TL.

TLATŌCQUI sower / sembrador (Z) [(2)Zp.114,216]. This contrasts with TLAHTOHQUI 'ruler.'

TLATŌC-TLI something planted, sown, buried / cosa enterrada, plantada, o sembrada (M) [(2)Tp.183,237]. See TŌCA.

TLATOHTOMALIZ-TLI action of loosening something / acción de desatar (Z) [(1)Zp.216]. See TOHTOM(A).

TLATOHTOMAL-LI something loosened, undone / desatado (Z) [(2)Zp.41,216]. See TOHTOM(A).

TLATOHTON-TLI something loosened, undone / cosa desatada, desabrochada, desnudada o desenvuelta (M) [(1)Tp.236]. See TOHTOM(A).

TLATOMĀHUAL-LI something fattened, fatness / cebón o cosa engordada (M), gordura (Z) [(2)Zp.63,216]. See TOMĀHUA.

TLATŌPALHUIĀ to collect rent, taxes / cobra (Z) [(2)Zp.28,216].

TLATŌPALHUIHQUI tax collector / cobrador (Z) [(2)Zp.28,216]. See TLATŌPALHUIĀ.

TLATOPŌN firearm / arma de fuego (Z) [(7)Zp.13,27,122,125,216,229]. See TOPŌN(I).

TLATOPŌN(I) for it to thunder / truena (Z) [(1)Zp.216]. See TOPŌN(I).

TLATOPŌNIĀ to shoot off a firearm / tira (con arma) (Z) [(2)Zp.122,216]. See TOPŌNIĀ.

TLATOPŌNILIZ-TLI barrage of gunfire or thunder / tronadero (Z) [(2)Zp.125,216]. See TOPŌN(I).

TLATOQUIHQUI stoker, fireman / fogonero (Z) [(2)Zp.60,216]. M has synonymous *tlatoquiani*. See TOQUIĀ.

TLATOTŌNĪLLŌ-TL summer / verano (Z) [(2)Zp.128,216]. M has *tlatotonilli*

'something warmed, sunburned.' See TOTŌNIĀ, -YŌ.

TLATŌTOQUIXOC-TLI cooking pot / olla para poner carne, frijoles (T) [(1)Tp.237]. See TOQUIĀ, XOC-TLI.

TLATQUIHUAH proprietor / dueño o señor (C) [(3)Cf.55r,87v]. See TLATQUI-TL.

TLATQUITIĀ *vt* to make something the property of someone / enajenar algo o enviar alguna cosa a otro (M) [(2)Cf.58r]. M has this with a direct object prefix plus an oblique reflexive prefix, meaning 'to appropriate something.' See TLATQUI-TL.

TLATQUITILIĀ applic. TLATQUITIĀ

TLATQUI-TL property, belongings / hacienda o vestidos (M) This is conventionally paired with ĀXCĀ(I)-TL 'property,' the whole phrase referring to one's property, wealth, estate. See (I)TQUI.

-TLATTAYA *necessarily possessed form* one's vision / mi vista, mi potencia visiva (C for first pers. sg. possessor) [(2)Cf.50r]. See (I)TTA.

TLATZACCĀN at the end, conclusion, last of all / al cabo, a fin, o a la postre (M) [(3)Cf.96r,107v,131v]. The final consonant of the second syllable has lost its labiality. See TZACU(A), -CĀN.

TLATZACU(A) to close, to make restitution, to suffer punishment for something / cierro, o pago y lasto algo (C for first pers. sg. subject), pagar por otro, expiar la falta de alguien (S) [(2)Cf.17v,62v]. See TZACU(A).

TLATZACUILTIĀ to punish someone / castigar o justiciar a alguno (M) [(4)Cf.45r,62v,90v,113r]. caus. TLATZACU(A)

TLATZACUILTILIZ-TLI punishment / castigo, coraje (Z) [(2)Zp.26,216]. See TLATZACUILTIĀ.

TLATZACUILTILŌNI someone deserving of punishment / digno y merecedor de castigo (M) [(2)Cf.45r]. See TLATZACUILTIĀ.

TLATZCAN cypress / ciprés (M), cedro o ciprés (C) This is abundantly attested in C. It also appears in Z with the absolutive suffix -TLI, but this is idiosyncratic to Z.

TLATZCANCAYŌ-TL something pertaining to cypress trees / lo concerniente a

los cipreses (S for TLATZCANYŌ-TL)
[(1)Cf.53v]. This appears in C as an example of a derivational process and without a gloss, but according to C it is synonymous with TLATZCANYŌ-TL, which is glossed in S. See TLATZCAN, -YŌ.

TLATZCANEH someone who possesses a cypress tree / dueño de un ciprés (S) [(1)Cf.55v, (1)Rp.45]. See TLATZCAN.

TLATZCANHUAH someone who possesses cypress trees / dueño, poseedor de cipreses (S) [(1)Cf.55v, (1)Rp.45]. See TLATZCAN.

TLATZCANTI to turn into a cypress / volverse ciprés (C) [(1)Cf.58v, Rp.47]. See TLATZCAN.

TLATZCANYŌ-TL something pertaining to cypress trees / lo concerniente a los cipreses (S) [(1)Cf.53v]. This is synonymous with TLATZCANCAYŌ-TL. See TLATZCAN, -YŌ.

TLATZCOTŌN(A) vt to break, snap something / quebrar hilo, cordel o soga (M), lo revienta, lo rompe (T) [(3)Tp.210]. See TLATZĪN(I), COTŌN(A).

TLATZCOTŌNALŌ nonact. TLATZ-COTŌN(A)

TLATZCOTŌN(I) to break, snap / quebrarse el hilo (M), se revienta (T) [(1)Tp.237]. See TLATZCOTŌN(A).

TLATZCOTŌNILIĀ applic. TLATZ-COTŌN(A)

TLATZCUEPŌNILIĀ vt to beat something or someone hard / le pega fuerte (T) [(3)Tp.210]. See TLATZĪN(I), CUEPŌNIĀ.

TLATZCUEPŌNILILIĀ applic. TLATZ-CUEPŌNILIĀ

TLATZCUEPŌNILĪLŌ nonact. TLATZ-CUEPŌNILIĀ

TLATZETZELOLIZ-TLI shaking, sifting / cernidura o sacudimiento (M) [(2)Zp.112,216]. In one of two attestations the vowel of the fourth syllable is marked long. See TZETZELOĀ.

TLATZETZELŌL-LI something sifted, strained, filtered, shaken / cosa cernida o sacudida (M) [(2)Zp.27,216]. See TZETZELOĀ.

TLATZETZELŌNI strainer, sieve / cedazo, coladera (Z) [(2)Zp.26,216]. See TZETZELOĀ.

TLATZHUĪTEQU(I) vt; pret: **TLATZ-HUĪTEC** to beat someone / le pega (T) [(3)Tp.210]. See HUĪTEQU(I).

TLATZHUĪTEQUĪHUA nonact. TLATZ-HUĪTEQU(I)

TLATZHUĪTEQUILIĀ applic. TLATZ-HUĪTEQU(I)

TLATZIHU(I) to be lazy, slothful, idle / tener pereza o ser perezoso (M)

TLATZIHUILIĀ vt for something to make someone apathetic or disgusted / le da flojera, pereza (T) [(1)Cf.64r, (3)Tp.210]. C glosses this as synonymous with TLA-TZIHUIĀ. altern. applic. TLATZIHU(I)

TLATZIHUILILIĀ applic. TLATZIHUILIĀ

TLATZIHUILĪLŌ nonact. TLATZIHUILIĀ

TLATZIHUILIZ-TLI laziness, sloth, apathy / pereza (M) [(1)Tp.237, (2)Zp.60,217]. See TLATZIHU(I).

TLATZIHUĪTIĀ caus. TLATZIHU(I)

TLATZILHUIĀ vt to be weary of something or someone, to be apathetic about or disgusted by something / aborrecer a otro (M), aborrecer algo que de en rostro, como la comida el enfermo (C) [(2)Cf.64r]. altern. applic. TLATZIHU(I)

TLATZILĪN jingle bell / cascabel (Z) [(2)Zp.26,217]. M has tlatzilinilli referring to a bell. See TZILĪN(I).

TLATZĪN(I) to make an explosive sound, to thunder, to sizzle / sonar algo reventado así como huevo cuando lo asan o cosa semejante (M), truena (Z) [(1)Zp.217]. Z also has impersonal TLATLATZĪN(I) with the sense 'to thunder.'

TLATZĪNIĀ vt to hit or spank someone / le pega, le da sus nalgadas (T) [(3)Tp.210]. See TLATZĪN(I).

TLATZĪNILIĀ applic. TLATZĪNIĀ

TLATZĪNILŌ nonact. TLATZĪNIĀ

TLATZĪNTLAN below, beneath, underneath / abajo o debajo (M) T has the additional gloss 'in the south,' reflecting local geography, since Tetelcingo is situated on land that drops away to lower altitudes to the south. See TZĪN-TLI, -TLAN.

TLATZIUH someone idle, lazy, slothful / haragán, flojo, zonzo, zoquete (Z) [(3)Zp.66,132,217]. See TLATZIHU(I).

TLATZIUHCĀMĀHU(A) vt to infect someone with one's laziness / lo entretiene, contagia a otro con la pereza (T) [(3)Tp.210]. See TLATZIHU(I), MĀHU(A).

TLATZIUHCĀYŌ-TL sloth, laziness / pereza (M) [(1)Tp.134]. See TLATZIHU(I), -YŌ.

TLATZIUHQUI someone lazy, slothful / perezoso (M) X shortens this to TLATZQUI. See TLATZIHU(I).

TLATZMOLĪN(I) for everything to sprout anew / todo retoñece (C) [(1)Cf.36v]. See (I)TZMOLĪN(I).

TLATZOĀ vt to beat something / lo bate (T) [(3)Tp.210].

TLATZOHYĀYALIZ-TLI stench, something disgusting / apestilencia (Z) [(2)Zp.12,217]. M has tzoyayaliztli 'smell of burnt feathers or cloth.' See TZO-TL, (I)HYĀYA.

TLATZŌLCĀN narrow place / lugar reducido (Z) [(3)Zp.77,107,217]. See TZŌLOĀ, -CĀN.

TLATZOLHUIĀ applic. TLATZOĀ

TLATZŌLIHUI narrow place / lugar reducido, angosto (T) [(1)Tp.237]. See TZŌLIHU(I).

TLATZŌLŌ nonact. TLATZOĀ

TLATZONICZALIZ-TLI the act of trampling / pisada (Z) [(2)Zp.99,217]. See TZONICZA.

TLATZONTEC-TLI judgement / cosa juzgada y sentenciada (M) [(1)Bf.10r]. See TZONTEQU(I).

TLATZOPITĪLŌNI punch, awl / puya, punzón (Z) [(2)Zp.104,217]. See TZOPITIĀ.

TLATZOTZONALIZ-TLI the act of making music by striking or plucking an instrument, the act of striking something / el acto de tañer atabales, órganos, harpa, etc., o el acto de dar golpes con alguna cosa (M) [(2)Zp.87,217]. See TZOTZON(A).

TLATZOTZONALŌNI musical instrument / instrumento (Z) [(1)Zp.217]. See TZOTZON(A).

TLATZOTZONANIH group of musicians / grupo de músicos (Z) [(2)Zp.64,217]. This nonstandard plural form implies TLATZOTZONANI 'musician,' the regular plural form of which would be formed by adding -MEH. See TZOTZON(A).

TLATZOTZONĪL-LI music / música (X) [(3)Xp.95]. See TZOTZON(A).

TLATZOTZONQUI musician / atabalero o tañedor de órganos (M), músico (Z) [(2)Zp.87,217]. See TLATZOTZONANIH.

TLATZOTZON-TLI something, someone beaten upon; a type of drum / atabal tañido, o persona apuñeada, o cosa golpeada, o cosa tupida y apretada (M), instrumento (de música) (Z) [(2)Zp.72,217]. In both attestations Z marks the vowel of the third syllable long, but it should not be. See TZOTZON(A).

TLATZOYŌNĪL-LI something fried / cosa frita (M) [(2)Zp.61,217]. Z also has a short form TLATZOYŌN. Both attestations mark the vowel of the second syllable long, but it should not be. See TZOYŌNIĀ.

TLĀUHQUECHŌL rich red plumage; bird of such plumage, roseate spoonbill or flamingo / pluma rica y bermeja (M) ave acuática muy parecida al pato y notable por el esplandor de sus plumas rojas (S) [(1)Cf.76v]. See TLĀHU(I)-TL, QUECHŌL-LI.

TLAXAMĀNĪL-LI something cracked or splintered, or something split (such as a shingle) / cabeza machucada, etc., tablas menudas, o astillas largas (M), tejamanil (Z) [(4)Zp.120,217,223]. Under influence from Spanish teja 'roof tile,' Z has the variant TEXAMĀNĪL-LI. See XAMĀNIĀ.

TLAXCALCHĪHU(A) to make tortillas or bread / hacer tortillas o pan (K) [(2)Cf.511]. See TLAXCAL-LI, CHĪHU(A).

TLAXCALCHĪHUALŌYĀN bakery / lugar donde se hace pan, panadería (C) [(1)Cf.511]. See TLAXCALCHĪHU(A), -YĀN.

TLAXCALCHĪHUCĀN bakery / panadería (C) [(1)Cf.51v]. See TLAXCALCHĪHU(A), -CĀN.

TLAXCALHUIĀ vt to make tortillas for someone / hacer tortillas de maíz para otro (M) [(3)Tp.192]. applic. TLAXCALOĀ

TLAXCALHUILIĀ applic. TLAXCALHUIĀ

TLAXCALHUĪLŌ nonact. TLAXCALHUIĀ

TLAXCALĪXCHĪLLOH enchilada, tortilla covered with chili-seasoned sauce / enchilada (Z) [(2)Zp.51,217]. See TLAXCAL-LI, ĪX-TLI, CHĪL-LI, -YOH.

TLAXCALLĀN place name Tlaxcala This is

implied by TLAXCALTĒCA-TL 'person from Tlaxcala.' See TLAXCAL-LI, -TLĀN.

TLAXCAL-LI tortilla, baked bread / tortillas de maíz, o pan generalmente (M) In older texts TLAXCAL-LI often refers to bread in general; more recently it has increasingly been used to distinguish maize tortillas from raised wheat bread. See (I)XCA.

TLAXCALMAN(A) to make tortillas / hace tortilla, echa tortilla, tortillea (T) [(3)Tp.238]. See TLAXCAL-LI, MAN(A).

TLAXCALMANALŌ nonact. TLAX-CALMAN(A)

TLAXCALMANILIĀ applic. TLAX-CALMAN(A)

TLAXCALNAMACA See TLAXCAL-LI, NAMACA.

TLAXCALNAMACAC seller of bread, tortillas / vendedor de pan (C) [(1)Cf.51v]. See TLAXCAL-LI, NAMACA.

TLAXCALNAMACŌYĀN place where bread is sold / lugar donde venden pan (M) [(1)Cf.51r]. See TLAXCAL-LI, NAMACA, -YĀN.

TLAXCALOĀ to make tortillas / hacer tortillas (M) See TLAXCAL-LI.

TLAXCALŌLŌ nonact. TLAXCALOĀ

TLAXCALPĪQUILŌNI napkin for wrapping up tortillas / servilleta (Z) [(2)Zp.115,217]. See TLAXCAL-LI, PĪQUILŌNI.

TLAXCALPŌPOZŌN dish of shredded tortillas boiled in broth / chilaquiles (T) [(1)Tp.238]. Because of the general loss of final N in T, the final one here is not attested but can be restored from the related verb. See TLAXCAL-LI, POZŌN(I).

TLAXCALTĒCA-TL pl: **TLAXCAL-TĒCAH** someone from Tlaxcala / natural de Tlaxcala (K) [(1)Bf.11r, (1)Cf.120v]. See TLAXCAL-LI.

TLAXCALTOTŌNIĀ to heat tortillas / calienta tortillas (T) [(3)Tp.238]. See TLAXCAL-LI, TOTŌNIĀ.

TLAXCALTOTOPOCH-TLI tostada, fried tortilla / tortilla tostada (T) [(1)Tp.238]. See TLAXCAL-LI, TOTOPOCH-TLI.

TLAXCALZOL-LI old dry tortilla / tortilla seca (T) [(1)Tp.238]. T is missing the internal L in the Nahuatl-to-Spanish side of the dictionary but has it in the Spanish-to-Nahuatl side. See TLAXCAL-LI, -ZOL-LI.

TLAXĒLOĀ for a chicken to scratch, scattering earth around / rasca (gallina) (Z) [(2)Zp.105,217]. See XĒLOĀ.

TLAXELŌLIZ-TLI division, appointment / el acto de dividir y partir alguna cosa o partija (M), separación, división (Z) [(3)Zp.47,115,217]. See XELOĀ.

TLAXHUIZ-TLI boil, tumor / divieso, incordio, o nacido (M) [(5)Zp.28,47,87,123,218]. In two of five attestations Z marks the vowel of the second syllable long. See (I)XHUI.

TLAXĪCŌLIZ-TLI support / soporte (Z) [(2)Zp.117,217]. This seems to be related to XĪCOĀ, but the only sense they have in common would seem to be one of endurance or tolerance of a burden.

TLĀXILIĀ vrefl,vt to abort, to cast something off; to throw something away from someone, to cause someone to abort / abortar, deshacerse de algo, dimitar de un cargo (S), hacer abortar a una mujer (S) applic. TLĀZ(A)

TLĀXILILIĀ applic. TLĀXILIĀ

TLĀXILĪLŌ nonact. TLĀXILIĀ

TLAXĪPĒHUAL-LI something peeled, the bark or shell of something / cosa desollada o descortezada, mazorca de maíz deshojada, o cortezas de pino y de oyametl para hacer buena brasa (M), cáscara de encino (Z) [(1)Zp.217]. See XĪPĒHU(A).

TLAXITĪNILIZ-TLI great fall, ruin, chasm, precipice / precipicio (Z) [(2)Zp.101,217]. See XITĪN(I).

TLAXITĪNĪLLŌ-TL precipice, falling of something, collapse / derrumbe [(2)Zp.41,217]. See XITĪNIĀ, -YŌ.

TLAXIUHTLATLA to be hot / hace calor (Z) [(2)Zp.24,217]. See XIUHTLATLA.

TLĀXŌ altern. nonact. TLĀZ(A)

TLAXOCOLIĀ to make things go sour, curdle, ferment / el que aceda o hace agria alguna cosa (M) lo hace acedo (T) [(1)Tp.238]. See XOCOYA.

TLAXOCOLTILŌNI leavening / levadura, se hace fuerza (Z) [(2)Zp.76,218]. In one of two attestations Z marks the vowel of the second syllable long. See TLAXOCOLIĀ.

TLAXOLOPIHHUILIĀ vt to slander someone / lo calumnia (Z) [(2)Zp.24,196]. See XOLOPIH-TLI, -HUIĀ.

TLAXONĒPALHUIĀ *vrefl,vt* to braid one's hair; to braid someone's hair / se hace trenzas (T), le hace sus trenzas (T) [(6)Tp.160,210]. See TLAXONĒPAL-LI, -HUIĀ.

TLAXONĒPALHUILIĀ applic. TLA-XONĒPALHUIĀ

TLAXONĒPALHUĪLŌ nonact. TLA-XONĒPALHUIĀ

TLAXONĒPAL-LI *pl:* **-TIN** braid, plait / trenza (T) [(7)Tp.238].

TLAXOPOCH-TLI *pl:* **-MEH** bird's nest / nido de gallina (T) [(1)Tp.238]. This specifically refers to a nest made in a depression on the ground. See XOPOCHTIC.

TLAXOXŌHUIYA for things to get green, for leaves to come out / verdeguear el prado que se está riendo (M) [(1)Cf.36v]. See XOXŌHUIYA.

TLAXQUI-TL something roasted in coals / cosa asada en las brasas o en el rescoldo (M) [(1)Cf.47r, (1)Rp.41]. See (I)XCA.

TLAXTLĀHU(A) *vt* to pay for something / pagar (X) [(3)Xp.77]. See (I)XTLĀHU(A).

TLAXTLĀHUALIZ-TLI payment, restitution / el acto de pagar o restituir algo (M) [(2)Zp.93,218]. See (I)XTLĀHU(A).

TLAXTLĀHUIĀ *vrefl,vt* to be self-satisfied; to pay for something / pagarse, o satisfacer así mismo (M), galardonar o restituir lo que debo a otro (M), lo paga, lo recompensa (Z) [(3)Cf.27v, (3)Zp.93,106,196]. X gives the truncated form TLAXTLĀHUI as an expression of thanks. See (I)XTLĀHU(A).

TLAXTLĀHUĪL-LI payment, restitution, wages / paga, jornal, soldada, restitución, o galardón (M) [(2)Tp.134,238, (5)Zp.93,113,118,218]. See (I)XTLĀHU(A).

TLAXTLĀUHQUI one who makes payment / pagador (Z) [(2)Zp.93,218]. See (I)XTLĀHU(A).

TLAXXĪM(A) *pret:* **TLAXXĪN** to commit adultery / adulterar [(2)Bf.11r]. M has this with a single *x*, but B has *xx*, which makes it contrast with TLA-XĪM(A) 'to plane something'< XĪM(A).

TLAYACAC at the beginning / al principio (C) [(1)Cf.108r]. M has several items with

tlayaca as an element sharing the sense of 'to go first.' See YAC(A)-TL, -C(O).

TLAYACĀNALIZ-TLI privilege, advantage, power, authority / primado o ventaja (M), poder, autoridad, gobernación, reino (Z) [(5)Zp.17,63,100,107,218]. See YACĀN(A).

TLAYACĀNALTIĀ *vt* to advance something / lo adelanta (T,Z) [(3)Tp.211, (2)Zp.5,196]. See YACĀN(A).

TLAYACĀNCĀUH constable, councilman / alguacil, regidor (Z) [(1)Zp.218]. See TLAYACĀNQUI.

TLAYACĀNQUETZ(A) *vrefl* to advance, to take the lead / se adelanta (Z) [(2)Zp.5,173]. See YACĀN(A), QUETZ(A).

TLAYACĀNQUI *pl:* **TLĀTLA-YACĀNQUIH** person in authority, leader, boss / autoridad, mayor, jefe, patrón, superior, gobernador (Z) [(1)Tp.238, (2)Zp.63,218]. M has synonymous *teyacanqui*. T gives a reduplicated plural rather than the regular -QUEH plural for this type of derived noun. The final glottal stop is given here by analogy with other reduplicated plurals. Because of T's general loss of glottal stops in word-final position, it is not directly attested. See YACĀN(A).

TLAYAHUALOĀ to go in a procession around something / rodear algo andando alrededor de el (C) [(3)Cf.62v]. M appears to have this as a transitive verb, but M's gloss shows the extra *tla* to be not the nonspecific object prefix TLA- but a distributive reduplication of the first syllable of the verb, TLAHTLAYAHUALOĀ 'to take many turns, to rotate.' See YAHUALOĀ.

TLAYAHUALŌCHTIĀ altern. caus. TLAYAHUALOĀ

TLAYAHUALŌLTIĀ caus. TLAYAHUALOĀ

TLAYĒCCĀMPA to the right-hand side / a mano derecha (M) [(3)Cf.93v,94v,131r]. See YĒCCĀN, -PA.

TLAYECOLTIĀ *vrefl,vt* to provide for oneself, to earn one's living; to serve others / buscar o grangear lo necesario a la vida (M), servir a otros (M) [(2)Cf.91r,108v]. See YECOĀ.

TLAYECOLTILIĀ applic. TLAYECOLTIĀ

-TLAYECOLTILŌCA *necessarily possessed form* the service of someone / servicio de alguien (K) [(1)Bf.3r]. See TLAYECOLTIĀ.

TLAYEHYECŌLIZ-TLI test, proof, evidence / ensaye o prueba del que se impone o ensaya (M) [(3)Zp.41,103,206]. See YEHYECOĀ.

TLĀY(I) to break ground for planting / labrar la tierra para sembrarla (M) [(2)Zp.18,207]. This is attested as an element of the synonymous compound TLAĪXTLĀY(I).

TLAYŌCOX-TLI something created, invented / cosa inventada (M) [(1)Bf.2r]. See YŌCOY(A).

TLAYŌCOYANI inventor, creator / inventador ... o inventor e industrioso (M) [(2)Bf.5v,9r]. See YŌCOY(A).

TLAYOCXITĪL-LI something cooked / cocido (Z) [(2)Zp.28,218]. This corresponds to T's TLAHUICXITĪL-LI. See YOCXITIĀ.

TLAYOHUA to get dark / anochecer (K) See YOHUA.

TLAYOHUAC last night / anoche (Z) [(3)Zp.11,89,218]. In both attestations Z marks the vowel of the second syllable long, but it should not be. See YOHUAC.

TLAYOHUAQUILIĀ to get dark, for night to fall / anochece (T) [(1)Tp.239]. See TLAYOHUA.

TLAYOHUAQUILIZ-TLI darkness / obscuridad, tineblas (T) [(1)Tp.239]. See TLAYOHUAQUILIĀ.

TLAYOHUATICAH to be getting dark / está obscureciendo (T) [(2)Tp.239]. See TLAYOHUA, the verb CĀ.

TLAYOHUAYĀN obscurity, place of darkness / en tinieblas (C), obscuridad, obscuro (Z) [(1)Cf.99r, (3)Zp.90,218]. See TLAYOHUA, -YĀN.

TLAYOHUAYĀNĪLLŌ-TL darkness, obscurity / obscuridad, tinieablas (Z) [(2)Zp.90,218]. See TLAYOHUAYĀN.

TLAYOHUAYĀNTIĀ to get dark, for night to fall / se hace de noche, anochece (Z) [(3)Zp.11,89,218]. See TLAYOHUAYĀN.

TLAYŌLCUĪTILIZ-TLI confession / confesión (Z) [(2)Zp.32,218]. M has synonymous *teyolcuitiliztli*. See YŌLCUĪTIĀ.

TLAYŌLCUĪTĪLŌNI confessional guide / confesionario (Z) [(2)Zp.32,218]. M has synonymous *teyolcuitiloni*. See YŌLCUĪTIĀ.

TLAYŌLĒHUALIZ-TLI invitation / invitación (Z) [(2)Zp.72,218]. M has *teyoleualiztli* with the somewhat different gloss 'the incitement or provocation of someone.' See YŌLĒHU(A).

TLAYŌLITIĀ to give birth / da a luz, se pare (Z) [(2)Zp.39,218]. See YŌL(I).

TLAYŌLLOHCĒHUIĀ to satisfy someone, to put someone to rest / lo contenta (Z) [(2)Zp.33,218]. See YŌLCĒHUIĀ.

TLAYŌLLOHPACHOHQUI someone who brings consolation / consolador (Z) [(2)Zp.32,164]. See YŌLLOH-TLI, PACHOĀ.

TLAYŌLLOH-TLI core, center, pith / corazón, centro del maíz o madero (T) [(2)Tp.239]. See YŌLLOH-TLI.

TLĀZ(A) *vrefl,vt* to fling oneself down; to cast or hurl someone down, to put someone out of office, to evict someone, to throw something aside, for a chicken to lay eggs / echarse por esos suelos o de alto abajo despeñándose (M), echar a otro en el suelo o derribarlo, o deponer y privar a alguno del oficio o señorío que tiene (M), tirar tiro, o arrojar algo, o poner huevos la gallina (M) In the case of 'to lay eggs,' the nonspecific object prefix TLA- can be seen as fused with the verb stem forming an intransitive verb TLATLĀZ(A).

TLAZĀLIZTĀC bed sheet / sábana (Z) [(2)Zp.112,214]. See TLAZĀL-LI, IZTĀC.

TLAZĀL-LI something sticky such as bird lime; clothing, cloth / liga para cazar o prender pájaros (M), ropa, trapo, tela, género (Z) [(8)Zp.104,111,120,125,172, 184,214]. This is abundantly attested in Z with the sense of 'clothing, cloth.' M has only the 'bird lime' sense, which in the sources for this dictionary are supported by derivations from ZĀLOĀ 'to glue, join something.'

TLĀZALŌ altern. nonact. TLĀZ(A)

TLAZĀLŌLIZ-TLI act of joining or glueing two things together, mosaic work / pegadura de una cosa con otra, o el acto de pegar alguna cosa a otra (M) [(1)Bf.10v]. See ZĀLOĀ.

TLAZĀLŌLTIĀ *vt* to adjust, augment something / lo ajusta, lo añade (T) [(3)Tp.210]. See ZĀLOĀ.

TLAZĀLŌLTILIĀ applic. TLAZĀLŌLTIĀ

TLAZĀLŌLTĪLŌ nonact. TLAZĀLŌLTIĀ

TLĀZALTIĀ *vt* to force someone to give something up / hacer dejar algo a otro con fuerza (M) [(1)Cf.62r]. caus. TLĀZ(A)

TLAZCALTĪL-LI child placed under the care of a tutor, someone adopted / prohijado, ahijado (Z) [(3)Zp.7,102,161]. Literally this just means 'someone reared.' See (I)ZCALTIĀ.

*TLAZOĀ This verb is nowhere attested as a free form but is the derivational base of the element TLAZOH-, which combines with other verbs by means of the ligature -CĀ- and has to do with value, love, and affection.

TLAZOHCĀMACHILIĀ *vt* to thank someone for something / recompensa un favor, le da gracias (Z) [(1)Tp.209, (3)Zp.64,106,196]. T has this applicative form but also has synonymous TLAZOHCĀMATILIĀ. applic. TLAZOHCĀMAT(I)

TLAZOHCĀMĀCHILTIĀ altern. caus. TLAZOHCĀMAT(I)

TLAZOHCĀMACHĪTIĀ altern. caus. TLAZOHCĀMAT(I)

TLAZOHCĀMAT(I) *vt; pret:* **TLAZOH-CĀMAH** to thank someone for something / ser agradecido o agradecer algo a otro (M) See TLAZOĀ, MAT(I).

TLAZOHCĀMATI *expression of thanks* gracias, muchas gracias (Z) [(1)Tp.235, (2)Zp.64,214]. In Z this has a final -C. See TLAZOHCĀMAT(I).

TLAZOHCĀMATILIĀ *vt* to thank someone / le da gracias (T) [(3)Tp.210]. See TLAZOHCĀMACHILIĀ.

TLAZOHCĀMATILILIĀ applic. TLAZOHCĀMATILIĀ

TLAZOHCĀMATILĪLŌ nonact. TLAZOHCĀMATILIĀ

TLAZOHPIL-LI someone of noble, legitimate birth / hijo o hija legítimos (M), un principal (C) [(1)Cf.117v]. See TLAZOH-TLI, PIL-LI.

TLAZOHTI for something to be rare, precious, for merchandise to be high priced / valer caro lo que se vende (M), escaso, escasea (Z) [(1)Bf.9r, (2)Zp.55,214]. See TLAZOH-TLI.

TLAZOHTILIĀ *vrefl,vt* to hold oneself in high regard; to value something highly, to put a high price on one's merchandise / tenerse en mucho y estimarse (M), tener y estimar en mucho alguna cosa o vender caro (M), encarecer algo ... lo que se compra y vende (M) T gives TLAZOHTLA as the derivational source for this, in which case TL is replaced by T before the applicative suffix. applic. TLAZOHTLA

TLAZOHTILIZ-TLI preciousness, expensiveness, love, affection / careza (M), amor, cariño (T) [(1)Tp.235]. See TLAZOHTI.

TLAZOHTLA *vrefl,vt* to love oneself; to love someone / amarse así mismo (M), amar a otro (M) See TLAZOH-TLI.

TLAZOHTLALIZ-TLI love, affection / cariño (Z) [(2)Zp.25,178,214,222,232]. M has this in a phrase about being worthy of love. See TLAZOHTLA.

TLAZOHTLALŌ nonact. TLAZOHTLA

-TLAZOHTLALŌCĀ *necessarily possessed form* the love with which one is loved / el amor con que yo soy amado (C for first pers. sg. possessor) [(1)Cf.48v]. This appears in a discussion of the distinction between derivations based on the nonactive form plus -CĀ and requiring a possessive prefix and those based on the active form with -LIZ-TLI, in this case TLAZOHTLALIZ-TLI 'love toward someone else.'

TLAZOHTLALŌNI someone, something lovable / cosa amable (M) See TLAZOHTLA.

TLAZOHTLALTIĀ *vt* to reconcile enemies / hacer amigos a los enemistados (M) [(1)Cf.63r]. caus. TLAZOHTLA

TLAZOHTLANQUI fair, fine, well-finished / muy linda (C for compound with HUEL) [(1)Cf.117v]. See TLAZOH-TLI, TLAM(I).

TLAZOHTLAPŌLOĀ *vt* to love someone out of the depths of one's unworthiness / yo pecador y malo amo a alguno (M for first pers. sg. subject) See TLAZOHTLA, -PŌLOĀ.

TLAZOH-TLI someone or something beloved, rare, or expensive / cosa preciosa o cara (M), querido (Z) T has what appears to be a plural form of this with -TIN, meaning 'drought.' See TLAZOĀ.

TLAZŌ-TL something perforated and strung

on a thread, something pierced and bled / cosa ensartada (M), cosa punzada (C), cosa sangrada (R) [(1)Cf.47r, (1)Rp.41]. See ZŌ.

TLAZŌZŌ-TL a string or series of beads or other perforated objects / cuentas ensartadas o cosa semejante (M), cosas ensartadas como perlas y cuentas (C) [(1)Cf.47r, (1)Rp.41]. See TLAZŌ-TL.

TLAZTALĒHUALLI rosy / color encarnado o rosado (M) [(1)Cf.76v]

TLE See TLE(H).

TLECĀHUIĀ *vt* to set fire to something / pegar fuego a alguna cosa (M) [(1)Cf.128v]. This contrasts with TLEHCAHUIĀ 'to ascend something.' See TLE-TL.

TLECAL-LI chimney, smoke vent, inferno / chimenea o humero (M), infierno (T) [(1)Bf.7r, (1)Tp.239]. See TLE-TL, CAL-LI.

TLECŌM(I)-TL *possessed form:* **-TLECŌN** fire pit, hearth, crucible / crisol para fundir oro (M), hornilla, fogón (Z), hornillo (Z) [(3)Zp.60,69,223]. Z also has the variant TLECŌN without an absolutive suffix. See TLE-TL, CŌM(I)-TL.

TLECUAHU(I)-TL *pl:* **-MEH** firebrand, coals, embers, firewood / artificio de palo para sacar fuego o tizón (M), brasas (T), leña (X) See TLE-TL, CUAHU(I)-TL.

TLECUEZALLŌ-TL spark, ember, blaze / llama de fuego (M), chispa (Z) [(2)Zp.39,223]. See TLE-TL.

TLECUIL(I)-TL *pl:* **-MEH** fire pit with three stones to support cooking vessels, hearth, oven / tlecuil, fogón, hornillo (T) [(1)Tp.239, (2)Zp.69,219]. M has *tlecuilli* 'hearth.' See TLE-TL, CUI.

TLECUĪLTIĀ *vt* to set something afire, to light something / prender (fuego, lumbre, vela, luz) [(3)Xp.77]. See TLE-TL, CUI.

TLE(H) *pl:* **TLEIHQUEH** what? / ¿qué? o ¿qué cosa? (C) According to C, this has a final glottal stop in phrases when the following word begins with a consonant and drops the glottal stop elsewhere. In some contexts it does not sustain its interrogative sense. With negation it means 'nothing.'

TLEHCAHUIĀ *vt* to raise something / subir algo arriba o en alto (M), lo sube, lo alza, lo levanta, lo eleva (T) This contrasts with TLECĀHUIĀ 'to set fire to something.' applic. TLEHCŌ

TLEHCAHUĪHUA nonact. TLEHCAHUIĀ

TLEHCAHUILIĀ *vt* to raise something for someone / se lo sube (T) [(4)Tp.211]. applic. TLEHCAHUIĀ

TLEHCAHUILILIĀ applic. TLEHCAHUILIĀ

TLEHCAHUILĪLŌ nonact. TLEHCAHUILIĀ

TLEHCŌ to ascend / subir arriba (M) In abundant attestation across sources the vowel of the second syllable is marked long only in two preterit forms in X. By form and meaning TLEHCŌ would seem to belong to a group of verbs ending in Ō such as PANŌ 'to cross a river' and TEMŌ 'to descend.' See AHCO.

TLEHCŌHUA nonact. TLEHCŌ

TLEHCŌLIZ-TLI ascent / el acto de subir (M), subida (Z) [(3)Zp.118,220]. Z does not mark the O long in either attestation. See TLEHCŌ.

TLEHCŌLTIĀ *vt* to raise something / subir alguna cosa arriba (M) [(2)Zp.118,196, (3)Xp.77]. caus. TLEHCŌ

TLEHUĀCQUI something toasted / tostado (T) [(1)Tp.239, (3)Xp.96]. See TLEHUĀQU(I).

TLEHUĀQU(I) *pret:* **TLEHUĀC** to toast or broil over a fire / tostarse, asarse (K) [(3)Cf.92v, (1)Tp.239, (3)Xp.96]. T has the reflex of a short vowel in the second syllable, despite having the reflex of a long vowel in the corresponding syllable of TLEHUĀCQUI. C marks the vowel long. See TLE-TL, HUĀQU(I).

TLEHUĀTZ(A) *vrefl,vt* se asa, se tuesta (tortilla, carne) (T), asar algo en asador o en parrillas (M) See TLE-TL, HUĀTZ(A).

TLEHZĀ something / algo, cosa, alguna cosa (Z) [(4)Zp.8,34,220]. See TLE(H), ZĀ.

TLEHZANNĒN to what end? what use? / ¿que provecho se sigue? o ¿que aprovecho ... lo que sea trabajado? [(3)Cf.112v,113r, 131v]. See TLE(H), ZANNĒN.

TLEIC, TLEĪCA to what end? why? / ¿a qué? o ¿para qué? (M), ¿por qué? (M), ¿de qué provecho? (C) [(2)Cf.113r]. C does not mark the I long in either of two attestations of TLEĪC. According to C TLEĪC is used only with the verb ĀY(I)) 'to do something.' See TLE(H), ĪC, ĪCA.

TLEĪCNĒN to what end? what use? / ¿de qué sirve? (C) [(2)Cf.113r]. See TLEĪC, NĒN.

TLEIHQUEH See TLE(H).

TLEIN what? / ¿qué? (M), ¿qué?, o ¿qué cosa? (C) Although M gives only an interrogative sense, there are abundant attestations in which TLEIN has a noninterrogative, relative sense. This has shortened to TLEN in Z and in many other Nahuatl speech communities. See TLE(H), IN.

TLEINMACH what in the world? what the devil? / ¿qué diablos ... ? (C) [(2)Cf.115v,116v]. See TLEIN, MACH.

TLEINMAH what? what may it be? / ¿qué cosa? (C) [(1)Cf.123v]. See TLEIN, MAH.

TLEĪPAMPA why? / ¿por qué? ¿por qué razón? o ¿por qué causa?, o ¿a qué propósito? ¿a qué? o ¿para qué? (M) [(1)Bf.9v, (1)Cf.122v]. See TLE(H), -PAMPA.

TLEMICOHUA nonact. TLEMIQU(I)

TLEMIQU(I) *pret:* **TLEMIC** to be hot, to suffer from the heat / abrasarse de calor (M), tiene calor (T) [(1)Cf.101r, (3)Tp.239]. See TLE-TL, MIQU(I).

TLEMIQUĪTIĀ caus. TLEMIQU(I)

TLEMŌL-LI stew, mole / guisado (C), mole colorado (T) [(2)Cf.118r,122v, (1)Tp.239]. See TLE-TL, MŌL-LI.

TLEMŌYŌ-TL *pl:* **-MEH** spark, ember / centella (M), chispa (T,Z) [(1)Tp.239, (2)Zp.39,223, (3)Xp.96]. See TLE-TL, MŌYŌ-TL.

TLEPACHIHU(I) to have a fever / tener gran calentura (M) [(1)Tp.239]. See TLE-TL, PACHIHU(I).

TLEPŌCHĒHU(A) *vt* to blacken something, to smut something / lo tizna (T) [(3)Tp.211]. See TLE-TL, PŌCHĒHU(A).

TLEPŌCHĒHUALŌ nonact. TLE-PŌCHĒHU(A)

TLEPŌCHĒHUILIĀ applic. TLE-PŌCHĒHU(A)

TLEQUIQUIZ-TLI firearm / arcabuz o escopeta, etc. (M), armas de fuego (C) [(3)Cf.104r,109r,120r]. See TLE-TL, QUIQUIZ-TLI.

TLE-TL fire / fuego (M) Z has I for E. See TLATLA.

TLETZIN-TLI flame, fire / lumbre, fuego, infierno (T) [(4)Tp.239]. T has this to the exclusion of TLE-TL. See TLE-TL.

TLEXĪC-TLI fire pit, hearth / hornillo (Z) [(2)Zp.69,219]. See TLE-TL, XĪC-TLI.

TLEYOH someone invested with honor, fame / afamado y esclarecido (M) [(1)Cf.119r]. M also has *tleyotl* 'fame, honor,' which represents contrasting TLEYŌ-TL.

TLEYŌ-TL See TLEYOH.

TLĪLCŌĀ-TL a type of black snake / culebra carbonera (Z) [(2)Zp.37,223]. See TLĪL-LI, CŌĀ-TL.

TLĪL-LI black ink, soot / tinta (M)

TLĪLLŌ-TL blackness / negrura (C) [(1)Cf.53r]. See TLĪL-LI, -YŌ.

TLĪLTIC *possessed form:* **-TLĪL-TICĀUH** something black / cosa negra de etiopia (M), negro (Z) C has an example in which this refers to an African, which is common in texts from the early colonial period onward. See TLĪL-LI.

TLĪLTICĀZCA-TL black ant / hormiga negra (Z) [(2)Zp.68,223]. See TLĪLTIC, ĀZCA-TL.

TLĪLTIQUE-TL black bean / frijol negro (Z) [(2)Zp.61,223]. See TLĪLTIC, E-TL.

TLĪLTZAPO-TL *pl:* **-MEH** black sapota, a fruit with black flesh / zapote negro (T,Z), zapote prieto, fruta regalada y común del reino de México (R) [(1)Tp.239, (2)Zp.131,223, (1)Rp.150]. See TLĪL-LI, TZAPO-TL.

TLĪLXŌCHI-TL vanilla orchid / ciertas vainicas de olores (M), la vanilla, fruto americano conocido en toda la Europa (R) [(1)Rp.150]. Although this literally means 'black flower,' the blossom is yellow, while the pod, or vanilla bean, is black. R fails to mark the long vowels. See TLĪL-LI, XŌCHI-TL.

-TLOC *postposition* adjacent to, close to / par de ... junto a (C) T has A for O. According to C, this is synonymous with -NĀHUAC.

-TLOCPA *compound postposition* to the vicinity of, toward / hacia mí (M for first pers. sg. possessor), hacia nosotros (M for first pers. plural possessor) This appears to have some affinity of meaning to TLACPA-, an element in terms such as TLACPACONĒ-TL 'stepchild,' TLACPATAH-TLI 'stepfather,' etc. See -TLOC, -PA.

TLOH-TLI hawk, especially the sparrow

hawk / gavilán, halcón, azor (M) [(1)Tp.241, (1)Rp.151]. T has the variant TOH-TLI, while R has both.

TLOQUEH This possessor derivation from -TLOC is conventionally paired with a possessor derivation from -NĀHUAC, the whole phrase TLOQUEH NĀHUAQUEH referring to the universal and all-pervading deity. See -TLOC.

TZ

TZACTOC something closed / cerrado (Z) [(2)Zp.27,225]. See TZACU(I), the verb O.

TZACU(A) *vt* to close, enclose, lock up something or someone; to pay a penalty / atapar o cerrar algo, o lastar y pagar la pena puesta por la ley (M), encerrar a alguno (M)

TZACUAL-LI small hill; temple, pyramid / cerrito, y cu (C) [(2)Bf.4r,9v, (1)Cf.58r].

TZACUALŌ nonact. TZACU(A)

TZACUALTIĀ caus. TZACU(A)

TZACU(I) to close, to get closed / cerrarse (K) This intransitive form is implied by Z's NACAZTZACU(I) 'to go deaf' and TOZCATZACU(I) 'to get hoarse.' See TZACU(A).

TZACUILIĀ *vt* to hold someone up, to pin someone down, to detain someone, to impede someone / lo ataja, lo detiene, lo estorba, lo impide, le niega, le prohibe (T) [(3)Tp.213]. applic. TZACU(A)

TZACUILILIĀ applic. TZACUILIĀ

TZACUILĪLŌ nonact. TZACUILIĀ

TZACUILTIĀ *vt* to punish someone / castigar o justiciar a alguno (M) In B and Z this is abundantly attested with the vowel of the second syllable long, while in C it is exceptionlessly attested with the vowel unmarked for length. By general rule it should be short. caus. TZACU(A)

TZAHTZACTICAH for something to be locked / cerrado (T) [(1)Tp.243]. M has a different construction with the same sense, *tzatzacutimani* 'for doors or the like to be closed.' There is a loss of labialization before the linking element -TI- here. See TZACU(A), the verb CĀ.

TZAHTZACU(A) *vrefl, vt* to enclose or lock up someone or something / encerrarse en alguna cámara o en otra parte (M), encerrar o encarcelar y recoger a otro (M), cerrar las puertas o las ventanas, o ensilar o encerrar maíz o trigo (M) [(3)Tp.213]. redup. TZACU(A)

TZAHTZAPAL-IN *pl*: **-MEH** sea bass and several other types of fish / mojarra (pescado corriente que hay en la barranca) (T) [(1)Tp.243, (1)Xp.97].

TZAHTZI to shout, proclaim, bray, crow, etc. / pregonar, dar voces, balar la oveja, bramar el toro, o cantar el gallo de Castilla (M)

TZAHTZĪHUA nonact. TZAHTZI

TZAHTZILIĀ applic. TZAHTZI

TZAHTZILIZ-TLI act of shouting, braying, crowing, etc. / voz, balido de oveja, o canto de aves (M), grito, gritería (Z) [(2)Zp.64,226]. See TZAHTZI.

TZAHTZĪTIĀ caus. TZAHTZI

TZĀHU(A) *vt* to spin / hilar (M) [(2)Tp.215,245, (5)Zp.67,120,123,216,225]. In M this is given as an intransitive verb, but T has it as both transitive and intransitive, and Z has it only as transitive.

TZĀHUAL-LI spider's web / tela de araña, telaraña (Z) [(2)Zp.120,225]. Z inverts the vowel length values in one attestation, and marks both vowels long in the other. See TZĀHU(A).

TZĀHUALŌ nonact. TZĀHU(A)

TZĀHUALTIA caus. TZĀHU(A)

TZĀHUĀNITTZIN green grasshopper / grillo verde (Z) [(2)Zp.64,226]. See TZĀHU(A).

-TZĀLAN *postposition* between, among / entre algunos, o por medio dellos (M) This is abundantly attested in C with the vowel of the first syllable long and that of the second syllable never marked long. T has long vowels in both syllables, but the final N is missing. Z has both vowels long. See TZĀLAN-TLI.

TZĀLANHUIĀ *vt* to cause trouble between others / lo entremete, lo revuelve (T) [(3)Tp.215]. T has lost the final N of the second syllable and has the reflex of a long vowel. C has the phrase *tetzālan, tenepantlà tinemi* 'you spread tales among others' (f.20v). See TZĀLAN-TLI, -HUIĀ.

TZĀLANHUILIĀ applic. TZĀLANHUIĀ
TZĀLANHUĪLŌ nonact. TZĀLANHUIĀ
TZĀLAN-TLI passageway, opening between
things / abra, quebrada de sierras o cañada
(M) [(2)Cf.20r]. M gives this as *tzallantli*
with geminate LL contrasting with single L
in the postposition -TZĀLAN.

TZANA-TL *pl:* **-MEH** grackle / pájaro negro
de pico encorvado, de tamaño del estor-
nino; su carne no sirve para comer (S)
[(3)Xp.79]. X has initial Z for TZ.

TZAPO-TL *pl:* **-MEH** sapota, a type of fruit /
cierta fruta conocida (M), zapote (X)

TZATZA *pl:* **-MEH** someone deaf / sordo (T)
[(1)Tp.243, (2)Zp.117,175, (2)Xp.97].

TZĀTZAHTZI to cry out, to shout repeatedly, to crow / dar muchas voces, o
gritar (M), cacarea (gallina) (T) [(1)Cf.121v,
(1)Tp.245]. redup. TZAHTZI

TZATZATI to go deaf / ensordecer (M) This
is indirectly attested by its applicative
form TZATZATILIĀ and in TZATZA. See
TZATZATILIĀ.

TZATZATILIĀ *vrefl,vt* to go deaf; to deafen
someone / se ensordece (T), lo ensordece
(T) [(6)Tp.162,214]. applic. TZATZATI

TZATZATILILIĀ applic. TZATZATILIĀ
TZATZATILĪLŌ nonact. TZATZATILIĀ
TZATZAYACA for cloth or the like to be
torn to shreds / rasgarse estas cosas (la
ropa, el lienzo) mucho (C) [(1)Cf.75r]. See
TZAYĀN(I).

TZATZAYATZ(A) *vt* to tear cloth or clothing to shreds / rasgarlas (la ropa, el lienzo) de esta manera (C) [(1)Cf.75r]. See
TZAYĀN(I).

TZAUC-TLI glue / engrudo (M) This is
indirectly attested in the sources for this
dictionary in forms built on TZACU(A)
and TZACU(I).

TZAUCTOC something closed / cerrado (X)
[(2)Xp.97]. See TZACU(I).

TZAYACTIC something torn, shredded /
roto, rasgado (Z) [(2)Zp.111,226]. See
TZAYĀN(I).

TZAYĀN(A) *vt* to tear something / rasgar,
romper, o hender algo, o desgajar rama de
árbol (M) See TZAYĀN(I).

TZAYĀNALŌ nonact. TZAYĀN(I)
TZAYĀN(I) for something to tear / ras-
garse algo (M) [(1)Cf.75r, (1)Tp.243]. See
TZAYĀN(A).

TZAYĀNILIĀ applic. TZAYĀN(A)
TZAYĀNQUI something torn / cosa rasgada
(M) [(1)Tp.243]. See TZAYĀN(I).

TZETZELHUIĀ *vt* to shake out or beat
something for someone / cerner algo
a otro o sacudirle la ropa (M) applic.
TZETZELOĀ

TZETZELOĀ *vt* to shake, wave something;
to sift something / sacudir la ropa, o el
árbol de fruta para derrocarla, o cernir algo,
cribar, o zarandar (M)

TZETZELŌLŌ nonact. TZETZELOĀ
TZICAHUĀZHUIĀ *vrefl,vt* to comb one's
hair; to comb something / peinarse (M),
lo peina (Z) [(4)Zp.96,198,217]. M also
has a variant *tziquauazuia.* See TZICA-
HUĀZ-TLI, -HUIĀ.

TZICAHUĀZ-TLI comb / peine (M)
[(6)Zp.96,198,217,226]. M also has a variant
tziquauaztli. Z has a shortened variant
TZICUĀZ-TLI.

TZICALHUIĀ *vt* to fasten, affix something
to something else, to keep something
belonging to someone else / se lo pegar, se
lo fija (T), detener alguna cosa a otro (M)
[(5)Tp.182,214]. applic. TZICOĀ

TZICALHUILIĀ applic. TZICALHUIĀ
TZICALHUĪLŌ nonact. TZICALHUIĀ
TZICATICAH for something to be fastened,
stuck together / pegado, está pegado (T)
[(1)Tp.243]. See TZICOĀ, the verb CĀ.

TZĪCA-TL *pl:* **-MEH** large stinging ant /
hormiga grande y ponzoñosa que pica (M)
This is abundantly attested in T and also
appears in B.

TZICNOĀ to have hiccups / tiene hipo, hipa
(T) [(3)Tp.243, (3)Zp.68,121,226, (3)Xp.97].
This is a variant form of TZIUCNOĀ with
delabialization before N. See TZIUCNOĀ.

TZICNŌLIZ-TLI hiccups / hipo (T,Z)
[(1)Tp.243, (2)Zp.68,226]. See TZICNOĀ.

TZICNŌLŌ nonact. TZICNOĀ
TZICNŌLTIĀ caus. TZICNOĀ
TZICOĀ *vt* to stick, fasten one thing to
another; to take hold of something / asir o
pegar algo a otra cosa (M) See TZIC-TLI.

TZICŌLŌ nonact. TZICOĀ
TZICTIC something sticky / chicle,
melcocha (Z) [(3)Zp.38,83,226]. In one
attestation the final C is missing. See
TZICOĀ.

TZIC-TLI chicle, gum of the sapodilla used

for chewing gum / chicle (T) [(1)Tp.243].
See TZICOĀ.
TZICUAHUĀZHUIĀ See TZICA-
HUĀZHUIĀ.
TZICUAHUĀZ-TLI See TZICAHUĀZ-TLI.
TZICUĀZ-TLI See TZICAHUĀZ-TLI.
TZĪCUĒHU(A) [(4)Bf.2r,4r,5r,6r]. This is only
attested paired with TLAPĀN(I), the sense
of the phrase being 'for children to be
born.' The construction also appears in the
grammar of Olmos with the same sense.
TLAPĀN(I) alone can mean 'for eggs to
hatch,' and TZĪCUĒHU(A) probably has a
similar meaning. M has *tentzicueua* 'to
nick the rim of a container' and *quauhtzic-
eualli* 'large splinters of wood,' suggesting
that the basic meaning of the verb is 'to
chip or splinter off.' It may also be related
to TZITZĪCA, having to do with becoming
full. In three out of four attestations in B
the vowel of the first syllable is marked
long. In the fourth it is specifically marked
short.
TZICUĪNALTIĀ *vt* to make someone,
something leap, run / le hace brincarlo, lo
salta (T), lo lleva corriendo, le hace correr
(T) caus. TZICUĪN(I)
TZICUĪNALTILIĀ applic. TZICUĪNALTIĀ
TZICUĪNALTĪLŌ nonact. TZICUĪNALTIĀ
TZICUĪN(I) to leap, jump, run; to splash /
corre, brinca, salta (T), salpicar cualquier
cosa líquida (M)
TZICUĪNĪHUA T gives this as the
nonactive form of the loan blend *cruz*
-TZICUĪN(I) 'to jump in a cross' (Tp.180).
Elsewhere the nonactive of TZICUĪN(I) is
TZICUĪNOHUA.
TZICUĪNOHUA nonact. TZICUĪN(I)
TZIHTZICNOĀ to sob, sigh, hiccup /
suspira (llora) (Z) [(3)Zp.119,226, (3)Xp.97].
X lacks the internal glottal stop. redup.
TZICNOĀ
TZIHTZĪTZQUIĀ redup. TZĪTZQUIĀ
TZILACAYOH-TLI *pl:* **-MEH** chilacayote, a
soft squash / calabaza tierna, chilacayote
(Z) [(3)Zp.23,38,226, (3)Xp.42, (1)Rp.143].
This squash has a variety of similar names.
R and X have CHILACAYOH-TLI. T has
TZIQUILAYOH-TLI, a form suggestive
of metathesis, but see TZIQUIL. See
AYOH-TLI.
TZILĪN(I) for a bell to ring, for something

metallic to sound / sonar o reteñir el metal
(M)
TZILĪNIĀ *vt* to ring a bell / tañer campana o
otra cosa semejante (M) See TZILĪN(I).
TZILĪNILIĀ applic. TZILĪNIĀ
TZILĪNĪLŌ nonact. TZILĪNIĀ
TZINĀCAN-TLI *pl:* **-MEH** bat / murciélago
que muerde (M) [(2)Zp.87,226, (5)Xp.97,
(3)Rp.154]. Z has a long vowel in the first
syllable and is missing the final N. X
agrees with M in having the final N and
gives a short vowel in the first syllable. T
has the variant TZONĀCA-TL. R gives
this both with and without an absolutive
suffix, but M gives it only without.
TZĪNĀNAH-TLI a type of plant, possibly
milkweed / una clase de planta (tiene la
vaina con semilla que vuela en el aire) (T)
[(1)Tp.243]. Because of the ambiguity of
syllable-final -H and -UH in T, it is possible that this should be -NAUH-TLI.
-TZINCO The honorific of postpositions is
formed by adding not simply -TZIN but
-TZINCO. See -TZIN-TLI, -C(O).
TZĪNCO *pl:* **-MEH** anus / ano (X) [(2)Xp.97].
See TZĪN-TLI, -C(O).
-TZĪNCOCOX *only attested in possessed
form* hip, posterior / su cadera, nalga,
asentadera (T) [(1)Tp.135]. See TZĪN-TLI,
TZĪNCUĀLCAX.
TZĪNCUĀLCAX *pl:* **-MEH** ~ **-TIN** hip /
cadera (X) [(4)Xp.97]. This seems to have
CAX(I)-TL as a component element. See
TZĪN-TLI, -TZĪNCOCOX.
TZĪNCUAUHYŌ-TL stalk, hilt / cabos de
cuchillos, o de otra cosa así (M), el rabo (de
la planta) (T) [(1)Tp.135]. See TZĪN-TLI,
CUAHU(I)-TL, -YŌ.
TZĪNCUEP(A) *vrefl,vt* to change sides; to
turn something over / cambiar de partido
(S) [(6)Tp.118,166]. In T this is attested
in compounds meaning to flip oneself
or something else over. See TZĪN-TLI,
CUEP(A).
TZĪNCUĒTIĀ *vt* to put something un-
derneath something, to lay a foundation
for something / le pone una cosa abajo
(adobe o chinámil a una casa, pañal a un
niño, etc.) (T) [(3)Tp.214]. See TZĪN-TLI,
CUĒ(I)-TL.
TZĪNCUĒTILIĀ applic. TZĪNCUĒTIĀ
TZĪNCUĒTĪLŌ nonact. TZĪNCUĒTIĀ

TZĪNCUITLAHUIY(A) *pret:* **-HUIX** for a plant to rot at the base / se pudre la planta (T) [(1)Tp.243]. See TZĪN-TLI, CUITL(A)-TL.

TZĪNĒHU(A) to begin / principia (Z) [(5)Zp.30,162,199,226]. M has this as a transitive verb with the sense of 'to hurl down from a high place, defeat, destroy something, someone' and indicates that the sense is metaphorical. The sense in Z is synonymous with TZĪNTI in C. See TZĪN-TLI, ĒHU(A).

TZĪNĒHUALIZ-TLI the beginning of something / principio (Z) [(2)Zp.102,226]. See TZĪNĒHU(A).

TZĪNĒHUALTIĀ caus. TZĪNĒHU(A)

-TZĪNĒUHCA *necessarily possessed form* the beginning of something / principio (Z) [(1)Zp.162]. See TZĪNĒHU(A).

-TZINOĀ *compounding verbal element used to form the honorific of reflexive verbs* The same vowel length problems across sources discussed under -TZIN-TLI apply to -TZINOĀ, since the latter is a derivation of the former. See the discussion under -TZIN-TLI.

-TZĪNPAN *necessarily possessed form* one's waist / su cintura (T) [(1)Tp.135]. T has characteristically lost the final N. See TZĪN-TLI, -PAN.

TZĪNPĒHUALTIĀ *vt* to begin something from scratch / apenas lo comienza (Z) [(2)Zp.30,199]. See TZĪN-TLI, PĒHU(A).

TZĪNPIHPĪTZCUAUHTI to get tired in one's rump, to get tired of sitting down / se cansa de las nalgas, se cansa de estar sentado (T) [(3)Tp.243]. See TZĪN-TLI, PIHPĪTZCUA, CUAUHTI.

TZĪNQUETZ(A) *vrefl,vt* to turn upside down; to turn something upside down / se empina (T), lo pone en cuatro pies, lo empina (T) [(7)Tp.162,214]. M has this only with a sexual sense, for a man to copulate with a woman from behind, or for her to present herself for that purpose. See TZĪN-TLI, QUETZ(A).

TZĪNQUETZTICAH *vrefl* to be elevated, steep / empinado (T) [(1)Tp.162]. See TZĪNQUETZ(A), the verb CĀ.

TZĪNQUĪXTIĀ *vrefl,vt* to retire, withdraw; to withdraw or reduce something / desistir, separarse, retroceder por miedo, ceder ...

(disminuir, desgravar un impuesto), cortar, cercenar, rebajar, disminuir una cosa (S) M has several more extended senses. See TZĪNQUĪZ(A).

TZĪNQUĪXTILIĀ applic. TZĪNQUĪZ(A)

TZĪNQUĪZ(A) to retire, to retreat, for a price to drop / retrocede para atrás, se abarata, se rebaja (el precio) (T) See TZĪN-TLI, QUĪZ(A).

TZĪNQUĪZTOC something inexpensive / cómodo (de precio) (Z) [(2)Zp.30,226]. See TZĪNQUĪZ(A), the verb O.

TZĪNTAMAL-LI *pl:* **-TIN** ~ **-MEH** buttocks / nalga (M) [(4)Tp.135,162, (5)Xp.97]. See TZĪN-TLI, TAMAL-LI.

TZĪNTAMALTEHTEQU(I) See TZĪNTAMAL-LI, TEHTEQU(I).

TZĪNTATAPAH-TLI *pl:* **-MEH** diaper / pañal (T) [(1)Tp.243]. See TZĪN-TLI, TATAPAH-TLI.

-TZĪNTECH *postposition* next to the base of something / junto a la base de, al tronco de (T) [(1)Tp.135]. See TZĪN-TLI, -TECH.

TZĪNTEHTEQU(I) See TZĪN-TLI, TEHTEQU(I).

TZĪNTELAQUIĀ *vrefl,vt* to sit down hard; to make someone sit down hard / se da un sentón (T), le da un sentón (T) [(6)Tp.162,214]. M has *tzintelaquitihuetzi* 'to slip and fall on one's rump' and several verbs with *tel* as the first element with the sense of kicking or shoving.

TZĪNTEMŌ for a price to decline; to descend something steep / se rebaja (el precio); baja en declive (T) [(1)Tp.243]. See TZĪN-TLI, TEMŌ.

TZĪNTEPOLTIC something bobtailed / rabón (T) [(1)Tp.243]. See TZĪN-TLI, TEPOLTIC.

TZĪNTEQU(I) See TZĪN-TLI, TEQU(I).

TZĪNTE-TL *possessed form:* **-TZĪN-TEYŌ** foundation, base, buttocks / cimiento de pared (M), nalgas (T) [(4)Tp.135, 214]. T has this incorporated into a verb, the whole construction meaning 'to spank.' It also occurs in X referring to the contents of a pot. See TZĪN-TLI, TE-TL.

TZĪNTETLAHTLATZCUEPŌNIĀ *vt* to spank someone / le pega en las nalgas, le da nalgadas (T) [(3)Tp.214]. See TZĪNTE-TL, TLAHTLATZCUEPŌNIĀ.

TZĪNTI to originate / tener comienzo o principio de ser (M) [(5)Cf.31v,75v,84v,99r]. See TZĪN-TLI.

TZĪNTILIZ-TLI the beginning or foundation of something / principio, comienzo o fundamento de alguna cosa (M) [(2)Cf.75v]. See TZĪNTI, TZĪN-TLI.

TZĪNTLAHTLAXCALOĀ *vt* to spank someone / le da nalgadas (T) [(3)Tp.214]. See TZĪN-TLI, TLAXCALOĀ.

TZĪNTLĀHUĪL-LI *pl:* **-TIN ~ -MEH** black widow spider / capulina, araña capulina (T) [(1)Tp.243]. See TZĪN-TLI, TLĀHUĪL-LI.

TZĪNTLĀLIĀ *vrefl* to sit on one's haunches / se sienta en cuclillas (Z) [(2)Zp.114,174]. See TZĪN-TLI, TLĀLIĀ.

-TZĪNTLAN *compound postposition* beneath / debajo de algo (C) See TZĪN-TLI, -TLAN.

TZĪNTLAN-TLI buttocks, base / nalga (M), su nalga, su cadera, sus asentaderas, su cimiento (Z) [(5)Zp.15,23,28,88,162]. See -TZĪNTLAN.

TZĪN-TLI base, foundation; buttocks, anus / el ojo del salvohonor (M), ano, colon, cimiento, base (S) In the sources for this dictionary this appears only in compounds, but it is given as a free form in M.

-TZIN-TLI *compounding element with honorific or diminutive sense; pl:* **-TZI-TZINTIN;** *vocative* **-TZINE ~ -TZE** (*stress on* E) Although necessarily bound, this behaves in a manner distinct from suffixes and postpositions. It has its own absolutive suffix, and it forms the plural by reduplication of itself plus the addition of the plural suffix -TIN; ICHCA-TL 'sheep,' ICHCATZIN-TLI, ICHCATZITZIN-TIN 'sheep (pl.).' If the item it compounds with does not take an absolutive suffix, then the compound does not either, and -TIN is omitted in the plural; ILAMA 'old woman,' ILAMATZIN, ILAMATZITZIN 'old women' (Cf.8r). Personal names with -TZIN often do not take the absolutive suffix. C is consistent in contrasting this bound -TZIN-TLI with the noun TZĪN-TLI 'base, foundation, buttocks' by vowel length. T, Z, and X all have long vowels in both, and this seems to be generally true of modern Nahuatl. B, with only a single attestation of TZĪN-TLI, has a complex and possibly transitional pattern for -TZIN-TLI. In B word-final -TZIN (in possessed forms and where absolutive -TLI is omitted) is never attested with a long vowel. It is as though the general rule which shortens word-final long vowels was extended to the vowel of -TZIN in spite of the final -N. Where -TLI is present, the vowel of -TZIN is marked long in about half the attestations. The I of the full vocative -TZINE is never attested with a long vowel, and in the special possessed honorific form NOPILTZINTZINE 'my lord,' the vowel of the second TZIN is specifically marked short twice, while the vowel of the first TZIN is marked long in four out of six attestations. In all other constructions, including -TZINCO, -TZINHUĀN, -TZITZINTIN, and -TZINTLE, the vowel of -TZIN is marked long in more than half the attestations and unmarked for length in the others. Aside from the special case of NOPILTZINTZINE, the vowel of -TZIN is never specifically marked short. This suggests that -TZIN-TLI and TZĪN-TLI were originally homophonous and that differentiation of them has been a local phenomenon. In C the differentiation is lexical; -TZIN-TLI has a short vowel and TZĪN-TLI has a long one. In B it appears that shortening applies to -TZIN exceptionlessly in word-final position, while the length of the vowel is ambiguous if it carries stress itself or precedes the main stressed syllable. A glottal stop is sometimes attested between -TZIN and the element with which it compounds, as in ACHIHTZIN< ACHI. This is generally true when -TZIN is added to possessed forms of kinship terms, as in ĪCIHUĀHUAHTZIN 'his wife'< CIHUĀ-TL 'woman, wife' plus the possessive suffix -HU(A).

TZĪNTZACUĪL-LI wall of a house / pared de la casa (Z) [(1)Zp.226]. See TZĪN-TLI, TZACU(A).

TZĪNYAHUALTIĀ *vt* to encircle the base of something / lo pone alrededor de la base de una cosa (T) [(3)Tp.214]. T characteristically has YE for YA. See TZĪN-TLI, YAHUALTIĀ.

TZĪPI-TL *pl:* **TZĪTZĪPIMEH** the child who is youngest when a new sibling is born / la criatura que está enferma o desgañada a causa de estar su madre preñada (M), el niño que es más chico cuando nace otro (T) [(1)Tp.243].

TZIQUI a bit of something / poquito, chiquito, chaparrito, pequeño, bajo (de estatura) (T for reduplicated form) [(3)Cf.125v, (1)Tp.244]. This is only attested bound to the additional diminutives -TZIN and -TŌN. The form TZIQUITŌN is so close to Spanish *chiquito* that it suggests a loan formation, but this is not necessarily the case.

TZIQUILAYOH-TLI *pl:* **-MEH** chilacayote, a soft squash / chilacayote (calabaza pinta) (T) [(2)Tp.109,243]. See TZILACAYOH-TLI.

TZIQUIL a morsel, bit of something / un poquito (T for TZIQUILTZITZIN) [(3)Tp.109,243,244]. Two of these attestations are as part of the name for the chilacayote squash. See TZIQUILOĀ.

TZIQUILOĀ to cut something off for someone / cortar una cosa a alguien (S) This is indirectly attested in the sources for this dictionary in constructions including TZIQUIL and TZIQUI.

TZITZĪCA *vt* to stuff something tight, to compress something in a container / atorar o meter algo muy apretado en algún agujero (M) [(1)Cf.84v].

TZITZICALHUIĀ applic. TZITZICOĀ

TZĪTZICĀZHUIĀ *vt* to punish someone by stinging him with nettles / ortigar a otro con ortigas (M) [(1)Bf.10r]. See TZĪTZICĀZ-TLI, -HUIĀ.

TZĪTZICĀZ-TLI nettle / ortiga (M), chichicastle, mal hombre (planta) (Z)

TZITZICOĀ *vt* to detain someone / lo entretiene (T) [(3)Tp.214]. redup. TZICOĀ

TZITZICŌLŌ nonact. TZITZICOĀ

TZITZICUICA to spatter / salpica (Z) [(1)Tp.107, (2)Zp.113,226, (3)Xp.98]. See TZICUĪN(I).

TZITZICUITZ(A) *vt* to spatter something / lo salpica (Z) [(2)Zp.113,199]. See TZICUĪN(I).

TZITZILICA for something to jingle / sonar los reales o la moneda cuando la cuentan (M), el ruido que hacen las campanas

cuando las repican (C) [(3)Cf.74r,77r]. See TZILĪN(I).

TZITZILITZ(A) *vt* to ring bells / repicar campanas (M) [(1)Cf.74r]. See TZILĪN(I).

TZITZĪNQUĪZ(A) to stagger / tambalea (Z) [(2)Zp.119,226]. redup. TZĪNQUĪZ(A)

TZĪTZIQUI something very small / muy pequeño (K) [(1)Cf.125v, (1)Tp.244]. According to C, reduplication of diminutives with a long vowel in the reduplicated syllable renders them even more diminutive (f.125v). redup. TZIQUI

TZĪTZQUIĀ *vt* to grip someone or something with the hand, to take hold of something / asir o tener algo en la mano (M), asir de alguna persona (M) [(4)Cf.64r].

TZĪTZQUILIĀ applic. TZĪTZQUIĀ

TZIUCNOĀ to sob or hiccup / sollozar o hipar (M) [(2)Cf.61v, (3)Xp.97]. Z and X have reduplicated TZIHTZICNOĀ 'to sob or to sigh.' See TZICNOĀ.

TZIUCNOLTIĀ caus. TZIUCNOĀ

TZOCO something very small / pequeño o pequeñuelo (M for *tzocoton*) [(1)Bf.6r, (3)Cf.125v, (1)Tp.165]. All attestations of this are with one or the other of the additional diminutives -TZIN, -TŌN. It may be related to XŌCOH, XŌCOYŌ-TL 'youngest (smallest) child.' It only appears in the Spanish-to-Nahuatl side of M.

TZOHCUILOĀ *vt* to stain something / lo mancha (Z) [(3)Zp.81,164,199]. See TZO-TL, (I)HCUILOĀ.

TZOHCUILTIC something dirty, stained / sucio, manchado, chorreado (Z) [(5)Zp.39,81,118,164,226, (2)Xp.98]. See TZOHCUILOĀ.

TZOHTZOCOLTIC something studded with protrusions / botonudo, palo que tiene tronquitos de ramas (T) [(1)Tp.244]. M has *tzotzocolli* 'large clay pitcher.'

TZOHTZOLTIC something thick and sticky like cooked oatmeal / espeso (como avena cocida) (T) [(2)Tp.244]. T has variants of this with and without the internal glottal stop.

TZOHTZOMAH-TLI *pl:* **-MEH** rag, worn out clothing / trapo o andrajo (M), ropa, tela, trapo, velo (T) T lacks the internal glottal stop, and it is not marked in the attestations in B and R, but it does appear in C. See (I)HTZOM(A).

TZOHTZON(A) *vt* to pat someone or something / dar palmadita con la mano, alagando a un muchacho o a un caballo (C) [(1)Cf.129r, (1)Rp.155]. C contrasts this with TZOTZON(A) 'to strike something, to play an instrument.'

TZOHUAHCAL-LI gourd cup / jícara (Z) [(2)Zp.73,226]. M has *tzoacati* meaning among other things for a squash to become damaged by mildew and *tzoacatl*, a fruit so damaged. The Z attestations lack an absolutive suffix. One attestation is spelled with medial -HU-, the other without.

TZŌLAQU(I) *pret:* **-AC** to fit / cabe (Z) [(2)Zp.22,227]. Only one of the attestations marks the vowel of the first syllable long. See TZŌL-LI, AQU(I).

TZŌLIHU(I) to narrow, to taper / estrecharse (M) [(1)Tp.237]. See TZŌLOĀ.

TZŌL-LI something narrow / cosa estrecha (K) This is an element in a number of compounds with the sense 'narrow.' See TZŌLOĀ.

TZŌLOĀ *vt* to narrow, compress, tighten something / estrechar o enangostar algo (M) This is indirectly attested in the sources for this dictionary. Although the vowel of the first syllable of this item is not marked long in the attestations of TZOTZŌLOĀ, it is supported by the forms TLATZŌLIHUI, TLATZŌLCĀN 'constricted place' and TZŌLTIC 'something narrow, constricted.'

TZŌLTIC something narrow, constricted / cosa estrecha o angosta (M) [(1)Tp.245, (2)Xp.98]. See TZŌLOĀ.

TZOM(A) *vt* to sew something / coser algo, o cubrir de paja el bohío (M) This verb is only attested in the sources for this dictionary in derived forms. M has it as a free form, but in view of M's entries *chpana.nitla* for (I)CHPĀN(A) 'to sweep something' and *cuiloa.nitla* for (I)HCUILOĀ 'to write something,' M's *tzoma.nitla* may represent (I)HTZOM(A). On the other hand, the derived form TZOHTZOMAH-TLI implies TZOM(A).

TZOM(I)-TL fleece, bristles, mane / lana, seda, crin (S) [(1)Bf.7r]. TZOM(I)-TL is a variant of TZON-TLI. The form of the single attestation is ambiguous between

TZOM(I)-TL and TZON-TLI. It is in the possessed construction ĪQUECHTETZON 'his shawl, his neck protection.' If there is semantic differentiation between TZOM(I)-TL and TZON-TLI 'head of hair,' then TZOM(I)-TL is slightly more appropriate. Otherwise, this does not constitute a genuine attestation of TZOM(I)-TL, as distinct from TZON-TLI.

TZOMOC something broken, scraped up / cosa rota y rasgada, o persona solícita y diligente, recia y fuerte (M for *tzomoctic*) [(1)Bf.11r]. M has several compounds with TZOMOC as an element with the sense of working hard at something, scraping away at it. TZOMOCNEM(I) has the sense of 'to scrape along in life.' See TZOMŌN(I).

TZOMŌN(I) for something to break / se rompe (T) [(2)Tp.244]. X has this as a transitive verb.

TZOMŌNIĀ *vt* to break something / romper o rasgar alguna cosa (M) [(3)Tp.214]. See TZOMŌN(I).

TZOMŌNILIĀ See TZOMŌNIĀ.

TZOMŌNĪLŌ nonact. TZOMŌNIĀ.

TZOMŌNQUI something broken / roto (T) [(1)Tp.244]. See TZOMŌN(I).

TZOMPĀM(I)-TL coral tree (Erythrina coralloides, Erythrina americana) / colorín, zompancle, gáspara (árbol) (T) [(2)Tp.244]. A common variant of this is TZOMPĀN-TLI. The length of the vowel in the second syllable distinguishes it from *tzompantli* 'skull rack,' which is a construction of TZON-TLI and locative -PAN. See TZON-TLI, PĀM(I)-TL.

TZOMPĀNCUAHU(I)-TL *pl:* **-MEH** coral tree (Erythrina coralloides, Erythrina americana) / colorín, zompancle, gáspara (árbol) (T) [(1)Tp.244]. See TZOMPĀM(I)-TL, CUAHU(I)-TL.

TZOMPĪLIHU(I) to have a cold / tener romadizo (M), se pega el catarro, tiene catarro (T) [(3)Tp.244]. See TZOMPĪL-LI.

TZOMPĪLIHUĪHUA nonact. TZOMPĪLIHU(I)

TZOMPĪLIHUĪTIĀ caus. TZOMPĪLIHU(I)

TZOMPĪL-LI respiratory infection, cold / catarro (T) [(4)Tp.244, (2)Zp.26,227, (2)Xp.98]. See TZON-TLI.

TZOMPOL-LI *pl:* **-MEH** ~ **-TIN** plant that

produces seeds used in making mole /
chompola que da semillas para mole (T)
[(2)Tp.109,244].

TZONĀCA-TL *pl:* **-MEH** bat / murciélago
(T) [(1)Tp.244]. This is peculiar to T; elsewhere it is TZINĀCAN-TLI.

TZONCAYĀHU(A) *vrefl,vt* to muss
one's hair; to groom someone / despeina
el cabello (T), lo peina (al otro) (T)
[(6)Tp.162,214]. The senses of the reflexive
and transitive uses of this verb appear to be
opposite. See TZON-TLI, CAYĀHU(A).

TZONCUAHCUĀ *vt* to chew something / lo
masca, lo mastica (Z) [(2)Zp.82,199]. See
TZON-TLI, CUAHCUĀ.

TZONCUĒLOĀ *vrefl* for a snake or worm
to coil / (gusano, culebra) se tuerce (T)
[(1)Tp.162]. See TZON-TLI, CUĒLOĀ.

TZONCUEP(A) *vrefl,vt* to turn somer-
saults; to turn something upside
down / da maromas (Z), vuelca (Z)
[(4)Zp.82,130,174,199]. See TZON-TLI,
CUEP(A).

TZONCUI *vrefl* to avenge oneself, to take
vengeance / vengarse (M) [(1)Cf.96v].
See TZON-TLI, CUI.

TZONHUĀZ-TLI snareline for hunting / lazo para cazar algo (M) [(1)Bf.10r,
(2)Cf.18r]. See TZON-TLI.

TZONICA- head down / cabeza abajo (M
from gloss for *tzonicpilcac* 'to hang head
down') This element is abundantly attested
in Z where the final vowel is marked long
in two attestations. It appears in a number
of constructions in M without the final
vowel. See TZON-TLI.

TZONICAIHCATOC something inclined /
empinado (Z) [(2)Zp.50,227]. M has *tzonic-
quicac* 'to hang by the feet' with IHCA as
the second element but without the verb
O. See TZONICA-, IHCA, the verb O.

TZONICANŌQUIĀ *vt* to overturn something / lo vuelca (Z) [(2)Zp.130,199]. See
TZONICA-, NŌQUIĀ.

TZONICAQUEP(A) *vt* to overturn something / lo trabuca (Z) [(2)Zp.124,199]. One
of the two attestations has a final -C. See
TZONICA-, QUEP(A).

TZONICAQUETZ(A) *vt* to turn something,
someone upside down, to throw someone
out headlong / vaciar el cántaro de agua en

la tinaja, o poner boca bajo la vasija, o
volver maderos o cestos lo de arriba abajo,
o echar a otro de cabeza en el agua o des-
peñarlo (M for *tzonicquetza*), echar a empujones a alguno de casa aunque le pese
(M for *tzonicquetza*) [(2)Zp.71,174]. See
TZONICA-, QUETZ(A).

TZONICZA *vt* to tread on something,
trample something / lo pisa (Z)
[(2)Zp.99,199]. See TZON-TLI, ICZA.

TZONILPIĀ *vrefl* to braid one's hair / hace
trenzas (Z) [(2)Zp.125,174]. See TZON-TLI,
(I)LPIĀ.

TZONIZTĀC someone with gray hair /
persona cana (M) [(2)Zp.25,162]. See
TZON-TLI, IZTĀC.

TZONMĀCĀUHTOC someone giddy,
lightheaded / suelto de la cabeza (Z)
[(1)Zp.227]. In MĀCĀHU(A) Z has MAH
for MĀ, but in the single attestation of this
item, the vowel is not marked long or
followed by a glottal stop either. See
TZON-TLI, MĀCĀHU(A), the verb O.

TZONPACHIUHTOC something bent
over / agachado (X) [(1)Xp.98]. See
TZONPACHOĀ.

TZONPACHOĀ *vrefl* to bend over /
agacharse (X) [(3)Xp.60]. See TZON-TLI,
PACHOĀ.

TZONPOCHICTIC someone with gray hair
/ canoso, cano (Z) [(2)Zp.25,162]. See
TZON-TLI, POCHICTIC.

TZONQUĪXTIĀ *vt* to finish doing something or to shave / acabar de hacer o de
concluir algo (M), rasura, se afeita (Z)
[(1)Cf.96r, (2)Zp.105,217]. See TZON-TLI,
QUĪXTIĀ.

TZONQUĪZ(A) for something to conclude,
end, or to grow hair / acabarse y concluirse
la obra (M), nacerme el cabello o el pelo, o
fenecer la vida (M), ya se acabó (C for
preterit) [(2)Cf.96r,113r]. See TZON-TLI,
QUĪZ(A).

TZONTECOM(A)-TL *pl:* **-MEH;** *possessed
form:* **-TECON** head, skull / cabeza cortada y apartada del cuerpo (M), cabeza (C),
cráneo (T) Z has an idiosyncratic possessed
form -TZONTECOMAT where the absolutive suffix appears to be present. Z also
has another possessed form ending in
-TECŌN, where the absolutive is not

present, but the long vowel of the final
syllable makes it appear to be derived from
CŌM(I)-TL rather than COM(A)-TL. See
TZON-TLI, TECOM(A)-TL, CŌM(I)-TL.
TZONTECOMEH one who has a head / el
que tiene cabeza (K) [(1)Cf.55v, (1)Rp.45].
For both C and R this is just one unglossed
example in a list illustrating the posses-
sor construction. R has N for M. See
TZONTECOM(A)-TL.
TZONTECOMPANILHUIĀ applic.
TZONTECOMPANOĀ
TZONTECOMPANOĀ vt to carry some-
thing on one's head / lo lleva en la cabeza
(T) [(3)Tp.214]. T has lost the final M of the
first element. The expected form of the
second element would be PANŌLTIĀ from
the verb PANŌ, which T has elsewhere.
See TZONTECOM(A)-TL, PANŌ.
TZONTECOMPANŌLŌ nonact. TZON-
TECOMPANOĀ
TZONTECONTEHTEQU(I) See TZON-
TECOM(A)-TL, TEHTEQU(I).
TZONTECONTLAPĀN(A) vt to break
someone's head / yo te quiebro la cabeza
(C for first pers. sg. subject) [(1)Cf.63v]. See
TZONTECOM(A)-TL, TLAPĀN(A).
TZONTECONTLAPĀNALIZ-TLI headache
/ dolor de cabeza (T) [(1)Tp.244]. See
TZONTECONTLAPĀN(A).
TZONTECONTLAPĀN(I) to have a
headache / tiene dolor de cabeza,
punza la cabeza (T) [(3)Tp.244]. See
TZONTECOM(A)-TL, TLAPĀN(I).
TZONTEQU(I) vt; pret: -TEC to judge or
sentence something / juzgar o sentenciar
algo (M) [(1)Bf.10r, (1)Cf.101v]. The attestation in B is partially illegible. It appears to be part of TLATZONTEC-TLI
'judgement.' See TZON-TLI, TEQU(I).
TZONTEQUILIĀ vt to judge or sentence
someone / juzgar o sentenciar a alguno (M)
[(1)Cf.101v]. applic. TZONTEQU(I)
TZONTE-TL pl: -MEH someone stubborn
and defiant, a piece of something that
sticks up / rebelde y pertinaz (M), pedazo (T), hormiga arriera (X) [(1)Tp.120,
(6)Xp.38,98]. T and X have this compounded with CUAHU(I)-TL 'tree' to mean
'stump.' X also has this as the name of a
type of ant. See TZON-TLI, TE-TL.

TZONTLAM(I) pret: -TLAN to come to an
end / extremo, término (Z for phrase)
[(5)Zp.58,121,144,227]. This is attested in
the phrase CĀMPA TZONTLAMI 'end,
terminus,' literally 'at the place where it
ends.' See TZON-TLI, TLAM(I).
-TZONTLAN compound postposition at the
head of one's bed / a la cabecera de la cama
(M) [(1)Cf.96v]. See TZON-TLI, -TLAN.
TZON-TLI head of hair / cabello o pelo
(M) Z has TZŌN, while all other sources
have a short vowel. There is a variant
TZOM(I)-TL recorded in S of which there
is a possible, but ambiguous attestation in
the sources for this dictionary. In compounds this sometimes has the sense of
'hair' and sometimes the sense of 'head.'
See TZOM(I)-TL.
TZONTZAPO-TL a type of sapota with
narcotic qualities (Lucuma salicifolia), a
name also used for a member of the plum
family / zapote cabello (Z) [(2)Zp.131,227].
See TZON-TLI, TZAPO-TL.
TZONXĪM(A) vrefl; pret: -XĪN to shave / se
afeita, se rasura (Z) [(2)Zp.6,174]. See
TZON-TLI, XĪM(A).
TZOP(A) vt to finish weaving something, to
finish constructing something / acabar y
concluir de tejer la tela o la bóveda, el
maderamiento de la casa, o cosa semejante
(M) This is implied by TZŌTZOPĀZ-TLI
'weaver's reed.'
TZOP(I) for a piece of weaving or other
construction to get finished / acabarse de
concluir la tela (M) This is implied by
TZŌTZOPĀZ-TLI 'weaver's reed.'
TZOPĒC something sweet / dulce, miel (Z)
[(6)Zp.48,84,179,210,227]. See TZOPĒLIC.
TZOPĒLIĀ vt to sweeten something / lo
endulza (T) This contrasts with intransitive TZOPĒLIY(A) 'to become sweet.'
TZOPĒLIC something sweet / cosa dulce
(M) See TZOPĒLIY(A).
-TZOPĒLICĀ necessarily possessed form
the sweetness of something / la dulzura (de
la miel) (C) [(2)Cf.49v,129r]. M has tzopeli-
cayotl 'sweetness.'
TZOPĒLICXIHU(I)-TL verbena, a plant
with fragrant leaves / hierba dulce (Z)
[(2)Zp.67,227]. See TZOPĒLIC, XIHU(I)-TL.
TZOPĒLILIĀ applic. TZOPĒLIĀ

TZOPĒLĬLŌ nonact. TZOPĒLIĀ
TZOPĒLIY(A) *pret:* **TZOPĒLĬX** ~ **TZOPĒLIYAC** to become sweet / endulcecerse (M) [(3)Cf.32r]. This contrasts with transitive TZOPĒLIĀ 'to sweeten something.'

TZOPĪLŌ-TL *pl:* **-MEH** buzzard / aura (M), zopilote, águila (T), zopilote de cabeza negra (X) [(1)Tp.244, (2)Zp.132,226, (3)Xp.98].

TZOPĪNALIZ-TLI pain, prick / dolor (T) [(1)Tp.244]. See TZOPĪNIĀ.

TZOPĪNIĀ *vt* to prick, jab, puncture something or someone / punzar, picar, o dar herronada (M), punzar a otro así (M) This is synonymous with CHOPĪNIĀ, both being descriptive of the puncturing action of beak, fangs, or talons. See TZOPITIĀ, TZOPŌNIĀ.

TZOPĪNILIĀ applic. TZOPĪNIĀ
TZOPĪNĪLŌ nonact. TZOPĪNIĀ

TZOPITIĀ *vt* to prick something / lo pica (Z) [(3)Zp.98,199,217]. This seems to be a Z variant of TZOPĪNIĀ. Z also has TZOPŌNIĀ, which M glosses as synonymous with TZOPĪNIĀ. See TZOPĪNIĀ.

TZOPŌNIĀ *vt* to prick something or someone / punzar, picar, o dar herronada (M), punzar a otro así (M), lo pica (Z) [(3)Tp.160, (2)Zp.98,199]. See TZOPĪNIĀ.

TZOPŌNĪLŌ nonact. TZOPŌNIĀ

TZO-TL sweat, bodily waste, filth / sudor espeso del cuerpo (M), sudor, suciedad, inmundicia (S) In the sources for this dictionary this is found only as an element of compounds, and with the sense of 'foulness, rottenness,' but M has it as a free form.

TZOTZOCA-TL *pl:* **-MEH** someone miserly and avaricious / verruga, o persona lacerada, apretada y escasa (M), mezquino, verruga, grano que no tiene pus (T) [(1)Tp.244, (3)Zp.84,85,227, (6)Xp.98,99]. There is a gender distinction in current Spanish *verrugo* 'miser' and *verruga* 'pimple.' The latter can also be a disparaging term for a person. T seems to use TZOTZOCA-TL both ways. M also has unreduplicated *tzocatl*.

TZŌTZOCOL-LI large pitcher / cántaro grande de barro (M) [(4)Zp.25,142,227].

TZOTZŌLOĀ *vt* to crumple, wrinkle something / lo arruga (Z) [(2)Zp.14,199]. redup. TZŌLOĀ

TZOTZŌLTIC something thick, crumpled, wrinkled / espeso (T), arrugado (Z) [(1)Tp.244, (2)Zp.14,227, (2)Xp.37]. The vowel of the second syllable is not given long in any attestation, but it should be if TZOTZŌLOĀ is correct and if this is related to TZŌLTIC. See TZOTZŌLOĀ, TZŌLTIC.

TZOTZOMAHTATAPAH-TLI old clothes / ropa vieja (T) [(1)Tp.135]. T has lost the glottal stop of the third syllable and possibly one from the initial syllable as well. See TZOHTZOMAH-TLI, TATAPAH-TLI.

TZOTZOMAHTIĀ *vrefl* to dress oneself / se viste (T) [(3)Tp.162]. T may have lost a glottal stop from the intitial syllable. See TZOHTZOMAH-TLI.

TZOTZOMAHTĪLŌ nonact. TZOTZOMAHTIĀ

TZOTZOMAH-TLI See TZOHTZOMAH-TLI.

TZOTZOMOCA for things to get torn / partirse, henderse, estallar, hablando de un objeto (S) This is implied by TZOTZOMOTZ(A) and TZOMŌN(I). See TZOMŌN(I).

TZOTZOMOCHILIĀ applic. TZOTZOMOTZ(A)

TZOTZOMOTZ(A) *vt* to tear something like cloth or paper / lo rompe (ropa, papel, etc.) (T) [(3)Tp.215]. M has *tzotzomoni*, the reduplicated form of TZOMŌN(I) with the same sense. See TZOMŌN(I).

TZOTZOMOTZALŌ nonact. TZOTZOMOTZ(A)

TZOTZON(A) *vt* to strike someone, to beat something, to play an instrument / golpear algo, o tañer instrumento (C), tañer atabales, o órganos, dar golpes o batir oro (M), apuñear o dar golpe a otro (M), lo toca (un instrumento de música) (T) C contrasts TZOTZON(A) with TZOHTZON(A) 'to beat something, someone with repeated blows.'

TZOTZONALŌ nonact. TZOTZON(A)
TZOTZONCUĒLOĀ *vrefl* to wriggle, move

in a serpentine manner / culebrea (Z)
[(2)Zp.37,174]. This seems to be a reduplicated form of TZONCUĒLOĀ, but the N
is missing from both attestations. See
TZONCUĒLOĀ.

TZOTZONILIĀ applic. TZOTZON(A)

TZŌTZOPĀZ-TLI weaver's reed, stick to
push down and tighten the weft / palo
ancho como cuchilla con que tupen y
aprietan la tela que se teje (M) [(2)Bf.2r,10v,
(1)Tp.245, (2)Zp.96,227]. One of the two
attestations in B has the vowel of the first
syllable specifically marked short, but the
other attestation in B has it marked long,
as it is in T and Z. This implies the verbs
TZOP(A) 'to finish weaving something'
and intransitive TZOP(I) 'for a piece of
weaving to get finished,' both of which are
in M.

TZOTZOPOCA to bubble during
fermentation / levanta burbujas cuando
fermenta (T) [(1)Tp.244]. Z has CHO-
CHOPOCA with the sense of 'to boil
furiously.' See CHOCHOPOCA.

TZŌTZŌ-TL pustule, eruption of the skin /
grano, viruela (X) [(3)Xp.99].

TZOTZOTLAC(A) to glitter, reflect / relucir,
relumbrar, o resplandecer (M) [(1)Tp.245].

TZOYŌN(I) to fry, for water to boil away /
freírse (M), se consume (el agua) por tanto
hervir (T), se fríe (T)

TZOYŌNIĀ vt to fry something / lo fríe
(T,Z) [(3)Tp.215, (2)Zp.61,199]. See
TZOYŌN(I).

TZOYŌNILIĀ applic. TZOYŌNIĀ

TZOYŌNĪLŌ nonact. TZOYŌNIĀ

TZOYŌNQUI something fried / frito (T)
[(1)Tp.245]. See TZOYŌN(I).

X

XĀCO something dark, dusky / pardo (Z) [(2)Zp.94,227].

XĀCOTIC something dark, oscure, muddy / turbio (Z) [(2)Zp.94,227]. See XĀCO.

XACUALHUIĀ applic. XACUALOĀ

XACUALIHU(I) to soften, melt, cook / ablanda, cocina, magulla (T) [(2)Tp.245, 248]. See XACUALOĀ.

XACUALOĀ *vt* to rub, mash or grind something, to cook something / desgranar semillas o cosa semejante, estregándolas con las manos, o sobar masa o cosa así (M), lo frota, lo friega, lo restriega, lo cocina (T) [(3)Tp.215]. See XACUALIHU(I).

XACUALŌLŌ nonact. XACUALOĀ

XAHCAL-LI jacal, house of poles and thatch / choza, bohío o casa de paja (M) See CAL-LI.

XAHCALMŌYŌ-TL mosquito / zancudo, mosco, mosquito (Z) [(1)Zp.227]. This literal meaning of this is 'jacal-fly.' See XAHCAL-LI, MŌYŌ-TL.

XAHUĀN(I) for water or other liquid to fall in a mass / caer golpe de agua, u otras cosas líquidas (C) [(1)Cf.75r].

XAHUĀNIĀ to empty out water or other liquids / vaciar agua o cosas líquidas (M) This is indirectly attested by XAHUĀN(I). See XAHUĀN(I).

XĀHUIĀ *vt* to wash, rinse something / lo enjuaga, lo lava (T) [(3)Tp.217]. This is probably from XĀNHUIĀ with loss of the syllable-final N. See XĀMIĀ.

XĀHUILIĀ applic. XĀHUIĀ

XĀHUĪLŌ nonact. XĀHUIĀ

XAHXAMĀN(I) redup. XAMĀN(I)

XĀLCAMAC sandy place / arenal, arenoso, lugar arenoso (T) [(1)Tp.247]. See XĀL-LI, -CAMAC.

XĀLHUIĀ *vt* to throw sand at someone / le echa arena (T) [(1)Tp.217]. See XĀL-LI, -HUIĀ.

XĀLHUILIĀ applic. XĀLHUIĀ

XĀLHUĪLŌ nonact. XĀLHUIĀ

XĀLLAH sandy place, beach / arenal (M) [(2)Zp.13,227]. See XĀL-LI, -TLAH.

XĀLLĀL-LI sandy land / tierra arenosa (Z) [(2)Zp.122,208]. See XĀL-LI, TLĀL-LI.

XĀL-LI sand / arena, o cierta piedra arenisca (M)

XĀLMŌYŌ-TL *pl:* **-MEH** a type of small mosquito / zancudo de arena, mosquito chico (X) [(3)Xp.102]. The literal meaning of this is 'sand fly.' See XĀL-LI, MŌYŌ-TL.

XĀLOCUIL-IN *pl:* **-TIN** a type of maize worm / gusano que come la caña del maíz (T) [(1)Tp.247]. See XĀL-LI, OCUIL-IN.

XĀLTE-TL *pl:* **-MEH** whetstone, pumice; gizzard / piedra arenosa (para filar), poma (T), su molleja (Z for possessed form), piedra poma (Z) [(1)Tp.247, (4)Zp.85,98,163]. See XĀL-LI, TE-TL.

XĀLTOCAMĒCA-TL someone from Xaltocan / natural de Xaltocan (K) [(1)Cf.56v]. See XĀLTOCĀN.

XĀLTOCĀN *place name* Xaltocan [(1)Cf.56v]. See XĀL-LI, -CĀN.

XĀLTOHTOPOCA for something to be crunchy, to have sand in it / está arenoso, tiene arena (p.ej. una comida) (T) [(1)Tp.247]. This attested form implies *TOHTOPOCA, but the regular form associated with TOPŌN(I) is TOTOPOCA with no glottal stop. TOPŌN(I), TOTOPOCA, and associated forms all involve crunchiness. See XĀL-LI, TOTOPOCHTIC.

XĀLTOMA-TL *pl:* **-MEH** a type of fruit (Saracha jaltomate) / cierta fruta como tomates (M) [(3)Xp.102]. The literal meaning of this is 'sand tomato.' See XĀL-LI, TOMA-TL.

XĀLXOCO-TL *pl:* **-MEH** guava / guayaba (Z) [(2)Zp.65,227, (6)Xp.102]. X has lost the internal L. The literal meaning of this is 'sand fruit.' See XĀL-LI, XOCO-TL, XOXOCO-TL.

XAMĀN(I) for certain brittle things to break

/ quebrarse huevos, tecomates, guitarras, etc., y no cosas de barro (C)

XAMĀNIĀ *vt* to crack, break someone's head or a gourd vessel / cascar o quebrantar cabeza o vaso de jical (M) This is not directly attested but is implied by XAMĀN(I) and TLAXAMĀNĪL-LI. See XAMĀN(I).

XĀMIĀ *vt* to wash one's face / le lava la cara (T)

XĀMILIĀ applic. XĀMIĀ

XĀMĪLŌ nonact. XĀMIĀ

XĀM(I)-TL *possessed form:* **-XĀN**; *pl:* **XĀMIH** adobe / adobe (M) [(2)Tp.247, (3)Xp.102].

XĀNCOTOC-TLI *pl:* **-MEH** piece of adobe / pedazo de adobe o de tabique (T) [(1)Tp.247]. See XĀM(I)-TL, COTOC-TLI.

XAXACA owl / tecolote, buho (Z) [(3)Zp.21,120,150].

XAXACACHTIC rough, rugged, craggy / rasposo, escabroso, áspero, burdo (Z) [(4)Zp.15,54,105,228].

XAXAHUACA for water or other liquid to fall in great quantity / caer en gran cantidad (agua) (C) [(1)Cf.75r]. See XAHUĀN(I).

XAXAHUATZ(A) *vt* to cause water or other liquid to fall in great quantity / hacerlas caer de esta manera (C referring to XAXAHUACA) [(1)Cf.75r]. See XAHUĀN(I).

XAXALTIC something loosely or thinly interwoven, as in open-textured weaving / cosa rala, así como manta, estera, o cosa semejante (M), tejido abierto (de tela, ayate, etc.) (T)

XAXAMACA for numbers of certain brittle things to break noisily / quebrarse muchas de estas cosas (huevos, tecomates, guitarras, etc., y no cosas de barro) con ruido (C) [(1)Cf.75r]. See XAMĀN(I).

XAXAMACHILIĀ applic. XAXAMATZ(A)

XAXAMĀN(A) *vt* to pound, bruise something / lo machuca (carrizo, etc.) (T) [(3)Tp.215]. See XAMĀN(I).

XAXAMĀNALŌ nonact. XAXAMĀN(A)

XAXAMĀNILIĀ applic. XAXAMĀN(A)

XAXAMATZ(A) *vt* to break certain brittle things into pieces; to route one's enemies, inflicting great casualties / quebrar y hacer

pedazos estas cosas (huevos, tecomates, guitarras, etc.) (C), hacer pedazos a los enemigos, haciendo gran estrago en ellos (M) [(3)Cf.75r]. See XAMĀN(I), XAXAMACA.

XĀXAPOHTZIN *pl:* **-MEH** Palma Christi, castor-oil plant / higuerilla (T) [(1)Tp.247].

XĀYACATEHTEQU(I) See XĀYAC(A)-TL, TEHTEQU(I).

XĀYAC(A)-TL face; mask / cara o rostro, carátula o máscara (M) Z has the variant XĀYAC-TLI, while X has a reduplicated form with the same sense. When -TZIN is added to this reduplicated form in X, it is used to mean 'horsefly.'

XĀYACAXOLOCHAHU(I) to have a wrinkled face, to frown / tiene la cara arrugada (T) [(3)Tp.247]. See XĀYAC(A)-TL, XOLOCHAHU(I).

XĀYAC-TLI See XĀYAC(A)-TL.

XĀYŌ-TL dregs; excrement / heces (M) [(1)Bf.11r].

XEHXELHUIĀ applic. XEHXELOĀ

XEHXELOĀ *vt* to divide something up into portions / repartir, dividir, o partir en partes (M) [(2)Cf.72v]. C contrasts this with XEHXĒLOĀ, the corresponding reduplicated form of XĒLOĀ 'to scatter something.' redup. XELOĀ

XEHXĒLOĀ *vt* to scatter something in various different directions and into different piles / extiendo (el maíz) en varias partes, y de varios montones (C) [(2)Cf.72v]. C contrasts this with XEHXELOĀ, the corresponding reduplicated form of XELOĀ 'to divide something.' redup. XĒLOĀ

XELHUĀZ-TLI *pl:* **-TIN** ~ **-MEH** small brush / cepillo, escobeta (para desenredarse el cabello) (T) Z has XIL for XEL, and X has XĀL. The vowel of instrumental -(HU)ĀZ-TLI is long, as Z and X have it, but T has it short in this item. See XELOĀ.

XELHUIĀ *vt* to divide something with someone, to relieve someone by taking part of his burden / partir con otro alguna cosa, o aliviar quitando parte de la carga o del tributo (M) applic. XELOĀ

XĒLHUIĀ *vt* to tousle someone's hair, to rake grass for someone, to scatter something for someone / le abre (el cabello, la yerba, etc.), lo derrama (como gallina el maíz) (T) [(3)Tp.216]. applic. XĒLOĀ

XELIHU(I) to split, divide in two / partirse o henderse por medio (M) See XELOĀ.

-XELIHUIYĀN *necessarily possessed form* the dividing place of something / a medio (C referring to midday) [(1)Cf.95v]. See XELIHU(I), -YĀN.

XELIUHTOC something divided up / dividido (Z) [(4)Zp.47,207,228, (2)Xp.102]. X has this glossed as 'something empty.' See XELIHU(I), the verb O.

XELOĀ *vt* to divide, split something up / partir, rajar, o dividir algo (M) This contrasts with XĒLOĀ 'to scatter something' They are easily confused because of the proximity of their senses.

XĒLOĀ *vt* to scatter something, to spread something out / extender algo, como maíz o trigo en paja, para que se seque (C) This contrasts with XELOĀ 'to divide something' They are easily confused because of the proximity of their senses.

XELŌLŌ nonact. XELOĀ

*XĒLŌLŌ This is not attested in the sources for this dictionary but is predicted by general rule. It contrasts with XELŌLŌ, the nonactive form of XELOĀ. nonact. XĒLOĀ

XELTIC change from currency of a larger denomination / cambio, vuelto (T) [(1)Tp.246]. See XELOĀ, XELIHU(I).

XĒXELHUIĀ applic. XĒXELOĀ

XĒXĒLHUIĀ applic. XĒXĒLOĀ

XĒXELOĀ *vt* to slice something, to carve something up / descuartizar al ahorcado (C), lo reparte (T) [(3)Cf.72v,129r]. C contrasts XĒXELOĀ 'to slice something' and XEHXELOĀ 'to divide something up into discrete portions.' This is one of the clearest contrastive uses of long-vowel reduplication versus vowel-glottal stop reduplication. C also contrasts XĒXELOĀ with XĒXĒLOĀ, the corresponding reduplicated form of the verb XĒLOĀ 'to scatter something.' redup. XELOĀ

XĒXĒLOĀ *vt* to scatter something or to spread something out continuously in a single direction / extiendo (el maíz) continuadamente en una parte (C), desparramar paja maíz (C) [(2)Cf.72v,129r, (1)Rp.156]. C

contrasts XĒXĒLOĀ 'to scatter, spread things in one continuous direction' with XEHXĒLOĀ 'to scatter, spread something in several directions.' This is one of the clearest contrastive uses of long-vowel reduplication versus vowel-glottal stop reduplication. XĒXĒLOĀ also contrasts with XĒXELOĀ, the corresponding reduplicated form of the verb XELOĀ 'to divide something.' redup. XĒLOĀ

XEYŌT(I) to have mange / tiene sarna (T) [(3)Tp.246]. See XEYŌ-TL.

XEYŌTĪHUA nonact. XEYŌT(I)

XEYŌTILIĀ applic. XEYŌT(I)

XEYŌ-TL mange / jiote, roña, sarna (T) [(4)Tp.246]. See XIYŌ-TL.

XĪCAHU(I) for something to get worse / se empeora (Z) [(2)Zp.49,228]. See XĪCOĀ.

XĪCALĀHUĀ-TL oak kindling wood / leña de encino (Z) [(1)Zp.228]. See XĪCALOĀ, ĀHUĀ-TL.

XĪCALECTIC something plucked bare / está pelado (T) [(1)Tp.246]. T has O for A. See XĪCALTIC.

XĪCALĒHU(A) *vt* to peel, shell something / lo pela, lo descascara (T) [(1)Tp.216]. T has O for A. See XĪCALOĀ, ĒHU(A).

XĪCALĒHU(I) for something to be peeled, shelled / se pela, se descascara (T) [(1)Tp.246]. T has O for A. See XĪCALĒHU(A).

XĪCALHUIĀ applic. XĪCOĀ

XĪCAL-LI *pl:* **-TIN ~ -MEH** gourd vessel / vaso de calabaza (M), recipiente para guardar tortillas (Z)

XĪCALOĀ *vt* to strip, denude something / lo desnuda (Z) [(2)Zp.43,199]. See XĪP-.

XĪCALTIC something bare; a bald head / calvo, pelón, cabeza de jícara (T), desnudo (Z) [(1)Tp.123, (2)Zp.43,228]. See XĪCALOĀ.

XĪCAMA-TL *pl:* **-MEH** jícama, a type of edible root (Pachyrhizus angulatus) / cierta raíz que se come cruda y es muy dulce (M) [(1)Tp.246]. M gives this both with an absolutive suffix and without. The T attestation is without.

XICCĀHU(A) *vrefl,vt* to be neglectful of oneself, to lose out through neglect, not to take oneself seriously; to abandon someone in disgust, to lose something through neglect / perder algo por descuido y negligencia, o no curar de su persona, o no hacer cuenta de sí (M), desamparar a otro con desdén y enojo, perder algo por su culpa y negligencia (M) [(3)Bf.11,1v,61, (1)Cf.121v]. See CĀHU(A).

XICCĀHUILIĀ applic. XICCĀHU(A)

XĪCOĀ vrefl,vt to feel envy; to suffer, endure something, to deceive someone / tener envidia o enojo, o agraviarse de algo (M), lo aguanta, lo soporta (T), engañar o burlar a otro (M)

XĪCOHCUITLAPĪLOĀ to wax thread / del sastre o zapatero, que encera el hilo, se dice (C) [(1)Cf.127v]. See XĪCOHCUITL(A)-TL, PĪLOĀ.

XĪCOHCUITL(A)-TL beeswax / cera (M) [(1)Cf.127v]. See XĪCOH-TLI, CUITL(A)-TL.

XĪCOH-TLI pl: -TIN ~ -MEH large bee, bumblebee / abeja grande de miel que horada los árboles, o abejón (M), abejorro, abejarrón (Z) T has CH for X.

XĪCŌL a self-centered, inconsiderate person / es desconsiderado, uno que no quiere hacer un favor, egoísta (T) [(1)Tp.246]. This is not attested with an absolutive suffix. See XĪCOĀ.

XĪCŌLŌ nonact. XĪCOĀ

XĪCOPĪN(A) vrefl, vt to joke; to tease someone / se chispa (T), lo chispa (T) [(4)Tp.162,216]. See XĪCOPĪN(I).

XĪCOPĪNALŌ nonact. XĪCOPĪN(A)

XĪCOPĪN(I) to make jokes / se zafa, se chispa (T) [(1)Tp.246]. See XĪCOPĪN(A).

XĪCOPĪNILIĀ applic. XĪCOPĪN(A)

XĪCTIĀ vt to hold someone in low esteem, to make bold with someone / tenerme otro en poco, o atrevérseme (M for first pers. sg. object) [(1)Cf.102v].

XĪC-TLI navel; peephole / ombligo o brújula para tirar derecho (M)

XIHU(I)-TL year / año (M,C) According to C, XIHU(I)-TL in this sense differs from XIHU(I)-TL 'grass; green stone' in forming the abstract derivation -XIUHCAYŌ-TL where the other forms XIUHYŌ-TL. M combines both in a single entry together with XĪHU(I)-TL 'comet.'

XIHU(I)-TL grass; green stone, turquoise / turquesa y yerba (M) XIHU(I)-TL in its

'turquoise' sense sometimes appears as TEŌXIHU(I)-TL, but the simple form XIUH is used in compounds to convey the sense of greenness. It also serves as a modifier for heat, indicating intensity, as white and blue do in English. According to C, this item differs from XIHU(I)-TL 'year' in that it forms the abstract derivation XIUHYŌ-TL, while the 'year' item is associated with the abstract form -XIUHCAYŌ-TL (which is always prefixed with a number). M combines both in a single entry with XĪHU(I)-TL 'comet.'

XĪHU(I)-TL comet / cometa (M,C) [(1)Cf.129r, (1)Rp.156]. C and R contrast XĪHU(I)-TL with XIHU(I)-TL 'grass; turquoise; year.' M combines them in a single entry.

XIHXICUIN glutton, big eater or self-centered person / glotón (M), ambicioso, codicia, egoísta (Z) [(4)Zp.10,29,48,228]. See XIHXICUINOĀ.

XIHXICUINOĀ to practice gluttony / glotonear (M) [(1)Bf.11v]. B does not attest the glottal stop, but C does in the related noun XIHXICUINYŌ-TL 'gluttony.'

XIHXICUINYŌ-TL excessive eating, gluttony / glotonería (M) [(2)Cf.72r]. M lacks the final N of CUIN. See XIHXICUIN, -YŌ.

XIHXIL(I) vt to trample, to tamp something down / pisar con pisón, o henchir recalcando (M) [(1)Cf.91v].

XIHXIPINTIC something rough, coarse, nubby / rasposo, tosco, áspero, burdo, rudo (Z) [(5)Zp.15,105,112,124,228]. All attestations have a long vowel in the third syllable, but see the note under XIPIN-TLI. redup. XIPINTIC

XILHUĀZ-TLI See XELHUĀZ-TLI.

XILHUIĀ See XELHUIĀ.

XILLĀNCUĀ vt; pret: -CUAH for the stomach to growl / gruñe la barriga (T) [(1)Tp.216]. See XILLĀN-TLI, CUĀ.

XILLĀNMALĪN(A) vt for someone's intestines to cramp / le retuerce las tripas (T) [(3)Tp.216]. See XILLĀN-TLI, MALĪN(A).

XILLĀNPĪQU(I) vt; pret: -PĪC to tuck something away in one's bosom / lo mete en el seno (T) [(3)Tp.216]. See XILLĀN-TLI, PĪQU(I).

XILLĀN-TLI womb, belly / vientre o barriga (M) There is disagreement across sources on vowel-length patterning for this item. It is attested twice in B, both times with the vowel of the second syllable marked long, once with the first vowel specifically marked short. C follows suit once in marking the vowel of the second syllable long but in four other attestations leaves both vowels of the stem unmarked. T consistently has the reflex of a long vowel in the first sýllable and a short vowel in the second, XĪLLAN-TLI. If the second element is the postposition -TLAN 'beneath,' the A should be short.

XĪLŌ-TL *pl:* **-MEH** tender ear of green maize before it solidifies / mazorca de maíz tierna y por cuajar (M) This contrasts with ĒLŌ-TL, which is the ear after the kernels form.

XĪLŌTZON-TLI corn tassel / raspa de espiga (M), cabello de elote (T) [(1)Tp.246, (3)Zp.22,228, (2)Xp.103]. T and X have the variant form XĪLŌMOTZON-TLI. See XĪLŌ-TL, TZON-TLI.

XĪLŌXŌCHI-TL silk-cotton tree / ciertas flores grandes y hermosas formadas de hilos o estambres semejantes a las garzotas de vidrio (R), pochote (K) [(1)Rp.156]. This appears in R without diacritics, but the component parts are elsewhere attested with them. See XĪLŌ-TL, XŌCHI-TL.

XĪM(A) *vt; pret:* **XĪN** to smooth, shave, plane wood or stone; to do carpentry / carpintear o dolar (M) See XĪP-.

XĪMALŌ nonact. XĪM(A)

XĪMILIĀ applic. XĪM(A)

XIMMĪL-LI unirrigated field / sementera de temporal (C) [(1)Cf.118v]. The first element of this is probably XIHU(I)-TL 'grass' with assimilation of UH to M. See XIHU(I)-TL, MĪL-LI.

XĪMŌHUAYĀN place of the dead, realm where the human body is shaved free of flesh / el lugar de los descarnados (K) [(1)Bf.6v]. See XĪM(A), -YĀN.

XINĀCHILHUIĀ applic. XINĀCHOĀ

XINĀCHOĀ *vrefl,vt* to multiply; to multiply something / asementarse (M), se multiplica (T), lo multiplica (T) See XINĀCH-TLI.

XINĀCHŌLŌ nonact. XINĀCHOĀ

XINĀCHPEHPEN(A) See XINĀCH-TLI, PEHPEN(A).

XINĀCH-TLI seed / semilla de hortaliza (M)

-XINĀCHYŌ *necessarily possessed form* one's semen / el semen genital (C) [(3)Cf.83r]. See XINĀCH-TLI.

XĪNIĀ *vt* to sprinkle, water something / lo esparce, lo riega (Z) [(3)Zp.55,107,199]. M has *xini* 'to fall down,' and S has that and also *xinia* 'to knock down, demolish, unravel something.' This is possibly the same verb by some extreme extension of meaning. The verbs in M and S are synonymous with XITĪN(I) and XITĪNIĀ. See XITĪN(I), XITĪNIĀ.

*XĪP- This is an element in numerous compounds and derivations and refers to peeling, flaying, shaving, etc. It appears to have a variant form *XĪ- in some words.

XĪPAL-LI *pl:* **-TIN ~ -MEH** lip / labio (X) [(2)Tp.134,159, (5)Xp.85]. See XĪP-.

XĪPĒHU(A) *vt* to flay, skin, peel something / desollar, o descortezar, o mondar habas, etc. (M) See XĪP-, ĒHU(A).

XĪPĒHUALŌ nonact. XĪPĒHU(A)

XĪPĒHU(I) for something to peel, to come off / se pela (T) [(1)Tp.246]. See XĪPĒHU(A).

XĪPĒHUILIĀ applic. XĪPĒHU(A)

XĪPETZILHUIĀ applic. XĪPETZOĀ

XĪPETZOĀ *vrefl,vt* to strip; to take off clothes / se desviste, se quita la ropa, se desnuda (T), lo encuera, lo desviste (T) See XĪP-.

XĪPETZŌLŌ nonact. XĪPETZOĀ

XĪPETZTIC something smooth, bare, bald / cosa lisa (M), pelado, encuerado (T) [(2)Tp.123,246]. See XĪPETZOĀ.

XĪPETZYŌ-TL misery / miseria (T) [(1)Tp.246]. See XĪPETZOĀ, -YŌ.

XĪPĒUH-TLI something hairless; a bald person / pelado (T) [(1)Tp.238]. See XĪPĒHU(A).

XIPINQUETZ(A) *vrefl* to break out in pimples, pumps / queda boludo (Z) [(1)Zp.175]. See XIPIPI, XIPINTIC, QUETZ(A).

XIPINTIC knot in a tree, bump / nudo de árbol (Z) [(2)Zp.89,228]. In one attestation the vowels of the second and third syllables are marked long. In the other none of the vowels are so marked. See XIPIN-TLI, XIHXIPINTIC.

XIPIN-TLI prepuce, foreskin of the penis / prepucio, o capullo del miembro (M) This is only attested in compounds and derived forms, all sharing the sense of 'bump, protrusion.' The attestations are divided between marking the vowels of the first and second syllables long or leaving them unmarked. The most common pattern is with a short vowel in the first syllable and a long vowel in the second. See XIPINTIC, XIPIPI.

XIPIPI pimple, wart / verruga (Z) [(2)Zp.129,228]. In one of the attestations the vowel of the first syllable is marked long, and in the other it is not. See XIPINTIC.

XIQUIPIL-LI *pl:* **-TIN** purse, pouch, sack / costal, talega, alforja, o bolsa (M) [(3)Xp.103, (1)Rp.74]. This is used symbolically in the vigesimal counting system to represent the unit 'eight thousand.'

XIQUITIC paunch, big belly / barrigón, panzón (Z) [(2)Zp.19,228].

XITĪN(I) for something to collapse (of a concrete object or an agreement) / caerse o deshacerse la pared o sierra, o cosa semejante, o desbaratarse la gente (M) M has a typographical error and gives *xitmi* for *xitini*. XITĪN(I) implies that M's *xitinia* 'to knock down a wall, abrogate an agreement, etc.' is XITĪNIĀ.

XITĪNIĀ *vt* to knock down a wall, to destroy something, to decimate the encampment of one's enemies / derrocar o deshacer pared, etc., o destruir algo (M), desbaratar real de enemigos (M) This is indirectly attested in the sources for this dictionary. See XITĪN(I).

XĪTLATZTIC naked / desnudo (Z) [(2)Zp.43,228]. See XĪP-.

XĪTOM(A) *vt; pret:* **-TON** to scrape something, to remove the skin of something / lo raspa, quita la piel (Z) [(3)Zp.104,105,199]. This appears to be synonymous with XĪPĒHU(A). See XĪP-, TOM(A).

XĪTOMAĒHU(A) *vrefl* to harvest tomatoes / corta jitomate (T) [(3)Tp.246]. See XĪTOMA-TL, ĒHU(A).

XĪTOMANAMACA See XĪTOMA-TL, NAMACA.

XĪTOMAPEHPEN(A) See XĪTOMA-TL, PEHPEN(A).

XĪTOMAPIY(A) *pret:* **-PIX ~ -PĪX** to tend tomatoes / cuida jitomate (T) [(2)Tp.231,246]. See XĪTOMA-TL, PIY(A).

XĪTOMATEQU(I) See XĪTOMA-TL, TEQU(I).

XĪTOMA-TL *pl:* **-MEH** large red or yellow tomato (as contrasted with the green husk tomato) / tomates grandes colorados, amarillos, y blancos (M), jitomate (T) See XĪTOM(A), TOMA-TL.

XITŌN(I) to get disarranged / descompone (T) [(1)Tp.246].

XITŌNIĀ *vt* to unravel, disarrange, destroy something / lo desenvuelve, lo descompone, lo desbarata (T) See XITŌN(I).

XITŌNILIĀ applic. XITŌNIĀ

XITŌNĪLŌ nonact. XITŌNIĀ

XITTOMŌN(I) to make a sound on bursting; to form a blister / reventando sonar (M), se ampolla (T in construction with 'hand') [(3)Tp.165]. This is attested in the sources for this dictionary only in the compound MĀXITTOMŌN(I). The corresponding transitive verb in M would be XITTOMŌNIĀ.

XITTOMŌNIĀ *vrefl,vt* to make an explosive sound; to cause something to make an explosive sound / hacer rueda el gallo de la tierra, etc. (M), hacer sonar algo reventando (M) This is indirectly attested by XITTOMŌN(I). M attests the unusual medial TT. See XITTOMŌN(I).

XITTOMŌNĪHUA nonact. XITTOMŌN(I)

XITTOMŌNTIĀ caus. XITTOMŌN(I)

XIUHCĀHUĀL-LI stubble / rastrojo (Z) [(2)Zp.105,228]. One of the attestations has the vowel-length values reversed. See XIHU(I)-TL, CĀHU(A).

XIUHCAL-LI bower / casa enramada (Z) [(2)Zp.52,228]. One of the attestations has the vowel of the first syllable marked long. See XIHU(I)-TL, CAL-LI.

XIUHCAMAC a grassy place / yerboso (T) [(1)Tp.246]. See XIHU(I)-TL, -CAMAC.

XIUHCAMOH-TLI *pl:* **-TIN** sweet potato greens / hierba de camote (X) [(3)Xp.103]. See XIHU(I)-TL, CAMOH-TLI.

-XIUHCAYŌ-TL *necessarily prefixed with a number* a matter of a certain number of years / cosa de un año (C for *cēxiuhcáyōtl*) [(2)Cf.53v]. See XIHU(I)-TL, -YŌ.

XIUHCOYOLTZITZILICA to tinkle like turquoise bells / suena como cascabeles de turquesa (C) [Cf.77r]. See XIHU(I)-TL, COYOL-LI, TZITZILICA.

XIUHEH to be of a certain age / tiene edad (Z) [(2)Zp.48,229]. The literal sense is 'possessor of years.' Z has an intrusive Y before the possessor suffix -EH. See XIHU(I)-TL.

XIUHMĀTĒCA *vt* to pull up plants, to clear ground / arranca yerba, roza (T) [(3)Tp.238]. See XIHU(I)-TL, MĀTĒCA.

XIUHMĀTĒCALŌ nonact. XIUHMĀTĒCA

XIUHMĀTĒQUILIĀ applic. XIUHMĀTĒCA

XIUHOCUIL-IN *pl:* -**TIN** caterpillar / oruga (gusano) (T) [(1)Tp.246]. The literal meaning of this is 'grass-worm.' See XIHU(I)-TL, OCUIL-IN.

XIUHPAN a year's time / año (T) [(1)Tp.246, (3)Xp.103,106]. See XIHU(I)-TL, -PAN.

XIUHQUILCŌĀ-TL a type of snake / culebra chirrionera (Z) [(2)Zp.37,228]. See XIHU(I)-TL, QUIL(I)-TL, CŌĀ-TL.

-XIUHTIĀ *necessarily prefixed with a number, the whole acts as an intransitive verb* to attain a certain age (number of years) / debía yo de tener hasta diez años (C for first pers. sg. subject imperfect with the number ten prefixed to the verb) [(4)Cf.96r,104r,107v]. See XIHU(I)-TL.

XIUHTIC last year, a year ago / hace el año (Z) [(2)Zp.66,229]. In one of the attestations the vowel of the first syllable is marked long. See XIHU(I)-TL.

XIUHTLAH a grassy place / yerboso (Z) [(2)Zp.131,228]. See XIHU(I)-TL, -TLAH.

XIUHTLATIĀ *vrefl,vt* to tire, to get impatient; to irritate someone / enfadarse o cansarse (M), enfadar a otro con importunidades (M)

XIUHTLATILIĀ applic. XIUHTLATIĀ

XIUHTLATĪLŌ nonact. XIUHTLATIĀ

XIUHTLATLA to be hot, to be burning with hunger / hambrear (M), tiene calor (Z) [(4)Zp.24,121,217,229]. See TLAXIUHTLATLA, XIHU(I)-TL, TLATLA.

XIUHYOH something grassy, leaf / yerboso (Z), hoja (X) [(2)Zp.131,229, (2)Xp.103]. See XIHU(I)-TL, -YOH.

XIUHYŌHUA for something to become grassy / se enyerba (Z) [(3)Zp.54,218,229]. See XIUHYŌ-TL.

XIUHYŌHUAC something overgrown with grass / enyerbado (Z) [(2)Zp.54,218]. See XIUHYŌHUA.

XIUHYŌ-TL grassiness / abstracto (de) yerba (C) [(1)Cf.53v]. This is from XIHU(I)-TL 'grass' and contrasts with the abstract derivation from XIHU(I)-TL 'year,' which is -XIUHCAYŌ-TL. See XIHU(I)-TL, -YŌ.

XIUHZĀLŌLIZ-TLI the art of mosaic work, sticking together green stones / cubrir con mosaicos (S for *xiuhçalolmana*) [(1)Bf.10v]. See XIHU(I)-TL, ZĀLOĀ.

XIUHZĀYŌL-IN *pl:* -**MEH** green fly / mosca verde, mosca filaria (X) [(3)Xp.103]. See XIHU(I)-TL, ZĀYŌL-IN.

XĪX(A) *vrefl* to urinate or defecate / proveerse o hacer cámara (M), cagar (M), orina (T) When this is compounded with Ā-TL 'water,' it still can mean to defecate as well as to urinate.

XĪXALŌ nonact. XĪX(A)

XIXĪCOĀ *vt* to deceive someone, win out over someone, to defeat someone / enganar y burlar a otro (M), le gana, le persuade, lo vence (T) See XĪCOĀ.

XIXIHCUEPŌN(I) to blister, break out in sores / se ampolla, se hace llagas (T) [(1)Tp.246]. See CUEPŌN(I).

XĪXILIĀ applic. XĪX(A)

XĪXIPINTŌL *pl:* -**TIN** ~ -**MEH** glowworm / luciérnaga (T) [(1)Tp.246]. See XIPIN-TLI.

XIXITICA for all of something (such as a wall) to crumble, come apart / desmoronarse, o deshacerse alguna cosa (M), cuando se desmorona y desbarata todo (C) [(2)Cf.74r,102r]. See XITĪN(I).

XIXITITZ(A) *vt* to cause all of something (such as a wall) to crumble / desbaratar algo (todo) (C) [(1)Cf.74r]. See XITĪN(I).

XIXITTOMŌN(I) to blister, to break out in sores / se ampolla, se hace llagas (T) [(1)Tp.246]. M has *xittomonalli* 'blister.' M also has *xittomoni* with the sense of 'to make an explosive noise.' See TOMŌN(I).

XIXĪX(A) *vrefl* to urinate / orinar

[(2)Zp.92,175]. In both attestations the vowel of the first syllable is short. redup. XĪX(A)

XIYŌ-TL itch, mange / empeine, o sarna (M), jiote, empeine (Z) [(1)Tp.197, (3)Zp.49,73,228]. T has E for I.

*XO- element with the sense 'foot' in many compoundsThis is an element of XOCPAL-LI 'sole' and XOPIL-LI 'toe.' There are many XO- compounds in M.

*XŌ- element with the sense 'green' in many compounds; see XŌPAN, XŌTLA, etc. XOXOCTIC also contains a XO element and the sense 'green' but has a short rather than a long vowel.

XOCATETLĀLIĀ *vrefl* to swell, for a raised swelling to form / se hincha (en forma de bola — como el piquete de abeja) (T) [(1)Tp.163]. Despite the different vowel in the second syllable, this may be related to XOCOTETIC 'something with a round shape.' See TLĀLIĀ.

XŌCHIAQUIĀ *vt* to plant flowers / plantar flores (K) [(1)Bf.10v]. There is no attested gloss of this, but it is parallel to M's *quauhaquia* 'to plant trees.' See XŌCHI-TL, AQUIĀ.

XŌCHICUAUHTŌPĪL-LI *pl: -MEH* cross decorated with flowers / cruz floreada (que usan en el casamiento) (T) [(2)Tp.120,247]. See XŌCHI-TL, CUAHU(I)-TL, TŌPĪL-LI.

XŌCHICUEPŌN(I) to bloom in the manner of a flower / brota como flor (C) [(1)Cf.76r]. See XŌCHI-TL, CUEPŌN(I).

XŌCHIHCUAL-LI fruit in general; banana / fruta generalmente (M), plátano (Z) In C and Z this is abundantly attested and consistently with a glottal stop between the two component elements. In T it is attested only once and without the glottal stop, but the loss of internal glottal stops is characteristic of T. The specific sense 'banana' is common to Z and Nahuatl of the Huasteca, areas where bananas are intensively cultivated. See XŌCHI-TL, CUAL-LI.

-XŌCHIHCUALLŌ *necessarily possessed form* the crop of fruit (of a tree) / fruta ... del árbol (C) [(1)Cf.83r]. See XŌCHIHCUAL-LI.

XŌCHIHCUALMĪL-LI banana plantation / platanar (Z) [(2)Zp.99,229]. See XŌCHIHCUAL-LI, MĪL-LI.

XŌCHIPEHPEN(A) to gather flowers / junta flores (T) [(1)Cf.76r, (2)Tp.196,247]. C contrasts this case where XŌCHI is the incorporated object with where it functions as a manner adverbial. In the latter case, an object prefix precedes XŌCHI; *nixōchipèpena* 'I gather flowers' and *nicxōchipèpena cuīcatl* 'I gather songs as I would flowers.' See XŌCHI-TL, PEHPEN(A).

XŌCHIPEHPEN(A) *vt* to gather something as one would gather flowers. / busco y escojo (algo) como las rosas (C) [(1)Cf.76r, (2)Rp.48,49]. See the discussion under XŌCHIPEHPEN(A) with incorporated object. See XŌCHI-TL, PEHPEN(A).

XŌCHIPOLOĀ *vrefl* to indulge oneself with delicacies / golosinear (M) [(1)Cf.71v]. M has the variant *xochpoloa*. In this construction XŌCHI has the extended sense of 'something precious, delicate' rather than its literal sense of 'flower.' See XŌCHI-TL, POLOĀ.

XŌCHITĒMOĀ to seek flowers / busco flores (C for first pers. sg. subject) [(2)Cf.76r]. C contrasts this in the case where XŌCHI is the incorporated object and where it functions as a manner adverbial. In the latter case, an object prefix precedes XŌCHI, *nixōchitēmoa* 'I seek flowers' and *nicxōchitēmoa cuīcatl* 'I seek songs as I would flowers.' See XŌCHI-TL, TĒMOĀ.

XŌCHITĒMOĀ *vt* to seek something as one seeks flowers / busco y escojo (algo) como flores (C for first pers. sg. subject) [(2)Cf.76r, (1)Rp.49]. See the discussion under XŌCHITĒMOĀ with incorporated object. See XŌCHI-TL, TĒMOĀ.

XŌCHITEQU(I) See XŌCHI-TL, TEQU(I).

XŌCHITIĀ to utter witticisms and bons mots; to make people laugh / decir gracias o donaires para hacer reir (M) [(1)Cf.101r]. M has the variant *xochtia*. XŌCHI here has a metaphorical sense of something delicate, precious rather than its literal sense. See XŌCHI-TL.

XŌCHI-TL *pl:* **-MEH** flower / rosa, o flor (M) As a modifier this has the sense 'something precious, delicate.' It is also conventionally paired with CUĪCA-TL 'song' to refer to poetry.

XŌCHITLAH flower garden / jardín (M) M also gives the reduplicated form of this, XOHXŌCHITLAH, with the same gloss. See XŌCHI-TL, -TLAH.

-XŌCHIYŌ *necessarily possessed form* the flowers (of a plant, tree) / la flor (del árbol) (C) [(1)Cf.83r]. See XŌCHI-TL, -YŌ.

XŌCHIYOĀ to flower / brotar o florecer el rosal (M) [(1)Tp.248, (1)Zp.60,229]. It is not clear whether this is the general form or a T variant. In T the preterit is formed regularly after the pattern of -OĀ verbs, but the Z form suggests it may be a -HUA verb forming the preterit as -HUAC. In this case, one would expect the O to be long. M gives the verb once as *xochyoua* and once as *xuchioa* with no preterit form. See XŌCHIYŌ-TL, XŌCHI-TL.

XŌCHIYŌTIĀ *vt* to decorate something with flowers / enrosar o adornar algo con flores (M) caus. XŌCHIYOĀ

XŌCHIYŌTILIĀ applic. XŌCHIYŌTIĀ

XŌCHIYŌTĪLŌ nonact. XŌCHIYŌTIĀ

XŌCHIYŌ-TL suet, grease / grasa, grosura, o enjundia (M) [(1)Cf.53r]. This is homophonous with the abstract derivation XŌCHIYŌ-TL 'essence of flowers' from XŌCHI-TL, but it should not be taken as necessarily an extension of it. It may be derivationally related to CHIYAN-TLI 'chia, oilseed.'

XŌCHIYŌ-TL the essence or being of flowers, matters having to do with flowers / el ser de las flores (C) [(2)Cf.53r,83r]. See XŌCHI-TL, -YŌ.

XŌCOĀ *vt* to hurl something or someone down in scorn / echar por ahí a otro con menosprecio (M) This is indirectly attested in XŌCŌLTITOC 'bruised' and XŌCŌLIĀ 'to damage something.'

XOCOĀTŌL-LI cornstarch beverage flavored with plum / atole de ciruela (T), atole agrio que beben en Todos Santos (Z) [(1)Tp.108, (1)Zp.229]. See XOCOTEĀTŌL-LI.

XOCOC something sour / cosa agria (M) [(1)Tp.246, (2)Zp.6,229]. In both attestations in Z the vowel of the second syllable is marked long, but it is short in T. See XOCO-TL.

XOCOCUAHU(I)-TL fruit tree / árbol de fruta (Z) [(1)Zp.229]. See XOCO-TL, CUAHU(I)-TL.

XOCOCUAUHTLAH orchard / naranjal (Z) [(2)Zp.88,229]. See XOCOCUAHU(I)-TL, -TLAH.

XŌCOH youngest child / el último niño (T) [(5)Tp.247,248]. See XŌCOYŌ-TL, TZOCO.

XŌCŌLIĀ *vt* to damage something / dañar (X) [(3)Xp.78]. See XŌCOĀ.

XŌCŌLTITOC bruised, worn out / magullado (Z) [(2)Zp.80,229]. Z does not mark the vowels of the first two syllables long. See XŌCOĀ.

XOCOPALTIC something sour / agrio (Z) [(2)Zp.6,229]. In one of the attestations the vowel of the second syllable is marked long, and the other is not. See XOCOC.

XOCOTEĀTŌL-LI cornstarch beverage seasoned with plum / atole de ciruela (es agrio) (T) [(1)Tp.246]. See XOCOTE-TL, ĀTŌL-LI.

XOCOTECUAHU(I)-TL *pl:* **-MEH** plum tree / ciruelo (T) [(1)Tp.246]. See XOCOTE-TL, CUAHU(I)-TL.

XOCOTETIC something with a round shape, something shaped like a plum / forma redonda, forma de bola (T) [(1)Tp.246]. See XOCOTE-TL.

XOCOTE-TL a type of sour plum / fruta muy verde y por sazonar (M), ciruela (T) [(3)Tp.247]. T has I for E. See XOCO-TL, TE-TL.

XOCO-TL fruit, plum / fruta (M), ciruela (X) This appears to be used as a more generic term for fruit, while XOCOTE-TL is specifically 'plum.' Most derivations from XOCO-TL have to do with sourness, unripeness, or immaturity.

XOCOTLAH place where fruit abounds / lugar abundante de fruta (R) [(1)Rp.138]. See XOCO-TL, -TLAH.

XOCOYA for something to sour, ferment, spoil / acedarse o avinagrarse (M), fermenta, agria, se echa a perder (comida) (T) [(1)Tp.247, (3)Zp.6,48,229]. See XOCOC.

XŌCOYŌ-TL *pl:* **-MEH** youngest child / hijo o hija menor o postrera (M) This frequently occurs as a possessed plural, NOXŌCOYŌHUĀNE 'my children' (vocative) meaning literally 'my youngest children.' See XŌCOH.

XOCPAL-LI sole of the foot / planta del pie (M) In T this is used as the name of a red wasp. See XO-, (I)CPAL-LI.

XOC-TLI *pl:* **-MEH** pot / olla (M) [(3)Tp.223,237,247, (3)Zp.18,25,229]. Z glosses this as 'babosa, caracol,' 'slug, snail.' This may be the same item in some extended sense, or it may be a loan extension involving XONAC(A)-TL, since Spanish *babosa* has both the sense of 'slug' and of 'green onion.'

XOHUIL-IN *pl:* **-MEH** catfish / pescado de a palmo que parece trucha (M), badre, bagre (X) [(3)Xp.104].

XOHXŌCHITLAH flower garden / jardín (M) [(1)Cf.18v]. This is the distributive of XŌCHITLAH, which has the same sense. redup. XŌCHITLAH

XŌICPŌXIHU(I)-TL indigo plant / muite (planta) (Z) (more commonly known as muicle) [(2)Zp.87,229]. the XŌ- here probably has the same 'green' sense it has in XŌTLA 'to bud,' XŌPANTLAH 'green time of the year,' etc. The second element may be derived from (I)CPOĀ 'to reseed something.' See XIHU(I)-TL.

XOLĀHU(A) *vrefl,vt* to slip; to make something slip / resbalar (M) [(3)Zp.109,200,218]. See XOLOĀ.

XOLĒHU(A) *vrefl,vt* to get skinned up by a blow; to peel something / rozarse o desollarse con golpe (M), lo pela (T) See EHU(A).

XOLĒHUALŌ nonact. XOLĒHU(A)

XOLĒHUILIĀ applic. XOLĒHU(A)

XŌLĒPITZĀHUAC a type of mushroom that is long and thin in shape / hongo angosto (T) [(1)Tp.248]. See XŌLĒ-TL, PITZĀHUAC.

XŌLĒ-TL *pl:* **-MEH** mushroom / hongo (T) [(4)Tp.120,220,248].

XOLOĀ *vrefl,vt* to slip; to make something slip / se resbala (T), lo resbala (T) [(6)Tp.163,217]. See XOLĀHU(A).

XOLOCHAHU(I) to get wrinkled / arrugarse de vejez (M) [(3)Tp.247]. See XOLOCHOĀ.

XOLOCHAHUĪHUA nonact. XOLOCHAHU(I)

XOLOCHAHUĪTIĀ caus. XOLOCHAHUĪTIĀ

XOLOCHALHUIĀ applic. XOLOCHOĀ

XOLOCHILHUIĀ applic. XOLOCHOĀ

XOLOCHOĀ *vt* to wrinkle, fold something / arrugar o plegar algo (M)

XOLOCHŌLŌ nonact. XOLOCHOĀ

XOLOCHTIC something wrinkled / arrugada cosa (M) [(1)Tp.247]. See XOLOCHAHU(I), XOLOCHOĀ.

XOLOLHUIĀ applic. XOLOĀ

XOLŌLŌ nonact. XOLOĀ

XOLOPIHTI *pret:* **XOLOPIHTIC** to be foolish, to joke and lie like a fool / volverse tonto (M), chismea, calumnia, miente (Z) [(4)Zp.24,39,84,229]. See XOLOPIH-TLI.

XOLOPIHTILIZ-TLI lie, falsehood / mentira (Z) [(2)Zp.84,229]. See XOLOPIH-TLI.

XOLOPIH-TLI *pl:* **-TIN** idiot, fool, dolt / bobo o tonto (M)

XOLOPIHYŌ-TL foolery, deceit / chisme, picardía (Z) [(3)Zp.39,98,229]. See XOLOPIH-TLI, -YŌ.

XŌLŌ-TL page, male servant / paje, mozo, criado, o esclavo (M) [(2)Bf.8r,8v]. This has the same form as the second element of ĀXŌLŌ-TL 'edible salamander' and HUEHXŌLŌ-TL 'turkey cock,' but there is no obvious connection in sense. It is distinct in vowel-length patterning from the first two syllables of XOLOPIH-TLI 'fool.'

XŌMĒ-TL elder tree / saúco (M) [(2)Zp.114,229].

XŌMĒTLATOPŌN blowgun, blowpipe / cerbatana (Z) [(2)Zp.27,229]. See XŌMĒ-TL, TLATOPŌN, TOPŌN(I).

XŌMIL-IN *pl:* **-TIN ~ -MEH** a type of edible insect (Hemiptera) / jumil (insecto comestible), chomil (T) [(2)Tp.247, (5)Xp.31,104]. T has variants XOHMIL-IN and XOMIL-IN.

XONACAPILŌL-LI small pitcher with handle for hanging / cantarito que se cuelga de su propia oreja (T) [(1)Tp.247]. See XONAC(A)-TL, PILŌL-LI.

XONAC(A)-TL *pl:* **-MEH** onion / cebolla (M)

This invites analysis into XO- 'foot' and NAC(A)-TL 'flesh.'

XONECUIL-LI staff used in offerings; a type of cactus / palo como bordón con muescas que ofrecían a los ídolos (M), nopal de monte (flor) (Z) [(2)Zp.89,229]. See XO-, NECUILOĀ.

XONELHUA-TL chaff / tamo (T) [(1)Tp.237]. See NELHUA-TL.

XŌNŌ-TL a type of tree (Heliocarpus americanus) / jonote (árbol) (Z) [(2)Zp.73,229].

XŌPAN green time of the year / verano (M) [(1)Cf.88r, (1)Tp.248, (1)Xp.104]. See XŌ-, -PAN.

XŌPANTLAH green time of the year, rainy season, summer / temporal, temporada, tiempo de las aguas, las aguas (T) [(1)Cf.88r, (1)Tp.248, (1)Xp.104]. X has -TLAN for -TLAH. See XŌPAN, -TLAH.

XOPEPE cockroach / cucaracha (Z) [(2)Zp.36,230]. This is a Totonac loanword, but Z also has XIPIPI 'wart, pimple,' which does appear to be of native lexical stock.

XOPILCUI vt to take a lot / coge mucho (T) [(3)Tp.217]. The literal sense of this seems to be 'to take with one's toes.' The Spanish gloss is a euphemism for engaging in intercourse, and M has a reduplicated form of the verb CUI with that sense. This may be yet another euphemism. See XOPIL-LI, CUI.

XOPIL-LI toe / dedo de pie (M) [(3)Tp.217]. This contrasts with XOPĪL-LI 'spoon.' See XO-, MAHPIL-LI.

XOPĪL-LI pl: -TIN spoon / cuchara (X) [(3)Xp.104]. This contrasts with XOPIL-LI 'toe.'

XOPITZA mushroom / hongo (Z) [(2)Zp.68,230]. M has xopitzactli 'shank,' literally 'thin leg.' Possibly this refers to a mushroom that has a long, slender stalk. See XŌLĒPITZĀHUAC.

XOPOCHCO piece of jewelry / joya (T) [(1)Tp.247].

XOPOCHTIC something sunken / sumido (T) [(1)Tp.247].

XŌTLA pret: XŌTLAC to burn, to catch fire, to run a fever; for flowers to burst into bloom / abrasarse la tierra, o encenderse los carbones o brotar las flores (M), tener gran calentura (M) Nahuatl also associates blooming with giving off a glow or exploding in CUEPŌN(I).

-XŌTLACA necessarily possessed form blooming (of flowers) / el brotar de las flores (C) [(1)Cf.49r]. M has xotlac 'flowers already full blown, open.' See XŌTLA.

XŌTLALTIĀ vt to burn something, to set fire to something / encender carbones (M), lo quema, lo enciende, lo prende (T) caus. XŌTLA

XŌTLALTILIĀ applic. XŌTLALTIĀ

XŌTLALTĪLŌ nonact. XŌTLALTIĀ

XŌX(A) vt to give someone the evil eye, to bewitch someone / aojar o hechizar o ojear a otro (M) [(1)Cf.1v].

XOXOCALĀ-TL tree frog / rana arbórea (Z) [(2)Zp.105,230]. See XOXOCTIC, CALĀ-TL.

XOXOCOCUAHU(I)-TL guava tree / guayabo (T) [(1)Tp.247]. See XOXOCO-TL, CUAHU(I)-TL.

XŌXŌCOHTZIN youngest child / el último niño (T) [(2)Tp.247,248]. See XŌCOYŌ-TL, XŌCOH.

XOXOCO-TL guava / guayaba, pomarrosa [(2)Tp.247]. See XOCO-TL, XĀLXOCO-TL.

XŌXOCPALTŌN pl: -TOTŌN red hornet / avispera colorada (son malas) (T) [(1)Tp.248]. See XOCPAL-LI.

XOXOCTIC something blue-green, green, unripe / cosa verde o descolorida por enfermedad, o cosa cruda (M), verde, azul (T), verde (no maduro) (T) Although the vowels of the first two syllables here are short, this is related to other constructions involving XŌ- with a sense of 'green.' See XOCO-TL.

XŌXOHCONĒTZIN pl: XŌXOH-CŌCONEH small jug / jarrito (T) [(1)Tp.248]. See XŌXŌCOHTZIN, XŌCOYŌ-TL, CONĒ-TL.

XOXŌHUIC something green, unripe / crudo, verde (no maduro) (T,Z) [(1)Tp.247, (2)Zp.128,230, (5)Xp.104]. X has the variant form XOXŌUHQUI. See XOXŌHUIYA, XOXOCTIC.

XOXŌHUIYA for something to turn green / pararse verdinegro de enfermedad, o descolorido, o pararse algo verde (M)

[(2)Cf.36v]. In both attestations C specifically marks the vowel of the first syllable short and that of the second syllable long. See XŌ-, XOXŌHUIC.

XŌXOLOCHTIC something wrinkled / arrugado (T) [(1)Tp.248]. See XOLOCHOĀ.

XŌXOLOCH-TLI wrinkle / arruga (T) [(2)Tp.248]. See XOLOCHOĀ.

XOXOQUĒHU(I) to turn green / enverdece, se pone verde (T) [(2)Tp.238,247]. See XOXOCTIC, -EHU(I).

XOXŌTLANI glowworm, firefly / cocuyo, luciérnaga (Z) [(2)Zp.77,230, (3)Xp.105]. X has MĒTZ for NI and adds final -TZIN. See XŌTLA.

XOXŌUHCACATZIN green frog / rana verde (X) [(3)Xp.104]. See XOXŌHUIC, CACA.

Y

YA This is a variant of YE 'already.'

YĀ *suppletive verb; sing. pres:* YAUH; *pret:* YAH to go / ir a alguna parte (M) This verb is suppletive with HU(I). In the dialects on which classical grammars were based, HU(I) is used for the present plural, the imperfect, the optative plural and the nonactive. It is also an element of the present progressive construction -TI-HU(I). There are variant forms of the imperfect and the nonactive based on YĀ. YĀ and HU(I), which are elsewhere suppletive, are compounded for the present tense singular, and many dialects have some reflex of YĀ and HU(I) in the present plural as well. Whenever they are compounded, the vowel of YĀ is shortened. The paradigm of YĀ is otherwise regular in the pattern of verbs that alternate a long final vowel with vowel plus glottal stop. See HU(I).

YACACUEP(A) *vrefl,vt* to change direction / da media vuelta y regresa (T), le cambia la dirección en que va (T) [(6)Tp.163,218]. See YAC(A)-TL, CUEP(A).

YACACUITL(A)-TL snot / mocos (M) See YAC(A)-TL, CUITL(A)-TL.

YACAHUĪTEQU(I) *vrefl; pret:* -TEC to strike one's own nose / se golpea en la nariz (T) [(3)Tp.163]. See YAC(A)-TL, HUĪTEQU(I).

YACAĪXĪCA to have a runny nose / se le escurre la nariz (T) [(3)Tp.248]. See YAC(A)-TL, ĪXĪCA.

YACAMOMOYOCA for one's nose to tickle / le hace cosquillas en la nariz (T) [(3)Tp.248]. See YAC(A)-TL, MOMOYOCA.

YACĀN(A) *vt* to govern someone, to lead someone / guiar a otro, o gobernar pueblo, o adiestrar al ciego (M) T has YE for YA. See YAC(A)-TL, ĀN(A).

YACĀNALTIĀ *caus.* YACĀN(A)

-YACAPAN *postposition* in front of, facing / enfrente de (X) [(3)Xp.49]. See YAC(A)-TL, -PAN.

YACAPANTLATQUI-TL estate of the eldest, entailed estate / mayorazgo (C) [(1)Cf.125v]. See YACAPAN-TLI, TLATQUI-TL.

YACAPAN-TLI someone firstborn / primogénito o primogénita (M) [(2)Cf.125v, (2)Tp.134,227]. This appears in C only as an element of two compounds. T only has it prefixed with TĒ-, but M has it both without the prefix and as *tiacapan* with the vowel of TĒ- reduced. See -YACAPAN.

YACAPĪLOĀ *vt* to draw something out into a point / le adelgazo la punta, torciéndole (C referring to threading a needle) [(1)Cf.127v]. See YAC(A)-TL, PĪLOĀ.

YACAPITZTIC something pointed / puntiagudo (Z) [(2)Zp.103,230]. M has *yacapitzauac* 'something slender.' Z has inconsistency of vowel length marking between attestations, but all vowels should be short. See YACAPITZ-TLI.

YACAPITZ-TLI *possessed form:* -YACAPITZ ~ -YACAPITZYŌ point / punta, la punta de aguja (X) [(2)Xp.49]. This is only attested in alternative possessed forms without the absolutive suffix. See YAC(A)-TL, PITZAC-TLI.

YACAPOHPŌHU(A) *vrefl* to clean one's nose / limpiarse las narices (M) [(1)Bf.11v, (3)Tp.218]. See POHPŌHU(A).

YAC(A)-TL nose, point, ridge / nariz, o punta de algo (M) T and X have YE for YA.

YACATLAHTZŌMIĀ *vrefl* to blow one's nose / sopla con la nariz (T) [(3)Tp.248]. See YAC(A)-TL, IHTZŌMIĀ.

YACATOLCUITL(A)-TL snot / moco (de la nariz) (T) [(1)Bf.11v, (2)Tp.138,248]. See YACATOL-LI, CUITL(A)-TL.

YACATOL-LI snot / mocos (M) [(1)Bf.11v, (2)Tp.138,248]. YAC(A)-TL

YACATTO See ACATTO.

YACATTOPA See ACATTOPA.

YACATZACU(A) *vrefl,vt* for one's nose to get obstructed; to obstruct someone's nose

/ se le tapan las narices (T), le tapa la nariz (T) [(6)Tp.163,218]. See YAC(A)-TL, TZACU(A).

YACATZŌLCOYOC nostril / ventana de la nariz (Z) [(2)Zp.88,164]. In one attestation no vowels are marked long, and in the other the vowels of the first and fourth syllables are marked long. See YACATZŌL-LI, COYOC-TLI.

YACATZŌL-LI nose / su nariz (T for possessed form) If the second element of this is TZŌL-LI 'something narrow,' then the vowel should be long, as it is in X, but it is abundantly attested with the reflex of a short vowel in T and inconsistently attested in Z. See YAC(A)-TL, TZŌL-LI.

YACATZŌLTEHTEQU(I) See YACATZŌL-LI, TEHTEQU(I).

YACAXITOLCUITL(A)-TL wattles (of a turkey) / su moco (de guajolote) (T) [(1)Tp.138]. See YAC(A)-TL, CUITL(A)-TL.

YACAXOLOCHOĀ vrefl,vt to wrinkle one's nose; to crease someone's nose / arruga la nariz (T); le arruga la nariz (T) See YAC(A)-TL, XOLOCHOĀ.

YACAZTEMOHMOLŌNIĀ vrefl to hit one's nose so that one has a nosebleed / se trompea, se golpea en las narices y sale sangre (T) [(3)Tp.163]. See YAC(A)-TL, MOLŌN(I).

YAHUALOĀ vt to go around something, to go in procession / cercar a otros, o irse a quejar primero que otros (M), andar en procesión o alrededor, o rodear (M) T has the variant YEHUALOĀ and Z YOHUALOĀ, but C agrees with M on YAHUALOĀ (f.95r). In the 1892 reprinting of C, however, the attestation is printed with e rather than a. R has a reduplicated form YAHYAHUALOĀ. R also has alternative causatives formed with -LTIĀ and -CHTIĀ but does not indicate the vowel length of the vowel preceding them.

YAHUALŌLŌ nonact. YAHUALOĀ

YAHUALTIĀ vt to put something around something / lo pone alrededor de la base de una cosa (T for TZĪNYAHUALTIĀ) [(3)Tp.214]. T has YE for YA. See YAHUALOĀ.

YAHUALTIC something round / cosa redonda como luna o rodela (M)

[(2)Tp.138,249, (2)Zp.107,231]. Z has YO for YA, while T has YE. See YAHUALOĀ.

YAHUALTILIĀ applic. YAHUALTIĀ

YAHUALTĪLŌ nonact. YAHUALTIĀ

YAHUI someone who has been on a long journey / peregrino de largo tiempo (M), 'va (de ir), viaja, asiste (Z) [(5) Zp.15,72,127,129,231]. YA and HU(I) 'to go' are generally suppletive. Here there seems to be a compound of the two. In Z it is glossed as a verb, but M glosses it as a nominal. Z has O for A. See YĀ.

YĀHUI-TL a type of maize with darkcolored kernels / maíz moreno o negro (M), maíz azul (Z) [(2)Tp.237, (2)Zp.80,230]. T has the reduplicated form YĀYĀHUI-TL

YAHYĀ to go / ir (K) [(1)Cf.71r, (1)Rp.36]. C uses this as an example of reduplication with a distributive sense; inchàchan ōyàyàquê 'each of them went to his own home.' redup. YĀ

YĀLHUA yesterday / ayer (M) Z has ĪYĀLHUATICA 'the other day.'

-YAMĀNCĀ necessarily possessed form one's softness / su blandura (C) [(1)Cf.21v]. See YAMĀNQUI.

YAMĀNCĀYŌ-TL softness, richness / blandura, y per metaphoram quiere decir riqueza y prosperidad (M) [(1)Cf.53r]. See YAMĀNQUI.

YAMĀNIĀ vt to soften something / ablandar o adobar cueros, o entibiar lo que está muy caliente, o ablandar cera o cosa semejante al fuego (M) This is indirectly attested by the applicative form YAMĀNILIĀ. T has YE for YA. See YAMĀNIY(A).

YAMĀNILIĀ vrefl,vt for something to soften; to soften something / se ablanda, se suaviza (T), amollentar algo, o entibiarlo (M) [(6)Tp.163,219]. T has YE for YA. applic. YAMĀNIĀ

YAMĀNILILIĀ applic. YAMĀNILIĀ

YAMĀNILĪLŌ nonact. YAMĀNILIĀ

YAMĀNIY(A) pret: YAMĀNIX for one's body to be neither warm nor cold; for something to soften, become smooth / estar templado el cuerpo (M), se ablanda, se suaviza (T) [(1)Tp.249]. T has YE for YA. See YAMĀNIĀ.

YAMĀNQUI something soft, delicate /

cosa blanda y muelle (M) [(2)Cf.53r,96r, (1)Tp.249]. T has YE for YA. Z has a variant form YEMĀNIC. See YAMĀNIY(A).

YAMĀXTZIN something soft, delicate (diminutive) / blandito, suavecito (Z) [(1)Zp.20,117,231]. See YAMĀNQUI.

-YĀN place where something is habitually done / el lugar y a veces el tiempo donde uno ejercita la acción del verbo (C) This suffixed element occurs in many set constructions with extended senses of place and duration. C analyzes it into suffixal -N added to deverbal instrumental nouns ending in -YĀ (f.50r). These nouns are otherwise identical in form with imperfects, and this in turn suggests that the imperfect suffix is -YĀ with a long vowel, although the vowel is shortened in the singular imperfect by virtue of being word-final and in the plural because it precedes a glottal stop.

YANCUIC something new, recent / cosa nueva o reciente (M) See YANCUIY(A).

YANCUICĀN newly, for the first time / nuevamente (M) See YANCUIY(A), -CĀN.

YANCUILIĀ vt to renovate something / renovar alguna cosa (M) See YANCUIY(A).

YANCUILILIĀ applic. YANCUILIĀ

YANCUILĪLŌ nonact. YANCUIY(A)

YANCUIY(A) pret: YANCUIX for something to be renovated, restored / se renueva (C) [(2)Cf.79r].

YĀŌCHIHCHĪHU(A) vrefl to arm oneself for battle / armarse para la guerra (M) [(1)Rp.159]. See YĀŌ-TL, CHIHCHĪHU(A).

YĀŌHUĒHUĔ-TL war drum / tambor (C) [(1)Cf.120r]. See YĀŌ-TL, HUĒHUĔ-TL.

YĀŌNĀMIQU(I) vt; pret: -MIC to meet someone in battle / les saldremos al encuentro de pelea (C for first pers. plural subject) [(1)Cf.121v]. See YĀŌ-TL, NĀMIQU(I).

YĀŌPAN in war / en la guerra (C) [(1)Cf.58v]. See YĀŌ-TL, -PAN.

YĀŌ-TL enemy / enemigo (M) In compounds YĀŌ also means 'war, battle,' but as a free form 'war' is YĀŌYŌ-TL, contrasting with YĀŌ-TL 'enemy.'

YĀŌTLA vt to make war on others / hacer guerra a otros (M) [(4)Cf.81v]. C gives as one example a reduplicated form used when many are involved in the fighting or by children at play when there are two opposing sides moyàyāōtlâ. See YĀŌ-TL.

YĀŌXŌCHI-TL pl: -MEH a type of flower / flor de pericón (X) [(8)Xp.105,227]. In one set of attestations X fails to mark the vowel of the first syllable long, but it is so marked elsewhere in X. The literal meaning of this is 'enemy flower' or 'war flower.' See YĀŌ-TL, XŌCHI-TL.

YĀŌYŌ-TL war, battle / guerra o batalla (M) [(3)Cf.211,107v,109v]. In compounds this drops the -YŌ and appears simply as YĀŌ. See YĀŌ-TL, -YŌ.

YAUH See YĀ.

YAYĀCTIC something dirty / sucio (Z) [(2)Zp.118,230]. This is probably related to (I)HYĀYA 'to stink' and -IHYĀCA 'the stench of something.'

YĀYAHTINEM(I) pret: -NEN to stroll / pasearse (M) [(1)Cf.93r]. See YĀ, NEM(I).

YĀYĀHUI-TL See YĀHUI-TL.

YĀYATIHU(I) sing. pres: -TIUH to walk, go along a bit at a time / andar o ir andando poco a poco (M) [(2)Cf.93r,94r]. In one of the two attestations the vowel of the third syllable is marked long as though this were formed with purposive -TĪHU(I). See YĀ, IHU(I).

YE suppletive verb to be (in the sense of Spanish estar) / estar, o ser (M under ca) This verb is suppletive with the verb CĀ. CĀ is used for the present and past tenses, YE elsewhere. The form YETZ- is used in the causative derivation YETZTIĀ and in the honorific construction YETZTICAH 'to be.' The nonactive YELOHUA has the form ĪLOHUA in T. C, T, and Z share an admonitive phrase 'be quiet,' the shared elements of which are ZAN XIYE, and it appears to be built on the verb YE, the phrase literally meaning 'just be.' See the verb CĀ.

YE already / ya, adverbio de tiempo (M) This particle combines with many other particles, sometimes written solid and sometimes spaced apart. Among these combinations where YE is initial are YE CUĒL 'already, soon,' YE IMMAN 'a while ago,' YE IUH (often written yeyuh) 'afterwards,' YE NECHCA 'formerly,' YE

NĒPA 'formerly,' YE HUEHCĀUH 'on the other side,' YE ĪC 'ready.'

YĒC- *modifying prefix* well, thoroughly, good, right / bien (K) See YĒC-TLI.

YECĀHUIĀ *vrefl* for something to be rinsed out, dried / se enjuaga (se saca jabón) (T) [(1)Tp.163]. Diphthongization of Ē and initial glide-formation leads to an ambiguity in T. The single attestation may have a reflex of a long vowel in the initial syllable.

YECĀHUĪLŌ nonact. YECĀHUIĀ

YĒCALHUIĀ *vt* to finish something for someone / acabo algo a otro (C) [(1)Cf.65r]. applic. YĒCOĀ

YECAPAXIHU(I)-TL night jasmine (Cestrum nocturnum) / huele de noche (árbol) (T) [(1)Tp.131]. The name of this fragrant flower may be derived from YAC(A)-TL 'nose' or -IHYĀCA 'the stench of something' Another name in T for the same tree is IHYĀCXIHU(I)-TL. See XIHU(I)-TL.

YECAPIXTLĀN *place name* Yecapixtla [(1)Tp.114]. The name of this town is spelled in many different ways in Nahuatl and Spanish sources. It is possibly derived from YAC(A)-TL 'nose, point, ridge' and PIY(A) 'to have,' but it is not certain. Such a derivation would be consistent with T's consistent YE for YA, but in the single attestation T drops the first syllable altogether.

YĒCCĀN (at) a good place or time / lugar bueno y abrigado (M), a buen tiempo (M) See YĒC-TLI, -CĀN.

YĒCCHĪHU(A) *vrefl,vt* for something to set itself aright, to be in good order; to order, arrange, correct something / se arregla, se compone, lo corrige, lo repara (T) See YĒC-TLI, CHĪHU(A).

YĒCCHĪUHQUI someone reliable and trustworthy / cumplidor, hace bien (Z) [(1)Zp.218]. See YĒC-TLI, CHĪHU(A).

YĒCCUĀTLAMATI someone intelligent / inteligente (Z) [(2)Zp.72,230]. See YĒC-TLI, CUĀ(I)-TL, MAT(I).

YĒCCUAUHNELOĀ *vrefl* for something to be beaten or scrambled well / se revuelve muy bien (T) [(1)Tp.163]. See YĒC-TLI, CUAHU(I)-TL, NELOĀ.

YĒCCUĒCHOĀ *vt* to grind something a second time, to grind something very fine / lo remuele (T) [(3)Tp.219]. See YĒC-TLI, CUĒCHOĀ.

YĒCEH but, however / empero o mas (M), pero (C) In C this is attested equally often with the vowel of the first syllable marked long and unmarked. Considering C's tendency to omit vowel-length marking in frequently used words when they are not central to the example, YĒCEH is probably correct.

YĒCHUĪCA *vt* to govern someone / gobierna (Z) [(2)Zp.63,191]. See YĒC-TLI, HUĪCA.

YĒCHUICXITIĀ *vt* to cook something well / lo coce bien, lo cocina bien (T) [(6)Tp.218,238]. See YĒC-TLI, HUICXITIĀ, IUCCI.

-YĒCMĀCOPA *necessarily possessed form* to or on one's right-hand side / derecha (X), a la derecha (X) [(2)Xp.49]. See YĒCMĀ(I)-TL, -COPA.

YĒCMĀ(I)-TL the right hand / la mano derecha (S) See YĒC-TLI, MĀ(I)-TL, MĀYĒCCĀN-TLI.

YĒCMELĀHUAC truly, certainly, clearly / cierto, verdadero, claramente, seguramente (Z) [(2)Zp.230]. Z characteristically lacks the final -C, as it does in several other similar items. Z also has four attestations of YĒC MELĀN with the same sense (p.28,114,128,230) with -N replacing -HUAC. See YĒC-TLI, MELĀHUAC.

YĒCNAC(A)-TL firm meat / carne maciza (T,Z) [(2)Tp.166,248, (3)Zp.25,79,230]. See YĒC-TLI, NAC(A)-TL.

YĒCNĒC(I) *pret:* **-NĒZ** to be, appear well / parece bien, se va bien (T) [(1)Tp.248]. See YĒC-TLI, NĒC(I).

YĒCNEM(I) *pret:* **-NEN** to live well, honorably / vives bien (C for second pers. sg. subject), honrado (Z) [(1)Cf.76v, (2)Zp.68,230]. M has derivations from YĒCNEM(I) but not the verb itself. Z treats this as a substantive 'someone honorable.' See YĒC-TLI, NEM(I).

YĒCNĒZTOC something clear / claro (Z) [(2)Zp.28,230]. See YĒCNĒC(I).

YĒCNŌTZ(A) *vrefl,vt* for something to be said respectfully; to speak to someone properly, respectfully [(6)Tp.163,218]. See YĒC-TLI, NŌTZ(A).

YECŌ for a river to rise / crece el río (T) [(1)Tp.248]. The long final vowel is not attested and is hypothesized here on the pattern of other verbs such as TEMŌ 'to descend.'

YECOĀ *vt* to taste, sample food or drink; to copulate with someone / probar el manjar (M), hacerlo a él o a ella (M) M has the 'taste' gloss of YECOĀ combined with the gloss of YĒCOĀ 'to conclude something' in a single entry. C points out that the 'taste' sense of YECOĀ is generally expressed with the reduplicated form of the verb YEHYECOĀ (f.127r).

YĒCOĀ *vt* to finish, conclude something / concluir o acabar obra (M) M combines this with YECOĀ 'to sample food or drink' in a single entry.

YĒCOHMACALIZ-TLI advice, direction / consejo (Z) [(2) Zp.32,231]. The literal sense of this is 'good road-giving.' See YĒC-TLI, OHMACALIZ-TLI.

YĒCPETZIHU(I) to become very smooth / se alisa muy bien (T) [(1)Tp.248]. See YĒC-TLI, PETZIHU(I).

YĒCPIY(A) *vt; pret:* **-PIX** ~ **-PĪX** to take good care of something / lo tiene bien, lo ahorra (T) [(3)Tp.219]. See YĒC-TLI, PIY(A).

YĒCQUĪZ(A) to turn out well / si ... tengamos buena cosecha (C in phrase referring to crops) [(1)Cf.113r]. See YĒC-TLI, QUĪZ(A).

YECTEL a while ago / días ha (M for *hace días*), los días pasados (C), el otro día (C) [(6)Cf.100v,103v,104r,131r]. Although this would appear to be a compound of YĒC-TLI and TĒL, the vowels are unmarked for length in all attestations.

YECTELTLAMATQUI a wise person / sabio (Z) [(2)Zp.112,231]. If the vowel length pattern is correct, this has the literal sense of 'knower of the things of old,' but Z in one attestation marks the vowel of the first syllable long and in the other the vowels of the first and second syllables long. Z also has QUITĒLMATI 'someone competent,' and this may interact with YĒC-TLI 'something good, pure, clean' in some way. See YECTEL, MAT(I).

YĒCTĒM(A) *vt; pret:* **-TĒN** to tune something / lo afina (guitarra, etc) [(3)Tp.219]. See YĒC-TLI, TĒM(A).

YĒCTĒM(I) *pret:* **-TĒN** for something to fill up / amontona (T) [(1)Tp.248]. See YĒC-TLI, TĒM(I).

YĒCTĒMIĀ *vt* to fill something full / lo llena bien, lo empaca bien lleno (T) [(3)Tp.238]. See YĒC-TLI, TĒMIĀ.

YĒCTĒMILIĀ applic. YĒCTĒMIĀ

YĒCTĒNĒHU(A) *vt* to praise someone, something / alabar a otro (M), alabar alguna cosa (M) [(4)Tp.219,248]. See YĒC-TLI, TĒNĒHU(A).

YĒCTĒNĒHUALIZPAN something holy / santo (T) [(1)Tp.248]. This seems to be a locative despite its gloss in T. See YĒCTĒNĒHU(A), -PAN.

YĒCTI to become good / hacerse bueno (C) [(3)Cf.57v,60r]. See YĒC-TLI.

YĒCTIC holy, perfect / recto, santo, perfecto (T) [(1)Tp.248]. See YĒCTI.

YĒCTILIĀ *vt* to restore, perfect something / restaurar (C), lo perfecciona (T) [(1)Cf.60r, (3)Tp.219]. applic. YĒCTI

YĒCTILILIĀ applic. YĒCTILIĀ

YĒCTILĪLŌ nonact. YĒCTILIĀ

YĒCTIY(A) *pret:* **YĒCTIX** ~ **YĒCTĪX** ~ **YĒCTIYAC** to become good / hacerse bueno (M) [(6)Cf.32r,57v, Rp.47]. See YĒCTI.

YĒCTLĀCAMELĀUHQUI someone honest, upright / honesto (T) [(1)Tp.248]. See YĒC-TLI, TLĀCA-TL, MELĀHU(A).

YĒCTLAHTOĀ to speak clearly / habla claramente (Z) [(2)Zp.28,231]. See YĒC-TLI, TLAHTOĀ.

YĒCTLĀLIĀ *vrefl,vt* to arrange, prepare, order oneself, someone, something / se compone, se prepara, se arregla, se corrige, se mejora (T), lo compone, lo prepara, lo arregla, lo corrige, lo mejora, lo repara (T), guarda (Z) See YĒC-TLI, TLĀLIĀ.

YĒCTLAMACHILIZ-TLI intelligence, knowing something well / inteligencia (Z) [(2)Zp.72,231]. In both attestations Z marks the vowel of CHI long, but it should be short. See YĒC-TLI, MAT(I).

YĒCTLAMATCĀYETŌLIZ-TLI peace / paz [(2)Zp.95,231]. The element YETŌLIZ appears to be equivalent to M's *yeliztli* 'state of being.' M has the construction *tlamatcayeliztli* 'peace and quiet.' See YĒC-TLI, TLAMATCĀ, the verb YE.

YĒCTLAMATQUI an intelligent, wise

person / inteligente, prudente, sabio (Z)
[(3)Zp.72,103,231]. See YĒC-TLI,
TLAMATQUI.

YĒCTLAPALTILIĀ vrefl,vt to get soaked; to
soak something / se empapa (T), lo empapa
(T) [(6)Tp.163,219]. See YĒC-TLI, PALTIĀ.

YĒC-TLI something good, pure, clean / cosa
buena (M)

YĒCTZICATICAH for something to
be secure, permanent / está fijo (T)
[(1)Tp.248]. See YĒC-TLI, TZICATICAH.

YECUĒL already, presently / ya (C) This is
more often written as two words. See YE,
CUĒL.

YĒCXACUALIHU(I) to cook through, to
become well-cooked / se cuece bien (T)
[(1)Tp.248]. See YĒC-TLI, XACUALIHU(I).

(Y)EH that one / aquél (M) This particle has
alternate forms YEH ~ EH (Cf.88r) and
is a constituent of several types of construction. As a free element it serves as a
minimal third person pronoun and as a
grammatical referent standing for a whole
proposition (as it, what, and that do in
various English constructions). This same
particle seems to be a constituent of
the Nahuatl pronominal system, NEH,
NEHHUĀ-TL, etc., being derived from
the personal prefixes plus EH; N-EH,
N-EH-HUĀ-TL 'I,' etc. A third use of
(Y)EH is as a sort of anchor at the end of
particle clusters; NŌCUĒLYEH 'on the
other hand,' QUĒNOCYEH 'all the more,'
MĀNOCEH< MĀ NO ZO (Y)EH 'nor
even, if only,' CUIXAHZOYEH 'I don't
know whether.' These clusters are sometimes written spaced as separate words and
sometimes solid with internal assimilation, but the entitive sense of (Y)EH
remains plausible in even the most lexicalized of them.

(Y)EHHUĀ-TL pl: **(Y)EHHUĀN** ~ **(Y)EH-
HUĀNTIN** he, she, it, they, etc. (independent third person pronoun) / aquél,
aquella, aquello (M) This is the long form
of the third person referent YEH ~ EH. It
sometimes appears as EHHUĀ-TL, but
YEHHUĀ-TL is more common. This also
appears without the absolutive, and when
honorific -TZIN is attached, the absolutive
is not used. See (Y)EH.

YĒHUA beforehand, some time ago /
denantes o ahora poco ha (M), endenan-
tes (C), hace buen rato (C) The form
YEYĒHUA indicates a longer space of
time, YECUĒL YĒHUA even longer, and
YEHUEL YĒHUA still longer (Cf.96v).

YEHYE redup. the verb YE

YEHYECALHUIĀ applic. YEHYECOĀ

YEHYECOĀ vrefl,vt to experience something; to test, sample, taste something /
ensayarse o esgrimir (M), probar o experimentar algo (M) Z has the variant
EHECOĀ. See YECOĀ.

(Y)EHYĒILHUITICA every three days / cada
tres días (C) [(2)Cf.19v,107r, (1)Rp.37]. In
attestations of this construction with other
numbers the reduplication is of the long
vowel type, not the vowel glottal stop type.
Perhaps the glottal stop here is a reflex of
stem-final Y. R marks the glottal stop on
the second syllable instead of the first. See
(Y)ĒY(I), ILHUI-TL.

YEHYELOHUA redup. YELOHUA

-YEHYEYĀN necessarily possessed form
one's customary place / en su lugar (C)
[(1)Cf.94r]. See YEYĀN-TLI.

YEĪCONYA a good while ago / buen rato há
(C), hace buen rato (K) [(3)Cf.126r]. The
component parts of this cluster are YE, ĪC,
and ONYA. The last part is not readily
analyzable, but it appears to be the directional prefix ON- and a verb, possibly some
reduction of YAUH< YĀ.

YELIZ-TLI state of being / ser o estado de
cada cosa (M) [(1)Bf.10v, (2)Cf.84r]. See the
verb YE.

YELMOYĀHU(I) to be nauseated / tiene asco
(T) [(3)Tp.249]. See MOYĀHU(A).

YELOHUA nonact. the verb YE

YEŌHUĪPTLA day before yesterday / an-
teayer (M), antes de ayer (C) [(3)Cf.95r,
(1)Zp.231]. This is constructed of YE
'already,' antecessive Ō and HUĪPTLA,
which alone has the sense of 'day after
tomorrow.' See YE, HUĪPTLA.

YEPA-TL See EPA-TL.

YĒPPA previously, some time ago / de antes,
o antes de ahora (M) Of eleven attestations
of this, only three have the vowel of the
first syllable marked long. In the others it
is unmarked, but the apparent relationship

of YĒPPA and YĒHUA adds support for the vowel being long.

YĒQUENEH finally, moreover / y más, y también (M), finalmente, ultimamente (C)

YĒQUIHTOĀ vt to praise someone or something, to declare something, to explain something / alabar a otro (M), lo afirma, lo declara, lo explica (T) [(3)Tp.219]. See YĒC-TLI, (I)HTOĀ.

YĒQUĪMPA a while ago, recently / hace poco, poco tiempo, recién, reciente (Z) [(4)Zp.100,106,122,231]. See YĒQUĪN.

YĒQUĪN just (referring to time) / apenas (Z) [(5)Zp.12,231]. This Z form seems related to YE and QUIN and also to YĒQUENEH 'finally, moreover,' although the vowel length and and quality do not agree. Z consistently has the vowel of the second syllable long in YĒQUĪN and YĒQUĪMPA and marks the vowel of the first syllable long half the time. See YE, QUIN, YĒQUENEH.

YETOC This is a characteristic Z progressive construction of the verb YE and the verb O.

YETZ- See the verb YE.

YETZTIĀ caus. YETZ-

YETZTICAH This compound verb construction involving both YE and CĀ of the suppletive complex meaning 'to be' is used in formal speech in place of the simple verb. See the verb YE.

(Y)ĒXCĀMPA See ĒXCĀMPA, (Y)ĒXCĀN, -PA.

(Y)ĒXCĀN in three places / en tres partes o lugares (M) [(2)Cf.91r]. There is a variant ĒXCĀN. See (Y)ĒY(I), -CĀN.

-YĒXCĀNIXTI See ĒXCĀNIXTI.

(Y)ĒXPA three times / trez veces (M) See (Y)ĒY(I), -PA.

YEYĀNTIĀ vt to take care of something / lo guarda, lo asegura (T) [(3)Tp.219]. See YEYĀN-TLI.

YEYĀNTILIĀ applic. YEYĀNTIĀ

YEYĀNTĪLŌ nonact. YEYĀNTIĀ

YEYĀN-TLI one's customary place of being / lugar o asiento (M) See the verb YE, -YĀN.

YEYĒHUA a good while ago / buen rato há (C) [(1)Cf.126r]. This may be a reduplicated form of YĒHUA or the phrase YE YĒHUA 'already a while ago.'

(Y)ĒY(I) three / tres (M) This has a variant ĒY(I). In some constructions the internal Y spirantizes, yielding YĒX. In other compounds this has the form YĒ with no final consonant.

YEZŌTLA vt to vomit something / lo vomito, lo asquea (T) [(3)Tp.219]. This is a variant of IHZŌTLA See IHZŌTLA.

YEZŌTLALHUIĀ applic. YEZŌTLA

YEZŌTLAL-LI vomit / vómito (T) [(1)Tp.249]. See YEZŌTLA.

YEZŌTLALŌ nonact. YEZŌTLA

-YŌ derivational suffix forming abstract nouns -ness, -hood, -ship / se hacen nombres abstractos (C) This suffix is pervasive in Nahuatl. In addition to its sense of 'abstract quality,' it is used with many possessed nouns to indicate inalienable possession; NAC(A)-TL 'flesh,' NONAC 'my flesh, meat' (from the market, for the table), NONACAYŌ 'the flesh of my body' (Cf.82r). Membership in the class of nouns that take -YŌ in the possessed form is arbitrary and extends to nonliteral cases such as TĒUC-TLI 'lord,' NOTĒUCYŌ ~ NOTĒCUIYŌ 'my lord, my lordship.' The Y assimilates to preceding L and Z to produce such forms as YŌLLŌ-TL 'heart, life, spirit'< YOL-YŌ and MAHUIZZŌ-TL 'honor'< MAHUIZ-YŌ. Derivations with -YŌ take the absolutive suffix -TL. See -YOH.

YOCCI to ripen, to cook / madurarse la fruta o cocerse algo (M) [(3)Zp.29,79,231]. Z has reorganized the first syllable of this item from IUC to YOC. The CC sequence here represents [ks], not [kk]. See IUCCI.

YOCCIC something ripe or cooked / cosa madura, o cosa cocida (M) [(3)Zp.28,79, 231]. See IUCCIC, YOCCI.

YŌCOLIĀ vt to make something for someone / formar algo a otro (C) applic. YŌCOY(A)

YŌCOXCĀ in a calm, peaceful manner / mansa o pacíficamente (M) This is derived from YŌCOY(A) with considerable extension of meaning.

YŌCOY(A) vt; pret: YŌCOX to make, construct, create something / fabricar o componer algo (M)

YOCXITIĀ This Z variant corresponds to

M's IUCXITIĀ and T's HUICXITIĀ, both with specifically marked short vowels in the second syllable where a long vowel is to be expected. Z does not mark the vowel long, although X has a long vowel in its variant of this causative form. caus. YOCCI

-YOH *derivational suffix* There is a relationship between the abstract derivational suffix -YŌ and this suffix, which is not incompatible with deriving -YOH by adding the possessor suffix -HUAH to -YŌ and reducing the result. In general -YŌ refers to a quality and -YOH to a concrete thing invested with or embodying that quality. In the case of contrasting YŌLLŌ-TL and YŌLLOH-TLI, both< YŌL-LI 'heart' by -YŌ and -YOH respectively, there seems to have been a confusion of the two derivations which has led to a suppletive relationship. -YŌLLŌ is used in simple possessed forms and YŌLLOH when followed by -TZIN and -TŌN (Cf.83v). The Y of -YOH assimilates to preceding L and Z to produce such forms as YŌLLOH-TLI 'heart (something filled with life)'< YŌL-YOH and MAHUIZZOH 'person replete with honor' < MAHUIZ-YOH. Aside from YŌLLOH-TLI 'heart,' -YOH derivations in general do not take an absolute suffix.

-YOHCĀUH *necessarily possessed form* one's possession, something for oneself alone / cosa mía (M for first pers. sg. possessor) [(1)Bf.10v, (2)Tp.138]. This is related to M's *yocatia* 'to take possession of, appropriate something' T has YŌ in place of YOH. See IYOH.

YOHTZIN single, without siblings / único, unigénito (Z) [(3)Zp.126,231]. See IYOH.

YOHUA to get dark, for night to fall / anochecer (M)

YOHUAC at night / de noche (M) See YOHUA.

YOHUAL-LI night / noche (M) See YOHUA.

YOHUALNEPANTLAH at midnight / media noche, o a media noche (M) [(2)Cf.95r]. See YOHUAL-LI, NEPANTLAH.

YOHUALTIĀ caus. YOHUA

YOHUALTICA at night / de noche (M)

[(4)Cf.95r,106r,124r]. See YOHUAL-LI, -CA.

YOHUATIMAN(I) for night to fall, to be night / todo se pone oscuro (C for *tlayohuatimomana*) [(4)Bf.6v,7r]. See YOHUA, MAN(I).

YOHUATZINCO in the morning, early in the morning / de mañana, o por la mañana, o mañana, o de madrugada (M) See YOHUA.

YOHYOHUAC to be dark in several places, everywhere / en todas partes está oscuro (C) [(1)Cf.73r, (1)Rp.161]. redup. YOHUAC

YOHYOHUATOC to be dark in several places, everywhere / en todas partes está oscuro (C) [(2)Cf.73r]. See YOHUA, the verb O.

YŌL- *modifying element incorporated in verbs and referring to volition, emotions* Although attestation of the noun YŌL-LI 'heart' is limited to X, this related modifying element is highly productive. With transitive verbs there can be ambiguity between YŌL-LI as an incorporated object and modifying YŌL-. The ambiguity parallels that discussed under XŌCHITĒMOĀ and XŌCHIPEHPEN(A). YŌL-, YŌLLŌ-TL, and YŌLLOH-TLI seem to have largely fallen together so that distinction among them is more functional than semantic, with YŌL- used adverbially, -YŌLLŌ in simple possessed forms, and YŌLLOH elsewhere, all with an extended sense that encompasses emotion, volition, strength, valor, and heart. This distribution is by no means exceptionless, as demonstrated by such doublets as YŌLCĒHUIĀ ~ TLAYŌLLOHCĒHUIĀ both with the sense of 'to placate, satisfy someone.' See YŌL-LI.

YŌLAHCI to become bored, weary, disgusted / se aburre, se fastidia (Z) [(3)Zp.4,59,231]. See YŌL-, AHCI.

YŌLAHCIC someone bored, weary, disgusted / fastidiado, aburrido (Z) [(2)Zp.4,231]. See YŌLAHCI.

-YŌLCĀ *necessarily possessed form* one's sustenance / sustento y mantenimiento (C) [(2)Cf.49r]. This occurs as part of the phrase -YŌLCĀ -NENCĀ (both possessed) with 'sustenance' as the sense of the whole construction. It is a different item from M's *yolcatl* 'vermin.' The long vowel of the second syllable is not directly attested, but it is implied by the related item YŌLCĀYŌ-TL. See YŌLCĀYŌ-TL.

-YŌLCĀN *necessarily possessed form* homeland, birthplace / patria o tierra natural de alguno (M) [(1)Bf.9v]. See YŌL(I), -CĀN.

YŌLCĀYŌ-TL one's sustenance, that by which one lives / el mantenimiento y sustento con que vivimos (C) This is a different item from M's *yolcayotl* 'snail, slug,' which is related to M's *yolcatl* 'vermin.' See YŌL(I).

YŌLCĒHU(I) to be calmed, placated, satisfied / aplacarse (M) This is indirectly attested in YŌLCĒHUIĀ.

YŌLCĒHUIĀ *vrefl,vt* to calm down; to calm, placate, satisfy someone [(6)Tp.164,220]. This implies intransitive YŌLCĒHU(I). Z has TLAYŌLLOHCĒHUIĀ with the same sense. See YŌL-, CĒHUIĀ.

YŌLCĒUHTOC someone happy, content / contento (Z) [(2)Zp.33,232]. See YŌLCĒHU(I), the verb O.

YŌLCHICĀHU(A) *vrefl,vt* to take courage, to incite oneself to bravery; to incite someone to bravery / animarse y esforzarse (M), animar a otro de esta manera (M) See YŌL-, CHICĀHU(A).

YŌLCHICĀHUAC someone brave, valiant / valeroso, valiente (Z) [(2)Zp.127,232]. See YŌLCHICĀHU(A).

YŌLCHICĀHUALIZ-TLI courage, vivacity, vitality / esfuerzo (M), esfuerzo, excitación, animación (S), paciente, pacífico (Z) [(2)Zp.92,232]. See YŌLCHICĀHU(A).

YŌLCHICHIC someone shy, antisocial / huraño (Z) [(2)Zp.70,232]. See YŌL-LI, CHICHIC.

YŌLCHIPĀHUAC someone purehearted, honorable / corazón limpio, honrado, justo (Z) [(4)Zp.34,68,74,232]. See YŌL-LI, CHIPĀHU(A).

YŌLCHIPĀHUALIZ-TLI perfection of spirit / perfección (Z) [(2)Zp.97,232]. See YŌL-LI, CHIPĀHU(A).

YŌLCOCOĀ *vrefl,vt* to be in pain, to grieve, to suffer envy; to feel sorry for someone /

tener pena o arrepentimiento, o tener envidia de algo (M), tiene duelo, tiene lástima, tiene tristeza, tiene sentimiento (T), le da lástima (T) See YŌL-, COCOĀ.

YŌLCOCŌLEH someone furious, excitable, impatient / hombre bravo e impaciente (M) [(1)Cf.87v]. See YŌL-, COCŌLEH.

YŌLCOCOLIĀ *vt* to aggravate someone, to hurt someone's feelings / insulto (Z in phrase) [(2)Zp.72,153]. Both attestations are short one CO syllable. applic. YŌLCOCOĀ

YŌLCUAL-LI someone trustworthy, honest, faithful / fiel, honrado, justo, honesto, simpático (Z) [(6)Zp.60,68,74,116,231]. See YŌL-LI, CUAL-LI.

YŌLCUĒCUEP(A) *vrefl* to be uneasy, upset / se turba (T) [(3)Tp.164]. See YŌLCUEP(A).

YŌLCUEHMOLĪHUIC worried / preocupado (Z) [(2)Zp.101,232]. See YŌL-, CUEHMOLĪHUIC.

YŌLCUEHMOLĬUHTOC someone impatient / impaciente (Z) [(2)Zp.70,232]. See YŌL-, CUEHMOLĬUHTOC.

YŌLCUEHMOLOĀ *vrefl* to worry / se preocupa (Z) [(2)Zp.101,175]. See YŌL-, CUEHMOLOĀ.

YŌLCUEHMOLŌLIZ-TLI anxiety, trouble / afán, molestia (Z) [(3)Zp.6,85,232]. See YŌLCUEHMOLOĀ.

YŌLCUEP(A) *vrefl,vt* to change one's mind; to change someone else's mind / mudar el parecer y propósito que tenía (M), hacer a otro que mude el propósito o parecer que tenía (M) See YŌL-, CUEP(A).

YŌLCUETLAHU(I) to faint / se desmaya (Z) [(2)Zp.43,232]. See YŌL-LI, CUETLAHU(I).

YŌLCUĪTIĀ *vrefl,vt* to confess, make confession; to confess someone / confesarse (M), confesar a otro (M) See YŌL-, CUĪTIĀ.

YŌLĒHU(A) *vrefl,vt* for one's emotions to be stirred, to fall in love; to excite someone / provocarse o incitarse a algo, o enamorarse (M), provocar así a otro (M) Z has this with the sense 'to invite someone.' See YŌL-, ĒHU(A).

YŌL(I) to live; to come to life, to hatch / vivir, resucitar, avivar, o empollarse el huevo (M)

YŌLIC tranquilly, gently, measuredly /

mansamente (C), despacio, poco a poco (Z)
YŌLICĀCENTILIĀ *vrefl* to come together
gently / se junta despacio (Z) [(1)Zp.175].
See YŌLIC, CENTILIĀ.
-YŌLĬCAHTZIN *necessarily possessed
form* polite phrase for greeting or pass-
ing / (seas) bien venido (C) [(1)Bf.1v, (6)
Cf.86r,120r]. The literal sense of this is
very close to 'take it easy.' See YŌLIC.
YŌLICNĪUH-TLI *pl:* **-MEH** bosom
friend / amigos de corazón (Z for plural)
[(1)Zp.232]. Z only gives this in the plural,
M only in possessed form. See YŌL-LI,
(I)CNĪUH-TLI.
YŌLIHCATOC someone excited / excitado
(Z) [(2)Zp.58,232]. See YŌL-, IHCA.
YŌLIHTLACALHUIĀ *vt* to offend
someone / ofender a alguno (M) applic.
YŌLIHTLACOĀ
YŌLIHTLACOĀ *vrefl,vt* to suffer; to hurt or
offend others / recibir pena (M), dar pena o
ofender a otro (M) See YŌL-, (I)HTLACOĀ.
YŌLĬHUA nonact. YŌL(I)
YŌLĬHUANI something that sustains life /
instrumento para vivir (C), que da vida (C)
[(2)Cf.45v,46r]. See YŌLĬHUA.
YŌLIHUĪTIĀ *vt* to revive, resuscitate
someone / lo resucita (T) [(3)Tp.219].
There is a simpler causative derivation
YŌLĪTIĀ< YŌL(I). See YŌL(I).
YŌLIHUĪTILIĀ applic. YŌLIHUĪTIĀ
YŌLIHUĪTĪLŌ nonact. YŌLIHUĪTIĀ
YŌLILICEH possessor of life / el que tiene
vida (C) [(1)Cf.55v]. See YŌLILIZ-TLI.
YŌLILIZ-TLI life / vida (M) [(3)Cf.47v,55v].
See YŌL(I).
-YŌLĬPAN *compound postposition* in one's
heart / en su corazón (T) [(1)Tp.138]. See
YŌL-LI, -PAN.
YŌLĬPANTIĀ *vrefl,vt* to give notice, to
announce; to announce, proclaim some-
thing / avisa, anuncia (T), le avisa, le advi-
erte, le anuncia (T) [(6)Tp.164,220]. T
specifically marks the vowel of the first
syllable of ĪPANTIĀ short, but ĪPANTILIĀ
in C has it marked long. See YŌL-,
ĪPANTIĀ.
YŌLĬPANTILIĀ applic. YŌLĬPANTIĀ
YŌLĬPANTĬLŌ nonact. YŌLĬPANTIĀ
YŌLĪTIĀ caus. YŌL(I)
YŌLIUHQUI someone simplehearted /

simple de corazón (Z) [(1)Zp.232]. See
YŌL-LI, IHU(I).
YŌLĪX-TLI stomach / estómago (T)
[(1)Tp.138, (4)Zp.71,130,175,186]. See
YŌL-LI, ĪX-TLI.
YŌLLĀLIĀ *vrefl,vt* to be consoled, content,
happy; to console, cheer someone / consolarse (M), consolar a otro (M) See YŌL-,
TLĀLIĀ.
YŌL-LI *pl:* **-TIN** heart / corazón (X). This is
abundantly attested as a free form in X but
not elsewhere. M has only *yoli, yuli* 'living
thing,' which is a different word. The
related verb-modifying element YŌL-,
which implies volition or emotional
involvement, is highly productive, and
there is potential ambiguity between it and
YŌL-LI as an incorporated object. YŌL-LI,
YŌLLŌ-TL, and YŌLLOH-TLI are virtually synonymous but tend to different
grammatical functions. See YŌL(I), YŌL-.
YŌLLOHPACHŌLIZ-TLI consolation /
consuelo (Z) [(2)Zp.33,232]. See
YŌLLOH-TLI, PACHOĀ.
YŌLLOHTLAHUĒLĪLŌCĀCUEP(A) *vt* to be
enraged at someone / os enfurece (C for
first pers. plural object) [(1)Cf.113v]. See
YŌLLOH-TLI, TLAHUĒLĪLŌC, CUEP(A).
YŌLLOH-TLI heart, pith, core / corazón (M)
See YŌL-LI, -YOH.
YŌLLOHTZETZELOĀ *vt* to empty
out, cleanse someone's heart / le sacude
el corazón, le limpia el corazón (T)
[(3)Tp.220]. T has characteristically lost a
glottal stop in the second syllable but
leaves evidence of it in the syllable's short
O. If YŌLLŌ-TL were the initial component, there would be the reflex of Ō
instead. See YŌLLOH-TLI, TZETZELOĀ.
YŌLLOHXŌCHI-TL magnolia / flor muy
olorosa de hechura de corazón (M), flor de
corazón (K) [(1)Cf.76r]. See YŌLLOH-TLI,
XŌCHI-TL.
YŌLLŌTIĀ *vt* to confide in a friend; to
inspire someone / descubrir algo al amigo
(M), inspirar algo a otro (M) [(1)Bf.2r]. See
YŌLLŌ-TL.
YŌLLŌ-TL heart, life, spirits / corazón o
meollo de fruta seca (M), su corazón, su
alma, su ánima (Z) This is almost always
possessed. -YŌLLŌ seems to serve as the

possessed form of both the abstraction here
and the more concrete YŌLLOH-TLI,
except when the latter is suffixed with
-TZIN or -TŌN. This is discussed in C on
f.83v. See YŌL-LI, -YŌ.

YŌLMALACACHILHUIĀ applic. YŌL-
MALACACHOĀ

YŌLMALACACHOĀ *vrefl,vt* to lose one's
bearings, to change one's mind; to confuse,
deceive, bewitch someone / desatinarse o
volverse de otro parecer (M), desatinar a
otro, o traerlo al retortero, o ligarlo con
hechizos (M) [(2)Cf.65v]. See YŌL-,
MALACACHOĀ.

YŌLMELĀHUAC someone honest, honorable, meek / humilde, justo, honrado,
honesto (Z) [(5)Zp.68,69,74,232]. This is
different in sense from M's *yolmelaua*,
which has to do with confession. See
YŌL-LI, MELĀHUAC.

YŌLMICTOC someone apathetic, dis-
couraged / desanimado (Z) [(2)Zp.41,232].
M has *yolmiqui* 'one who has fainted'
with a similar derivation. Both are
from YŌLMIQU(I) 'to be faint of heart,
dispirited, depressed.'

YŌLMIQU(I) *pret:* **-MIC** to be faint of heart,
dispirited, depressed / desmayarse o
amortecerse, o tener comezón, o espantarse (M) This is indirectly attested in
YŌLMICTOC. See YŌL-, MIQU(I).

YŌLNEHCIHU(I) to sigh / suspira (Z)
[(2)Zp.119,232]. See YŌL-, ĒLCIHCIHU(I).

YŌLNĒNTOC someone inconsistent,
unreliable / variable, inconstante (Z)
[(3)Zp.71,128,232]. See YŌL-LI, NĒN, the
verb O.

YŌLNŌTZ(A) *vt* to have affection for
someone / le tiene cariño (T) [(3)Tp.220].
See YŌL-, NŌTZ(A).

YŌLPAHZOLOĀ *vrefl,vt* to suffer; to
trouble someone / se aflige (de molestia), se molesta (T), lo molesta (T)
[(6)Tp.164,220]. See YŌL-, PAHZOLOĀ.

YŌLPĀQUIC someone happy, content /
alegre, contento, gozoso (Z) [(3)Zp.8,
33,232]. Only one of three attestations has
the final -C. See YŌL-, PĀQU(I).

YŌLPĀQUILIZ-TLI happiness, enjoyment /
alegría, gozo (Z) [(3)Zp.8,64,232]. See
YŌLPĀQUIC.

YŌLPATLA *vrefl* to repent / se arrepiente (Z)
[(2)Zp.14,175]. See YŌL-, PATLA.

YŌLPEHPEN(A) *vrefl* to think / piensa (T)
[(3)Tp.164]. See YŌL-, PEHPEN(A).

YŌLPIPĪCTIC someone hardhearted /
duro de corazón, sin conciencia (Z)
[(3)Zp.31,48,232]. YŌL-LI, PIPĪCTIC

YŌLPOLIHUILIZ-TLI trouble, confusion /
molestia, confusión (Z) [(3)Zp.32,85,232].
See YŌL-, POLIHU(I).

YŌLQUEPTOC someone crazy / loco (Z)
[(2)Zp.77,232]. See YŌL-, QUEPTOC.

YŌLQUETZ(A) *vrefl* to despair, lose hope /
se desespera (Z) [(2)Zp.42,175]. The gloss of
this item seems contrary to the sense of
its constituent parts. See YŌL-, QUETZ(A).

YŌLQUI a living thing, something brought
to life / animal bruto, o cosa viva, o huevo
empollado, o el resucitado de muerte a
vida (M) [(2)Bf.31,3v, (6)Xp.82,108]. B forms
the plural in regular fashion, YŌLQUEH,
while X adds -MEH. See YŌL(I).

YŌLQUĪZAC someone cheerful, happy,
content / alegre, contento (Z), gozoso (Z)
[(5)Zp.8,33,64,,232]. This is opposite in
sense from M's verb *yolquixtia* 'to annoy
someone very much.' Of five attestations,
three have final -C and two do not. On
Zp.232 both forms are given as separate
entries, although the glosses do not contrast. See YŌL-LI, QUĪZ(A).

YŌLTEQUIPACHOĀ *vrefl* to become sad, to
be regretful / tener pesar de lo que hizo (M)
[(2)Zp.125,175]. See YŌL-, TEQUI-
PACHOĀ.

YŌLTIHTICUĪN(I) to beat, throb, palpitate /
palpita (Z) [(1)Zp.232]. This is only attested
once; TI should probably be TZI. See
YŌL-LI, TZICUĪN(I).

YŌLTITLAN stomach / estómago (X)
[(2)Xp.108]. See YŌL-LI, -TLAN.

YŌLTLAMATQUI someone wise / sabio (Z)
[(2)Zp.112,232]. See YŌL-, TLAMATQUI.

YŌLTLAŌCOY(A) *pret:* **-COX** to be sad /
tiene tristeza (Z) [(2)Zp.125,232]. See YŌL-,
TLAŌCOY(A).

YŌLTLAZOHTLALIZ-TLI love / cariño (Z)
[(2)Zp.25,232]. See YŌL-, TLAZOHTLA.

YŌLTOC someone alive, among the living /
vivente (Z) [(4)Zp.130,232]. See YŌL(I),
the verb O.

YŌLTOTOMOCATOC someone excited /
excitado (Z) [(2)Zp.58,232]. See YŌL-,
TOTOMOCA, the verb O.

YŌLTZACUĪZ-TLI for someone's breathing
to be cut off / su resuello se le cierra (Z)
[(1)Zp.232]. The second element of this
is a contraction of *TZACUILIZ-TLI<
TZACUILIĀ 'to impede something.' See
YŌL-LI, TZACU(A).

YŌLTZAHTZI to cry out / grita (Z)
[(2)Zp.64,232]. See YŌL-, TZAHTZI.

YŌLYAMĀNIC someone benevolent, kind,
just / justo, benigno, benévolo, manso,
suave, tierno (Z) [(5)Zp.19,74,81,117,232].
See YŌL-, YAMĀNQUI.

YŌLYAMĀNILIZ-TLI consideration,
tenderheartedness / blandura de corazón
(M), consideración (Z) [(2)Zp.32,232]. Z has
YE for YA and NAL for NIL. See YŌL-,
YAMĀNIĀ.

YŌMOHTLAN-TLI flank / costado de
persona o de sierra (M) [(1)Cf.92v].

-YŌ-TL See -YŌ.

YŌYOHUA redup. YOHUA

YŌYOHUAC every night, every early
morning / todas las madrugadas (C)
[(2)Cf.73r,106r]. redup. YOHUAC

Z

ZĀ only / solamente (C) C distinguishes ZĀ from ZAN, which appears synonymous. According to C, ZĀ implies that the matter in question was not always as it is but has come to be so, whereas ZAN carries no such presupposition (Cf.110r). In T the reflex of ZĀ alternates in about equal numbers with ZA with a short vowel, which is the reflex of ZAN by T's regular loss of word-final nasals. Z alternates between ZĀ and ZAH.

ZACA *vt* to transport, convey something / acarrear algo (M)

ZACACAL-LI thatched house / casa de zacate (T) [(1)Tp.220]. See ZACA-TL, CAL-LI.

ZACACOPĪN(A) to pull up grass / arranca zacate (T) [(1)Tp.220]. See ZACA-TL, COPĪN(A).

ZACALŌ nonact. ZACA

ZACAMĪL-LI grassland / zacatal (Z) [(2)Zp.112,201]. See ZACA-TL, MĪL-LI.

ZACAMOĀ break ground, clear land, weed / abrir o labrar de nuevo la tierra, rozar la yerba (M) [(2) Cf.65v]. See ZACA-TL.

ZACAMOLHUIĀ applic. ZACAMOĀ

ZACAPEHPEN(A) See ZACA-TL, PEHPEN(A).

ZACAPIHPĪTZTŌN a type of bird / una especie de pájaro (T) [(1)Tp.220]. See ZACA-TL, PĪTZ(A).

ZACATEQU(I) See ZACA-TL, TEQU(I).

ZACATETEZ-TLI a type of grass, hay / zacate chino (T) [(1)Tp.220]. This may refer to chopped or ground up hay. See ZACA-TL, TETEZTIC.

ZACA-TL grass, hay / paja (M), pasto, zacate, maleza, rastrojo (T)

ZACAXŌLĒ-TL *pl:* -MEH a type of mushroom / hongo (T) [(1)Tp.220]. See ZACA-TL, XŌLĒ-TL.

ZĀCEH ultimately, once and for all / finalmente (C) [(2)Cf.117r]. This is a contraction of the sequence ZĀ ZO (Y)EH.

ZACŌ-TL *pl:* -MEH marten, ferret / marta (animal), hurón (T) [(1)Tp.220].

ZAHCANOHPAL-LI a type of nopal cactus / cacto, nopal silvestre (T) [(2)Tp.221]. T has variants with and without the glottal stop in the third syllable. T also has a stem-final I, which in turn takes the -TL form of the absolutive suffix, -NOHPALI-TL, but elsewhere NOHPAL-LI is the conventional form. See NOHPAL-LI.

ZAHU(A) to fast, to abstain / ayunar (M)

ZAHUACOCO-TL *pl:* -MEH fleabite, rash / sarpullido, erupción (Z) [(2)Zp.114,201]. This is attested only in plural form. See ZAHUA-TL, COCO-TL.

ZAHUALIZ-TLI fast / ayuno (Z) [(3)Zp.17,201]. Z marks the vowel of the second syllable long, but it should not be. This is attested eight times as an element of personal names in B, always with both stem vowels short. See ZAHU(A).

ZAHUAN(A) to be hoarse / está ronco (T) [(3)Tp.221]. See ZAHUAN(I).

ZAHUANALŌ nonact. ZAHUAN(A)

ZAHUANALTIĀ caus. ZAHUAN(A)

ZAHUAN(I) to be hoarse / está ronco (T) [(3)Tp.221]. See ZAHUAN(I).

ZAHUANĪHUA nonact. ZAHUAN(I)

ZAHUANITIĀ The vowel of the third syllable of this form should be long but is specifically marked short. caus. ZAHUAN(I)

ZAHUA-TL *pl:* -MEH pox, rash / roña, tiña, viruelas (S), grano, llaga, erupción, sarpullido, viruela (T) [(1)Cf.127r, (3)Tp.223, (2)Zp.130,166]. C specifically marks the vowel of the first syllable short, while T and Z have it long, hence contrasting with the verb ZAHU(A) 'to fast.' C contrasts this with the place name ZĀHUĀ-TL, where both vowels are long. See ZAHU(A).

ZĀHUĀ-TL *place name* the name of a river in Tlaxcala / río de Tlaxcala (C)

[(1)Cf.127r]. C contrasts this with
ZAHUA-TL 'pox, itch.'

ZAHUATLAHUEPĀUHQUI rubella /
viruela loca (T) [(1)Tp.223]. See
ZAHUA-TL, HUAPĀHU(A).

ZAHZACA *vt* to transport something from
various places / acarrear algo (M), darse
priesa en acarrear de varias partes (C)
[(2)Cf.72r]. redup. ZACA

ZAHZĀLIUHYĀN-TLI the joints of the
body / coyunturas de los miembros del
cuerpo (M) [(1)Cf.94r, (2)Zp.14,159]. This is
the distributive form of ZĀLIUHYĀN-TLI
'joint.' redup. ZĀLIUHYĀN-TLI

ZAHZĀLOĀ *vt* to align something, to patch
something together / pone en línea (Z),
remienda (Z) [(4)Zp.11,108,193,214]. redup.
ZĀLOĀ

ZĀLHUIĀ applic. ZĀLOĀ

ZĀLIHU(I) *vt* to stick to something / pe-
garse una cosa a otra (M) See ZĀLOĀ.

ZĀLIUHTOC in order / en orden (Z)
[(2)Zp.91,201]. See ZĀLIHU(I), the verb O.

ZĀLIUHYĀN-TLI place where things fit
properly, joint / coyunturas de los miembros del cuerpo (M), en su lugar y en
caja (C) [(1)Cf.94r, (2)Zp.14,159]. Z has
the variant form ZĀLIHUIYĀN. See
ZĀLIHU(I), -YĀN.

ZĀLOĀ *vt* to glue, solder something, to
make something stick to something else /
pegar algo, engrudar, hacer pared, o soldar
con plomo, etc. (M)

ZĀLŌLŌ nonact. ZĀLOĀ

ZĀLŌLTIĀ caus. ZĀLOĀ

ZAMĀHUALTIĀ to swell, ripen something (maize) / lo hincha (maíz) (Z)
[(2)Zp.67,193].

ZAN only / solamente (M) See ZĀ.

ZANCĒ only one / solamente uno (C) Variants include ZAZCĒ and ZANCEN. See
ZAN, CEM.

ZANCUĒL just a moment; frequently / un
momento, un pequeño instante; frecuentemente, muy a menudo (S) [(1)Cf.131v].
This is often written as two words. See
ZAN, CUĒL.

ZĀNĒN *dubitative particle* I wonder if ...
(with respect to something expected or
desired) / por ventura, querrá Dios (C) C
contrasts ZĀNĒN with ZANNĒN, the
latter being an emphatic expression of

NĒN 'in vain' (Cf.112v,113r). See ZĀ,
NĒN.

ZĀNĪL-LI *pl:* **-TIN** tale, fable; conversation /
consejuelas para hacer reír (M for reduplicated form), cuento, plática, conversación
(Z) [(6)Zp.33,36,99,201]. This is commonly
found in reduplicated form, but there are
no attestations of it in the sources for this
dictionary which would show whether the
reduplication is of the short-vowel, long-
vowel, or vowel-glottal stop type. See
ZĀNĪLOĀ.

ZĀNĪLOĀ to talk, converse / lo platica (Z)
[(2)Zp.99,201]. M has the applicative form
of this verb in reduplicated form *çaçanil-
huia*. See ZĀNĪL-LI.

ZĀNĪPAN something moderate; moderately
/ cosa manual o mediana, o algún tanto, o
en alguna manera (M), medianamente, de
buena manera (C) [(8)Cf.122r,123r,131v]. Of
eight attestations C marks the vowel of
the first syllable long five times and leaves
three unmarked. Apparently this is not a
compound of ZAN and ĪPAN. It is often
found in the phrases ZĀNĪPAN CUAL-LI
and ZĀNĪPAN YĒC-TLI, both of which
appear in M with the same sense of
ZĀNĪPAN alone.

ZANIYOH only, alone / solamente, o solo
(M) Other elements can intervene between
ZAN and IYOH. In Z this is reduced to
ZĀYOH. See ZAN, IYOĀ.

ZANMACH See ZAN, MACH.

ZANMACHEH See ZAN, MACHEH.

ZANNĒN in vain / en vano, o por demás (M)
See ZAN, NĒN, note under ZĀNĒN.

ZANNŌ likewise, also, by the same token
(often indicating identity of time or place) /
identidad de lugar o tiempo (C), el mismo
o los mismo (M for *çannoye*)

ZANQUĒZQUICĀN only in a few places /
solamente en pocas (partes o lugares) (C)
[(1)Cf.91v]. See ZAN, QUĒZQUICĀN.

ZANYENŌ particle indicating identity of
time or place / identidad de lugar o tiempo
(C) [(4)Cf.89v,90r]. See ZANNŌ, YE.

ZAQUILIĀ applic. ZACA

ZĀTĒPAN later, afterwards, at the last /
después, a la postre, o al cabo (M), después,
más tarde, luego (T) See ZĀ, TĒPAN.

ZĀTĒPANYAHUI someone younger / menor
(T) [(2)Tp.64,223]. The literal sense of this

is 'to go afterwards.' T characteristically
drops word-final nasals, and when such an
element compounds, the nasal sometimes
does not appear, even though it is no
longer in word-final position, and this is
the case with this item. See ZĀTĒPAN,
YĀ.

ZĀYŌL-IN *pl:* **-MEH** fly / mosca (M) C uses
ZĀYŌL-IN as an example of how nouns
with the -IN absolute suffix can form the
possessor derivation with -EH or -HUAH
in free variation, ZĀYŌLEH ~ ZĀYŌL-
HUAH 'one who has flies.'

ZĀYŌLTĒN-TLI fly bite / grano de mosco,
piquete de mosco (T) [(1)Tp.223]. See
ZĀYŌL-IN, TĒN-TLI.

ZAZACA redup. ZACA

ZĀZAHUATIC someone hoarse / estar
ronco o zumbar, o follar las fuelles (M for
çaçauaca), ronco (Z) [(4)Zp.111,201,225].
See ZAHUAN(A), ZAHUAN(I).

ZĀZAHUAYOH itch, mange / sarna (T)
[(1)Tp.223]. See ZAHUA-TL, -YOH.

ZAZĀLIC something sticky or adhesive /
cosa pegajosa, como engrudo o cosa semejante (M) [(2)Xp.80]. See ZAZĀLTIC,
ZĀLOĀ.

-ZĀZĀLŌL *only attested in possessed
form* one's joint / su conyuntura (T)
[(1)Tp.133]. T has O for the reflex of Ā
here. See ZĀLOĀ.

-ZĀZĀLIUHYŌ *only attested in possessed
form* one's joint / su conyuntura (T)
[(1)Tp.133]. T has O for the reflex of Ā
here. See ZĀLIHU(I).

ZAZĀLTIC something sticky, viscous / cosa
pegajosa como engrudo, o cosa semejante
(M) [(1)Tp.221, (3)Zp.95,130,201]. M gives
as synonymns *çaçaltic* and *çaçalic*. T has a
short vowel in ZAL despite the clear
relationship to ZĀLIHU(I) and ZĀLOĀ. In
one of three attestations Z marks the
vowel long. See ZĀLOĀ.

ZĀZAN any which way, without coherence
or sense / sin traza, disparatada y ne-
ciamente (C) C has a discussion of this
with repeated examples (f.115v). T has
ZĀZAN-TLI with an absolutive suffix and
the sense 'many things.'

ZAZCĒ See ZANCĒ.

ZAZCEMI at one and the same time / de
una vez (C) [(3)Cf.126r]. M has *ça cemi* as a

phrase glossed as 'finally, just this once, or
something said upon departure.' See ZAN,
CEMI.

ZĀZO -ever / cualquiera (C) This particle
placed before an interrogative particle
replaces its interrogative sense with the
sense of -ever constructions in English;
whatever, whenever, whoever, etc.

-ZO This is a necessarily bound particle that
adheres to other particles without any
overt sense of its own. The vowel is often
lost in particle clusters.

ZŌ *vrefl,vt; pret:* **ZŌC** to pierce oneself; to
draw blood by piercing someone / san-
grarse (M), punzar y sangrar (C), pinchar,
sangrar a alguien (S)

ZŌC-TLI corn husk / tamo, cascarita del
maíz (Z) [(2)Zp.119,203].

ZŌHU(A) *vrefl,vt* to stretch or spread out; to
extend, spread out, open something / se
estira (ropa, etc.), se tiende (T), tender o
desplegar ropa, o abrir libro (M)

ZOHUACHICHI female dog, bitch / perra
(T) [(1)Tp.222]. See ZOHUA-TL, CHICHI.

ZOHUAEHĒCA-TL the weeping woman
(a ghost) / llorona, mal aire que se cambia
en forma de mujer (T) [(1)Tp.223]. See
ZOHUA-TL, EHĒCA-TL.

ZOHUAHTIĀ *vt* for a man to marry a
woman / lo casa (hombre con mujer) (T)
[(3)Tp.202]. Here a glottal stop intervenes
between ZOHUA and the verbal suffix
-TIĀ. See ZOHUA-TL.

ZOHUAHTILIĀ applic. ZOHUAHTIĀ

ZOHUAHTILĪLŌ nonact. ZOHUAHTIĀ

ZOHUĀHUAH one who has a wife, a
married man / ya está casado (T)
[(2)Tp.223]. This is the only instance in T
in which the vowel of the second syllable
of ZOHUA-TL is given as the reflex of a
long vowel. The short vowel of the other
attestations of ZOHUA-TL contrasts with
that of CIHUĀ-TL, which is consistently
attested long.

ZOHUAHUEHXŌLŌ-TL turkey hen /
guajolote, totola, pava (T) [(1)Tp.222]. This
is contradictory, since HUEHXŌLŌ-TL in
general specifically means 'turkey cock.'
See ZOHUA-TL, HUEHXŌLŌ-TL.

ZŌHUALŌ nonact. ZŌHU(A)

ZOHUAMIZTŌN female cat / gata (T)
[(1)Tp.222]. See ZOHUA-TL, MIZ-TLI.

ZOHUAMŌN-TLI daughter-in-law, bride, fiancée / novia (T) [(1)Tp.222]. In the Spanish-to-Nahuatl side, T gives this as a gloss for *nuera* 'daughter-in-law.' In terms pertaining to in-law relationships the vowel of the MŌN element is consistently short in T and consistently long elsewhere. See ZOHUA-TL, MŌN-TLI.

ZOHUA-TL *pl: -MEH* woman / mujer (M) Although CIHUĀ-TL is the standard form for the Valley of Mexico, M also gives *çouatl*. ZOHUA-TL is the standard form in T and is widely spread in modern Nahuatl. Although the vowel of the second syllable of CIHUĀ-TL is long, T does not have the reflex of a long vowel in ZOHUA-TL or in any of its derivations with the exception of ZOHUĀHUAH 'one who has a wife.' See CIHUĀ-TL.

ZOHUATŌTOL turkey hen / guajolota, totola, pava (T) [(1)Tp.222]. This is only attested without an absolutive prefix. See ZOHUA-TL, TŌTOL-IN.

ZŌHUILIĀ applic. ZŌHU(A)

ZOHZŌ *vt; pret:* **ZOHZŌC** to string things together by piercing and threading them. / ensartar cuentas, ají, flores, o cosas semejantes (M) In T there has been characteristic loss of the internal glottal stop. See ZŌ.

ZOHZŌHU(A) *vrefl,vt* to spread open one's arms; to spread something out / abrir los brazos]; tender o desplegar mantas, o abrir libros (M)(K) [(2)Bf.6v,7r]. redup. ZŌHU(A)

ZOHZŌHUA *vt* to nail something, to pierce something / lo clava...lo martilla (Z) [(3)Zp.28,82,194]. See ZŌ.

ZOHZŌLHUIĀ T has the reflex of a short vowel in the second syllable where a long vowel is to be expected. applic. ZOHZŌ

ZOHZŌLŌ nonact. ZOHZŌ

ZOHZOQUIHUIĀ T is missing the glottal stop of the initial reduplicated syllable, but short vowel reduplication is unlikely here. redup. ZOQUIHUIĀ

ZOHZŌTIMAN(I) *vt* to touch and pierce something such as the sky / que tocan y punzan (el cielo) (C) [(2)Cf.71r]. This is derived from ZŌ, but C does not mark the vowel of the second syllable long in one attestation and in the other marks it short. See ZŌ, MAN(I).

ZOLHUIĀ applic. ZOLOĀ

ZŌL-IN *pl: -TIN* quail / codorniz (M) [(1)Tp.223].

-ZOL-LI *compounding element for nouns* something old, worn out / traída, vieja, y maltratada (C) Unlike -TZIN-TLI, -TŌN-TLI, etc., this has no reduplicated plural, since it is only used with inanimate objects (Cf.8r). See ZOLOĀ.

ZOLOĀ *vrefl,vt* to exhaust oneself; to wear something out / envejecer ropa o cosa semejante (M) [(3)Zp.45,169,189]. Z has one attestation of ZOLHUIĀ and two of ZOLOĀ, all with the sense of 'to exhaust, tire someone.' See MĀZOLHUIĀ, COCHIHZOLOĀ.

ZOLŌN(I) for something to rush along with a great noise / ir con gran ímpetu y ruído el río (M) [(1)Cf.74v].

ZOLTIC something old / antiguo, viejo (T) [(2)Tp.223, (3)Zp.11,129,203, (2)Xp.47]. See -ZOL-LI.

ZŌMĀ *vrefl; pret:* **ZŌMAH** to frown in anger / yo tengo ceño como enojado (C for first pers. sg. subject)

ZŌMĀLIĀ *vrefl* to become angry, to work oneself into a rage / enojarse, encolerizarse (S) [(2)Cf.64v,65v]. The vowel of the second syllable should be long but is not so marked in the two attestations. applic. ZŌMĀ

ZŌMĀL-LI anger / coraje, ira, mohina (T) [(1)Bf.9v, (1)Cf.40r, (1)Tp.223]. See ZŌMĀ.

ZŌNECTIC something spongy / cosa fofa, esponjada, o liviana (M) [(1)Tp.223]. See ZŌNĒHU(A).

ZŌNĒHU(A) *vrefl,vt* for something to swell, puff up; to make something swell or puff up / azorarse el ave (M), alterar o alborotar la gente (M), apitonarse o azorarse o crecer mucho el agua de río, o azorarse el perro o el gato, etc. (M), se infla, se esponja (T) See ZŌNĒHU(I).

ZŌNĒHUALŌ nonact. ZŌNĒHU(A)

ZŌNĒHUALTIĀ *vt* to cause something to swell; to suffocate / lo esponja (T), sofoca (Z) [(3)Tp.202, (2)Zp.116,214]. caus. ZŌNĒHU(A)

ZŌNĒHU(I) to inflate / infla (Z) [(4)Tp.130, (2)Zp.71,203]. See ZŌNĒHU(A).

ZŌNĒHUILIĀ applic. ZŌNĒHU(A)

ZŌNĒHUALIZ-TLI swelling, expansion, inflation, flood / crecimiento de río, etc. (M) [(1)Tp.130]. T has I for A. See ZŌNĒHU(A).

ZOQUIAQUIĀ vrefl,vt to bury oneself in mud; to bury someone or something in mud / se entierra en lodo (T), lo mete al lodo (piedra, etc.) (T) [(5)Tp.157,202]. See ZOQUI-TL, ĀQUIĀ.

ZOQUIĀ-TL marsh, pool / cieno (M), charco (Z) [(2)Zp.38,203]. See ZOQUI-TL, Ā-TL.

ZOQUICAX(I)-TL flat earthen bowl / cajete de barro (Z) [(2)Zp.23,203]. See ZOQUI-TL, CAX(I)-TL.

ZOQUICHĪHU(A) to mix mud for foundations and adobe / hacer barro para edificar pared o para hacer adobes, etc. (M) This is indirectly attested by ZOQUICHĪUHQUI. See ZOQUI-TL, CHĪHU(A).

ZOQUICHĪUHQUI potter, someone who works clay / ollero (C) According to M, this is 'one who makes said clay' for foundations and adobe. See ZOQUICHĪHU(A).

ZOQUIHUIĀ vrefl,vt to get soiled with mud; to soil something with mud / se enloda (Z), enlodar algo (M) [(2)Zp.52,172]. See ZOQUI-TL, -HUIĀ.

ZOQUINELOĀ vrefl,vt to soil oneself; to soil someone with mud / enlodarse (M), enlodar a otro (M) See ZOQUI-TL, NELOĀ.

ZOQUIPACHOĀ vrefl,vt to sink into mud; to spread mud over something / se entierra dentro del lodo (T), estercolar la tierra en cierta manera (M) See ZOQUI-TL, PACHOĀ.

ZOQUIPĀTLA to mix, beat mud / bate el lodo (T) [(3)Tp.223]. See ZOQUI-TL, PĀTLA.

ZOQUITI to become boggy, muddy / mojarse, hacerse una sopa de agua (M), volver cieno (C) [(1)Cf.58v]. See ZOQUI-TL.

ZOQUI-TL clay, mud / barro, lodo (M)

ZOQUITLAH bog, muddy place / lodazal (M) [(1)Tp.223, (2)Zp.16,203]. The vowels of the second and third syllables are marked long in one of the attestations

in Z, but they should all be short. See ZOQUI-TL, -TLAH.

ZOQUITŌCA vrefl,vt to stick something in mud, to bury something in mud / se atasca, se entierra en lodo (T), lo entierra dentro el lodo (T) See ZOQUI-TL, TŌCA.

ZOQUIYOH something covered with clay / cosa enlodada (M) [(1)Cf.54r,82r, (1)Rp.44]. This conventionally pairs with TLĀLLOH, both possessed, to refer to one's earthly body. See ZOQUI-TL, -YOH.

ZOTLĀHUA to faint / desmayarse o amortecerse (M) [(1)Cf.88r].

ZŌTOC something nailed / clavado [(2)Zp.28,203]. In one of the attestations both vowels are marked long and in the other neither. See ZŌ, the verb O.

ZŌTŌL-IN palm tree / palma (M); planta para hacer tenates, canasta (Z) [(2)Zp.203].

ZŌYĀ-TL palm tree / palma (M) [(1)Tp.173,(2)Zp.93,203, (2)Xp.82]. T has this with a short vowel in the first syllable and the reflex of Ō in the second.

ZOZOLCA to snore, grunt / ronca (Z) [(3)Zp.64,111,203]. This seems to be a truncated variant of ZOZOLOCA 'to make a rumbling noise.'

ZOZOLCAHUIĀ vt to grunt at someone / le gruñe (Z) [(2)Zp.64,194]. One of the attestations marks the vowels of the second and third syllables long, but they should not be.

ZOZOLOCA to make a rumbling or roaring noise / follar o zumbar las fuelles, o anhelar el que está muriendo (M), hace ruido (como frijol hirviendo) (T) [(3)Cf.74v,129r, (1)Tp.223]. See ZOLŌN(I).

ZOZOLOCATIHU(I) present singular: **-TIUH** to make a whizzing sound / de la piedra tirada con fuerza o de la codorniz que se levanta y vuela se dice (C) [(2)Cf.74v,129r]. See ZOZOLOCA, HU(I).

ZOZOLOTZ(A) vt to cause something to make a rumbling, roaring sound / hacer ruido el chorro de agua que cae sobre otra agua (M) [(2)Cf.74v,129r]. See ZOLŌN(I).